Botanica's Pocket

GARDENING
ENCYCLOPEDIA

Botanica's Pocket

GARDENING
ENCYCLOPEDIA

Over 1000 pages & over 2000 plants listed

Photos © Random House Australia Pty Ltd 2001
From the Random House Photo Library
Text © Random House Australia Pty Ltd 2001
Original ISBN 1 74051 434 3

Publisher: James Mills-Hicks
Managing Editor: Susan Page
Assembly: Sarah Elworthy
Production Manager: Linda Watchorn
Publishing Assistant: Anabel Pandiella

'Design your garden': Michael Bligh
'Caring for your garden': Geoffrey Burnie

© 2007 for this edition:
Tandem Verlag GmbH
h. f. ullmann is an imprint of
Tandem Verlag GmbH

Printed in China

ISBN 978-3-8331-2939-1

10 9 8 7 6 5 4 3 2 1
X IX VIII VII VI V IV III II I

Contents

Chapter 1

CREATING YOUR GARDEN

DESIGNING YOUR GARDEN

Getting the concept right

Whether you are starting from scratch or redesigning an existing garden, whether you live in the city, town or country, putting time and thought into the design of your garden is vital. When you begin, before thinking about where you will plant that favorite flowering shrub or perennial, you must first look at the 'big picture'.

Developing the basic layout and structure

If selecting a site for a new house and garden, be sure to consider a few basic things that will affect greatly the success of your new home. Aspect is one, as it can be such an advantage to have both house and garden sited where they receive the winter sun. Wind protection is another. No matter how good the view is it is generally well worth sacrificing by screening with an effective windbreak to protect the house and garden from the strong prevailing winds.

Although views are important, if you don't have one, remember that superb views can always be created within your garden by clever design.

Ideally the site should be reasonably level, otherwise expensive earthworks may be required.

Once you have selected your site or garden you wish to redo, other basic layout and structural decisions need to be considered. The best way to analyze

these is to start at the beginning, at the property entrance and then work through to the house.

In the case of a country garden, the link between the main road and your house site needs to be carefully looked at, especially in terms of the location of the property entrance, the alignment of the property drive, whether you have a parkland of trees to drive through before reaching the garden and then the ideal location to enter the garden to ensure an appropriate approach to the house. Once within the garden, and this applies to town gardens as well, the position of the garden drive needs to be determined, as well as how your guest vehicles will be accommodated, where best to garage your own vehicles and how to link the visitor car park with the house to encourage guests to use the front door.

You then need to look at the best way to utilize the garden areas about the house. One way of doing this is to break up the garden into distinct areas such as the entrance garden, the outdoor living area, an area for active recreation such as swimming and tennis and finally, but not least, the utility area may include a clothes line, compost heap, garden shed and vegetable garden.

At this early stage, it is the functional and aesthetic considerations that are so important to get right. For example, when considering tree planting, before you even think about including your favorite species, you need to think more in terms of their location, height, shape, color of summer and autumn foliage, their flower color and whether deciduous or evergreen species are appropriate. When considering garden beds, before thinking about where you will plant those favorite perennials, think more in terms of where garden beds will be required, what size they will be, their shape, what height should the planting be in various locations within the beds and whether deciduous or evergreen species should be included. By thinking in these terms the basic layout and structure of your garden should develop correctly.

Determining the style of garden

Think carefully about what style of garden suits best your site and your own taste. Your preferred style of garden will be considerably influenced by the character and style of your house. For example, if your house is of a formal, classical style, a garden that would further enhance and complement the architecture would be appropriate. On the other hand, if your house is an informal cottage, a cottage-style garden would further strengthen the character of the house.

Your chosen style must also suit your lifestyle. It is essential that you design a garden that you can easily maintain. At different stages in life, priorities change and this needs to be reflected in the design of your garden. For example, if you are a young working couple, time for the garden can be very limited. If your children are older, and you have money available, you

may choose to incorporate those recreational facilities such as a swimming pool and tennis court, which greatly impact on the structure and layout of the garden. And if you are retired with occasional visits from grandchildren, those outdoor living spaces become especially important as you may have more time to spend enjoying your garden.

The environmental conditions of your site can play a big part in determining the appropriate style of garden. It is greatly influenced by the trees, shrubs and groundcovers that will grow on your site easily. To help determine what best to grow, drive about your area and have a good look at established gardens and see what has survived over time and in particular, what trees and plants are thriving in

Putting a lot of time and thought into planning your garden will bring great rewards.

A well-designed and well-placed gazebo can provide year-round interest.

your local area. Later as your garden matures and you begin to create a microclimate within your garden area, you may well be able to grow other plants that normally would not grow easily in your area. Be patient, as things do change within a garden and new opportunities arise as the garden develops.

The topography of your site is also important. If your site is on steeply sloping terrain, a certain amount of terracing may be required to create more useable outdoor spaces. This provides excellent opportunities for attractive steps, retaining walls and planted banks. In the case of a very flat site, you may create variations in height in the garden in terms of a sunken garden, raised beds, mounding or even ensuring that clear changes of level are appreciated through appropriate evergreen plantings of different heights. Finally, do consider the financial cost of creat-

ing the style of garden you desire, both in terms of construction and maintenance. A highly structured, formal style of garden, to be successful, may require certain structures and materials that are expensive, as compared to a more informal style of garden that may be far less expensive to establish. Obviously the size of your garden also plays a major role.

Ensuring year-round color and interest

When designing your garden, it is also important to think about creating a garden that looks good, not just in the spring when so much is flowering, but through all seasons. A good indicator of a well-designed garden is one that looks attractive during the most difficult times of the year. Winter, for example, can be a dull time in the garden, but if well designed, it can be superb.

One of the major roles of creating a garden is to enhance your lifestyle. Your garden should be designed to encourage your family and friends to enjoy it, to admire it and to sit within it to soak up its peace and beauty. It is also important to satisfy you the designer, as there is no doubt that the more attractive the garden looks, the more inspired you are to get out there and work it, to get it exactly the way you want it. Finally, a garden that looks good year round will add value to your property.

Designing a garden that has good color and interest year round takes more than simply choosing plants that flower or look good for every season. We also need to be aware of the contribution of the structure and layout of the garden, the inclusion of built structures, ornamentation and the role of water within the garden.

The layout and structure of the garden becomes most apparent in winter. Defined vistas within the garden in the form of paved walkways flanked with trees and features to focus on provide strong visual interest, as do vistas that focus on the landscape beyond. Spaces created within the garden, such as a canopy of trees, give a three-dimensional look to the garden. Level changes in the form of retaining walls, steps and banks also contribute to the structure of a garden, providing interest throughout the year.

The gazebo, summerhouse or pavilion, if well designed and well placed within the garden, can be a feature year round. A pergola may link one lawn space to another through a large garden bed, or an arbor may announce the entrance to a pathway. All provide good structural interest without requiring maintenance. Ornamentation such as urns, pots and tubs, a birdbath, sundial or dovecote, even sculpture and certainly a bench seat are all worth considering. They can provide a focus within an enclosed space such as a courtyard or at the end of a vista, but should be very carefully placed to ensure that they do not compete with each other.

Water is another effective and low-maintenance feature available. In a town garden, a small pond might be discovered surrounded by shade-loving flowering shrubs beneath tall trees within a hidden part of the garden, or a tumbling stream could be found. A wall fountain could be set up in a smaller garden, or a more formal raised pond may act as a central feature. In a country garden, a lake may form the boundary between the garden and the area beyond.

The careful selection and location of particular trees, shrubs and perennials can provide a succession of color and interest throughout the year. As well as flower color, the color, form and texture of foliage, the fruit and berries of particular species and even the trunks and stems of especially trees can contribute greatly towards year-round interest. Although most plants flower in spring, there are many that flower at other times. For example, after the

Ornaments such as this dovecote can add interest to the garden.

leaves of the photinias that initially turn bright red and later green, and in winter the evergreen trees come into their own providing structure during the cold months.

In autumn, certain trees and shrubs provide a spectacular show of fruit and berries. Shrubs such as cotoneasters and pyracanthas, although considered weeds in some areas, are excellent hardy species that provide brilliant color in autumn, along with trees such as the Mexican hawthorn *(Crataegus pubescens)* and blueberry ash *(Mahonia aquifolium)* which have delightful fruits.

The bark on the trunks and stems of trees and shrubs at certain times f the year can also be spectacular. An example familiar to many is the silver birch *(Betula pendula)* with its beautiful dappled white trunk that, when seen as a grove underplanted with daffodils creates a classic winter scene in a cool-climate garden. Even more striking is the pure white bark of the Japanese white birch *(Betula platyphylla)*. In warmer areas, the leopard-wood *(Caesalpinia ferrea)* has a similar display to the silver birch and looks equally as good either as a specimen tree or as a grove. Many of the eucalypts also have superb bark such as the ribbon gum *(Eucalyptus viminalis)* with its ribbons of bark, and the lemon-scented gum *(Eucalyptus citriodora)* with its smooth white trunk.

spring flush of crabapples *(Malus* sp.) and so many others, the repeat flowering roses such as 'Iceberg' continue to flower throughout summer and deep into autumn. Of the perennials, the Japanese wind flowers *(Anemone hupehensis)* flower beautifully in autumn and then in the cold winter months we discover the beautiful Chinese witch hazel *(Hamamelis mollis)* with its fragrant yellow flowers on display.

In terms of foliage, we tend to immediately think of the brilliant autumn colors of deciduous trees and shrubs, particularly in the colder regions where their colors are often much stronger. However, in summer when they are full with leaf, there is a huge palette of foliage colors that can be used to create beautiful scenes. The fresh green of the Manchurian pear *(Pyrus ussuriensis)*, the soft gray of the wormwood *(Artemisia* sp.), the red tones of the barberry *(Berberis* sp.) and the golden yellow of the golden robinia *(Robinia pseudoacacia* 'Frisia') are all good examples of such strong color variations. In the spring we think of the fresh new

You can also provide year-round interest by creating a garden that appeals to all the senses. Visually, a succession of attractive garden scenes can be made using plantings, ornamentation and water. As one explores such a garden, the fragrance of flowers and foliage further enhances the experience, especially when scented plants are strategically located beside pathways, bench seats and beneath windows of the house. Certain plants also entice people to touch them, for example, the smooth white bark of a lemon-scented gum can be irresistible. And if we listen carefully, the many sounds of the garden can be delightful—the rustling of leaves in the breeze, the buzz of bees in summer, the singing of birds at dawn and the tinkling of water from a fountain.

Basic Principles to Consider

Whether you have a small town garden, a Mediterranean garden in a warm climate or a cold-climate garden; whether your garden is on the coast or inland, whether it is a formal classical garden or an informal rambling garden—the basic principles of good design apply equally. Every garden has particular opportunities and constraints to respond to, but often the only major difference in terms of structure and layout is the scale of what you are playing with; the dimensions of trees, garden beds and spaces.

An effective way to determine what design ideas should be implemented is to pretend you are a guest arriving for lunch when the sun is shining and the house, garden and the landscape beyond are all clearly seen. If you have a town garden, you should start at the front gate and move on to examine the garden and house. In the case of a country garden, start at the property entrance. As you travel slowly up the drive, you critically analyze all that you see, progressing from the property entrance to the house and eventually about the garden. Let me take you on such a journey, by exploring some of the most important aspects of good garden design, some of the basic principles to consider.

The property entrance

In the case of a country garden, whether it be a small area of land on the outskirts of town or a very large property, the area between the property entrance off the street or main road and the house should be carefully considered. Is it safe in terms of other

The property drive should be attractive and welcoming.

A typical plan for a property entrance.

traffic when turning into or pulling out of the entrance, especially if the road is busy? It is essential that a clear view in both directions of the main road is gained from the entrance.

If there are well-established trees growing along the boundary fence, it may be an advantage to place the entrance through the center of two well-established trees or a group of trees. If your intention though is to frame the entrance with introduced trees, a clear site will be required. Choose a place where minimal earthworks would be needed to link the road level to your property.

It is important that the entrance looks like the main front entrance. Make it clear that you care about the presentation of your property by announcing the entrance in an appropriate way. Be careful not to design an entrance that might be somewhat

ostentatious, rather it should be understated, with simple clean lines and in character with the local area.

The two main elements to consider are the wings of the entrance and the framework of the trees about the entrance. In most country situations, the boundary fence is usually a simple affair, parallel to the main road. It is best to place the actual entrance a short distance inside your property and then link either side of the entrance with wings using a different form of fencing; you can choose either a gate or a grid. The choice of fencing to form the wings depends on personal taste, however, a simple post and rail fence is often the most appropriate. Consider constructing the wings from the same material as the house. If stone is chosen, use the indigenous stone of the local area as this will make it feel as though it belongs to the district. In terms of dimensions, the wings should be a minimum of 6 feet (3 meters) long and ideally about 30 feet (10 meters), set at a 45 degree angle to the boundary fence and at the same height as the normal fence.

Frame the entrance with trees that suit the scale of the surrounding landscape—large, clean trunked canopy trees. The trees may be either introduced or native species. If your entrance site is surrounded with native vegetation, however, usually the best solution is to strengthen the existing character by planting more of the same.

The property drive

The area between the property entrance and the house is also important; the drive to the house should be attractive and welcoming.

A major consideration is the alignment of the drive, where it is to run and whether it be straight or meandering. Generally, a meandering drive is considerably more interesting than a straight one, but sometimes this is not possible. You may be able to sweep the drive up onto a ridge line to gain a view to the landscape on the other side or down beside a pond or river to enjoy a water view.

One of the biggest opportunities to enhance the look of the drive is to strategically place trees to create a sense of driving through a parkland of trees. Such planting can be done as large individual trees or as groups of 3 or 5 smaller trees placed naturally. When young, such trees will require protection. To determine the location of the trees, always design as seen from the drive. There may be a view that can be enhanced by framing with large canopy trees, there may be another view that is unattractive and therefore can be screened with a selection of hardy evergreen trees.

You may choose to place an avenue of trees along the drive. Often the property drive is simply too long to allow this to be practical, but in some cases, the drive can be fenced off as a laneway and large, clean trunked trees evenly spaced, parallel to the drive, can look quite spectacular. Usually the one species of tree should be used in such avenues, planted about 10 feet (3 meters) from the edge of the drive and approximately 30 feet (10 meters) apart.

Hostas are excellent shade plants for beneath trees.

To significantly enhance the visual quality of the area through which a property drive may run, consider the creation of a body of water such as a pond or lake. To ensure that it looks good, make it look more like a naturally occurring body of water by having the pond wall very low above the high water mark and well covered in topsoil to support a strong cover of grass.

Other attractive, naturally occurring landscape elements may exist which should be taken advantage of. A stand of large native trees or a particularly attractive and interesting rock outcrop could be better appreciated by taking the drive near them.

As the property drive gets closer to the home, provide for a clear view of it long before you actually reach the house and garden, so it can be appreciated within its landscape setting. This helps to build a sense of anticipation. This may be achieved by simply removing some trees that block the view or taking the drive over a slight knoll to discover the view.

The entrance parkland

For those with plenty of space to play with, a subtle but effective way to enhance the experience of approaching the home is to create a transition zone in the form of a defined parkland of trees through which to drive before entering the garden. This is an excellent opportunity to link the broader rural landscape with the property and the detailed 'gardenesque' landscape of the garden and needs to be very carefully considered. Whether the drive is meandering or straight, the opportunity is here to have an avenue of trees that helps to create a subtle sense of formality and consequently builds the anticipation before reaching the garden. Generally, such an avenue should be made up of just the one species of tree, of large scale, clean trunked and planted approximately 6 feet (2 meters) from the edge of the drive, 25 feet (8 meters) apart to eventually form an archway of foliage over the drive.

Outside the avenue, the rest of the area should be carefully planted to create a natural parkland of a variety of trees that grow easily within your environment, especially in regard to soil, climate and drainage. One of the secrets of a well-designed parkland is the creation of space using the canopy of the trees. Such spaces can allow a clear view of many of the trees used and may extend right through the parkland to a distant mountain or hill to form a vista. Other surrounding views that are unattractive should be screened with evergreen trees. Ensure there is a good proportion of evergreen trees to provide adequate structure throughout the winter months when the deciduous trees have lost their leaves. You also need to decide what character of planting is desired. You may choose to use a variety of native trees, or a variety of introduced deciduous, evergreen and flowering trees.

The entrance parkland provides an excellent opportunity to create beautiful scenes utilizing the color, form and

The entrance parkland provides a good opportunity to create beautiful scenes by, for example, contrasting foliage colors of various tree species.

texture of the canopy of trees. A tapestry of different shades of green can be excellent, however, to create a more dramatic scene, consider contrasting the colors of the various species such as placing a yellow-foliaged tree beside red foliage. Contrasting the forms of the canopy of trees can also create dramatic effect, for example, when an upright tree is placed beside a rounded tree. When we speak of the texture of trees, we are talking about the size of leaf of the canopy. For example, contrast can be created by placing a fine-leafed tree beside a large-leafed tree.

Further visual interest can be created by including copses of the same species of tree together, and in other parts of the parkland it may be appropriate to simply have one large individual tree grown as a specimen. Generally in a parkland situation, shrub planting is not necessary. However, clever design can allow the growing of large drifts of bulbs, especially daffodils and jonquils *(Narcissus* sp.) and bluebells *(Hyacinthoides* sp.) which can be beautifully laid out as natural drifts linked to the base of deciduous trees.

In some situations, a parkland can be used to surround the garden, which has the advantage of softening the boundary between the garden and the broad rural landscape and thereby helping to integrate the garden within its surrounding landscape.

The garden entrance

It is equally important for a town garden as for a country garden that its entrance is very carefully considered. First impressions do count, and it should look as though it is the main entrance. It should be appropriately announced in an understated and welcoming way.

The garden entrance may be either a pedestrian or vehicular entrance. For most town gardens, it is clear that people are invited to park in the street and to walk through the front gate towards the house. However, in a country garden situation, many choose not to invite people to drive in to the garden, but instead to park outside the garden boundary. Whichever situation is designed for, it must be made clear to guests where they are invited to park. Shade trees should be provided and the parking area located close to the entrance gate.

To ensure your guests enter where you want them to, place a pergola or arbor at the front gate to announce the entrance. The design should relate to the architecture of the house by, for example, having the posts the same size and material as the posts of the verandah. An appropriate size for such a pergola is 6 feet (2 meters) wide and 10 feet (3 meters) long, which could then be clothed in a flowering climber.

Where vehicles are invited to enter the garden, make it clear to guests by creating an attractive and welcoming entrance. Certainly don't place a pedestrian gate nearby, which may only confuse people. The wings of the garden entrance should be similar to those at the property entrance, although on a smaller scale.

The garden drive

For too long, people have allowed that dreaded necessity the vehicle to dominate what should be the best part of the garden! The entrance garden is so important to get right as it provides the foreground to the front facade of your house, it is that part of the garden that is usually seen most clearly from the street or road and it is the first part of your garden your guests see when they arrive. So don't ruin it by expanses of stark gravel or paving.

Minimize the visual impact of the drive by locating it, instead of up the middle of the front entrance garden, round the perimeter of the garden. By following this principle more generous areas of lawn or garden can be designed for the center of the front garden, a more appropriate layout of garden can be designed to enhance the front facade of the house and the view from within the house is not spoilt. There are always exceptions to the rule, however, especially in the case of a traditional house with a symmetrical front facade that can often be complemented by a circular drive.

In a smaller garden, it may be economical to put down a hard paved drive such as brick paving or asphalt. The main advantage of a hard paved drive is the reduced maintenance required, especially after heavy rain when a gravel surface can be scoured. When low maintenance is important but the softer gravel drive look is desired, have an asphalt drive with a washed gravel rolled into the surface resulting in only about 10 per cent of the gravel being loose on the drive.

The most practical surface for the garden drive in larger gardens is usually gravel. However, it is important that a clean line is created between the edge of the drive and the adjacent lawn or garden bed. This can be achieved by using an edge of bricks placed end to end. Further, it is important to ensure that weeds do not grow up the center of the drive.

The other main consideration is drainage. In most instances it is acceptable to allow the surface run-off to flow off the surface onto a lawn space adjacent. However, where the drive is steep and is cut into the side of the slope, it is necessary to have a simple brick or stone gutter on the top side of the drive that drains into regular culverts.

Gravel is a practical surface for the drive in larger gardens.

An attractive front entrance path.

Parking of vehicles

Some of the most beautiful houses are ruined by the sight of cars parked across their front. Too often people spend weeks getting the house and garden looking good for a lunch party, only to see their guests park their cars all over the place, ruining the look of both the house and garden.

As pointed out earlier, it is essential to make it clear to people where they are invited to park. Locate the visitor parking area to the side of the house, not far from the front door. In the case of a circular drive, actively encourage people not to park on the turning circle but in a visitor's parking area located to the edge of the turning circle. Ensure that the width of the turning circle is narrow so that your guests are not tempted to park on the drive.

Your vehicle should be accommodated within an area located close to the house further along the drive past the visitor's parking area. Ensure there is a comfortable backing bay.

The front entrance path

Once people reach the visitor car park, it should be made very clear where they are invited to enter the house. The car park should be linked to the front door by a well-defined front entrance path that is so inviting that people will feel uncomfortable using any other pathway. Carefully position the front entrance path so that it takes full advantage of the best angle of approach to the front of your house. Often this angle may be approximately 45 degrees to the front of the house. For clarity, build an attractive pergola or place a pair of attractive urns at the path entrance. The path should be wide enough so that two people can walk comfortably side by side, and generally it should be of a hard paving such as brick or stone so as to provide convenient access during all types of weather.

In terms of planting beside the path, as you will have guests every season, it is important to ensure there is something of color and interest throughout the year. Incorporate scented plants that will be appreciated as people walk along the path.

Designing from within the house

It is now time to assess the garden design from within the house. When you analyze the view through your windows to the garden beyond, try treating the frame of the windows as the frame of a picture. By doing this you can study what you see and then design accordingly.

Ideally the scene from every window within the house should be as good as it can be, however, the views particularly from the family room, the kitchen, the master bedroom and the dining room should be considered priorities. Such views must be considered not by simply standing by the window looking out but from the angle of view that is appropriate for each particular room. For example, the view from the family room should be assessed from the sitting position on a couch, from the kitchen standing at the kitchen sink, from the master bedroom sitting up in bed, and from the dining room sitting at the dining room table. When analyzing such views, many opportunities may become apparent. For example, there may be a vista to a distant landscape which could be further enhanced by simply removing a tree or shrub that impedes the view; there may be a clear view of your neighbor's house which could be effectively screened by the strategic placement of an evergreen tree or shrub; there may be the opportunity for a feature such as a bird bath, dovecote or sundial that would draw focus to the end of a vista within the garden; and within a house of classic symmetrical layout, when standing in the central hallway looking out the front door, there may be the opportunity to place a feature directly opposite the middle of

the hallway to form a central axis that runs through into a formal garden.

Next assess the views from the main vantage points at the exterior of the house such as a verandah, terrace or patio. In the same way these views should be assessed, not by standing beside the balustrade, but by sitting on the outdoor furniture and assessing the view from that angle.

Enhancing the architecture of the house

Having assessed the views from within the house, the next most important angle of view is to walk out of the house and look back towards it to assess the layout and planting of the garden. These should be designed primarily to enhance the architecture of the building. A good approach to take is to treat the house as an integral part of your whole garden scheme. It is clearly the largest structure within your garden, and therefore needs to be well integrated within its garden setting.

It's important to frame each facade of the house with appropriate tree planting, placed diagonally opposite the corners of the house. The size of such trees depends on the size of the house so, in the case of a two-storeyed house, a taller tree would be required placed a little further out from the corner of the house so that eventually, when the tree is mature, the height of the tree will reach approximately the height of the roof, the width of the canopy just reaching the edge of the roof. Generally such trees need to be

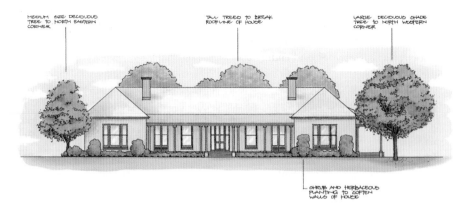

MEDIUM SIZE DECIDUOUS
TREE TO NORTH EASTERN
CORNER

TALL TREES TO BREAK
ROOFLINE OF HOUSE

LARGE DECIDUOUS SHADE
TREE TO NORTH WESTERN
CORNER

SHRUB AND HERBACEOUS
PLANTING TO SOFTEN
WALLS OF HOUSE

This elevation of a house illustrates how tree and shrub plantings can enhance the architecture of a house.

deciduous to provide adequate shade throughout the heat of summer but to allow plenty of sun during the cold winter months.

Another opportunity to enhance the architecture of the house is to soften the stark walls of the house with foliage by the strategic placement of trees and shrubs beside the walls of the house. Foliage should not be allowed to grow taller than the window ledges, however, between windows and doors the foliage should be taller to effectively soften. An excellent example of such planting is the use of evergreen shrubs to fill the gap between the ground level and the level of a verandah that nearly always looks so much better when softened with foliage.

One further step to enhance the house is to ensure that some tall tree planting is established to the back of the house that, when looking from the front garden towards the house, breaks up the roof line and thereby helps to nestle the house within its setting.

The layout and structure of the garden about the house should directly relate to the architecture of the house. If the house is small and cottage-like, generally the beds about the house should be of an appropriate scale and would therefore be about 3 to 5 feet (1 to 1.5 meters) wide. For a larger house with a larger garden, the scale of garden beds must respond to the scale of house and consequently, could be as wide as 6 to 10 feet (2 to 3 meters) to achieve an appropriate proportion. The shape of such beds is also important as generally, multi-curved beds are inappropriate and beds that are parallel to the line of the house tend to look better. To break up this straight line, the opportunity to sweep the beds out at the corners of the house forming peninsular beds is worth considering.

An excellent example of the layout of the garden relating to and complementing the architecture of a house is the case of a symmetrical front facade where a central axis runs from the hall-way, across the verandah, down the front steps, along a path, into the center of a circular rose garden and ending at a feature tree to the far end of the axis.

Further relationships can be dis-covered between the house and garden by the careful choice of appropriate planting about the house. For example, the colors used within the house may be complemented by the careful choice of colored flowers and foliage adjacent to windows.

Creating space within the garden

One of the most important principles for the design of any garden is the cre-ation of space. The canopy of trees, the edge of garden beds and the structures of walls and hedges all contribute to the creation of space within a garden.

Such garden spaces vary greatly in size and character. For example, a small city garden may consist of only one important space, say of an area of paving surrounded by the walls of adja-cent buildings and softened by the care-ful placement of garden beds to the perimeter of the space, and incorporat-ing one single canopy tree creating a greater sense of enclosure for the space. In a larger garden there may be a series of spaces of various sizes and characters that may be inter-linked with lawned walks and paved pathways. A generous lawn space may be defined by sweeping beds of perennials, shrubs and trees. Off this space a pathway may be

Garden layout and plantings should be designed primarily to enhance the architecture of the house. You can do this by treating your house as part of the whole garden scheme.

discovered which leads into a small enclosed space where a pond is found beneath the canopy of trees, surrounded by water-loving plants. In another direction off the main lawn space there may be a vista to the landscape beyond, framed by the canopy of trees that draws the eye to a distant line of hills.

You could consider creating island beds away from the house. Such a bed could be kidney-shaped and separate the garden from the parkland beyond; through the center of this bed may be a pergola which links the two. You may also be able to create an attractive courtyard or lawn spaces enclosed by the wings of the house, especially if you have a U- or H-shaped house.

Greater interest can be created within the garden by developing a distinct character for each space. This can be done by incorporating a distinctive feature such as a pond, a feature tree, a piece of sculpture or simply a bench seat. Such a feature may be designed to be seen from within the house and therefore becomes the focus at the end of a vista from the house.

One of the easiest ways to go wrong in designing your garden is to add more than your garden really needs to look good. An excellent example of this is the way a spacious lawn can be cluttered by the inappropriate planting of individual shrubs within the lawn space. Not only do these shrubs create a

A lawn space that has been defined by both perimeter and circular flower beds as well as by trees.

maintenance hazard as it is so difficult to stop the grass from growing through the shrub, they also clog up valuable space. In a courtyard environment, the space may be cluttered by too many pots or unnecessary furniture. So, the 'KISS' method often applies when you are designing a garden or courtyard: Keep It Simple, Stupid!

Utilizing the borrowed landscape

Often a property is purchased or a house built because of the view from that position. Such views should be further enhanced by the appropriate layout and planting of the garden. The view from your house and garden may be some excellent trees growing in your neighbor's backyard, a range of hills, an open plain, a lake or harbor, or even a magnificent mountain.

As it is from within the house that the garden is most admired, it is from here that the view of the landscape beyond should be carefully considered. The next most important angles of view are from your outdoor entertaining areas and then from the various vantage points within the garden.

One of the best opportunities to enhance the view to the borrowed landscape is to frame it with appropriate tree planting to create a vista, thus creating a stronger focus towards the particular view and, if the view is panoramic, effectively defining each vista and concentrating the view to the most attractive features of the landscape. An integral part of this framing is the screening of unattractive views.

Another opportunity is to complement the immediate landscape bordering your garden area with the appropriate layout and planting. For example, if your garden is surrounded with native plants, it would be appropriate to mass plant the perimeters of your garden with a variety of native trees and shrubs that would help integrate your new garden with the landscape beyond. If your neighbor has attractive trees in her/his backyard, you could complement these by screening the boundary fence and planting smaller trees with contrasting foliage.

A most important principle to consider is what type of boundary is to be used for the garden. In a country garden situation, often the best boundary fence is one that is as visually insignificant as possible—a simple wire fence is a good choice—so that the eye simply flows through the fence rather than having to jump the fence to get to the landscape beyond. You could also use a ha ha, a retaining wall that forms the edge of a sweeping lawn usually running from the house to the edge of the garden that then adjoins a parkland area. As seen from the house, the front lawn blends with the area beyond and creates the illusion that there is no boundary fence at all. Water can also be used effectively. A pond, strategically placed with the boundary fence of the garden running into either side of it, could form the boundary between the parkland beyond and the garden itself. This can form a beautiful scene, especially when the body of water is enclosed with tree planting to create a vista leading from the house, across a green lawn, over the water to the landscape beyond.

The garden beds

The layout and planting of garden beds is what largely determines a garden's character and style. It is here that the personality of the designer becomes apparent, especially in regard to the degree of formality.

The priority location for garden beds is adjacent to the house, especially at the front of the house. Such planting provides a garden setting for the house and, if appropriately planted and laid out, can significantly enhance the architecture of the building. The next priority location is along the perimeter of the garden boundary. In a town garden where there are neighbors, it can

become a priority to establish beds along all boundaries to provide effective privacy, screening of unattractive views and to soften boundary fences.

Garden beds are required to integrate some of the larger structures in a garden. For example, a swimming pool or tennis court needs to be effectively integrated within its garden setting by strategically placing beds about the perimeter. Also, structures such as a gazebo and garden shed need to be carefully integrated to enhance their architecture or to screen.

Every garden needs to have a utility area. Such an area should not be seen from the main parts of the garden, especially from the house, and so garden beds of evergreen foliage should be used to screen such an area.

To break a large garden into smaller spaces, island beds within a sea of lawn

Garden style is largely determined by the layout and planting of garden beds, which should be integrated with the house.

can be appropriate, especially to define one part of the garden from the next and to frame vistas from within the garden and to the landscape beyond.

Paved areas such as courtyards, driveways and pathways can often be enhanced by the softening effect of foliage established within beds to the edge of such hard paved surfaces. In a courtyard, often large urns and troughs can be used to reduce the starkness, especially at the junction of the paved surface with the courtyard walls. However, well-prepared beds beside the walls of the courtyard are often a better solution than large numbers of containers that can easily dry out in hot weather.

Maintenance can often be reduced by the appropriate placement of beds to accommodate mass planting of groundcovers and shrubs. For example, a steep bank where it is difficult to cut the grass, beneath trees where any other planting would find it difficult to grow and where individual shrubs are grown, it is often an advantage to accommodate such planting within a garden bed.

There should be a good reason for the choice and placement of every plant. By all means, plant species of perennials and shrubs that appeal, but they must be placed to suit the functional and aesthetic considerations that will contribute to the overall design. Two important considerations are the mature height and foliage color of the species chosen.

For most situations it is best to have a clear view of the plants within a bed.

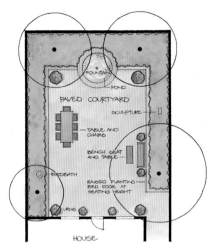

A typical courtyard design.

The lowest plants should be towards the front of the bed with the taller shrubs towards the back. The eventual height of the tallest plants will depend greatly on whether you want to screen a view or enhance it. The taller the foliage, the greater sense of enclosure created, which should also be considered when defining a space.

Although flower color is important, usually perennials and shrubs are only flowering for a short time of the year, and consequently the foliage color of such plants is more significant in terms of creating beautiful scenes. Not only the color but the form and texture of the foliage of the plants should be carefully considered and used to create interest. For example, gray foliage can be contrasted with green, upright foliage with rounded foliage and large-leafed foliage with small-leafed foliage.

It's important to create balanced foliage and flower color. When, for

Including a sunken garden in the overall garden design is a creative way to use changes of level.

example, looking from the house into the garden, ensure that any strong foliage or flower color is balanced by repeating such plants in strategic positions throughout the garden.

The colors of flower and foliage you choose for your garden are very much based on personal taste, and there is no doubt that a garden of mainly pastel colors such as soft blues, pinks and silver foliage can create a very relaxed scene. However, you mustn't hesitate to use some bright colors as long as they are well balanced by adjacent complementary colors. Plants with hot, bright flowers of red or yellow can look excellent when planted in association with plants of cool colors such as blue and purple respectively.

Generally, a garden that has generous drifts of the same plant growing together seems to look more attractive than a garden with a host of individual plants that together create a fussy and spotty look. When planting out perennials, such smaller plants are seen best in groups of at least 5 or 7; when planting medium height shrubs, don't hesitate to plant 2 or 3 of the same species together to form a sweep of foliage and flower; and then larger shrubs can be planted as individual specimens throughout the garden.

Ensure that there is adequate structure within garden beds of predominantly herbaceous perennials in the form of shrub foliage. It is important that your beds look good in every season and consequently, at least a fifth of the shrubs throughout a bed should be evergreen to ensure that there is good structure provided in the cold winter months when deciduous shrubs have lost their leaves and many of the perennials are dormant.

Finally, remember that garden beds are there to present the foliage and flower of plants, not to display mulch or tan bark. So by all means mulch your beds when possible, but the over-all intent is to create a complete ground-cover of attractive foliage.

Utilizing changes of level

Level changes within the garden are an opportunity to add interest in the form of steps, retaining walls and slopes. If well designed and positioned, they can be an attractive feature.

In the case of a sloping site, it is important to create leveled areas about the house and within the garden to make more usable spaces. Especially for outdoor eating, it is convenient to have a leveled lawn space for a table and bench seating; ball games for children can be much easier to play on leveled ground; and a leveled plain of lawn or gravel can look more attractive than a sloping plain.

To create leveled spaces, a balanced cut and fill of the slope is usually the most practical solution. However, there are some circumstances where only one or the other job is needed.

Throughout many areas gardens are created on flat sites. In most cases, it is unnecessary to create changes of level within such sites, for unless it is done very carefully, the creation of mounds and undulations can look contrived as it is not the natural landform of the area. The careful use of plants to create varying heights of foliage within garden beds is usually sufficient to create height differences.

Where mounding is appropriate, it is important to make it look as natural as possible by having mounds rise very gradually to a height no more than 3 to 6 feet (1 to 2 meters) depending on their width and breadth. A good example of where mounding is appropriate is where the natural soil is particularly poor, shallow or mainly clay. In these situations it can be a great advantage to import the soil, especially for the garden beds, so that the proposed planting depends more on the imported soil than the natural soil of the site. This form of mounding is also particularly appropriate to areas that are badly drained as it allows the plants to get above the poorly drained natural soil by having the majority of their feeder roots within the mounded bed.

In a town garden where the traffic of a busy road is adjacent to the garden, mounding is an effective way of reducing traffic noise. Where a strong sense of enclosure is desired for a particular space within the garden, mounding can add to this in association with appropriate shrub and tree planting.

A more subtle approach is the creation of gentle undulations within the garden. This is particularly appropriate in well-drained soil where gentle rises and depressions can be created to complement the overall design of the garden without causing poorly drained depressions. In areas where the soil is not well draining it is important to add soil to the site to create the rises that then form the illusion of depressions as well. To emphasize the slight rise in the garden, it can be mass planted with shrubs and trees to add to its height. Sweeping undulations can be complemented by the sweeping curves of garden beds of the same scale.

You could also create a sunken garden. This could be a rectangular, circular or oval shape which may be approximately 3 feet (1 meter) deep, 15 feet (5 meters) wide and about 30 feet (10 meters) long, depending on the available space. Such a garden provides the opportunity to have a set of attractive steps leading down into it and a retaining wall to form the boundary of the garden.

When linking one level to another with a set of steps, it's important to ensure that the steps are of generous proportions to make them more inviting and comfortable to use. In most small gardens, steps of about 5 feet (1.5 meters) wide can be appropriate, but in larger gardens steps of up to 10 feet (3 meters) wide can look excellent. The choice of material depends largely on what is available and what suits the style of garden you are creating. Stone can be excellent as long as it has good flat surfaces that are comfortable to walk on. Sometimes the material is governed by what the house is built of, which is an opportunity to relate the garden to the house.

To enhance a set of steps, place appropriate urns on either side at the top to indicate the start of the steps. It is important to fill what is usually a fairly unattractive space between the sides of steps and the adjacent retaining wall. This space should be filled with a dense evergreen shrub, preferably the same shrub on both sides, and ideally a scented shrub.

Retaining walls can be an attractive feature in the garden. Generally it is

These steps are designed to merge with the garden.

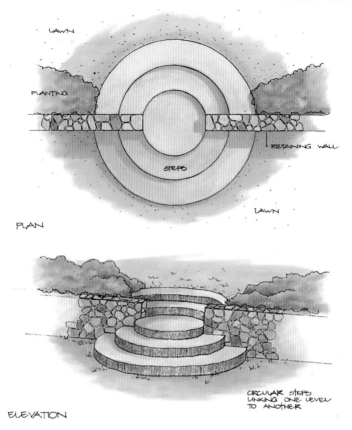

LAWN

PLANTING

RETAINING WALL

STEPS

LAWN

PLAN

ELEVATION

CIRCULAR STEPS
LINKING ONE LEVEL
TO ANOTHER

A plan for circular garden steps that link one level of the garden to another.

more desirable to have retaining walls no taller than approximately 3 feet (1 meter); if the slope requires it, a series of retaining walls to form terraces could be constructed. Such retaining walls are built from a variety of materials and can be softened with plantings at their base and especially from above where it can be allowed to cascade down.

A revetment may be appropriate in your garden. This is similar to a retaining wall except that the slope of the wall is at an angle and that the material the revetment is made from does not actually support the earth behind it but simply covers the steep slope to prevent soil erosion. Such revetments are particularly effective when built of stone.

In many cases where there is a change of level in a garden, it is unnecessary to construct a retaining wall or revetment. The best option may be to form a sloping bank that may be stabilized against erosion by a groundcover of grass or other groundcover that will bind the soil with its root

This colorful planting welcomes the visitor.

system. When such a bank faces the house, the slope presents the plants as seen from the house. Consequently, an attractive tapestry of a variety of flowering groundcovers can be created.

Structures within the garden

An important part of good garden design is the integration of built structures that can most effectively complement and strengthen the overall layout and structure of your garden. Structures such as a gazebo, pavilion or summerhouse; a free-standing pergola, arbor or arch; a colonnade or a wall can all add tremendous interest to your garden.

The pergola, arbor and arch are designed for people to walk beneath and usually designed to support a flowering climber. Pergolas tend to be quite large with a length of at least 10 feet

(3 meters) or more, while an arbor usually has a length of no more than 3 feet (1 meter) and an arch tends to be similar but is curved instead of squared. Such structures can be designed in a multitude of styles. For example, a pergola may be built of columns to suit a formal classical house, another built of sawn timber to suit a more modest timber house and another built of natural un-sawn timbers to suit a less formal house. Structures such as these are excellent value as once they are constructed and an appropriate climber allowed to grow over them, they can become a major feature of the garden and yet take little work to maintain.

Gazebos come in many shapes and sizes and, depending upon their style and use, may be called a pavilion, summerhouse, rotunda or even slab hut.

There is something rather special about being able to sit in the garden surrounded by flowering shrubs and trees with the rain pouring down while you are warm and dry sitting within your gazebo. Gazebos provide an excellent opportunity for outdoor eating and entertaining or just sitting to take in the delights of your garden.

It is important to place structures well away from the main house so they do not compete architecturally with the house. Generally, the style of the structure should be similar to the house, using similar architectural elements such as the same roof and wall cladding. They can often be used to great effect to take full advantage of an especially good vista that may look back towards the house or out to the landscape beyond. A gazebo may be placed

primarily for its visual impact as a feature within the garden to be seen from the house or its primary function may be to help draw people to a particular part of the garden such as the top of the hill where otherwise people may not bother to walk.

The colonnade and garden wall are both structures that can effectively separate one part of the garden from the next. The colonnade is traditionally built of columns, but it can also be simply built of sawn or natural timber posts, which are linked across the top by timber that is then clothed in an attractive climber. The garden wall is obviously a more solid structure that may not only be used to separate one space from another, but also to assist in providing wind protection. Such a wall provides an opportunity for growing

Structures add interest and beauty to the garden.

A peaceful place to sit and contemplate.

espaliered trees on its face or planting flowering climbers to soften the wall's starkness.

Ornamentation in the garden

One of the best opportunities to add year-round interest to your garden and particularly to strengthen your chosen style, is to carefully integrate ornamentation such as urns, a birdbath, sundial and bench seating. Such furnishings are available in a vast array of shapes, sizes and styles, and need to be carefully chosen and placed in strategic positions about the garden to complement and enhance your garden design.

One of the main roles of such ornamentation is to provide focus in the garden, helping to draw the eye into a space as well as physically drawing people into a space to explore it. For

example, a space created by the canopy of trees in a parkland can be greatly enhanced by incorporating to the edge of the canopy within an enclosed part of the space, a dovecote or bench seat.

To ensure ornaments look comfortable, place them in a garden bed where foliage can provide a backdrop and a subtle sense of enclosure for the feature. For example, a bench seat is often best placed to the edge of a bed where it does not need to be moved when the lawn is mown and where people are enticed to sit. A bird bath, decorative urn or piece of sculpture should also be placed reasonably close to the edge of a bed where the planting tends to be lower. And a sundial should be close to the edge of a bed so the time can be read, and in full sun so that it becomes more than a decorative feature.

When choosing the color and size of an ornament, keep in mind the importance of being able to see the feature within its garden setting. If, for example, the backdrop for a seat is dark green foliage, then show off the attractive lines of the seat design by having it a contrasting color such as cream or even a shade of blue. The further away the ornament from view, the clearer this contrast should be and larger the size.

Such features are effective in providing interest and focus throughout the cold winter months when few plants are flowering and there is less foliage about. A sundial to the center of a rose garden is an excellent example in this case for the winter months.

A typical design for a pergola.

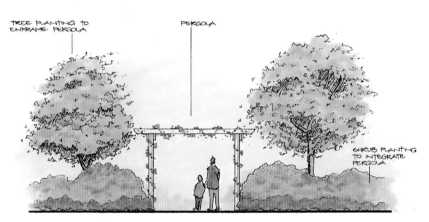

TREE PLANTING TO ENFRAME PERGOLA

PERGOLA

SHRUB PLANTING TO INTEGRATE PERGOLA

ELEVATION

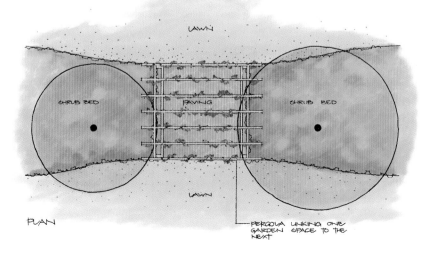

LAWN

SHRUB BED

PAVING

SHRUB BED

LAWN

PLAN

PERGOLA LINKING ONE GARDEN SPACE TO THE NEXT

Urns, tubs, pots and troughs are all containers that can add tremendous interest and style to your garden. Some are quite ornate, others very simple, so they need to be carefully chosen to suit your style. Such containers can draw focus to the entrance of a pathway, indicate the position of steps as seen from above, act as a feature in a garden bed or complement a bench seat by flanking it. Containers are effective where it is impractical to incorporate garden beds to the perimeter of a paved courtyard. Large urns and pots can be carefully placed and planted to provide foliage to soften especially the junction between the paving surface and the wall of the courtyard. Troughs are very effective, especially where space is restricted. The planting of such containers needs to be carefully considered as they do tend to dry out quickly; plants that will withstand dry conditions occasionally are generally preferable.

No matter how large or small your garden is, bench seating should be incorporated; it is so important to invite people to sit and relax in your garden, as it is extraordinary how much more one can observe when sitting as compared to even strolling about a garden. In a courtyard often a table and chairs are provided, but the best designed courtyards are often those where there is also a comfortable bench seat for people to sit in a more casual way. Another opportunity for a bench seat is to take advantage of a particular vista that may not be discovered unless you encourage people to sit.

Ornaments such as this urn need to be carefully selected and placed to complement the garden design.

Sculpture is something that many people shy away from, but if you visit some of the better galleries you may be surprised to discover a piece that really appeals and would look comfortable in your garden. Often bronze or molded stone sculptures of children and/or animals can be easily incorporated.

A note of warning: try to resist the temptation to add more ornaments than is really necessary thus avoiding a contrived look. Generally, a space in the garden should not have more than one piece of ornamentation. Pieces should not be seen too close together as they will only compete with each other visually.

Integrating the swimming pool and tennis court

Some of the most beautiful gardens have been ruined by swimming pools and tennis courts. Too often aesthetic considerations have been overpowered by the convenience of having a pool or tennis court near the house, thereby spoiling a lovely view to the landscape beyond or clogging up a generous space of lawn in front of the main facade of the house.

Yes, you can design a beautiful garden including such things, but it needs to be carefully done. If you are fortunate enough to be able to have a pool and tennis court, place them together so that an active recreational part of the garden is created where both the sight and sounds will not spoil the rest of the garden. When this is done, they can be further complemented by placing a pavilion from which both the tennis and the swimming can be seen and which can provide storage facilities and other conveniences for the pool and court.

Keep in mind that it is as much the noise as the sight of the swimming pool and tennis court that can spoil the garden. There are certain parts of the garden that must be avoided, the entrance garden especially and where an important vista from the house may be spoilt. The best position for this recreational area is where it is well sheltered from the prevailing winds and where the opportunity to watch the tennis looking from the western

This swimming pool blends well with its garden surrounds.

side is possible so that the afternoon sun is not in one's eyes. Space is critical: there is an advantage in having a pool long enough to be able to get some exercise from it by doing laps; and the space obviously must be big enough to accommodate a tennis court, which must run north–south if any serious tennis player is to join you.

The swimming pool itself can be an attractive feature. It is the surrounding child proof safety fence that is the problem. Consequently, the challenge is to make the fence as visually insignificant as possible. This can be achieved by placing the fence well away from the pool, thereby creating a generous sized pool precinct. This area could include both paved and lawn spaces for outdoor entertaining, furniture such as bench seating and tables, a shade structure such as a pergola covered in a deciduous climber or an Italian market umbrella, all surrounded by a generous garden bed that incorporates the pool fence with foliage tall enough on both sides to screen the fence completely. To further reduce the visual impact of the fence, it should be painted black and be of a very simple design, certainly not one with fancy bits along its top that only attract attention to the fence. The planting about the pool should be primarily evergreen to reduce the amount of leaf drop into the pool, particularly during autumn.

Finally, another consideration is the color of the lining of the pool. It is often an attractive option to consider, instead of the traditional sky blue color, a deep blue or bottle green. A black lining is also an option that significantly enhances the reflection of cloud and surrounding trees off the surface of the water.

To effectively integrate the tennis court in your garden, soften the high fence line with tree and shrub planting surrounding its perimeter, except of course to its viewing side where low planting should be placed to soften the junction between the edge of the court and the adjoining garden. To further reduce the visual impact of the court fence, paint both the chain mesh and the posts black, and don't make the fence higher than 3 feet (1 meter) on the viewing side. The surface of the court can successfully be gravel or a dark green super grass.

The utility area

The best designed gardens are those that allow you to invite people for lunch and still leave the laundry on the line. Every garden should have a utility area of some sort that accommodates such necessities as the clothes line, garden shed, compost bins, worm farm and those inevitable bits and pieces that need to be stored somewhere out of the way.

The utility area must not be seen from the house or other parts of the garden. It should be effectively screened by either a bank of evergreen foliage, a tall fence of lattice or a garden wall. The tall bank of foliage could be in the form of a clipped hedge of evergreen shrubs or a wider bed of a variety of evergreen shrubs forming an attractive display. Especially where space is quite limited or if the screening is desired as soon as possible, a lattice fence can be most appropriate. Such can be further enhanced by climbing on it, an attractive flowering evergreen climber. A garden wall also provides opportunities to not only screen the utility area, but to provide the option of growing an espalier on its face. This could be further enhanced by establishing a flower bed to its base.

The location of the utility area needs to be carefully chosen as it is important that, for example, for the convenient use of the clothes line, it has easy access from the laundry, is in a sunny position and it will receive a breeze for drying the clothes. The rest of the facilities in the utility area should be located close to the center of the garden.

The orchard, vegetable and herb garden

There is nothing better than home grown fruit and vegetables. For those who have the space, the work involved in having an orchard, vegetable and herb garden is well worth it.

An orchard of fruit and nut trees can play an integral part in the overall design of your garden. In a town garden the orchard may have only 2 or 3 trees, but in a larger garden it could be as many as 10 to 15 trees. Orchards are usually placed in the back or side garden. Most fruit trees require full sun and excellent drainage to ensure vigorous growth and ripening of the fruit.

The orchard should be made up of fruit trees that do best in your particular climate and soil conditions. For example, in cold climates the dependable fruit trees would include apple, pear, plum and two fruits that are not often seen enough, the fig and mulberry. Of the nut

An apple tree displaying its bountiful supply of fresh fruit.

A well-laid out vegetable garden.

trees, chestnut and walnut may well be worthwhile. In warmer climates the citrus trees do particularly well such as orange, grapefruit, cumquat and lemon, and of the nuts the macadamia and pecan may be grown. Keep in mind that some fruits such as apple and pear require two of the same species for cross pollination.

The vegetable garden should be located closer to the house, in easy reach of the kitchen. A gravel path may link the kitchen door with the vegetable garden and unless designed as a decorative kitchen garden, it should be hidden away from the rest of the garden in the utility area. To ensure good growth of vegetables, the garden should be located

in full sun, well away from root competition from nearby trees and have excellent drainage. For convenience grow each type of vegetable in its own compartment, which may be separated by pathways. Gravel tends not to be good for this as it is difficult to keep the gravel clean when weeding the vegetable garden.

Where space is not an issue, the vegetable garden presents the opportunity to create an impressive feature within the back garden in the form of a decorative kitchen garden. This could be laid out as a large circular garden, divided into radiating segments containing a designed planting of vegetables, herbs and even roses, cut flowers and small fruit trees. As a centerpiece, a sundial could be placed with its pedestal emerging from a sea of thyme.

The herb garden should be located very close to the kitchen where one can dash out and pick a few herbs for the summer salad. Like the vegetables, herbs require full sun and excellent drainage, so an appropriate herb garden may be established in a raised bed or even a series of large pots in a sunny position near the kitchen door.

Water in the garden

One of the most beautiful elements in any landscape is water. People seem to be naturally attracted to water, whether it be still or moving. Since very early times, water has played a major role in the design of gardens, especially in hot climates. If there is the slightest opportunity to include a water feature in your garden, then it should be considered.

There are numerous ways that water can be displayed, so your challenge is to determine what shape, size and style of water feature will best complement your garden design. If the garden has strong formal lines, these can be strengthened by the integration of a circular, square or rectangular pond constructed of molded stone that may feature a jet of water or a tiered fountain in its center. Alternatively, if your design is more informal, this can be strengthened by the inclusion of a more natural kidney-shaped pond that may be edged in rock and generous foliage and overhanging trees with drifts of waterlilies and water iris breaking the surface.

A splendid wall fountain provides an excellent opportunity to break up a stark wall of a house or courtyard. A classic form is where the water appears from the mouth of a lion's head, which falls into a half urn and overflows into a larger pond below. Another water feature particularly suited to a courtyard garden is a raised pond that may be of seating height where people can sit beside the water and dabble their fingers to enjoy the coolness of the water. Such a pond may be square, circular or rectangular and may well integrate with other raised garden beds in the courtyard. Goldfish, waterlilies and water irises would complete the scene.

To enhance a lawn space, a formal pond at may be incorporated. It could be

The challenge is to design a water feature that will best complement your garden design.

round, square or rectangular, large or small depending on the shape and size of the space. A tiered fountain, a tall jet of water or a classic urn on a pedestal brimming with water can make a good central feature.

An unusual but stunning feature is a formal cascade of water that uses a gentle lawn slope within the garden and forms a central axis. Depending on the scale of garden, such a cascade could be 6 to 13 feet (2 to 4 meters) wide and up to 65 feet (20 meters) long.

A fantasy of many a gardener is to have a gentle tumbling stream running through their garden. This is indeed a beautiful scene but must be done carefully otherwise it can look contrived. It may begin at the top of a gentle slope within the garden as a natural spring appearing from beneath rocks, then gently fall through boulders and stone in the form of a series of cascades and waterfalls and end at the bottom in a large natural pond filled with fish and water plants. Even a length of 6 feet (2 meters) can look lovely but one of over 65 feet (20 meters) can be quite spectacular.

Generally such a water feature looks more comfortable located at the lowest part of the landscape. Even a formal pond can look less contrived if placed in the lowest part of its garden setting. If such a low point does not exist, it can be created by careful excavation.

Most water features can be softened by the use of foliage.

Whether they be formal or informal, still or moving, most water bodies can be enhanced by the softening of foliage, either to the edge with shrub and herbaceous planting, or in the water in the form of water iris and waterlilies. Water iris is particularly good because it provides an excellent contrast in form, with its vertical foliage contrasting with the horizontal plain of the water. When establishing such plants, do keep in mind that the water feature is there mainly to display water not foliage, so as a rule of thumb no more than a third of the water surface should be covered in foliage.

Natural looking ponds nearly always look their best when well enclosed with foliage and overhanging trees. People should be able to walk to the water's edge to take a close look and so it is a good idea to have one edge of the pond where the adjacent lawn or paving runs down to it.

A swimming pool can be designed to be an attractive water feature in the garden, especially when the child safety fence is well concealed. The style of your garden may suit a natural swimming hole complete with a cascade of water flowing down rocks surrounded with evergreen foliage to the edge. If your garden is more structured, a simple rectangular pool with carefully chosen paving to its edge and a well-designed summerhouse placed to one end may be appropriate.

One of the great classic country garden scenes is to enjoy a view from the the house, looking across a sweeping lawn to a large pond or small lake that forms a boundary to the garden with parkland on the far side. Such a body of water replaces the need for a fence or even a ha ha, and may be enclosed by the canopy of water-loving trees that frames the view to form a vista to the landscape beyond.

By incorporating a water feature, especially a large natural looking pond, you are also helping to create a healthier and self-sustaining ecosystem in your garden. By having a combination of trees, shrubs, groundcovers and water, you create a habitat for (especially) birds and insects that can help to minimize the problems of pests and diseases within the garden. It provides the opportunity to have ducks that will enjoy your pond as well as the snails in your garden.

Water is not only good for the wildlife but also for you, your family and friends. The sight and sound of still or tumbling water can be so soothing and peaceful in this otherwise bustling world. During the heat of summer, a body of water can have a definite cooling effect both physically and psychologically. To take full advantage of the many attributes that water provides within the garden, a strategically placed bench seat should nearly always accompany a water feature.

The rose garden

The rose is one of the most loved of all flowers. A massed garden of roses can be spectacular. One of the great attributes of roses is that many of those available today will repeat flower from early spring to late autumn, providing excellent value in terms of color throughout much of the year.

However, the rose garden in winter can be very bare and stark, but there are ways to ensure that it continues to look attractive even when there is not a leaf or flower upon the rose bushes. One way is to establish evergreen borders along the edge of the beds of roses using traditional edging plants such as catmint *(Nepeta* sp.), lavender *(Lavandula* sp.), erigeron and box *(Buxus* sp.). This can be taken further in the form of a parterre rose garden where these plants are grown among the roses as well to form a geometric shape. The other main way is to provide a strong structural layout in terms of its shape. Contributing to this layout can be paved pathways within the rose garden, which may be laid out in a symmetrical shape. A central feature may be incorporated such as a sundial on a pedestal or a fountain in the center of a pond.

The formal rose garden may form part of a border to a lawn space that may be rectangular in shape and have a backdrop incorporating a colonnade draped in climbing roses to complement the shrub roses in front. However, a classic way of displaying roses is to design a rose garden that forms a central feature of a large lawn space or even at the center of a circular drive. Depending on the situation, such a rose garden may form an axis that relates directly with the house and then with the rest of the garden. For example, a pathway may extend from the front steps of the house leading into the rose garden and then radiating out in three or four directions. Bench seating may then be incorporated to the edge of the paving between each path.

As flower color is such a dominant characteristic of the rose, you need to be careful that neighboring colors do not clash—such as bright yellow and deep pink—but instead complement each other. Often a blending of colors seems to work well, for example, yellow can be seen beside cream that then blends to white, then to pink, red, apricot and then back to yellow. Such colors should be seen as drifts or blocks of colors within a rose garden to create a tapestry of color. The planting of a formal symmetrical rose garden needs to be especially carefully done to ensure the symmetry is respected and so, often only 2 or 3 colors is appropriate. Also consider the eventual height of the rose bush when planting so that all roses can be seen.

The character of the rose is also a factor to bear in mind. If you have a modern contemporary house and garden, for example, the modern hybrids can look appropriate; however, an older style of house may have its character strengthened by incorporating old garden roses.

Think about placing a bench in the rose garden so that you, your family and friends can sit down and soak up the fragrance and to enjoy the color and form of the roses.

Flower color and the 'character' of a rose are factors to consider when planting a rose garden.

If you decide against a formal rose garden, then integrate them with other shrubs in the garden. This can make it more difficult to maintain the rose bushes. Random and informal pockets of roses can be quite successful in sunny locations. A dense evergreen backdrop will help display the flowers to best advantage.

Children in the garden

One of the main roles of the garden is to provide a safe and pleasant environment for your family and friends. If young children are part of your family, they should be seriously considered in terms of the layout and planting.

One of the most important spaces in a young family's garden is the children's play area. Children love to have their very own special place where they can make a mess with their toys and sandpits without bothering anybody else. So that such a space does not spoil the rest of your beautiful garden, it can be cleverly screened by the strategic planting of evergreen shrubs that can be allowed to grow to a height that hides the untidy toys but still allows a view of the children as they play. One of the best angles of view to determine the height of screening is from the kitchen window. Within this play space, popular equipment such as a log fort, sandpit, a climbing frame and swings could be incorporated and, if the children are very young, it could be convenient to fence off the area to contain the toddlers. To ensure this space is safe and comfortable, deciduous shade should be provided in the form of a tree or pergola, especially to protect against the hot afternoon summer sun. Wind shelter is also necessary and you should avoid growing any thorny shrubs such as roses in the space.

Most children get a real kick out of growing their own flowers and vegetables, especially when the flowers are put on display indoors or the

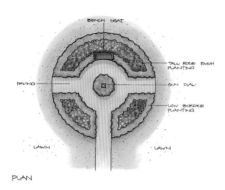

PLAN

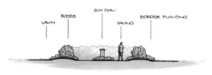

A typical rose garden design.

eventually provide excellent enclosed spaces beneath their canopies where play-houses can be created and where children can hide when playing hide-and-seek. Shrub species that have long thorns or spiky leaves that may be dangerous to little eyes and tender skin should be avoided. Children love brightly colored and scented flowers that, if a bit too bright, could be planted predominantly in their play area.

Birds and butterflies intrigue children by their movement and color, and can be encouraged to be in the garden by growing shrubs that attract them. There is always great excitement when a new nest of eggs is found among the shrubs and trees, particularly when the babies hatch.

Older children love climbing trees, and appropriate trees should be planted with branches that grow close to the ground and are not brittle.

Another opportunity to encourage children to use the garden is to incorporate a large pond, ideally once they have learnt to swim, where they can sail their boats. Such a water feature will also attract birds and encourage them to make their home in your garden. One of the very real dangers of a garden with water is accidental drowning. This risk can be greatly minimized by fencing off a large pond or if it is small, placing a strong black steel mesh cover across the pond, positioned about 50 mm below the surface so as not to spoil the look of the pond. Even this is not safe for toddlers, but is safer than no cover at all.

vegetables reach the dining room table. They should be given their own special little plot where they can get involved with their own garden.

Children love a garden with a great sense of mystery and enchantment. To strengthen a sense of mystery integrate a number of small enclosed spaces where they can hide away and pretend to be in their own little world. Small meandering pathways through large garden beds are exciting to explore and may lead to a bench seat, a piece of sculpture or a decorative urn. Easy access right round the house that can act as a bike or running circuit is something kids love to use, and for their ball games it is crucial that somewhere in the garden there is open lawn space where these games can be played.

You could also grow shrubs that

Toddlers are great explorers and will get anywhere and eat anything. So, do not grow poisonous plants such as oleanders. And don't spread snail bait about the garden.

Putting it all Together

For any worthwhile project, one of the secrets of success is good planning. Although most gardens are planned in a fairly ad hoc manner, a great deal of time and money can be saved by getting it right the first time. You only have to speak to those who have spent a lifetime creating a garden—most regret not having put more time into the initial planning of their garden.

Having considered your desired concept of garden in terms of its basic layout and structure and preferred style,

These roses add charm and beauty to this pergola.

and then considered some of the basic principles of good garden design, it is now time to put it all together as a coherent, integrated design that is perfectly suited to your site and your family.

You may think you have it worked out in your head and that your garden will gradually evolve into a beautiful creation, but the best way to make sure is to put it all on paper first, to illustrate all your ideas on a plan. Your ideas need to be seen in context with other ideas, and sometimes a little compromise is required to ensure it all fits well together.

Preparing the landscape survey plan

The first step is to prepare a drawing that clearly illustrates all the existing features of the area to be developed as a garden. The drawing, drawn to scale, should include all existing trees, rock outcrops, drainage lines, steep slopes, aerial and underground services and any other physical features that may affect your design. Ideally, levels should also be illustrated, but this is not always necessary at the initial planning stage.

Illustrating the priorities as a concept plan

Based on the landscape survey, a concept plan can be prepared that broadly illustrates in bubble diagram form the main use areas. This includes the approximate position of the house and garden boundaries, the entrance garden, the area for the swimming pool and/or tennis court, the utility area, windbreaks, open areas to retain vistas to the landscape beyond, and the position of a water feature.

Developing ideas for the master plan

Having determined the conceptual layout of your garden, it's time to start illustrating to scale the actual location of the main elements of the garden in the form of a master plan. Elements such as the garden entrance, drive, guest's car park, front entrance path, swimming pool and/or tennis court, utility area, all garden beds, the position of trees, lawn, gravel and hard paved areas, structures and water features can all be illustrated.

This can be a gradual process; as design elements are integrated, the garden gradually comes alive to eventually illustrate the complete picture.

Getting the details right for the planting plans

Once you feel you have developed the master plan sufficiently and are happy with the overall design, you can proceed to the next stage of preparing planting plans, drawn to scale, illustrating the planting schemes for each garden bed. The choice of tree species and some of the more detailed decisions such as the choice and position of ornamentation and garden structures can also be illustrated.

It is not until this stage is reached, that you should reach for the shovel to start constructing your garden with confidence.

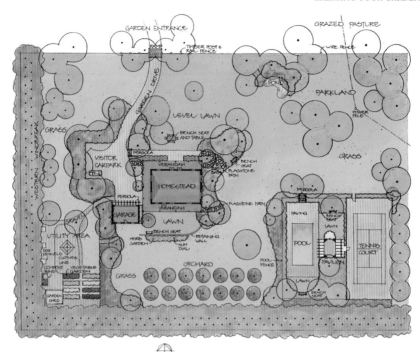

A typical master plan.

Now you are ready to get your thoughts in order and start planning, planting, caring for and enjoying a garden that is the fruit of your labors.

CARING FOR YOUR GARDEN

Healthy, harmless and fun—that's gardening, one of the most creative and rewarding pastimes anyone can do. When you decide to make a garden, you create a living system: a community of individuals brought together from all over the globe, to live with you in your little patch of the world. The fact that plants are as alive as you, they need food and water to live, and they can get sick and need care, is what makes gardening so different from other leisure activities. When you paint a picture, stitch a tapestry or decoupage a box, the materials you use have no life, and when the project is done, your job is finished. But with gardening, you've chosen to become a manager of life, and that's a role that has no end.

A garden is never finished. To look its best and to provide you with the surroundings you dream of, it will always need you. A good garden, even a native garden, cannot look after itself and still remain beautiful and within the bounds you have set for it. It needs a gardener to provide water in the dry

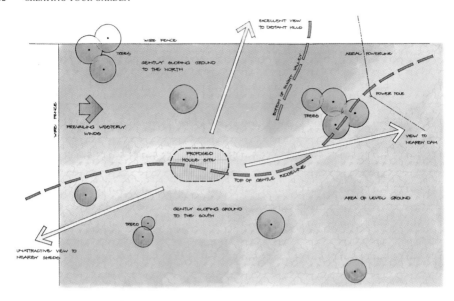

A typical landscape survey plan.

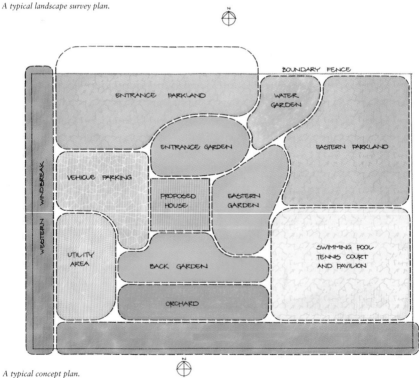

A typical concept plan.

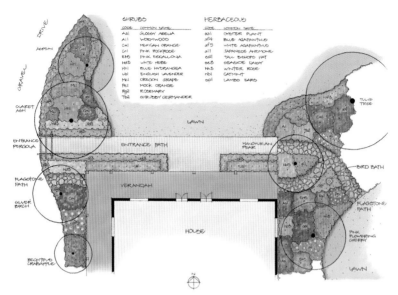

A typical planting plan.

times, to replace used up organic matter and soil nutrients, to prune excessive growth, to control damaging pests and to do countless other little jobs. But when you see the results of what you do, that cool, lush foliage, those exquisite blooms, that ever-improving panorama that adds beauty, amenity and value to your home, you won't wish for the mythical low maintenance garden. In fact, you won't think of gardening as work at all—it will be what you do for enjoyment.

From the Ground, Up

No matter what type of garden you want, the foundation for its success lies in the quality of your soil. Most plants will always grow and look best in deep, fertile, well-drained soil, and this may call for some soil improvements.

Although you will be keen to get planting, it is a mistake to rush into it without first examining the soil and making changes if need be. You can waste a lot of money and growing time by planting up a garden in soil that's just no good.

Soil consists of broken down rocks and the rotted remains of plants and animals, known as organic matter. The rock particles can be very fine, like in clay; medium sized, as in silt; or coarse, such as those in sand. A good soil has a perfect mixture of all these particles held together by the rotted organic matter, which helps the particles clump together into bigger crumbs. This crumbly soil has plenty of space between the particles, into which rainwater seeps and air can penetrate. The roots of plants need both water *and* air,

A spectacular display of summer bedding plants.

and that's why plants do best in a deep, crumbly soil.

If a soil has too many fine particles, they press together tightly and leave little space for water and air. This is known as a clay or heavy soil, and may prove to be awkward. The roots of plants find it physically hard to penetrate clay, and they are also discouraged by the lack of air down there. When dry, a clay soil can set hard, and when a heavy soil finally does get wet, the water it contains is slow to drain away and roots can literally drown. Whether wet or dry, a clay soil will always be heavy and difficult to dig. On the plus side, clay contains a lot of minerals that plants need, so a soil that contains a proportion of clay is highly fertile and desirable. Clay also helps bigger, sandy particles to clump together.

At the other extreme, if a soil has too many coarse particles, it will resemble sand. Sandy soils are very easy to dig and have the advantage of being very well drained so there's no chance of roots drowning through overwatering or excessive rain. But sand is not particularly nutritious for plants, and is so free-draining there's the constant danger of plants dying through lack of water. You have to water a sandy soil often to keep the garden going, but because frequent watering washes nutrients down through the soil and out of reach of the roots, you also have to fertilize much more often. Sand particles, being coarse, will open up and aerate clay.

To find out what type of soil you have, and whether or not it has enough organic matter, use a spade to dig up a section about 4 inches (10 centimeters) deep. Is it easy to dig or hard and stony? Easy digging is a good sign. If it contains adequate organic matter, it will be quite dark and moist, and there may be worms or tunnels to indicate their recent presence. Your soil should also have a pleasant, earthy smell: a sour smell could mean it drains badly.

Next, take a handful of the soil, moisten and rub between the fingers. If it feels very gritty, it contains a lot of sand, but if it is smooth and silky, it will have a high clay content. Another test is to try and form a long cylinder from the moistened soil. The more clay the soil contains, the easier it will be to form a plasticine-like ribbon—sandy soils just fall apart. If you can form some sort of cylinder, but not a long one, and if the soil seems crumbly, but doesn't fall apart completely, you could be in luck and have good soil that will only need annual mulching with rotted organic matter to keep it that way.

How to improve soil

No matter what kind of soil you have, the most important thing you can do to improve it, is to add organic matter. And the worse the condition of the soil, the more you should add before you plant anything.

Organic matter is the vital ingredient of all fertile soils. Without it, your garden won't grow well. Organic matter is anything that was once alive and, in soils, is usually the rotted fallen remains of plants (leaves, bark, flowers or fruit) and animal droppings. When

these things fall to the ground and rot, they provide food for countless soil organisms, such as worms and bacteria, the actions of which further enrich and aerate the soil. Eventually, organic matter rots into humus, a black, slightly greasy substance that binds the soil particles together into the desirable bigger crumbs when worked into the soil by worms and other organisms. Humus also improves the moisture holding capacity of the soil and provides plants with essential nutrients.

Unfortunately, adding organic matter is not a once-only process. You will find that one application will not be enough to turn heavy clay into healthy, friable soil, or dry sand into moist, crumbly earth, because as organic matter rots it greatly decreases in volume. It is also depleted from soils by the action of plants and soil organisms. To create a fertile base on which to build a garden, applications each 2 or 3 months apart may be needed, but this is most easily done before any plants are placed in position. Another application and then another and another will begin the process that turns bad soil into good, but it requires patience on your part and may mean delaying your visit to the nursery.

If you have heavy clay soil, it can be worth treating it with natural gypsum. This is a powdery mineral that, when applied to some clays and watered in, makes the clay particles clump together into crumbs that are easier to work. You must use natural gypsum, which is a sandy brown color, not builders gypsum, which is white. Do remember that gypsum does not work on all types of clay. To find out whether or not it will have any effect on your clay, try the following. Firstly, place a small piece of dry clay into a glass of distilled water or rainwater, and leave undisturbed for 24 hours. Secondly, if the the water turns cloudy around the fragment, gypsum will help. Thirdly, if the water stays clear, do the test again but use a moist fragment of clay. Fourthly, If the water turns cloudy this time, gypsum will help prevent the clay soil disintegrating in wet weather. Finally, if no discoloration occurs, gypsum will not help.

You do not have to dig the gypsum in, watering it in will do. Alternatively, there are liquid products that can be watered onto clay soil, which do a similar job. They are sold under a number of brand names, and take about 8 weeks to be fully effective. If you use either gypsum or the liquid products, adding organic matter afterwards is still necessary.

What organic matter to use

There are many types of commercial organic matter available and most nurseries will have a selection of bagged material. Trouble is, it's quite expensive to buy it this way, especially in the volume you will need. It is better to buy it in bulk from a landscape supply company, or load up your trailer with free supplies that are sometimes available.

Horse, cow or sheep manure are all good, as is compost, lucerne hay, grass clippings, chipped-up prunings and fallen leaves. Waste from food processing plants, such as pea trash, rice hulls, peanut shells and sugar cane waste is sometimes available in regional areas for little or no cost. Riding schools, racetracks and stables can be a good, often free source of horse manure, and if you're friendly with a livestock farmer, you'll get all the manure you want, so long as you do the shovelling.

As a rule, don't apply organic matter while it is fresh or green. Instead, pile it up and let it rot down for a month or

Below: Three samples of mulch: from left to right, cow manure, blood and bone, and compost.

Bottom: Keeping the soil mulched is the best and most natural way to keep it fertile, free-draining and healthy.

more. This makes it more beneficial to the soil and won't cause nutrient deficiencies, which can happen if you use unrotted organic matter.

Apply organic matter over moist soil and try to build it up in layers of different material, each layer about 2 inches (5 centimeters) thick. It isn't necessary to dig it in, soil organisms will take care of that, but if you plan to apply a lot of organic matter, over a poor clay soil for example, you will eventually raise the level of your garden and may need to build low retaining walls. In general, building up over clay is a better idea than digging down into it, but you do have to consider retaining the new soil level.

If you already have good soil and an existing garden, mulch around your plants with rotted organic matter at least once a year, but preferably twice, in spring and summer. Keep the mulch away from the trunks of plants, since it can cause problems with some species.

Remember, no matter what type of soil you have, keeping it mulched with rotted organic matter is the best and most natural way to keep it fertile, free-draining and healthy. It will also reduce or eliminate the need to apply fertilizer.

Compost: the mulch you make yourself

In nature, organic matter is added to the soil with every falling leaf and twig. You too can use your own garden and kitchen waste as the raw materials for making compost—probably the best soil improving mulch there is. By composting garden and kitchen waste you will also help reduce the mountains of garbage the city authorities have to dispose of every day, and that's good for taxpayers and for the environment.

Compost is fully decayed organic matter. It is dark, crumbly, sweet smelling and bears no resemblance to the ingredients that were used to make it. Your garden can supply lawn clippings and fallen leaves, flowers and fruit, and if you invest in a power shredder or mulcher you'll also be able to turn woody prunings and twigs into useable compost. Sticks, twigs or prunings should not be used without shredding them first, because they take too

Diversity in plantings attracts a diversity of wildlife.

long to break down. From your kitchen, you can recycle vegetable and fruit waste, coffee grounds, tea leaves and even the contents of your vacuum cleaner, but don't include bones, meat scraps or dairy products.

To make compost, you can use one of the many commercial tumblers or bins on the market, or simply pile the material up on a patch of soil in a corner out of the way. If you choose the latter, it is a good idea to have a pile of soil nearby, so that you can cover the material you add with a thin layer of earth. This helps produce better compost by introducing another ingredient; it also prevents smells and deters flies and animals. You should also cover the heap to prevent it from becoming too wet during rainy weather, and to retain moisture when it's dry.

The best compost is made from a number of different materials laid thinly on top of each other. For example, a layer of shredded prunings covered with a layer of grass clippings, followed by layers of leaves, manure, kitchen scraps, more prunings, soil, straw and so on. Periodically turn the heap so that everything gets a chance to be inside where all the serious rotting goes on. While turning, check the moisture level. If it is sodden, it is too wet, and if it is dry it should be moistened. Heaps that are too wet will smell, while dry heaps take forever to rot.

The bigger and faster you can build your heap, the sooner it will decay into compost. That is because big heaps generate their own heat as they rot

(you can see them steaming), which not only speeds the decomposition process, but also destroys harmful organisms within the heap. Then when a heap is as big as it should be, you can start another while the first is rotting down.

You can use the compost when it is completely broken down into a soil-like consistency. You should not be able to identify any remains of the ingredients used. Spread it thinly, about 2 inches (5 centimeters) deep, but be careful not to pile it up against the trunks or stems as this can be harmful to some plants.

If you only have a small garden or don't produce a lot of green and kitchen waste, a worm farm can be a viable alternative to a compost heap. A worm farm will not produce large quantities of compost, perhaps only the equivalent of a bag or two a year, but it is a good way to get rid of leafy kitchen waste without filling up your bin.

Essentially, all that is involved is the feeding of compost worms with cut-up or shredded kitchen waste. As the worms consume the organic matter, it is passed out as worm castings that fall to the base of the farm. A rich liquid is also produced and this can be collected and watered onto plants. Eventually, the castings build up and can be spread out around the garden. The worm farm itself is about the size of a fruit box, although bigger models are available.

Which plants to grow?

Choosing plants is always exciting and fun, but what you choose now will have a big impact on the later look and performance of the garden. It is a mistake to rush into planting without a clear idea of the look or style you want to achieve. If you were putting in a new kitchen, you would never go out and buy the fittings without measuring first and without an idea of the colors and style you wanted, and it should be the same with your garden. How to plan your garden is covered elsewhere in this book, and you should read that section before buying any plants.

When you do get to the nursery, the choice will probably be huge, but just because something is available in the nursery does not necessarily make it a good choice for you. The thousands of plants gardeners can select come from all over the world, very often from climates very different from our own. Climate is important to plants: they cannot escape from it, and the climate of their natural range will often have caused them to grow the way they do. For example, if a plant comes from a climate where most of the rain falls in winter but summers are very hot and dry, most likely it will grow during autumn, winter and early spring, and go completely or partially dormant in summer to escape the extreme heat and dryness. If you live in a place where summers are rainy and humid but winters are dry, the plant won't

Plants that come from your own region or other parts of the world with a similar climate will be the best plants to grow in your garden.

grow very well. It will become stressed and weakened by the crazy climate, and such plants are much more liable to attacks by pests and diseases.

The very best plants for you will be those that come from your own region or other parts of the world with a similar climate. They will expect the rainfall you get, when you get it, and will not be put out too much by the highest and lowest temperatures you experience. On the opposite page and overleaf there is a Hardiness Zone Map that divides the world into zones based on the average minimum temperature experienced. The zones were originally devised by the US Department of Agriculture, but have been widely adopted around the world. Many gardening books, including this one, refer to the zones in which individual plants will succeed, and you should familiarize yourself with your zone number for future reference.

Another good way to determine which plants will succeed in your garden is to take a walk around your neighborhood. Plants that are thriving in neighboring gardens will obviously do well for you too. Most gardeners will be more than happy to tell you the name of a plant, if they know it, and would certainly let you take a piece of it to a nursery for identification if they don't. Botanic gardens and nature reserves are also excellent places to see plants, and because they are usually labeled, identification is no problem. Take notepad and pen with you so that you can write down the dimensions of

any plants you like, because their ultimate size may prove not fit the use you have in mind.

Do not underestimate the size to which a plant will grow, and remember that it is not just the height but also the spread that you must take into account. When shopping for plants, keep it clear in your head how much space you have available: the plan you made will be invaluable at this point. All plants look small and harmless in the nursery, but don't forget that gardening is about managing living things that will grow bigger, sometimes much, much bigger. If you put a lot of small plants together in a given space so that it looks full, you will soon have an overgrown mess, much of which will have to be pulled out to make room for the remainder to grow. That is a lot of work, not to mention a waste of money. Better to plant widely, with the ultimate size in mind—you can always fill the gaps with short-lived annual flowers while the permanent plants are growing.

A good garden isn't just pretty to look at, it serves to make the land around the house more liveable by providing privacy, shelter and shade. It can even make a home more comfortable by shading an otherwise hot wall for example, or directing cold, blustery winds away from the house. Trees will be essential for many of these structural uses, whether they are big specimens or just tree-like shrubs. Again, think carefully before you choose. If you live in the country or on a large property,

HARDINESS ZONE MAPS

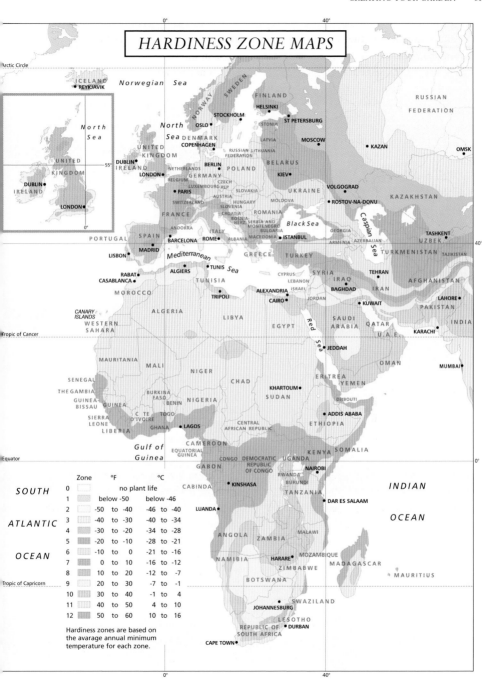

Zone	°F	°C
0	no plant life	
1	below -50	below -46
2	-50 to -40	-46 to -40
3	-40 to -30	-40 to -34
4	-30 to -20	-34 to -28
5	-20 to -10	-28 to -21
6	-10 to 0	-21 to -16
7	0 to 10	-16 to -12
8	10 to 20	-12 to -7
9	20 to 30	-7 to -1
10	30 to 40	-1 to 4
11	40 to 50	4 to 10
12	50 to 60	10 to 16

Hardiness zones are based on
the avarage annual minimum
temperature for each zone.

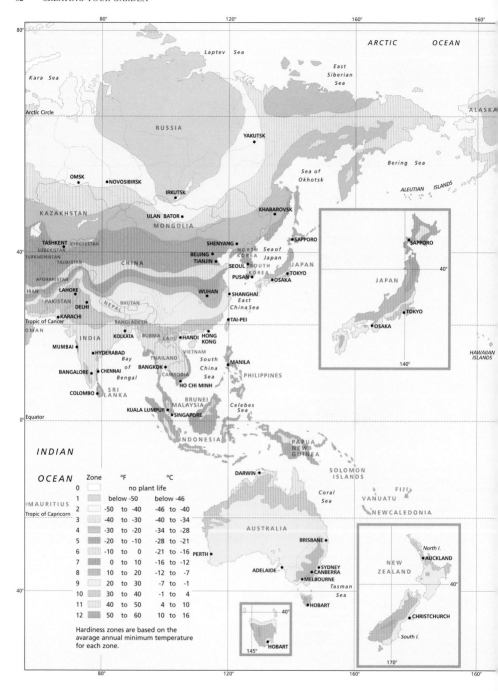

Zone	°F			°C		
0	no plant life					
1	below -50			below -46		
2	-50	to	-40	-46	to	-40
3	-40	to	-30	-40	to	-34
4	-30	to	-20	-34	to	-28
5	-20	to	-10	-28	to	-21
6	-10	to	0	-21	to	-16
7	0	to	10	-16	to	-12
8	10	to	20	-12	to	-7
9	20	to	30	-7	to	-1
10	30	to	40	-1	to	4
11	40	to	50	4	to	10
12	50	to	60	10	to	16

Hardiness zones are based on the
avarage annual minimum temperature
for each zone.

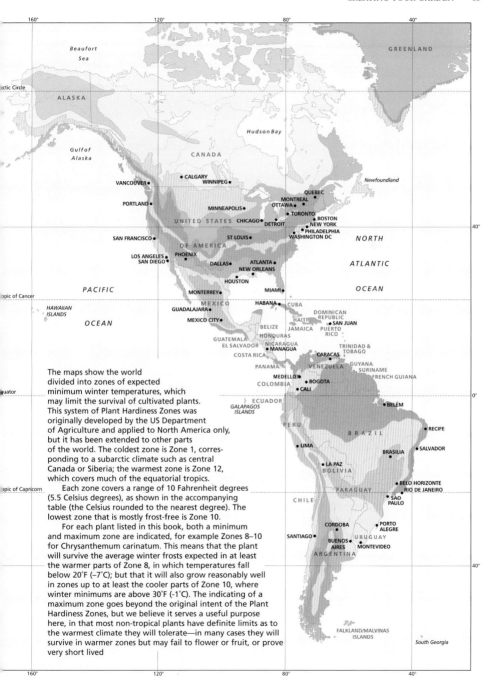

The maps show the world divided into zones of expected minimum winter temperatures, which may limit the survival of cultivated plants. This system of Plant Hardiness Zones was originally developed by the US Department of Agriculture and applied to North America only, but it has been extended to other parts of the world. The coldest zone is Zone 1, corresponding to a subarctic climate such as central Canada or Siberia; the warmest zone is Zone 12, which covers much of the equatorial tropics.

Each zone covers a range of 10 Fahrenheit degrees (5.5 Celsius degrees), as shown in the accompanying table (the Celsius rounded to the nearest degree). The lowest zone that is mostly frost-free is Zone 10.

For each plant listed in this book, both a minimum and maximum zone are indicated, for example Zones 8–10 for Chrysanthemum carinatum. This means that the plant will survive the average winter frosts expected in at least the warmer parts of Zone 8, in which temperatures fall below 20°F (–7°C); but that it will also grow reasonably well in zones up to at least the cooler parts of Zone 10, where winter minimums are above 30°F (-1°C). The indicating of a maximum zone goes beyond the original intent of the Plant Hardiness Zones, but we believe it serves a useful purpose here, in that most non-tropical plants have definite limits as to the warmest climate they will tolerate—in many cases they will survive in warmer zones but may fail to flower or fruit, or prove very short lived

Here, the house and garden are well integrated.

huge trees won't cause you or your neighbors any problems, so long as they are wisely sited, but in the suburbs things are different. Trees that are too big will cast a lot of shade, possibly unwanted shade onto your land or your neighbor's land. They can also block views and light, which can lead to nasty disputes. In most instances, there is no need to plant very big trees in the suburbs anyway. Small to medium-sized trees or shrubs can usually provide all the privacy, shelter and shade you need without causing problems for anyone.

The amount of sun or shade an area gets can often determine which plants you should grow there. Some plants demand full sun, others like full shade and the remainder like something in between. It is vital, therefore, that you familiarize yourself with the parts of the garden that are shady, and note how long the shade lasts and when it occurs. Remember that the sun moves

from east to west during the day and is higher in the sky during the summer; areas that are shady now may not be later in the season, and vice versa.

As the garden grows, some of the areas that were once sunny will fall into shade, and the plants that you put there may begin to suffer. Those specimens that expect full sun will grow long and spindly in shade and they will hardly flower at all. If you want to avoid the expense of replacing failing sun lovers with shade lovers, it is quite easy to predict where shade will begin to develop as the garden matures. If you plant a tree, or group of trees and shrubs, sooner or later an area of shade will be created. Anticipate that eventuality by planting cheap, disposable plants, such as annual flowers or vegetables, between the trees and shrubs. As the shade increases these can be replaced with permanent shade lovers. A final thing to consider when choosing plants is their flower color and the appearance of their foliage. If you buy plants at random, just because you like the look of them in the nursery, the finished result is likely to be a gaudy garden with an unappealing mix of clashing colors. However, if at the planning stage you decide on a color scheme for the whole garden or just for different parts of it, you will have some guideline when you go to the nursery. It is also worth remembering that most nurseries sell plants when they are in flower. If all your plants are bought at the same time, based only on the flower display you can see, your garden will only ever flower at that time of year. There will be nothing in bloom for the rest of the year.

The color, shape and texture of foliage should also be kept in mind. Foliage is with us when the flowers fade, and very appealing patterns can be created in the garden by combining various types of foliage in the one area.

What makes a good plant?

In the nursery, look for plants that are in proportion to the size of their pots, which are well clothed with healthy looking leaves. The bigger a plant the bigger its roots, and when a root system of a big plant is crammed into a small pot, it becomes congested and may never develop properly when planted out in the garden. Very often, the smaller, cheaper version of the same plant, the roots of which are not congested, will establish itself more quickly in the ground than the bigger, more expensive specimen with pot-bound roots. So how do you tell if a plant is potbound? Look at its overall condition. It should not be yellow or

A well-designed garden will provide shade, shelter and privacy.

sparse, and there should be no roots protruding from the drain hole. The plant itself should not be much bigger than the pot.

The foliage should look healthy, but what constitutes the right shade of green can depend on the plant itself—some types have lighter colored foliage than others, so compare the plant with others of the same species. Finally, beware of bargain or sale-priced plants. Often they are too far gone to be saved—you will always be better off with a quality plant.

Make your own plants

It is possible to grow a garden without spending a lot of money. With a little practice, you can propagate your own plants by taking cuttings, sowing seeds, making layers or dividing existing plants.

Clearly, it is slower than buying existing plants, but it's a lot cheaper, and many people enjoy the satisfaction that comes from creating and growing a new plant. Before you can do this, however, you have to begin with the plant you want to propagate. It might be in a friend or neighbor's garden, or it might be a plant you already have. If you intend to create a mass planting or a hedge, you could buy a single plant from a nursery, then make many more plants from that.

CUTTINGS
Most plants are propagated by cuttings, which involves taking a small section of stem and inducing it to form roots of its own. The best times to take cuttings of most plants is spring, early summer and early autumn, but those species that lose their leaves in winter can also be rooted in winter.

To take cuttings, you will need a pair of clean, sharp secateurs, a bag of seed-raising or propagating mix (available from nurseries), hormone rooting powder or gel, a slim stick, clean pots, clear plastic bottles or bags and some small stakes or coat-hanger wire.

The target plant should be well watered the day before so that its stems are firm. You should take the cuttings early in the day. Before you start, have everything you need set up in a shady place, with the pots already filled with the moistened seed-raising or propagating mix. Then, using the secateurs, make the cuttings about 6 inches (15 centimeters) long, taking pieces from strong healthy growth. Next, take a mixture of tips and side-shoots, and take more than you think you need to allow for failures, and work quickly. When you have gathered the cuttings, process them immediately.

To process, strip the lower foliage away, to leave just a few sets of leaves at the top. Then, remove any flowers, flower buds or seeds, and if the remaining leaves are big, cut them in half crosswise to reduce water loss. Dip the severed ends of the cuttings into the rooting hormone, then use the slim stick to make little holes in the propagating mix. Next, insert the cutting into the hole about a quarter of its length deep, firm down the soil, and if the pot is very small, place one cutting

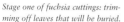

Stage one of fuchsia cuttings: trimming off leaves that will be buried.

Stage two: inserting the cuttings in a pot of sharp sand with just a little compost.

Stage three: covering the cuttings with a mini-greenhouse—a plastic bottle.

in it only. In a big pot, you can place several cuttings together, but do not cram them—they must be separated later. Water the cuttings in well, then cover with the clear plastic bags or bottles. Finally, use the stakes or coat hanger wire to make a supporting framework that will keep the plastic bag or bottle away from the cuttings.

The cuttings should be placed in a sheltered, warm spot that stays shady all day, but is well lit. They will require very little water, but check them periodically to ensure that the propagating mix remains lightly moist, not sodden. It will take 4 to 6 weeks for roots to develop, and a sure sign of success is new growth. When roots have formed, gently unpot the cuttings, and then pot them up individually into bigger containers so that they can be grown on to planting size. Gradually expose the rooted cuttings to greater amounts of sun, but be patient and do not put

them straight into full sun, even if they are sun lovers, or they will burn.

Should the plant you want to strike from cuttings be a long way from your home, here's a way to keep them fresh during the trip back. Take the cuttings as usual and as quickly as you can, then gather them together and place them on a few sheets of wet newspaper. Wrap up the paper and place the whole package in a plastic bag. If you have one, place the parcel of cuttings inside a cooler with some ice, and take them home. If you have no cooler, put the parcel of cuttings under the seat of the car, or on the floor that is kept in the shade. On your arrival home, the cuttings should be processed immediately.

SEED

Some plants don't strike easily from cuttings, but may grow readily from seed. To propagate from seed, you will need a bag of seed-raising mix, and pots, punnets or seedlings trays. Collect the seed when it is fully ripe, and remove it from its outer casing. Typically, this is a fleshy fruit, a pod or a hard shell, but some plants, for example, palms, retain their seeds in woody capsules that can be hard to open. Before leaving the pod or shell to propagate, try to crack them slightly.

Sow the seed into pots, punnets or trays of seed-raising mix, then cover thinly with some mix—by no more than the thickness of the seed. Moisten them with a fine mist spray and place the container in a warm and sheltered, but not sunny spot. Keep the seed-raising mix lightly and evenly moist. Most seeds germinate within 2 weeks, but some species are much slower.

When the seedlings emerge, allow them to grow until they are big enough to handle. Then, using the handle of a teaspoon, very gently lift each seedling out, and pot them up into small individual pots for growing on. Gradually expose them to more and more sun if they are sun-loving plants.

This series of photographs shows the way a courtyard garden changes across the four seasons. Clockwise from top left: Spring, Summer, Winter, Autumn.

LAYERING

This process yields a few, relatively big plants, which are ready to go straight into the garden. Layering exploits the ability of many plants to make roots where their branches touch the ground, but it is only suitable for plants with pliable, arching branches or those with low branches.

To make a layer, select a branch that can be bent to the ground. Where it touches the ground, use a sharp knife to make a cut part way through the stem. Don't cut the stem off. Next, bend the stem up to open the wound and push a matchstick into the cut to hold it open. Finally, bury the wounded section and hold it down with a brick or tent pegs. Because the stem is not cut through, the branch is still fed by the parent plant, and remains alive and healthy. Leave it for at least 3 months, then check for roots by removing the brick and gently tugging on the branch. If it remains fast, roots have formed. The stem can be detached from the parent and the rooted layer dug up for immediate planting elsewhere.

Another form of layering, called air layering, is useful where the stem cannot be brought down to ground level. With this method, select a reasonably large branch, not too huge or the root system produced will not be able to support all the foliage, then use a razor-sharp knife to cut thin, vertical strips of bark from the stem. Each strip should be 1–2 inches (25–50 millimeters) long, and 1 inch (25 millimeters) wide. Do this carefully, since your aim is to remove only the top layer of bark so that the green cambium tissue beneath the surface is exposed. You must leave strips of uncut bark between the strips as this will support the top growth while roots grow in the cut sections.

After the cuts have been made, wrap the wounded section with moist sphagnum moss, available from nurseries, and hold the moss in place with a sheet of clear plastic that is tied firmly to the branch above and below the wounded area. You should end up with a bulge of moist sphagnum beneath the plastic cover, which should be left in place for 6 weeks in summer, or several months in winter, until plenty of roots can be seen in the sphagnum moss. When the roots are clearly visible, detach the rooted section with secateurs or loppers, and pot the new plant up. Place it in shade at first, and keep it moist and misted with water as its root system will be fairly small. Once it displays strong growth, it can be planted out.

DIVISION

Many small, non-woody plants and some multi-stemmed shrubs multiply themselves into an expanding clump. When these clumps are a good size, they can be dug up and divided into many smaller plants: each division has its own roots and is ready for replanting. The best time to divide a plant is when it is dormant, usually from late autumn to late winter. In the case of evergreens, division is best just before the new growing season begins. Use a garden fork and spade to dig up the clump, shake off as much soil as possible and divide the plant into smaller sections. Some can be simply pulled apart, others need to be cut, but it will be clear where the divisions are. The new plants should be replanted immediately, or can be potted up for later planting. Clump-forming plants bought at a nursery can also be divided before planting into the garden, and this can be a good way to get a lot of plants cheaply. Division is useful if you want to grow a border of one particular plant or a large area of it.

How to plant

If plants are not placed in the soil properly, there's a good chance that they won't grow well or they will become unstable. Since it's the topsoil that contains most of the nutrients, air and water that plants need, this is where most of the feeder roots will be found—spread out sideways in the top 12 inches (30 centimeters) of soil. Allow for this by always digging a wide planting hole, about 3 times wider than the pot in which you bought the plant. The hole need be no deeper than the pot, but it's a good idea to break up and loosen the soil in the bottom of the hole to allow for easy root penetration. Similarly, you should scar the sides of the hole, especially if the digging has caused a shiny, almost glazed surface on the walls of the hole.

Unpot the plant by holding its main stem in one hand and punching down on the rim of the pot with the fist of the other. First, check the rootball. If roots circle around the base and the sides of the rootball, and it seems jammed with roots, it is vital that they are released before planting. Any circling roots should be pulled out and uncurled, and any that are overlong or have been damaged by the process should be trimmed. Next, use a sharp knife to score several vertical cuts down the sides of the rootball as this encourages new roots that will grow laterally into the soil. Some of the excavated soil should then be crumbled into a mound in the center of the hole, and the rootball placed on top. Spread the freed roots downwards and outwards and adjust the height of the mound so that the plant's mainstem will be the same depth in the soil as it was in the pot. Finally, refill the hole with the crumbled, excavated soil, tamping down as you go so as not to leave air pockets. Do not compress the soil heavily.

Now the hole has been refilled, sprinkle a sparse ration of slow release fertilizer below the outer edge of the foliage canopy, and water in well. If you like, use some of the excavated soil to form a raised wall around the plant to act as a temporary reservoir. To finish, cover the soil with a layer of rotted organic matter such as old manure, compost or straw. It is not a good idea to refill the hole with organic matter or to mix a lot of organic matter in with the excavated soil, because in nature, organic matter is found on top of the soil, not under it. If your soil is too poor to support the plant, improve all

Layering a magnolia; the branch chosen is one growing from the base of the tree.

Bending the branch to the ground, so that a short section can be buried.

The layer needs to be held immobile; here bent wires are pinning it to the ground.

of the soil—don't just create wells of fertility in the planting hole or the roots will have no inclination to spread out through the soil. Worse still, if you have clay soil that drains slowly, filling the planting hole with organic matter, which is water retentive, could create a puddle and drown the plant.

After planting, water in well and keep the soil evenly moist for at least the first year until the plant is well established. Staking is neither a necessity nor a good idea, because by providing support against natural wind action, the plant is not encouraged to develop a stronger trunk or root system. When the stake is removed, the plant could blow over in even a moderate wind. If you live in a very windy area, staking could be considered necessary but the plant should be tied loosely to the stake using a stretchable material such as a stocking. Aim to remove the stake as soon as the plant is established. In

exposed places, plants respond to wind by growing away from it, and you should expect and accept the same.

Garden care

WATERING

There is no formula that tells you how often you should water. Watering depends on a number of outside influences that change from garden to garden. These influences include how well the soil drains and how moisture retentive it is, the slope of your land, the amount of sun it receives, the warmth of your climate, how much rainfall you get and when you get it, the types of plants you are growing, and the strength and frequency of wind.

In general, you should always aim to keep the soil evenly moist. But that is a lot easier said than done. You don't want to waste water by watering unnecessarily, but neither do you want to stress the garden by keeping it in

Digging the planting hole, deep and wide enough to hold the roots of the rose bush without crowding.

With the bush in place, soil is being filled around its roots. The next stage is to water it.

After watering, the bush is being given a mulch of compost. This is a warm-climate planting.

permanent drought. Luckily, plants do not just drop dead from lack of water, they warn you with their appearance. Wilting is the most obvious sign. Also, leaves will lose luster or begin to shrivel, and the lowest leaves may start to die. Wilting point will naturally be reached more quickly in summer than in winter, but if you take the time to observe your garden's behaviour between waterings, you will soon get a good idea of how long it takes to dry out.

Water needs to be applied generously so that the soil is wetted deep down. Infrequent, deep waterings, equivalent to say 1–2 inches (25–50 millimeters) of rain, is both more water efficient and better for the plants than light sprinklings, which only wet the surface layers. Water that does not penetrate deeply is wasted, as it quickly evaporates from the soil. Furthermore, it encourages plants to develop surface roots, which are then vulnerable to drying out.

The best way to water deeply is to use a sprinkler or a fixed watering system. Watering by a hand held hose usually results in light watering because it just isn't practical to stand there long enough to deliver the amount of water needed. If you are patient and enjoy hand watering, go ahead, but do the following test to ensure that you are applying enough water. Before you water, dig down into the soil at several places around the garden. Make the holes about 8 inches (20 centimeters) deep. Look carefully at the exposed soil from all levels, and remember its condition. If it is already moist you need not water. After this, refill the holes and water as usual, and keep a note of your start and finish time. An hour after you finish watering, dig more holes of the same depth in different places, and compare the condition of the soil. See how far the water has penetrated. If it goes down deep, you are doing the right thing.

You should also do a time and volume test if you use sprinklers. With this test you will learn how long your sprinkler must run to deliver a known depth of water. Place several straight-sided glass jars on level ground in various places within the sprinkler's reach, putting some of the jars in the open and some under foliage. Before you turn the sprinkler on, take note of the time and whether the tap is turned on full or not. Exactly one hour later, turn the sprinkler off and measure the depth of water in each of the jars. This will tell you how much water you are applying per hour, and which parts of the garden it is reaching. Next time you water, you will know how long to run the sprinkler to apply a certain amount of water.

To minimize water wastage, only use sprinklers during the cooler parts of a still day, ideally in the morning. Be careful to place the sprinkler where it will throw water onto plants only, not walls, paths or drives. Sprinklers that throw water in a circular pattern are the least efficient as there are always corners that are not watered. Oscillating sprinklers, which throw in an infinitely variable rectangle, can be set quite precisely, so wastage is minimized. Once you know how long your sprinkler needs to run to deliver the required depth of water, fitting a timer to the tap lets you set the required time and go away. The time tap will turn the water off after the period has elapsed, so there's no wastage if you are the forgetful type.

A fixed watering system is another way to water efficiently and, when laid out properly, it can dramatically reduce water use. Manufacturers of these systems produce detailed brochures that describe how to plan a system for your garden and how to install it. A specialist irrigation retailer or a large garden center will supply the brochures and also offer you expert advice.

However, do not imagine that a watering system is a work-free, once and for all solution to the job of watering—they do require regular maintenance. The tiny sprinklers, sprays and drippers they use are very often blocked and need clearing, and it is common for ants to build nests within the lines, requiring the system to be flushed through. Also, as plants grow, foliage can intercept sprayed water, which results in dry patches, so it's important to check each outlet often while the system is running, but it is not hard to reposition outlets or raise or lower them if need be. One final point to consider with watering systems is the lines themselves. Since they are made out of plastic, they are easily cut by digging tools, so whenever you dig in the garden you have to be mindful of the irrigation lines.

If minimizing water use is a priority for you, careful plant selection in the first place will help achieve that aim. As a guideline, avoid plants with dense, glossy green foliage and any that have pointed drip-tips to their leaves. These are signs that the plants come from high rainfall areas, and you do not want to plant a rainforest garden. Instead, look for plants that have evolved in drier regions. They will often have small leaves that may be leathery or stiff and usually olive green, gray-green, gray or silvery in appearance. If some of your favorite plants need regular water, then try not to scatter them throughout the garden; instead, grow them all together in one area. That way, you can water them as deeply and often as they need, and water the rest of the garden much less frequently. It is a mistake to place a plant that needs a lot of water next to one that expects dryness, because the watering needs of one will harm the other.

Another way to conserve water in the soil, and therefore reduce the frequency of watering, is to apply a thick layer of mulch. Mulch keeps the soil beneath it cool, so there will be less evaporation and as it rots it creates humus, an absorbent material that holds water for long periods. Lucerne

hay is an ideal mulch for this purpose, but any rotted organic matter will do. If possible, apply the mulch right after soaking rain or deep watering, and reapply when the mulch begins to rot.

There are also products available on the market that can be watered onto the soil and condense humidity from the air between the soil particles. These are called humectants. They are effective for about 3 months, after which they must be reapplied. In the garden, they are best applied at the beginning of the warm weather, and reapplied once or twice during the summer. Water crystals are an alternative product. For maximum effect, these have to be dug into the soil prior to planting, whereupon they absorb soil water and change from a crystal into a much bigger lump of jelly. The plant roots are then able to extract the water from this

Don't use sprinklers on windy days, or during the hottest times of the day.

jelly during dry times. The crystals are effective for about 5 years, although they will not be easy to replace in a garden that will be full of plants by then.

Many soils and potting mixes can become water repellent if allowed to dry out, and they may be almost impossible to re-wet. When soils reach this stage, even prolonged heavy rain will be unable to re-wet them, so you are faced with a garden that is in a state of permanent drought. Unfortunately, it is not easy to tell, just by looking, if your soil is in this condition. The thin top layer may look damp after a watering, but the only way to tell for sure is to dig down into the soil a few minutes after this. If the soil beneath is dry, then you are just wasting water every time you apply it.

To correct this, apply a wetting agent. These are sold as liquids and are available under a number of brand names. They are either watered or sprinkled on to the soil, and then watered in properly. Wetting agents are effective for 3–6 months, and need to be reapplied each spring and then again in early and late summer.

FEEDING

All plants need feeding, but if you improved your soil with organic matter before planting and you remulch regularly with rotted organic matter, you may not need to provide any other type of fertilizer at all. You should certainly aim to minimize the use of fertilizer, because it is both quite expensive and can be a pollutant. Excessive fertilizer

washed out of the soil by rain or watering just ends up in rivers and oceans where it can cause serious algal blooms. Just go easy with it, and you can't go wrong.

Fertilizer can be organic or inorganic. Organic fertilizer is made from plants or animals. It is more expensive than inorganic fertilizer and is not so concentrated, but it often lasts longer in the soil and has the advantage of containing substances that improve the condition of the soil. Inorganic fertilizers are purely the elements, minerals and salts that plants need in a soluble, concentrated form. They are relatively cheap and effective, but can be leached out of the soil quickly by water. They do not improve the condition of the soil and, in excess, can harm some soil organisms, notably worms. Fertilizer must always be used strictly in accordance with the dosage instructions on the pack, or simply use less than recommended. More fertilizer will not make plants grow better, in fact, in some cases, it can kill them.

Fertilizer always contains nitrogen (N), phosphorus (P) and potassium (K), which are the three most important (but not the only) plant foods. Different fertilizers are formulated with different relative amounts of N, P and K, and are formulated to benefit different types of plants. Sometimes the NPK ratio is stated prominently on the front of a fertilizer pack, otherwise it will always be listed somewhere, along with the other ingredients. There is little need, however, for you to have all the

Sprinkle granular fertilizers on when they are dry, then let them slowly dissolve as you water.

different fertilizers. For the average garden, with its diverse range of plants, a pack of 'complete' or 'all purpose' fertilizer is perfectly adequate. If you grow a lot of one type of plant, roses, citrus trees or vegetables for example, you could look for a fertilizer that is formulated for those plants.

Fertilizers can be mixed in water (soluble fertilizers) or sprinkled as granules (granular fertilizers). There are also formulations that release their nutrients slowly over a number of months, which is a good way to be sure of continuous feeding over a long period. These slow release fertilizers are much more expensive than either soluble or granular types, so it is definitely worth reading and following the application instructions on the pack.

Soluble fertilizers are fast acting and are absorbed through the leaves as well as the plant roots. They are good for giving plants a quick boost, or to correct yellowing of leaves caused by lack of nitrogen. They are washed out of the soil fast, so should not be overused.

Granular fertilizers are also soluble,

but you sprinkle them on when they are dry and let them slowly dissolve as you water. Because they are soluble, it also means that they can be quickly leached out of the soil.

The best time to fertilize is at the beginning of the growing season. This will be spring for most plants, but for those species that come from places with hot, dry summers, the growing season may begin in autumn. If possible, only apply fertilizer after rain or watering, since it is important to always feed plants when the soil is moist. After feeding, the fertilizer must be watered in properly.

It is much better to feed your plants naturally with rotted organic matter than to become dependent on inorganic fertilizer. Some plants, particularly Australian and South African natives, are very sensitive to fertilizers, and can be killed by them. If you only use fertilizers sparingly, you will not lose plants in this way, nor will you be adding to the pollution load in our waterways.

WEEDING

Few gardeners enjoy weeding, but it is an essential job because weeds compete with plants for water, space, light and nutrients, and they can also harbor pests and diseases. Moreover, if they are not controlled, your garden will soon look messy and quite uninviting.

The best way to keep weeds under control is to tackle them before you do much planting, ideally at the same time as improving the soil. It will then be much easier to keep them down when the garden is installed. If you don't have many in the garden, you can spray whatever comes up with the herbicide glyphosate. This is not a dangerous poison and is safe to use when applied in accordance with directions. It is, however, a total herbicide, which means that it kills or damages whatever green plant it touches. That is why it is best to use it before you begin to plant the garden.

Faced with a big weed problem, it is important to remember that the problem does not end once you have simply destroyed all of the weeds you can see. There will be a bank of weed seeds, bulbs, tubers or perennial roots lying dormant in the soil, some of which

may not germinate or grow until a certain season arrives. For example, if you kill off all the weeds you have in early autumn, the garden may look clear of weeds until the end of winter, and you might think you have won. But come spring, a whole new crop of weeds will appear, and if you have filled the garden with plants in the meantime, it will be much more difficult to use herbicide and you may have to laboriously weed by hand. A better strategy is to keep the garden empty and improve the soil, which helps to encourage the weeds to grow, then treat the weeds periodically as they come up. Once you have minimized the weed problem, you can start to plant up.

A healthy show of bedding plants.

If you already have an established garden, but also a weed problem, then it is possible to paint herbicide on to individual weeds. Spray methods are tricky because the herbicide can easily drift on to a valued plant. If you accidentally spray an ornamental plant with herbicide, either immediately prune off the affected foliage or hose the plant down. If you have to weed by hand, start in the most weed-free areas of the garden and work outwards. If possible, remove the weeds before they flower and set seed, and try to dig out the whole plant, roots, bulbs and tubers included. Keep a rubbish bag with you and put the pulled weeds straight into the bag—do not carry them through the garden or you may be unwittingly spreading weed seeds. Once you have an area cleared of weeds, keep it clear by pulling new weeds out as soon as they appear.

An alternative weed control strategy is to deprive weeds of light so they die. Smother the weeds with either several sheets of newspaper or a commercial weedmat, and cover this with a layer of mulch. The process is most successful on seasonal, annual weeds. Weeds that arise from bulbs, tubers or perennial roots are not so easily eradicated, and simply come up again when the newspaper rots away. In this case, the permanent weedmat is a better idea, but the inherent problem with weedmats is that you have to slit a hole in them in order to plant anything. Over time, the mat can become very cut up, and each cut is a possible exit for weeds.

Furthermore, as both weedmats and newspaper are covered with mulch, weed seeds blown in from other places or those dropped by birds will grow in the mulch. Remove these as they appear so you will not be faced with a big weeding job in the future.

A simple strategy that does work, is to plant densely. Use this method after you have made a concerted attack on the weeds or in conjunction with the weedmat method. Plant the area out with thickly foliaged shrubs that will grow taller than the weeds. It is vital that the shrubs grow together to form one continuous canopy, because this will exclude light from the ground thereby killing or discouraging the weeds.

If weeds in the lawn are your biggest problem, you may be able to use a selective lawn herbicide to control them. However, this depends on the type of grass you have and also the type of weeds. Some grasses are damaged by lawn herbicides, and some common lawn weeds will survive unaffected. Before you buy a herbicide for your lawn, know what type of grass you have. Also know the types of weeds you are trying to control; the relevant information should be listed on the herbicide label.

One non-toxic method to control lawn weeds with broad leaves is to make a 2:1 mixture of sulphate of ammonia and sulphate of iron. In the early morning of a fine, sunny day in late winter, sprinkle the dry mix directly on to the weeds—be careful not to broadcast it as it will burn the grass as well. The two chemicals will burn the weed away and because both are lawn fertilizers, they will feed the grass that grows into the space previously taken up by the weeds.

Lawn weeds that cannot be killed by either of the above two methods should be dug out by hand before they flower. Once the lawn is weed free, you can help keep it that way by watering, feeding and aerating the grass every 2 or 3 months in the growing season. You can hire a spiked roller to aerate a lawn.

If you are about to start a new lawn, either from seed, sprigs, runners or by laying turf, ensure that the ground below is well-prepared and free of weeds. Whatever weeds you leave will soon be disfiguring your new lawn.

Spray herbicides should never be used on a windy day. Even in calm weather, the chances of spray drift can be minimized by applying a coarse rather than a fine spray (sprayers have an adjustable nozzle), and hold the nozzle as close to the weed as possible. If you ever intend to use the spray equipment to apply insecticide, fungicide or foliar fertilizer to plants, ensure that you wash the equipment out thoroughly with hot, soapy water after using herbicide.

PRUNING

Pruning is one of the most important jobs in the garden: it allows you to shape the garden to your needs. Unpruned plants may grow too tall

A thriving, well looked after garden.

The old-fashioned curved pruning saw lets you get in close in tight corners like this one.

Keeping your tools sharp will mean you can always make a clean cut.

or too wide for their allotted spaces, which can cause them to grow over paths or block light entering windows or they may have dead or diseased branches, or simply have adopted an unattractive shape. Pruning lets you correct all this without harming the plants at all. It also improves the look of plants and their flowering performance, giving you the very best out of the plants you grow. By keeping plants more compact, it also allows you to squeeze in a greater number of plants into your garden.

But of course, not all plants need pruning. Many grow naturally dense and neat, and if you are happy with the appearance and of a plant and it is not causing any problems, don't prune it. Even plants that do benefit from pruning may not need to be pruned every year, although there are many that are improved by an annual trim. Your own observations and experiences will soon identify these plants.

Before you can begin, there are a number of tools that are needed. A pair of good quality secateurs (right and left-handed models are available) is essential, but secateurs can only cut relatively thin branches and twigs. You should never force them to cut a branch thicker than their design allows. For thicker and/or higher placed branches, you will need a pair of long-handled loppers. These are basically secateurs with much longer handles, and are operated with both hands. The extra length gives greater leverage, but these should also not be used on branches that are too thick for them. For those, a pruning saw is the best piece of equipment. This tool has a curved blade and sharp teeth that make short work of thick branches. A final requirement is a pair of shears, used to clip hedges or to shear shrubs lightly. Like huge scissors, shears are for cutting and shaping soft, non-woody growth.

All tools should be kept sharp. Blunt blades crush and tear stems, and such wounds do not heal as quickly as clean cuts. Just as in people, open wounds on plants are an invitation to disease. It is also a good idea to disinfect cutting blades with a wipe of bleach or methylated spirits before they are used, and before moving from one plant to another. Plant diseases are easily spread around the garden on dirty tools.

If you ever need to thin branches from a tree or tall shrub that are too high to reach buy an extension handle that will allow you to reach up to 15 feet (4.5 meters) with both feet firmly and safely on the ground. Some brands allow you to easily fit and remove different cutting heads, so you will only ever need the one handle. If at all possible, do not climb ladders. If there's no alternative, have someone with you at all times to hold the ladder steady, to pass tools to you and to help take down the cut branches. Place the ladder on level ground only, and never climb higher than the second rung from the top. Falling from ladders is a common cause of serious injury in the garden, which is why we recommend the very long handled tools.

Pruning can have a number of different objectives. If you want to make a young plant grow dense and compact, just use your fingers to pinch out the growing tip of each stem. You may want to reinvigorate and compact a plant that has grown too big or too open. To do that, you need to cut it back hard to a basic framework of branches. Perhaps the problem is lack of light under a tree, and selective removal of whole branches from the canopy will fix that. Or maybe you want the leaves to grow more densely and restore the plant's neat outline, and then you would shear it lightly all over. If your aim is to change the shape of a plant for aesthetic or practical reasons, you might remove some branches, shorten others and then shear the plant all over. With pruning, you can have a garden that grows exactly how you would like it to, and if you follow a few simple rules and don't just hack away, both you and your plants will be very happy.

There is no best time to prune that can be applied to all plants, simply because different species grow, flower and fruit at different times of the year. If you prune a particular plant at the right time of year, it need not result in the loss of that year's flowers or fruit. As a general rule deciduous, woody plants (those that drop their leaves for the winter) that bloom later in spring or early summer produce flowers on new growth, which is formed after winter. These plants should be pruned while they are bare in winter, since you will not cut off any flowers because the flowering wood is not produced until the spring. Some deciduous trees and shrubs, however, flower on old wood, and these are typically plants that bloom before mid-spring. If you prune these specimens in winter, when bare, you will cut off the very branches that produce the flowers early in the growing season. Instead, prune these plants right after flowering ends. If you have deciduous plants and you don't know whether they flower on new or old wood, prune after bloom, but note the plant's behaviour for next year.

Evergreens are best pruned right after bloom, as this gives them a full year to regrow the flowering stems. You can also prune them in late winter just before the new spring growth, but do not do this to evergreens that flower in early spring.

Little pruning jobs can be done at anytime. For example, the removal of a branch that is in the way, the shortening of overlong growth or the cutting of damaged, dead or diseased branches.

How much growth you should cut back depends on the plant. Some

This quite formal garden, featuring an ivy archway, requires regular pruning to keep it looking good.

shrubs can be cut right back to the ground in order to encourage a mass of vigorous new growth and a brilliant floral display. Others need to have the older stems removed to make way for new growth, while others simply need to be trimmed all over. Before you decide what to do, take a good look at how the plant produces its stems, and at its natural habit of growth. Your aim should be to preserve that natural habit, while reducing the size of the plant.

If the plant has a definite framework of branches, such as in fuchsias, hibiscus and tibouchinas, aim to preserve this and reduce or remove the smaller, outer branches. On shrubs that produce many upright stems from the base, remove about a quarter of the canes at ground level, which will make way for new growth. Cut out the oldest stems first, and leave the younger, more vigorous canes, which will produce the best flowers. Shrubs and trees that are naturally dense and compact may never need pruning, but if they do, just shear them lightly all over.

Always remove dead, diseased or damaged stems first. Next, look for branches that rub against each other and remove the weakest branch or the one that is growing in the least desirable direction. Finally, you can also cut out any weak, spindly growth or branches that head in towards the center of the plant. Remove all these branches cleanly where they meet another branch. Do not leave stubs.

Remember that buds will continue to grow in the direction they are pointing,

If you want to make a young plant grow dense and compact, just use your fingers to pinch out the growing tip of each stem.

so make cuts that will encourage new shoots to grow upwards and outwards, not in towards the center. Long branches can be shortened back to growth buds, which are usually found where leaves join stems. Make pruning cuts on a slant so that water runs off and, if you like, you can paint larger wounds (those over 1 inch [25 millimeters] in diameter) with a tree wound sealant, although there is some debate as to whether or not these products are helpful. Some authorities believe that they do nothing to speed up the healing process, but others are convinced that the sealants prevent or minimize the entry of disease-causing organisms.

When you have finished pruning, you will have a pile of raw material that is ideal for making soil-enriching mulch. The prunings will have to be shredded first, then piled up and composted, before they can be spread on the garden. Unless you own a power mulcher, consider renting one. If you get together with a couple of neighbors for a weekend of pruning and mulching, you will get the best use out of the hiring cost.

Wildlife in the garden

Plants attract animals. They feed, house and shelter a huge range of birds, lizards, insects and spiders, and the bushier and more diverse the plantings in your garden, the greater the range of wildlife you will attract. However, few gardeners object to birds, and the smaller lizards, but insects and spiders are often treated as enemies. This is misguided as most of these creatures are not just harmless, they're quite helpful!

It is certainly true that some insects attack plants, but if you reach for the poison sprays every time you see an insect on a plant, you will not only be killing the enemies, but also the insects and spiders that feed on them, which are your allies in the garden. Furthermore, the regular use of sprays discourages birds, pollutes the air and may be dangerous to you and your family. Major infestations of insect pests should certainly be promptly controlled, but you will find that if you are sparing with the sprays and put up with the odd outbreak of minor damage, a rising population of birds and predatory insects will keep the garden in balance.

Spiders are almost universally loathed and ruthlessly killed, even though most of those that set up home in your garden are harmless. Their webs trap all sorts of insects, and the spiders themselves eventually become bird food. If they build webs over paths or doors, just knock that part of the web down and the spider will build elsewhere.

Most gardeners want to attract native birds into their gardens. The best and most natural way to do it is to plant up the garden with a good range of dense trees and shrubs. These will provide the food, shelter and cover that small birds need, and although native plants are the most natural choices, many introduced species will also feed native birds. Large expanses of lawn are not particularly attractive to many birds, since there is little food there, and no cover from bigger, more aggressive birds.

As a rule, you should not feed birds artificially. They can become dependent on you for food, and what you supply them with may not meet all their nutritional needs. If you go on holidays, the birds can starve, and cats are attracted to congregations of birds flapping around a feeder at any time. It is better to let the birds feed themselves on the different plants in your garden.

Water is another matter. Reliable supplies of fresh, clean water can be hard to come by in the suburbs, and if you want more birds, 2 or 3 birdbaths spaced in the garden will do the trick. You must, however, keep the water clean, and scrub out the birdbath occasionally; a position in shade also helps to keep the water cool. In summer, when bird activity is greatest, and demand for water high, it is essential to change the water every morning or evening. If you can also change it once more during the day, you will have birds in the garden from dawn to dusk. Mount the birdbath as high as possible, as wet birds are vulnerable to attack from cats. If possible, place it among

This garden has clearly been well cared for.

spiny or prickly shrubs because these offer small birds the best protection. Birds also enjoy a nearby perch onto which they can fly to preen themselves.

Another way to attract birds is to provide safe nesting sites. Many smaller birds build their own nests, but need dense shrubbery in which to build it. Plants that have branches all the way to the ground are ideal, and if they also have spiny or prickly foliage, so much the better. Small birds can dart in and out of this foliage, but larger predatory birds cannot get in, and neither can cats. Bird houses rarely attract anything but pest birds such as sparrows and pigeons, because they are either set too close to the ground for native birds or they are the wrong shape. A number of birds do nest in hollows of trees and could conceivably nest in some sort of nest box, but if you are serious about providing this sort of home, a number of instructional books on how to build nest boxes for various birds have been produced.

Pests and diseases

Because your garden is a living community, from time to time some of its members will get sick. In many cases the plant will simply recover by itself, or the weather may change and the problem will lessen. Only if the problem persists or if the plant shows signs of serious damage should you resort to chemical control. Even then, you should make sure that you can't control the problem by simply picking off and squashing the offending pest.

It is worth remembering that insects and plant diseases are part of the system. In their natural habitat, healthy plants are able to resist and outgrow the insects and pathogens that occur; weak plants succumb, as they are meant to, and the same system works in gardens. Because many of the plants in our garden are from many different parts of the world, it is only natural that some will dislike the change in climate or soil from that which they evolved to live in. These plants could be stressed by their new home, and consequently become magnets for pests and diseases. If you find that a plant is frequently damaged by pests and requires spraying with a poison, ask yourself is it worth keeping? Wouldn't a plant that lives happily in your garden with few or no problems be a better choice? Unfortunately, we cannot grow everything we would like to: our own climate and environment has a direct effect, and it may be an ill-effect.

Pests can be classified by the way they eat, and therefore the damage they cause. Sucking pests, which include aphids, bugs and mites, pierce leaves, stems and fruit, then suck the sap. This can cause stem tips and flower buds to wither, leaves to become mottled or discolored, and fruit to fall prematurely. It can destroy the ornamental value of a plant, and weaken it to the stage where it becomes an easy target for other pests and diseases. Sucking pests can also transmit diseases from one plant to another.

Chewing pests, which include grubs, caterpillars, beetles and grasshoppers, eat holes in foliage and flowers. This destroys the appearance of the plant. In severe infestations, whole plants can be defoliated, which prevents them from manufacturing food from sunlight, thereby weakening them considerably.

Rasping pests, notably snails and slugs, do not chew holes but rasp away at the surface of leaves, flowers and fruit with file-like mouth parts. The end re-sult is similar to that of a chewing pest, but the control methods are different.

Diseases can be caused by bacteria or fungi. They often show up as brown or black spotting or edging, die-back or wilting of foliage, water-soaked areas on leaves, rust-like spots, or a powdery white coating on leaves or flowers. Diseases can kill plants outright or be passing afflictions that recur at certain times of the year, often as a result of climatic conditions. On the whole, dis-eases are harder to treat than pests because the cause is not always obvious and some diseases are simply impos-sible to cure.

Never spray a plant without first knowing what it is you are trying to control. Some chemicals are designed to control specific pests and diseases. To spray a fungus with a chemical designed to kill bugs will be ineffective, and possibly more harmful to yourself. Similarly, if snails have caused damage and you spray with a product designed to kill caterpillars, you are just need-lessly polluting the garden.

At first you may not know what is causing the damage, although it is pos-sible to use the process of deduction.

Start with an examination of the dam-age. Holes mean a chewer or a rasper, tiny spots or wilting could mean a sucker or a disease. Look on and under the leaves, especially near the damage. You may find the culprit there and then, and can squash it. If you suspect a chewer, look for droppings on the lower leaves. Round balls are a sure sign of caterpillars, and the bigger the balls the bigger the caterpillar you are looking for. Long, slender cylinders, which may be spiralled or partly so, are deposits left by snails and slugs. These pests also leave a silvery trail of slime.

Sucking pests are usually clearly vis-ible as in the case of aphids and most bugs, but mites are very small. Their presence is given away by fine webbing where the leaves join the stems.

If you still cannot find a likely cause, take a piece of the damage to a nursery, and ask a horticulturalist to advise you. If a chemical control is recommended, read the label thoroughly because it will tell you exactly what pests or dis-eases the chemical will target and on what types of plant. It will also give instructions on how to apply it and what safety equipment is needed. Take this advice seriously, as many garden chemicals are toxic to humans if applied carelessly. Always store chemicals in their original bottles, well out of the reach of children. If you need to dilute a concentrate, mix it up using the exact proportions stated on the bottle, and in a quantity enough for the job at hand—mixed up chemicals usually do not last, and should not be stored.

COMMON PESTS AND HOW TO CONTROL THEM

Aphids

About pinhead size, aphids may be black, green or pink. They are most common during the warmer months, and cluster in thick colonies on the tips of young shoots and on flower buds. Sometimes they will cluster beneath new leaves. The sweet, sticky substance they excrete attracts ants, and columns of ants on plants may indicate the presence of aphids or other sucking pests. Aphids cause wilting of new shoots, and wilting or deformation of flowers. They can transmit diseases from plant to plant.

Aphids have natural enemies which help to control them. These include the larvae of ladybird beetles, wasps, lace-wings and hoverflies. You can also squash them by hand.

If the infestation remains or becomes severe, spray the aphids with a pyreth-rum based insecticide. This will control the aphids, but has no residual effect.

Above: A Rose attacked by aphids.

Top: A close-up view of aphids, which cluster in thick colonies on the tips of young shoots and on flower buds.

Beetles

There are many different varieties of beetles, and not all are pests. Beetles chew holes in foliage, or eat the roots of plants whilst in their grub stage. However, if the plant is well-fed and watered, it usually recovers.

To control beetles, spray the foliage with carbaryl or another suitable poison that leaves a residue on the leaves. Lawn beetles, which eat the roots of grasses and cause dead patches to appear on the lawn, can be treated with a water-on lawn grub killer.

Bugs

There are many different varieties and sizes of bugs, and not all of them are pests. Bugs that are pests include, the tarnished plant bug, reddish brown, mottled green; and the common green capsid, green with reddish bronze markings. The sap-sucking antics of these bugs can cause both fruit and flower drop and deformities. The bugs also attack all parts of the foliage, which can result in the wilting of shoots and the curling of leaves.

Bugs have few natural enemies. Use a systemic insecticide to control them.

Caterpillars

These are the larval stage of moths and butterflies. They chew holes in foliage and flowers, and can rapidly defoliate plants if present in large numbers. Caterpillars are troublesome pests on vegetables and many ornamental plants. Hand control is possible on smaller outbreaks, but you will have to inspect plants frequently.

For easy control of caterpillars, use a bacterial spray containing *Bacillus thuringiensis*, which transmits a fatal disease to the grubs. It is harmless to people, other types of insects and birds.

Grasshoppers and katydids

Voracious chewers, these pests can do great damage, even in small numbers. They vary in size from 1–3 inches (25–70 millimeters), are usually green, brown or green and black, and jump when approached. They commonly chew into flower stems and devour tender flower buds. Pick off and squash them when seen or spray plants with carbaryl, which leaves a toxic residue on the leaves.

Mealybugs

Like little blobs of cotton wool, slow-moving mealybugs gather in cracks and crevices, especially where leaves join stems. They can also live on the roots of plants, and if they are present in numbers above ground, it is likely they will also be infesting the roots. Mealybugs are common on indoor plants, but

Rose growers need to keep an eye out for black spot, a common fungal disease.

also affect a wide range of outdoor plants—typically palms grown in areas that are too cool. Mealybugs suck sap and can weaken plants. They also distort and deform emerging leaves.

The best chemical control involves using a systemic insecticide (spraying and drenching) as this will also kill mealybugs on the roots.

Mites

Related to spiders, mites are very small sucking pests that cause spotting and yellowing of leaves. Severe infestations can kill plants. They are most prevalent during the warmer months, and the common two-spotted or red spider mite is especially troublesome during hot, dry weather. They attack both garden and indoor plants. Use a magnifying glass to look under foliage that has become yellow or finely spotted for signs of the presence of mites. Fine webbing is an indicator.

Predatory mites, which eat other mites, are available, but once released, miticides must not be used. Chemical control is difficult because mites have developed a resistance to the chemicals available to home gardeners. An increase in humidity around affected plants helps discourage mites: spray water under the foliage and wet the areas around affected plants.

Scale

Immobile, scale insects live under hard or soft, waxy, hemispherical shells attached to leaves and stems. They may be brown, black, pink or white, and vary in size from a tiny fleck to about ½ inch (12 millimeters). Scale suck sap, and are common on both indoor and many garden plants.

They can be scraped off with the fingernail or wiped off with a cloth, which has been moistened with white oil. These are both good methods of control for relatively small infestations. If chemical control is necessary, spray with white oil (not highly toxic) to smother the scale insects. Alternatively, you could use a systemic insecticide.

Snails and slugs

Very common in spring and autumn, snails and slugs can appear in large numbers after periods of rain. They destroy foliage, and newly planted seedlings are especially vulnerable. Snails and slugs are most active at night, favoring dewy or rainy nights. Silvery trails of slime are a sure indicator of their presence.

Snails and slugs are easily controlled by hand if you are persistent. Go into the garden in the early morning with a bucket of very salty water to collect them. Look under and in among foliage, under fence rails, under pots, anywhere they can seek shelter. Drop collected snails and slugs into the water. If you do this for 2 or 3 mornings in a row, you can clear the garden for many weeks.

Snail and slug bait is a chemical alternative, but most bait is attractive and toxic to dogs. Scatter thinly and as directed to minimize this danger and store packs safely. Iron-based snail baits are alleged to be the safest of all, because they do not contain poison.

Thrips

These tiny flying insects often appear in spring. They are discouraged by humidity, and watering under and over the foliage can reduce greatly their numbers. Thrips suck sap and like to find their way into unopened flower buds, which destroys the bloom before it opens. They can also cause streaking and flecking of the foliage, which will turn brown and dry in severe cases.

If necessary, spray with a systemic insecticide when the fast-moving insects are first seen, with follow-up sprays at fortnightly intervals.

COMMON DISEASES AND HOW TO CONTROL THEM

Black spot

This disease is very common on roses, especially when grown in humid areas, although orchids and other plants are also affected. Black spot is caused by a fungus and appears as a black spot. Leaves later turn yellow and fall. In severe cases the plant can be almost defoliated.

To control black spot, remove the affected leaves and place them in a bag in a bin. Spray with a fungicide that is suitable for the plant—check the details on the label.

Collar rot

Caused by a fungus, collar rot occurs around the base of the plant and is fatal if not treated. It is fairly common on citrus, but also affects other plants especially if mulch or soil is piled up around the main stem. Signs of infection include gum oozing from the base of the plant and spongy wet-looking, bark. This eventually dries and flakes.

To treat, use a sharp, clean knife to cut away all the infected tissue so that only healthy green wood remains. Then, paint the wound with copper oxychloride. Saturate the ground with a suitable fungicide, and in future keep mulch well away from the main stem.

Mildew

These powdery white spots or powdery coating are common in humid weather, especially on roses, daisies and vegetables such as zucchini and squash. Mildew is a fungus that debilitates plants by weakening their foliage, and some plants are much more susceptible than others. The best control is simply not to grow species that are prone to this disease.

Control mildew with a suitable fungicide (choose a fungicide recommended for the particular plant affected); spraying should begin at the first sign of infection. Respray regularly until the warm, humid weather has passed.

Petal blight

This affects azaleas, and first appears as brown spots on the flowers. Within days, the whole flower collapses as if wilted, then turns into a soggy mass, which later dries brown and hangs on the plant. Petal blight is caused by a fungus.

Once an azalea has had petal blight it will return every year, and control must begin just as the flower buds start to show color. Spray all over and under the foliage and flower buds with a fungicide. Spray the ground under the plant as well. Repeat every 2 weeks until flowering is finished.

Root rot

Several types of fungus cause roots to rot, and the above ground parts of the plant will suddenly wilt and die back. Root rots are hard to control, and it is often better to replace affected plants with an unrelated variety, since some species are much more resistant to it than others.

An expensive option is to drench the soil beneath and beyond the foliage canopy with a suitable fungicide, although this is not a once and for all cure. A preventative is to improve the drainage and fertility of the soil with rotted organic matter, which can help minimize the risk of root rot.

Rust

This appears as small yellow spots on the upper-sides of leaves, with corresponding rusty colored lumps on the undersides. Rust is a fungal disease that affects a wide range of plants, and causes leaf fall and weakness.

If rust is a problem on a particular plant, replace it either with a rust-resistant variety of the same plant, if available, or with another plant altogether. Several fungicides are available—choose one that is suitable for that particular plant.

Sooty mold

Sooty mold is a black, soot-like fungus that can cover foliage and stems. The fungus grows on the sticky secretions of sap-sucking insects such as scale, mealybugs and aphids. It is more unsightly than damaging, and does not actually harm the plant except to reduce the light that reaches the leaves.

If sooty mold is present, the problem is a sap-sucking pest. Spray the plant with a systemic insecticide to destroy the insects, and the sooty mold will slowly disappear.

Mixed planting acts as a deterrent to pests and diseases.

Chapter 2

ANNUALS & PERENNIALS

Cushion-forming perennials planted with upright annuals are pleasing to the eye.

In the popularity stakes, annuals and perennials are hard to beat. They are spritely plants that dazzle their pollinators with bright, welcoming blooms. Much to the joy of gardeners, who delight in their fleeting seasonal display, they bring tremendous boosts of color and vitality to a garden.

The difference between annuals and perennials

In nature, annuals are found mainly in open spaces, where harsh environmental conditions, either heat or extreme cold, dictate that these plants grow, bloom and set seed all within a short growing season. Perennials are longer lived than annuals, but are equally demonstrative in their eye-catching displays. They have evolved stocky root systems or other mechanisms to help them survive even really cold winters and be revived when their cyclical bell tinkles. To confuse beginner gardeners even further there are also biennials; mostly cool-climate plants that normally grow in their first year and then flower, set seed and die in their second. Many of the wild species have been improved by plant breeders, although annuals and perennials are still governed by the seasons and best results occur when we follow their natural cycle.

Annuals inspire creative gardening

Many gardeners are surprised to learn that there is much more to annuals than simply colorful, low-growing hybrids reminiscent of massed park and public garden displays. Trailing or climbing annuals such as nasturtiums (*Tropaeolum* species) and sweet peas (*Lathyrus odoratus*) can be interspersed with more permanent growers to invigorate a display, or there are tall and slender annuals like cosmos, which wave their welcome in the softest breeze. If you want cut flowers, there are annuals with long stems, while others produce masses of flowers that look most effective when grown for potted indoor display.

Most annuals, some more than others, demand a gardener's time in the form of deadheading. It's really quite remarkable how this undemanding and pleasurable evening task can extend the flowering season: the poor plants become quite determined to set seed, and so continue to produce beautiful flower buds for us to pick. Remember, however, that this continual beauty

parade needs to be nourished if it is to be sustained—you will need a quick acting liquid fertilizer designed to promote the flowers rather than the green growth.

Annuals allow us to try new plants because the displays are short lived. Since we know they won't last, there is plenty of room for experimenting. There's nothing so beguiling as a splash of bright-eyed pansies (*Viola* species) when many surrounding shrubs have either entered into a barren dormancy or have foliage with that lackluster winter look about it, but there's many a keen gardener all ready with an experimental plan for the next round; new color combinations, or perhaps an entirely new staging. You may well be astounded when you break some stuffy

Drifts of colour created by planting a single species, such as these primulas, give an appealing effect.

rules about color, trail the sweet peas up a twiggy deciduous shrub, replace a lawn with a blanket of *Lobelia erinus* or plant a packet of sunflower seeds in the twisting fashion of a maze. With little effort or cost involved, especially if growing from seed, we can behave like the professional landscapers and change the entire look of a garden each season using these versatile plants.

Annuals together with perennials

Who has the space or time these days to spend hours digging large garden beds, plant tiny seedlings regimental fashion and look at bare earth waiting for them to flower? Cottage garden devotees taught us long ago to spot plant some annuals between perennial drifts to create a living tapestry that often repeats through self-seeding. For less than the cost of a bunch of flowers, nurseries supply pots of colorful annuals to wave an instant wand across a bare patch, to intersperse between more permanent plants, or to place in tubs or hanging baskets.

On the nursery shelves you will also find punnets of bedding plants; perennials to plant in drifts. These often include perennials with decorative foliage, such as gray-green or variegated forms,

Taller annuals and perennials should be planted near the back of a bed. Fragrant plants are best appreciated close to paths.

that can be used to great effect along-side your annuals. They will make attractive eye-rests or punctuation marks between a contrasting colorful combination.

How to grow annuals and perennials

Most annuals and perennials demand full sun, the better to help them pro-duce flowers, seeds and offsets for their continued existence into the next year. In warmer climates, however, many perennials are best treated as annuals, while in cooler areas they will happily submit to a trim at the season's end.

As with any gardening endeavour, the quality of the soil is the next most important ingredient. Initial preparation will repay the gardener many times over. First of all, ensure the bed is free of weeds, which romp away and swamp newly planted seedlings when given extra attention in the form of digging or nourishment. Then dig the garden over, and incorporate humus, humus and more humus. The addition of humus, such as rotted animal manure, home-made compost or a commercially packaged material will always be ben-eficial to your soil, whether it be clay based or of a sandy nature.

Annuals are raised by seed. Some can be sown directly onto the soil, but many are better sown in trays where a tighter control can be exercised, es-pecially in colder climates where they can be started earlier in a sheltered position away from frosts or heavy rain. Either way, the soil in which seeds

or young seedlings are to be planted needs to be very fine to allow the tiny roots of the emerging seedlings easy penetration. So bring out the rake and ensure an even, friable surface.

Perennials can be grown from seed, but it can take them a few years to flower. Most are easily propagated by division, which involves the separation of either their crowns or rhizomes. Perennials are best regenerated in this manner every 3 or 5 years depending on the species. Since the divided plants are usually quite established, with well developed roots and foliage, there is no need to prepare garden beds to the same fine tilth required for tiny annuals.

Unlike annuals, perennials will be in the same position for some years. As most are voracious feeders, it is essen-tial to provide them with ample nutri-ents to boost their progress. Spread a complete fertilizer before you plant: this can mean the difference between a humdrum or spectacular first season display.

Through division of perennials, which are then planted out in great drifts of the same species, and adequate fertilizing, gardeners can quickly and cheaply establish a mature garden at-mosphere that is to their liking. How-ever, if your local nursery is unable to help you find the plants that you are looking for, it is worth knowing that there is an increasingly vast industry devoted to mail order. Perennials travel very well in dormancy, so there is no longer reason not to grow exactly what you want.

Acanthus spinosus

ACANTHUS

BEAR'S BREECHES

Around 30 species of perennials and shrubs from tropical Africa and Asia as well as Mediterranean Europe make up this genus. The genus name goes back to ancient Greek, and the large and colorful family Acanthaceae (mainly tropical) takes its name from the genus. The deeply lobed and toothed leaves of *Acanthus mollis* and *A. spinosus* have lent their shape to the carved motifs used to decorate the capitals of Corinthian columns. It is only the more temperate perennial species that have been much cultivated, valued for their erect spikes of bracted, curiously shaped flowers, as well as their handsome foliage. The flowers appear in spring and early summer, after which the leaves may die back but sprout again before winter.

CULTIVATION
Frost hardy, they do best in full sun or light shade. They prefer a rich, well-drained soil with adequate moisture in winter and spring. Spent flower stems and leaves can be removed if they offend. Snails and caterpillars can damage the new leaves. Propagation is normally by division in autumn, or from seed.

Acanthus mollis

Occurring on both sides of the Mediterranean, this well-known species is somewhat variable, the form grown in gardens having broader, softer leaves and taller flowering stems than most wild plants. It is more of a woodland plant than other acanthuses, appreciating shelter and deep, moist soil. The large leaves are a deep, glossy green and rather soft, inclined to droop in hot dry weather. Flower spikes can be over 6 ft (1.8 m) tall, the purple-pink bracts contrasting sharply with the crinkled white flowers. Spreading by deeply buried rhizomes, it can be hard to eradicate once established. 'Candelabrus' is one of several cultivars of *Acanthus mollis*. **ZONES 7–10.**

Acanthus spinosus

This eastern Mediterranean species has large leaves that are deeply divided, the segments having coarse, spine-tipped teeth. In summer it sends up flower spikes to about 4 ft (1.2 m) high, the individual flowers and bracts being very similar to those of *Acanthus mollis*. **ZONES 7–10.**

Acanthus mollis

ACHILLEA

Achillea millefolium 'Apfelblüte'

YARROW, MILFOIL, SNEEZEWORT

There are about 85 species of *Achillea*, most native to Europe and temperate Asia, with a handful in North America. Foliage is fern-like, aromatic and often hairy. Most species bear masses of large, flat heads of tiny daisy flowers from late spring to autumn in shades of white, yellow, orange, pink or red. Achilleas are suitable for massed border planting and rockeries, and flowerheads can be dried—retaining their color—for winter decoration. This genus is named after Achilles, who, in Greek mythology, used the plant to heal wounds.

CULTIVATION

These hardy perennials are easily grown and tolerant of poor soils, but they do best in sunny, well-drained sites in temperate climates. They multiply rapidly by deep rhizomes and are easily propagated by division in late winter or spring, or from cuttings in early summer. Flowering stems may be cut when spent or left to die down naturally in winter, when the clumps should be pruned to stimulate strong spring growth. Fertilize in spring.

Achillea filipendulina 'Gold Plate'

Achillea filipendulina

This species, native to the Caucasus, bears brilliant, deep yellow flowers over a long summer season. It grows to 4 ft (1.2 m) with flowerheads up to 6 in (15 cm) wide and is one of the most drought resistant of summer flowers. 'Gold Plate', a strong-growing, erect cultivar reaching 4 ft (1.2 m), has aromatic, bright green foliage, and flat, rounded heads of golden-yellow flowers, 4–6 in (10–15 cm) wide. 'Parker's Variety' has yellow flowers. ZONES 3–10.

Achillea millefolium

MILFOIL, YARROW

Widely distributed in Europe and temperate Asia, this common species is hardy and vigorous to the point of weediness, and naturalizes freely. It grows to 24 in (60 cm) tall with soft, feathery, dark green foliage and white to pink flowers in summer. Cultivars include 'Cerise Queen', cherry red with pale colors; 'Fanal' (syn. 'The Beacon'), bright red; 'Red Beauty', silvery leaves and rose-red flowers; the pink 'Rosea'; and 'Apfelblüte', deep rose pink. Once established, plants can be difficult to eradicate. Most *Achillea* hybrids have this species as one parent. 'Paprika' has orange-red flowerheads that fade with age. ZONES 3–10.

Achillea 'Moonshine'

A cultivar of hybrid origin, this plant bears pretty flattened heads of pale sulfur yellow to bright yellow flowers throughout summer. It is a good species for cut flowers. It has delicate, feathery, silvery gray leaves and an upright habit, reaching a height of 24 in (60 cm). It should be divided regularly in spring to promote strong growth. ZONES 3–10.

Achillea 'Moonshine'

Acinos alpinus

syn. *Calamintha alpina*

ALPINE CALAMINT

Spikes of violet flowers 1 in (25 mm) wide and with white marks on the lower lips are borne on this spreading, short-lived perennial, a native of central and southern Europe. Growing 4–8 in (10–20 cm) in height, it has rounded leaves with either pointed or blunt tips. **ZONES 6–9.**

ACINOS

CALAMINT

This genus of 10 species of annuals and woody, evergreen perennials gets its name from the Greek word *akinos*, the name of a small aromatic plant. Usually small, tufted, bushy or spreading plants growing to 8 in (20 cm), they come from central and southern Europe and western Asia. The 2-lipped, tubular flowers are borne on erect spikes in mid-summer.

CULTIVATION

Mostly quite frost hardy, they will grow in poor soil as long as it is well drained (they do not like wet conditions) and need full sun. Propagate from seed or cuttings in spring.

Acinos alpinus

ACONITUM

ACONITE, MONKSHOOD, WOLFSBANE

Consisting of around 100 species of perennials scattered across temperate regions of the northern hemisphere, this genus is renowned for the virulent poisons contained in the sap of many. From ancient times until quite recently they were widely employed for deliberate poisoning, from execution of criminals to baiting wolves, or placing in an enemy's water supply. The poison has also been used medicinally in carefully controlled doses and continues to attract the interest of pharmaceutical researchers. The plants themselves are instantly recognizable by their flowers, mostly in shades of deep blue or purple or less commonly white, pink or yellow, with 5 petals of which the upper one bulges up into a prominent helmet-like shape. In growth habit and leaves, the monkshoods show a strong resemblance to their relatives the delphiniums.

CULTIVATION

Monkshoods make attractive additions to herbaceous borders and woodland gardens. They prefer deep, moist soil and a sheltered position, partly shaded if summers are hot and dry. Propagate by division after the leaves die back in autumn, or from seed.

Aconitum carmichaelii 'Arendsii'

Aconitum carmichaelii
syn. *Aconitum fischeri*

A native of northern and western China, this has become one of the most popular monks-hoods by virtue of the rich violet-blue flowers, which are densely packed on the spikes in late summer. The leaves, thick, glossy and deeply veined, grow on rather woody stems. Several races and selections are cultivated, varying in stature from 3 to 6 ft (1 to 1.8 m), including 'Arendsii' (syn. 'Arends'), a striking blue-flowered cultivar. **ZONES 4–9.**

Aconitum napellus
ACONITE, MONKSHOOD

Of wide distribution in Europe and temperate Asia, this is the monkshood species most widely grown in gardens and is as handsome as any when well grown. The stems are erect, to 4 ft (1.2 m) high, with large leaves divided into very narrow segments and a tall, open spike of deep blue to purplish flowers. A vigorous grower, it likes damp woodland or stream bank conditions. **ZONES 5–9.**

Aconitum napellus

ADENOPHORA

This genus of around 40 species of herbaceous perennials is closely related to *Campanula*, in fact distinguished from it only by an internal feature of flower structure. Most are native to eastern Asia but 2 species occur wild in Europe. One species is grown in Japan for its edible roots.

CULTIVATION

Cultivation requirements and mode of propagation are the same as for *Campanula*.

Adenophora uehatae

Native to eastern Asia, this is a charming dwarf species with large, pendulous pale mauve-blue bells borne on short leafy stems. It makes a fine rock-garden subject. **ZONES 5–9.**

Adenophora uehatae

ADONIS

This genus consists of 20 species of annuals and perennials from Europe and cooler parts of Asia, with brightly colored flowers similar to *Anemone*, to which it is closely related. The Greek god Adonis, beloved of Aphrodite, gave his name to the original annual species, whose red flowers were said to have sprung from drops of his blood when he was killed by a boar. The leaves are mostly finely divided, the uppermost ones on each stem forming a sort of 'nest' on which the single bowl-shaped flower rests. It is only the perennial species that are much cultivated, used in herbaceous borders and rock gardens.

CULTIVATION

Adonis require a cool climate with warm dry summers. They are best grown in a sheltered spot in full sun, and in moist, fertile soil with a high humus content. Propagate from fresh seed or by division of clumps.

Adonis annua

Adonis annua
PHEASANT'S EYE

Quite different from most species, this is a summer-flowering annual with finely divided foliage and branching stems 12–15 in (30–38 cm) tall. The bright red, 5- to 8-petalled flowers are about 1 in (25 mm) wide with black centers. It occurs naturally in southern Europe and south-west Asia. **ZONES 6–9.**

Adonis vernalis

This European perennial species is rather like *Adonis amurensis* but has very narrow, almost needle-like, finely divided leaflets. Its 12- to 20-petalled, bright yellow flowers are large, up to 3 in (8 cm) across, and open in early spring. Both this species and *A. annua* have been used medicinally, but are now regarded as too toxic for general use. **ZONES 3–9.**

Aethionema coridifolium
LEBANESE STONE CRESS

This perennial, native to the eastern Mediterranean region, bears prolific heads of rose pink flowers from spring to mid-summer. It has a branching, low habit with slender reddish brown stems and narrow, grayish blue leaves. It reaches a height and spread of about 10 in (25 cm). **ZONES 7–9.**

Aethionema 'Mavis Holmes'

AETHIONEMA

Ranging through the Mediterranean region and into western Asia, the 30 or more species of this genus include evergreen perennials, subshrubs and low shrubs, all with small, narrow leaves and producing spikes or clusters of 4-petalled pink to white flowers in spring and summer. The genus belongs to the mustard family, falling into the same tribe as *Arabis* and *Alyssum*. A number of species are cultivated, prized mainly by rock-garden enthusiasts for their compact habit and profuse display of bloom such as the mauve-pink cultivar 'Mavis Holmes'.

CULTIVATION

Aethionemas thrive best in a climate with a cool, moist winter and a warm, dry summer. They should be grown in raised beds or rockeries in gritty, free-draining soil and exposed to full sun. Propagate from seed or cuttings.

Agapanthus praecox subsp. *Orientalis*

AGAPANTHUS

AFRICAN LILY, AGAPANTHUS, LILY-OF-THE-NILE

Native to southern Africa, these strong-growing perennials are popular for their fine foliage and showy flowers produced in abundance over summer. Arching, strap-shaped leaves spring from short rhizomes with dense, fleshy roots. Flowers are various shades of blue (white in some cultivars) in many flowered umbels, borne on a long erect stem, often 3 ft (1 m) or more tall. Agapanthus are ideal for background plants or for edging along a wall, fence or driveway, some hybrid examples are 'Irving Cantor' and 'Storm Cloud'. Headbourne Hybrids are especially vigorous and hardy. They grow to 3 ft (1 m) and come in a range of bright colors.

Agapanthus species

CULTIVATION
Agapanthus can thrive in conditions of neglect, on sites such as dry slopes and near the coast. They enjoy full sun but will tolerate some shade, and will grow in any soil as long as they get water in spring and summer. They naturalize readily, soon forming large clumps; they also make excellent tub and container specimens. Remove spent flower stems and dead leaves at the end of winter. Agapanthus are frost hardy to marginally frost hardy. Propagate by division in late winter, or from seed in spring or autumn.

Agapanthus campanulatus
Native to KwaZulu Natal in South Africa, this species makes a large clump of narrow, grayish leaves that die back in autumn. In mid- to late summer, crowded umbels of pale blue flowers with broadly spreading petals are borne on 3 ft (1 m) stems. It is the most frost-hardy species. *Agapanthus campanulatus* var. *patens*, smaller and more slender, is one of the daintiest of all the forms. ZONES 7–11.

Agapanthus praecox
This commonly grown species bears glorious starbursts of lavender-blue flowers in summer, and its densely clumped evergreen foliage is handsome in the garden all year round. It is also available in white. *Agapanthus praecox* subsp. *orientalis* has large dense umbels of blue flowers. It prefers full sun, moist soil and is marginally frost hardy. ZONES 9–11.

Agapanthus campanulatus

AGERATUM
FLOSS FLOWER

While undoubtedly best known for the annual bedding plants derived from *Ageratum houstonianum*, this genus includes some 43 species of annuals and perennials mostly native to warmer regions of the Americas. They are clump-forming or mounding plants up to 30 in (75 cm) tall with felted or hairy, roughly oval to heart-shaped leaves with shallowly toothed or serrated edges. The flowerheads are a mass of fine filaments, usually dusky blue, lavender or pink and crowded in terminal clusters.

CULTIVATION
Best grown in full sun in moist, well-drained soil. Regular dead-heading is essential to prolong the flowering. Propagate by spring-sown seed, either raised indoors in containers or sown directly in the garden.

Ageratum houstonianum

Ageratum houstonianum
Native to Central America and the West Indies, this annual species is popular as a summer-bedding plant. It is available in 3 sizes, tall: 12 in (30 cm), medium: 8 in (20 cm) and dwarf: 6 in (15 cm). It forms clumps of foliage with fluffy flowers in an unusual dusky blue that blends effectively with many other bedding plants. Pink and white forms are also available. **ZONES 9–12.**

Ajania pacifica

Ajania pacifica
syns *Chrysanthemum pacificum, Dendranthema pacificum*
An attractive plant, occurring wild in far eastern Asia, this species makes a spreading, loose mound of evergreen foliage up to about 18 in (45 cm) high. The leaves are deep green on the upper side and clothed in dense white hairs beneath; the white shows at the coarsely scalloped edges, making a striking contrast with the green. Sprays of brilliant gold flowerheads in autumn further enhance the effect. **ZONES 4–10.**

AJANIA

This genus, consisting of 30 or so species from eastern and central Asia, is one of a number of genera now recognized in place of *Chrysanthemum* in its older, broader sense. *Ajania* is closest to *Dendranthema* and its species have similar bluntly lobed leaves mostly with whitish-woolly hairs on the undersides. But their flowerheads are small and button-like, lacking ray florets and arranged in flat-tish panicles at the tips of branches. The plants have extensively branching under-ground rhizomes, sending up numerous tough, wiry stems. Only one species, *Ajania pacifica*, has been widely cultivated for ornament in gardens and parks.

CULTIVATION
The plants are very hardy and easily grown in a wide range of situations, thriving in both poor and fertile soils, though preferring good drainage and full sun. If not cut back hard after flowering, including the rhizome, they may spread so rapidly that adjacent plants are smothered. Propagate from rhizome divisions.

Ajuga reptans

EUROPEAN BUGLE, COMMON BUGLE,
BLUE BUGLE

The commonly grown ajuga, native to Europe, spreads by surface runners in the same way as a strawberry plant, making a mat of leafy rosettes only 2–3 in (5–8 cm) high and indefinite spread. In spring it sends up spikes of deep blue flowers, up to 8 in (20 cm) high in some cultivars. The most familiar versions are: 'Atropurpurea' (syn. 'Purpurea') which has dark purple to bronze leaves; 'Burgundy Glow', with cream and maroon variegated leaves; 'Multicolor', with white, pink and purple leaves; and 'Variegata', with light green and cream leaves. Rather different is 'Jungle Beauty', which is much larger, spreads more rapidly, and has dark green leaves tinged with purple. 'Catlin's Giant' has much larger leaves and longer, to 8 in (20 cm), inflorescences. 'Pink Elf' is a compact form with dark pink flowers. **ZONES 3–10.**

Ajuga reptans 'Atropurpurea'

AJUGA

BUGLE

About 50 species of low-growing annuals and perennials make up this genus, which ranges through Europe, Asia, Africa and Australia, mainly in cooler regions. Although belonging to the mint family, their foliage is hardly aromatic. Rosettes of soft, spatulate leaves lengthen into spikes of blue, purple or pink (rarely yellow) 2-lipped flowers. In most perennial species the plants spread by runners or underground rhizomes, some forming extensive carpets. They make attractive groundcovers, especially for shady places such as corners of courtyards.

Ajuga reptans 'Atropurpurea'

CULTIVATION

These are frost-hardy, trouble-free plants requiring little but moist soil and shelter from strong sun, though the bronze and variegated forms develop best color in sun. The commonly grown species thrive in a range of climates, from severe cold to subtropical. Propagate by division.

ALCEA

HOLLYHOCK

The botanical name *Alcea* is the old Roman one; Linnaeus adopted it although he also used the name *Althaea*, from the Greek *altheo*, to cure, in allusion to the plant's use in traditional medicine. Native to the eastern Mediterranean, hollyhocks were originally called holy hock or holy mallow; it is said that plants were taken to England from the Holy Land during the Crusades. There are about 60 species in the genus, all from western and central Asia. They bear flowers on spikes which may be 6 ft (1.8 m) or more high, making them far too tall for the average flower-bed; even 'dwarf' cultivars grow to 3 ft (1 m) tall.

CULTIVATION

Hollyhocks are quite frost hardy but need shelter from wind, benefiting from staking in exposed positions. They prefer sun, a rich, heavy well-drained soil and frequent watering in dry weather. Propagate from seed in late summer or spring. Rust disease can be a problem; spray with fungicide.

Alcea rosea

Alcea rosea
syn. Althaea rosea

HOLLYHOCK

This biennial, believed originally to have come from Turkey or Palestine, is popular for its tall spikes of flowers which appear in summer and early autumn, and come in a range of colors including pink, purple, cream and yellow; they can be either single, flat circles of color 4 in (10 cm) across, or so lavishly double that they are like spheres of ruffled petals. Foliage is roundish and rough and the plants may be as much as 10 ft (3 m) tall, erect and generally unbranched. The **Chater's Double Group** of cultivars have peony-shaped, double flowers that may be any color from purple-blue, purple, red, yellow and white to pink or apricot. There are many other cultivars and series including **Pinafore Mixed** and **Majorette Mixed** with lacy, semi-double flowers in pastel shades. **ZONES 4–10.**

Alchemilla mollis

LADY'S MANTLE

Sometimes sold as *Alchemilla vulgaris*, this is the most widely cultivated species in the genus. It is a low-growing perennial ideal for ground-cover, the front of borders or for rock gardens. It is clump forming, growing to a height and spread of about 16 in (40 cm). It has decorative, wavy edged leaves which hold dew or raindrops to give a sparkling effect. In summer, it bears masses of small sprays of greenish yellow flowers. *A. speciosa* is very like *A. mollis* except that its leaves are more deeply lobed and the leaf stems have a covering of fine hairs. **ZONES 4–9.**

ALCHEMILLA

LADY'S MANTLE

There are around 300 species of herbaceous perennials in this Eurasian genus. There are also a few alpine species in Australia and New Zealand, but it is not clear if they are natives or naturalized introductions. They form clumps of palmate (hand-shaped) or rounded, lobed, gray-green leaves often covered with fine hairs. Their spreading stems often root as they grow. Branched inflorescences of tiny yellow-green flowers develop in summer. Their sizes range from 6 to 30 in (15 to 75 cm) tall and wide. Many species have medicinal properties.

CULTIVATION

They are easily grown in well-drained, humus-rich soil, with some afternoon shade in warm climates. Propagate from seed or division in late winter to early spring.

Alchemilla mollis

Alstroemeria aurea

syn. *Alstroemeria aurantiaca*

Native to Chile and the most common and easily grown species, this has heads of orange flowers, tipped with green and streaked with maroon. Leaves are twisted, narrow and lance-shaped. Several cultivars exist; 'Majestic' and 'Bronze Beauty' both have deep orange or bronzy orange flowers; they grow to 2–3 ft (0.6–1 m) with a similar spread. **ZONES 7–9.**

Alstroemeria, Ligtu Hybrids

The well-known Ligtu Hybrids first appeared in Britain in the late 1920s, when *Alstroemeria ligtu* was crossed with *A. haemantha*. They come in a range of colors from cream to orange, red and yellow, but have been overshadowed in recent years as cut flowers by other hybrid strains derived from *A. aurea*. The plants die down soon after flowering. **ZONES 7–9.**

ALSTROEMERIA

PERUVIAN LILY

Native to South America where they occur mostly in the Andes, the 50 or so species of tuberous and rhizomatous plants are among the finest of all perennials for cutting, but they do drop their petals. Erect, wiry stems bear scattered, thin, twisted leaves concentrated on the upper half, and terminate in umbels of out-ward-facing flowers, usually with flaring petals that are variously spotted or streaked. They flower profusely from spring to summer.

CULTIVATION

All grow well in sun or light shade in a well-enriched, well-drained acidic soil. They soon form large clumps, bearing dozens of flowerheads. Propagate from seed or by division in early spring. They are frost hardy, but in cold winters protect the dormant tubers by covering with loose peat or dry bracken. Best left undisturbed when established, but one-year-old seedlings transplant well. Alstroemerias do well naturalized under trees or on sloping banks.

Alstroemeria aurea

ALYSSUM

MADWORT

The commonly grown bedding alyssum is now classified under *Lobularia*, but there are still some 170 species of annuals, perennials and subshrubs in this genus and many of them are superb rockery plants. They are mainly low spreaders with small elliptical leaves. In spring and early summer they are smothered in heads of tiny white, cream, yellow or pink flowers. Most are less than 8 in (20 cm) tall with a few of the shrubbier species reaching 24 in (60 cm).

CULTIVATION

Plant in full sun with gritty, well-drained soil. Alyssums are ideal for growing in rock crevices and as dry-stone wall plants, though it is important that they are given an occasional soaking in spring and summer. Most species are fairly frost hardy and are propagated from seed or small cuttings.

Alyssum murale

YELLOW TUFT

One of the taller species, this native of southeastern Europe grows to around 18 in (45 cm) tall. Its leaves are gray-green and ½–1 in (12–25 mm) long. The flowers are yellow. **ZONES 7–9.**

Alyssum murale

Alyssum spinosum

Found naturally in southern France and south-eastern Spain, this species is a twiggy subshrub that grows to 24 in (60 cm) tall. It has gray-green to silver foliage and the branches are spiny tipped. In spring to early summer, the flowers open white and become purple tinted as they age. *Alyssum spinosum* var. *roseum* has light to deep pink flowers. **ZONES 8–9.**

Alyssum spinosum

Amaranthus tricolor 'Joseph's Coat'

AMARANTHUS

The 60 or so species of annuals and short-lived perennials that make up this genus range through most warmer parts of the world and include weeds, leaf vegetables and grain crops as well as a few ornamentals, grown for their brilliant foliage, curious flowers and adaptability to hot, dry conditions. They are popular bedding plants, with large and attractively colored leaves and minute flowers borne in drooping tassel-like spikes.

CULTIVATION

A sunny, dry position with protection from strong winds is essential, and these plants enjoy a fertile, well-drained soil, mulched during hot weather. They are marginally frost hardy and in cool climates are usually brought on under glass before planting out in late spring. Prune when young to thicken growth. Prepare soil for planting with plenty of manure, and water seedlings regularly. Protect from snails when young and watch for caterpillars and aphids. Propagation is normally from seed.

Amaranthus caudatus

LOVE-LIES-BLEEDING, TASSEL FLOWER

This species, growing to 4 ft (1.2 m) or more high, has oval, dull green leaves and dark red flowers in long, drooping cords, their ends often touching the ground. Flowers appear in summer through to autumn. In many old gardens this plant was used to give height in the center of circular beds. **ZONES 8–11.**

Amaranthus tricolor

Native to tropical Africa and Asia, this quick-growing annual has given rise to many culti-vated strains, some used as leaf vegetables (Chinese spinach), others as bedding plants with brilliantly colored leaves. They are bushy annuals, reaching about 3 ft (1 m) high and 18 in (45 cm) wide. Tiny red flowers appear in summer. 'Flaming Fountain' has leaves that are deep green at the base, then bronze tinted higher up, and then entirely blood red at the top. 'Joseph's Coat', has brilliant bronze, gold, orange and red variegated leaves which retain their coloring into late autumn. **ZONES 8–11.**

Amaranthus tricolor 'Flaming Fountain'

AMMI

Six species of carrot-like perennials belong to this genus, occurring wild in the Mediterranean region, western Asia and the Canary Islands. They are fairly typical umbellifers with large, ferny basal leaves and flowering stems bearing large umbels of numerous small white flowers. One species *(Ammi majus)* is sometimes grown for cut flowers or as a cottage-garden plant, and a second *(A. visnaga)* has long been used medicinally in the Middle East. *Ammi* was the classical Greek and Latin name for a plant of this type, though its exact identity is uncertain.

Ammi majus

CULTIVATION

Usually treated as annuals, they are easily grown in a sheltered but sunny position in any reasonable garden soil, kept fairly moist. Propagate from seed in spring. They usually self-seed once established.

Ammi majus
BISHOP'S WEED

Native to the Mediterranean region and western Asia, this species has become widely naturalized in other continents. It grows to 24–36 in (60–90 cm) tall, producing a succession of large, lacy flowering heads in summer and autumn. **ZONES 6–10.**

Amsonia tabernaemontana

AMSONIA
BLUE STAR

A genus of around 20 species of perennials and subshrubs native to southern Europe, western Asia, Japan and North America. They grow to around 3 ft (1 m) tall and have bright to deep green, narrow, lance-shaped leaves. Stems and leaves bleed milky sap when cut. The flowers, borne mainly in summer, are tubular with widely flared mouths. They are carried in phlox-like heads.

CULTIVATION

Amsonias are easily grown in any moist, well-drained soil that does not dry out in summer. Plant in full sun or part-shade. They are moderately to very frost hardy and generally die back to the rootstock in winter. Propagation is from seed, early summer cuttings or by division in late winter.

Amsonia tabernaemontana
BLUE STAR, BLUE DOGBANE

Amsonia tabernaemontana is a delightful perennial from northeastern and central USA. Stiff stems, 24–36 in (60–90 cm) tall, are topped by pyramidal clusters of small, star-shaped flowers of pale blue from late spring to summer, flowering along with peonies and irises. The leaves are narrow to elliptical and about 2½ in (6 cm) long. This species needs minimal care if given a moist, fertile soil in full sun to light shade. It is good in the perennial border or in a damp wildflower meadow. The species name commemorates a famous sixteenth-century German herbalist, who latinized his name as Tabernaemontanus. **ZONES 3–9.**

Anagallis monellii

ANAGALLIS
PIMPERNEL

These are low-growing, often mat-forming annuals and perennials with small, heart-shaped to elliptical, bright green leaves arranged in opposite pairs. In spring and summer small, 5-petalled flowers appear in profusion on short stems. The flowers usually arise from the leaf axils or occasionally in small racemes at the stem tips. They come in a variety of colors.

CULTIVATION
Plant in full sun in any well-drained soil that does not dry out entirely in summer. The more attractive, less vigorous species are excellent rockery plants. Propagate annuals from seed; perennials from seed, by division or from small tip cuttings. Some of the weedy species self-sow only too readily.

Anagallis monellii
syns *Anagallis linifolia,*
A. collina

This charming little plant is grown for its brilliant blue or scarlet flowers of ½ in (12 mm) diameter, which appear during summer. This species grows to under 18 in (45 cm), with a spread of 6 in (15 cm) or more. **ZONES 7–10.**

ANCHUSA
ALKANET, SUMMER FORGET-ME-NOT

This genus consists of about 50 species of annuals, biennials and perennials occurring in Europe, North and South Africa and western Asia. Although many have a rather weedy habit and undistinguished foliage, they bear flowers of a wonderful sapphire blue, which though individually not large are carried in clusters over a long spring and early summer season and do not fade easily. Anchusas are also suitable for containers; dwarf perennial species are more at home in the rock garden.

CULTIVATION
Frost hardy, plant in a sunny position in deep, rich, well-drained soil. In hot areas, plant in part-shade to maintain flower color. Feed sparingly and water generously. Taller species benefit from staking. Cut the flower stalks after blooming to promote new growth. Propagate perennials by division in winter, annuals and biennials from seed in autumn or spring. It is best to transplant the perennials when they are dormant in winter.

Anchusa azurea 'Loddon Royalist'

Anchusa azurea
syn. *Anchusa italica*
ITALIAN ALKANET

Occurring wild around the Mediterranean and the Black Sea, this species is an upright perennial up to 3–4 ft (1–1.2 m) high and 24 in (60 cm) wide. Anchusa azurea has coarse, hairy leaves and an erect habit with tiers of brilliant blue flowers borne in spring to summer. Its several cultivars differ in their precise shade of blue: rich blue **'Morning Glory'**, light blue **'Opal'** and the intense deep blue of **'Loddon Royalist'**. **ZONES 3–9.**

A. × *hybrida* 'Honorine Jobert'

ANEMONE

WINDFLOWER

This genus of over 100 species of perennials occurs widely in the northern hemisphere, but with the majority in temperate Asia. Species include a diverse range of woodland plants as well as the common florist's anemone (*Anemone coronaria*). All have tufts of basal leaves that are divided in palmate fashion into few to many leaflets. The starry or bowl-shaped flowers have 5 or more petals, their colors covering almost the whole range of flower colors. Anemones can be divided into the autumn flowering species with fiberous roots, such as *A. hupehensis* and *A.* × *hybrida*, and the tuberous and rhizomatous types, usually spring flowering, which include the ground-hugging *A. blanda* and *A. nemorosa*. There are other rhizomatous species which tolerate less moisture and more open conditions. Given the right conditions and left undisturbed for many years, many of these will form wonderful carpets of both leaf texture and color through their delicate flowers. The tuberous-rooted types, of which *A. coronaria* is best known, flower in spring and are best replaced every 1–2 years.

CULTIVATION
Most woodland species are very frost hardy and do well in rich, moist yet well-drained soil in a lightly shaded position. Propagate from seed planted in summer or divide established clumps in early winter when dormant. The tuberous-rooted types appreciate full sun, well-drained soil, and a dry dormancy period. However, they are more prone to frost damage and the tubers tend to become weakened after blooming, so they are often treated as annuals.

Anemone hupehensis

JAPANESE WIND FLOWER

A perennial with fiberous roots, this species from central and western China (long cultivated in Japan), can be almost evergreen in milder climates where, if conditions are to its liking it may spread and provide good ground-cover, producing its single white to mauve flowers on tall, openly branched stems during the early autumn. 'Hadspen Abundance' has deep pink petals edged with pale pink to almost white. 'September Charm' has large pale pink flowers with 5 to 6 petals, while *Anemone hupehensis* var. *japonica* is taller and has more petals than the wild Chinese plants. It includes 'Prinz Heinrich' (Prince Henry) with 10 or more deep rose-pink petals, paler on the undersides. Most of the cultivars ascribed to this species are now placed under *Anemone* × *hybrida*. **ZONES 6–10.**

Anemone × hybrida

These popular hybrids are believed to have arisen as crosses between *Anemone hupehensis* and its close relative the Himalayan *A. vitifolia*, the latter distinguished by the dense woolly hair on its leaf undersides and usually white flowers. The hybrids generally have leaves that are hairier beneath than in *A. hupehensis*, and flowers in all shades from white to deepest rose, the petals numbering from 5 to over 30. They generally lack fertile pollen. The robust plants may reach heights of 5 ft (1.5 m) in flower. There are over 30 cultivars, among the most common being 'Honorine Jobert', with pure white, 6–9-petalled flowers and very dark green leaves. Most nurseries do not list cultivar names but just sell the plants in flower, when they are easy to select both for color and flower type. **ZONES 6–10.**

A. hupehensis 'Hadspen Abundance'

Anemone nemorosa
WOOD ANEMONE

As its common name implies, this European species is happiest in a moist, shaded position where its delicate creamy white early spring flowers delight passersby. Usually under 4 in (10 cm) high, it has fine creeping rhizomes that will quickly cover a wanted area if conditions are suitable. Many named cultivars exist including 'Allenii', a rich lilac blue on the outside of the petals and pale lilac on the insides; 'Robinsoniana', with lavender-blue petals; and 'Vestal', a late-blooming white variety. **ZONES 5–9.**

Anemone nemorosa

Anigozanthos,
Bush Gems Series

The best of the kangaroo paws for their resistance to ink disease, the Bush Gems' hybrids are mostly of compact size, with flowers ranging from yellow, gold and green through to orange, red and burgundy. 'Bush Heritage' is a small cultivar of 12–20 in (30–50 cm) in height with flowers of burnt terracotta and olive green. 'Bush Twilight' grows 8–15 in (20–40 cm) tall, has prolific flowers in muted orange, yellow and green tones, appearing mainly in spring above the dull green, very narrow leaves. Other popular cultivars in the Series are 'Bush Glow', sunset red, and 'Bush Gold', golden yellow. **ZONES 9–11.**

ANIGOZANTHOS
KANGAROO PAW

Native to southwestern Australia, these evergreen perennials are noted for their unique bird-attracting tubular flowers, the outsides coated with dense shaggy hairs and opening at the apex into 6 'claws', the whole resembling an animal's paw. Foliage is somewhat grass-like, and the various species can range in height from 1 to 6 ft (0.3 to 1.8 m). Flowers come in many colors including green, gold, deep red and orange-red; some species and hybrids are bicolored. In recent years many hybrids have been produced, meeting the demands of the cut-flower industry and the florists' trade in potted flowers—an example is *Anigozanthos* 'Red Cross'—though most will grow outdoors equally well in mild areas.

Anigozanthos, Bush Gems Series, 'Bush Glow'

CULTIVATION

They prefer warm, very well-drained sandy or gravelly soil and a hot, sunny, open position. Water well during dry seasons. Most will tolerate very light frosts and do well in coastal regions. Most tolerate drought, although flowering will be prolonged with summer water. Propagate by division in spring or from fresh seed. Kangaroo paws are often affected by ink disease, a fungus which blackens the foliage. Watch for snails which can shred younger leaves overnight.

Anigozanthos flavidus
YELLOW KANGAROO PAW

Regarded as the hardiest of the kangaroo paws, this species has a vigorous clumping growth habit to 3 ft (1 m) across. With long, dull green leaves, flowering stems 3–5 ft (1–1.5 m) tall, and flowers in green, yellow or soft red tones, this species has proved adaptable to a range of soils and climates. Native to the far southwestern corner of Australia, where it is attractive to native birds, it is used extensively in hybridization programs. **ZONES 9–11.**

Anigozanthos flavidus

Anigozanthos manglesii
RED-AND-GREEN KANGAROO PAW

This striking plant has blue-green, strap-like leaves. Flowers are a deep green, contrasting vividly with a red base and stem, and appear mainly in spring. Flowering stems are 18–36 in (45–90 cm) in height and the plant has a spread at the base of about 18 in (45 cm). Unfortunately this spectacular species is one of the most difficult to cultivate, being very susceptible to ink disease as well as summer root rot. **ZONES 9–10.**

Anigozanthos manglesii

ANTHEMIS

In suitable conditions the 100 or so species of this genus of annuals and perennials from the Mediterranean region and western Asia are prolific in their flowering and this is what prompted the name, from the Greek *anthemon*. Belonging to the larger daisy family, the flowerheads have the typical daisy shape and are generally white, cream or yellow with distinctive contrasting disc florets; a typical example is *Anthemis* 'Moonlight'. Even when not in flower most species have somewhat aromatic, finely dissected foliage in shades of green or silver gray, which can be used to advantage in the mixed border or rockery. Formerly *Anthemis* was taken in a broader sense to include the herbal chamomile, which belongs to the genus *Chamaemelum*.

Anthemis tinctoria
DYER'S CHAMOMILE, GOLDEN MARGUERITE

Native to Europe and western Asia, this is a very hardy, easily grown perennial that is covered in late spring and summer with a dazzling display of daisy flowers above fern-like, crinkled green leaves. The plant mounds to as much as 3 ft (1 m) high if supported on a rockery or a bank. The epithet *tinctoria* signifies a dye plant, and indeed the flowers of this species were once used to make a yellow dye. The typical form with bright golden flowers is now less popular than some of the cultivars, notably 'E. C. Buxton' with subtle soft yellow blooms blending beautifully with the fine foliage. **ZONES 4–10.**

CULTIVATION
These plants flower best in full sun and like well-drained soil. The perennials can be short-lived and often become untidy, but cutting back after flowering in the autumn ensures a more shapely plant. They are easily replaced by cuttings taken in the warmer months or by division in autumn or spring. Annual species can be grown from seed.

Anthemis tinctoria

Antirrhinum majus

ANTIRRHINUM

SNAPDRAGON

The resemblance of snapdragon flowers to the face of a beast was noted by the ancient Greeks, who called them Antirrhinon, nose-like. In French they are gueule de loup, wolf's mouth, and in German and Italian the name means lion's mouth. Closely related to the toadflaxes *(Linaria)*, the genus consists of about 40 species, most from the western Mediterranean region but with a few from western North America. They include annuals, perennials and evergreen subshrubs. The common snapdragon *(Antirrhinum majus)* is a perennial but it is normally treated as an annual in gardens.

CULTIVATION
They prefer fertile, well-drained soil in full sun. Propagate the garden snapdragon from seed in spring or early autumn.

Antirrhinum majus Liberty Series

Antirrhinum majus
GARDEN SNAPDRAGON

This bushy short-lived perennial is valued for its showy flowers, borne over a long period from spring to autumn. The many named cultivars, usually grown as annuals, spread of 12–18 in (30–45 cm) and may be tall, 30 in (75 cm); medium: 18 in (45 cm); or dwarf: 10 in (25 cm). Plant breeders have developed snapdragons with wide open or double flowers, but none have the charm of the traditional form, as exemplified by the strain called Liberty. Treat these garden snapdragons as annuals—they rarely flower well after the first year, and old plants are apt to succumb to the fungus, antirrhinum rust. Deadhead to prolong flowering and pinch out early buds to increase branching. The Coronette Series of F1 hybrids, bred as bedding plants, exemplifies some of the qualities plant geneticists are injecting into their breeding programs. These include tolerance of bad weather, extra large blooms on heavy spikes and uniformity from seedling stage. They can grow to 24 in (60 cm) or more tall and a number of individual colors are available, from bronze through shades of pink to deep red to yellows and white. Two popular cultivars are 'Flower Carpet' and 'Madame Butterfly'.
ZONES 6–10.

Aponogeton distachyos

Aponogeton distachyos
WATER HAWTHORN

From southern Africa, this plant makes an interesting ornamental for garden ponds, but is best not grown too close to waterlilies (*Nymphaea*), as its densely massed foliage tends to smother them. Hawthorn-scented white flower spikes, 2–4 in (5–10 cm) long and of a curious Y-shape, are produced from late spring to autumn and sometimes into winter, turning green as they age and bend into the water, where the fruit ripens. It will grow in temperate climates provided the water does not freeze. **ZONES 8–10.**

AQUILEGIA
COLUMBINE

The common name comes from the Latin for dove, as the flowers were thought to resemble a cluster of doves. Native to Europe, North America and temperate regions of Asia, these graceful, clump-forming perennials are grown for their spurred, bell-shaped—single and double forms—flowers in a varied color range, and for their fern-like foliage. Some are also useful as cut flowers, and the dwarf and alpine species make good rock garden plants. They flower mostly in late spring and early summer, and look best in bold clumps with a foreground planting of annuals.

CULTIVATION
Frost hardy, they prefer a well-drained light soil, enriched with manure, and a sunny site protected from strong winds and with some shade in hot areas. In cold climates columbines are perennials and need to be cut to the ground in late winter, but growing the larger-flowered cultivars as annuals usually gives best results. Propagate by division or from seed in autumn and spring; many of them self-seed readily.

APONOGETON
WATER HAWTHORN

This genus of aquatic plants consists of 40-odd species, found wild in streams and lakes through tropical and subtropical regions of Africa, Asia and Australasia, but with the greatest concentration in Madagascar. The leaves are long-stalked, oval to narrowly oblong, with a close network of veining; they may be fully submerged, or most of the leaves may float on the surface. Long-stalked flowering heads emerge just above water, branched into short fleshy spikes of curious small white, pink or purplish flowers. The tuberous roots and flower buds are sometimes eaten in their native countries.

CULTIVATION
Aponogetons fall into 2 groups as far as cultivation is concerned. The larger group consists of choice subjects for the tropical aquarium, notably the magnificent *Aponogeton madagascariensis*, with its lattice-like submerged leaves—not quite typical of this group, its requirements being very specialized—these require a fairly deep tank, the water kept to at least 60°F (16°C) in winter, higher in summer. The smaller group, typified by *A. distachyos*, are more cold hardy and vigorous, and are grown outdoors in temperate climates so long as the water has no more than a thin crust of ice from time to time in winter. They are easily grown, planted into the bottom mud or sand. Propagate by division of the tubers, or from seed.

Aquilegia,
Aquilegia caerulea
McKana Hybrids

This, the best known strain of long-spurred columbines, is derived from North American species, chiefly *Aquilegia caerulea*, *A. chrysantha* and *A. formosa*. They bear flowers in a wide assortment of colors in late spring and early summer. Whatever the color of the sepals, the 5 petals that carry the spurs are usually white or yellow. Pinching off spent flowers will prolong the season. The plants grow to 3 ft (1 m) or more. **ZONES 3–10.**

Aquilegia vulgaris
GRANNY'S BONNETS, COLUMBINE

Aquilegia McKana Hybrids

This is the true columbine of Europe, one of the parents of many hybrids. It grows to 3 ft (1 m) high with a spread of 18 in (45 cm) or more. On long stems from the center of a loose rosette of gray-green foliage, it bears funnel-shaped, short-spurred flowers, typically dull blue in wild plants but ranging through pink, crimson, white and purple in garden varieties. The cultivar 'Nora Barlow' has double flowers of a curious form, with many narrow, greenish sepals and pink petals that lack spurs. **ZONES 3–10.**

Aquilegia vulgaris Hybrid

ARABIS
ROCK CRESS

Arabis caucasica

Over 120 species make up this northern hemisphere genus of annuals and perennials, the latter mostly evergreen. Although some can reach as much as 3 ft (1 m) in height, species grown in gardens are dwarf, often mat-forming perennials suited to the rock garden, dry walls and crevices. They spread by short rhizomes, producing crowded tufts of spatula-shaped leaves. Short sprays of delicate, 4-petalled flowers are held above the foliage in spring and summer.

Arabis blepharophylla

CULTIVATION
They grow best in very well-drained soil in a sunny position. Propagation is from seed or from cuttings taken in summer, or by division.

Arabis blepharophylla
CALIFORNIA ROCK CRESS

This is a moderately frost-hardy Californian native, which grows at low altitudes, and forms a compact clump 4– 6 in (10–15 cm) high. Tufts of toothed green leaves extend into short, leafy spikes of pink to purple flowers during spring. It is best in a rockery or crevice where it will not be overrun. An award-winning cultivar is 'Frühlingzauber' (syn. 'Spring Charm'), with rich rose-purple flowers. **ZONES 7–10.**

Arabis caucasica
syn. Arabis albida
WALL ROCK CRESS

This tough, evergreen perennial is sometimes used to overplant spring-flowering bulbs. Easily grown, it forms dense clusters of thick foliage up to 6 in (15 cm) high and 18 in (45 cm) wide. In spring it has white flowers on loose racemes above gray-green leaf rosettes. There are various forms of *Arabis caucasica* such as 'Pinkie', *A. c.* var. *brevifolia* and double-flowered forms such as 'Flore Pleno' (syn. 'Plena'). **ZONES 4–10.**

CULTIVATION

Given plenty of space in a sunny position and well-drained, sandy soil, arctotises may be used as bedding plants or to cover a large area of dry bank. Flowering can be prolonged if blooms are dead-headed after the first flush of early summer. They can be grown in containers. Propagate from seed or cuttings, which can be rooted at any time of year.

Arctotis Hybrids

These very pretty plants were known until recently as × *Venidioarctotis* hybrids, one of the main parent species having being placed in the genus *Venidium* (now combined with *Arctotis*). They are grown as annual bedding plants in frost-prone areas but will overwinter in milder climates. Growing to a height and spread of around 18 in (45 cm), these hybrids have gray, lobed leaves that are quite downy beneath. In summer and autumn they produce a long succession of showy blooms, to 3 in (8 cm) across in a very wide range of colors, often 2-toned. 'Gold Bi-Color', 'Apricot', 'Flame', 'Dream Coat' and 'Wine' are among the more popular of the named hybrids. **ZONES 9–11.**

ARCTOTIS

syns *Venidium*, × *Venidioarctotis*

AFRICAN DAISY

This genus consists of about 50 species of annuals and evergreen perennials from South Africa. The stems and leaves are to varying degrees coated in matted downy hairs, giving them a gray-green or silvery gray color. The showy flowers are typical of the daisy family. They rely on the sun to open fully and come in a range of colors from creamy yellow often through orange to deep pinks and claret reds. Many hybrids are now available, their blooms with rings of darker color towards the center. Growth habit varies from compact and shrubby to quite prostrate, plants of the latter type making a faster-spreading and colorful groundcover. Some of the more distinctive *Arctotis* species include *A. arctotoides*, with narrow, deeply lobed leaves, and *A. cumbletonii* which has quite narrow disc florets.

Arctotis Hybrid 'Dream Coat'

Arctotis Hybrid 'Wine'

Arctotis cumbletonii

ARMERIA
THRIFT, SEA PINK

This genus of about 35 species of low-growing, tufted, early summer-flowering perennials is found in a wide variety of environments in the temperate zones of Eurasia, Africa and the Americas—from salt marshes and storm-swept headlands of the seashores to alpine meadows. The plants have crowded, narrow, mostly evergreen leaves, usually forming a dense mound, and small flowers crowded into globular heads, each atop a slender stalk.

Armeria maritima

CULTIVATION
They are suitable for rock gardens or borders and prefer exposed, sunny positions and rather dry soil with good drainage. They are generally frost hardy. Propagate from seed or cuttings in spring or autumn.

Armeria maritima
COMMON THRIFT, SEA PINK

Native around much of the northern hemisphere and consisting of many wild races, thrift was in cultivation as early as 1578. Growing to 4 in (10 cm) high and spreading to 8 in (20 cm), it has a mound-like mass of narrow, dark green leaves, and dense flowerheads of small, white to pink flowers are produced in spring and summer. Most *Armeria* cultivars are derived from this species. 'Vindictive' has vibrant rose-pink flowers. 'Alba' has small white flowers. **ZONES 4–9.**

Artemisia ludoviciana
syn. **Artemisia purshiana**
WESTERN MUGWORT, WHITE SAGE

Native to western North America and Mexico, this rhizomatous species is grown for its lance-shaped, sometimes coarsely toothed leaves, which are densely white-felted beneath and gray- to white-haired above. Bell-shaped, grayish flowerheads are produced in summer. A spreading, invasive species, it reaches a height of 4 ft (1.2 m) and is very frost hardy. 'Valerie Finnis', with its jagged margined leaves, together with 'Silver Queen' are 2 of several popular cultivars, while *Artemisia ludoviciana* var. **albula**, found naturally in California, has much smaller leaves. **ZONES 4–10.**

Artemisia ludoviciana 'Silver Queen'

ARTEMISIA
WORMWOOD

This is a large genus of perennials and shrubs native to temperate regions of the northern hemisphere, many from arid and semi-arid environments. They are grown mainly for their decorative foliage which is often aromatic and sometimes repellent to insects; in many species it is coated with whitish hairs. An attractive addition to a flower border, the feathery foliage provides interest throughout the year. The small yellowish flowerheads are not showy. There are both evergreen and deciduous species.

CULTIVATION
Mostly quite frost hardy, they prefer an open, sunny situation with light, well-drained soil. Prune back lightly in spring to stimulate growth. Propagate from cuttings in summer or by division in spring. Transplant during winter.

ARUNCUS
GOAT'S BEARD

There are 3 species in this genus of rhizomatous perennials, occurring widely over temperate and subarctic regions of the northern hemisphere. Their appearance is very much that of a giant astilbe, with ferny basal leaves up to 3 ft (1 m) long, and summer plumes of tiny cream flowers in 8–18 in (20–45 cm) long, pyramidal panicles carried on wiry stems that hold them well above the foliage.

CULTIVATION
They are best grown in sun or part-shade in moist, humus-rich, well-drained soil around edges of ponds. Goat's beard is very frost hardy and is propagated from seed or by division.

Aruncus dioicus
syns Aruncus sylvestris, Spiraea aruncus

A graceful, woodland perennial, this clump-forming plant produces a mass of rich green, fern-like foliage and arching plumes of tiny, greenish or creamy white flowers in summer. It grows 6 ft (1.8 m) tall and 4 ft (1.2 m) wide. Cut flowering stems back hard in autumn. 'Kneiffii' reaches about 3 ft (1 m) and has cream-colored flowers. **ZONES 3–9.**

ASTER
MICHAELMAS OR EASTER DAISY, ASTER

Native to temperate regions of the northern hemisphere (most numerous in North America), this large genus of perennials and deciduous or evergreen subshrubs contains over 250 species, ranging in height from miniatures suitable for rock gardens to 6 ft (1.8 m) giants. The leaves are simple and mostly smooth-edged, sometimes hairy, often quite small. Showy, daisy-like flowerheads are usually produced in late summer or autumn in a wide range of colors, including blue, violet, purple, pink, red and white, all with a central disc of yellow or purple. There are many aster cultivars once listed under the parent species, but this has become too complex and many now stand alone. A typical example is Aster 'Coombe's Violet'. The 'China asters' grown as bedding annuals are now placed in the genus Callistephus.

Aruncus dioicus

CULTIVATION
Easily grown, they prefer sun (or part-shade in hot areas) in a well-drained soil, preferably enriched with compost. Keep moist at all times and shelter from strong winds and stake the taller species. Cut the long stems down to ground level and tidy the clumps when the flowers have faded. Propagate by division in spring or late autumn, or from softwood cuttings in spring. Divide plants every 2 to 3 years, using the most vigorous outer part. Powdery mildew, rust, aphids and snails can be a problem.

Aster alpinus

Aster 'Coombe's Violet'

From the higher mountains of Europe, this clump-forming plant, usually 6–12 in (15–30 cm) high and spreading to 18 in (45 cm), bears large, violet-blue, daisy flowers with yellow centers from late spring until mid-summer; the foliage is dark green. It is a popular rock-garden plant and is fully frost hardy. There are a number of named cultivars. The cultivar '**Trimix**' grows to 8 in (20 cm) and has pretty flowers that are a tricolor mix of pink, blue and white. **ZONES 3–9.**

Aster alpinus cultivar

Aster ericoides

HEATH ASTER

The specific name means 'with leaves like those of Erica', the heath genus, and indeed this species from eastern and central USA and northern Mexico has very small, narrow leaves, at least on the upper stems. With flowering stems rising up to 3 ft (1 m) high from tufted basal shoots towards mid-summer and into autumn, it provides a wonderful display of massed, small, white flowerheads as does one of its more compact cultivars, '**White Heather**'. There are a number of cultivars of varied heights, mostly with pale pinkish or yellowish blooms. The cut flowers are popular with florists. **ZONES 4–10.**

Aster ericoides

Aster divaricatus

Aster divaricatus

WHITE WOOD ASTER

Also from eastern North America, this is a distinctive species with slender, wiry, dark mahogany stems to about 24 in (60 cm) tall that tend to twist and wander, broad-based leaves tapering to fine points, and delicate, open sprays of small, white flowerheads. Spreading by rhizomes to form loose clumps, it is essentially a plant for the woodland garden. Some forms of *Aster divaricatus* are taller and more robust. **ZONES 3–9.**

Aster novae-angliae
NEW ENGLAND ASTER

Originally native over a wide area of the
eastern and central USA, this species is
represented in cultivation by many cultivars, showing much variation in form
and color of blooms. Vigorous clumps of
mostly vertical, 3–5 ft (1–1.5 m) stems are
likely to lean with the weight of large,
loose clusters of daisies, making staking
necessary. Cultivars include the late-
blooming, clear pink 'Harrington's Pink';
the rose-pink, mildew-resistant 'Barr's
Pink'; and the cerise 'September Ruby';
while 'Andenken an Alma Pötschke',
often shortened to 'Alma Pötschke', is a
compact-growing, though 4 ft (1.2 m) tall
plant with bright rose-pink blooms, and
'Hella Lacy'. These popular asters prefer
a moist, rich soil in full sun. ZONES 4–9.

Aster novae-angliae 'Andenken an Alma Pötschke'

Aster novi-belgii
NEW YORK ASTER

Novi-belgii is Linnaeus' attempt to
translate New Amsterdam (now New
York) into Latin; the Belgii were the tribe
encountered by Julius Caesar in the Low
Countries. The New York aster in its wild
form is native to the east coast, from
Newfoundland to Georgia. It has given
rise to innumerable garden forms in
colors ranging from the palest mauve to
violet and deep pink, and with varying
degrees of 'doubling' of the flowerheads.
They are among the most useful plants
for the perennial border in cooler-
temperate climates, responding to generous feeding and watering in spring and
summer. It is, however, subject to mildew.
Cultivars include 'Court Herald', and the
popular 'Mulberry' which has large,
semi-double, rich mulberry-red blooms.
'Ernest Ballard', named for a leading
aster breeder, grows to 3 ft (1 m) with
large, purple-red blooms. 'Audrey'
is a very pretty cultivar; it grows to a
compact 12 in (30 cm) with double,
lavender-blue autumn flowers. ZONES 3–9.

Aster novae-angliae 'Barr's Pink'

ASTILBE

FALSE SPIRAEA

This genus of 14 species of pretty, early to late summer perennials comes mostly from eastern Asia, where they grow in the moist ground beside woodland streams, though there are also 2 species occurring in the eastern USA. All astilbes have basal tufts of ferny, compound leaves, the leaflets usually sharply toothed. Pointed, plume-like panicles of tiny, white to pink or red flowers rise well above the foliage. Most usual in cultivation are the hybrids grouped under the name *Astilbe* × *arendsii*, though there are many recent hybrid cultivars of different parentage. The name 'spiraea' was mistakenly attached to this genus when they were introduced to England in the 1820s.

CULTIVATION
They need a lightly shaded place with rich, leafy soil that never dries out, though they do not like being actually flooded, especially in winter. Cooler climates suit them best; in hot summers they need constant watering to keep their roots cool. Good cut flowers, they also make pretty pot plants for bringing indoors for a while when the flowers are at their best. In a heated greenhouse they will flower early. Propagate by division in winter.

Astilbe, Arendsii Hybrids

This hybrid group, derived from four east Asian species, *Astilbe astilboides*, *A. japonica*, *A. davidii* and *A. thunbergii*, is named after German horticulturalist Georg Arends (1863–1952) to whom many of the finest cultivars are credited. Heights vary, usually 18–48 in (0.45–1.2 m), with a spread of 18–30 in (45–75 cm). They produce feathery spikes in a wide color range from late spring to early summer. Cultivars are available in a range of colors from red through pink to white and include 'Amethyst', with pale purple to pink flowers; 'Fanal', with long-lasting scarlet flowers; 'Brautschleier' ('Bridal Veil'), white; 'Rheinland', deep rose; and 'Europa', pale pink flowers. **ZONES 6–10.**

Astilbe, Arendsii Hybrid, 'Brautschleier'

Astilbe chinensis

A late-summer-flowering species native to China, Korea and eastern Siberia, this is an attractive, clump-forming plant reaching 24 in (60 cm) with toothed, hairy, dark green leaflets and dense, fluffy spikes of tiny, star-shaped, white, flushed pink blooms. 'Pumila', a dwarf form growing to 12 in (30 cm) with pinkish mauve flowers, doesn't mind heavier clay soils and will spread quickly if conditions are to its liking. *Astilbe chinensis* var. *davidii* grows to 6 ft (1.8 m) with purple-pink flowers crowded on long, slender panicles; this variety has the added interest of bronze-toned new foliage, while *A. c.* var. *taquetii* has lavender-pink flowers on a plant about 3 ft (1 m) tall. **ZONES 6–10.**

Astilbe chinensis 'Pumila'

Astilbe, Arendsii Hybrid 'Europa'

AUBRIETA
ROCK CRESS

Although mountain flowers, aubrietas are not diminutive and temperamental as are many alpine plants. Rather they make carpets of color at the front of flowerbeds, or down retaining walls. Not very tall—6 in (15 cm) or so at most—they will happily sprawl to several times their height and in spring cover themselves with 4-petalled flowers, mainly in shades of purple. About a dozen species are native to stony hillsides and mountains from the Mediterranean area to as far east as Iran. The plants most often seen in gardens are hybrids mainly derived from *Aubrieta deltoidea*. The genus name honors the French botanical painter Claude Aubriet (1668–1743); it has sometimes been spelt Aubrietia.

CULTIVATION
They are easy to grow in cool-temperate climates (flowering is erratic in warm ones), asking only sunshine or a little shade and fertile, well-drained soil. They are short lived and it is wise to take a few cuttings in summer every 3 or 4 years; they are readily propagated also by division of the rhizomatous rootstock.

Aubrieta deltoidea

AURINIA

This is a genus of 7 species of biennials and evergreen perennials, formerly included in *Alyssum*, found from central and southern Europe to the Ukraine and Turkey. They are mainly small, spreading, mound-forming plants. The leaves are initially in basal rosettes, mostly fairly narrow. They bear elongated sprays of tiny yellow or white flowers in spring and early summer.

CULTIVATION
Plant in light, gritty, well-drained soil in full sun. They are ideal for rockeries, rock crevices or dry-stone walls. Most species are very frost hardy and are propagated from seed or small tip cuttings; they will self-sow in suitable locations.

Aurinia saxatilis 'Citrina'

Aubrieta deltoidea

Native to southeastern Europe and Turkey, this compact, mat-forming perennial has greenish gray leaves and masses of starry, mauve-pink flowers borne over a long period in spring. The species itself is now rare in gardens, most cultivated aubrietas being hybrids now known collectively as *Aubrieta* × *cultorum*, though they are often listed as *A. deltoidea*. **ZONES 4–9.**

Aurinia saxatilis

Aurinia saxatilis
syn. *Alyssum saxatile*
BASKET OF GOLD, YELLOW ALYSSUM

The only commonly grown species, it is a native of central and southeastern Europe. It has hairy, gray-green leaves, forms rather loose mounds to 10 in (25 cm) high and is smothered in bright yellow flowers in spring and early summer. It is very popular as a rockery or wall plant. There are a number of cultivars, including '**Argentea**', with silvery leaves; '**Citrina**', with lemon-yellow flowers; '**Gold Dust**', up to 12 in (30 cm) mounds with deep golden-yellow flowers; '**Sulphurea**', with glowing yellow flowers; and '**Tom Thumb**', a 4 in (10 cm) high dwarf with small leaves. **ZONES 4–9.**

Baptisia australis

Baptisia australis

FALSE INDIGO

This summer-flowering perennial is attractive in both flower and foliage. The leaves are blue-green and form a loose mound up to about 5 ft.(1.5 m) high and 3 ft (1 m) across. The lupin-like flowers are borne on erect spikes from early to mid-summer and are an unusual shade of purplish blue. The seed pods can be dried for indoor decoration. **ZONES 3–10.**

BAPTISIA

FALSE INDIGO

Baptisia is a genus of 20–30 species of pea-flowered perennials that grow naturally among the tall grasses of the prairies and woodlands of eastern and central USA. The common name arises from the former use of some species by dyers as a substitute for true indigo (*Indigofera*). Few of the species are grown much in gardens. Most are somewhat shrubby in habit, and the leaves are divided into 3 leaflets like a clover or a medic. The blue, purple, yellow or white pea-flowers are borne in terminal spikes over a fairly long summer season.

CULTIVATION

The plants prefer full sun and neutral, well-drained soil. They are not bothered by frost, nor do they resent very dry conditions in summer. As they have a deep root system they should not be transplanted or disturbed. Propagation is best done from seed in autumn or by division.

BEGONIA

BEGONIA

Begonias are native to moist tropical and subtropical regions of all continents except Australia, and are most diverse in South America. There are over 1,500 known species, ranging from rhizomatous perennials a few inches (centimeters) high to 3 ft (1 m) shrubs. Many are grown indoors, prized for their beautifully colored and textured foliage or showy flowers, sometimes both present in the one species or cultivar. Mostly evergreen, their broad, usually asymmetrical leaves have a rather brittle and waxy texture. Female flowers, as distinct from male flowers that are on the same plant, have broad, colored flanges on the ovaries which develop into winged fruits.

Begonia enthusiasts divide the species and cultivars into a number of classes depending on growth habit and type of rootstock. The cane-stemmed begonias are erect growers, sometimes quite tall, with straight stems, fiberous roots, and usually pendent clusters of showy flowers; somewhat similar are some shrubby begonias, with a more closely branched habit (the bedding begonias belong here); another similar group but with lower, softer stems are known as the winter-flowering begonias, grown for their profuse and colorful flowers that peak in winter; the rhizomatous begonias are a large and varied class, with leaves arising directly from creeping, knotty rhizomes—they include the Rex begonias with attractively variegated leaves and many others grown for foliage; finally the tuberous begonias, now largely represented by hybrids of the Tuber-hybrida Group, which die back to tubers in winter and bear large, showy, often double flowers in summer, for instance 'Mandy Henschke'.

CULTIVATION

Many of the cane-stemmed, winter-flowering, shrubby and rhizomatous types can be grown outdoors in frost-free climates and make fine garden plants, though rhizomatous kinds in particular are prone to slug and snail attack. As indoor plants they do well in standard potting mix with peat moss or leafmold added to increase acidity. Grow in bright to moderate light, with good ventilation and above-average humidity, which can be maintained by standing pots on a tray of pebbles and water. Pinch back young plants of the shrubby type to keep them compact and to encourage flowers. Tuberous begonias require special treatment: tubers must be forced into growth in early spring at a temperature of 65°F (18°C) in peat moss or sphagnum, and kept in a cool, well-ventilated greenhouse for the summer-flowering season. After flowering, plants die back and tubers are lifted in mid-autumn and stored dry. Propagate from tubers in the case of tuberous begonias. Other begonias may be propagated from stem or leaf cuttings (laying the cut leaf blades flat on damp sand and weighing them down with pebbles), or by division of rhizomes, or from seed. Begonias are susceptible to gray mold, powdery mildew and botrytis in the warmer part of the year if conditions are too damp.

Begonia 'Cleopatra'

This rhizomatous begonia is a popular, easy-to-grow plant with a dense mass of shortly creeping rhizomes that support crowded, sharply lobed, yellow-green and purplish brown leaves. Profuse, long-stalked sprays of pale pink flowers bloom in early spring. In warm climates it is a popular balcony plant, thriving in hot sun. **ZONES 10–12.**

Begonia fuchsioides

Begonia fuchsioides

Native to Venezuela, this shrubby begonia has small, crowded, oval leaves, flushed pink on new growths. Small coral-red to pale pink flowers are borne in numerous short sprays over a long season from autumn to spring. Suitable for outdoor use in warm areas, it grows to 3 ft (1 m) tall with an erect, closely branched habit and gracefully drooping branchlets. It also makes a good pot plant. It prefers good light. **ZONES 10–12.**

Begonia, Semperflorens-cultorum Group

BEDDING BEGONIA, WAX BEGONIA

Derived largely from the Brazilian *Begonia semperflorens,* the dwarf, shrubby begonias of this group are often grown as bedding annuals, for example, 'Ernst Benary', or for borders in shaded gardens, and are also popular as potted plants for window boxes or patio tubs. Freely branching plants with soft, succulent stems, they have rounded, glossy green (bronze or variegated in some cultivars) leaves about 2 in (5 cm) long. The flowers are profuse, opening progressively at the branch tips over a long summer and early autumn season (most of the

Begonia, Tuberhybrida Group 'Mandy Henschke'

Begonia 'Cleopatra'

year in warmer climates). The numerous cultivars include singles and doubles in colors of bright rose pink, light pink, white or red; they are generally released as a series, with mixed colors. They are grown from seed or stem cuttings and planted out in late spring in cooler climates; pinch out growing tips to encourage bushy growth. **Cocktail Series** are bushy miniatures with bronzy foliage and single flowers: **'Gin'** has metallic black-green leaves and deep pink flowers; **'Vodka'** produces deep red flowers against very dark green leaves; and the pale bronze leaves of **'Whiskey'** are offset by white flowers. **Thousand Wonders** is an older series consisting of compact, sun-hardy plants in mixed shades of pink and white. **ZONES 9–11.**

B. Semperflorens-cultorum Group

Bellis perennis, Pomponette Series

BELLIS

DAISY

The pretty little white flower that spangles lawns in spring is one of the best loved of European wildflowers. These, the true daisies, belong to the genus *Bellis* which consists of 15 species of small perennials that occur wild in Europe, North Africa and Turkey. *Bellis* is from the Latin *bellus* which means 'pretty' or 'charming', while the English 'daisy' is a corruption of 'day's eye', arising from the way the flower closes up at night, opening once again to greet the new sunrise. The plants form rosettes with small oval to spoon-shaped leaves; each rosette produces a succession of flowerheads on individual stalks in shades of white, pink, blue or crimson. Only one of the species is widely cultivated, mostly in the form of improved strains.

CULTIVATION

Daisies have long been favorite flowers for edging flowerbeds in spring and, while they are perennial in cool-temperate climates, it is usual to treat them as annuals or biennials, sowing seed in autumn. They will thrive in any good garden soil in sun or part-shade; make sure to keep soil moist in winter and spring. Propagation is from seed or by division.

Bellis perennis

ENGLISH DAISY, COMMON DAISY

This lovely daisy has become widely naturalized in temperate parts of most continents. The wild plants are small, forming carpets of crowded rosettes that spread through lawns by short runners. The 1 in (25 mm) wide flowerheads, appearing from late winter to early summer, are white with golden centers and pale purplish undersides. **'Medicis White'** is a white cultivar and a favorite with many gardeners. The garden strains mostly have double flowerheads of red, crimson, pink or white, all with a gold center. **'Alba Plena'** is an old double white cultivar, very different from the **Pomponette Series** daisies now popular as bedding plants and cut flowers; these are a far cry from the wild flowers, making neat hemispherical flowerheads 1½ in (35 mm) wide with curled petals, on stems up to 10 in (25 cm) high. They come in mixed colors. **ZONES 3–10.**

Bergenia cordifolia

BERGENIA

Consisting of 6 or 7 species of rhizomatous, semi-evergreen perennials in the saxifrage family from eastern and central Asia, this genus is characterized by large, handsome, paddle-shaped leaves, arising from the ground on short stalks to form loose clumps. There are also many garden hybrids that have been developed over the last 100 years or so. Large clusters of flowers—mostly pale pink, but also white and dark pink—are borne on short, stout stems in winter and spring. An example is 'Eroica', with deep pink flowers. The foliage often develops attractive red tints in winter.

CULTIVATION

Bergenias make excellent rockery plants, thriving in sun or shade and tolerant of exposed sites as well as moist ground beside streams or ponds, but leaves color most strongly when plants are grown under drier conditions. Some are good as groundcover when planted en masse. Water well in hot conditions and remove spent flowerheads to prolong flowering. Propagate by division in spring after flowering, when the plants have become crowded.

Bergenia × schmidtii

Bergenia cordifolia
HEARTLEAF SAXIFRAGE

Native to Siberia's Altai Mountains, this tough perennial has crinkly edged, more or less heart-shaped leaves up to 8 in (20 cm) wide, and produces panicles of drooping purple-pink flowers on 12–15 in (30–38 cm) stems in late winter and early spring. The plant is long flowering and the leaves remain green in winter. 'Purpurea' has magenta-pink flowers and leaves tinged purple. **ZONES 3–9.**

Bergenia × schmidtii

Arguably the most vigorous and most widely planted bergenia, this old hybrid between *Bergenia ciliata* and *B. crassifolia* has large, rounded, fleshy, dull green leaves. Set among the foliage are rose-pink blooms on stalks up to 12 in (30 cm) long. The main flush of flowers occurs in late winter and early spring; frosts may damage blooms, but it often flowers sporadically at other times. The plant spreads to make a fine groundcover, and adapts well to warm-temperate humid climates. **ZONES 5–10.**

Bergenia 'Eroica'

BIDENS

TICKSEED, BEGGAR'S TICKS, BURR-MARIGOLD

This is a genus of around 200 species of annuals, perennials, subshrubs and shrubs that is closely related to *Cosmos* and occurs in most parts of the world except very cold regions. In most countries this genus is represented only by a weedy species. The majority are native to Mexico and adjacent regions of the Americas. The plants have erect leafy stems, usually much branched, with opposite pairs of leaves that are generally compound or deeply divided. Yellow daisy flowers (occasionally red to purple, for example, the purplish pink *Bidens aequisquamea*), mostly with very few but broad ray florets, open in a long succession and are followed by burr-like seedheads containing narrow seeds, each tipped with 2-barbed bristles (*Bidens* means 'two-toothed') that can stick to clothing and fur.

CULTIVATION

These plants are very easily grown in any well-drained soil. Plant in full sun or morning shade, and water well in summer. Although hardiness varies with the species, most will withstand moderate frosts. Propagate from seed or cuttings, or by division, depending on the growth form.

Bidens ferulifolia

BOYKINIA

syn. *Telesonix*

A North American and Japanese genus of 9 species of woodland and alpine perennials, these plants spread by shortly creeping rhizomes. They resemble the closely related genera *Heuchera* and *Tiarella*, and have lobed and toothed, roughly heart- or kidney-shaped hairy leaves, varying in size depending on the species. Stalked panicles of small, 5-petalled, white, cream or reddish flowers open through spring or summer. While not spectacular, they are graceful plants that help to lighten shady corners. Botanists differ on the question of whether *Telesonix* should be united with *Boykinia*.

CULTIVATION

Plant in moist, humus-rich, well-drained soil in dappled shade. Hardiness varies, though all species will tolerate at least moderate frosts. Propagate by division in late winter.

Bidens ferulifolia

Native to Mexico and Arizona, *Bidens ferulifolia* is a bushy, evergreen perennial 18–24 in (45–60 cm) tall, usually short lived. The leaves are small and fern-like, divided into narrow segments, and it bears golden-yellow, few-rayed flowerheads to 1½ in (35 mm) wide in a long succession from late spring to autumn. 'Arizona' and 'Golden Goddess' are both popular cultivars. **ZONES 8–10.**

Boykinia jamesii

Boykinia jamesii

syns *Boykinia heucheriformis*, *Telesonix jamesii*

A native of Colorado, this cold-hardy species is one of the smallest boykinias. Its kidney-shaped leaves are usually less than 2 in (5 cm) wide and the plant forms a compact mound of fresh green foliage around 4 in (10 cm) high and up to 6 in (15 cm) in diameter. Its narrow 6 in (15 cm) stems bear purple-red flowers, larger than those of other boykinias, and it needs to be treated as an alpine. **ZONES 5–8.**

BRACHYCOME
syn. *Brachyscome*

Native to Australia, the low-growing annuals and evergreen perennials of this genus are attractive groundcover or rockery plants. Many of the perennials are mound-forming, spreading by underground runners and having finely divided, soft, fern-like foliage. They bear a profusion of daisy-like flowerheads in shades of blue, mauve, pink and yellow, with orange or brownish centers or yellow as in the hybrids 'Sunburst' and 'Outback Sunburst', both with white ray florets. Botanists have disputed the spelling of this genus, the debate hinging on whether the nineteenth-century botanist who spelt it *Brachyscome* had the right to subsequently correct his bad Greek, as he did (it combines *brachys*, short, with *kome*, hair, referring to a seed feature, but the 's' is dropped when they are joined).

Brachycome iberidifolia 'Blue Star'

Brachycome 'Outback Sunburst'

Brachycome multifida

CULTIVATION

Brachycome species require a sunny situation and a light, well-drained garden soil. Many are moderately frost hardy and some will tolerate coastal salt spray. Be careful not to overwater as they prefer dry conditions. Pinch out early shoots to encourage branching. Propagate from ripe seed or stem cuttings or by division in spring or autumn.

Brachycome iberidifolia
SWAN RIVER DAISY

This daisy is a weak-stemmed annual, long grown as a bedding or border plant, that grows to a height and spread of around 12 in (30 cm), sometimes taller. It has deeply dissected leaves with very narrow segments. Small, fragrant, daisy-like flowerheads, normally mauve-blue but sometimes white, pink or purple, appear in great profusion in summer and early autumn. 'Blue Star' is a cultivar with massed small mauve to purple-blue flowers. **ZONES 9–11.**

Brachycome multifida

This perennial species is a charming groundcover in warm-temperate climates, though it is not long lived and should be renewed every few years. It grows to 4–6 in (10–15 cm) high and spreads to about 18 in (45 cm). The mauve-pink flowerheads bloom for weeks in late spring and summer. It likes sunshine and perfect drainage and is propagated by layers or from cuttings. 'Break O' Day' is a selected form with finer leaves, profuse mauve-blue flowers and a very compact habit. **ZONES 9–11.**

Bracteantha bracteata 'Diamond Head'

BRACTEANTHA
syn. Helichrysum
STRAWFLOWER, EVERLASTING DAISY

This Australian genus consists of 7 species of annuals and perennials, until recently classified under *Helichrysum*. They differ from true helichrysums in their large, decorative flowerheads carried singly or a few together at the end of the flowering branches, each consisting of golden yellow to white bracts of straw-like texture surrounding a disc of tiny yellow or brownish florets. The leaves, mostly broad and thin, are often downy on their undersides, or can be very sticky in some species. Most of the cultivated forms and seedling strains are treated as forms of *Bracteantha bracteata*, but further botanical study is likely to result in new species being recognized.

CULTIVATION

Plant in moist, well-drained soil in full sun. The summer-flowering annuals may be planted from late winter for an early display. Provided they are not waterlogged, most species will tolerate light to moderate frosts. Propagate annuals from seed and perennials from seed or tip cuttings.

Bracteantha bracteata
syn. Helichrysum bracteatum

This annual or short-lived perennial has an erect habit and grows to a height of around 3 ft (1 m). It has weak, hollow stems, thin green leaves and from summer to early autumn bears golden-yellow blooms up to 2 in (5 cm) in diameter at the branch tips. In the mid-nineteenth century annual strains with larger flowerheads in shades of pink, bronze red, cream, purple and yellow were developed; these plants were generally more vigorous; **Bright Bikinis Series** is a modern descendant of these. Some more spreading, shrubby perennial plants from eastern Australia, which may be recognized as distinct species, have been named as cultivars. These include the popular **'Dargan Hill Monarch'**, with rich yellow blooms up to 3 in (8 cm) across, emerging over several months; and **'Diamond Head'**, which is similar but lower and more compact. **ZONES 8–11.**

Bracteantha bracteata

BROWALLIA
BUSH VIOLET

This is a genus of 6 species of bushy annuals and evergreen perennials, all native to tropical South America and the West Indies. They are densely foliaged with a compact habit, soft stems and simple, strongly veined, deep green leaves. The flowers, carried singly in the leaf axils, are like smaller versions of nicotianas (to which they are related) but with shorter tubes and generally in shades of blue, purple or white; they can be quite profuse on well-grown plants.

CULTIVATION
In cool climates browallias are grown as conservatory plants or treated as summer annuals. In frost-free climates they will grow well outdoors in moist, humus-rich, well-drained soil in a warm, part-shaded position sheltered from drying winds. Regular feeding with liquid fertilizer will keep the foliage lush and ensure steady flowering. Pinch back the stem tips to keep the plants bushy. Propagate the annuals from seed in spring, the perennials from seed or tip cuttings.

Browallia Americana

Browallia americana
syn. *Browallia elata*

This annual makes a bushy plant of up to 24 in (60 cm) tall. In summer and early autumn it bears showy 2 in (5 cm) wide flowers, their color varying from a rare shade of intense blue through paler violet to white. It makes a good pot or basket plant and also grows well outdoors. 'Vanja' has deep blue flowers with white eyes; 'White Bells' has ice white flowers. **ZONES 9–11.**

CALAMINTHA
CALAMINT

This genus is described in the Vegetables and Herbs chapter, but the species below is often grown in perennial gardens.

Calamintha grandiflora
LARGE-FLOWERED CALAMINT

With 1–1½ in (25–35 mm) long bright pink flowers, this species is used both as an ornament and as a herb. A woodland plant, it occurs wild in southern Europe, North Africa and Asia as far east as Iran. The tall stems spring from creeping rhizomes and bear pale green serrated leaves. The flowers are borne in summer in the uppermost leaf axils. **ZONES 7–10.**

Calceolaria, Herbeohybrida Group

CALCEOLARIA

LADIES' PURSE, SLIPPER FLOWER, POCKETBOOK FLOWER

Gardeners who know this genus only in the form of the gaudy 'slipper flowers' sold by florists may be surprised to learn that it contains upward of 300 species, ranging from tiny annuals to herbaceous perennials and even scrambling climbers and quite woody shrubs. All are native to the Americas, from Mexico southward to Tierra del Fuego, and all share the same curious flower structure, with a lower lip inflated like a rather bulbous slipper. Flower colors are mainly yellows and oranges, often with red or purple spots.

CULTIVATION
Calceolarias come from a wide range of habitats and vary greatly in cold hardiness. When grown outdoors they prefer a shady, cool site in moist, well-drained soil with added compost. Provide shelter from heavy winds as the flowers are easily damaged. Shrubby species may benefit from being pruned back by half in winter. Propagate from seed or softwood cuttings in summer or late spring. The Herbeohybrida Group, grown mainly in cool greenhouses, are fed and watered liberally in the summer growing season; they are subject to a number of diseases and pest infestations.

Calceolaria, Herbeohybrida Group

These are the popular florists' calceolarias, a group of hybrids derived from 3 Chilean species. They are soft-stemmed, compact, bushy biennials often treated as annuals, producing in spring and summer blooms in a range of bright colors from yellow to deep red and so densely massed they almost hide the soft green foliage. Innumerable named varieties have appeared over the years, and they are now mostly sold as mixed-color seedling strains and series. Marginally frost hardy, they can be used for summer bedding but do not tolerate very hot, dry weather. Normally 12–18 in (30–45 cm) tall, dwarf strains can be as small as 6 in (15 cm). 'Sunset Mixed' are bushy F1 hybrids 12 in (30 cm) tall with flowers in vibrant shades of red, orange and mixes of these two; they are useful in massed bedding. 'Sunshine' is also an F1 hybrid of compact form around 10 in (25 cm) high, with bright golden-yellow blooms, bred for planting in massed displays or for use in borders. **ZONES 9–11.**

Calceolaria, Herbeohybrida Group, 'Sunset Mixed'

CALENDULA

MARIGOLD

It is thought that St Hildegard of Bingen (1098–1179) dedicated *Calendula officinalis* to the Virgin Mary and gave the flowers the name Mary's gold, or marigold. To gardeners of today 'marigold' generally signifies the unrelated *Tagetes* from Mexico (the so-called 'African' and 'French' marigolds). In the Middle Ages marigolds were considered a certain remedy for all sorts of ills ranging from smallpox to indigestion and 'evil humors of the head', and even today the marigold is a favorite of herbalists. The genus *Calendula* consists of about 20 species of bushy annuals and evergreen perennials, occurring wild from the Canary Islands through the Mediterranean region to Iran in the east. They have simple, somewhat aromatic leaves and daisy-like, orange or yellow flowers.

CULTIVATION

Calendulas are mostly fairly frost-hardy plants and are readily grown in well-drained soil of any quality in sun or part-shade. Flowering will be prolonged with regular deadheading. Propagate from seed, and watch for aphids and powdery mildew.

Calendula arvensis

FIELD MARIGOLD

This sprawling annual is a common wildflower in Mediter-ranean countries, where it grows among the long grass of fields and displays its golden flowers from spring to autumn and on into winter if the weather is mild. The name *Calendula* comes from the same root as calendar and refers to the almost all-year blooming. It is rarely cultivated but, transplanted to gardens, it can make a bright show. **ZONES 6–10.**

Calendula officinalis

Calendula officinalis

POT MARIGOLD, ENGLISH MARIGOLD

Originally native to southern Europe and long valued for its medicinal qualities, this species is known in gardens only by its many cultivars and seedling strains, popular winter- and spring-flowering annuals that remain in bloom for a long time. There are tall and dwarf forms, all of bushy habit, the tall growing to a height and spread of 24 in (60 cm) and the dwarf to 12 in (30 cm). All forms have lance-shaped, strongly scented, pale green leaves and single or double flowerheads. Tall cultivars include **'Geisha Girl'**, with double orange flowers; the **Pacific Beauty Series**, with double flowers in a number of different colors including bi-colors; **'Princess'**, with crested orange, gold or yellow flowers; and the **Touch of Red Series**, with double flowers in tones of deep orange-red. Dwarf cultivars include **'Fiesta Gitana'**, with double flowers in colors ranging from cream to orange, and **'Honey Babe'**, with apricot, yellow and orange flowers. **ZONES 6–10.**

Calendula arvensis

CALLISTEPHUS
CHINA ASTER

This genus contains one annual species, native to China and once included in the genus *Aster*. It is a colorful garden flower, with summer blooms in a wonderful array of shades from white to pink, blue, red and purple, popular both for bedding and as a cut flower. Long cultivation has given rise to many variants, and plant breeders add new strains almost every year. The 3–4 in (8–10 cm) flowerheads can be either yellow-centered single daisies or fully double. The doubles can have petals that are plume-like and shaggy, more formal and straight or very short, making the blooms like perfect pompons.

Callistephus chinensis

CULTIVATION

China aster is usually sown in spring to flower during summer, but the season of bloom is not long and it is usual to make successive sowings to prolong it. It is superlative for cutting and will grow in any climate, from the coolest temperate to subtropical. Give it sunshine and fertile, well-drained soil, and do not plant it in the same bed 2 years in a row—a rest of 2 or 3 years between plantings is desirable to guard against aster wilt, a soilborne fungus.

Callistephus chinensis
syn. *Aster chinensis*

This erect, bushy, fast-growing annual has oval, toothed, mid-green leaves and long-stalked flowerheads. There are very many seedling strains available, ranging from tall, up to 3 ft (1 m), to dwarf, about 8 in (20 cm). Stake tall cultivars and remove spent flowers regularly. The **Milady Series** are vigorous cultivars to 12 in (30 cm) in height with double flowerheads in pinks, reds, white, purplish blue and mixed colors. **ZONES 6–10.**

Campanula medium

CAMPANULA
BELLFLOWER, BLUEBELL

Native to the temperate parts of the northern hemisphere, this large genus includes about 250 species of showy herbaceous plants, mostly perennials but a few annual or biennial. The leaves vary in shape and size, occasionally arising mainly from upright stems or sometimes only in basal clusters. The flowers are mostly bell-shaped but in some species are more tubular, urn-shaped or star-shaped, and come in shades of blue and purple with some pinks and whites.

CULTIVATION

Campanulas are useful for rockeries, borders, wild gardens and hanging baskets. All do best in a moderately rich, moist, well-drained soil. They grow in sun or shade, but flower color remains brightest in shady situations. Protect from drying winds and stake the taller varieties, which make good cut flowers. Remove spent flower stems. Propagate from seed in spring (sow seed for alpines in autumn), by division in spring or autumn, or from basal cuttings in spring. They are very frost hardy to frost tender. Transplant during winter and protect from slugs.

Campanula carpatica
CARPATHIAN BELLFLOWER, TUSSOCK BELLFLOWER

The slowly spreading clumps of basal leaves of this species make it well suited for use as an edging or rock-garden plant. From late spring through summer, 8–12 in (20–30 cm) stems rise above the foliage, carrying upward-facing, 1–2 in (2.5–5 cm) wide, bowl-shaped flowers in blue, lavender or white. The most common cultivars available are the compact-growing 'Blue Clips' and 'White Clips', and the bright violet-blue 'Wedgwood Blue'. ZONES 3–9.

Campanula glomerata
CLUSTERED BELLFLOWER

This variable species is found throughout Europe and temperate Asia. The violet-blue flowers are grouped in almost globular clusters on 10–15 in (25–38 cm) tall stems in early summer and again later if the old flower stems are removed. 'Superba' grows to 24 in (60 cm); *Campanula glomerata* var. *dahurica* is a deeper violet than the species. There are also double-flowered and white versions. ZONES 3–9.

Campanula glomerata 'Superba'

Campanula medium
CANTERBURY BELL

A biennial species from southern Europe, this is a slow-growing, erect plant with narrow basal leaves. In spring and early summer it has stout spires reaching 4 ft (1.2 m) tall of crowded, white, pink or blue, bell-shaped flowers with recurved rims and prominent large green calyces. Dwarf cultivars grow to 24 in (60 cm), and double forms have a colored calyx like a second petal tube. Grow as border plants in part-shade. ZONES 6–10.

Campanula portenschlagiana
syn. *Campanula muralis*
DALMATIAN BELLFLOWER

Native to a small area of the Dalmatian limestone mountains of Croatia, this is a dwarf, evergreen perennial growing to a maximum height of 6 in (15 cm) with an indefinite spread. It has crowded small violet-like leaves and a profusion of small, star-shaped, violet flowers in late spring and early summer. Best suited to rockeries and wall crevices, this species likes a cool, partially shaded site with good drainage. ZONES 5–10.

Campanula portenschlagiana

CANNA

This genus of robust rhizomatous perennials consists of about 25 species, all native to tropical and South America. Belonging to the same broad grouping as gingers and bananas, they resemble these in that their apparent aboveground stems are not true stems but collections of tightly furled leaf bases, rising from the thick knotty rhizomes. Slender flowering stems grow up through the centers of these false stems, emerging at the top with showy flowers of asymmetrical structure. Most of the wild species have rather narrow-petalled flowers in shades of yellow, red or purple. All garden cannas are hybrids with much broader petals, originating as crosses between several species in the mid-nineteenth century. Early hybrids had fairly smooth petals in single colors but the addition of *Canna flaccida* genes resulted in larger, crumpled flowers with striking variegations ('orchid-flowered cannas'). Cannas range from the common reds, oranges and yellows through to apricots, creams and pinks. The leaves can be green, bronze or purple, or sometimes white- or yellow-striped. Plants range in height from 18 in (45 cm) to 8 ft (2.4 m).

CULTIVATION

Cannas thrive outdoors in frost-free, warm climates but if grown outside in colder areas the roots need to be protected with thick mulch in winter, or else the rhizomes may be lifted in autumn and stored until spring—alternatively they can be grown in containers in a conservatory or greenhouse. They are sun-loving plants and thrive in hot dry weather as long as roots are kept moist, and they respond well to heavy feeding. Cut back to the ground after flowers finish. Propagate in spring by division.

Canna × generalis

Canna × generalis is a large, highly variable group of canna hybrids of unknown or complex parentage. Plants are extremely variable, ranging from dwarfs less than 3 ft (1 m) to large growers that reach 6 ft (1.8 m). Foliage is also variable and may be plain green, reddish, purple or variegated. Flowers come in all the warm shades, either in plain single colors like the orange-red 'Brandywine' or spotted or streaked as in the yellow and red 'King Numbert'. 'Königin Charlotte' has dazzling red flowers. 'Lenape' is a dwarf hybrid with bright yellow flowers with a red throat and brownish red spots; it grows to a height of only 30 in (75 cm). 'Lucifer' is a most attractive hybrid with yellow-edged red petals and purple-toned leaves. It is one of the newer dwarf types, growing to 3 ft (1 m). **ZONES 9–12.**

Canna × generalis 'Lucifer'

Canna × generalis 'Lenape'

CARDAMINE

BITTERCRESS

This genus of the mustard family includes 150 or more species of annuals and perennials from most parts of the world, usually with dissected or compound leaves forming basal tufts and on lower parts of the flowering stems. Small, 4-petalled, white, pink or purple flowers like small stocks open progressively up the stem and are followed by slender pods that split apart suddenly, flinging the minute seeds a short distance. They are found in shady, moist habitats, some forming large mats, but the genus also includes several common small weeds, for example *Cardamine hirsuta* which can be eaten like watercress.

CULTIVATION

Given moist soil and full or part shade, these soft-leafed plants can be planted in a woodland garden or in an informal border, where their foliage makes an attractive groundcover.

Cardamine raphanifolia

Cardamine raphanifolia

syn. **Cardamine latifolia**

The botanical name of this species, native to southern Europe and western Asia, means 'radish-leafed' and its leaves do resemble those of a small radish plant. It is a perennial of up to about 24 in (60 cm) tall, the stems springing from a creeping rhizome. The flowers are pinkish purple, borne from late spring to mid-summer. Coming from stream banks and damp woodland, it will take sun as long as its roots are kept moist. **ZONES 7–9.**

CARTHAMUS

This genus of prickly composites of the thistle tribe consists of 14 species of annuals and perennials from the Mediterranean region and western Asia. Some are troublesome weeds but one species, safflower, is of commercial importance as an oil seed, and was also the source of red and yellow dyes used for rouge and food coloring. They are plants of upright growth with very sharp spines bordering the parchment-textured leaves; the thistle-like flowerheads are smallish, mostly with yellow florets surrounded by a ring of fiercely spiny bracts.

Carthamus tinctorius

CULTIVATION

Not fussy as to soil but enjoying a full sun position, these plants need little care and their flowers make good, though not long lasting, cut flowers that can be easily dried. Propagate from seed in spring.

Carthamus tinctorius

SAFFLOWER, FALSE SAFFRON

A fast-growing annual 24–36 in (60–90 cm) tall, this plant is valued for its orange-yellow flowers in summer and for the oil contained in its seeds. Its leaves are spiny and oblong, running down the stems. Safflower is frost hardy and grows best in fertile, well-drained soil. **ZONES 7–11.**

CELMISIA

SNOW DAISY, MOUNTAIN DAISY, NEW ZEALAND DAISY

Sixty or so species of rhizomatous perennials and subshrubs with white daisy-like flowerheads make up this genus, the majority native to New Zealand but with a smaller number native to Tasmania and southeastern mainland Australia. Mostly occurring in higher mountain grasslands, meadows and rocky places, they are attractive evergreen plants with tufts of narrow silvery gray leaves and a profuse display of yellow-centered white flowers, mostly solitary on scaly stalks. The leaf undersides of most species are covered with a thick silvery white fur.

CULTIVATION

Most celmisias are true alpine plants that resent lowland conditions, but a few will grow successfully in rockeries, peat beds or scree gardens in temperate climates. They can be planted in full sun or part-shade and require moist, well-drained, gritty, acid soil. Protect from hot sun in drier areas and from excessive moisture in cool climates. Propagate from seed in autumn or by division in late spring.

Celmisia hookeri

Celmisia hookeri

From the South Island of New Zealand where it occurs in dry grasslands from the sea coast to lower mountain slopes, this is one of the larger-leafed species, with leaves up to 12 in (30 cm) long and 3 in (8 cm) wide, glossy deep green above and with thick white felt beneath. The flowerheads are up to 4 in (10 cm) across on short, thick stems, with a wide disc and a rather narrow rim of ray florets. **ZONES 7–9.**

CELOSIA

COCKSCOMB, CHINESE WOOLFLOWER

This genus of erect annuals, perennials and shrubs in the amaranthus family contains 50 or more species from warmer parts of Asia, Africa and the Americas, but only one *(Celosia argentea)* is widely cultivated as a bedding annual and for cut flowers. It has evolved in cultivation into several different forms, hardly recognizable as belonging to the one species. It has simple, soft, strongly veined leaves; the variation is almost wholly in the structure of the heads of the small flowers, which have undergone proliferation and deformation in the two major cultivated races.

CULTIVATION

In cool climates celosias are treated as conservatory plants, or planted out for summer bedding after raising seedlings under glass in spring. They are better adapted to hot climates, withstanding the fiercest summer heat. They require full sun, rich, well-drained soil and constant moisture. Propagate from seed in spring.

Celosia argentea
syns *Celosia cristata, C. pyramidalis*

Probably native to tropical Asia, this erect, summer-flowering annual can reach 3 ft (1 m) or more in height. The leaves are mid-green; the silvery white flowers appear in summer in dense, erect, pointed spikes with a silvery sheen. The species is best known in the guise of two strikingly different cultivar groups, which in turn are hardly recognizable as belonging to the species. These are the **Plumosa Group**, with erect, plume-like heads of tiny deformed flowers in a range of hot colors, and the **Cristata Group** (cockscombs), with bizarre wavy crests of fused flower stalks also in many colors. Both have been developed in cultivation with a range of seedling strains, differing in height as well as size and the color of the flowerheads. The Plumosa Group in particular are favored for cut flowers and sale in pots for indoor decoration. Some dwarf strains are no more than 6 in (15 cm) tall, while the old-fashioned bedding strains are about 24 in (60 cm). Most strains are sold as mixed colors. **ZONES 10–12.**

CENIA

This genus of low-growing annuals and perennials in the daisy family is closely related to *Cotula*, in which they were formerly included. The plants have rather the aspect of *Anthemis* but the yellow flowerheads lack ray florets, appearing like large buttons, borne singly on slender stalks. The finely divided leaves are softly hairy and slightly aromatic.

CULTIVATION

Easily grown as rock-garden or edging plants, they produce a succession of cheerful blooms though the plants can become rather straggly as they age. Sow seed in autumn, planting out in a sunny spot when seedlings are 1 in (25 mm) high.

Cenia turbinata

Cenia turbinata

syn. *Cotula turbinata*
BACHELOR'S BUTTONS

Native to coastal areas of South Africa's Cape Province, this species is a short-lived perennial but in the garden is most often treated as an annual. The sprawling stems radiate from a central rootstock, concealed beneath the pale green, dissected, hairy foliage. In spring it produces a succession of bright yellow 'buttons' about 1¼ in (30 mm) in diameter on short, weak stalks. The plant grows 4–6 in (10–15 cm) high and spreads to about 24 in (60 cm). **ZONES 8–10.**

CENTAUREA

CORNFLOWER, KNAPWEED

This genus, belonging to the thistle tribe of composites, is a huge one with around 450 species scattered all over the temperate, grassy regions of Eurasia and north Africa, with one or two strays in America. It includes annuals, biennials and perennials. Some spiny-leafed species are troublesome weeds in some parts of the world. Apart from the common annual cornflower, some of the perennial species are desirable garden plants; they come in various colors, from white through shades of blue, red, pink, purple and yellow. The flowerheads typically have an urn-shaped receptacle of fringed or spiny bracts, from the mouth of which radiate the quite large florets, each deeply divided into 5 colored petals; smaller florets occupy the center of the head, but do not form a distinct disc as in other members of the daisy or Compositae family.

CULTIVATION

Cornflowers do well in well-drained soil in a sunny position. Propagate from seed in spring or autumn; perennials can also be divided in spring or autumn.

Centaurea cineraria

Centaurea cineraria

syns *Centaurea candidissima* of gardens, *C. gymnocarpa*
DUSTY MILLER

A shrubby perennial from the Mediterranean region, *Centaurea cineraria* is grown mainly for its beautiful, much divided silvery white foliage. When not in flower the plant is easily mistaken for the unrelated *Senecio cineraria*, also known as dusty miller. Small thistle-like, lilac-pink flowerheads held on much-branched flower stems reveal delicate symmetry and color. The silveriness of the foliage can vary from plant to plant, the best being selected for propagation. **ZONES 7–10.**

Centaurea cyanus

BLUE-BOTTLE, BACHELOR'S BUTTON,
CORNFLOWER

One of the best known wild-flowers of Europe and northern Asia, this species is also a common weed of cereal crops. It is a weak-stemmed erect annual 24–36 in (60–90 cm) tall with very narrow leaves and small, rather untidy flowerheads that are typically a slightly purplish shade of blue. Garden varieties have been developed with larger flowers in shades of pale and deep pink, cerise, crimson, white, purple and blue, some of them dwarf and more compact. Best displayed in large clumps, it will flower for months if deadheads are removed regularly. **ZONES 5–10.**

Centaurea macrocephala

GLOBE CORNFLOWER

With foliage somewhat like a large dandelion, this perennial species originates in the sub-alpine fields of Armenia and nearby parts of Turkey. In summer, stout leafy stems, up to 3 ft (1 m) tall, carry yellow flowerheads about 2 in (5 cm) across with a club-like base of shiny brown bracts. **ZONES 4–9.**

Centaurea cyanus

Centaurea macrocephala

Centranthus ruber
RED VALERIAN, JUPITER'S BEARD, KISS-ME-QUICK

This perennial is often seen as a naturalized plant on dry banks and is ideal for dry rock gardens as well as borders. It forms loose clumps of somewhat fleshy leaves and grows to a height of 24–36 in (60–90 cm). From late spring to autumn it produces dense clusters of small, star-shaped, deep reddish pink to pale pink flowers that last for a long time. The cultivar **'Albus'** has white flowers. One of the easiest plants to grow, *Centranthus ruber* requires sun and good drainage and will tolerate exposed positions and poor alkaline soil. **ZONES 5–10.**

CENTRANTHUS
VALERIAN

Around 10 species belong to this genus of annual and perennial herbs, native to the Mediterranean region and western Asia, but only one, *Centranthus ruber*, is widely planted for ornament. They make tufts of soft leaves that may be simple and smooth edged or less commonly dissected, and the leafy, branched flowering stems bear many irregular heads of tiny tubular flowers.

CULTIVATION
Grow in full sun in moderately fertile, chalk or lime soil that is well drained. Deadhead regularly. These plants are not long lived and are best divided every 3 years to ensure a good display. Propagate from seed or by division.

Centranthus ruber

CHELIDONIUM
GREATER CELANDINE, SWALLOWWORT

A single species of short-lived perennial belongs to this genus of the poppy family, native to Europe and western Asia. It forms a clump of leafy stems, the slightly brittle leaves divided into several irregular leaflets with scalloped edges. Short sprays of small 4-petalled bright yellow flowers are produced over a long season, each flower soon succeeded by a slender pod that splits to release tiny black seeds. Broken leaves and stems bleed an orange latex which is irritating to the skin and has been used to cure warts; the plant has many other traditional medicinal uses but is quite poisonous.

CULTIVATION
The plant is very frost hardy and is easily grown in sun or light shade, adapting to all except very wet soils. Its duration may be only biennial, but it self-seeds readily and can become invasive. Propagate from seed or by division in autumn and cut back after flowering to keep under control.

Chelidonium majus

Chelidonium majus

This quick-growing perennial can form an effective groundcover if planted closely. It is an erect to rather sprawling plant to 2–4 ft (0.6–1.2 m) high and wide, with attractive pale green foliage. From midspring to mid-autumn it produces a continuous scatter of bright golden-yellow flowers about 1 in (25 mm) across; the slender seed capsules are 2 in (5 cm) long. **'Flore Pleno'** has double flowers. **ZONES 6–9.**

CHELONE

TURTLEHEAD

This genus of 6 species of rather coarse but showy perennials from North America is related to *Penstemon*, which they resemble in growth habit and foliage. The name comes from the Greek *kelone* meaning a tortoise or turtle, and refers to the hooded, gaping flowers, borne in short terminal spikes. Leaves are toothed and shiny in most species.

CULTIVATION

They are best along streams or pond edges, but also adapt to a moist border planting with rich soil in full sun or part-shade. Propagate by dividing clumps in early spring, from cuttings in summer or from seed in spring or autumn.

Chelone lyonii

Chelone lyonii

PINK TURTLEHEAD

This species from mountains of south-eastern USA grows to a height of at least 3 ft (1 m), with erect, angled stems and dark green leaves up to 6 in (15 cm) long. The summer flowers are rosy purple and are produced in axillary and terminal spikes terminating the stems, and in upper leaf axils. **ZONES 6–9.**

Chrysanthemum carinatum

Chrysanthemum carinatum

syn. **Chrysanthemum tricolor**
PAINTED DAISY, SUMMER CHRYSANTHEMUM,
TRICOLOR CHRYSANTHEMUM

This spectacular annual species is from Morocco and grows to 24 in (60 cm), spreading to 12 in (30 cm) with much-divided, rather fleshy leaves and banded, multicolored flowers in spring and early summer. 'Monarch Court Jesters' comes in red with yellow centers or white with red centers, and the Tricolor Series has many color combinations. They are excellent as bedding plants and cut flowers. **ZONES 8–10.**

CHRYSANTHEMUM

CHRYSANTHEMUM

As now recognized by most botanists, this once large and varied genus is a shadow of its former self, reduced to a mere 5 species of annuals from Europe and North Africa. As a common name, though, 'chrysanthemum' will always be understood by gardeners to refer to the group of showy hybrid plants derived from east Asian species now classified under *Dendranthema*. The situation arose because Linnaeus' original or 'type' species of his genus *Chrysanthemum* was the European corn marigold, *C. segetum*— when the genus was later split up, it was with this and its close relatives that the name *Chrysanthemum* had to stick. Genus headings under which the former 'chrysanthemums' should be sought, in order of horticultural importance follow: *Dendranthema, Argyranthemum, Leucanthemum, Tanacetum, Pyrethropsis* and *Ajania*.

CULTIVATION

The true chrysanthemums are easily grown annuals, requiring little more than a moist, fertile, well-prepared soil and a sunny position. They prefer coolish summers but in warmer, drier climates can be timed to bloom in winter. Propagate from seed, sown in autumn or early spring.

CLARKIA

syn. *Godetia*

This genus, allied to the evening primroses *(Oenothera)* and consisting of about 36 species, was named in honor of Captain William Clark, of the famous Lewis and Clark expedition that crossed the American continent in 1806. They are bushy annuals, undistinguished in foliage but spectacular in their all too short flowering season when they are covered in showy funnel-shaped flowers in various shades of pink, white and carmine. The flowers can be 4 in (10 cm) across, and they look a little like azaleas—in Germany they are called *Sommerazalee*, the summer azalea. They are very good as cut flowers, borne on long stems and lasting a week in water.

CULTIVATION

They are easily grown in full sun in any temperate climate. They prefer moist but well-drained, slightly acid soil; soil that is too fertile will see good foliage but poor flower production. Propagate from seed in autumn or spring.

Clarkia amoena

syn. *Clarkia grandiflora*

FAREWELL-TO-SPRING

A free-flowering annual, this Californian native is fast growing to a height of 24 in (60 cm) and spread of 12 in (30 cm). It has lance-shaped, mid-green leaves, thin upright stems, and in summer bears spikes of open, cup-like, single or double flowers in shades of pink; a number of cultivars have been produced from this species. Allow it to dry out between watering and watch for signs of botrytis.
ZONES 7–11.

Clarkia amoena

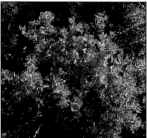

CLEOME

SPIDER FLOWER, SPIDER PLANT

This genus of 150 species of bushy annuals and short-lived evergreen shrubs, from subtropical and tropical zones all over the world, is characterized by its spidery flowers with 4 petals that narrow into basal stalks and mostly long, spidery stamens and styles. The leaves are composed of from 5 to 7 palmate leaflets. One species is widely grown as a background bedding plant, useful for its rapid growth and delicate floral effect.

Cleome hassleriana

syn. *Cleome spinosa* of gardens

Native to subtropical South America, this fast-growing, bushy annual is valued for its unusual spidery flowers. An erect plant, it grows to 4 ft (1.2 m) tall with a spread of 18 in (45 cm). It has large palmate leaves and the hairy, slightly prickly stems are topped in summer with heads of airy, pink and white flowers with long, protruding stamens. Several strains are available as seed, ranging in color from pure white to purple. **ZONES 9–11.**

Cleome hassleriana

CULTIVATION

Marginally frost hardy, they require full sun and fertile, well-drained soil, regular water and shelter from strong winds. Taller growth can be encouraged by removing side branches, and dead flowers should also be removed. Propagate from seed in spring or early summer. Check for aphids.

Clintonia borealis

CORN LILY, BLUEBEARD

From eastern and central North America, this species has loose clusters of yellowish white flowers with recurving petals and protruding stamens, followed by blue berries. It reaches a height of 6–12 in (15–30 cm) and blooms in late spring and early summer. **ZONES 3–9.**

Clintonia umbellulata

SPECKLED WOOD-LILY

From eastern USA, this is one of the prettiest species with dense umbels of fragrant white flowers, often speckled green or purplish, rising on stems up to 15 in (40 cm) tall above dense patches of luxuriant foliage. The flowers appear in late spring and early summer and are followed by black berries. **ZONES 4–9.**

CLINTONIA

Five species of woodland lilies from North America and eastern Asia make up this genus, all rhizomatous perennials with rich green smooth foliage rather like that of *Convallaria*, and erect spikes or umbels (solitary in one species) of small, starry 6-petalled flowers.

Clintonia borealis

CULTIVATION

All species need a cool, peaty, lime-free soil and a shaded, humid position, and so are best suited to a woodland garden. Winter mulching will protect from frost. Propagate from seed or division of rhizomes.

CONSOLIDA

LARKSPUR

Botanists in the past often treated these annuals as species of *Delphinium*, but the consensus now is that the 40 or so species constitute a distinct genus, occurring in the Mediterranean region and west and central Asia. The name *Consolida* was bestowed in the Middle Ages in recognition of the plants' use in the healing of wounds; they were believed to help the clotting (consolidating) of the blood. The larkspurs grown in gardens are mostly derived from the one species, *Consolida ajacis*, and include many strains, mostly grown as mixed colors. The flowers of the taller kinds will last a long time when cut. They have finely divided, feather-like leaves and poisonous seeds.

CULTIVATION

They are not difficult to grow, succeeding in any temperate or even mildly subtropical climate and liking full sun and rich, well-drained soil. Tall cultivars need to be staked. Propagate from seed and watch for snails and slugs and for powdery mildew.

Consolida ajacis

syns *Consolida ambigua, Delphinium consolida*

The name larkspur comes from the nectar spur at the back of the flowers, hidden in the open blooms but clearly visible on the unopened buds. This Mediterranean species originally had blue flowers. Present-day garden larkspurs are the result of hybrid-izing this species with *Consolida orientalis* to give the 'rocket larkspurs', or may be derived mainly from *C. regalis* in the case of the 'forking larkspurs'. Their blooms may be pink, white or purple and are usually double, borne mainly in summer. Some can reach a height of 4 ft (1.2 m). **ZONES 7–11.**

Consolida ajacis

Convallaria majalis

Renowned for its glorious perfume, this beautiful plant does best in cool climates. It is low growing, 8–12 in (20–30 cm) high but of indefinite spread, with dark green leaves. The dainty white bell-shaped flowers are ¼–½ in (6–12 mm) across and appear in spring. Pink-flowered variants are known, collectively referred to as *Convallaria majalis* var. *rosea*, and there are several cultivars with variegated or gold foliage. **ZONES 3–9.**

CONVALLARIA
LILY-OF-THE-VALLEY

Convallaria majalis

Some botanists have recognized several species of *Convallaria*, but most believe there is only one, occurring wild in forests from France to Siberia, also cooler parts of North America. The plant spreads over the forest floor by slender underground rhizomes which at intervals send up pointed oval leaves and slender flowering stems adorned with little white bells, shining like pearls against the dull green of the foliage. The red berries that follow have their uses in medicine, but they are poisonous—dangerously so, as they are sweet enough to tempt children.

CULTIVATION

The rhizomes, or 'pips' as they are commonly known from their growing tips, should be planted in autumn in a part-shaded position. Given the right conditions, lily-of-the-valley spreads quite freely and in a confined space sometimes becomes overcrowded, when it will benefit from lifting and thinning. Grow in fertile, humus-rich, moist soil. They can be potted for display indoors, then replanted outdoors after flowering. Propagation is normally from seed or by division.

Convolvulus tricolor 'Blue Ensign'

CONVOLVULUS

This genus contains about 250 species of mainly slender, twining creepers and small herbaceous plants. The genus is described in more detail in the chapter on Lawns, Groundcovers, Ornamental Grasses and Bamboos.

Convolvulus cneorum
BUSH MORNING GLORY

This attractive plant from Mediterranean Europe has crowded, weak, upcurving stems sprouting from the base to a height of 2–4 ft (0.6–1.2 m). The leaves, in tufts along the stems, are soft and narrow with a coating of silky hairs which gives them a silvery sheen. The stems terminate in dense clusters of silky buds, each producing a long succession of flowers through spring and summer, flesh-pink in bud but opening a dazzling white with a small yellow eye. **ZONES 8–10.**

Convolvulus tricolor
syn. **Convolvulus minor**

This bedding annual from the Mediterranean bears profuse deep purple-blue or white flowers with banded yellow and white throats. The small leaves are lance-shaped and mid-green. A slender, few-branched plant, it grows to a height of 8–12 in (20–30 cm) and blooms continuously from late spring to early autumn, but individual flowers last only one day. '**Blue Ensign**' is a popular cultivar. **ZONES 8–11.**

Coreopsis lanceolata

COREOPSIS

Around 80 species of annuals and perennials from cooler or drier regions of the Americas make up this genus of the daisy family. The flowerheads, borne on slender stems mainly in summer, are mostly shades of gold or yellow, some bicolored. Leaves vary from simple and narrow, usually toothed, to deeply divided, and may be basal or scattered up the stems.

CULTIVATION

The annuals are grown as bedding plants, while the perennials are excellent for herbaceous borders. Perennials prefer full sun and a fertile, well-drained soil but also grow well in coastal regions and in poor, stony soil. Propagate by division of old clumps in winter or spring, or by spring cuttings. Annuals also prefer full sun and a fertile, well-drained soil; they will not tolerate a heavy clay soil. Taller varieties may need staking. Propagate from seed in spring or autumn.

Coreopsis lanceolata

Also from southeastern and central USA, this is a tufted perennial with long-stalked, lance-shaped basal leaves and bright golden-yellow flowerheads on leafy stems up to about 24 in (60 cm) high. It is extremely floriferous and when mass planted can make sheets of gold in spring and early summer. Short lived, it is very free-seeding, to the point that it has become an environmental weed in parts of Australia, on very poor soils. Double forms are sometimes grown. **'Baby Sun'** is a compact long blooming cultivar about 12 in (30 cm) high; suitable for bedding. **ZONES 3–11.**

Coreopsis tinctoria

TICKSEED, PLAINS COREOPSIS, CALLIOPSIS

This fast-growing, showy annual produces clusters of bright yellow flowerheads with red centers throughout summer and autumn. Of slender, weak habit, it grows to a height of 24–36 in (60–90 cm). The plants tend to incline over and may need staking. It provides good cut flowers. The species has a wide natural distribution in North America. **ZONES 4–10.**

Coreopsis verticillata

From southeastern USA, this perennial species produces crowded erect stems to 30 in (75 cm) tall from a tangled mass of thin rhizomes; the leaves, in whorls of 3, are divided into very narrow segments. The abundant bright yellow flowerheads are borne from late spring until autumn. This species does best in light soil of low fertility. **'Moonbeam'** is slightly lower and more compact with lemon-yellow blooms. **ZONES 6–10.**

Coreopsis verticillata 'Moonbeam'

Coronilla varia
syn. *Securigera varia*
CROWN VETCH

A sprawling perennial from Europe, crown vetch has run wild in some parts of the USA. It can spread quite rapidly by a deep network of thin rhizomes, the weak leafy stems rising to about 24 in (60 cm) tall. The soft pinnate leaves resemble those of the true vetches *(Vicia)* and the clover-like heads of pink to lilac-pink flowers appear throughout summer. Not suited to a formal garden, it can be rather invasive, but makes a good soil-binding plant for a sunny bank, stopping erosion while slower plants take hold. Some botanists now place it in the genus *Securigera*. **ZONES 6–10.**

Coronilla varia

CORONILLA
CROWN VETCH

A legume genus of 20 or so species of annuals, perennials and low, wiry shrubs, native to Europe, western Asia and northern Africa. They have pinnate leaves with small, thin or somewhat fleshy leaflets, and stalked umbels of small pea-flowers a little like some clover or medic flowers. Certain perennial and shrub species are grown as ornamentals, valued for their profuse flowers blooming over a long season, though not especially showy. *Coronilla* is Latin for 'little crown', referring to the neat circular umbels of some species.

CULTIVATION
They need full sun, moderately fertile, well-drained soil and protection from cold winds. Cut leggy plants back to the base in spring. Propagate from seed, cuttings, or division of rootstock.

CORYDALIS

The 300 or so species that make up this genus, occur widely as natives in temperate regions of the northern hemisphere. They include some annuals but are mostly perennials, with basal tufts of ferny, deeply dissected leaves springing from fleshy rhizomes or tubers. The smallish tubular flowers have a short backward-pointing spur that may be curved; they are usually grouped in short spikes or clusters and come in a range of colors, mostly creams, yellows, pinks and purples but a few have clear blue flowers.

CULTIVATION
The sun-loving species do very well in rock gardens, while the shade lovers are best planted beneath shrubs in a border, or in a woodland garden. Soil should be well drained but moisture-retentive, rich in humus for the woodland species. Several species, such as *Corydalis lutea*, self-seed freely, coming up in cracks between paving or on walls. Propagate from seed or by division.

Corydalis lutea
YELLOW CORYDALIS

The most easily cultivated species, this native of Europe's southern Alps region is widely naturalized in temperate climates around the world. A rhizomatous perennial, it makes broad clumps or mounds of fresh green foliage, to about 12 in (30 cm) high, and is dotted from spring to autumn with short sprays of soft yellow flowers. It will grow in many situations but often self-seeds in wall crevices or moist chinks in rockeries. In a woodland garden it makes an attractive groundcover. **ZONES 6–10.**

Corydalis lutea

Cosmos bipinnatus 'Sea Shells'

COSMOS

MEXICAN ASTER

This genus of annuals and perennials, allied to *Dahlia*, contains 25 species native to warmer parts of the Americas but mostly to Mexico. Two of the species are well known garden flowers, grown around the world, and two or three others are occasionally grown. They have erect but weak, leafy stems and the leaves are variously lobed or deeply and finely dissected. Flowerheads, on slender stalks terminating branches, are daisy-like with showy, broad ray-florets surrounding a small disc; they range in color from white through pinks, yellows, oranges, reds and purples to deep maroon.

CULTIVATION

They are only moderately frost hardy and in cold climates need protection in winter. Seedlings should be planted out only after all danger of frost has passed. They require a sunny situation with protection from strong winds and will grow in any well-drained soil as long as it is not over-rich. Mulch with compost and water well in hot, dry weather. Propagate annuals from seed in spring or autumn, the perennials from basal cuttings in spring. Deadhead regularly, and in humid weather check for insect pests and mildew.

Cosmos bipinnatus

COMMON COSMOS, MEXICAN ASTER

This feathery-leafed annual from Mexico and far southern USA reaches 5–6 ft (1.5–1.8 m) in height with showy daisy-like flowerheads in summer and autumn, in shades of pink, red, purple or white. Taller plants may need staking. Newer strains are usually more compact and can have double flowers and striped petals. **'Sea Shells'** has pink, sometimes crimson or white flowerheads with edges of ray-florets curled into a tube. **ZONES 8–11.**

Cosmos bipinnatus

CYNOGLOSSUM

A genus of 55 species of annuals, biennials and perennials from most temperate regions of the world. All species are frost hardy and valued for their long flowering period. They are related to the common forget-me-not, which many resemble.

CULTIVATION

All species need a fertile but not over rich soil; if over-nourished the plants tend to flop over. Propagation is from seed sown in autumn or spring or, in the case of perennial species, by division.

Cynoglossum amabile

CHINESE FORGET-ME-NOT

This upright annual or biennial, growing to a height of about 20 in (50 cm) has dull green hairy lanceolate leaves and flowers in racemes, generally blue although white and pink forms can occur. Flowers are produced in spring and early summer. It self-seeds very readily. 'Firmament' has pendulous sky-blue flowers. **ZONES 5–9.**

Cynoglossum amabile 'Firmament'

DAHLIA

Most of the species in this genus have tuberous roots, and detailed information on the genus is given in the Bulbs, Corms and Tubers chapter. However, *Dahlia* Hybrids can be treated as perennials.

Dahlia, Group 1, 'Yellow Hammer'

Dahlia, Group 3, cultivar

Dahlia, Group 4, 'Gerrie Hoek'

Dahlia Hybrids

The following are the 10 main classification groups of Dahlia hybrids.

Single-flowered (Group 1): As the name suggests, these hybrids have a single ring of ray petals (sometimes 2) with an open center. Most singles are small plants usually growing no more than 18 in (45 cm) high, so they are ideal for bedding and are often sold as seed strains. **'Yellow Hammer'** is a popular cultivar.

Anemone-flowered (Group 2): This group includes fewer cultivars than most of the others. They have one or more rows of outer ray florets; instead of the yellow center, these tiny flowers have mutated into outward-pointing tubular florets.

Collarette (Group 3): This group, once again becoming popular, has a single row of 8 outer large florets, usually flat and rounded at the tips. Then comes a row of shorter tubular, wavy florets often in a contrasting color and finally the normally yellow center.

Waterlily or nymphaea-flowered (Group 4): Fully double-flowered with slightly cupped petals, these dahlias resemble the waterlilies. The overall effect is of a flattish flower. **'Cameo'** and **'Gerrie Hoek'** are popular cultivars.

Decorative (Group 5): This group are fully double-flowered dahlias with no central disc showing. The petals are more numerous and slightly twisted making the flower look fuller than the waterlily types. This group, which can produce some truly giant forms, may be subdivided into formal decoratives and informal ones. Informal decoratives have petals that are twisted or pointed and of an irregular arrangement. 'Hamari Gold' and 'Evening Mail' are giant decoratives. 'Majuba' is a medium-sized decorative. Large informal decorative types include 'Almand's Climax', 'Alva's Supreme', 'Golden Ballade' and 'Suffolk Punch'.

Ball (Group 6): As the name suggests these dahlias are full doubles and almost ball-shaped. Miniature, small, medium and large forms are available. 'Rose Cupid' is a medium-sized ball dahlia and 'Wotton Cupid' is a miniature.

Pompon (Group 7): These are similar to ball dahlias but even more globose and usually not much more than 2 in (5 cm)

Dahlia, Group 6, 'Rose Cupid'

across. They are sometimes called 'Drum Stick' dahlias. 'Buttercup' is a pompon form.

Cactus-flowered (Group 8): These fully double-flowered dahlias have long, narrow rolled petals which give the flowers a spidery look. This group can be divided further by size as well as into classes with straight petals, incurved petals or recurved petals. 'Hamari Bride' is a medium-sized form.

Semi-cactus (Group 9): As the name suggests this group is close to Group 8 but the petals are broader at the base and less rolled back at the edges. 'So Dainty' is a miniature; 'Brandaris' is a medium form; 'Hayley Jane' is small; and 'Salmon Keene' has large flowers.

Miscellaneous (Group 10): This category consists of small groups and unique forms of dahlias that do not fit into any of the above groups. If breeders increase the numbers in any of the forms in this category, they will probably be split off to form new groups. Under this heading can be found such forms as orchid types which are single with revolute petals: 'Giraffe' is an example. The star dahlias are also single in appearance and produce very pointed, widely spaced petals. Peony-flowered

Dahlia, Group 5, 'Majuba'

dahlias, which are still kept as a separate group in some countries, usually have one or two rows of flat petals with a center that can be open or partly covered by small twisted petals; examples of this form include 'Bishop of Llandaff', 'Fascination' and 'Tally Ho'. ZONES 7–10.

Delphinium elatum × *D. grandiflorum*

DELPHINIUM

This genus contains 250 or so species native to mainly northern hemisphere temperate zones, with a few found in scattered, high-altitude areas of Africa. They range from attractive self-seeding annuals or dwarf alpine plants up to statuesque perennials that can exceed 8 ft (2.4 m) in height. Nearly all start growth as a tuft of long-stalked basal leaves, their blades divided into 3 to 7 radiating lobes or segments. The tufts elongate into erect, sometimes branched flowering stems bearing stalked 5-petalled flowers each with a backward-pointing nectar spur. Garden delphiniums are mainly derived from *Delphinium elatum* and its hybrids. Recognized groups include the Belladonna, Elatum and Pacific hybrids. The annual larkspurs have now been placed in the genus *Consolida*.

Dahlia, Group 9, 'Salmon Keene'

CULTIVATION

Very frost hardy, most like a cool to cold winter. They prefer full sun with shelter from strong winds, and well-drained, fertile soil with plenty of organic matter. Stake tall cultivars. Apply a liquid fertilizer at 2–3 weekly intervals. To maintain type, propagate from cuttings or by division though some species have been bred to come true from seed.

Delphinium, Belladonna Group

These frost-hardy perennials *(Delphinium elatum* × *D. grandiflorum)* have an upright, loosely branching form. Their widely-spaced blue or white flowers, 1 in (25 mm) or more wide, are single or sometimes semi-double and borne on loose spikes ranging in height up to 4 ft (1.2 m). They bloom in early and late summer. Propagate by division or from basal cuttings in spring. ZONES 3–9.

Delphinium, Belladonna Group

Delphinium grandiflorum 'Blue Butterfly'

Delphinium grandiflorum

syn. *Delphinium chinense*

BUTTERFLY DELPHINIUM, CHINESE DELPHINIUM

Native to China, Siberia, Japan and Mongolia, this tufted perennial grows to a height of 18 in (45 cm) and a spread of 12 in (30 cm), the leaf segments further divided into narrow lobes. Its large bright blue flowers, with the long spurs finely warted, bloom over a long period in summer. It is fully frost hardy. **'Azure Fairy'** is a pale blue-flowering form; **'Blue Butterfly'** has bright blue flowers. **ZONES 3–9.**

Delphinium, Pacific Hybrid 'Galahad'

Delphinium, Pacific Hybrids

These short-lived perennials, usually grown as biennials, were bred in California with the main parent being the perennial *Delphinium elatum*. They are stately plants to 5 ft (1.5 m) or more in height with star-like single, semi-double or double flowers of mostly blue, purple or white, clustered on erect rigid spikes. Some of the named cultivars are: **'Astolat'**, a perennial with lavender-mauve flowers with dark eyes; **'Black Knight'**, with deep rich purple flowers with black eyes; **'Galahad'** has pure white flowers. **'Guinevere'** bears pale purple flowers with a pinkish tinge and white eyes; **'King Arthur'** has purple flowers with white eyes; and **'Summer Skies'** has pale sky-blue flowers. **ZONES 7–9.**

Dendranthema × *grandiflorum*, single form

DENDRANTHEMA

This genus of about 20 species of upright perennials is native to Europe and Asia. The species were previously included in the genus Chrysanthemum and include the beautiful florists' chrysanthemums. Few of the wild species are seen in gardens. The florists' chrysanthemums are very variable hybrid cultivars, now grouped under the name *Dendranthema* × *grandiflorum* (syn. *Chrysanthemum morifolium*). They originated in China before 500 BC. These chrysanthemums are grown for garden decoration and for cutting. They will naturally form several smallish blooms per stem, known as sprays. Disbudded chrysanthemums are formed by removing the lateral buds of spray types at an early stage. This leaves a single terminal bud to form on each stem and produces much larger, individual blooms that are suitable for exhibition. With continuous hybridization the flowerheads have diversified in size, shape, and disposition of the florets in the blooms. There are 10 main groups of classification based largely upon floral characteristics. All but a few flower in mid- to late autumn. The following are the 10 main groups.

Anemone-centered: A daisy-like bloom which has a pin-cushion center and a single or double row of radiating flat florets, often in contrasting colors. They are normally grown as sprays rather than single blooms.

Incurved: Fully double globular blooms formed of firm-textured florets curving inwards and packed closely together. The flowers are excellent cut flowers. They are used extensively for show work and floral art exhibitions.

Intermediate: Fully double blooms with an incurving shaggy form, the florets curling to form a ball. Some varieties have outcurving florets at the base of the flowerhead.

Pompon: Fully double, globe-shaped blooms formed of numerous, tightly packed florets. Normally grown as sprays.

Quill-shaped: Double blooms with narrow tubular florets, opening out at the tip.

Reflexed: Rounded double blooms, formed of florets that curve out and down, often with a curl or twist.

Fully reflexed: Perfectly rounded, double blooms with florets that curve out and down with the lowermost florets touching the stem.

Single: These have well-formed daisy-like blooms with up to 5 rows of radiating florets arranged around a flattened yellow disc. They are excellent for massed planting and are available in a wide variety of colors.

Spiders: Double blooms with long, narrow tubular florets that spread out in all directions in a spider-like formation.

Spoon-shaped: Double blooms with very narrow radiating florets with the tips expanded to form spoon shapes.

CULTIVATION

Mostly frost hardy, though some forms may be somewhat frost tender. Grow in sun in a well-drained slightly acidic soil, improved with compost and manure. Pinch out tips to promote flowering lateral stems. Removing surplus buds influences the size and quality of the flowers. Stake tall plants and tie stems. Propagate from seed, by division or cuttings.

Dendranthema × *grandiflorum*, single form

Dendranthema × grandiflorum
'Yellow Nightingale'

Dendranthema × grandiflorum, spider form

Dianthus barbatus

Dendranthema × grandiflorum
syns Chrysanthemum indicum, C. morifolium
FLORISTS' CHRYSANTHEMUM

This hybrid is thought to be of Chinese origin and is the parent of hundreds of cultivars. Traditionally treated as a perennial, it is a vigorous subshrub to 5 ft (1.5 m) tall with thick, strongly aromatic lobed leaves to 3 in (8 cm) in length with a gray felted underside. The single blooms have yellow centers and spreading ray florets in white, yellow, bronze, pink, red or purple. Numerous cultivars of various shapes and sizes are listed by specialist nurseries and new ones are being raised annually. The following lists some of the more popular cultivars and their type.

An example of an anemone-centered florists' chrysanthemum is **'Raymond Mounsey'**, which has red blooms, while incurved examples include **'Gillette'** with cream flowers. Among the intermediate types are **'Crimson Tide'** with pale bronze blooms and **'Elizabeth Shoesmith'**, which bears large deep pink to purple flowers. The pompon type includes **'Maria'**, which is pink, while quill-shaped includes **'Yellow Nightingale'**, which has yellow flowers. The following are reflexed types: **'Flame Symbol'**, with burnt orange double flowers; **'Matthew Scaelle'**, with deep pink blooms; and **'Yellow Symbol'**, with bright golden-yellow blooms. Among the fully reflexed types is **'George Griffiths'**, with rich red flowerheads. An example of the single type is **'Mason's Bronze'**, which has bronze colored blooms. The spider form counts among its members **'Dusky Queen'**, which bears double golden-orange blooms and **'Sterling Silver'**, with white blooms. An example of the spoon-shaped type is **'Pennine Alfie'**, which produces double blooms with tubular bronze and yellow ray florets. **ZONES 4-10.**

DIANTHUS
CARNATION, PINK

This large genus consists of some 300 species. They mostly occur in Europe and Asia with a single species in Arctic North America and a few extending to southern Africa. Most are plants for the rock garden or edges of garden beds. Much hybridizing has created several different groups of pinks and carnations bred for specific purposes. Border Carnations are annual or perennial plants up to 24 in (60 cm) used as the name suggests as well as for cut flowers. Perpetual-flowering Carnations are mainly grown in the open but may be grown under cover to produce unblemished blooms; these are often disbudded leaving only the top bud to develop. American Spray Carnations are treated like perpetuals except that no disbudding is carried out. Malmaison Carnations, now undergoing a revival in popularity, are so-called because of their supposed resemblance to the Bourbon rose 'Souvenir de la Malmaison'; highly perfumed, they are grown in the same way as the perpetuals but need more care. Other groups of hybrids for the garden and cutting are the Modern Pinks and the Old-fashioned Pinks. Finally comes the Alpine or Rock Pinks bred from alpine species and used mostly in rock gardens. In all hybrid groups there are some cultivars that are self-colored (all the same color), and others that are flecked, picotee or laced, the latter two types having petals narrowly edged with a different color.

CULTIVATION

Ranging from fully to marginally frost hardy, *Dianthus* species like a sunny position, protection from strong winds, and well-drained, slightly alkaline soil. Stake taller varieties. Prune stems after flowering. Propagate perennials by layering or from cuttings in summer; annuals and biennials from seed in autumn or early spring. Watch for aphids, thrips and caterpillars, rust and virus infections.

Dianthus, Alpine Pinks

Also known as Rock Pinks, the cultivars of this hybrid group are compact plants forming mounds or mats of crowded fine leaves. The flowers come in many colors and shapes and are usually held 6–12 in (15–30 cm) above the foliage. **'La Bourboule'** (syn. 'La Bourbille') bears a profusion of single clove-scented pink flowers with fringed petals; **'Pike's Pink'** has gray-green foliage and rounded double pink flowers with a darker zone at the base; **'Nancy Colman'** is very similar but without the darker zone. **ZONES 4–9.**

Dianthus barbatus

SWEET WILLIAM

A slow-growing, frost-hardy perennial usually treated as a biennial, sweet William self-sows readily and grows to a height of 18 in (45 cm) and spread of 6 in (15 cm). The crowded, flattened heads of fragrant flowers range from white through pinks to carmine and crimson-purple and are often zoned in two tones. They flower in late spring and early summer and are ideal for massed planting. The dwarf cultivars,

Dianthus, Alpine Pink, 'Pike's Pink'

about 4 in (10 cm) tall, are usually treated as annuals. It has been crossed with Modern Pinks to produce a strain of hybrids, known as 'Sweet Wivelsfield'. **ZONES 4–10.**

Dianthus, Modern Pinks

These densely leafed, mound-forming perennials are derived from crosses between cultivars of *Dianthus plumarius* and *D. caryophyllus*. The earlier hybrids were called *D.* × *allwoodii* but these hardly stand apart from the rest of the Modern Pinks now. Modern Pinks have gray-green foliage and many erect flowering stems, each carrying 4 to 6 fragrant, single to fully double flowers in shades of white, pink or crimson, often with dark centers and with plain or fringed petals. Most are 12–18 in (30–45 cm) tall with a spread of 18 in (45 cm) and flower from late spring until early autumn; some are clove-scented. There are many Modern Pinks to choose from. **'Allwoodii'** bears fringed, pale purple-pink flowers with deep red central zones; **'Becky Robinson'** bears laced pink, clove-scented double blooms with ruby centers and margins; **'Dick Portman'** bears double crimson flowers with pinkish cream centers and margins; **'Doris'** is a scented pale pink double with deep pink center; **'Gran's Favorite'** is a sweetly scented, short-stemmed double, white with maroon centers and margins; **'Houndspool Ruby'** (syns 'Ruby', 'Ruby Doris') has rich pink double flowers with darker pink centers; 'Joy' is a great favorite. It has semi-double carmine-pink flowers on strong upright stems; 'Laced Monarch' bears deep pink to cerise double flowers with pale pink markings; 'Monica Wyatt' has very attractive full double clove-scented pale pink flowers with dark centers; 'Valda Wyatt' has clove-scented, rich pink double flowers with darker centers; and 'Warrior' has double pink flowers with deep red centers and margins. **ZONES 5–10.**

Diascia barberae

This low-growing, rather fragile perennial has small, heart-shaped, pale green leaves; it bears clusters of twin-spurred, salmon-pink flowers from spring to early autumn. It grows 6–12 in (15–30 cm) tall with a spread of 8 in (20 cm). 'Ruby Field' has salmon pink, wide-lipped, flowers produced over a long period from summer to autumn. **ZONES 8–10.**

Diascia vigilis
syn. *Diascia elegans*

A vigorous plant with a strongly stoloniferous habit, it grows to 20 in (50 cm) tall. The foliage is light green and glossy. It produces loose racemes of clear pink flowers from summer into early winter with incurved spurs. This is one of the most frost hardy and floriferous species. **ZONES 8–10.**

Dianthus, Old-fashioned Pinks

These are tuft-forming perennials that grow to 18 in (45 cm) high. In late spring and early summer they bear single to fully double, clove-scented flowers to 2½ in (6 cm) across from white, through pale pink and magenta to red, often fringed and with contrasting centers. 'Mrs Sinkins' is highly perfumed with pure white shaggy flowers prone to split at the calyx; and 'Pink Mrs Sinkins' is a pale pink form of Mrs Sinkins. 'Clare' produces bicolored, clove-scented, double pink-fringed flowers with maroon centers; and the delightful 'Rose de Mai' bears clove-scented, single pink flowers with deep pink eyes. **ZONES 5–9.**

Dianthus, Old-fashioned Pink, 'Clare'

DIASCIA
TWINSPUR

This is a genus of about 50 species of delicate but long-blooming perennials from South Africa that are popular in rockeries and borders and as potted specimens. They bear terminal racemes of flat, generally pink flowers with double nectar spurs on the back, and have erect or prostrate stems with toothed, mid-green leaves. A number of attractive cultivars are available including 'Kelly's Eye', and 'Rose Queen', which is an excellent bedding plant.

CULTIVATION
Full sun is best, with afternoon shade in hot areas; most are frost hardy, but they dislike humidity. A fertile, moist but well-drained soil and regular summer watering are vital. Pinch out tips to increase bushiness and cut back old stems after flowering. In autumn, propagate from seed or take cuttings to overwinter in a cool greenhouse.

Diascia vigilis

Dicentra formosa
WESTERN BLEEDING HEART

This spreading plant grows to about 18 in (45 cm) high with a spread of 12 in (30 cm). Dainty pink and red flowers appear on slender arching stems throughout spring and summer. 'Alba' is a white-flowered form. **ZONES 3–9.**

Dicentra formosa 'Alba'

DICTAMNUS
BURNING BUSH

The Book of Exodus tells how God spoke to Moses on Mount Sinai from a bush that burned yet was not consumed by the fire. Theologians point out that since this was a miracle the species is irrelevant. Gardeners insist that it must have been *Dictamnus albus*, the only species in its genus and indeed indigenous to the Mediterranean and temperate Asia. In still, warm conditions so much aromatic oil evaporates from the leaves that if you strike a match near it the vapor ignites and the bush is engulfed in flame, but so briefly that it is not damaged.

CULTIVATION
This perennial needs full sun and fertile, well-drained soil. It resents disturbance. Propagate from fresh seed in summer.

Dictamnus albus
syn. *Dictamnus fraxinella*
BURNING BUSH, DITTANY, GAS PLANT

This herbaceous, woody-stemmed perennial bears early summer spikes of fragrant, star-shaped, white, pink or lilac flowers with long stamens. It grows to 3 ft (1 m) tall with a spread of 36 in (90 cm) and has glossy light green leaves. It is quite frost hardy. *Dictamnus albus* var. *purpureus* (syn. *D. a.* var. *rubra*) bears purple-pink flowers with purple veins. **ZONES 3–9.**

DICENTRA
BLEEDING HEART

This genus consists of about 20 species of annuals and perennials much admired for their feathery leaves and the graceful carriage of their flowers, although they do not grow or flower well without a period of winter chill. The flowers, pendent and heart-shaped, come in red, pink, white, purple and yellow. They flower from mid-spring into early summer, though potted plants can be gently forced into early spring bloom if taken into a mildly warmed greenhouse at mid-winter. From Asia and North America, they are usually found in woodland and mountainous areas.

CULTIVATION
Mostly quite frost hardy, dicentras love humus-rich, moist but well-drained soil and some light shade. Propagate from seed in autumn or by division in late winter.

Dictamnus albus

Digitalis purpurea f. albiflora

Digitalis × mertonensis

DIGITALIS
FOXGLOVE

Natives of Europe, northern Africa and western Asia, these 22 species of biennials and perennials, some of them evergreen, are grown for their tall spikes of tubular, 2-lipped flowers which come in many colors including magenta, purple, white, cream, yellow, pink and lavender. The leaves are simple, mid-green and entire or toothed. The medicinal properties of digitalis have been known since ancient times, and these plants are still used in the treatment of heart ailments.

CULTIVATION
Marginally frost hardy to fully frost hardy, digitalis grow in most sheltered conditions, doing best in cool climates in part-shade and humus-rich, well-drained soil. Cut flowering stems down to the ground after spring flowering to encourage secondary spikes. Propagate from seed in autumn or by division; they self-seed readily.

Digitalis purpurea

Digitalis × mertonensis
A hybrid of *Digitalis grandiflora* and *D. purpurea*, this frost-hardy perennial forms a clump about 3 ft (1 m) tall and 12 in (30 cm) wide. Summer flowering, it bears spikes of tubular, pink to salmon flowers above a rosette of soft, hairy, oval leaves. Divide after flowering. **ZONES 4–9.**

Digitalis purpurea
This is the common foxglove, a short-lived, frost-hardy perennial with an upright habit, a height of 3–5 ft (1–1.5 m) and a spread of 24 in (60 cm). The flowers come in purple, pink, rosy magenta, white or pale yellow, above a rosette of rough, oval, deep green leaves. All parts of the plant, especially the leaves, are poisonous. Many seedling strains are available, grown as bedding annuals, the **Excelsior Hybrids** in mixed colors being very popular. *Digitalis purpurea* f. *albiflora* has pure white flowers sometimes lightly spotted brown inside; it will usually come true from seed especially if it is isolated from other colored forms. **ZONES 5–10.**

Dimorphotheca pluvialis

syn. *Dimorphotheca annua*

RAIN DAISY

This lovely bedding annual produces small flowerheads in late winter and spring that are snow white above, purple beneath, with brownish purple centers. Low growing, it reaches 8–12 in (20–30 cm) in height with a similar spread. *Dimorphotheca pluvialis* may also be successfully grown in containers. **ZONES 8–10.**

DIMORPHOTHECA

AFRICAN DAISY, CAPE MARIGOLD

These 7 species of annuals, perennials and evergreen subshrubs from South Africa have colorful, daisy-like flowers from late winter. Related to *Osteospermum*, they are useful for rock gardens and borders.

CULTIVATION

They need an open sunny situation and fertile, well-drained soil; they are salt tolerant. The flowers only open in sunshine. Prune lightly after flowering; deadheading prolongs flowering. Propagate annuals from seed in spring and perennials from cuttings in summer. Watch for fungal diseases in summer rainfall areas.

Dimorphotheca pluvialis

Dodecatheon meadia

From eastern North America, this is the best-known species, bearing white, rose pink or cyclamen pink, nodding flowers. It has primula-like, clumped rosettes of pale green leaves, and grows 6–18 in (15–45 cm) high with a spread of 18 in (45 cm). It was named for English scientist Richard Mead (1673–1754), a patron of American botanical studies. **ZONES 3–9.**

Dodecatheon pulchellum

syns *Dodecatheon amethystinum,*
D. pauciflorum, D. radicatum

Native to the mountains of western North America, this clump-forming perennial has mid-green 8 in (20 cm) long leaves in rosettes and produces up to 30 deep cerise to lilac flowers per stem. White forms are known as well as a form named **'Red Wings'** which has magenta-pink flowers on strong stems in late spring and early summer. **ZONES 4–9.**

DODECATHEON

SHOOTING STAR

The shooting stars (about 14 species) are western North America's equivalent to Europe's cyclamens and, like them, they are perennials and cousins of the primrose. Most are rosette-forming and grow to about 15 in (38 cm) high, with pink or white flower clusters. They have swept-back petals and protruding stamens.

CULTIVATION

Fully frost hardy, they prefer part-shade in moist, well-drained acidic soil. Most require a dry dormant summer period after flowering. They resent disturbance. Propagate from seed in autumn or by division in winter.

Dodecatheon meadia

Dorotheanthus bellidiformis

ICE PLANT, LIVINGSTONE DAISY, BOKBAAIVYGIE

This small succulent annual has daisy-like flowerheads in dazzling shades of yellow, white, red or pink in summer sun, although the flowers close in dull weather. It grows to 6 in (15 cm) tall and spreads to 12 in (30 cm) and has fleshy light green leaves to 3 in (7 cm) long with glistening surface cells. **ZONES 9–11.**

DOROTHEANTHUS

ICE PLANT, LIVINGSTONE DAISY

A genus of about 10 species of succulent annuals from South Africa, these mat-forming plants bear masses of daisy-like flowers in bright shades of red, pink, white or bicolored with dark centers in summer. Ideal for borders and massed displays.

CULTIVATION

Marginally frost hardy, grow in well-drained soil in a sunny spot. Deadhead to improve appearance and prolong flowering. In frost-prone areas plant after the likelihood of frost has passed. Propagate from seed.

Dorotheanthus bellidiformis

Doryanthes palmeri

DORYANTHES

The 2 species of *Doryanthes* are large evergreen perennials indigenous to the east coast of Australia. Somewhat resembling agaves in growth habit, they have loose rosettes of sword-shaped leaves and bear large red flowers with spreading petals, at the end of very tall stalks. The nectar attracts birds. They require up to 10 years to bloom.

CULTIVATION

Frost tender, they do best in full sun or part-shade in warm, frost-free conditions in light, humus-rich, well-drained soil. Water well during the growing season. Propagate from seed or by division.

Doryanthes excelsa

Doryanthes excelsa

GYMEA LILY

The larger and more common of the 2 species, *Doryanthes excelsa* is one of the largest lilies in the world. The large rounded head of deep red, torch-like flowers is borne terminally on a stem that can reach 20 ft (6 m) tall, arising from a rosette of sword-shaped leaves that can spread to about 8 ft (2.4 m) wide. It makes a spectacular feature plant for a large garden. **ZONES 9–11.**

Doryanthes palmeri

This species forms a dense rosette of lance-shaped, bright green leaves up to 10 ft (3 m) long. The flower stalk, up to 18 ft (5 m) tall, carries numerous scarlet, funnel-shaped flowers with white throats. They are arranged along the upper part of the stalk and appear in spring. **ZONES 9–11.**

ECHINACEA

CONEFLOWER

The 9 coneflower species, all native to the USA, share their common name with their close cousins the rudbeckias; some botanists still prefer to include them in that genus. They are clump-forming plants with thick edible roots. The daisy-like flowerheads are usually mauve-pink or purple, with darker and paler garden forms available. The dried root and rhizome of *Echinacea angustifolia* and *E. purpurea* are used in herbal medicine and allegedly increase the body's resistance to infection.

CULTIVATION

Very frost hardy, they like full sun and fertile soil, and resent disturbance—divide only to increase stock, otherwise leave alone; mulch each spring. Deadhead regularly to prolong flowering. Propagate by division or from root cuttings from winter to early spring.

ECHINOPS

GLOBE THISTLE

This is a genus, related to thistles, which contains about 120 species of erect perennials, biennials and annuals. The perennials are most commonly grown in gardens. They are native to southern Europe, central Asia as well as some of the mountainous areas of tropical Africa. The cultivated species are considered bold attractive additions to mixed or herbaceous borders and many are used in dried flower arrangements. The foliage is usually gray-green and thistle-like though usually not as spiny. The ball-shaped flowerheads can be blue, blue-gray or white, the rich blues being the most favored, and up to 2 in (5 cm) in diameter. Most cultivated species grow to 4 ft (1.2 m) or more.

CULTIVATION

These plants are usually fully frost hardy and heat tolerant, requiring nothing more than a sunny aspect with well-drained soil of any quality. Like most herbaceous perennials, cut them to the ground in autumn or early winter. Propagate by division or from seed.

Echinacea purpurea

Echinacea purpurea
syn. *Rudbeckia purpurea*
PURPLE CONEFLOWER

This showy, summer-flowering perennial has dark green, lance-shaped leaves and large, daisy-like, rosy purple flowers with high, orange-brown central cones. The flowerheads, about 4 in (10 cm) wide, are borne singly on strong stems and are useful for cutting. Of upright habit, it grows to 4 ft (1.2 m) tall and spreads about 18 in (45 cm). 'Robert Bloom' has dark pink flowers with orange-brown centers, while 'White Swan' has large, pure white flowers with orange-brown centers. **ZONES 3–10.**

Echinops ritro

Echinops ritro

This perennial is a useful plant for the herbaceous border, and its globe-like, spiky flowers can be cut and dried for winter decoration. It has large, deeply cut, prickly leaves with downy undersides, silvery white stems and round, thistle-like, purplish blue flowerheads in summer. Of upright habit, it grows 30 in (75 cm) tall and wide. **ZONES 3–10.**

ECHIUM

Indigenous to the Mediterranean, Canary Islands and Madeira in western Europe, the 40 or so species of annuals, perennials and shrubs in this genus are grown for their spectacular bright blue, purple or pink flowers that appear in late spring and summer. The hairy leaves form rosettes at the bases of the flowering stems. They look best in mixed borders. Ingestion of the plants can cause stomach upsets.

CULTIVATION

Very frost hardy to frost tender, they require a dry climate, full sun and a light to medium, well-drained soil. They become unwieldy in soil that is too rich or damp. Prune gently after flowering to keep them compact. Coastal planting is ideal. Propagate from seed or cuttings in spring or summer. In mild climates they self-seed readily.

Echium plantagineum

Epilobium angustifolium

EPILOBIUM

syn. **Chamaenerion**

WILLOW HERB

This is a large genus of about 200 species of annuals, biennials, perennials and subshrubs in the evening primrose family, widely distributed throughout the temperate and cold zones of both hemispheres. Most species are invasive, but some are valued in cultivation for their pretty deep pink or white flowers produced over a long period from summer to autumn.

CULTIVATION

Plant in sun or shade in moist, well-drained soil. They are mostly quite frost hardy. Remove spent flowers to prevent seeding. Propagate from seed in spring or autumn, or from cuttings.

Echium plantagineum

syn. **Echium lycopsis**

This annual or biennial to 24 in (60 cm) and native to warm, dry areas of Europe produces a basal rosette of bristly leaves up to 6 in (15 cm) long. The flower stems produced in late spring and summer form a panicle of rich blue-purple, occasionally red flowers. This is an attractive bedding plant but it tends to self-seed in dry climates; in southern Australia it has become a notorious weed known as Paterson's curse. **ZONES 9–10.**

Echium vulgare

VIPER'S BUGLOSS

This spectacular European biennial to 3 ft (1 m) tall has erect leafy stems. The funnel-shaped flowers, borne in spikes or panicles, are usually a rich violet, although white and pink forms exist. A dwarf form is available with white, blue, pink or purple flowers. **ZONES 7–10.**

Epilobium angustifolium

syn. **Chamaenerion angustifolium**

FIREWEED, ROSE BAY WILLOW HERB

This is a tall, vigorous perennial to 5 ft (1.5 m) found throughout the northern and mountainous parts of Eurasia and North America, most widespread in areas that have been recently burned or logged. Drifts of rose-pink flowering spikes are produced in late summer. It will spread indefinitely unless confined by pruning or containing the root system; it self-seeds freely. **ZONES 2–9.**

EREMURUS

FOXTAIL LILY, DESERT CANDLE

This is a genus of 50 or so species, all native to the cold, high plains of central and western Asia. Among the most dramatic of early summer perennials, they are mainly clump forming with a rosette of strap-shaped leaves. Their flower spikes, each of which can contain hundreds of flowers in pale shades of white, yellow or pink, rise to well over head height. The foliage is luxuriant but low so the flower stems rise almost naked, which makes them all the more imposing.

CULTIVATION

In the wild these cool- to cold-climate plants are protected from the winter cold by a thick blanket of snow; in milder climates they must be given a winter mulch to ensure the soil does not freeze. The other requirements are sun, a well-drained soil and shelter from strong winds. Propagate from fresh seed in autumn or by careful division after flowering.

Eremurus stenophyllus

Eremurus stenophyllus

This species from southwestern or central Asia has tufted basal leaves that are gray-green in color. The flowers are bright yellow and produced on spikes up to 3 ft (1 m) tall. **ZONES 5–9.**

Erigeron glaucus

Erigeron glaucus 'Cape Sebastian'

ERIGERON

FLEABANE

This genus contains about 200 species of annuals, biennials and perennials. The genus is described in more detail in the chapter on Lawns, Groundcovers, Ornamental Grasses and Bamboos.

Erigeron glaucus

SEASIDE DAISY, BEACH ASTER

This clump-forming perennial grows to about 10 in (25 cm) in height with a spread of about 8 in (20 cm). The spoon-shaped leaves are glaucous. Lilac-pink flowers are borne in summer. 'Cape Sebastian' has compact growth and flowers profusely. **ZONES 3–10.**

Eryngium 'Jos Eijking'

ERYNGIUM
SEA HOLLY

Eryngium bourgatii

This striking herbaceous perennial from the eastern Mediterranean has basal leaves that are leathery, gray-green and silver veined. Its flower spikes rise up to 30 in (75 cm) tall and support numerous blue or gray-green flowers surrounded by silvery spiny bracts. 'Othello' is a compact form that produces shorter flowers on strong, thick stems. **ZONES 5–9.**

Mostly native to South America and Europe, these 230 species of biennials and perennials are members of the same family as the carrot, and are grown for their interesting foliage and spiny collared flowerheads that usually have a bluish metallic sheen. They flower over a long period in summer and may be cut before they fully open, and dried for winter decoration. The spiny margins of the strongly colored, thistle-like bracts that surround the central flower give rise to the common name 'holly'. A number of named hybrids are available including the rather striking 'Jos Eijking'.

CULTIVATION
Mostly frost hardy, they need sun, good drainage and sandy soil. Plants tend to collapse in wet, heavy ground in winter. Propagate species from fresh seed; selected forms by root cuttings in winter or by division in spring.

Eryngium bourgatii

Erysimum × allionii
syn. *Cheiranthus × allionii*
SIBERIAN WALLFLOWER

This slow-growing but short-
lived hybrid is a bushy evergreen suitable for rock gardens,
banks and borders. It has
toothed, mid-green leaves and
bears bright yellow or orange
flowers in spring, putting on
a dazzling display for a long
period. It reaches a height and
spread of 12–18 in (30–45 cm).
ZONES 3–10.

Erysimum cheiri
syn. *Cheiranthus cheiri*
ENGLISH WALLFLOWER

This bushy species from
southern Europe is grown as
an annual or biennial and has
been part of the cottage garden
for centuries. Cultivars vary
in height from 8 to 24 in
(20 to 60 cm) and spread to
15 in (38 cm). Fragrant, 4-
petalled flowers appear in
spring, or during winter in
mild-winter regions. Colors
range from pastel pink and
yellow to deep brown, bronze,
orange, bright yellow, dark
red and scarlet. All have
lance-shaped leaves. They do
best where summers are cool.
'Monarch Fair Lady', to 18 in
(45 cm) high, has single, deep
orange to bright yellow
flowers; 'Orange Bedder', to
12 in (30 cm) high, is grown
as a biennial and has abundant, scented, brilliant orange
flowers. **ZONES 7–10.**

Erysimum cheiri 'Monarch Fair Lady'

ERYSIMUM
syn. *Cheiranthus*
WALLFLOWER

These 80 species of annuals and perennials range in the wild
from Europe to central Asia, with a smaller number in North
America. Some are suitable for rock gardens, such as the hybrid
'Orange Flame', others fit nicely into the border. Short-lived
species are best grown as biennials. Some form woody bases and
become leggy after a few years, at which time they are best
replaced with younger specimens. A number are fine winter to
spring flowerers, while some flower all winter or all year in very
mild regions. The older types are sweetly scented, while the
newer cultivars have no fragrance but bloom well over a long
season. Botanists have now placed all species of *Cheiranthus*
into this genus.

CULTIVATION
Mostly frost hardy, they do best in well-drained, fertile soil in
an open, sunny position. Cut back perennials after flowering so
only a few leaves remain on each stem. Propagate from seed in
spring or cuttings in summer.

Erysimum × allionii

Erysimum cheiri

ESCHSCHOLZIA

CALIFORNIA POPPY

This genus from western North America was named by botanist and poet, Adalbert von Chamisso (1781–1838) in honor of his friend, Johan Friedrich Eschscholz. It is a genus of 8 to 10 annuals and perennials with deeply dissected leaves. They bear capsular fruits and yellow to orange poppy-like flowers that close up in dull weather.

Eschscholzia californica

CULTIVATION

Species of *Eschscholzia* thrive in warm, dry climates but will tolerate quite severe frosts. They do not like transplanting so should be sown directly where they are to grow. Grow in poor, well-drained soil and deadhead regularly to prolong flowering. Propagate from seed sown in spring.

EUPHORBIA

Many members of this very large genus are succulents, and detailed information on the genus is given in the Cacti and Succulents chapter. However, the ones included here can be treated as perennials.

Euphorbia amygdaloides var. *robbiae*

Eschscholzia californica

This short-lived perennial, the official floral emblem of California, has cup-shaped flowers that open out from gray-green feathery foliage into vivid shades of orange, though cultivated strains have extended the color range to bronze, yellow, cream, scarlet, mauve and rose. It flowers in spring with intermittent blooms in summer and autumn; the flowers close on cloudy days. Of rounded habit, it grows to 12 in (30 cm) high with a similar or wider spread. 'Mission Bells Mixed' is a seedling strain with double and semi-double blooms in both pastel and strong colors; 'Ballerina' is also semi-double or double, in yellow, orange, red and pink; 'Thai Silk Series' consists of compact plants with large single or semi-double flowers with fluted and striped petals in orange, pink and bronze-red. **ZONES 6–11.**

Euphorbia griffithii

Euphorbia amygdaloides

WOOD SPURGE

Native to much of Europe and also Asia Minor, this erect perennial to 3 ft (1 m) high has dark green leaves to 3 in (8 cm) long and flowerheads with yellowish green bracts from mid-spring to early summer. It is generally represented in cultivation by its frost-hardy, selected, colorful varieties and forms. *Euphorbia amygdaloides* var. *robbiae* (syn. *E. robbiae*), Mrs Robb's bonnet, forms spreading rosettes of dark green leaves to 24 in (60 cm) high and wide and bears rounded heads of lime-green floral bracts; and 'Rubra' has light green leaves heavily suffused with burgundy and acid green floral bracts. *E. amygdaloides* can also be grown as a pot plant. **ZONES 7–9.**

Euphorbia griffithii

This perennial from the eastern Himalayas, which grows to a height of 3 ft (1 m), produces small, yellow flowers surrounded by brilliant orange bracts in summer. The lanceolate, green leaves have prominent pinkish midribs and turn red and yellow in autumn. 'Fireglow' produces orange-red floral bracts in early summer. **ZONES 6–9.**

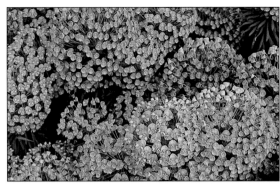

Euphorbia griffithii 'Fireglow'

Euphorbia californica subsp. *Wulfenii*

Euphorbia marginata
SNOW ON THE MOUNTAIN, GHOSTWEED

Native to central areas of North America, this bushy annual makes an excellent foil for brighter flowers. It has pointed oval, bright green leaves, sharply margined with white, and broad, petal-like white bracts surrounding small flowers in summer. *Euphorbia marginata* is fairly fast growing to about 24 in (60 cm) tall with a spread of about 12 in (30 cm). It will endure cold conditions. **ZONES 4–10.**

Euphorbia marginata

EXACUM

Like *Eustoma*, this genus belongs to the gentian family; it consists of about 25 species of annuals, biennials or perennials, widely distributed through tropical Africa and Asia. They have mostly yellow, white, blue or purple flowers that are often broadly cup-shaped or flat, unlike the tubular flowers of gentians. Only one species, *Exacum affine*, has become widely cultivated, a miniature from the hot dry island of Socotra that sits just off the horn of Africa at the mouth of the Red Sea; it is usually grown as an indoor plant, and is popular for its neat shrub-like growth habit and long succession of pretty flowers.

CULTIVATION

These plants can only be grown outdoors in warm, frost-free climates, where they do best in a sunny position in rich, moist but well-drained soil. Indoors they like diffused sun and a night temperature not below 50°F (10°C). Do not overwater. Propagate from seed in early spring.

Exacum affine

Exacum affine
PERSIAN VIOLET, GERMAN VIOLET

This showy miniature has shiny, oval leaves and bears a profusion of small, 5-petalled, saucer-shaped, usually purple-blue flowers with yellow stamens throughout summer. A biennial usually treated as an annual, *Exacum affine* grows to a height and spread of 8–12 in (20–30 cm). 'Blue Midget' grows to only half as big and has lavender-blue flowers, while 'White Midget' has white flowers. **ZONES 10–12.**

FARFUGIUM

From temperate Asia and closely allied to *Ligularia*, the 2 species of evergreen perennials in this genus are grown for their large, leathery foliage and daisy-like, yellow flowerheads. They are suitable for containers.

CULTIVATION

These frost-hardy plants do best in part-shade in fertile, moist but well-drained soil. Propagate from seed in spring or by division of variegated cultivars in spring.

Farfugium japonicum

Farfugium japonicum

syns *Farfugium tussilagineum,*
Ligularia tussilaginea

Native to Japan, this clump-forming perennial to 24 in (60 cm) high has glossy, kidney-shaped leaves on long stalks, above which arise downy branched stems bearing clusters of flowers from autumn to winter. '**Aureo-maculatum**', the leopard plant, has variegated leaves with circular yellow blotches. **ZONES 7–10.**

Felicia amelloides

FELICIA

BLUE DAISY

This genus, which ranges from southern Africa to Arabia, consists of 80 species of annuals, perennials and evergreen subshrubs. Named after Herr Felix, mayor of Regensburg on the Danube (about 1845), they are sprawling plants with aromatic foliage; in mild climates they flower on and off almost all year. The daisy-like, usually blue flowerheads with yellow disc florets are borne in masses.

CULTIVATION

They are fully frost hardy to frost tender and require full sun and well-drained, humus-rich, gravelly soil; they do not tolerate wet conditions. In all but the mildest areas the frost-tender perennial species need protection in winter with open-ended cloches. Deadheading prolongs the flowering season. Prune straggly shoots regularly. Propagate from cuttings taken in late summer or autumn or from seed in spring.

Felicia amelloides

BLUE MARGUERITE

This bushy, evergreen perennial has a spreading habit, growing to 24 in (60 cm) in height and twice as wide. It has roundish, bright green leaves and sky blue flowerheads with bright yellow centers borne on long stalks from late spring to autumn. Frost tender, it is fast growing in temperate climates and is suitable for seaside gardens. It is often grown as an annual in cool areas. 'Santa Anita' has extra large blue flowers and 'Alba' is a white form. *Felicia pappei* is like a miniature version of *F. amelloides* in growth, foliage and flower except that the flowerheads are an even richer, purer blue. It reaches 20 in (50 cm) in height. **ZONES 9–11.**

Filipendula vulgaris

Filipendula vulgaris
syn. *Filipendula hexapetala*

DROPWORT

From Europe and Asia, this species grows to 24–36 in (60–90 cm) high and has fleshy swollen roots. It is grown for its attractive, deeply cut, fern-like foliage, and crowded heads of tiny white flowers; some garden varieties are pink. This species will tolerate fairly dry conditions and must have good drainage. **ZONES 3–9.**

FILIPENDULA

This is a genus of 10 species of herbaceous perennials from northern temperate regions. All except *Filipendula vulgaris* occur naturally in moist waterside habitats. They have alternate pinnate leaves and erect stems bearing large panicle-like clusters of tiny, 5-petalled flowers with fluffy stamens. They do well at the back of large perennial borders and in waterside positions.

CULTIVATION
Grow these fully frost-hardy plants in full sun or part-shade in any moisture-retentive but well-drained soil. *F. rubra* and *F. ulmaria* will thrive in swampy, boggy sites. Propagate from seed or by division in spring or autumn. Check for powdery mildew.

GAILLARDIA

BLANKET FLOWER

Gaillardia × grandiflora 'Kobold'

This genus of around 30 species of annuals, perennials and bien-nials are all native to the USA, with the exception of 2 South American species. The perennials are better suited to cool-temperate climates. All plants bloom for a very long season from summer until the first frosts. The daisy-like flowers are either single, like small sunflowers, or double and as much as 6 in (15 cm) wide. The common name arose because the colors of the flowers resemble the bright yellows, oranges and reds of the blankets traditionally worn by Native Americans. Gaillardias are a colorful addition to the flower border and meadow garden, they are also very good for cutting.

CULTIVATION

Among the hardiest of garden flowers, they tolerate extreme heat, cold, dryness, strong winds and poor soils. Plant in full sun in well-drained soil and stake if necessary. In cool climates the stems of peren-nials should be cut back in late summer in order to re-cover before frosts. Propagate from seed in spring or early summer. Perennials may be divided in spring.

Gaillardia × grandiflora

Gaillardia × grandiflora

These hybrids of *Gaillardia aristata* and *G. pulchella* are the most commonly grown of the blanket flowers. The plants form mounds up to 3 ft (1 m) high and wide and have narrow, slightly lobed hairy leaves. The flowerheads, 3–4 in (8–10 cm) in diameter, come in hot colors: red, yel-low, orange and burgundy. They are propagated by division or from cuttings. There are several named cultivars. **'Burgunder'** ('Burgundy') has deep maroon-colored flowers; **'Dazzler'** has bright orange-yellow flowers with maroon centers; **'Kobold'** ('Goblin') has compact growth to 12 in (30 cm) high and rich red flowers with yellow tips. **ZONES 5–10.**

GALIUM
BEDSTRAW

This genus contains about 400 species of annuals and perennials of cosmopolitan distribution, of which some have become naturalized beyond their native regions and are weeds. They have weak sprawling stems and whorls of narrow green leaves. Many species spread by slender, much-branched rhizomes. The small star-shaped flowers are white, pink or yellow.

CULTIVATION
Grow these frost-hardy plants in part-shade in well-drained but moist soil. Propagate from fresh ripe seed or by division in early spring or autumn.

Galium verum
LADY'S BEDSTRAW

This sprawling perennial from temperate Eurasia and North America grows to about 12 in (30 cm) high forming a dense mass of fine foliage up to 4 ft (1.2 m) across. It has linear leaves arranged in whorls and tiny bright yellow flowers borne in dense terminal heads in summer and early autumn. **ZONES 3–10.**

Galium verum

GAURA

Related to the evening primrose *(Oenothera)*, this genus of about 20 species of annuals, biennials, perennials and subshrubs from North America are apt to be weedy, despite their showy flowers and the genus name that translates as 'gorgeous'. They have simple, narrow leaves and either racemes or panicles of flat, star-shaped, pink or white flowers.

CULTIVATION
They prefer full sun and light, well-drained soil. Cut ruthlessly to the ground when flowering has finished. Propagate from seed in autumn or spring, or from cuttings in summer.

Gaura lindheimeri

Native to the USA–Mexico border region, this clump-forming, long-flowering perennial is useful for backgrounds and mixed flower borders. It has loosely branched stems covered with tiny hairs, and from spring to autumn produces long sprays of beautiful flowers which open white from pink buds. It grows to 4 ft (1.2 m) in height with a spread of 3 ft (1 m). **ZONES 5–10.**

Gaura lindheimeri

GAZANIA

Gazania rigens var. leucolaena

From tropical and southern Africa, this genus consists of about 16 species of low-growing annuals and perennials grown for their bright colorful flowers. The genus name honors the medieval scholar Theodore of Gaza (1398–1478). The leaves are entire or deeply lobed, long and narrow, often dark green on top and white- or silver-gray felted beneath or in some species silvery haired on both sides. The flowerheads borne singly on short stalks range from cream to yellow, gold, pink, red, buff, brown and intermediate shades, usually with contrasting bands or spots at the petal bases. They appear from early spring until summer. Most modern varieties are hybrids from several South African species; they are marginally frost hardy and useful for coastal areas for bedding, rock gardens, pots and tubs and for binding soil on slopes. Cultivars include 'Double Orange' bearing large orange flowers with double centers on short stems just above the leaves; 'Flore Pleno' with bright yellow double flowers; and 'Gwen's Pink' with salmon pink single flowers with yellow centers and dark brown rings. Plants in the Chansonette Series are strong but low growers, reaching just 8 in (20 cm) in height. There are many color varieties, mostly with contrasting dark centers.

CULTIVATION

Grow in full sun in sandy, fairly dry, well-drained soil. Mulch with compost and water during dry periods. Propagate by division or from cuttings in autumn, or from seed in late winter to early spring.

Gazania rigens

This perennial species grows to a height of 12 in (30 cm) with a similar spread. It is a mat-forming plant with crowded rosettes of mostly unlobed leaves that are green above and whitish beneath, and orange flowerheads with a black eye spot at petal bases. The leaves of *Gazania rigens* var. *leucolaena* are silvery green on both sides and the flowers are yellow; *G. r.* var. *uniflora* has flowers that are smaller and short stalked. **ZONES 9–11.**

Gazania, Sunshine Hybrids

These mat-forming perennials may be grown as annuals. The height and spread is around 8 in (20 cm) and solitary flowers, which are borne in summer, range in color with the disc florets usually ringed in a darker color. **ZONES 9–11.**

Gazania, 'Gwen's Pink'

GENTIANA
GENTIAN

Occurring worldwide, mostly in alpine meadows and occasionally in woodlands, this is a genus of around 400 species of annuals, biennials and perennials, some of them evergreen. Intense deep blues and sky blues are the usual flower colors, but whites, creams, yellows and even red are also found. The mostly trumpet-shaped flowers are borne from spring to autumn. They are useful in rock gardens and sloping hillside gardens.

CULTIVATION

They prefer cooler regions and well-drained, but moisture-retentive soil rich in humus. Some species grow naturally in limestone soil. Plant in either sun or semi-shade. Propagate by division in spring or from fresh seed in autumn. Divide autumn-flowering species every 3 years in early spring, planting out in fresh soil.

Gentiana acaulis
syns Gentiana excisa, G. kochiana
STEMLESS GENTIAN, TRUMPET GENTIAN

The stemless gentian is an evergreen, rhizomatous perennial from southern Europe. It makes a striking carpet of small, crowded leaves and disproportionately large vivid blue trumpet flowers with green-spotted throats in spring and early summer. The foliage is only about 1 in (25 mm) high. It needs a deep root run and benefits from a light application of lime. **ZONES 3–9.**

Gentiana sino-ornata

This evergreen perennial from western China flowers in autumn, bearing deep blue trumpet flowers that are paler at the base and banded purplish blue. It has a prostrate, spreading habit, reaching 2 in (5 cm) tall and 12 in (30 cm) wide. 'Alba' has white flowers. **ZONES 6–9.**

Gentiana acaulis

Gentiana sino-ornata 'Alba'

GERANIUM
CRANESBILL

Over 300 species of annual, biennial and perennial geraniums, some evergreen, grow all over the world mainly in cool-temperate regions. The leaves are on long stalks, broadly circular in outline but usually palmately lobed. They make small, showy clumps with pink to blue or purple and white, 5-petalled flowers. The true geraniums or cranesbills, so-called for the shape of their small, dry fruitlets, are often confused with species of the genus *Pelargonium*, also commonly known as 'geraniums'. Symmetrical flowers are their chief point of distinction from pelargoniums, which produce irregularly shaped or marked flowers. With their attractive flowers they are useful for rock gardens, groundcovers and borders. Compact species and hybrids such as 'Brookside' and *Geranium gold-manii* are also good for containers.

CULTIVATION

Mostly quite frost hardy, they prefer a sunny situation and damp, well-drained soil. Transplant during winter. Propagate from seed in spring, cuttings in summer, or by division in autumn.

Geranium 'Brookside'

Geranium cinereum subsp. *subcaulescans*

Geranium cinereum 'Ballerina'

Geranium cinereum

From southern Europe, this small, tufted perennial to 6 in (15 cm) tall forms a basal rosette of soft, deeply divided leaves. The cup-shaped flowers, white or pale pink often with purple veins, are produced in late spring or early summer. **'Ballerina'** bears purplish pink flowers with distinct purple veins; *Geranium cinereum* **subsp.** *subcaulescens* has darker green leaves and vivid magenta flowers with a striking black center. **ZONES 5–9.**

Geranium himalayense

syn. *Geranium grandiflorum*

This clump-forming perennial has cushions of neatly cut leaves and grows to 18 in (45 cm) high and 24 in (60 cm) wide. In summer large cup-shaped violet-blue flowers with white centers appear on long stalks. **'Gravetye'** (syn. *Geranium grandiflorum* var. *alpinum*) has lilac-blue flowers with reddish centers and leaves that turn russet before dying down in autumn. **'Plenum'** (syn. 'Birch Double') has double, purplish pink flowers with darker veins. **ZONES 4–9.**

Geranium himalayense

Geranium macrorrhizum

Geranium macrorrhizum

This clump-forming perennial often forms large colonies in its shady mountain habitats of southern Europe. The sticky, deeply lobed leaves are aromatic, often turning red or bronze in autumn. The flowers appear on 12 in (30 cm) stems above the foliage in spring and early summer. Flower color varies from pink or purplish to pure white. It makes an excellent groundcover for a dry, shady site. 'Album' has white petals with reddish calyces; 'Ingwersen's Variety' has pale pink flowers and smoother glossy leaves. 'Spessart' is an attractive German cultivar. **ZONES 4–9.**

Geranium psilostemon

syn. Geranium armenum
ARMENIAN CRANESBILL

This robust clump-forming perennial grows 2–4 ft (0.6–1.2 m) high and 24 in (60 cm) wide; it has lobed, deeply toothed leaves, often reddish in autumn. Striking, large cup-shaped magenta flowers with a black eye appear in summer. **ZONES 6–9.**

Geranium psilostemon

Geum chiloense 'Lady Stratheden'

Geum chiloense

**syns Geum coccineum of gardens,
G. quellyon**
SCARLET AVENS

This Chilean native reaches a height of 24 in (60 cm) with a spread of 12 in (30 cm). It forms a basal rosette of deep green, pinnate leaves to 12 in (30 cm) long. The vivid scarlet, cup-shaped flowers appear in terminal panicles in summer. 'Lady Stratheden' (syn. 'Goldball') has semi-double, golden-yellow flowers. 'Mrs Bradshaw' bears rounded semi-double scarlet flowers. **ZONES 5–9.**

GEUM
AVENS

This genus of 50 or so herbaceous perennials is from the temperate and colder zones of both northern and southern hemispheres. Species form basal rosettes of hairy, lobed leaves and bear masses of red, orange and yellow flowers with prominent stamens from late spring until early autumn, and almost all year in frost-free areas. They suit mixed herbaceous borders and rock gardens, but may require a lot of room.

CULTIVATION

Frost hardy, they prefer a sunny, open position and moist, well-drained soil. Propagate from seed in autumn or by division in autumn or spring.

Gillenia trifoliata

GILLENIA

This genus of the rose family consists of 2 species of rhizomatous perennials from temperate North America. They are clump forming with stalkless leaves consisting of 3 leaflets and starry, 5-petalled flowers. After flowering the sepals enlarge and turn red. They are easy to grow in a shady position and make good cut flowers.

CULTIVATION

Very frost hardy, they prefer humus-rich, moist but well-drained soil, preferably in part-shade. Propagate from seed in spring or by division in spring or autumn.

GLOBULARIA

GLOBE DAISY

The 20 or so species of this genus of mainly evergreen, tufted or sometimes mat-forming perennials or subshrubs are grown for their neat rounded habit and compact heads of many tiny tubular flowers in shades of blue. Many species are suitable for a rock garden or for container growing, such as the tight, cushion-forming 'Hort's Variety'. The bushy subshrubs such as *Globularia × indubia* and *G. sarcophylla* are attractive planted among other small shrubs or against low walls.

CULTIVATION

Most of the cultivated species are only moderately frost hardy. Plant them in full sun in well-drained soil. Water sparingly and keep dry in winter. Propagate from seed in autumn or by division in spring and early summer.

Gillenia trifoliata

INDIAN PHYSIC, BOWMAN'S ROOT

This species is up to 4 ft (1.2 m) tall and has reddish stems and bronze green leaves composed of 3 oval toothed leaflets, each 3 in (8 cm) long. Open panicles of white or pale pink starry flowers are produced throughout summer. **ZONES 3–9.**

Globularia cordifolia

This evergreen miniature subshrub, found in central and southern Europe, has creeping woody stems with unusual tiny, spoon-shaped leaves, and produces solitary, stemless, fluffy blue to pale mauve flowerheads from late spring to early summer. *Globularia cordifolia* forms a dense mat or hummock, growing to a height of only 1–5 in (2.5–12 cm) and gradually spreading to 8 in (20 cm) or more. **ZONES 6–9.**

Globularia cordifolia

GUNNERA

This is a genus of around 45 species of rhizomatous perennials from temperate regions of Africa, Australasia and South America. Occurring in moist habitats, they range in size from small, mat-forming plants to very large, clump-forming plants with some of the largest leaves of any broad-leafed plants. They are grown mainly for their striking foliage, although some species have attractive flower spikes and fruits.

CULTIVATION
Most species enjoy moist but well-aerated soil at the edge of a pond or stream. Plant in rich soil in full sun, although they may need shelter from very hot sun (which can scorch the leaves) and wind (which can reduce the leaves to tatters). Propagate from seed in autumn or spring, or by division in early spring. Protect from slugs and snails.

Gunnera manicata
syn. *Gunnera brasiliensis*
GIANT ORNAMENTAL RHUBARB

Native to the high mountain swamps of Colombia and Brazil, this huge plant thrives in boggy soil and is usually grown on the margins of a pond. The massive leaves quickly unfurl in spring to as wide as 8 ft (2.4 m) on prickly stalks about 6 ft (1.8 m) high. Long spikes of greenish red flowers are borne in summer. Give the dormant crown a protective mulch of straw in winter. **ZONES 7–9.**

Gunnera manicata

Gypsophila paniculata

GYPSOPHILA

Native to Europe, Asia and North Africa, there are over 100 species of these annuals and perennials, some of which are semi-evergreen. They are grown for their masses of small, dainty, white or pink flowers, often used by florists as a foil for bolder flowers or foliage. The narrow leaves are borne in opposite pairs.

CULTIVATION

Plant in full sun with shelter from strong winds. Fully frost hardy, they will tolerate most soils but do best in deep, well-drained soil lightened with compost or peat and grow well in limy soil. Cut back after flowering to encourage a second flush. Transplant when dormant during winter. Propagate from cuttings in summer or from seed in spring or autumn.

Gypsophila repens

Gypsophila paniculata
BABY'S BREATH

This short-lived perennial, mostly treated as an annual, has small, dark green leaves and sprays of tiny white spring flowers. It reaches a height and spread of 3 ft (1 m) or more. **'Bristol Fairy'** has double white flowers. **'Compact Plena'** has double white or soft pink flowers. **ZONES 4–10.**

Gypsophila paniculata 'Bristol Fairy'

Gypsophila repens

This prostrate perennial has stems forming low mounds up to 8 in (20 cm) high and 18 in (45 cm) wide. It has narrow, bluish green leaves and bears panicles of star-shaped white, lilac or pale purple flowers in summer. It is an ideal plant for trailing over rocks. **'Dorothy Teacher'** has abundant pale pink flowers ageing to deep pink. **ZONES 4–9.**

Hacquetia epipactis

HACQUETIA
syn. *Dondia*

There is one species only in this genus: a tiny perennial from the woodlands of eastern Europe. At most it grows to 4 in (10 cm) tall, spreading very slowly into a small mat. The flowers appear in spring before the leaves and the plant is usually grown in rock gardens or in small pots in collections of alpine plants. It requires a cold winter for success.

CULTIVATION

Grow in porous, gritty soil that contains leafmold or other rotted organic matter in part- or dappled shade. Keep moist but give more water from the time the flower buds appear until the leaves begin to yellow in autumn. Propagate from seed sown as soon as it is ripe or by division of clumps in late winter, before flower buds appear. Divide infrequently as it resents root disturbance.

Hacquetia epipactis
syn. *Dondia epipactis*

The pinhead-sized, bright yellow flowers of this species are surrounded by glossy green bracts, giving the effect of a most unusual bright green flower. Appearing straight from the ground in earliest spring, they are followed by 3-lobed leaves. This is a most unusual and desirable plant for cooler areas. **ZONES 6–9.**

HELENIUM

SNEEZEWEED, HELEN'S FLOWER

This genus, native to the Americas, consists of about 40 species of annual, biennial or perennial herbs. The mid-green leaves, which are alternate on erect stems, are oval to lance-shaped. The daisy-like flowerheads appear in summer and have yellow, red-brown or orange ray florets and yellow, yellow-green, red or brown disc florets. The flowers make a good border and are ideal for cutting.

CULTIVATION

Frost hardy, heleniums are easy to grow in any temperate climate as long as they get sun. The soil should be moist and well drained. Remove spent flowers regularly to prolong the flowering period. Propagate by division of old clumps in winter or from seed in spring or autumn.

Helenium autumnale

COMMON SNEEZEWEED

This perennial from North America grows about 5 ft (1.5 m) tall. The flowers occur from late summer to mid-autumn. This species has given rise to a number of named garden forms whose flowers range from yellow to maroon, with many being a blend of yellow and russet tones. **ZONES 3–9.**

Helenium autumnale

HELIANTHUS

This genus of the daisy family includes one of the world's most important oilseed plants, also used for livestock fodder, as well as the Jerusalem artichoke with edible tubers, and many ornamentals. Consisting of around 70 species of annuals and perennials, all native to the Americas, they have large daisy-like, mostly golden-yellow flowerheads, which are on prolonged display from summer to autumn. The plants have hairy, often sticky leaves and tall, rough stems. They make very good cut flowers.

CULTIVATION

Frost hardy, they prefer full sun and protection from wind. The soil should be well drained. Fertilize in spring to promote large blooms and water generously in dry conditions. Perennials should be cut down to the base when they finish flowering. Propagate from seed or by division in autumn or early spring.

Helianthus annuus

Helianthus × multiflorus

Helianthus annuus

COMMON SUNFLOWER

This fast-growing, upright annual can reach a height of 10 ft (3 m) or more. Large, daisy-like, 12 in (30 cm) wide yellow flowerheads with brown centers are borne in summer. They are tall, leggy plants with broad, mid-green leaves. This species produces one of the world's most important oilseeds. It can be a little large for small gardens, but newer varieties have been developed that grow to a more manageable size, about 6 ft (1.8 m), including **'Autumn Beauty'** with medium-sized flowers usually brownish red, deep red, light yellow or golden yellow; and **'Teddy Bear'**, a compact grower with double, dark yellow flowers. **ZONES 4–11.**

Helianthus × m. 'Loddon Gold'

Helianthus × multiflorus

Helianthus × multiflorus is a clump-forming perennial to 6 ft (1.8 m) in height and 3 ft (1 m) in spread. The domed flowers can be up to 6 in (15 cm) across and appear in late summer to mid-autumn. Some popular cultivars include 'Capenoch Star', 'Loddon Gold', 'Triomphe de Gand' and 'Soleil d'Or'. **ZONES 5–9.**

Helianthus × multiflorus

Heliopsis helianthoides

This species grows to 5 ft (1.5 m) tall and 3 ft (1 m) in spread. It has coarse, hairy leaves and golden-yellow-flowers in summer. The cultivar 'Patula' has semi-double orange flowers. 'Light of Loddon' has rough, hairy leaves and strong stems that carry dahlia-like, bright yellow, double flowers in late summer; it grows to a height of 3 ft (1 m) and a spread of 24 in (60 cm). **ZONES 4–9.**

Heliopsis h., 'Light of Loddon'

HELIOPSIS

ORANGE SUNFLOWER, OX EYE

The name *Heliopsis* means resembling a sunflower, and these perennials from the North American prairies do look like sunflowers, though on a rather reduced and more manageable scale. There are about 12 species, with stiff, branching stems and toothed, mid- to dark green leaves. The solitary, usually yellow flowers are up to 3 in (8 cm) wide and make good cut flowers.

CULTIVATION

These plants are easily grown, and for a while will even tolerate poor conditions. However, they thrive in fertile, moist but well-drained soil and a sunny position. They are all very frost hardy. Deadhead regularly to prolong the flower display and cut back to ground level after flowering finishes. Propagate from seed or cuttings in spring, or by division in spring or autumn.

Heliotropium arborescens

Heliotropium arborescens
syn. *Heliotropium peruvianum*
CHERRY PIE, COMMON HELIOTROPE

Traditionally treated as a perennial, this attractive, soft-wooded evergreen shrub bears clusters of fragrant, purple to lavender flowers, with a delicate scent similar to stewed cherries, from late spring to autumn. From the Peruvian Andes, it grows fast to 30 in (75 cm) tall and 3 ft (1 m) wide. It has dark green, wrinkled leaves, golden to lime-green in the cultivar 'Aurea' and dark purplish green in 'Lord Robert'. In cold climates it is grown as a conservatory or summer bedding plant. **ZONES 9–11.**

HELIOTROPIUM

HELIOTROPE

This genus consists of over 250 species of annuals, perennials, shrubs and subshrubs from most warmer parts of the world. The leaves are simple and usually alternate. The clusters of flowers can be purple, blue, white or yellow and are deliciously scented. They appear in summer and are attractive to butterflies. The smaller varieties make excellent pot plants and hanging baskets.

CULTIVATION

Heliotropes grow wild in both subtropical and cooler temperate climates and hence vary in frost hardiness. They prefer moist, well-drained, moderately fertile soil. Cut plants back by about half in early spring to promote bushiness. Propagate from seed in spring or cuttings in early autumn.

HELLEBORUS

Helleborus argutifolius

HELLEBORE

Native to areas of Europe and western Asia, these 15 perennial or evergreen species are useful winter- and spring-flowering plants for cooler climates. They bear beautiful, open flowers in white or shades of green, red and purple and are effective planted in drifts or massed in the shade of deciduous trees. All hellebores are poisonous.

CULTIVATION

Grow in part-shade and moist, well-drained, humus-rich soil; do not let them completely dry out in summer. Cut off old leaves from deciduous species just as the buds start to appear. Remove flowerheads after seeds drop. A top-dressing of compost or manure after flowering is beneficial. Propagate from seed or by division in autumn or early spring. Check the plants for aphids.

Helleborus argutifolius

syns *Helleborus corsicus, H. lividus* subsp. *corsicus*

CORSICAN HELLEBORE

This is one of the earliest flowering hellebores, with blooms appearing in late winter and early spring. It is a robust evergreen that produces large clusters of cup-shaped, nodding, 2 in (5 cm) wide green flowers on an upright spike above divided, spiny, margined, deep green foliage. It has a clump-forming habit, growing to a height of 24 in (60 cm) and a spread of 24–36 in (60–90 cm). This is the most sun- and drought-tolerant species of the genus. **ZONES 6–9.**

Helleborus foetidus

STINKING HELLEBORE

This clump-forming perennial has attractive, dark green, divided leaves that remain all year. In winter or early spring the clusters of pale green, bell-shaped flowers, delicately edged with red, are borne on short stems. Established plants will often self-seed readily. **ZONES 6–10.**

Helleborus lividus

This species from the islands of the western Mediterranean has deep green or bluish green leaves and bowl-shaped, creamy green flowers from winter to spring. It is slow to establish after being transplanted. **ZONES 7–9.**

Helleborus niger

CHRISTMAS ROSE

Popular for its white, mid-winter flowers, often appearing in the snow, this is one of the more temperamental species. It is often worth covering the plant with a cloche before the flowers open, to protect them from the winter weather. The mid-green, deeply lobed leaves are evergreen; mounds are 12 in (30 cm) high with a spread of 12–18 in (30–45 cm). They need steady moisture. **ZONES 3–9.**

Helleborus orientalis

Helleborus purpurascens

Helleborus orientalis

LENTEN ROSE

The most widely grown of the genus, this evergreen, clump-forming species from Greece, Turkey and the Caucasus grows to 24 in (60 cm) high and wide. The large nodding flowers come in a great variety of colors from white, green, pink and rose to purple, sometimes with dark spots. Very frost hardy, it flowers in winter or early spring. The dense foliage fades and can be trimmed back before flowering. **ZONES 6–10.**

Helleborus purpurascens

Flowering from about mid-winter, even in cool climates, this frost-hardy, deciduous perennial from eastern Europe blooms before the new season's leaves appear. Plants grow anywhere up to 12 in (30 cm) tall but often less and the clumps spread at least 12 in (30 cm) across. The compound leaves are big and lobed and the flowers are an odd gray-green-pink combination. **ZONES 6–9.**

HEMEROCALLIS

DAYLILY

Native to temperate east Asia, these perennials, some of which are semi-evergreen or evergreen, are grown for their showy, often fragrant flowers which come in a vibrant range of colors. Individual blooms last only for a day, but are borne in great numbers on strong stems above tall, grassy foliage and continue flowering from early summer to autumn. The flower size varies from 3 in (8 cm) miniatures to giants of 6 in (15 cm) or more, single or double; and plant height ranges from about 24 in (60 cm) to 3 ft (1 m). Grow in the herbaceous border, among shrubs or naturalize in grassy woodland areas.

Hemerocallis fulva

TAWNY DAYLILY

This clump-forming species to 3 ft (1 m). high and 30 in (75 cm) wide, bears rich orange-red, trumpet-shaped, 3–6 in (8–15 cm) wide flowers from mid- to late summer. It has been in cultivation for centuries and in China and Japan the flower buds are sold as food. The cultivar 'Flore Pleno' (syn. 'Kwanzo') has 6 in (15 cm) double orange flowers with sepals curved back and a red eye. 'Kwanzo Variegata' bears similar flowers to 'Flore Pleno' and has pretty leaves with a white margin. **ZONES 4–11.**

Hemerocallis fulva

CULTIVATION

Position carefully when planting as the flowers turn their heads towards the sun and the equator. Most daylilies are fully hardy; they prefer sun but will grow well and give brighter colors in part-shade. Plant in a reasonably good soil that does not dry out. Propagate by division in autumn or spring and divide clumps every 3 or 4 years. Cultivars raised from seed do not come true to type. Check for slugs and snails in early spring. Plants may also suffer from aphid or spider mite attack.

Hemerocallis lilioasphodelus

Hemerocallis lilioasphodelus

syn. Hemerocallis flava

PALE DAYLILY, LEMON DAYLILY

This is one of the first daylilies used for breeding and is found across China. It forms large spreading clumps with leaves up to 30 in (75 cm) long. The lemon-yellow flowers are sweetly scented and borne in a cluster of 3 to 9 blooms. It has a range of uses in Chinese herbal medicine: some parts may be eaten, while others may be hallucinogenic. **ZONES 4–9.**

HEUCHERA

ALUM ROOT, CORAL BELLS

There are about 55 species of these evergreen and semi-evergreen perennials, native to North America and Mexico. They form neat clumps of scalloped leaves, often tinted bronze or purple, from which arise stems bearing masses of dainty, nodding, white, crimson or pink bell flowers often over a long flowering season. They make useful groundcovers and woodland plants, or they may be used as rock garden or edging plants.

CULTIVATION

Mostly very frost hardy, they grow well in either full sun or semi-shade and like well-drained, coarse, moisture-retentive soil. Propagate species from seed in autumn or by division in spring or autumn; cultivars by division in autumn or early spring. Remove spent flower stems and divide established clumps every 3 or 4 years.

Heuchera sanguinea

Heuchera × brizoides

This group are all complex hybrids involving *Heuchera sanguinea* and several other species. Highly attractive plants, they produce mounds of rounded, lobed leaves that are prettily marbled. Above these rise tall, slender, arching stems bearing dainty bell-like flowers in white, as in '**June Bride**', or shades of pink or red. Foliage mounds are about 12 in (30 cm) tall with flower stems rising at least another 12 in (30 cm). **ZONES 3–10.**

Heuchera sanguinea

CORAL BELLS

This is the most commonly grown species, and occurs naturally from Arizona to New Mexico. It grows to 18 in (45 cm) tall and has sprays of scarlet or coral-red flowers above toothed, deeply lobed leaves. British and American gardeners have developed cultivars with a wider color range—from pale pink to deep red—and slightly larger flowers. The **Bressingham Hybrids** are typical. **ZONES 6–10.**

Heuchera × brizoides 'June Bride'

HIBISCUS

Most of the species belonging to this genus are shrubs, and detailed information on the genus is given in the Shrubs chapter. However, *Hibiscus moscheutos* is treated here as a perennial.

Hibiscus moscheutos

Hibiscus moscheutos

COMMON ROSE MALLOW,
SWAMP ROSE MALLOW

This herbaceous perennial grows to 8 ft (2.4 m) high and 3–5 ft (1–1.5 m) wide. Single, hollyhock-like flowers 4–8 in (10–20 cm) wide are carried on robust, unbranched stems in late summer and autumn. Colors vary from white to pink, some with deeper throat markings. The leaves are large, toothed and softly hairy beneath. A range of lower-growing cultivars with dramatic large flowers has been bred from this species, including 'Southern Belle' with rose-pink blooms up to 10 in (25 cm) across. **ZONES 5–9.**

Hibiscus moscheutos 'Southern Belle'

Hosta fortunei

This strong-growing perennial has given rise to many hybrids. It has ovate or broad lanceolate, pleated and pointed leaves that are a dull mid-green. In summer tall flower stems are produced from which hang lavender flowers. Plants grow at least 18 in (45 cm) tall but spread nearly twice as wide. '**Albomarginata**' has gray-green leaves with creamy yellow to white margins; '**Albopicta**' has leaves marbled or irregularly marked in 2 shades of green; '**Aurea**' is a luminous golden green; and '**Aureomarginata**' has leaves edged in yellow. **ZONES 6–10.**

HOSTA

PLANTAIN LILY

Natives of Japan and China, the 40 species in this genus of easily grown, frost-hardy perennials are valued for their decorative foliage. They all produce wide, handsome leaves, some being marbled or marked with white and others a bluish green. All-yellow foliage forms are also available. They do well in large pots or planters, are excellent for groundcover, and add an exotic touch planted on the margins of lily ponds or in bog gardens. Tall stems to about 18 in (45 cm) tall, bear nodding white, pink or shades of purple and blue, bell- or trumpet-shaped flowers during warmer weather. Both the leaves and the flowers are popular for floral arrangements.

CULTIVATION

They grow well in shade and rich, moist, neutral, well-drained soil. Feed regularly during the growing season. Propagate by division in early spring, and guard against snails and slugs.

Hosta sieboldiana

This robust, clump-forming plant grows to 3 ft (1 m) high and 5 ft (1.5 m) wide. It has puckered, heart-shaped, bluish gray leaves and bears racemes of mauve buds opening to trumpet-shaped white flowers in early summer. 'Frances Williams' has heart-shaped, puckered blue-green leaves with yellowish green margins. *Hosta sieboldiana* var. *elegans* also has heart-shaped, puckered leaves.
ZONES 6–10.

Hosta ventricosa

BLUE PLANTAIN LILY

From China and Korea, this plant forms a tall clump of shiny, dark green leaves that are strongly veined and broadly heart-shaped. Tall stems of purple flowers appear in summer. **ZONES 6–10.**

Hosta sieboldiana

Hosta fortunei 'Albopicta'

Hosta fortunei 'Aureomarginata'

HOUTTUYNIA

There is only one species in this genus, a wide-spreading, creeping herbaceous perennial native to eastern Asia. It grows in moist or wet, part- or fully shaded areas. It makes a good groundcover in moist, woodland gardens or beside ponds and is also happy growing in shallow water or boggy ground. The wild form has dark green, heart-shaped, red-margined, plain green leaves, and in summer bears spikes of tiny yellowish flowers with 4 pure white bracts at the base of each spike.

CULTIVATION

Grow this frost-hardy plant in moist, rich soil. In cooler climates the plant will tolerate sun so long as the ground is moist, but in hotter places some shade is desirable. Where winters are always cold, reduce water in winter or cover the roots with a thick layer of straw. Propagate from ripe seed or from cuttings in late spring and early summer, or by division in spring.

Houttuynia cordata

Ranging from the Himalayas to Japan, this water-loving deciduous perennial makes a good groundcover but may become invasive. It is a vigorous plant, growing to 12 in (30 cm) in height with an indefinite spread. It grows from underground runners which send up bright red branched stems bearing aromatic green leaves. However, the most popular form, 'Chameleon' (syns 'Tricolor', 'Variegata') is strikingly variegated in red, cream, pink and green. **ZONES 5–11.**

HYPERICUM

Many of the species belonging to this genus are shrubs, and detailed information on the genus is given in the Shrubs chapter. However, *Hypericum cerastoides* is treated here as a perennial.

Houttuynia cordata 'Chameleon'

Hypericum cerastoides

Hypericum cerastoides

syn. *Hypericum rhodoppeum*

This densely mounding perennial has oval, gray-green leaves and terminal clusters of bright yellow, cup-shaped flowers in late spring and early summer. It has an upright, slightly spreading habit and grows to 12 in (30 cm) tall with an 18 in (45 cm) spread. Frost hardy, it is useful in rock gardens. **ZONES 6–9.**

Iberis amara

CANDYTUFT, HYACINTH-FLOWERED
CANDYTUFT

This frost-hardy, fast-growing
and erect bushy annual has
lance-shaped mid-green leaves
and reaches a height of 12 in
(30 cm), with a spread of 6 in
(15 cm). It produces large
racemes of small, fragrant,
pure white flowers in early
spring and summer. Various
strains are available. The
Hyacinth-flowered Series has
large fragrant flowers in
varying shades of pink; these
are sometimes used as cut
flowers. **ZONES 7–11.**

Iberis sempervirens

CANDYTUFT, EVERGREEN CANDYTUFT

A low, spreading, evergreen
perennial, this species from
southern Europe is ideal for
rock gardens. It has narrow,
dark green leaves and dense,
rounded heads of unscented
white flowers in spring and
early summer. It is frost hardy,
and grows 6–12 in (15–30 cm)
high with a spread of 18–24 in
(45–60 cm). The cultivar
'**Snowflake**' is most attractive,
with glossy, dark green leaves
and semi-spherical heads of
white flowers. Lightly trim
after flowering. **ZONES 4–11.**

Impatiens, New Guinea Hybrid 'Tango'

IBERIS

This genus consists of around 50 species of annuals, perennials
and evergreen subshrubs are mainly from southern Europe,
northern Africa and western Asia. Highly regarded as decorative
plants they are excellent for rock gardens, bedding and borders.
Showy flowers are borne in either flattish heads in white, red
and purple, or in erect racemes of pure white flowers.

CULTIVATION
Fully to marginally frost hardy, they require a warm, sunny
position and a well-drained, light soil, preferably with added
lime or dolomite. Propagate from seed in spring or autumn—
they may self-sow, but are unlikely to become invasive—or cuttings in summer.

Iberis sempervirens   *Iberis amara*

IMPATIENS

This large genus of around 850 species of succulent-stemmed
annuals, evergreen perennials and subshrubs is widely distributed, especially in the subtropics and tropics of Asia and Africa.
They are useful for colorful summer bedding displays and for
indoor and patio plants. The flowers come in an ever-increasing
range of colors. Many hybrid strains are perennial in mild climates, but in colder climates are usually grown as annuals.
Their botanical name, *Impatiens,* refers to the impatience with
which they grow and multiply.

CULTIVATION
Frost hardy to frost tender, they will grow in sun or part-shade;
many species do well under overhanging trees. They prefer a
moist but freely drained soil, and need protection from strong
winds. Tip prune the fast-growing shoots to encourage shrubby
growth and more abundant flowers. Propagate from seed or
stem cuttings in spring and summer.

Impatiens, New Guinea Hybrids

Hybrids from a New Guinean species, members of this group of fast-growing perennials are also grown as annuals in cool climates. They are frost tender and grow to a height and spread of 12–18 in (30–45 cm). The leaves are oval, pointed and bronze green, or may be variegated with cream, white or yellow. The flat, spurred flowers are pink, orange, red or cerise, sometimes with white markings. Cultivars include '**Cheers**', with its coral flowers and yellow leaves; '**Concerto**', with crimson-centered deep pink flowers; '**Tango**', with deep orange flowers; and '**Red Magic**', which has scarlet flowers and bronze-red leaves. They do well in brightly lit positions indoors in cooler climates, or on enclosed verandahs or patios in warmer areas. **ZONES 10–12.**

Impatiens, New Guinea Hybrid 'Concerto'

Impatiens usambarensis

This tropical African species gets its name from the Usambara Mountains on the borders of Kenya and Tanzania, where it was first discovered. It is related to the better known *Impatiens walleriana* and has been used in the breeding of the many colorful 'busy lizzie' hybrids in this group. *I. u ×walleriana,* seen here, displays just one of the many possible color outcomes in such crosses. **ZONES 10–12.**

Impatiens u. × walleriana

Impatiens, New Guinea Hybrid cultivar

Incarvillea delavayi
PRIDE OF CHINA, HARDY GLOXINIA

This fleshy-rooted, clump-forming perennial is useful for rock gardens and borders. It has handsome, fern-like foliage and erect stems bearing large, trumpet-shaped, rosy purple flowers in summer. It grows to a height of 24 in (60 cm) with a spread of 12 in (30 cm), but dies down early in autumn. It is very frost hardy, but should be protected with a compost mulch during cold winters.
ZONES 6–10.

Inula helenium

INCARVILLEA

This genus of the bignonia family (Bignoniaceae) consists of 14 species native to central and east Asia, including the Himalayas, and are suitable for rock gardens and borders. The taller species are more at home in herbaceous borders. Some species are annuals, although those in cultivation are usually perennial. From mountain habitats, some of the shorter growing species from higher altitudes have, strangely enough, the largest and most exotic flowers. Most species flower in shades of magenta and deep rose pink although there are 1 or 2 which have flowers in shades of yellow or white.

CULTIVATION

Most species of *Incarvillea* are frost hardy, but do not tolerate overly wet or waterlogged soil in winter. They usually require an aspect that has rich, moisture-retentive, well-drained soil, in a position that receives ample sun except in the very hottest part of the day. These plants prefer cold to temperate climates. Propagation is usually by seed in autumn or spring; division in spring or autumn is possible, but difficult, as mature plants resent disturbance.

Incarvillea delavayi

INULA

Native to Asia, Africa and Europe, this genus of about 90 species in the daisy family are mostly herbaceous perennials, although some are subshrubs, biennials or annuals. The different species vary in size from quite tiny plants suited to the rock garden up to towering perennials that can exceed 10 ft (3 m) tall. Often in the case of the larger species, the leaves can also be impressive if somewhat rank. Inulas are well known for their fine-petalled, invariably yellow daisies, some species of which are quite large and showy. Several species have been in cultivated since ancient times and the name *Inula* was used by the Roman.

CULTIVATION

Inulas are frost hardy plants. They will grow in any deep, fertile, well-drained or moist soil but not one that is wet. They prefer a sunny to part-shaded aspect. Propagation is usually from seed or by division in spring or autumn.

Inula helenium
ELECAMPANE, SCABWORT

Believed to have originated in central Asia, this plant has become widely naturalized. It is one of the largest *Inula* species at 8 ft (2.4 m) tall with a spread of 3 ft (1 m). As it is rhizomatous, it is also one of the most invasive. It produces its large, yellow daisy-like flowers in summer and should be planted with due deference to its invasive potential. *Inula helenium* was used in medicine as a tonic, astringent, demulcent and diuretic. Because of this, it is often planted in herb gardens.
ZONES 5–10.

Iresine herbstii 'Brilliantissima'

IRESINE

Belonging to the amaranthus family, these tropical perennials from the Americas and Australia—some 80 species in all—are sometimes treated as annuals. They vary in habit from upright to ground-hugging. The flowers are insignificant and not the reason for which these plants are grown. It is for their often brilliantly colored leaves that they merit attention.

CULTIVATION

These frost-tender plants only make permanent garden plants in tropical to warm temperate climates where there is no incidence of frost. In cooler areas they can be grown in greenhouses and planted out once all chance of frost has passed. They prefer good loamy, well-drained soil and must be kept moist during the growth period. They also need bright light, with some direct sun, to retain the brilliant color in their leaves. Tips should be pinched out in the growing season to encourage bushy plants. Propagate from cuttings in spring.

Iresine herbstii
syn. *Iresine reticulata*
BEEFSTEAK PLANT, BLOODLEAF

Native to Brazil, this species makes an attractive tropical bedding or pot plant. Although perennial, it is often treated as an annual that is overwintered as struck cuttings in a greenhouse in cold areas. It grows to 24 in (60 cm) tall with a spread of 18 in (45 cm), but usually much less if grown as an annual. It has red stems and rounded purple-red leaves up to 4 in (10 cm) long, with notches at the tips and yellowish red veins. Garden forms have a range of colors: from bright green leaves with bright yellow veins through to cultivars such as 'Brilliantissima' with its rich purple-green leaves with beetroot-pink veins. **ZONES 10–12.**

IRIS

This wide-ranging genus of more than 200 species, native to the temperate regions of the northern hemisphere, is named for the Greek goddess of the rainbow, and is valued for its beautiful and distinctive flowers. Each flower has 6 petals: 3 outer petals, called 'falls', which droop away from the center and alternate with the inner petals, called 'standards'. There are many hybrids. Irises are divided into 2 main groups, rhizomatous and bulbous.

Rhizomatous irises have sword-shaped leaves, are sometimes evergreen, and are subdivided into 3 groups: bearded (or flag) irises, with a tuft of hairs (the 'beard') on the 3 lower petals; beardless irises, without the tuft; crested or Evansia irises, with a raised crest instead of a beard.

The bearded types include the rare and beautiful Oncocyclus and Regelia irises, native to the eastern Mediterranean and Central Asia; they need cold winters and hot, dry summers to flourish. Hybrids between these 2 groups are called Regeliocyclus irises, while hybrids between either of them and other bearded irises are called Arilbred irises. But the main group of bearded irises consists of numerous species with thick, creeping rhizomes, mainly from temperate Eurasia, and countless hybrids bred from these: both species and hybrids can be subdivided into the 3 classes Tall Bearded, Intermediate Bearded and Dwarf Bearded irises, depending mainly on the plant's height but some other characteristics as well. Tall bearded irises have the largest number of hybrid cultivars.

The beardless irises mostly have long narrow leaves and include several identifiable groups of species and hybrids, notably the east Asian Laevigatae or Water irises, including the large-flowered 'Kaempferi' irises derived from *I. ensata*, the Louisiana irises from southeastern USA and their hybrids, the Pacific Coast irises from the west side of North America, also with many hybrids, and the Eurasian Spuria and Siberian irises, consisting of numerous species and a scattering of hybrids.

The bulbous irises are also divided into 3 groups, the Juno, Reticulata and Xiphium irises, the first 2 consisting of beautiful but mostly difficult bulbs from west and central Asia. The Xiphium irises, centered on the Mediterranean, are more easily grown; they have given rise to a group of bulbous hybrids including the so-called English, Spanish and Dutch irises; it is the latter that are commonly seen in flower shops.

CULTIVATION

Growing conditions vary greatly. As a rule, rhizomatous irises, with the exception of the crested or Evansia irises, are very frost hardy and prefer a sunny position; some of the beardless types like very moist soil. Bulbous irises are also very frost hardy, and prefer a sunny position with ample moisture during growth, but very little during their summer dormancy. Bulbous irises should be planted in autumn and are prone to virus infection and so need to be kept free of aphids, which will spread the infection. Propagate irises by division in late summer after flowering or from seed in autumn. Named cultivars should only be divided.

Iris, Tall Bearded Hybrid 'Supreme Sultan'

Iris, Bearded Hybrids

Often classed under *Iris germanica* or *I. pallida*, which are only 2 of their ancestral species, the bearded irises are among the most widely grown of late-spring flowers. They have fat creeping rhizomes, handsome sword-shaped, grayish foliage and stems bearing several large flowers. They are available in an enormous range of colors—everything but true red—with many varieties featuring blended colors, contrasting standards and falls, or a broad band of color around basically white flowers (this pattern is called 'plicata'). Some of the newer varieties, described as 'remontant', flower again in late summer or autumn, though rather erratically. All prefer a temperate climate, sun and mildly alkaline, well-drained soil, and flower most freely if not over-watered in summer. Bearded irises are subdivided into 3 groups:

Dwarf Bearded, which grow 6–15 in (15–40 cm) tall and flower earlier than the others.

Intermediate Bearded, about 24 in (60 cm) tall, which flower a fortnight or so later than the dwarf varieties. **'Sunny Dawn'** is typical, with yellow flowers with red beards.

Tall Bearded irises are the last to bloom and grow to 3 ft (1 m) tall or slightly higher. Cultivars include **'Almaden'**, **'Blue Shimmer'**, **'Dancer's Veil'**, **'Light Beam'**, **'Orange Celebrity'**, **'Cannington Skies'** and **'Supreme Sultan'**. **ZONES 5–10.**

Iris japonica

Iris, Tall Bearded, 'Light Beam'

Iris, Tall Bearded, 'Dancer's Veil'

Iris, Louisiana Hybrid

Iris japonica
syn. Iris fimbriata
CRESTED IRIS

This is the best known of the crested or Evansia species. It grows to 18–32 in (45–80 cm) in height, forming large clumps of almost evergreen, glossy mid-green leaves. In late winter and spring, it bears sprays of 2½ in (6 cm) wide, ruffled, pale blue or white flowers; each fall has a violet patch around an orange crest. It prefers an acidic soil, a lightly shaded position, and a mild climate. It must be kept shaded from afternoon sun. A variety with white-striped leaves, it is rather shy flowering. **ZONES 8–11.**

Iris, Louisiana Hybrids

This extremely colorful group of rhizomatous, beardless hybrid irises include *Iris fulva* and *I. brevicaulis* among their ancestral species. They are evergreen with fine strap-like foliage and can build into substantial clumps; divide after 2 to 3 years. The Louisiana hybrids are not fully frost hardy in very cold climates, but are becoming increasingly popular in Australia and southern parts of the USA. Although basically swamp or water irises, they will happily grow in the garden if kept very well watered. They do best in a sunny position with average to damp, humus-rich garden soil. This group rarely exceeds 3 ft (1 m) in height and is usually much shorter. Some of the available hybrids include 'Art World', 'Bluebonnet Sue', 'Exclusive Label' and 'Guessing Game'. **ZONES 7–10.**

Iris unguicularis

syn. Iris stylosa

WINTER IRIS, ALGERIAN IRIS

This evergreen, beardless species from northern Africa is notable for bearing its flowers deep down among the clumps of grassy, dark green leaves, on stems no more than 8 in (20 cm) long. The flowers are typically pale blue, but white and darker blue to purple varieties are also available; the falls have yellow centers. It blooms from autumn to spring and the flowers are primrose-scented. Although moderately frost hardy, it does best in a warm, sheltered, sunny position, in slightly alkaline soil. To make the flowers more conspicuous cut the tough foliage back in early winter. **ZONES 7–10.**

Iris, Louisiana, 'Impressioned'

Iris unguicularis

KNAUTIA

Consisting of 60 species of annuals and perennials, this genus is found extensively throughout temperate Eurasia, from the Mediterranean to Siberia. Their flowers are very like the related *Scabiosa*, but few are ornamental enough to be grown in gardens except for the two species discussed here. These have a rosette of basal leaves through which the flower stems grow; these are branched and support some leaves.

Knautia macedonica

A showy species from the central Balkans to Romania, this makes an attractive subject for herbaceous borders. Its habit is similar to *Knautia arvensis*, but it grows to only 30 in (75 cm) tall, although it has larger and more attractive flowers which are usually deep purple-red, and occasionally pale pink or white. The darker shades are the best. **ZONES 6–10.**

CULTIVATION

Occurring in meadows, hedgerows and open woodland, these frost-hardy plants prefer sun or part-shade. Although often found growing in limy soil in their natural habitat, they will grow happily in any well-drained loam, but require staking. Propagate from seed in autumn or by basal cuttings in spring.

Knautia macedonica

Kniphofia × praecox

KNIPHOFIA
RED-HOT POKER, TORCH LILY, TRITOMA

The 68 species in this genus of stately perennials, some of which are evergreen, are native to southern and eastern Africa. Upright, tufted plants with long leaves, in summer they carry showy, brightly colored, tubular flowers in dense spikes on tall bare stems; some cultivars flower in winter and early spring. Originally the flowers were mostly flame colored (the common name, red-hot poker, dates from the days of coal fires), but due to the work of German plant breeder Max Leichtlin (1831–1910) and others, the flowers can also be pink, orange or yellow. Ranging from head-high to miniature types growing to 24 in (60 cm) or less, they are attractive to nectar-feeding birds.

CULTIVATION
Frost hardy to somewhat frost tender, they require an open position in full sun, well-drained soil and plenty of water in summer. In areas with winter temperatures below 5°F (–15°C) they can be carefully lifted and stored indoors to be planted again in spring, although heavy mulching is preferable. They will tolerate wind and coastal conditions. From spring onwards, fertilize monthly. Remove dead flower stems and leaves in late autumn. Propagate species from seed or by division in spring; cultivars by division in spring.

Kniphofia 'Little Maid'

'Little Maid' is a dwarf form that reaches a height of 24 in (60 cm). It has buff-tinted soft yellow flowers opening from pale green buds. **ZONES 7–10.**

Kniphofia × *praecox*
RED-HOT POKER

This South African perennial is the most common species in the wild and reaches up to 5 ft (1.5 m) tall when in bloom. Its slender leaves, up to 24 in (60 cm) long, are heavily keeled and serrated. Vivid red or yellow flowers appear in early summer. It is able to survive long dry periods and enjoys full sun. **ZONES 7–10.**

Kniphofia 'Little Maid'

LAMIUM
syns *Galeobdolon, Lamiastrum*
DEAD NETTLE

This genus of over 50 species of annuals and rhizomatous perennials, native to Europe, Asia and North Africa, belongs to the mint family, not the nettle family as the common name would seem to indicate. They include some common weeds and hedgerow plants as well as a handful cultivated for ornament. Some have astringent properties and have been used in folk medicine, or have been grown as pot herbs in parts of Europe. Some are an important source of nectar for bees. They have leaves with toothed margins, arranged in opposite pairs and sometimes splashed with paler gray-green or white, and short spikes or axillary whorls of white, yellow, pink or purple 2-lipped flowers, the upper lip curved over in a helmet-like shape.

CULTIVATION

Lamiums are frost hardy and grow well in most soils. Flower color determines planting season and light requirement: white- and purple-flowered species are planted in spring and prefer full sun; the yellow-flowered ones are planted in autumn and prefer shade. They often have invasive habits and need plenty of room. Propagate from seed or by division in early spring.

Lamium galeobdolon

syns *Galeobdolon luteum, G. argentatum, Lamiastrum galeobdolon*
YELLOW ARCHANGEL

This perennial species from Europe and western Asia spreads both by rhizomes and surface runners to form extensive, loose mats of foliage usually about 12 in (30 cm) deep, spreading over moist, shady areas beneath trees. Its leaves are variably splashed with silvery gray and in summer it bears leafy spikes of bright yellow flowers each about ¾ in (18 mm) long. 'Florentinum' has leaves splashed with silver that becomes purple-tinged in winter. 'Hermann's Pride' is densely mat forming and has narrow leaves streaked and spotted with silver. **ZONES 6–10.**

Lamium galeobdolon

Lamium maculatum 'Beacon's Silver'

Lamium maculatum

SPOTTED DEADNETTLE

Its wild forms often regarded almost as weeds, this semi-evergreen perennial is native to Europe and western Asia and naturalized in North America. A variable species, it may have erect stems to 24 in (60 cm) tall, or have a lower, more spreading habit. The strongly toothed leaves have a central blotch or stripe of pale silvery green, and leafy whorled spikes of very pale pink to deep rose flowers appear in spring and summer. The cultivars are more desirable garden plants, mostly with a compact mat-forming habit and not more than 6 in (15 cm) high. 'Pink Pewter' has silvery leaves which highlight the beautiful pink flowers; 'Beacon's Silver' has purplish flowers with silvery green leaves edged dark green; 'Roseum' has silver-striped foliage and pinkish lilac flowers; and 'White Nancy' has silvery green leaves and white flowers. **ZONES 4–10.**

LATHYRUS

Closely allied to the garden peas (*Pisum*) and vetches (*Vicia*), this genus consists of 150 or so species of annuals and perennials, many of them tendril climbers and some of them edible. They are native mainly in temperate northern hemisphere regions but with a significant number of species also in Andean South America. The leaves are pinnate with the uppermost pair of leaflets usually modified into tendrils. The pea-shaped flowers come in a wide range of colors, from red, mauve and white to blue and even pale yellow. Flat seed pods follow the flowers. *Lathyrus odoratus*, the sweet pea, has a proud place in the history of science, for it was one of the chief plants used by Gregor Mendel (1822–84) in his hybridizing experiments which laid the foundations for the science of genetics.

CULTIVATION

Plant these frost-hardy plants in fertile, well-drained soil in full sun. Stake or train on wires and deadhead regularly. Propagate annuals from seed in early summer or early autumn, and perennials from seed in autumn or by division in spring. They may be affected by mildew and botrytis.

Lathyrus odoratus Supersnoop Group

Lathyrus odoratus

Lathyrus odoratus

SWEET PEA

Native to Italy but much improved upon by gardeners, this vigorous, climbing annual is grown for its abundant, sweetly scented flowers. The 1½ in (35 mm) wide flowers, in white, cream, pink, blue, mauve, lavender, maroon and scarlet, bloom several to the stem from late winter to early summer and make excellent cut flowers. The plant grows to 6 ft (1.8 m) or more in height, although there are dwarf, non-climbing cultivars available. The climbers will need a good support, such as wire netting or lattice, and are ideal for covering sunny walls or fences. Over many years of development sweet peas have become less scented. Also, mixed color seedling strains, for example, 'Carnival', tended to predominate. With the resurgence of interest in cottage gardens, breeders, mainly in the UK and New Zealand, developed a range of very fragrant cultivars in single colors. These include 'Apricot Sprite', deep apricot fading with age; 'Bandaid', pale pink flowers; 'Elegance', pure white flowers; 'Esther Ranson', mauve flowers; 'Felicity Kendall', deep purplish pink flowers; 'Hampton Court', purple to mauve flowers; 'Katherine', bright red-pink flowers; 'Kiri Te Kanawa', pinkish purple flowers; and 'Lucy', with apricot-pink flowers. The Knee-hi Group, although a little taller than the name suggests—around 24–30 in (60–75 cm) high—is a bushy strain that flowers heavily in white through red to blue. Cultivars in the Supersnoop Group have no tendrils and may be grown as bushes rather than as climbers. ZONES 4–10.

Lathyrus odoratus 'Hampton Court'

Lavatera trimestris
ANNUAL MALLOW

This shrubby annual, native to the Mediterranean, is grown mainly for its silken, trumpet-shaped, brilliant white or pink flowers. The flowers are 3 in (8 cm) wide and appear from summer to early autumn. They are short lived but are borne in profusion, benefiting from regular deadheading. The annual mallow has an erect, branching habit and is moderately fast growing to a height of 24 in (60 cm) and a spread of 18 in (45 cm). The cultivar **'Mont Blanc'** (syn. *Lavatera* 'Mont Blanc') has pure white flowers; **'Silver Cup'** has lovely dark pink flowers. **ZONES 8–11.**

Lavatera trimestris 'Mont Blanc'

Lavatera trimestris

LAVATERA

Closely related to the mallows and hollyhocks, this genus of 25 species of annuals, biennials, perennials and softwooded shrubs has a scattered, patchy distribution around temperate regions of the world, mostly in Mediterranean or similar climates; some of them favor seashores. A few species are cultivated for their colorful mallow flowers, generally produced over a long season. These plants are upright in habit with simple to palmately lobed leaves, often downy to the touch. The shrubs and perennials in this genus are not very long-lived.

CULTIVATION

Moderately to very frost-hardy, these plants prefer a sunny site with any well-drained soil. Prune after a flush of blooms to encourage branching and more flowers. Propagate annuals, biennials and perennials in spring or early autumn from seed sown *in situ* (cuttings do not strike well), and shrubs from cuttings in early spring or summer.

LEONTOPODIUM

EDELWEISS

Occurring wild in the mountains of Europe and temperate Asia, this genus consists of about 35 species of short-lived, downy perennials in the daisy family. Their distinctive feature is the flowerheads, with a central disc of rather inconspicuous cream florets surrounded by a ring of overlapping, pointed bracts of unequal length and coated with sparse to dense white wool. The simple, lance-shaped leaves are also covered with white hairs, which protect the plant from cold and from intense ultraviolet sunlight. They are suitable for rock gardens in cool to cold climates.

Leontopodium alpinum

CULTIVATION

Plant in full sun or part-shade (in hot climates) in gritty, well-drained soil. They are very frost hardy but need shelter from winter rain. Propagate from fresh seed or by division in spring.

Leontopodium alpinum

Much loved by the Swiss, the European edelweiss is often regarded as a symbol of the Alps. It reaches a height and spread of around 8 in (20 cm). Each silvery white flowerhead is 2–3 in (5–8 cm) across, the bracts so thickly felted they look like strips of flannel. It blooms in spring or early summer. **ZONES 5–9.**

LEUCANTHEMUM

There are about 25 species of annuals or perennials in this genus from Europe and temperate Asia, all previously included in *Chrysanthemum* by many botanists, though some botanists always treated them as a distinct genus. They are clump-forming plants with variably toothed or lobed leaves that are neither grayish hairy nor aromatic, unlike those of other chrysanthemum relatives. Long-stalked daisy-like flowerheads arise from leafy stems, with white or yellow ray florets and yellow disc florets. They are mostly vigorous, adaptable plants.

CULTIVATION

These plants are largely undemanding, growing well in a perennial border or garden bed in full sun or morning shade in moderately fertile, moist but well-drained soil. Propagate from seed or cuttings, or by division.

Leucanthemum × *superbum* 'Tinkerbell'

Leucanthemum × *superbum*

syns *Chrysanthemum maximum* of gardens, *C.* × *superbum*
SHASTA DAISY

Growing to a height and spread of 2–3 ft (60–90 cm), this robust perennial has large, daisy-like white flowerheads with pale golden centers; these may be 3 in (8 cm) across and are carried high above the dark, shiny, toothed leaves in summer and early autumn. The Shasta daisies were once thought to be *Leucanthemum maximum*, a native of the Pyrenees but are now believed to be hybrids between that species and the Portuguese *L. lacustre*; they were first noticed naturalized on the slopes of Mount Shasta in California, USA and attracted the attention of the famous plant breeder Luther Burbank. There are now many cultivars, always white-flowered, but including doubles as well as singles, some with fringed petals. Some of the more popular include **'Aglaia'**, which grows to 12 in (30 cm) tall and has semi-double flowers that last throughout summer; **'Esther Read'** grows 3 ft (1 m) tall with a mass of semi-double flowers; **'Wirral Pride'** grows 30 in (75 cm) with double white flowerheads; and **'Wirral Supreme'** has anemone-centered double flowers. **'Tinker-bell'** is a low-growing form with single flowers. **ZONES 5–10.**

Leucanthemum × superbum

Leucogenes grandiceps

Leucogenes grandiceps has felty, white bracts enclosing golden-yellow flowerheads and downy silver leaves. It is dense and low growing, reaching a height and spread of 6 in (15 cm). **ZONES 7–9.**

Leucogenes grandiceps

LEUCOGENES
NEW ZEALAND EDELWEISS

This very small genus consists of 3 or 4 species of evergreen, woody based perennials, first cousins of the helichrysums or everlasting daisies. Although not closely related to the European edelweiss, they resemble it both in their mountain habitat and small, furry, white flowers. The resemblance is close enough that the name *Leucogenes* is the Greek translation of the German word edelweiss, meaning 'the noble white flower'. They are excellent rock-garden plants.

CULTIVATION
The mountains of New Zealand being less frigid than the Alps, *Leucogenes* species are a little less dependent on cold winters to flourish than their European counterparts. Winter-wet feet are their enemy, so they need very good drainage. Plant in full or filtered sun in gritty, peaty soil. Propagate from fresh, ripe seed or from cuttings in late spring or early summer.

LIATRIS

BLAZING STAR

These 40 species of perennials come from the central and eastern regions of North America. In summer they shoot up tall, cylindrical spikes of fluffy flowers from a knobby rootstock that remains visible during the rest of the year. They belong to the daisy or composite family but their spike-like inflorescences, with crowded small flowerheads opening from the top downward, are so unlike those of other daisies that it is hard to recognize their affinity.

CULTIVATION

These plants will grow in most soils and conditions including damp places such as on the banks of streams, although they do best in climates with low humidity. They thrive with minimum care and attention, making excellent border plants. Propagation is from seed or by division of old clumps in winter.

Liatris spicata 'Kobold'

Liatris spicata

syn. **Liatris callilepis** of gardens

GAY FEATHER, SPIKE GAY FEATHER

This low-growing species is a desirable cut flower and a good butterfly-bee-attracting plant. The flowers are lilac purple, although they can occur in pink and white. They are produced in crowded, fluffy spikes—like a feather duster—in late summer, opening from the top downwards, the opposite of most flowering spikes. It grows to a height of 24 in (60 cm), with thickened, corm-like rootstocks and basal tufts of grassy, mid-green foliage. 'Floristan' is a seedling strain growing to 5 ft (1.5 m) tall; it is available in 2 colors: deep violet ('**Floristan Violett**') and white ('**Floristan Weiss**'). '**Kobold**' is a dwarf cultivar reaching 15 in (38 cm) and producing bright purple flowers. **ZONES 3–10.**

LIGULARIA

There are at least 150 species of perennials in this genus which is closely related to *Senecio* and is found mainly in temperate eastern Asia, though a smaller number occur in northern Asia and Europe. Many species are large-leafed, clump-forming plants that produce tall spires of daisy-like flowerheads, mostly in shades of yellow or orange. The cultivated ligularias are stately plants and vigorous growers, adapted to moist, sheltered sites such as stream banks and woodland glades and flowering mainly in summer and early autumn. The spring foliage can be almost as ornamental as the summer blooms.

CULTIVATION

Quite frost hardy, they prefer moist, well-drained soil and will grow in either sun or part-shade. Propagate by division in spring or from seed in spring or autumn. They are prone to attack by slugs and snails.

Ligularia dentata

Ligularia dentata

syns *Ligularia clivorum*, *Senecio clivorum*

This compact species from China and Japan is grown for its striking foliage and showy flowerheads. It grows to a height of 4 ft (1.2 m) and a spread of 3 ft (1 m). It has kidney-shaped, long-stalked, leathery, brownish green leaves and bears clusters of large, 3 in (8 cm) wide, orange-yellow flowerheads on long branching stems in summer. It will grow happily at the edge of ponds. Cultivars worth growing are '**Othello**' and '**Desdemona**', which has green leaves heavily overlaid with bronze and maroon. '**Gregynog Gold**' has round green leaves and orange flowers. **ZONES 4–9.**

Ligularia stenocephala

This pretty species from Japan, China and Taiwan grows to 5 ft (1.5 m). It has dark purple stems and bears slender racemes of yellow flowers in summer. The leaves are triangular and toothed. **ZONES 5–10.**

Ligularia stenocephala

LIMNANTHES

MEADOW FOAM, POACHED EGG FLOWER

These western North American meadow plants are annuals more often cultivated in other countries. The genus consists of 7 species of plants with 5-petalled, cup-shaped flowers and bright green leaves and can be relied on to provide color from spring to autumn.

CULTIVATION

They prefer damp soil and full sun as long as the roots are cool. Sow seed directly in autumn or early spring and lightly cover. Staggered sowing ensures a constant display best suited to the rockery or along the pavement edge.

Limnanthes douglasii

MEADOW FOAM

Delightful and delicate, this 6 in (15 cm) tall plant has pale green fern-like foliage and masses of 1 in (25 mm) slightly perfumed, white-edged, golden-centered flowers. There is also a pure gold form. It is named after the early nineteenth-century collector David Douglas, who made many important finds in western North America. **ZONES 8–10.**

LIMONIUM

STATICE, SEA LAVENDER

Statice is an obsolete botanical name of this genus of around 150 species, scattered around the world's temperate regions mostly in saline coastal and desert environments, with major concentrations in the Mediterranean, central Asia and the Canary Islands. They include evergreen and deciduous sub-shrubs, perennials, biennials and annuals, some of the latter grown as border plants and popular for their many-colored heads of small papery flowers which can be cut and dried for decoration. The flowers should be cut just as they open and hung upside down to dry in a cool, airy place. The tapering, almost stalkless leaves appear in basal rosettes.

CULTIVATION

Statices are easily grown in full sun and well-drained, sandy soil. Their tolerance to sea spray and low rainfall make them a good choice for seaside and low-maintenance holiday-house gardens. Plants will benefit from light fertilizing in spring, while the flower-heads are developing. Propagate by division in spring, from seed in early spring or autumn or from root cuttings in late winter. Transplant during winter or early spring.

Limonium latifolium

syn. **Limonium platyphyllum**

From eastern Europe, this tall-stemmed perennial bears clusters of lavender-blue or white flowers over summer. Clump forming and large leafed, it grows 24 in (60 cm) tall and spreads 18 in (45 cm). The dried flower stems have a delicate appearance. **ZONES 5–10.**

Limonium latifolium

LINARIA
EGGS AND BACON, TOADFLAX

Native mainly in the Mediterranean region and western Europe, these 100 species of adaptable annuals, biennials and perennials are related to snapdragons and have naturalized in many places. They grow to 18 in (45 cm) with masses of tiny snapdragon-like blooms in many colors. The erect stems have stalkless, usually gray-green leaves. They are ideally suited to rock gardens, borders and cottage gardens.

CULTIVATION

They require rich, well-drained, preferably sandy soil, moderate water and full sun. Seed sown directly in autumn or very early spring will germinate in 2 weeks. Seedlings need to be thinned to a 6 in (15 cm) spacing and weeded to ensure no over-shadowing of these fine plants. Cutting back after the first flush will produce more flowers.

Linaria purpurea
PURPLE TOADFLAX

This perennial from Italy and now naturalized elsewhere in Europe, reaches 3 ft (1 m) tall. In summer it bears violet flowers tinged with purple. 'Canon J. Went' is a tall example of the species with tiny pale pink flowers. **ZONES 6–10.**

Linaria purpurea 'Canon J. Went'

Linum narbonense

LINUM
FLAX

This genus contains 200 species of annuals, biennials, perennials, subshrubs and shrubs, some of which are evergreen, distributed widely in temperate regions. It includes the commercial flax, *Linum usitatissimum*, grown for fiber and oilseed. Several ornamental species are grown for their profusely blooming, 5-petalled flowers, which can be yellow, white, blue, red or pink. They are useful plants in a rock garden or border.

CULTIVATION

They are mostly quite frost hardy; some need shelter in cool climates. Grow in a sunny spot in humus-rich, well-drained, peaty soil. After perennial species flower, prune them back hard. Propagate the annuals, biennials and perennials from seed in autumn and perennials by division in spring or autumn. Most self-sow readily. Transplant from late autumn until early spring.

Linum narbonense

A perennial native of the Mediterranean region, this most handsome of all the blue flaxes has violet, funnel-shaped flowers borne on slender stems. The flowers last for many weeks in summer. It has soft, green leaves and forms clumps 18 in (45 cm) high and wide. **ZONES 5–10.**

LIRIOPE

This genus contains 5 species of clump-forming, rhizomatous, evergreen perennials native to Vietnam, China, Taiwan and Japan. Some cultivars are so dark in leaf they are practically black, a most unusual color for the designer to play with. They do not creep, and for ground-cover have to be planted 6 in (15 cm) apart. *Liriope* flowers range from white through to pale purple.

CULTIVATION

Grow in full sun or part-shade in well-drained soil. In early spring cut back shabby leaves, just before the new ones appear. Propagate from seed in autumn or by division in early spring.

Liriope muscari

syns Liriope platyphylla, L. graminifolia

This clumping, evergreen perennial is a useful casual groundcover or path edging. It has grass-like, shining, dark green leaves and bears erect spikes of rounded, bell-shaped, violet flowers in late summer. It grows to a height of 12–24 in (30–60 cm) with a spread of 18 in (45 cm), with flower spikes held just above the foliage. 'Lilac Beauty' comes from China and Japan and is a larger example of the species; the leaves are 1 in (25 mm) wide and 12–18 in (30–45 cm) long with stiff lilac flowers rising above the foliage. '**Majestic**' has large violet-blue flowers. '**Variegata**' is the most common of the variegated forms—the leaf margins are lined with cream and it has lovely lilac flowers. **ZONES 6–10.**

Liriope muscari

Lobelia erinus 'Crystal Palace'

LOBELIA

This genus of 370 species of annuals, perennials and shrubs is widely distributed in temperate regions, particularly the Americas and Africa. Growth habits vary from low bedding plants to tall herbaceous perennials or shrubs. They are all grown for their ornamental flowers and neat foliage and make excellent edging, flower box, hanging basket and rock-garden specimens. Some are suitable in wild gardens or by the waterside.

CULTIVATION

These frost-hardy to somewhat frost-tender plants are best grown in well-drained, moist, light loam enriched with animal manure or compost. Most grow in sun or part-shade but resent wet conditions in winter. Prune after the first flush of flowers to encourage repeat flowering, and fertilize weekly with a liquid manure during the season. Propagate annuals from seed in spring, perennial species from seed or by division in spring or autumn and perennial cultivars by division only. Transplant from late autumn until early spring.

Lobelia erinus

EDGING LOBELIA

This slow-growing, compact annual is native to South Africa and grows to a height of 4–8 in (10–20 cm) and spread of 4–6 in (10–15 cm). It has a tufted, often semi-trailing habit, with dense oval to lance-shaped leaves tapering at the base. It bears small, 2-lipped pinkish purple flowers continuously from spring to early autumn. '**Cambridge Blue**' is a popular hybrid along with '**Color Cascade**', with a mass of blue to violet to pink and white flowers. '**Crystal Palace**' is a very small variety with dense foliage and is smothered in deep violet-blue flowers. **ZONES 7–11.**

LOBULARIA

This genus consists of 5 species of frost-hardy, dwarf plants from the Mediterranean and the Canary Islands; they are useful for rockeries, window boxes and borders. Although there are both annual and perennial forms, the annuals are most commonly grown. They bear tiny 4-petalled, fragrant flowers in compact, terminal racemes in summer and early autumn.

Lobularia maritima

CULTIVATION
Grow in full sun in fertile, well-drained soil. Continuous flowering can be encouraged by regular deadheading. Propagate from seed in spring or, if used outdoors, from late spring to autumn.

Lobularia maritima
syn. *Alyssum maritimum*
SWEET ALYSSUM, SWEET ALICE

This fast-growing, spreading annual is a widely popular edging, rock-garden or window box plant. It produces masses of tiny, honey-scented, 4-petalled white flowers over a long season, from spring to early autumn. Lilac, pink and violet shades are also available. It has a low, rounded, compact habit with lance-shaped, grayish green leaves, and grows to a height of 3–12 in (8–30 cm) and a spread of 8–12 in (20–30 cm). 'Violet Queen' is the darkest of the garden varieties of sweet Alice. **ZONES 7–10.**

LUNARIA
HONESTY

Allied to stocks *(Matthiola)*, the origin of the common name for this genus of 3 species of annuals, biennials and perennials is uncertain. It could be from the way the silver lining of the seed pods is concealed in the brown husk like a silver coin, the reward of virtue that does not flaunt itself. Sprays of honesty have been popular as dried flower arrangements since the eighteenth century.

CULTIVATION
Plant in full sun or part-shade in fertile, moist but well-drained soil. Propagate perennials from seed or by division in autumn or spring, biennials from seed. They self-seed readily.

Lunaria annua
syn. *Lunaria biennis*

This fast-growing biennial, native to southern Europe and the Mediterranean coast, is grown for its attractive flowers and curious fruit. It has pointed, oval, serrated, bright green leaves and bears heads of scented, 4-petalled, rosy magenta, white or violet-purple flowers throughout spring and early summer. These are followed by circular seed pods with a silvery, translucent membrane. Erect in habit, it grows to a height of 30 in (75 cm) and a spread of 12 in (30 cm). **ZONES 8–10.**

Lunaria annua

LUPINUS
LUPIN, LUPINE

This legume genus of 200 species of annuals, perennials and
semi-evergreen and evergreen shrubs and subshrubs, is mainly
native to North America, southern Europe and North Africa.
They are popular for their ease of culture, rapid growth and
long, erect spikes of showy pea-flowers in a range of colors
including blue, purple, pink, white, yellow, orange and red.
Apart from being ornamentals, they are used for animal fodder,
as a 'green manure' crop because of their nitrogen-fixing capacity.
A few species are grown for grain, used as food by both humans
and livestock. The compound leaves are distinct among legumes
in being palmate, with 5 or more leaflets radiating from a common stalk, rather than the usual pinnate arrangement.

CULTIVATION

Most lupins prefer climates with cool wet winters and long dry
summers. Plant in full sun in well-drained, moderately fertile,
slightly acidic, sandy soil. Water well in the growing season and
mulch in dry areas. Spent flowers should be cut away to prolong
plant life and to prevent self-seeding. The foliage adds nitrogen
to the soil when dug in. Propagate species from seed in autumn
and Russell hybrids from cuttings or by division in early spring.

Lupinus hartwegii

Lupinus, Russell Hybrid 'Troop the Colour'

Lupinus hartwegii
HAIRY LUPIN

Native to Mexico, this fast-
growing annual has a
compact, erect growth habit
and reaches 30 in (75 cm) in
height with a spread of 15 in
(38 cm). It has hairy dark
green leaves, and slender
spikes of flowers in shades of
blue, white or pink are borne
abundantly in late winter,
spring and early summer.
ZONES 7–11.

Lupinus, Russell Hybrids

George Russell was a gardener
fond of growing lupins, and
over the years selected the
best seedlings from open-
pollinated plants of *Lupinus
polyphyllus*. Around 1937 a
colorful selection of his
perennial lupins was released
and rapidly became popular,
known as 'Russell lupins'. It is
thought that they are hybrids,
the other major parent being
the annual *L. hartwegii*. This
fine strain of strong-growing

lupins bears long spikes of large, strongly colored flowers in cream, pink, orange, blue or violet, some varieties bicolored, in late spring and summer. They produce a magnificent clump of deeply divided, mid-green leaves, growing to a height of 3 ft (1 m). 'Noble Maiden', one of the Band of Nobles series, has cream flowers; 'Polar Princess' has white flowers; and the blooms of 'Troop the Color' are bright red. There are also dwarf strains, such as the 24 in (60 cm) high 'Lulu'. ZONES 3–9.

Lupinus, Russell, 'Polar Princess'

Lychnis chalcedonica

Lychnis coronaria 'Alba'

LYCHNIS
CAMPION, CATCHFLY

Native to temperate regions of the northern hemisphere, these 15 to 20 species of biennials and perennials include some that have been cultivated for many centuries, grown for their summer flowers that range in color from white through pinks and oranges to deep red. All have flat 5-petalled flowers but in many species the petals are notched or deeply forked or sometimes divided into narrow teeth. The genus is related to *Silene*, and the boundary between the 2 genera has shifted with varying botanical opinion.

CULTIVATION

They are frost hardy and easily grown in cool climates, preferably in sunny sites, and in any well-drained soil. The higher mountain species do best in soil that is protected from being excessively warmed by the sun. Remove spent stems after flowering and deadhead frequently to prolong the flowering period. Propagate by division or from seed in autumn or early spring. Some species self-seed readily.

Lychnis chalcedonica
MALTESE CROSS

This perennial species from far eastern Europe has been a favorite with gardeners since the seventeenth century. Its color is such a dazzling orange-red that its garden companions should be chosen with care. It flowers for a rather short season in early summer, grows about 4 ft (1.2 m) tall, and takes its common name from the shape of the flower. White and pink varieties and one with double flowers exist, but these are fairly rare. ZONES 4–10.

Lychnis coronaria
ROSE CAMPION, DUSTY MILLER, MULLEIN PINK

A clump-forming perennial sometimes grown as a biennial, this striking plant grows to a height of 30 in (75 cm) and a spread of 18 in (45 cm). It forms a dense clump of silvery white downy leaves, and many-branched gray stems carry large, deep rose-pink to scarlet flowers throughout summer. **'Alba'** is a white-flowered cultivar. In ancient times the flowers were used for garlands and crowns. It is drought tolerant, requires little or no cultivation or watering, and often self-seeds. **ZONES 4–10.**

Lychnis × haageana 'Vesuvius'

Lychnis coronaria

Lychnis × haageana 'Vesuvius'
syn. *Lychnis × arkwrightii* **'Vesuvius'**

This hybrid is probably a cross between two Asian species, *Lychnis fulgens* and *L. sieboldii*, though *L. chalcedonica* is also a possible parent, and its exact origin is unclear. What is beyond doubt, however, is that it is a singularly striking perennial in all respects. Often short-lived, it is nonetheless worth growing for its deep bronze green foliage and its large vivid orange flowers. It reaches around 24 in (60 cm) high and blooms from mid-summer. It is a spectacular plant to contrast against light green foliage and pale flowers. **ZONES 6–10.**

Lysichiton americanus

LYSICHITON
syn. *Lysichitum*
SKUNK CABBAGE

This unusual genus of the arum family is composed of 2 species of rhizomatous perennials, one from northeastern Asia, the other from western North America. They flower in spring as or before the new foliage develops. The stout-stemmed, pointed, heart-shaped leaves are quite large, sometimes as much as 4 ft (1.2 m) long when fully expanded. The spathes, white or yellow depending on the species, are around 15 in (38 cm) long and partially enclose the flower spike (spadix). The flowers have a musky smell that is nowhere near as bad as the common name suggests.

CULTIVATION

Skunk cabbages are frost-hardy plants suited only to cool climates. They normally grow in damp or boggy ground and are best positioned at the edges of ponds or streams. Propagate from seed or by division.

Lysichiton americanus
YELLOW SKUNK CABBAGE

This species ranges in the wild from coastal Alaska to northern California and east to Montana. It has large butter-yellow spathes that appear in mid-spring before the leaves, though still present when the leaves have expanded, making a dramatic contrast. It grows to a height of around 3 ft (1 m).
ZONES 5–9.

Lysimachia vulgaris

LYSIMACHIA
LOOSESTRIFE

This genus contains around 150 species of mainly evergreen perennials and shrubs from the northern hemisphere. The genus is described in more detail in the chapter on Lawns, Groundcovers, Ornamental Grasses and Bamboos.

Lysimachia vulgaris
YELLOW LOOSESTRIFE

This perennial is a common wildflower in Europe and western Asia, growing in wet meadows and along streams. It has creeping rhizomes with erect stems that can be 4 ft (1.2 m) or more in height, with broad green leaves in whorls of three or four. The starry golden-yellow flowers, about ¾ in (18 mm) wide, are borne in loose terminal spikes in summer. **ZONES 5–10.**

LYTHRUM
LOOSESTRIFE

This genus of around 35 species of annuals, perennials and sub-shrubs is scattered through all continents except South America. They vary from small creeping plants with stems rooting in the mud of ditches, to plants 6 ft (1.8 m) or more tall with showy spikes of pink to purple flowers.

Lythrum salicaria

CULTIVATION
These plants will grow in most soil conditions as long as moisture is adequate, and in bogs and other wetlands some species can be quite invasive. Propagation is very easy from seed or by division.

MACLEAYA
PLUME POPPY

This genus honors the services to botany of Alexander Macleay (1767–1848), for many years Colonial Secretary of New South Wales, Australia. The plants are sometimes offered under the name *Bocconia*, a closely allied genus whose members are all American. The genus consists of 2 or so species of rhizomatous perennials from China and Japan that in fact do not really resemble poppies; the deception arises because the tubular flowers shed their petals as they open. The heart-shaped leaves are gray-green to olive green.

CULTIVATION
These fully frost-hardy plants prefer full sun and moderately fertile, moist but well-drained soil. Protect from cold winds. Propagate from seed or cuttings or by division.

Lythrum salicaria
PURPLE LOOSESTRIFE

A native of Europe, North Africa and western Asia, this perennial always grows in wet ground, often spreading into the shallow water at the edges of ponds. Erect stems arise from a knotty rhizome to a height varying from 3–6 ft (1–1.8 m) depending on soil moisture and fertility. It produces showy long spikes of pink to magenta flowers from mid-summer to autumn. In eastern North America it has become widely naturalized and in some areas is detested as a weed, displacing native wildflowers. Purple loosestrife was used in folk medicine for centuries; its tannins have coagulent properties, hence staunching the flow of blood; treatment of cholera was one of its uses. There are a number of garden forms, with flowers in the deep rose-red to deep pink range, some double-flowered. 'Feuerkerze' ('Fire-candle') is a cultivar with more reddish flowers. **ZONES 3–10.**

Macleaya cordata
syn. *Bocconia cordata*

This tall perennial, growing to 5–8 ft (1.5–2.4 m) in height, has large, rounded, deeply veined, heart-shaped, gray-green leaves. Large, feathery, terminal flower spikes of cream tinted with pink are borne in summer. It is one of the most attractive foliage plants for the herbaceous border. It exudes a yellow sap when cut. This plant spreads from rhizomes and may become invasive. **ZONES 3–10.**

Macleaya cordata

MALVA

MALLOW

This genus is made up of 30 species of annuals, biennials and perennials that originate in Europe, North Africa and Asia, but have in some cases naturalized elsewhere. The flowers are similar to but smaller than the popular *Lavatera* to which the malvas are related; they are single, 5-petalled flowers in shades of white, pink, blue or purple. Although they may not be quite as showy as those of *Lavatera*, they do make attractive subjects for the border or wild garden.

CULTIVATION

These plants flourish in sunny, well-drained aspects and tend to be more robust and longer lived in not too rich soil. They are fully frost hardy. Cut plants back after the first flowers have faded. Propagate from cuttings or seed in spring; the perennials often self-seed. Watch for rust disease in spring.

Matthiola incana

Matthiola incana

This upright biennial or short-lived perennial is best grown as an annual. It has a bushy habit and grows up to 24 in (60 cm) in height with a spread of 30 cm (12 in). Fully frost hardy, it has lance-shaped, gray-green leaves and fragrant, 3–6 in (8–15 cm) long spikes of mauve flowers borne in spring. Many varieties and strains are available, the best selected for a high percentage of double flowers. 'Mammoth Column' grows taller, reaching 30 in (75 cm) in height, and produces a single, 12–15 in (30–38 cm) tall spike of scented flowers in spring in mixed or separate colors. **ZONES 6–10.**

Malva moschata

MUSK MALLOW

Useful for naturalizing in a wild garden or odd corner, this perennial has narrow, lobed, divided leaves with a sticky, hairy texture which emit a musky, cheesy odor when crushed. A native of Europe, *Malva moschata* bears profuse spikes of saucer-shaped pink flowers in summer. 'Alba', a white cultivar, is also very popular. It has a bushy, branching habit and can grow to a height of 3 ft (1 m). **ZONES 3–10.**

Malva moschata

MATTHIOLA

STOCK, GILLYFLOWER

This is a genus of some 55 species of annuals, biennials and subshrubby perennials, few of which are grown in gardens with the exceptions of the night-scented stock *Matthiola longipetala* subsp. *bicornis* and the cultivars of *M. incana*, the much-loved stock that has many forms in both double and single flowers. The species are native to Europe, central and southwestern Asia and North Africa. The leaves are usually gray-green and the perfumed flowers can be produced from spring to autumn. They are attractive both for bedding out and as cut flowers but be warned, stocks are prone to quite a few pests and diseases, including downy mildew, club-root, gray mold and cabbage root fly.

CULTIVATION

Matthiola prefer a sunny aspect in moist but well-drained, neutral or alkaline soil. Shelter from strong winds and stake some of the larger forms and the top-heavy large doubles. Propagate from seed sown *in situ* for night-scented stock—this should be staggered to increase flowering season—or in spring sow seed of *M. incana* types into seed trays and prick out into beds later.

Meconopsis betonicifolia
syn. *Meconopsis baileyi*
BLUE POPPY, TIBETAN POPPY,
HIMALAYAN POPPY

This clump-forming woodland species bears sky blue, saucer-shaped, 2–3 in (5–8 cm) wide satiny flowers with yellow stamens in late spring and early summer. Oblong, mid-green leaves occur in basal rosettes. It grows 3–5 ft (1–1.5 m) tall and 18 in (45 cm) wide. It does not bloom in the first season, and dies down completely over winter. **ZONES 7–9.**

Meconopsis betonicifolia

MECONOPSIS

This genus consists of about 45 species of annuals, biennials and short-lived perennials that are mostly native to the Himalayas. They bear large, exotic flowers with papery petals and a bold, central boss of stamens on tall stems. The flower stalks lengthen after flowering as the fruits develop. The hairy leaves are either simple or pinnate.

CULTIVATION
Mostly frost hardy, they need a moist but not over-wet, lime-free, humus-rich soil and a cool site in part-or full shade with shelter from strong winds. Propagate from seed in late summer.

MENYANTHES

There is only one species in this genus, with a very wide distri-bution through Europe, northern Asia, northwestern India and North America. It is an aquatic or marginal water plant with creeping rhizomes to 4 ft (1.2 m) long. This plant has long been used in herbal medicine to relieve gout and fever. The Inuit ground it into a flour and the leaves have been used in Scandinavia to make beer.

CULTIVATION
This plant is fully frost hardy and is happy grown in wet mud in, or on the edge of, water. Propagate from seed sown in wet soil or cuttings of pre-rooted rhizomes in spring.

Menyanthes trifoliata
BOG BEAN

This plant has attractive foliage divided into 3 leaflets of rich green supported by dark-colored stems. The tiny fringed flowers are produced in erect spikes and are white, but pink in bud. This species grows to about 12 in (30 cm) tall and spreads out over a considerable area of water. **ZONES 3–10.**

Menyanthes trifoliata

MIMULUS

syn. *Diplacus*

MONKEY FLOWER, MUSK

The 180 or so species of annuals, perennials and shrubs are characterized by tubular flowers with flared mouths, often curiously spotted and mottled, which have been likened to grinning monkey faces. The flowers come in a large range of colors, including brown, orange, yellow, red, pink and crimson. Mainly native to the cool Pacific coastal areas of Chile and the USA, most species are suited to bog gardens or other moist situations, although some are excellent rock garden plants.

CULTIVATION

Grow these plants in full sun or part-shade in wet or moist soil. Propagate perennials by division in spring and annuals from seed in autumn or early spring.

Mimulus moschatus

Mimulus cardinalis

MONARDA

BERGAMOT, HORSEMINT

This is a genus of 15 species of perennials or annuals from North America with green, sometimes purple-tinged, veined, aromatic leaves. They are much loved by bees and are used for flavoring teas and in potpourris, as well as for their ornamental value, flower color and scent. Plants can be single stemmed or sparsely branching, and bear 2-lipped, tubular flowers from mid-summer to early autumn.

CULTIVATION

They are very frost-hardy plants best planted in full sun although some shade is acceptable. They must be well drained; in fact the annual species do best on sandy soil. The perennials are happy in moist soil and in some climates like a good feed of manure or compost. Annuals are sown directly into their permanent spot, and perennials are usually grown by division of established clumps.

Mimulus cardinalis

CARDINAL MONKEY FLOWER,

SCARLET MONKEY FLOWER

From southwestern USA and Mexico, this herbaceous perennial grows at least 3 ft (1 m) tall and 12 in (30 cm) wide. It has sharply toothed, hairy, mid-green leaves and produces racemes of yellow-throated scarlet flowers from summer through to autumn. Found on banks of streams and ponds, it needs a sheltered position as it tends to sprawl if battered by rain and wind. ZONES 7–11.

Mimulus moschatus

MONKEY MUSK

This small, creeping, water-loving perennial grows to a height and spread of 6–12 in (15–30 cm). It bears pale yellow flowers, lightly dotted with brown, in summer to autumn. It is very frost hardy. This plant was once grown for its musk scent but, mysteriously, it has been odorless for many years. ZONES 7–10.

Monarda didyma 'Aquarius'

Monarda didyma

BEE BALM, OSWEGO TEA

This plant was used by the Native Americans and early colonists as a herbal tea. With its spidery white, pink or red flowers borne in late summer, it is one of the showiest of the culinary herbs. The young leaves may be used in salads or as a stuffing for roast meat.

Monarda didyma grows 3 ft (1 m) or more tall. '**Aquarius**' has deep, purple-lilac flowers with purplish green bracts. '**Cambridge Scarlet**' is a vigorous perennial to 3 ft (1 m) with dark green, slightly toothed leaves that when crushed or brushed against emit an exotic, citrus-like scent. '**Croftway Pink**' grows to 30 in (75 cm) tall and has rose-pink flowers from mid-summer to early autumn. **ZONES 4–10.**

Monarda didyma

Myosotis alpestris
ALPINE FORGET-ME-NOT

This short-lived perennial from Europe (usually grown as an annual or biennial) forms clumps to a height and spread of 4–6 in (10–15 cm). In late spring and early summer, it bears clusters of dainty, bright blue, pink or white flowers with creamy yellow eyes. **ZONES 4–10.**

Myosotis sylvatica
GARDEN FORGET-ME-NOT

This European biennial or short-lived perennial is usually grown as an annual for its bright lavender-blue, yellow-eyed flowers in spring and early summer. It forms mounds of fuzzy foliage 18 in (45 cm) tall and 12 in (30 cm) wide, with taller stems uncurling as the flower buds open. There are many named selections; some more compact, some pink or white. '**Blue Ball**' has tiny, deep blue flowers and is good for edging. **ZONES 5–10.**

Myosotis sylvatica

MYOSOTIS
FORGET-ME-NOT

This genus of annuals and perennials includes 34 New Zealand natives among its 50 or so species, but the most commonly cultivated are from the temperate regions of Europe, Asia and the Americas. Their dainty blue (sometimes pink or white) flowers bloom in spring, and most species are useful in rock gardens and borders, or as groundcover under trees and shrubs. The plants fade after flowering. *Myosotis*, from the Greek for 'mouse ear', refers to the pointed leaves. The flowers have long been associated with love and remembrance.

Myosotis alpestris

CULTIVATION

Mostly quite frost hardy, they prefer a semi-shaded setting or a sunny spot protected by larger plants, and fertile, well-drained soil. They are rarely affected by pests or diseases and like fertilizing before the flowering period. Propagate from seed in autumn. Once established, they self-seed freely.

Myrrhis odorata

This graceful perennial to 6 ft (1.8 m) high is excellent as a background plant in the herb garden or mixed flower border. It will tolerate shade and can be sited beneath garden trees. It self-seeds readily and the strongest seedlings may be transplanted. **ZONES 5–10.**

MYRRHIS
SWEET CICELY, MYRRH

This is a genus of only one species, an attractive long-lived perennial in the carrot family, native to southern Europe. It has aromatic, fern-like leaves and fragrant creamy white flowers in flattened heads in early summer, followed by ribbed, shiny brown seeds that have a very brief viability. The leaves and seeds have a sweet aniseed flavor and are cooked with fruit as a sugar substitute. They are also good in raw vegetable juices.

CULTIVATION

Fully frost hardy, they should be grown in part-shade in moist but well-drained, fertile soil. Propagate from fresh seed in autumn or spring or by division in autumn or early spring.

Myrrhis odorata

NEMESIA

This genus of 50-odd species of annuals, perennials and subshrubs comes from South Africa. Their flowering period is short, although if they are cut back hard when flowering slows down they will flower again. The flowers are showy, being trumpet-shaped and 2-lipped, and are borne singly in the upper leaf axils or in terminal racemes. The leaves are opposite and simple.

CULTIVATION

These plants need a protected, sunny position and fertile, well-drained soil. They cannot tolerate very hot, humid climates. Pinch out growing shoots on young plants to ensure a bushy habit. Propagate from seed in early autumn or early spring in cool areas.

Nemesia caerulea 'Elliott's Variety'

Nemesia caerulea
syn. *Nemesia fruticans*

This perennial can grow up
to 24 in (60 cm) in height if
conditions are to its liking.
Becoming slightly woody at
the base, it tends to sprawl,
branching into erect stems
holding small mid-green
leaves and terminal heads of
soft pink, lavender or blue
flowers. **'Elliott's Variety'** is
very free-flowering, with
bright mauve-blue flowers
with a white eye. **ZONES 8–10.**

Nemesia strumosa

Nemesia strumosa 'Prince of Orange'

Nemesia strumosa

Nemesia strumosa is a colorful, fast-growing, bushy annual,
popular as a bedding plant. It has lance-shaped, pale green,
prominently toothed leaves, and grows to a height of 8–12 in
(20–30 cm) and a spread of 10 in (25 cm). Large flowers in
yellow, white, red or orange are borne in spring on short
terminal racemes. **'Blue Gem'** is a compact cultivar to 8 in
(20 cm), with small, clear blue flowers. **'Prince of Orange'** also
grows to about 8 in (20 cm), but has orange flowers with purple
veins. **'Red and White'** has flowers strikingly bicolored, the
upper lip bright red and the lower lip white. **ZONES 9–11.**

Nemesia strumosa 'Red and White'

NEMOPHILA

This is a group of 11 species of annuals grown for their bright, open, 5-petalled flowers. Originating from western USA, these annuals make good borders and are attractive in window boxes. They produce colorful spring–summer blooms in a range of mainly blues.

Nemophila menziesii

Nemophila maculata

CULTIVATION

These quick-growing annuals grow best in full sun or part-shade in friable, moisture-retentive soil. As the foliage is rather soft, provide protection from wind and position plants away from high-traffic pathways. Regular watering will help prolong blooming. Check for aphids. Propagate from seed which can be sown *in situ* during the autumn months.

Nemophila maculata
FIVE SPOT

Commonly referred to as five spot because each veined, white petal has a prominent deep purple blotch at its tip, this plant grows to about 12 in (30 cm) tall. It is used extensively in massed displays as plants hold their profusion of blooms above the ferny foliage over a long period during summer. **ZONES 7–11.**

Nemophila menziesii
syn. **Nemophila insignis**
BABY BLUE-EYES

A charming little Californian wildflower, this spreading annual is a useful groundcover under shrubs such as roses, as well as in rock gardens and around edges; it is particularly effective overplanted in a bed with spring bulbs. It bears small, bowl-shaped, sapphire-blue flowers with a well-defined concentric ring of white in the center. It has dainty, serrated foliage, and grows to a height and width of 6–10 in (15–25 cm). These plants dislike heat and transplanting. **ZONES 7–11.**

Nepeta × faassenii

NEPETA

This large genus of more than 200 species of perennial, rarely annual, plants is used extensively in herbaceous borders and for edgings or as groundcover plants. Some species have highly aromatic silver-gray foliage and are naturally compact, while others tend to be taller growing plants and may benefit from staking. Originating from a wide area of Eurasia, North Africa and the mountains of tropical Africa, many species have been extensively hybridized to produce exceptional garden plants.

Nepeta cataria

CULTIVATION

Provide a well-drained soil in a sunny position. Some of the vigorous herbaceous species make good single species groundcovers as they have a tendency to overpower less robust plants. However, they can be kept in check by light trimming during the growing season and can be cut back each year to prevent the plants from becoming too straggly. Propagation is by division, from cuttings taken during late spring or from seed.

Nepeta cataria

CATNIP, CATMINT

Catnip is a frost-hardy perennial with branching, upright stems growing up to 3 ft (1 m). It has aromatic, green leaves and whorls of white flowers from late spring through to autumn. Cats are attracted to this plant and will lie in it or play in it and sometimes dig it up. A tea made from the leaves is said to be relaxing. **ZONES 3–10.**

Nepeta clarkei

This species from Pakistan and Kashmir forms large clumps up to 30 in (75 cm) high. The leaves are green and the upright flowering stems hold masses of lilac-blue blooms, each with a white patch on the lower lip. This is a very cold-hardy species. **ZONES 3–9.**

N. × faassenii 'Dropmore Blue'

Nepeta × faassenii

CATMINT

This is a bushy, clump-forming perennial, useful for separating strong colors in the shrub or flower border. It is very effective when used with stone, either in walls, paving or rock gardens or as an edging plant. It forms spreading mounds of grayish green leaves that are aromatic when crushed, and the numerous flower stems carry hundreds of small, violet-blue flowers throughout summer. It grows to a height and spread of 18 in (45 cm). Many cultivars are available, including **'Dropmore Blue'**, with upright, tall flower spikes of lavender blue; and **'Six Hills Giant'**, a robust plant growing to around 18 in (45 cm) with gray foliage complemented by tall spikes of lavender-blue flowers that will bloom continuously throughout the summer if spent flowers are kept clipped. **'Walker's Blue'** has finer foliage and flowers than the other two hybrids. **ZONES 3–10.**

Nepeta clarkei

Nepeta nervosa

Nepeta nervosa

This showy species forms a bushy habit to 24 in (60 cm) tall. It has long, narrow, deeply veined leaves and dense spikes of purplish blue flowers, although they can occasionally be yellow in the wilds of its native Kashmir. **ZONES 5–9.**

Nepeta racemosa
syn. Nepeta mussinii

Native to the Caucasus region and northern
Iran, this ornamental species has generally been
known as *Nepeta mussinii* in gardens, though
many of the plants sold under that name are in
fact the hybrid *N. × faassenii*. It is a vigorous
perennial up to about 12 in (30 cm) high with
gray-green, densely hairy leaves and lavender-
blue summer flowers in long racemes. '**Blue
Wonder**' is a very free-flowering form of
spreading habit with violet-blue flowers;
'**Snowflake**' has pure white flowers.
ZONES 3–10.

Nepeta racemosa 'Blue Wonder'

Nicotiana × *sanderae* 'Falling Star'

NICOTIANA
FLOWERING TOBACCO

The 67 species of annuals, biennials, perennials and shrubs in this genus
from America and Australia include the commercial tobacco plant. Other
species are grown for the fragrance of their warm-weather flowers,
which usually open at night. The flowers of modern strains remain open
all day, but have limited perfume. They are good for cutting, although
the plants are sticky to handle.

CULTIVATION
Marginally frost hardy to frost tender, they need full sun or light shade
and fertile, moist but well-drained soil. Propagate from seed in early
spring. Check carefully for snails and caterpillars.

Nicotiana × sanderae

This species is a slow-growing, bushy annual reaching a height of 15 in (38 cm) and spread of 8 in (20 cm). In summer and early autumn, it bears long, trumpet-shaped flowers in shades of white, pink, red, cerise, bright crimson and purple. The flowers stay open during the day and are fragrant in the evening. Many cultivars have been developed from this garden hybrid, including 'Lime Green', which has abundant, vivid lime-green blooms held over a long summer season. The flowers of 'Falling Star' range from white to pale pink to deep pink. **ZONES 8–11.**

Nicotiana tabacum

Nicotiana sylvestris

This is one of the few summer-flowering annuals that thrive in shade. It is also one of the taller-growing species, with flowers that remain open even in deep shade or on overcast days. It is robust, though tender, and grows to 5 ft (1.5 m) or more, and bears tall, stately flowering stems that arise from a mass of large, bright green lush foliage. The long, tubular, white flowers are particularly fragrant on warm summer evenings, so plant it where the scent can be appreciated. **ZONES 8–11.**

Nicotiana tabacum

TOBACCO

The flowers of this plant are pretty and offer a pleasant, if faint, perfume. They are rather small, about 1 in (25 mm) wide, and they are borne atop a head-high plant with coarse leaves. The plant is scarcely decorative enough for a flower garden, but the leaves make tobacco. Although different cultivars have been developed for processing into cigarettes, pipe tobacco or cigars, it is the way the leaves are processed that determines their ultimate use. **ZONES 8–11.**

Nigella damascena 'Miss Jekyll'

Nigella damascena

LOVE-IN-A-MIST, DEVIL-IN-A-BUSH

This fully frost-hardy annual bears spurred, many-petalled, pale to lilac-blue or white flowers in spring and early summer. They are almost hidden by the bright green, feathery foliage, and are followed by rounded, green seed pods that mature to brown. Upright and fast growing, it reaches 24 in (60 cm) in height with a spread of 8 in (20 cm). 'Miss Jekyll' is a double blue form. **ZONES 6–10.**

NIGELLA

Nigellas are a genus of about 15 species of annuals from the Mediterranean region and western Asia. The flowers and ornamental seed pods are attractive and are popular for flower arrangements.

CULTIVATION

Nigella seedlings hate being transplanted, but if seeds are sown where the plants are to grow, and some of the flowers are allowed to go to seed, new plants will come up of their own accord for years. Plant in full sun in fertile, well-drained soil and deadhead to prolong flowering if the seed pods are not needed. Propagate from seed in autumn or spring.

Nigella damascena

Nuphar lutea
YELLOW POND LILY

This species is native to eastern USA, the West Indies, northern Africa and large tracts of Eurasia. It thrives in deep water and has large orbicular leaves that emerge when the water is shallow or float when planted in deeper ponds. Summer-flowering, deep yellow-orange blooms held just above the surface emit a distinct odor. This is a vigorous species. **ZONES 4–11.**

Nuphar lutea

NUPHAR
SPATTERDOCK, POND LILY, YELLOW POND LILY

Made up of 25 species of perennial aquatic herbs with creeping rhizomes, these pond lilies from the temperate northern hemisphere have large, floating and submerged leaves. The flowers, usually in yellow or green tones, are held on stalks above the water surface.

CULTIVATION
Requirements are very similar to the hardy species of *Nymphaea* with the additional benefit that they will flower in shade and some are suited to being planted in slow-moving water. They prefer to be planted in pots of rich soil and carefully submerged to around 24 in (60 cm) deep, depending on the species. Propagation is by division and best carried out in spring.

NYMPHAEA
WATERLILY

Nymphaea, Hardy Hybrid, 'Attraction'

This genus of 50 species of deciduous and evergreen perennial aquatic plants with fleshy roots is named after the Greek goddess Nymphe. They are grown for their rounded, floating leaves that are cleft at the base and for their attractive large flowers which come in shades of white and cream, brilliant yellows and oranges, pinks and deep reds, blues and purple. They may be night blooming, depending on species, and sometimes fragrant. The berry-like fruits mature underwater. There are both frost-hardy and tropical varieties.

CULTIVATION

Frost-hardy waterlilies grow in most climates and flower freely throughout summer. Faded foliage should be removed. Divide the tuber-like rhizomes and replant in spring or summer every 3 or 4 years. Tropical waterlilies are all frost tender, and require a very warm, sunny situation. They flower from mid-summer into autumn. In cooler areas, the tubers of tropical waterlilies should be lifted and stored in moist sand over winter. All species need still water and annual fertilizing as they are gross feeders. Propagate from seed or by separating plantlets in spring or early autumn. Check for insects, particularly aphids; goldfish kept in the pool will eat most pests.

Nymphaea, Hardy Hybrid, 'Formosa'

Nymphaea, Hardy Hybrid, 'Rosea'

Nymphaea, Hardy Hybrids

These cold-hardy and colorful hybrids have been bred from several European and North American species, principally *Nymphaea alba,* *N. odorata* and *N. mexicana.* The day-blooming flowers are 3–6 in (8–15 cm) across, mostly in shades of white, yellow, pink or red, set on or just above the surface of the water. **'Atropurpurea'** has reddish purple foliage complementing its dark red, wide-open flowers with golden stamens. **'Attraction'** will grow in quite deep water. Its crimson-red flowers with contrasting white sepals deepen to a rich garnet red as they age. **'Formosa'** is a profuse bloomer, producing many large flowers in a soft rosy pink shade on opening, becoming deeper in color as the flowers age. **'Lucida'** has large green leaves and attractive, deep red flowers with paler outer petals, 5–6 in (12–15 cm) across. The compact **Laydeckeri hybrids** are very free flowering yet produce comparatively little foliage. Colors range from soft rose pink to deep pink and rosy crimson, and they have a spread of around 24 in (60 cm). **'Fulgens'** has star-shaped, semi-double, crimson to magenta flowers. The **Marliacea hybrids** are among the most elegant of all the hardy waterlilies, raised by M. Latour-Marliac in the 1880s. They have dark green leaves and star-shaped, semi-double, soft pink flowers with golden centers, which appear in summer. The large flowers stand slightly above the water. **'Albida'** is a strong-growing plant that bears free-blooming white flowers. **'Rosea'** is also very popular. **ZONES 5–10.**

Nymphaea odorata
POND LILY, WHITE WATERLILY

This native of North and tropical America has white fragrant, many-petalled flowers 3–5 in (8–12 cm) across, appearing by day in summer. The leaves are thick, glossy and mid-green. The plant spreads to 4 ft (1.2 m). **ZONES 3–11.**

Nymphaea tetragona 'Helvola'

Nymphaea tetragona 'Helvola'

This true miniature waterlily bears soft yellow, star-shaped, semi-double flowers only 2–3 in (5–8 cm) across. The leaves are handsome, too, being dark olive green splashed with maroon. The species is widely distributed around the temperate northern hemisphere. Plant with around 10 in (25 cm) of water over the crown of the plant. It is the smallest of the miniature waterlilies. **ZONES 7–10.**

Nymphoides peltata

NYMPHOIDES

FAIRY WATERLILY, WATER SNOWFLAKE

Resembling miniature waterlilies, the 20 species of rhizomatous, aquatic perennials in this genus are distributed throughout the world. Their rootstocks embed in the pond bottom while the long-stalked, oval, round or kidney-shaped, wavy-edged leaves float on the surface. The foliage ranges in diameter from 1 to 6 in (2.5 to 15 cm), and is usually slightly glossy and olive green, occasionally purple mottled. The ½–1 in (12–25 mm) diameter flowers, with 5 often fimbriated (fringed) petals, may be white or yellow; they appear in summer and are held just above the foliage.

CULTIVATION

Plant *Nymphoides* species in soil with a water depth of 4–18 in (10–45 cm) in full or half-day sun. The runners can often spread to 6 ft (1.8 m), so allow plenty of room for development. Propagation is usually by division of the rootstock in late winter or early spring.

Nymphoides peltata

WATER FRINGE, YELLOW FLOATING HEART

This is a very hardy species from a vast area of Eurasia and Japan. The small, heart-shaped submerged leaves grow near the very long rhizomes, while surface leaves are bright green with blackish markings on their upper sides and reddish tinges below. The flowers are bright golden yellow. **ZONES 6–10.**

OENOTHERA

EVENING PRIMROSE

Native to temperate regions of both North and South America but widely naturalized elsewhere, this genus consists of more than 120 species of annuals, biennials and perennials. Their short-lived flowers, borne during summer, have 4 delicate petals, yellow, red, white or (less commonly) pink, and a long basal tube. Most species are pollinated by nocturnal insects and only release their fragrance at night. Some do not even open their petals during the day. Evening primrose oil is extracted from the tiny seeds. It contains certain fatty acids believed to be beneficial to health if consumed regularly in modest quantities.

CULTIVATION

They are mostly frost hardy and grow best in a well-drained, sandy soil in an open, sunny situation. They will tolerate dry conditions. Propagate from seed or by division in spring or autumn, or from softwood cuttings in late spring.

Oenothera speciosa 'Rosea'

Oenothera macrocarpa

Oenothera macrocarpa

syn. *Oenothera missouriensis*

OZARK SUNDROPS, MISSOURI PRIMROSE, FLUTTERMILLS

This perennial is usually almost stemless with large rosettes of narrow tapering leaves. The flowers are large, reaching 4 in (10 cm) in diameter, lemon yellow in color and open in the evening in summer. This plant reaches a height of no more than 6 in (15 cm), but spreads to 24 in (60 cm) or more across, the flowers appearing singly from between the leaves. **ZONES 5–9.**

Oenothera speciosa

WHITE EVENING PRIMROSE, SHOWY EVENING PRIMROSE

This short-lived, rhizomatous perennial native to southern USA and Mexico bears spikes of profuse, fragrant, saucer-shaped, pink-tinted white flowers. Fresh flowerheads open daily during summer. The small leaves often turn red in hot or cold weather. Clump forming, it grows to 18–24 in (45–60 cm) in height with a spread of 18 in (45 cm) or more. **'Rosea'** (syns 'Childsii', *Oenothera berlandieri*) is lower growing, with flowers edged and heavily veined rose pink, yellow in the center. **'Siskiyou'** is similar but with larger flowers. These pink forms have often been confused with *O. rosea*, which has much smaller flowers. **ZONES 5–10.**

OMPHALODES

NAVELWORT

From Europe, Asia and Mexico, this genus consists of 28 species of forget-me-not–like annuals and perennials that are either evergreen or semi-evergreen. These plants make excellent groundcovers, and they are most suited to rock gardens.

These plants prefer shade or part-shade with moist but well-drained soil (except for *Omphalodes linifolia*, which prefers a sunny position). They are mostly frost hardy. Propagate from seed in spring or by division in autumn.

Omphalodes cappadocica

Omphalodes cappadocica

This spreading perennial from Turkey has creeping underground stems. It produces numerous sprays of flat, bright purple-blue flowers in spring that arise from clumps of densely hairy, oval to heart-shaped leaves that are found at the base of the plant. This plant reaches a height of 6–8 in (15–20 cm) and a spread of 10 in (25 cm) and is fully frost hardy. 'Cherry Ingram' is a vigorous grower to 10 in (25 cm) in height with purplish blue flowers. 'Starry Eyes' has relatively big flowers, with each blue petal edged white giving a pretty, starry effect. **ZONES 6–9.**

Paeonia lactiflora Hybrid
'Bowl of Beauty'

PAEONIA
PEONY

There are 33 species in this genus of beautiful perennials and shrubs. The genus name goes back to classical Greek and arose from the supposed medicinal properties of some species. Peonies are all deciduous and have long-lived, rather woody rootstocks with swollen roots, and large compound leaves with the leaflets usually toothed or lobed. Each new stem in spring terminates in one to several large, rose-like flowers. Their centers are a mass of short stamens that almost conceal the 2 to 5 large ovaries, which develop into short pods containing large seeds. The flowers are mostly in shades of pink or red, but there are also white and yellow-flowered species. The great majority of peonies are herbaceous, dying back to the ground in autumn, but there is a small group of Chinese species, known as the 'tree peonies' that have woody stems, although no more than about 8 ft (2.4 m) in height, so strictly they are shrubs. Cultivars of this tree peony group produce the largest and most magnificent of all peony flowers, some approaching a diameter of 12 in (30 cm), mostly double and often beautifully frilled or ruffled.

CULTIVATION
Most peonies will only succeed in climates with a cold winter, allowing dormancy and initiation of flower buds, but new foliage and flower buds can be damaged by late frosts. Plant in a sheltered position in full or slightly filtered sunlight, in cool, moist soil. Mulch and feed with well-rotted manure when leaf growth starts, but avoid disturbing roots. Pruning of the tree peonies should be minimal, consisting of trimming out weaker side shoots. Propagate from seed in autumn, or by division in the case of named cultivars. Tree peony cultivars are best propagated from basal suckers, but few are produced. Hence, plants on their own roots are very expensive. A faster and cheaper method is to graft them onto herbaceous rootstocks, but the resulting plants are often short lived.

Paeonia lactiflora Hybrid 'President Roosevelt'

Paeonia lactiflora Hybrids

These herbaceous Chinese peonies are derived mainly from *Paeonia lactiflora*. They have handsome foliage, which is maroon tinted when it first appears in spring, and usually scented flowers in a huge range of colors and forms. **'Beacon Flame'** has deep red, semi-double flowers. **'Bowl of Beauty'** grows to 3 ft (1 m) tall and between late spring and mid-summer bears dense clusters of slender, creamy white petaloids nesting in the center of broad, pink outer petals. **'Coral Charm'** has deep apricot buds fading to soft orange-pink as they mature. **'Cora Stubbs'** has broad outer petals and smaller central ones in contrasting tones. **'Duchesse de Nemours'** is a fairly tall grower with fragrant, white to soft yellow flowers with frilled incurving petals. **'Félix Crousse'** is a deep pink double with a red center. **'Festiva Maxima'** has large, fully double, scented flowers with frilled petals that are white with red flecks. **'Inspecteur Lavergne'** is late-flowering and fully double red. **'Kelway's Glorious'** has highly scented, creamy white, double flowers. **'Miss America'** has large, highly scented white flowers with gold stamens. **'Monsieur Jules Elie'** has very deep cerise-pink single flowers. **'President Roosevelt'** is a luxuriant 'rose' or 'bomb' double peony. **'Sarah Bernhardt'** has scented, double, rose-pink flowers with silvery margins. **'Whitleyi Major'** has single, ivory-white flowers with yellow stamens. **ZONES 6–9.**

Paeonia lactiflora Hybrid 'Beacon Flame'

Paeonia lactiflora Hybrid 'Cora Stubbs'

Papaver nudicaule
ICELAND POPPY

This tuft-forming perennial
from North America and Asia
Minor is almost always grown
as an annual. It is good for
rock gardens and for cutting.
Large scented flowers, borne
in winter and spring, are
white, yellow, orange or pink,
and have a crinkled texture.
The leaves are pale green, and
the stems are long and hairy.
It grows 12–24 in (30–60 cm)
tall with a 6–8 in (15–20 cm)
spread. **ZONES 2–10.**

Papaver orientale

PAPAVER
POPPY

The 50 or so annual, biennial or perennial species of the genus
Papaver are mainly from the temperate parts of Eurasia and
Africa, with a couple from eastern USA. Their characteristic
cupped petals and nodding buds that turn skywards upon opening make them popular bedding flowers. Several of their close
relatives take their name in common usage, such as the tree
poppy *(Romneya)*, the Californian poppy *(Eschscholzia)* or the
blue poppy *(Meconopsis)*.

CULTIVATION
Poppies are fully frost hardy and prefer little or no shade and
deep, moist, well-drained soil. Sow seed in spring or autumn;
many species self-seed readily.

Papaver orientale
ORIENTAL POPPY

This herbaceous perennial is
native to southwest Asia. In
summer, it bears spectacular
flowers as big as peonies in
shades of pink through to red
with dark centers to 4 in
(10 cm) in diameter. The
cultivated varieties, sometimes
double, come in a wide range
of colors and many feature a
dark basal blotch on each
petal. It has hairy, lance-like,
bluish green leaves and can
become straggly. According
to the variety, it grows from
18 in (45 cm) to more than
3 ft (1 m) tall. **'Cedric Morris'**
is a big-flowered form with
individual blooms up to 6 in
(15 cm) across. Its shell-pink
flowers have frilly petals, each
with an almost black blotch
at the base. **'Mrs Perry'** has
large, coral-pink flowers.
ZONES 3–9.

Papaver nudicaule

Papaver rhoeas

CORN POPPY, FIELD POPPY, FLANDERS POPPY

The cupped flowers on this fast-growing annual are small, delicate, scarlet and single. The cultivated varieties (**Shirley Series**) come in reds, pinks, whites and bicolors. They have a pale heart instead of the black cross that marks the center of the wild poppy. The leaves are light green and lobed. This species grows to 24 in (60 cm) high with a 12 in (30 cm) spread. Double-flowered strains are also available. '**Mother of Pearl**' has gray, pink or blue-purple flowers. **ZONES 5–9.**

Papaver rhoeas

Papaver rhoeas 'Mother of Pearl'

Papaver somniferum

OPIUM POPPY

The grayish green leaves on this fast-growing annual from the Middle East are lobed and elliptical with serrated edges. It blooms in summer, to display big flowers in white, pink, red or purple, usually as doubles. Opium poppies are cultivated for the milky sap produced in their seed capsules, which is the source of the narcotic drug opium and its derivatives. **ZONES 7–10.**

Papaver somniferum

PARNASSIA

BOG STAR, PARNASSUS GRASS

This is a genus of around 15 species of perennials found over much of the northern temperate zone. They have long-stemmed, kidney-shaped to near round, 1–4 in (2.5–10cm) long leaves in basal rosettes. The wiry flowers stem, which grow up to 24 in (60 cm) tall, bear a single, 5-petalled, 1–1½ in (25–35 mm) wide flower backed by a single bract. The flowers open in summer.

CULTIVATION

Plant in moist, well-drained soil in sun or part-shade and do not allow to become dry in summer. Some species are very difficult to cultivate and will only grow well in naturally damp, grassy meadows or damp, peaty soil. All species are very hardy. Propagate from seed in autumn or by very careful division of established clumps.

Parnassia grandifolia

Parnassia grandifolia

This species from central and south-eastern USA grows to 24 in (60 cm) tall. It has rounded 1½– 4 in (3.5–10 cm) long leaves on 1½– 6 in (3.5–15 cm) stems. Its flowers are white with very narrow petals. **ZONES 6–10.**

PARONYCHIA

WHITLOW WORT

This widespread genus consists of around 50 species of usually mat- or clump-forming, dianthus- or thyme-like annuals or perennials. Most occur naturally in the Mediterranean region and have wiry stems and tiny linear to rounded leaves, often in pairs. The minute flower inflorescences, in themselves quite inconspicuous, smother the plants in early summer and are highlighted by the surrounding silvery bracts.

CULTIVATION

These are very much plants for well-drained, sunny positions and are at home in rockeries or alpine houses. Most are quite frost hardy, but suffer if kept wet and cold in winter. Propagate from seed or by layering (they are often self-layering) or by division.

Paronychia capitata

Paronychia argentea

This species from southern Europe, North Africa and southwest Asia forms a mat of wiry stems with rounded leaves. In summer, it is smothered in small, dull yellow inflorescences partially covered by silvery bracts. **ZONES 7–11.**

Paronychia capitata

This Mediterranean species is very similar to *Paronychia argentea*. However, its leaves are linear to lance-shaped rather than rounded and its bracts are an even brighter silver. **ZONES 6–10.**

PELARGONIUM

The widely grown hybrid pelargoniums are popularly known as 'geraniums', but should not be confused with members of the genus *Geranium*, which is in the same plant family. The genus *Pelargonium* consists of perhaps 280 species, the vast majority endemic to South Africa and adjacent Namibia. Although pelargoniums are mostly soft-wooded shrubs and subshrubs, some are herbaceous perennials or even annuals. There is also a large but little known group of species that have succulent stems, leaves or roots and are grown by succulent collectors. The leaves of pelargoniums are often as broad as they are long, and are variously toothed, scalloped, lobed or dissected, depending on the species. The foliage is usually aromatic, containing a wide range of essential oils, and may secrete resin that give the leaves a sticky feel. Flowers of the wild species have the 2 upper petals differently colored or marked from the 3 lower ones, a feature that distinguishes pelargoniums from true geraniums.

Their seeds are plumed like thistledown, another distinguishing feature.

Only a few groups of hybrid pelargoniums are widely grown in gardens and as indoor plants. The common garden and pot 'geraniums' are the Zonal pelargoniums, once known as *Pelargonium* × *hortorum* (described in detail in the chapter on Shrubs). This group has the largest number of cultivars including 'Caroline Schmidt', 'Flower of Spring', 'Frank Headley' and 'Mrs Parker'. Somewhat similar are the Ivy-leafed pelargoniums, with their semi-scrambling habit and leaves that are fleshier with more pointed lobes. These are also the subject of intensive breeding, and tend to merge with Zonals in some of their characteristics. Another major group is the Regal pelargoniums, sometimes known as the Martha Washington geraniums or *Pelargonium* × *domesticum* (also described in detail in the chapter on Shrubs). Popular cultivars in this group include 'Rosmaroy' and 'Lord Bute'.

Pelargonium, Zonal Hybrid, 'Caroline Schmidt'

Pelargonium, Regal Hybrid, 'Rosmaroy'

Other smaller groups of hybrids bred for their flowers include Unique and Angel pelargoniums, which are the most significant. 'Captain Starlight' is a popular Angel hybrid, and 'Scarlet Pet' is a good example of a Unique hybrid. And then there is a large and varied group, Scented-leafed pelargoniums, grown primarily for their foliage, a typical example of this group is 'Fragrans'. Scented-leafed pelargoniums are described in more detail in the chapter on Shrubs.

Pelargonium, Angel Hybrid, 'Captain Starlight'

CULTIVATION

These frost-tender plants are often treated like annuals for summer bedding in colder climates. In warmer climates with long hours of daylight, they flower almost all the time, although they do not do well in extreme heat and humidity. Plant in pots or beds. The site should be sunny with light, well-drained, neutral soil. If grown in pots, fertilize regularly and remove dead heads. Avoid overwatering: Zonals in particular rot at the base if soil remains wet, although stems re-root higher up (but weaker plants result). Propagate from softwood cuttings from spring to autumn.

Pelargonium, Regal Hybrid, 'Lord Bute'

Pelargonium, Unique Hybrid, 'Scarlet Pet'

Pelargonium, Ivy-leafed Hybrids

These are derived mainly from the South
African *Pelargonium peltatum*, which has a
scrambling or trailing habit with fleshy,
pointed-lobed, hairless leaves and small pink
flowers. The many cultivars retain the leaf
characteristics, but have larger flowers in
conspicuous long-stalked heads, often double
and in a wide range of colors. Easily grown,
they tolerate wetter conditions than the Zonals,
and are especially suited to hanging baskets
and the tops of retaining walls. Recent
developments include variegated leaves and
compact or miniature plants. Hybridization of
Ivy-leafed and Zonal pelargoniums has resulted
in plants with leaves like the former, and
flowers more like the latter. The popular
'**Amethyst**' has massed clusters of semi-double,
purple-pink flowers. '**Blooming Gem**' has
bright pink flowers. The **Cascade Series** of
miniature Ivy-leafed pelargoniums have small
leaves and masses of small flowers. It includes
'**Laced Red Cascade**', with red flowers flecked
with white, and '**Lilac Cascade**', with lavender-
pink flowers. '**Chic**' has deep pink, double
flowers. '**Crocetta**' has red-edged, semi-double,
white flowers. '**Galilee**', one of the best known
Ivy-leafed cultivars, is compact and has leaves
that may be variegated with cream or cream
and pink; its densely massed double flowers are
flesh pink. '**Harlequin Mahogany**' has flowers

Pelargonium, Scented-leafed Hybrid, 'Fragrans'

with white variegations caused by a virus
transmitted through the seed. This has enabled
the breeding of a range of colors from pink and
white to red and white. '**Mutzel**' has bright red
flowers and pale green variegated leaves.
ZONES 9–11.

Pelargonium, Ivy-leafed Hybrid, 'Crocetta'

Pelargonium, Ivy-leafed Hybrid, 'Galilee'

Pelargonium tomentosum

Pelargonium tomentosum
PEPPERMINT GERANIUM

A strong, refreshing smell of peppermint comes from the large, pale green, velvety leaves of this sprawling, soft-stemmed pelargonium. It produces tiny, insignificant, purple-veined white flowers in clusters. It reaches 24 in (60 cm) in height, and spreads widely or can be hung over a ledge. It is shade tolerant but will also grow in full sun if sheltered from wind. If required, its spread can be limited by pinching out the growing tips, but older plants are better replaced.
ZONES 10–11.

Pelargonium, Ivy-leafed Hybrid, 'Harlequin Mahogany'

Pelargonium 'Splendide'

Believed to be a hybrid between the South African species *Pelargonium tricolor* and *P. ovale*, this subshrubby 6–12 in (15–30 cm) tall plant, often sold as *P. tricolor* 'Arborea', has knotted woody stems with toothed, long-stalked, oval, hairy, gray-green leaves. It produces branched flowering stems ending in 2- to 3-flowered clusters of striking bicolored flowers. They have red upper petals, dark purple at the base, and pure white lower petals, about 1½ in (35 mm) wide. **'Pretty Lady'** is similar.
ZONES 9–11.

Pelargonium 'Splendide'

Penstemon barbatus

PENSTEMON

This large genus consists of 250 species of deciduous, evergreen or semi-evergreen subshrubs and perennials, mostly native to Central and North America. The leaves appear in opposite pairs in whorls, while the flowers have 2 lobes on the upper lip and 3 on the lower. Hybrids are valued for their showy flower spikes in blues, reds, whites, and bicolors. Tall varieties suit sheltered borders, and dwarf strains brighten up bedding schemes. 'Bev Jensen' is red and 'Holly's White' is a favorite in the USA.

CULTIVATION

These marginally to very frost-hardy plants do best in fertile, well-drained soil and full sun. Cut plants back hard after flowering. They can be propagated from seed in spring or autumn, by division in spring, or from cuttings of non-flowering shoots in late summer (the only method for cultivars).

Penstemon 'Firebird'

P. 'Andenken an Friedrich Hahn'

Penstemon 'Andenken an Friedrich Hahn'
syn. Penstemon 'Garnet'

This very frost-hardy perennial, which grows to 30 in (75 cm) with a 24 in (60 cm) spread, bears its dark pink flowers from mid-summer to autumn. **ZONES 7–10.**

Penstemon barbatus
syn. Chelone barbata
CORAL PENSTEMON,
BEARD-LIP PENSTEMON

The scarlet flowers on this semi-evergreen, very frost-hardy perennial are tubular with 2 lips. They bloom on racemes from mid-summer to early autumn above narrow, lance-shaped, green leaves. The plant grows to 3 ft (1 m) high, with a spread of 12 in (30 cm). **ZONES 3–10.**

Penstemon digitalis

Native to eastern North America, this very frost-hardy perennial species is usually seen with white or pale lavender flowers, neither particularly exciting. **'Husker's Red'**, however, is notable for its deep reddish purple foliage. A robust plant, it reaches a height of 30 in (75 cm) and spread of 24 in (60 cm), and is attractive to hummingbirds. **ZONES 3–9.**

Penstemon 'Evelyn'

This is a 30 in (75 cm) tall perennial hybrid with very narrow leaves and masses of slightly curved pale pink flowers. It is very frost hardy. **ZONES 7–10.**

Penstemon 'Firebird'
syn. Penstemon 'Schoenholzen'

This cultivar grows to around 30 in (75 cm) and has vivid orange-red flowers. **ZONES 7–10.**

Penstemon ×
gloxinioides
BORDER PENSTEMON

This name applies to a group
of hybrids raised in the middle
of the nineteenth century from
Penstemon cobaea and
P. hartwegii. They have some
of the largest and showiest
flowers of any penstemons,
mainly in rich reds and pinks
and usually with a white
throat. However, they are
often short lived and not so
cold hardy as other pen-
stemons, and have declined
in popularity. **ZONES 7–9.**

Penstemon × gloxinioides

Pericallis × hybrida
syns Senecio cruentus, S. × hybrida

This hybrid reaches 12 in
(30 cm) tall and wide. It is a
multi-purpose bloomer for
grouping or for formal bedding in part-shaded spots. It
is ideal for window boxes, for
containers on balconies or in
courtyards. The color of the
daisy-like flowers ranges from
pink, red, purple and crimson
through to white, as well as
the traditional blue. They are
very tolerant of heat, salt air
and poor soil, but suffer in
high humidity or excessive
rain. **ZONES 9–11.**

PERICALLIS
CINERARIA

This genus has about 15 species of perennials and subshrubs
closely allied to *Senecio,* where they were once included. They
are distributed throughout the mid-latitude islands of the
Atlantic Ocean. Best known in cultivation for the florist's
cineraria (*Pericallis × hybrida*), the wild species are nowhere
near as fancy. The leaves, which form basal rosettes in the
perennials, are usually oval to lance-shaped, 2–6 in (5–15 cm)
long, with finely toothed edges and covered in small hairs. The
flowers are usually pink, mauve or purple, ½–2 in (1.2–5 cm)
wide and carried in open heads.

CULTIVATION
Although easily cultivated in any moist, well-drained soil in
part- to full shade, few species will tolerate anything other than
very light frosts. The florist's strains are often used as winter-
flowering house plants. Propagate from seed or cuttings or by
division, depending on the growth form.

Persicaria bistorta 'Superba'

PERSICARIA

syns *Aconogonon, Bistorta, Tovara*

KNOTWEED

This genus contains 50 to 80 species of annuals, perennials and subshrubs. The genus is described in more detail in the chapter on Lawns, Groundcovers, Ornamental Grasses and Bamboos.

Persicaria bistorta

syn. *Polygonum bistorta*

BISTORT, SNAKEWEED

A vigorous perennial with heavy rootstock, *Persicaria bistorta* is found from Europe to western Asia. This species grows to 24 in (60 cm) tall. Its leaves are oblong with wavy margins and grow 4–8 in (10–20 cm) long. The white or pink flowers open in summer. '**Superba**' has densely packed spikes of pink flowers. **ZONES 4–9.**

Persicaria filiformis

syn. *Polygonum filiforme*

Up to 4 ft (1.2 m) tall, *Persicaria filiformis* comes from Japan, the Himalayas and northeastern USA. It has 3–6 in (8–15 cm) long elliptical leaves with a covering of short, rough hairs and often marked with rows of chocolate-brown flecks. The flower spikes are slender and the green-white or pale pink flowers are not particularly showy. **ZONES 5–10.**

Persicaria macrophylla

syn. *Polygonum macrophyllum*

This spreading Himalayan and western Chinese semi-evergreen perennial rarely exceeds 6 in (15 cm) in height, but has leaves up to 4 in (10 cm) long. The foliage forms a basal clump that slowly enlarges and spreads. The pink or red flowers open in summer. **ZONES 5–9.**

Persicaria macrophylla

Persicaria filiformis

Petunia, Celebrity Series, 'Pink Morn'

PETUNIA

PETUNIA

'*Petun*' means 'tobacco' in a South American Indian dialect, and petunias are indeed relatives of the tobaccos *(Nicotiana)*. Their leaves have a similar narcotic effect on humans, and both genera belong to the same family as potatoes (Solanaceae). There are around 35 species in the genus, occurring in warmer parts of South America. They include annuals, biennials and shrubby perennials. The leaves are dark green, rather hairy and smooth-edged and the trumpet-shaped flowers are white, purple, red, blue, pink or mixed hues. It is doubtful whether any other group of garden annuals has been the subject of such intense selection by plant breeders over such a long period as the petunias. Interestingly, from what has been revealed of their work, it seems to have been concentrated almost entirely on the one hybrid combination, *Petunia* × *hybrida*.

CULTIVATION

The garden petunias are frost-tender plants always grown as annuals. They are popular as bedding plants and for window boxes, hanging baskets and planters. Fairly fast growing, they like well-drained, fertile soil and a sunny spot and thrive where summers are hot. Provide shelter from wind. Flowers of some of the larger Grandiflora hybrids are damaged by rain, but others, mainly the Multiflora hybrids, are more resistant. Sow seed under glass in early spring, or plant purchased seedlings at beginning of summer. Fertilize every month until flowering is well advanced. Pinch back hard to encourage branching and deadhead regularly. Watch for cucumber mosaic and tomato spotted wilt.

Petunia × *hybrida* 'Frenzy Rose'

They include the **Plum Series,** with delightfully veined flowers and **Bonanza Series** with frilly, trumpet-shaped double flowers in a multitude of colors. The **Celebrity Series,** including cultivars such as **'Pink Morn'**, also covers a wide color range, and are mainly in pastel shades. They can be distinguished by their light-throated flowers. The **Madness Series** have small single-color flowers. **'Purple Wave'** is a seedling strain with prolific flowers of a single, magenta-purple color. It has a cascading growth habit and is similar to the vegetatively propagated **'Colorwave'** petunias. **ZONES 9–11.**

Petunia × *hybrida* cultivar

Petunia × *hybrida*

Believed to have originated as a cross between the white-flowered *Petunia axillaris* and the pink to purple-flowered *P. integrifolia*, the garden petunia was a well-known summer bedding plant in Europe by the middle of the nineteenth century. From an early stage, the garden petunias were divided into four groups of cultivars and seedling strains, designated by Latin names, and this classification still survives. The two most important groups are the **Grandiflora** and **Multiflora** petunias, both with plants around 12 in (30 cm) tall at maturity. Flowers of the former are very wide and shallow, scattered over the somewhat sprawling plants, while Multifloras are more compact in growth with densely massed and somewhat narrower blooms. The **Nana Compacta** petunias are generally less than 6 in (15 cm) high, of compact habit, and with profuse small flowers. The **Pendula** petunias have prostrate, trailing stems and are grown mainly in hanging baskets. It is the Grandiflora petunias that are now the most popular, with a dazzling range of newer F1 hybrids, although they are more easily rain damaged and susceptible to disfiguring botrytis rot. They include the **Cascade** and **Supercascade Series** (or Magic Series), available in a wide range of colors, with single flowers and somewhat trailing stems suitable for hanging baskets. **'Giants of California'** is not so profusely blooming, but individual blossoms are very large with ruffled edges and are white, pink or mauve. The Multifloras have smaller blooms but are more prolific flowerers.

Petunia × *hybrida* 'Pink Vein'

Petunia integrifolia
syn. *Petunia violacea*

Sometimes sold as 'Burgundy Pet', this Argentinian species is a short-lived shrubby perennial that produces masses of small, dark-throated, rose purple flowers on sprawling plants. It is a weather- and disease-tolerant species that is being increasingly used in hybridizing. Some very free-flowering cultivars recently released under the trade name **Million Bells** may belong to this species. **ZONES 9–11.**

Petunia × hybrida 'Pink Flamingo'

Petunia integrifolia

PHLOMIS

This genus consists of around 100 species of often downy-leafed perennials, subshrubs and shrubs found from the Mediterranean region to China. Although variable, in most cases their leaves are large, over 4 in (10 cm) long, and densely covered with hair-like felting. Typical of members of the nettle family, the leaves occur in whorls on upright stems. The tubular flowers, borne on upright verticillasters, curl downwards and have 2 lips at the tip, the upper lip hooded over the lower. They occur in clusters of 2 to 40 blooms, depending on the species, and are usually in shades of cream, yellow, pink, mauve or purple.

CULTIVATION

Hardiness varies, though most will tolerate moderate frosts. Species with heavily felted foliage suffer in prolonged wet weather and are best grown in exposed positions where the foliage dries quickly after rain. Plant in moist, well-drained soil in full sun or part-shade. Propagate from seed or from small cuttings of non-flowering shoots, or by division where possible.

Phlomis russeliana

Phlomis russeliana

This easily grown perennial thrives in any ordinary soil given a reasonable amount of sun. The large, heart-shaped, fresh green leaves make excellent groundcover if planted in quantity, forming clumps around 12 in (30 cm) high and up to 24 in (60 cm) across. In summer, it bears stout stems 3 ft (1 m) high topped with several whorls of hooded, butter-yellow flowers. **ZONES 7–10.**

Phlox paniculata

PHLOX

This genus contains more than 60 species of evergreen and semi-evergreen annuals and perennials, mostly native to North America. They are grown for their profuse, fragrant flowers and the symmetry of the flower clusters. The name *phlox* means 'flame', appropriate for these brightly colored, showy flowers popular in bedding and border displays. *Phlox purpurea × lutea* has deep pink flowers with pale yellow centers.

CULTIVATION

Perennials are easily grown in any temperate climate, and need a lot of water while they grow. Annuals grow in almost any climate. Plant in fertile, moist but well-drained soil in a sunny or part-shaded position. Propagate from seed or cuttings or by division. Watch out for red spider mite, eelworm and powdery mildew.

Phlox drummondii
ANNUAL PHLOX

This bushy annual grows quickly to 15 in (38 cm) tall and half that in spread. In summer and autumn, it bears closely clustered, small, flattish flowers with 5 petals in reds, pinks, purples and creams. It has lanceolate, light green leaves and is frost resistant. 'Sternenzauber' (syn. 'Twinkle') bears star-like flowers that have pointed petals. There are dwarf strains that grow to 4 in (10 cm). **ZONES 6–10.**

Phlox drummondii 'Sternenzauber'

Phlox paniculata 'Mother of Pearl'

Phlox paniculata
SUMMER PHLOX, PERENNIAL PHLOX

This tall perennial to 3 ft (1 m) bears long-lasting flowerheads of many small flowers in summer. 'Amethyst' has violet flowers. 'Brigadier' has very deep green leaves and pink flowers suffused with orange. 'Bright Eyes' has pink flowers with red eyes. 'Eventide' has light mauve or lavender-blue flowers. 'Fujiyama' has pure white flowers on stems up to 30 in (75 cm) tall. 'Graf Zeppelin' has white flowers with pinkish red centers. 'Mother of Pearl' has white to pale pink flowers suffused pink on stems up to 30 in (75 cm) tall. 'Prince of Orange' has deep pink flowers flushed with orange on stems up to 3 ft (1 m) tall. 'Prospero' is an award-winning cultivar with white-edged, mauve flowers. 'Sir John Falstaff' has salmon-pink flowers. 'Snow Hare' has snowy white flowers. 'White Admiral' bears pure white flowers. 'Windsor' has deep pink flowers. ZONES 4–10.

Phlox paniculata 'Prince of Orange'

PHORMIUM
NEW ZEALAND FLAX

Valued for the dramatic effect of their stiff, vertical leaves, these 2 species of large, clumping plants from New Zealand grow well in most conditions. In summer, they produce panicles of flowers that attract nectar-feeding birds. The large, arching, striped leaves appear in clumps and can be anything from dark green to green-yellow. There are many cultivars with variegated or brightly colored foliage. They range in height from 3 ft (1 m) to 6 ft (1.8 m). The fiber of these flaxes has been used commercially, but is now largely confined to traditional Maori crafts.

CULTIVATION

They make splendid container plants as well as useful garden specimens in almost any climate. They are fairly frost hardy, and respond well to generous watering and permanently moist conditions. Propagate from seed or by division in spring.

Phormium cookianum 'Sundowner'

Phormium Hybrid 'Rainbow Warrior'

Phormium Hybrids

'**Rainbow Warrior**' is a recently released cultivar that makes a luxuriant clump of foliage. It has long arching and drooping leaves that are predominantly pinkish red and irregularly striped with bronze green. **ZONES 8–11.**

Phormium cookianum
syn. *Phormium colensoi*

Found throughout New Zealand in a wide range of conditions, this species has leaves 2–5 ft (0.6–1.5 m) long and up to 2½ in (6 cm) wide. Its flowers are yellow to red-brown with yellow interiors, and are carried on stiffly erect stems that extend well above the foliage clump. '**Dark Delight**' has deep wine-red leaves up to 4 ft (1.2 m) long. '**Duet**' is a 12 in (30 cm) tall dwarf cultivar with cream and green foliage. '**Maori Maiden**' (syn. 'Rainbow Maiden') is an upright grower with 3 ft (1 m) long bronze leaves striped red. '**Sundowner**' has extremely long leaves, almost 6 ft (1.8 m), that are bronze-green with cream or pinkish edges. '**Tricolor**' is an evergreen, upright perennial with bold spiky leaves prettily striped with red, yellow and green, and panicles of tubular, pale yellowish green flowers. **ZONES 8–11.**

Phormium tenax

Phormium tenax 'Variegatum'

PHUOPSIS

This is a genus of just one species, a small clump- or mat-forming perennial native to the Caucasus and northern Iran. Its whorled foliage is reminiscent of the closely related woodruff *(Galium odoratum)* with tiny, narrow leaves in starry clusters at intervals along the 6–8 in (15–20cm) stems. Its flowers are bright pink, ½ in (12 mm) long, 5-petalled tubes with a protruding style. They are massed in rounded heads of 30 to 50 blooms and open in summer.

CULTIVATION

This plant is very frost hardy and is best grown in gritty, humus-rich, moist soil in sun or part-shade. Propagate from seed or cuttings of non-flowering shoots or by division.

Phuopsis stylosa

This charming little plant is most at home in a corner of a rockery that doesn't get too hot and dry in summer. Remove the heads of small pink flowers as they deteriorate and the display should last well into autumn. **ZONES 7–9.**

Phormium tenax

The larger of the flax species, this has olive green, strap-like leaves 6–10 ft (1.8–3 m) tall in clumps about 6 ft (1.8 m) across. It grows well by the sea. Hybrids of *Phormium tenax* and *P. cookianum* are often more compact than their parents, and their foliage varies from bronze or purplish chartreuse to pink and salmon. The leaves may also be variegated with vertical stripes of 2 or more colors. **'Bronze Baby'** has wide, fiberous, copper-toned leaves with sharply pointed tips. In summer, it bears tubular, bronze-red flowers on a strong stem from the base of the clump. **'Dazzler'** has red leaves edged with plum-purple. **'Purpureum'** has stiff, pointed, plum-purple to dark copper leaves and in summer bears reddish flowers on purplish blue stems. **'Variegatum'** has foliage marked with a lighter colored stripe. **'Maori Chief'** has green and rose red-striped leaves growing to 5 ft (1.5 m). **'Tom Thumb'** has green leaves with bronze margins growing to 24 in (60 cm). **'Coffee'** is another popular cultivar. **ZONES 8–11.**

Phuopsis stylosa

Physalis alkekengi
CHINESE LANTERN, WINTER CHERRY

This 24 in (60 cm) tall perennial found from southern Europe to Japan is most notable for the vivid orange calyx that surrounds the ripening fruit, giving rise to one of its common names. The narrow leaves, about 3 in (8 cm) long, are mid-green. The flowers are small and white with yellow centers. The fruiting stems are often used fresh in floral arrangements or dried for winter decoration. *Physalis alkekengi* var. *franchetii* has minute, creamy white flowers. **ZONES 6–10.**

Physostegia virginiana

Physostegia virginiana

The showy flowers of this herbaceous perennial, which bloom in erect terminal spikes late in summer, are tubular, have 2 lips and are available in pale pink, magenta ('**Vivid**') or white. It grows to 3 ft (1 m) and give a striking display suitable for a mixed border. '**Summer Snow**' has white flowers. '**Summer Spire**' is around 24 in (60 cm) tall with deep pink flowers. **ZONES 3–10.**

PHYSALIS
GROUND CHERRY

Physalis contains about 80 species of moderately frost-hardy annuals and perennials. The genus is described in more detail in the chapter on Fruit Trees, Nut Trees and Other Fruits.

Physalis alkekengi var. *franchetii*

PHYSOSTEGIA
OBEDIENT PLANT, FALSE DRAGON HEAD

This is a North American genus of some 12 species of rhizomatous perennials. They are vigorous growers and quickly develop in spring to form clumps of unbranched, upright stems clothed in narrow, lance-shaped, long leaves with toothed edges. Plant size varies from 2 to 6 ft (0.6 to 1.8 m) tall and the leaves are 2 to 6 in (5 to 15 cm) long. From mid-summer, spikes of flowers develop at the stem tips. The flowers are tubular to bell-shaped with 2 upper lobes and 3 lower lobes. They are usually less than ½ in (12 mm) long and in shades of lavender, pink or purple and white. If a flower is moved, it will not spring back into position but will stay put, owing to a stalk with a hinge-like structure.

CULTIVATION
Obedient plants prefer moist, well-drained soil in sun or very light shade. They are very easy to grow and can be slightly invasive. Hardiness varies, though all species tolerate at least moderate frosts. Propagate from seed, from small basal cuttings or by division.

PHYTEUMA

HORNED RAMPION

This Eurasian genus of around 40 species of small perennials is instantly recognizable for the unusually structured flowerheads. The plants vary in size from 4 to 30 in (10 to 75 cm) tall. Their basal leaves are usually heart-shaped, while the upper leaves are oval to lance-shaped. The leaves are sometimes sharply toothed. The flowers are borne on rounded heads and are tubular, often swelling at the base, with scarcely open tips from which the stigma protrudes; they are usually in lavender, blue or purple shades tinged with white.

CULTIVATION

The small alpine species should be grown in light, gritty soil with added humus in a rockery or alpine house; the large species will grow in a normal perennial border, but take care that they do not become overgrown by more vigorous plants. Plant in sun or part-shade. Propagate from seed or by division where possible.

Phyteuma comosum

syn. Physoplexis comosa

Native to the European Alps, this tufted perennial rarely exceeds 4 in (10 cm) in height. It has toothed, heart-shaped leaves and heads of violet-blue flowers. A favorite of alpine enthusiasts, it requires a gritty soil with added humus for moisture retention. **ZONES 6–9.**

Phyteuma comosum

PLATYCODON

BALLOON FLOWER, CHINESE BELLFLOWER

The sole species in this genus is a semi-tuberous perennial with flower stems up to 30 in (75 cm) tall. It is native to China, Japan, Korea and eastern Siberia. In spring it forms a clump of 2–3 in (5–8 cm) long, toothed-edged, elliptical to lance-shaped light blue-green foliage. The leafy flower stems develop quickly from mid-summer, and are topped with heads of inflated buds that open into broad, bell-shaped, white, pink, blue or purple flowers up to 2 in (5 cm) wide.

Platycodon grandiflorus

On this species, balloon-like buds open out into 5-petalled summer flowers like bells, colored blue, purple, pink or white. The serrated, elliptical leaves with a silvery blue cast form in a neat clump up to 24 in (60 cm) high and half that in spread. 'Fuji Blue' is very erect to 30 in (75 cm) tall with large blue flowers. *Platycodon grandiflorus* var. *mariesii* is more compact than the species, and grows to 18 in (45 cm) tall and with glossy, lance-shaped leaves. **ZONES 4–10.**

CULTIVATION

Very frost hardy and easily grown in any well-drained soil in full sun, this plant may take a few years to become established. Propagate from seed or by division. Because it resents disturbance, divide it as little as possible.

Platycodon grandiflorus 'Fuji Blue'

POLEMONIUM

JACOB'S LADDER

This genus of around 25 species of annuals and perennials is distributed over the Arctic and temperate regions of the northern hemisphere. They form clumps of soft, bright green, ferny, pinnate leaves from which emerge upright stems topped with heads of short, tubular, bell- or funnel-shaped flowers usually in white or shades of blue or pink. Completely dormant in winter, they develop quickly in spring and are in flower by early summer.

CULTIVATION

Most species are very frost hardy and easily cultivated in moist, well-drained soil in sun or part-shade. Propagate annuals from seed and perennials from seed or cuttings of young shoots or by division. Some species self-sow freely.

Polemonium caeruleum

Polemonium caeruleum

Yellowy orange stamens provide a colorful contrast against the light purplish blue of this perennial's bell-shaped flowers when they open in summer. The flowers cluster among lance-shaped leaflets arranged in many pairs like the rungs of a ladder. The plant grows in a clump to a height and spread of up to 24 in (60 cm) or more. The stem is hollow and upright. A native of temperate Europe, it suits cooler climates. **ZONES 2–9.**

POLYGONATUM

SOLOMON'S SEAL

The 30 or so species in this genus of forest-floor perennials are distributed all over the temperate zones of the northern hemisphere. The most likely explanation of the common name is that the scars left on the creeping rhizomes, after the flowering stems die off in autumn, are thought to resemble the 6-pointed star associated with kings Solomon and David. King Solomon is thought to have first discovered the medicinal qualities of the plants, which are credited with healing wounds. The distilled sap of the rhizomes is still used in the cosmetics industry. The plants' fresh greenery and delicate white flowers make them favorites for planting in woodland gardens.

CULTIVATION

They need rich, moist soil and a shady spot. Cut back to the rhizome in autumn as they are completely dormant in winter. Propagate from seed or by division of the rhizomes in spring or autumn.

Polygonatum × hybridum

Polygonatum × hybridum

This hybrid species does best in cool to cold areas. In spring, the white, green-tipped, tubular flowers hang down from the drooping 3 ft (1 m) stems at the leaf axils. It is difficult to grow from seed. **ZONES 6–9.**

Pontederia cordata

PONTEDERIA

PICKEREL WEED

The 5 or so aquatic perennials in this genus are all native to river shallows in North and South America. They have distinctive, lance-shaped leaves and bell-shaped, usually blue flowers in terminal spikes. The Latin name has nothing to do with ponds; it honors Guilio Pontedera (1688–1757), who was a professor of botany at the University of Padua in Italy.

CULTIVATION

Easily grown, pickerel weed flourishes in almost any climate, from cold to subtropical. Plant it in full sun in up to 10 in (25 cm) of water. Only the spent flower stems need pruning, to encourage successive batches of flowers from spring to autumn. Propagate from seed or by division in spring.

Pontederia cordata

PICKEREL RUSH

This species grows on the east coast of North America. A very frost-hardy, marginal water plant, it grows to 30 in (75 cm) with a 18 in (45 cm) spread. Its tapered, heart-shaped leaves are dark green and shiny. In summer, it produces intense blue flowers in dense, terminal spikes.
ZONES 3–10.

PORTULACA

There are about 100 species of semi-succulent annuals or perennials in this genus, indigenous to the warm, dry regions of the world. The fleshy leaves vary in color from white to green or red, but it is for their cup-shaped flowers that they are grown, which are white, yellow, apricot, pink, purple or scarlet and resembling roses in form.

Portulaca grandiflora

CULTIVATION

They are easily grown in all climates. In cooler areas they should not be planted out until the danger of frost has passed. Because they are plants of the deserts they need sun, well-drained soil and only occasional watering. Propagate from seed in spring or cuttings in summer. Check for aphids.

Portulaca grandiflora
ROSE MOSS, SUN PLANT

Native to South America and one of the few annual succulents, this low-growing plant reaches 8 in (20 cm) high and spreads to 6 in (15 cm). It has small, lance-shaped, fleshy, bright green leaves like beads on their reddish stems. Its large, open flowers, usually double and borne in summer, are 3 in (8 cm) wide and come in bright colors including yellow, pink, red or orange. The flowers close at night and on cloudy days. It is suitable as a groundcover or in a rockery or border. **ZONES 10–11.**

POTENTILLA
CINQUEFOIL

This genus of approximately 500 perennials, annuals, biennials and deciduous shrubs is indigenous mainly to the northern hemisphere, from temperate to Arctic regions. Most species have 5-parted leaves (hence the common name cinquefoil), and range from only 1 in (25 mm) or so tall to about 18 in (45 cm). They bear clusters of 1 in (25 mm), rounded, bright flowers in profusion through spring and summer. Some *Potentilla* species are used medicinally: the root bark of one species is said to stop nose bleeds and even internal bleeding.

CULTIVATION

Plant all species in well-drained, fertile soil. Although the species all thrive in full sun in temperate climates, the colors of pink, red and orange cultivars will be brighter if protected from very strong sun. Perennials are generally frost hardy. Propagate by division in spring, or from seed or by division in autumn. Shrubs can be propagated from seed in autumn or from cuttings in summer.

Potentilla nepalensis

A profusion of flowers in shades of pink or apricot with cherry red centers appears throughout summer on the slim branching stems of this Himalayan perennial. With bright green, strawberry-like leaves, this species grows to 12 in (30 cm) or more high and twice that in width. **'Miss Willmott'** is an 18 in (45 cm) high cultivar with deep pink flowers. **ZONES 5–9.**

Potentilla nepalensis 'Miss Willmott'

Primula auricula

This small, central European perennial has yellow flowers in spring and furry leaves (hence the old common name, bear's ear—*auricula* means a 'little ear'). Garden varieties come in a wide range of colors. In the mid-eighteenth century a mutation resulted in flowers in shades of gray, pale green and almost black with centers covered with a white powder called 'paste'. Such flowers, called show auriculas, were once great favorites, but now have few devotees. **ZONES 3–9.**

Primula elatior

OXLIP

This European species has 2–8 in (5–20 cm) long leaves with finely hairy undersides. Its 10–30 cm (4–12 in) flower stems carry a heavy crop of long-tubed 1 in (5 mm) wide yellow to orange-yellow flowers. **ZONES 5–9.**

Primula auricula

PRIMULA

PRIMROSE

This well-known and much-loved genus of perennials has about 400 species, found throughout the temperate regions of the northern hemisphere, although most densely concentrated in China and the Himalayas. They also occur on high mountains in the tropics, extending as far south as Papua New Guinea. They are mainly rhizomatous, though some have poorly developed rhizomes and are short lived (*Primula malacoides*, for example). The foliage is usually crowded into a basal tuft or rosette, and the leaves are mostly broadest toward their tips, with toothed or scalloped margins. The flowering stems vary in form, but most often carry successive whorls or a single umbel of flowers. In a few species, the flowers are tightly crowded into a terminal head or a short spike, or they emerge singly or in small groups from among the leaves on short stalks. Flower shape, size and color vary so much that it is hard to generalize, though basically all have tubular flowers that open into a funnel or flat disc with five or more petals that are often notched at their tips.

CULTIVATION

Primulas like fertile, well-drained soil, part-shade and ample water. Propagate from seed in spring, early summer or autumn, by division or from root cuttings. Remove dead heads and old foliage after blooming. There is a primula for virtually every position and purpose.

Primula elatior

Primula japonica
JAPANESE PRIMROSE

Primula japonica

Forming a clump up to 24 in (60 cm) high and 18 in (45 cm) across, this fully frost-hardy perennial flowers in tiers on tall, sturdy stems like a candelabra. Its shiny flowers are borne in spring and early summer, and range through pink, crimson and purple to nearly pure white, usually with a distinct eye of another color. The leaves are elliptical, serrated and pale green. This species does best in a moist situation. **'Postford White'** offers a white, flattish round flower. **ZONES 5–10.**

Primula malacoides
FAIRY PRIMROSE

This is a native of China. Small, open flowers bloom in spiral masses on this frost-tender perennial, sometimes grown as an annual. The single or double flowers range from white to pink to magenta. Its oval, light green leaves and erect stem have a hairy texture. It reaches a height and spread of 12 in (30 cm) or more. **ZONES 8–11.**

Primula obconica
POISON PRIMROSE

Dense flower clusters grow in an umbellate arrangement on hairy, erect stems of this perennial. Native to China, it grows to 12 in (30 cm) high and wide and flowers from winter through spring. The yellow-eyed, flattish flowers, 1 in (25 mm) across, range from white to pink to purple. The light green leaves are elliptical and serrated. **ZONES 8–11.**

Primula,
Polyanthus Group
syn. *Primula × polyantha*

These fully frost-hardy perennials, sometimes grown as annuals, reach 12 in (30 cm) in spread and height. Large, flat, scented flowers in every color but green bloom on dense umbels from winter to spring. Polyanthus are cultivars derived from *Primula vulgaris* crossed with *P. veris*, and have been grown since the seventeenth century. **ZONES 6–10.**

Primula obconica

Primula malacoides

Primula vulgaris
ENGLISH PRIMROSE, COMMON PRIMROSE

This common European wildflower likes its cultivated conditions to resemble the cool woodland of its native environment. Low growing to 8 in (20 cm) and usually frost hardy, it produces a carpet of bright flowers in spring. The flattish flowers are pale yellow with dark eyes (but the garden forms come in every color), and bloom singly on hairy stems above rosettes of crinkled, lance-shaped, serrated leaves. Both the leaves and flowers are edible. 'Gigha White' has white flowers with yellow centers. **ZONES 6–9.**

Primula vulgaris

Primula, Polyanthus Group

Primula vulgaris 'Gigha White'

Psylliostachys suworowii

PSYLLIOSTACHYS
STATICE

This genus of 6 to 8 species of annuals was once included with *Statice (Limonium)*, but are now classified separately. Rarely over 15 in (38 cm) tall in flower, they form a clump of basal leaves, sometimes hairy, that are often deeply cut so they are almost pinnate. The tiny, papery flowers are white, pink or mauve, and borne on upright spikes that only rarely branch. They are dried or used fresh in floral arrangements.

CULTIVATION

Plant *Psylliostachys* species in moist, well-drained soil in full sun and allow to dry off after flowering. Propagate from seed.

Psylliostachys suworowii
syn. **Limonium suworowii**
RUSSIAN STATICE, RAT'S TAIL STATICE

Native to Iran, Afghanistan and central Asia, *Psylliostachys suworowii* has sticky 2–6 in (5–15 cm) leaves and relatively large pink flowers which are borne on wavy, 6 in (15 cm) spikes. **ZONES 6–10.**

PULMONARIA
LUNGWORT

This is a Eurasian genus that consists of 14 species of perennial, rhizomatous, forget-me-not-like plants. The common name refers to their former medicinal use, not their appearance. The most common species are low, spreading plants 6–10 in (15–25 cm) high with a spread of 24 in (60 cm) or more. The simple, oval to lance-shaped leaves are sometimes slightly downy and often spotted silver-white. From very early spring, small deep blue, pink or white flowers open from pink or white buds.

CULTIVATION
These woodland plants are easily grown in cool, moist, humus-rich soil in light shade. All species are very frost hardy. Propagation is normally from seed or cuttings or by division.

Pulmonaria saccharata 'Highdown'

PULSATILLA
PASQUE FLOWER

This genus contains 30 species of spring-flowering, deciduous perennials from Eurasia and North America. They are closely related to anemones and were once included in that genus. They form mounds of very finely divided, almost ferny foliaged rosettes. The leaves and flower stems are covered with downy silver-gray hairs. The general effect is that of a hairy anemone with simple large flowers. The flower color range includes white, pink, purple and red.

CULTIVATION
Most often grown in rockeries, these very frost-hardy plants are also suitable for borders and troughs and prefer a moist, gritty, scree soil in sun or part-shade. They do best with cool to cold winters and cool summers and tend to be short lived in mild areas. Propagate from seed or by division.

Pulmonaria angustifolia
BLUE COWSLIP, BLUE LUNGWORT

Dark blue flowers, sometimes tinged pink, bloom throughout spring on this frost-resistant European, deciduous perennial. The flower-heads have a 5-lobed tubular shape and are held above basal rosettes of mid-green foliage. The plant grows to a height and spread of 10–12 in (25–30 cm). The cultivar 'Blaues Meer' produces an extra generous display of big, very bright blue flowers. **ZONES 3–9.**

Pulmonaria saccharata
JERUSALEM SAGE, BETHLEHEM SAGE

This evergreen perennial has heavily spotted, hairy, 10 in (25 cm) leaves and has given rise to numerous cultivars with flowers in white and all shades of pink and blue. 'Highdown' is one of the more popular cultivars. It is 12 in (30 cm) tall with silver-frosted leaves and pendulous clusters of blue flowers. The cultivars of the **Argentea Group** have silver leaves and red flowers that age to dark purple. **ZONES 3–9.**

Pulsatilla vulgaris 'Alba'

Pulsatilla vulgaris
syns Anemone pulsatilla, A. vulgaris

Nodding, 6-petalled flowers bloom in spring on this species from Europe. The yellow centers of the flowers are a stark color contrast to the petals, which can range through white, pink and red to purple. The finely divided leaves are pale green and very hairy. Reaching 10 in (25 cm) in height and spread, the species makes a wonderful rock-garden plant. Avoid disturbing the roots. There are a number of popular cultivars available. 'Alba' has pure white flowers and needs protection from sun and frost for the flowers to last. 'Rode Klokke' (syn. 'Rote Glocke') is a free-flowering form with dark red blooms. 'Rubra' has purplish red or rusty flowers. **ZONES 5–9.**

Ramonda nathaliae

This species, which reaches a height and spread of 4 in (10 cm), bears panicles of flat, 4-petalled, deep purple flowers with orange-yellow centers. The mid- to dark green leaves, hairier on the undersides than on top, grow to 2 in (5 cm) in length. **ZONES 6–9.**

RAMONDA

This genus from Spain, the Pyrenees and the Balkans contains 3 species of evergreen perennials that have rosettes of hairy, usually wrinkled leaves with toothed, wavy edges. They do well in rock gardens or even in cracks in stone walls. They are also grown for their brightly colored, 4- to 5-petalled flowers, which appear in late spring and early summer.

CULTIVATION

Excessive water in the leaf rosettes may cause rotting, so these plants are best grown on an angle in part-shade and very well-drained, humus-rich soil. Propagate from seed or cuttings.

Ramonda nathaliae

Ranunculus gramineus

Ranunculus gramineus

With hairy, bluish green leaves shaped like grass, this clump-forming perennial from south-western Europe has a compact spread and grows 18 in (45 cm) tall. In late spring and early summer it produces yellow, cup-shaped flowers. Plant it in rich soil. **ZONES 7–10.**

RANUNCULUS

BUTTERCUP

This genus of some 400 annuals and perennials is distributed throughout temperate regions worldwide. They are grown for their colorful flowers, which are bowl- or cup-shaped, 5-petalled and yellow, white, red, orange or pink. The name derives from the Latin for 'frog', due to the tendency of some species to grow in bogs or shallow water. Two species of buttercups are popular folk cures for arthritis, sciatica, rheumatism and skin conditions, including the removal of warts.

CULTIVATION

Most species of *Ranunculus* are easy to grow and thrive in well-drained soil, cool, moist conditions and sunny or shady locations. They are mostly fully frost hardy. Propagate from fresh seed or by division in spring or autumn. Water well through the growing season and allow to dry out after flowering. Keep an eye out for powdery mildew and for attacks by slugs, snails and aphids.

Ranunculus lyallii

Ranunculus lyallii

MT COOK LILY, GIANT MOUNTAIN BUTTER-
CUP, MOUNTAIN LILY

Native to New Zealand's South
Island, this thicket-forming
perennial grows to 3 ft (1 m)
tall. Its broad, leathery leaves
can reach 8 in (20 cm) wide
and are lustrous deep green.
Glossy, white, cup-shaped
flowers appear in clusters in
summer. Moderately frost
hardy, this species can sometimes be a bit difficult to
grow. **ZONES 7–9.**

Reseda odorata

COMMON MIGNONETTE

From northern Africa, this
moderately fast-growing
annual is renowned for the
strong fragrance of its flowers.
The conical heads of tiny
greenish flowers with touches
of red, have dark orange
stamens, but are otherwise
unspectacular. They appear
from summer to early autumn.
The plants grow to 24 in
(60 cm) high and about half
that in spread. **ZONES 6–10.**

RESEDA

MIGNONETTE

This genus from Asia, Africa and Europe contains about 60
species of erect or spreading, branching annuals and perennials.
They bear star-shaped, greenish white or greenish yellow flowers
in spike-like racemes from spring to autumn. These are attractive to bees. Mignonette used to be a favorite with perfumers
and the plant is still cultivated in France for its essential oils.

CULTIVATION
Plant in full sun or part-
shade in well-drained,
fertile, preferably alkaline
soil. Deadheading will prolong flowering. Propagate
from seed in late winter.

Reseda odorata

Rheum palmatum
CHINESE RHUBARB

This species bears panicles of small, dark red to creamy green flowers that open early in summer. It has deep green leaves with decoratively cut edges, and reaches up to 8 ft (2.4 m) in height and 6 ft (1.8 m) in spread. 'Atrosanguineum' has dark pink flowers and crimson leaves that fade to dark green.
ZONES 6–10.

Rheum palmatum 'Atrosanguineum'

RHEUM

This genus contains 50 species of rhizomatous perennials, including the edible rhubarb and several ornamental plants. From eastern Europe and central Asia to the Himalayas and China, they are grown for their striking appearance and for their large basal leaves, which are coarsely toothed and have prominent midribs and veins. The minute, star-shaped flowers appear in summer.

CULTIVATION
These very frost-hardy plants prefer full sun or part-shade and deep, moist, humus-rich soil. Propagate from seed or by division, and watch out for slugs and crown rot.

RHODIOLA

Similar to *Hylotelephium* and the larger *Sedum* species, this genus includes around 50 species of fleshy leafed, rhizomatous perennials widely distributed in the northern hemisphere. The plants are composed of a mass of thickened stems clothed with simple, often toothed, gray-green leaves. The individual, star-shaped flowers, in shades of yellow, orange, red, occasionally green or white, appear in dense, rounded heads.

CULTIVATION
Most *Rhodiola* species are frost-hardy and undemanding. Plant in an area that remains moist in summer but which is not boggy in winter. A sunny rock garden is ideal. Propagate by division in spring or take cuttings of the young growth. They may be attacked by aphids.

Rhodiola kirilowii

Rhodiola kirilowii
syn. *Sedum kirilowii*

Found from central Asia to Mongolia, this species has heavy, branched rhizomes from which develop stout, upright stems that grow to 3 ft (1 m) tall. The narrow to lance-shaped leaves are unusually large, sometimes over 10 ft (3 m) long. The attractive flowers are yellow-green to rusty red, and open from early summer.
ZONES 5–10.

Rhodiola rosea

syn. Sedum rosea

ROSEROOT

The tightly massed heads of pink buds produced by this perennial in late spring or early summer open to small, star-shaped flowers in pale purple, green or yellow. The saw-edged, elliptical leaves are fleshy. This species grows into a clump 12 in (30 cm) in height and spread. The name comes from the scent of the fleshy roots, used in making perfume. It is a highly sociable species that occurs right around the temperate northern hemisphere. **ZONES 2–9.**

Rhodiola stephanii

syn. Sedum stephanii

This rhizomatous, branching species from eastern Siberia has bright yellow-green, deeply toothed leaves. The flowering stems, to 10 in (25 cm) in length, bear their creamy white flowers in summer. **ZONES 5–10.**

Rhodiola stephanii

Rhodiola rosea

ROMNEYA

TREE POPPY

The 2 species in this genus from North America are summer-flowering, woody based perennials and deciduous subshrubs. They have blue-green foliage composed of alternate leaves and poppy-like, 6-petalled flowers with glossy yellow stamens.

CULTIVATION

They prefer a warm, sunny position and fertile, well-drained soil. They are difficult to establish (although once established they may become invasive), and they resent transplanting. Protect the roots in very cold areas in winter. Propagate from seed or from cuttings.

Romneya coulteri

Romneya coulteri

CALIFORNIA TREE POPPY, MATILIJA POPPY

This shrubby Californian perennial produces large, sweetly scented, poppy-like white flowers highlighted with fluffy gold stamens. The silvery green leaves are deeply divided, their edges sparsely fringed with hairs. Fully frost hardy, it forms a bush up to 8 ft (2.4 m) high with a spread of 3 ft (1 m) *Romneya coulteri* var. *trichocalyx* has pointed, rather bristly sepals. **ZONES 7–10.**

Rudbeckia fulgida var. *s.* 'Goldsturm'

RUDBECKIA
CONEFLOWER

This popular genus from North America has about 15 species of annuals, biennials and perennials. The plants in this genus have bright, daisy-like, composite flowers with prominent central cones (hence the common name). The single, double or semi-double flowers are usually in tones of yellow. The cones, however, vary from green through rust, purple and black. Species range in height from 24 in (60 cm) to 10 ft (3 m). A number of rudbeckias make excellent cut flowers.

CULTIVATION
Coneflowers prefer loamy, moisture-retentive soil in full sun or part-shade. Propagate from seed or by division in spring or autumn. They are moderately to fully frost hardy. Aphids may be a problem.

Rudbeckia fulgida
BLACK-EYED SUSAN, ORANGE CONEFLOWER

This rhizomatous perennial, to 3 ft (1 m) tall, has branched stems, mid-green, slightly hairy leaves with prominent veins, and daisy-like, orange-yellow flowers with dark brown centers. *Rudbeckia fulgida* var. *deamii* has very hairy stems and is free flowering; *R. f.* var. *speciosa* has elliptic to lance-shaped basal leaves and toothed stem leaves; *R. f.* var. *sullivantii* 'Goldsturm' (syn. *R.* 'Goldsturm') grows to 24 in (60 cm) tall and has crowded stems that bear lanceolate leaves. ZONES 3–10.

Rudbeckia hirta
BLACK-EYED SUSAN

The flowerheads on this biennial or short-lived perennial are bright yellow, with central cones of purplish brown, and its lanceolate leaves are mid-green and hairy. It reaches 12–36 in (30–90 cm) tall, with a spread of 12 in (30 cm). 'Irish Eyes' is noteworthy for its olive green center. 'Marmalade' has large flowerheads with golden-orange ray florets. Many dwarf cultivars such as 'Becky Mixed' are available in a range of colors from pale lemon to orange and red. They are usually treated as annuals. ZONES 3–10.

Rudbeckia laciniata
CUTLEAF CONEFLOWER

This species is a splendid summer-flowering perennial that can reach 10 ft (3 m) tall, though 6 ft (1.8 m) is more usual. The drooping ray florets give the flowerhead an informal elegance. 'Golden Glow' is a striking, if somewhat floppy, double cultivar. 'Goldquelle' grows to around 30 in (75 cm) tall and has large, bright yellow, double flowers. ZONES 3–10.

Rudbeckia hirta 'Irish Eyes'

Rudbeckia laciniata 'Goldquelle'

SALPIGLOSSIS

These species from the southern Andes are not seen very often in gardens as they can be tricky to grow, but patient gardeners who live in mild climates with fairly cool summers will be rewarded by a short but beautiful display of flowers like petunias (they are related). They come in rich shades of crimson, scarlet, orange, blue, purple and white, all veined and laced with gold. There are 2 species of annuals and perennials providing color in borders or as greenhouse plants in cold climates.

CULTIVATION

Plant in full sun in rich, well-drained soil. Deadhead regularly. *Salpiglossis* species are best sown in early spring directly in the place they are to grow, as seedlings do not always survive transplanting. They are prone to attack by aphids.

Salpiglossis sinuata

SALVIA

SAGE

The largest genus of the mint family, *Salvia* consists of as many as 900 species of annuals, perennials and soft-wooded shrubs, distributed through most parts of the world except very cold regions and tropical rainforests. Their tubular, 2-lipped flowers are very distinctive. The lower lip is flat but the upper lip helmet- or boat-shaped; the calyx is also 2-lipped and may be colored. The flowers come in a wide range of colors, including some of the brightest blues and scarlets of any plants, though yellows are rare. Many beautiful sage species are grown as garden plants, including some with aromatic leaves grown primarily as culinary herbs, but even these can be grown for their ornamental value alone. The genus name goes back to Roman times and derives from the Latin *salvus*, 'safe' or 'well', referring to the supposed healing properties of *Salvia officinalis*.

CULTIVATION

Most of the shrubby Mexican and South American species will tolerate only light frosts, but some of the perennials are more frost-hardy. Sages generally do best planted in full sun in well drained, light-textured soil with adequate watering in summer. Propagate from seed in spring, cuttings in early summer, or division of rhizomatous species at almost any time. Foliage of many species is attacked by snails, slugs and caterpillars.

Salpiglossis sinuata

PAINTED TONGUE

Offering a variety of flower colors including red, orange, yellow, blue and purple, this annual from Peru and Argentina blooms in summer and early autumn. The 2 in (5 cm) wide, heavily veined flowers are like small flaring trumpets, while the lanceolate leaves are light green. A fast grower, it reaches a height of 18–24 in (45–60 cm) and a spread of at least 15 in (38 cm). It is frost tender and dislikes dry conditions. **ZONES 8–11.**

Salvia coccinea 'Coral Nymph'

Salvia coccinea

RED TEXAS SAGE

This compact, bushy, short-lived perennial from South America is treated as an annual in colder climates. It has small mid-green leaves and an abundance of scarlet flowers from early summer to late autumn. It is normally grown in full sun, but when placed in light shade and protected from frost it can survive another season or two. Many forms are known, including a pure white and a lovely salmon pink and white bicolor. 'Coral Nymph' is a compact form with coral-pink flowers; 'Lady in Red' is also compact, growing just 15 in (38 cm) tall with bright red flowers. **ZONES 8–11.**

Salvia involucrata 'Bethellii'

Salvia splendens
SCARLET SAGE

This native of Brazil, which is grown as an annual, produces dense terminal spikes of scarlet flowers in summer through early autumn. The leaves are toothed and elliptical. It grows 3–4 ft (1–1.2 m) tall and wide. In hotter climates, give some shade; it is moderately frost hardy. '**Salsa Burgundy**' has deep burgundy flowers, while '**Van Houttei**' has a deep dull red calyx with large lighter red flowers; both prefer a little shade. **ZONES 9–12.**

Salvia sclarea

Salvia involucrata
ROSELEAF SAGE

This is a charming tall perennial that remains evergreen in mild climates but even so, is best cut back to the ground every year to promote flowering. From the highlands of central Mexico, it has erect cane-like stems to about 5 ft (1.5 m) high and broad, long-stalked leaves that often develop red veining. The loose flower spikes terminate in groups of large mauve to magenta bracts, which are shed one by one to reveal a trio of developing flowers of the same or deeper color; each flower is up to 2 in (5 cm) long, tubular but swollen in the middle, and the small upper lip is covered in velvety hairs. It blooms over a long summer–autumn season, and appreciates sun and rich, well drained soil. In the UK, it has been known as '**Bethellii**', a superior selection from the wild. **ZONES 9–10.**

Salvia splendens 'Salsa Burgundy'

Salvia sclarea
BIENNIAL CLARY, CLARY SAGE

This native of southern Europe and Syria is a biennial and grows 3 ft (1 m) tall. Clary sage has been used medicinally and as a flavoring for beverages. Moderately fast growing and erect, it has long, loose, terminal spikes of tubular, greenish white tinged with purple flowers in summer, and velvety, heart-shaped leaves. *Salvia sclarea* var. *turkestanica* has pink stems and white, pink-flecked flowers. **ZONES 5–10.**

Salvia × sylvestris 'Ostfriesland'

Salvia viridis

This is an erect annual or biennial plant with oval or oblong leaves up to 2 in (5 cm) long. The green or purple calyx bears ½ in (12 mm) flowers which may be white to lilac to purple. It occurs around the Mediterranean and flowers in summer. There are several named color forms available. **ZONES 7–11.**

Salvia viridis

Salvia × sylvestris

This leafy perennial to 12–36 in (30–90 cm) high is a hybrid between *Salvia pratensis* and *S. nemorosa*. It has hairy oblong heart-shaped leaves 2–4 in (5–10 cm) long. The summer flowers are purplish violet in long-branched heads. It comes from western Asia and Europe but is naturalized in North America. There are many cultivars, some of uncertain origin. **'Blauhügel'** ('Blue Mound') is a compact grower with clear blue flowers; **'Ostfriesland'** ('East Friesland') is deep purple; **'Mainacht'** is lower growing with blackish purple tones; and **'Wesuwe'** is an early bloomer with dark violet flowers. **ZONES 5–10.**

SARRACENIA
PITCHER PLANT

The *Sarracenia* genus consists of about 8 insectivorous evergreen or perennial species from the eastern part of North America; although they cover a wide area, they prefer to grow in peat bogs or in the sodden ground at the edges of pools. All the species have curious, many-petalled flowers whose styles develop into a sort of umbrella that shelters the stamens. The flowers are usually purple-red or greenish yellow or a blend of these colors, and the same tints are found in the modified leaves, called pitchers, which are nearly as decorative as the flowers. Insects are attracted to the foliage colors and slide down the slippery sides, drowning in the rainwater that accumulates at the bottom.

CULTIVATION
These moderately to fully frost-hardy plants need sun or part-shade and moist, peaty soil. Keep very wet during the growth period, and cool and moist in winter. Propagate from seed or by division in spring.

Sarracenia leucophylla

Saxifraga stolonifera

syn. **Saxifraga sarmentosa**

MOTHER OF THOUSANDS, STRAWBERRY
BEGONIA

Geranium-like leaves are a
feature of this perennial,
which has rounded, glossy
leaves that are olive green
with silver veins, purplish
pink on the undersides. In
spring through early summer,
oddly petalled white flowers
are borne in delicate panicles
on thin, erect stalks. One petal
on the tiny flowers seems to
outgrow its 4 companion
petals. Frost tender, it grows
to a height of 6–8 in (15–
20 cm) and spreads to 12 in
(30 cm) by runners. 'Tricolor'
has deeply cut, green leaves
patterned with red and white.
ZONES 5–10.

Sarracenia leucophylla

syn. **Sarracenia drummondii**

This semi-evergreen perennial bears purple-red flowers in spring
and has erect, slender pitchers up to 4 ft (1.2 m) long with
narrow wings and erect lids with wavy margins. These are
usually white and have light purple-red netting, gradually
merging into green bases. **ZONES 7–11.**

SAXIFRAGA

SAXIFRAGE

Both the foliage and blooms on these perennials, biennials and
annuals are equally appealing. The genus comprises some 440
species of evergreens and semi-evergreens. Their natural territory
includes temperate, alpine and subarctic regions, mostly in the
northern hemisphere, but many garden hybrids have been cultivated. They serve well in rock gardens and as groundcover. The
flowers are mostly white, sometimes spotted with pink, but
other colors are also available. The genus name combines two
Latin terms, 'rock' and 'to break', suggestive of either the hardiness of their rooting system or their reputed medicinal effect on
bladder stones.

CULTIVATION

Soil and light requirements vary greatly depending on the species;
they also vary from being very frost hardy to marginally frost
hardy. Propagate from seed in autumn, by division or from
rooted offsets in winter.

Saxifraga paniculata

syn. **Saxifraga aizoon**

LIVELONG SAXIFRAGE

This summer-flowering evergreen perennial from central Europe
bears terminal clusters of 5-petalled white, pale pink or yellow
flowers, often with spots of reddish purple. The bluish green
leaves form a rosette below the flower stems. *Saxifraga
paniculata* grows to a height and spread of 8–10 in (20–25 cm).
Grow in full sun in well-drained, alkaline soil. Many forms have
variations in flower
size and color. 'Rosea'
has bright pink
flowers. 'Minima' has
very small foliage and
flowers. *Saxifraga
paniculata* var.
baldensis has very
small rosettes of leaves
and red-tinged flower
stems. **ZONES 3–9.**

Saxifraga p. var. *baldensis*

Scabiosa columbaria 'Butterfly Blue'

SCABIOSA

SCABIOUS, PINCUSHION FLOWER

This genus of 80 annuals, biennials and perennials from temperate climates, bears tall-stemmed, honey-scented flowers ideal for cutting. The blooms, bearing multiple florets with protruding filaments giving a pincushion effect, range from white, yellow, red, blue and mauve to deep purple.

CULTIVATION

Best in full sun in well-drained, alkaline soil. Propagate annuals from seed in spring, and perennials from cuttings in summer, seed in autumn or by division in early spring.

Scabiosa caucasica

This perennial bears summer flowerheads in many hues with centers often in a contrasting color. It reaches a height and spread of 18–24 in (45–60 cm). 'Clive Greaves' has lilac-blue flowers; 'Miss Wilmott' has white flowers; 'Staefa' is a strong grower with blue flowers; and 'Mrs Isaac House' has creamy white flowers. ZONES 4–10.

Scabiosa columbaria

This biennial or perennial grows to 24 in (60 cm) tall with a spread of 3 ft (1 m). Slender, erect, hairy stems produce globular heads of reddish purple to lilac-blue flowers in 1½ in (35 mm) wide heads during summer and autumn. 'Butterfly Blue' is a lower growing, dense, fuzzy leafed cultivar with lavender-blue pincushion flowers over a very long period. ZONES 6–10.

Scabiosa caucasica 'Staefa'

SCAEVOLA

FAN FLOWER

This genus from Australia and the Pacific region contains 96 species of mainly temperate origin. Most are evergreen perennials, shrubs, subshrubs and small trees, with a number of groundcovering varieties that have proved adaptable to a wide range of garden conditions, including seaside gardens. Most have leaves that are fleshy, often hairy and occasionally succulent, borne on stout, sometimes brittle stems. Fan-shaped flowers, while generally fairly small at ½–1 in (12–25 mm) across, are profuse and are held on the plant for long periods. The flower color ranges from white to blue, mauve and deep purple.

CULTIVATION

Species of *Scaevola* tolerate a wide range of soils but prefer them light and well drained; they do best in sun or part-shade. Propagate from seed or cuttings in spring or summer.

Scaevola aemula

syn. *Scaevola humilis*

FAIRY FAN FLOWER

The thick, coarsely toothed, dark green leaves on this perennial herb grow along spreading stems to form ground-hugging cover not more than 18 in (45 cm) high with a similar spread. Spikes of large, purple-blue flowers with yellow throats continue to elongate as new flowers open, blooming from early spring to late summer. Native to the sandy coast and near coastal woodlands of Australia, it resists dry conditions, frost and salt spray. 'Blue Wonder' bears lilac-blue flowers almost continuously in great profusion. **ZONES 9–11.**

Scaevola aemula

SCHIZANTHUS
POOR MAN'S ORCHID, BUTTERFLY FLOWER

This genus contains 12 to 15 species of annuals from the Chilean mountains. Although the blooms do look like miniature orchids, *Schizanthus* are in fact related to petunias. They come in shades of pink, mauve, red, purple and white, all with gold-speckled throats. They grow to about 3 ft (1 m) high and 12 in (30 cm) wide. Most of the flowers seen in gardens are hybrids, and give a colorful display over a short spring to summer season.

CULTIVATION

These subtropical mountain plants do not like extremes of heat or cold. They grow best outdoors in a mild, frost-free climate. In colder climates they need the controlled, even temperature of a greenhouse. Grow in full sun in fertile, well-drained soil and pinch out growing tips of young plants to ensure bushy growth. Propagate from seed in summer or autumn.

Schizanthus × wisetonensis

Schizanthus × wisetonensis

This erect species bears tubular to flared, 2-lipped, white, blue, pink or reddish brown flowers often flushed with yellow from spring to summer. It has lance-shaped, light green leaves and grows to 18 in (45 cm) high with a spread of 12 in (30 cm). Most garden strains are derived from this species. **ZONES 7–11.**

Scutellaria indica

This is an upright, slowly spreading perennial around 12 in (30 cm) high with light gray-green oval leaves and clumped heads of soft blue-gray, tubular flowers. *Scutellaria indica* var. *parvifolia* (syn. *S. i.* var. *japonica*) is lower growing to 4 in (10 cm) and clumps more rapidly. It has crowded heads of blue-mauve, shortish tubular flowers in late spring. If deadheaded immediately it will flower again in late summer. **ZONES 5–10.**

SCUTELLARIA
SKULLCAP, HELMET FLOWER

Scutellaria indica var. *parvifolia*

The name of this genus comes from the Latin *scutella*, meaning a small shield or cup, which is a rough description of the pouch of the upper calyx. There are some 300 known species that consist mainly of summer-flowering perennials, most on a rhizomatous root system, though a few are annuals and rarely subshrubs. Most species occur in temperate regions throughout the northern hemisphere.

CULTIVATION

They are easily grown in full sun in most reasonable garden soil. None would be happy with parched soil in summer, but they are content with ordinary watering throughout dry weather. Propagation is by division in winter or from seed sown fresh in autumn. Cuttings may be taken in summer.

SIDALCEA
PRAIRIE MALLOW, CHECKER MALLOW

These 20 to 25 species of upright annuals or perennials with lobed, rounded leaves are found in open grasslands and mountain forests of western USA. Pink, purple or white flowers have a silky appearance and feel, and last well when cut.

CULTIVATION

They prefer cool summers and mild winters in good, deep, moisture-retentive soil. They will tolerate a little shade in hot climates. If cut back after flowering they will produce a second flush of blooms. Propagate from seed or by division.

Sidalcea malviflora

Sidalcea malviflora
CHECKERBLOOM

This erect perennial plant grows to 4 ft (1.2 m) tall with spreading fiberous roots. It has lobed leaves and loose heads of pink or white flowers resembling hollyhocks during spring and summer. Most cultivars included under this name are now believed to be hybrids with other species. **ZONES 6–10.**

Silene armeria

SILENE
CAMPION, CATCHFLY

This genus contains over 500 species of annuals, biennials and deciduous or evergreen perennials. They all feature 5-petalled summer flowers, baggy calyces and a multitude of small, elliptical, often silky leaves. Some of the species do well potted and others make good groundcovers, with numerous stems forming a mound. Many of the weedier species open their flowers only at night, when they can be quite pretty, though all that is seen during the day are shrivelled petals. Some exude gum from their stems; passing flies get stuck to this, hence the common name catchfly.

CULTIVATION

Widely distributed throughout temperate and cold climates of the northern hemisphere, these marginally to fully frost-hardy plants like fertile, well-drained soil and full or part-sun. Propagate from seed in spring or early autumn or from cuttings in spring.

Silene armeria

This European annual or biennial has pink, bell-shaped flowers with 5 notched petals. Growing to a height of 12 in (30 cm) with a spread of 6 in (15 cm), it has slender, erect, branching stems and linear leaves. **ZONES 6–10.**

Silene uniflora

syn. *Silene vulgaris* subsp. *maritima*

SEA CAMPION

This deep-rooted perennial bears a multitude of white flowers like pompons on branched stems in spring or summer. Its calyces are greenish and balloon like, and its lanceolate leaves have a grayish cast. Reaching about 8 in (20 cm) in height and spread, it can be grown on top of walls, in beds or containers and grows wild on cliffs along the European seaboard. **'Flore Pleno'** has double white flowers with deeply cut petals. **ZONES 3–10.**

Silene uniflora 'Flore Pleno'

Sisyrinchium graminoides

syn. *Sisyrinchium angustifolium*

BLUE-EYED GRASS

This semi-evergreen perennial blooms in spring, producing terminal clusters of small pale to dark purple flowers like irises, with yellow throats. The stalks are flattened and winged. **ZONES 3–10.**

Sisyrinchium striatum

syn. *Phaiophleps nigricans*

SATIN FLOWER

Long, narrow and sword-shaped, the leaves on this fully frost-hardy, evergreen perennial are gray-green. In summer it bears slender spikes of small cream flowers, striped purple. The species, which originates in Chile and Argentina, grows 18–24 in (45–60 cm) high with a 12 in (30 cm) spread. There is also an attractive variegated form. **ZONES 8–10.**

Sisyrinchium graminoides

SISYRINCHIUM

The genus includes 90 marginally to fully frost-hardy species of annuals and rhizomatous perennials. They often self-destruct in seasons of prolific blooming, because the flower stem kills off the leaf stem from which it sprouts.

Sisyrinchium striatum

CULTIVATION

Establish them in poor to moderately fertile, moist but well-drained soil. Although tolerant of part-shade, they prefer sun. They readily self-seed, otherwise they can be propagated by division in late summer.

Soldanella montana

Soldanella montana

Growing to about 12 in (30 cm) tall, this mound-forming species comes from the Alps but prefers the alpine woodlands to the bare rocks higher up. It flowers in early spring, often before the snows have quite melted, producing long, pendent, bell-shaped, lavender-blue blossoms with fringed mouths. It has shallow-toothed, rounded leaves. **ZONES 6–9.**

SOLDANELLA
SNOWBELL

The soldanellas are elegant relatives of the primrose. They come from the mountains of Europe and flower at the end of spring. There are 10 species of evergreen perennials, all rather alike and interbreeding freely both in the wild and in gardens much to the irritation of those who like to be certain of their plants' names. They have nodding to pendent purple to white flowers and leathery leaves and are good plants for rock gardens and tubs.

CULTIVATION
These plants are mostly fully frost hardy, although the flower buds may be destroyed by frost. They need part-shade and humus-rich, well-drained, peaty soil. Propagate from seed in spring or by division in late summer. Watch out for slugs.

SOLIDAGO

GOLDENROD

The goldenrods are a genus of about 100 species of woody based perennials, almost all indigenous to the meadows and prairies of North America, with a few species in South America and Eurasia. They are related to the asters and, like them, flower in autumn. Their effect is quite different, however, as the individual flowers are very much smaller and are bright yellow. Most of the species are too weedy to be allowed into even the wildest garden, but some are worth cultivating for their big flower clusters and there are some very attractive hybrids.

CULTIVATION

These fully frost-hardy plants grow well in sun or shade in any fertile, well-drained soil. Most species self-seed, or they can be propagated by dividing the clumps in autumn or spring.

Solidago 'Golden Wings'

This perennial grows to 5 ft (1.5 m) high with a spread of 3 ft (1 m). It has downy, lance-shaped leaves with serrated margins, and produces small, bright yellow flowers in feathery panicles early in autumn. **ZONES 5–10.**

Solidago virgaurea

This 3 ft (1 m) tall plant from Europe blooms in summer and autumn, with dense heads of yellow flowers. *Solidago virgaurea* subsp. *minuta* only grows to 4 in (10 cm) high. **ZONES 5–10.**

Solidago virgaurea

Solidago 'Golden Wings'

Stachys byzantina 'Cotton Boll'

STACHYS

BETONY, WOUNDWORT, HEDGE NETTLE

This genus of the mint family, contains about 300 species of annuals, perennials and evergreen shrubs. They have long been used in herb gardens and many of them have supposed medicinal value. They come from a range of habitats mostly in northern temperate regions. Many species are aromatic, and most are attractive to bees and butterflies. They bear tubular, 2-lipped, purple, red, pink, yellow or white flowers.

CULTIVATION

They all like well-drained, moderately fertile soil in full sun. Propagate from seed or cuttings or by division.

Stachys byzantina

syns *Stachys lanata, S. olympica*

LAMBS' EARS, LAMBS' TAILS, LAMBS' TONGUES

The leaves give this perennial its common names: they are lance-shaped and have the same white, downy feel of a lamb. Unfortunately, the leaves turn to mush in very cold, humid or wet weather. It makes a good groundcover or border plant, growing 12–18 in

(30–45 cm) high, with a 24 in (60 cm) spread. Mauve-pink flowers appear in summer. **'Silver Carpet'** seldom flowers, remaining more compact than the species; **'Cotton Boll'** (syn. 'Sheila McQueen') has flowers that look like cottonwool balls; **'Primrose Heron'** has yellowish green leaves; and **'Big Ears'** (syn. 'Countess Helen von Stein') is a large-growing cultivar that bears tall spikes of purple flowers. **ZONES 5–10.**

Stachys byzantina 'Big Ears'

Stachys coccinea

Stachys coccinea
SCARLET HEDGE NETTLE

This long-flowering perennial native to southwest USA and Mexico bears red flowers, although pink and white forms are now available. The flowers are almost irresistible to humming-birds. Flowering continues from spring through autumn on plants that grow 12–36 in (30–90 cm) tall and 18 in (45 cm) wide. **ZONES 6–10.**

Stachys officinalis
BISHOP'S WORT, WOOD BETONY

This stately erect perennial from Europe grows to 3 ft (1 m) in height. The basal rosette leaves are oblong or heart-shaped. The red-purple flowers are held in dense spikes, although white and pink forms also occur. **ZONES 5–10.**

Stachys officinalis

STOKESIA

STOKES' ASTER

This genus of a single perennial species native to the southeastern states of the USA was named after Englishman Dr Jonathan Stokes (1755–1831). One of the most attractive late-flowering perennials, it grows to about 18 in (45 cm) high and flowers from late summer to autumn if the spent flower stems are promptly removed. It is very good for cutting.

CULTIVATION

Plant in full sun or part-shade and fertile, well-drained soil. Water well in summer. Propagate from seed in autumn or by division in spring.

Stokesia laevis

syn. *Stokesia cyanea*

This fully frost-hardy perennial has evergreen rosettes of narrow, mid-green, basal and divided leaves. The blue-mauve or white blooms have a shaggy appearance reminiscent of cornflowers, and are borne freely on erect stems. **ZONES 7–10.**

Stokesia laevis

Symphytum asperum

Symphytum asperum

PRICKLY COMFREY

This thick-rooted perennial from Europe, Turkey and Iran has oval, heart-shaped or oblong leaves covered with stiff prickly hairs. The flower stems grow up to 5 ft (1.5 m) tall and are openly branched with few hairs. There are many flowers in the head; they open a rose color, soon changing to lilac or blue, and are ½ in (12 mm) long. It has become naturalized in North America where it has been grown as a fodder plant. **ZONES 5–10.**

SYMPHYTUM

COMFREY

This genus comprises 25 to 35 species of hairy perennials from damp and shaded places in Europe, North Africa and western Asia. They grow rapidly and may become invasive in the garden. The leaves are alternate and rather crowded at the base of the plant. The flowers are held in shortly branched heads of pink, blue, white or cream. Each flower consists of a tube terminating in 5 triangular lobes.

CULTIVATION

They are easily grown in sun or part-shade in moist, well-dug soil with added manure. Propagate from seed, cuttings, or by division.

Symphytum caucasicum

This is a smaller, softly hairy branched perennial growing 24 in (60 cm) tall. The leaves are hairy on both sides and oval to oblong up to 8 in (20 cm) long; they run back a short way down the stem. The flowers are at first red-purple, changing to blue, and ¾ in (18 mm) long in terminal paired heads. **ZONES 5–10.**

Symphytum caucasicum

Symphytum 'Goldsmith'

syn. Symphytum 'Jubilee'

'Goldsmith' grows to 12 in (30 cm) and has leaves edged and blotched with cream and gold; the flowers are blue, pink or white. **ZONES 5–10.**

Symphytum 'Goldsmith'

Symphytum officinale

COMMON COMFREY, BONESET, HEALING HERB

This robust, clump-forming species from Europe and western Asia grows to 5 ft (1.5 m) with large, lance-shaped leaves and clusters of pretty white, pink or mauve pendent flowers in spring and summer. It is used as a companion plant because it keeps the surrounding soil rich and moist. However, it often becomes invasive. Wilted leaves are used as a mulch and help activate decomposition in compost heaps; they are rich in nitrogen. In the Middle Ages, comfrey was used as an aid in setting broken bones; it is moderately poisonous if too much is eaten. **ZONES 5–10.**

Symphytum × uplandicum

RUSSIAN COMFREY

This coarse, hairy perennial hybrid between *Symphytum asperum* and *S. officinale* grows to 6 ft (1.8 m) tall. Leaves are oblong and run a short distance down the stem. Flowers are ¾ in (18 mm) long, rosy at first then becoming purple or blue. 'Variegatum' has attractive cream leaf variegation, but flower color is poor and they are often removed. **ZONES 5–10.**

Symphytum × uplandicum 'Variegatum'

Tagetes 'Disco Orange'

TAGETES
MARIGOLD

These annuals were rare at the time of their discovery in the seventeenth century; today, they are among the most familiar of summer plants and are useful as bedding plants or for edging. The single or double flowers come in cheerful shades of orange, yellow, mahogany, brown and red and contrast brightly with the deep green leaves. Some of the 50 or so species have aromatic foliage, hence *Tagetes minuta*'s common name of stinking Roger. It is also said that the roots exude substances fatal to soil-borne pests, leading to their extensive use as companion plants.

CULTIVATION
These fast-growing plants thrive in warm, frost-free climates, but the young plants may need to be raised in a greenhouse in cooler climates. Grow in full sun in fertile, well-drained soil. Deadhead regularly to prolong flowering. Propagate from seed in spring after the danger of frost has passed. Watch for slugs and snails.

Tagetes 'Disco Orange'
Judging by the cultivar name, it's a safe bet that 'Disco Orange' first appeared sometime in the 1970s. It is a cheerful dwarf marigold suitable for the front of a summer border, and produces single, weather-resistant flowerheads from late spring to early autumn. **ZONES 9–11.**

Tagetes patula
FRENCH MARIGOLD

This fast-growing, bushy annual reaches 12 in (30 cm) in height and spread. It was introduced to European gardens from its native Mexico via France—hence its common name. The double flowerheads, produced in summer and early autumn, resemble carnations. They bloom in red, yellow and orange. The leaves are deep green and aromatic. **'Dainty Marietta'** is an all-yellow cultivar with single flowerheads; **Naughty Marietta'** bears single, golden-yellow flowerheads with dark red-brown markings on the petal bases; and **'Honeycomb'** has large, mahogany-red flowers edged with gold. **ZONES 9–11.**

Tagetes patula 'Dainty Marietta'

Tagetes patula

Tagetes tenuifolia 'Tangerine Gem'

Tagetes tenuifolia

SIGNET MARIGOLD

More delicate in its lacy foliage than other
Tagetes species, the signet marigold grows to
a height and spread of only 8 in (20 cm),
making it suitable for edgings and bedding.
The summer and early autumn flowers are
also small and are soft yellow or orange.
'Tangerine Gem' bears small, single, rich
orange flowerheads. **ZONES 9–11.**

Tagetes tenuifolia 'Tangerine Gem'

TANACETUM

Tanacetum coccineum

syn. **Pyrethrum**

In classical Greek mythology, immortality came to Ganymede as a result of drinking tansy, a species of this genus of rhizomatous perennial daisies. Even in recent times, it has been used (despite being potentially quite poisonous even when applied externally) for treating hysteria, skin conditions, sprains, bruises, rheumatism, to name but a few. Confined mainly to temperate regions of the northern hemisphere, the 70 or so species of this genus, relatives of the chrysanthemum, are today more appreciated for their daisy-like flowers and their foliage, which is often white-hairy and in many cases finely dissected.

CULTIVATION

Moderately to very frost hardy, they prefer full sun in well-drained, dryish soil; in fact, any soil that is not wet and heavy. Do not overwater. A second flowering may be encouraged if faded flowers are cut back. These plants spread readily and need to be kept under control. Propagate by division in spring or from seed in late winter or early spring.

Tanacetum coccineum

syns **Chrysanthemum coccineum, Pyrethrum roseum**

PAINTED DAISY, PYRETHRUM

This frost-hardy, erect perennial has dark green, feathery, scented leaves that are finely dissected. Its single, or sometimes double, long-stalked flowerheads may be pink, red, purple or white, and appear from late spring to early summer. The species grows 2–3 ft (60–90 cm) tall with a spread of 18 in (45 cm) or more. 'Brenda' has striking magenta single flowers. 'Eileen May Robinson' is one of the best single pinks. 'James Kelway' has deep crimson-pink flowers. It is a native of western Asia. ZONES 5–9.

Tanacetum parthenium

syn. **Chrysanthemum parthenium**

FEVERFEW

Feverfew is one of those aromatic plants with a long history of medicinal use. It was once used to dispel fevers and agues, and as an antidote for over-indulgence in opium. These days it is admired for its pretty clusters of single or double, ½ in (12 mm) wide, white-petalled, daisy-like flowers. These are borne over a long period in summer. Frost hardy, it has yellow-green leaves up to 3 in (8 cm) long. This species reaches 24 in (60 cm) in height with a spread of 18 in (45 cm). Although perennial, it is short lived, and many gardeners prefer to sow it afresh each spring. 'Aureum' has bright golden foliage. 'Golden Moss' is a dwarf cultivar with a height and spread of 6 in (15 cm). It has golden, moss-like foliage and is often grown as an edging or bedding plant. The cultivar 'Snowball' has pom-pon flowers and grows to 12 in (30 cm) tall. ZONES 6–10.

Tanacetum ptarmiciflorum

syn. **Chrysanthemum ptarmiciflorum**

DUSTY MILLER, SILVER LACE

This bushy perennial from the Canary Islands spreads from a woody tap root. Its silvery, lanceolate leaves are strongly divided. Marginally frost-hardy and with a maximum height and spread of 15 in (38 cm), it is good for the rock garden. White flowerheads in terminal clusters are borne in summer. It is very useful in floral arrangements. ZONES 9–11.

Tanacetum ptarmiciflorum

Thalictrum aquilegiifolium

THALICTRUM

MEADOW RUE

Over 300 species make up this genus of perennials known for their fluffy, showy flowers. The branches of their slender, upstanding stems often intertwine. The leaves are finely divided. Blooming in spring and summer, the flowers have no petals, but instead have 4 or 5 sepals and conspicuous stamen tufts. They serve well in borders, particularly as a contrast to perennials with bolder blooms and foliage.

CULTIVATION

Grow these frost-hardy plants in sun or part-shade in any well-drained soil. Some species need cool conditions. Propagate from fresh seed in autumn or by division in spring.

Thalictrum aquilegiifolium

GREATER MEADOW RUE

This clump-forming Eurasian perennial grows to 3 ft (1 m) tall and has a spread of 18 in (45 cm). Pink, lilac or greenish white flowers in fluffy clusters on strong stems appear in summer. Each gray-green leaf comprises 3 to 7 small, elliptical, toothed leaflets in a feather-like arrangement. ZONES 6–10.

Thalictrum delavayi

syn. *Thalictrum dipterocarpum* of gardens

LAVENDER SHOWER

Rather than fluffy heads, this graceful, clump-forming perennial bears a multitude of nodding, lilac flowers in loose panicles, with prominent yellow stamens. The flowers are borne from the middle to the end of summer. The finely divided leaves give the mid-green foliage a dainty appearance. Reaching 4 ft (1.2 m) high, this species has a spread of 24 in (60 cm). ZONES 7–10.

Thalictrum delavayi

Tiarella wherryi

An almost evergreen perennial, this slow-growing, clump-forming species reaches 8 in (20 cm) high and wide. The late spring flowers make a decorative mass of soft pink or white star shapes and last quite well when cut. The hairy, green leaves turn crimson in autumn.
ZONES 6–10.

TIARELLA
FOAMFLOWER

The foamflowers are a genus of 5 species of forest-floor perennials, all of which are native to North America. They resemble their relatives, the heucheras, and can be hybridized with them. They all grow from thick rootstocks, with their decorative leaves growing close to the ground. The airy sprays of small white flowers are borne on bare stems about 30 cm (12 in) tall; pale pink forms occur rarely.

CULTIVATION

Very frost hardy, they are easy to grow in cool-temperate climates, and make good groundcovers for a woodland-style garden. Plant in part- to deep shade in moist, well-drained soil. Propagate from seed or by division in early spring.

Tiarella wherryi

Tithonia rotundifolia

TITHONIA
MEXICAN SUNFLOWER

This genus of 10 species consists mainly of tall, somewhat woody annuals, biennials and perennials. Originating in Central America and the West Indies, they are related to sunflowers and bear large, vivid yellow, orange or scarlet daisy-like flowerheads in summer and autumn. The leaves are often hairy on the undersides and sharply lobed.

CULTIVATION

Marginally frost hardy, these plants thrive in hot, dry conditions, but require a plentiful supply of water. They grow best in well-drained soil and need full sun. They may need staking. Dead-head regularly to promote a longer flowering season and prune hard after flowering to encourage new growth. Propagate from seed sown under glass in late winter or early spring.

Tithonia rotundifolia

This bulky annual needs plenty of room in the garden as it can easily grow to 5 ft (1.5 m) tall with a spread of 3 ft (1 m). Its leaves are heart-shaped. It is great for hot color schemes, both in the garden and as a cut flower, with its 4 in (10 cm) wide, zinnia-like flowers of orange or scarlet. 'Torch' bears bright orange or red flowerheads and grows to 3 ft (1 m).
ZONES 8–11.

TOLMIEA

PIGGYBACK PLANT, YOUTH-ON-AGE, MOTHER-OF-THOUSANDS

A relative of *Heuchera* and *Saxifraga*, this genus consists of a single species of evergreen perennial from the west coast of North America. Its dark green leaves are very like those of some heucheras, heart-shaped and coarsely toothed, but the plant's most distinctive feature is the production, on some leaves, of a plantlet at the point where the leaf joins its stalk. As the leaves age and droop, these plantlets take root and grow, which allows the plant to spread quite extensively over the shaded forest floor of its normal habitat. The slender, erect flowering stems bear inconspicuous flowers, again very like those of some heucheras.

CULTIVATION
It is a popular indoor plant as well as being a useful ground-cover for shade in regions of mild, moist climate. It adapts well to hanging baskets, making a ball of luxuriant foliage. Keep soil moist but not soggy and water sparingly in winter. Feed every 2 months in the warmer season with half-strength soluble ferti-lizer. Attacks by spider mites cause browning of the leaves, and require immediate treatment. It is easily propagated by detach-ing well-developed plantlets.

Tolmiea menziesii

The pale green leaves of this perennial are speckled with gold and somewhat hairy, 2–4 in (5–10 cm) long, and arise in dense clumps from short surface rhizomes. In late spring and early summer it produces sparse flowering stems 12–24 in (30–60 cm) tall bearing dull red-brown flowers with tiny narrow petals. **ZONES 7–10.**

Tolmiea menziesii

CULTIVATION
Most species are extremely hardy alpines that prefer to grow in well-drained soil that stays moist in summer. Plant in sun or morning shade. De-spite their hardiness, they tend to be short lived and often do better in alpine houses, where they are protected from cold, wet conditions that may cause rotting. Propagate from seed.

Townsendia exscapa

Probably the most widely cultivated species and a favorite of rockery enthusiasts, this little white-flowered, silver-leafed daisy occurs natu-rally from central Canada to Mexico. It demands perfectly drained soil and shelter from winter rain, protection it receives in the wild from a covering of snow. **ZONES 3–9.**

Townsendia exscapa

TOWNSENDIA

This North American genus comprises around 20 species of annual, biennial and perennial daisies. They form mats of nar-row or spatula-shaped leaves, often silvery to gray-green in color. Most species are less than 6 in (15 cm) high and less than 18 in (45 cm) wide. The ½–1½ in (12–35 mm) diameter flowers, which open in spring and summer, resemble a single-flowered Michaelmas daisy. They are white, pink, mauve or purple, with a yellow central disc.

TRADESCANTIA

syns Rhoeo, Setcreasea, Zebrina

SPIDERWORT

This genus consists of 50 or more species of perennials, some of them evergreen, from North and South America. Some are rather weedy, but the creeping species (wandering jew) make useful groundcovers and are grown for their attractive foliage. Some of the upright species are cherished for their pure blue flowers, a color not easy to find for the late-summer garden. Most of the trailing types are rather frost tender and are usually grown as greenhouse pot plants. In mild-winter climates they make good groundcover, admired for their richly toned foliage.

CULTIVATION

Grow in full sun or part-shade in fertile, moist to dry soil. Cut back ruthlessly as they become straggly. Propagate by division or from tip cuttings in spring, summer or autumn.

Tragopogon dubius

TRAGOPOGON

Widely distributed over Europe and temperate Asia, this genus consists of over 100 species of annuals, biennials and perennials belonging to the daisy family. They have solitary or sparsely branched stems, grass-like leaves and terminal, star-shaped flowerheads that are followed by large heads of thistle down.

CULTIVATION

Most species are frost hardy and adaptable to most soils. All prefer a sunny position. Propagate from seed sown in spring.

Tradescantia, Andersoniana Group

This group covers a range of plants formerly listed under *Tradescantia × andersoniana* or *T. virginiana*. They are mainly low-growing perennials with fleshy, strap-like leaves and heads of 3-petalled flowers. Although the foliage clump seldom exceeds 18 in (45 cm) high, the flower stems can reach 24 in (60 cm). There are many hybrids in a range of white, mauve, pink and purple flower shades. Those of 'Alba' are white; 'J. C. Weguelin' has lavender-blue flowers; 'Jazz' has magenta flowers; and 'Red Cloud' is cerise-red flowers. **ZONES 7–10.**

Tradescantia, Andersoniana Group, 'Red Cloud'

Tragopogon dubius

GOATSBEARD

This European species is an erect biennial herb that grows to 3 ft (1 m) tall. It has basal grass-like leaves that half sheathe the base of the stem. The lemon-yellow, star-shaped flowerheads open in the morning and close during the day. **ZONES 5–10.**

Tricyrtis hirta

This upright species bears 2 in (5 cm) wide, star-shaped white flowers spotted with purple from late summer to autumn. The branching stems are about 3 ft (1 m) long. **ZONES 5–9.**

Tricyrtis hirta

Trillium chloropetalum
GIANT TRILLIUM

The giant trillium is found from California to Washington in western USA, in wooded or streamside situations. Growing up to 24 in (60 cm) tall, its flowers may be green, white, pink or maroon, with the 3 petals held upright. This species is more tolerant of dry shade than others. **ZONES 6–9.**

TRICYRTIS
TOAD LILIES

The common name of this genus of about 20 species seems to have biased gardeners against the toad lilies—no one thinks of toads as attractive—but these clumping rhizomatous summer-flowering perennials from the woodlands of Asia are really quite attractive in their quiet colorings and markings. The flowers, which are star-, bell- or funnel-shaped, with opened-out tips, are held in the axils of the leaves. The leaves are pointed and pale to dark green, appearing on erect or arching, hairy stems.

CULTIVATION

Grow these very frost-hardy plants in part-shade in humus-rich, moist soil; in areas with cool summers, they need a warm spot. Propagate from seed in autumn or by division in spring.

TRILLIUM
WAKE ROBIN, WOOD LILY

Among North America's most beautiful wild-flowers, this genus in the lily family contains 30 species of rhizomatous, deciduous perennials; they also occur naturally in northeastern Asia. Upright or nodding, solitary, funnel-shaped flowers with 3 simple petals are held just above a whorl of 3 leaves. The numerous species are found in woodland habitats, flowering in spring before the deciduous leaves which remain green until autumn. They make good ornamentals.

CULTIVATION

Frost hardy, they prefer a cool, moist soil with ample water and shade from hot afternoon sun. Slow to propagate from seed in autumn or by division in summer, they are long lived once established.

Trillium chloropetalum

VALERIANA

VALERIAN

This genus consists of more than 150 species of herbaceous perennials, herbs and subshrubs, but few of the plants are of any ornamental value. Those that are may be good border and rock-garden plants. The name derives from the Latin *valere*, meaning 'keep well', in recognition of the medicinal properties of some species: before modern tranquilizers were introduced, the root from *Valeriana officinalis* was used to treat a range of nervous conditions.

CULTIVATION

Very frost hardy, they will thrive in almost any soil, in sun or part-shade. Propagate from seed or by division of estab-lished plants in autumn.

Valeriana officinalis

Valeriana officinalis

CAT'S VALERIAN, COMMON VALERIAN, GARDEN HELIOTROPE

This clump-forming, fleshy perennial, which is attractive to cats, grows to 4 ft (1.2 m) tall with a spread of 3 ft (1 m). It occurs naturally throughout Europe and eastwards to Russia and western Asia. It bears rounded flowerheads of white to dark pink flowers in summer on erect, hollow, hairy stems. The leaves are opposite with serrated margins. **ZONES 3–9.**

Verbascum bombyciferum

This biennial from Asia Minor has silvery gray, furry, large leaves and grows 6 ft (1.8 m) tall. It bears golden-yellow, cup-shaped flowers in summer, sometimes in terminal spikes. **ZONES 6–10.**

Verbascum bombyciferum

VERBASCUM

MULLEIN

This genus consists of semi-evergreen to evergreen perennials, biennials and shrubs from Europe and the more temperate zones of Asia. Including some very large and some very coarse species, the genus offers much variety in the foliage with leaves rang-ing from glossy to velvety. They develop large, often complex, basal rosettes. Many of the 250 or so species are scarcely better than weeds. However, several are desirable in the garden for their stately habit, gray foliage and long summer-flowering season. The flowers do not open from the bottom up as, for example, delphiniums or foxgloves do, but a few at a time along the spike.

CULTIVATION

These plants are fully to moderately frost hardy but will not tolerate winter-wet conditions. Establish all species in well-drained soil and an open, sunny location, although they do tolerate shade. Propagate from seed in spring or late summer or by division in winter. Some species self-seed readily.

Verbena canadensis

VERBENA

Originating in Europe, South America and North America, this genus of 250 or more species of biennials and perennials is characterized by small, dark, irregularly shaped and toothed leaves. They bloom in late spring, summer and autumn. An agreeably spicy aroma is associated with most verbenas.

CULTIVATION

Marginally frost hardy to frost tender, they do best where winters are not severe. Establish in medium, well-drained soil in full sun or at most part-shade. Propagate from seed in autumn or spring, stem cuttings in summer or autumn, or by division. They can also be propagated in spring by division of young shoots.

Verbena bonariensis

This tall South American perennial is often grown as an annual, primarily for its deep purple flowers which top the sparsely foliaged 4–5 ft (1.2–1.5 m) stems from summer to autumn. The deeply toothed leaves cluster in a mounded rosette, which easily fits in the front of a border; the floral stems give a vertical line without much mass. Frost-hardy, it self-seeds readily and survives with only minimal water, even in dry areas. **ZONES 7–10.**

Verbena bonariensis

Verbena canadensis
ROSE VERBENA, CREEPING VERVAIN

This native of eastern North America is a trailing or sprawling, short-lived perennial easily grown as an annual. It grows to 18 in (45 cm) in height with a spread of 24 in (60 cm). The dark purplish pink flowers appear from summer through autumn. **ZONES 5–10.**

Veronica spicata 'Blue Peter'

VERONICA

SPEEDWELL

Saint Veronica was the woman who, pious legend relates, wiped the face of Christ with her veil and was rewarded with having his image imprinted on it. Her connection with this flower is that the savants of the Middle Ages thought they could see a face in it. They must have peered rather closely, because veronica flowers are not exactly large— ½ in (12 mm) wide is big for the genus. The shrubby species are now given a genus of their own, *Hebe*, and all the remaining 200 or so are herbaceous perennials. They range from prostrate, creeping plants suitable for the rock garden to 6 ft (1.8 m) high giants. Small as the flowers are, they make quite an impact, being gathered in clusters of various sizes and coming in great abundance in summer. Blue is the predominant color, although white and pink versions are also common.

CULTIVATION

Fully to moderately frost hardy, these plants are easy to grow in any temperate climate, and are not fussy about soil or position. Propagate from seed in autumn or spring, from cuttings in summer or by division.

Veronica longifolia 'Rosea'

Veronica gentianoides

Veronica gentianoides
GENTIAN SPEEDWELL

This mat-forming perennial has wide, dark green leaves from which rise spikes of pale blue or white flowers in late spring. It reaches 18 in (45 cm) in height and spread. **ZONES 4–9.**

Veronica longifolia
BEACH SPEEDWELL

From northern and central Europe and Asia, this perennial plant grows up to 3 ft (1 m) tall. Its narrow, tapering leaves are arranged in whorls and toothed on the edges. The flowers are lilac-blue and closely packed on a long, erect infloresence. '**Rosea**' has pink flowers and branched stems. **ZONES 4–9.**

Veronica spicata
DIGGER'S SPEEDWELL, SPIKE SPEEDWELL

This very frost-hardy European perennial reaches a height of 24 in (60 cm) and spreads up to 3 ft (1 m). Its stems are erect, hairy and branching. Spikes of small, star-shaped, blue flowers with purple stamens bloom in summer. The leaves are mid-green, linear to lanceolate. *Veronica spicata* subsp. *incana* is notable for its spreading clumps of silvery, felty leaves and deep violet-blue flowers. '**Blaufuchs**' is bright lavender blue; '**Blue Peter**' has dark blue flowers in very compact spikes; '**Heidekind**', a compact form to 12–15 in (30–38 cm) tall, has hot pink flowers and silver-gray foliage; '**Red Fox**' has crimson flowers; and '**Rosea**' is a pink-flowered form. **ZONES 3–9.**

VIOLA
VIOLET, HEARTSEASE, PANSY

This well-known and much-loved genus of
annuals, perennials and subshrubs consists
of as many as 500 species. They are found in
most temperate regions of the world including
high mountains of the tropics, though with the
greatest concentrations of species in North
America, the Andes and Japan. Most are creeping plants, either deciduous or evergreen, with
slender to thick rhizomes and leaves most often
kidney-shaped or heart-shaped, though in some
species they are divided into narrow lobes.
Flowers of the wild species are seldom more
than 1 in (25 mm) across and characteristically
have 3 spreading lower petals and 2 erect
upper petals, with a short nectar spur projecting to the rear of the flower. Many species also
produce *cleistogamous* flowers, with smaller
petals that do not open properly, and able to
set seed without cross-pollination. A few
Eurasian species have been hybridized extensively to produce the garden pansies, violas and
violettas, with showy flowers in very bright or
deep colors. These are nearly always grown as
annuals, though potentially some are short-
lived perennials.

CULTIVATION
Most of the cultivated *Viola* species will tolerate light frosts at least, and many are fully frost
hardy. The more compact perennial species suit
rock gardens where they do best in cooler,
moister spots, while the more spreading species
make effective groundcovers beneath trees and
taller shrubs, requiring little or no attention.
Pansies and violas *(Viola × wittrockiana)* are
grown as annuals or pot plants in full sun, but
appreciate shelter from drying winds. Sow seed
in late winter or early spring, under glass if
necessary, planting out in late spring in soil
that is well-drained but not too rich. Water
well and feed sparingly as flowers develop.
Propagate by division or from cuttings.

Viola cornuta
HORNED VIOLET

Native to the Pyrenees, this is a broad-faced
violet with a short spur at the back, in shades
of pale blue to deeper violet and borne in spring
and summer. The plants spread by rhizomes,

Viola cornuta

sending up flowering stems to 6 in (15 cm)
long. The horned violet is one of the major
parent species of pansies and violas. 'Minor'
has smaller leaves and flowers. **ZONES 6–9.**

Viola labradorica
LABRADOR VIOLET

Native to North America through to Greenland, this low-growing, spreading species has
light purple flowers in spring. *Viola labradorica*
does well in shady places, but can become
invasive. **ZONES 2–9.**

Viola odorata
SWEET VIOLET

A sweet perfume wafts from the flowers of this
much-loved species, which are the well-known
florists' violets. This viola is a spreading,
rhizomatous perennial from Europe, which
grows 3 in (8 cm) tall and may spread indefinitely on cool, moist ground. Its dark green
leaves are a pointed kidney shape with shallowly toothed edges. Spurred, flat-faced flowers
in violet, white or rose appear from late winter
through early spring. It boasts many cultivars.
ZONES 6–10.

Viola labradorica

Viola sororia
syn. *Viola papilionacea*
WOOLLY BLUE VIOLET

This stemless, herbaceous perennial has scalloped, thickly hairy leaves 4 in (10 cm) long. It bears short-spurred white flowers heavily speckled with violet blue from spring to summer; the flowers are sometimes deep violet blue. **'Freckles'** has white flowers speckled with violet purple. Both the species and the cultivar reach 4–6 in (10–15 cm) in height. ***Viola sororia* var. *priceana*** has grayish white flowers with violet-blue stems. **ZONES 4–10.**

Viola sororia

Viola tricolor
WILD PANSY, JOHNNY JUMP UP,
LOVE-IN-IDLENESS

Of wide occurrence in Europe and temperate Asia, this annual, biennial or short-lived perennial produces neat flowers in autumn and winter in mild climates if cut back in late summer. They have appealing faces, in shades of yellow, blue, violet and white. It has lobed, oval to lance-shaped leaves. It grows to a height and spread of 6 in (15 cm) and self-seeds readily. *Viola tricolor* **'Bowles' Black'** is a striking cultivar with black velvety petals and a yellow center. **ZONES 4–10.**

Viola × wittrockiana

Viola × wittrockiana
PANSY, VIOLA

This hybrid group of compactly branched perennials are almost always grown as biennials or annuals. Offering flowers of a great many hues, the numerous cultivars bloom in late winter through spring and possibly into summer in cooler climates. The flowers are up to 4 in (10 cm) across and have 5 petals in a somewhat flat-faced arrangement. The mid-green leaves are elliptical, with bluntly toothed margins. The plants grow slowly, reaching about 8 in (20 cm) in height and spread. This is a complex hybrid group, including both pansies and violas, the latter traditionally distinguished by the flowers lacking dark blotches, but there are now intermediate types with pale-colored markings. Hybrids in the **Imperial Series** are large-flowered pansies. **'Gold Princess'** is a good example, producing bicolored flowers in golden yellow and red. The **Joker Series** are of an intermediate type, with a range of very bright contrasting colors such as orange and purple. The **Accord Series** of pansies covers most colors and has a very dark central blotch. **'Padparadja'** has vibrant orange flowers. **'Magic'** has purple flowers with a bright face. Other seedling strains include the **Universal** and **Sky Series. ZONES 5–10.**

Viola tricolor

Wahlenbergia communis
syn. Wahlenbergia bicolor

TUFTED BLUEBELL, GRASS-LEAF BLUEBELL

This tufted perennial is native to Australia where it occurs in all mainland states, sometimes in fairly arid areas. It grows up to 30 in (75 cm) high and has linear leaves to 3 in (8 cm) long, sometimes with small teeth. Masses of star-shaped, light blue flowers are borne in spring and summer. **ZONES 8–11.**

Wahlenbergia gloriosa

ROYAL BLUEBELL, AUSTRALIAN BLUEBELL

This perennial with spreading rhizomes and erect stems to about 8 in (20 cm) high is a native of Australian alpine regions and is the floral emblem of the Australian Capital Territory. It has dark green, lance-shaped leaves to 1½ in (35 mm) long with wavy, toothed margins and bears a profusion of royal-blue or purple, bell-shaped flowers on separate fine stems in summer. **ZONES 8–10.**

Wahlenbergia communis

Wahlenbergia gloriosa

WAHLENBERGIA

BLUEBELLS

This is a genus of about 200 species of annuals or perennials with a wide distribution, mostly in the southern hemisphere. They have variable foliage and the flowers range from wide open stars to tubular bells, all with 5 prominent lobes, in shades of blue, purple or white. They are usually small in stature and are suitable for a rock garden or border.

CULTIVATION

Unless otherwise stated, the species described are fully frost hardy. Grow in a well-drained, humus-rich soil in full sun or light shade. Propagate from seed or by division in spring.

Wulfenia carinthiaca

WULFENIA

This is a genus of about 6 species of small evergreen tufted perennials, native to southeastern Europe, western Asia and the Himalayas. Leaves are usually rough-textured with scalloped margins, set from a basal point on long stalks. Flowers are borne on spike-like racemes from the base of the plant—these are blue to purple, tubular in shape with 4 lobes. The fruits are capsules.

CULTIVATION

Fully frost hardy and suited to cold climates, plants resent high humidity and excessive moisture in winter. They prefer full sun and moist, but well-drained soil. Propagate from seed or by division in spring.

XERANTHEMUM
IMMORTELLE

The 5 or 6 annuals in this genus are natives of the Mediterranean region, extending to Iran. They are known as immortelles or everlasting flowers because their dried flowerheads retain their color and form for many years. The upright, branching stems have narrow, woolly leaves. The flowerheads are solitary on long stems and the small fertile flowers are surrounded by papery bracts which may be white, purple or pink.

CULTIVATION

Moderately frost hardy, they grow best in a sunny position in fertile, well-drained soil. Propagate in spring from seed sown *in situ*.

Wulfenia carinthiaca

Native to the Alps and the Balkan Peninsula, this species has a height and spread of about 8 in (20 cm). Leaves are in a basal rosette and are lance-shaped to oval, about 7 in (18 cm) long, toothed, dark green and hairy underneath. The top quarter of the flower stem is a one-sided spike of tubular flowers; violet blue with rounded lobes, which are borne in summer.
ZONES 5–9.

Xeranthemum annuum
IMMORTELLE

A good source of dried flowers, this annual blooms in summer, producing heads of purple, daisy-like flowers; whites, pinks and mauves, some with a 'double' appearance are also available. The leaves are silvery and lance-shaped and the plants grow to around 24 in (60 cm) high and 18 in (45 cm) wide.
Mixed Hybrids include singles and doubles in shades of pink, purple, mauve, red or white.
ZONES 7–10.

Xeranthemum annuum, Mixed Hybrids

Zinnia elegans
YOUTH-AND-OLD-AGE

This sturdy Mexican annual is the best known of the zinnias. The wild form has purple flowerheads, and blooms from summer to autumn. It grows fairly rapidly to 24–30 in (60–75 cm), with a smaller spread. Garden varieties offer hues of white, red, pink, yellow, violet, orange or crimson in flowers up to 6 in (15 cm) across. '**Envy**' has pale green semi-double flowers. The **Dreamland** series is compact and heavy flowering, which is typical of F1 Hybrid bedding zinnias. '**Dreamland Ivy**' has pale greenish yellow flowers. The **Thumbelina** series has 2 in (5 cm) wide flowerheads on plants that are only 6 in (15 cm) high. **ZONES 8–11.**

Zinnia elegans 'Dreamland Ivy'

Zinnia elegans

ZINNIA
ZINNIA

This genus of 20 species of erect to spreading annuals, perennials and subshrubs has daisy-like, terminal flowerheads in many colors including white, yellow, orange, red, purple and lilac. Found throughout Mexico and Central and South America, some are grown for cut flowers and in mixed borders.

CULTIVATION
These plants are marginally frost hardy and are best in a sunny position in fertile soil that drains well. They need frequent deadheading. Propagate from seed sown under glass early in spring.

Chapter 3

SHRUBS

The foliage and flowers of shrubs bring color to a garden. Their foliage can also act as a foil to bright flowers.

Where would gardens be without shrubs? Regardless of climate considerations, shrubs form a vast and hugely variable group, which includes the most hardy and easy care of all plants available. Even with only shrubs to choose from, a gardener would be able to keep a colorful and interesting garden all year round.

What is a shrub?

Gardeners are often confused by the word shrub. It can mean a low-growing, even trailing plant, but the term can be as easily applied to medium or tall growers. When the various types of shrubs are well combined, they can provide a tapestry effect in a border or can be used to unite a house with its garden.

Shrubs are either evergreen or deciduous, although in more temperate climates some, which are deciduous in colder areas, will tend to be semi-deciduous. A semi-deciduous plant does not become completely dormant in winter, nor will it probably color as well in autumn. However, there is usually no detrimental effect to the plant's overall flowering or growth performance.

Shrubs as a part of the garden landscape

In the shrub border, it is the happy mixture of both evergreen and deciduous types that add to its appeal. A solid row of deep green foliage could look rather somber if not enlivened by the numerous shades and textures of evergreens. More interest can be created by the addition of the changing foliage of deciduous shrubs.

The variable growth habits of shrubs are of particular relevance when these plants are added to a garden landscape.

There is more to a successful shrubbery than to have tall shrubs towards the back, and the medium and lower growers in the foreground. Shrubs have different shapes and forms as well as heights: some, like camellias, have a naturally neat form, others, usually those with multiple climbing stems, spread out in a vase-like fashion and need room to show off their decorative canes in spring.

Also consider the flowering times, but more specifically the seasonal variations of the colors and tonings of both the foliage and flowers. Wonderful displays are possible in wildly differing themes. With the right combination of shrubs, a successive display throughout the year can be achieved. In spring, bare branches can become veiled in the delicate soft pinks of blossom before the greening takes place. Then, in high summer, a tropical effect can suddenly burst upon the scene with hibiscus dripping orbs of reds, yellows and oranges, backed with fragrant frangipani. As cooler days and nights bring an end to summer, berries and autumn leaves can extend the color well into winter.

It is clever planning rather than impulse buying that makes this sort of line-up possible. Arrange chosen plants on a paper plan, and remember to intersperse deciduous species with evergreens to avoid bare spaces in winter. Landscapers are past masters at this magical trick, since they get to try out new ideas and combinations with each new garden. We one-off gardeners, however, only get a single chance, but don't let that be a worry—shrubs are easily transplanted!

Another point to borrow from the landscape designers is the way in which they use plants to great effect. They usually group plants in numbers of three upwards, in odd numbers. This is an impressive way to give prominence to a favorite flower or to highlight a sculptured, highly textured leaf form. It certainly gives substance to a planting. Use this ploy to unite a large garden bed that could otherwise look mundane and patchy. Be guided by the particular species that grow well in neighborhood gardens, as well as seeking expertise from a local nursery.

How to choose a shrub

The choice of plants is just as important as a garden's preparation. Shrubs are long-lived plants and will repay your initial consideration

The attractive pink blooms of Daphne mezereum *complement the mid-green leaves, adding interest to the garden.*

through the pleasurable seasons. First of all, compile a list of shrubs that you would like to grow. Do your homework, with books such as this, to research not only height and width of a plant, but also its colors, overall shape, leaf tex-ture and flowering times. As you recall old favorites, add them to your list as well. Finally, when you are happy with the result, go and visit the nursery. Try to find a nursery that carries plants other than those that bloom to perfection the weekend you visit. You may be surprised that most nurseries do not

Versatile fuchsias can grow in pots and hanging baskets and in the garden. Some like 'Leonara' can be trained as standards.

have everything you want. Nurseries know that gardeners are easily seduced by a pretty flower, so don't bother to stock anything else. Be firm, however, and try to resist accepting a flowering substitute there and then. A reputable horticulturist will tell you when your choice is likely to be available, and you will be quite busy in the meantime planting out the shrubs you have bought.

Always choose plants that suit your climate and soil type. With soil, take into consideration its pH as well as whether it is sandy or more of a clay consistency. Shrubs such as ericas, rhododendrons and pieris to name but a few, are happiest in acidic sites, while others prefer more neutral or alkaline soils. As with all your plants, the climate of your garden should match that of the shrub's natural environment. If the climatic difference is too extreme, your work load will increase as you try to maintain the health and vigor of your plants.

Currently it is the vogue to dominate a planting scheme with just one species; in effect, hedging your bets on one type of shrub that is particularly suited to your neighborhood. Who can say how long this fashion will prevail, but it certainly gives an air of tidy formality to a garden even if only a small area is planted in this manner. Similarly, a neatly clipped shrub gives a sense of this formal tradition, often planted as an alternative to an ornamental object.

The best hedge shrubs are those with smallish leaves, coupled with strong fiberous roots and branching habits. They will become more dense as they are continually clipped. To quickly achieve a hedge effect, and to form a dense barrier, they need to be planted much closer together than shrubs in the general garden.

Hedge shrubs also make ideal topiary subjects. It is simply a matter of carefully clipping and training a shrub, often around a wire frame. The result of this constant pruning will be a conversation point for a pot on a terrace. Other popular pot plants include standardized shrubs, which have had all the side shoots stripped off a staked, straight trunk during early growth, until a particular height is reached. Standards are often seen in a formal setting, but select a plant with a slight twist to its trunk for a more relaxed approach. Through gentle training, borrowing some of the techniques used in bonsai, anyone can produce a standard specimen that is very attractive in both shape and form, as well as in flower.

Fragrance is another unforgettable ingredient that should be considered when shrubs are chosen. Anybody who has unexpectedly been delighted by a fragrance while walking through a garden will realize how evocative it is to have something similar in our own domain. Regardless of the climatic zone, there are many shrubs that will impart this extra dimension, adding another fleeting pleasure to a garden. Most scented shrubs, such as sweet osmanthus (*Osmanthus fragrans*) have quite inconspicuous flowers, but since their scent carries, it is unnecessary for them to occupy prime planting positions right beside a path or patio. It is often the very fact that fragrance is so transient that makes a perfumed garden so appealing.

One of the charms of gardening today is that the old rules are being broken by innovative people who are keen to try new approaches. For example: once, stiff rose bushes were singled out in a specially alloted strip of garden beside the drive or front path; now these charmers are seen to perfection in sunny mixed borders where they blend beautifully with their surroundings. Plant breeders helped here with new varieties, so that practical gardeners can experiment.

Abelia schumannii

ABELIA

A genus of about 30 species of deciduous and evergreen shrubs from eastern Asia and Mexico, abelias are elegant and bear abundant small tubular or trumpet-shaped flowers throughout summer. They grow to about 6 ft (1.8 m) tall and have dark green foliage on arching canes.

CULTIVATION

Species vary from moderately frost hardy to somewhat tender. Frost-hardy species are trouble-free plants, capable of surviving harsh conditions. Abelias prefer sun or light shade, and need a well-drained soil with regular water in summer. Easily propagated from cuttings, they can withstand heavy pruning, for example, for low hedging.

Abelia × grandiflora

Abelia × grandiflora

This hybrid between *Abelia chinensis* and *A. uniflora* grows 6–8 ft (1.8–2.4 m) tall and wide. It has arching reddish brown canes and small, glossy dark green leaves. Small mauve and white flowers appear in early summer, usually with a second flush at the end of summer. The dull pink calyces persist after the flowers fall, contrasting with the leaves which turn purplish bronze. The cultivar '**Francis Mason**' has yellow or yellow-edged leaves but it has a tendency to revert to plain green. **ZONES 7–10.**

Abelia schumannii

Less vigorous than *Abelia × grandiflora*, this deciduous shrub likes a sheltered situation. It has arching red canes and small pointed leaves; the upper part of each cane produces a succession of showy bell-shaped flowers from late spring to early autumn. Flowers are rose pink with an orange blotch in the throat; the pale reddish calyx persists on the shrub after the flower falls. **ZONES 7–10.**

Abeliophyllum distichum

In spring, this spreading shrub bears attractive, scented white flowers which are sometimes tinged pink. It grows well against a sunny wall and will reach a height of about 5 ft (1.5 m). **ZONES 5–9.**

ABELIOPHYLLUM

WHITE FORSYTHIA

This genus, related to *Forsythia* contains only one species—a deciduous shrub from Korea. It bears fragrant flowers from late winter and into spring.

CULTIVATION

Abeliophyllum distichum is hardy and likes fertile, well-drained soil and a position in full sun. Protect from late frosts which can damage the blooms. Propagate from semi-ripe cuttings in summer.

Abutilon × *hybridum* 'Orange King'

ABUTILON

syn. *Corynabutilon*

CHINESE LANTERN, FLOWERING MAPLE

There are 100 or more species of mostly evergreen shrubs in this genus but only a few truly merit the name 'Chinese lantern'; that is only a few have flowers pendent on weak stalks and an inflated calyx above a bell of 5 overlapping petals. Such a flower type is adapted to pollination by hummingbirds. Most species, however, have a wide open flower like a small hibiscus, with petals most commonly yellow or orange. Distributed widely through warmer countries, South America is home to most species. A small group of species from the cooler parts of Chile has mauve flowers and deciduous foliage, and is sometimes placed in a separate genus, *Corynabutilon*.

CULTIVATION

They need well-drained soil and full sun or part-shade. In cooler climates they can be grown in containers in sheltered, sunny spots or in greenhouses. They need good watering, especially if in containers (in which they bloom best if root-bound). Propagate from cuttings in late summer. Flea-beetles, aphids and caterpillars can be problems in the garden.

Abutilon × *hybridum*

CHINESE LANTERN

Abutilon × *hybridum* is a collective name for cultivars derived from hybridizing some South American species. The lantern-like flowers, borne from spring to autumn, come in yellow, white, orange, pink, mauve and scarlet. Named cultivars include '**Nabob**'; '**Golden Fleece**', with rich golden-yellow flowers; '**Kentish Belle**', with brilliant orange flowers; '**Orange King**'; '**Ruby Glow**'; '**Ashford Red**'; and '**Souvenir de Bonn**', with variegated foliage and red-veined orange flowers. In warm climates they grow to 8 ft (2.4 m), some with a similar spread, and an open growth habit. Prune hard in early spring; tip prune to promote bushiness and flower-ing. These cultivars can be grown indoors in a cool but sunny room. **ZONES 9–11.**

Abutilon vitifolium

Abutilon megapotamicum

Abutilon megapotamicum
BRAZILIAN BELL-FLOWER

This species from southern Brazil and Uruguay comes in two growth forms: an almost prostrate shrub with branches that may self-layer, making it a good groundcover or rock-garden plant, and a vigorous shrub of up to 8 ft (2.4 m) with arching cane-like branches. Both have smallish, pendent, bell-shaped flowers with a deep red calyx and pale yellow petals. In cooler climates it is usually grown as a pot plant but in zone 8 it can be grown outdoors against a warm wall. Cultivars include 'Marianne', 'Thomsonii', 'Super', 'Wisley Red' and 'Variegatum'. The latter has leaves heavily blotched yellow and a prostrate growth habit. **ZONES 8–11.**

Abutilon × *suntense*

This cool-climate hybrid will tolerate lower temperatures than *Abutilon vitifolium*; its other parent is *A. ochsenii* from the colder south of Chile. It reaches 12 ft (3.5 m) tall and about 8 ft (2.4 m) wide, has dark green leaves and profuse purple or mauve flowers from spring to early summer. The cultivar 'Jermyns' has deep mauve flowers fading with age. This moderately frost hardy plant requires shelter from strong winds. **ZONES 8–9.**

Abutilon vitifolium
syn. *Corynabutilon vitifolium*

This soft-wooded, short-lived, deciduous shrub from Chile reaches 10–12 ft (3–3.5 m). In summer, it bears profuse clusters of mauve-purple to white flowers up to 3 in (8 cm) wide. While needing a cool moist climate, it is one of the most cold hardy abutilons, but does best against a sheltered house wall or in a courtyard. Prune hard in early spring to prevent the shrub becoming straggly. Named cultivars include 'Veronica Tennant' with fine, very pale lavender flowers; and 'Album' with white flowers. **ZONES 8–9.**

Abutilon × *suntense*

Acalypha hispida
CHENILLE PLANT, RED-HOT CAT-TAIL

Thought to be from Malaysia, this upright, soft-stemmed shrub has striking, tiny, bright red flowers that in summer hang in pendulous, tassel-like spikes on the female plants. The leaves are large, oval and bright green to reddish bronze. It grows to 6 ft (1.8 m) high and wide. Regular pruning will maintain a bushy shape. It does best in sheltered sites in full sun; in cool climates it needs a heated conservatory.
ZONES 11–12.

Acalypha wilkesiana
FIJIAN FIRE PLANT, COPPER LEAF

Originating in Fiji and nearby islands, this shrub grows to a height and spread of 10 ft (3 m). With erect stems branching from the base, it has large, serrated, oval leaves in a wide color range, some with contrasting margins. Inconspicuous tassel-like catkins of reddish bronze flowers appear in summer and autumn. It prefers a warm, sheltered position. Foliage colors are best in full sun. Cultivars include **'Macrophylla'** with large leaves, each differently variegated with bronze, copper, red, cream and yellow blotches; **'Godseffiana'** with narrow, drooping green leaves edged with cream; **'Macafeeana'** with deep bronze leaves splashed with coppery red; and **'Marginata'** with bronze-red leaves edged with cream or pale pink.
ZONES 10–11.

Acalypha hispida

ACALYPHA

This genus of evergreen shrubs and subshrubs consists of over 400 species from most warmer countries of the world; only a few are grown as ornamentals. Some of these are valued for the decorative, narrow spikes of crowded, feathery flowers on the female plants (males are on different plants), while one species is grown only for its showy variegated foliage.

CULTIVATION

They need a sunny to semi-shaded position, well-drained, light soil, plenty of water in summer, and protection from wind. Plants are frost tender. Prune lightly to shape in late winter, then feed and water. Propagate from cuttings in summer. Watch for mealybug, red spider mite and white fly.

Acalypha wilkesiana 'Macrophylla'

Aloysia triphylla
syn. Lippia citriodora
LEMON-SCENTED VERBENA

Grown for its heavily lemon-scented, crinkly, pale to mid-green leaves, this shrub has an open, rather straggling habit. It can reach a height and spread of 10 ft (3 m), and racemes of dainty, light lavender flowers appear through summer and autumn. It needs regular pruning to improve its shape. Oil of verbena is produced from the leaves. It needs protection in winter and is suitable for container growing. **ZONES 8–11.**

ALOYSIA

This genus consists of around 40 species of evergreen shrubs from North, Central and South America, grown for their attractive and strongly aromatic foliage. The branches are soft and cane-like with leaves arranged in opposite pairs or in whorls of three. Tiny flowers are borne in panicles terminating the branches.

CULTIVATION
They prefer a well-drained, loamy or light-textured soil and plenty of summer watering. Tolerant of only mild frosts, they do best in a sunny position in a warm, coastal environment. In cold areas, new specimens should be planted out each year. Remove dead wood in early summer, and prune well in late winter to maintain a bushy shape and encourage the flowers, which are borne on the current season's growth. Propagate by semi-hardwood cuttings in summer or soft-tip cuttings in spring.

Aloysia triphylla

AMELANCHIER
SERVICEBERRY, SNOWY MESPILUS, JUNEBERRY

These shrubs and small trees, mostly native to cool climates of North America, belong to the pome-fruit group of trees and shrubs in the rose family, which includes apples, pears and quinces as well as many 'berry' shrubs. Most *Amelanchier* species are deciduous, with simple oval leaves, clusters of white flowers, frequently with long narrow petals, and small rounded fruit ripening to purple or black and often sweet and edible. Some species make attractive, graceful trees, valued for the display of snowy white flowers in spring and for their autumn coloring.

Amelanchier alnifolia

CULTIVATION

They do best in moist, fertile soil in a grassy glade in the shelter of other trees but receiving ample sun. Propagation is normally from seed or by layering.

Amelanchier alnifolia
SASKATOON SERVICEBERRY, WESTERN SERVICEBERRY

Native to a wide area from central Alaska down the Rocky Mountains to Colorado, this species is commonly a shrub of 6 ft (1.8 m) or more, branching from the base. Clusters of white flowers, borne among its small, coarsely toothed leaves in late spring are followed by small, sweet, blue-black fruit. It is of limited value as an ornamental, but extremely cold hardy. 'Pembina' is one of its cultivars. **ZONES 4–9.**

Amelanchier arborea

Amelanchier arborea
syn. *Amelanchier canadensis* of gardens
DOWNY SERVICEBERRY

Occurring naturally in the eastern USA, this easily grown tree reaches about 20 ft (6 m) in gardens, usually with a narrowish crown and drooping lower branches. The finely toothed, pointed leaves are covered with white down as they emerge in spring. Profuse flowers, in short, upright sprays, are followed in early summer by small fleshy fruit. In autumn, the foliage turns red, orange or yellow. **ZONES 4–9.**

Amelanchier lamarckii

The origin of this species has been the subject of speculation: in the past it has been much confused with *Amelanchier canadensis* and *A. laevis*. It makes a spreading shrub or small tree to 30 ft (9 m). The leaves are broad and deep green, with a coating of silky hairs when young. White flowers appear in spring in drooping clusters; small edible fruit ripen to black. **ZONES 6–9.**

Amelanchier lamarckii

Andromeda polifolia

Andromeda polifolia

Growing to about 24 in (60 cm) high and wide, this species has narrow, deep green 1 in (25 mm) long leaves with pale undersides. The tiny white to pink flowers appear in sprays in spring. 'Compacta' has a denser, more compact habit, with grayish leaves and pink flowers. **ZONES 2–9.**

ANDROMEDA

BOG ROSEMARY

Only 2 species of low evergreen shrubs make up this genus from the colder parts of the northern hemisphere. They have tough short branches that root along the ground and small oblong leathery leaves. The small flowers, in short terminal sprays, are urn-shaped with a narrow aperture.

CULTIVATION

These shrubs are best grown in a shaded rockery. They prefer moist yet well-drained, acid conditions. They will tolerate any frosts and prefer a cold climate. Propagate from seed or small tip cuttings.

ANISODONTEA

This genus of shrubby mallows from southern Africa have tough, wiry stems and small flowers like miniature hibiscus, carried on slender stalks from short lateral shoots near the tips of the branches. The leaves are small and irregularly lobed. Recently rediscovered and popularized as free-blooming indoor plants, or in warm-temperate climates as garden shrubs. However, if grown indoors they must receive some sun or very strong reflected light.

CULTIVATION

They need frequent watering in the warmer part of the year, little in the cooler. Light pruning after flowers finish produces a more compact plant and encourages subsequent flowering. Propagation is normally from summer cuttings, which strike readily. Grow them in a cold frame.

Anisodontea capensis
syn. *Malvastrum capensis*

This species will quickly grow to a shrub about 6 ft (1.8 m) high with long straggling branches and rather sparse foliage. Flowers, ¾ in (18 mm) in diameter, appear in successive flushes from spring through summer or almost the whole year in warmer climates; flesh pink with darker veining on opening, they age to very pale pink. It needs protection in winter and is suitable for container growing. **ZONES 9–11.**

Anisodontea capensis

Arctostaphylos uva-ursi

Arctostaphylos uva-ursi
BEARBERRY, KINNIKINNICK

Found in the wild in the colder regions of the northern hemisphere, this species is best known as a completely prostrate form that can cascade over walls or embankments to form curtains of neat, dark green foliage that develops intense red tones in autumn and winter. In late spring it bears small clusters of dull pink, almost globular flowers, followed by green berries that ripen to red; it is readily propagated from cuttings. Cultivars include 'Massachusetts'; 'Radiant'; and 'Wood's Red', which is a dwarf cultivar. 'Vancouver Jade' is an exceptionally vigorous and disease-resistant selection. 'Point Reyes' is tolerant of coastal conditions. **ZONES 4–9.**

ARCTOSTAPHYLOS
BEARBERRY, MANZANITA

Allied to *Arbutus*, this genus of around 50 species of evergreen shrubs or, rarely, small trees includes 2 species widely distributed through cool climates of the northern hemisphere; all others are native to western North America or Mexico. They are tough plants with very woody stems, smallish, leathery leaves and small clusters of white or pink, bell-shaped flowers. Some of the Californian species from the 'chaparral' evergreen scrub of the coastal ranges can survive the fires that periodically ravage it. They mostly have very ornamental bark, purple, red or orange and peeling in thin shreds or flakes.

CULTIVATION

They need full sun or part-shade and moist but well-drained, fertile, lime-free soil. The seed, enclosed in a small fleshy fruit, is difficult to germinate, which explains why manzanitas are propagated from tip cuttings hardened off in winter; treatment with smoke may assist germination.

Argyranthemum frutescens

ARGYRANTHEMUM

MARGUERITE

One of several horticulturally important genera now recognized in place of the once more broadly defined *Chrysanthemum*, this genus consists of 22 species of evergreen subshrubs from the Canary Islands and Madeira. They tend to be upright, rarely over 3 ft (1 m) tall, and bushy with deeply lobed or divided, bright green to blue-green leaves. From spring to autumn in cool climates but mainly in winter–spring in warmer climates, the bushes are covered in 1–3 in (2.5–8 cm) wide daisies in white and a wide range of pink and yellow shades. Marguerites make good cut flowers and large numbers are sold potted by florists. In recent years there has been a renewed interest in breeding, resulting in many new cultivars.

CULTIVATION

Marguerites are very easy to cultivate in any light, well-drained soil in full sun. They grow particularly well near the sea and have naturalized in some coastal areas of the world. They should be cut back either in late winter or late summer to encourage fresh growth. Most species and cultivars tolerate light, irregular frosts only. Propagate from seed or cuttings.

Argyranthemum frutescens
syn. *Chrysanthemum frutescens*

Although the true species, a 3 ft (1 m) tall, white-flowered shrub from the Canary Islands, is now rarely cultivated, most of the commonly seen garden cultivars are classified under this name though many may in fact be hybrids with other species. There are numerous cultivars with a huge range of flower forms and sizes in a range of colors from white to deep pink and yellow. Some notable examples include 'Bridesmaid', 'California Gold', 'Harvest Gold', 'Jamaica Primrose', 'Little Rex', 'Margaret', 'Pink Lady', 'Rising Sun', 'Silver Leaf', 'Snow Man', 'Tauranga Star' and 'Weymouth Pink'. Provide winter protection. They grow well in hanging baskets. **ZONES 8–11.**

Argyranthemum frutescens 'California Gold'

Argyranthemum frutescens 'Bridesmaid'

Aronia arbutifolia
RED CHOKEBERRY

Native to eastern North America, where it is a common understorey plant, this species grows to 6 ft (1.8 m) with many vertical stems forming spreading clumps. White flowers in spring are followed by bright red berries in autumn and early winter, popular with birds. Narrow, oval leaves turn bright red in autumn—this is best in 'Brilliant' (sometimes listed as 'Brilliantissima'). **ZONES 4–9.**

Aronia melanocarpa
BLACK CHOKEBERRY

Very similar in foliage and flowers to the red chokeberry (*Aronia arbutifolia*) and originating in the same region of the USA, the black chokeberry is a lower, more spreading shrub with more densely crowded stems. The leaves are less glossy and the berries, ripening a brilliantly glossy black, do not last long into autumn but drop soon after they ripen. 'Nero' and 'Viking' are well-known cultivars of *A. melanocarpa*. **ZONES 5–9.**

ARONIA
CHOKEBERRY

A member of the pome-fruit group of the rose family, *Aronia* consists of only 3 deciduous shrub species from North America, but all these make fine garden shrubs of compact size with abundant displays of glossy red or black berries in late summer and autumn. They have oval leaves with finely toothed margins, and bear small umbels of flowers like miniature apple blossoms in spring.

CULTIVATION

Frost hardy and not demanding as to soil, they will grow well in part-shade but respond to full sun with more profuse fruit and brighter autumn foliage. Cut the oldest stems to the ground to encourage new growth. Propagate from seed or cuttings. The foliage is prone to disfigurement by the pear and cherry slug, sawfly larvae.

Aronia melanocarpa

AUCUBA
AUCUBA, SPOTTED LAUREL

This is an east Asian genus consisting of 3 species of shrubs, valued for their tolerance of heavy shade and large, often colorful, evergreen leaves. Clusters of large red berries appear in autumn but, with flowers of different sexes on different plants, it is only the females that fruit. One commonly grown species has given rise to many cultivars with a range of variegated leaves.

CULTIVATION

They are tough and resilient, tolerant of frost, neglect, pollution and heavy shading but responding to better treatment and stronger light with more luxuriant growth. The long-lasting but tender leaves should be protected from wind damage. Grow in full sun or part- or full shade, with filtered light for the variegated species, in any soil. Propagate from seed or cuttings.

Aucuba japonica 'Crotonifolia'

Aucuba japonica
JAPANESE AUCUBA

Usually a shrub of 4–6 ft (1.2–1.8 m), this species will continue to spread by basal sprouting and self-layering of its weak, soft-wooded stems and, as it thickens up, the mass of stems will support one another, allowing it to reach 10 ft (3 m). The thick, soft, glossy leaves are up to 10 in (25 cm) long and very variably toothed. Sprays of small, reddish flowers in spring may be followed by drooping clusters of ½ in (12 mm) long, red berries in early autumn. **'Variegata'** (female) has leaves densely spotted with yellow, and **'Crotonifolia'** (male) has leaves heavily splashed with yellow. **ZONES 7–10.**

Baccharis pilularis 'Twin Peaks'

Baccharis pilularis
DWARF COYOTE BUSH

A native of California and Oregon, this evergreen shrub grows to a height of 24–36 in (60–90 cm). It has small, oval, bright green leaves on spreading branches and tiny white flowers. It is adaptable to most soils in any sunny position and is resistant to frost and to very dry conditions. 'Twin Peaks' is a selected compact form under 30 in (75 cm) high and 10 ft (3 m) wide. It is valued as a hardy cover on dry slopes and for its fire-retardant qualities. **ZONES 7–10.**

BACCHARIS

This genus of approximately 350 species of perennials and shrubs in the Compositae (daisy) family is native to the Americas. Most are evergreen, densely foliaged, wiry-stemmed plants, many from drier regions or locations with saline soil or exposed to salt spray. The leaves, arranged alternately on the branches, are mostly tough and leathery, very variable in shape but mostly toothed or lobed and often slightly resinous and sticky. The small, usually white or grayish flowerheads, which grow in panicles at the ends of branches, lack the ray-like flowers of typical daisies. Most species are rank-growing plants of no ornamental value but a few are useful in the garden.

CULTIVATION

Any sunny location with reasonable soil will do. Some salt-resistant species are ideal plants for coastal gardens. Some, too, will tolerate moderate to severe frosts but most are frost tender. Propagate from small tip cuttings or seed.

Berberis darwinii
DARWIN BARBERRY

The showiest of several evergreen species from Chile and
Argentina, all with small
leaves and neat clusters of
deep yellow to orange flowers.
Berberis darwinii has dark
green, glossy leaves with
holly-like toothing and dense
short sprays of bright golden-
yellow flowers in late winter
and spring. These are followed by bluish berries. It
grows 6 ft (1.8 m) or more
high and wide with an irregular, open branching habit;
branches are less spiny than
most other species.
ZONES 7–10.

Berberis julianae

The leaves of this evergreen
shrub are glossy with spined
edges. In late spring, the shrub
comes alive with yellow
flowers, sometimes tinged red.
These are borne in attractive
clusters. Rectangular shaped
fruit follow. It reaches a height
of 10 ft (3 m). **ZONES 4–10.**

Berberis darwinii

BERBERIS
BARBERRY

This is a large genus of well over 400 species of hardy shrubs,
both evergreen and deciduous, mostly branching from below the
ground into densely massed canes and with weak to quite fierce
spines where the leaves join the stems. The leaves are generally
rather leathery, of small to medium size and often with prickly
marginal teeth. Clusters of small yellow, cream, orange or reddish flowers are followed by small fleshy fruits. Most species
come from temperate east Asia, a
few from Europe and several from
Andean South America. North
American species once placed in
Berberis are now referred to
Mahonia.

CULTIVATION
Barberries are easy to grow and
thrive in most soil types. Withstanding hard pruning, they are
useful for hedges. Propagate from
seed or cuttings. In some countries
there are restrictions on growing
barberries because some species can
harbor the overwintering phase of
the wheat rust fungus.

Berberis julianae

Berberis × ottawensis

This hybrid is best known in the form of the clone **'Superba'** (syn. 'Purpurea'), which is similar to and often confused with *B. thunbergii* 'Atropurpurea' but is taller, around 6 ft (1.8 m), and more vigorous, with the new growths bronze red rather than dark purplish. Its red berries appear in autumn. It is a popular and very hardy, deciduous shrub with densely massed stems, useful for hedging or to provide contrast amongst green-leafed shrubs. It is also prized by flower arrangers. **ZONES 3–10.**

Berberis × ottawensis 'Superba'

Berberis thunbergii 'Red Pillar'

Berberis thunbergii

THUNBERG BARBERRY, JAPANESE BARBERRY

This is one of the most widely planted barberries, usually in the guise of one of its cultivars. Native to Japan, it is a low-growing deciduous shrub (almost evergreen in warmer climates) only 5 ft (1.5 m) in height, with densely massed stems and small, neatly rounded leaves. Its spines are not particularly fierce. The small, not very decorative, bell-shaped flowers that appear in mid-spring are greenish yellow with dull red stripes. **'Atropurpurea'** has deep purplish brown foliage turning a metallic bronze black in late autumn. **'Atropurpurea Nana'** (syns 'Crimson Pygmy', 'Little Favorite') is a neat, bun-shaped plant only 12–18 in (30–45 cm) high, with similar toning plus green tints. **'Keller's Surprise'** is compact and rather narrow, with green or bronze leaves splashed with pink. **'Rose Glow'** has rich purple leaves, variously marked pink, with green margins. **'Red Pillar'** is an improved form of the earlier cultivar **'Erecta'** and has purple-red foliage and a very upright growth habit to 4–5 ft (1.2–1.5 m) tall. **ZONES 4–10.**

Berberis verrucolosa

Berberis verrucolosa

WARTY BARBERRY

This slow-growing, evergreen shrub from western China is normally about 5 ft (1.5 m) high with masses of strongly arching stems, their bark covered in small warty brown protuberances. The small, glossy leaves are crowded along the stems. Yellow flowers appear in late spring scattered singly among the leaves, followed by cylindrical purple-black berries with a blue bloom. **ZONES 5–9.**

Brachyglottis, Dunedin Hybrids

Of mixed parentage involving 3 species, the Dunedin Hybrids resulted from a chance crossing early in the twentieth century at Dunedin in New Zealand. They are bushy, if somewhat open, shrubs to 5 ft (1.5 m) with dark green leaves having the characteristic felty white undersurface of the genus and the daisy-like yellow flowerheads. '**Sunshine**' has neat elliptical leaves and bright yellow flowerheads in large, loose terminal clusters. **ZONES 7–9.**

Brachyglottis greyi

syn. *Senecio greyi*

This many-branched evergreen shrub grows into a large mound, anything up to 6 ft (1.8 m) high and greater than this in spread. Its small, bright yellow, daisy-like flowers appear in summer and autumn and are less interesting than its hair-covered leathery, green-gray leaves. This moderately frost-hardy species has long been grown in the UK. **ZONES 7–9.**

Brachyglottis, Dunedin Hybrid 'Sunshine'

BRACHYGLOTTIS

This genus of low evergreen shrubs and small trees includes about 30 species. Most are New Zealand natives, but one or two occur in Tasmania. Apart from their flowers, many are valued for their attractive foliage. The flowerheads are in small to rather large panicles at the branch tips, and may be white or golden yellow with conspicuous petals (actually ray florets), or small and greenish white with no ray florets.

CULTIVATION

These are rewarding garden plants in a suitable climate—they do best in cool but mild and rainy climates. Plant in a sunny position in well-drained soil. The shrubby species respond to heavy pruning. Propagate from cuttings in late summer. Keep them in shape by cutting back.

Brachyglottis greyi

BRUGMANSIA

syn. Datura

ANGEL'S TRUMPET

The large shrubs or small trees of this genus are grown for their very large, fragrant, pendent trumpet flowers. They are still often found under the name *Datura*, but the true daturas are short lived, herbaceous plants with smaller, more upright flowers and capsular fruits that are usually prickly (brugmansias have fleshy, unarmed fruit that may be very long and narrow). Five or more species are currently attributed to *Brugmansia*, most originating in the Andes of northern South America, though even there they seem always to be associated with human habitation. They are evergreen or semi-evergreen and their leaves are large and soft, rather like tobacco leaves but smaller, and all parts of the plant are narcotic and poisonous.

CULTIVATION

Frost tender to marginally frost hardy, the plants prefer a warm to hot climate, a sunny sheltered site and a light, fertile, well-drained soil. Provide winter protection. Best grown as small trees, they can be shaped when young to obtain a single trunk or can be kept trimmed as dense, rounded shrubs. They can also be grown in containers. Water well during the growing season. Propagate from tip cuttings in spring or summer. Whitefly and spider mite can cause problems, as can snails.

Brugmansia × *candida*

Brugmansia sanguinea

Brugmansia × *candida*

syn. Datura candida

This rather untidy large shrub or small tree, 10–15 ft (3–4.5 m) high, branches low from a short trunk; the long, oval, velvety leaves are confined to the branch tips. The pendulous white flowers, strongly scented at night, are up to 12 in (30 cm) long and have a widely flared mouth. They appear in summer and autumn but also at other times. *Brugmansia* × *candida* is now believed to be a hybrid between *B. aurea* and *B. versicolor*. 'Plena' has an extra frill of petals inside the main trumpet. **ZONES 10–12.**

Brugmansia sanguinea

syn. Datura sanguinea

RED ANGEL'S TRUMPET

This is the most distinctive of the brugmansias because of its usually orange-red flowers with yellow veins, narrower across the mouth than other species or hybrids. Reported to grow at altitudes up to 12,000 ft (3,600 m) in its native Andes and to become a tree as much as 40 ft (12 m) high, this is the most cold hardy of the brugmansias. It is normally seen in gardens as a many-stemmed shrub to about 8 ft (2.4 m) high. Flower color varies, some forms having paler orange or yellow flowers. **ZONES 9–11.**

Brugmansia suaveolens

syn. *Datura suaveolens*

This many-branched, spreading evergreen shrub or small tree, which reaches 15 ft (4.5 m), has downy, oval leaves up to 12 in (30 cm) long. The flowers are narrower than in *Brugmansia* × *candida*, and their tubes are heavily striped with green. They are profuse at various times of the year. Widely grown in tropical gardens, it is sometimes seen pruned to a round-headed shrub. In cool climates it does well in moderately heated greenhouses. 'Plena' has semi-double blooms. **ZONES 10–12.**

Brugmansia suaveolens

Buddleja alternifolia

BUDDLEJA

Buddleja davidii 'Dubonnet'

Often spelt *Buddleia* (after seventeenth-century English botanist Adam Buddle), *Buddleja* is now ruled the correct form. This genus consists of shrubs and small, mostly short-lived trees, both evergreen and deciduous. Most of the cultivated species originate in China, but the genus also occurs in Africa, Madagascar, southern Asia and South America and includes many tropical and subtropical species. The leaves are large, pointed and often crepe-textured, usually in opposite pairs. The spice-scented flowers are small and tubular, and occur in dense spikes at the branch tips or sometimes in smaller clusters along the branches. They range through pinks, mauves, reddish purples, oranges and yellows.

CULTIVATION

Buddlejas prefer full sun and good drainage, but thrive in any soil type. Fairly hard pruning in early spring controls their straggly appearance. Propagate from cuttings in summer.

Buddleja alternifolia

In full bloom in late spring and early summer, this tall deciduous shrub from north-western China is transformed into a fountain of fragrant, mauve-pink blossom, the small individual flowers strung in clusters along its arching branches. It looks best trained to a single trunk so the branches can weep effectively from above, and should not be pruned back hard as it flowers on the previous summer's wood. **ZONES 6–9.**

Buddleja davidii

BUTTERFLY BUSH

The common buddleja of gardens, *Buddleja davidii* is native to central and western China. It is a deciduous or semi-evergreen shrub of about

Buddleja globosa

12 ft (3.5 m) with gray-green foliage. In late summer and early autumn its arching canes bear at their tips long, narrow cones of densely packed flowers, mauve with an orange eye in the original form. These are attractive to butterflies, which feed on the scented nectar. Prune in late winter to encourage strong canes with larger flower spikes. Cultivars with flowers in larger spikes and richer tones include 'Cardinal', rich purple-pink; 'Black Knight', dark purple; 'Empire Blue', purple-blue with an orange eye; 'Royal Red', magenta; and 'White Bouquet', cream with an orange eye. 'Dubonnet' has large spikes of purple-pink flowers, and 'Pink Delight' has long narrow spikes of bright pink ones. The flowers of 'White Profusion' are white with golden-yellow centers. **ZONES 5–10.**

Buddleja globosa
ORANGE BALL TREE

Deep golden-orange balls of tiny flowers, hanging like baubles from the branch tips in late spring and summer, make this deciduous or semi-evergreen species from temperate Chile and Argentina strikingly different from other buddlejas. The strongly veined leaves are soft and covered in white felty hairs, as are the twigs and flower stalks. It is a tall shrub of 10–15 ft (3–4.5 m), making fast growth under suitably sheltered conditions but inclined to be short lived. In cool but mild, moist climates it will do well close to the sea. **ZONES 7–10.**

Buddleja davidii 'Cardinal'

Buddleja × weyeriana

This name applies to hybrids between *Buddleja davidii* and *B. globosa*. In growth habit they resemble *B. davidii* though taller and with longer canes, but the flower spikes are broken up into globular bunches of cream or orange-yellow flowers reminiscent of the heads of *B. globosa*. 'Golden Glow' has gold flowers, deep orange in the throat. 'Wattle Bird' is a recent hybrid with pale to rich yellow flowers in elongated spikes. **ZONES 7–10.**

Buddleja × weyeriana 'Wattle Bird'

Bupleurum fruticosum

BUPLEURUM

Over 100 species belong to this genus of the carrot family, and they include annuals, perennials and shrubs ranging through Europe, Africa, Asia and some cooler parts of North America. They differ from most members of the family in their undivided, untoothed leaves, mostly rather long and narrow but broader or even almost circular in some species. The small greenish or yellowish flowers are borne in rounded umbels, often with a circle or cup of pointed bracts, and the primary umbels are generally grouped into compound umbels. 'Thorow-wax', the common name, is sometimes used for the genus as a whole, but correctly applies only to the western European annual *Bupleurum rotundifolium*, which has curious large, teardrop-shaped leaves through which the slender stems appear to grow.

CULTIVATION

Some of the more shrubby evergreen species with leathery, salt-resistant foliage are useful plants for seaside gardens, while several herbaceous perennial species are sometimes grown as rockery plants. Plant in a sunny position in light, well-drained soil. Propagate shrub species from cuttings or by root division, herbaceous species from seed or by division.

Bupleurum fruticosum
SHRUBBY HARE'S-EAR

This southern European species is a 6–10 ft (1.8–3 m) tall, spreading evergreen shrub, though only 3 ft (1 m) or less in exposed positions. Its leaves are narrow and leathery with rounded tips, bluish green, especially on the undersides, and up to 3 in (8 cm) long with prominent midribs. From mid-summer it develops umbels of small, fleshy, yellow flowers at the branch tips. **ZONES 7–10.**

Buxus microphylla var. *japonica*

BUXUS

BOX

Traditional evergreens of cool-climate gardens, boxes are grown for their small, neat, leathery leaves and dense, long-lived growth habit. The genus consists of around 30 species, only a few of which originate in Europe and temperate Asia; most in fact are tropical and subtropical plants that come from Central America, the West Indies or southern Africa, most of them larger leafed and unknown in cultivation. The cultivated boxes, though regarded as shrubs, are capable (except for some dwarf cultivars) of growing into small trees with strong, contorted trunks and branches. Creamy yellow boxwood was once used for fine woodcut blocks for printing. The small flowers are greenish yellow and appear in small clusters in the leaf axils in spring; they are profuse and attract bees.

CULTIVATION

These tough plants have very simple requirements, thriving in most soils in sun or shade and adapting well to warmer climates. Boxes withstand regular close clipping, making them ideal for topiary, formal hedges and mazes. Pruning can be continued throughout the year. Propagate from cuttings.

Buxus microphylla

JAPANESE BOX

This east Asian box, long grown in Japan but unknown in the wild, first came to Western gardens as a dwarf cultivar with distorted leaves. Later, wild forms were discovered in Japan, Korea and China and named as varieties: **Buxus microphylla var. japonica** (syn. *B. japonica*), **B. m. var. koreana** and **B. m. var. sinica** respectively. In leaf size and shape they are all quite similar to the European box but the leaves are slightly glossier and usually more rounded at the tip, with the broadest part somewhat above the middle. A characteristic feature is the way the leaves turn a pale yellow-brown in frosty winters. In North America *B. m.* var. *koreana* is popular for its compact, low-growing habit and cold hardiness. In milder climates *B. m.* var. *japonica*, with slightly larger, rounder leaves, sometimes reaches 10 ft (3 m). **ZONES 6–10.**

Buxus microphylla

Buxus sempervirens
EUROPEAN BOX, COMMON BOX

The common box can grow as tall as 30 ft (9 m) with a trunk 12 in (30 cm) thick, but as a garden shrub it is commonly only 3–6 ft (1–1.8 m) high and is represented by a bewildering range of forms and cultivars, including the mound-forming '**Vardar Valley**'. The edging box, '**Suffruticosa**', has a very dense, bushy habit and can be maintained as a dwarf hedge of 12 in (30 cm) or less. There are also many variegated clones, including '**Marginata**', which has yellow-margined leaves, and '**Argenteo-variegata**', with white-edged leaves. **ZONES 5–10.**

Buxus sempervirens

Buxus sempervirens 'Suffruticosa'

Calceolaria integrifolia

Native to Chile, this is a spreading shrub of rather loose and untidy habit though easily kept in shape by pruning, reaching a height of 6 ft (1.8 m). It has closely veined, slightly sticky leaves with an attractive, fine 'seersucker' texture, but is prone to insect damage. From late spring to early autumn a succession of bright yellow or bronzy yellow flowers appear in long-stalked clusters from the branch tips. It is the main parent of a group of hybrids, the **Fruticohybrida Group**. It needs protection in winter and is suitable for container growing. **ZONES 8–10.**

Calceolaria integrifolia

CALCEOLARIA

Most of the species in this genus are annuals, biennials or perennials, and detailed information on the genus is given in the Annuals and Perennials chapter. However, *Calceolaria integrifolia* is treated here as a shrub.

Callicarpa americana

Callicarpa americana
AMERICAN BEAUTY BERRY

Not as commonly grown as it deserves, this deciduous species from southeastern and central USA makes a low, spreading shrub to 3–6 ft (1–1.8 m) in height. *Callicarpa americana* has broad, strongly veined leaves with downy undersides. The pink to violet-purple flowers are small but the brilliant mauve-magenta fruit are showy, in tight clusters like miniature bunches of grapes, and the fruit persist well into winter. **ZONES 7–10.**

CALLICARPA
BEAUTY BERRY

Deciduous and evergreen shrubs and small trees occurring in tropical regions around the world as well as more temperate regions of east Asia and North America, the 140 or so *Callicarpa* species can be untidy in growth but appealing in flower and especially in fruit. The branches are long and cane-like; the leaves, in opposite pairs, are usually downy on their undersides. In the popular deciduous species, sprays of small pink to purple summer flowers are followed in autumn by dense clusters of small shiny berries, white or mauve to purple, which may persist into winter on the bare branches. Fruiting branches are often cut for indoor decoration.

CULTIVATION

Only 3 or 4 species are commonly grown in cool climates but others from subtropical and tropical regions make good garden subjects. *Callicarpa* species do best in full sun and fertile soil. Cut back older branches in late winter to encourage strong flowering canes. Propagate from tip cuttings.

Callistemon citrinus

syn. Callistemon lanceolatus
SCARLET BOTTLEBRUSH,
LEMON BOTTLEBRUSH

Widely distributed through coastal southeastern Australia, this stiff-leafed, bushy shrub was among the first bottle-brushes to be taken into cultivation. Its botanical epithet refers to a lemon scent in the crushed leaves, but this is barely detectable. A tough and vigorous plant, it usually grows quite rapidly to 10 ft (3 m) but may remain at much the same size for decades after, with a short basal trunk. The scarlet to crimson spikes are 4 in (10 cm) long and held erect, appearing in late spring and summer, often with an autumn flush as well. A variable species, it has a number of wild races as well as many cultivars, including 'Burgundy', with clustered, wine-colored brushes and leaves an attractive pinkish red when young; 'Mauve Mist', also with colored new leaves and abundant brushes that start mauve and age to a deeper magenta; 'Reeves Pink', a denser shrub with clear pink flowers; 'Splendens' (syn. 'Endeavour'), an early cultivar making a compact bush bearing bright scarlet brushes over a long period; and 'White Anzac' (syn. 'Albus'), with white flowers. Protect from winter frosts. It also makes a nice pot plant. **ZONES 8–11.**

Callistemon citrinus 'Burgundy'

CALLISTEMON

BOTTLEBRUSH

These evergreen Australian shrubs and small trees bear magnificent long-stamened, mostly red flowers in dense cylindrical spikes. The tips of the flower spikes continue to grow as leafy shoots, leaving long-lasting, woody seed capsules that eventually become half embedded in the thickening branch. Many species have a somewhat weeping habit and a few have striking papery bark, like that in the related genus *Melaleuca*. The flowers are nectar rich and attract birds, including small parrots in their native regions. The 25 species hybridize freely and seed from mixed stands cannot be trusted to come true. In recent decades many hybrid cultivars have been named, most of uncertain parentage, with flowers in a variety of hues in the white, pink to red range.

CULTIVATION

Shrubby callistemons make a fine addition to the shrub border, where they attract birds. Larger species are popular as compact street and park trees for mild climates. In general, they are only marginally frost tolerant and prefer full sun and moist soil; some, however, will tolerate poor drainage. A light pruning after flowering will prevent seed capsules forming and help promote bushiness. Prune to make a single trunk on tree-like species. Propagation of species is from seed (preferably wild collected), cultivars and selected clones from tip cuttings.

Callistemon citrinus 'White Anzac'

CALLUNA

HEATHER, LING

The sole species of this genus, heather, is an evergreen shrub and is the dominant moorland plant of the colder parts of the UK and northern Europe; it is closely related to the heath genus *Erica*. White, pink, red or purple are the usual colors for the small bell-shaped flowers, borne in dense clusters. In winter the foliage turns brownish or dull purple. Mostly grown in gardens are the numerous cultivars, selected for dwarf or compact growth and for flower or foliage color.

CULTIVATION

It is an extremely frost-hardy plant, thriving in very exposed situations and often performing poorly under kinder conditions. The soil should be acidic, gritty, and of low fertility. Cut back after flowering to keep bushes compact. In areas with warm, humid summers it is prone to root- and stem-rot. Propagation is usually from tip cuttings or rooted branches can be detached.

Calluna vulgaris 'Orange Queen'

Calluna vulgaris

Common heather makes a spreading shrub 12–36 in (30–90 cm) high. The flowers of wild plants are pale pink to a strong purplish pink, occasionally white. Flowering time is variable: some races and cultivars flower through summer, others from midsummer to early autumn. With over 400 cultivars available it is hard to decide which to mention, but the following are representative and will add interest and diversity to the garden. 'H. E. Beale' is quite a tall specimen to 30 in (75 cm) with grayish green foliage and long racemes of silvery pink double flowers held late in the season. 'Multicolor' is 4 in (10 cm) tall with a 10 in (25 cm) spread and is a compact variety with interesting yellow-green foliage tinged orange and red with racemes of mauve blooms. 'Orange Queen' is a very compact plant grown for its foliage, golden yellow in summer changing to deep burnt-orange in winter; it has single pink flowers. **ZONES 4–9.**

Calluna vulgaris 'Multicolor'

CALYCANTHUS

ALLSPICE

Calycanthus occidentalis

Only 2 or 3 species make up this genus of deciduous, cool-climate shrubs from North America. The leaves, bark and wood all have a spicy aroma when they are cut or bruised. They are grown for their curiously colored flowers, which appear singly among the leaves in late spring or summer and resemble small magnolia flowers with narrow petals that are deep red-brown or dull reddish purple; the flowers make interesting indoor decorations.

CULTIVATION
Undemanding shrubs, they flower best in a sunny but sheltered position in fertile, humus-rich, moist soil. Propagation is usually by layering branches, or from the seeds which are contained in soft, fig-like fruits.

Calycanthus floridus

Calycanthus floridus
CAROLINA ALLSPICE, SWEET SHRUB

A shrub from southeastern USA, it grows 6–9 ft (1.8–2.7 m) and has broad, glossy, pale green leaves with downy undersides. Its 2 in (5 cm) wide, early summer flowers consist of many petals that are dull brownish red, often with paler tips. **ZONES 6–10.**

Calycanthus occidentalis
SPICE BUSH, CALIFORNIAN ALLSPICE

This species, from the ranges of northern California, makes a shrub of rather irregular growth up to 12 ft (3.5 m) tall. The leaves are larger than those of *Calycanthus floridus* and their undersides are not downy. The flowers are also larger, sometimes 3 in (8 cm) across, but with similar coloring to those of *C. floridus*. **ZONES 7–10.**

CAMELLIA

Camellias are among the most popular of flowering shrubs and a profusion of beautiful garden varieties has been produced. Most of the many thousands of cultivars now listed are descended from *Camellia japonica*, introduced to Europe in the early eighteenth century from China. Two other species, *C. sasanqua* and *C. reticulata*, have also produced many cultivars. The genus of *Camellia*, however, has numerous additional species, most of which have never been cultivated. In the wild they are restricted to eastern Asia, ranging from Japan through southern and central China into Indochina, with a few outliers in the eastern Himalayas and the Malay Archipelago. Southern China accounts for the great majority of species, and discoveries by Chinese botanists in recent decades have tripled the number of known species, from under 100 in 1960 to almost 300 at the present time. All species are evergreen shrubs or small trees. The majority have small flowers of no great ornamental value, but there are nonetheless many beautiful species still awaiting introduction to gardens; some with appealing foliage or bark, rather than flowers, as their chief attraction. The flower color of camellias is always in the white-pink-red range, except for a small group of southern Chinese and Vietnamese species that have pale yellow to bronze-yellow flowers—their introduction to cultivation, which started in the 1970s, gave hope of introducing yellow into hybrid cultivars, but success has so far been elusive. Hybridization between other species, however, has increased from a trickle in the 1930s (with the *C.* × *williamsii* hybrids) to an avalanche at the present time, and hybrid camellias (as opposed to straight japonicas, reticulatas or sasanquas) now account for a large proportion of new releases.

Apart from the ornamental species, there are camellias with economic importance of other kinds. Tea is the dried and cured young leaves of *C. sinensis*, now grown in many parts of the world in addition to its native southern China. Also from China is *C. oleifera*, grown there in plantations for the valuable oil pressed from its seeds, used in cooking and cosmetics; several other species are also grown for their oil.

CULTIVATION

Most camellias grow best in mild, humid climates and some species are very frost tender, but most of the cultivars are moderately frost hardy. They prefer well-drained, slightly acidic soil enriched with organic matter and generally grow best in part-shade, though some cultivars are quite sun tolerant. Good drainage is important to prevent phytophthora root rot, but they like to be kept moist. Many varieties are suited to pot culture and make handsome tub specimens. Pruning is unnecessary, but trim them after flowering or cut back harder if rejuvenation is required. Propagate from cuttings in late summer or winter, or by grafting.

Camellia Hybrids

Few attempts were made to cross the different species of camellia in the nineteenth century, although hybrids in many other genera were being produced. There were some accidental camellia hybrids from China and Japan, but no successful deliberate cross was raised until the *Camellia* × *williamsii* hybrids were released around 1940. Hybrids slowly gained in popularity through the 1960s and 1970s and now make up a substantial proportion of new releases. The most widely used parents are *C. japonica*, *C. sasanqua* and *C. reticulata* but many others have also been used, including *C. saluenensis, C. pitardii, C. cuspidata, C. lutchuensis* and more recently some of the small-flowered species such as *C. tsaii*. In this way the diversity of foliage, flower and growth form is being extended. The addition of fragrance to camellia blooms

Camellia Hybrid 'Cornish Snow'

Camellia Hybrid 'Scentuous'

is one direction breeders are taking. Some representative cultivars are **'Brian'** *(C. saluenensis × reticulata)*, which has rose pink pointed petals in a hose-in-hose arrangement up to 4 in (10 cm) across, with a vigorous, upright habit; **'Cornish Snow'** *(C. cuspidata × saluenensis)* with profuse, delicate, small single white flowers sometimes flushed pink, a tall, open habit and very cold hardy; **'Scentuous'** *(C. japonica* 'Tiffany × *lutchuensis)* with semi-double white petals flushed pink on the reverse, the fragrance of *C. lutchuensis*, an open habit and bright green leaves. **'Baby Bear'** *(C. rosiflora × tsaii)* is a small-flowered dwarf form with light pink blooms and a dense habit ideal for bonsai or rockery use. **ZONES 7–10.**

Camellia japonica

Wild plants of this best known camellia species are small, scraggy trees 20–30 ft (6–9 m) tall in their natural habitats in Japan, Korea and China, usually with red, somewhat funnel-shaped, 5-petalled flowers only 2–3 in (5–8 cm) across. In Japan the typical form, **Camellia japonica** subsp. *japonica*, is found in coastal scrubs of the south and is replaced in north-western Honshu by the more cold-tolerant **C. j.** subsp. *rusticana*, known as the 'snow camellia'. Selection of desirable garden forms of *Camellia japonica* began at least 300 years ago in both China and Japan, the Chinese favoring double flowers and the Japanese singles. After its introduction to Europe in about 1745 an increasing number of these cultivars were imported, mostly renamed with Latin names such as **'Alba Plena'** and **'Anemoni-flora'** on their arrival, and in the early nine-teenth century many new cultivars were raised there. It was discovered that new flower types could be obtained by seedling selection and by watching for branch sports (vegetative mutations). By the late nineteenth–early twentieth century thousands of cultivars had arisen, not only in Europe but in California, Australia and New Zealand not to mention Japan, where new cultivars were actively being produced. Camellias fell from fashion to some degree during the period between World War I and World War II, but the 1950s saw them come back strongly and the majority of known cultivars date from this time and later. Even though hybrid camellias make up an increasing proportion of new listings, cultivars of pure *C. japonica* origin remain as popular as ever.

Camellia japonica 'Desire'

Camellia japonica 'Chandleri'

Camellia japonica 'Betty Sheffield Pink'

Camellia enthusiasts have devised classifications of the cultivars based on flower size and form: sizes run from **miniature** (under 2½ in [6 cm]) through **small**, **medium**, **medium-large** and **large** to **very large** (over 5 in [12 cm]); forms of flower are divided into **single**, **semi-double**, **anemone-form**, **informal double or peony-form**, **rose-form double** and **formal double**. By specifying their size class and form and describing the coloring, most cultivars can be pinned down at least to a small group. A subgroup of japonicas that deserve special mention are the **Higo camellias**, a collection of distinctively beautiful single cultivars from the southern Japanese island of Kyushu. *Camellia japonica* cultivars vary in flowering time from late autumn to early spring in mild climates, and from early to late spring in cooler climates. They will not survive outdoors where winter temperatures drop much below 15°F (–10°C). Among representative cultivars, some old favorites are **'Adolphe Audusson'**, with large saucer-shaped, semi-double, dark red flowers sometimes with white markings and prominent yellow stamens; **'Chandleri'**, a bright red, anemone-form double of medium size; **'Magnoliiflora'** (syn. 'Hagoromo'), an elegant semi-double with blush pink blooms of medium size; **'Virginia Franco Rosea'**, a small formal double with many-rowed petals in soft pink with faint lines. Significant newer cultivars include **'Betty Sheffield Pink'**, a medium-large incomplete double anemone-form with wavy pink petals sometimes irregularly splashed

white; **'Guilio Nuccio'**, a very large semi-double with very broad, irregular coral red petals and prominent yellow stamens; **'Desire'**, a medium-large formal double with pale pink, shading to darker pink or lilac on the outside; **'Erin Farmer'**, a large semi-double in orchid pink, shading to almost white with golden stamens in the center. The best known miniature is **'Bokuhan'** (syn. 'Tinsie'), the tiny flowers having a ring of dark red petals surrounding a white bulb of petaloids; it is a very old Japanese cultivar. A fine Higo cultivar is **'Yamato Nishiki'** (syn. 'Brocade of Old Japan'), with large, single white flowers broadly streaked pink and red, and a very wide circle of gold stamens. Representing a group of cultivars with curious foliage is **'Kingyo-Tsubaki'** (syns 'Fishtail', 'Mermaid'), with leaves mostly 3-lobed; the flowers are medium-small, single and rose pink. **ZONES 5–10.**

Camellia japonica 'Erin Farmer'

Camellia japonica 'Guilio Nuccio'

Camellia reticulata

This species includes some of the largest flowered camellia cultivars, and many of these were cultivated for centuries in southern China before one was brought to England in 1820. Not until much later a far smaller flowered plant was discovered growing wild in Yunnan and determined by botanists to be the wild ancestor of these early Chinese cultivars. Many additional cultivars have since been documented, mostly in Yunnan and often as temple trees up to 40 ft (12 m) tall and hundreds of years old—they are known as the **'Yunnan camellias'**. *Camellia reticulata* makes a more upright plant than *C. japonica,* with an open framework of sparser foliage and large, leathery leaves. They are late blooming for camellias, flowering from late winter to mid-spring. The wild form is sold as **'Wild Type'** and has rather irregularly cup-shaped single reddish pink flowers about 3 in (8 cm) wide. The original introduction from 1820, **'Captain Rawes'**, is still admired, with 6 in (15 cm) semi-double blooms of rich carmine-pink, the petals coarsely fluted. Newer cultivars are more compact, for example, the American **'Lila Naff'**, a single but with multiple broad petals of a most delicate pink, and **'William Hertrich'**, a very large semi-double with deep red petals. Many cultivars that are usually treated as reticulatas are in fact hybrids, with influence from other species. **ZONES 8–10.**

Camellia sasanqua 'Paradise Belinda'

Camellia sasanqua

Originating in southern Japan, this small-leafed species has given rise to many hundreds of cultivars. The most versatile camellias from the landscaping point of view, the sasanquas have greatly increased in popularity recently. They are densely leafed plants that can be grown as hedges and even as street trees, and some cultivars are suited to espaliering against a wall or fence. They have small, shiny, dark green leaves and small to medium-sized, delicately fragrant, mostly single or semi-double flowers in a variety of colors, profusely borne but individually short lived. Different cultivars extend the flowering season from early autumn to mid-winter. Sasanquas are faster growing and more sun tolerant than most camellias, performing better in mild climates. Among superior cultivars are **'Jennifer Susan'**, with clear pink semi-double flowers; **'Plantation Pink'**, an Australian-raised cultivar with larger single, saucer-shaped, soft pink flowers, excellent for hedging; **'Paradise Belinda'**, semi-double with the outer

Camellia reticulata 'Lila Naff'

Camellia reticulata 'William Hertrich'

stamens bearing small petal-like organs to give it an unusual effect; and **'Mine-no-yuki'** (syn. 'White Doves'), a creamy semi-double that can be espaliered. **ZONES 9–11.**

Camellia sinensis
TEA

Camellia sasanqua 'Plantation Pink'

All the world's tea comes from this species, grown mainly in plantations in the highlands of tropical Asia but also in southern China (its original home) and Japan, and more recently in other parts of the world where the climate is suitably mild and humid. Tender new shoots are plucked, fermented and dried in different ways to give black or green tea. It normally makes a shrub of 6–10 ft (1.8– 3 m) tall with thin, serrated leaves and rather insignificant, white to cream flowers about 1 in (25 mm) across borne on recurved stalks from the leaf axils; when grown for tea the plants are kept trimmed to about chest height and flowers are rarely seen. *Camellia sinensis* **var. assamica** is the Assam tea now grown universally in India and Sri Lanka, with larger leaves and more vigorous growth. **ZONES 9–11.**

Camellia sinensis

Camellia × williamsii

Although hybrid camellias are dealt with separately under a general heading, this group is so well known it merits its own heading. All these hybrids are crosses between *C. japonica* and the western Chinese mountain species *C. saluenensis*, or seedlings of succeeding generations. The original *C. × williamsii* was raised in Britain in the 1930s and several cultivars became available in the 1940s, soon achieving popularity for their cold hardiness and profuse blooms in clear colors borne over a long winter and spring season. One of the earliest and best known is **'Donation'** with large orchid-pink, semi-double flowers. **'Caerhays'** has medium-sized, semi-double, lilac-rose flowers on somewhat pendulous branches. **'E. G. Waterhouse'** has an erect habit with matt green foliage and formal double flowers of a rich fuchsia pink. **ZONES 7–10.**

Camellia × williamsii 'E. G. Waterhouse'

Camellia × williamsii 'Donation'

Carpenteria californica

CARPENTERIA

TREE ANEMONE, BUSH ANEMONE

Carpenteria californica

In the wild this very attractive shrub is known only from a small area of central California, on dry mountain slopes. It can grow to 20 ft (6 m) tall but in gardens it is usually a sprawling shrub of 6–8 ft (1.8–2.4 m) tall that may need support, and is best grown against a sunny wall. The flowers, solitary or in small groups, are normally 2–2½ in (5–6 cm) wide but may be up to 4 in (10 cm) wide with broadly overlapping petals. **ZONES 7–9.**

Only one species from California belongs to this genus, an evergreen shrub with pure white flowers like those of *Philadelphus* but with 5 to 7 petals rather than 4, and a more conspicuous cluster of golden stamens. The leaves are narrow and soft, deep green above but paler and felty beneath, arranged in opposite pairs on the soft-wooded branches. It is a beautiful shrub when in full flower in late spring and early summer. Named for the American Professor Carpenter, it should not be confused with the palm genus *Carpentaria*.

CULTIVATION

Although requiring a fairly cool climate, this species only flowers well in regions with warm dry summers and needs ample sunshine, well-drained, gritty soil that must not dry out too much and protection from strong winds. Propagation is usually from seed, as cuttings do not root easily.

Caryopteris incana

CARYOPTERIS

BLUEBEARD

This is a genus of 6 species of deciduous, erect subshrubs or woody perennials in the verbena family, all native to eastern Asia. They have slender, cane-like stems with thin, toothed leaves arranged in opposite pairs, and bear small blue or purple flowers in dense stalked clusters in the leaf axils. Only 2 species have been grown much in gardens and even these are now largely replaced by the hybrid between them, represented by a number of cultivars.

CULTIVATION

These plants are often included in shrub borders where their grayish foliage and white or blue flowers blend well with plants of more robust color. They need to be placed in a full sun position, in well-drained, humus-rich soil. Cut well back in early spring to ensure a good framework for the new season's growth and consequent late summer to autumn flowering. Seed can be used for propagation, but in the case of the many cultivars it is necessary to take soft-tip or semi-ripe cuttings.

Caryopteris × *clandonensis*

HYBRID BLUEBEARD, BLUE-MIST SHRUB

This subshrub, a cross between *Caryopteris incana* and *C. mongolica*, is prized for its masses of delicate, purple-blue flowers borne from late summer to autumn. It grows to a height and spread of 3 ft (1 m), and the oval leaves are gray-green and irregularly serrated. '**Ferndown**' a popular choice among the many cultivars, with dark violet-blue flowers, while '**Heavenly Blue**' has blooms of deep blue. '**Kew Blue**' has darker green leaves and dark blue flowers. **ZONES 5–9.**

Caryopteris incana

syn. *Caryopteris mastacanthus*
BLUEBEARD

This soft-stemmed shrub from China and Japan is often treated as a perennial in gardens. It reaches around 5 ft (1.5 m) in height with upright, leafy stems. The leaves are soft grayish, coarsely serrated and the clusters of bluish purple flowers display prominent stamen filaments, prompting the common name. **ZONES 7–10.**

Caryopteris × *clandonensis* 'Ferndown'

Cassiope 'Edinburgh'

CASSIOPE

Cassiope 'Edinburgh'

This cultivar originated as a hybrid between *Cassiope fastigiata* and *C. lycopodioides*. It reaches a height of about 12 in (30 cm), with many stems from the base. In late spring, it bears small white bells in rather tight clusters on short stalks. **ZONES 4–8.**

Closely allied to the heathers, this genus of 12 species of dwarf evergreen shrubs is found in the Arctic and alpine regions of the northern hemisphere; consequently it is only suited to gardens assured of moist, cool summers and moisture-retentive soil imitating the wild conditions. Cassiopes are low-growing plants, many stemmed from the base, with scale-like leaves and nodding, small, white or pink flowers. The name is taken from Greek mythology, Cassiope being the mother of Andromeda—her name was chosen for this genus because of its close relationship to the genus *Andromeda*. It should be pronounced with four syllables, like Penelope.

CULTIVATION

Cassiopes need to be grown in rather peaty soil to supply the required acidity and moisture, and although they enjoy an open position they need to be protected from the sun and from reflected heat if growing in containers or among rocks. Propagation is from cuttings in summer, while the mat-forming types can be increased from self-rooted stems.

Ceanothus thyrsiflorus

CEANOTHUS

CALIFORNIA LILAC

Brilliant displays of blue, violet, or occasionally pink or white flowers are the chief attraction of most of the 50 or more species of this genus of evergreen and deciduous shrubs (some reaching small tree size), all of them North American but the vast majority confined to the coast ranges of California. Some species that grow on coastal cliffs develop dense, prostrate forms highly resistant to salt spray. The leaves are small to medium sized, blunt tipped and usually toothed. The flowers, individually tiny with thread-like stalks, are massed in dense clusters at the branch ends; they appear in spring in most species.

CULTIVATION

As garden plants these shrubs can be outstandingly ornamental but often short-lived, especially prone to sudden death in climates with warm, wet summers. They require full sun and prefer shelter, particularly from strong winds, in well-drained soil. Propagate from seed, often freely produced in small round capsules, or from cuttings.

Ceanothus impressus

SANTA BARBARA CEANOTHUS

A free-flowering, small-leafed, evergreen species of dense, spreading habit, this is a first-class garden shrub under suitable conditions. The leaves are ½ in (12 mm) long or less, very thick and with the veins deeply impressed into the upper surface. In spring it produces a profuse display of small clusters of deep blue flowers. From 6–10 ft (1.8–3 m) in height, this coastal Californian species prefers tough, exposed conditions. 'Puget Blue' features stunning blue flowers and is probably a hybrid with *C. papillosus*. **ZONES 8–10.**

Ceanothus thyrsiflorus

BLUE BLOSSOM CEANOTHUS

This is an evergreen shrub or small tree that grows to over 20 ft (6 m) in its native moist coastal forests of California, but the forms grown in gardens include some, for example *Ceanothus thyrsiflorus* var. *repens,* that are more compact shrubs of only 3–10 ft (1–3 m) with vigorous spreading branches. The shiny, oval, medium-sized leaves have 3 prominent longitudinal veins. In late spring and early summer the plant produces dense cylindrical clusters of lavender-blue to almost white flowers. 'Blue Mound' is a low-growing hybrid of *C. thyrsiflorus* reaching 5 ft (1.5 m) in height and spreading to over 6 ft (1.8 m) wide, with medium blue flowers. 'Cascade' on the other hand can grow to 25 ft (8 m) with broadly arching branches and pale blue flowers. **ZONES 7–9.**

Cephalotaxus harringtonia
JAPANESE PLUM YEW

First known from Japan, this variable species also occurs in Korea and parts of China. The typical form is a spreading, bushy shrub 6–10 ft (1.8–3 m) tall with leaves up to 2½ in (6 cm) long. More commonly grown is *Cephalotaxus harringtonia* var. *drupacea*, a dome-like shrub to about 10 ft (3 m) with short blunt leaves in 2 erect rows. The most remarkable and attractive form is 'Fastigiata': very erect, it sends up a dense mass of long, straight stems from the base, with radiating whorls of recurving leaves. It forms a tight column 6 ft (1.8 m) or more high and 24–36 in (60–90 cm) across. 'Nana' is a low-growing form, generally under 3 ft (1 m) high but spreading widely with almost prostrate branches, often self-layering. 'Prostrata' forms a cushion of generally ascending branches to 24 in (60 cm) tall and spreads about 4 ft (1.2 m). **ZONES 6–10.**

Cephalotaxus harringtonia 'Prostrata'

CEPHALOTAXUS
PLUM YEW

This is an interesting genus of conifers consisting of around 10 species of shrubs or small trees from eastern Asia, mostly with many stems sprouting from the base. The deep green, leathery leaves are rather like those of the true yews *(Taxus)*, though usually longer. The fleshy 'fruits' develop in stalked globular heads and are more like olives than plums, ripening reddish brown. Male pollen sacs are grouped in small, globular clusters on separate trees.

CULTIVATION

They are tough, resilient plants, but do best in cool, fairly humid climates and in sheltered spots. The occasional free-seeding specimen can cause minor problems by the quantity of 'fruit' dropping to rot on the ground. Propagate from seed, which may take 2 years to germinate, or from cuttings.

Cephalotaxus harringtonia 'Fastigiata'

CERATOSTIGMA

This genus of 8 species of herbaceous perennials and small shrubs is primarily of Himalayan and east Asian origin, with one species endemic to the Horn of Africa. Most of the species grown in gardens are small deciduous shrubs and from spring to autumn they produce loose heads of blue flowers. The small leaves are deep green, turning to bronze or crimson in autumn before dropping.

CULTIVATION

Ceratostigma species will grow in any moist, well-drained soil in sun or part-shade. Propagate from seed or semi-ripe cuttings, or by division. In cold climates they will reshoot from the roots even though the top growth may die right back.

Ceratostigma willmottianum

CHINESE PLUMBAGO

This 2–4 ft (0.6–1.2 m), deciduous shrub from western Sichuan, China, is prized for its small lilac-blue flowers that open from late summer to autumn. The leaves are deep green, roughly diamond-shaped and around 2 in (5 cm) long. **ZONES 6–10.**

Ceratostigma willmottianum

CESTRUM

This genus of the potato family is made up of almost 200 species of mostly evergreen shrubs native to Central and South America and the West Indies. The leaves are simple and smooth edged, often with a rank smell when bruised, and the smallish flowers are tubular or urn-shaped, gathered in clusters at the branch tips. The flowers vary in color from white to green, yellow, red and dull purplish, and some are night scented. Small round berries follow the flowers; these and other parts of plants are poisonous.

CULTIVATION

Cestrums make rather straggly bushes but can be pruned hard to shape by removing older stems each year after flowering. In frost-free climates they grow easily in full sun and moderately fertile, well-drained soil with plentiful water in summer and regular fertilizing. In cooler climates grow in a conservatory or against a wall for frost protection. They are excellent container plants. Some species are free seeding and invasive. Propagate from soft tip cuttings.

Cestrum 'Newellii'

Cestrum 'Newellii'

This is a popular cultivar of hybrid origin, possibly between *Cestrum elegans* and *C. fasciculatum*—it takes an expert eye, in fact, to distinguish between these and *C.* 'Newellii'. It reaches about 6 ft (1.8 m) high and produces clusters of crimson, unscented flowers through much of the year, followed by matching berries. Tougher than most cestrums, it is regarded as a weed in some mild areas. **ZONES 9–11.**

Cestrum nocturnum

NIGHT-SCENTED JESSAMINE,
LADY OF THE NIGHT

A somewhat untidy evergreen shrub to 12 ft (3.5 m) tall and almost as wide, this species has long, slender, arching branches springing densely from the base. Clusters of slender, pale green flowers appear in late summer and autumn, strongly and sweetly perfumed at night but scentless during the day. The green berries that follow turn a glossy china white in early winter. **ZONES 10–12.**

Cestrum nocturnum

Chaenomeles speciosa
'Apple Blossom'

CHAENOMELES

FLOWERING QUINCE

Related to the edible quince *(Cydonia)* with similar large, hard fruits, these many-stemmed deciduous shrubs bear red, pink or white flowers on a tangle of bare branches in early spring or even late winter. Originating in China, Japan and Korea, they are very frost hardy and adaptable. The tough, springy branches are often thorny on vigorous shoots; the leaves are simple and finely toothed. The flowers appear in stalkless clusters on the previous year's wood, followed in summer by yellow-green fruits with waxy, strongly perfumed skins that make fine jams and jellies. The wild forms have been superseded by a large selection of cultivars.

CULTIVATION

They do best in a sunny spot in well-drained but not too rich soil and a dry atmosphere. Cut back hard each year. Propagate from cuttings.

Chaenomeles × superba

Chaenomeles japonica

syn. *Chaenomeles maulei*
JAPANESE FLOWERING QUINCE

This low-growing species, native to Japan, is usually no more than 3 ft (1 m) high, making a dense mass of horizontally spreading, thorny branches. The flowers, appearing long after the plant has come into leaf, are about 1½ in (25 mm) across and usually orange-red but sometimes crimson. Produced from spring to summer, they are followed by small, round yellow fruit that have a pleasant fragrance. *Chaenomeles japonica* var. *alpina* is a dwarf form with semi-prostrate stems and small orange flowers. **ZONES 4–9.**

Chaenomeles japonica

Chaenomeles speciosa

CHINESE FLOWERING QUINCE, JAPONICA

This species and its hybrids are the most commonly grown flowering quinces. Shrubs 5–10 ft (1.5–3 m) high, they spread by basal suckers to form dense thickets of stems. Their leaves are larger than in *Chaenomeles japonica*, up to 4 in (10 cm) long and 1½ in (35 mm) wide, and the scarlet to deep red flowers, opening from late winter to mid-spring, are also larger. Modern cultivars vary in availability, but several older ones still widely grown include 'Apple Blossom', white, flushed pink; 'Nivalis', white; 'Moerloosii', white flushed and blotched pink and carmine; and 'Rubra Grandiflora', crimson. **ZONES 6–10.**

Chaenomeles × superba

This is a hybrid between *Chaenomeles japonica* and *C. speciosa* with a height about midway between that of the two parents. It has given rise to a number of first-class cultivars like 'Knap Hill Scarlet' with bright orange-scarlet flowers; 'Crimson and Gold' with deep crimson petals and gold anthers; 'Nicoline', which has a rather sprawling habit and scarlet flowers; 'Pink Lady' with large, bright rose-pink flowers; and 'Rowallane' with deep crimson flowers. **ZONES 6–10.**

Chamaecytisus purpureus

CHAMAECYTISUS

A broom genus consisting of about 30 species of deciduous and evergreen shrubs from the Mediterranean region and the Canary Islands, *Chamaecytisus* is closely related to *Cytisus* and its species were formerly included in the latter genus. They range from dwarf to quite tall shrubs but all have leaves consisting of 3 leaflets and produce clusters of white, yellow, pink or purple pea-flowers. Some are attractive rock-garden subjects, while at least one taller species is grown as a fodder and green manure plant.

CULTIVATION

The smaller species should be grown in full sun in very well-drained soil, preferably in a raised position such as a rock garden. They seldom survive transplanting. The taller species are less fussy and will grow in most soils, fertile or infertile, and in a range of situations. Propagate from seed or cuttings.

Chamaecytisus purpureus
syn. *Cytisus purpureus*
PURPLE BROOM

Native to southeastern Europe this is a low-growing deciduous shrub reaching a height of about 18 in (45 cm), with a broadly spreading habit. Showy lilac-purple flowers about ¾ in (18 mm) in length are produced in late spring and early summer, in clusters of one to three at each leaf axil. Flowering in the next season is promoted by cutting back as soon as flowering has finished. **ZONES 6–9.**

Chimonanthus praecox
syn. Chimonanthus fragrans

The wintersweet makes a thicket of stiff, angular stems 10–15 ft (3–4.5 m) high and wide, with harsh-textured, mid-green leaves. The flowers appear in abundance on bare winter branches or, in milder climates, among the last leaves of autumn; the petals are pale yellow to off-white with a dull pink or red basal zone showing on the inside. The fruits are yellowish brown when ripe. The cultivar 'Luteus' has late blooming, buttercup-yellow flowers. **ZONES 6–10.**

CHIMONANTHUS
WINTERSWEET

This small genus of 6 species of deciduous shrubs from China belongs to a primitive flowering-plant family allied to the magnolia family; one species is popular in gardens for its deliciously scented flowers produced from early to mid-winter. The leaves are simple and thin textured, clustered at the ends of the stiff branches. Smallish flowers are clustered just below branch tips; they are multi-petalled and cup-shaped, with a translucent waxy texture, and are followed by leathery-skinned fruit of a strange shape, like little bags stuffed with balls, which turn out to be the large seeds.

CULTIVATION

Quite frost hardy, it will grow in most positions. In cold climates position against a warm wall to protect the flowers. Immediately after flowering thin out weaker stems and, if desired, shorten larger stems. Propagate from seed or layer multiple stems by mounding with soil.

Chimonanthus praecox

CHOISYA

This genus of 8 species of evergreen shrubs belongs to the same family as citrus, and is from Mexico and the far south of the USA. One species is widely cultivated as an ornamental in warm-temperate climates. Their leaves are compound with 3 to 7 leaflets radiating from the stalk apex; from the leaf axils arise clusters of fragrant star-shaped white flowers, resembling orange-blossoms. The crushed or bruised leaves are also aromatic.

CULTIVATION

They are excellent hedging plants as well as being attractive additions to shrub borders, growing best in full sun or part shade and a slightly acid, humus-rich, well-drained soil. Protect from strong winds, fertilize in spring and trim lightly after flowering to keep foliage dense and ground-hugging. Propagate from tip cuttings in autumn.

Choisya ternata
MEXICAN ORANGE BLOSSOM

One of the most frost hardy evergreens to come from the highlands of Mexico, this popular species makes a compact, rounded
bush to 6 ft (1.8 m) or more. Its attractive leaves consist of 3
glossy deep green leaflets (*ternata* means 'grouped in 3s'). Tight
clusters of small white, fragrant flowers appear among the
leaves in spring, and sometimes again in late summer. The cultivar **'Sundance'** has golden-yellow foliage when young, maturing
to yellow-green. **ZONES 7–11.**

Choisya ternata

CISTUS
ROCK ROSE

These evergreen shrubs from around the Mediterranean and the
Canary Islands are valued for their attractive, saucer-shaped
flowers, which have crinkled petals in shades of pink, purple or
white and a central boss of golden stamens, like a single rose.
Although short-lived, most bloom over a long season, some for
almost the whole year, and they do very well in shrub borders,
on banks or in pots; some examples include 'Peggy Sammons',
'Santa Cruz', 'Snow Mound' and 'Warley Rose'. Some species
exude an aromatic resin which the ancient Greeks and Romans
called *labdanum* and used for incense and perfume, as well as
medicinally.

Cistus ladanifer

CULTIVATION

These shrubs are easily cultivated provided they are given a warm, sunny position and very well-drained, even rather dry soil; they like being among large rocks or other rubble where their roots can seek out deep moisture. If necessary they can be tip pruned to promote bushiness, or main branches shortened by about a third after flowering. Most species are moderately frost hardy; all are resistant to very dry conditions. They will thrive in countries with cool- to warm-temperate climates, but not in subtropical regions with hot, humid summers. Propagation is normally from cuttings, although seed is readily germinated.

Cistus albidus
WHITE-LEAFED ROCKROSE

This attractive species, with felty, gray-green foliage and large, lilac-pink flowers with a small yellow blotch at the base of each petal, is very sensitive to excess moisture. From the far southwest of Europe and northwest Africa, it grows to 4 ft (1.2 m) high and 8 ft (2.4 m) wide with foliage right down to the ground, concealing thick, twisted branches. The flowers appear mainly in spring. **ZONES 7–9.**

Cistus albidus

Cistus ladanifer
CRIMSON-SPOT ROCKROSE

The most upright and slender species, *Cistus ladanifer* grows 5–6 ft (1.5–1.8 m) tall but quickly becomes sparse and leggy and does not take well to pruning. The whole plant, apart from the flower petals, is coated with a shiny resin that in the heat of the day becomes semi-liquid and very aromatic. Its leaves are narrow and dark green and the flowers, among the largest in the genus at 3–4 in (8–10 m) across, have pure white petals each with a reddish choco-late basal blotch—they are borne from mid-spring to early summer. The cultivar 'Albi-florus' has pure white petals. **ZONES 8–10.**

Cistus × purpureus 'Brilliancy'

Cistus laurifolius

The laurel-leafed cistus from southwestern Europe and Morocco is not one of the largest in flower—the blooms are only about 2½ in (6 cm) wide—but it is a very beautiful, free-flowering plant. It has pure white flowers that are in gleaming contrast all through the summer against the leathery deep green leaves. Capable of growing to 6 ft (1.8 m) high, it has the best reputation for cold hardiness of any *Cistus*. **ZONES 7–9**.

Cistus 'Snow Mound'

Cistus 'Peggy Sammons'

Cistus × purpureus

ORCHID ROCK ROSE

This hybrid between *Cistus ladanifer* and *C. creticus* has deep pink flowers with prominent, dark reddish chocolate blotches on the petals. It is frost hardy and free flowering. Several clones have been named including **'Brilliancy'**, with clear pink petals, and **'Betty Taudevin'**, a deeper reddish pink. **ZONES 7–9**.

Cistus laurifolius

CLERODENDRUM

Clerodendrum trichotomum

This genus of over 400 species ranges through the world's tropics and warmer climates. It contains trees, shrubs, climbers and herbaceous plants, both deciduous and evergreen, some with very showy flowers. The features that unite them are leaves in opposite pairs; tubular flowers, usually flared or bowl-shaped at the mouth with 4 long stamens and a style protruding well beyond the tube; and fruit, a shiny berry sitting at the center of the calyx that usually becomes larger and thicker after flowering.

CULTIVATION

They vary greatly in their cold hardiness, though only a few species from China and Japan are suited to cool climates. They all appreciate a sunny position, though sheltered from strong wind and the hottest summer sun, and deep, moist, fertile soil. Propagate from cuttings, which strike readily under heat. Many species sucker quickly from the roots.

Clerodendrum bungei

Clerodendrum bungei
syn. Clerodendrum foetidum
GLORY FLOWER

This suckering shrub from China and the Himalayas has many vertical stems topped in summer with wonderfully fragrant heads of rose-pink flowers. The leaves are large and coarse, and have an unpleasant smell if crushed or bruised. The stems will reach 6 ft (1.8 m) unless cut to the ground each spring; new growths will then flower on 3 ft (1 m) stems. It will spread rapidly if not contained or controlled. **ZONES 7–10.**

Clerodendrum trichotomum
HARLEQUIN GLORY BOWER

Native to Japan and China, this is one of the most frost-hardy species. It makes an elegant deciduous shrub or tree to 15–20 ft (4.5–6 m) in height, of erect growth and sparse branching habit, drooping lower branches and thin, downy leaves. In late summer, it produces at the branch tips gracefully drooping panicles of slightly up-turned, sweet-scented white flowers, that age to pale mauve with large, dull pinkish calyces that are sharply ribbed. The small blue fruit, cupped in enlarged red calyces, can make quite a display. **ZONES 7–10.**

COLLETIA
ANCHOR PLANT

This unusual genus consists of 17 species of stiff, woody, ever-green shrubs from temperate and subtropical South America with leaves and branchlets arranged in opposite pairs. The leaves are very small and in most species are present only on new growths; their photosynthetic function is taken over by the green branchlets, each tipped by a fierce spine. Small white bell-shaped flowers appear in clusters at the branchlet junctions and have a sweet, honey-like smell. Colletias are curious plants.

CULTIVATION

They can be grown in any average garden soil and prefer full sun. Few shrubs are so well suited to forming an intruder-proof barrier. Propagation is from cuttings or seed, produced in small, globular capsules. Plants can be pruned back to encourage denser growth.

Colletia paradoxa

CORNUS

CORNEL, DOGWOOD

This genus of 45 species of evergreen and deciduous trees and shrubs from the northern hemisphere is discussed in detail in the chapter on Trees. The following species are shrubs.

Cornus alba

RED-BARKED DOGWOOD, TATARIAN DOGWOOD

Shiny red branches and twigs, brightest in winter or late autumn, are the feature of this northeast Asian deciduous shrub. It makes a dense thicket of slender stems 6–10 ft (1.8–3 m) high and often twice that in spread, with lower branches suckering or taking root on the ground. In late spring and summer it bears small clusters of creamy yellow flowers, followed by pea-sized white or blue-tinted fruit. It thrives in damp ground and is effective by lakes and streams. Cultivars include 'Elegantissima', with gray-green leaves partly white on their margins; 'Sibirica', with bright red leaves and stems; and 'Spaethii', with brilliantly gold-variegated leaves. **ZONES 4–9.**

Cornus stolonifera

Colletia paradoxa

syn. *Colletia cruciata*

Indigenous to Uruguay, Argentina and southern Brazil, this shrub grows to about 10 ft (3 m) tall with an erect, very irregular growth habit. Its leafless branchlets are deep gray-green with a slight waxy bloom and mostly flattened in the vertical plane, but sometimes it produces branches with shorter, narrower branchlets as well. The texture of the plant is remarkable—tapping it with a fingernail is like tapping a sheet of plywood. The flowers are white and appear in great abundance in autumn. They are fairly long lasting. **ZONES 7–10.**

Cornus alba 'Elegantissima'

Cornus stolonifera

syn. *Cornus sericea*

RED-OSIER DOGWOOD

This shrubby species is similar to *Cornus alba* but native to eastern North America and has a tendency to spread faster into large clumps. The winter stems are bright red, as are the fruit, while the flowers are white. Both species make excellent winter accent plants against white snow or dark evergreens. 'Flaviramea' has yellow winter stems; 'Kelsey Gold' has bright yellowish green leaves; 'Silver and Gold' has variegated leaves with yellow winter stems. **ZONES 2–10.**

CORONILLA
CROWN VETCH

This is a legume genus of 20 or so species of annuals, perennials and low shrubs. They have been described in the Annuals and Perennials chapter. The species described here is a popular shrub.

Coronilla emerus

Coronilla emerus
SCORPION SENNA, FALSE SENNA

Of wide natural distribution in Europe, this low, somewhat sprawling deciduous shrub has bright yellow flowers borne in small groups from the leaf axils in spring. They are followed by slender seed pods that are articulated, like a scorpion's tail. The leaves are small with few, rounded, bright green leaflets. Normally less than 3 ft (1 m) high it will sometimes reach twice this height. **ZONES 6–9.**

Corylopsis glabrescens

CORYLOPSIS
WINTER HAZEL

These deciduous shrubs from China and Japan produce short, usually pendulous spikes of fragrant, 5-petalled, pale yellow or greenish flowers on the bare branches before the blunt-toothed leaves appear in late spring. The fruits, ripening in summer among the leaves, are small, woody capsules each containing 2 black seeds. The subtle appeal of these shrubs lies mostly in the repetitive pattern of flower spikes on the bare branches.

CULTIVATION
Corylopsis species are best suited to a woodland setting in a reasonably moist, cool climate, providing a bold foil for bolder shrubs such as rhododendrons. The soil should be fertile, moist but well-drained and acid. Propagation is normally from seed.

Corylopsis glabrescens
FRAGRANT WINTER HAZEL

Native to Japan where it grows in the mountains, this attractive species makes a broadly spreading shrub of 15 ft (4.5 m) tall, sometimes even higher. The small flowers are lemon yellow in color with rather narrow petals and appear in mid-spring.
ZONES 6–9.

Corylopsis spicata
SPIKE WINTER HAZEL

This species from Japan was
the first one known in the
West. It is low growing, seldom exceeding 6 ft (1.8 m)
and often less, and broadly
spreading. The narrow, pale
greenish yellow, spring flowers
have red anthers, the short
spikes bursting from particularly large, pale green bracts
which persist on the spikes.
The arrangement of flowers is
more informal than that of
some other species. **ZONES 6–9**.

Corylopsis spicata

Corylus maxima

CORYLUS
HAZEL, FILBERT

The 10 or more deciduous trees and large shrubs in this genus
are best known for their edible nuts. The commonly grown
species have massed stems that spring from ground level, but
some others have a well-developed trunk. The branches are
tough and supple, and bear broad, toothed leaves that are somewhat heart-shaped and strongly veined. Male and female flowers
grow on the same plant; the males in slender catkins that appear
before the leaves expand; and the females are inconspicuous.
The latter develop into the distinctive nuts, each enclosed in a
fringed green husk and ripening in summer.

CULTIVATION
Provide ample space, full sun or part-shade and fertile, moist but
well-drained, chalky soil. Propagate by detaching suckers, or by
fresh nuts. For fruit set, there is a cold requirement of about
1,000 hours below 45°F (7°C). Cool, moist summers also assist
nut production.

Corylus maxima
FILBERT

The filbert, a native of
southern Europe, is similar in
most respects to the hazel but
is more inclined to become
tree-like and has sticky hairs
on the young twigs. The most
obvious difference, though, is
the much longer tubular husk
completely enclosing each nut,
which is also more elongated.
As an ornamental it is best
known by the cultivar
'Purpurea', which has deep,
dark purple, spring foliage,
softening to a dull greenish
purple in summer. **ZONES 4–9**.

COTINUS

Cotinus coggygria

SMOKE BUSH, SMOKE TREE

Only 3 species make up this genus of deciduous shrubs or small trees: one is from temperate Eurasia, one from eastern North America, and one confined to southwestern China. They have simple, oval, untoothed leaves. A striking feature is the inflorescences, much-branched with delicate, thread-like dull purplish branchlets, only a few of which carry the small flowers; they produce a curiously ornamental effect like fine puffs of smoke scattered over the foliage. Both flowers and fruits are tiny and inconspicuous. The foliage is another attraction, coloring deeply in autumn, and in some cultivars the spring foliage offers good color. In earlier times a commercial yellow dye was extracted from the wood of these trees.

CULTIVATION
Smoke bushes are easily grown, adapting to a range of temperate climates but most at home where summers are moderately warm and dry. Soil that is too moist or fertile discourages free flowering. Propagate from softwood cuttings in summer or seed in autumn.

Cotinus coggygria 'Velvet Cloak'

Cotinus coggygria
syn. *Rhus cotinus*
VENETIAN SUMAC, SMOKE TREE

Of wide distribution from southern Europe to central China, this bushy shrub is usually 10–15 ft (3–4 m) in height and spread, and has oval, long-stalked leaves. The inflorescences appear in early summer and are pale pinkish bronze, ageing to a duller purple-gray. Some of the flowers produce small, dry, flattened fruit in late summer. Autumn foliage has strong orange and bronze tones. **'Purpureus'** is widely grown—it has rich, purplish spring foliage becoming greener in summer and glowing orange and purple in autumn; **'Royal Purple'** is very similar but spring and summer foliage is deeper purple; the leaves of **'Velvet Cloak'** are purple and turn dark reddish purple in autumn.
ZONES 6–10.

Cotinus obovatus
syns *Cotinus americanus*, *Rhus cotinoides*
AMERICAN SMOKE TREE

From southeastern USA, this species can make a small tree of up to 30 ft (9 m), though may remain a tall shrub. The leaves are larger than those of *Cotinus coggygria* and bronze pink when young, turning mid-green in summer and finally orange-scarlet to purple in autumn. The inflorescences are also larger but sparser, and male and female flowers are on different trees.
ZONES 5–10.

Cotinus obovatus

COTONEASTER

This temperate Eurasian genus of shrubs (rarely small trees) includes both deciduous and evergreen species and is one of the small-fruited genera of the pome-fruit group of the rose family, that includes *Pyracantha*, *Crataegus* and *Amelanchier*. The name dates from Roman times, and means something like 'useless quince'. The lower-growing species are popular for rockeries, embankments and foundation plantings. They are mostly very frost hardy, often of dense, spreading habit, and provide a good display of red berries. Some species make good hedges and espaliers.

CULTIVATION

The evergreen species especially provide fine displays of berries, even in warmer temperate climates. All do best in full sun in moderately fertile, well-drained soil. They are prone to the bacterial disease fireblight. Propagate from seed or cuttings.

Cotoneaster dammeri

BEARBERRY COTONEASTER

Most distinctive of the fully prostrate cotoneasters, this central Chinese evergreen species has relatively large, round-tipped leaves with the veins deeply impressed into their dark green upper surfaces; the scattered starry white flowers appear through summer and are followed by solitary red fruit that last well into winter, when the leaves turn bronze. The varietal name *radicans* is often added, but there is confusion as to which form of the species it belongs; all cultivated forms have very similar qualities. 'Coral Beauty' has profuse, bright orange fruit. **ZONES 5–10.**

Cotoneaster dammeri 'Coral Beauty'

Cotoneaster franchetii

Cotoneaster franchetii

This attractive evergreen from western China grows to about 10 ft (3 m) tall, with long, cane-like branches. The smallish, pointed leaves have curved veins strongly impressed into the glossy upper surface and woolly undersides. In early summer it bears small clusters of pink-tinged white flowers, followed by tight groups of salmon-pink to pale orange berries which last into winter. A reliable shrub, it adapts to most garden conditions, in both warm and cool climates. **ZONES 6–10.**

Cotoneaster glaucophyllus

syn. **Cotoneaster serotinus**

GRAY-LEAFED COTONEASTER

This large shrub species is variable in the wild in its native west and central China, but an evergreen (or semi-evergreen) form, *Cotoneaster glaucophyllus* f. *serotinus* is best known in western gardens. Branching low, it forms an irregularly shaped, 10–12 ft (3–3.5 m) shrub. The leaves are broad, at first coated in woolly white hairs on the underside, but these soon wear off leaving only a thin bluish waxy bloom. Profuse but undistinguished white flowers appear in early summer, followed by an abundance of small, glossy red fruit that may persist through winter. Self-sown seedlings are often plentiful. **ZONES 6–11.**

Cotoneaster glaucophyllus

Cotoneaster horizontalis
ROCK COTONEASTER

Popular in cooler areas where its fine foliage
takes on bronze purple, orange and reddish
autumn hues, this semi-prostrate shrub has
horizontal, flattened sprays of branches building up in stiff tiers with age to 3 ft (1 m) high
and up to 8 ft (2.4 m) wide. The small flesh
pink summer flowers are followed by much
showier, deep red fruit. Native to mountain
areas of western China, it is deciduous in cool
climates but only semi-deciduous in warmer
climates. The named forms include 'Variegatus'
with leaves edged with white; *Cotoneaster
horizontalis* var. *perpusillus* is a more compact,
dwarf plant with tiny leaves. ZONES 5–10.

Cotoneaster 'Hybridus Pendulus'

This semi-deciduous hybrid is a shrub of high
ornamental value, with weak, pendulous
branches and rather narrow leaves, enlivened
from late summer onward by loose bunches of
bright red berries. Planted on its own roots, it
mounds up eventually to about 3 ft (1 m) tall,
and the branches can trail effectively over walls
or rocks. Alternatively, grafted onto a standard
of one of the taller species, it can make an
attractive weeping specimen with curtains of
foliage. ZONES 5–9.

Cotoneaster lacteus
syn. **Cotoneaster parneyi**
ROCKSPRAY COTONEASTER

This evergreen Chinese shrub is similar to
Cotoneaster glaucophyllus but has a more
persistent coating of wool on its leaf undersides, and more conspicuous veining on the
upper. The white flowers appear early in
summer, followed by large bunches of orange-
red fruits that persist through winter. It adapts
well to warmer climates. ZONES 7–11.

Cotoneaster salicifolius

Cotoneaster microphyllus

This compact, densely twiggy species from the
Himalayas has small, thick, glossy evergreen
leaves and plump crimson to purplish red fruit
from late summer to winter. Its growth habit
varies from completely prostrate to upright or
mound-like, 3–4 ft (1–1.2 m) in height; mature
plants have a framework of tough, woody
branches. Vigorous and very frost hardy, it
needs a fairly exposed location in full sun. For
a formal look, and to display its fruit more
effectively, it can be clipped into dense mounds.
Cotoneaster microphyllus var. *cochleatus* (syn.
Cotoneaster cochleatus) is almost prostrate,
with profuse fruit. *C. m.* var. *thymifolius* is a
stiffly upright shrub to 24 in (60 cm) with a
finely twiggy habit and narrow, wedge-shaped
leaves. ZONES 5–10.

Cotoneaster salicifolius
WILLOWLEAF COTONEASTER

This attractive evergreen species from western
China features narrow leaves with a network
of veins deeply impressed into their convex,
glossy upper surfaces. The profuse large
bunches of bright red berries last long into
winter, when the leaves may also take on
bronze and yellow tones. It is variable in habit;
some forms are low and spreading, others
reach 10–15 ft (3–4.5 m) with long, arching
growths. It takes well to trimming and makes a
fine hedge plant. 'Herbstfeuer' ('Autumn Fire')
is low and spreading and bears abundant
orange-red fruit. ZONES 6–10.

Cotoneaster lacteus

Cotoneaster splendens

Cotoneaster splendens

An attractive small-leafed but very vigorous deciduous shrub from northwestern China, this species was initially introduced to Sweden in the 1930s by the Swedish collector Harry Smith and was only popularized elsewhere in the West much more recently. It is a medium-sized shrub growing to 5–10 ft (1.5–3 m) with arching shoots, grayish green, glossy leaves that turn red in autumn, solitary pinkish flowers in summer and reddish orange fruit up to almost ½ in (12 mm) long. **ZONES 5–9.**

Cuphea ignea
syn. *Cuphea platycentra*
CIGAR FLOWER, CIGARETTE PLANT

This species from Mexico and the West Indies gets its common names from the flowers, which are small, orange and tubular. Each has a white tip with a touch of black, suggesting the ash at the tip of a cigar or cigarette. The leaves are small, elliptical and bright green. A bushy subshrub, it grows to about 24 in (60 cm) high; it benefits from the occasional trimming to keep it compact. **ZONES 10–12.**

Cuphea micropetala

This attractive Mexican species is like a larger version of *Cuphea ignea*. The leaves are up to 2½ in (6 cm) long, bright green and elliptical with a prominent midrib. The 1½–2 in (3.5–5 cm) tubular flowers occur in rows at the branch tips and are orange-red with golden yellow tones, tipped with greenish yellow. Tougher than most, this species will withstand the occasional light frosts. Although in the wild *C. micropetala* occurs on streamsides, it grows well in normal garden soils. **ZONES 9–11.**

CUPHEA

Cuphea micropetala

From Central and South America, this genus consists of over 250 species of annuals, evergreen perennials, subshrubs and shrubs. They are mostly rather low growing with weak stems and smallish, simple leaves. The flowers have a long tubular calyx and small circular red, pink, yellow or white petals, the latter sometimes hardly visible. Most species are quite frost tender, but as they are fast growing they are often treated as annuals. The many species vary quite considerably. They bloom almost throughout the year.

CULTIVATION

They prefer moist, well-drained soil in sun or very light shade. Provide protection in winter. These plants are also suitable for container growing. Propagation is usually from small tip cuttings, though seed is easily raised.

Cuphea ignea

Cyrilla racemiflora

Cyrilla racemiflora

This shrub often only grows to about 5 ft (1.5 m) high, but under good conditions it can reach 20 ft (6 m) or more, with a central woody stem and open branching habit, the lateral branches wiry and tending to curve upward. The rather sparse leaves are glossy green and turn dull red one by one before falling in late autumn. The white flower spikes start opening in early summer and may continue almost to autumn. The flowers are followed by tiny, dry fruit. **ZONES 6–11.**

CYRILLA

AMERICAN LEATHERWOOD, SWAMP CYRILLA

This genus consists of only one species of small tree or often only a shrub that includes both deciduous and evergreen races. This fact is partly explained by its very wide climatic range, from Virginia in eastern USA south through Florida and the West Indies, and into South America as far as Brazil. The plants usually grown in gardens are the northern, deciduous forms. They are tall shrubs with spatula-shaped leaves, producing many long, tapering racemes of tiny, white, fragrant flowers from just below the new leaves.

CULTIVATION

In the wild, cyrilla forms dense thickets along the margins of swamps, while in gardens it is an undemanding shrub worth growing for the elegance of its flowers. It does best in a sunny but sheltered spot in fertile, humus-rich, moist but well-drained soil. Propagation is normally from seed.

CYTISUS

BROOM

The brooms are a diverse group of usually yellow-flowered, leguminous shrubs and sub-shrubs from Europe and the Mediterranean region, which include a number of genera—the most important are *Cytisus* and *Genista*. *Cytisus* alone is a large and variable genus, in habit ranging from tall and erect to prostrate. Some of the 30 species have well-developed leaves, either simple and narrow or composed of 3 leaflets, while others are almost leafless with photosynthesis performed by the green, angled branchlets. All have pea-flowers in small, profuse clusters along new growth.

CULTIVATION

Generally easy garden subjects, they flower well under most conditions except deep shade, tolerating both dry and boggy soils, fertile or quite infertile. Some smaller species demand warm dry positions in a rock garden in pockets of well-drained soil. They are easily propagated from seed, cuttings or, in the case of some named cultivars, by grafting.

Cytisus × praecox

WARMINSTER BROOM, MOONLIGHT BROOM

This hybrid between the tall *Cytisus multiflorus* and the lower-growing *C. purgans* includes several popular cultivars, all making free-flowering shrubs of 3–4 ft (1–1.2 m), with massed, slender branchlets arising from ground level and spreading gracefully. The original hybrid has cream and yellow flowers, with a heavy fragrance, borne in mid- to late spring. More recent cultivars include **'Allgold'**, with cascading sprays of soft, golden-yellow blossom, and **'Goldspear'**, a lower and broader shrub with deeper gold flowers. **ZONES 5–9.**

Cytisus × praecox 'Allgold'

Cytisus scoparius

COMMON BROOM, SCOTCH BROOM

Widely distributed in central and western Europe including the UK, this is one of the taller and most vigorous species of *Cytisus*, reaching 6–8 ft (1.8–2.4 m) in height and making a great show of golden-yellow blossoms in late spring and early summer. The black seed pods may be abundant, ripening in mid-summer and scattering their seed with a sharp, cracking sound in hot, dry weather. In cooler areas of some southern hemisphere countries it has become a troublesome weed. 'Pendulus' is a rare cultivar with pendulous branches. **ZONES 5–9.**

Cytisus scoparius

Cytisus scoparius 'Pendulus'

DABOECIA

ST DABEOC'S HEATH, IRISH HEATH

Only 2 species make up this genus of small-leafed, evergreen shrubs native to areas of western Europe and the Azores Islands. Low and spreading, they are commonly grouped with the heaths and heathers *(Erica* and *Calluna)* as suitable for heather gardens, rock gardens and retaining walls. Conspicuous white to purple urn-shaped flowers, which contract to a small mouth, are borne on nodding stalks along bare stems that stand above the foliage. The petal tube falls after flowering, unlike that of many heaths and heathers.

CULTIVATION

Frost hardy to marginally frost hardy, they require permanently moist, acidic soil in a sunny position. Trim after flowering. Named varieties normally require propagation from cuttings, but they do produce fertile seed which may breed true to type.

Daboecia cantabrica

Daboecia cantabrica

Dispersed along the Atlantic coasts of France and Ireland, this species grows to 24 in (60 cm) high and has narrow, lance-shaped, dark green leaves with white hairs beneath. The rose-purple flowers, borne throughout summer and autumn, are about ½ in (12 mm) long. 'Alba' has pointed dark green leaves and white flowers; 'Atropurpurea' has deep rosy purple flowers; 'Bicolor' has white, purple and some striped flowers; 'Creeping White' has white flowers and a low creeping habit. **ZONES 7–9.**

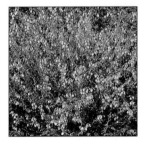

Daboecia cantabrica 'Creeping White'

Danäe racemosa

ALEXANDRIAN LAUREL

This native of Turkey and Iran makes an elegant evergreen plant to 3 ft (1 m) high and across. Its tiny greenish white flowers are produced in summer and are followed by red berries that can persist well into winter. Whole branches can be cut and last well in a vase. **ZONES 7–10.**

DANÄE

Danäe racemosa

This genus consists of only one species of evergreen clump-forming perennial from western Asia. It is grown for its elegant arching stems and its attractive foliage and fruit.

CULTIVATION

Frost hardy, it grows in a humus-rich, moist but well-drained soil in sun or shade. Old or damaged stems can be cut back to ground level if necessary in spring. Propagate from seed or by division.

Daphne bholua

DAPHNE

DAPHNE

Indigenous to Europe, North Africa and temperate Asia, this genus includes 50 or so deciduous and evergreen shrubs. They have simple, leathery leaves and small, highly fragrant flowers clustered at the shoot tips or leaf axils. Although the flower parts are not differentiated into true petals and sepals, for the sake of simplicity here they are called 'petals', of which there are always 4, characteristically pointed, recurving and rather fleshy. In the wild many daphnes occur on mountains in stony ground, often on limestone.

CULTIVATION

They prefer cool, well-aerated, gritty, humus-rich soil; intolerant of root disturbance, they are best planted out while small. The taller species are better adapted to sheltered woodlands, the smaller ones to rock gardens. Propagate from cuttings or layers. Fresh seed usually germinates readily but many species fail to fruit.

Daphne cneorum

Daphne × burkwoodii

Daphne bholua

This species from the eastern Himalayas can be evergreen or deciduous depending on the form selected. It usually grows into an upright shrub up to 12 ft (3.5 m) tall and 5 ft (1.5 m) wide. It has clusters of highly scented soft pink flowers in late winter. Selected forms include 'Gurkha', which is deciduous, and 'Jacqueline Postill', which is evergreen. ZONES 6–9.

Daphne × burkwoodii

This popular hybrid *(Daphne cneorum × D. caucasica)* was raised early in the twentieth century by the Burkwood brothers, well-known English nurserymen. It is a low, rounded semi-evergreen shrub up to 3 ft (1 m) tall. Its pale pink flowers, darker in bud, appear in mid- to late spring, sometimes through summer. The most easily grown deciduous daphne, it flowers best in full sun. 'Somerset' is slightly more vigorous and has deep pink flowers with pale pink lobes. ZONES 5–9.

Daphne cneorum

GARLAND FLOWER, ROSE DAPHNE

This low-growing, to 16 in (40 cm), evergreen shrub from southern Europe has a loose, semi-prostrate habit, with trailing main shoots and dense lateral branches. It has small dark green leaves and bears fragrant rose-pink flowers in mid-spring. It is a sun-loving plant but requires moist, well-drained soil. ZONES 4–9.

Daphne mezereum

Daphne mezereum
MEZEREON, FEBRUARY DAPHNE

This slow-growing, short-lived, deciduous shrub grows to 5 ft (1.5 m) tall, and has long narrow leaves and purplish pink to purplish red, fragrant flowers clustering along bare twigs in early spring. Below the leaves, poisonous red fruit ripen in late summer. It needs moisture and shelter. **ZONES 5–9.**

Daphne retusa

This species may be a form of *Daphne tangutica*; authorities vary in their opinions. It makes a compact shrub to 30 in (75 cm) high with fragrant pale pink flowers in spring and glossy rich green foliage. **ZONES 6–9.**

Daphne genkwa
LILAC DAPHNE

Indigenous to China but long cultivated in Japan, this small deciduous shrub tends to be short lived in cultivation. It is sparsely branched, producing long, wiry growths in summer which, next spring while still leafless, bear clusters of delicate, long-tubed, lilac flowers at every leaf axil. It prefers sheltered, sunny, frost-free conditions. **ZONES 5–9.**

Daphne retusa

Daphne genkwa

DEUTZIA

Deutzia × elegantissima

These summer-flowering, deciduous shrubs from east Asia and the Himalayas are closely related to *Philadelphus* but they bear their smaller, white or pink flowers in more crowded sprays, with 5, rather than 4, pointed petals. Like *Philadelphus,* the plants have long, straight, cane-like stems. The leaves occur in opposite pairs and are mostly finely toothed. There are many frost-hardy species and fine hybrids available, especially those bred by the Lémoine nursery at Nancy, France, from 1890 to 1940.

CULTIVATION

Deutzias prefer a sheltered position, moist fertile soil and some sun during the day. Avoid pruning the previous year's short lateral shoots; thin out canes and shorten some of the thickest old stems after flowering. Propagate from seed or cuttings in late spring.

Deutzia crenata var. *nakaiana* 'Nikko'

Deutzia gracilis

Deutzia crenata var. nakaiana 'Nikko'

syn. *Deutzia gracilis* 'Nikko'

One of the smallest deutzias, it makes a low spreading mound often rooting as it spreads. It is a good rock garden plant or groundcover in a shrub border, growing to about 24 in (60 cm) tall and as much as 4 ft (1.2 m) wide. The starry white flowers are produced in summer in spikes and the pale green foliage often turns burgundy before shedding. **ZONES 5–9.**

Deutzia × elegantissima

ELEGANT DEUTZIA

Including some of the finest and largest-flowered pinks among its clones, this hybrid of *Deutzia purpurascens* and D. *sieboldiana* reaches 4–6 ft (1.2–1.8 m) with purplish red twigs and flower stalks. The Lémoine nursery released the 2 original cultivars: 'Elegantissima', near-white inside and rose pink outside; and 'Fasciculata', with a slightly deeper rose flush. The Irish hybrid 'Rosealind' has deeper flesh pink flowers. **ZONES 5–9.**

Deutzia gracilis

SLENDER DEUTZIA

A native of Japan, this popular species has a graceful, spreading habit and pure white flowers in slender, arching sprays during late spring and early summer. It grows 3–6 ft (1–1.8 m) tall, and is one of the chief parents of hybrid deutzias. **ZONES 4–10.**

Deutzia purpurascens

Deutzia purpurascens

A graceful species from Yunnan discovered by
the famous missionary-botanist Abbé Delavay,
this slender arching shrub to 5 ft (1.5 m) tall
has flowers that are white inside and purple
on the outside. This species has been used
extensively in hybridization. **ZONES 5–9.**

Deutzia × rosea

One of the earliest Lémoine crosses between
Deutzia gracilis and *D. purpurascens*, it reaches
a height and spread of 30 in (75 cm) and has
the low, spreading habit of the former species
with the pink coloration of the latter. The
original clone has flowers of the palest pink,
in shorter, broader sprays than in *D. gracilis*.
'**Carminea**' has larger panicles of pink flowers
with a stronger carmine pink on the back.
ZONES 5–9.

Deutzia × rosea

Deutzia × rosea 'Carminea'

Deutzia scabra

This, the longest established and most robust, cold-hardy species in Western gardens, has thick canes to about 10 ft (3 m), and long, dull green, rough-textured leaves. Large panicles of white, bell-shaped flowers terminate upper branches from mid-spring to early summer. 'Flore Pleno' has double flowers, striped dull pink on the outside; 'Candidissima' is a pure white double; 'Pride of Rochester', another double, has larger flowers faintly tinted mauve outside. **ZONES 5–10.**

Deutzia scabra

Deutzia scabra 'Pride of Rochester'

Dipelta floribunda

Dipelta floribunda

From the lower mountains of China, this shrub grows to about 10 ft (3 m), with woody stems and pale peeling bark. It bears broad, soft leaves and large, drooping clusters of pale pink, fragrant flowers, 1½ in (35 mm) long; these are deeper pink on the outside of the tube and have orange-yellow markings in the throat. **ZONES 6–9.**

DIPELTA

Four species from China make up this genus of deciduous shrubs, and only one is well established in Western gardens, however, even that is uncommon. They are related to and resemble *Weigela* and *Kolkwitzia*, with richly marked, bell-shaped flowers in large clusters. The fruits are partly concealed by two rounded bracts enlarging at their base after the flowers are shed.

CULTIVATION

They are frost hardy, and prefer a sunny position with moist, fertile, well-drained soil and shelter from strong winds. Propagate from seed or cuttings.

Dracaena marginata

A slow-growing tree or shrub from Madagascar, this species reaches 15–20 ft (4.5–6 m) in warm climates. Its narrow, sword-like leaves have red margins. The cultivar '**Tricolor**' with a cream stripe and red edge is commonly grown as a house plant. This species tolerates some shade and quite low winter temperatures but not frost. **ZONES 10–12.**

Dracaena marginata

Dracaena marginata 'Tricolor'

DRACAENA
syn. **Pleomele**

This genus of some 40 species of evergreen trees and shrubs, many originating from equatorial Africa and Asia, is grown for foliage, often as greenhouse or indoor plants. Those grown indoors are sometimes confused with species of *Cordyline* and are often termed 'false palms' because of their cane-like stems and crowns of sword-like leaves.

CULTIVATION

Outdoors, dracaenas need warm-temperate to subtropical conditions, full sun or part-shade and well-drained soil. Cut back to almost soil level in spring. In cooler climates they are best as container plants. Propagate from seed or by air-layering in spring or from stem cuttings in summer. Watch out for mealybugs.

ELAEAGNUS

This genus of about 45 species of deciduous and evergreen shrubs, small trees and scrambling climbers comes from Europe, Asia and North America, with one species extending to Australia. All have alternate, entire leaves which, together with the young stems, flower buds and fruits, glisten with tiny silvery or rusty brown scales. Small flowers, clustered in leaf axils, are tubular at the base with 4 spreading petals. The fruits, pale fleshy drupes, are edible in some species.

Elaeagnus pungens 'Variegata'

Elaeagnus pungens

CULTIVATION

Frost hardy and generally vigorous and trouble-free, they thrive in most soils and positions. The evergreen species will tolerate shade. Most species can be cut back heavily if a bushy shape is desired. Propagation is usually from seed for deciduous species and from cuttings for the evergreens.

Elaeagnus angustifolia

OLEASTER, RUSSIAN OLIVE

This deciduous species extends from southern Europe to China. A large shrub or small tree, it grows to 30 ft (9 m) high, the new branches and the undersides of the narrow leaves coated in silvery scales. In late spring and early summer clusters of small, perfumed, pale yellow flowers appear. These are followed in late summer by edible yellowish fruit, which is also coated in silvery scales. It makes a striking ornamental but needs warm, dry summers to bring out its silvery foliage. **ZONES 7–9.**

Elaeagnus pungens

SILVERBERRY, THORNY ELAEAGNUS

The most common species of the genus, this frost-hardy, evergreen bush or scrambling climber has long, prickly, horizontal branches and glossy, oval leaves which are dark green above and silvery beneath. It is excellent for hedges, growing to a height and width of 10–15 ft (3–4.5 m). In autumn *Elaeagnus pungens* bears fragrant, tiny, bell-shaped, cream flowers. The cultivar '**Variegata**' has narrow, irregular, cream-margined leaves; and '**Maculata**' has leaves with a central splash of gold. **ZONES 7–10.**

Elaeagnus umbellata

AUTUMN ELAEAGNUS, AUTUMN-OLIVE

From the Himalayas, China and Japan, this deciduous or semi-deciduous species is a large, spreading shrub 12–15 ft (3.5–4.5 m) high with broad, green leaves that may have wavy margins and silvery, reflective undersides. In late spring and early summer it bears numerous clusters of scented cream flowers in the upper leaf axils, followed by crowded, small, berry-like fruit that ripen to pale red, blending attractively with the pale yellow autumn foliage. **ZONES 7–10.**

Elaeagnus umbellata

Enkianthus campanulatus

REDVEIN ENKIANTHUS

From Japan and southern China, this is the most popular species, reaching 8–12 ft (2.4–3.5 m) high, of narrow, open habit and rather slow growing. Abundant flowers, cream but heavily striped and tipped dull crimson, appear in spring. In autumn the leaves turn to shades of gold, scarlet and dull purple. *Enkianthus campanulatus* var. *palibinii* has more reddish flowers. **ZONES 6–9.**

Enkianthus perulatus

WHITE ENKIANTHUS

From Japan, this is rather distinctive among *Enkianthus* species in its lower, bushier habit and more sparsely scattered urn-shaped flowers that are pure white or greenish white, without markings and contracted at the mouth. They are borne on nodding stalks in early spring. This species likes a very cool, sheltered position and has brilliant red autumn foliage. **ZONES 6–9.**

Enkianthus perulatus

ENKIANTHUS

About 10 species of deciduous shrubs from eastern Asia make up this genus, valued for their small, bell-shaped flowers, densely clustered and prettily marked in most species, and fine autumn foliage colors. Growth is rather open and the smallish leaves are clustered at the end of each season's growth, producing a layered effect. The stalked, pendulous flowers are produced in numerous short sprays.

CULTIVATION

Very frost hardy, they like similar conditions to many rhododendrons and azaleas: moist woodland with humus-rich but not too fertile, acid soil. They will not thrive in heavy shade. Avoid pruning to a rounded shape as the flowers will not be so well displayed. Propagate from seed or cuttings in summer.

Enkianthus campanulatus   *Enkianthus campanulatus* var. *palibinii*

EPHEDRA

JOINT-FIR, MORMON TEA

Ephedra is a genus of around 40 species of gymnosperms from southern Europe, North Africa, temperate Asia and the Americas. They show no close relationship with other major plant groups and are presumed to be an evolutionary dead end. These near-leafless shrubs form a mass of slim, dull green, jointed stems—such as those of *Ephedra californica*—and are tolerant of dry conditions. Tiny scale-like leaves are present for a brief period after rain. They do not produce true flowers but have separate male and female, yellow, flower-like cones (strobili) that are usually followed by berry-like fruits. This genus is best known for its association with ephedrine, used as an allergy and asthma treatment, a stimulant and a metabolic accelerator. Some herbal extracts of ephedrine are known as Ma Huang or Mormon tea.

CULTIVATION

Very frost hardy to marginally frost hardy, they demand a light, stony or sandy soil with good drainage and full sun. No pests or diseases are known. Propagate from seed.

Ephedra gerardiana

Ephedra americana
Var. *andina*

syn. *Ephedra chilensis*

This variety is native to the Andes mountain range, from Ecuador to Patagonia, and is usually a sprawling shrub to 8 ft (2.4 m), although it is sometimes a small tree to 12 ft (3.5 m) high. The young shoots are green and finely ridged. The leaves when present are small, no more than ¼ in (6 mm). Its berries are vivid red to orange. **ZONES 6–9.**

Ephedra gerardiana

This species, native to China and the Himalayas, can be a tiny creeping shrub as low as 2 in (5 cm) in height, al-though it can be found up to 24 in (60 cm) high with a spread of up to 10 ft (3 m). The fruit are red and to ¼ in (6 mm) long. **ZONES 7–10.**

Erica carnea 'Springwood White'

ERICA

HEATH

This large genus is made up of more than 800 species of small-leafed, free-flowering, evergreen shrubs. The vast majority are native to South Africa, but a relatively small number of species occur in Europe and elsewhere in Africa. In Europe, several *Erica* species plus the closely related *Calluna* (heather) dominate moorland vegetation. The Cape heaths from South Africa, often with long, tubular flowers, are fine garden plants in mild-winter climates where summer humidity is low. The European species bear smaller, bell-shaped flowers in a more limited white to deep pink color range but are frost hardy and are very popular garden plants.

CULTIVATION

Most heaths like full sun, well-drained, neutral to acid soil and dislike lime and animal manure. Prune after flowering to keep plants bushy and compact. Propagate from seed or from cuttings in late summer.

Erica carnea

syn. *Erica herbacea*

WINTER HEATH, SNOW HEATH

From the mountains of central and southern Europe, this frost-hardy species and its numerous cultivars are among the few heaths that will thrive in chalk soils. It forms a low, spreading subshrub usually less than 12 in (30 cm) high with densely crowded branches. Through most of winter and into early spring it produces a fine display of small, urn-shaped, purple-pink flowers with protruding darker stamens. This is an ideal groundcover between taller shrubs or beneath deciduous trees, or in rock gardens. Well-known cultivars include '**December Red**' with purplish pink flowers and '**March Seedling**', which flowers until late spring. Others are '**Myretoun Ruby**', with very dark green leaves against bright rose-pink flowers; '**Ruby Glow**' with deep rose-red flowers; '**Springwood Pink**' with a vigorous trailing habit and rose-pink flowers; and '**Springwood White**' with a spreading habit, vigorous growth and white flowers. **ZONES 5–9.**

Erica carnea 'March Seedling'

Erica cinerea
BELL HEATHER, TWISTED HEATH

Native throughout western Europe including the British Isles, this heather is one of the prettiest of the frost-hardy heaths. Its small, crowded, rose-pink bells are produced over a long season from early summer to early autumn. Low and spreading, the stiff ends of the twisted branches ascend to 12–18 in (30–45 cm). Bell heather dislikes hot summer weather, which scorches its foliage and may kill the plant. The many named cultivars vary chiefly in flower color from white to rich rose purple; some also have golden or coppery foliage. '**Kerry Cherry**' has deep pink flowers, '**Crimson King**' is crimson; '**Golden Drop**' has summer foliage gold with coppery tints, turning red in winter. **ZONES 5–9.**

Erica cinerea 'Kerry Cherry'

Erica × darleyensis
DARLEY DALE HEATH

Erica × darleyensis is a hybrid of the two frost-hardy species *Erica erigena* and *E. carnea* and has proved to be a valuable garden plant. It forms a dense, bushy shrub to 24 in (60 cm) high with dark green foliage, and from late autumn through spring is covered in crowded, short spikes of cylindrical, pale rose flowers with protruding, darker stamens. It tolerates chalk soils. The original clone is now known as '**Darley Dale**' but others, with flowers ranging from white to deep pink, are listed: '**Dunwood Splendour**' spreads widely and produces a spectacular display of mauve-pink flowers; '**George Rendall**' is a compact grower with purplish pink flowers throughout winter; '**Jack H. Brummage**' has golden to red-tinted winter foliage and purplish pink flowers; and '**White Perfection**' has bright green foliage and pure white flowers. **ZONES 6–9.**

Erica × darleyensis 'Darley Dale'

Erica erigena 'Alba Compacta'

Erica erigena

syns Erica hibernica, E. mediterranea

IRISH HEATH, MEDITERRANEAN HEATH

This western European species has deep green foliage and massed, urn-shaped, bright pink flowers in winter and spring. It grows to 6 ft (1.8 m) high and 3 ft (1 m) wide. Cultivars include **'Alba Compacta'**, a compact, white-flowered form; **'Ewan Jones'**, a vigorous grower with mauve-pink flowers set against dark green leaves; **'Hibernica'** with shell-pink flowers; **'Hibernica Alba'**, a spectacular white-flowered form growing about 3 ft (1 m) tall. **'Irish Dusk'** with rose-pink flowers and gray-green leaves; **'Mrs Parris Lavender'** an upright form to 18 in (45 cm) tall with mauve flowers; **'Mrs Parris White'**, an albino form of the previous cultivar; **'Silver Bells'** with white, scented flowers; **'Superba'** with pale pink, perfumed flowers; and **'W. T. Rackliff'**, a compact grower with white flowers. **ZONES 7–9.**

Erica erigena 'Mrs Parris Lavender'

Erica mackaiana

syns Erica crawfordii, E. mackaii, E. mackayana

MACKAY'S HEATH

This neat little shrub from Spain and Ireland grows to about 18 in (45 cm) tall and 30 in (75 cm) wide. Its branches are hairy while young and its dark green leaves are arranged in whorls of four. The flowers are usually pink and produced in terminal clusters from summer to early autumn, although many different colors have been selected and named. **'Galicia'** grows less than 8 in (20 cm) tall and has mauve-pink flowers opening from orange buds; **'Maura'** is a small form to 6 in (15 cm) tall with gray-green foliage and semi-double purple flowers; and **'Shining Light'** grows to 10 in (25 cm) tall by 24 in (60 cm) wide and has pure white flowers. **ZONES 6–9.**

Erica mackaiana 'Galicia'

Erica mammosa

RED SIGNAL HEATH

This South African species has bright green foliage and massed terminal clusters of red to deep pink tubular flowers, 1 in (25 mm) long, in spring. It grows to about 3 ft (1 m) high and 18 in (45 cm) wide. **'Coccinea'** and **'Jubilee'** are just two of its many attractive cultivars. **ZONES 9–10.**

Erica mammosa

Erica × stuartii

Erica × stuartii 'Irish Lemon'

Erica × stuartii is a cross between Erica mackaiana and E. tetralix. This small, upright shrub to 18 in (45 cm) tall with gray-green foliage bears pink flowers through summer and autumn. 'Irish Lemon' produces brilliant yellow spring growth which greens later. The urn-shaped flowers are mauve and are borne from late spring well into summer. **ZONES 6–9.**

ERIOGONUM
WILD BUCKWHEAT, UMBRELLA PLANT

This is a large genus of the polygonum family, of some 150 species of annuals, perennials or small shrubs native to North America, mainly the western side. Some of the smaller ones are ideal rock-garden plants and many of the taller species make good cut flowers, both fresh and dried. The long-lasting flowers are small but are produced in clusters surrounded by attractive toothed or lobed bracts. Most species come from mountain habitats or alkaline desert areas.

Erica mammosa 'Jubilee'

CULTIVATION
Frost tolerance varies, but all like a sunny, well-drained site. If kept dry in winter they will stand more cold than if damp. Cut back after flowering unless seed is required. Propagate from seed in spring or autumn, or by division in spring or early summer.

Eriogonum umbellatum
SULFUR BUCKWHEAT

This woody-based perennial is from the Rocky Mountains in British Columbia. In summer it bears attractive heads of tiny, bright yellow flowers that turn copper with age. A useful rock-garden plant, it grows to a height of 12 in (30 cm) and a spread of 24 in (60 cm), with dense green leaves with white, downy undersides. In cooler, wetter areas some shelter is required. *Erigonum umbellatum* var. *subalpinum* has creamy yellow flowers that turn dull mauve with age. **ZONES 6–9.**

Eriogonum umbellatum

ERYTHRINA

The 108 species of deciduous and semi-evergreen trees and shrubs in this genus occur wild in tropical and subtropical regions of the world, though with most species in Africa and the Americas. Belonging to the bean tribe of legumes, they are grown as ornamentals for their vividly hued flowers; their trunks and branches are protected by short sharp prickles. The leaves are compound with 3 broad, often diamond-shaped leaflets. Bean-like flowers in crimson, scarlet and orange are borne in racemes towards the ends of the branches at varying times of the year (some species in mid-winter), followed by narrow seed pods that dry and brown as they ripen.

CULTIVATION

Most species are not frost hardy. They enjoy full sun and well-drained soil. Propagate from seed in spring or cuttings in summer.

Erythrina crista-galli

COMMON CORAL TREE, COCK'S COMB

This species from South America is the best known coral tree in temperate climates, where it is treated almost as an herbaceous plant, being cut back almost to the ground in autumn, transferred to a large pot and overwintered under glass. It is also grown permanently in the greenhouse, particularly in very cool areas, and again pruned quite severely in late autumn. It grows about 6 ft (1.8 m) tall under these conditions. In subtropical climates the coral tree grows into a gnarled, wide-crowned tree 15–30 ft (4.5–9 m) tall and bears scarlet or coral-red flowers in spring and summer. **ZONES 8–11.**

Erythrina crista-galli

EUONYMUS

SPINDLE TREE

Euonymus alatus

This genus of about 175 species consists of both deciduous and evergreen trees, shrubs and creepers from the northern hemisphere, centered mainly in east Asia including the Himalayas. All have simple leaves in opposite pairs, usually with toothed margins. Flowers are inconspicuous, greenish or yellowish, in small groups along the lower parts of the current year's growth. While deciduous plants, such as 'Red Chief', have rich autumn foliage, it is the capsular fruits that provide the main interest, splitting open in autumn to reveal bright yellow, red or orange seeds. Birds, attracted to the oily outer layer, distribute the seeds.

CULTIVATION

Mostly frost hardy, spindle trees grow best in a sheltered position with ample sun and fertile, well-drained soil. Propagate from seed or cuttings.

Euonymus alatus

WINGED SPINDLE, WINGED EUONYMUS

From Japan, China and Korea, this decorative, spreading, much-branched, deciduous shrub grows 6–8 ft (1.8–2.4 m) tall, the small branches distinctive for the broad 'wings' of corky tissue attached to either side of the green twig. In late spring it bears small, green flowers in inconspicuous sprays and by autumn the small, purplish, 4-lobed capsules split to reveal orange-red seeds. At the same time the leaves turn vivid deep red, sometimes showing paler scarlet tones before falling. *Euonymus alatus* var. *apterus* has a more lax habit and rarely produces the corky wings of bark. **ZONES 5–9.**

Euonymus fortunei 'Emerald 'n' Gold'

Euonymus europaeus

EUROPEAN SPINDLE TREE

This deciduous shrub or small tree is usually single stemmed at the base and occasionally reaches 20 ft (6 m). It is native to Europe, including the UK, and can be found growing in woodlands and often on limestone or chalk soils. The wood of this and the few other European species was once used to make spindles, used in spinning wool. It has inconspicuous flowers followed in autumn by pink or red fruit that split open to reveal the large orange seeds. At the same time the leaves turn to shades of yellow and scarlet. 'Aldenhamensis' is a form selected for the larger size and brilliant pink coloring of its fruits; 'Red Cascade' is often pendulous with the weight of its large red, orange-seeded berries. **ZONES 6–9.**

Euonymus fortunei

syn. *Euonymus radicans*

WINTERCREEPER EUONYMUS

This prostrate to shrubby creeper spreads or climbs by aerial roots and can climb a wall as high as 20 ft (6 m). As a groundcover it has an indefinite spread, but it is mostly more compact forms that are grown in gardens. From early to mid-summer it bears greenish white flowers on the branching, non-clinging adult stems. 'Emerald Gaiety' is a small, compact cultivar with dark green leaves margined with white and often pink-tinged in winter; it grows to 3 ft (1 m) tall and 5 ft (1.5 m) wide. 'Emerald 'n' Gold' is a very bushy, small form with broad gold edges to its green leaves often tinged pink in winter; it grows to about 12 in (30 cm) tall and 3 ft (1 m) wide. 'Silver Queen' has broad white margins to its leaves which are pink-tinged in winter; it is a bushy shrub up to 6 ft (1.8 m) tall and wider than its height. 'Variegatus' (syn. 'Gracilis') is a climbing or trailing form with larger leaves with white margins, often tinted pink. **ZONES 5–9.**

Euonymus europaeus

Eupatorium purpureum
JOE PYE WEED

This robust perennial grows to a height of 5–8 ft (1.5–2.4 m) with a spread of about 4 ft (1.2 m) or more. It provides a bold accent for the autumn garden, with 12 in (30 cm) long leaves and large heads of tiny, purplish flowers. Native to eastern and central North America, it is usually found where there is plenty of water and needs lots of moisture for full growth. **ZONES 4–9.**

EUPATORIUM

This genus contains about 40 species of perennials and sub-shrubs, mainly from the Americas but a few from Asia and Europe. Only a few are cultivated for their large terminal panicles of small flowerheads, which come in white or shades of purple, mauve or pink.

CULTIVATION

Mostly quite frost hardy, they need full sun or part-shade and moist but well-drained soil. The shrubs should be pruned lightly in spring or after flowering. Propagate from seed in spring, from cuttings in summer or by division in early spring or autumn.

Eupatorium purpureum

EURYOPS

Part of the large daisy family, this genus consists of around 100 species of annuals, perennials and evergreen shrubs, most of which come from southern Africa. They are grown for their colorful yellow to orange flowerheads which are held above fern-like foliage.

CULTIVATION

Frost hardiness varies between species. Generally, a well-drained soil and a position in full sun are the main requirements of these attractive plants, otherwise the shrubs tend to grow leggy and the flowers are not as plentiful. Lightly prune after the flowers have faded but do not disturb the roots. Propagate from seed in spring or cuttings in summer.

Euryops chrysanthemoides
syn. *Gamolepis chrysanthemoides*
PARIS DAISY

Growing to around 3 ft (1 m) high, this shrub has soft, ir-regularly serrated leaves and in winter is covered with yel-low daisy-like flowerheads; these continue sporadically through most of the year. It does well in warm, dry cli-mates; in cool areas it makes an attractive pot plant. **ZONES 9–11.**

Euryops chrysanthemoides

Exochorda × macrantha

This hybrid was raised in France around 1900 by crossing *Exochorda racemosa* with *E. korolkowii*. Sometimes reaching 10 ft (3 m) tall, in mid- to late spring it produces elongated clusters of pure white flowers, each about 1½ in (35 mm) across, from every branch tip. 'The Bride', is one of the loveliest varieties of pearl bush. It makes a weeping shrub of up to 6 ft (1.8 m) or so tall and about as much in width. 'The Bride' produces masses of large white flowers on arching stems in spring. **ZONES 6–9.**

Exochorda racemosa

This species from northern China, long established in Western gardens, makes a lovely display when well grown. It grows to about 10 ft (3 m) high with arching branches and has narrow, pale green leaves to 3 in (8 cm) long. The flowers are borne in late spring, with loose, slender sprays appearing from the branch tips, each flower being 1½ in (35 mm) wide with narrow petals. **ZONES 6–9.**

Exochorda × macrantha

EXOCHORDA

PEARL BUSH

There are 4 species of deciduous shrubs in this genus from central Asia and northern China. They have weak, pithy branches and thin-textured, paddle-shaped leaves. In spring the branch ends are clustered with 5-petalled, white flowers of delicate, informal beauty. The fruits are capsules with wing-like segments, splitting apart when ripe to release flattened seeds.

CULTIVATION

Exochorda racemosa

Species of *Exochorda* are quite frost hardy but they prefer climates with sharply defined seasons and dry summers for the best display of flowers. A sheltered position in full sun and well-drained soil are desirable. Prune older stems back to their bases after flowering for vigorous new growth and abundant flowers. Propagate from seed in autumn or from cuttings.

× FATSHEDERA

TREE IVY

The one species of this hybrid genus, combining *Fatsia* and *Hedera*, is an evergreen erect or scrambling shrub grown mainly for its foliage and often used as a conservatory or house plant in cool climates. It grows to 6 ft (1.8 m) or more high with palmately 5- or 7-lobed lusterous dark green leaves. Rounded heads of small greenish white flowers are borne in terminal panicles in autumn.

CULTIVATION

Grow this frost-hardy plant in fertile, well-drained soil in full sun or part-shade. It will withstand coastal exposure and can be grown in seaside gardens. Propagate from cuttings in summer.

× *Fatshedera lizei*

This is a spreading open shrub with glossy lobed leaves to 10 in (25 cm) across. It is used extensively as groundcover, or it can be trained against a wall or tree trunk. 'Variegata' is a popular cultivar. It has leaves with a narrow, creamy white edge. For bushy growth, regularly pinch back when young. **ZONES 7–11.**

× *Fatshedera lizei*

FORSYTHIA

Since their introduction to Western gardens from China and Japan in the nineteenth century, the 7 species of forsythia have been popular shrubs valued for their brilliant yellow or gold blossoms in mid-spring. They make excellent cut flowers. Deciduous or sometimes semi-evergreen and of medium stature, they have soft-wooded stems branching from near the ground. The rather narrow, bluntly toothed leaves appear after the 4-petalled flowers, which are paired or clustered at the twig nodes.

CULTIVATION

Fully frost hardy, they are not fussy about soil type but fertilizer and compost encourage growth. They prefer a sunny position, but climate is crucial: they seldom flower in warm climates, requiring winter temperatures well below freezing point. Prune only to remove older branches. Propagation is normally from cuttings in early summer.

Forsythia × intermedia
BORDER FORSYTHIA

An arching or spreading deciduous shrub with dark
green, lance-shaped leaves,
this species grows 8–10 ft
(2.4–3 m) tall and slightly
wider. A hybrid between
Forsythia suspensa and *F.
viridissima*, it was first recorded in Germany circa 1885.
Some fine cultivars include
'Lynwood' and 'Spectabilis'. In
1939 Karl Sax at the Arnold
Arboretum in Massachusetts
created the first artificial tetraploid, 'Arnold Giant', and subsequently bred 'Beatrix
Farrand' and 'Karl Sax', all
carrying large, brilliant gold
flowers.
ZONES 5–9.

Forsythia suspensa
WEEPING FORSYTHIA

Indigenous to China, this
deciduous species was cultivated for centuries in Japan
before being taken to Europe.
It makes a shrub of 8–10 ft
(2.4–3 m), or taller if supported, with dense, slender,
arching branches. From early
to mid-spring the branches
carry profuse golden flowers
with narrow petals.
ZONES 4–9.

Forsythia suspensa

Forsythia × intermedia

Forsythia × intermedia 'Lynwood'

FOTHERGILLA

From southeastern USA, this genus consists of 2 species of deciduous shrubs grown for their spring flowers and autumn
foliage color. The fragrant, petal-less flowers are in upright, conical, brush-like spikes with conspicuous creamy white stamens.
They appear before the foliage, which is roughly diamond-
shaped, heavily ribbed and hazel-like. The leaves start out bright
green, mature to deep green and develop intense yellow, orange
and red autumn tones.

CULTIVATION
Frost hardy, they do best in humus-rich, moist but well-drained,
acidic soil in sun or light shade and can be trimmed to shape
after flowering if necessary. Propagate from seed or cuttings or
by layering.

Fothergilla gardenii

Fothergilla gardenii

WITCH ALDER, DWARF FOTHERGILLA

A small bushy shrub 24–36 in (60–90 cm) high
from coastal plain areas of eastern USA, this
species thrives in a cool climate with moist,
well-drained soil. It produces fragrant white
flowers 1½ in (35 mm) long in early spring,
and the 2–3 in (5–8 cm) long leaves that follow
develop brilliant autumn colors. **ZONES 5–10.**

Fothergilla major

syn. *Fothergilla monticola*

MOUNTAIN WITCH HAZEL, ALABAMA FOTHERGILLA

This shrub thrives in cool, shady mountain
areas. The best known of the genus, it grows
to 6–10 ft (1.8–3 m) tall and nearly as wide.
Fragrant, white, puffball flowers appear in
spring and again in autumn. The dark green
leaves, slightly blue beneath, turn vibrant
yellows, oranges and reds in autumn. **ZONES 5–9.**

Fothergilla major

Fremontodendron californicum

This is the best known and hardiest species, ranging along California's Sierra Nevada foothills and coast ranges. It can reach 30 ft (9 m), but is usually a sparse, crooked shrub 20 ft (6 m) tall with dark brown bark. It produces a succession of 2 in (5 cm) wide golden flowers from mid- to late spring. *Fremontodendron californicum* subsp. *decumbens* has a dwarf habit and orange-yellow flowers. **ZONES 8–10.**

FREMONTODENDRON

syn. Fremontia

FLANNEL BUSH

This unusual small genus consists of 2 species of evergreen or semi-evergreen shrubs or small trees from the far southwestern USA and Mexico. The young stems have a felty coating of hairs, as do the lobed leaves on their pale undersides. The large bowl-shaped flowers consist of 5 petal-like, large golden sepals. They are named after Major-General John Charles Fremont (1813–90), an American explorer and distinguished amateur botanist.

CULTIVATION

Frost hardy, these plants are not difficult to grow in a sheltered, sunny position with neutral to alkaline, well-drained soil, but they tend to be short lived. Plant out in spring when the danger of frost has passed. They do not perform well in climates with hot, wet summers. Propagate from seed in spring or cuttings in summer.

Fremontodendron californicum

Fuchsia 'Jack of Hearts'

FUCHSIA

This genus consists of about 100 species and thousands of hybrids and cultivars developed for their pendulous flowers, which come in a fascinating variety of forms (though usually with a long or short perianth tube, spreading sepals and 4 broad petals) and a wonderful range of colors. They are deciduous or evergreen trees, shrubs or perennials treated almost as herbaceous plants. The genus is confined to South and Central America except for 4 species in New Zealand and one in Tahiti. Most of the larger-flowered American species inhabit areas of very high rainfall, sometimes growing as epiphytes or on boulders in moss forests: they are pollinated by hummingbirds. Habit varies from upright shrubs to spreading bushes. Trailing lax varieties are ideal for hanging baskets. Strong upright types may be trained as compact bushes, standards or espaliers.

CULTIVATION

Moderately frost hardy to frost tender, these plants require moist but well-drained, fertile soil in sun or partial shade and shelter from hot winds and afternoon sun. In most cases, pinching back at an early age and then pruning after flowering will improve shape and flower yield. Propagate from seed or cuttings, and check for white fly, spider mite, rust and gray mold.

Fuchsia 'Baby Blue Eyes'

Fuchsia Hybrids
syn. Fuchsia × hybrida

This name covers the thousands of modern large-flowered hybrid cultivars derived mainly from *Fuchsia magellanica*, *F. fulgens* and *F. triphylla*. '**Baby Blue Eyes**', '**Blue Satin**', '**Jack of Hearts**' and '**Tango Queen**' are typical hybrids. All may be grown in pots, hanging baskets or planted in the garden. Those of upright habit may be trained as standards, while trailing cultivars suit hanging baskets and window boxes. **ZONES 8–11.**

Fuchsia 'Tango Queen'

Fuchsia 'Blue Satin'

Fuchsia magellanica 'Versicolor'

Fuchsia magellanica
LADIES' EARDROPS, HARDY FUCHSIA

From Chile and Argentina, this vigorous erect shrub grows up
to 10 ft (3 m) tall. It has lance-shaped to ovate leaves usually
held in whorls of three. The pendulous red tubular flowers with
red sepals and purple petals are produced over a long period in
summer; black fruit follow. Prune it back to maintain its shape.
'Alba' can grow to a considerable size and bears white flowers.
'Thompsonii' has scarlet tubes and sepals and pale purplish
petals; although the flowers are smaller than type, they are more
profuse. 'Versicolor' (syn. 'Tricolor') has gray-green leaves that
are flushed red when immature and irregularly white-splotched
margins when mature; the flowers are small and deep red.
ZONES 7–10.

Fuchsia magellanica

Fuchsia triphylla
HONEYSUCKLE FUCHSIA

From the West Indies, this
evergreen shrub grows to a
height of 30 in (75 cm) and
has pairs or whorls of lance-
shaped leaves with a purple
undersurface. The orange-
scarlet flowers have a slender
tapered tube and small petals.
They are borne in dense
terminal clusters. The leaf
color is most intense if the
plant is grown in light shade.
The honeysuckle fuchsia
grows best in a frost-free
climate. **ZONES 10–11.**

GAULTHERIA
syns × *Gaulnettya, Pernettya*

Named after Dr Gaultier, an eighteenth-century physician, this
genus of 170 or so species of evergreen shrubs are widely distributed in moist temperate regions of the world, also in higher
mountain areas of the tropics. They have attractive glossy leaves
which may be aromatic when crushed. The flowers are pink or
white and are usually bell- or urn-shaped. The fruits, though
capsules, are berry-like and aromatic.

CULTIVATION

Marginally to very frost hardy, they prefer well-drained, humus-
rich, acid soil, and a sheltered position in part-shade. Propagate
from seed in autumn or cuttings in summer, or by division of
suckers in autumn or spring.

Gaultheria shallon

Gaultheria mucronata

syn. **Pernettya mucronata**

PRICKLY HEATH

This thicket-forming, suckering shrub from Chile and Argentina grows to 5 ft (1.5 m) high and wide and has deep green, glossy leaves ½ in (12 mm) long with sharp tips. It bears clusters of small, white, pendulous flowers and small, fleshy, pinkish purple fruit. There are separate male and female plants. Cultivars include 'Bell's Seedling', with deep dusky pink berries; 'Mother of Pearl', with pale pink berries; 'Mulberry Wine' with purple berries; and 'White Pearl' with white berries. 'Wintertime' has pure white berries. **ZONES 7–9.**

Gaultheria shallon

SHALLON

From northwestern North America, this suckering shrub grows to 4–10 ft (1.2–3 m) high and wide. In spring it produces terminal panicles of small, pinkish white, lily-of-the-valley flowers. These are followed by ½ in (12 mm) fleshy, purple fruit. **ZONES 5–9.**

Gaultheria × wisleyensis

syn. × **Gaulnettya wisleyensis**

These vigorous hybrids, bred in England from *Gaultheria shallon* and *G. mucronata*, though variable are usually dense and less than 6 ft (1.8 m) high. They have small leathery leaves, white flowers and large bunches of dark red berries that persist until late winter. Several named culti-vars are available. **ZONES 7–9.**

Gaultheria mucronata 'Bell's Seedling'

Gaultheria × wisleyensis

Genista hispanica

GENISTA
syns *Chamaespartium, Teline*
BROOM

From Europe and the Mediterranean to western Asia, this legume genus consists of about 90 species of deciduous and evergreen shrubs, grown for their profuse, fragrant, pea-like flowers. Many of the species have very reduced leaves, sometimes bearing their flowers on leafless green branches. In ancient times their flowers were used to make dyes.

CULTIVATION
Many are only marginally frost hardy; they prefer a temperate climate and some are good seaside plants. Full sun and a not-too-rich, well-drained soil suit them best. The frost-tender species can be grown in a well-ventilated greenhouse. They resent being transplanted. Prune to encourage a compact, bushy shape. Propagate from seed in spring or cuttings in summer.

Genista pilosa

Genista hispanica
SPANISH GORSE

From southwestern Europe, this dwarf deciduous shrub is ideal for rockeries and dry, sunny banks. It has few leaves and many spines. It grows 30 in (75 cm) tall and 5 ft (1.5 m) wide, forming a neat dome covered in spring and early summer with dense clusters of tiny, golden-yellow flowers. **ZONES 6–10.**

Genista lydia

This mound-forming, deciduous shrub from the Balkans reaches 24–36 in (60–90 cm) tall and wide; it has arching branches and bluish green leaves. Bright yellow pea-like flowers are borne in abundance in early summer. Fully frost hardy, this is an excellent plant for rockeries, banks and for trailing over walls. **ZONES 7–9.**

Genista lydia

Genista pilosa

This deciduous, prostrate to erect European species grows to 16 in (40 cm) high and twice as wide. Fully frost hardy, it bears small, narrow, lance-shaped, dark green leaves with a silky under-surface and profuse small yellow pea-flowers in early summer. 'Vancouver Gold' has a domed habit to 18 in (45 cm) high and golden-yellow flowers. **ZONES 5–9.**

Genista tinctoria
DYER'S BROOM, WOADWAXEN

Used as a medicinal herb and as a source of yellow dye, this tough, deciduous, green-stemmed 3 ft (1 m) shrub ranges from Europe to Siberia. It has 1 in (25 mm) long leaves with fine hairs beneath. Golden-yellow, pea-flowers appear in summer after other brooms have finished flowering. 'Flore Pleno' (syn. 'Plena') is a dwarf cultivar, 12 in (30 cm) high, with double flowers. 'Royal Gold' has golden-yellow flowers arranged in conical panicles to 3 in (8 cm) long. **ZONES 5–9.**

Genista tinctoria

Grevillea 'Canberra Gem'

GREVILLEA

Some 250 species of evergreen shrubs and trees in the protea family make up this genus. Variable in habit, foliage and flowers, most grevilleas are native to Australia with a few from New Caledonia and Papua New Guinea. The small flowers are mostly densely crowded into heads or spikes, their most conspicuous feature being the long styles which are at first bent over like a hairpin and then straighten out. Many are adaptable and easy to grow, with a long flowering period, and are popular with nectar-seeking birds. The leaves are commonly deeply divided and may be very decorative in their own right, the foliage of some species being grown for cutting. In the last several decades hundreds of hybrid grevillea cultivars have been bred, nearly all in Australia, and many are extremely floriferous. Some of the most beautiful species are low growing or prostrate; these may be planted in a rock garden, as groundcover or in pots.

CULTIVATION

Moderately frost hardy to frost tender, grevilleas do best in well-drained, slightly dry, neutral to acid soil in full sun. Strong roots develop early and it is important not to disturb these when planting out. Pruning of shrubby species and cultivars is recommended immediately after flowering to promote healthy new growth and a compact habit. They are generally pest free although scale insects and leaf spot may pose a problem. Propagate from seed in spring, from cuttings in late summer, or by grafting for some of the species most prone to root-rot.

Grevillea 'Canberra Gem'
syn. *Grevillea juniperina* 'Pink Pearl'

This dense, bushy shrub grows to 8 ft (2.4 m) with a similar spread, its erect stems crowded in a hedge-like form. It has narrow, pointed, dark green leaves and is irregularly scattered with small clusters of bright pink and red flowers from winter to late summer. A hybrid between *Grevillea juniperina* and *G. rosmarinifolia*, it is moderately frost hardy and responds well to hard pruning. It can be grown as a hedge, though not very long-lived. **ZONES 7–10.**

Grevillea victoriae

Grevillea lanigera
'Mt Tamboritha'

Grevillea lanigera
WOOLLY GREVILLEA

This species from mountains of southeastern Australia has narrow, grayish, furry leaves and red and cream flower clusters from late winter to spring. It varies in size—some forms are prostrate and others grow to about 3 ft (1 m) tall and wide. This is one of the more frost-hardy species, but it does resent summer humidity. **'Mt Tamboritha'** is a popular, small, prostrate form with soft gray-green foliage and reddish pink and cream flowers. **ZONES 7–9.**

Grevillea victoriae
ROYAL GREVILLEA

This variable species from the mountains of southeastern Australia makes an upright, spreading shrub to 6 ft (1.8 m) high and 10 ft (3 m) across. It has ovate gray-green leaves to 6 in (15 cm) long with silvery undersides. Pendent clusters of rusty red, spider-type flowerheads appear in spring and again in late summer and autumn. Occurring at elevations of up to 6,000 ft (1,800 m), it is one of the more frost-hardy grevilleas. **ZONES 7–9.**

Hamamelis × intermedia 'Ruby Glow'

HAMAMELIS

WITCH HAZEL

This genus contains 5 species of deciduous shrubs or small trees from east Asia and North America. They are prized for their fragrant flowers, borne on bare stems through winter, and for their foliage, which turns yellow with red and orange tints in autumn. The fruits are small capsules containing 2 black seeds.

CULTIVATION

Hamamelis are good shrubs for cool-climate gardens, preferring an open, sunny position (although they will tolerate semi-shade) in fertile, moist but well-drained, loamy, acid soil. Propagate selected forms by grafting in winter, from heeled cuttings in summer or by budding in late summer. Species can be raised from seed, but germination may take a full year. Check for coral spot and honey fungus.

Hamamelis × intermedia

The name covers a group of cultivars derived from *Hamamelis japonica* and *H. mollis*, deciduous shrubs with oval leaves 3–6 in (8–15 cm) long that color well in autumn. Fragrant flowers appear on bare twigs in winter, their color varying from light yellow to deep orange depending on the cultivar. **'Arnold Promise'** has bright yellow flowers; **'Diane'** has fragrant, spidery, deep red flowers in late winter and large leaves that turn red and yellow in autumn; **'Jelena'** is bright orange; and **'Ruby Glow'** (syn. *H. japonica* 'Rubra Superba') has coppery red flowers and rich foliage colors in autumn. **ZONES 4–9.**

Hamamelis × intermedia 'Jelena'

Hamamelis mollis

Hamamelis mollis
CHINESE WITCH HAZEL

This upright, open shrub has extremely fragrant, golden-yellow flowers, borne on bare branches from mid-winter to early spring. It grows to a height and spread of 10–15 ft (3–4.5 m) and the large, thick leaves are mid-green above and downy beneath; they turn deep golden yellow in autumn. 'Coombe Wood' has slightly larger flowers; 'Pallida' has dense clusters of large, sweetly scented sulfur-yellow flowers and yellow leaves in autumn. **ZONES 4–9.**

Hamamelis japonica
JAPANESE WITCH HAZEL

This open, upright shrub grows to a height of 10–15 ft (3–4.5 m) and about as wide. Its perfumed yellow flowers with twisted petals are carried in clusters on the bare branches from mid- to late winter. Flowering branches are often cut for indoor decoration. The oval, mid-green leaves appear in spring and turn yellow before dropping in autumn. **ZONES 4–9.**

Hamamelis virginiana
VIRGINIAN WITCH HAZEL, COMMON WITCH HAZEL

This species has an open, up-right habit and grows to a height and spread of 12–20 ft (3.5–6 m) but can be readily adapted to tree-like form by training to a single trunk in its early years. Small, fragrant, curled and twisted yellow flowers appear in autumn as the leaves fall. The dark green, broadly oval leaves turn a bright buttercup yellow in autumn. **ZONES 7–9.**

Hamamelis virginiana

Hamamelis japonica

Hebe ochracea 'James Stirling'

HEBE

VERONICA

The large genus *Veronica* used to be interpreted more broadly to include all these shrubby species (native to New Zealand and nearby islands, with a couple in Chile). With over 100 species of evergreen shrubs, the hebes include many first-rate garden plants. They have neat, attractive leaves and often showy flower-spikes, which arise in the axils of the leaves, as in *Hebe* 'Wiri Joy', 'Autumn Beauty' and 'Pamela Joy'. There are 2 main groups: the broad-leafed hebes, fast-growing shrubs with pleasing foliage and abundant spikes of small flowers ranging from white through pink to violet and blue over a long summer to autumn season; and the whipcord hebes with small leaves that give them the appearance of dwarf conifers, and white or pale mauve flowers.

CULTIVATION

Most hebes are best suited to temperate to warm climates. In warm climates they grow equally well in sun or shade; in cooler climates sun is preferred. They like moist but well-drained soil and the broad-leafed types benefit from a post-flowering trim. Many mountain whipcord hebes are not easy to grow at low altitudes. Protect from strong winds. They should be propagated from cuttings in summer.

Hebe armstrongii

syn. *Hebe lycopodioides*

From summer to early winter this frost-hardy, rounded, bushy shrub bears dense clusters of tiny, 4-petalled, white flowers. One of the whipcord group, its narrow oval leaves are bronze when young and the twigs are a distinctive greenish gold. *Hebe armstrongii* has a height and spread of less than 3 ft (1 m). It makes a wonderful addition to the garden. **ZONES 8–10.**

Hebe ochracea

A frost-hardy whipcord species with olive-green to golden-brown stems, *Hebe ochracea* is most commonly represented by '**James Stirling**', a particularly bright golden cultivar. The shrub grows to about 18 in (45 cm) high and 3 ft (1 m) wide. The inflorescences of about 10 white flowers are rarely seen in cultivation. It is not advisable to prune this species unless absolutely necessary as pruning may lead to dieback. **ZONES 6–10.**

Hebe armstrongii

Hebe salicifolia
KOROMIKO, KOKOMUKA

This frost-hardy, spreading evergreen shrub, up to about 10 ft (3 m) tall and wide, is from New Zealand's South Island and Chile and is tolerant of pollution and salt winds. Of dense habit, it makes an effective screen. The narrow, waxy leaves may be up to 6 in (15 cm) long. The fragrant white flowers, tinged with lilac, are produced in showy spikes up to 8 in (20 cm) long. **ZONES 7–9.**

Hebe 'Autumn Beauty'

Hebe pinguifolia

Hebe pinguifolia

This variable and adaptable small shrub from the drier mountain districts of the South Island of New Zealand can grow to 3 ft (1 m) high and wide. The pale blue-green leaves are margined with red, and the white flowers are borne in small dense terminal spikes. It can tolerate a wide range of growing conditions and is frost hardy. **'Pagei'** is a low, spreading form with small, blue-gray leaves and many small white flowers in spring. It is an ideal rock-garden plant. **ZONES 6–10.**

Hebe salicifolia

Helianthemum 'Fire King'

HELIANTHEMUM

ROCK ROSE, SUN ROSE

Helianthemum means flower of sunshine, an appropriate name
for flowers that only open in bright sunlight. Allied to *Cistus*,
the genus contains over 100 species found on rocky and scrubby
ground in temperate zones around the world. Sun roses are sturdy,
short-lived, evergreen or semi-evergreen shrubs or subshrubs.
Their bushy foliage ranges in color from silver to mid-green.
There are many garden forms, mostly of low, spreading habit.
Wild plants have flowers resembling 1 in (25 mm) wide wild
roses, but garden forms can be anything from white through yellow and salmon-pink to red and orange, and some varieties have
double flowers.

CULTIVATION

Plant in full sun in freely
draining, coarse soil with a
little peat or compost added
during dry periods. As the
flowers fade, they should be
cut back lightly to encourage
a second flush of bloom in
autumn. Propagate from seed
or cuttings.

Helianthemum
'Fire King'

This popular, vibrant cultivar
is similar to *Helianthemum*
'Fire Dragon' but its flowers
are a brighter orange. This
plant forms low, spreading
mounds of gray-green leaves.
It reaches 12–18 ft (30–45 cm)
high. **ZONES 6–10.**

Helianthemum
nummularium

A variable species from
Europe and Turkey, *Helianthemum nummularium* has
a neat, prostrate habit and
grayish foliage. Its small but
profuse flowers vary in color
from yellow or cream to pink
or orange. Most of the cultivars traditionally listed under
this name are in fact of hybrid
origin. **ZONES 5–10.**

Helianthemum nummularium

HELICHRYSUM

EVERLASTING, PAPER DAISY, STRAWFLOWER

The genus has been described in detail in the chapter on Lawns, Groundcovers, Ornamental Grasses and Bamboos. The following species is a shrub.

Helichrysum splendidum

syns Helichrysum alveolatum, H. trilineatum

This dense evergreen shrub occurs in the mountains of Africa from Ethiopia to the Cape. It grows to 5 ft (1.5 m) high and wide. It has crowded narrow leaves clothed in cobweb-like white hairs. Profuse small heads of golden-yellow flowers are borne from summer through autumn. Frost hardy, it should be kept compact with regular pruning. **ZONES 7–10.**

Helichrysum splendidum

HIBISCUS

While the genus name conjures up the innumerable cultivars of *Hibiscus rosa-sinensis*, the genus of around 220 species is quite diverse, including hot-climate evergreen shrubs and small trees and also a few deciduous, temperate-zone shrubs and some annuals and perennials. The leaves are mostly toothed or lobed and the flowers, borne singly or in terminal spikes, are of characteristic shape with a funnel of 5 overlapping petals and a central column of fused stamens.

CULTIVATION

Easy to grow, the shrubby species thrive in sun and slightly acid, well-drained soil. Water regularly and feed during the flowering period. Trim after flowering to maintain shape. Propagate from seed or cuttings or by division, depending on the species. Check for aphids, mealybugs and white fly. The *H. rosa-sinensis* cultivars make good greenhouse subjects in frosty climates, and compact-growing cultivars are gaining popularity as house plants.

Hibiscus rosa-sinensis

Hibiscus coccineus

This tall perennial species from the marshes of Georgia and Florida in the USA has distinctively shaped petals, each petal narrowing at the base to a slender basal stalk. The elegant flower, up to 8 in (20 cm) wide, also has the long column of stamens typical of many hibiscus, which dusts the head and back of birds with pollen. **ZONES 7–11.**

Hibiscus coccineus

Hibiscus rosa-sinensis
CHINESE HIBISCUS, RED HIBISCUS, SHOEFLOWER

The name shoeflower is Jamaican, from the unromantic use of crushed flowers to polish black shoes. The species itself is of ancient hybrid origin from the Indian Ocean region and is a glossy leafed evergreen shrub, sometimes as much as 15 ft (4.5 m) high and wide, with blood red flowers borne just about all year. It is less often seen than its numerous garden cultivars, some pure bred and others, like the enormous blooming Hawaiian hybrids, carrying the genes of other species. These plants grow 3–10 ft (1–3 m) high, and the flowers can be 5-petalled singles, semi-double or fully double, the colors ranging from white through pinks to red; the Hawaiian hybrids offer yellow, coral and orange, often with 2 or 3 shades in each flower. The flowers range upwards in size from about 5 in (12 cm): some of the Hawaiian hybrids are as large as dinner plates. Each flower only lasts a day, opening in the morning and withering by evening, but they appear in long succession as long as the weather is warm. All the *Hibiscus rosa-sinensis* cultivars like a frost-free climate. They include 'Surfrider' with single flowers that are deep orange with a red center; 'Fiesta' with dark apricot flowers with red and white centers; 'Covakanic' with flowers in beautiful varying tones of orange and apricot; as well as 'Apple Blossom', 'Cooperi', 'Madonna' and 'Sabrina'. **ZONES 10–12.**

Hibiscus syriacus

BLUE HIBISCUS, ROSE OF SHARON

This upright, deciduous shrub (evergreen in warmer climates) from temperate Asia is the most frost hardy of the genus. It flowers freely in summer in varying shades of white, pink, soft red, mauve and violet blue. The single, semi-double and double flowers are bell-shaped and are borne in the axils of the leaves. The plant has small, hairless leaves and grows to 12 ft (3.5 m) tall with a spread of 3–6 ft (1–1.8 m). Prune to shape in the first 2 years of growth, trimming lightly thereafter to maintain compact form. Popular cultivars include 'Ardens' with large, mauve flowers with crimson centers; 'Blue Bird' with single, violet blue flowers with red centers; 'Diana' with broad, pure white flowers; and 'Woodbridge' with 2-toned pink blooms at least 4 in (10 cm) across. **ZONES 5–10.**

Hibiscus rosa-sinensis 'Covakanic'

Hibiscus rosa-sinensis Hawaiian Hybrid

Hibiscus syriacus 'Woodbridge'

Hibiscus syriacus 'Blue Bird'

HIPPOPHAË

These 3 species of thorny, deciduous shrubs and trees are valued for their toughness and their showy autumn berries. Both male and female plants must be grown together to obtain the fruit. Inconspicuous flowers appear in spring. Indigenous to cold-climate regions of Asia and northern Europe, they are found along the coast or river banks and in sandy woodlands. They are wind and salt resistant and make excellent hedges for coastal areas.

CULTIVATION
Species of *Hippophaë* grow best in full sun and tolerate dry or very sandy soil. Propagation is from seed in autumn or from cuttings in summer.

Hippophaë rhamnoides

Hippophaë rhamnoides
SEA BUCKTHORN

Growing to a height and spread of about 20 ft (6 m) with a bushy, arching habit, this shrub or small tree has very narrow, gray-green leaves with paler undersides. Insignificant, yellowish flowers appear in clusters in spring, before the leaf growth. The bright orange berries are borne in dense clusters on the shoots of female plants and usually persist through winter. **ZONES 2–9.**

HYDRANGEA

These deciduous or evergreen shrubs, climbers and sometimes small trees occur over a wide area of temperate Asia and North and South America. Most species have large oval leaves with serrated edges; some develop good autumn foliage color. The flower clusters contain tiny fertile flowers and showy sterile ones with 4 petal-like sepals. Although most species produce panicles of flowers with few sterile flowers, many cultivated forms have heads composed almost entirely of sterile flowers and are called by gardeners mobcaps, mopheads or hortensias (for *Hydrangea macrophylla* cultivars only). Intermediate forms with a ring of sterile flowers surrounding fertile flowers are called lacecaps. Flower color may vary with the acidity or alkalinity of the soil: blue in acid soil, pink or red in alkaline; white cultivars do not change. In some but not all cultivars the old flowers gradually fade to shades of green and pink, this color being independent of soil type.

CULTIVATION
Except in cool, moist climates, they need shade or part-shade or both leaves and flowers will scorch; and though soil should be constantly moist and rich in humus, it should be well drained. Pruning is best done immediately after bloom. Propagation is usually from cuttings or seed. Check regularly for powdery mildew, leaf spot, honey fungus and aphids, scale insects and spider mites.

Hydrangea aspera

Hydrangea arborescens

SNOWHILL HYDRANGEA, SMOOTH HYDRANGEA

This frost-hardy, shade-loving shrub from eastern USA grows 6–8 ft (1.8–2.4 m) tall, usually with a greater spread. It forms a lax mound from many suckering stems which are clothed in big, simple, serrated leaves up to 6 in (15 cm) long. Hemispherical heads of many small white flowers are produced in late spring and summer; these turn green as they age. '**Grandiflora**' is commonly sold but '**Annabelle**' is an improved variety with bigger blooms that are produced about 2 weeks later. **ZONES 6–9.**

Hydrangea arborescens 'Annabelle'

Hydrangea heteromalla 'Bretschneideri'

Hydrangea aspera

This species occurs naturally over much of southern and eastern Asia, showing much variation in the wild. In cultivation it grows to around 10 ft (3 m) high and wide. Its serrated-edged leaves vary from narrow to oval, and are 3–10 in (8–25 cm) long. The large flowerheads that occur in summer are lacecap style with pale, sterile flowers and tiny, purplish blue, fertile flowers. The flower color varies little with soil type. The **Villosa Group** bear broad heads of blue or purple flowers in the center of the shrubs and larger white flowers towards the periphery. Deciduous and upright, they grow to a height and spread of 10 ft (3 m) and are very frost hardy. **ZONES 7–10.**

Hydrangea heteromalla

Growing to a height of 10 ft (3 m), this deciduous shrub from western China and Tibet produces many stems from ground level to form a loose, rounded shrub. The leaves are broadly lanceolate or narrowly ovate, pointy and toothed along their edges. The flowers are of the lacecap variety with a cluster of tiny fertile flowers surrounded by bigger, more showy infertile, white or pink flowers. Blooming occurs in summer. The cultivar '**Bretschneideri**' is shrubbier than the species and has narrower leaves, peeling, reddish brown bark and flatter flower sprays. **ZONES 6–9.**

Hydrangea macrophylla

Hydrangea macrophylla 'Sunset'

Hydrangea macrophylla 'Altona'

Hydrangea macrophylla

BIGLEAF HYDRANGEA,
GARDEN HYDRANGEA

This species in its typical wild form comes from Japan and is rather rare in cultivation. The name also covers a large race of garden varieties derived from it, though in fact many of these may have originated as hybrids between *Hydrangea macrophylla* and *H. aspera*. The major group known as 'hortensias' (once *H. hortensia)* have flowerheads of the 'mophead' type, with densely massed sterile florets. A smaller group are the 'lacecaps'; examples are **'Blue Sky'** and **'Blue Wave'**. There are many named cultivars, ranging in growth from less than 3 ft (1 m) tall and wide to twice that size; 5 ft (1.5 m) is the average. As a rule, the deeper the color the smaller the growth. **'Geoffrey Chadbund'** is a lacecap form with rich, bright red flowers; **'Libelle'** (also a lacecap) has extra large, pure white

infertile flowers that give the head a crowded, full look; 'Altona' is a hortensia form with flowers that vary from deep pink to purplish blue; 'Générale Vicomtesse de Vibraye' (also a hortensia) bears large flowerheads in pink or pale blue. 'Lilacina' (lacecap) has pink flowers that may be tinged purple; 'Shower' (lacecap) produces elegant heads of clear, hot pink; 'Sir Joseph Banks' (hortensia) is pink flowered; 'Sunset' (lacecap) is a big, vigorous shrub which often grows to over 5 ft (1.5 m) across and produces many heads of rich pinkish scarlet blooms; 'Taube' is similar to 'Sunset' but does not grow quite as large and has softer pink blooms; and 'Veitchii' (lacecap) bears flowers that open white but as they age they turn soft pink.
ZONES 6–10.

Hydrangea macrophylla 'Blue Sky'

Hydrangea macrophylla 'Sir Joseph Banks'

Hydrangea paniculata

Hydrangea paniculata
PANICLE HYDRANGEA

This large deciduous shrub from China and Japan grows to 15 ft (4.5 m) or more, with a broad, dome-shaped crown the same in width. It has large, oval, dark green leaves and in mid-summer bears small cream, fertile flowers and larger flat, creamy white,

Hydrangea paniculata 'Grandiflora'

Hydrangea quercifolia

Hydrangea serrata 'Bluebird'

sterile flowers that turn rose purple as they age. Prune back hard in late winter or spring for larger flowerheads. **'Grandiflora'** is the form most commonly grown. **'Tardiva'** does not flower until autumn. **ZONES 5–9.**

Hydrangea quercifolia
OAK-LEAF HYDRANGEA

Native to the USA, this deciduous shrub grows to a height of 6–8 ft (1.8–2.4 m), spreading by stolons to 12 ft (3.5 m) or more. Deeply lobed, dark green leaves turn orange-scarlet in autumn. The flowers, borne from mid-summer to mid-autumn, are a mixture of small, fertile and sterile flowers. The white, sterile flowers fade to pink and violet. It performs best in dappled shade. **ZONES 5–9.**

Hydrangea serrata

This species, a lacecap style hydrangea, is closely allied to *Hydrangea macrophylla* and sometimes included there as a subspecies. It grows into a rounded shrub to 5 ft (1.5 m) tall with a similar spread. The leaves are more narrowly ovate than in *H. macrophylla* and are prominently toothed. **'Bluebird'** is typical of the species with wide, flattish flowerheads over most of summer. **ZONES 6–10.**

Hypericum frondosum
GOLDEN ST JOHN'S WORT

A rounded deciduous shrub from the southeastern States of the USA, golden St John's wort grows up to 4 ft (1.2 m) tall with a similar spread. The many stems are upright and densely clothed with curving, oblong leaves that are a blue-green color with a powdery bloom. In summer clusters of showy, bright yellow flowers are borne. '**Sunburst**' is an improvement on the species and worth seeking out. **ZONES 5–10.**

Hypericum 'Hidcote'

This dense bushy shrub grows 4 ft (1.2 m) in height and has a spread of 5 ft (1.5 m). It bears large, cup-shaped, 2½ in (6 cm) golden-yellow flowers from mid-summer to early autumn and has lance-shaped, dark green leaves. **ZONES 7–10.**

Hypericum beanii 'Gold Cup'

Hypericum 'Hidcote'

HYPERICUM
ST JOHN'S WORT

This is a large and varied genus of 400 species of annuals, perennials, shrubs and a few small trees, some evergreen but mostly deciduous, grown for their showy flowers in shades of yellow with a central mass of prominent golden stamens. They are found throughout the world in a broad range of habitats. Species range in size from tiny perennials for rockeries to over 10 ft (3 m) tall.

CULTIVATION

Mostly cool-climate plants, they prefer full sun but will tolerate some shade. They do best in fertile, well-drained soil, with plentiful water in late spring and summer. Remove seed capsules after flowering and prune in winter to maintain a rounded shape. Cultivars are propagated from cuttings in summer, and species from seed in autumn or from cuttings in summer. Some species are susceptible to rust.

Hypericum beanii

A vigorous, evergreen shrub from western China, this variable species may grow to 6 ft (1.8 m) tall with dense, arching branches. The mid-green leaves are usually elliptical and paler beneath. Large, star-shaped, golden-yellow flowers with showy stamens appear in summer. This species is often used for bank retention. '**Gold Cup**' (syn. *Hypericum* × *cyathiflorum* 'Gold Cup') produces 2 in (5 cm) wide, cup-shaped, golden-yellow flowers in summer. **ZONES 7–10.**

Hypericum frondosum

Hypericum kouytchense

This broad semi-evergreen shrub grows to 5 ft (1.5 m) tall, spreading to 6 ft (1.8 m). Golden-yellow flattish flowers with showy long styles and stamens are carried in profusion on drooping branchlets in summer. **ZONES 6–10.**

Hypericum × moserianum

GOLD FLOWER

This species bears star-shaped, bright yellow flowers. 'Tricolor', with its green, cream and pink leaves, is one of the most desirable of variegated-leafed shrubs; it grows 24–36 in (60–90 cm) tall and rather wider, bearing modest bowl-shaped flowers from summer to autumn. **ZONES 7–10.**

Hypericum × moserianum
'Tricolor'

Hypericum kouytchense

IBERIS

Fifty species of decorative annuals, perennials and subshrubs make up this genus, which is described in more detail in the chapter on Annuals and Perennials. The following species is treated as a small shrub.

Iberis gibraltarica

GIBRALTAR CANDYTUFT

This species, a sprawling, bushy perennial from Gibraltar and southern Spain grows to 12 in (30 cm) in height. It has narrow, dark green leaves and produces clusters of pink- or red-tinged white flowers in summer. Although normally frost hardy, it is susceptible to damage when frost is combined with wet winter conditions. **ZONES 7–11.**

ILEX

Ilex crenata 'Green Lustre'

Most members of this genus are trees; details on the genus are given in the Trees chapter. Those included here can be treated as shrubs.

Ilex cornuta
CHINESE HOLLY

Self-fertile and well suited to mild-winter climates, this fully frost-hardy, dense, rounded shrub from China, grows to 12 ft (3.5 m) with a spread of 15 ft (4.5 m). The thick glossy leaves are almost rectangular, with spiny points; the berries, while not as profuse as on English holly, are larger and are borne throughout summer. **ZONES 6–10.**

Ilex crenata
JAPANESE HOLLY

From Japan, this frost-hardy, compact, evergreen shrub has stiff branches, small scalloped leaves, dull white flowers and glossy black berries. Often used for hedges and topiary, it can grow to 15 ft (4.5 m) with a spread of 10 ft (3 m), but is usually smaller. Cultivars include **'Convexa'**, with almost spineless, glossy black-green leaves and purplish stems; **'Golden Gem'**, a compact but rarely flowering shrub, with soft yellow foliage; **'Green Lustre'**, a compact male shrub with very dark green leaves and no fruit; **'Helleri'**, a female clone of spreading habit that can reach 5 ft (1.5 m) in height and spread, with sparsely spined leaves and black fruit; and **'Schwoebel's Compact'**, a low-spreading dwarf form to 3 ft (1 m) tall. Variegated or pale-leafed forms do best in full sun; green-leafed forms do well in partial shade. **ZONES 6–10.**

Ilex verticillata
WINTERBERRY, BLACK ALDER, CORAL BERRY

From eastern USA, this deciduous shrub grows 6–10 ft (1.8–3 m) high and has a spread of 4–10 ft (1.2–3 m). The toothed leaves are purple-tinged in spring and turn yellow in autumn. The bright red berries stay on the bare branches for a long period, persisting until spring. This shrub tolerates wet conditions. Cultivars include **'Cacapon'**, a female, which produces abundant berries when grown with a male; **'Nana'** (syn. 'Red Sprite'), a dwarf female which reaches 4 ft (1.2 m) tall and has a spread of 5 ft (1.5 m); and **'Winter Red'**, an extra vigorous female with a height and spread of 10 ft (3 m) and good crops of bright red berries when grown with a male plant. **ZONES 3–9.**

Ilex verticillata

Ilex cornuta

Indigofera decora

Indigofera decora
syn. *Indigofera incarnata*

This bushy deciduous shrub from China and Japan grows to 24 in (60 cm) and spreads to 3 ft (1 m); wider in mild climates. Moderately frost hardy, stems may die back to ground level, but the plant usually shoots again from the rootstock. The glossy, dark green, pinnate leaves, up to 10 in (25 cm) long, are composed of 7 to 13 oval leaflets. Long wisteria-like spikes of mauve-pink pea-shaped flowers appear through the warmer months. The cultivar '**Alba**' is a white-flowering form. **ZONES 7–11.**

INDIGOFERA

More than 700 species of annuals, perennials, shrubs and small trees make up this large leguminous genus. Mostly from tropical and subtropical regions, species are found in both hemispheres. Cultivated species are generally subshrubs or small, deciduous, woody plants with smallish pinnate leaves and panicles of pea-like flowers, usually in summer.

CULTIVATION

Frost-tender to moderately frost hardy, they prefer light, moist, well-drained soil in sun or part-shade. Propagate from seed in autumn or cuttings or basal suckers in summer.

Indigofera decora 'Alba'

IOCHROMA

Members of the nightshade family, these brittle-wooded, tropical and subtropical, evergreen shrubs from Central and South America are suited to warm, humid climates. Usually erect, with softwooded, arching branches, clusters of long tubular blue, purple, red or white flowers appear through summer and autumn. They are suitable for the garden, the greenhouse or as potted plants.

CULTIVATION

These frost-tender plants need full sun to part-shade and fertile, well-drained soil. In the garden, a sheltered position is best for protection from wind. Young plants can be pruned lightly to make them bushy, and flowered stems should be cut back heavily in early spring. Propagate from cuttings or seed. Potted plants should be watered well in summer. Watch for white fly and spider mites.

Iochroma cyaneum

ITEA

Of the 10 species of evergreen and deciduous shrubs and trees in this genus, most are from tropical and temperate Asia but one species is native to North America. They are grown for their showy, fragrant autumn flowers. They are frost hardy, although in some colder areas they need the protection of a wall. These are useful plants for specimens or for growing in a shrubbery. The botanical name *Itea* comes from the Greek, meaning 'willow', to which some species bear a slight resemblance.

CULTIVATION

They will thrive in anything but very dry soil and prefer a part-shaded position, but will tolerate full sun. Propagate from cuttings in summer and plant out in autumn or spring.

Iochroma cyaneum
syns *Iochroma tubulosum,*
I. lanceolatum
VIOLET TUBEFLOWER

This fast-growing, semi-erect shrub grows to 10 ft (3 m) high with a spread of 5 ft (1.5 m). It brings a deep purple accent to the warm-climate garden; it can be grown in a greenhouse in cooler areas. It has gray-green felty leaves; deep purple-blue flowers are borne in large pendent clusters through summer and autumn. Prune to shape in early spring. **ZONES 9–11.**

Iochroma grandiflorum

Indigenous to Ecuador, this shrub or small tree grows 10–20 ft (3–6 m) high and 6–12 ft (1.8–3.5 m) wide. Its soft, deep green, pointed oval leaves are up to 8 in (20 cm) long and are slightly downy when young. The flowers, borne in late summer and autumn, are long, pendent, bright purple tubes with widely flared mouths. Pulpy, purplish green, berry-like fruit follow. **ZONES 9–12.**

Itea virginica

Itea virginica
SWEETSPIRE, VIRGINIA WILLOW

The best known member of the genus, this deciduous North American shrub of upright, slender form grows 3–5 ft (1–1.5 m) tall and in summer bears fragrant, creamy white flowers in semi-erect panicles. Its finely toothed, deciduous, bright green leaves do not fall until early winter, when they sometimes turn red. It is suitable for mass planting, particularly in wet, low places and is more frost hardy than *Itea ilicifolia*. **ZONES 5–9.**

JASMINUM

Most of the species belonging to this genus are climbers, and detailed information on the genus is given in the Climbers and Creepers chapter. However, the species below are treated as shrubs.

Jasminum mesnyi
syn. Jasminum primulinum
YELLOW JASMINE, PRIMROSE JASMINE

This marginally frost-hardy evergreen shrub from western China grows to 6–10 ft (1.8–3 m) in height and spread. Its long, arching canes eventually form a wide, fountain shape. The deep green leaves are made up of 3 leaflets, and bright yellow, scented blooms appear during late winter and early spring. Remove old canes to thin crowded plants. It is suitable for a hanging basket. **ZONES 8–10.**

Jasminum nudiflorum

Jasminum mesnyi

Juniperus × media 'Dandelight'

Jasminum nudiflorum
WINTER JASMINE

This rambling, deciduous, arching shrub from China has oval, dark green foliage and grows 6–10 ft (1.8–3 m) tall with a similar spread. It is best suited to a cool or cold climate, where it will bear masses of bright yellow flowers on slender, leafless, green shoots in winter and early spring. Frost hardy, it prefers a well-drained soil and full sun. **ZONES 6–9.**

Jasminum officinale
COMMON JASMINE, POET'S JASMINE, JESSAMINE

Introduced to Europe from China in the sixteenth century, this deciduous or semi-evergreen shrubby climber can be maintained as a neat 3–5 ft (1–1.5 m) shrub or allowed to ramble. The dark green leaves have 7 to 9 leaflets; clusters of deep pink buds followed by very fragrant, starry white flowers occur through summer and autumn. This frost-hardy species likes full sun, well-drained, fertile soil and ample water in warmer months. It is an excellent container plant for a sunny terrace. The essential oil of this species is used in perfume and as a food flavoring, such as in maraschino cherries. Pink-flowered and variegated-foliage forms are also available. **ZONES 6–10.**

JUNIPERUS

Most of the species belonging to this genus are trees, and detailed information on the genus is given in the Trees chapter. However, *Juniperus × media* is treated here as a shrub.

Juniperus × media

This group of cultivars, mainly derived from *Juniperus chinensis* and valued in cool to cold climates for their foliage, are all spreading shrubs, 1 or 2 being semi-prostrate. Their mainly scale-like, gray-green leaves have an unpleasant smell when crushed; the berries are white or blue-black. **'Blaauw'** grows to a height and spread of 6 ft (1.8 m) with blue-green foliage; **'Gold Coast'**, possibly the finest golden form of this group, makes a neat, spreading groundcover shrub to 3 ft (1 m) in height and spread; **'Dandelight'** to 24 in (60 cm) with a 6 ft (1.8 m) spread has golden yellow new growth ageing to yellow-green; **'Old Gold'**, a

sport of 'Pfitzeriana Aurea', is a neat plant
ideal for large rock gardens or as a groundcover reaching 30 in (75 cm) tall with a spread
of 5 ft (1.5 m) and attractive golden foliage;
'Pfitzeriana', by far the best known cultivar,
grows to 10 ft (3 m) tall with a spread of
10–15 ft (3–4.5 m) and is broadly pyramidal
with wide-spreading branches with weeping
tips and gray-green leaves; 'Pfitzeriana Aurea',
only for those with plenty of space, is a hardy
juniper with spray-like branches that reach up
to 3 ft (1m) in height with a spread of more
than 10 ft (3 m); '**Plumosa Aurea**' reaches a
height of 3 ft (1 m) and spread of 6 ft (1.8 m)
with arched, weeping tips to the branches and
green-gold foliage turning bronze in winter;
and '**Plumosa Aurea-Variegata**' will grow to
12 in (30 cm) tall with a spread of more than
3 ft (1 m) and has gray foliage with sprays of
creamy yellow foliage splashed throughout.
ZONES 4–10.

Kalmia latifolia

KALMIA

From North America, this genus of 6 poisonous
species contains some beautiful spring-flowering evergreen shrubs. The 2 common species
are quite different in general appearance, but
both bloom in late spring and early summer
and bear heads of pink flowers that open from
buds that look almost like cake decorations.

CULTIVATION

They prefer a cool, moist climate in lime-free,
humus-rich, well-drained soil and a position in
part-shade. They are among the hardiest of
broad-leafed evergreens. Propagate from seed
in autumn or cuttings in summer, or by layering.

Kalmia angustifolia

Kalmia angustifolia
SHEEP LAUREL, HOBBLE BUSH, LAMBKILL

This open, twiggy shrub growing to 3 ft (1 m)
tall and 4 ft (1.2 m) wide can be kept in a neat,
compact shape suitable for shrubberies, rockeries or containers if trimmed after flowering.
The leaves are 1–2 in (2.5–5 cm) long, and
bright green to bluish green. The flowerheads,
usually bright reddish pink, appear in late
spring and early summer. In its native USA,
it acquired its common names because sheep
were often caught in the low, sprawling
branches. Propagate by layering. *Kalmia
angustifolia* f. *rubra* has deeper, almost red
flowers. **ZONES 2–9.**

Kalmia latifolia
MOUNTAIN LAUREL, CALICO BUSH

From late spring to early summer, this shrub
bears clusters of distinctive, bright pink buds
that open to small, pale pink flowers with
stamens arranged like umbrella ribs. In cultivation, they usually grow to 5 ft (1.5 m) high
and wide. 'Ostbo Red' has deeper pink flowers
which open from red buds; 'Carousel' has
purple-striped white flowers; and 'Elf' is a
pink-flowered dwarf form. **ZONES 3–9.**

KERRIA

JAPANESE ROSE

Kerria japonica

This genus from China and Japan contains one species, a deciduous shrub with many upright 6 ft (1.8 m), deep green stems emerging directly from the ground. The leaves are 1 in (25 mm) long, bright green and roughly diamond-shaped with finely serrated edges. The true species has simple, bright golden-yellow flowers up to 2 in (5 cm) across.

CULTIVATION
A very tough, fully frost-hardy, adaptable plant, it does well in moist, well-drained soil in dappled shade. Trim lightly after flowering to thin out the older canes. Propagate from basal suckers or cuttings in summer or by division in autumn.

KOLKWITZIA

BEAUTY BUSH

This genus consists of a single species of deciduous shrub from China, much admired in temperate and cool-climate gardens for its lavish spring display. However, as its foliage is undistinguished during summer, it should be placed where other plants can attract the eye.

CULTIVATION
Fully frost hardy, *Kolkwitzia* grows in any well-drained soil and does well in sun or light shade. It can become very untidy if old wood is not removed from time to time; winter pruning will simply cut away the flowering wood. Propagation is from cuttings in summer.

Kerria japonica

The golden blossoms of this shrub, which appear in spring, make good cut flowers; the small leaves that follow sparsely clothe the arching branches. Although *Kerria japonica* is single-flowered, the double form '**Pleniflora**' is more common in gardens. **ZONES 5–10.**

Kolkwitzia amabilis

Kolkwitzia amabilis

This bushy shrub develops into a mass of upright, cane-like stems to 12 ft (3.5 m) high. The leaves are in opposite pairs, oval, 1½ in (35 mm) long and deep green. The pale pink, trumpet-shaped flowers, which open in spring, form profuse clusters at the ends of the side branches. They are followed by small fruit covered with bristles. '**Pink Cloud**' has clear pink flowers and is slightly larger than the type. **ZONES 4–9.**

LAVANDULA

LAVENDER

These fragrant, evergreen, aromatic shrubs, of which there are around 25 species, are valued for their attractive lacy, fragrant, usually grayish foliage. They occur naturally from the Mediterranean region through the Middle East to India. Most species grow 24–36 in (60–90 cm) high and a similar width. The small mauve-purple or bluish purple flowers emerge from between bracts in erect, short spikes held on stalks above the foliage, mostly in spring. There are oil glands at the bases of the flowers that produce the pungent oil of lavender, obtained commercially by distillation from *Lavandula angustifolia* and *L. stoechas*.

CULTIVATION

These plants prefer full sun and fertile, well-drained soil; they will thrive in both acid and alkaline soils. The woodier species such as *L. dentata* are excellent as low hedges, and a light trim after blooming keeps them neat. Hardiness varies with the species, although most are moderately frost hardy if the growth is well ripened by warm autumn weather. Propagate from seed or cuttings in summer.

Lavandula angustifolia 'Alba'

Lavandula angustifolia

syns *Lavandula officinalis*,
L. spica, L. vera
LAVENDER

This dense, bushy subshrub grows to about 3 ft (1 m) tall though usually lower, with narrow, furry gray leaves. It is grown mainly for the long-stemmed heads of purple, scented flowers that appear in summer and through the warm months; these are easily dried for lavender sachets, potpourri and the like. *Lavandula angustifolia* makes an attractive low hedge and can be trimmed after flowering. There are a number of selected cultivars, of which 'Munstead' and the dwarf 'Hidcote' are outstanding. 'Alba' grows to 24 in (60 cm) with a 3 ft (1 m) spread; it has yellowish gray bark on its woody stems, pale gray-green foliage and white flowers in whorls. 'Jean Davis' grows to 15–18 in (38–45 cm) and has blue-green foliage and tall pinkish white flowers. **ZONES 6–10.**

Lavandula × intermedia

ENGLISH LAVENDER, LAVANDIN

These naturally occurring and cultivated hybrids between *Lavandula angustifolia* and *L. latifolia* show considerable variation in plant size and flower form. Few exceed 3 ft (1 m) tall but they are otherwise something of a catch-all group. The cultivar 'Provence' has green foliage and small-bracted spikes of mauve-pink flowers. **ZONES 6–10.**

Lavandula × intermedia 'Provence'

Lavandula stoechas

Lavandula latifolia

SPIKE LAVENDER

This subshrubby species is very like *Lavandula angustifolia*, differing in its slightly wider leaves but narrower floral bracts. A rounded clump rarely reaching 3 ft (1 m) high and wide, its gray stems and foliage are downy and fragrant. The heavily scented, light purple flowers of the shrub appear in spikes in summer. Its compact form makes *L. latifolia* an ideal specimen for growing in containers and as dwarf hedges. **ZONES 7–10.**

Lavandula stoechas 'Merle'

Lavandula stoechas

SPANISH LAVENDER, FRENCH LAVENDER

Native to the western Mediterranean, this marginally frost-hardy species is the most striking in flower of all lavenders, at least in some of its varied forms. A small neat shrub 20–30 in (50–75 cm) high, it has pine-scented, narrow silvery green leaves with inward-curling edges. In late spring and summer it is covered with spikes of deep purple flowers. Several bracts at the apex of each spike are elongated into pinkish purple 'rabbit ears' of varying size. **'Merle'** is a compact bush with long-eared, magenta-purple flowerheads. **'Marshwood'** is a particularly heavy flowering, long-blooming cultivar. *Lavandula stoechas* subsp. *lusitanica* has very narrow leaves and dark purple flowers with paler 'rabbit ear' bracts. *L. s.* subsp. *pedunculata* (syn. *L. pedunculata*) from Spain, North Africa and the Balkans, grows 18–24 in (45–60 cm) tall. It has flower stalks that grow to 2–3 in (5–8 cm). The shrub has greenish foliage and the flower spikes are plump and pale green after the flowers have dropped. *L. s.* subsp. *luisieri*, which is a native of Portugal, is an upright bush with green rather than silver-gray foliage and large purple flower spikes. **ZONES 7–10.**

Lavandula latifolia

Ledum groenlandicum
LABRADOR TEA

One of the few shrubs to survive the rigorous climate of Greenland, this species is also found in northern North America. It grows 3 ft (1 m) high and 4 ft (1.2 m) wide. The wiry branches are covered in red-brown hair, as are the undersides of the 1–2½ in (2.5–6 cm) long leaves. Clusters of flowers open at the branch tips from late spring. The leaves and stems are used in folk medicine as inhalants or insect repellents.
ZONES 2–8.

LEDUM

Resembling small examples of their close relatives the rhododendrons, the 4 species in this genus are bushy evergreen shrubs. They range widely around the cooler northern temperate regions and into subarctic territories. They vary in height from 1 to 6 ft (0.3 to 1.8 m) depending on the harshness of the environment in which they are grown. In spring and summer they are covered in small, 5-petalled white flowers with protruding stamens.

CULTIVATION

Treat in the same way as a cool-climate rhododendron: plant in cool, humus-rich, moist but well-drained soil in shade or morning sun. They are among the frost hardiest of broad-leafed evergreen plants. Propagate from seed or cuttings or by layering.

LEUCOTHOË

Ledum groenlandicum

This genus, containing about 50 species of deciduous and evergreen shrubs allied to *Pieris*, is widely distributed in cool- to warm-climate regions from southern USA to the mountains of South America, with a few in east Asia. They have simple, alternate leaves and produce white or pink flowers in short axillary or terminal spikes. The fruits are small capsules containing many seeds.

Leucothoë davisiae
SIERRA LAUREL

An evergreen shrub from the USA, this species reaches a height of 3 ft (1 m) with a spread of 5 ft (1.5 m). In summer it has 6 in (15 cm) long clusters of white, bell-shaped flowers. Water regularly during the growing season. **ZONES 5–10.**

Leucothoë fontanesiana
syn. *Leucothoë catesbaei*
PEARL FLOWER, DROOPING LEUCOTHOE

Indigenous to the southeastern states of the USA, this evergreen shrub grows 3–5 ft (1–1.5 m) tall. The arching stems bear leathery, long-pointed dark green leaves and pendulous spikes of small bell-shaped white or pinkish flowers through spring. '**Rainbow**' (or 'Golden Rainbow'), is a very popular cultivar, with cream and pink-mottled green leaves.
ZONES 6–10.

CULTIVATION

These shrubs prefer moist, acidic, well-drained soil and a sheltered position in sun or part-shade. Propagation is from seed, cuttings or from the suckering root sections of the plant, or by division.

Leucothoë fontanesiana

Ligustrum japonicum
'Rotundifolium'

LIGUSTRUM
PRIVET

For many temperate-climate gardeners the words 'hedge' and 'privet' are synonymous, but this genus of some 50 or so species of shrubs and trees from temperate Asia, Europe and North Africa offers more than simply the ability to grow in almost any soil or position and to take regular clipping without protest; some species are in fact rather decorative. They range from shrubs to small trees, some evergreen, others deciduous; all grow very rapidly and bear abundant sprays of small white flowers in summer, almost always scented, though sometimes unpleasantly. The flowers are followed by black berries, which can look very striking against the gold-splashed leaves of the variegated cultivars. Birds feast on these and can easily overpopulate the whole district with privet seedlings. In parts of the USA, Australia and New Zealand several privet species have become detested weeds.

CULTIVATION

Grow in sun or part-shade in moist, well-drained soil. The roots are very greedy, usually making growing anything else within their reach a frustrating exercise. Privets grow all too easily from seed in autumn or spring or by division, but selected varieties need to be propagated from cuttings.

Ligustrum japonicum
JAPANESE PRIVET

This bushy, evergreen shrub with a dense habit reaches 10 ft (3 m) tall with a spread of 8 ft (2.4 m). From Asia, it has oval, glossy, dark green leaves and bears large conical panicles of flowers from mid-summer to early autumn, followed by blue-black berries. It can be used as a hedge plant. 'Rotundifolium' is dense and slow growing, with thick, rounded leaves. **ZONES 7–11.**

Ligustrum obtusifolium

This deciduous Japanese shrub reaches 10 ft (3 m) in height. It has graceful mid-green foliage and white flowers in summer. *Ligustrum obtusifolium* var. *regelianum* is frost hardy and has a horizontal branching pattern, growing 5–6 ft (1.5–1.8 m) tall. Its leaves may turn purplish in spring and autumn, and the white flowers produce black berries that last into winter. **ZONES 3–10.**

Ligustrum ovalifolium
CALIFORNIA PRIVET

Although native to Japan, this shrub is so entrenched in parts of the USA that it is known as California privet. This species and *Ligustrum japonicum* are now weeds in New Zealand. Growing to about 12 ft (3.5 m) tall, it is mostly seen in its variegated form: 'Aureum'. Partly deciduous, it can form a thick mass of upright branches and is often used as hedging. The leaves need full sun to become variegated yellow; if green-leafed shoots appear, cut them out or they will eventually take over. **ZONES 5–10.**

Ligustrum vulgare
EUROPEAN PRIVET, COMMON PRIVET

This bushy shrub from Europe, North Africa and temperate Asia is deciduous or semi-evergreen and reaches a height and spread of 10 ft (3 m). It has dark green, pointed, oval leaves and bears panicles of small, strongly perfumed white flowers from early to mid-summer, followed by black berries. There are several cultivars with variegated leaves. If using as a hedge, prune back hard for the first few years of growth. **ZONES 4–10.**

Ligustrum vulgare

Lonicera nitida
BOX HONEYSUCKLE

An evergreen shrub endemic to Yunnan and Sichuan, China, this is possibly the smallest-leafed honeysuckle, forming a dense bush composed of masses of fine twigs bearing tightly packed, ½ in (12 mm) long, leathery, dark green glossy leaves. Gold- and variegated-foliage forms, such as **'Aurea'**, are available. The small, creamy white, spring-borne flowers are not showy and the purple fruit are rarely seen in cultivation, so it is best regarded as a foliage plant. It withstands heavy trimming and is often used for hedging. **'Baggesen's Gold'** has tiny, bright yellow leaves, insignificant yellowish green flowers and mauve fruit. **ZONES 6–10.**

Lonicera nitida 'Baggesen's Gold'

LONICERA

Most of the species belonging to this genus are creepers, and detailed information on the genus is given in the Climbers and Creepers chapter. However, the ones included here can be treated as shrubs.

Lonicera tatarica
TATARIAN HONEYSUCKLE

This deciduous, medium-sized shrub grows to a height of 12 ft (3.5 m) and spreads to 10 ft (3 m). In late spring and early summer the dark green foliage is covered with trumpet-shaped flowers in shades from white to deep pink; these are followed by red berries. **ZONES 2–9.**

Lonicera fragrantissima
WINTER HONEYSUCKLE

From China, this bushy, deciduous or semi-evergreen shrub reaches a height of 6–8 ft (1.8–2.4 m) with a spread of 10 ft (3 m). The most fragrant of the shrubby species, winter honeysuckle bears short, creamy white flowers in pairs, in some forms stained with rose carmine, in winter and early spring. The berries are dark red. The new dark green oval leaves appear shortly after the flowers and except in the coldest climates, many of these will hang on the plant through winter. **ZONES 4–10.**

Lonicera tatarica

Lonicera fragrantissima

Magnolia liliiflora

Magnolia stellata
STAR MAGNOLIA

This compact, many-branched, deciduous shrub from Japan grows 10–15 ft (3–4.5 m) tall and wide, with aromatic bark when young, and narrow dark green leaves. Fragrant, star-like, pure white flowers open from silky buds in late winter and early spring, before the leaves. It flowers when quite young, and has several cultivars in shades of pink, including **'Rosea'**. **'Waterlily'**, the most prolific flowerer, has more petals and slightly larger white flowers. **ZONES 5–9.**

MAGNOLIA

Most of the species belonging to this genus are trees, and detailed information on the genus is given in the Trees chapter. However, the ones included here can be treated as shrubs.

Magnolia liliiflora
syn. *Magnolia quinquepeta*
LILY MAGNOLIA

A deciduous, bushy shrub, this Chinese species reaches 10 ft (3 m) tall and 15 ft (4.5 m) wide. The mid- to dark green leaves, downy on the undersides, taper to a point. Fragrant, narrow, purplish pink flowers, whitish inside, are borne among the leaves from mid-spring until mid-summer. **'Nigra'** has large, dark wine purple flowers that are pale purple inside. **ZONES 6–10.**

Magnolia stellata

Mahonia aquifolium

MAHONIA

The 70 species of evergreen, low-growing to tall-flowering shrubs that make up this genus come from east Asia, and North and Central America. They have beautiful foliage, often fragrant yellow flowers, blue-black, dark red or purplish fruits that mostly have a bloom of whitish or blue-gray wax on some taller species and cultivars, and interesting bark. The berries resemble miniature grapes and make an excellent jelly. They make useful hedges, windbreaks and groundcovers. Some botanists still include these plants in the genus *Berberis*.

CULTIVATION

Cool-climate shrubs, they require a sunny aspect and well-drained, fertile soil with adequate water. In warmer climates they do better in shade or part-shade. They seldom need pruning, but old canes can be cut out at ground level. Propagate species from cuttings, basal suckers or seed; selected forms from cuttings or basal suckers.

Mahonia aquifolium
OREGON GRAPE, HOLLY GRAPE

From western North America, this dense, bushy species grows 6 ft (1.8 m) high and wide. Its 8 in (20 cm) long deep green pinnate leaves each consist of 5 to 9 holly-like leaflets; in the cooler months, these develop purple tones. Clustered heads of small, bright yellow flowers appear in spring, before the fruit. 'Compacta' is a more compact form growing to about half the size of the species.
ZONES 5–10.

Mahonia bealei
LEATHERLEAF MAHONIA

This species is sometimes listed as a form of *Mahonia japonica* and differs mainly in its shorter, stiffer flower spikes and the fact that its leaflets often overlap and have a broader base. The leaf color is also deeper. It is native to western China. **ZONES 6–10.**

Mahonia bealei

Mahonia lomariifolia

From central and western China, this is one of the tallest
and most elegant mahonias, growing 10–15 ft (3–4.5 m)
tall and 6–10 ft (1.8–3 m) wide. Its long, dark green
leaves, borne mostly at the ends of the bamboo-like
shoots, have narrow, holly-like spiny leaflets. Dense, upright racemes of fragrant, bright yellow flowers appear
during late autumn and winter, before the purplish fruit.
ZONES 7–10.

Mahonia × media

This hybrid between *Mahonia japonica* and *M. lomariifolia*
is one of several named cultivars of this cross that has
been repeated several times in England to produce plants
with the good foliage of the latter and the hardiness of
the former. **'Charity'** has flowers in densely clustered
racemes; **'Buckland'** bears its flowers in arching racemes.
ZONES 6–10.

Mahonia lomariifolia

Mahonia × media

Malus × *purpurea* 'Aldenhamensis'

MALUS

Most of the species belonging to this genus are trees, and detailed information on the genus is given in the Trees chapter. However, the ones included here can be treated as shrubs.

Malus sieboldii 'Gorgeous'

Malus floribunda
JAPANESE CRAB

This parent of many hybrids grows 25 ft (8 m) tall with a broad 30 ft (9 m) crown and arching branches. It bears profuse, pale pink flowers, red in bud, and tiny, pea-shaped, yellowish blushed red fruit. *Malus floribunda* is thought to have been introduced to Japan from China. **ZONES 4–9.**

Malus × purpurea

These hybrid shrubs have very dark, sometimes glossy, bark and bronze or purple-red foliage. The flowers are large, red to purple-red, followed by small fruit of a similar color. Cultivars include '**Aldenhamensis**', a spreading tree to 25 ft (8 m) with semi-double, wine-red flowers and purple-red fruit; and '**Eleyi**', with purple leaves, deep crimson flowers and purple-red fruit. **ZONES 4–9.**

Malus sieboldii 'Gorgeous'

A cultivar whose breeder had no modesty, this green-leafed form has white blossoms from pink buds followed by good crops of green-red to deep red crabapples. This variety is considered a good one to harvest for jellies and preserves. **ZONES 5–10.**

Malus floribunda

MYRICA

Myrica is a genus of about 50 species of evergreen or deciduous shrubs and trees of worldwide distribution ranging in height from 5 ft (1.5m) to 100 ft (30 m). Their fruits are clusters of bluish black berries enclosed in a white waxy crust. Tiny flowers appear in late spring; both sexes are borne on the one plant, the males in elongated catkins and the females in globular clusters.

Myrica californica

CULTIVATION

Moderately frost hardy to frost tender, they thrive in part-shade, but will not grow in alkaline or chalky conditions, and must never be allowed to dry out. Propagate from seed or cuttings, or by layering in summer.

Myrica californica
PACIFIC WAX MYRTLE

An evergreen shrub or small tree, this native of the West Coast of the USA has dark green leaves and a decidedly upright habit, except where sheared by coastal winds. *Myrica californica* grows 25 ft (8 m) or more in height, less in spread. **ZONES 7–10.**

Myrica cerifera
WAX MYRTLE

This evergreen shrub flourishes in southeastern North America, in swampy conditions, peaty soil and the shade of taller trees. Reaching 30 ft (9 m) tall, it bears narrow, glossy dark green leaves with unusual downy undersides. Its golden-brown catkins are followed by the fruit, the wax on which is used in the manufacture of candles. **ZONES 6–10.**

Myrica cerifera

MYRTUS
MYRTLE

The Ancient Greeks and Romans knew these shrubs as *Myrtus*, from which 'myrtle' derives, via Old French. Contemporary botanists classify the southern hemisphere myrtles into several other genera, including *Lophomyrtus*, *Luma* and *Ugni*, leaving *Myrtus* with only 2 Mediterranean species. Myrtles are usually dense, evergreen shrubs with small, deep green, pointed leaves and starry white flowers in spring, sometimes followed by purple-black berries.

CULTIVATION

True myrtles prefer moist, well-drained soil and grow in sun or light shade. Trimming keeps them compact. They can be used for hedging or as container plants, clipped into a ball or pyramid. In cooler areas, container plants need protection during winter. Some foliage cultivars are available, but there is little variation in the flowers. Propagate from cuttings or from seed.

Myrtus communis
TRUE MYRTLE

This erect shrub, to around 10 ft (3 m), has highly perfumed white flowers in spring, followed by edible berries ripening to blue-black with a delicate whitish, waxy bloom. The leaves, when crushed, are also very fragrant. It needs protection in winter and is suitable for container growing. Several cultivars exist including 'Compacta', a dwarf form with smallish leaves; 'Flore Pleno' with double white flowers; 'Microphylla' with tiny leaves and flowers; 'Variegata' with leaves edged white; and 'Tarentina' with creamy white flowers and needle-like leaves. **ZONES 8–11.**

Myrtus communis

Nandina domestica

NANDINA
SACRED BAMBOO, HEAVENLY BAMBOO

This is a single species genus from China and Japan. Despite its rather bamboo-like habit and the elegance of its leaves it is actually related to the barberries. It grows as a clump of thin, upright stems, and bears sprays of white flowers in summer and red berries in autumn and winter. Plants are either male or female, and both are needed for the berries to develop; hermaphrodite cultivars are available. The scientific name is a corruption of the Japanese name *nanten*, and the common name comes from the Oriental tradition of planting it in temple gardens; it is also popular in secular gardens.

CULTIVATION

This moderately frost-hardy species likes some shade, fertile soil and a warm-temperate or subtropical climate. In spring, prune straggly stems to the base on established plants. Propagate from seed or cuttings in summer.

Nandina domestica

This shrub has strongly upright, cane-like stems and grows to 6 ft (1.8 m) high. The evergreen foliage is usually bipinnate and composed of many 1 in (25 mm), elliptical leaflets. These are red when young, becoming green and then developing intense yellow, orange and red tones when the cold weather arrives. The small white flowers appear in terminal panicles in summer. 'Nana' (syns 'Compacta', 'Pygmaea') is a widely grown dwarf form, making a rounded shrub about 18 in (45 cm) in height and width, often taking on deep scarlet and red tones in autumn and winter; 'Firepower' is similar in form, with bright pink or red winter foliage; 'Harbor Dwarf' is a cultivar no more than 24 in (60 cm) high that spreads extensively by rhizomes to make a useful groundcover; 'Richmond' is an erect hermaphrodite raised in New Zealand that produces abundant dense clusters of fruit without the need of a pollinating plant; 'Umpqua Chief' is a vigorous plant 5–6 ft (1.5–1.8 m) tall with good winter color. **ZONES 5–10.**

Nerium oleander 'Algiers'

NERIUM

ROSE LAUREL, OLEANDER

This small genus consists of one or two species of evergreen shrubs native to northern Africa and southwestern Asia. They bear brightly colored, funnel-shaped flowers with 5 broad petals; these are followed by bean-like seed pods containing plumed seeds. The leaves are narrow, leathery and lance-shaped. *Nerium oleander* and its cultivars are those plants most commonly seen in gardens. All neriums are very poisonous; all parts of the plant are so very bitter that even goats will not eat them.

CULTIVATION

Plant these shrubs in full sun and in well-drained soil. If they get overgrown and leggy, they can be rejuvenated by severe pruning in spring. In frosty climates, they can be grown in containers and overwintered under glass. Protect from frosts in winter. Propagate from seed in spring or from summer cuttings.

Nerium oleander

Depending on the cultivar selected, these plants can grow from 6–12 ft (1.8–3.5 m) tall. As the species is often used for hedging, it is wise to keep the varying growth habits of the cultivars in mind if a uniform appearance is wanted. The blooms can be single or double, and some cultivars have variegated foliage. Some popular cultivars include: **'Album'**, with single, white flowers and a cream center; **'Little Red'**, with single red flowers; **'Luteum Plenum'**, with creamy yellow double flowers; **'Mrs Fred Roeding'**, with salmon-pink double blooms and a relatively small growth habit; **'Petite Pink'**, with single pale pink flowers and growing only 3–6 ft (1–1.8 m) tall; **'Punctatum'**, a vigorous plant with single, pale pink blooms; **'Splendens Variegatum'**, with pink double flowers and variegated gold-green foliage borne at the expense of the profuse flowering habit of its parent 'Splendens'; **'Algiers'**, with its flowers of the darkest red; and **'Madonna Grandiflora'**, which has white double flowers. **'Casablanca'** (syn. 'Monica') has single, very pale pink, almost white flowers. **ZONES 9–11.**

Nerium oleander 'Album'

NEVIUSIA

SNOW-WREATH

This genus of only 2 species, is found on the cliffs above the Black Warrior River in Alabama, USA. A member of the rose family, it is a very frost-hardy plant, admired for its beautiful spring flowers.

CULTIVATION

This plant prefers reasonably fertile, well-drained soil but appreciates extra water in dry periods. After flowering, remove old wood by cutting back to the lowest outward-facing bud. Propagate by division or from cuttings or seed.

Neviusia alabamensis

Neviusia alabamensis

ALABAMA SNOW-WREATH

This deciduous shrub grows to around 5 ft (1.5 m) and has a stoloniferous root system. This means that it has a spreading, multi-stemmed habit, and needs ample room to develop. The spring-borne flowers, with distinctive spreading stamens, are pure white in their natural habitat, but usually creamy white in cultivation unless grown under glass. **ZONES 5–10.**

OSMANTHUS

syn. *Siphonosmanthus*

Except for one from the Caucasus region, all 30 or so species of evergreen shrubs and trees in this genus are native to the Himalayas, China and Japan. Several are prized for the fragrance of their flowers, which some consider the sweetest and most attractive of all flowers. The white or cream flowers of most species are rather inconspicuous, but their fragrance is reminiscent of jasmine or gardenia. The Chinese use the flowers to enhance the scent of tea. Many Chinese species have longer tubular flowers that are more decorative. Belonging to the olive family, they are slow growing, with some eventually reaching 50 ft (15 m). The thick, rigid leaves may be edged with stout, even hooked, spiny teeth.

CULTIVATION
Plants should be clipped after flowering to
maintain their compact shape. Plant in rich,
well-drained soil in a sheltered position in
either sun or part-shade. Propagate from seed
or cuttings or by layering.

Osmanthus delavayi
syn. Siphonosmanthus delavayi
DELAVAY OSMANTHUS

This species grows to a height and spread of
around 6 ft (1.8 m). It has serrated, oval, dark
green leaves, 1 in (25 mm) long, held on arching branches. The white flowers are tubular,
about ½ in (12 mm) long, and are borne
profusely in the leaf axils and at ends of
branches during summer. **ZONES 7–9.**

Osmanthus heterophyllus 'Variegatus'

Osmanthus fragrans

Osmanthus fragrans
SWEET OSMANTHUS, SWEET OLIVE

Usually seen as a shrub with a height of around
10 ft (3 m), this species can be trained as a
small tree and can also be grown in containers.
Its broad, deep green leaves act as a foil to the
clusters of very small creamy white or yellow
flowers, which are held towards the ends of the
branches. It flowers intermittently from spring
to autumn. *Osmanthus fragrans* f. *aurantiacus*
has dull orange flowers. **ZONES 7–11.**

Osmanthus heterophyllus
syn. Osmanthus ilicifolius
HOLLY OSMANTHUS, HOLLY TEA OLIVE

Native to Japan and Taiwan, this shrub
produces leaves of rather variable shape, some
toothed like holly leaves and others only
toothed at the tip. It grows to a height and
spread of some 15 ft (4.5 m), and is sometimes
grown as a hedge. It bears sparse rather
inconspicuous white flowers in early summer.
'Gulftide' has very spiny leaves; 'Purpureus' has
very dark purple leaves; and 'Variegatus' has
leaves irregularly edged in white. **ZONES 7–10.**

Osmanthus delavayi

PACHYSTEGIA

The status of this New Zealand genus is somewhat confused. Some botanists include it with *Olearia*; some suggest there are up to 5 species while others regard it as just one highly variable species. It is closely allied to the New Zealand bush daisies and is found in the coastal region of the northeast of the South Island. The large, thick, leathery leaves have glossy, wax-coated upper surfaces and felted undersides—superb protection against salt spray and coastal storms. The showy, white, daisy-like flowers, produced in summer, are followed by rounded fluffy, brown seedheads.

Pachystegia insignis

CULTIVATION

Moderately frost hardy, they grow in any well-drained soil in sun or light shade, and are ideal for exposed coastal gardens. Propagate from seed or cuttings.

Pachystegia insignis

syn. *Olearia insignis*

MARLBOROUGH ROCK DAISY

This evergreen shrub ranges in height from 1–5 ft (0.3–1.5 m) and can spread to 3 ft (1 m). White flowerheads with golden-yellow central florets open in summer. Its leaves, 3–8 in (8–20 cm) long, are deep glossy green above with white or beige felting below. **ZONES 8–11.**

Paeonia suffruticosa

Paeonia lutea

PAEONIA

Most of the species belonging to this genus are perennials, and detailed information on the genus is given in the Annuals and Perennials chapter. However, the ones included here can be treated as shrubs.

Paeonia lutea

YELLOW TREE PEONY

This shrub from western China was introduced to the West in the late nineteenth century. It grows to a height and spread of 5 ft (1.5 m) and from late spring to early summer bears single, clear yellow flowers about 6 in (15 cm) across. The leaves are dark green with saw-toothed margins. *Paeonia lutea* var. *ludlowii* grows to 8 ft (2.4 m) tall and produces bright yellow flowers in late spring. **ZONES 6–9.**

Paeonia suffruticosa

TREE PEONY, MOUTAN

Native to China, this handsome deciduous shrub has been so enthusiastically transplanted into gardens it is probably extinct in the wild. It reaches a height and width of 3–6 ft (1–1.8 m) and produces very large single or double cup-shaped flowers in spring. Depending on the variety, these are white, pink, red or yellow, and are set among attractive, large, midgreen leaves. *Paeonia suffruticosa* subsp. *rockii* has semi-double white flowers with a maroon blotch at the base of each petal. **ZONES 4–9.**

PELARGONIUM

Many of the species belonging to this genus are perennials, and detailed information on the genus is given in the Annuals and Perennials chapter. However, the ones included here can be treated as shrubs. They need protection in winter, and all are suitable for container growing.

Pelargonium quercifolium
OAK-LEAFED GERANIUM, ALMOND GERANIUM

This scented-leafed species is an erect shrub growing to around 5 ft (1.5 m) tall. It has deeply lobed and serrated-edged, dark green leaves that are perhaps, as the name suggests, slightly reminiscent of oak leaves. The leaves and stems are sticky and highly aromatic. The pretty flowers are purple-pink with the 2 upper petals bearing darker markings. **ZONES 9–11.**

Pelargonium , Regal Hybrid, 'White Glory'

Pelargonium, Regal Hybrid, 'Kimono'

Pelargonium, Regal Hybrids
MARTHA WASHINGTON GERANIUMS, REGAL GERANIUMS, REGAL PELARGONIUMS

The spectacular large blooms of these hybrids originally derived from the South African mauve-flowered *Pelargonium cucullatum*, further breeding brought in red, purple and white coloring from *P. fulgidum*, *P. angulosum* and *P. grandiflorum* respectively. Sprawling shrubs about 24 in (60 cm) high, they have strong woody stems and stiff, pleated, sharply toothed leaves. In late spring and summer, they bear clusters of large flowers, wide open and often blotched or bicolored. Frost tender, in cool areas they need a greenhouse. Cut back hard after blooming to keep the bushes compact. There are a multitude of eye-catching, named forms available, including '**Kimono**', bright pink with darker markings and a white center; '**White Glory**' a pure white form; and '**Starlight Magic**', with velvety purple-pink petals on the top half of the flower, and a paler shade on the bottom half. **ZONES 9–11.**

Pelargonium quercifolium

Pelargonium, Scented-leafed Hybrids

This varied group of hybrids derives from quite a few wild South African species. Many of them are primary hybrids whose origins go back to the early nineteenth century, although there are also a good number of more recent cultivars. Most are vigorous shrubs with dense branches and shallowly to deeply lobed or dissected leaves that in some are quite hairy. The range of essential oils in the leaves is very large, their scents ranging through peppermint, eucalyptus, lemon, cloves, aniseed, apple, rose and even coconut. Often a hot day will bring out the aroma, but it is released most strongly when the foliage is bruised or crushed. Some have quite showy flowers, in others they are small but still pretty. **'Fragrans'** (apple geranium) is a bushy, many-branched shrub reaching 12 in (30 cm) high and wide. A strong spicy smell like green apples comes off the small, roughly heart-shaped, lobed, gray-green leaves. Its flowers are small and white, sometimes with red veining on the upper petals. **'Mabel Gray'**, a vigorous cultivar, has lemon-scented leaves that are rough, serrated-edged and deeply lobed, and pale purple flowers with red markings. Considered to be the most strongly scented pelargonium, it grows to 15 in (38 cm) high. **ZONES 8–11.**

Pelargonium, Scented-leafed Hybrid, 'Fragrans'

Pelargonium, Zonal Hybrid, 'Frank Headley'

Pelargonium, Zonal Hybrids

ZONAL PELARGONIUM, BEDDING GERANIUM

This large group of hybrids, which have been known collectively as *Pelargonium* × *hortorum*, are derived principally from *P. inquinans*, which occurs wild in southeastern South Africa, but their parentage includes several other species as well, including *P. zonale* and *P. frutetorum*. They are compact plants, usually less than 24 in (60 cm) tall, with succulent green to pale bronze stems and almost circular to kidney-shaped, undulating leaves that have distinctive darker markings or 'zones'. The flowers, massed on long-stemmed heads, may be single or double, are usually brightly colored and appear over a long season. Although shrubs, Zonal pelargoniums may be treated as bedding annuals. Besides the vast number of typical Zonal cultivars, there are a number of distinct subgroups that are recognized by enthusiasts. **Variegated** or **Fancy-leafed** zonals have foliage banded and dappled with red, purple, orange and yellow, sometimes with all these colors showing; **Miniature** and **Dwarf** varieties are compact plants, the leaves sometimes quite small and often purple tinged; flowers vary, but include some with narrow petals, some of these are referred to as **Frutetorums**, reflecting the dominance of this parent species. **Stellars** (or 'Staphs') are an increasingly popular group with narrow, pointed, sometimes forked petals giving the flowers a very distinctive appearance; they come in both singles and doubles, in many colors. **Formosums** have very narrow petals and deeply lobed leaves. **Rosebuds** are a double with, as the name suggests, double flowers like a miniature rose bloom in bud. **Cactus-flowered** zonals have flowers with quilled petals like the cactus-flowered dahlias. Another recent development has been the appearance of Zonal pelargoniums sold as seed, usually as mixed-color series. The following is just a selection of the thousands of zonal cultivars available. 'Caroline Schmidt' (syn. 'Wilhelm Langguth') is a compact plant with white-edged, pale-centered, bright green leaves and bright red double flowers. 'Dolly Varden' is a fancy-leafed cultivar with cream, bronze and green foliage and single red flowers. 'Flower of Spring' is an upright grower with cream-edged leaves and vermilion single flowers. 'Francis Parrett' is a miniature with deep green leaves and tight clusters of double fuchsia-pink flowers. 'Frank Headley' is a miniature with cream-edged leaves and soft pink single flowers. 'Irene', which gives its name to a group of hybrids, has red semi-double flowers and clearly zonal, downy green leaves. 'Mr Henry Cox' (syn. 'Mrs Henry Cox') is a fancy-leafed type with dark-zoned leaves edged in gold and shadowed with red; the flowers are dark-centered bright pink singles. 'Mrs Parker' has white-edged gray-green leaves with darker markings and deep pink double flowers in tight heads. 'Orange Ricard' is a compact plant with tight heads of orange-red flowers. 'Apple Blossom Rosebud' is one of the most popular rosebud zonals, the flowers are white, and pink-flushed white and the foliage bright green with little zonation; 'Gemini' is a stellar cultivar with white-centered, pink flowers. 'The Boar' is a miniature of the Frutetorum group with small salmon-pink flowers and toothed-edged, rounded leaves. **ZONES 10–11.**

Pelargonium, Zonal Hybrid, 'Flower of Spring'

Perovskia abrotanoides

PEROVSKIA

Found in western Asia and the Himalayan region, the 7 species of deciduous subshrubs in this genus have gray-white stems and aromatic leaves that are covered with gray felt when young. As they mature, the deeply lobed, 2–3 in (5–8 cm) long leaves lose their felting and become gray-green. They form large clumps to 3–5 ft (1–1.5 m) tall and are topped in late summer with 12–18 in (30–45 cm) panicles of tiny violet to pink flowers.

CULTIVATION

They are very easily grown in any well-drained, rather dry soil in a sunny position. It is often best to contain their growth by planting them beside a path, wall or border edge. If allowed free rein, smaller, less vigorous plants may be smothered. They are very frost hardy and may be propagated from seed, or by cuttings of non-flowering stems.

Perovskia abrotanoides

Native to Afghanistan and the western Himalayas, this 3 ft (1 m) tall species has 3 in (8 cm) long, deeply cut, oval, gray-green leaves. The small tubular flowers, in whorls of 4 to 6 blooms on 15 in (38 cm) panicles, are violet to pink. It blooms in late summer. **ZONES 8–11.**

Philadelphus coronarius

PHILADELPHUS

MOCK ORANGE, SYRINGA

This genus of 60 species of deciduous shrubs comes from the temperate regions of the northern hemisphere, mainly from east Asia and North America. The cultivated species are all quite similar. They grow to a height and spread of 10 ft (3 m) and have light green, roughly elliptical leaves about 3 in (8 cm) long. They flower in late spring and early summer, bearing 4-petalled white or cream flowers in loose clusters. The flower scent strongly resembles that of orange blossom, hence the common name. *Philadelphus* 'Miniature Snowflake' is a dwarf cultivar of the popular 'Snowflake'. 'Natchez' is another cultivar often grown.

CULTIVATION

Moderately to very frost hardy, they are easily grown, preferring moist, well-drained soil and a position in sun or light shade. They may be pruned after flowering and can be used for informal hedging. Propagate from seed or from cuttings taken in summer.

Philadelphus coronarius

From southern Europe and Asia Minor, this species grows to 6 ft (1.8 m) tall and has very fragrant 2 in (5 cm) wide white flowers. Its oval, bright green leaves are slightly hairy on the undersides. '**Aureus**' has bright yellow new growth and smaller flowers; '**Variegatus**' bears white flowers and has white-edged leaves. **ZONES 2–9.**

Philadelphus 'Lemoinei'

syn. *Philadelphus* × *lemoinei*

This hybrid between *Philadelphus coronarius* and *P. microphyllus* was bred in the late 1880s by the famous French hybridist Lémoine, who also raised many hydrangeas and lilacs. It grows to 6 ft (1.8 m) and has arching branches. The 1 in (25 mm) flowers are white, very fragrant and are usually carried in clusters of up to 7 blooms. **ZONES 3–9.**

Philadelphus 'Lemoinei'

Philadelphus pendulifolius

Possibly a hybrid rather than a true species, this plant grows to about 8 ft (2.4 cm) high and wide and bears racemes of cup-shaped white flowers. **ZONES 5–9.**

Philadelphus 'Virginal'

Very frost hardy, this vigorous, upright shrub grows to a height and spread of a little under 10 ft (3 m). From late spring to early summer, it bears large, fragrant, semi-double flowers set among dark green, oval leaves. **ZONES 3–9.**

Philadelphus 'Virginal'

Philadelphus pendulifolius

Phillyrea angustifolia

This species from the dry hills around the Mediterranean has an olive-like appearance with narrow, lance-shaped leaves up to 3 in (8 cm) long and clusters of tiny greenish cream flowers in spring. It develops into a dense shrub up to 10 ft (3 m) tall. **ZONES 7–10.**

PHILLYREA
MOCK PRIVET

Phillyrea angustifolia

Closely related and very similar to *Osmanthus*, this genus of 4 evergreen shrubs or small trees is found in the Mediterranean region and the Middle East. They grow 10–30 ft (3–9 m) tall, depending on the species, and have small, leathery leaves, sometimes with toothed edges. Their flowers are very small but fragrant. They are white to greenish cream, clustered in the leaf axils and open in spring, and are followed by small blue-black drupes.

CULTIVATION
Reasonably frost hardy, these plants are easily grown in moist, well-drained soil in full sun or part-shade. They will tolerate dry conditions once established and are tough, adaptable plants. Able to withstand frequent trimming, they are suitable for hedging. Propagate from cuttings.

PHLOMIS

Most of the species belonging to this genus are perennials, and detailed information on the genus is given in the Annuals and Perennials chapter. However, *Phlomis fruticosa* is treated here as a shrub.

Phlomis fruticosa

Phlomis fruticosa

JERUSALEM SAGE

This evergreen shrub, a native of southern Europe, is grown for the strikingly beautiful yellow flowers it bears in whorls from early to mid-summer, among wrinkled, oval, felty green leaves. It tolerates coastal areas quite well and grows to a height and spread of 30 in (75 cm). To keep its habit neat, prune to about half its size in autumn. **ZONES 7–10.**

Photinia serratifolia

PHOTINIA

These 60 species of evergreen or deciduous shrubs and small trees from the Himalayas, Southeast and eastern Asia are mostly fast growing. They are cultivated for their brilliant young foliage and, if deciduous, for their autumn color. The leaves are alternate and the flowers, mostly white, are followed by either red or dark blue berries. The genus takes its name from a Greek word meaning 'shining'; this is a reference to the gleaming foliage.

CULTIVATION

Plant in sun or part-shade in fertile, well-drained soil with protection from strong winds. They make excellent hedges and should be pruned to promote bushiness and new growth. Propagate from seed or cuttings in summer, or by grafting onto hawthorn or quince stock.

Photinia serratifolia

syn. **Photinia serrulata**

CHINESE HAWTHORN, CHINESE PHOTINIA

From China, this evergreen shrub or small tree grows to a height of 20 ft (6 m) with a bushy crown, but can also be kept lower and clipped to form a hedge. The glossy oval leaves are large, serrated and bronze tinted in spring. The small, white spring flowers are followed by small, red berries. **ZONES 7–10.**

× *Phylliopsis hillieri* 'Pinocchio'

× *Phylliopsis hillieri*

Growing to a height of 12 in (30 cm), this shrub produces its small racemes of tiny, 5-lobed, red-purple flowers in spring. **'Coppelia'** has relatively large, open lavender-pink flowers. **'Pinocchio'** is a very compact cultivar with small glossy leaves and spikes of bright pink flowers. **ZONES 3–9.**

× *PHYLLIOPSIS*

This intergeneric hybrid genus resulted from crossing 2 North American shrubs of the erica family (*Phyllodoce breweri* and *Kalmiopsis leachiana*), which produced dwarf, evergreen shrubs with ½–1½ in (12–25 mm) long glossy dark green, oblong leaves and bell-shaped flowers.

CULTIVATION

Plant in moist, humus-rich, well-drained soil in dappled shade. They are ideal for moist, shaded rockeries or in pots in a cool alpine house. These plants are very frost hardy and they can be easily propagated from small tip cuttings or by layering.

Physocarpus opulifolius

PHYSOCARPUS

NINEBARK

Physocarpus monogynus

MOUNTAIN NINEBARK

This species from central USA grows to around 3–6 ft (1–1.8 m) tall with arching, spreading stems. The new stems are bright brown, sticky, often with fine hairs; the young leaves are light green. The 2 in (5 cm) wide foliage is 3- to 5-lobed with serrated edges. Flat 2 in (5 cm) wide heads of small white flowers open from late spring. **ZONES 5–10.**

The unusual inflated fruits of this genus of deciduous shrubs from Asia and North America are not edible—the 12 or so species are admired for their flowers and attractive foliage. In the wild, they reach a maximum height of 10 ft (3 m). The leaves are prominently veined, lobed and serrated, and change to a dull yellow in autumn. The 5-petalled white or pink flowers, appearing in spring or early summer, are small but are displayed in decorative clusters along the branches.

CULTIVATION

Physocarpus species require fertile, well-drained soil in a sunny position. They are easy to grow in temperate climates, but resent soil with a high lime content and dry roots. Thin out crowded plants by cutting back some of the arching canes after flowering. Propagate from seed or cuttings of semi-ripened wood in summer.

Physocarpus opulifolius

Native to eastern USA, this shrub has a height and spread of 5–10 ft (1.5–3 m) and a graceful arching habit. The yellowish green, rounded, heart-shaped leaves complement the dense, pink-tipped white flowers, which are at their best in early summer. Reddish pods with yellow seeds contrast well with the bright autumn foliage and the dark brown bark that peels off in layers. 'Aureus' has bright greenish yellow leaves and white flowers. 'Dart's Gold', to 4 ft (1.2 m) tall, has bright golden foliage and white flowers flushed pink. ZONES 2–10.

Physocarpus monogynus

Pieris formosa

This dense, bushy shrub from China carries glossy, dark green leathery leaves and bears sprays of small white flowers in mid-spring. Frost resistant, it grows well in cool or mild climates but is not tolerant of dry conditions. It is one of the taller species, growing to 12 ft (3.5 m). The red-leaf pearl flower, *Pieris formosa* var. *forrestii* (syn. *P. forrestii*), is usually smaller, growing to a height and spread of 6 ft (1.8 m) with scarlet-bronze young growth against which the flowers gleam in striking contrast. *P. f.* var. *forrestii* 'Wakehurst' is a tall shrub that can reach 15 ft (4.5 m) and has large clusters of white flowers and red new growth that fades to pink before greening. ZONES 6–9.

Pieris formosa var. *forrestii*

PIERIS

This genus consists of 7 species of evergreen shrubs and, more rarely, small trees from North America, east Asia and the Himalayas. The shrubby species are valued for their neat compact habit, attractive foliage and flowers, their height rarely exceeding 12 ft (3.5 m) and often less. The flower buds are held throughout the winter, and in spring open into clusters of small, bell-shaped, waxy, usually white flowers.

CULTIVATION

These plants require a temperate climate, soil that is moist, peaty and acidic, and a part-shaded site. They appreciate humidity. Propagate from seed in spring or from cuttings in summer, or by layering.

Pieris japonica 'Bert Chandler'

Pieris japonica
LILY-OF-THE-VALLEY SHRUB

This Japanese shrub can grow to 12 ft (3.5 m) high but usually reaches only 6 ft (1.8 m) in cultivation. Its pointed, elliptical, deep green leaves, to 4 in (10 cm) long, are reddish copper when young. Panicles of small, white, bell-shaped flowers appear from early spring. The many cultivars include '**Bert Chandler**', with pink and cream new growth; '**Christmas Cheer**', with early, pale pink flowers; '**Flamingo**', with bright pink flowers; '**Mountain Fire**', with vivid red new growth and white flowers; '**Purity**' has large, pure white flowers; '**Red Mill**' is a vigorous, late-flowering cultivar; '**Tickled Pink**' has pale red new growth and pink-tinted to pale pink flowers; and '**Variegata**' has cream-edged foliage. **ZONES 4–10.**

Pieris japonica 'Mountain Fire'

Plectranthus fruticosus

PLECTRANTHUS

This genus contains more than 350 species of annuals, perennials and shrubs native to Africa, Asia and Australia. Most are rather frost tender and several species are grown as house plants, others are garden ornamentals or herbs. They generally have succulent or semi-succulent stems. The leaves, too, are often fleshy and frequently oval to heart-shaped. The flowers are small and tubular, but are borne in sometimes showy spikes that extend above the foliage.

CULTIVATION
Plant in moist, well-drained soil in part-shade. Protect from frost and prolonged dry conditions. Propagate from seed or cuttings or by layering. Many species are spreading and will self-layer.

Plectranthus coleoides
syn. *Plectranthus forsteri*

This perennial, found in subtropical eastern Australia, New Caledonia, Fiji and nearby Pacific islands, has straggling stems that take root as they spread. It has toothed, oval leaves up to 1½ in (35 mm) long and if able to mound up, it can reach 3 ft (1 m) high. It is more often known as *P. forsteri*. It has pale blue to mauve flowers in heads of 6–10 blooms. It is suitable for container growing and needs protection in the winter months.
ZONES 10–12.

Plectranthus fruticosus

From South Africa, this erect shrub, up to 7 ft (2 m) tall, has sparsely hairy stems and large, toothed leaves with purplish brown undersides. The flowers occur in shades of blue and mauve speckled with purple. It needs protection from winter frosts.
ZONES 10–11.

Plumbago auriculata

Plumbago auriculata 'Royal Cape'

Plumbago auriculata
syn. *Plumbago capensis*
BLUE PLUMBAGO, CAPE PLUMBAGO

This fast-growing species from South Africa grows to 6 ft (1.8 m) tall with a similar spread and carries its prolific sky-blue flowers through the warmer months. The pale green, oblong leaves are 2 in (5 cm) long. It suckers readily, and grows higher on supports or by climbing nearby shrubs. It is cultivated as an informal hedge or as a trimmed, formal hedge. 'Alba' has clear white blooms. 'Royal Cape' has flowers of a more intense blue and is slightly more tolerant of frost and dry conditions.
ZONES 9–11.

PLUMBAGO
LEADWORT

This genus consists of 10 to 15 species of annuals, perennials, evergreen shrubs and scrambling climbers and semi-climbers, which are found in warm-temperate to tropical regions of the world. The blue, white or red flowers have 5 petals narrowing to a long slender tube and are massed on short stems near the tips of the arching branches. The leaves are arranged alternately.

CULTIVATION

Plumbagos are reliable plants. They only require well-drained soil, perhaps enriched with a little organic matter. They grow best in warm climates; in frost-prone areas they do well in a mildly warmed greenhouse. Established plants are tolerant of dry conditions, but soil should be kept moist during summer for a good flowering display. Pruning in late winter is recommended to tidy their vigorous stems and remove old wood. This stimulates new growth and next season's flowers. Propagate from tip cuttings in the warmer months or from semi-hardwood cuttings in autumn.

PODOCARPUS

PLUM PINE

Podocarpus contains about 100 fast-growing, evergreen species popular for their dense foliage and attractive habit. The genus is described in more detail in the chapter on Trees. The following species is considered a shrub.

Podocarpus lawrencii

Podocarpus lawrencii

syn. *Podocarpus alpinus*

MOUNTAIN PLUM PINE

This fairly slow-growing Australian shrub or small tree can withstand frost but requires a sunny position. It ranges in height from 24 in (60 cm) in mountain areas to 25 ft (8 m) in lower woodlands. The trunk is gnarled and twisted and the small, grayish green leaves contrast well with the red, fleshy berries. This species is suitable for container planting. **ZONES 7–9.**

Potentilla fruticosa 'Goldfinger'

POTENTILLA

Potentilla fruticosa 'Elizabeth'

Most of the species belonging to this genus are perennials, and detailed information on the genus is given in the Annuals and Perennials chapter. However, *Potentilla fruticosa* is treated here as a shrub.

Potentilla fruticosa

BUSH CINQUEFOIL

This dense, deciduous shrub, found in many parts of the temperate northern hemisphere, grows to over 3 ft (1 m) tall with a spread of 4 ft (1.2 m) or more. From early summer to autumn garden varieties bear 1 in (25 mm) wide flowers in shades from white to yellow and orange, the orange ones often fading to salmon pink in the sunshine. The flat, mid-green leaves comprise 5 or 7 narrow elliptical leaflets arranged palmately. There are many popular cultivars available. **'Tangerine'** has golden-orange flowers; **'Goldstar'** is an upright shrub with large, deep yellow flowers; **'Maanleys'** grows up to 4 ft (1.2 m) tall with blue-green foliage and pale yellow flowers; and **'Red Ace'**, a low grower with small leaves and bright orange-red flowers, is inclined to be untidy and short lived. **'Abbotswood'** is a very attractive, spreading, 24 in (60 cm) tall shrub with white flowers; **'Beesii'** grows to 24 in (60 cm) tall with very silvery leaves and bright yellow flowers; **'Daydawn'** is a 3 ft (1 m) tall shrub with salmon-pink flowers; **'Elizabeth'** is a dense, bushy, 3 ft (1 m) shrub with bright yellow flowers; **'Goldfinger'** is a low grower with narrow, bright green leaflets and very bright yellow flowers; and **'Primrose Beauty'**, up to 3 ft (1 m) tall and 5 ft (1.5 m) wide, has primrose-yellow flowers very reminiscent of a small wild rose. **ZONES 2–9.**

Prunus glandulosa 'Sinensis'

PRUNUS

Most of the species belonging to this large genus from the northern hemisphere are trees, and detailed information on the genus is given in the Trees chapter. However, the species described below are treated as shrubs.

Prunus glandulosa
DWARF FLOWERING ALMOND, ALMOND-CHERRY

This deciduous shrub from China and Japan belongs to a group of dwarf Prunus species that belong in the cherry subgenus *(Cerasus)* but show some of the characteristics of almonds and peaches. It makes a showy late spring-flowering shrub of up to 5 ft (1.5 m) with thin, wiry branches, small leaves, and profuse white to pale pink flowers, borne along the stems. The dark red fruit about half the size of a cherry are edible though rather sour. It is common practice to cut the bushes back almost to ground level as soon as flowering finishes, producing a thicket of strong vertical shoots that bloom very freely the next spring. 'Sinensis' (syn. 'Rosa Plena') bears double pink flowers. 'Alba Plena' has double white flowers. **ZONES 6–10.**

Prunus spinosa
SLOE, BLACKTHORN

A species of plum, this 12–15 ft (3.5–4.5 m) thorny shrub or small tree is found throughout temperate Eurasia and in North Africa. It has toothed 2 in (5 cm) long leaves and profuse small white flowers borne singly or occasionally in pairs on the leafless branches in early spring. The flowers are followed in summer by ½ in (12 mm) diameter, prune-like fruit that can be used to make a very tart jam or conserve. **ZONES 4–9.**

PYRACANTHA
FIRETHORN

Native to temperate Asia and the Mediterranean, these 7 species of large shrubs are grown for their evergreen foliage and abundant, bright red, orange or yellow berries in autumn and winter. Although tasteless, the berries are edible and much enjoyed by birds. Growing up to 20 ft (6 m), the branches are armed with spines; the foliage is usually glossy green. Clusters of small, white flowers are borne on short spurs along the branches in spring.

CULTIVATION
These temperate-climate plants adapt to a wide range of soils. Firethorns need a sunny position for the brightest berry display, and adequate moisture in dry weather. Propagate from seed or cuttings. Pruning is often necessary to control size, but bear in mind that fruits are produced on second-year wood. They can be espaliered and also make dense, informal hedges and screens. They tend to naturalize and become invasive in favorable conditions. Check for fireblight and scab.

Pyracantha angustifolia
ORANGE FIRETHORN

From western China, this dense shrub with graceful, horizontal branches can reach a height and width of 10 ft (3 m) or more. Its narrow, oblong, dark green leaves, 2 in (5 cm) long, have gray downy undersides and are clustered in rosettes on the flowering twigs but arranged spirally on new shoots. It bears clusters of small white flowers from late spring to early summer. Yellow or orange berries persist for most of winter; the flesh has a floury texture. **ZONES 6–11.**

Pyracantha crenatoserrata

syn. **Pyracantha fortuneana**
YUNNAN FIRETHORN

Native to central and western China, this species has dense, deep green foliage. The rather broad leaves are glossy and hairless on both sides. Its berries are orange, ripening to crimson red. It grows to a height and spread of 12 ft (3.5 m) and looks particularly effective if trained against a brick wall. **'Gold Rush'** bears orange-yellow berries. **ZONES 6–10.**

Pyracantha coccinea 'Lalandei'

Pyracantha coccinea

SCARLET FIRETHORN

Pyracantha crenatoserrata

This species, originally from southern Europe, Turkey and the Caucasus, produces a spectacular display of fiery scarlet fruit that resemble tiny apples. Both fruit and foliage become darker if grown in cool climates. It grows to 15 ft (4.5 m) with arching branches spreading to 6 ft (1.8 m). Its narrow leaves are up to 1½ in (35 mm) long, held on slender stalks. Young leaves and twigs are finely downy. **'Kasan'** carries striking orange-red fruit. **'Lalandei'**, developed in France in the 1870s, is a vigorous plant with erect branches that display abundant fruit which ripen to bright orange-red. **'Fructo Luteo'** has bright yellow berries ripening to golden yellow. **ZONES 5–9.**

Pyracantha crenatoserrata
'Gold Rush' and
Pyracantha 'Orange Glow'

Pyracantha crenulata
syn. Crataegus crenulata
NEPAL FIRETHORN

Native to Nepal and China, this sturdy, erect, marginally frost-hardy shrub grows rapidly to a height and spread of 10–12 ft (3–3.5 m). Numerous white, open flowers in early summer are followed by a profusion of small, dark red berries. The glossy leaves are narrow and blunt. **ZONES 7–10.**

Pyracantha 'Mohave'

This bushy shrub grows to 12 ft (3.5 m) and has dark green leaves, small white flowers and long-lasting orange-red berries. **ZONES 7–10.**

Pyracantha 'Mohave'

Pyracantha 'Orange Glow'

This upright cultivar, to 10 ft (3 m) in height, is well suited to espaliering. It has vivid orange berries that are very attractive to birds. **ZONES 7–10.**

Pyracantha crenulata

Pyracantha 'Orange Glow'

Rhamnus californica

RHAMNUS
syn. *Frangula*
BUCKTHORN

This genus of 125 species of deciduous and evergreen shrubs and small trees occurs in a range of climates, mostly in the northern hemisphere. It tolerates dry conditions and salt-laden atmospheres. They are distinguished by smooth, dark bark and simple green leaves, often with serrated edges. The flowers, borne in clusters, are insignificant. The fruits are fleshy, pea-sized berries popular with birds. Some species are thorny, some produce dyes that are used commercially, and the bark of some species is the source of the purgative cascara sagrada.

CULTIVATION
These versatile plants require moderately fertile, well-drained soil and full sun or part-shade in hot areas. Propagate the deciduous species from seed and the evergreen species from cuttings in summer.

Rhamnus alaternus
'Argenteovariegatus'

Rhamnus alaternus
ITALIAN BUCKTHORN, ALATERNUS

This large, evergreen, multi-stemmed shrub from the Mediterranean region is valued in its native lands for its tolerance of dry conditions and polluted environments. The plant grows quickly to 15 ft (4.5 m) and its thorny branches bear a mass of small, glossy dark green leaves. These hide the tiny greenish yellow flowers, which attract all kinds of insects. Its berries are purple-black. It can become invasive in certain areas. The cultivar 'Argenteo-variegatus', which is more decorative than its parent but is less frost hardy, has leaves that are marbled with gray and edged with creamy white. **ZONES 7–10.**

Rhamnus californica
syn. *Frangula californica*
COFFEEBERRY, CALIFORNIA BUCKTHORN

This evergreen or semi-evergreen shrub from western North America bears finely toothed oval leaves up to 2 in (5 cm) long with 12 pairs of veins. It grows to 12 ft (3.5 m) with a 10 ft (3 m) spread. Honey-bees are attracted to the greenish flowers. The fruit change from red to black as they ripen. 'Eve Case', 'Sea View' and 'Curly' have full-flavored fruit. **ZONES 7–10.**

Rhododendron 'Bibiani'

RHODODENDRON
syn. *Azalea*

Rhododendrons are a diverse genus of deciduous, semi-evergreen and evergreen trees and shrubs, numbering some 800 species with thousands of cultivars. There are 3 divisions: azaleas, Vireyas and 'true' rhododendrons, ranging from miniature shrubs to small trees. Flowers come in a range of colors. The bell- to funnel-shaped flowers have 5 or more petals and are usually held in clusters at the branch tips. In some cultivars either the calyx or stamens develop into petal-like structures known as 'hose in hose'.

Rhododendron augustinii

CULTIVATION
Most require part-shade and prefer light, well-drained but moist soil with slightly acid pH, enriched with organic matter with a cool root run. They do not tolerate lime. Protect from afternoon sun and strong winds. They are prone to infestation by thrips, two-spotted mite (red spider mite) and powdery mildew in humid areas. Propagate from cuttings, or by layering or grafting.

Rhododendron 'Alice'
This is a *Rhododendron griffithianum* hybrid with 6 in (15 cm) long leaves that becomes large with age. Its large trusses of bright pink blooms with lighter centers appear mid-season. **ZONE 6–9.**

Rhododendron augustinii
This species has unusually small evergreen leaves that are dark green and tapered, with a prominent mid-vein. A medium-sized shrub reaching a height and width of 5 ft (1.5 m), *Rhododendron augustinii* is covered in late spring by a profusion of tubular blue or violet flowers, ranging from pale to deep hues—the deeper the color, the more tender the plant. The flowers occur in clusters of three or five. It performs best in dappled shade. It is the parent of many blue-flowered hybrids. **ZONE 6–9.**

Rhododendron 'Bibiani'
This is a medium-sized *Rhododendron arboreum* hybrid raised in 1934 by the famous English breeder Lionel de Rothschild. It has 4–6 in (10–15 cm) long, dark green, heavy textured leaves and early, deep red, 2 in (5 cm) wide, bell-shaped flowers held in trusses of 11 to 15 blooms. 'Gibraltar' is a hybrid seedling of 'Bibiani' with similar blooms of very deep red. **ZONE 7–10.**

Rhododendron 'Alice'

Rhododendron 'Blue Peter'

Probably a *Rhododendron ponticum* hybrid, *R*. 'Blue Peter' is a medium-sized bush, which was introduced by the English company Waterer in 1933. It has glossy deep green leaves and frilled trusses of lavender-blue flowers with a prominent purple flare. It flowers in the middle of the season. **ZONE 6–9.**

Rhododendron 'Blue Peter'

Rhododendron 'Brickdust'

Typical of a *Rhododendron williamsianum* hybrid, this small plant forms a dense mound of 2 in (5 cm) long, rounded leaves with masses of loose trusses of bell-shaped flowers. The blooms are dusky orange and appear mid-season. **ZONE 6–9.**

Rhododendron calendulaceum

FLAME AZALEA

This deciduous azalea, found from West Virginia to Georgia, USA develops into a spreading bush around 12 ft (3.5 m) tall and wide. Its orange to red (rarely yellow) funnel-shaped flowers open in late spring and are carried in trusses of 5 to 7 blooms. The flower color varies with the season, location and climate. Many orange to flame azaleas derive their color from this species. **ZONE 5–9.**

Rhododendron 'Brickdust'

Rhododendron calendulaceum

Rhododendron catawbiense

CATAWBA RHODODENDRON,
MOUNTAIN ROSEBAY

This shrub from eastern USA is one of the most influential species in the development of frost-hardy hybrids. It grows to around 10 ft (3 m) tall and develops into a dense thicket of shiny, deep green foliage. Its cup-shaped flowers, which open from late spring, are pink, rosy pink, lilac-purple or white and carried in trusses of up to 20 blooms. **'Album'** is a heat-resistant form with white flowers that open from pink buds. **ZONE 4–9.**

Rhododendron catawbiense

Rhododendron 'Cherry Custard'

This small Canadian hybrid shows its 'Fabia' heritage in its flat 10- to 12-flowered trusses of yellow blooms that open from orange-red buds. It is a low, spreading plant with narrow, pointed elliptical leaves. **ZONE 7–9.**

Rhododendron 'Cherry Custard'

Rhododendron ciliatum

Rhododendron ciliatum

Native to the Himalayan region, this species is a compact 4–6 ft (1.2–1.8 m) shrub. It has 2–3 in (5–8 cm) long, shiny deep green leaves with bluish undersides. The bark is red-brown and peeling. From early spring it produces white or white flushed rose, bell-shaped flowers and is an easily grown shrub that tolerates slightly alkaline soil. **ZONES 7–9.**

Rhododendron cinnabarinum

Native to the Himalayan region and northern Burma, this aromatic species is an upright shrub or small tree 5–20 ft (1.5–6 m) tall. Its peeling red-brown bark and narrowly oval, deep green to blue-green leaves are very attractive, as are the 2 in (5 cm) long, pendulous, tubular flowers that open from mid-spring. Usually orange, the 3- to 5-flowered trusses may be red, salmon pink, pink, yellow, apricot or combinations of colors. *Rhododendron cinnabarinum* subsp. *cinnabarinum* 'Mount Everest' has apricot flowers that are more widely open than usual. **ZONES 6–9.**

Rhododendron cinnabarinum
subsp. *cinnabarinum* 'Mount Everest'

Rhododendron 'Crest'

Raised in England in 1953, this medium-sized shrub was one of the first hybrids to use *Rhododendron wardii* rather than *R. burmanicum* to produce yellow flowers with frost hardiness. It is an open grower with bronze-green foliage and flowers mid-season. **ZONES 6–9.**

Rhododendron 'Crest'

Rhododendron degronianum

Rhododendron degronianum

This rhododendron grows into a neat small shrub, 4–6 ft (1.2–1.8 m) high, with a domed crown. It produces dark green leaves up to 6 in (15 cm) long with light brown, fuzzy undersides. Its bell-shaped flowers are a delicate, soft pink and appear in late spring. *Rhododendron degronianum* subsp. *yakushimanum*, is a dense, mounding, 3–8 ft (1–2.4 m) tall shrub with 3–4 in (8–10 cm) long, deep green leathery leaves with rolled edges and heavy fawn indumentum. The flowers appear quite early and are white or pale pink opening from deep pink buds and carried in rounded trusses of up to 10 blooms. 'Exbury Form' makes a perfect dome of deep green, heavily indumented foliage with light pink flowers. 'Koichiro Wada' is similar to 'Exbury Form' but has white flowers opening from deep pink buds. **ZONE 7–9.**

Rhododendron 'Dido'

Rhododendron 'Dido'

Rhododendron 'Dido', raised in England in 1934, has had more influence as a parent plant than as a garden specimen. Used as one of the parents of 'Lem's Cameo', it has greatly influenced modern American rhododendron development. It grows to 4 ft (1.2 m) and has rounded, light green leaves and lax trusses of yellow-centered, orange-pink, trumpet-shaped flowers. ZONES 7–9.

Rhododendron 'Elisabeth Hobbie'

Rhododendron 'Elisabeth Hobbie'

This is a small *Rhododendron forrestii* hybrid with rounded, 2 in (5 cm) long, deep green leaves. The petioles and new growth are red tinted. Bright to deep red, bell-shaped flowers in clusters of 5 to 7 blooms open mid-season. ZONES 6–10.

Rhododendron 'Elizabeth'

This hybrid shows considerable *Rhododendron griersonianum* influence. It is a medium-sized, rather open bush with 3–4 in (8–10 cm) long, narrow pointed leaves and bright red 3 in (8 cm) wide, funnel-shaped flowers in lax 6- to 8-bloom trusses from early mid-season. ZONES 7–9.

Rhododendron 'Elizabeth'

Rhododendron Fabia

This collection of sister seedlings resulted from a 1934 *Rhododendron dichroanthum* and *R. griersonianum* cross by the Welsh breeder Aberconway. This grex has had enormous influence in the development of modern frost-hardy hybrids in yellow and orange shades. The plants grow to around 3 ft (1 m) tall and slightly wider with 3 in (8 cm) pointed elliptical leaves. The mid-season flowers are in soft orange tones, bell-shaped, and carried in open trusses of 3 to 7 blooms. **'Roman Pottery'** has unusual terracotta-colored flowers. ZONES 7–9.

Rhododendron 'Elisabeth Hobbie'

Rhododendron fastigiatum

In the wild this alpine species from Yunnan Province, China, grows at altitudes of up to 15,000 ft (4,500 m). It has ½ in (12 mm) long, blue-gray leaves and is a dense, wiry stemmed, 18–30 in (45–75 cm) tall shrub. It flowers in mid-spring when it is smothered in ½ in (12 mm) purple or lavender blooms, and is a superb plant for a rockery or alpine house. **ZONES 7–9.**

Rhododendron fastigiatum

Rhododendron 'Fastuosum Flore Pleno'

Rhododendron 'Fastuosum Flore Pleno'

Dating from before 1846 and still one of the few double-flowered 'true' rhododendrons, this large shrub has mid-green, 4–6 in (10–15 cm) long leaves. They open mid-season to late and are semi-double, deep lavender with greenish yellow throat markings in trusses of 7 to 15 blooms. **ZONES 5–8.**

Rhododendron fortunei

This Chinese species has been extremely in-fluential in the development of garden hybrids. It is a shrub or small tree 4–30 ft (1.2–9 m) tall with matt mid-green oval leaves up to 8 in (20 cm) long. Its 4 in (10 cm) wide flowers open pink, fade to white and are fragrant. They open from mid-spring and are carried in large rounded trusses. *Rhododendron fortunei* subsp. *discolor* has flowers with a yellow-green throat blotch; *R. f.* subsp. *fortunei* has scented, pale pink to lavender flowers. **ZONES 6–9.**

Rhododendron fortunei subsp. *fortunei*

Rhododendron 'Hydon Dawn'

Rhododendron
'Hydon Dawn'

This is a *Rhododendron yakushi-manum* hybrid of the same cross as the better known 'Hydon Hunter'. It is a small bush that develops into a mound of glossy, bright green foliage. The flowers, borne in small rounded trusses, open mid-season and are pink, lightening at the edges. **ZONES 7–9.**

Rhododendron 'Impi'

'Impi' combines dark green foliage with very deep purple-red flowers. It is a medium-sized bush that blooms from late mid-season. Its flowers are carried in small rounded trusses. **ZONES 7–9.**

Rhododendron 'Impi'

Rhododendron 'Irene Stead'

Rhododendron 'Irene Stead'

Of Loderi parentage and very similar to the plants of that grex, this New Zealand-raised hybrid is a large bush with mid-green leaves around 8 in (20 cm) long. Its mid-season, pale pink and white flowers are somewhat waxy and carried in large conical trusses. **ZONES 6–9.**

Rhododendron 'Jingle Bells'

This Fabia hybrid is a neat, small bush with a dense covering of narrow deep green, 3–4 in (8–10 cm) long leaves. Orange, bell-shaped flowers in lax trusses of 5 to 9 blooms open from orange-red buds and fade to yellow. They smother the plant in mid-season. **ZONES 7–9.**

Rhododendron johnstoneanum

Rhododendron johnstoneanum

From northern India, this 8–15 ft (2.4–4.5 m) tall shrub, sometimes epiphytic in the wild, has bristly elliptical leaves up to 3 in (8 cm) long. Its flowers are scented, 3 in (8 cm) long, funnel-shaped, creamy white or pale yellow, sometimes with red or yellow spots, and open from early spring. **'Double Diamond'** has creamy yellow double flowers, often with darker markings. **ZONES 7–9.**

Rhododendron kaempferi

Rhododendron kaempferi

This 4–10 ft (1.2–3 m) tall evergreen azalea
from Japan is fully frost hardy, though it loses
much of its foliage in very cold conditions. The
hairy, elliptical leaves are 1½ in (35 mm) long.
Funnel-shaped flowers open from mid-spring
and are red to orange-pink, occasionally white,
sometimes with purple or red flecks. It is
extensively used in hybridizing for frost
hardiness. **ZONES 5–9.**

Rhododendron kiusianum

Rhododendron kiusianum

The foliage of this azalea develops yellow, red
and purple tones as it ages and then most of
the oval, hairy leaves are dropped by the end of
winter, despite its classification as an evergreen.
A very dense, twiggy bush that forms a
rounded hummock to around 3 ft (1 m) high
and 5 ft (1.5 m) wide, from early spring it is
hidden beneath masses of tiny pinkish purple
flowers. White and light pink-flowered forms
are also available. This is one of the parents of
the Kurume azalea hybrids. **ZONE 6–10.**

Rhododendron
'Kubla Khan'

This medium-sized plant has
bright green foliage and striking flowers with calyces so
large they create a hose-in-
hose effect. The color is a
combination of pink, orange
and red on a cream back-
ground with a large red flare
on the upper lobes and calyx.
It blooms from late mid-
season and needs cool conditions for the flowers to last.
ZONE 6–9.

Rhododendron 'Kubla Khan'

Rhododendron
'Lemon Lodge'

Very distinctive foliage and soft pastel yellow flowers distinguish 'Lemon Lodge', a medium to large New Zealand-raised *Rhododendron wardii* hybrid. The leaves are a bright light to mid-green, oval, 3–4 in (8–10 cm) with a waxy texture. The flowers are in rather flat trusses that open mid-season. **ZONE 7–10.**

Rhododendron 'Lemon Lodge'

Rhododendron 'Lem's Aurora'

Rhododendron 'Lem's Aurora'

This is a compact small to medium-sized bush with dark green, 4 in (10 cm) leaves and rounded trusses of crimson flowers with light golden-yellow centers and calyces. It blooms mid-season. **ZONE 6–9.**

Rhododendron 'Lem's Cameo'

This beautiful and very influential hybrid is a medium-sized mound of deep green, glossy 3–4 in (8–10 cm) long leaves with rich bronze new growth. The mid-season flowers, borne in trusses of up to 20 blooms, are delicate shades of apricot-pink and creamy yellow and funnel-shaped. **ZONE 7–9.**

Rhododendron 'Lem's Cameo'

Rhododendron 'Lem's Monarch'

This impressive large shrub is densely foliaged with rounded, bright mid-green leaves up to 8 in (20 cm) long. The flowers, carried in large conical trusses of 9 to 15 blooms, are funnel-shaped and white to pale pink flushed and edged deep pink to crimson. **ZONE 6–9.**

Rhododendron 'Lem's Monarch'

Rhododendron Loderi 'King George'

Rhododendron 'Mrs G. W. Leak'

Rhododendron Loderi

This grex consists of a large group of *Rhododendron griffithianum* × *R. fortunei* seedlings that date from around 1900. They are all very similar to one another and have 6–8 in (15–20 cm) long, mid-green to slightly glaucous leaves and large trusses of white to mid-pink, funnel-shaped, fragrant flowers. They are large, tree-like plants that are very impressive in full bloom. **'King George'** has white flowers opening from pink buds. **'Sir Edmond'** has very large pale pink flowers. **'Sir Joseph Hooker'** has light to mid-pink flowers. **ZONES 6–9.**

Rhododendron luteum

This deciduous azalea grows to 12 ft (3.5 m) and has 2–4 in (5–10 cm) long, bristly, lance-shaped leaves. Its flowers are bright yellow and sweetly scented. They are long, funnel-shaped with a narrow tube in trusses of up to 12 blooms. **ZONES 5–9.**

Rhododendron 'Moonstone'

A small to medium-sized shrub, this *Rhododendron williamsianum* hybrid has 2–3 in (5–8 cm) long, rounded mid-green leaves. From early spring it is smothered in 3- to 5-flowered clusters of greenish white to pale cream, slightly pendulous, bell-shaped flowers. **ZONES 6–9.**

Rhododendron 'Mrs G. W. Leak'

This medium to large bush is in-stantly recognizable when in bloom. Its light pink, funnel-shaped flowers have a beautiful red flare and spot-ting that stands out from a great distance. They are borne in upright trusses of 9 to 12 blooms from early mid-season. The leaves are mid-green, 4–6 in (10–15 cm) long and very sticky, especially when young. **ZONES 6–9.**

Rhododendron luteum hybrids

Rhododendron nakaharai

Rhododendron nakaharai

This evergreen Taiwanese azalea is a near-prostrate shrub usually under 12 in (30 cm) tall. The pointed elliptical leaves are hairy and a little under 1 in (25 mm) long. The 1 in (25 mm) long orange-red funnel-shaped flowers open in early summer. This rhododendron is a good rockery, bonsai or ground-cover plant. 'Mt Steven Star' is a densely foliaged, prostrate form with large deep orange-red flowers. **ZONES 5–10.**

Rhododendron molle

This deciduous azalea is found in eastern and central China. It grows 4–6 ft (1.2–1.8 m) tall and bears large, densely packed trusses of 2½ in (6 m) long, funnel-shaped yellow or orange flowers from mid-spring. The flowers are sometimes fragrant. *Rhododendron molle* **subsp. *japonicum*** (syn. *R. japonicum*), from Japan, is a 3–10 ft (1–3 m) tall shrub with bright red, orange-red, pink or yellow flowers and brightly colored autumn foliage. This subspecies is the principal parent of the deciduous Mollis Azaleas. **ZONES 7–9.**

Rhododendron molle subsp. *japonicum*

Rhododendron occidentale

Rhododendron occidentale

From western USA, this species is a 6–15 ft (1.8–4.5 m) tall deciduous azalea with slightly hairy, 4 in (10 cm) long elliptical leaves. The fragrant 3 in (8 cm) wide, funnel-shaped flowers are carried in trusses of up to 12 blooms, and are usually white or pale pink with a yellow, occasionally maroon, flare, although it may be red, yellow or orange-pink. The foliage turns red and copper in autumn. The cultivar 'Leonard Frisbie' has large, frilled, fragrant flowers that are white suffused pink with a yellow flare. **ZONES 6–10.**

Rhododendron 'Olin O. Dobbs'

Rhododendron 'Olin O. Dobbs'

Famed for its heavy, waxy flowers of intense red-purple, this medium-sized American hybrid also has lusterous deep green leaves up to 6 in (15 cm) long. The flowers are funnel-shaped and carried in conical trusses of 11 to 15 blooms that open from mid-season. **ZONES 5–9.**

Rhododendron 'Patty Bee'

This pretty little dwarf hybrid develops into a mound of bright green elliptical leaves. From early mid-season it is smothered in 6-flowered clusters of soft yellow, funnel-shaped flowers up to 2 in (5 cm) wide. It is ideal for rockeries or containers. **ZONE 6–10.**

Rhododendron 'Patty Bee'

Rhododendron ponticum

Rhododendron ponticum

From Europe and the Middle East to Russia, this 6–20 ft (1.8–6 m) shrub has glossy deep green, oblong to lance-shaped leaves up to 8 in (20 cm) long. The 10- to 15-flowered trusses open in late spring and are 2 in (5 cm) long, funnel-shaped, purple, lavender, pink or rarely maroon or white flushed pink, often with yellow, ocher or brown flecks. It is used in hybridizing. **'Variegatum'** has dark green leaves with cream edges and occasional stripes or flecks. **ZONES 6–10.**

Rhododendron 'President Roosevelt'

This old medium-sized Dutch hybrid is still one
of the few rhododendrons with boldly variegated foliage. The leaves are deep green with
a central yellow splash and 4–6 in (10–15 cm)
long. The flowers, which open early and are
carried in conical trusses of 5 to 11 blooms, are
funnel-shaped and white, edged and flushed
with red. **ZONES 7–9.**

Rhododendron 'President Roosevelt'

Rhododendron 'Rubicon'

This densely foliaged, medium-sized bush has
lush, somewhat puckered, glossy green leaves
up to 4 in (10 cm) long. 'Rubicon' has funnel-
shaped, attractive deep rich red flowers which
are carried in trusses of 9 to 17 blooms. The
flowers open early to mid-season. **ZONES 7–9.**

Rhododendron 'Rubicon'

Rhododendron 'Sappho'

Rhododendron 'Sappho' was raised before
1847 but it is still a very distinctive plant today. When not in flower this cultivar looks
much like any other large rhododendron but
in bloom it cannot be mistaken for any other.
Its funnel-shaped flowers, carried in upright
conical trusses of 5 to 11 blooms, are pure
white with a large, sharply contrasting,
blackish purple flare. **ZONES 5–8.**

Rhododendron 'Sappho'

Rhododendron 'Seta'

Rhododendron 'Seta'

Among the earliest rhododendrons to bloom,
'Seta' has 2 in (5 cm) long, slightly blue-green
pointed leaves and develops into an open,
medium-sized bush. Its flowers, which are tubular
to bell-shaped and carried in small clusters, are
palest pink with a darker edge. **ZONES 7–8.**

Rhododendron wardii var. *wardii*

Rhododendron williamsianum

This densely foliaged shrub from Sichuan, China grows 2–5 ft (0.6–1.5 m) tall and has rounded to heart-shaped, matt mid-green leaves up to 2 in (5 cm) long. The new growth is a contrasting bronze color. The flowers, which appear in mid-spring, are bell-shaped, 2 in (5 cm) long, mid-pink to rose, sometimes with darker flecks and carried in loose clusters of 2 to 3 blooms. **ZONES 7–9.**

Rhododendron 'Winsome'

Rhododendron yakushimanum

Rhododendron wardii

Named after collector and explorer Frank Kingdon Ward, this species from western China is variable and ranges from 3–25 ft (1–8 m) tall. It has deep green, oval, 4 in (10 cm) long leaves and saucer-shaped white to pale yellow, sometimes crimson-blotched flowers in trusses of 7 to 14 blooms from mid-spring. *Rhododendron wardii* var. *wardii* has bright yellow flowers, sometimes with a purple blotch, and is used extensively in hybridizing. **ZONES 7–9.**

Rhododendron williamsianum

Rhododendron 'Winsome'

This small to medium-sized bush is attractive throughout the year. From early mid-season the foliage disappears under 5- to 9-flowered clusters of deep pink bell-shaped flowers. **ZONES 7–9.**

Rhododendron yakushimanum

Native to Yakushima Island, Japan, this dense, mounding, 3–8 ft (1–2.4 m) tall shrub has 3–4 in (8–10 cm) long, deep green leathery leaves with rolled edges and heavy fawn indumentum. The flowers appear quite early and are white or pale pink opening from deep pink buds and carried in rounded trusses of up to 10 blooms. 'Exbury Form' makes a perfect dome of deep green, heavily indumented foliage with light pink flowers. 'Koichiro Wada' is similar to 'Exbury Form' but has white flowers opening from deep pink buds. **ZONES 5–9.**

Rhododendron, Azaleas

Azaleas are spectacular cool-temperate flowering shrubs. Flowers are white, yellow through pink and orange to flame blaze undiluted with green. Most shrubs in gardens are deciduous hybrids, grouped as **Mollis, Ghent, Knap Hill, Exbury, Occidentale, Ilam** and others. They make wide-spreading shrubs up to 10 ft (3 m) tall. The most popular deciduous azalea cultivars include **'Exquisita'** (Occidentale), **'Homebush'** (Knap Hill) and **'Louie Williams'** (Ilam). **ZONE 6–9.**

Rhododendron, Ilam Azalea 'Louie Williams'

Rhododendron, Ghent Azaleas

In the early 1800s Ghent, Belgium, was the main center for azalea breeding. The earliest hybrids were raised from *Rhododendron calendulaceum, R. nudiflorum, R. luteum* and *R. viscosum.* Later, *R. molle* was crossed with *R. viscosum* to produce the Viscosepalum hybrids, which have now largely disappeared. Further developments include the double Ghent or Rustica strain. Introduced from the late 1850s, they were followed in 1890 by a similar group of double-flowered hybrids known as Rustica Flore Pleno hybrids. Ghent azaleas tend to be large, late-flowering plants with small flowers in large heads. They are often fragrant. At the height of their popularity over 500 Ghent cultivars were available. Today they have been largely superseded by later styles. **'Coccinea Speciosa'** has bright orange-pink flowers with a striking orange blotch. **'Daviesii'** is a tall, upright Viscosepalum hybrid with fragrant, white to pale yellow flowers late in the season. **'Nancy Waterer'** has large, bright yellow, scented flowers from late spring. **'Narcissiflora'** is a tall, upright hybrid with

small, double, fragrant, pale yellow flowers from late spring. **'Norma'** is a Rustica Flore Pleno hybrid with small pink-edged orange-red, double flowers. **'Phebe'** (syn. 'Phoebe') is a Rustica Flore Pleno hybrid with yellow double flowers. **'Vulcan'** is an upright bush with deep red flowers that have an orange-yellow blotch. **ZONES 5–9.**

Rhododendron, Knap Hill, Exbury and Ilam Azaleas

The Knap Hill, Exbury and Ilam hybrids are the most widely grown deciduous azaleas. The original plants were developed from about 1870 at the Knap Hill (England) nursery of Anthony Waterer. Starting with Ghent azaleas, he crossbred extensively and selected only the best of the resultant hybrids. Waterer named only one of his plants, **'Nancy Waterer'** (officially a Ghent hybrid), and it was not until the seedlings were acquired by Sunningdale Nurseries in 1924 that plants started to be made available to the public. Lionel de Rothschild of Exbury developed the Exbury strain from Knap Hill seedlings. The first of these, **'Hotspur'**, was introduced in 1934. The collection was almost lost during World War II and relatively few hybrids were introduced until the 1950s. Edgar Stead of Ilam, Christchurch, New Zealand, working with various species and Ghent and Knap Hill hybrids, further refined the strain. Stead's work was continued by Dr. J. S. Yeates. Most are large bushes with vividly colored single flowers. Frost hardiness varies. **'Brazil'**, an Exbury hybrid, has bright orange-red flowers. **'Cannon's Double'**, a low-growing Exbury hybrid, has light yellow and cream double flowers. **'Carmen'** (syn. 'Ilam Carmen'), an early-flowering Ilam hybrid, has apricot flowers with a yellow-orange blotch. **'Cecile'**, an Exbury hybrid, has red flowers with an orange-yellow blotch. **'Chaffinch'**, a Knap Hill hybrid, has deep pink flowers and is often sold as a seedling as it is quite variable. **'Gallipoli'**, an Exbury hybrid, has apricot-pink flowers with an orange blotch. **'Gibraltar'**, an Exbury hybrid, has bright orange-red flowers from mid-spring. **'Homebush'**, a Knap Hill hybrid, has semi-double purplish red flowers. **'Hotspur'**, an Exbury hybrid, has bright orange-red flowers. **'Klondyke'**, an Exbury hybrid, has bright orange flowers with an orange-yellow blotch. **'Louie Williams'** (syn. 'Ilam Louis Williams'), an Ilam hybrid, has large, light pink and soft yellow flowers with an orange blotch. **'Maori'**, a low-growing Ilam hybrid, has bright orange-red flowers in large trusses. **'Ming'** (syn. 'Ilam Ming'), an Ilam hybrid, has large orange flowers with a yellow blotch and is among the first to flower. **'Persil'**, a Knap Hill hybrid, has white flowers with a soft yellow blotch. **'Red Rag'**, an Ilam hybrid, has slightly frilled, bright orange-red flowers. **'Strawberry Ice'**, an Exbury hybrid, has yellow-ish pink flushed mid-pink flowers with an orange blotch. **'Yellow Giant'** (syn. 'Ilam Yellow Giant'), an Ilam hybrid, has large bright yellow flowers. **ZONES 5–9.**

Rhododendron, Knap Hill Azalea, 'Homebush'

Rhodotypos scandens

Rhodotypos scandens

This upright or slightly arching shrub bears its shallowly cupped, single, 4-petalled flowers in late spring and early summer. The sharply toothed leaves are most appealing when young. **ZONES 5–9.**

RHODOTYPOS

This genus, closely allied to *Kerria*, contains one species, a 15 ft (4.5 m) deciduous shrub native to China and Japan with soft mid-green leaves and simple, 2 in (5 cm) diameter white flowers. The calyces remain after the flowers fall and enclose ¼–½ in (6–12 mm) glossy black berries. As the sepals dry they fold back to reveal the pea-shaped fruit, which appear to be unattractive to birds and lasts well into winter.

CULTIVATION

This plant grows happily in any well-drained soil in sun or light shade. It is fully frost hardy and may be propagated from cuttings or seed, or by layering.

RHUS

Rhus is a large, diverse genus consisting of 200 species of deciduous and evergreen shrubs, trees and scrambling vines found in many parts of the world. One group of species, now separated into a new genus, *Toxicodendron*, contains trees and shrubs notorious for causing allergies. Some deciduous species turn brilliant shades of red, purple, orange, yellow and bronze in autumn; others bear reddish or brownish velvety fruit. Many produce male and female flowers on different trees. Some of the many evergreen species are moderately frost tolerant. Many species tolerate pollution.

CULTIVATION

They like a sunny position, moderately fertile, moist but well-drained soil and protection from wind. Propagate from seed or cuttings, or by dividing root suckers.

Rhus aromatica
FRAGRANT SUMAC

This sprawling, deciduous species from eastern USA reaches 3 ft (1 m) tall and 5 ft (1.5 m) wide. Tiny yellow flowers, borne in spikes on bare stems, are followed by downy, deep green, coarsely toothed and aromatic foliage maturing to spectacular shades of orange and purple in autumn. Small red berries appear in mid-summer. 'Gro-Low' is a very low-growing form with fragrant flowers that are a deeper yellow than those of the species. **ZONES 2–9.**

RIBES

Many of the species belonging to this genus bear fruit, and detailed information on the genus is given in the Fruit Trees, Nut Trees and Other Fruits chapter. However, the species named here are treated as shrubs.

Rhus typhina
syn. **Rhus hirta**
STAG'S HORN SUMAC

This deciduous shrub or small tree from temperate eastern North America makes a brilliant autumn display. It grows a slender erect trunk or thicket of stems up to 15 ft (4.5 m) high and spreads to 12 ft (3.5 m). It bears pinnate leaves with toothed, 6 in (15 cm) leaflets, yellowish green flower clusters and striking 'candles' of velvety red fruit. '**Dissecta**' (syns *Rhus typhina* 'Laciniata', *R. hirta* 'Laciniata') carries its dark fruit well into winter and has deeply dissected, fern-like foliage. **ZONES 3–9.**

Rhus aromatica

Ribes alpinum
MOUNTAIN CURRANT, ALPINE CURRANT

This dense, twiggy, deciduous shrub from northern Europe to Russia grows 6 ft (1.8 m) tall and wide. Reddish purple, smooth stems bear 3- to 5-lobed rounded, serrated leaves. The pale, greenish yellow flower clusters carry 7 to 15 blossoms. These are followed by large bunches of scarlet berries, provided both male and female plants are grown. *Ribes alpinum* is a neat and versatile shrub that tolerates heavy shade. **ZONES 5–9.**

Ribes alpinum

Ribes odoratum

syn. Ribes aureum of gardens

CLOVE CURRANT, BUFFALO CURRANT

A spreading 8 ft (2.4 m) shrub with prickle-free stems, this species is native to the prairies and high plains of midwestern USA. The shiny, 3-lobed leaves color well in autumn. The large, down-turned flowerheads are greenish yellow, deepening with age and followed by black berries. The plant is grown mainly for the spicy, clove-like fragrance of its leaves. **ZONES 6–9.**

Ribes sanguineum

RED FLOWERING CURRANT, WINTER CURRANT, FLOWERING CURRANT

This prickle-free, deciduous shrub from western North America has aromatic, lobed leaves that are held on 12 ft (3.5 m) stems. The deep pink or red flowers, appearing in late spring, are borne on erect to drooping spikes. Bluish black berries follow in summer. There are several named cultivars, including '**King Edward VII**', which bears carmine flowers; '**Brocklebankii**', with golden leaves and pink flowers; '**Tydeman's White**', with white flowers; '**White Icicle**' has pure white clusters of flowers; and '**Pulborough Scarlet**' carries a mass of deep red flowers. *Ribes sanguineum* var. *glutinosum* has hanging clusters of pink flowers and leaves that are more sparsely

Ribes odoratum

pubescent than *R. sanguineum*. '**Barrie Coate**' was found on Fremont Peak in California growing in full sun and has deep rose-colored, pendent clusters of flowers. '**Spring Showers**' is a bushy, vase-shaped shrub with downy bright green leaves and hanging clusters of pink flowers. **ZONES 6–10.**

Ribes speciosum

FUCHSIA FLOWERING GOOSEBERRY

This deciduous, spiny, bushy shrub from California in the USA reaches 6 ft (1.8 m) in height and spread. Fully frost hardy, it has red juvenile shoots and oval, 3- to 5-lobed glossy green leaves. Its slender, drooping red flowers, which open in late winter, have long red stamens; they are followed by spherical red fruit. **ZONES 7–10.**

Ribes sanguineum

ROBINIA

BLACK LOCUST

This genus, comprising 20 species of deciduous shrubs and trees, is described in more detail in the chapter on Trees. The following species is a shrub.

Robinia hispida

ROSE ACACIA

Robinia hispida is a deciduous shrub from the dry woods and scrub of southeastern USA. It has pinnate leaves that are fresh green, long and fern-like; the erect stems and branches are clothed in brown bristles. In summer, rose-pink pea-flowers are followed by bristly seed pods up to 3 in (8 cm) long. In favorable conditions the plant quickly reaches 6 ft (1.8 m). This species is sometimes grafted on to stems of *R. pseudo-acacia* to produce a small, mop-headed tree. On *Robinia hispida* var. *kelseyi* (syn. *R. kelseyi*) only the flower stalks and raceme axes have bristles; it bears glossy rose-pink flowers. **ZONES 5–10.**

ROSA

ROSE

Roses have been popular since ancient times. Most of the roses grown today are hybrids many generations removed from their wild parent species. They come in a variety of flower forms and colors. Fragrance is variable, some cultivars are intensely fragrant, others not at all. Roses range from only a few inches (centimeters) high to giant climbers.

CULTIVATION

Roses prefer cool to cool-temperate conditions and sunny positions, which reduces the incidence of fungal diseases such as mildew, black spot and rust. They prefer a fairly rich soil with regular spring watering and occasional mulching. They are prone to aphids, mites and thrips. Most may be propagated from stratified seed or cuttings.

Rosa bracteata

Rosa bracteata
syns 'Chicksaw Rose',
'Macartney Rose'

A dense shrub or wall plant to 10 ft (3 m), *Rosa bracteata* has long, grayish brown stems that are well armed with hooked thorns, often arranged in pairs. There is a plentiful covering of dark green, round-ish and glossy leaves that have tomentose undersides. There are nine leaflets. The white flowers, with pronounced stamens, sometimes have a hint of cream showing through. They are borne singly on the end of stubby laterals through-out summer, and are followed by plumply rounded, orange hips. Although it is not suit-able for cold climates, it makes an excellent shrub in temperate zones; it has, in fact become naturalized in the southern states of the USA. This is a superb wall plant, as it is evergreen and easy going. 'Mermaid' is a famous off-spring of this species and is much hardier. **ZONE 7–11.**

Rosa foetida

Rosa chinensis

A near-evergreen shrub or scrambler, this rose grows to around 15 ft (5 m) high and wide. It bears widely spaced prickles; its leaves are divided into 3 or 5 leaflets. The 5-petalled flowers, usually borne in small groups, open pink and rapidly age to red, followed by orange hips. Its repeat-flowering habit was a vital ingredient in the development of modern garden roses. **ZONE 7–11.**

Rosa foetida

AUSTRIAN BRIAR

This deciduous species de-velops into a dense, twiggy shrub up to 10 ft (3 m) high and wide with numer-ous prickles. The branches carry pinnate leaves with between 5 and 9 leaflets. Flowers are 5-petalled and bright yellow. 'Bicolor' has flowers that are yellow on the outside and coppery red inside. **ZONE 4–9.**

Rosa gallica
FRENCH ROSE, RED ROSE

A suckering species, this is a dense, low-growing, 3 ft (1 m) tall shrub that bears few prickles. The leaves are divided into 3 or 5 leathery leaflets, and the slightly scented flowers are pink. Because of its tendency to produce double flowers, it has been an important species in the development of modern roses. 'Officinalis' has semi-double deep pink flowers. **ZONE 5–9.**

Rosa gallica

Rosa moschata
syn. 'The Musk Rose'

A tall shrub or small climber to 10 ft (3 m) tall with firm, grayish green wood, *Rosa moschata* is sparsely populated with brown, hooked thorns. The gray-green leaves are soft to touch, downy on the undersides, especially on its prominent veins, inclined to droop and made up of 5 to 7 leaflets. The flowers are fragrant and creamy white, with well-spaced single petals; on hot days they reflex backward. Each flower is about 1½ in (35 mm) across and loosely arranged in large corymbs that first appear in late summer, and repeat well into autumn. *R. moschata* is an ancestor of many Modern Garden Roses. Until it was redis-covered by Graham Stuart Thomas in 1963, the species was thought to be lost to cultivation. Prior to then, *R. brunonii* had been erroneously distributed through nurseries as *R. moschata*, a confusion that is still prevalent in some parts of the world. It is an excellent small climber or shrub. *R. moschata* 'Plena' is a seldom-seen, double form. **ZONE 4–10.**

Rosa moschata nepalensis

Rosa moyesii 'Fargesii'

Rosa moyesii

This densely suckering rose bears rich crimson flowers in a single summertime flush. The branches carry straight prickles and the dark green leaves are divided into between 7 and 13 leaflets. This plant can reach 10 ft (3 m). The pendent, deep scarlet flask-shaped hips may persist into winter. A popular hybrid is 'Geranium' with paler leaves, carmine-red petals and an eye-catching display of scarlet hips. This grows to about 1.8 m (6 ft) high and wide. 'Fargesii' has flowers of exceptionally vivid color. **ZONE 5–9.**

Rosa roxburghii 'Plena'

Rosa rugosa

Rosa pimpinellifolia

syns *Rosa spinosissima*, 'Altaica',
'Burnet Rose', 'Scots Rose'

This short-growing, dense and prickly shrub suckers freely when grown on its own roots. The branches are upright or only slightly arching and greenish brown, thickly populated with both sharp thorns and bristles. There are 5 to 11 heavily serrated and broadly oval leaflets per leaf, which look almost fern-like en masse. They are darkish green, changing to russet-brown in autumn. The flowers are produced in great profusion in late spring to early summer, and they are creamy white, single and quite beautiful with golden-brown stamens. The globular hips are mahogany to black when ripe. *Rosa pimpinellifolia altaica*, (syn. *R. p.* 'Grandiflora'), introduced from western Asia in 1820, is a taller grower with larger, soft primrose flowers. It is a superior plant to the species, but both are worthwhile in any type of garden. In Victorian times, *R. spinosissima* was extensively used as a parent,

giving rise to many double and single, short-growing shrub roses in a variety of colors. They include such varieties as 'Mary Queen of Scots' and 'William III'. In the 1950s some excellent shrub roses were raised in Germany from this species, such as 'Frühlingsgold'. **ZONE 3–11.**

Rosa roxburghii 'Plena'

syn. *Rosa roxburghii*

CHESTNUT ROSE, BURR ROSE

This large, suckering shrub grows to 6 ft (1.8 m) tall and wide, with many upright light silvery brown stems with flaking bark (giving off a pungent aroma) and very sharp, straight thorns in pairs at the nodes. The mid-green foliage is quite striking. The summer flowers are very double, opening flat and reflexing, with upwards of 80 petals, the color of the petals varying from white to deep mauve pink. **ZONES 5–10.**

Rosa rugosa

This hardy, sprawling shrub has thick, glossy, deep green, heavily veined leaves that are divided into as many as 9 leaflets. Its habit is dense and bushy to about 5 ft (1.5 m) high and wide, with branches thickly covered with prickles and bristles. It blooms in repeated flushes over a long season. The 5-petalled, white to deep pink flowers are followed by showy, large, pinkish orange-red hips. This disease-resistant species has given rise to a group of hybrids known collectively as Rugosas. '**Alba**' is a white-flowered cultivar. **ZONE 3–10.**

Rosa rugosa 'Alba'

Rosa sericea ssp. omeiensis var. pteracantha

Rosa sericea ssp. omeiensis var. pteracantha
BROAD-SPINED ROSE

This large, cool-climate rose bush reaches about 10 ft (3 m). It has huge, broad-based prickles, deep red on young shoots. As the shoot matures, the prickles turn pale gray and opaque. Its leaves are divided into as many as 17 leaflets. The single burst of charming, white, 4-petalled flowers appears in late spring and is followed by small, oval, orange-red hips and attractive autumnal foliage.
ZONE 6–10.

Rosa xanthina
This angular, cool-climate shrub, reaching a height of 10 ft (3 m), rarely performs or displays well in frost-free climates. The scented, yellow flowers are small, semi-double and appear in a single flush in late spring. The wood and fern-like leaves are dark. Closely allied is the cultivar **'Canary Bird'**, which has a stronger yellow flower color and is very free flowering. Although described after *Rosa xanthina*, *R. x.* f. *spontanea*, a vigorous grower with single flowers, is thought to be the true wild species. **ZONE 5–9.**

Rosa xanthina f. spontanea

Rosa, OGR, Centifolia
'Petite de Hollande'

Roses, Old Garden Roses
These are the groups that were developed before the rather arbitrary date 1867, when the first of the Large-flowered roses (Hybrid Teas) was introduced. There are literally hundreds to choose from.

Old garden roses are classified as **Gallicas** (such as 'Anaïs Ségales', a small bush with deep pink, double flowers); **Albas** (such as 'Alba Maxima' up to 8 ft [2.4 m] tall with white, double flowers); **Damasks** (such as 'Omar Khayyam' and 'Ispahan', fragrant mid-pink doubles dating from the 1800s, and 'York and Lancaster', another popular Damask); **Centifolias** (like 'Petite de Hollande', a small bush with masses of strongly scented pink blooms; and 'Fantin Latour', another popular Centifolia); **Moss** (such as 'Chapeau de Napoleon' with fragrant mid-pink, double flowers); **China** (such as 'Mutabilis', with light yellow-orange flowers that age to crimson); **Tea** (such as 'Lady Hillingdon', with loose double, golden-yellow flowers); **Bourbon** (such as 'Boule de Neige', with white double flowers opening from red buds, and '**Bourbon Queen**' and 'Souvenir de St Anne's', other popular Bourbons); **Portland** (such as 'Comte de Chambord' with sweetly scented, pink, double flowers); **Hybrid Perpetual** (such as '**Champion of the World**', a deep pink double that is always one of the first to bloom); **Noisette** (such as 'Alister Stella Gray', with light golden-yellow, fragrant double blooms).

Rosa, OGR, Tea, 'Lady Hillingdon'

Rosa, OGR, Portland, 'Comte de Chambord'

Rosa, OGR, 'Mutabilis'

Rosa, Modern Garden Roses

Most roses grown today are modern roses. Again, there are many hundreds to choose from, so make sure you choose the right one for your garden. Modern garden roses are classed as **Bush** roses (**Large-**, **Cluster-flowered** or **Polyantha**) which make compact, upright bushes about 3 ft (1 m) tall (often more in mild climates). 'Peace' is a Large-flowered rose with perfectly formed, soft yellow flowers edged rose pink. '**Double Delight**', '**Just Joey**', '**Loving Memory**', '**Mme Caroline Testout**' and '**Tequila Sunrise**' are other popular Large-flowered roses. 'Iceberg', a Cluster-flowered rose, is covered in heads of pure

Rosa, MGR, Cluster-flowered, 'Peace'

white blooms over a long season. **'Auckland Metro'**, **'Burma Star'**, **'Jacqueline du Pré'**, **'Playboy'**, **'Ripples'** and **'Rock 'n' Roll'** are other popular Cluster-flowered roses. **'Strawberry Ice'** is a Polyantha rose with white and cerise double flowers.

Shrub roses are taller, less upright growers, mostly

Rosa, MGR, English Rose, 'Constance Spry'

Rosa, MGR, Miniature, 'Anita Charles'

Rosa, MGR, Large-flowered, 'Loving Memory'

repeat flowering, and include **'Buff Beauty'**, a **Hybrid Musk**, with soft yellow, ageing to cream flowers, and **'Autumn Delight'**, another popular Hybrid Musk; **'Sarah van Fleet'**, a **Hybrid Rugosa**, a tall, prickly bush with scented, double, deep pink flowers, and **'Roseraie de L'Haÿ'**, another popular Hybrid Rugosa; **'Charles Austin'**, an **English Rose**, with large, fragrant

Rosa, MGR, Hybrid Musk, 'Autumn Delight'

Rosa, MGR, English Rose, 'Charles Austin'

Rosa, MGR, Cluster-flowered, 'Iceberg'

blooms in a dusky buff to yellow shade, and **'Constance Spry'**, another popular English rose; **'Fritz Nobis'**, growing to 1.8 m (6 ft) with clusters of pale pink to white, semi-double flowers.

Miniature roses make lovely shrubs. **'Anita Charles'** has deep pink, double flowers with an amber reverse to the petals; and **'Si'**, the smallest of all roses, has tiny, perfectly formed pink rosebuds.

Rosa, MGR, 'Jacqueline du Pré'

Rosa, MGR, Hybrid Musk, 'Buff Beauty'

Rosa, MGR, Cluster-flowered, 'Double Delight'

Rubus 'Benenden'

This deciduous, arching, thornless shrub has peeling bark and lobed, deep green leaves. Reaching 10 ft (3 m) in height and spread, it bears its large, pure white flowers in late spring and early summer. **ZONES 5–9.**

Rubus cockburnianus

This deciduous shrub from China grows to 8 ft (2.4 m) in height and spread. The black fruit, while edible, are unpalatable; they follow the racemes of purple flowers, which appear in summer. The ovate leaves are deep green above and felty white beneath. **ZONES 6–10.**

Rubus 'Benenden'

RUBUS

Many of the species belonging to this genus bear fruit, and detailed information on the genus is given in the Fruit Trees, Nut Trees and Other Fruits chapter. However, those named here are treated as shrubs.

Rubus cockburnianus

Rubus odoratus

Rubus odoratus

ORNAMENTAL RASPBERRY, FLOWERING RASPBERRY, THIMBLEBERRY

This vigorous, thicket-forming, deciduous, prickle-free shrub is from eastern North America. It has peeling stems and can grow to 6 ft (1.8 m) tall. The vine-like leaves are dark green and velvety; the fragrant flower sprays which are produced all through the warmer months, are a warm rose pink, sometimes white. The red fruit are tasteless. **ZONES 2–8.**

Rubus thibetanus

This deciduous, arching shrub from western China has white-bloomed, brownish purple young shoots in winter and fern-like, glossy deep green foliage that is white beneath. Growing to 8 ft (2.4 m) in height and spread, *Rubus thibetanus* bears its small pink flowers from mid- to late summer; the flowers are followed by the black fruit. **ZONES 6–10.**

Rubus thibetanus 'Silver Fern'

Ruscus aculeatus

Ruscus aculeatus

BUTCHER'S BROOM, BOX HOLLY

A tough, erect, branching evergreen subshrub, *Ruscus aculeatus* is native to northern Africa. Its spring flowers are followed by bright red berries. The leaves end in spines, and the flowers and fruit are borne in the center. Moderately frost hardy, it grows to a height of 30 in (75 cm) and a spread of 3 ft (1 m). Butcher's broom is so called because in days gone by, butchers used the brush of the spiky stems to brush down their chopping blocks. **ZONES 7–10.**

RUSCUS

BROOM

This genus from the Mediterranean region, Madeira and the Azores consists of 6 species of evergreen, clump-forming sub-shrubs grown for their foliage and fruits. The leaves are actually flattened shoots, on which flowers and fruits are borne. The flowers are tiny, star-shaped and green to greenish white and the fruits, for which both male and female plants are required, are red and showy.

CULTIVATION

These plants will tolerate anything from full sun to part-shade and any soil as long as it is not waterlogged. Propagate from seed or by division.

Salix gracilistyla
ROSE-GOLD PUSSY WILLOW

This vigorous shrub to 10 ft
(3 m) has gray downy leaves
and young shoots. The leaves
are oblong, up to 4 in (10 cm)
long, at first silky but the
upper surface becoming
smooth. The silky gray male
catkins can be up to 2 in
(5 cm) long, appearing in
spring before the leaves. It is
found naturally in eastern
Asia. 'Melanostachys' has
black bracts over the catkins,
so that the whole catkin
appears black. **ZONES 6–10.**

Salix gracilistyla 'Melanostachys'

Salix lanata
WOOLLY WILLOW

This small shrub from northern Europe grows to 3 ft (1 m)
tall and is of slow, spreading
habit, becoming gnarled with
age. The silvery gray rounded
leaves, up to 2 in (5 cm) long,
mature to a dull green on top
and become slightly wavy.
Erect, felty yellow-gray catkins appear in spring after the
leaves. **ZONES 2–9.**

Salix purpurea
PURPLE OSIER, PURPLE WILLOW,
BASKET WILLOW

This species from Europe,
North Africa to central Asia
and Japan grows to about
15 ft (4.5 m) high. In its
darkest forms the catkins are
an intense reddish purple. The
leaves are silver gray, often
with a hint of purple on the
undersides, and the stems are
tinted purple. 'Nana' is a
compact form to 3 ft (1 m)
with slender shoots and gray-
green leaves. **ZONES 5–10.**

SALIX

Most of the species belonging to this genus are trees, and
detailed information on the genus is given in the Trees chapter.
However, the species named here are treated as shrubs.

Salix purpurea 'Nana'

Salix lanata

Sambucus canadensis
AMERICAN ELDER, SWEET ELDER

An upright, deciduous shrub from cold-climate regions in the northeast of North America, this fast-growing species reaches about 10 ft (3 m) tall with a similar spread and has soft pithy stems. The compound leaves have 5 to 11 leaflets and the tiny, white, starry flowers appear in spring, borne in large sprays about 8 in (20 cm) across; they are followed by purple-black berries. **'Aurea'** features golden-yellow foliage and red berries. **'York'** was raised in New York State in 1964 and is considered among the best cultivars; it is a large bush with large fruit and requires cross-pollination by another cultivar to produce its best crops. **ZONES 2–10.**

Sambucus nigra
EUROPEAN ELDER, BLACK ELDER, COMMON ELDER

Although the common elder is sometimes regarded as a weed, it is cultivated for its large, spring-borne sprays of tiny white flowers and the clusters of purple-black berries that follow. Originally from Europe, northern Africa and western Asia, it is a deciduous shrub or small tree to 20 ft (6 m) high with pinnate leaves made up of 5 to 9 deep green, serrated leaflets. The berries are used in pies, the flowers and fruit to make wine or liqueurs. **'Aurea'** has creamy white, star-shaped, fragrant flowers and yellow leaves; **'Laciniata'** has irregularly, finely cut leaves. **ZONES 4–10.**

SAMBUCUS
ELDERBERRY, ELDER

Sambucus canadensis

This genus includes about 25 species of perennials, deciduous shrubs and softwooded trees, with representatives spread widely over the temperate regions of the world. Although most are rarely cultivated because of their tendency to be somewhat weedy and invasive, some species are useful for their edible flowers and berries and are attractive in foliage and flower. Most have pinnate leaves and in late spring and early summer bear large radiating sprays of tiny white or creamy flowers followed by clusters of usually purple-black, blue or red berries.

CULTIVATION
Usually undemanding, Sambucus thrive in any reasonably well-drained, fertile soil in sun or shade. Prune out old shoots and cut young shoots by half. Propagate from seed in autumn or cuttings in summer or winter.

Sambucus nigra

Sambucus nigra 'Aurea'

Santolina rosmarinifolia

SANTOLINA

Small, aromatic, frost-hardy evergreens from the Mediterranean region, the 18 shrub species in this genus are grown for their scented, usually silvery gray foliage and dainty, button-like yellow flowerheads. They are useful for covering banks and as a groundcover.

CULTIVATION

They require well-drained soil and a sunny situation. Cut back old wood to encourage new growth from the base immediately after flowering, and remove dead flowerheads and stems in autumn. Propagate from cuttings in summer.

Santolina chamaecyparissus

COTTON LAVENDER, LAVENDER COTTON

This low-spreading, aromatic shrub, native to mild, coastal areas of the Mediterranean, grows to a height of 18 in (45 cm) and spread of 3 ft (1 m). It bears bright yellow, rounded flowerheads on long stalks in summer, set among oblong, grayish green leaves divided into tiny segments. **'Lemon Queen'** is a compact form—to 24 in (60 cm)—with lemon-yellow flowerheads. **ZONES 7–10.**

Santolina rosmarinifolia

syn. **Santolina virens**

HOLY FLAX

Native to Spain, Portugal and southern France, this species has green, thread-like, 1½ in (35 mm) long leaves and bears heads of bright yellow flowers in mid-summer. It has a dense bushy habit, reaching a height of 24 in (60 cm) with a spread of 3 ft (1 m). **'Morning Mist'** has golden-yellow flowers; **'Primrose Gem'** has paler yellow flowers. **ZONES 7–10.**

Santolina chamaecyparissus

Santolina chamaecyparissus 'Lemon Queen'

SARCOCOCCA
SWEET BOX, CHRISTMAS BOX

This is a genus of 11 species of wiry stemmed, evergreen shrubs from India, China and Southeast Asia with glossy, deep green, elliptical leaves. They produce small white to pink flowers that are not very showy but are sweetly scented. The flowers are followed by conspicuous berries.

Sarcococca confusa

CULTIVATION
While often grown in difficult, dry, shady areas, sweet boxes look better with a little care and attention. They prefer a relatively cool, moist climate with well-drained soil. Propagate from seed in autumn, from cuttings in summer or by layers. They are largely trouble free.

Sarcococca confusa
This dense species with multiple basal green branches slowly grows 6 ft (1.8 m) tall and bears smooth shiny dark green leaves 1½–2 in (3.5–5 cm) long. The small white flowers occur in clusters along the stems during late autumn and winter. Shiny black berries follow. The origin of this species remains unknown; it could be from China but it has not been found in the wild. It may be a natural hybrid. **ZONES 5–10.**

Senecio cineraria

Senecio cineraria
syns *Cineraria maritima,*
Senecio candicans, S. maritimus
DUSTY MILLER

This evergreen subshrub or
shrub, which grows 24 in
(60 cm) tall and wide, is a
multi-purpose bloomer for
grouping or for formal bedding in semi-shaded spots,
window boxes, containers
on balconies or in protected
courtyards. The daisy-like
flowers are mustard yellow in
color. *Senecio cineraria* is very
tolerant of heat, salt air and
poor soil, but does poorly in
high humidity or excessive
rain. '**Silver Dust**' has lacy,
almost white leaves.
ZONES 8–11.

SENECIO

This large genus of vigorous leafy plants includes some 1,000
species from all over the world. Plants range from annuals, biennials and perennials to evergreen tree-like shrubs and climbers,
some of the species being succulent. The daisy-like flowers, mostly
yellow but sometimes red, orange, blue or purple, are arranged
in small to large clusters at the tops of the plants. Some species
contain alkaloids and are poisonous to humans and animals.

CULTIVATION
Reasonably fertile, well-drained soil suits these frost-tender to
fully frost-hardy plants, as well as a sunny location. Regular tip
pruning encourages a bushy habit. Propagate shrubs from cuttings in summer, annuals from seed in autumn and perennials by
division in spring.

SKIMMIA

Spread over much of eastern Asia from the Himalayan region to eastern Siberia, Japan, Taiwan and the Philippines, this genus includes 4 species of evergreen shrubs and trees. They have glossy deep green, oval leaves about 4–6 in (10–15 cm) long and about half as wide. The small starry flowers, which open from late winter, are white or cream and densely packed in conical clusters. They are followed by red or black berries depending on the species. Most species require male and female plants to be present for pollination.

CULTIVATION

Skimmias are plants for shade or part-shade and grow very well with rhododendrons, azaleas and camellias. Like them, they prefer moist, humus-rich, well-drained soil. They can be raised from seed in autumn but are commonly grown from cuttings in late summer.

Skimmia japonica

Skimmia japonica

JAPANESE SKIMMIA

This fully frost-hardy shrub grows to about 20 ft (6 m) high and wide. It has 4 in (10 cm) long, glossy, deep green, leathery, oval leaves. In spring, terminal clusters of slightly fragrant, creamy white flowers are borne, followed by ½ in (12 mm) long, bright red berries. Both male and female plants are required to obtain berries. '**Rubella**' has red-margined leaves and dark red flower buds. *Skimmia japonica* subsp. *reevesiana* '**Robert Fortune**' is a hermaphrodite with pale green leaves margined in dark green. **ZONES 7–10.**

Solanum rantonnetii

syn. *Lycianthes rantonnetii*
PARAGUAY NIGHTSHADE,
BLUE POTATO BUSH

This South American relative of the potato is a valuable long-blooming shrub or scrambling vine for warm-climate gardens. Simple green leaves cover the branches and provide a good foil for the summer-long profusion of deep violet-blue flowers. It can be used as a 6–8 ft (1.8–2.4 m) tall background shrub or trained on a trellis or arbor, where it may reach 12 ft (3.5 m) or more. It needs protection in winter in cool climates, and is suitable for container growing. '**Royal Robe**' has deeper purple flowers and nearly year-round bloom in mild-winter areas. **ZONES 9–11.**

SOLANUM

Many of the species belonging to this genus are climbers, and detailed information on the genus is given in the Climbers and Creepers chapter. However, the *Solanum rantonnetii* included here can be treated as a shrub.

Solanum rantonnetii

SORBARIA

The 10 shrub species of this genus originate from the cool- to cold-mountain regions of Asia. All are deciduous and have pinnate leaves with serrated leaflets. The small, starry white flowers, usually in large terminal panicles, have a cup-shaped calyx, 5 reflexed petals and many prominent stamens. The fruits are berries.

CULTIVATION

Most species sucker freely; they thrive in full sun in rich, moist soil and prefer cool climates. Prune in winter to restrict size; remove some older canes if necessary. Propagate from seed or cuttings in late winter or summer, or by division in autumn.

Sorbus reducta

SORBUS

ROWAN, SERVICE TREE, MOUNTAIN ASH

This genus of about 100 species of trees and shrubs from the northern hemisphere is described in more detail in the chapter on Trees. The following species is a small shrub.

Sorbus reducta

This small shrub to 5 ft (1.5 m) forms a thicket by suckering. The elliptical leaflets become bronze and purplish in autumn. The flowers are white but sparse, and white or ruby fruit follow. It comes from western China. 'Gnome' is a smaller, tighter form. **ZONES 6–9.**

Sorbaria kirilowii

syns **Sorbaria arborea, Spiraea arborea**
FALSE SPIRAEA

This large, spreading shrub from China and Tibet grows to 20 ft (6 m) tall with cane-like stems and compound leaves consisting of up to 17 long, narrow leaflets. The flowers are held in upright fluffy panicles 12 in (30 cm) long. The young growth is often covered in masses of hair. **ZONES 4–10.**

Sorbaria kirilowii

Sorbus vilmorinii

This shrub or small tree grows 20 ft (6 m) tall and spreads 13–16 ft (4–5 m). The buds and shoots are downy and reddish brow. The many leaflets are grayish underneath, becoming red and purple in the autumn. The white flowers are followed by drooping clusters of rosy berries that fade to pinkish white. It is native to China. **ZONES 6–9.**

Sorbus vilmorinii

SPARRMANNIA

This small genus of 3 to 7 species of evergreen trees and shrubs is indigenous to tropical and temperate southern Africa and Madagascar. The stems and leaves are covered with soft hairs. The large, soft leaves have a toothed edge and may be lobed. Its attractive flowers, on long stalks, are arranged in clusters near the shoot tips or arise from the leaf axils. The fruits are spiny capsules.

CULTIVATION

These plants need a sunny position with shelter from wind and frost, and well-drained soil enriched with organic matter. Keep the soil moist during the active growth period. These are plants for warm climates, often grown in greenhouses in cooler areas. Propagate from cuttings in late spring.

Sparrmannia africana
AFRICAN HEMP, WILD HOLLYHOCK, AFRICAN LINDEN

This fast-growing shrub or small tree reaches 20 ft (6 m) and bears clusters of striking white flowers with prominent purple and gold stamens. Flowering peaks in winter to early spring but the species flowers sporadically throughout most of the year. The large leaves may be oval to heart-shaped with a pointed tip, or have several finger-like lobes. The stems are erect and woody with many spreading branches. The fruit are rounded. 'Flore Plena' has double flowers. **ZONES 9–11.**

Spartium junceum

SPARTIUM
BROOM, SPANISH BROOM

This genus includes just one species, a deciduous, almost leafless shrub that is indigenous to the Mediterranean region but has naturalized in a few areas with a similar climate. A yellow dye is derived from the flowers.

CULTIVATION

This adaptable plant thrives in well-drained soil enriched with a little organic matter. Full sun is best; it is a shrub for warm to coolish climates. Pruning after flowering will maintain compact, well-shaped bushes. Propagate from seed or cuttings.

Spartium junceum

This shrub bears masses of large, golden-yellow, fragrant pea-flowers carried in loose, 18 in (45 cm) long spikes at the shoot tips. It flowers profusely through spring into early summer. The leaves are bluish green, lance-shaped to linear and up to 1 in (25 mm) long; they are shed from the new growth soon after they appear. The broom makes a bushy shrub 6–10 ft (1.8–3 m) tall; on older specimens the stems arch downwards. The fruit are flat, silvery pods maturing to brown.
ZONES 6–11.

SPIRAEA

This genus consists of 80 species of deciduous or semi-evergreen shrubs, mostly from Europe, Asia and North America to Mexico, that are valued for their spring and summer flower display and autumn foliage color. Spiraeas form clumps of wiry stems that shoot up from the base and are densely covered with narrow, toothed leaves. They belong to the rose family, and under a magnifying glass the flowers do resemble tiny roses but they are so small that the individual flower is lost among the mass of blooms carried on each cluster.

CULTIVATION

Spiraeas are adaptable plants that thrive under most garden conditions in temperate climates, though they prefer a warm summer. They thrive in moist, well-drained soil and a position sheltered from the hottest sun, especially in warm-summer areas where the foliage may burn. Most should be pruned after flowering. Propagate from cuttings in summer.

Spiraea cantoniensis
REEVES' SPIRAEA

This deciduous or semi-evergreen shrub is very showy when in flower in spring, with rounded 2 in (5 cm) clusters of small, white, 5-petalled flowers densely clothing the reddish, gracefully arching branches. The narrow leaves are dark green above and blue-green below. A 3–6 ft (1–1.8 m) tall species, it originated in China. It can be used for hedging and is the best spiraea for warmer temperate regions. The double-flowered form is the most popular in gardens. **ZONES 5–11.**

Spiraea cantoniensis

Spiraea japonica 'Anthony Waterer'

Spiraea japonica
JAPANESE SPIRAEA

This low, mounding, deciduous shrub bears rose-pink to red flowers from late spring to mid-summer. It grows to a height and spread of about 6 ft (1.8 m). The cream and pink variegated new leaves turn green as they mature. It has the best foliage of any in the genus and many varieties and cultivars, including: 'Little Princess', to 3 ft

(1 m) tall; **'Anthony Waterer'**, the most commonly cultivated selection; **'Goldflame'**, popular for its bronze new growth which turns golden as it matures; **'Nyewoods'**, with small leaves and dark pink flowers; **'Shirobana'**, with both dark pink and white flowers on one plant; and **'Nana'** (syn. 'Alpina'), more compact at only 18 in (45 cm). **ZONES 3–10.**

Spiraea japonica 'Goldflame'

Spiraea japonica

Spiraea japonica 'Nana'

Spiraea nipponica

Spiraea nipponica

From Japan, this upright to spreading deciduous shrub reaches 6 ft (1.8 m) high and wide. Its rounded leaves are finely serrated and in early summer it bears pure white flowers in neat, round heads crowded along the branches. **'Snowmound'** is a particularly vigorous cultivar. **ZONES 5–10.**

Spiraea prunifolia

This deciduous shrub from China, Taiwan and Japan grows to 6 ft (1.8 m) tall. Snowy white, 5-petalled flowers with greenish centers are arranged in small clusters of 3 to 6 all along its pendulous branches in early spring before the leaves appear. These turn red in autumn. The double-flowered 'Plena' is the only form commonly grown. **ZONES 4–10.**

Spiraea prunifolia 'Plena'

Stachyurus praecox

A 6 ft (1.8 m) high and wide deciduous shrub indigenous to Japan, this species is noted for its early flowering habit. Its gracefully drooping, 3 in (8 cm) long racemes of buds appear on the bare branches in autumn, opening as small pale yellow flowers in late winter or early spring. The leaves that follow are up to 6 in (15 cm) long and are carried on somewhat tiered, reddish brown stems. **ZONES 5–10.**

Stachyurus praecox

STACHYURUS

This genus includes some 6 species of deciduous or semi-ever-green shrubs and trees from the Himalayas and eastern Asia. Although reminiscent of the witch hazels and *Corylopsis,* they belong in a different family. They are generally not spectacular plants though one species, *Stachyurus praecox,* is fairly widely grown. They bloom in late winter or early spring before or just as the leaves are developing, and produce small cream to pale yellow flowers in drooping racemes at every leaf bud. They also have broadly lance-shaped leaves.

CULTIVATION

These plants prefer humus-rich, well-drained, acidic soil in sun or light shade and are usually propagated from seed or cuttings in summer.

Stephanandra incisa

Stephanandra incisa
LACE SHRUB, CUTLEAF STEPHANANDRA

Occurring naturally in Japan, Taiwan and Korea, this shrub grows to about 6 ft (1.8 m) tall with a similar spread. The lace shrub has graceful arching branches with diamond-shaped, deeply toothed leaves. The tiny greenish white flowers appear in summer. This shrub tolerates neglect. 'Crispa' is a dwarf-growing cultivar with slightly curled leaves. **ZONES 4–10.**

STEPHANANDRA

This genus is made up of 4 species of deciduous shrubs related to *Spiraea*. From the eastern Asian region, they tolerate low temperatures. The toothed and lobed mid-green leaves, which turn orange and gold in autumn, are very ornamental, as are the sepia-tinted bare stems in winter. Tiny, star-shaped, white or greenish flowers appear in summer in soft panicles; each has many stamens.

CULTIVATION
Species of *Stephanandra* grow well in sun or part-shade, preferring rich, moist, loamy soil and, if necessary, can be pruned to shape in winter. Propagate from cuttings or by division in autumn.

Stephanandra tanakae

Valued for its decorative, arching growth habit and attractive leaves, this shrub from Japan grows to about 10 ft (3 m) tall with a similar spread. The plant's leaves are 2–4 in (5–10 cm) long with shallowly toothed lobes with long points. The new foliage is pinkish brown. The tiny white flowers are borne through summer. **ZONES 4–10.**

Stephanandra tanakae

Streptosolen jamesonii
syn. *Browallia jamesonii*

This fast-growing, evergreen
shrub reaches 6 ft (1.8 m)
high, with long flexible stems
that arch slightly under the
weight of the flowerheads.
Flowering peaks in spring to
summer but continues for
much of the year. Individual,
bright orange flowers are on
a thin stalk, and strangely
twisted; they form large dense
clusters at the branch tips.
The leaves are neat, oval and
shiny dark green above, paler
underneath. Both foliage and
flowers bear fine hairs.
ZONES 9–11.

STREPTOSOLEN
MARMALADE BUSH

This genus consists of only one species, a loosely scrambling
shrub with alternate, simple leaves occurring in parts of the
northern Andes. It is cultivated mainly for its clusters of brightly
colored, long-tubed, funnel-shaped flowers.

CULTIVATION

In the garden it does best in full sun with shelter from strong
winds. A light, well-drained soil is ideal, preferably enriched
with organic matter, and it needs adequate moisture during
warmer months. Light pruning after flowering will keep it
compact. Propagate from cuttings in summer.

Symphoricarpos orbiculatus

Symphoricarpos × chenaultii

Symphoricarpos orbiculatus
INDIAN CURRANT, CORAL BERRY

This tough, adaptable shrub
from the USA and Mexico
grows to about 6 ft (1.8 m)
high and wide. It is very dense
and twiggy, with oval leaves
around 1½ in (35 mm) long.
The fruit are small, under
¼ in (6 mm) in diameter, but
abundant and a conspicuous
bright pink. The berries last
long after the leaves have
fallen. A hot summer will
yield a heavier crop of berries.
ZONES 3–9.

SYMPHORICARPOS
SNOWBERRY

This genus is made up of about 17 species of deciduous shrubs
allied to *Lonicera* and from North America, with one rare and
obscure species from China. They have elliptical to nearly round
leaves and very small, bell-shaped, pink or white flowers in
spring. They are mostly grown for their large crops of distinctive berries, which stand out clearly in winter when the branches
are bare.

CULTIVATION

They are easily grown in any moist, well-drained soil in sun
or shade and are usually propagated from open-ground winter
hardwood cuttings. Being resistant to shade, poor soil and pollution, they are very suitable for city gardens.

Symphoricarpos × chenaultii
CHENAULT CORALBERRY

This hybrid is an arching, many-branched shrub with pinkish
flowers in spring followed by white fruit tinged pink. It reaches
a height and spread of 3–6 ft (1–1.8 m). 'Hancock' is a dwarf
selection only 12 in (30 cm) tall; it is a good groundcover for
shaded area. **ZONES 5–9.**

SYRINGA

LILAC

Lilacs are prized for their upright to arching panicles of small, highly fragrant flowers, which are massed in loose heads. They appear from mid-spring and range in color from white and pale yellow to all shades of pink, mauve and purple. Most of the common garden varieties of *Syringa vulgaris* were raised in France in the late 1800s to early 1900s, though new forms appear from time to time; not all cultivars are fragrant. The genus contains about 20 species, all deciduous shrubs and trees from Europe and northeastern Asia. Most reach about 8 ft (2.4 m) high and 6 ft (1.8 m) wide, with opposite leaves that sometimes color well in autumn.

CULTIVATION

Lilacs prefer moist, humus-rich, well-drained soil in sun or light shade. They do best where winters are cold because they require at least a few frosts in order to flower well. Any pruning is best done immediately after flowering. Species may be raised from seed or cuttings. Named cultivars are usually grafted but can sometimes be struck from hardwood or semi-ripe cuttings. Established plants produce suckers that can be used for propagation.

Syringa josikaea

Syringa josikaea

HUNGARIAN LILAC

This is an erect shrub to 12 ft (3.5 m) with rigid warty branches. The leaves are glossy on top and gray underneath with felted veins. The richly colored flowers are held upright in loose heads in summer. **ZONES 5–9.**

Syringa laciniata

CUT-LEAF LILAC

This species, a graceful form with prettily dissected 3- to 9-lobed leaves, produces small heads of lilac flowers 4 in (10 cm) long in mid-spring and is a spreading shrub that grows to 6 ft (1.8 m) with a spread of 10 ft (3 m). **ZONES 5–9.**

Syringa laciniata

Syringa meyeri 'Superba'

Syringa meyeri

Syringa meyeri 'Palibin'

From China, this small spreading shrub grows to about 6 ft
(1.8 m) tall and wide. The leaves are elliptical and the deep
purplish mauve flowers appear in spring in dense heads.
'Palibin' is a slow-growing dwarf cultivar with violet to rose-
pink flowers in small dense clusters. 'Superba' has dark pink
flowers that fade as they mature; it is a long-flowering form
with some flowers produced from mid-spring to mid-summer.
All forms of *Syringa meyeri* may have a lesser flowering in
autumn. **ZONES 4–9.**

Syringa × persica 'Alba'

Syringa × persica

PERSIAN LILAC

This is thought to be a hybrid
of *Syringa laciniata* and
S. afghanica or else a stable
juvenile form of *S. laciniata*.
Probably native to Afghanistan,
it is a deciduous, bushy, compact shrub. In spring it bears
profuse heads of small, delightfully fragrant flowers set
amid narrow, pointed, dark
green leaves. It grows to a
height and spread of just
under 6 ft (1.8 m) and will
grow in warmer winter climates than most lilacs. 'Alba'
has dainty, sweetly scented
white flowers. **ZONES 5–9.**

Syringa pubescens ssp. *patula* 'Miss Kim'

Syringa reticulata
JAPANESE TREE LILAC

This Japanese lilac has comparatively small flowers, but they produce a wonderful spring display of creamy white flowerheads at the ends of the branches. Sweetly fragrant, they stand out against the dark green foliage and make excellent cut flowers. Whilst the Japanese tree lilac can grow to 30 ft (9 m), forming a squat, wide-crowned tree, it is usually seen as a large shrub. **ZONES 3–9.**

Syringa pubescens subsp. *patula*
syn. *Syringa patula*
MISS KIM LILAC

Syringa pubescens subsp. *patula* is a compact selection of an excellent lilac notable for its late-season flowering. It has relatively large leaves and fragrant flowers that are pale lilac pink. This plant will reach a height of 6–8 ft (1.8–2.4 m) with a similar spread, but is slow growing and will remain only 3–4 ft (1–1.2 m) tall for many years. **ZONES 4–9.**

Syringa reticulata

Syringa vulgaris
COMMON LILAC

This is the species from which most garden
cultivars derive. It is native to southeastern
Europe and grows to about 20 ft (6 m) high
with pointed, oval or heart-shaped leaves up
to 4 in (10 cm) long. The flowers are borne
in dense pyramidal heads and are strongly
fragrant, white or pale mauve. **'Andenken an
Ludwig Späth'** (syn. 'Souvenir de Louis Spaeth')
has single, deep purple, large heads in mid-
season; **'Katherine Havemeyer'** has fully
double, large-flowered heads of lavender-purple
buds opening to a soft mauve-pink; **'Mme
Lemoine'** is a double white with medium-sized
tight flowerheads on a free-flowering and
compact shrub; and **'Primrose'** has single, soft
lemon flowers on a compact shrub, early in the
season. **ZONES 5–9.**

Syringa vulgaris
'Mme Lemoine'

Syringa vulgaris
'Andenken an Ludwig Späth'

Syringa vulgaris

TAMARIX

Tamarix parviflora

TAMARISK

The 50 or so species of tough shrubs and small trees in this genus occur naturally in southern Europe, North Africa and temperate Asia in dry riverbeds, often in saline soils. Most *Tamarix* species are deciduous, but a few are evergreen. They develop a short trunk and a graceful dense canopy of drooping branchlets. The leaves are minute and scale-like, and have salt-secreting glands. The flowers are small and white or pink, occurring in abundant, slender spikes; the fruits are capsules.

CULTIVATION

Grown for ornament and as windbreaks, these trees adapt to a wide range of soils and climates and can cope with salt spray and very dry conditions. Very to moderately frost hardy, they do best in deep, sandy soil with good drainage and can be pruned after flowering. Propagate from ripe seed or from hardwood cuttings in winter and semi-ripe cuttings in late spring or autumn. They are prone to attack by stem borers in poorly drained soil.

Tamarix ramosissima 'Pink Cascade'

Tamarix parviflora

syn. *Tamarix tetrandra* var. *purpurea*

EARLY TAMARISK

This species grows well in mild climates; it is frost hardy but drought sensitive. A deciduous, spreading shrub or small tree up to 15 ft (4.5 m) in height, it is a pretty sight when smothered in spring with a haze of tiny, pale pink flowers, which are carried in small spikes along the previous year's growth. The toothed, mid-green leaves are small and narrow, and turn orange-red in autumn. This tree is often confused with the similar *Tamarix gallica*. **ZONES 5–10.**

Tamarix ramosissima

syn. *Tamarix pentandra*

LATE TAMARISK

Perhaps the most widely grown *Tamarix* species, this elegant, deciduous shrub grows to about 15 ft (4.5 m) with a spread of about 10 ft (3 m). Occurring from eastern Europe to central Asia and very frost hardy, it has tiny blue-green leaves, and dark red-brown branches and twigs. Clusters up to 6 in (15 cm) long of profuse, small pink flowers are borne in plumes during late summer and early autumn. 'Pink Cascade' is a vigorous cultivar which bears rich rose-pink flowers. **ZONES 2–10.**

Tamarix tetrandra

Tamarix tetrandra grows to 10 ft (3 m) with arching purplish brown shoots and needle-like leaves. In spring, it bears lateral racemes of 4-petalled, pink flowers on the previous year's growth. **ZONES 6–10.**

Tamarix tetrandra

TEUCRIUM
GERMANDER

Mainly native to the Mediterranean, this genus of around 100 species in the mint family was named for King Teucer of Troy, who reputedly used the plants medicinally. Evergreen or deciduous shrubs, subshrubs and perennials, they have 2-lipped flowers and slightly aromatic foliage. These plants are able to withstand hot, dry conditions and poor soils. They can be used as hedges and will grow in sheltered maritime conditions.

CULTIVATION
Mostly fairly frost hardy, they prefer light, well-drained soil and sun. Low-growing species do best in poor soils. Propagate shrubs and subshrubs from cuttings in summer; perennials are propagated by division in autumn or from seed in spring.

Teucrium polium
This deciduous subshrub with procumbent stems forms low hummocks 1–2 in (2.5–5 cm) in height. Its narrow, gray, felted leaves have scalloped margins and white to yellow or pinkish purple flowers in terminal heads are produced in summer. It is moderately frost hardy. '**Aureum**' has leaves edged with creamy yellow. **ZONES 7–10**.

Teucrium chamaedrys
WALL GERMANDER

This hardy, evergreen alpine species of subshrub is native to Europe and southwestern Asia. It grows 1–2 ft (30–60 cm) tall with a spread of 2–3 ft (60–90 cm). The toothed, ovate leaves are glossy deep green above and gray beneath. It is suitable for walls, steep banks and edging, and has long been used as a medicinal herb. Spikes of pale to deep rosy purple flowers are produced in summer and autumn. '**Prostratum**' is, as its name suggests, a prostrate form. **ZONES 5–10**.

Teucrium chamaedrys

Teucrium polium 'Aureum'

TIBOUCHINA

LASIANDRA, GLORY BUSH

There are more than 300 species in this genus of evergreen perennials, shrubs, small trees and scrambling climbers from South America. The flowers are large and vivid, commonly purple, pink or white, with 5 satiny petals. They are borne either singly or in clusters at the shoot tips, and sometimes the whole plant is smothered with blooms over several months, usually from late summer to early winter. The flower buds are rounded and fat, while the leaves are simple and hairy, deeply marked with 3 to 7 veins. New growth is often a contrasting reddish bronze, and stems are square; the fruits are capsules.

CULTIVATION

They prefer full sun and do best in light soil with added organic matter and a slightly acidic to neutral pH. Keep plants moist during the growing season. Prune after flowering. They have brittle stems and need shelter from wind; they do not like frost. Propagate from cuttings in late spring or summer.

Tibouchina urvilleana

Tibouchina urvilleana

syns *Lasiandra semidecandra,*
Tibouchina semidecandra
PRINCESS FLOWER, GLORY BUSH

This slender-branched species develops a short trunk topped by a bushy rounded crown and reaches 15 ft (4.5 m) in height. The young stems are reddish and slightly hairy, turning brown later. The oval to slightly oblong leaves are 2–4 in (5–10 cm) long, shiny dark green above and slightly hairy below. The rich purple to violet, satiny flowers, 3 in (8 cm) wide with purple stamens, are borne singly or in small groups. The flower buds are large, reddish and hairy. **ZONES 9–12.**

ULEX

GORSE

This genus consists of about 20 species of leafless or almost leafless, densely spiny shrubs from western Europe and North Africa. It belongs to the broom tribe of legumes along with *Cytisus, Genista* and *Spartium.* Young plants have small, compound leaves with 3 leaflets, but on mature plants the leaves are reduced to sharp spines, as are the branch tips. The flowers are profuse, mostly golden yellow and fragrant, borne singly or in small clusters. Small, hairy pods release their seeds explosively in mid-summer. Gorses are valued for their ability to thrive on sites too exposed or infertile for most other shrubs. Common gorse, *Ulex europaeus,* is apt to become a nuisance, however, especially in regions other than its native Europe.

CULTIVATION

Fully frost hardy, gorses thrive under most conditions (though not in the tropics or subtropics) as long as they receive full sun. They are tolerant of very poor sandy soils and exposure to salt-laden winds. In more sheltered positions, they may need pruning to keep a compact form. Propagate from seed in autumn or spring, or from cuttings in summer.

Ulex europaeus

COMMON GORSE, FURZE

This species is a broad, mound-like shrub which reaches about 6 ft (1.8 m) in height. When it blooms in spring, it is completely covered in pea-flowers in groups of twos or threes; their fragrance resembles that of coconut. The double-flowered form, 'Flore Pleno', has rather distorted blooms, but is more compact; it is also preferred for cultivation because it cannot form seeds and is thus not invasive. **ZONES 6–9.**

Ulex europaeus

VIBURNUM

This important genus is made up of some 150 species of evergreen, semi-evergreen and deciduous cool-climate shrubs or small trees, primarily of Asian origin with fewer species from North America, Europe and northern Africa. Many of the cultivated species and forms are noted for their fragrant, showy flowers and may also produce colorful berries or bright autumn foliage. In several species, flowers are arranged in a similar way to those of the lacecap hydrangeas, with small fertile flowers and large sterile ones on the same plant; these have all given rise to cultivars with all-sterile flowerheads known as 'snowball viburnums'. The evergreen species are often used for hedging.

CULTIVATION

Fully to moderately frost hardy, most species are remarkably trouble-free plants, growing in any well-drained soil in sun or light shade. They can be trimmed heavily after flowering, even though this will prevent fruit forming. They are usually propagated from cuttings in summer or from seed in autumn.

Viburnum × *bodnantense*

Viburnum × *burkwoodii*

Viburnum × bodnantense

A hybrid between *Viburnum farreri* and *V. grandiflorum*, this deciduous shrub reaches 10 ft (3 m) in height. It has slightly glossy, deep green, oval leaves that are pale green on the undersides. Before they drop in autumn, they develop intense orange, red and purple tones. The heavily scented flowers, which bloom from autumn to early spring depending on the climate, are bright pink in the bud, open pale pink and fade to white. **'Dawn'** has slightly darker flowers, especially those that open in spring; and **'Deben'** has light pink to white, somewhat tubular flowers. **ZONES 7–10.**

Viburnum × *burkwoodii* 'Park Farm'

Viburnum × burkwoodii

BURKWOOD VIBURNUM

A hybrid between *Viburnum carlesii* and *V. utile*, this 8–10 ft (2.4–3 m) high semi-evergreen shrub has glossy, deep green, pointed oval leaves to about 3 in (8 cm) long. They are pale sage green on the undersides and those that drop in autumn develop bright yellow and red tones. From early to late spring ball-shaped clusters of small, starry, fragrant flowers open; they are pink in the bud, opening white. **'Anne Russell'**, the result of a backcross with *V. carlesii*, has clusters of fragrant flowers. **'Park Farm'** has a more spreading habit and larger flowers. **'Mohawk'** has dark glossy leaves that turn to orange in autumn and fragrant red-blotched white flowers that open from red buds. **ZONES 5–10.**

Viburnum davidii
DAVID VIBURNUM

This evergreen species from Sichuan, China, grows 3–5 ft (1–1.5 m) tall and spreads slowly to form a densely foliaged shrub up to 6 ft (1.8 m) across. If massed, it makes an excellent, large-scale groundcover. The pointed oval leaves are bright glossy green and up to 6 in (15 cm) long; leaf petioles and new wood are reddish brown. The spring-borne clusters of white flowers are not spectacular, but are followed by turquoise blue berries. 'Femina' is a reliable, heavy-fruiting cultivar. **ZONES 7–10.**

Viburnum davidii 'Femina'

Viburnum davidii

Viburnum dilatatum
LINDEN VIBURNUM

From Japan and China, this 10 ft (3 m) tall deciduous shrub has coarsely toothed, hairy oval leaves. Its flowers are white and abundant and carried in heads 4–6 in (10–15 m) wide; bright red fruit follow. **'Iroquois'** is slightly smaller and bushier than the species with flowers more of a creamy white. **ZONES 5–10.**

Viburnum dilatatum 'Iroquois'

Viburnum farreri 'Candidissimum'

Viburnum farreri
syn. Viburnum fragrans

Discovered in mountain regions of western
China at the beginning of the twentieth century
by Reginald Farrer, this deciduous shrub grows
to 8–10 ft (2.4–3 m) tall. Its lightly arching
branches are clad in oval, deeply toothed leaves
with prominent veins; bronze when young, they
mature to rich green and turn red before
falling. The pink buds open to white, sweetly
smelling flowers clustered at the branch tips in
early spring before the leaves appear. Glossy
red fruit are produced only occasionally.
'Candidissimum' has pure white flowers and
buds, and bright green leaves. **ZONES 6–10.**

Viburnum lantana 'Rugosum'

Viburnum lantana
WAYFARING TREE

Often used as hedging, this deciduous species
from Europe and northwestern Asia is tolerant
of cold climates. *Viburnum lantana* forms a
tall, branching shrub 15 ft (4.5 m) high and is
distinguished by its new shoots, which are
unusually furry for a viburnum. The oval leaves
have hairy undersides and turn burgundy red in
autumn. In early summer, small, creamy white
flowers are profusely borne in flat clusters. The
oblong red fruit ripen to black. The cultivar
'Rugosum' has larger and more wrinkled leaves
and larger flower clusters. **ZONES 3–9.**

Viburnum lantana

Viburnum macrocephalum
CHINESE SNOWBALL TREE

The distinctive characteristic of this species native to China is the presence of small, fertile flowers and large sterile ones, but the cultivar 'Sterile' has all-sterile flowers. Huge, rounded trusses of white flowers, up to 6 in (15 cm) across, give a spectacular display in early summer on this upright shrub. The dark green, leathery leaves are oval, 4 in (10 cm) long and tinted red and yellow in autumn; normally deciduous, this species may be semi-evergreen in milder climates. It grows to 6–10 ft (1.8–3 m) tall. **ZONES 6–10.**

Viburnum macrocephalum

Viburnum opulus 'Pink Sensation'

Viburnum opulus 'Compactum'

Viburnum opulus
GUELDER ROSE, EUROPEAN
CRANBERRY BUSH

This lovely deciduous shrub from Europe and North Africa produces splendid clusters of snowy white, lacy flowers in summer. It has attractive fruit and autumn color, and can be grown in wet or boggy situations. A large shrub growing to 12 ft (3.5 m) tall, it has gray bark

and a spreading habit with long, pale green shoots. Its leaves turn deep crimson in autumn. Generous bunches of shiny, translucent, orange-red fruit remain on the bush until well into winter. **'Aureum'** has bronze-colored shoots turning yellow then green, and yellowish leaves which may burn in the sun; **'Compactum'** is a dense, compact shrub bearing large quantities of flowers and fruit; **'Nanum'** has small leaves and seldom flowers or fruits; **'Roseum'** (syn. *Viburnum opulus* 'Sterile'), the snowball bush, has snowball-like heads of pale green to white, sterile flowers so large they weigh the branches down; **'Pink Sensation'** is similar to 'Roseum' except the flowers have a pinkish hue; and **'Xanthocarpum'** has clear yellow fruit which are quite translucent when ripe.
ZONES 2–10.

Viburnum opulus 'Aureum'

Viburnum opulus

Viburnum opulus 'Pink Sensation'

Viburnum plicatum 'Pink Beauty'

Viburnum plicatum 'Rosace'

Viburnum plicatum 'Mariessi'

Viburnum plicatum

syn. *Viburnum tomentosum*

This deciduous shrub from Japan and China grows to about 15 ft (4.5 m) tall with a similar spread. It has hazel-like, 3 in (8 cm) long, mid-green, pointed oval leaves with serrated edges and a somewhat tiered growth habit, a feature emphasized in the cultivar '**Mariesii**'. The large, creamy white flower clusters with a mass of tiny fertile flowers in the center, enclosed by large sterile flowers, open in spring; they are followed by small red berries that ripen black. **'Lanarth'** is a fine cultivar, with branches less arching than the species; **'Pink Beauty'** has a pale pink tinge to the flowers; and **'Sterile'** (syn. *Viburnum plicatum* var. *plicatum*) is a sterile form. **'Rosace'** has sterile heads of mixed white and pink flowers and bronze spring foliage. **ZONES 4–9.**

Viburnum plicatum

Viburnum rhytidophyllum
LEATHERLEAF VIBURNUM

This fast-growing, evergreen shrub from China has distinctive, handsome foliage. Its long leaves are corrugated, deeply veined and dark glossy green, with gray felted undersides. Growing to 10–15 ft (3–4.5 m) tall and almost as wide, it tolerates alkaline soil. Small, creamy white spring flowers appear in large, flat clusters at the ends of branches; the fruit are oval berries, red at first, later turning black. Plant in groups to ensure fruiting. **ZONES 6–10.**

Viburnum sargentii
SARGENT VIBURNUM

From northeastern Asia, this 10–15 ft (3–4.5 m) deciduous shrub has 4 in (10 cm) wide, 3-lobed leaves, yellow-green when young, ageing to dark brown. The large, individual flowers are carried on heads up to 4 in (10 cm) wide. The berries are red. **'Onondaga'** has maroon young growth that becomes purple-red in autumn. **ZONES 4–9.**

Viburnum rhytidophyllum

Viburnum sargentii 'Onondaga'

Viburnum tinus
LAURUSTINUS

This densely foliaged ever-green shrub from the Mediterranean region may eventually grow to 15 ft (4.5 m) tall and 20 ft (6 m) wide, although it is usually kept smaller through trimming. The dark green, pointed elliptical leaves are up to 4 in (10 cm) long and develop purplish tones in cold weather. Cream and yellow variegated foliage forms are available. Clusters of white flowers open from pink buds from late winter, followed by blue-black berries. **'Compactum'** (syn. 'Spring Bouquet') is a smaller form with dense compact growth; **'Eve Price'** has smaller leaves, carmine buds and pink-tinged flowers; **'Gwenllian'** has pink buds that open into pinkish white flowers followed by clusters of blackish seeds; and **'Pink Prelude'** has white flowers becoming deep pink. **ZONES 7–10.**

Viburnum tinus

Viburnum trilobum

Viburnum trilobum
syns *Viburnum americanum*, *V. opulus* var. *americanum*
HIGHBUSH CRANBERRY, AMERICAN CRANBERRY BUSH

The North American equivalent of *Viburnum opulus*, this species has showy flowers, fruit and autumn foliage. Growing 8–12 ft (2.4–3.5 m) tall and wide, it is useful as a hedge or screening plant. The white flowers appear in spring in flat-topped clusters. The bright red fruit appear in autumn and last through winter. **'Wentworth'** has a very heavy crop of fruit. **ZONES 3–9.**

VITEX

This genus is made up of about 250 mainly tropical and sub-tropical trees and shrubs—some evergreen, some deciduous. The leaves are compound with 3 to 7 leaflets radiating from the stalk—less commonly, the leaves are simple. Highlights are the sprays of tubular flowers in shades of white, yellow, red, blue or purple; the fleshy drupes are usually not a feature. In some species, both the leaves and the flowers are aromatic.

CULTIVATION

Moderately to marginally frost hardy, *Vitex* adapt to most soils, but do best in fertile soil with good drainage and with plenty of summer moisture. A sheltered spot in full sun is ideal. Propagate from seed in autumn or spring or cuttings in summer.

Vitex agnus-castus

Vitex agnus-castus
CHASTE TREE

This moderately frost-hardy shrub, indigenous to southern Europe and western Asia, has aromatic leaves; these are 6–8 in (15–20 cm) long with 5 to 7 lance-shaped to rounded leaflets, deep green on top and felty gray underneath. The chaste tree is a deciduous, rounded shrub or small tree, 10–20 ft (3–6 m) tall with an upright, branching, woody stem. From early summer to autumn it bears dense, erect sprays of faintly perfumed, lavender flowers up to 12 in (30 cm) long. Small purple fruit follow. White-flowered and variegated-leaf forms are also available. *Vitex agnus-castus* var. *latifolia* has shorter, broader leaves.
ZONES 7–10.

WEIGELA

This genus includes about 12 species of arching deciduous shrubs from Japan, Korea and northeastern China. Most grow 6–10 ft (1.8–3 m) high and wide, and have pointed, elliptical, deep green leaves about 4 in (10 cm) long. The foliage often develops orange, red and purple tones in autumn. Masses of white, pink or crimson, sometimes yellowish, 1½ in (35 mm) long, bell- or trumpet-shaped flowers appear in spring,

Weigela floribunda

CULTIVATION
Fully frost hardy, most species prefer full
sun or light shade in moist, fertile, well-
drained soil. Prune out older branches after
flowering to maintain vigor. Propagate
from summer cuttings.

Weigela 'Bristol Ruby'
This erect hybrid, bred from *Weigela
florida* and *W. coraeensis*, is grown for the
profusion of crimson flowers which adorn
the shrub from late spring to early summer.
It grows to 6 ft (1.8 m) tall, with slender,
arching branches and dark green oval
leaves. **ZONES 4–10.**

Weigela floribunda
syn. *Diervilla floribunda*
From Japan, this deciduous shrub reaches
about 10 ft (3 m) in height and has slender,
pointed leaves which are hairy on both
sides. Young shoots are also hairy, as are
the outsides of the flowers. These are deep
crimson, crowded on short lateral branchlets, tubular in form with the style projecting out from the opened petals.
ZONES 6–10.

Weigela florida 'Eva Rathke'

Weigela florida 'Aureovariegata'

Weigela florida

This arching, deciduous shrub from Japan, Korea and northeastern China, which grows up to 10 ft (3 m) or so, is grown for its lavish spring display of rose-pink, trumpet-shaped flowers. **'Appleblossom'**, with variegated leaves, has flowers that open white and age to pink. **'Aureovariegata'** has bright green, cream-edged leaves and wide, bright pink, trumpet-shaped flowers to 1½ in (35 mm) wide. **'Eva Rathke'** bears crimson flowers from purplish red buds. Fully frost hardy, it grows 5 ft (1.5 m) tall and wide with a dense, erect habit. **'Foliis Purpureis'** has purplish green leaves. The flowers are deep pink, paler inside the tube and appear from late spring to early summer. **ZONES 4–10.**

Weigela florida

Xanthoceras sorbifolium

Xanthoceras sorbifolium

This deciduous upright shrub or small tree to about 15 ft (4.5 m) is native to China. The bright green leaves are composed of many sharply toothed leaflets. The white flowers are borne in erect sprays from the leaf axils in late spring and summer; each flower has a carmine red blotch at the base of the petals. The common name refers to the horn-like growths between the petals. The large fruiting capsules are pear-shaped and contain small seeds like chestnuts. It has thick, fleshy yellow roots. **ZONES 6–10.**

XANTHOCERAS
YELLOW HORN

Native to China, this genus consists of only one species. Even though related to *Koelreuteria*, it is very different in general appearance. Except for its vulnerability to occasional injury by late spring frosts, this deciduous shrub or small tree is easily grown. The fragrant, erect flower spikes recall those of the horse chestnut.

CULTIVATION
While it tolerates low winter temperatures, the yellow horn should be protected from late frosts and needs long hot summers to flower well. It prefers well-drained, good loamy soil and will tolerate mild alkalinity. It requires plenty of sunshine but does well in cooler areas if sited in a warm sheltered position. Propagate from stratified seed in spring or root cuttings or suckers in late winter; prune lightly to maintain shape. It is susceptible to coral spot fungus.

Chapter 4

TREES

The intrinsic beauty of trees dominates a garden. Regardless of the size of a garden, whether it is a grand park with an avenue of stately conifers or a sub-urban plot with just a lone specimen, it is trees that create the atmosphere.

What is a tree?

By definition, a tree is a single, woody stemmed plant at least 15 ft (4.5 m) high at maturity. Trees are divided into two main types: conifers and broad-leafed trees, either of which can be deciduous or ever-green. A myriad of ex-ceptions include the mallee type, trees with more than one trunk, and then there are palms and tree ferns—used in a similar horticultural manner, but have a different type of trunk. Gardeners need not concern themselves with these technicalities: their quest for the perfect tree for a particular site is a different matter.

Trees have a huge variety of form and features. Acer saccharum *and* Acer rubrum *are known for their glorious autumn colors.*

Decide what is best before planting a tree

Factors that are worth considering be-fore a tree is planted include its eventual height, shape and density. More often than not, there are also neighborly con-siderations to ponder.

In today's environment, this does not just mean careful planting along a boundary so as not to cast unwanted shade next door, but also accounting for the neighboring wildlife; whether those decorative seeds will be eaten by birds and deposited, to detrimental effect, in nearby bush or woodland.

Luckily for gardeners on smaller sites, plant breeders have developed more socially acceptable, compact cul-tivars of many species. Trees such as the magnificent towering evergreen magnolia *(Magnolia grandiflora)* are now available in smaller growing forms like 'Little Gem'. It is wise, however, to check carefully when you consider cultivars of well-known species. The tree mentioned above, for example, beloved by many as a huge-canopied evergreen with large, creamy white, perfumed flowers, has a number of cultivars with different growth characteristics. Even though the foliage or flower variation may not be obvious when a cultivar is seen in the nursery container, a young tree may develop into something quite dissimilar to the original species.

If you feel there is room for a tree in your garden, take into consideration that it may be many years before it reaches its full maturity, and you may have moved on before this time. However, who hasn't relaxed in the shade of a mature tree in the heat of summer and thanked the person who planted it for their foresight? So be heartened, you can watch a tree grow and usually within ten years, the vision becomes a reality. And if care was taken in its choosing, it will continue to give pleasure.

Always select a tree that is suitable to both the climate and soil of your garden. Anyone who admires a particular tree while on holidays beside the sea, then tries to coax the same species along in a gar-den above the snowline, is heading for disaster. Although a great number of trees have the capacity to acclimatize to a wide zonal range, they may be slower to mature, differ in size or produce fewer fruits or flowers.

Do you choose an evergreen or deciduous tree? Many gardeners grow evergreen specimens simply because they don't like to sweep up fallen leaves every autumn. Beyond a colorful autumn display, however, a deciduous tree that has dropped its leaves will also allow the weaker winter sun to

This bristle cone pine in Nevada, USA, is said to be the oldest tree in the world—it's nearly 5,000 years old.

The silver birch (Betula pendula) *is popular for its spring and autumn foliage.*

warm a patio or terrace. It will also shade this favorite outdoor spot in the heat of summer. Likewise, many understorey plants appreciate the extra light that filters through in winter and early spring, which boosts their spring flowering, then to be covered by a cooling canopy during summer, followed by a free mulch as the leaves fall in autumn.

Evergreens are firm favorites when it comes to screens. Whether the screen is to provide shelter from wind or to hide unsightly distractions beyond the boundary fence, always keep aspect in mind. It makes little sense to clothe a

garden in deep shade throughout the year just to screen a distant power line, whereas there may not be much choice if a 3-storey apartment block already takes the sun away from your yard.

Like height, the mature shape of a tree can be a governing factor. First ask questions of yourself and fellow users of the garden. Is it necessary to have dense foliage from ground level to act as a sight and sound barrier? If not, a couple of spreading, leafy, deciduous trees may be a better alternative to a row of conical-shaped conifers. Do you have the space for a broad canopy under which to place outdoor furniture? If yes, then do you want it to be a deciduous or evergreen canopy? And remember, the mature look of most species can be manipulated as they grow. In a courtyard garden, for example, a smaller tree can be induced to supply a leafy canopy by stripping the trunk of any side branches until head height is reached. Then, as these upper branches grow, tie them with a weight and string so they are trained into graceful, arching limbs.

A decision about what tree to plant is really a matter of priorities. First, compile a list of governing factors; what is required of the tree in the sense of height, shade, root performance, suitability to soil type, foliage color and quite importantly, the overall performance rating. To make the choice less difficult, some trees are in the 5-star performance rating category, which means they flower, fruit, produce good leaf coloring, have textured decorative bark, are attractive to birds and wildlife and bear inherently interesting leaf shapes. In short, these are bonus point plants—a 5-star plant for temperate regions is the crepe myrtle (*Lagerstroemia indica*).

An instant effect

Everybody likes an instant effect, especially in a new garden. Rather than buying a knee-high tree from your local nursery only to wait years for it to grow, it may be worth putting some money towards an advanced or semi-advanced specimen. Specialist nurseries are able to supply any number of advanced trees, which have been grown especially for this purpose. These will, of course, be more expensive, but they will give many years of pleasure as they continue to mature.

Planting and pruning

There is always a temptation to rush from nursery to garden with spade in hand to produce the instant garden. It will pay dividends, however, to be patient and prepare the position well in advance. Thoroughly dig and improve the soil, see to any drainage or irrigation requirements and add the necessary fertilizer and mulch before you bring a tree home. Evergreens can be planted year round, but do best if planted in either autumn or early spring, and deciduous trees are best planted during the winter months when they are dormant. Quite large, bare rooted specimens, which can be purchased through mail order catalogues, are a considerably cheaper way of buying deciduous trees.

Except for irrigation, which is particularly important in hot, dry areas, a tree will need very little further maintenance once it has been planted. So long as the correct tree has been chosen for a particular position, there should be very little need to prune. Unless it suffers storm damage your tree should be among the longest-surviving plants in the garden framework.

Abies cephalonica
GREEK FIR, CEPHALONIAN FIR

This fir belongs to a group of
Mediterranean firs with short,
stiff, outward-pointing,
prickly needles, and occurs
naturally in the mountains
of Greece and the Balkans.
Widely grown, hardy and
vigorous, it was introduced
into Britain in the early 1800s,
where native specimens have
reached heights equal to those
in the wild, about 120 ft
(36 m). The brown cones are
roughly cylindrical and about
4 in (10 cm) long. **ZONES 6–9.**

Abies balsamea 'Hudsonia'

ABIES
FIR

The true firs, sometimes known as silver firs to distinguish them
from *Picea* (which have pendent, not upright, cones), comprise
40-odd species of evergreen conifers. Among the most stately
of all conifers, firs come from cool- to cold-climate mountain
areas of the northern hemisphere. The majority are from China
and western North America, but a few species extend into the
tropics on the high mountains of Central America and Southeast
Asia. The short, stiff needles usually have 2 longitudinal blue
bands on their undersides.

CULTIVATION

Their narrow shape and often slow growth allow many *Abies*
species to fit comfortably into the larger suburban garden, but
they will not tolerate urban pollution and prefer a moist climate
without extremes of heat. They should be planted in soil which
has adequate depth, drainage and moisture retention.
Propagation is from seed. Grafting is used for selected clones,
including named cultivars. The only pruning or shaping needed
is the removal of twin leading shoots as soon as they appear.

Abies balsamea
BALSAM FIR

The 'balsam' in this fir's name is a clear, thin resin in its bark,
once commercially important. The most widespread North
American species, it extends from Canada (where it is a major
source of paper pulp) south through the mountains of eastern
USA as far as West Virginia. In cultivation, a short-lived slender
tree, grown for its spicy fragrance, bluish green foliage and
Christmas tree shape. Dwarf cultivars are most often seen in
gardens with the most popular being '**Hudsonia**', a compact
miniature shrub up to 24 in (60 cm) high and '**Nana**', a neat
rounded shrub of similar size. **ZONES 3–8.**

Abies cephalonica

Abies concolor var. *lowiana*

Abies concolor

COLORADO FIR, WHITE FIR

This species grows wild in the Rocky Mountains of western USA, where it reaches 150 ft (45 m), with a taller race, *Abies concolor* var. *lowiana* (Pacific fir), found closer to the coast in Oregon and northern California. The needles, which are bluish green on both sides and blunt tipped, exude a lemon scent when bruised. Cones range from deep dull purple to pale brown. A fine ornamental fir, it is also hardy and vigorous. Seedlings vary in the blueness of their foliage. Some of the best blue forms, propagated by grafting, are sold under the name '**Glauca**'; even more striking is the rare and slower-growing pale blue cultivar '**Candicans**'. '**Compacta**' also has quite blue foliage but is a dwarf cultivar, hardly exceeding 3 ft (1 m). **ZONES 5–9.**

Abies firma

Abies firma

MOMI FIR, JAPANESE FIR

With foliage of a deep shiny green, this species reaches 150 ft (45 m) in the mountains of southern Japan. It is densely branched with stiff, leathery needles, up to 1½ in (35 mm) long, in 2 rows forming a wide V-shape on twigs of the lower branches. The brown, egg-shaped cones are up to 4 in (10 cm) long. **ZONES 6–9.**

Abies homolepis

NIKKO FIR

Native to central Japan, this species grows well in Europe and North America and is more tolerant of urban pollution than most firs. It can exceed 100 ft (30 m) in height, and is broadly conical when young. Its crowded needles, up to 1½ in (35 mm) long, are dark green with broad blue-white bands on the undersides and blunt tips. The bark on young trees and immature cones is purplish gray. The shrub-sized cultivar '**Prostrata**' lacks erect leading shoots and is propagated from cuttings. **ZONES 5–9.**

Abies homolepis

Abies homolepis 'Prostrata'

Abies koreana

Abies koreana
KOREAN FIR

In the wild known only from mountains in the
far south of Korea, this fir has been grown in
the West from the early 1900s. It is valued for
its compact size, seldom exceeding 20–30 ft
(6–9 m), and its early coning—it may produce
its attractive small bluish cones when as little
as 3 ft (1 m) high. The crowded needles are
short and broad with notched tips and wide
blue bands on the undersides. It is ideal for
smaller gardens, or for a large rock garden.
ZONES 5–9.

Abies lasiocarpa
SUBALPINE FIR, ROCKY MOUNTAIN FIR

This species grows up to the tree line in the
Rocky Mountains, from Arizona to southern
Alaska. It may be a 100 ft (30 m) tall tree or
a horizontal spreading shrub. The needles are
crowded and overlapping, with bluish stripes
on both surfaces. Cones are fat and dark
purple. To the southeast of its range the typical
species is replaced by *Abies lasiocarpa* var.
arizonica, the corkbark fir, which has thick,
corky, pale bark and blue-gray foliage. Selections
of this variety valued as garden plants include
'**Compacta**', silver-blue and slow growing but
difficult to obtain as it is propagated by grafting, and '**Aurea**', which has yellowish foliage.
ZONES 4–9.

Abies lasiocarpa

Abies nordmanniana

Abies nordmanniana
CAUCASIAN FIR, NORDMANN FIR

This handsome fir can grow to 200 ft (60 m)
and is native to the mountains of the Caucasus.
Its densely crowded needles are dark glossy
green, with rounded and slightly notched tips
and whitish bands on the undersides. When
crushed they smell like orange peel. The long
fat cones ripen to reddish brown. Vigorous and
adaptable, with a narrow shape and a long
straight leading shoot, it is widely grown as
an ornamental. **ZONES 4–9.**

Abies pinsapo

Abies pinsapo
SPANISH FIR

A handsome column-shaped tree reaching 100 ft (30 m), often with multiple leaders and densely crowded branches, this fir adapts to a wide range of soils and climates. The very short, rigid needles are less flattened than in most firs, and have fine bluish white stripes on both surfaces. In spring small purple pollen cones appear on the lower branch tips. The seed cones, produced near the top of the tree, are brown when ripe. Seedlings are selected for bluish foliage, collectively referred to under the cultivar name 'Glauca'. **ZONES 5–9.**

Abies pinsapo 'Glauca'

Abies procera 'Glauca'

ACACIA
WATTLE

This large genus contains over 1,200 species of trees and shrubs from warm climates. Some are deciduous but most are evergreen. Over 700 are indigenous to Australia. They range from low-growing shrubs to tall trees and many have been introduced to other countries for economic and ornamental purposes. Acacias are also common in tropical and subtropical Africa; most African species are characterized by vicious spines and referred to as 'thorn trees'. Acacias have either bipinnate leaves or their leaves are replaced by flattened leaf stalks, known as phyllodes, which perform the function of photosynthesis. The tiny flowers, ranging from deep golden yellow to cream or white, and crowded into globular heads or cylindrical spikes, are often fragrant and produce abundant, bee-attracting pollen. Fruit are either round or flattened pods.

CULTIVATION
The hard-coated seeds remain viable for up to 30 years. They should be treated by heating and soaking for germination in spring. Some need fire to germinate. In cultivation many species are fast-growing but short-lived (10–15 years). In their native regions they are often disfigured by insect or fungus attack. They do best in full sun and well-drained soil. Some will take part-shade.

Abies procera
syn. Abies nobilis
NOBLE FIR

A very tall conifer from the high-rainfall coastal region of northwestern USA, this species reaches over 250 ft (75 m). Smooth-barked and broadly conical when young, it develops a mast-like trunk and a high, pointed crown with foliage in horizontal tiers. The narrow, bluntly pointed needles vary from bluish green to strong silvery blue. Cones are large, fat and purplish brown. It adapts well to cultivation in a cool, moist climate and good, deep soil. It is susceptible to aphid attacks in warmer climates. Blue-foliaged 'Glauca' cultivars are usually grown. **ZONES 4–9.**

Acacia greggii

Acacia greggii
CATCLAW ACACIA

A native of southwestern North America, this deciduous shrub reaches 6–8 ft (1.8–2.4 m) in height and spread and can be shaped into a small tree for patio gardens. Tiny, gray-green leaves appear in mid-spring, followed by fuzzy yellow catkins in late spring. The branches are covered with thorns, making the catclaw acacia useful as a barrier planting. It loves heat and is very drought tolerant once established. **ZONES 7–11.**

ACER

MAPLE

Maples are unrivaled for their autumn foliage coloring and variety of leaf shape and texture. They are also grown for shade and for timber. Many are compact enough for the average garden. The distinctive 2-winged fruit (samaras) are more noticeable than the flowers, which in most species are inconspicuous. Bark is a feature of some maples. Although usually smooth and gray or greenish, in the group known as the 'snakebark maples' it has longitudinal gray or red-brown stripes and in others it is flaky or papery. Most species come from eastern Asia; nine species are native to North America and a few to Europe.

CULTIVATION

Most maples prefer a cool, moist climate with ample rainfall in spring and summer. Shelter from strong winds. For best autumn color, grow them in a neutral to acid soil. Propagation is generally from seed for the species, by grafting for cultivars. Cuttings are difficult to root, but layering of low branches can be successful. Seed germination can be aided by overwintering in damp litter, or by refrigeration.

Acer cappadocicum 'Aureum'

Acer buergerianum

TRIDENT MAPLE

Although tall in its native forests of eastern China, in cultivation this species usually makes a bushy-topped small tree with a thick, strong trunk. The bark is pale brown and dappled and the smallish leaves usually have 3 short lobes close together at the upper end. Autumn coloring is often two-toned, with scarlet patches on a green or yellowish background. It tolerates exposed positions and poor soils. **ZONES 6–10.**

Acer campestre

FIELD MAPLE, HEDGE MAPLE

A small to medium bushy-crowned tree, this European maple also occurs in western Asia and north Africa. In the UK it is also known as hedge maple, for its use in the traditional hedges that divide fields. It withstands heavy pruning and can be trimmed into dense, regular shapes. It has thick, furrowed, corky bark; autumn brings golden yellow or slightly bronze tints to the foliage. **ZONES 4–9.**

Acer cappadocicum

COLISEUM MAPLE

This maple is found from southern Europe across temperate Asia to central China, with a number of geographic subspecies. Its smooth green leaves have regular, radiating triangular lobes, each lobe drawn out into a slender point. Fast growing, it can reach 100 ft (30 m) in the wild and is better suited to parks and streets rather than suburban gardens. The autumn color is a brilliant golden yellow. 'Rubrum' has dark red new shoots, the young leaves expanding bright red before turning green. **ZONES 5–9.**

Acer × *freemanii*

This hybrid between *Acer rubrum* (the red maple) and *Acer saccharinum* (the silver maple) was raised by O. M. Freeman at the US National Arboretum in 1933, but has since frequently been found to occur spontaneously. In foliage it is intermediate between these species, growing to 50 ft (15 m) or more quite rapidly with erect branches and a rounded crown. A half-dozen cultivars of *A.* × *freemanii* have been named including the colorful 'Autumn Blaze'. They are suitable specimens for street planting. They are normally propagated by layering. **ZONES 5–9.**

Acer × freemanii 'Autumn Blaze'

Acer japonicum

Acer monspessulanum

MONTPELIER MAPLE, FRENCH MAPLE

Related to *Acer campestre* and occurring on stony hillsides around the Mediterranean, this bushy small tree of up to 30 ft (9 m) has dark green, rather thick leaves 1½–2 in (35 mm–5 cm) long with 3 blunt lobes. It is tolerant of dry conditions and its compact crown makes it well suited for streets and suburban lawns. It turns reddish in autumn. **ZONES 5–10.**

Acer griseum

PAPERBARK MAPLE

Prized for its bark—chestnut brown with paler corky dots which it sheds each year in wide curling strips—this narrow-crowned tree grows to 30 ft (9 m) with a fairly straight trunk. In autumn its small, dark green leaves turn deep scarlet. Under moist, sheltered conditions in good soil, growth can be rapid. No longer common in the wild in its native China, in cultivation it produces mostly infertile seed, so can be hard to obtain. **ZONES 5–9.**

Acer japonicum

FULL-MOON MAPLE

This maple's new growth is distinctive—very pale green with a coating of silky white hairs that disappear as the leaves mature into olive green tones. In autumn some leaves change early to orange or red, while others retain their summer colors into late autumn. Slow growing and of narrow, shrubby habit, it is intolerant of drying winds and likes a moist, sheltered position. It has long been cultivated in Japan. Its many cultivars include '**Aconitifolium**', with ferny leaves that turn crimson in autumn, and '**Vitifolium**', with leaves slightly more deeply lobed than the normal species and coloring more brilliant scarlet, orange or yellow. **ZONES 5–9.**

Acer griseum

Acer negundo
BOX-ELDER MAPLE, BOX ELDER

The only North American maple to have compound leaves (consisting of 3 to 7 leaflets), this species can reach 50 ft (15 m) with a thick trunk and upright branching habit, but is more often seen as a smaller tree with cane-like, bright green branches. It is fast growing and tolerates poor conditions but its branches break easily in high winds. In some areas it is regarded as a weed because of its free-seeding habits. Its several subspecies extend south into Mexico and Guatemala. Favorite cultivars include **'Elegans'**, **'Variegatum'** and **'Aureomarginatum'**, with leaflets that are edged white or gold respectively; **'Aureo-variegatum'** has leaflets with broader, deeper yellow margins, retaining this coloring into autumn; the newer **'Flamingo'** is similar to 'Variegatum' but with leaves that are strongly flushed with pink on the new growth. The male clone **'Violaceum'** has purplish new shoots and twigs; the male flower tassels are also pale purple. None of these cultivars reach much more than half the size of the wild, green-leafed type.
ZONES 4–10.

Acer negundo

Acer palmatum 'Bloodgood'

Acer palmatum

Acer palmatum
JAPANESE MAPLE

The Japanese maple is the most widely grown maple in gardens. It is valued for its compact size, delicate ferny foliage, and brilliant autumn coloring, from rich gold to deepest blood-red. In a garden it grows to 12–15 ft (3.5–4.5 m), branching low, with strong sinuous branches and a dense, rounded crown. Although more tolerant of warmer climates than most maples, it needs shade and shelter or leaves may shrivel. The more than 300 cultivars range from rock-garden miniatures to vigorous small trees, with a great variety of leaf shape, size and coloration. Nearly all need to be grafted to preserve their characteristics, so they are expensive. The most popular cultivar of tree size is **'Atropurpureum'**, dense and spreading, with dark purple spring foliage giving way to paler olive-purple in summer and deep scarlet tones in autumn; it largely comes true from seed. '**Sangokaku**' ('Senkaki') has coral-red branches and twigs, which are displayed bare in winter; in autumn leaves have brilliant gold tones. '**Atrolineare**' has foliage color like 'Atropurpureum' but leaves divided almost to the base into narrow lobes. In the **Dissectum Group**, the primary leaf lobes are deeply cut into a filigree pattern; their fine, drooping twigs grow down rather than upward, so they are grafted onto a standard. The height of the standard determines the height of the dome-shaped shrub. '**Dissectum**' is a small cultivar with leaves turning yellow tinged with orange in autumn. '**Dissectum Viridis**', the original green cut-leaf maple, is slightly more able to withstand the sun than is '**Dissectum Atropurpureum**' ('Ornatum') which has purple leaves that are green in summer . Some other cultivars that are well-known include '**Bloodgood**', '**Butterfly**', '**Chitoseyama**', '**Koreanum**', '**Osakazuki**' and '**Shigitatsu Sawa**'. The finely cut leaves of '**Crimson Queen**' are red-purple, as are those of '**Garnet**' which persist through autumn. '**Red Pygmy**' is a vase-shaped cultivar with red leaves in spring, turning to gold in autumn. Some other popular forms include '**Linearilobum Rubrum**', '**Trompenburg**' , '**Hessei**' and '**Lutescens**'. **ZONES 5–10.**

Acer pensylvanicum

Acer palmatum 'Dissectum Viridis'

Acer palmatum 'Dissectum Atropurpureum'

Acer pensylvanicum
STRIPED MAPLE, MOOSEWOOD

Erect, vigorous and with a single main trunk, the striped maple is native to eastern North America. The bark striping on younger limbs is the most richly colored of any of the snakebark maples, suffused with red as well as olive and white. Autumn color is a bright golden yellow. The popular cultivar '**Erythrocladum**' has striking red branches in winter. **ZONES 5–9.**

Acer platanoides
NORWAY MAPLE

This maple ranges from north of the Arctic Circle in Scandinavia (reduced almost to a shrub) across Europe from France to the Urals but not to the Mediterranean or the British Isles, though cultivated there for centuries. A large, round-headed tree, it thrives in a wide range of soils and situations, but not in warm climates. Yellow flowers appear before the leaves; autumn color is gold to reddish orange. Popular cultivars include **'Oregon Pride'**, **'Cleveland'**, **'Summershade'** and **'Drummondii'**, which has variegated leaves. Cultivars with deep purplish foliage include **'Schwedleri'**, **'Faasen's Black'** and **'Crimson King'**. **'Columnare'**, with plain green leaves, has a narrow column shape. All except 'Oregon Pride' are slow growing, and so suit smaller gardens. **ZONES 4–9.**

Acer platanoides 'Drummondii'

Acer platanoides 'Schwedleri'

Acer platanoides

Acer platanoides

Acer pseudoplatanus
SYCAMORE MAPLE

This species, which occurs naturally from Portugal to the Caspian Sea and has been long established in England and North America, seeds so profusely as to be regarded a weed. Cultivated trees are usually 40–60 ft (12–18 m) tall and form a broad, dense crown of dark green. The thick, scaly bark is pale gray. A useful park and street tree, it prefers a sheltered situation with deep moist soil, but tolerates more exposed sites. The cultivar **'Purpureum'** has leaf undersides of a deep plum, uppersides also slightly purplish. **'Erythrocarpum'** has red fruit in conspicuous clusters. The spring foliage of **'Brilliantissimum'** is pale creamy yellow flushed pink, changing in summer to whitish with green veining; it is slow growing and suits smaller gardens; **'Rubicundum'** has leaves flecked deep pink. **'Variegatum'** has cream markings. **ZONES 4–9.**

Acer pseudoplatanus 'Brilliantissimum'

Acer rubrum
RED MAPLE, SCARLET MAPLE

This large maple from eastern North America displays brilliant autumn tones of deep red, contrasting with the blue-white undersides. In the wild it grows to 30 m (100 ft) in forests on deep alluvial soil. As a planted tree it makes rapid growth, with a straight trunk and narrow crown at first, but spreading broadly with age. Its timber is prized for furniture making. There are numerous popular cultivars including 'Bowhall', 'Red Sunset', 'Schlesingeri', the conical 'Scanlon' and 'October Glory', which has glossy green foliage that turns a brilliant crimson in autumn. **ZONES 4–9.**

Acer saccharinum
syn. Acer dasycarpum
SILVER MAPLE

Ranging over eastern USA and Canada (except the Arctic north), the silver maple grows large, branching low into several trunks with a broad crown of foliage. As an ornamental it is popular for its hardiness, rapid growth and rich golden autumn color. The cane-like branches are easily damaged by storms and heavy snow, but quickly grow back. American and European nurseries have developed many cultivars. **ZONES 4–9.**

Acer pseudoplatanus 'Erythrocarpum'

Acer rubrum

Acer saccharum
SUGAR MAPLE

Commercially important for its sap (maple syrup) and durable timber, this maple ranges across eastern North America from Newfoundland and Manitoba in the north to Florida in the south, and west to Utah. In the south and west, regional sub-species occur, including *Acer saccharum subspp. floridanum*, *grandidentatum*, *leucoderme* and *nigrum*: all have been treated as distinct species by some botanists. Its leaf adorns the Canadian flag. Often slow growing in the first 10 years, in the garden it makes a low-branching, broad-crowned tree of 40–50 ft (12–15 m), though it will grow much taller in forests. Autumn color varies from tree to tree, with yellow, orange, scarlet and crimson all common. **A. s. subsp. *grandidentatum*** (bigtooth maple) is widely distributed in western North America. It has thicker leaves, and the bluish white undersides contrast with the deep green upper, and blunter, lobes. It makes a small, bushy-topped tree to 40 ft (12 m), and has pale bark. Attractive cultivars include **'Globosum'**, **'Green Mountain'**, **'Legacy'** and **'Monumentale'**. **ZONES 4–9.**

Acer saccharinum

Acer tataricum
TATARIAN MAPLE, AMUR MAPLE

As now recognized, this is the maple species with the widest east–west distribution, occurring wild from Austria eastward across Europe and temperate Asia all the way to Japan and far eastern Siberia. Tataria was the name used in the eighteenth century for central Asia and eastern Russia, where it is a common tree. The species is divided into 4 geographic subspecies of which the most commonly cultivated is ***Acer tataricum*** subsp. ***ginnala*** (syn. *Acer ginnala*) from northeastern China, Japan, Korea and eastern Siberia: a large shrub or small tree of 15–30 ft (4.5–9 m), it often branches from the base into several long cane-like stems; leaves are long pointed and irregularly lobed, turning red in autumn and falling rapidly; red fruits are a summer feature. A quick grower, it is fully frost hardy; **'Flame'** is one of its cultivars. **ZONES 4–9.**

Acer tataricum

Aesculus × carnea

Aesculus × carnea

RED HORSE-CHESTNUT

This hybrid tree, thought to
have originated by chance in
Germany in the early 1800s,
grows to about 30 ft (9 m)
and often comes true from
seed. It gets the reddish pink
of its flowers (produced in
late spring) from one parent,
Aesculus pavia; the other
parent is *A. hippocastanum*.
It adapts to warmer and drier
climates than *A. hippocastanum*. The cultivar 'Briotii'
has larger spikes of brighter
pink flowers. **ZONES 6–9.**

Aesculus flava

syn. *Aesculus octandra*

YELLOW BUCKEYE, SWEET BUCKEYE

This ornamental tree is native
to fertile valleys in central-
eastern USA, and grows to 90 ft
(27 m) in the wild. Smallish
creamy yellow or occasionally
pinkish flowers appear in 6 in
(15 cm) panicles from late
spring to early summer, followed by fruit each with 2 to
4 seeds. The dark green leaves
turn yellow before falling. The
bark is dark brown, becoming
furrowed with age. **ZONES 4–9.**

AESCULUS

HORSE-CHESTNUT, BUCKEYE

These deciduous trees and shrubs have a finger-like arrangement
of leaflets of their compound leaves, and eye-catching spikes of
cream to reddish flowers at branch ends in spring or summer.
The large, nut-like seeds, released from round capsules, resemble
chestnuts but are bitter and inedible. At least half of the 20 or
so species occur in North America, the remainder are scattered
across temperate Asia and Europe. Renowned as majestic park
and avenue trees in European cities, in the wild they are primarily
trees of valley floors, where they grow in sheltered positions in
deep soil with good moisture.

CULTIVATION

Although most are frost hardy, they perform best in those cool
climates where seasons are sharply demarcated and summers are
warm. They are propagated from seed or, in the case of selected
clones and hybrids, by bud grafting.

Aesculus × carnea 'Briotii'

Aesculus indica
INDIAN HORSE CHESTNUT

From the northwest Hima-layas, this tree tends to branch very low and produce a thick trunk and spreading crown when planted in the open. In early to mid-summer it produces 12–15 in (30–38 cm) spikes of white flowers with petals tinged yellow or red. The shiny leaves turn yellow in autumn; the large fruit, brownish and slightly rough, lack prickles. It requires a sheltered but sunny position and reliable soil moisture. **ZONES 6–9.**

Aesculus parviflora
BOTTLEBRUSH BUCKEYE

This many-stemmed shrub, native to the southeastern USA, grows 6–10 ft (1.8–3 m) tall, spreading into a broad clump by new growths from the roots. The five large, strongly veined leaflets are downy on the undersides. In late summer it produces spikes of spidery flowers with small white petals and long, pinkish stamens. This species likes a hot humid summer, deep moist soil and a sheltered position. **ZONES 7–10.**

Aesculus hippocastanum

Aesculus hippocastanum
HORSE CHESTNUT

This tree originated in the mountain valleys of the Greece–Albania border region and is now widely planted in parks, avenues and large gardens in Europe. It can reach 100 ft (30 m), though is usually half that and bears striking 'candles' of bloom in spring and early summer; individual flowers have white, crumpled petals with a yellow basal patch which ages to dull red. The fruit have a leathery case covered with short prickles and in autumn they release large seeds, known as 'conkers' to British children. The dark green foliage turns yellow-brown in autumn. **'Baumannii'** has longer-lasting double flowers. **ZONES 6–9.**

Aesculus parviflora

AILANTHUS
TREE OF HEAVEN, SIRIS

This tree genus from eastern Asia and the Pacific region includes both winter-deciduous and dry-season-deciduous species, though only the former are generally known in cultivation. They are vigorous growers of medium size with long pinnate leaves and branches terminating in large flower clusters—male and female flowers are on separate trees and neither is very conspicuous, but those on female trees develop in summer into masses of winged, papery fruits that are very decorative. The winter-deciduous species are frost-hardy trees that adapt well to urban areas, even coming up from self-sown seed in the cracks of paving. They tolerate hard pruning, responding with vigorous new growths.

CULTIVATION
They do best in warm-temperate areas but will survive in most climates, preferring full sun or partial shade and deep, rich soil. Propagation is by means of seed in autumn and suckers or root cuttings from the female tree in winter.

Ailanthus altissima
syn. Ailanthus glandulosa
TREE OF HEAVEN

Native to China, in some cities this tree is valued for its ability to withstand urban pollution, in other areas it is scorned as a weed. Planted on a large lawn it shows little inclination to sucker, growing to 50 ft (15 m), its dome-shaped crown is scattered with bunches of pale reddish brown fruits in summer. The deep green, pinnate leaves, up to 24 in (60 cm) long on young trees, smell unpleasant if bruised. **ZONES 6–10.**

Ailanthus altissima

Albizia julibrissin

ALBIZIA

For the most part *Albizia* species are quick growing tropical trees and shrubs with globular clusters of long-stamened flowers, rather like those of many *Mimosa* and *Acacia* species but larger. They have feathery leaves and densely clustered small flowers in which the stamens are far longer and more conspicuous than the petals. In nature they are often rather weedy small trees and frequently short lived, but can be shapely.

CULTIVATION
Springing up quickly from seed, *Albizia* species are easy to cultivate; their main requirements are summer warmth and moisture and a reasonably sheltered site.

Albizia julibrissin
SILK TREE

Ranging from Iran east to China, this deciduous tree is named for the long, silky stamens, creamy white to deep pink, the visible part of the flowerheads, borne in summer. Often less than 6 ft (1.8 m) tall, though flowering freely, in ideal conditions it becomes a flat-crowned tree of 20–25 ft (6–8 m) with luxuriant feathery foliage. It likes a warm-temperate climate and does very well in large containers but seldom lives beyond 30 years. Exceptionally richly colored specimens are usually given the name *Albizia julibrissin* var. *rosea*. They make good container plants.
ZONES 8–10.

ALNUS

ALDER

Alnus firma

Upright trees related to the birches *(Betula)*, alders come mainly from cool to cold climates of the northern hemisphere. Though less attractive than the birches, they are very fast growing and their roots contain micro-organisms that can fix nitrogen from the air, adding to soil fertility. Light-loving trees themselves, alders act as nurse trees for slower-growing conifers but die after they are overtopped by them and shaded out. The female catkins are egg-shaped, hanging in groups at branch tips, becoming hard and woody in the seeding stage. The bark is brown or blackish and sometimes furrowed. Alders from cool-temperate regions are deciduous but produce little autumn color. A few species from subtropical mountain areas are evergreen or semi-evergreen.

CULTIVATION

Most alders require a cool-temperate climate, or one in which winters are distinctly cold. They do best in permanently moist soil, and some species (notably *A. glutinosa*) thrive in valley floors where soil is too waterlogged for most other trees; many alders will also grow in very infertile or polluted soils. When planted for ornament or shade the trees should be shaped early to a single trunk, and branches trimmed to above head height. Propagate from seed or hardwood cuttings.

Alnus firma

JAPANESE ALDER

This beautiful alder from the mountains of Japan has narrow, sharply toothed and beautifully textured leaves on gracefully arching branches. It may remain a large shrub to 10 ft (3 m) for many years, though it can ultimately reach 30 ft (9 m). It has attractive bark, with older squares of gray flaking off to reveal reddish new bark. The leaves often remain green late into autumn. This alder is not widely planted outside Japan. **ZONES 5–9.**

Alnus glutinosa

BLACK ALDER, COMMON ALDER

In cold, bleak climates and on poor, boggy soils the common alder of Europe is sometimes the only tree apart from certain willows that will thrive. It can reach heights of 60 ft (18 m) in the wild but planted trees are seldom more than half that. The dark brown bark becomes deeply furrowed and checkered and the high crown of the tree is often irregular and rather open. The leaves of the cultivar '**Imperialis**' are dissected into narrow, pointed lobes. **ZONES 4–9.**

Alnus rubra

syn. *Alnus oregona*

RED ALDER

Ranging from Alaska to central California, this tree grows to 40–50 ft (12–15 m), usually branching into several trunks with pendulous lower branches. Bark is thin and pale gray. The large leaves have coarse marginal teeth and are dark green above with paler gray-green undersides often covered with orange down. This alder produces profuse yellow male catkins at the branch tips in early spring. Reasonably frost hardy, it will soon outgrow a small garden. **ZONES 6–9.**

Alnus rubra

Aralia chinensis

Aralia chinensis

CHINESE ARALIA

As a young tree of up to about 10 ft (3 m), this species is usually single-stemmed with an irregular, umbrella-like crown of dark green leaves each about 4 ft (1.2 m) long, consisting of large, oval leaflets with closely toothed margins. It flowers in early autumn, producing large panicles of creamy yellow umbels that droop over the foliage. With age it branches into smaller crowns, with smaller leaves and flower sprays, and may reach as much as 30 ft (9 m) in height. The leaves turn yellowish in autumn. **ZONES 7–10.**

Aralia elata

JAPANESE ANGELICA TREE

Native to Japan and mainland northeast Asia, this highly ornamental, frost-hardy species can grow to a spreading tree of up to 30 ft (9 m) but is most commonly seen as a shrub with few branches. Large sprays of tiny white flowers are carried into early autumn, when the leaves have yellow and reddish tones. The leaflets of the cultivar 'Variegata' have whitish markings. **ZONES 5–9.**

ARALIA

This genus of around 40 species of evergreen and deciduous shrubs and small trees and a few herbaceous perennials has a wide distribution in eastern and tropical Asia and the Americas. They have prickly stems, handsome, large, compound leaves consisting of numerous leaflets, and large, terminal panicles of densely packed, small cream flowers. Younger plants of these woody species often make single, unbranched trunks with the leaves confined to the top, but as they age lateral branches develop and multiply to give a broad-headed small tree. Aralias can be eye-catching specimens when in full flower.

CULTIVATION

They need shelter from strong, drying winds and will tolerate full sun or part-shade beneath taller trees. While a moist, fertile soil suits them well, poorer soils are said to produce hardier, longer-lived specimens. Propagate from seed sown in autumn or suckers in spring.

Aralia elata

Arbutus menziesii

ARBUTUS
STRAWBERRY TREE, MADRONE

A dozen or more species of evergreen tree belong to this genus, the majority from Mexico and the remainder found in the Mediterranean region and North America. Most are smallish trees with thick trunks and somewhat sinuous limbs; the bark often peels attractively. The thick-textured leaves are usually finely toothed and the flowers are small, white or pinkish bells in compact clusters at the branch ends. A small proportion of flowers develop into fleshy but hard, reddish yellow globular fruit, often with wrinkled surfaces, which take almost a year to ripen. The 'strawberry' in the name refers to the fruit, which are edible but hardly palatable.

CULTIVATION

All *Arbutus* species prefer cool, humid climates, but tolerate dry conditions in summer; continental climates with extreme heat and cold do not suit them. They adapt equally to peaty, acid soils and limestone soil. Propagation is normally from seed, easily extracted from the fleshy fruit. Plant young: they dislike root disturbance.

Arbutus unedo

Arbutus menziesii
MADRONE

Native from California to British Columbia, the madrone is the giant of the genus, reaching 100 ft (30 m) in height and 6 ft (1.8 m) in trunk diameter. In the wild it grows mostly in humid areas among tall conifers such as redwoods. It has beautiful, smooth, orange-brown bark and smooth-edged, glossy green leaves with whitish undersides, and produces large clusters of pure white flowers and profuse small, orange-red fruit. The common name is a corruption of madroño, the Spanish name for *Arbutus unedo*. **ZONES 5–9.**

Arbutus unedo
ARBUTUS, STRAWBERRY TREE

Native to the western Mediterranean and Ireland, this bushy-crowned, small tree can attain 30 ft (9 m), though 10–15 ft (3–4.5 m) is more usual in gardens. The bark is dark gray-brown, rather fiberous and scaly, and the smaller branches and twigs have a reddish hue. In autumn the white or pinkish flower clusters, along with the 1 in (25 mm) orange fruit from the previous year, contrast with the dark foliage. It is fairly frost hardy and will tolerate neglect, but dislikes shade and damp ground. 'Compacta' is a smaller cultivar. **ZONES 7–10.**

Austrocedrus chilensis

Austrocedrus chilensis

Native to the Andean slopes of Chile and Argentina at altitudes of 3,000–6,000 ft (900–1,800 m), this moderately fast-growing species can reach 80 ft (24 m); young trees have a densely columnar habit but with age the crown lifts higher above a bare trunk and narrow cone of branches. The gray bark is finely scaled; some trees have more bluish foliage than others.
ZONES 7–9.

AUSTROCEDRUS

CHILEAN CEDAR

The only member of this temperate South American genus is a conifer of the *Thuja* type, with flattened sprays of branchlets that are themselves strongly flattened and with small, narrow cones consisting of weak, woody scales. In *Austrocedrus* the branchlets are quite fine and fern-like, attractively marked with bluish bands on the undersides. It is valued as a timber tree in its native Chile, where its fragrant, durable, easily worked, reddish wood is in demand for fine cabinet work.

CULTIVATION

It is a fairly frost-hardy conifer, able to survive in exposed positions but appreciating some shelter and deep, moist soil. Propagate from seed or cuttings.

AZARA

The 15 or so species of this temperate South American
genus of shrubs and small trees are characterized by neat,
glossy, evergreen foliage and massed, small, yellow flowers
and include trees from the Chilean subantarctic rainforests
of the south as well as some from drier evergreen scrubs
of the lower Andean slopes further north. A characteristic
feature is the way each branch node has one small and one
larger leaf. While they are quite attractive plants, azaras
develop a certain 'legginess' with age.

CULTIVATION

Azaras prefer cool but mild and humid climates and grow
best in sheltered sites in moist soil. In colder areas they
can be trained against walls to protect them from severe
frosts. Propagate from cuttings in summer.

Azara microphylla

Azara microphylla

This fairly erect, small tree may reach 20 ft (6 m)
in the garden, more in the wild in its native Chile
and western Argentina. A vigorous grower with
fine foliage, in late winter it produces numerous
clusters of tiny, fragrant flowers half-hidden under
the leaf sprays. The most adaptable member of
the genus, but sometimes damaged by frost in
southern England, **'Variegata'** has attractive
cream variegations. **ZONES 7–9.**

Betula albosinensis

CHINESE RED BIRCH

The most beautiful
feature of this west-
ern Chinese birch is
its pale coppery,
orange-red bark; a
thin bloom of white
powder coats the new
bark, which is re-
vealed as large, loose
plates of the shiny
older bark layer peel-
off. *Betula albosinensis*
is a medium-sized tree
of 30–40 ft (9–12 m),
often branching low.
Its jaggedly toothed
leaves are up to 3 in
(8 cm) long. A shel-
tered, sunny spot with
moist soil suits it
best. **ZONES 6–9.**

BETULA

BIRCH

Betula albosinensis

Deciduous trees extending to the far northern regions of the globe as
well as lower-latitude mountains of the northern hemisphere, birches are
among the most admired of all trees as landscape subjects despite having
fairly inconspicuous flowers and fruits. Their appeal lies in their sparkling white to pinkish brown trunks, combined with vivid green spring
foliage and delicate tracery of winter twigs. The short, broad, serrated
leaves mostly turn gold in autumn before dropping. Their fast early
growth, yet fairly modest final height, are added advantages for use in
gardens or streets. In nature, birches often grow in dense stands rather
than scattered among other trees.

CULTIVATION

To grow birches successfully, a climate cool enough for at least the occasional winter snowfall is needed. Birches are shallow-rooted and will
need watering during dry periods. They grow best in full sun or dappled
shade in deep, well-drained soil, but some adapt to poorer, shallower,
even boggy soil. Propagation is normally from the small winged seeds,
produced in vast numbers from the cylindrical female catkins.

Betula nigra

Betula nigra

RIVER BIRCH

Widespread in warmer parts of eastern USA, this species' natural habitat is riverbanks. With maturity it becomes broader crowned, forking 10–20 ft (3–6 m) above ground into several arching limbs. Older trunks have dark, furrowed bark at the base, but in young trees the bark is smooth and whitish. The luxuriant leaves are triangular, with irregularly toothed edges. Though most at home beside water, the river birch thrives in well-drained soil and reaches 30 ft (9 m). 'Heritage' has striking smooth bark—cream, salmon pink or pale brown, that peels off in large curling plates. **ZONES 4–9.**

Betula papyrifera

Betula papyrifera

PAPER BIRCH, CANOE BIRCH

Famed for its tough papery bark, once used by Native Americans for their light but strong canoes, the paper birch is one of the most wide-ranging North American species and is extremely cold hardy. It reaches 60 ft (18 m) in cultivation, and has a sparse crown. The largish leaves are broadly heart-shaped or egg-shaped. The white or cream bark peels off in thin, curling layers, exposing new bark of a pale orange-brown. Its chief ornamental value is in the bark. From southern Alaska is a smaller-growing tree, *Betula papyrifera* **var. *kenaica***—up to 40 ft (12 m) with slightly smaller leaves and fissured bark at the base of older trees. **ZONES 2–9.**

Betula pendula 'Tristis'

Betula pendula

syns *Betula alba*, *B. verrucosa*

SILVER BIRCH, WHITE BIRCH

The common birch of northern Europe, the silver birch is also one of the most elegant species, with smooth gray-white bark and fine arching branchlets bearing small shimmering leaves. It is the most widely cultivated birch, ideal as a windbreak and generally trouble free in terms of pests and diseases. It reaches around 30–50 ft (9–15 m) in temperate climates; however, in Scandinavia it can reach 70–80 ft (21–24 m) and is an important timber tree there. Many cultivars have been named, including '**Purpurea**', with rich, dark purple leaves, '**Laciniata**'

Betula pendula

(commonly misidentified as 'Dalecarlica') with deeply incised leaves and weeping branches; '**Tristis**' with an erect trunk but weeping branchlets; and '**Youngii**' with growth like a weeping willow and no leading shoot, requiring it to be grafted on a standard. **ZONES 2–9.**

Betula platyphylla

Betula utilis
HIMALAYAN BIRCH

From the middle altitudes of the Himalayas, this tree up to 60 ft (18 m) has pale, smooth, peeling bark and a broadly domed crown. The leaves, dark green with paler undersides and irregularly toothed, are up to 3 in (8 cm) long. Most widely grown is **Betula utilis var. jacquemontii** with dazzling white or cream bark that peels in horizontal bands. Several clones of this variety with outstanding bark qualities have been named as cultivars. There are also forms with darker orange-brown bark. **B. u. var. occidentalis** normally has duller grayish white bark. '**Jermyns**' is a cultivar selected for the whiteness of its bark, uninterrupted by any darker markings or bands. **ZONES 7–9.**

Betula platyphylla
JAPANESE WHITE BIRCH

Occurring widely through western and northern China, Japan, Korea, Mongolia and eastern Siberia, this species has several geographical varieties, of which the one common in the West is **Betula platyphylla var. japonica** (syn. *B. japonica*) from Japan and Siberia. In leaves and fruit this birch is similar to the silver birch, but it has dazzling pure white bark. A vigorous grower, it is a shapely tree of 40 ft (12 m) or more. '**Whitespire**' is a cultivar of very upright growth with clean white bark. **ZONES 4–9.**

Betula pubescens
DOWNY BIRCH

Similar to the silver birch in geographic range, habitat and stature, this birch is less ornamental, usually with a more brownish cream bark (sometimes more whitish) and less pendulous branchlets. Its main distinction is the fine down on young twigs and it also tolerates more poorly drained soil. **Betula pubescens subsp. carpatica** is smaller with a more densely branched crown. **ZONES 2–9.**

Betula pubescens

Betula utilis

Calocedrus decurrens

CALOCEDRUS

Calocedrus means 'beautiful cedar' and its 3 species, from western USA, Taiwan, western China and adjacent Burma, are indeed beautiful trees, though only the American one is well known in gardens. The branchlets are arranged in strongly flattened sprays, each branchlet with small scale leaves that alternate between large (lateral) and small (facial) pairs. The cones have only 4 seed-bearing scales, lying parallel in 2 opposite pairs, each scale with only 2 winged seeds.

CULTIVATION

These trees do best in cool, moist mountain areas in full sun or part-shade and in deep, moderately fertile soil, but may still grow well under poorer conditions as small, bushy but attractive trees. If liberally watered when young they will cope better with dry conditions when larger. Propagate from seed in spring or cuttings in late summer.

Calocedrus decurrens

syn. *Libocedrus decurrens*
INCENSE CEDAR

Valued for its shapely, conical habit and attractive foliage, this species is fully frost hardy and grows slowly to 40–70 ft (12–21 m). The foliage is a glossy dark green and the cylindrical cones open with 3 splayed segments. 'Intricata' is a compact dwarf cultivar; its twisted branches turn brown in winter. **ZONES 5–9.**

Caragana arborescens

CARAGANA

PEA SHRUB

About 80 species belong to this genus of pea-flowered deciduous shrubs and small trees from central and eastern Asia, of which several have been established in cultivation in Europe and North America. They are curious plants of a rather subdued attraction, with lemon-yellow, orange or reddish flowers and small, pinnate leaves. Slender, straw-colored pods appear in autumn after the flowers.

CULTIVATION

Although at their best in climates with cold winters and hot, dry summers, caraganas are adaptable in this respect with root systems not prone to rot diseases. Most are very frost hardy. They set plenty of seed in the pods, which ripen in mid-summer and provide an easy means of propagation.

Caragana arborescens

SIBERIAN PEA TREE

This is the tallest species, attaining a height of 12–20 ft (3.5–6 m). A native of central Asia, Siberia and Mongolia, it has been cultivated in western Europe for almost 250 years and is valued for its frost hardiness and tolerance of poor conditions. The leaves are soft and spineless, consisting of 8 to 12 fresh green leaflets. Loose clusters of slender-stalked, pale yellow flowers hang among the leaves from late spring to early summer. Several cultivars have been named, including 'Lorbergii' with long narrow leaves and small flowers; 'Pendula' with weeping branches, which is usually grafted onto a standard; and 'Walker', a dwarf spreading plant used as a groundcover. **ZONES 3–9.**

CARPINUS

HORNBEAM

The subtle beauty of hornbeams lies in their usually smoothly fluted trunks and limbs, their neatly veined, small, simple leaves that color attractively in autumn, and their bunches of dry, winged fruit hanging from the twigs. *Carpinus* is a small genus of catkin-bearing, deciduous trees scattered across cool-climate areas of the northern hemisphere. In foliage and fruits there is not a huge variation between the species, though overall size and growth habit are distinct for each. Most, and in particular the European *Carpinus betulus*, yield a timber that is exceptionally strong, hard and close grained; it is much used in the mechanism

Carpinus betulus

of pianos. Long lived and often slow growing, hornbeams are useful small to medium-sized trees for parks, streets and lawns.

CULTIVATION

These grow best in well-drained, moderately fertile soil in a sunny or part-shaded position. Propagation is from seed except for certain named clones, which must be grafted.

Carpinus japonica

Carpinus betulus
COMMON HORNBEAM,
EUROPEAN HORNBEAM

Ranging from Asia Minor across Europe to eastern England, this species can grow to 80 ft (24 m) although 30 ft (9 m) is an average garden height. The common horn-beam has a broad, rounded crown and pale gray bark, fairly smooth and often fluted. The ovate leaves are ribbed and serrated, downy when young, and change from dark green in summer to yellow in autumn. Inconspicuous flowers in early spring are followed by clusters of pale yellow winged fruit. It likes cool, moist conditions. 'Columnaris' is a compact grower to 30 ft (9 m) high and 20 ft (6 m) wide; 'Fastigiata' (syn. 'Pyramidalis') develops into a taller, broadly conical tree. **ZONES 6–9.**

Carpinus japonica
JAPANESE HORNBEAM

This species makes a medium-sized tree 30–40 ft (9–12 m) tall, forking rather low with broadly ascending branches. The smooth, dark gray bark often has lighter streaks and becomes scaly and furrowed with age. The leaves are larger than those of the common hornbeam, up to 4 in (10 cm) long and more closely veined, with edges more finely but sharply toothed and heart-shaped bases. The fruiting catkins are compact with broad, overlapping, jaggedly toothed bracts. **ZONES 5–9.**

Catalpa speciosa

CATALPA

CATALPA, INDIAN BEAN TREE

This genus consists of 11 species of fast-growing, deciduous trees from eastern Asia and North America. Catalpas have large, ovate leaves in opposite pairs, sprays of showy, bell-shaped flowers at the end of the branches, and extraordinarily long, thin fruits that open to release quantities of very light, winged seeds that float away on the breeze. At their best they are beautiful trees with a dense canopy of luxuriant foliage dotted with flower sprays and are capable of very fast growth, but may look scrappy if exposed to cold or dry winds or if the soil is too poor. Some species yield valuable timber.

CULTIVATION

Grow in moist, well-drained soil in a sunny but sheltered position. Propagate from seed in autumn or cuttings in late spring or summer, or by budding in late summer or grafting in winter.

Catalpa bignonioides

SOUTHERN CATALPA

This species comes from the warmer southeast of the USA, from Florida west to Mississippi, where it grows along riverbanks and around the edges of swamps. It makes a reasonably compact tree of 25–50 ft (8–15 m) with a rounded, irregularly shaped crown and is cultivated as an ornamental tree for streets, large gardens and parks. The heart-shaped leaves taper to a fine point and have downy undersides; they turn black before dropping in autumn. Sprays of 2 in (5 cm), white flowers with frilled edges and orange blotches and purple spots on their lower lips appear in summer. 'Aurea' has lime-yellow leaves. ZONES 5–10.

Catalpa speciosa

NORTHERN CATALPA, WESTERN CATALPA

This handsome, fast-growing tree reaches over 100 ft (30 m) in its home region, the central Mississippi basin between Arkansas and Indiana, where it grows in forests in rich, moist soil in valley bottoms and on lower slopes. It is sometimes planted for its timber. The leaves are larger than those of *Catalpa bignonioides* but the flowers, borne in mid-summer, are similar though individually slightly larger. Northern catalpa is usually regarded as less decorative overall than the southern species. ZONES 4–10.

Far left: *Catalpa bignonioides*
Left: *Catalpa bignonioides* 'Aurea'

CEDRUS

CEDAR

Cedrus atlantica 'Glauca Pendula'

This is a renowned genus of conifers belonging to the pine family; the 4 very similar species, from northwest Africa, Cyprus, Asia Minor and the Himalayas, are so similar that some botanists prefer to treat them as subspecies or varieties of a single species. All have needle-like leaves arranged in rosettes on the short but long-lasting lateral shoots, which arise from axils of the longer needles on stronger growths. The pollen cones, shaped like small bananas and up to 4 in (10 cm) long, release large clouds of pollen in early spring. The seed cones are broadly egg- or barrel-shaped, pale bluish or brownish; they eventually shatter to release seeds with broad papery wings. Cedars are valued for the fine architectural effects of their branching, the texture and color of their foliage, and their vigorous growth.

CULTIVATION
In suitable climatic conditions these conifers are long lived and trouble-free trees, growing quite massive with age. They need full sun and well-drained, chalky soil. Propagation is normally from seed, though cuttings, layering and grafting are used for certain cultivars.

Cedrus atlantica

Cedrus atlantica

syn. **Cedrus libani** subsp. **atlantica**

ATLAS CEDAR

Native to the Atlas Mountains (*atlantica* is the adjectival form) of Morocco and Algeria, this tree in its younger stages has a neat, pyramidal shape with stiffly ascending branches, but with age it spreads into a broadly flat-topped tree with massive limbs up to 100 ft (30 m) or more high on good sites. The densely clustered needles are never more than 1 in (25 mm) long and vary from dark green to bluish, though it is mainly the bluish forms that are seen in gardens. This species prefers moderately cool climates. The collective cultivar name '**Glauca**' is used for selected seedling plants with bluish foliage. '**Glauca Pendula**' has long, pendulous branches and no leading shoot and is usually grafted onto a standard.

ZONES 6–9.

Cedrus deodara

DEODAR, DEODAR CEDAR

The deodar (its Indian name) occurs in the western Himalayas, reaching over 200 ft (60 m) in the wild, but is now almost extinct over much of its former range. In cultivation it makes fast early growth.

Cedrus deodara

The long leading shoots nod over slightly, and smaller branches are quite pendulous. The foliage is a dark, slightly grayish green, with needles about 1½ in (35 mm) long on strong shoots. The deodar is at its best in milder, humid climates in deep soil, making luxuriant growth and reaching 30 ft (9 m) in about 10 years. The most popular cultivar is 'Aurea', with golden branch tips. **ZONES 7–10.**

Cedrus libani 'Pendula'

Cedrus deodara 'Aurea'

Cedrus libani
CEDAR OF LEBANON, LEBANON CEDAR

This magnificent tree has been all but wiped out in Lebanon, with only a few small groves surviving on Mount Lebanon; larger populations survive in Turkey. It was introduced to western Europe centuries ago, and trees in England are up to 120 ft (36 m) in height and 8 ft (2.4 m) in trunk diameter. As a young tree it has a narrow, erect habit but with age adopts a flat-topped shape with massive spreading limbs. The dark green needles are up to 1½ in (35 mm) long. It prefers a moist, cool climate. 'Aurea-Prostrata' is a dwarf form with golden foliage; 'Nana' is a very dwarf, slow-growing cultivar of semi-prostrate habit suited to rock gardens; **'Pendula'** is a weeping form, usually grafted onto a standard. *Cedrus libani* subsp. *stenocoma* is the geographical race from mountains of southwestern Turkey; it has a more narrowly conical or columnar growth habit. **ZONES 6–9.**

Cedrus libani

CELTIS

NETTLE TREE, HACKBERRY

This large genus of 70 species includes many evergreens, occurring mainly in the tropics, but the cool-climate, deciduous species from North America, Europe and Asia are the ones mostly cultivated. They are medium to fairly large trees with smooth or slightly rough bark. The leaves are smallish, oval and pointed at the tip, with few or many marginal teeth. Insignificant flowers, of different sexes and lacking petals, appear with the new leaves, and the fruits are small, hard drupes carried singly in the leaf axils. Birds eat the fruits and disperse the seeds, and some species self-seed and can become a nuisance. *Celtis* species are planted mainly as shade trees in streets and parks, where they make shapely, long-lived and trouble-free specimens.

CULTIVATION

In cooler climates, these fully frost-hardy trees like dry soil and full sun; in warmer areas they prefer rich, moist, well-drained soil and part-shade. Propagate from seed in autumn.

CERCIDIPHYLLUM

KATSURA TREE

Consisting of a single species of deciduous tree native to Japan and China, this genus is placed in a family of its own, allied to the magnolia family. The dull red flowers are rather insignificant, with different sexes on different trees. On female trees clusters of small greenish pod-like fruit follow the flowers. The katsura tree is valued chiefly for its foliage, which is reddish when first expanding in spring, then dark green, changing in autumn to various mixtures of yellow, pink, orange and red. Katsura is its Japanese name.

CULTIVATION

This tree prefers rich, moist but well-drained soil in a sunny or part-shaded position. It is fully frost hardy but the spring foliage is easily damaged by late frost, very dry conditions or drying winds. Propagate from seed or cuttings.

Cercidiphyllum japonicum

In cultivation in the West *Cercidiphyllum japonicum* is known as a small, rather slender tree to about 40 ft (12 m) high, but in Japan and China it is the largest native deciduous tree—ancient specimens up to 130 ft (40 m) tall, with trunks over 15 ft (4.5 m) in diameter, are known. The trunk often forks at a narrow angle and the short branches spread horizontally in tiers. The heart-shaped leaves are mostly under 3 in (8 cm) wide, but larger in *C. j.* var. *magnificum*; the Chinese *C. j.* var. *sinense* has slightly different leaves and flowers. 'Pendulum' has a dome-shaped crown and pendulous branches. **ZONES 6–9.**

Celtis occidentalis

Celtis occidentalis

AMERICAN HACKBERRY

This species comes from the east of the USA, the Mississippi Basin and eastern Canada. In its preferred habitat of forests in deep, rich, alluvial soils it can reach a very large size, but when planted in the open it makes a shapely, spreading tree of 40–60 ft (12–18 m). The bark, smooth on saplings, becomes rough as the tree matures. The pea-sized fruit ripen through red to dull purple. The foliage turns pale yellow in autumn; it can become a pest along riverbanks and channels in some countries. **ZONES 3–10.**

Cercidiphyllum japonicum 'Pendulum'

CERCIS

JUDAS TREE, REDBUD

Cercis siliquastrum

This genus is made up of small, deciduous trees or shrubs from North America, Asia and southern Europe. Their profuse clusters of pea-like flowers, bright rose pink to crimson, line the bare branches in spring; even the neat, pointed buds, slightly deeper in color, make an elegant display, hence the American name redbud. The handsome, heart-shaped to almost circular leaves follow, along with flat seed pods up to 4 in (10 cm) long.

CULTIVATION

All 7 or 8 species are worth cultivating, though not all are easily obtained. They resent disturbance to their roots, especially transplanting. A sunny position suits them best and they thrive in hot, dry summer weather, as long as the soil moisture is adequate in winter and spring. They are easily propagated from seed, though growth is often slow and it may take many years for them to become larger than shrub size.

Cercis canadensis

EASTERN REDBUD

Native to eastern and central USA, this tree can reach 40 ft (12 m) in the wild and is strikingly beautiful in flower. In gardens it rarely exceeds 12 ft (3.5 m), branching close to the ground. The leaves are heart-shaped with a distinct point, and appear after the flowers. The buds are deep rose, and the paler rose flowers are profuse and showy; flowering may continue from spring into early summer. 'Forest Pansy' has purple-colored leaves. In the southwestern part of its range the typical form is replaced by *Cercis canadensis* var. *texensis*, whose leaf undersides have a waxy bluish coating. **ZONES 5–9.**

Cercis siliquastrum

JUDAS TREE, LOVE TREE

Native to regions close to the Mediterranean and Black Sea coasts, this tree seldom exceeds 25 ft (8 m) even after several decades. The leaves are slightly bluish green with rounded tips, and the late spring flowers, larger and deeper pinkish magenta than in other species, arise in clusters on previous years' growths. It is the most reliable ornamental species in regions where winters are mild. Forms with distinct flower coloration include the white 'Alba' and the deeper reddish 'Rubra'. **ZONES 7–9.**

Cercis canadensis 'Forest Pansy'

Chamaecyparis lawsoniana 'Golden Wonder'

CHAMAECYPARIS

FALSE CYPRESS

In the nineteenth century botanists classified these conifers as *Cupressus* (true cypresses), and indeed the differences are slight—the latter genus has its tiny branchlets more flattened with the scale-like leaves of two types, and the cones are smaller and release their seed earlier. Nearly all the 8 *Chamaecyparis* species occur in cooler, moister, more northerly regions in North America and eastern Asia, while the true cypresses mostly occur further south and in drier regions. Several species have many cultivars, which feature colored foliage (usually gold, bluish or bronze); narrow, fastigiate, columnar or dwarf habit; bizarre foliage traits; or needle-like juvenile foliage.

CULTIVATION

These frost-hardy trees grow well in a cool, moist climate; they respond with fast growth to deep, rich, well-drained soil and a sheltered position. Cultivars are easily propagated from cuttings, the typical tree forms from seed.

Chamaecyparis lawsoniana 'Erecta Aurea'

Chamaecyparis lawsoniana

Chamaecyparis lawsoniana

PORT ORFORD CEDAR, LAWSON CYPRESS

From the humid coastal forests of northwestern USA, this is the most widely planted member of the genus in its typical form, as well having given rise to a larger number of cultivars than almost any other conifer species. Planted trees are up to120 ft (36 m) tall with trunks up to 4 ft (1.2 m) in diameter, narrowly conical with pendulous side branches producing rippling curtains of bluish green to deep green foliage. Over 180 cultivars are currently available and many more have been named. 'Alumii', of erect, conical habit with very bluish, dense foliage, grows to 10–25 ft (3–4.5 m) or more. 'Argentea Compacta' is a dwarf shrub with green foliage variegated with cream. 'Aurea Densa' has golden-yellow foliage. 'Croftway' has gray foliage fading to dark green. 'Ellwoodii' is a dense, conical shrub with blue-tinged foliage. 'Erecta' is plain green with very erect, narrow sprays of foliage tightly crowded together; it can reach 30 ft (9 m) with age. 'Erecta Aurea' grows upright and has bright yellow foliage. 'Fletcheri' has gray-blue foliage in smaller, less regular sprays and is semi-juvenile, the leaves somewhat needle-like. 'Green Globe' is a dense dwarf cultivar to 18 in (45 cm) with fine, dark green foliage. 'Lane' makes a narrower column with lemony yellow foliage in late spring and summer changing to bronze-gold in winter. 'Lemon Queen' has pale yellow foliage and 'Golden Wonder' is very similar. 'Pembury Blue' bears pendent sprays of silvery blue foliage. 'Stewartii', a golden cultivar, rapidly reaches 15–25 ft (4.5–8 m), with a broad base and crowded nodding sprays of rich buttery foliage; it is often used in landscaping for a gold effect on a large scale. 'Wisselii' grows to 80 ft (24 m) and is a narrowly conical tree with bluish green foliage. 'Winston Churchill' is a popular recent cultivar; it has a pronounced conical growth habit and golden-yellow foliage. **ZONES 6–10.**

Chamaecyparis nootkatensis

NOOTKA CYPRESS, ALASKA CEDAR,

From western North America, this cypress ranges much further north than *Chamaecyparis lawsoniana*, up through the west coast of Canada right into Alaska. A large, conical, forest tree, growing to about 100 ft (30 m) in height and 25 ft (8 m) in spread; the small blue-green cones have a recurved, pointed flap at the center of each scale. *C. nootkatensis* is an attractive tree and thrives under more adverse conditions of soil and climate. 'Pendula' has vertically hanging sprays of foliage and an open crown in maturity. **ZONES 4–9.**

Chamaecyparis nootkatensis

Chamaecyparis obtusa 'Crippsii'

Chamaecyparis obtusa 'Nana Gracilis'

Chamaecyparis obtusa

HINOKI CYPRESS, HINOKI FALSE CYPRESS

The normal, tall form of this fine tree from Japan, with richly textured, deep green foliage, is seldom seen in gardens; the species is usually represented by its dwarf or colored cultivars. One of Japan's most valued timber trees, it reaches 120 ft (36 m) in the wild with a trunk to 4 ft (1.2 m) in diameter and thick, red-brown bark. In cultivation it grows 60 ft (18 m) high, broadly columnar with dense, spreading branches that touch the ground. 'Crippsii' makes a broad, golden pyramid with a vigorous leading shoot and is usually about 10–15 ft (3–4.5 m) tall. 'Tetragona' and 'Tetragona Aurea' are of similar height but narrower and more irregularly branched, their scale leaves in 4 equal ranks and branchlets tightly crowded; the former is a deep, slightly bluish green, the latter green and gold. Of the dwarf cultivars, the smallest under 12 in (30 cm) in height, the best known are 'Flabelliformis', with pale green leaves to 6 in (15 cm); 'Kosteri' with apple-green foliage; 'Minima', under 4 in (10 cm) after 20 years and with mid-green foliage; 'Nana', a spreading tree to 3 ft (1 m) in height; 'Nana Gracilis' and its many variants, little bun-shaped plants normally 12–24 in (30–60 cm) high with crowded fans of tiny branchlets producing a richly textured effect; 'Nana Aurea', which has golden tips to the fans and more of a bronze tone in winter; and 'Verdon' with yellow-green young growth. **ZONES 5–10.**

Chamaecyparis pisifera

SAWARA CYPRESS, SAWARA FALSE CYPRESS

Chamaecyparis pisifera 'Nana'

Growing to 150 ft (45 m) in the wild, this vigorous Japanese species makes a broad, conical tree; the lower sides of the branchlets are strongly marked bluish white and the tiny scale leaves on juvenile growth are quite prickly. The cultivars fall into 4 groups: the **Squarrosa Group**, the **Plumosa Group** (the largest group), the **Filifera Group** and the **Nana Group**. 'Squarrosa' itself is a broadly pyramidal tree to 65 ft (20 m) with pale bluish gray juvenile foliage that turns dull purple in winter. 'Squarrosa Intermedia' is a dwarf cultivar. 'Boulevard' is narrowly conical, to 10 ft (3 m), with foliage of a bright steel blue mixed with green. The Plumosa Group includes 'Plumosa', a conical or columnar tree to 20 ft (6 m) with mid-green foliage, the leaves shorter and less prickly than 'Squarrosa'; '**Plumosa Aurea**' with yellow-green foliage; and '**Plumosa Compressa**', a dwarf cultivar to 18 in (45 cm) with yellowish green foliage. Of the Filifera Group, the best known are: '**Filifera**', with slender shoots and dark green leaves, seldom grown now; '**Filifera Aurea**', a broadly pyramidal shrub of up to 10 ft (3 m); its bright gold and green foliage has flattened fans of branchlets mixed with elongated 'rat's tail' branch-lets that arch gracefully. 'Nana' is a hemispherical shrub with very crowded, tiny sprays of foliage; it can take 10 years or more to reach 12 in (30 cm). **ZONES 5–10.**

Chamaecyparis thyoides

Chamaecyparis thyoides

ATLANTIC WHITE CEDAR, SOUTHERN WHITE CEDAR

From eastern North America, this very frost-hardy tree reaches about 60 ft (18 m) in the wild, less in cultivation. It is narrowly columnar when young. The dull gray-green branchlets are grouped into very small fans crowded irregularly on the branches and do not produce the rippled foliage effect of most other species. '**Andelyensis**' is a conical form with bluish green leaves. '**Ericoides**' makes a broad pyramid 6–8 ft (1.8–2.4 m) high; its soft, persistent, juvenile foliage is bronze-green in spring and summer, changing to deep plum tones in winter. '**Red Star**' is a compact tree to 6 ft (1.8 m) with soft, feathery, silvery green foliage turning rich purple in winter. **ZONES 4–9.**

Chamaecyparis pisifera 'Plumosa'

CHIONANTHUS

Chionanthus virginicus

FRINGE TREE

Belonging to the olive family, the genus *Chionanthus* used to be regarded as consisting of only 2 species of deciduous trees, one from temperate North America and one from China, but botanists have now transferred to it a large number of tropical evergreens from the genus *Linociera*. The deciduous species, though, are of most interest to gardeners. In late spring the crowns of these small trees are sprinkled with clusters of delicate white flowers—each slender-stalked flower has 4 narrow, diverging white petals. A good specimen in full flower is outstandingly beautiful. The smooth-margined leaves are in opposite pairs, and the summer fruits are like small olives.

CULTIVATION

These cool-climate trees are easily grown but may be slow to increase in size and can take 10 years to flower. A sunny but sheltered position with good soil and drainage suits them best. Propagate from seed in autumn.

Chionanthus retusus

CHINESE FRINGE TREE

Native to China and Taiwan, this tree can reach 30 ft (9 m), developing a broad, umbrella-like crown with age. The shiny leaves vary in shape and size on the one tree. The flowers, with petals about 1 in (25 mm) long, are borne in profuse, upright clusters that stand above the foliage in late spring or early summer. This seems to be the more climatically adaptable of the 2 species, flowering equally well in both cool and warm, even subtropical regions. **ZONES 6–10.**

Chionanthus virginicus

AMERICAN FRINGE TREE

The individual flowers of this species are similar to those of *Chionanthus retusus*, but the leaves are larger and less shiny and the longer, drooping flower sprays appear among the foliage rather than standing above it. In its native forests of southeastern USA it grows in rich, moist soil close to streams, occasionally 30 ft (9 m) tall but often only a shrub. Away from its native regions it can be a bit of a shy bloomer, performing better in continental climates of central Europe than in the UK and not doing so well in climates warmer than that. **ZONES 5–9.**

Chionanthus retusus

Cladrastis lutea
syn. Cladrastis kentukea
AMERICAN YELLOWWOOD

The natural range of this species is from North Carolina to Alabama and Missouri, in rich soils on hill slopes or along ravines near streams. There it grows to 60 ft (18 m) with a trunk diameter to 3 ft (1 m), forking not far above the ground with steeply angled limbs. In cultivation it rarely exceeds 30 ft (9 m). The leaves consist of 5 to 9 broad, veined leaflets that are a fresh, rich green in summer turning yellow in autumn. White flowers appear in early summer. Some trees flower only every second year. **ZONES 6–10.**

CLADRASTIS
YELLOWWOOD

This genus of 5 species of deciduous small leguminous trees occurs wild in eastern USA, Japan and China. The pinnate leaves have rather few leaflets and the pendulous sprays of small to medium-sized, fragrant white or pinkish pea-flowers that appear in summer are slightly reminiscent of *Wisteria* flowers. The flowers are followed by flattened pods, each containing a row of small, hard seeds. They are elegant trees, valued for their late flowering and, in the case of the American species, for their autumn foliage.

CULTIVATION

Fully frost hardy, they prefer full sun and fertile, well-drained soil. They need protection from strong winds as the wood is brittle. Propagate from seed in autumn or from cuttings in winter.

Cladrastis lutea

Clethra barbinervis

CLETHRA

A scattering of deciduous tree and shrub species across North America and eastern Asia, plus a larger number of evergreens in warmer climates, principally Southeast Asia, and one outlying species on the island of Madeira make up the total of 30 species in this genus. The frost-hardy deciduous species mostly behave as spreading shrubs in cultivation, producing a thicket of stems concealed by dense foliage. The leaves are thin textured with closely toothed margins. In summer and autumn, small white flowers are borne in delicate loose sprays among the leaves, followed by numerous, tiny seed capsules.

CULTIVATION

Clethras prefer sheltered, moist spots half-shaded by taller trees and peaty, acid, moist but well-drained soil. They can be propagated from seed, cuttings or layers.

Clethra barbinervis
JAPANESE CLETHRA

This species from mountain woodlands of Japan can make a 30 ft (9 m) tree in the wild with peeling orange-brown bark. In gardens it usually makes a shrub of less than 10 ft (3 m) with crowded stems that tend to lean outward and strongly veined leaves with a fuzz of very short hairs on the veins. The attractive flowers appear in short panicles at the branch tips. **ZONES 6–9.**

CORNUS

CORNEL, DOGWOOD

Cornus controversa

About 45 species of shrubs, trees and even 1 or 2 herbaceous perennials make up this genus, widely distributed in temperate regions of the northern hemisphere. They include deciduous and evergreen species, all with simple, smooth-edged leaves that characteristically have prominent, inward-curving veins. Flowers are small, mostly greenish, yellowish or dull purplish: few are decorative, but in one group of species they are arranged in dense heads surrounded by large white, pink or yellow bracts that can be showy. Another shrubby group has small panicles of flowers that are not at all showy, but the stems and twigs are often bright red or yellow, giving a decorative effect especially when leafless in winter. One such species is the common European dogwood, *Cornus sanguinea*. The fleshy fruits are also ornamental.

CULTIVATION

The various species all do best in sun or very light shade. Most appreciate a rich, fertile, well-drained soil, though some of the multi-stemmed shrub species will grow well in boggy ground. Many are quite frost hardy but *Cornus capitata* will tolerate only light frosts. The species with decorative red stems can be cut back annually almost to ground level to encourage new growths, which have the best color. Propagate from seed or rooted layers struck in a moist sand-peat mixture.

Cornus controversa 'Variegata'

Cornus controversa

TABLE DOGWOOD, GIANT DOGWOOD

Native to China, Korea and Japan, this handsome deciduous species grows about 40 ft (12 m), with a straight trunk and horizontal tiers of foliage. The glossy, strongly veined leaves are arranged alternately on the reddish twigs, a feature shared by *Cornus alternifolia* only. In bloom it is one of the showiest of the species lacking large bracts, with white flowers in flat clusters about 4 in (10 cm) across borne in early summer. The fruit are shiny black, and autumn foliage is red to purplish. 'Variegata' has leaves with creamy white margins. **ZONES 6–9.**

Cornus florida

FLOWERING DOGWOOD

Popular for its beauty and reliability, this species reaches 20 ft (6 m) or more tall with a single, somewhat crooked trunk, and in mid-spring bears an abundance of flowerheads, each with 4 large white or rose-pink bracts. In late summer the scattered red fruit make a fine showing, and in autumn the foliage is scarlet and deep purple with a whitish bloom on the leaf undersides. It prefers a warm summer and may not flower well in cool-summer climates. 'Rubra' has dark rose bracts that are paler at the base. 'Apple Blossom' has pale pink flower bracts. **ZONES 5–9.**

Cornus florida 'Rubra'

Cornus kousa

Cornus kousa
JAPANESE FLOWERING DOGWOOD, KOUSA

Occurring wild in Japan, China and Korea, *Cornus kousa* can reach 20 ft (6 m) or more at maturity with dense, deep green foliage and tiered lower branches. In early summer when the leaves have fully expanded, the flowerheads with large, pure white bracts appear, each bract tapering to an acute point. The small compound fruit are dull red. As popular in gardens as the typical Japanese race is, *C. k.* var. *chinensis* has slightly larger 'flowers' and more vigorous growth. **ZONES 6–9.**

Cornus mas

Cornus mas
CORNELIAN CHERRY

When it flowers in late winter or early spring on the leafless branches, this tree species looks unlike most other dogwoods. The flowers are tiny and golden yellow, grouped in small clusters without decorative bracts, but so profuse on the small twigs as well as on thicker branches, that they make a fine display. Stiff and rather narrow at first, with maturity it becomes a spreading tree of 25 ft (8 m) or so. Edible fruit ripen bright red in late summer. Native to central and southeastern Europe, *Cornus mas* provides winter color for streets, parks and gardens. '**Variegata**' has white-margined leaves. **ZONES 6–9.**

Cornus nuttallii
PACIFIC DOGWOOD

In the wild, in the Pacific Northwest of North America, this is a slender tree to 50 ft (15 m), but in gardens is often only a tall shrub. The flowerheads are 4–5 in (10–12 cm) across with 4 to 7 pure white bracts, ageing pinkish, and the small cluster of flowers at their center is dull purple. Flowering occurs from mid-spring to early summer. The autumn foliage is yellow and red. This beautiful but short-lived tree is somewhat frost tender, but thrives in a cool, rainy climate in a part-shaded position. **ZONES 7–9.**

Crataegus diffusa

CRATAEGUS

HAWTHORN, MAY

Native to cool-climate areas of the northern hemisphere, this genus belongs to the pome-fruit group of the rose family and the resemblance of the fruits to miniature apples obvious. Most of the 200 species have long, sharp thorns on the summer growths; the leaves are either toothed or lobed, and the white or rarely pink flowers are clustered in flat to rounded umbels in late spring or summer. They are followed in autumn by fruits mostly in shades of red, often also with attractive foliage colors.

CULTIVATION

Hawthorns are robust, frost-hardy, deciduous trees, most of them compact enough even for quite small gardens. They are sun-lovers and not very fussy about soil type or drainage. Some species sucker from the base, but suckers can be removed to produce a tree form. Some hawthorns are prone to fireblight, controlled only by prompt removal and burning of affected branches. Foliage may also be disfigured by the 'pear and cherry slug' (larva of a sawfly); spray severe attacks with an insecticide. Propagate from cold-stratified seed, or by grafting of named clones. In winter they are easily transplanted.

Crataegus diffusa

Another species from the northeastern USA, it grows up to 30 ft (10 m), the branches armed with long spines. Leaves are pale green and shallowly lobed. Umbels of smallish white flowers in late spring or early summer are followed by red fruit about ⅜ in (9 mm) in diameter. **ZONES 4–9.**

Crataegus flava

YELLOW HAW, SUMMER HAW

This species is believed native to eastern USA, but is not now found in the wild. It is a tree with smallish, smooth, toothed or shallowly lobed leaves, fairly large white flowers borne in early summer, and greenish yellow fruit about ⅝ in (15 mm) in diameter. It is not one of the more ornamental hawthorns. **ZONES 4–9.**

Crataegus laevigata

syn. *Crataegus oxyacantha*

MIDLAND HAWTHORN, MAY, ENGLISH HAWTHORN

This small tree reaches 25 ft (8 m) or more in height and spread. Native to Europe and North Africa, *Crataegus laevigata* is easily confused with the English may *(C. monogyna)*, both these species having once been called *C. oxyacantha*. It has mid- to dark green, glossy leaves with shallow, rounded lobes and produces few thorns. In late spring, the plant comes truly alive, when an abundance of vibrant white flowers open. The cultivar **'Paul's Scarlet'** has bright crimson, double flowers opening in late spring; **'Punicea'** has deep pink single flowers with white centers; **'Punicea Flore Pleno'** is similar but with double flowers. The flowers last well when cut for indoor decoration. **ZONES 4–9.**

Crataegus laevigata 'Punicea Flore Pleno'

Crataegus phaenopyrum

Crataegus × lavallei

Crataegus × lavallei

syn. Crataegus × carrierei
LAVALLE HAWTHORN, CARRIERE HAWTHORN

This hybrid originated in France in about 1880, the result of a cross between *Crataegus crus-galli* and *C. pubescens*. It forms a densely branched, almost thornless tree of 15–20 ft (4.5–6 m). The broad, irregularly toothed leaves are darker glossy green than most hawthorns and are semi-evergreen in warmer climates. The white flowers with red stamens open in loose clusters in early summer, and are followed by large yellow fruit, ripening to orange-red. Its autumn foliage tones intensify after the first hard frost. **ZONES 6–10.**

Crataegus monogyna subsp. azarella

Crataegus monogyna

HAWTHORN, MAY

Native to Europe, this small tree is most commonly cultivated as a hedgerow, but when growing wild it can reach 30 ft (9 m). The leaves have 5 to 7 jagged lobes, and turn yellow-brown in autumn. The fragrant, single white flowers open in late spring, mid-May in England though according to the old calendar they opened around May Day (1 May). The small dark red fruit that follow hang onto the twigs into winter. *Crataegus laevigata* is very similar, but *C. monogyna* is easily distinguished by its single style and fruit stone. *C. monogyna* subsp. *azarella* has leaves with very downy undersides. **ZONES 4–9.**

Crataegus phaenopyrum

syn. Crataegus cordata
WASHINGTON THORN

From southeastern USA, this elegant though very thorny tree reaches 20–30 ft (6–9 m), forming a round-headed, densely branched tree with long, sharp thorns. The leaves have 3 to 5 sharply toothed lobes, and are glossy green. Fragrant white flowers in mid-summer are followed in autumn by profuse clusters of small, shiny orange-red berries. **ZONES 4–10.**

Crataegus pubescens
syns *Crataegus mexicana*,
C. stipulacea
MEXICAN HAWTHORN

This semi-evergreen species from the mountains of Mexico reaches 15–30 ft (4.5–9 m) and is often entirely thornless. The oblong, leathery leaves are coarsely toothed and dark satiny green with downy undersides. Clusters of white flowers with pink stamens are produced in mid-spring, followed in autumn by large edible fruit that ripen to butter yellow; they are sold in markets in some Mexican towns. **ZONES 7–10.**

Crataegus punctata
THICKET HAWTHORN

This species from eastern USA makes an attractive tree, growing to about 30 ft (9 m) with a stout trunk and crown of horizontally spreading branches. It has broad dark green leaves with toothed or slightly lobed margins and downy on the undersides. In early summer it produces clusters of white blossom up to 4 in (10 cm) wide. The fruit are large, slightly pear-shaped, dull crimson with paler dots. It is one of the most ornamental of the North American species. **'Aurea'** has yellow fruit. **ZONES 5–9.**

Crataegus punctata

Crataegus viridis
GREEN HAWTHORN

Making a small tree of up to about 30 ft (9 m), this species from southeastern USA has fairly broad, glossy dark green leaves that are toothed or lobed in the upper half; in late spring–early summer it bears white flowers in small and rather sparse clusters, followed by smallish red fruit. **'Winter King'** is a superior cultivar with silvery bark, a vase-like form with relatively few thorns, good red autumn color and bright red fruit that last well into winter. **ZONES 4–9.**

Crataegus viridis 'Winter King'

Crataegus pubescens

CRYPTOMERIA

JAPANESE CEDAR, SUGI

Only one species is generally accepted in this conifer genus from China and Japan, though many variations have been named. Often fast-growing, the branches and branchlets of this evergreen are clothed in short, leathery needle leaves that are densely overlapping and curve inward slightly. Male (pollen) and female (seed) cones are on the same tree, the former in profuse clusters and releasing clouds of pollen in spring, the latter in sparser groups behind the branch tips. Its handsome shape and uniformity of growth make it highly suitable for windbreaks, hedges and avenues. In Japan it is grown for its timber, but is also venerated in historic groves and avenues.

CULTIVATION

Very frost hardy, it prefers full sun or part-shade and deep, fertile, moist but well-drained soil. It likes plenty of water. Propagation is from seed, or from cuttings for the cultivars.

Cryptomeria japonica 'Elegans'

Cryptomeria japonica 'Elegans Nana'

Cryptomeria japonica 'Globosa Nana'

Cryptomeria japonica

This species can make rapid growth, to 20–25 ft (6–8 m) in 10 years; old trees in Japan are up to 150 ft (45 m) high, with massive trunks. The bark is thick and brown with straight, vertical furrows. Growth habit is conical with a long, pointed leader. The Japanese race has thicker branchlets and stiffer habit than the Chinese one, *Cryptomeria japonica* var. *sinensis*. There are at least 50 cultivars, most dwarf but a few approaching the wild types in size. The best known of the taller ones is '**Elegans**', which makes a solid column of foliage of up to 30 ft (9 m) high and 8 ft (2.4 m) across; the needles remain long and soft, and in winter the whole tree turns a striking dull bronze or plum color. '**Elegans Nana**' is similar but a dwarf form. '**Araucarioides**', with a bizarre tangle of long rat's tail branches, reaches 10 ft (3 m) and makes an interesting foliage contrast in a mixed conifer planting. '**Globosa Nana**', the most popular lower-growing cultivar, makes a dense ball with intricate branching that is soft to the touch; it is plain green, with paler green new growth in spring and summer. While listed as a dwarf, in good soil it may grow to 10 ft (3 m) across in only 15 years. '**Bandai-Sugi**' makes a globose plant that becomes irregular in shape after a time, to 6 ft (1.8 m); the foliage is thick and turns dull bronze in winter. '**Jindai-Sugi**' is a slow-growing bush, irregularly shaped with a flattish top; foliage is bright green and dense. The very tiny '**Vilmoriniana**' grows to about 12 in (30 cm) high and is suitable for rockeries. It has also been successfully grown in containers. **ZONES 7–10.**

CUNNINGHAMIA

CHINESE CEDAR, CHINA FIR

This unusual conifer genus is native to China, Taiwan and Indo-china. The stiff, springy, curved leaves taper to prickly points and have glossy upper surfaces. Dead leaves remain attached to the branches, making the interior of the trees untidy and prickly, but a well-grown specimen is among the more attractive conifers. Although quite handsome and not difficult to grow, *Cunninghamia* species are found mostly in botanical gardens and larger private collections.

CULTIVATION

Fully frost hardy, they require adequate rainfall and deep, fertile soil. Propagation is normally from seed, though seed set may be poor, or from cuttings.

Cunninghamia lanceolata

Cunninghamia lanceolata

COFFIN PINE, COFFIN FIR, CHINA FIR

In China, where it once had an extensive natural distribution, this tree provided a valued timber for coffins (it was thought the aromatic timber prevented bodies from decomposing), resulting in its over-exploitation. Trees of 150 ft (45 m) tall were recorded there, but in parks and gardens elsewhere it is mainly seen as a tree of 20–40 ft (6–12 m), sometimes multi-trunked and widest at the top, sometimes narrower with a single, straight trunk and scattered clumps of lateral branches. The growth rate is likewise unpredictable, and it may remain shrubby for many years. **ZONES 6–10.**

× CUPRESSOCYPARIS

The '×' in front of the name indicates that this is a bigeneric hybrid, that is, a hybrid between 2 different genera, in this case *Cupressus* and *Chamaecyparis*. Although the name applies to any hybrid between these genera (including later generations and backcrosses), it is best known in the form of the one which first appeared in England in 1888 as a chance hybrid between the frost-hardy *Chamaecyparis nootkatensis* and the less hardy *Cupressus macrocarpa*. Two additional hybrids have since been raised, their *Cupressus* parents being *C. glabra* and *C. lusitanica* respectively.

CULTIVATION

These conifers combine rapid growth with reasonable frost hardiness, and adapt well to poorly drained soil but not to arid climates. They are widely planted for fast-growing hedges as they respond well to frequent trimming. However, if they are left untrimmed they rapidly grow to tree size. Propagate from cuttings, which strike readily under nursery conditions. Although seed is fertile, the resulting seedlings might vary.

× *Cupressocyparis leylandii*

LEYLAND CYPRESS

Representing the original cross between *Chamaecyparis nootkatensis* and *Cupressus macrocarpa*, this name encompasses a number of seedling clones, some of which have been named as cultivars. When used without specifying a cultivar name it usually refers to 'Haggerston Grey' or 'Leighton Green', which both make very vigorous, upright trees with a long, open leading shoot and slightly irregular outline; foliage is deep green or slightly grayish. In good soil it will reach 30 ft (9 m) in 10 years and double that in 30 years, ultimately growing to 100 ft (30 m) or more. 'Naylor's Blue' has more strongly bluish green foliage and is more columnar in habit. **ZONES 5–10.**

× Cupressocyparis leylandii

CUPRESSUS

Cupressus arizonica

CYPRESS

This important conifer genus has been cultivated since Classical times but its species are seldom planted where winters are severe due to their limited cold tolerance. The majority of the 20 or so species occur wild in western USA, Mexico and Guatemala, with a smaller number in the Himalayas and western China and a single species in the Mediterranean region. As well as the wild forms the cypresses include many cultivars. They are handsome ornamentals that come in many foliage hues; they range from tall to dwarf, from columnar to weeping or high-crowned and spreading. Their dense foliage and rapid growth makes them especially useful for screens and windbreaks.

CULTIVATION

Some species are very tolerant of dry conditions, others need a moister climate. Soil and sunlight requirements vary, although generally they prefer full sun, well-drained soil and protection from cold winds. They are easy to propagate from seed, always plentiful on adult trees, and cultivars are almost as easily raised from cuttings. However, some cypress species suffer from the disease cypress canker, which disfigures the trees and finally kills them.

Cupressus arizonica
ARIZONA CYPRESS, ROUGH-BARKED ARIZONA CYPRESS

Originating in Arizona, USA, and sometimes confused with *Cupressus glabra*, this pyramidal species will grow to 50 ft (15 m). Its mature foliage is gray-green and does not display the white spots of the smooth Arizona cypress. It has short-stalked, large, round cones, up to 1 in (25 mm) across, and a brown, stringy and furrowed bark. It is grown both as a specimen tree and as a hedge. **ZONES 7–10.**

Cupressus macrocarpa

Cupressus glabra
syn. **Cupressus arizonica** var. **glabra**
SMOOTH ARIZONA CYPRESS

This species comes from the mountains of western Arizona, an area of low rainfall and quite low winter temperatures. With compact blue-gray foliage marked with white resin dots, waxy whitish twigs and reddish, flaking bark, it is highly ornamental; it is especially popular in warm regions with hot dry summers. Under such conditions it makes vigorous growth, is long lived, and is resistant to pests and diseases. There are different forms in cultivation, some fairly narrowly conical and others with much broader, looser crowns. It varies also in the blueness of its foliage, and seedlings can be selected for this character. Mature specimens are usually 30–40 ft (9–12 m) in height. **ZONES 7–10.**

Cupressus macrocarpa
MONTEREY CYPRESS

Endemic to a very short stretch of the central Californian coast near Monterey, this grows into one of the largest of all cypresses, reaching 120 ft (36 m) tall with a trunk diameter of 8 ft (2.4 m). When planted in a grove it forms a tall, straight trunk, but in the open in good soil it branches low with massive, spreading limbs, producing a broad, dense crown of deep green with a rather spiky outline. Close up, the foliage is rather coarse, and it has a slightly sour smell when bruised. The cones are large and wrinkled. It grows best in cool but mild climates with winter rainfall and takes only 10 years or so to form a dense 30–40 ft

(9–12 m) tree. It is one of the most popular farm hedging trees in New Zealand. Golden cultivars include 'Brunniana', somewhat columnar, the foliage ageing almost green; the vigorous 'Aurea', with long, golden spikes of foliage spreading almost horizontally; and 'Aurea Saligna' with remarkable weeping, gold-tipped branchlets and elongated scale leaves. A lower-growing cultivar to 4 ft (1.2 m) is 'Greenstead Magnificent', which spreads to form a flat-topped, dense mat of pale gray-green foliage, drooping around the edges; as the plant ages the whole becomes raised above the ground on a short trunk. 'Goldcrest' is a small conical form with golden foliage. **ZONES 7–10.**

Cupressus macrocarpa 'Greenstead Magnificent'

Cupressus torulosa
BHUTAN CYPRESS, HIMALAYAN CYPRESS

This tall conifer reaches 150 ft (45 m) in its native Himalayas, though in cultivation 50–80 ft (15–24 m) is more usual. An elegant tree with a long pointed crown broader at the base, it is valued for its fast growth and fragrant timber. Its small branchlets are slender and slightly curved, consisting of tiny deep green scale leaves that are blunt tipped. The small cones are purple when young but ripen shiny brown, and the brown fiberous bark peels into strips. It grows best in mild, very moist climates. **ZONES 8–10.**

Cupressus torulosa

Cupressus torulosa

DAVIDIA

DOVE TREE, HANDKERCHIEF TREE

This genus contains just one species, though some varieties occur. In China, it can reach over 60 ft (18 m), with a rounded crown, and in full flower it is one of the most striking of all deciduous trees outside the tropics. 'Like huge butterflies hovering' is how plant explorer E. H. Wilson described the long-stalked flowerheads, each nestled between 2 large, drooping white or cream bracts. The surface of the large, soft, toothed leaves is deeply creased by veins.

CULTIVATION

The tree is always raised from its large seeds, enclosed in a plum-like fruit about 1½ in (35 mm) long. Cold treatment assists germination. It is frost hardy, but the bracts need protecting from wind. It needs rich, porous soil and full sun or part-shade. Propagate from the whole fruit, which may take up to 3 years to germinate.

Dracaena draco

DRACAENA

Most of the species belonging to this genus are shrubs, and detailed information on the genus is given in the Shrubs chapter. However, *Dracaena draco* is treated here as a tree.

Davidia involucrata

This conical tree has broad leaves up to 6 in (15 cm) long, and small, deep set, brownish red flowers surrounded by 2 white bracts of unequal lengths. The greenish brown, pendent, ridged fruit are up to 2 in (5 cm) across. The more commonly cultivated form is *Davidia involucrata* var. *vilmoriniana*, which has paler and less downy leaf undersides. **ZONES 7–9.**

Davidia involucrata var. *vilmoriniana*

Dracaena draco

DRAGON'S-BLOOD TREE, DRAGON TREE

This slow-growing tree from the Canary Islands is long lived. It may reach 30 ft (9 m) high with a trunk to 3 ft (1 m) in diameter and a crown of rosettes of stiff, lance-shaped, blue-green leaves to 24 in (60 cm) long and nearly 2 in (5 cm) wide. It bears insignificant flowers followed by orange berries in summer. It needs protection from frosts and is suitable for container growing. **ZONES 10–11.**

Dracaena draco

Erica arborea 'Alpina'

ERICA

HEATH

The great majority of species in this large genus are shrubs and are described in detail in the chapter on Shrubs. The species described below is more usually treated as a tree.

Erica arborea

TREE HEATH, BRUYÈRE

The largest of the heaths, this frost-hardy species also has the widest distribution, from the Canary Islands and Portugal right across to Iran and south through the high mountains of Arabia, Ethiopia and equatorial Africa, where it forms mist-shrouded forests of trees 20 ft (6 m) high with stout trunks. It has contorted woody stems, finely fiberous bark and dark green needle-like leaves. It bears masses of small white flowers in spring. 'Alpina' is less than 6 ft (1.8 m) high, has bright green foliage and white flowers in dense cylindrical racemes. Protect from winter frosts. **ZONES 8–10.**

EUCALYPTUS

EUCALYPT, GUM TREE

Australia is the original home of all but a few of over 700 species that make up this genus of evergreen trees of the myrtle family. But eucalypts are possibly the world's most widely planted trees, especially in drier subtropical and tropical regions, for example in Africa, the Middle East, India, and South America. They are renowned for their fast height growth and ability to thrive on poor or degraded land, providing shelter, timber and fuel—even stands of 5-year-old saplings yield dead leaves, bark and twigs for fuel in places where other fuels are scarce. Against these benefits should be set the increasing complaints, notably in India, that widespread plantings of eucalypts creates environments hostile to other plant and animal life of importance in traditional rural culture.

Eucalypts are unusual trees, with leaves that tend to hang vertically so the foliage provides only partial shade; the leaves contain aromatic oil in small translucent cavities, eucalyptus oil being an important product of certain species. The nectar-rich flowers are abundant, mostly white, but yellow, pink or red in a minority of species, with the massed stamens the most conspicuous part. Petals and sepals are fused into a cap-like structure (operculum) that is shed as the stamens unfold; the fruits are woody capsules, mostly quite small. The bark of many eucalypts is smooth and shed annually, and the new and old bark can make a colorful contrast while this is happening. Other groups of eucalypts have persistent bark of varying texture, examples being the stringybark and ironbark groups. In cooler countries eucalypts are often seen only as cut foliage, sold by florists; this foliage is the juvenile type characteristic of many species, with rounded, stalkless, waxy-bluish leaves, and mostly gives way to adult leaves that are narrow, stalked, and greener. A distinctive growth form seen in many of the smaller-growing eucalypts is what Australians call a 'mallee', in which a large woody tuber gives rise to a number of slender trunks; it is characteristic of many species.

A recent development in the botanical study of eucalypts is the splitting off of 113 species into the newly named genus *Corymbia*, consisting mainly of the 'bloodwoods'. Only a small number of cultivated species are affected by this reclassification.

CULTIVATION

There are species to suit most climates except those where winter temperatures fall below about 10°F (–12°C), but the great majority of species will tolerate only the lightest frosts. Drought hardiness also varies greatly, some species requiring fairly moist conditions. With rare exceptions eucalypts are grown from seed, which germinates freely. They should be planted out into the ground when no more than 18 in (45 cm) high, ensuring that roots have not coiled in the container at any stage. They seldom survive transplanting, and are not long-lived as container plants. They prefer full sun at all stages of growth.

Eucalyptus globulus

Eucalyptus globulus

TASMANIAN BLUE GUM

The first eucalypt to be introduced to Europe and North America, this large tree can grow to over 200 ft (60 m), with a trunk to 6 ft (1.8 m) in diameter. The bluish bark is shed in long strips. Juvenile leaves are silvery blue and rectangular, while the adult form is deep green and sickle shaped, to 18 in (45 cm) long. A distinctive feature is the solitary, stalkless flowers in the leaf axils, with broad, wrinkled, bluish bud caps. Occurring naturally in coastal areas of Tasmania and far southern Victoria, it prefers moist conditions. It is used for timber, paper pulp and as a source of eucalyptus oil. '**Compacta**' reaches only 30 ft (10 m) and retains its silvery blue juvenile foliage for some years. **ZONES 8–10**.

Eucalyptus pauciflora

Eucalyptus gunnii
syn. **Eucalyptus divaricata**
ALPINE CIDER GUM

From the highlands of Tasmania, this 80 ft (24 m) tall tree is sometimes multi-trunked. It has light reddish brown bark that peels irregularly revealing white new bark. Young trees have the 'silver dollar' style foliage: opposite pairs of rounded, gray-green leaves. Mature trees have narrower stalked leaves. Small cream flowers in spring and summer are followed by tiny, goblet-shaped seed capsules. It is perhaps the most frost-hardy eucalypt and the most commonly grown in the British Isles. **ZONES 7–9**.

Eucalyptus pauciflora
syn. **Eucalyptus coriacea**
SNOW GUM

This 30–60 ft (9–18 m) tree is found in southeastern Australia, commonly growing in frost-prone highland valleys. It tends to have a rather twisted trunk, with reddish brown or gray bark peeling in irregular strips to reveal white and beige under-bark. Small cream flowers are borne in spring and summer. Alpine snow gum, *Eucalyptus pauciflora* subsp. *niphophila* (syn. *E. niphophila*), occurs at altitudes over 5,000 ft (1,500 m) where snow lies through most of winter; it is smaller and lower branching. **ZONES 7–9**.

FAGUS

BEECH

Although these long-lived, deciduous trees, to 130 ft (40 m), are scattered across Europe, the UK, Asia and North America, most of the 10 species are confined to China and Japan. They occur in a rather narrow climatic zone, being absent from far northern forests as well as the lowland Mediterranean-type forests. Most species have a rounded crown of delicate foliage that turns golden brown in autumn and smooth, gray bark. They bear brown-scaled, pointed winter buds and prominently veined, ovate to elliptic leaves. In spring, new leaves are briefly accompanied by small, individual clusters of male and female flowers. In early autumn, small shaggy fruit capsules split open to release angular, oil-rich seeds (beech nuts) that are a major food source for wildlife. Their valuable timber is close-grained and readily worked; it is used for flooring and furniture, and for making kitchen utensils.

CULTIVATION

Frost hardy, beeches require well-drained, reasonably fertile soil and some shelter from strong wind; they will do best in areas with long, warm summers. Purple-leafed forms prefer full sun and yellow-leafed forms a little shade. Propagate from seed as soon as it falls; cultivars must be grafted. They may be attacked by aphids and are prone to powdery mildew.

Fagus orientalis

ORIENTAL BEECH

This species once formed extensive forests in Greece, Turkey, northern Iran and the Caucasus, replacing *Fagus sylvatica* at low altitudes. It resembles that species except that it has noticeably longer leaves that turn brownish yellow in autumn and larger nuts. In a suitably warm climate it can grow vigorously to 70 ft (21 m) in height and 50 ft (15 m) in spread. **ZONES 5–10.**

Fagus orientalis

Fagus sylvatica

COMMON BEECH, EUROPEAN BEECH

Although regarded as one of the most 'English' natives, this species ranges across Europe and western Asia, with an average height of about 80 ft (24 m). In spring, it bears drooping balls of yellowish male flowers and greenish clusters of female flowers. Many cultivars have been selected for their habit, intricately cut leaves and colorful foliage, including 'Aspleniifolia', a fern-leafed beech with narrow, deeply cut leaves; 'Dawyck', with a narrow columnar habit to 50 ft (15 m) and dark purple foliage; 'Pendula' with branches that droop from a mushroom-shaped crown; *Fagus sylvatica* f. *purpurea* (syn. 'Atropunicea'), the copper beech, a round-headed form with purple-green leaves that turn copper and which does best in full sun; 'Riversii', the purple beech, with very dark purple leaves; 'Rohanii', with brownish purple deeply cut leaves; 'Rotundifolia', with strong upright growth and small rounded leaves; 'Tricolor' (syn. 'Roseo-marginata'), a smaller tree with purplish leaves edged and striped pink and cream; and 'Zlatia', which bears yellow young foliage that later becomes mid- to dark green. **ZONES 5–9.**

Fagus sylvatica 'Rotundifolia'

Fagus sylvatica

Franklinia alatamaha

Franklinia alatamaha

The name of this species is taken from the Altamaha River in Georgia, where this species was first discovered. It makes a small, spreading tree of about 15–20 ft (4.5–6 m), and is often multi-trunked. The glossy, bright green leaves turn scarlet in autumn, while the 3 in (8 cm) wide fragrant flowers open in late summer and early autumn. **ZONES 7–10.**

FRANKLINIA

FRANKLIN TREE

Named for Benjamin Franklin and consisting of a single species, this genus became extinct in the wild shortly after its discovery in about 1765 in Georgia, USA, due to the rapid spread of white settlement and clearing of the forests. It is a small deciduous tree with large white flowers with crinkled, overlapping petals and a central bunch of golden stamens similar to those of the closely related *Camellia*. The fruit, large woody capsules, have 5 compartments and split to release 2 flattened seeds.

CULTIVATION

Frost hardy, it prefers humus-rich, moist but well-drained soil and a sheltered, warm position in full sun. Growth is slow. Climates with long, hot, humid summers produce the best flowering. Propagation is normally from fresh ripe seed.

Fraxinus americana
WHITE ASH

The most valued ash in North America, this species occurs naturally through eastern USA and in southeastern Canada. In the wild it reaches about 80 ft (24 m), with a long straight bole and furrowed gray-brown bark and a somewhat domed canopy. The pinnate leaves have 7 to 9 large, dark green leaflets with silvery undersides. The inconspicuous flowers appear before the leaves. Autumn color is most commonly a fine yellow. A number of forms are available including *Fraxinus americana* var. *juglandifolia*, which has a slender, columnar habit, and '**Autumn Purple**', with leaves that turn reddish purple in autumn. **ZONES 4–10.**

FRAXINUS
ASH

This genus consists of 65 species of mainly deciduous, fast-growing trees, ranging throughout the northern hemisphere except for the coldest regions and lowland tropics. It differs from other woody members of the olive family (Oleaceae) in having pinnate leaves consisting of several leaflets, small insignificant flowers that in most species lack petals, and single-seeded, winged fruits botanically called samaras. One group of species known as the 'flowering ashes', typified by *Fraxinus ornus*, produces showier flowers with small petals in large terminal panicles at the tips of the branches. Several larger species are valued for their tough, pale timber.

CULTIVATION
Ashes are mostly quite frost hardy and can survive exposed or arid conditions, but thrive in shelter and in fertile, moist but well-drained soil. They are widely planted as street and park trees and are seldom affected by pests and diseases. Propagate from seed in autumn; for cultivars, graft onto seedling stock of the same species.

Fraxinus americana 'Autumn Purple'

Fraxinus angustifolia 'Raywood'

Fraxinus angustifolia
syn. *Fraxinus oxycarpa*
NARROW-LEAFED ASH

This species is related to *Fraxinus excelsior*, with similar foliage, flowers and fruit but darker bark and leaves in whorls of 3 to 4, not in pairs. It can grow in semi-arid climates and has a broadly columnar to rounded crown. *F. a.* subsp. *oxycarpa* (the desert ash), has leaves with up to 7 leaflets, hairy under the midribs. 'Raywood', apparently a clone of sub-species *oxycarpa*, is called the claret ash for its wine-purple autumn foliage. **ZONES 6–10.**

Fraxinus pennsylvanica

RED ASH, GREEN ASH

Similar to *Fraxinus americana*, this tree is also a fast-growing native of North America but is not as large; it reaches 70 ft (21 m) in height with a similar spread. Its green leaves are divided into 5 to 9 leaflets and are sometimes hairy, resembling stalks. This species prefers a moist soil. **'Summit'** has an upright, cylindrical habit with leaves turning yellow in autumn; *F. pennsylvanica* **var.** *subintegerrima* has long, narrow, sword-shaped leaves. **ZONES 4–10.**

Fraxinus ornus

Fraxinus excelsior

Fraxinus excelsior

EUROPEAN ASH, COMMON ASH

One of Europe's largest deciduous trees, this species can reach 140 ft (42 m); in the open it is usually 50–60 ft (15–18 m), with a broad crown. It bears dark green leaves with 9 to 11 narrow, toothed leaflets that turn yellow in autumn. Velvety, blackish flower buds are noticeable in winter. **'Aurea'** and the more vigorous **'Jaspidea'** have pale yellowish green summer foliage that deepens in autumn; the twigs turn yellow in winter. **'Pendula'**, the weeping ash, has branches often weeping to the ground. **ZONES 4–10.**

Fraxinus ornus

FLOWERING ASH, MANNA ASH

From southern Europe and Asia Minor, the widely cultivated flowering ash makes a round-topped tree of 30–50 ft (9–15 m) with a short, fluted trunk and smooth gray bark. The leaves have 5 to 9 oval leaflets, dull green with downy undersides. In late spring it bears foamy panicles of white blossoms all over the crown, and then small, narrow fruit. **ZONES 6–10.**

Fraxinus pennsylvanica

GINKGO
GINKGO, MAIDENHAIR TREE

The Ginkgoales, seed-bearing plants more primitive than the conifers and more ancient, first appeared in the Permian Period (about 300 million years ago) and flourished through the Jurassic and Cretaceous periods. About 100 million years ago they began to die out, leaving the maidenhair tree as the sole survivor—and then only in China. It is now unknown in a wild state, and probably would no longer exist if ancient trees had not been preserved in temple grounds and young ones planted there. The common name 'maidenhair' refers to the leaf shape and vein pattern, resembling some of the maidenhair fern (*Adiantum*) species. Male trees bear small spikes of pollen sacs, females solitary naked seeds ('fruits') with an oily flesh around the large kernel.

CULTIVATION

A tree of temperate climates, it resists pollution and seems to have outlived any pests it may have once had. It does, however, need shelter from strong winds and does best in deep, fertile soil. City authorities prefer to grow male trees, as females drop smelly fruit; in China female trees are preferred as the seeds are edible and nutritious. Fruit do not appear before the tree is at least 20 years old, however. Propagate from seed or autumn cuttings.

Ginkgo biloba

The ginkgo grows at least 80 ft (24 m) tall, upright when young and eventually spreading to 30 ft (9 m) or more. Deciduous, the 4 in (10 cm) long, matt green, fan-shaped leaves turn golden yellow in autumn. A fleshy, plum-like orange-brown fruit with an edible kernel appears in late summer and autumn if male and female trees are grown together. 'Fastigiata' is a slender, erect cultivar that reaches 30 ft (9 m). 'Princeton Sentry' has a narrow, upright habit and is male. **ZONES 3–10.**

Ginkgo biloba 'Fastigiata'

GLEDITSIA
LOCUST

Occurring in temperate and subtropical regions of North and South America as well as Africa and Asia, this genus of about 14 species of deciduous, broadly spreading, usually thorny trees is grown for attractive foliage, ease of cultivation and for shade. They have pinnate or bipinnate leaves, inconspicuous flowers and large, often twisted, hanging seed pods that are filled with a sweetish, edible pulp. The locust referred to in the Bible is the related *Ceratonia siliqua*, but in North America 'locust' has been used for both *Gleditsia* and *Robinia*, the latter not closely related.

CULTIVATION

Gleditsias grow best in full sun in rich, moist soil and tolerate poor drainage. They are fast growing and mostly frost hardy, although young plants may need protection from frost. Prune young trees to promote a single, straight trunk; thorns on the lower trunk can be removed. Propagate selected forms by budding in spring or summer and species from seed in autumn.

Gleditsia triacanthos
HONEY LOCUST

Native to eastern and central USA and reaching 100 ft (30 m), this species has an open, vase-shaped canopy and a thorny trunk. Fern-like, shiny, green bipinnate leaves with small leaflets turn deep yellow in autumn. Twisted black pods, up to 18 in (45 cm) long and 1½ in (35 mm) wide, hang from the branches in autumn and winter. *Gleditsia triacanthos* f. *inermis* is thornless as are most modern cultivars. '**Imperial**' has rounded leaves and few seed pods; '**Ruby Lace**' has reddish young growth turning bronze in autumn; '**Shademaster**' is fast growing and broadly conical with bright green leaves; '**Skyline**' has dark green leaves that turn yellow in autumn; '**Stevens**' is wide spreading with bright green leaves turning yellow in autumn; and '**Sunburst**' has bright yellow young leaves that turn pale green in summer. **ZONES 3–10.**

Gleditsia triacanthos f. *inermis*

Gymnocladus dioica

GYMNOCLADUS

Distinctive for their enormous, handsome bipinnate leaves, the 4 deciduous trees of this genus, allied to *Gleditsia*, come from North America and east Asia. Small, greenish white flowers appear only in prolonged warm weather. The seeds and pods of different species have been used for soap and as a coffee substitute. Only female trees bear fruits.

CULTIVATION

Cool-climate plants, they require full sun and deep, well-drained, fertile soil. Propagate from seed in autumn.

Gymnocladus dioica
KENTUCKY COFFEE TREE

From moist woodland areas of the eastern USA, this slow-growing tree reaches 70 ft (21 m) tall and 50 ft (15 m) wide. The large compound leaves, up to 3 ft (1 m) long, are pinkish bronze when young. The small, star-shaped white flowers are fragrant and are borne in early summer followed, on the female plants, by pendent reddish brown pods to 10 in (25 cm) long. The seeds were once roasted and ground for a coffee-like beverage. **ZONES 4–10.**

Halesia carolina

Halesia carolina
syn. *Halesia tetraptera*

CAROLINA SILVERBELL

This ornamental, spreading tree grows 25–40 ft (8–12 m) high and somewhat wider. It flowers profusely, even when young, producing masses of drooping, bell-shaped white or pink-flushed flowers in mid- to late spring. The flowers are followed by 4-winged green fruit that ripen to pale brown. The mid-green leaves are downy when they first appear and turn yellow in autumn. **ZONES 3–9.**

HALESIA
SILVERBELL, SNOWDROP TREE

The 5 species of this genus of deciduous trees and shrubs are found in eastern USA and in China in rich, moist woodlands and beside streams. They are grown mainly for their attractive bell-shaped flowers, opening in clusters as the leaves unfold, and the unusual winged fruit capsules that follow.

CULTIVATION

Cool-climate plants, they prefer a sheltered position in part- to full sun and grow best in well-drained, moist, neutral to acid soil. Propagation is from seed in autumn or from softwood cuttings in summer. Halesias have little trouble with pests and diseases.

Hoheria lyallii
syn. *Plagianthus lyallii*
LACEBARK

This attractive deciduous tree
from New Zealand can grow
to 20 ft (6 m) tall. It has
thick, fiberous bark, which
gives it its common name. The
toothed, oblong leaves are
gray-green with a felty white
underside; they are up to 4 in
(10 cm) long. Fragrant white
flowers appear in late summer
and are followed by leathery,
capsular fruit. The lacebark
prefers a sunny position and
soil rich in humus; it tolerates
alkaline soil. **ZONES 7–10.**

Hoheria sexstylosa
RIBBONWOOD

Narrowly conical in habit,
this evergreen tree grows to
20 ft (6 m) tall; it has an erect
trunk and main branches with
drooping branchlets. The
leaves are bright green and
oval, with sharply toothed
margins. Small clusters of
sweetly fragrant star-shaped
white flowers are borne
abundantly in late summer
and autumn, followed by
small, brown, winged fruit
capsules. When young the
plant is bushy and has more
deeply toothed leaves.
ZONES 7–10.

Hoheria lyallii

HOHERIA

This genus consists of 5 species of evergreen and deciduous
small trees native to the forests of New Zealand. Of slender,
upright habit, they are grown for their showy clusters of faintly
perfumed white flowers which appear in summer and autumn.
Plants can be anywhere between 20–50 ft (6–15 m) high and
flowering is usually followed by fruit capsules.

CULTIVATION
Happiest in warm-tem-
perate climates, they
grow in sun or semi-
shade in fertile, well-
drained soil in areas
with high summer
rainfall. Straggly plants
can be pruned by
about one-third in
winter and all plants
benefit from a light
annual pruning of the
outer branches to
maintain a tidy shape
and abundant foliage.
They are propagated
from seed in autumn
or from cuttings in
summer.

Hoheria sexstylosa

IDESIA

WONDER TREE, LIGIRI

This genus consists of a single species of deciduous tree. Indigenous to central and western China, Korea, Japan and neighboring islands, it is grown for its striking foliage and fruit, and makes a handsome shade tree. To obtain the fruit, both male and female plants are needed.

CULTIVATION

It will grow in either sun or part-shade. Moderately fertile, moist but well-drained neutral to acid soil and a cool to warm-temperate climate suit it best. It can be pruned when young to establish a single main trunk, which will promote a shapely crown. Propagate from seed in autumn or cuttings in summer.

Idesia polycarpa

ILEX

HOLLY

Ilex × *altaclerensis* 'Lawsoniana'

The 400 or so evergreen and deciduous trees and shrubs that make up this large genus come predominantly from the temperate regions of the northern hemisphere. They are grown for their foliage and clusters of small glossy berries. Hollies make excellent hedges, border and tub plants or screens for privacy according to their height. Male and female plants must be grown together to obtain the berries. Produced in summer, autumn or winter, the berries are either red, yellow or black, and clusters of small, insignificant, greenish white flowers precede them.

CULTIVATION

Hollies grow well in deep, friable, well-drained soils with high organic content. They are fully to marginally frost hardy. An open, sunny position is best in cool climates. Water in hot, dry summers. Hollies do not like transplanting. Prune carefully in spring to check vigorous growth. Propagate from seed or cuttings. Check for signs of holly aphid and holly leaf miner.

Idesia polycarpa

This fast-growing, shapely tree grows to a height of 40 ft (12 m), with a broadly conical crown spreading to 20 ft (6 m). It has large heart-shaped, red-stalked dark green leaves; fragrant, greenish flowers are borne in spring and summer. *Idesia polycarpa* is frost hardy, particularly after long, hot summers which promote well-ripened wood. The female plants produce large hanging clusters of pea-sized berries that turn deep red in autumn and are not eaten by birds. **ZONES 6–10.**

Ilex × altaclerensis

HIGHCLERE HOLLY

This group of evergreen hybrid hollies, reaching a height of about 50 ft (15 m), has larger, variable leaves and larger flowers and berries than the English holly *(Ilex aqui-folium)*. Its many cultivars include 'Belgica Aurea' (syn. 'Silver Sentinel'), an upright female with few-spined leaves, which have a gray-green center and irregular yellow margin; 'Camelliifolia', a female with purple-tinged shoots, leaf stems and petal bases, larger berries and long leaves with only a few spines; 'Golden King', a frost-hardy female with smooth-edged, deep green leaves with yellow margins which makes an excellent hedge (requires pollination with a male cultivar such as 'Silver Queen', a cultivar of *I. aquifolium*, to bear its red berries); 'Hendersonii', a compact female with long-lasting red berries and dull green foliage; 'Hodginsii', a robust male clone with dark purple twigs and glossy, very deep green foliage; '**Lawsoniana**' a sport of 'Hendersonii', which has good crops of red berries and sparsely spined leaves with irregular light green and gold centers; and '**Wilsonii**', a moderately frost-hardy female growing to 20 ft (6 m) with a spread of 12 ft (3.5 m), broad, spiny, dark green leaves and masses of large scarlet fruits which make it good for hedging. Able to resist pollution and harsh coastal conditions, this is a very useful plant for industrial and maritime areas. **ZONES 6–10.**

Ilex × *aquipernyi* 'Meschick'

Ilex aquifolium 'Golden Queen'

Ilex × *altaclerensis* 'Hendersonii'

Ilex aquifolium
ENGLISH HOLLY

Native to Europe, north Africa and western Asia, this evergreen species—a popular Christmas decoration in the northern hemisphere with its glossy, spiny-edged dark green leaves and bright red winter berries—reaches 40 ft (12 m) with a spread of about 15 ft (4.5 m) or more and has an erect, branching habit. The most commonly grown cultivars include '**Amber**', which has lovely yellow fruit and almost thornless leaves; '**Angustifolia**', which has green or purple twigs and lanceolate dark green foliage with a neat pyramidal shape; '**Aurea Marginata**', a small, bushy, silver holly with yellow margins on its spiny foliage and red berries on the female form; '**Ferox**', the hedgehog holly, a male with more compact growth to a height of 20 ft (6 m) and leaves with spines over their entire surface; '**Ferox Argentea**', a male with purple twigs and small, cream-edged dark green leaves; '**Golden Milkboy**', with variegated golden leaves; '**Golden Queen**', a dense male clone with spiny, dark green leaves with pale green and gray shadings and a substantial yellow margin; '**Handsworth New Silver**', a free-fruiting clone, with creamy white-margined leaves and purple twigs; '**J. C. van Tol**', which grows to 15 ft (4.5 m) tall with dark green, almost spineless leaves and crimson berries; '**Madame Briot**', a female clone with large, strongly spined, glossy green leaves, which are broadly edged in gold and scarlet berries; '**Pyramidalis**', a good fruit-bearing female clone that bears well and has a conical habit whilst young, but broadens with age; '**Pyramidalis Fructu Luteo**', much the same as the previous clone, but with yellow fruit; '**Silver Milkmaid**', with scarlet fruit and green-edged golden leaves, that are prone to revert to green and must be cut out if they do so; and '**Silver Queen**', a male, non-berrying shrub with leaves that are pink when young, maturing to a very dark green in the middle with creamy white margins and gray-green in between. **ZONES 6–10.**

Ilex aquifolium

Ilex × aquipernyi

This hybrid between *Ilex aquifolium* and *I. pernyi* is a conical evergreen small tree. It grows to 20 ft (6 m), with a spread of 12 ft (3.5 m). It has glossy, dark green spiny leaves and bears red fruit. '**Meschick**' colors a pinkish bronze. **ZONES 6–10.**

Ilex × meserveae
MESERVE HYBRID HOLLY

This group of hybrids was derived from *Ilex aquifolium* and *I. rugosa*. It is noted for the bluish green foliage, purple stems, red berries and frost hardiness of its members. Most have a dense, pyramidal shape and make attractive, strong-growing hedges. The cultivars '**Blue Girl**', '**Blue Boy**' and '**Blue Angel**' are the most commonly available. Others include '**Blue Prince**', a male plant of spreading habit, which grows to 10 ft (3 m) in height and spread, and has glossy bright green leaves; and '**Blue Princess**', with extra glossy foliage and very abundant red berries on a shrub up to 10 ft (3 m) tall. **ZONES 5–9.**

Ilex opaca
AMERICAN HOLLY

This evergreen tree grows to a height and spread of about 30 ft (9 m); it has an erect habit and produces red berries in winter. The leaves are dull green above and yellowish underneath, with spiny or smooth edges. It prefers a sunny position and acid soil, and does not do well near the sea. **ZONES 5–10.**

Ilex pernyi
PERNY'S HOLLY

From central and western China, this densely branched evergreen tree was named after the French missionary Paul Perny. It grows to a height of 30 ft (9 m), with distinctive, diamond-shaped, triangular-spined leaves and oval red berries. The flowers are yellowish. This species is very frost hardy, but does not tolerate dry conditions. **ZONES 5–10.**

Ilex opaca

Ilex × meserveae 'Blue Prince'

Ilex pernyi

JUNIPERUS
JUNIPER

Juniperus squamata 'Blue Carpet'

Slow growing and long lived, the 50 or so species of evergreen shrubs and trees in this conifer genus are occur throughout the northern hemisphere. Juvenile foliage is needle-like, but at maturity many species develop shorter scale-like leaves, closely pressed to the stem and exuding a pungent smell when crushed. Both types of foliage are found on adult trees of some species. Male and female cones usually occur on separate plants. The bluish black or reddish seed cones have fleshy, fused scales; known as berries, those of some junipers are used to flavor gin. The fragrant, pinkish, cedar-like timber is soft but durable. Various species of juniper are used medicinally with a range of applications from antiseptic to diuretic.

CULTIVATION
Easily cultivated in a cool climate, they prefer a sunny position and any well-drained soil. Prune to maintain shape or restrict size, but do not make visible pruning cuts as old, leafless wood rarely sprouts. Propagate from cuttings in winter, layers if low-growing, or from seed; cultivars can be propagated by grafting.

Juniperus chinensis 'Aurea'

Juniperus communis cultivar

Juniperus chinensis
CHINESE JUNIPER

Native to the Himalayas, China, Mongolia and Japan, this frost-hardy species usually matures to a conical tree up to 50 ft (15 m) in height with a spread of 6–10 ft (1.8–3 m). Sometimes, however, it forms a low-spreading shrub. Both adult and juvenile foliage may be found on adult trees. The berries are fleshy and glaucous white. 'Aurea' grows to at least 35 ft (11 m) tall, with a conical habit and soft, golden foliage; 'Blaauw' is somewhat spreading when young, but becomes an upright 5 ft (1.5 m) shrub; 'Kaizuka' is a small tree to 20 ft (6 m), with twisted spear-like branches; 'Obelisk' is an attractive plant of upright form that can reach 10 ft (3 m) in height and has bluish green juvenile foliage; 'Pyramidalis' grows to 15 ft (4.5 m) tall, with dense, blue-green leaves and a columnar habit; and 'Variegata' grows to 20 ft (6 m) tall, glaucous with white markings.
ZONES 4–9.

Juniperus communis
COMMON JUNIPER

Ranging widely through northern Europe, North America and western Asia, this is either an upright tree growing to 20 ft (6 m) or a sprawling shrub with a height and spread of 10–15 ft (3–4.5 m). It has brownish red bark and grayish green leaves. Fleshy, greenish berries take 2 to 3 years to ripen to black and are used for flavoring gin. Hardiness varies considerably depending on the subspecies or cultivar. Among popular cultivars are 'Compressa', a dwarf, erect form suitable for the rock garden, growing to 30 in (75 cm) tall and 6 in (15 cm) wide with silvery blue needles; 'Depressa Aurea', a dwarf form growing to 24 in (60 cm) tall and 6 ft (1.8 m) wide with bronze-gold foliage; 'Hibernica', growing 10–15 ft (3–4.5 m) tall and 2–4 ft (0.6–1.2 m) wide, forming a dense column of dull, blue-green foliage when young but becoming broader and conical with age; and 'Hornibrookii', an excellent prostrate shrub with gray-green foliage that rarely exceeds 10 in (25 cm) in height, but will spread to more than 4 ft (1.2 m) wide. **ZONES 2–9.**

Juniperus recurva
COFFIN JUNIPER, HIMALAYAN JUNIPER

Native to Burma, southwest China and the Himalayas, this shrub or tree grows to 50 ft (15 m) tall and 15 ft (4.5 m) wide. It has spreading, pendulous branches and needle-like, aromatic, gray- or blue-green incurved leaves. The reddish brown bark peels in vertical strips; its glossy berries are dark purple. Its aromatic wood was used in China to make coffins, hence the common name. *Juniperus recurva* var. *coxii* has smaller leaves. **ZONES 7–11.**

Juniperus rigida
NEEDLE JUNIPER

From Japan and Korea, this cool-climate tree grows to 20 ft (6 m) in height, although it often forms a shrub when grown in gardens. It has pendulous branches and needle-like leaves with a band of white on the upper surface. The fruit ripens through brown to blue-black. **ZONES 4–9.**

Juniperus squamata
HOLLYWOOD JUNIPER

This species ranges in height from 1–20 ft (0.3–6 m) with a spread of 3–15 ft (1–4.5 m) depending on the variety. Needle-like green or blue-green leaves clothe densely crowded branchlets and the bark is flaky and reddish brown; the berries are fleshy and black. 'Blue Carpet' is another blue-needled juniper which makes a mat of foliage about 10 in (25 cm) deep with a spread of up to 3 ft (1 m). 'Blue Star', a dense, rounded shrub with blue foliage, grows to 18 in (45 cm) tall and 24 in (60 cm) wide. 'Holger' is a lovely shrub with a spreading, star-shaped habit that grows up to 24 in (60 cm) tall and 6 ft (1.8 m) wide. Its steely blue needles are attractively ornamented in spring by its golden tips. 'Meyeri' has steely blue foliage with a rich silver sheen and reaches a height and spread of 15 ft (4.5 m). **ZONES 4–10.**

Juniperus virginiana
EASTERN RED CEDAR, PENCIL CEDAR

From North America, this is the tallest of the junipers commonly grown in gardens, reaching 50–60 ft (15–18 m) in height. It has a conical or broadly columnar habit and both scale- and needle-like, gray-green leaves. The berries are fleshy, small, glaucous and brownish violet. The wood is used in making lead pencils, hence the common name. 'Glauca', a columnar form with blue-green foliage, grows to 25 ft (8 m) tall with a spread of 8 ft (2.4 m); 'Hetzii' has layers of gray-green foliage and reaches 10–12 ft (3–3.5 m) high and wide. **ZONES 2–9.**

Juniperus rigida

Koelreuteria paniculata
GOLDEN RAIN TREE, VARNISH TREE

From China and Korea, this slow-growing, wide-spreading tree can reach 30–50 ft (9–15 m), but is often smaller in gardens. It has a convex crown and a single or divided main trunk. The bark is furrowed and the branches droop at the ends. The mid-green leaflets turn deep golden yellow to orange in autumn. Large clusters of clear yellow flowers are borne in summer and are followed by papery, bladder-like, pinkish brown pods. It does well in alkaline soil. '**September**' (syn. 'September Gold') is similar to the species, except that it flowers late in the season. **ZONES 4–10.**

Koelreuteria paniculata

KOELREUTERIA

Grown for their foliage, flowers and decorative fruit, this small genus of 3 species of deciduous trees is from dry valley woodlands in eastern Asia. They are useful small trees with pyramid-shaped panicles of long, bowl-shaped flowers followed by inflated fruit capsules.

CULTIVATION

Moderately frost hardy, they thrive in full sun in fertile, well-aerated soil with free drainage. They can withstand hot, dry summers, but seaside conditions do not suit them. Propagate from root cuttings in late winter or from seed in autumn. Prune in the early years to establish a single trunk.

Koelreuteria paniculata

Laburnum anagyroides
COMMON LABURNUM,
GOLDEN CHAIN TREE, GOLDEN RAIN

From the mountain regions of
central and southern Europe,
this small, spreading tree
grows to a height and spread
of 25 ft (8 m). The gray-green
leaves are downy on the undersides. The densely clustered
flowers are borne on 6–10 in
(15–25 cm) long pendulous
racemes in late spring and
early summer, and are followed by hairy brown pods
containing black seeds. The
cultivar **'Aureum'** has pale
yellowish green foliage.
ZONES 3–9.

Laburnum × watereri
VOSS LABURNUM, WATERER LABURNUM

Now the most commonly
grown laburnum, this hybrid
between *Laburnum ana-
gyroides* and *L. alpinum*
makes a tree of similar size
to the parent species. It has
dark green leaflets and in late
spring and early summer it
produces dense racemes up
to 18 in (45 cm) in length of
fragrant rich yellow flowers.
'Vossii', the cultivar most
commonly seen in nurseries,
produces rich, buttercup-
yellow flowers on racemes
up to 24 in (60 cm) in length.
ZONES 3–9.

LABURNUM
GOLDEN CHAIN TREE

Laburnum anagyroides

Two species of deciduous small trees from Europe and western
Asia make up this genus of legumes, allied to *Cytisus* and other
brooms. They have compound leaves with 3 leaflets that are
larger and thinner than other members of the broom tribe, and
the bright yellow pea-flowers borne in profuse pendulous sprays
are also relatively large; they are followed by brown seed pods.
All parts of the tree are very poisonous; handle with gloves.

CULTIVATION

Laburnum × watereri 'Vossii'

Cool-climate plants, they
prefer full sun, some
humidity and tolerate
any moderately fertile
soil with free drainage—
they do not like being
waterlogged. Prune com-
peting leaders in the
early years to establish a
tree-like form. Owners
of large gardens may
create 'laburnum arches'
of 2 rows of trees tied
down over a trellis, so
that the flower sprays
hang below like wis-
terias. Watch for leaf
miner insects; protect
young trees from snails.
Propagate species from
seed in autumn, cultivars
by budding in summer.

LAGERSTROEMIA
CRAPE (OR CREPE) MYRTLE

From southern and eastern Asia and ranging
as far as northern Australia, this is a genus of
around 50 species of evergreen and deciduous
small to large trees, a few grown in warm and
hot climates for their showy flowers. Their
most distinctive feature is the crinkly margin
and slender basal stalk of each of the 5 petals
that make up a flower; the flowers in turn are
massed into large, dense panicles at the branch
tips. The 'crape' (alternatively crepe) in the
name arose from the flowers' texture being
reminiscent of the once popular fabric crape,
while 'myrtle' alludes to their being close relatives to the large myrtle family. They make fine
garden plants and are easily grown. Some
species have attractive smooth bark, colored
green, brown or reddish. The timber of some
species is highly prized for shipbuilding.

CULTIVATION

They thrive in full sun in well-drained, humus-
rich soil. Shelter from strong summer winds,
which destroy the delicate flowers. Propagate
from cuttings in summer or from seed in
spring. Watch for powdery mildew.

Lagerstroemia indica

Lagerstroemia indica
CRAPE (OR CREPE) MYRTLE, PRIDE OF INDIA

This deciduous tree, now believed to have
originated in China, grows to about 25 ft (8 m)
tall with an open, spreading, rounded head and
smooth beige-colored bark streaked red-brown.
In mid- to late summer it bears large clusters of
frilly pink to deep red flowers. In cooler areas,
the small oval leaves turn gold in autumn.
Flowerheads appear at the tips of the current
season's growth; they are largest on strong
growths, encouraged by pruning the main
branches in winter; if not pruned, the tree develops an attractive, open shape, with massed
smaller heads. The typical form of this species
is now almost forgotten in cultivation, replaced
by an array of cultivars (including some of
dwarf habit), not all of which live up to the
claims of their promoters. 'Petite Snow', of
dwarf habit, has white flowers; 'Ruby Lace'
has frilly, deep red blooms. Some cultivars,
such as 'Eavesii', with its broad, open habit and
pale mauve flowers and 'Heliotrope Beauty'
with pale lilac-pink flowers, are believed to be
of hybrid origin: *Lagerstroemia indica* ×
L. speciosa hybrids re-crossed with *L. indica*.
Some modern American cultivars are hybrids
between *L. indica* and **L. fauriei**, such as
'Natchez' with creamy flowers; 'Seminole'
with mid-pink flowers; and 'Tuscarora' with
crimson flowers. **ZONES 6–11.**

Lagerstroemia indica 'Tuscarora'

Larix kaempferi

LARIX
LARCH

From cool mountainous regions of the northern hemisphere, these deciduous, fast-growing conifers have a handsome, graceful form and fresh green spring foliage as well as strong, durable timber; the bark also is used for tanning and dyeing. They lose their leaves in autumn, bursting into leaf in early spring. With the new foliage appear both drooping yellow male (pollen) cones and upright red female cones, which mature over the following summer to short, erect seed cones with thin scales; these persist on the tree after shedding their seeds. Up to 15 species of *Larix* have been recognized, but recent studies have merged some of these, reducing this number to as few as 9 species.

CULTIVATION
Cold-to cool-climate plants, they do best in well-drained, light or gravelly soil; most resent waterlogged soil. Propagate from seed. Check regularly for larch canker or blister and infestation by larch chermes.

Larix decidua
EUROPEAN LARCH

From the mountains of central and southern Europe, this tree reaches a height of 100 ft (30 m); it has a conical crown when young, spreading with maturity. The branches are widely spaced and the branchlets have a graceful, weeping habit. The soft, bright green, needle-like leaves turn yellow in autumn before dropping. The mature seed cones are egg-shaped, brown and upright. The gray bark becomes red-brown, fissured and scaly with age. **ZONES 2–9.**

Larix kaempferi
syn. *Larix leptolepis*
JAPANESE LARCH

This fast-growing Japanese species is widely used for ornamental landscaping and is grown in forestry plantations. Broadly conical, it grows to a height of 100 ft (30 m) and a spread of 20 ft (6 m). Its soft needle-like leaves are gray- to blue-green and the mature cones are brown and almost globular, their broad scales spreading at the tips to give a rosebud appearance. The scaly bark is reddish brown, or orange-red on older branches. **ZONES 4–9.**

Larix decidua

Liquidambar styraciflua 'Variegata'

LIQUIDAMBAR

Liquidambar styraciflua

This is a genus of 4 species of deciduous trees from Turkey, eastern Asia, North America and Mexico belonging to the witch-hazel family, grown for their shapely form, handsome foliage and superb autumn colors. The leaves are deeply lobed, resembling a typical maple leaf. Some species produce a resinous gum known as liquid storax that is used to scent soap, as an expectorant in cough remedies and in the treatment of some skin diseases.

CULTIVATION

They are temperate-climate plants, requiring sun or part-shade and fertile, deep, loamy soil with adequate water during spring and summer. They will not thrive in shallow, sandy soil. The trees are best allowed to develop their lower branches to ground level. Propagate by budding in spring or from seed in autumn.

Liquidambar formosana

From central and southeastern China and Taiwan, this broadly conical species grows to 40 ft (12 m) with a spread of 30 ft (10 m). Its single trunk is erect, and the horizontal branches bear large, 3-lobed, toothed leaves that are bronze when young, dark green when mature, then turn red, gold and purple in autumn. The bark is grayish white. Small, yellow-green flowers appear in spring, followed by spiky, globular fruit clusters. The wood is used for making tea chests. **ZONES 7–10.**

Liquidambar styraciflua
SWEET GUM

This widely grown deciduous tree is native to eastern USA and Mexico and reaches a height of 80 ft (24 m) and spread of 40 ft (12 m). The young branches and twigs often have distinctive ridges of corky bark and the wood of this species, known commercially as satin walnut, is used for furniture-making. It bears glossy dark green leaves that color orange to red and purple in autumn. Globular heads of small yellow-green flowers appear in spring, followed by spiky, ball-like fruit clusters. Some *Liquidamber styraciflua* cultivars valued for their rich autumn coloring include '**Moraine**'; '**Burgundy**': deep purple-red; '**Festival**': pink through yellow; '**Palo Alto**': orange-red; '**Rotundiloba**', an odd form with the leaves having very rounded lobes, as the name suggests; '**Variegata**': streaked yellow; and '**Worplesdon**': purple through orange-yellow. **ZONES 5–11.**

Liquidambar formosana

Liriodendron tulipifera

From eastern USA, this is
an outstanding tree for cool
climates, reaching 100 ft
(30 m) or more with a spread
of about 50 ft (15 m). A vigorous grower with a broadly
conical habit, it bears deep
green, lobed leaves that turn
rich golden yellow in autumn.
Its summer-blooming flowers
are followed by conical brown
fruit. The pale timber, called
'yellow poplar', is not very
hard or durable but is fairly
light and strong and much
used in furniture-making.
'Aureomarginatum' has green
leaves heavily edged with
yellow; **'Fastigiatum'** is about
half the size, with an erect,
columnar form.
ZONES 4–10.

LIRIODENDRON
TULIP TREE

Liriodendron tulipifera

Some botanists dispute there being 2 species in this genus; they
prefer to recognize only one, *Liriodendron tulipifera*, regarding
L. chinense as a variety of this. The majority, however, accept
the two. Their 4-lobed leaves distinguish them at once from all
other trees: they look as though someone has cut their ends off
with scissors. The flowers are distinctive too, in pale green with
orange at the bases of their petals and numerous stamens. They
do not, in fact, look very much like tulips, but are more like
their cousins the magnolias. They are both handsome trees, with
straight boles and symmetrical crowns, though they are too
large, and fast growing to be suitable for any but the largest
of gardens.

CULTIVATION
They prefer a tem-
perate climate, sun
or part-shade and
deep, fertile, well-
drained, slightly
acidic soil and are
propagated from
seed or by grafting.
They are difficult
to transplant.

Liriodendron tulipifera 'Aureomarginatum'

Maclura pomifera
OSAGE ORANGE

This deciduous tree from southern USA can reach 50 ft (15 m) in height with a spread of 40 ft (12 m). It has dark brown, fissured bark, and its thorny branches form an open, irregular crown with oval, dark green leaves. Tiny yellow flowers, borne in summer, are followed by large, wrinkled, pale green fruit. The hard, flexible timber is used for archery bows. Young plants may be susceptible to frost damage. **ZONES 7–10.**

MACLURA
syn. *Cudrania*

This genus of 15 species of deciduous and evergreen thorny trees, shrubs and scrambling climbers is scattered widely throughout warmer parts of the world. The usually green flowers appear in racemes or clusters. Both male and female trees bear flowers and both are needed for fruits to grow; on female trees, the flowers are followed by compound fruits.

CULTIVATION

Fully frost hardy, they do best in full sun and in areas with hot summers. They will grow well in a wide range of soils. They have spreading roots and are resistant to very dry conditions. Propagate from seed in autumn, or from cuttings in summer or late winter.

Maclura pomifera

MAGNOLIA

This large, varied genus of 100 or more species of deciduous and evergreen trees and shrubs from east Asia and the Americas was named after French botanist Pierre Magnol. Magnolia leaves are usually oval and smooth edged. The flowers are generally large, fragrant and solitary, come in white, yellow, pink or purple, and vary in shape from almost flat and saucer-like to a narrow goblet shape. The fruits are cone-like or roughly cylindrical.

CULTIVATION

Magnolias require deep, fertile, well-drained soil. Some species require alkaline soil while others prefer a mildly acid, humus-rich soil. The roots are fragile so the plants do not transplant readily. They thrive in sun or part-shade but need protection from strong or salty winds. The flower buds are frost sensitive. Propagate from cuttings in summer or seed in autumn, or by grafting in winter.

Magnolia acuminata
CUCUMBER TREE

This most stately of American deciduous magnolias reaches 90 ft (27 m) in the wild and develops a wide pyramid shape. The 10 in (25 cm) long, mid- to dark green leaves have downy undersides. The cup-shaped, slightly fragrant, greenish yellow flowers with erect petals appear singly in early summer; the green cucumber-shaped fruit ripen to red. **ZONES 4–9.**

Magnolia acuminata

Magnolia campbellii 'Lanarth'

Magnolia denudata

Magnolia campbellii

Magnolia campbellii

This deciduous Himalayan species grows 80 ft (24 m) tall with a 40 ft (12 m) wide crown. Slightly fragrant flowers appear on leafless branches from late winter to mid-spring. Plants raised from seed take 20 or more years to flower. 'Alba' has pure white flowers; 'Charles Raffill' is white and rose purple; 'Lanarth' is a deeper rose purple; and *Magnolia campbellii* subsp. *mollicomata* flowers at an earlier age. **ZONES 7–10.**

Magnolia denudata

syns *Magnolia conspicua, M. heptapeta*
YULAN MAGNOLIA

This small deciduous tree from central China grows 30 ft (9 m) in height and the same in width. Masses of scented, pure white flowers are borne from mid- to late spring before the mid-green leaves and rectangular cones containing orange seeds appear. The Chinese have cultivated the Yulan magnolia for centuries as a symbol of purity and candor. *Magnolia denudata* is closely related to **M. sprengeri** 'Diva', a taller plant bearing rose-pink flowers. **ZONES 6–10.**

Magnolia grandiflora
SOUTHERN MAGNOLIA, BULL BAY

One of the few cultivated evergreen magnolias, this southern USA species forms a dense 60–80 ft (18–24 m) dome of deep green leathery leaves, rust-colored underneath. Cup-shaped white or cream blooms 10 in (25 cm) across appear during late summer, followed by reddish brown cones. It usually prefers warm, moist conditions, but many cultivars (including the Freeman hybrids with *Magnolia virginiana*) are hardier; others, such as 'Exmouth', have a more conical habit and fragrant flowers from an early age. 'Edith Bogue' is renowned for its cold tolerance. 'Little Gem' is a narrow semi-dwarf selection with smaller flowers produced on young plants; it will reach up to 12 ft (3.5 m) tall or so in 15 years. 'Russett' was selected because of its compact upright habit and the beige suede-like undersides of the leaves; it also has comparatively large flowers to 12 in (30 cm) across. 'St Mary' is a slow-growing compact form with profuse blooms and shiny green leaves, rust colored underneath. **ZONES 6–11.**

Magnolia grandiflora

Magnolia sieboldii

Magnolia sieboldii
OYAMA MAGNOLIA

This smallish tree or large shrub is one representative of a group of deciduous, summer-flowering species from China. Their pendent flowers distinguish them from the upright ones of the better known spring-flowering species. The white blooms are beautifully fragrant. **ZONES 7–10.**

Magnolia × soulangeana 'Lennei'

Magnolia × soulangeana
SAUCER MAGNOLIA

This deciduous hybrid between *Magnolia denudata* and *M. liliiflora* first appeared in Europe in the 1820s and is now represented by many cultivars. It is an erect tree that grows to 25 ft (8 m) tall and 15 ft (4.5 m) wide, usually single trunked. The dark green leaves are

Magnolia × soulangeana

tapered at the base and rounded at the tip, with a short point. Blooms in goblet, cup or saucer shapes and in white, pink or deep purple-pink appear from late winter to mid-spring, before and after the leaves emerge. The flowers of **'Alexandrina'** are pure white inside, flushed rose purple outside; and **'Brozzonii'** has very large white flowers, purple at the base. Goblet-shaped cultivars include **'Lennei'**, purplish pink outside, white to pale purple inside; **'Lennei Alba'** with pure white flowers; and **'Rustica Rubra'**, rose red outside and pink and white inside.
ZONES 5–10.

Magnolia virginiana

Magnolia wilsonii
WILSON'S MAGNOLIA

From China, this spreading, deciduous shrub or small tree grows to 20 ft (6 m) high and wide. In late spring and early summer fragrant cup-shaped white flowers with red or magenta stamens hang from arching branches among narrow, mid- to dark green leaves that are velvety beneath. Pink fruit follow, ripening to release shiny red seeds. It tolerates alkaline soil. **ZONES 7–10.**

Magnolia virginiana
SWEET BAY

From eastern America, this evergreen to semi-evergreen tree reaches a height of 20 ft (6 m) in gardens. In cooler climates it may become deciduous. Fragrant, creamy white, goblet-shaped flowers are produced in summer and are followed by red fruit 2 in (5 cm) long with scarlet seeds. The leaves of this species are smaller than those of most other magnolias. **ZONES 5–10.**

Magnolia wilsonii

Malus ioensis

MALUS

APPLE, CRABAPPLE

This genus of 35 species of deciduous flowering and fruiting trees from the northern temperate zones contains the diverse crabapple as well as the many varieties of the long-cultivated edible apple, probably derived from crosses between several species and usually named *Malus × domestica* or *M. pumila*. The leaves are simple and toothed, sometimes lobed, and the flower clusters vary from white to deep rose pink or deep reddish purple. They are valued for their shapely form, moderate size and delicate spring blossom.

CULTIVATION

Very frost hardy, they prefer a cool, moist climate and full sun (but tolerate part-shade) and need fertile, well-drained, loamy soil with protection from strong winds. They grow in poorer soils if fertilized annually. Cut out dead wood in winter and prune for a balanced shape. Propagate by budding in summer or grafting in winter. Watch for aphids and fireblight.

Malus florentina

syn. × *Malosorbus florentina*

This species from northern Italy may be a natural hybrid between *Malus sylvestris* and *Sorbus torminalis*. It is a small round-headed tree with white flowers followed by small bright red berries. Its serrated gray-green foliage is similar to that of a hawthorn (*Crataegus*). **ZONES 6–9.**

Malus ioensis

IOWA CRAB

Growing 20 ft (6 m) tall and 25 ft (8 m) wide, this leafy tree has a shrubby habit and good autumn color. Its heavy crop of large, fragrant, pale pink flowers is borne in late spring—it is one of the last crabapples to flower, and one of the finest. 'Plena' has double flowers followed by green fruit; 'Prairiefire' has glossy bark, red-purple single flowers and deep purple-red fruit. **ZONES 2–9.**

Malus florentina

Malus, Ornamental crabapple, 'Pink Perfection'

Malus, Ornamental crabapples

This group includes 'Beverly', an upright spreading tree to 20 ft (6 m) high with white single flowers and excellent, small bright red fruit; 'Butterball', up to 25 ft (8 m) tall with pink-tinged white flowers and bright orange-yellow fruit; 'Candied Apple', a small, spreading tree with pink flowers and red fruit; 'Dolgo', to 40 ft (12 m), with white flowers and purple-red fruit; 'John Downie', conical when mature, with red-flushed orange fruit; 'Katherine', with semi-double pink flowers and rich red fruit blushed yellow; 'Naragansett', a good disease-resistant tree to 13 ft (4 m) high with showy red buds, white single flowers and pendulous clusters of cherry-red fruit; 'Pink Perfection', with pale pink and white double flowers; 'Prince Georges', with sterile, scented fully double pale pink flowers; 'Profusion', with rich, dark wine-red flowers and cherry-like, red-purple fruit; 'Radiant', to 25 ft (8 m) high with deep red buds, deep pink single flowers and bright red fruit; 'Red Jade', a weeping tree to 12 ft (3.5 m) with white- to pink-flushed flowers and glossy red fruit; and 'Strathmore', a narrow upright tree to 9 ft (3 m) that bears fragrant, dark pink flowers and purple fruit. **ZONES 3–9.**

Malus sargentii
SARGENT'S CRABAPPLE

Malus, Ornamental crabapple, 'Prince Georges'

A spreading shrub, this species reaches a height of 8–10 ft (2.4–3 m) and spread of 12–20 ft (3.5–6 m). It bears oval, dark green leaves with serrated margins, masses of white flowers and tiny, deep red fruit that last well into winter. Some branches may carry thorns. **ZONES 4–9.**

Malus sargentii

Malus sylvestris
WILD CRABAPPLE, COMMON CRABAPPLE

From Europe, this parent of orchard crabapples can grow 30 ft (9 m) tall and 10 ft (3 m) wide, and has a rounded crown and dark bark. It bears white flowers flushed with pink and its yellow, flushed orange-red fruit, although rather sour and bitter, make delicious conserves. The leaves have a partly red stalk and some branches may bear thorns. **ZONES 3–9.**

Malus sylvestris cultivar

Metasequoia glyptostroboides

Its gracefully conical outline and delicate foliage, light green in spring and summer, have made the dawn redwood a popular tree. It grows unusually fast in favorable conditions, and old trees may reach 200 ft (60 m) in height. As the tree matures, the rough-textured bark turns from reddish to dark brown to gray. It can be clipped to make a tall hedge.
ZONES 5–10.

METASEQUOIA

DAWN REDWOOD

Until shortly after World War II, *Metasequoia glyptostroboides*, the single species of the genus, was known only as a fossil conifer. Then a stand of living trees was discovered in western China; from these it has been propagated and widely planted in temperate-climate areas. It is notable for its gold and russet foliage in autumn—it is one of the few deciduous conifers. It grows very rapidly and, as the timber is durable and of fine quality, it is a very promising tree for cool-climate forestry.

CULTIVATION
It prefers full sun, deep fertile soil, good summer rainfall and shelter from strong winds. It is fully frost hardy. Propagate from seed or cuttings from side shoots in autumn.

Metasequoia glyptostroboides

Metasequoia glyptostroboides

Microbiota decussata

MICROBIOTA

There is just one species in this genus, a dwarf evergreen conifer that is excellent as a groundcover, as a specimen on its own, or grouped with other low-growing conifers or heathers. It also makes a good foil for other more colorful plants, such as bulbs.

CULTIVATION

Very frost hardy, it does best in free-draining soil with an open aspect, although it tolerates extremes of temperature and high altitudes. Prune only if absolutely necessary and then only into the new wood. Propagate from seed or from tip cuttings.

Microbiota decussata
RUSSIAN ARBORVITAE

This conifer from Siberia grows to only 18 in (45 cm) high with a spread of up to 10 ft (3 m). Its branches nod at the tips and bear flat sprays of scale-like, yellowish green leaves (bronze in winter). Its small, round cones are pale brown and contain one fertile seed each. **ZONES 3–9.**

Nothofagus fusca
NEW ZEALAND RED BEECH

This attractive, erect evergreen has a dome-shaped crown and averages 20–40 ft (6–12 m) in height when cultivated and up to 120 ft (36 m) in the wild. The egg-shaped, roughly serrated foliage is up to 2 in (5 cm) long; immature leaves turn reddish bronze in cooler weather. Small, green flowers are followed by seed cups, each containing 3 angular seeds. **ZONES 7–10.**

Nothofagus menziesii
NEW ZEALAND SILVER BEECH

Famed for its beautiful silver bark, this evergreen species from New Zealand bears a mass of small, dense leaves with coarsely serrated margins. Reaching a height of 70 ft (21 m), it needs plenty of sun and protection from wind. The flowers appear as small catkins in summer. **ZONES 7–10.**

Nothofagus solandri
BLACK BEECH

A 60 ft (18 m) high evergreen tree native to New Zealand, the black beech has small leaves, around ½ in (12 mm) long, but they are densely packed in fan-like sprays. The young growth is soft and downy. Small, reddish brown flowers, heavy with pollen, open in spring. Although individually the flowers are not very significant, when in full bloom the tree develops a reddish cast. *Nothofagus solandri* var. *cliffortioides* has twisted and more sharply pointed leaves. **ZONES 7–10.**

Nothofagus fusca

NOTHOFAGUS
SOUTHERN BEECH

Wide ranging in the southern hemisphere from South America to southeastern Australia, *Nothofagus* is a genus of more than 25 species of evergreen and deciduous trees. Fast growing, they have dark green leaves often with toothed margins. The foliage of several of the deciduous species displays rich bronze hues before dropping. The small fruits each contain 3 triangular seeds known as beechnuts.

CULTIVATION

Southern beeches can be cultivated in a variety of climates provided they have protection from strong winds. They prefer acidic soil deep enough to support their large root system and should be planted out when small and never transplanted. Position in full sun and water well when young. Propagate from cuttings in summer or seed in autumn.

Nothofagus menziesii

Nothofagus solandri

Nyssa sylvatica
BLACK TUPELO, SOUR GUM, PEPPERIDGE

This elegant tree is one of the most decorative and useful of all deciduous plants, as it flourishes in swampy conditions. The glossy, 4 in (10 cm) long leaves, which are slightly wider towards the tip, are dark or yellowish green then turn brilliant red, often with shades of orange and yellow as well, before dropping. It grows to 70 ft (21 m) with a broad columnar conical habit and has an unusual trunk covered with brownish gray bark, which breaks up into large pieces on mature specimens. **ZONES 3–10.**

NYSSA
TUPELO

Nyssa sylvatica

Occurring naturally in southern Asia and North America, this genus is named after Nyssa, the water nymph, because the trees insist on adequate year-round water to survive. Fast growing and wind tolerant, they must be left undisturbed after planting and may reach a maximum height of 120 ft (36 m) with a broad-based, conical shape. Small clusters of greenish white flowers appear during summer, to be followed by vivid, dark purple berries up to 1 in (25 mm) long which provide an effective contrast to the stunning foliage. Few trees attract as much attention as these when they are clad in their spectacular red, crimson, yellow and orange autumn foliage.

CULTIVATION

They need fertile, moist but well-drained, neutral to acidic soil, sun or part-shade and a cool climate. Prune only to remove dead or crowded branches. Propagate from cuttings in summer or from seed in autumn.

Ostrya carpinifolia
HOP-HORNBEAM

Native to southern Europe and Turkey, the hop-hornbeam forms a compact tree of up to 60 ft (18 m) with a conical crown. Its toothed, dark green leaves turn a clear yellow before falling and look very attractive against the smooth gray bark of its trunk. The pendent fruiting catkins are cream to straw-colored, about 2 in (5 cm) long. **ZONES 2–9.**

OSTRYA
HOP-HORNBEAM

There are 10 species of deciduous trees in this genus scattered through temperate regions of the northern hemisphere. Allied to the true hornbeams *(Carpinus)*, they have similar toothed leaves that are prominently veined and tapered to a point. In spring, the yellow male catkins look attractive against the bright green new leaves; these are followed in summer by the shorter fruiting catkins, each small nutlet enclosed in a bladder-like bract like those of hops *(Humulus)*, hence the common name. Hop-hornbeams may be rather slow growing in the early stages but are attractive small- to medium-sized trees, usually with a good autumn coloring.

CULTIVATION

To flourish, these frost-hardy trees need a sheltered position in full sun or part-shade and fertile, well-drained soil. Prune only to remove dead branches. Propagate from seed in spring.

Ostrya carpinifolia

Oxydendrum arboreum

Oxydendrum arboreum

Making a small, 20–40 ft (6–12 m) tree, this cool-climate species tolerates frost better than it does dry conditions. The trunk is slender and the crown pyramid-shaped. Streamers of small white lily-of-the-valley-like flowers appear in late summer sometimes prior to, sometimes coinciding with, the display of deep scarlet foliage. **ZONES 3–9.**

OXYDENDRUM

SORREL TREE, SOURWOOD

The single deciduous tree species in this genus is a native of eastern USA and is grown for its autumn foliage and flowers. The leaves are alternate and finely toothed; the fragrant, small urn-shaped flowers are held in drooping terminal panicles. The genus takes its name from Greek words meaning 'sour tree', a reference to the sour-tasting foliage.

CULTIVATION

For the best autumn colors, it should be planted in an open position in sun or part-shade in moist soil. An occasional dressing of iron and/or ammonia after flowering may be required. Propagate from cuttings in summer or seed in autumn.

PARROTIA

PERSIAN WITCH-HAZEL

This genus from Iran and the Caucasus was named after F. W. Parrot, a German botanist. It consists of a single tree species cultivated for its rich hues in autumn and unusual flowers. The petal-less flowers consist of upright, wiry, dark red stamens enclosed in brown bracts. They appear in early spring before the leaves, which are about 4 in (10 cm) long and have undulating edges. The branches on older trees dip down towards the ground.

CULTIVATION

A lime-tolerant tree, it is said to achieve its best colors when grown in slightly acid soil. It grows well in full sun, fertile soil and temperate climates. Propagate from softwood cuttings in summer or from seed in autumn—germination can take up to 18 months.

Parrotia persica

This spreading, short-trunked, deciduous tree with flaking bark can reach 40 ft (12 m) in the wild; in a garden it is unlikely to grow above 25 ft (7.5 m). The roughly diamond-shaped leaves turn magnificent shades of yellow, orange and crimson in autumn.
ZONES 5–9.

Parrotia persica

Paulownia fortunei

PAULOWNIA

Originating in eastern Asia, this genus of 17 species of deciduous trees is named for Anna Paulowna, daughter of Paul I, Tsar of Russia. Some fast-growing species reach 8 ft (2.4 m) in their first year, eventually growing to 50 ft (15 m). Their big, heart-shaped leaves and dense clusters of elegant flowers make them distinctive shade trees. Conspicuous, attractive buds appear in autumn, opening in spring to foxglove-like flower spikes; these are followed by the leaves and capsules containing winged seeds. Some species are grown for timber in China and Japan.

CULTIVATION

These very frost-hardy trees do best in well-drained, fertile soil, with ample moisture in summer and shelter from strong winds. Propagate from seed or root cuttings taken in late summer or winter.

Paulownia fortunei
POWTON

This spreading tree to 40 ft
(12 m) tall has broad, oval,
mid-green leaves, 6–8 in
(15–20 cm) long and half as
wide with the midribs and
major veins clearly visible
on the hairy undersides. The
leaves turn dull yellow before
dropping in autumn. Fragrant,
3 in (8 cm) long, bell-shaped
flowers, cream to pale mauve
with a creamy, purple-spotted
throat, are borne in clusters
in spring. **ZONES 6–10.**

Paulownia tomentosa
syn. *Paulownia imperialis*
PRINCESS TREE, EMPRESS TREE

This tree can reach a height
and width of 40 ft (12 m) and
is valued for its large, paired,
heart-shaped leaves, up to
12 in (30 cm) wide, and erect,
fragrant, pale violet flowers.
Grown in both cool- and
warm-temperate climates, it
can suffer frost damage to the
flower buds. If pruned almost
to the ground each winter, the
tree will develop branches
about 10 ft (3 m) long with
enormous leaves, but will not
flower. **ZONES 5–10.**

Paulownia tomentosa

PHELLODENDRON

Elegant, slender and requiring little maintenance, these 10
species of deciduous trees from east Asia grow to 50 ft (15 m)
tall with a crown spreading to 12 ft (3.5 m). The shiny, light
green pinnate leaves turn a rich shade of yellow in autumn.
Small, yellowish green flowers appear in late spring or early
summer, followed by blackberry-like fruits.

CULTIVATION

These trees are extremely hardy, tolerating both frost and harsh
sun, although they prefer protection from wind. They grow
best in full sun with fertile, well-drained soil. Seed may be germinated in spring, or propagate from cuttings or by grafting
or layering in summer.

Phellodendron amurense
AMUR CORK TREE

Originally from China and Japan, this is the most common species of the genus in cultivation and earns its common name from its corky older branches. Growing to 40 ft (12 m) tall, it prefers humus-rich soil and summer moisture. Its bright green leaves with 5 to 11 leaflets have an unusual heart-shaped base and a pungent aroma. The 5-petalled flowers, male and female on separate trees, produce berries that are held above the foliage in dense bunches. **ZONES 3–9.**

Phellodendron sachalinense
syn. *Phellodendron amurense* var. *sachalinense*
SAKHALIN CORK TREE

This 25 ft (8 m) tall tree from northeast Asia has thin, dark brown bark that, despite its common name, is not corky like many *Phellodendron* species. The young growth is rusty red and the leaves are up to 12 in (30 cm) long with 7 to 11 leaflets. They are deep green above, blue-green below. **ZONES 3–9.**

Phellodendron amurense
Top: *Phellodendron sachalinense*

PICEA
SPRUCE

The 30 to 40 members of this genus of evergreen conifers originate in the cool-temperate regions of the northern hemisphere where there are deep pockets of moist, rich, acidic, freely draining soil. Sometimes reaching an impressive 220 ft (66 m) in height, they develop a stiff, narrow, conical, sometimes columnar growth habit with short, horizontal to upward-pointing branches. The leaves are arranged spirally on short pegs and their color varies from bright green to glaucous blue. Able to withstand strong winds, they bear large cones which hang downwards, distinguishing the genus from the superficially similar firs *(Abies)*. The slow growth and contorted habit of some cultivars make them ideal bonsai specimens; others are prostrate and make excellent groundcovers. This genus produces valuable timber, plus pitch and turpentine.

CULTIVATION

Plant in full sun in deep, moist but well-drained, neutral to acid soil. Propagate from seed or cuttings in autumn or by grafting. They will not survive transplantation when large, nor grow well in heavily polluted environments. They may be prone to attack from aphids, red spider mites and, in warm, humid climates, fungal infections.

Picea abies

Picea abies

syn. *Picea excelsa*

NORWAY SPRUCE, COMMON SPRUCE

Native to Scandinavia where it can grow to nearly 200 ft (60 m), but less in cultivation, this is the traditional Christmas tree in Europe. Its straight trunk is covered in orange-brown, maturing to reddish, bark which it sheds in scales. The leaves are dark green and rectangular and the reddish cigar-shaped cones, erect at first, become pendulous and grow to 8 in (20 cm) long. Dwarf shrubby cultivars have usually been propagated from witches' brooms, a tight clump of congested foliage that sometimes appears on the plant. Shallow rooted, the Norway spruce can be upended by strong winds. **'Conica'** is a low-growing cultivar, less than 15 ft (4.5 m) with a broad, conical crown. **'Maxwellii'**, the Maxwell spruce, is a low-growing, compact form ideal for rockeries and borders. **'Pumila Glauca'** is a semi-erect dwarf form with bluish green foliage. **'Pygmaea'** is a slow-growing dwarf form. **'Reflexa'** is a weeping cultivar distinguished by growing tips that point upwards when young; it makes a beautiful prostrate shrub. **'Inversa'** is a spreading bush with downward-trailing branches. **'Little Gem'** is a flat-topped dwarf shrub that grows very slowly. **'Nidiformis'**, the bird's nest spruce, is a dwarf form with outward- and upward-curving branches that tend to make a nest-like bowl in the center of the plant. **ZONES 2–9.**

Picea abies 'Little Gem'

Picea breweriana

Picea breweriana

WEEPING SPRUCE,
BREWER'S WEEPING SPRUCE

The branchlets of this North American conifer hang its foliage in 3 ft (1 m) long, curtain-like streamers from its horizontally held branches. The needles are blue-green and flattened and the light brown cones grow to 4 in (10 cm) long. The tree forms a strong trunk, reaching a height of 100 ft (30 m) or more, with a broad conical shape that becomes narrow if the tree is grown in crowded conditions. **ZONES 2–9.**

Picea engelmannii
ENGELMANN SPRUCE

Growing slowly to 150 ft (45 m) or more, this is one of the most cold-tolerant evergreen trees; it also grows well in poor soil. The densely textured, pyramid-shaped crown, spreading to 15 ft (4.5 m), is made up of sharply pointed, 4-angled, soft gray to steel-blue needles up to 1 in (25 mm) long. The cones are cylindrical, green and tinged with purple. **ZONES 1–9.**

Picea engelmannii

Picea mariana
AMERICAN BLACK SPRUCE

From the USA, this 60 ft (18 m) conifer has a pyramidal crown spreading to 15 ft (4.5 m) composed of whorled branches bearing blunt, bluish green needles. The 1½ in (35 mm) long cones are purplish brown and remain on the tree for up to 30 years. *Picea mariana* prefers boggy soil and must have an open, sunny position to thrive. **'Nana'** is a popular slow-growing dwarf cultivar, suitable for smaller gardens. **ZONES 1–8.**

Picea mariana

Picea glauca
WHITE SPRUCE

From Canada and grown commercially for the paper industry, this slow-growing tree can reach 80 ft (24 m). Bright green shoots appear in spring, and the drooping branchlets carry aromatic, 4-angled needles up to ½ in (12 mm) long. The cones are small and narrow. The cultivar **'Echiniformis'** is a dwarf, mounding form with a spiky, needle-studded surface. *Picea glauca* var. *albertiana* 'Conica', the dwarf Alberta spruce, is a very densely foliaged, bright green, conical dwarf that is usually seen as a 3 ft (1 m) shrub, though with great age it can reach 10 ft (3 m). **ZONES 1–9.**

Picea glauca var. *albertiana* 'Conica'

Picea pungens 'Viridis'

Picea omorika

SERBIAN SPRUCE

Picea omorika

From Serbia and Bosnia, this spruce reaches 100 ft (30 m) or more with pendulous branches forming a narrow, spire-like crown. The bright green, flattened needles have a square tip and a grayish underside. The purplish cones mature to a deep brown. Happy in a range of soils from acid to limy and more tolerant of urban pollution than most species, it is one of the best *Picea* for large, temperate-climate gardens. *Picea omorika* × *breweriana* is a hybrid between the 2 popular, award-winning species. **ZONES 4–9.**

Picea orientalis

CAUCASIAN SPRUCE

Reaching 100 ft (30 m) in its native Turkey and Caucasus, this slow-growing spruce produces abundant, pendent branches from ground level up. The brilliant, glossy green foliage is short and neat; spectacular brick-red male cones appear in spring, and the purple female cones grow 3 in (8 cm) long. This spruce prefers a sheltered site. '**Atrovirens**' displays attractive rich green foliage that flushes to golden yellow in early summer. '**Aurea**' has golden-yellow juvenile foliage that greens as it ages but retains a hint of gold. **ZONES 3–9.**

Picea orientalis

Picea pungens

COLORADO SPRUCE

This frost-hardy species from the west coast of the USA grows to 100 ft (30 m) or more in the wild, although it is usually much smaller in gardens. It has a pyramid of bluish green foliage composed of stiff and sharply pointed needles; the bark is gray. Prune regularly as fresh growth will not bud from dead wood. The many cultivars include '**Aurea**', with golden leaves; '**Caerulea**', with bluish white leaves; '**Conica**', which grows into a cone-shaped cultivar; '**Glauca**', which is the commonly grown Colorado blue spruce with striking, steel-blue new foliage; '**Globosa**', which is a rounded, dwarf form with attractive bluish leaves that is very slow-growing, taking a decade or more to reach 24 in (60 cm) in height; '**Hoopsii**', which is prized for its even bluer foliage; '**Iseli Fastigiate**', with upward-pointing branches and very sharp needles; '**Koster**', with foliage maturing from silvery deep blue to green, spiralled branches and tubular, scaled cones about 4 in (10 cm) long; **'Pendens'**, a prostrate, blue cultivar; **'Royal Blue'**, another striking blue cultivar; **'Moerheimii'** from the Netherlands and bred to produce silvery blue foliage that is longer than other forms; and **'Viridis'**, with very dark green foliage. **ZONES 2–10.**

Picea pungens

Picea pungens 'Pendens'

Picea sitchensis

SITKA SPRUCE

Fast growing to 150 ft (45 m), this is one of the few trees in the genus that can survive being transplanted when young. It also enjoys humid sites but needs good summer rainfall. Its trunk has pale bark. The pyramidal crown becomes broader as the tree matures and is composed of whorled branches; the leaves are flattened, stiff and bluish gray. The 4 in (10 cm) long cones are covered with thin papery scales and they release their winged seeds on warm spring days. The timber is not very strong. **ZONES 4–9.**

Picea smithiana

Picea smithiana

MORINDA SPRUCE,
WEST HIMALAYAN SPRUCE

This 120 ft (36 m) spruce, found from Nepal to Afghanistan, develops graceful branches that hang in cascades. The foliage is dark green and composed of fine, 4-angled needles up to 1½ in (35 mm) long. Green cones maturing to shiny brown grow to 8 in (20 cm) long, often at the ends of the branches, accentuating their pendulous effect. **ZONES 6–9.**

Picea sitchensis

PINUS
PINE

In everyday speech 'pine' and 'conifer' are almost synonymous but to botanists and foresters the name pine means a tree of the genus *Pinus*, arguably the most important genus of conifers. Consisting of around 120 species of needle-leafed evergreens, *Pinus* is represented in most parts of the northern hemisphere, from northern Scandinavia and Alaska to the equator (in Sumatra), though absent from all but the far north of Africa. The greatest concentrations of species are in the Mexican highlands, southern USA and China—though the best-known species come from more northern regions, for example, the Scots pine *(P. sylvestris)* of northern Eurasia. Most pines are medium to tall forest trees but a few are small and bushy, though never true shrubs in their typical, wild forms unless stunted by extreme conditions. The characteristic feature of *Pinus* is the way the needles are grouped in bundles, the number per bundle, usually be-tween 2 and 7, is fairly constant for each species. Male (pollen) and female (seed) cones are borne on the same tree. The species of *Pinus* are divided into 2 major groups, namely the white pines (soft pines) with typically 5 needles and non-woody cone scales, and the black pines (hard pines) with typically 2 to 4 needles and woody cone scales, the cones taking 2 years or longer to mature their seeds. The white pines are typified by the North American *P. strobus* and include some of the tallest conifers; the black pines are typified by *P. sylvestris* or *P. radiata* and account for the majority of species, includ-ing nearly all those from the subtropics and tropics. Pines include many of the world's im-portant forest trees, especially in cool-temperate and subarctic regions, providing lumber for many everyday purposes including house con-struction, and much of the world's paper pulp. In the past their aromatic resins (pitch) and tur-pentines had many uses but these have largely been replaced by petroleum products. The seeds of several species (pine nuts) are important foods in some cultures. In recent times the bark of pines, once discarded as sawmill waste, has become widely used in horticultural growing mediums and as a mulch in landscaping. For smaller gardens the most suitable pines are some of the dwarf cultivars of species such as *P. sylvestris*, *P. thunbergii*, *P. strobus* and *P. mugo*, which can be grown as tub or rock-garden specimens. Many pines can also be used as bonsai subjects, or they can be grown for several years as Christmas trees and dis-carded when too large.

CULTIVATION

Most pines are easily grown in a wide range of conditions, though their tolerance of both cold and warmth varies and each species has its optimum climate. They are mostly very wind resistant and will thrive on soils of moderate to low fertility, but may need a symbiotic soil fungus to assist nutrient uptake on poorer soils—these fungi are likely to be present in the pines' native regions, but a handful of decaying needles from a pine forest can be added if planting pines where none have grown before. The majority of pines require well-drained soil, and resent soil disturbance. Seed is normally the only means of propagation, cuttings being almost impossible to strike, but cultivars may be grafted.

Pinus aristata
BRISTLE CONE PINE

Slow growing and long lived, this North American pine can reach 30 ft (9 m) or more in height. As a garden plant it forms a dense shrubby tree, making an effective informal windbreak. Its 2 in (5 cm) long, deep green needles flecked with resin press closely to the stem in groups of five. Its cones are glossy and 14 in (10 cm) long. **ZONES 5–9.**

Pinus aristata

Pinus cembra

AROLLA PINE, SWISS STONE PINE

Growing to 80 ft (24 m) in its native Alps, central Europe and
Siberia, this pine is appreciated for its neat, conical shape, dense
foliage and long-lived needles. It is tough and disease resistant,
but must be kept moist. The 6 in (15 cm) long, dark green,
glossy needles occur in groups of five. The 3 in (8 cm) cones
mature from purple to deep bluish brown. The seeds are edible.
ZONES 4–9.

Pinus contorta

SHORE PINE, BEACH PINE

This species from the west coast of North America grows quickly
to 30 ft (9 m) tall then develops horizontal branches and grows
slowly to 70 ft (21 m). It has pairs of dark green, 2 in (5 cm)
needles and small yellow-brown cones. It is easily trimmed to
shape and does well as a garden specimen but does not thrive in
hot, dry areas. *Pinus contorta* var. *latifolia*, the lodgepole pine,
is a straight-trunked, tapering tree to 80 ft (24 m) in its native
Rocky Mountains but is slow growing, low and bushy in cultivation. It has yellowish green, 2–3 in (5–8 cm) long needles in
pairs and small, oval cones that release fine seeds that are
carried by wind. **ZONES 7–9.**

Pinus cembra

Pinus contorta var. *latifolia*

Pinus densiflora

JAPANESE RED PINE

Used as a timber tree in its
native Japan, where it can
reach 100 ft (30 m), in cultivation this distinctive pine
with red bark and naturally
twisted shape is slow growing
and often multi-trunked. It
can be pruned and makes a
popular bonsai specimen.
Ovoid, yellow-purplish cones
stand out boldly from the
bright green, 4 in (10 cm)
long foliage. There are many
popular cultivars including
'Tanyosho Nana'. The dwarf
cultivar 'Umbraculifera' has
an umbrella-like canopy and
orange-red, flaky bark on its
multiple trunks; an extremely
slow grower, it eventually
reaches 15 ft (4.5 m). 'Oculus
Draconis', the dragon's eye
pine, has yellow-banded
needles. 'Pendula' is a strong-
growing, semi-prostrate
cultivar best grown near
ponds or on banks where its
weeping form can be most
appreciated. **ZONES 4–9.**

Pinus halepensis

ALEPPO PINE

From the eastern Mediterranean area, this pine is the most resistant to dry conditions, in fact tolerating most conditions except severe frost when young. Fast growing to 50 ft (15 m), it has a spreading crown and a distinctive rugged character. The young bark is ash gray, but ages to reddish brown. The soft, light green needles are 4 in (10 cm) long and are usually carried in pairs; the 3–4 in (8–10 cm) cones are reddish brown. **ZONES 7–10.**

Pinus halepensis

Pinus mugo

MOUNTAIN PINE, SWISS MOUNTAIN PINE

In the mountains of Europe this small tree grows slowly to 12 ft (3.5 m). Its windswept appearance reflects its habitat, making it an interesting bonsai and rock garden specimen. Its pairs of 2 in (5 cm) long, bright green needles develop from resinous buds. The oval, dark brown cones are 1–2 in (2–5 cm) long. This species does not tolerate extreme heat or dry conditions. **'Aurea'** has golden foliage. **'Gnom'**, a compact bush 6 ft (1.8 m) high with a similar spread, produces whitish new shoots against rich, black-green mature growth. **'Mops'** matures to 5 ft (1.5 m) over 10 years. *Pinus mugo* var. *pumilo*, the dwarf Swiss mountain pine, develops a compact bun shape, achieving 30 in (75 cm) in 10 years. **ZONES 2–9.**

Pinus mugo 'Mops'

Pinus nigra

AUSTRIAN BLACK PINE,
EUROPEAN BLACK PINE

From central and southern Europe, this pine grows to 120 ft (36 m) or more in the wild, though cultivated specimens rarely exceed 50 ft (15 m). It has an open, conical habit with a whitish brown trunk, whorled branches and a dense crown of dark green, 6 in (15 cm) long, paired needles; its cones are 3 in (8 cm) long. It grows in chalk and clay and tolerates coastal conditions. *Pinus nigra* var. *maritima*, the Corsican pine, forms a denser crown and is slower growing; its gray-green twisted needle pairs can exceed 6 in (15 cm) and it has cracking bark and a very straight trunk that is harvested for timber. **ZONES 4–9.**

Pinus nigra var. *maritima*

Pinus palustris

Pinus palustris

LONG-LEAF PINE

From eastern and central USA, this pine grows to 100 ft (30 m) with an open crown. It has blunt, bluish green needles up to 18 in (45 cm) long, arranged in groups of three. Its 6–10 in (15–25 cm) long, reddish brown cones have spines on the tips of their scales and are held on the tree for up to 20 years. This pine will not tolerate strong winds or dry conditions. **ZONES 4–11.**

Pinus parviflora

JAPANESE WHITE PINE

This pyramid-shaped pine usually grows to 40 ft (12 m) in culti-vation but in its native Japan can reach 80 ft (24 m) tall with a similar spread. It produces some of the shortest needles in the genus—1½ in (35 mm) long. Its dense, bluish green foliage and slow growth habit make it a popular bonsai or tub subject. '**Brevifolia**' is an upright, sparsely foliaged cultivar. The blue-foliaged '**Glauca**' takes many years to reach 5 ft (1.5 m); its needles have distinctive blue-white bands on their inner sides. '**Adcock's Dwarf**' is a bun-shaped cultivar that grows to 30 in (75 cm). **ZONES 3–9.**

Pinus pinaster

Pinus parviflora 'Brevifolia'

Pinus pinaster

MARITIME PINE, CLUSTER PINE

From the Mediterranean region and growing quickly to 100 ft (30 m), this pine does not tolerate dry con-ditions or frost but enjoys coastal locations and is a good windbreak. Its bright reddish brown bark is deeply furrowed. The paired green needles, up to 10 in (25 cm) long, are stiff and shiny. Rich brown, oval cones 6 in (15 cm) or more long persist on the branches for many years without opening. This pine is valued for timber and resin. **ZONES 7–10.**

Pinus ponderosa

PONDEROSA PINE, WESTERN YELLOW PINE

Abundant in its native western North America, this pine has a deeply fissured bark with a mosaic of broad, smooth, yellowish brown, reddish brown and pinkish gray plates. An important timber tree, it can reach 200 ft (60 m) but in cultivation is usually smaller. It has dark brown cones on spire-like branches. Its dark green needles, in bundles of 3, are up to 10 in (25 cm) long. **ZONES 5–9.**

Pinus strobus

Pinus strobus

EASTERN WHITE PINE, WEYMOUTH PINE

Occurring naturally in eastern North America, where it is valued for its timber, this species grows to 200 ft (60 m) in the wild but to less than 80 ft (24 m) in cultivation. It is characterized by deeply fissured, grayish brown bark and whorled branches. The conical crown becomes flattish with age. Its fine, 4 in (10 cm) long, bluish green needles are soft and are carried in groups of five. The pointed cones, clustered at the branch ends, produce copious amounts of white resin. This species develops rapidly if grown away from a polluted environment and, though cold hardy, it is susceptible to dry conditions and windburn. '**Fastigiata**' has vivid green growth on upward-pointing branches. '**Nana**' is a rounded dwarf cultivar with dense foliage that completely obscures the branches. '**Prostrata**' is a very low-growing, spreading cultivar that eventually mounds to around 18 in (45 cm) high at the center. '**Radiata**' is a dwarf cultivar that develops into a slowly spreading hummock of foliage up to 24 in (60 cm) high. **ZONES 3–9.**

Pinus sylvestris

SCOTS PINE

This fast-growing species, found throughout northern Europe and western Asia and the only pine indigenous to the UK, is the most commonly grown pine in Europe and is often used in forestry. It reaches 100 ft (30 m) with a rounded head of foliage and orange-red bark. Twisted, bluish green needles grow in pairs and are 3 in (8 cm) long. This pine grows well in poor sandy soil but will not tolerate dry conditions. Dwarf cultivars make attractive tub specimens. '**Aurea**' has gold-tinted foliage, especially the new growth and the winter foliage. '**Beuvronensis**' is a very densely foliaged dwarf cultivar with light blue-green needles that eventually reaches 6 ft (1.8 m) tall but is small for many years. '**Moseri**' is a small pyramidal cultivar with yellow foliage. '**Watereri**' only grows 2–3 in (5–8 cm) a year and can be thought of as a dwarf, blue-foliaged form of the Scots pine. It is ideal for rockeries or collections of dwarf conifers. **ZONES 4–9.**

Pinus sylvestris 'Moseri'

Pinus thunbergii

syn. *Pinus thunbergiana*

JAPANESE BLACK PINE

This pine has a rugged trunk, purplish black bark, pairs of thick needles, conspicuous white buds and an intricate framework of irregular, layered, horizontal branches. Widely grown in Japan as an ornamental, it has for centuries inspired artists and bonsai masters. It will stand any amount of pruning and trimming to shape; untrimmed it grows to 120 ft (36 m). It does very well in containers. '**Nishiki**' is a naturally dwarf, gnarled cultivar with corky bark very popular for bonsai. **ZONES 5–9.**

Pinus wallichiana
BHUTAN PINE, BLUE PINE

This ornamental pine is an effective centerpiece for a large lawn, with its conical shape, broad base and graceful long branches bearing drooping, gray-green needles 6–8 in (15–20 cm) long. Its 12 in (30 cm) long cones are eyecatching. If grown in moist, deep soil it can reach 150 ft (45 m). It is cold and disease resistant but suffers in hot, dry conditions. **ZONES 5–9.**

Pinus wallichiana

Pistacia chinensis

Pistacia chinensis
CHINESE PISTACHIO

Growing to 25 ft (8 m) in gardens, this deciduous species has glossy green leaves consisting of up to 10 pairs of leaflets that in autumn turn yellow, orange and scarlet. The inconspicuous flowers, borne in panicles, are followed in summer by small red spherical seed pods that turn blue in autumn and attract birds. An excellent street tree, it also makes a good canopy for shade-loving shrubs. It often forms a double trunk. **ZONES 5–10.**

PISTACIA
PISTACHIO

This small genus consists of 9 species of deciduous and evergreen trees and shrubs occurring naturally in the warm-temperate regions of the northern hemisphere. It includes the familiar edible pistachio nuts as well as ornamental deciduous species that develop vivid foliage tones in autumn, and species grown for their resins and oils. The tallest species grow to 80 ft (24 m). The leaf arrangements are compound, usually composed of an even number of leaflets. The flowers are generally inconspicuous, male and female flowers occurring on separate plants. Female plants display clusters of small berries or fleshy fruits in autumn and early winter.

CULTIVATION

A well-drained soil in full sun is preferred. Propagate from seed sown in autumn and winter, or by budding or grafting.

PITTOSPORUM

Pittosporum tenuifolium 'Variegatum'

This genus consists of some 200 species of evergreen trees and shrubs from the tropical and subtropical regions of Australasia, Africa, Asia and the Pacific Islands. They make good specimen plants, screens and windbreaks or dense hedges in mild-winter climates. The leaves are arranged alternately along the stems or in whorls. Several species have striking foliage prized by flower arrangers. The fragrant flowers are followed by fruits with a hard outer capsule enclosing round seeds with a sticky covering.

CULTIVATION

Grow in fertile, well-drained soil and keep moist over summer to maintain the foliage at its best. They need full sun or part-shade, and a sheltered position in colder areas. Some species are frost tolerant and many are excellent for seaside gardens. Propagate from seed in autumn or spring, or from tip cuttings in summer.

Pittosporum tenuifolium
'Tom Thumb'

Pittosporum tobira 'Variegatum'

Pittosporum tenuifolium
KOHUHU, TAWHIWHI

This New Zealand species can reach 30 ft (9 m); young plants are columnar, rounding as they mature. It has pale green oblong leaves, 3 in (8 cm) long, and black twigs and bark. Its small, dark brown flowers, borne in late spring, have an intense honey perfume at night. In late summer its round fruit ripen from green to almost black. It tolerates heavy pruning and prefers an open, sunny site. 'Silver Magic' has small, silver-gray leaves that develop pink tints, especially in winter. 'Tom Thumb' is a low-growing form usually under 3 ft (1 m) tall with deep purple-bronze leaves with wavy edges; 'Variegatum' has olive-green leaves with cream margins. **ZONES 9–11.**

Pittosporum tobira
JAPANESE MOCK ORANGE

From Japan and China, this shrubby species eventually reaches 8 ft (2.4 m). Its oval to oblong shiny green leaves, 4 in (10 cm) long, occur in whorls along the stems. Star-shaped, cream flowers with an orange blossom scent appear in late spring and summer. It thrives in mild climates in an open, sunny position. Provide protection in colder climates. *Pittosporum tobira* is a good hedge plant in coastal regions. 'Wheeler's Dwarf', a mound-like shrub, grows to 24 in (60 cm); 'Variegatum' has an irregular silvery white edge to its leaves. **ZONES 9–11.**

PLAGIANTHUS

This genus consists of *Plagianthus regius*, which is 40 ft (12 m) tall and is one of the few deciduous trees native to New Zealand, and *P. divaricatus*, a shrub that eventually reaches 6 ft (1.8 m) in height and spread. They have light olive-green leaves with serrated edges and greenish white flowers in summer. They are very tough and adaptable plants.

CULTIVATION

Plant in moist, well-drained soil with light shade when young. Propagate from seed or grow selected male forms from cuttings.

Plagianthus regius

Plagianthus regius
syn. *Plagianthus betulinus*
RIBBONWOOD

When young this tree is a densely twiggy, spreading shrub and stays in this form for several years. The leaves are up to 4 in (10 cm) long. There are separate male and female plants, both producing panicles of yellowish or greenish white flowers; those of the male are slightly larger and more decorative. The name ribbonwood comes from the lacy inner bark. **ZONES 7–9.**

Platanus orientalis

PLATANUS
PLANE, SYCAMORE

This genus consists of 6 species of large, vigorous, wide-crowned, deciduous trees from Eurasia, North America and Mexico. It contains some of the world's largest shade trees for dry-summer climates, many of which are widely used as street trees. They are called planes or plane trees in some countries, sycamores in others. The most conspicuous feature is the flaking, mottled bark, which is shed in winter. The 5-lobed leaves are large and maple-like, and the brown seed balls hang in clusters on the trees in winter. The flowers are insignificant.

CULTIVATION

They thrive in deep, rich, well-drained soil in a sunny site and can be transplanted. Propagate from seed or cuttings or by layering. Most tolerate severe pruning, air pollution and hard construction (e.g. paving) covering the roots.

Platanus orientalis

Platanus × acerifolia

syns *Platanus × hispanica,*
P. × hybrida
LONDON PLANE

Used as a street tree for many years, this fast-growing hybrid can reach 120 ft (36 m) in height. It can withstand poor conditions and is resistant to leaf blight; however, the roots can lift paving and the large, bright green, leathery leaves can block small drains. Its straight, erect trunk is attractively blotched in gray, brown and white. **ZONES 3–10.**

Platanus orientalis

CHINAR, CHENNAR, ORIENTAL PLANE

Ranging from Turkey to the western Himalayas, this large tree grows about 100 ft (30 m) tall with spreading branches. Fully frost hardy, it has a relatively short, stout trunk and flaking gray to greenish white bark. Its deeply incised leaves form 5 to 7 narrow, pointed lobes, and 3 to 5 round, brown seedheads hang like beads on a thread. It is used as a street tree in Australia, southern Africa and southern Europe. The leaves of **'Digitata'** have elongated, narrow lobes that are more deeply cut.
ZONES 3–10.

Platanus × acerifolia

Platycladus orientalis

syns Thuja orientalis, Biota orientalis

This densely branched large shrub or small tree grows to 40 ft (12 m) tall. Young plants are conical to columnar; older trees have a domed crown of upward-sweeping branches atop the short trunk. Some smaller varieties have very dense, crisp foliage and a symmetrical shape; others are more irregular. They are recognizable by the arrangement of their foliage in narrow, vertical planes. Some dwarf types keep their fuzzy, juvenile foliage. 'Aurea Nana' is a golden-foliaged cultivar with a low, rounded growth habit seldom more than 3 ft (1 m) tall. 'Blue Cone' is a dense, upright plant with a conical growth habit and blue-green foliage. 'Elegantissima' is a neat, 8 ft (2.4 m) tall shrub with a broad columnar growth habit and yellow-tipped foliage sprays that develop golden tones in winter. 'Filiformis Erecta' has thread-like foliage that droops slightly or lays flat along the stems and grows 5–6 ft (1.5–1.8 m) tall. 'Green Cone' is similar in shape to 'Blue Cone', but with green foliage. 'Hillieri' is another rounded dwarf cultivar. 'Raffles' is a dense, low-growing, rounded cultivar with bright yellow foliage. 'Rosedalis' looks prickly but feels soft and grows 3–5 ft (1–1.5 m) tall.
ZONES 6–11.

PLATYCLADUS

ORIENTAL ARBOR-VITAE

Platycladus is a genus from China and Korea that contains only a single species, an evergreen conifer featuring flat, fan-like sprays of aromatic foliage. You may also find it listed with the closely related *Thuja*. It is a slender, conical tree but the attraction for gardeners lies in the wide choice of selected small to dwarf cultivars. These offer a diversity of neat, conical or rounded bushes with changing foliage tones through the seasons. As all the branches are retained right down to the ground, they form excellent hedges and screens, rockery features or tub specimens. The leaves are tiny, scale-like needles that clasp the twigs. Female trees have small, erect, rather fleshy cones with overlapping scales, which ripen from waxy blue to brown. The species prefers warmer climates than many conifers.

CULTIVATION

Choose a spot sheltered from strong winds, although preferably in full sun. A partly shaded position will also be suitable. Most moist, well-drained soils are appropriate. Prune *Platycladus* lightly in spring, if desired, to shape. Propagate from seed in spring, or from cuttings taken in the cooler months.

Platycladus orientalis 'Green Cone'

PODOCARPUS

PLUM PINE

Occurring throughout the wet tropics and southern hemisphere continents extending also to Japan and Mexico, the 100 or so species in this coniferous genus are all moderately fast-growing evergreens, ranging from groundcovers of 3 ft (1 m) to trees up to 150 ft (45 m) in height. Grown for their dense foliage and attractive habit, they bear a slight resemblance to the yews *(Taxus)*. The flat, generally narrow leaves are spirally arranged. There are separate male and female plants: the males have catkin-like yellow pollen cones; the females have naked seeds held on short stalks that develop into the fleshy blue-black to red berry-like 'fruits' that give them their common name. Some species are harvested for softwood.

CULTIVATION

They are reliable in a range of soils from rich to poor either in full sun or part-shade, depending on the species, although warm-temperate climates, free from heavy frost, suit them best. In cooler areas, plum pines can be successfully grown indoors. Leave unpruned unless a hedge is desired. Propagate from seed or cuttings.

Podocarpus elatus

Podocarpus macrophyllus

Podocarpus macrophyllus 'Maki'

Podocarpus elatus
BROWN PINE

In its native eastern Australia, this species can grow to 120 ft (36 m) with a spreading crown, but is smaller when cultivated as a shade tree or clipped as a hedge. It has flaky, dark brown bark, and its shiny, dark green leaves, 4 in (10 cm) long, are oblong and sharply pointed. The edible fruit are rounded and purplish to black, and 1 in (25 mm) across. This species can tolerate mild frosts, but must be watered in dry periods. **ZONES 9–12.**

Podocarpus macrophyllus
KUSAMAKI, BUDDHIST PINE, YEW PINE

From the mountains of Japan and China, where it grows to 70 ft (21 m) tall with a spread of 12 ft (3.5 m), this cold-tolerant species prefers moist, rich soil. It has long, thick, dark green leaves up to 6 in (15 cm) long and responds well to pruning, making a good thick hedge. It is often grown in Japanese temple gardens and is also a suitable container plant. The berries are small and black. 'Maki', rarely bigger than a shrub, has a distinctly erect habit with almost vertical branches. **ZONES 7–11.**

Poncirus trifoliata

PONCIRUS

TRIFOLIATE ORANGE, BITTER ORANGE

This genus, closely related to *Citrus*, consists of a single species—a small, fast-growing, deciduous tree originally from China and Korea that looks most attractive in winter without its leaves. Although mainly used as a rootstock for oranges and some other *Citrus* species, it is an attractive plant in flower. It also makes an impenetrable thorny hedge.

CULTIVATION

This very frost-hardy plant prefers full sun and fertile, well-drained soil. Shelter it from cold winds. Propagate from seed or cuttings in summer.

Poncirus trifoliata

This species has flattened stems, long, stout spines and trifoliate leaves. It bears white, scented, 5-petalled flowers that open before or with the new growth in spring. These are followed by yellow fruit that become quite fragrant when ripe, but are inedible. Prune in early summer when used in hedging. **ZONES 5–11.**

Populus deltoides

Populus alba

WHITE POPLAR, SILVER POPLAR

From Europe and the Middle East, this species reaches 80 ft (24 m). The leaves have 3 to 5 lobes, and their undersides are covered with white, downy hairs that give a silvery effect in the wind. The leaves turn gold in autumn. In spring the tree carries reddish catkins; the bark is grayish white. It can withstand low moisture levels, salt winds and poor alkaline soils. Because of its suckering roots it grows best in open country. 'Pyramidalis' is conical, and 'Richardii' bears yellowish leaves. **ZONES 2–10.**

POPULUS

POPLAR, ASPEN, COTTONWOOD

This genus consists of some 35 species of fast-growing, deciduous trees all from temperate regions of the northern hemisphere. Many blaze with yellow or gold in autumn. Poplars are widely cultivated in parks and large gardens and as avenue trees, windbreaks and screens. Their soft white timber is used for making matches and packing cases. Male and female flowers, borne on separate trees, are hanging catkins and appear in late winter and early spring before the leaves, which are set on long, flexible stalks. The fruits are capsules containing seeds covered with cotton-like hairs. Most species are short lived—60 years or so.

CULTIVATION

Plant in deep, moist, well-drained, fertile soil in full sun; they dislike arid conditions. Many species have vigorous root systems notorious for blocking drains and lifting paving, and so are not suitable for small gardens; some species sucker freely from the roots. Propagate from cuttings in winter.

Populus alba 'Pyramidalis'

Populus deltoides
EASTERN COTTONWOOD, EASTERN POPLAR

An upright, broad-headed tree from eastern North America
growing to 100 ft (30 m), this species is less likely to sucker
than other poplars. It is short lived and brittle in high winds.
The triangular, glossy green leaves are up to 8 in (20 cm) long
and are coarsely toothed; the bark is gray and deeply corrugated.
The long catkins are yellow and red. The common name cottonwood refers to the copious quantities of fluff that surround the
seeds. This is a tough tree for extreme inland conditions.
Populus deltoides var. *monilifera*, the northern cottonwood,
bears slightly smaller leaves with the toothed margins more
sharply delineated. **ZONES 3–11.**

Populus nigra

Populus tremula

Populus nigra
BLACK POPLAR

At 100 ft (30 m), with a
suckering habit, this tree is
not for small gardens. It has
dark, deeply furrowed bark.
Its large, diamond-shaped
leaves, bronze when young,
become bright green, then
yellow in autumn; held on
thin stalks, they seem to
'dance' perpetually. Male
trees produce black catkins
in mid-winter. **'Italica'** (syn.
Populus pyramidalis), the
Lombardy poplar, is a male
cultivar popular for its narrow, columnar shape and fast
growth. **ZONES 6–10.**

Populus tremula
COMMON ASPEN, EUROPEAN ASPEN

A vigorous, spreading tree
from Europe suitable for cool
climates, this species grows
to about 50 ft (15 m). The
rounded, toothed leaves are
bronze red when young, gray-
green in maturity and turn a
clear yellow in autumn. They
are held on slim, flat stems
and quiver and rustle in the
slightest breeze. Long gray
catkins are carried in late
winter. In large gardens and
parks constant mowing will
control its suckering habit.
ZONES 1–9.

PRUNUS

Prunus campanulata

This large genus, mostly from the northern hemisphere, includes the edible stone fruits—cherries, plums, apricots, peaches, nectarines and almonds—but is also represented in gardens by ornamental species and cultivars with beautiful flowers. While the genus includes several shrubby species, most are trees growing on average to 15 ft (4.5 m), although some can reach as much as 100 ft (30 m). Most of the familiar species are deciduous and bloom in spring (or late winter in mild climates) with scented, 5-petalled, pink or white flowers. The leaves are simple and often serrated and all produce a fleshy fruit containing a single hard stone. Many have attractive foliage colors in autumn, and others have interesting bark. The timber of cherries and plums is sometimes used commercially.

The genus *Prunus* consists of about 430 species, and these are divided among 5 or 6 easily recognized subgenera, treated as distinct genera by botanists in some countries. They are: *Prunus* in the narrow sense, which includes all the plums; sometimes included in this subgenus but sometimes kept separate are *Armeniaca*, the apricots; *Amygdalus* includes peaches, nectarines and almonds as well as a few ornamental species with similar stalkless blossoms and pitted stones; *Cerasus* includes all the cherries and flowering cherries with few-flowered umbels; while *Padus* includes the bird cherries, mainly North American, with small flowers in long racemes; and finally there are the evergreens in subgenus *Laurocerasus*, also with flowers in racemes and including the well-known cherry laurel and its allies and a large group of tropical rainforest trees.

CULTIVATION

Plant in moist, well-drained soil in full sun but with some protection from strong wind for the spring blossom. Feed young trees with a high-nitrogen fertilizer. Many fruiting varieties respond well to espaliering. Propagate by grafting or from seed—named cultivars must be grafted or budded onto seedling stocks. Pests and diseases vary with locality.

Prunus × *blireana*
DOUBLE FLOWERING PLUM

This popular hybrid originated in the early twentieth century as a cross between the Japanese apricot *Prunus mume* and the purple-leafed plum *Prunus cerasifera* 'Pissardii'. A rounded shrub or small tree, it grows to around 12 ft (3.5 m) high and has slender, arching branches and thin, red-purple leaves that change to golden brown in autumn. In early spring it bears fragrant pale rose-pink, double flowers. **ZONES 5–10.**

Prunus campanulata
TAIWAN CHERRY, CARMINE CHERRY

This cherry species from Taiwan, south China and the Ryukyu Islands is less frost tolerant than most other deciduous *Prunus* species and does best in warm-temperate climates. It can reach 30 ft (9 m) in height though is mostly smaller in cultivation, with a vase-shaped habit. It comes into bloom in mid- to late winter in a warm climate, or early spring in cooler climates. The bare branches are festooned with clusters of bell-shaped flowers, bright carmine red in the commonly grown form. The foliage turns bronze red in autumn. Like most cherries, it responds poorly to pruning. **ZONES 7–11.**

Prunus × *blireana*

Prunus mume 'Geisha'

Prunus mume 'Pendula'

Prunus laurocerasus
CHERRY LAUREL, LAUREL CHERRY

Both the botanical and common names of this handsome evergreen reflect the resemblance of its foliage to that of the true laurel *(Laurus nobilis)* and the 2 plants are sometimes confused. Native to the Balkans, Turkey and the Caspian region, it grows 10–20 ft (3–6 m) in height. The shiny, bright green leaves are 6 in (15 cm) or more long; in mid- to late spring it bears upright sprays of small, sweetly scented white flowers, followed by red berries that ripen to black in autumn. One of the toughest of evergreens, cherry laurel tolerates alkaline soils and will grow in shade. 'Otto Luyken' is a free-flowering dwarf form growing to 3–4 ft (1–1.2 m) in height and spreading 5 ft (1.5 m). 'Zabeliana' is a horizontally branched cultivar, usually under 3 ft (1 m) in height and 12 ft (3.5 m) or more in width, with narrow, willow-like leaves. **ZONES 6–10.**

Prunus mume
JAPANESE APRICOT

Closely related to the common apricot, this very early flowering species is a native of China, but has been cultivated for many centuries in both China and Japan, and has given rise there to hundreds of named cultivars selected for both fruit and flower. It makes a round-headed tree of 15–30 ft (4.5–9 m) high with sharply pointed leaves up to 4 in (10 cm) long. The lightly scented, white to deep pink flowers, 1 in (25 mm) or more across, are carried in small clusters along the branches in late spring and are followed by yellowish, apricot-like fruit. Its blossoms feature in classical Chinese and Japanese paintings and it is also popular for bonsai work. Cultivars include **'Alboplena'** with white double flowers; **'Benishidori'**, a later flowerer with fragrant pink double flowers; **'Pendula'** with a weeping habit; and **'Geisha'** with semi-double deep rose flowers. **ZONES 6–9.**

Prunus, Sato-zakura Group 'Takasago'

Prunus, Sato-zakura Group

These are the main group of Japanese flowering cherries, believed to be derived mainly from the species *Prunus serrulata* (under which name they are commonly to be found), but with probable hybrid influence of several closely related species. Mostly small to medium-sized trees, they can be recognized by their large leaves with fine, even teeth ending in bristle-like points, and their loose umbels of flowers that are mostly over 1½ in (35 mm) in diameter; the bases of the umbels carry conspicuous, toothed bracts, like miniature leaves. They are among the most widely planted trees for spring blossom in cool climates but require good rainfall and a mild summer for the best display of blossom. The numerous cultivars are mostly of Japanese origin and there has been much confusion as to their names. Height and growth form vary with cultivar, as do the color, shape and size of the flowers and the color of the new leaves, which unfold with or just after the opening flowers. **'Shirofugen'**, strong growing to 20 ft (6 m), blooms late, and the purplish pink buds intermingle attractively with the young, copper leaves; clusters of double flowers open white and turn purplish pink. **'Takasago'**, the Naden cherry, with scented pink flowers, is thought by some to be a hybrid with *Prunus* × *yedoensis*. **'Ukon'**, an upright tree to 30 ft (9 m), bears large pink-tinged, greenish cream flowers in mid-spring. **ZONES 5–9.**

Prunus, Sato-zakura Group 'Shirofugen'

Prunus × *subhirtella* 'Pendula'

Prunus × *subhirtella*

HIGAN CHERRY, ROSEBUD CHERRY

This graceful cherry from Japan is now believed to be of hybrid origin. It grows to 30 ft (9 m) and produces a profusion of pale pink flowers early in spring. The leaves are dark green and pointed, and fade to shades of yellow before dropping. It thrives in cool climates but can be rather short-lived. **'Autumnalis'**, growing to 15 ft (4.5 m), bears pink-budded white flowers intermittently from late autumn through winter and into early spring; **'Autumnalis Rosea'** is similar but has pale pink flowers. **'Pendula'** has slender, vertically pendulous branches like a weeping willow and is usually grafted onto a standard; it bears a profusion of small pale pink, 5-petalled flowers from late winter into spring, followed by little spherical brown-red fruit. The spring-blooming **'Pendula Rubra'** bears rich pink flowers. **'Accolade'** is a presumed hybrid between *Prunus* × *subhirtella* and *P. sargentii*: it makes a spreading tree to about 25 ft (8 m), with quite large, pale pink semi-double flowers opening from deep pink buds in early spring. **ZONES 5–9.**

Prunus × *subhirtella* 'Accolade'

PSEUDOLARIX
GOLDEN LARCH

This genus consists of a single species, a deciduous conifer from China. Slow growing to 120 ft (36 m), in cultivation it seldom exceeds 70 ft (21 m). It grows almost as wide as it does high. It differs from the larch *(Larix)* in that the cone scales taper to a point; the male cones are held in clusters, not singly, and the scales on the female cones spread and drop off.

CULTIVATION
Plant in moist, rich, deep, well-drained, acid soil. It requires shelter from strong winds and abundant light. Propagate from seed.

Pseudolarix amabilis

PSEUDOTSUGA

Among the largest of all conifers, the 6 to 8 *Pseudotsuga* species are seldom seen at their maximum height outside their native North America, China, Taiwan, Japan and Mexico. They can reach 300 ft (90 m) with a cylindrical trunk supporting an attractive, broad pyramidal shape. The leaves are soft, green, flattened and tapered, with two bands of white on their undersides. The brown cones, 2 in (5 cm) long with pointed bracts, hang downwards; they take a year to mature.

CULTIVATION
These very frost-hardy trees prefer cold climates, cool, deep soil and sunny, open spaces. Propagate from seed or by grafting.

Pseudolarix amabilis
syn. *Pseudolarix kaempferi*

The horizontal branches on this species form a broad conical crown, held on a trunk with reddish brown bark that is fissured and scaly. Its fine leaves are soft and pale green with bluish undersides and are arranged in rosettes along slender twigs. The foliage turns golden yellow in the cooler months before dropping. Its flowers appear as catkins, followed by green cones that mature to yellow and persist on the tree. It makes an excellent bonsai specimen. **ZONES 3–9.**

Pseudotsuga menziesii
syns *Pseudotsuga douglasii*, *P. taxifolia*
DOUGLAS FIR, OREGON PINE

This fast-growing conifer can reach 300 ft (90 m) and live for 400 years. Its timber has long been valued in North America. Its sturdy trunk is covered with dark, reddish brown, thick, corky bark. The branch tips curve upwards and have dense, soft, fragrant, bluish green, needle-like foliage. At each branch tip wine-red buds form in winter, opening as apple-green rosettes of new growth in spring. Pendulous cones appear after the plant is 20 years old. **ZONES 4–9.**

Ptelea trifoliata

Ptelea trifoliata

HOP TREE, WATER ASH, STINKING ASH

This tree can grow to 25 ft (8 m), given the shade of taller trees and plenty of mulch in the warmer months to conserve soil moisture. The bark is a rich brown, and the oval, dark green leaflets are up to 4 in (10 cm) long. The fruit resemble bunches of keys. This tree makes an attractive ornamental for cool-temperate gardens. **'Aurea'** has soft yellow leaves when young that mature to lime green.
ZONES 2–9.

PTELEA

From the cooler parts of North America, this is a genus of 11 species of small, deciduous trees or large shrubs that grow slowly to an eventual height of 25 ft (8 m). The branching stems carry bushy foliage with leaves composed of 3 oblong leaflets. In common with the citrus family, to which they are related, the leaves have oily glands that release a scent when crushed. They turn a beautiful shade of gold in autumn. The small, greenish white flowers are fragrant and are borne from late spring to early summer.

CULTIVATION

Plant in a shady site in free-draining soil and keep well watered. Propagate from seed in autumn or by layering and grafting in spring.

PTEROCARYA
WING NUT

Ranging from the Caucasus to China, this genus consists of about 10 species of deciduous trees that are grown for their handsome leaves and pendent flowers. Reaching a height of 100 ft (30 m) or more, they have spreading crowns with abundant, pinnate, bright green leaves, each leaflet 4 in (10 cm) or more long. Members can be readily identified by the spring flowers, which appear as yellowish green catkins and grow to 18 in (45 cm) long. Winged nutlets, forming chains up to 18 in (45 cm) long, hang from the branches in ribbons and are an eye-catching feature.

CULTIVATION

These very frost-hardy trees prefer full sun and fertile, deep, moist but well-drained soil. Propagate from cuttings in summer or from suckers or seed in autumn.

Pterocarya fraxinifolia

Pterocarya carpinifolia

Pterocarya carpinifolia

Pterocarya carpinifolia

The name of this species means 'with leaves like *Carpinus*' (the hornbeam genus). This presumably refers to the conspicuous, regular veining of the leaflets—though the hornbeams, of course, differ in having simple, not compound leaves. In other respects *Pterocarya carpinifolia* resembles *P. fraxinifolia*. **ZONES 5–9.**

Pterocarya fraxinifolia
CAUCASIAN WING NUT

This large tree quickly reaches 100 ft (30 m) and has a wide crown adorned with numerous leaflets. Its flowers form long, pendulous, greenish golden catkins; these are followed by ribbons of winged fruit. This species needs a sheltered position and is an excellent shade tree for a large garden or park, especially near water. **ZONES 5–9.**

PTEROSTYRAX

This genus from Asia consists of 4 species of deciduous shrubs and trees that reach up to 50 ft (15 m) with a spread of 40 ft (12 m). The slender branches carry serrated leaves that are 6 in (15 cm) or more long, bright green and oval. Creamy white, fluffy flowers are produced in pendulous sprays up to 10 in (25 cm) long. The fruits are bristly seed capsules.

CULTIVATION

Plant in deep, moist, well-drained soil in sun or part-shade. Propagate from seed in the cooler months, from cuttings in summer or by layering. These useful shade trees should be pruned only to control shape and size.

Pterostyrax hispida

PYRUS

PEAR

The 30 or so species in this genus from temperate Eurasia and North Africa are related to the apple (Malus). Slow-growing, deciduous and semi-evergreen trees, they occasionally reach 80 ft (24 m) but are often smaller. They have been cultivated since antiquity for their grainy textured, sweet, juicy, yellowish green fruits, not all of which are pear-shaped. They are also valued for their attractive autumn foliage (for which they need plenty of sun) and their clusters of fragrant, 5-petalled, white flowers (sometimes tinged with pink), which appear with the new leaves, or just before them, in spring. The glossy leaves vary from almost round to quite narrow.

CULTIVATION

With their modest moisture requirements they suit coastal conditions and thrive in heavy, sandy loams with good drainage in a sunny position. They are ideal for cool-temperate climates. They must be cross-pollinated to produce fruit. Prune to remove damaged branches and to improve their shape in late winter or early spring. Propagate from seed or by grafting.

Pterostyrax hispida
EPAULETTE TREE,
FRAGRANT EPAULETTE TREE

This species from China and Japan grows to 50 ft (15 m). Rich green, oval leaves with wedge-shaped bases and downy undersides form a dense crown. In summer it displays fragrant white flowers in drooping sprays. Gray, furry, 10-ribbed fruit appear in early autumn and stay on the bare branches during winter. **ZONES 4–9.**

Pyrus calleryana
CALLERY PEAR

Grown as an ornamental, this shapely semi-evergreen tree from China reaches 60 ft (18 m) with a broad canopy. Showy clusters of white flowers appear in early spring and are often followed by small, brown, inedible fruit. The grayish green, 3 in (8 cm) long leaves stay on the tree until late autumn, when they turn shades of rich purplish claret, red, orange or yellow. Tolerating heat, dry conditions, wind and poor soil, it makes an ideal street tree. It is resistant to fire blight but is not very long lived. 'Bradford' is a common cultivar that flowers profusely and grows well in poor conditions. 'Aristocrat' is a pyramidal, thornless cultivar with glossy, wavy edged leaves that turn fiery red in autumn and yellow to red fruit. 'Chanticleer' is a narrow-crowned, spiny cultivar with red to magenta autumn foliage. **ZONES 5–9.**

Pyrus ussuriensis

Pyrus ussuriensis
MANCHURIAN PEAR, USSURI PEAR

This is the largest growing
pear species and can reach
70 ft (21 m) or more. With
a broad, pyramidal shape, it
makes a neat, attractive street
tree. In spring it is covered
with a profusion of small,
scented white flowers that
are followed by small, yellow-
brown fruit. Its almost heart-
shaped, dark shiny green
leaves are up to 4 in (10 cm)
wide and turn brilliant red
and coral in autumn.
ZONES 4–9.

Pyrus salicifolia
WILLOW-LEAFED PEAR, SILVER PEAR, WEEPING SILVER PEAR

This popular ornamental pear, growing to about 25 ft (8 m),
comes from the Caucasus and Iran. It has graceful, arching
branches and the willow-like foliage is long, silver-gray and
covered with silky down when young. Small, creamy white
flowers are somewhat hidden by the foliage. The small, brown,
pear-shaped fruit ripen in autumn. **'Pendula'** has a willowy habit
and is more popular than the species itself; its foliage is smaller
than that of its parent. Both are very frost hardy. **ZONES 4–9.**

Pyrus calleryana

Pyrus salicifolia 'Pendula'

QUERCUS

OAK

Quercus canariensis

Most oaks are from temperate regions but a surprisingly large number of the 600 or so evergreen, semi-evergreen and deciduous species come from tropical and subtropical regions of Mexico, Southeast Asia and even New Guinea. Oaks range from shrubs 3 ft (1 m) high to trees of 120 ft (36 m), and are mostly very long lived; some species have been used for centuries for their hardwood timber. Their leaves, mostly lobed and leathery but in some species thin and lustrous, provide a dense canopy for a multitude of animals, birds and insects and make wonderful compost for acid-loving plants. The leaves of some deciduous oaks develop magnificent hues during the cooler months before they drop. Oaks can be divided into 'white oaks' and 'red oaks', the former with rounded leaf lobes and edible acorns that mature in one year, the latter with pointed leaf lobes and acorns that mature in 2 years and are too bitter to eat. The female flowers are insignificant and greenish, while the male flowers appear as yellow catkins in spring.

CULTIVATION

They thrive in deep, damp, well-drained soil. Some species like full sun; others prefer part-shade when young. They have extensive root systems and do not like to be transplanted. Prune only to remove damaged limbs. Otherwise easy to maintain, oaks are susceptible to oak-leaf miner in humid climates, as well as oak root fungus and aphids. Propagate from fresh seed or by grafting in late winter just before new buds appear.

Quercus acutissima

syn. *Quercus serrata*

JAPANESE OAK, SAWTOOTH OAK

The 6 in (15 cm) long, narrow, glossy green leaves on this deciduous oak from China, Japan and Korea are similar to those of the chestnut and turn yellow in autumn. This slow-growing, lime-hating tree eventually reaches a height of 50 ft (15 m). The narrow foliage remains on the tree until well into winter and attractive long catkins appear in spring. The name sawtooth oak comes from the regular serration of the leaves. Its old name was *Quercus serrata*. **ZONES 5–10.**

Quercus canariensis

syns *Quercus lusitanica, Q. mirbeckii*

CANARY OAK, MIRBECK'S OAK

From North Africa and the Iberian Peninsula, this deciduous or semi-evergreen species keeps its 4 in (10 cm) long, coarsely toothed leaves until well into winter by which time they are a yellowish brown. It grows quickly to 40 ft (12 m) and its long acorns taper to a fine point. To a gardener, this is effectively a larger-leafed version of the English oak that can withstand drier conditions, though it is not suitable for really arid regions. In the wild it grows naturally in river valleys. **ZONES 7–10.**

Quercus acutissima

Quercus cerris

Quercus cerris
TURKEY OAK

Originating in central and southern Europe and Turkey, this deciduous oak is one of the grandest in the genus, reaching 120 ft (36 m) with a stout trunk. Its dark, rough bark is deeply fissured and its narrow leaves are gray-green and irregularly toothed, up to 4 in (10 cm) long. It can tolerate alkaline soils and seaside situations, though it rarely reaches its full size there. Its acorns are enclosed within shaggy cups and mature during their second year.
ZONES 7–10.

Quercus coccinea
SCARLET OAK

This deciduous eastern North American oak has deeply lobed, glossy bright green leaves with bristle tips. The 6 in (15 cm) long leaves turn brilliant scarlet in a cool, dry autumn and stay on the tree for a long time. It reaches 80 ft (24 m) on a strong central trunk and is distinguished by its drooping branches. The bark is gray and darkens as it matures. *Quercus coccinea* can tolerate pollution and makes a good specimen for urban environments. 'Splendens' has very deep red autumn foliage color. **ZONES 2–9.**

Quercus ilex

Quercus ilex
HOLM OAK, HOLLY OAK

Native to southern Europe and North Africa, near the Mediterranean coast, this round-headed, dense evergreen can grow to 90 ft (27 m). Its oval leaves are toothed (similar to holly) when young, but become entire with age, and are a lusterous dark green above and white and downy underneath. It grows well in an exposed position, particularly on the coast, and makes a good windbreak. **ZONES 7–10.**

Quercus ilex

Quercus coccinea

Quercus palustris

Quercus palustris
PIN OAK

From the eastern and central USA, this species tolerates dry, sandy soil though it is at its best in deep alluvial soils with plenty of water in summer. Moderately fast growing, it matures to 80 ft (24 m) high. Its smooth, gray trunk supports horizontal branches towards the top of the tree, while the lower branches droop gracefully. Its lusterous green leaves are 4 in (10 cm) long with deep, pointed lobes that turn crimson in autumn and persist on the tree well into winter. It has a shallow root system. **ZONES 3–10.**

Quercus petraea
syn. *Quercus sessiliflora*
DURMAST OAK, SESSILE OAK

A deciduous tree from central and southeastern Europe and western Asia, this species is closely allied to *Quercus robur* and grows to over 100 ft (30 m). Leaves are glossy green and leathery, and it often forms a broad crown. The bark is grayish and fissured and the trunk thick and stout, continuing to the crown of the tree, making it an important timber tree in Europe. This white oak has leaves with 5 to 8 rounded lobes. **ZONES 5–9.**

Quercus robur
COMMON OAK, ENGLISH OAK, PEDUNCULATE OAK

Arguably the most famous of all the oaks and with a life span of 600 to 700 years, this species has spreading, heavily leafed branches that provide good shade. Its 4 in (10 cm) long leaves are deciduous and remain dark green through autumn. It eventually reaches a height of 120 ft (36 m) and trunks with a circumference of more than 70 ft (21 m) have been recorded. It is one of Europe's most valuable timber trees. 'Fastigiata' is grown for its narrow, upright habit, while 'Concordia' is a rounded tree to 30 ft (9 m). **ZONES 3–10.**

Quercus robur

Quercus rubra
syn. *Quercus borealis*
RED OAK, NORTHERN RED OAK

Originating in eastern USA and eastern Canada, this robust deciduous tree reaches up to 90 ft (27 m) with a broad canopy formed by strong, straight branches. Its shiny gray bark forms flat-topped ridges that become dark brown as it ages. The matt green leaves with pointed lobes are up to 8 in (20 cm) in length and display rich scarlet and red-brown autumn hues. The large acorn is held in a shallow cup. The red oak grows relatively quickly and does well in sun or part-shade. The young leaves of 'Aurea' are bright yellow. **ZONES 3–9.**

Quercus rubra 'Aurea'

Quercus suber

CORK OAK

The thick, furrowed, gray bark of *Quercus suber*, principally from Spain and Portugal and growing elsewhere around the Mediterranean, is the source of commercial cork. A short, sturdy, often gnarled and twisted trunk gives the tree character. It reaches 60 ft (18 m) high with a broad, spreading canopy of 50 ft (15 m). The oval, evergreen leaves with a slightly toothed edge are up to 3 in (8 cm) long; they are a dark, shiny green on top and silvery beneath. Single or paired acorns mature to chocolate brown and are held loosely in a cup covering just over a third of the acorn. **ZONES 8–10.**

Quercus virginiana

syn. Quercus virens

LIVE OAK

This evergreen species is native to southeastern USA and Gulf States west to Mexico. It grows to 40–60 ft (12–18 m) tall with a short trunk that supports horizontally spreading branches and a dense, broad-domed crown. The dark green leaves are white and downy underneath, oblong to rounded in shape and up to 4 in (10 cm) long. The acorns are small, arranged singly or in twos or threes and ripen to very dark brown within a year, which is unusual for a red oak. **ZONES 7–11.**

Quercus virginiana

Rhododendron arboreum

RHODODENDRON

Most of the species belonging to this genus are shrubs, and detailed information on the genus is given in the Shrubs chapter. However, *Rhododendron arboreum* is treated here as a tree.

Rhododendron arboreum

From northern India to southern China and over 100 ft (30 m) tall in the wild, this species reaches 40 ft (12 m) in cultivation with a narrow, cylindrical crown. Its leathery, deep bronze-green, 8 in (20 cm) long leaves have whitish or rust-colored undersides. Red, white or deep pink bell-shaped flowers in globular heads of 15 to 20 blooms open in very early spring. *Rhododendron arboreum* was an early introduction and is a parent of many cultivars. **ZONES 7–11.**

ROBINIA
BLACK LOCUST

Robinia pseudoacacia 'Frisia'

These 20 species of leguminous deciduous shrubs and trees from the USA are fast growing and tolerate pollution well. Some *Robinia* species grow 80 ft (24 m) tall although many are shrub-like, reaching only 6 ft (1.8 m). Most of the species spread by suckers and are self-seeding. The pinnate leaves have small oval leaflets, sometimes turning buttery yellow in autumn. There is usually a pair of spines on the branch at each leaf base. They bear pendulous sprays of pink, purple or white, fragrant pea-blossoms in spring. The fruits are flat pods less than 4 in (10 cm) long. Cultivars have been grafted to produce a mop-like head of foliage.

CULTIVATION
Robinias prefer poor but moist soil in a sunny position sheltered from strong winds. Propagate from scarified seed, cuttings or suckers or by division. Cultivars must be grafted.

Robinia pseudoacacia
FALSE ACACIA, BLACK LOCUST

This fast-growing 80 ft (24 m) tree has dark, deeply grooved bark and prickly branches. The pinnate, fern-like leaves, with about 23 leaflets, turn yellow in autumn. The scented white pea-flowers appear in late spring or summer, followed by reddish brown pods containing black, kidney-shaped seeds. The cultivar 'Frisia' carries golden foliage deepening in autumn, and is thornless. 'Rozynskiana' is a large shrub or small tree with drooping branches and leaves. 'Tortuosa' has short, twisted branches. 'Umbraculifera', the mop-head acacia, is also thornless and rarely flowers. These cultivars rarely exceed 30 ft (9 m). **ZONES 3–10.**

Robinia × *slavinii* 'Hillieri'

Robinia × *slavinii* 'Hillieri' is a small tree with a compact, rounded head of foliage. Its fragrant flowers are lavender pink and open from early summer. It is ideal in large containers or as a feature plant for small gardens. **ZONES 5–10.**

Robinia × *slavinii* 'Hillieri'

Salix babylonica

SALIX

WILLOW, OSIER, SALLOW

This genus includes about 300 species of deciduous trees, shrubs and subshrubs mainly from cold and temperate regions in the northern hemisphere. The fast-growing but relatively short-lived trees are the most widely grown. They are largely grown for their timber, their twigs which are used in basket-making, and their strong suckering habit, which aids soil retention. Willow bark was the original source of aspirin. The leaves are usually bright green, lance-shaped and narrow. The flowers, which are borne in fluffy catkins, are conspicuous in some species, appearing before or with the new leaves; male and female catkins are usually borne on separate trees.

CULTIVATION

These frost-hardy plants do best in areas with clearly defined seasons and prefer cool, moist soil with sun or part-shade. Propagate from seed or cuttings in either winter or summer, or by layering. They are vulnerable to attack by caterpillars, aphids and gall mites as well as canker-causing fungal diseases.

Salix alba var. *sericea*

Salix alba
WHITE WILLOW

A very adaptable tree from Europe, northern Africa and central Asia, this species grows to about 80 ft (24 m) high. Its erect branches weep somewhat at the tips and are clothed with 3 in (8 cm) long, narrow leaves that are bright green above with flattened silky hairs on the undersides. The white willow makes a good windbreak tree, albeit with invasive roots. 'Britzensis' (syn. 'Chermesina') has bright red stems; 'Chrysostela' has yellow shoots tipped with orange; *Salix alba* var. *caerulea* has blue-green leaves and is the willow from which cricket bats are made; *S. a.* var. *sericea* has silvery foliage; and 'Vitellina', the golden willow, has young growth of a brilliant clear yellow. ZONES 2–10.

Salix babylonica
WEEPING WILLOW,
BABYLON WEEPING WILLOW

Probably the most widely grown and recognized willow, this Chinese species grows to about 50 ft (15 m) high and wide. The narrow, bright green leaves, 3–6 in (8–15 cm) long, densely cover flexible, arching branches that often droop right down to ground level. 'Crispa' has twisted leaves and a narrower growth habit. *Salix babylonica* var. *pekinensis* 'Tortuosa' has lance-shaped, serrated leaves that turn yellow in autumn. ZONES 4–10.

Salix caprea

Salix caprea

PUSSY WILLOW, GOAT WILLOW, GREAT WILLOW, FLORIST'S WILLOW

Native to Europe to northeast Asia, this dense shrub or tree grows 10–30 ft (3–9 m) tall. The oval mid-green leaves are 2–4 in (5–10 cm) long with a fleecy gray underside. The male plant has large yellow catkins called 'palm', the female has silvery catkins known as 'pussy willow', both appearing in spring before the foliage. This species grows well in brackish marshlands but its very strong suckering habit can cause great problems in a smaller garden. **'Kilmarnock'** is a stiffly pendulous weeping tree, with a dense head of yellow and brown shoots. **ZONES 5–10.**

Salix fragilis

CRACK WILLOW, BRITTLE WILLOW

This fast-growing, erect species from Europe and northwestern Asia can reach 50 ft (15 m) tall, its many branches forming a broad crown. The toothed leaves, to 6 in (15 cm) long, turn yellow in autumn. Its wood has been used to produce high-quality charcoal. This tree grows easily and can naturalize and become a problem, spreading along the banks of streams. Several cultivars are known. The common name brittle willow comes from the tree's brittle twigs; old trees rot easily and break apart in storms. **ZONES 5–10.**

Salix fragilis

SCIADOPITYS

JAPANESE UMBRELLA PINE

This genus consists of just one species, a very distinctive and handsome conifer from Japan. It is an upright, single-trunked, conical tree that eventually grows to over 100 ft (30 m) tall, though it is very slow growing. It can be kept in a container for long periods and is often used as a bonsai subject.

CULTIVATION

Japanese umbrella pines prefer a cool maritime climate with cool, moist, humus-rich soil and light shade when young. Propagate from seed.

Sciadopitys verticillata

Sciadopitys verticillata

The distinctive foliage of this species is composed of deep green, flattened needles up to 6 in (15 cm) long carried in stiff whorls of 20 to 30 and facing upwards, creating an effect like the ribs of an umbrella. Interestingly, the needles are not true leaves at all but they do photosynthesize; the true 'leaves' are the tiny scales that lie almost flat along the stems. The small oval cones take 2 years to mature. **ZONES 5–10.**

Sciadopitys verticillata

Sequoiadendron giganteum

syns Sequoia gigantea, Wellingtonia gigantea

This conifer can grow to 300 ft (90 m) tall, with a trunk up to 40 ft (12 m) in diameter at the base. It is an upright, single-trunked, conical tree with sprays of deep green, slightly prickly, cypress-like foliage. A specimen of this species in the Sequoia National Park in California is said to be 3,800 years old. 'Pendulum' has pendent side branches. **ZONES 7–10.**

Sequoiadendron giganteum

Sequoiadendron giganteum

SEQUOIADENDRON

GIANT SEQUOIA, BIG TREE

From the Sierra Nevada area of California, the only species in this genus is a true giant of a tree. While not quite as tall as the California redwood *(Sequoia sempervirens)*, it is far more heavily built and contains the largest timber volume of any tree. It is also very long lived, and is an impressive tree for large parks and gardens. Its huge trunk is covered in rough, deeply fissured, reddish brown bark.

CULTIVATION

Trees of this size need a solid base, so plant in deep, well-drained soil in an open, sunny position and water well when young; it is frost resistant but dislikes dry conditions. Propagate from seed or cuttings.

Sorbus americana

Sorbus americana
AMERICAN MOUNTAIN ASH

This is a vigorous tree to 30 ft (9 m) with ascending reddish branches and red sticky buds. The pinnate leaves are bright green, turning bright golden yellow in autumn. Large dense bunches of small red berries follow. It comes from eastern North America. **ZONES 3–9.**

Sorbus aria
WHITEBEAM

This European species is a 30 ft (9 m) tall tree with coarsely toothed, simple leaves 4 in (10 cm) long with white felting on the undersides. They develop orange and yellow autumn tones. The ½ in (12 mm) berries are red. This species is very tough, tolerating chalky soil, salt winds and air pollution. The cultivar **'Aurea'** has light yellowish green leaves; **'Chrysophylla'** has yellow leaves; **'Lutescens'** has young foliage covered with fine silvery hairs; **'Majestica'** has leaves and berries larger than those of the species; and **'Theophrasta'** has orange berries and glossy green foliage. **ZONES 2–9.**

Sorbus aria 'Theophrasta'

SORBUS
ROWAN, SERVICE TREE, MOUNTAIN ASH

This genus is made up of 100 species of deciduous trees and shrubs from cool-climate regions of the northern hemisphere, grown for their foliage, timber and decorative fruits. Most species have pinnate leaves and terminal clusters of small, creamy white flowers in spring. The flowers, which are often rather unpleasantly scented, are followed by showy berries. A few species have attractive autumn foliage.

CULTIVATION

Rowans are easily grown in sun or part-shade in any well-drained, fertile soil and are most at home in areas with distinct winters. The species may be raised from stratified seed; selected forms are usually grafted. They are susceptible to fireblight.

Sorbus aria

Sorbus hupehensis

Sorbus aucuparia

ROWAN, MOUNTAIN ASH, EUROPEAN MOUNTAIN ASH

The most commonly grown species, this tree grows to about 50 ft (15 m) high in gardens, much taller in its native European and Asian forests. The pinnate leaves, made up of 11 to 15 small, toothed leaflets, turn rich gold in autumn. The white spring flowers are followed by scarlet berries. 'Asplenifolia' has very finely cut leaves; 'Edulis' is a large-berried form used for jams and preserves; 'Fructu Luteo' has orange-yellow berries; 'Pendula' has wide-spreading growth and a weeping habit; 'Sheerwater Seedling' is narrowly upright; and 'Xanthocarpa' has yellow berries. **ZONES 2–9.**

Sorbus cashmiriana

KASHMIR MOUNTAIN ASH

Indigenous to the western Himalayas, this spreading tree reaches a height of 25 ft (8 m), although it is often smaller. Its mid-green leaves are made up of 17 to 19 elliptical leaflets that are gray-green underneath. The pendent clusters of white to pale pink flowers appear in early summer, followed by ½ in (12 mm) wide globular white fruit that endure into winter. **ZONES 5–9.**

Sorbus hupehensis

HUBEI ROWAN

Indigenous to Hubei province in central China, this tall, vigorous tree has blue-green pinnate leaves made up of 9 to 17 leaflets. The foliage develops orange, red and purple autumn tones. The berries are white, tinged pink, and are carried on red stems. **ZONES 5–9.**

Sorbus cashmiriana

Sorbus aucuparia

Sorbus 'Joseph Rock'

Sorbus 'Joseph Rock'

This vigorous upright tree of unknown east Asian origin grows to about 30 ft (9 m) high. Its leaves are made up of 15 to 21 sharply toothed leaflets that develop rich red, orange and purple tones in autumn. It produces large clusters of bright yellow berries. **ZONES 4–9.**

Sorbus pohuashanensis

Indigenous to mountainous regions of northern China where it reaches 70 ft (21 m) tall, this species is closely related to the European rowan *(Sorbus aucuparia)*. The pinnate leaves are up to 8 in (20 cm) long, green above but hairy and blue-green beneath; young shoots and flower buds are also covered in hair. The flat-topped clusters of flowers are held above the foliage, as are the shiny red fruit. The cultivar **'Pagoda Red'** has a fine display of fruit. **ZONES 4–9.**

Sorbus pohuashanensis 'Pagoda Red'

Sorbus pohuashanensis 'Pagoda Red'

Sorbus terminalis
WILD SERVICE TREE

This species from the Mediterranean grows to 50 ft (15 m) or more with a rounded crown. The twigs are felted when young, the leaves maple-shaped, dark green and glossy but white and downy beneath, becoming bronzed yellow in autumn. Reddish brown fruit follow the white flowers. **ZONES 6–9.**

Sorbus terminalis

Stewartia pseudocamellia
syn. *Stuartia pseudocamellia*
FALSE CAMELLIA, JAPANESE STEWARTIA

Indigenous to Japan (not Hokkaido) and Korea, this species can grow to 70 ft (21 m) high in the wild but is more commonly about 13 ft (4 m) in cultivation. It blooms from late spring to early summer and the white flowers are followed by small, spherical, nut-like seed capsules that are a prominent feature from mid-summer. It has attractive peeling bark and yellow, orange and red autumn foliage. *Stewartia pseudocamellia* var. *koreana* (syn. *Stewartia koreana)* hardly differs from the typical Japanese plants, the main distinction being that the petals spread more widely instead of being cupped and the leaves are broader and less silky when young. **ZONES 6–10.**

Stewartia sinensis
syn. *Stuartia sinensis*

A 30 ft (9 m) tall tree indigenous to China, this species blooms in late spring and summer with small, fragrant, rose-like, white flowers about 2 in (5 cm) across. The color of the flaking bark is a warm reddish brown to purple and the autumn foliage is crimson. **ZONES 6–10.**

Stewartia pseudocamellia

STEWARTIA
syn. *Stuartia*

This eastern Asian and North American genus consists of 15 to 20 species of deciduous or evergreen small trees or shrubs closely allied to the camellias. The flowers are usually white with prominent golden stamens, about 3 in (8 cm) across, and resemble single camellia blooms. The leaves are elliptical, 2–6 in (5–15 cm) long, and often develop bright orange and red autumn tones.

CULTIVATION
Species of *Stewartia* grow best in moist, humus-rich, well-drained, slightly acidic soil in sun or part-shade. Propagate from seed in autumn or from cuttings in summer.

Styrax japonicus

JAPANESE SNOWBELL,
JAPANESE SNOWDROP TREE

This species is a native of
Japan, Korea and China. It
grows to about 25 ft (8 m)
high and flowers from mid-
spring. Its branches, which are
clothed with rather narrow,
3 in (8 cm) long, deep green
shiny leaves, tend to be held
horizontally which creates a
somewhat tiered effect. Protect this species from hot sun.
ZONES 6–9.

Styrax obassia

FRAGRANT SNOWBELL

Indigenous to Japan, Korea
and northern China, this
species grows to 30 ft (9 m)
high. Its flowers, less pendulous than those of other
species, are slightly fragrant.
Large deep green, paddle-
shaped leaves, up to 8 in
(20 cm) long have whitish
down on the undersides. It is
worth growing for the foliage
alone. **ZONES 6–9.**

Styrax japonicus

STYRAX

SNOWBELL

This genus consists of about 100 species of deciduous and evergreen shrubs and small trees occurring naturally over a wide
area of the Americas and eastern Asia, with one species native to
Europe. Several cool-temperate, deciduous species are cultivated
for their neat growth habit and attractive spring display of
slightly drooping sprays of small, bell-shaped, white flowers,
which appear on the previous year's wood.

Styrax obassia

CULTIVATION

They prefer cool, moist,
well-drained soil and cool,
moist, summer climates.
Usually raised from stratified
seed in autumn, they can
also be grown from cuttings
in summer.

Taxodium ascendens
POND CYPRESS

Occurring mainly in the coastal sandy 'pine barrens' of eastern USA, this species grows in shallow pools in the wild. A narrowly conical tree, it reaches a height of 60 ft (18 m) in cultivation and has spirally arranged leaves on erect branchlets. The new spring growth is erect and fresh green, becoming rich brown in autumn. The small cones hang from the branch tips. As its common name suggests, this tree makes an excellent feature beside rivers, ponds and lakes. 'Nutans' has shoots that are erect at first, becoming nodding as they mature. **ZONES 7–10.**

Taxodium distichum
BALD CYPRESS, SWAMP CYPRESS

Found in the swamp regions of southeastern USA, this fast-growing tree reaches a height of 120 ft (36 m) in the wild, but only about 80 ft (24 m) in cultivation. It is distinguished by its deeply fissured, fiberous, reddish brown bark and knobbly 'knees'. These special structures are vertical woody growths sent up from the roots when the plant is standing in water and are thought to allow the tree to breathe with its root system submerged. It has tiny, light green, slender, pointed leaves which, as they mature, turn rusty red in autumn then golden brown before falling. It has resinous, round, purple cones, 1 in (25 mm) across. **ZONES 6–10.**

Taxodium distichum

TAXODIUM

This genus of deciduous or semi-evergreen conifers consists of 3 species, which occur naturally on the edges of rivers and lakes in eastern North America and parts of Mexico. The genus name comes from the supposed similarity of their foliage to that of the yews *(Taxus)*. *Taxodium* species develop large, spreading branches and shed their leaves in autumn, still attached to the small branchlets. These are feather-like and turn coppery brown. The male (pollen) cones are tiny; the female ones are globular, up to 1 in (25 mm) in diameter. The wood of *Taxodium* species is strong, tough and termite resistant.

CULTIVATION

These trees thrive in boggy soils in full sun and will even grow in shallow water. However, they will grow equally well in a normal well-drained soil that is sufficiently deep and moist. Propagate from seed or cuttings.

Taxodium ascendens

TAXUS
YEW

Taxus baccata 'Fastigiata'

The evergreen conifers of this small genus, from cool-climate regions of the northern hemisphere, are slow growing but very long lived. Young trees are conical in shape, but as they age—over the centuries—they develop a domed crown and a massive, thick trunk clothed in reddish brown or grayish brown bark which peels off in thin scales. The flat green leaves are shortish, needle-like and sharply pointed; male and female flowers appear on separate trees in spring. The single, small brown seed of the female plant is enclosed in a vivid red fleshy cup; this cup is the only part of the plant that is not poisonous to humans and animals. Yews make excellent dense hedges and are often used for topiary.

CULTIVATION
These frost-hardy trees tolerate a wide range of conditions, including heavy shade and chalky soil. However, they do not enjoy warm winters or hot, dry summers. Propagate from seed or cuttings or by grafting.

Taxus baccata
ENGLISH YEW, COMMON YEW

Indigenous to western Asia, North Africa and Europe, this dense, dark tree has had legendary and religious associations for centuries. The wood of this tree was once used for making longbows. It grows best in a moist alkaline soil in an open position. The dark-colored trunk is erect and very thick in maturity; the leaves are dark green. The male tree bears scaly cones, while the female tree bears cup-shaped, scarlet berries which encase a poisonous seed. Old trees may reach 50 ft (15 m), but cultivars rarely achieve this height. '**Aurea**' has golden yellow foliage when young, turning green in the second year. '**Dovastoniana**', known as the Westfelton yew because the original tree was planted in 1777 at Westfelton in Shropshire, England, is a distinct form with tiers of wide-spreading, horizontal branches; it normally is found only in the female form. '**Dovastoniana Aurea**' is similar in habit but the leaves are edged bright yellow. '**Fastigiata**', the Irish yew, is columnar, while '**Repandens**' has a spreading habit. '**Semperaurea**' is a slow-growing male bush with ascending branches and gold leaves that fade with age to a russet yellow. **ZONES 5–10.**

Taxus baccata 'Repandens'

Taxus cuspidata
JAPANESE YEW

Faster growing than *Taxus baccata*, this conifer is popular in cold climates and is tolerant of very dry and shady conditions. It forms a large shrub or small tree to 15 ft (4.5 m) or more in height and spread, with an erect trunk which is covered in grayish brown bark. The dense foliage is composed of small, narrow leaves arranged in V-shaped rows on the stem. The leaves are dull green above and lighter below. Tolerant of pollution, it is one of the few conifers that performs well in difficult urban environments. **'Aurescens'** is a low-growing compact form with deep yellow young leaves that turn green in the second year. Equally compact is the dwarf cultivar **'Densiformis'**, which forms a dense mound about 3 ft (1 m) high. **ZONES 4–9.**

Taxus baccata

Taxus cuspidata

Taxus × media

These hybrids between the English and Japanese yews offer a range of sizes and shapes for the garden. **'Brownii'**, a male form, and **'Everlow'** are low and rounded, eventually reaching 8 ft (2.4 m) tall and wide; they are easily kept smaller by pruning. **'Hatfield'** is the broad, upright male form, while **'Hicksii'** is narrow, upright and female; both are good for hedging. **ZONES 5–9.**

Taxus × media 'Everlow'

Thuja occidentalis 'Smaragd'

THUJA

ARBOR-VITAE

This small genus contains 5 evergreen conifers that come from high-rainfall, cool-temperate regions of northeastern Asia and North America. All are valuable timber trees, and several are widely cultivated on a commercial basis. They feature erect, straight trunks covered in deeply fissured, fiberous bark and are columnar to pyramidal. The aromatic foliage consists of sprays of scale-like leaves, often flattened. The egg-shaped cones are covered with overlapping scales and are green, maturing to brown; they are notably small for such large trees, mostly under ½ in (12 mm) long. Dwarf cultivars, some no more than 15 in (38 cm) high, make excellent rockery or container specimens; most are juvenile forms.

CULTIVATION

These plants tolerate cold and are not fussy about soil as long as it is well drained; most species prefer full sun and dislike dry conditions. Propagation is from seed or cuttings in winter.

Thuja occidentalis 'Rheingold'

Thuja occidentalis 'Micky'

Thuja occidentalis

AMERICAN ARBOR-VITAE, WHITE CEDAR

Growing to 50 ft (15 m) in height with a pyramidal crown, this species has attractive, reddish brown, peeling bark. Its dense foliage is composed of yellow-green glandular leaves with bluish undersides held on flat, spreading branchlets. The leaves turn bronze in autumn; it has tiny, yellow-green cones which ripen to brown. This species has given rise to more than 140 cultivars, ranging from dwarf shrubs to large trees. **'Ericoides'** is a small dense bush to 18 in (45 cm) tall and has soft, loose, bronze juvenile foliage which becomes brownish green as it matures. **'Lutea'** grows to 8 ft (2.4 m) in 10 years; its leaves become rich golden bronze in winter. **'Lutea Nana'** is a small conical bush, very dense, with golden-yellow foliage in winter. **'Micky'** is a bun-shaped, green-foliaged cultivar. Slow-growing **'Rheingold'** forms a spreading, semi-prostrate dome 30 in (75 cm) high and 5 ft (1.5 m) wide, and has leaves that turn rich golden brown in winter. **'Smaragd'**, with a compact pyramidal habit, has bright green foliage all year round and forms a dense hedge 6 ft (1.8 m) high. **ZONES 4–10.**

Thuja plicata

WESTERN RED CEDAR

This fast-growing conifer reaches about 80 ft (24 m) in cultivation, but is much taller in its natural habitat. It has long been harvested for its durable and versatile soft-wood timber. Of conical habit, it becomes columnar in maturity, with branches sweeping the ground. When the rich, coppery green foliage is crushed, it exudes a sweet, tangy aroma. The dwarf cultivar **'Rogersii'** forms a round bun shape 18 in (45 cm) across. Compact **'Zebrina'**, growing to 20 ft (6 m) high and 5 ft (1.5 m) wide, has glossy bright green foliage striped with yellow. **'Aurea'** has rich, old gold foliage. **'Stoneham Gold'** is slow growing, but eventually makes a large bush with dense foliage and a narrowly conical form; the foliage is bright gold topped with copper bronze. Similar to 'Stoneham Gold', and also slow growing, **'Collyer's Gold'** has brighter yellow foliage. **ZONES 5–10.**

Thuja plicata

Thuja plicata 'Collyer's Gold'

Thujopsis dolabrata

This evergreen conifer is variable in growth habit, from upright and pyramidal to spreading and bushy. It reaches a height of 20–50 ft (6–15 m) with a spread of 25–30 ft (8–9 m). Its foliage is composed of flattened, scale-like leaves which are dark green above with frosted white undersides. Its small cones are bluish gray, round and scaly. The dwarf cultivar 'Nana' forms a spreading, bun shape 24 in (60 cm) high by 5 ft (1.5 m) wide, with fresh green foliage, sometimes tinged bronze. The slow-growing 'Variegata' matures to a broad pyramid 10 ft (3 m) high and 5 ft (1.5 m) wide; its vivid green, shiny foliage is splashed with white. **ZONES 5–10.**

Thujopsis dolabrata

THUJOPSIS
MOCK THUJA, HIBA, FALSE ARBORVITAE

This genus from Japan contains only a single species, *Thujopsis dolabrata*. It resembles *Thuja*, but is distinguished by several important features, namely round, woody cones, winged seeds and larger leaves. It is the parent of several cultivars, which vary in habit and foliage color.

CULTIVATION
Tolerant of cold, this plant thrives in moist, well-drained, acidic or alkaline soil and an open, sunny position. Propagation is from seed, or cuttings for selected forms.

Thujopsis dolabrata 'Nana'

TILIA
LIME TREE, LINDEN

From temperate regions of Asia, Europe and North America, this genus consists of 45 species of tall, handsome, deciduous trees, often planted in avenues and streets because they are fast growing and withstand regular heavy pruning and atmospheric pollution. They are generally upright, with thick, buttressed trunks, and have a tendency to sucker. Rounded to heart-shaped leaves, held on thin stalks, briefly turn yellow in autumn. The small, fragrant, cup-shaped cream flowers are borne in clusters in summer; each cluster has a whitish bract which persists and helps to disperse the fruits on the wind. Both flowers and bracts are dried to make linden tea. The fruits are small, round, hard, green berries. Several species are valued for their pale, strong but lightweight wood.

CULTIVATION
Very frost hardy, they do best in cool climates and prefer full sun, neutral, well-drained soil and plenty of water in dry periods. Even quite large trees can be readily transplanted during their winter dormancy. Propagate from seed in autumn, from cuttings or by layering; selected forms and hybrids can be grafted in late summer.

Tilia americana
BASSWOOD, AMERICAN LINDEN

This attractive, sturdy tree from eastern-central
USA and Canada grows to 120 ft (36 m) tall. It
has an erect trunk with smooth gray bark which
becomes fissured with age. Its young branches
are green and form a compact, narrow crown.
The heart-shaped, dull green leaves are up to
6 in (15 cm) long and have toothed edges.
Yellowish white, fragrant flowers in pendent
clusters appear in summer, followed by small,
hairy fruit. 'Redmond', a selected form raised
in Nebraska in about 1926, has a dense conical
habit. **ZONES 3–9.**

Tilia cordata
syn. Tilia parvifolia
SMALL-LEAFED LINDEN, LITTLE-LEAF LINDEN

An inhabitant of European woodlands, this
species grows to 100 ft (30 m) tall with a
dome-shaped crown. Its leathery, round leaves,
2 in (5 cm) across, are bright green on top with
pale undersides. Its small flowers are pale yellow and sweetly scented; the fruit are gray.
This long-lived species can make a handsome
specimen for parks and formal gardens where
it has plenty of space. The soft whitish timber
is often used for wood carving and musical
instruments. 'Greenspire' is a fast-growing
American selection with an upright habit and
oval-shaped crown. '**June Bride**' is heavy-
flowering with conical growth and glossy
leaves. **ZONES 2–9.**

Tilia cordata

Tilia × europaea
syn. Tilia × vulgaris
EUROPEAN LINDEN, COMMON LIME TREE

Widely grown in Europe, this handsome,
vigorous hybrid between *Tilia cordata* and *T.
platyphyllos* grows to 100 ft (30 m) tall. It is
characterized by a dense, shapely crown held
on a stout trunk that has a strong tendency to
sucker. Shoots should be removed from the bur
at the base from time to time. The smooth
green shoots grow in a distinct zigzag pattern
and the bright green, rounded to heart-shaped
leaves have toothed edges. Its pale yellow
flowers appear among the leaves in early
summer; they are sometimes infused and drunk
as a tea. The rounded fruit are faintly ribbed.
The foliage of '**Wratislaviensis**' is golden yellow
when young, maturing to a dark green.
ZONES 3–9.

Tilia × europaea 'Wratislaviensis'

Tilia americana

Tilia platyphyllos
BROAD-LEAFED LINDEN, BIG-LEAF LINDEN

Reaching a height of 80 ft (24 m), this vigorous European species has a straight, rough, gray trunk and a rounded crown spreading to a broad shape. The young shoots are reddish brown and downy; the large, dark green leaves are heart-shaped and bluish underneath. Pale yellow flowers in groups of three are followed by hard, pear-shaped, ribbed fruit. In 'Rubra', the bark of the young twigs is a vivid red. **ZONES 5–9.**

Tilia platyphyllos

Tilia 'Petiolaris'

Tilia 'Petiolaris'
syn. *Tilia petiolaris*
WEEPING SILVER LINDEN, PENDENT SILVER LIME, WEEPING LIME

Possibly no more than a form of *Tilia tomentosa*, this weeping tree reaches 60–80 ft (18–24 m) in height. It has a spreading, conical form which expands with age. The pointed, cordate leaves are 2–4 in (5–10 cm) long, deep green on top and silver-felted underneath. Creamy yellow flowers bloom in terminal clusters and are followed by bumpy, nut-like seed pods. **ZONES 5–9.**

Tilia platyphyllos 'Rubra'

Tilia tomentosa
SILVER LINDEN, SILVER LIME

This graceful tree native to eastern Europe and
Turkey is distinguished by its young shoots, which
are pale gray and felted. Growing to 90 ft (27 m)
tall, its ascending branches are often pendulous at
the tips. Large round leaves, with serrated edges and
whitish undersides, seem to shimmer in the wind.
The highly fragrant, lime-green flowers, which are
borne in summer and are toxic to bees, are followed
by rough, oval fruit. **ZONES 5–9.**

Tilia tomentosa

Toona sinensis

TOONA

Previously included in the closely related genus *Cedrela*, the 4
or 5 species of deciduous and evergreen trees in this genus are
found naturally from China and the Himalayas to eastern
Australia. They are valued for their fine, often aromatic timber.
Attractive pinnate leaves have many oval to lance-shaped
leaflets.

CULTIVATION

Toona species grow best in moist climates with full sun and a
deep, rich soil; water regularly. Their cold tolerance depends on
their country of origin; *Toona ciliata* and *T. sinensis* thrive in
subtropical climates, with shelter from wind. Propagate from
fresh seed or suckers in late summer. Tip moth larvae and mites
attack some species.

Toona sinensis
syn. *Cedrela sinensis*
CHINESE TOON

Occurring in Southeast Asia
and China, this species is also
very variable, and only some
forms have found their way
into cultivation. It may become a large, single-trunked
tree, but is also seen as a
clump of stems to about 30 ft
(9 m) high. The leaves are up
to 24 in (60 cm) long, with
dark green leaflets and a
reddish central stalk. The
young shoots are used as a
vegetable in China, smelling
strongly of onions when
broken. In recent years there
has appeared in Western
gardens the striking cultivar
'Flamingo', which has brilliant
pink spring foliage turning
cream and finally green; first
noticed in Australia and New
Zealand, it spreads widely by
root suckers, sending up
slender stems to no more than
20 ft (6 m) high. **ZONES 6–11.**

Torreya nucifera

TORREYA

The yew-like evergreen coniferous trees and shrubs of this small genus of 6 or so species occur naturally in eastern Asia and North America. The spiny pointed leaves are spirally arranged on twisted shoots and are often paler on the undersides. The fruits are oval drupes which contain a single seed.

CULTIVATION

They adapt to a wide variety of soils, from chalk to heavy clay and poor sand, and are reasonably cold tolerant provided they are planted in a sheltered position. All demand adequate water during dry spells. Propagate from seed or by grafting.

Torreya californica

CALIFORNIA NUTMEG

This neat, erect tree grows to a height of 70 ft (21 m); conical in habit, its horizontal branches sweep the ground in maturity. The dark green, needle-like leaves, about 2½ in (6 cm) long, are yellowish green beneath. Male and female organs are borne on separate trees; woody, olive-like fruit, similar to the nutmeg of commerce, follow on female trees. **ZONES 7–10.**

Torreya nucifera

NAYA

This attractive, symmetrical conifer reaches about 70 ft (21 m) in height. Its stiff, spiky, yew-like foliage is dark gray-green and pleasantly pungent when crushed. The bark is a smooth reddish brown. The fruit are edible green drupes which ripen to purple with a white bloom. **ZONES 7–10.**

Torreya californica

TSUGA

HEMLOCK

Tsuga chinensis

The 10 or so species of elegant evergreen conifers from cool-temperate areas of North America and east Asia that make up this genus are widely grown as ornamentals in cool climates. They range from tall trees to (in the case of dwarf cultivars) small shrubs good for hedging and rockeries. Conical to pyramidal in habit, the spreading branches droop gracefully. Both male and female cones are small, the latter with thin scales and containing winged seeds. The common name hemlock has no link to the poisonous herb—the trees are not poisonous.

CULTIVATION

These frost-hardy trees are tolerant of shade and thrive in slightly acid, deep, well-drained soil containing plenty of organic matter. They do not enjoy urban environments or very exposed positions, and dislike being transplanted. Propagate from seed in spring or cuttings in autumn.

Tsuga canadensis
'Pendula'

Tsuga canadensis

EASTERN HEMLOCK, CANADIAN HEMLOCK

From the cool northeast of North America, this slow-growing tree reaches a height of 80 ft (24 m), with a trunk that is often forked at the base. It forms a broad pyramidal crown, the thin branches with pendulous tips. The short, oblong needles are arranged in 2 rows and are grayish brown and hairy when young, maturing to dark green with 2 grayish bands on the undersides. Oval cones 1 in (25 mm) long are borne at the ends of the branchlets and disperse their seeds in autumn. 'Pendula' forms a semi-prostrate mound to 6 ft (1.8 m) tall and wide; its lime-green juvenile foliage becomes grayish green with age. **ZONES 2–9.**

Tsuga chinensis

CHINESE HEMLOCK

This conifer reaches a height of 70 ft (21 m) in the wild, less in cultivation. It has been in cultivation for thousands of years and is often a feature of formal Japanese gardens. It forms a narrow crown with a spread of around 12 ft (3.5 m) and is one of the neatest members of the genus. Its yellowish young shoots precede glossy green needles that are distinctly notched at the tip. **ZONES 6–10.**

Tsuga canadensis

Tsuga heterophylla
WESTERN HEMLOCK

From northwestern North
America, this large, fast-
growing tree can reach nearly
200 ft (60 m) in the wild
(generally less in cultivation)
and is harvested commercially
for its pale yellow timber and
tannin-rich bark. As with
Sequoia, the harvest comes
almost entirely from natural
forests, to the great concern
of environmentalists. As a
specimen in parks and large
gardens it is particularly
elegant, with a spire-like
habit, weeping branchlets and
a rusty brown, fissured trunk.
New young shoots are grayish, and the flat needles are
deep green. **ZONES 6–10.**

Tsuga heterophylla

Ulmus glabra 'Camperdownii'

ULMUS
ELM

The 30 or so species in this genus of trees occur naturally in
temperate regions of the northern hemisphere. During the 1920s
and 1930s, and again in the 1960s and 1970s, elm trees in
Europe and North America were devastated by Dutch elm
disease, caused by the fungus *Ophiostoma ulmi*, which is transmitted by the elm bark beetle. Except for a few east Asian
species, they are deciduous, turning yellow in autumn. The
leaves are usually one-sided at the base, with prominent, parallel
lateral veins and regularly toothed margins; the small, disc-like
fruits have a membranous wing and are carried in clusters.
Most elms are large limbed with furrowed gray bark and high,
domed crowns.

CULTIVATION

Mostly very frost hardy, elms require cool to cold winters and prefer full sun and deep, moist, fertile soil. Propagate from semi-ripe cuttings in summer, from suckers or by grafting or budding in autumn. They can be propagated from seed in autumn, but the germination rate is often low.

Ulmus americana

Ulmus glabra

Ulmus americana

AMERICAN ELM, WHITE ELM

The largest North American elm, this species occurs naturally over eastern and central USA, and southern Canada. It can reach a height of 120 ft (36 m) in the wild—about half that in cultivation—and has high-arching limbs. Mature trees develop a broad crown and may become strongly buttressed at the base; the ash-gray bark is deeply fissured. The leaves, 4–6 in (10–15 cm) long, have smooth upper sides with slightly downy undersides, and unforked lateral veins. 'Delaware' is broadly vase-shaped, fast growing and claimed to be resistant to Dutch elm disease. 'Princeton' is also vase-shaped, and vigorous with some resistance to elm leaf beetle. 'Washington' is thought to be a hybrid of *Ulmus americana* and an unknown species. **ZONES 3–9.**

Ulmus glabra

syns *Ulmus montana*, *U. scabra*

SCOTCH ELM, WYCH ELM

One of the major European elms, this species can grow to more than 100 ft (30 m) high with a wide, spreading crown, and does not sucker from the roots. Its dull, dark green leaves, up to 6 in (15 cm) long and broadest near the apex, have a rough raspy upper surface. 'Camperdownii' forms a dome-like mound of weeping branches when grafted onto a standard; 'Lutescens', the common golden elm, has spring and summer foliage colored lime green and tipped with pale yellow. **ZONES 3–9.**

Ulmus glabra 'Camperdownii'

Ulmus × hollandica

DUTCH ELM, HYBRID ELM

Ulmus × hollandica

This hybrid name covers several clones believed to originate from crosses between *Ulmus glabra* and *U. minor*. Their glossy dark green leaves, yellowing in autumn, are mostly smaller and less raspy than *U. glabra* leaves, and broader and shorter stalked than those of *U. minor*. The original, now often referred to as 'Hollandica', has broad, rounded leaves. 'Jacqueline Hillier' is a small bushy shrub growing 8 ft (2.4 m) in height. 'Purpurascens', a vigorous, open tree, has purplish green new growth. 'Vegeta', the Huntingdon elm (an old clone), bears pale yellowish green leaves in flattened sprays. **ZONES 4–9.**

Ulmus minor

syn. *Ulmus carpinifolia*

FIELD ELM, SMOOTH-LEAFED ELM

Widespread throughout Europe, western Asia and North Africa, this deciduous species is usually smaller than the other European elms and the crown is pointed. It reaches a height of 100 ft (30 m) with a spread of up to 70 ft (21 m) in the wild. The leaves are also smaller, tapering at both ends, with smooth upper sides and a slender stalk. Due to its suckering habit, a single tree may form a small, dense grove. 'Variegata', with white-streaked leaves, is just as vigorous, but is less inclined to sucker. *Ulmus minor* 'Cornubiensis' (syn. *U. angustifolia* var. *cornubiensis*) is a tall, slender tree growing 60–70 ft (18–21 m) tall and 20 ft (6 m) wide. Commonly known as Cornish elm, it forms a dense conical head of ascending branches, later becoming more open and loose. The leaves are smooth and glossy above and conspicuously tufted beneath. It thrives in coastal situations. **ZONES 4–9.**

Ulmus procera

Ulmus minor

Ulmus minor 'Cornubiensis'

Ulmus parvifolia
CHINESE ELM, LACEBARK ELM

Native to China and Japan, this elm grows to 60 ft (18 m) tall and has a spreading, sinuous habit and bark mottled with dark gray, reddish brown and cream. It is semi-evergreen in mild climates. The small, leathery, dark green leaves, smooth and shiny on top, have small, blunt teeth. The fruit mature in autumn, much later than those of most other elms. It is relatively resistant to Dutch elm disease. **'Frosty'** is a shrubby, slow-growing form with small, neatly arranged leaves bearing white teeth. **ZONES 5–10.**

Ulmus parvifolia

Ulmus procera
ENGLISH ELM

This elm, which can reach 80 ft (24 m) in height, has a high-branched, billowing crown and straight or slightly sinuous trunk. In the UK, few have survived Dutch elm disease. Cultivated in the southern hemisphere, it produces a compact, rounded crown up to 80 ft (24 m) high. Its smallish, rounded leaves have a rough surface. Seldom setting fertile seed, it is usually propagated from suckers. The rare cultivar **'Louis van Houtte'** has very attractive golden-green leaves. **ZONES 4–9.**

YUCCA

The 40 or so species of unusual perennials, shrubs and trees in this genus are found in drier regions of North America. Often slow growing, they form rosettes of stiff, sword-like leaves usually tipped with a sharp spine; as they mature some species develop an upright trunk, often branched. Yuccas bear showy, tall panicles of drooping, white or cream, bell- to cup-shaped flowers. The fruits are either fleshy or dry capsules, but in most species are rarely seen away from the plants' native lands as the flowers must be pollinated by the yucca moth.

CULTIVATION

Yuccas do best in areas of low humidity; they prefer full sun and sandy soil with good drainage. Depending on the species, they are frost hardy to frost tender. Propagate from seed (if available), cuttings or suckers in spring.

Yucca brevifolia

Yucca brevifolia

JOSHUA TREE

Of striking if somewhat misshapen appearance, this well-known tree reaches 40 ft (12 m) tall in its natural habitat. The short leaves are narrow and sharply pointed, with minute teeth along the edges. Its greenish white flowers about 2½ in (6 cm) long, arranged on a long erect spike, are followed by dry capsules. Extremely slow growing, it can be difficult to cultivate, even in its native regions of southern USA and northern Mexico. Flowering is irregular and dependent on rain in the wild; in cultivation, late spring is the usual flowering season. **ZONES 7–10.**

Yucca filifera

Normally seen as a low clump of foliage, this Mexican species may eventually become tree-like, reaching up to 30 ft (9 m) in height and eventually much branched. When young it resembles *Yucca filamentosa*, but the leaves are shorter and thinner, with the margins sparsely threaded. The flowers on the tall summer panicles are creamy white and pendulous. **'Golden Sword'** has yellow leaf margins; **'Ivory'** has creamy white flowers tinged green. **ZONES 7–10.**

Yucca filifera 'Golden Sword'

Zelkova carpinifolia
ELM ZELKOVA

From the Caucasus and Asia Minor, this slow-growing tree can live to a great age, reaching 100 ft (30 m) high and 50 ft (15 m) wide. It has a dense, rounded head, slender upright branches and weeping branchlets. The pointed, mid-green, leaves have serrated edges; their upper sides are rough to the touch. Fragrant but insignificant flowers appear in spring. **ZONES 4–10.**

Zelkova serrata
JAPANESE ZELKOVA

This ornamental tree from Japan, Korea and Taiwan grows to a height of 80 ft (24 m) or more with a wide, spreading crown. It has smooth bark dappled gray and brown and new shoots are tinged purple. The pointed, oblong, sharply serrated leaves are light green and slightly hairy above, with shiny undersides. The foliage turns golden yellow to rusty brown in autumn. Cultivars include 'Village Green', and 'Green Vase' growing to 40 ft (12 m) tall in a graceful vase shape. **ZONES 3–10.**

Zelkova serrata

ZELKOVA

Occurring naturally from Asia Minor across cool-climate areas of western Asia to China and Japan, these deciduous trees are cultivated for their attractive habit and handsome foliage. They are important timber trees in China and Japan. The leaves resemble those of the English or American elms, but are smaller, giving an effect of airy elegance. Although related to the elms, they are not plagued by the same diseases and are becoming popular as elm substitutes. The small, greenish flowers, borne in spring, are sometimes perfumed; both the flowers and fruits are insignificant.

CULTIVATION

Although frost hardy, they prefer some shelter. They need full sun and deep, fertile, well-drained soil and plenty of water during summer. Propagate from seed or root cuttings in autumn, or by grafting.

Zelkova serrata

Zelkova carpinifolia

Chapter 5

LAWNS, GROUND-COVERS, ORNAMENTAL GRASSES & BAMBOOS

A lush lawn gives a verdant base to the surrounding shrubbery, but needs an occasional nutritional boost.

Lawns

To have played barefoot on a lawn is one of the joys remembered from childhood. Only when we become gardeners, though, do we realize how much energy is expended on this playground. Nevertheless, there is nothing as enticingly beautiful as a well-kept sward of grass, and those prepared to work towards this pleasure are amply rewarded, since a lawn is an integral part of a pleasing garden landscape.

Choose a lawn to suit your garden

Climatic and environmental conditions may prevent gardeners in some areas from enjoying the lush lawns of those regions with assured regular rain. However, there is a sufficiently wide range of species, including native grasses, to cater for the whole variety of conditions. Alternatively, consider not to have a lawn at all, at least in the traditional sense; there is a large choice of groundcovers that can release you from the tiresome, repetitive task of mowing.

Select a lawn grass carefully. Most successful seeded lawns are made up of more than one type of grass, which is apparent to anyone who reads the labels on the many packet mixes. Seed mixes are combined by specialists to provide year-round coverage for many different conditions, such as shady areas under established trees. Turf, on the other hand, consists mainly of one species renowned for its tough, almost year-round performance. Whichever type is finally chosen, be prepared to fertilize and water to encourage a dense, matted grass cover. Weeds are quick to invade thin, undernourished lawns and can give a patchy look.

Prepare the soil before the lawn is sown

Lawns are long term additions to the garden. They also tend to be the first part of the new landscape to be tackled after the builders have left, so the urge for a quick fix is strong. Unfortunately, there are no shortcuts, and soil preparation really pays off. Now is the time to consider underground irrigation systems or if extra piping is needed for a garden tap. As well as irrigation, drainage needs are paramount, both to ensure that excess surface water is guided away from the house as well as to fix any unusually boggy sections of the garden. A badly drained lawn will always be a pest to mow and can, over time, become quite uneven and covered with slippery moss. Think positive in a situation like this—there is a wide range of plants grouped under the term ornamental grasses that will thirstily soak up any excess, and it may be the

perfect position to incorporate a garden pond surrounded by these tussocked beauties.

Unfortunately, lawn preparation is often more than just a case of raking the surface even. Builder's rubble, as well as any larger stones that could damage a lawn mower need to be removed. In large gardens, a rotary hoe makes easy work of digging the soil, and they are readily hired. Smaller areas can be dug over with a fork, with new topsoil added if necessary. Next, allow the soil time to settle and remove any weed seedlings, before evenly spreading a pre-planting fertilizer.

Now is the time to add the grass. If turfing, be sure to lay it out as soon as possible after delivery. Grass seed, however, gives a little more leeway, just wait until rain is forecast before it is sown. Remember, though, that heavy

Pampas grass is a stately addition between colorful border plants.

A distinctive patch of flowering groundcover breaks the monotony of a large expanse of grass.

rain can cause run off, which takes newly sown seed to the bottom of the garden. Finally, water both newly planted turf and seeded lawns gently and frequently. As they become established, less frequent but thorough watering will encourage the roots to penetrate well down into the soil where they will be better insulated against weather variations.

Lawns will need the occasional nutritional boost, because the new growth is regularly stripped off by the mower. How often it is fed depends on the type of lawn that is desired. A lawn that gives a really verdant base to the surrounding shrubbery needs frequent fertilizing, otherwise relax, and simply spread a balanced fertilizer over the grass each spring.

Make a flower meadow

The really lazy or some would say imaginative gardener can have a good reason not to mow for months if bulbs are allowed to naturalize in a lawn. This is because bulb foliage should be left to grow for a month or more after flowering. Freesias give a perfumed carpet while daffodils glow with the very essence of spring. Grassed areas can also be planted with spring- and summer-flowering annuals, such as the Flanders poppy *(Papaver rhoeas)* and cornflower *(Centaurea cyana)*. Experiment with various species in a small area or sow a single species crop, such as the everlasting daisy (*Bracteantha* species). Many of the annuals will self seed, and give a repeat performance the following year.

Flower meadows are very effective and almost self-sufficient. Little or no fertilizer is needed since the grass needs little encouragement to outwit the flowers. In this more naturalistic treatment, choose a grass species of a less robust nature, rather than the ubiquitous kikuyu *(Pennisetum clandestinum)*. If the meadow becomes untidy, a quick trick is to cut a curving or a more formal straight path through it to lead to a focal point. A mown border around the meadow perimeter does wonders to define the 'wild' area. To repeat the effect the following year, just allow the annual flowers to drop their seed. Finally, pick the grass seedheads and mow the meadow down for winter.

Other groundcovers

As a lawn alternative, flower meadows make an ideal temporary show. Further alternatives include groundcover plants, which give year-round cover of a very dense, weed-suppressing nature. They include naturally low-growing shrubs, perennials and succulents and the lower-growing tufted grasses. Many of these are eminently suited as lawn replacements, but for visually open spaces rather than for walking or playing on.

Groundcovers are very easily propagated from cuttings or root division, which allows a great number to be quickly and economically reproduced by the gardener. Some have a root system that allows them to spread, while others are best planted close together to form an impenetrable mat. Like lawns, groundcovers benefit from thoughtful soil preparation and gentle care when young.

Some people feel that it is rather boring to have a large garden area given over to one particular plant. In this case, break the area with distinctive, well-defined patches of gravel, bark mulch or brick paths. Otherwise, groundcovers can be used in a tapestry effect, but care is needed here to prevent trailing types from becoming entangled with other species. Many groundcovers perform a dual function, like the carpeting roses, which provide a colorful display as well as thorns to discourage unwanted trespassers.

Ornamental grasses and bamboos

Large-growing relatives of the grasses, these structural plants can be used to great effect in the garden landscape. They can be grouped so that their leaves ripple in the wind, or scattered in perennial borders where their bold outlines arrest the eye. The late summer seedheads of the ornamental grasses look spectacular when placed against a backdrop of deep green or where they catch the lower rays of the setting sun. At the end of the season, it is wonderful to see them shrouded in the early morning mists of autumn. In winter, the seedheads are cut back both to tidy the plants and to use for indoor display.

Often thought of as low-maintenance plants, ornamental grasses and bamboos repay care and attention, especially in their early years. Prepare the ground well, water and fertilize regularly as they are becoming established, and control weeds by mulching. Many species form large clumps that may need to be divided every 3 or 4 years. For others, all that is required is to cut back the dying foliage.

LAWNS & GROUNDCOVERS

Acaena microphylla

NEW ZEALAND BURR

From the grasslands of New Zealand, this is one of the smallest-growing species. Forming a dense mat only about 1 in (25 mm) deep and usually no more than 12 in (30 cm) or so across, the stems run beneath the soil and root. The tiny leaflets are only ⅛ in (3 mm) across and are bronzy when young. Pink-spined fruiting heads add to the effect in autumn. **ZONES 7–10.**

Acaena novae-zelandiae

This popular species from New Zealand, southeast Australia and New Guinea may be prostrate or mounding with wiry stems reaching 6–24 in (15–60 cm) long. The bright green leaves (which are sometimes tinted red) are up to 4 in (10 cm) long and composed of 9 to 15 leaflets. The flowerhead is cream and the immature fruiting heads have bright red spines on the burrs. This species is quite a vigorous grower, sometimes becoming a nuisance. **ZONES 5–10.**

Acaena 'Blue Haze'

ACAENA

Around 100 species make up this genus of low-growing evergreen perennials. Those grown in gardens all have thin, creeping stems or buried rhizomes that bear at intervals tufts of small pinnate leaves with toothed margins. Flowers are rather insignificant, green or purple-brown, in dense stalked heads or spikes, but are followed by small dry fruit with barbed hooks that cling to socks at the slightest touch. Acaenas are grown as rock-garden plants or sometimes as groundcovers, valued for their pretty, intricate foliage. Some more vigorous species are regarded as weeds, even in their native countries.

CULTIVATION

They are tough little plants, thriving in exposed places and poor soil, but do demand good drainage and summer moisture. Propagate from seed or by division.

Acaena argentea

This species from Peru and Chile has prostrate stems that spread to form a 24 in (60 cm) wide mat. The leaves, which are up to 6 in (15 cm) long, are pinnate with 9 to 15 leaflets, blue-gray above with silvery undersides. The flower and seedheads are purple. **ZONES 7–10.**

Acaena argentea

Acaena 'Blue Haze'

Thought probably to be a form of *Acaena magellanica*, which comes from the southern Andes and sub-Antarctic islands, this vigorous plant can spread to an indefinite size, the stems rooting. The crowded leaves with roundish, toothed leaflets are an attractive pale blue-gray, and in summer it sends up 4 in (10 cm) high purplish flowerheads followed in autumn by red-spined fruit. A useful groundcover, it will spill over rocks or retaining walls. This is a tough plant and will tolerate poor soil, although it will do better with good drainage. **ZONES 7–10.**

Acaena novae-zelandiae

Agrostis capillaris
syn. *Agrostis tenuis*
BENT GRASS, BROWN TOP,
COLONIAL BENT

Regarded highly for its tolerance of the cold, this attractive and durable perennial species from Europe is widely grown as a lawn grass in areas where summers are not too hot and dry. Although frost resistant, it is drought tender. Left unmown, it grows to 16 in (40 cm) in height. The recommended mowing height is about ¾ in (20 mm). A prodigious spreader, it has a creeping stem, with bright green, narrow leaves. Compared with other bent grasses, this more erect species needs less care. **ZONES 5–10.**

ACANTHOLIMON
PRICKLY THRIFT

This genus consists of around 120 species of curious prickly leafed, dwarf, evergreen perennials and subshrubs from the eastern Mediterranean region and west and central Asia. Only a few have been successfully introduced to cultivation. These include some choice rock-garden plants. In the wild they inhabit dry mountain and desert areas, growing on screes, gravelly plains and the margins of salt lakes. Most species have crowded rosettes of stiff, harsh, needle-like leaves forming a mat or mound that may be very long lived, often with a thatch of old dead leaves built up beneath the living leaves. Some species have a whitish encrustation of mineral salts on the leaves. Related to armerias, acantho-limons have similar pink or white flowers but they are grouped into short spikes rather than rounded heads; they may either nestle among the leaves or be held on stalks well above them.

CULTIVATION
These plants have specialized requirements. They dislike wetness persisting around their bases, especially when dormant in winter, so plant them in very coarse, gritty soil with the stems sitting on stones or rocks. A very hot, dry position suits them best. Propagate from tip cuttings.

Acantholimon glumaceum
From the Caucasus Mountains and adjacent parts of Turkey, this species makes a low mound of densely crowded rosettes only 2–3 in (5–8 cm) high and up to 12 in (30 cm) across. The showy deep pink flowers are produced in summer on numerous very short spikes, barely emerging above the rigid, prickly leaves. Where conditions suit it, *Acantholimon glumaceum* makes a fine rock-garden subject. **ZONES 5–9.**

AGROSTIS
BENT GRASS, BROWN TOP

This is a near-worldwide genus of some 120 species of annual and perennial grasses, both tuft-forming and stoloniferous. Those most widely cultivated have long, fine stolons which produce roots at every node, thus developing a dense sod of roots and mat of fine leaves. If left unmown, most species grow 12–24 in (30–60 cm) tall with feathery inflorescences of tiny seedheads from spring to autumn. Various species of bent grass or browntop are widely used in cooler climates for lawns where a high-quality turf is required. They will grow even in light shade.

CULTIVATION
They need well-aerated and well-drained slightly acid to neutral soil (pH 5.6–7.0) with ample summer moisture and frequent feeding. They should be mown frequently and short. Propagate from seed. Brown patch and dollar spot are common diseases.

ANDROSACE
ROCK JASMINE

This genus consists of around 100 species of annuals and perennials from cooler regions of the northern hemisphere. It is mainly the low-growing perennials that are valued as garden plants, forming dense mats or cushions no more than 4 in (10 cm) high. Favorites for rock-garden planting, they are rarely spectacular but are appealing. Most species have light green or silvery gray, loose rosettes of foliage crowded along prostrate stems, topped with umbels of small white or pink 5-petalled flowers in spring and summer.

CULTIVATION

Best in sunny, well-drained scree or rockery conditions with free-draining gravel-based soil and additional humus. Most are quite frost hardy but some may require alpine-house conditions in areas subject to heavy winter rains. Propagate from seed, cuttings or self-rooted layers.

Asarum europaeum

ASARUM
WILD GINGER

This genus, belonging to the same family as *Aristolochia* (Dutchman's pipe), consists of over 70 species of rhizomatous perennials, both evergreen and deciduous, distributed widely through temperate areas of the northern hemisphere but most numerous in Japan and the USA. They are better known for their use in traditional medicine than as ornamental plants, though the foliage can make an attractive groundcover in shaded woodland gardens. The leaves are either kidney- or heart-shaped, and the small, bell-shaped flowers, which are usually hidden below the leaves, are mostly dull brownish or purplish and open at the mouth into 3 sharply reflexed sepals. Some examples include *Asarum chinense*, *A. maximum*, *A. muramatui* and *A. sieboldii*. All four species have very attractive foliage.

CULTIVATION

These plants prefer a shady site in moist, well-drained soil and can be planted out any time between autumn and spring. They spread rapidly; divide the clumps every few years in spring. They can also be propagated from seed. Watch for slugs and snails.

Androsace lanuginosa

A spreading groundcover or mat-forming perennial from the Himalayas, with small deep green leaves that appear somewhat silvery due to a covering of fine silky hairs. Only about 2 in (5 cm) high, the plants can spread rapidly to 18 in (45 cm) or more wide. Heads of light pink flowers appear profusely in summer and autumn. **ZONES 6–9.**

Androsace lanuginosa

Asarum europaeum
ASARABACCA

Widely distributed in European woodlands, this species has conspicuous shaggy hairs on both the creeping rhizomes and the 4–6 in (10–15 cm) long leaf stalks. The deep-green, glossy leaves are kidney-shaped to almost circular, up to 3 in (8 cm) wide. The dull purplish flowers, hidden under the leaves, are insignificant, only about 2 in (12 mm) long. Asarabacca was formerly used medicinally and as an ingredient of snuff powders, but is moderately toxic. **ZONES 6–9.**

Buglossoides purpurocaerulea
syn. *Lithospermum purpureocaeruleum*

This 30 in (75 cm) tall perennial species spreads to form a mat or clump of leafy stems 18–24 in (45–60 cm) tall with 3 in (8 cm) long, rather narrow leaves, and topped by small heads of ¾ in (20 mm) wide flowers that age to blue after opening purple-red. **ZONES 5–9.**

BUGLOSSOIDES

Buglossoides purpurocaerulea

This is a genus of around 15 species of annuals and perennials found over much of Europe and temperate Asia. The perennial species spread by rhizomes and may become slightly invasive. They have broad to narrow leaves on erect stems, mostly with bristly hairs. Small, starry, borage-like blue or purple flowers form in small heads at the top of the stems.

CULTIVATION
These plants prefer a warm, dry position in part-shade. Plant in a sheltered position for the best results. They are very frost hardy and are usually propagated by division in late winter. Annuals are raised from seed.

Campanula poscharskyana
SERBIAN BELLFLOWER

This bellflower is a native of Bosnia and Croatia. Low growing, it is a vigorous spreader with rounded hairy leaves and bears sprays of starry mauve-blue flowers from late spring onwards. It can mound up to 12 in (30 cm) high with an indefinite spread and is ideal as a groundcover, on walls, banks and in the front of mixed borders. Part-shade will prolong flowering. **ZONES 3–10.**

CAMPANULA

Campanula poscharskyana

Most of the species belonging to this genus are perennials, and detailed information on the genus is given in the Annuals and Perennials chapter. However, *Campanula poscharskyana* is treated here as a groundcover.

CERASTIUM

Sixty or so species of low-growing annuals and perennials belong to this genus, occurring in most temperate regions of the world though mainly in the northern hemisphere, where some extend into Arctic regions. The annuals include some common weeds of lawns (mouse-eared chickweeds), proliferating in winter and spring, but some of the perennials are useful garden plants grown as groundcovers or rock-garden subjects, for example, *Cerastium boissieri*. They have very weak stems from a network of thin rhizomes and small leaves, usually clothed in whitish hairs, tapering to narrow bases. The flowers are white with 5 petals, each notched at the apex, held in stalked clusters above the leaves.

CULTIVATION

Easily cultivated, some cerastiums can be quite invasive if planted in confined spaces in a rock garden. All are frost hardy and like full sun and well-drained soil. Their foliage should, if possible, be kept dry both in winter and during humid summer weather as the fine hairs on the leaves tend to retain moisture and become mildewed. They are easily propagated by division of rhizomes.

Cerastium tomentosum
SNOW-IN-SUMMER

A vigorous, fast-growing groundcover, this perennial is ideal for a well-drained, hot, dry bank or rockery. It has narrow silvery gray leaves, and masses of star-shaped white flowers, which are borne in loose heads in late spring and summer. It is particularly attractive when used as an underplanting against darker backgrounds. The foliage is dense and an effective weed suppressant. It grows to 6 in (15 cm) high, spreads indefinitely, and is very cold hardy. In the wild this species is variable and some botanists have split off a number of species from it. Taken in the broad sense, though, it has a wide distribution through the mountains of southern and eastern Europe and western Asia. **ZONES 3–10.**

Cerastium tomentosum

CERATOSTIGMA

This genus of 8 species of herbaceous perennials and small shrubs is primarily of Himalayan and east Asian origin, with one species endemic to the Horn of Africa. They are covered in detail in the chapter on Shrubs. The following species is a popular groundcover plant.

Ceratostigma plumbaginoides
syn. **Plumbago larpentae**
PERENNIAL LEADWORT, DWARF PLUMBAGO

Native to western China, this bushy perennial grows to 18 in (45 cm) high with rather erect, crowded stems arising from much-branched rhizomes. It has oval, mid-green leaves that turn a rich orange and red in autumn. The flowers are plumbago-like, with small clusters of single cornflower-blue blooms appearing on reddish, branched stems in late summer and autumn. **ZONES 6–9.**

Ceratostigma plumbaginoides

CONVOLVULUS

Found in many temperate regions of the world, this genus consists mainly of slender, twining creepers (the bindweeds) and small herbaceous plants. Only a few species are shrubby, and even these are soft stemmed and renewed by shooting from the base. They have simple, thin-textured, usually narrow leaves and the flowers are like morning glories, with a strongly flared tube that opens by unfurling 'pleats'. However, *Convolvulus* species differ from many true morning glories *(Ipomoea)* in having flowers that stay open all day, rather than shrivelling by early afternoon. Convolvulus flowers usually open in succession over a long season.

CULTIVATION

These easily grown plants adapt to most soils and to exposed as well as sheltered positions, but always prefer full sun. They can be cut back hard after flowering for thicker growth. Protect from winter frosts. Propagate from cuttings.

Convolvulus sabatius

syn. *Convolvulus mauritanicus*
MOROCCAN GLORY VINE, BINDWEED,
GROUND MORNING GLORY

Widely distributed in northern Africa with a foothold in southern Italy, this densely trailing perennial bears profuse lilac-blue flowers from spring to autumn. It has slender underground rhizomes, and its stems may twine around twigs, with small oval green leaves. An excellent plant for draping over walls and hanging baskets, it grows from 6 to 8 in (15 to 20 cm) and spreads extensively.
ZONES 8–11.

Convolvulus sabatius

DACTYLIS

COCKSFOOT, ORCHARD GRASS

This is a genus of 2 species of coarse perennial pasture grasses from Europe, North Africa and temperate Asia. The name comes from the Greek for 'finger', possibly a reference to the finger-thick aggregations of seedheads that are borne on tall stems. They make large, dense tussocks of foliage with flat, green leaf blades which often have a loosely tangled appearance. They are useful fodder when young but toughen with age and are difficult to mow. They are one of the more notorious hayfever grasses when flowering in spring.

CULTIVATION

Often sown in pastures to provide fodder, these grasses prefer fertile, moist soils and respond vigorously to fertilizer application. The foliage is killed by winter frosts, though light frosts can leave the plants still green when other grasses are frost-killed. Propagate by division.

Dactylis glomerata

This grass is usually a pasture grass, not an ornamental. However, in its variegated forms it can be attractive and will make a groundcover in sun or semi-shade. 'Variegata' has white-striped foliage and grows to about 10 in (25 cm) and 'Elegantissima' has similar variegation but only grows to a dwarf hummock of 6 in (15 cm). **ZONES 6–10.**

DRYAS

MOUNTAIN AVENS

Dryas octopetala 'Minor'

A small genus of 3 species from alpine and Arctic regions of the northern hemisphere, *Dryas* species make dense mats of evergreen foliage somewhat like tiny oak leaves; these often turn dark bronze in winter. Although the foliage and stems hug the ground, the showy flowers and seedheads sit up well above them.

CULTIVATION

Completely cold tolerant they may be less than satisfactory in warm climates. They make attractive rock-garden or ground-cover plants and are also useful between paving slabs. Grow in full sun or part-shade in a well-drained, humus-rich soil. Propagate from seed or cuttings.

Dryas octopetala

MOUNTAIN AVENS

This lovely European alpine plant can make evergreen mats up to 4 in (10 cm) tall in flower with a spread exceeding 3 ft (1 m). It has dark green scalloped leaves to 1½ in (4 cm) long. The pure white flowers, 1½ in (4 cm) across and with a boss of golden stamens in the center, are produced in late spring and early summer and followed by equally ornamental fluffy silver seedheads. *Dryas octopetala* var. *argentea* (syn. *lanata*) has felted leaves on both sides; 'Minor' has smaller flowers and leaves.
ZONES 2–9.

DUCHESNEA

INDIAN STRAWBERRY, MOCK STRAWBERRY

There are 6 species of these perennial plants, closely related to and very similar in appearance to the true strawberries. The leaves are divided into 3 to 5 leaflets and the plant spreads vegetatively with long fine stolons that produce more rosettes. Native to eastern and southern Asia, they differ from strawberries in having yellow flowers instead of white flowers and the red fruits are dry and unpalatable.

CULTIVATION

These frost-hardy plants can be quite aggressive so they should be placed with care; they are probably best as groundcovers in less cultivated parts of the garden. They prefer part-shade and are not really fussy about the soil. Propagate by division.

Duchesnea indica

syns *Fragaria indica, Potentilla indica*

A semi-evergreen trailing perennial, this species grows to a height of 4 in (10 cm) and multiplies rapidly by runners to an indefinite spread. It is useful as a groundcover and for bed edges, hanging baskets and pots. It has dark green leaves and bright, 1 in (25 cm) wide, yellow flowers from spring to early summer. Ornamental, strawberry-like small red fruits appear in late summer. **ZONES 5–11.**

Duchesnea indica

Epimedium pinnatum

EPIMEDIUM
BARRENWORT

This genus of about 40 species comes mainly from temperate Asia with a few species extending to the Mediterranean. Among the most useful low-growing perennials for shady situations, the barrenworts produce elegant foliage, sometimes evergreen, the compound leaves are composed of heart-shaped leaflets. Delightful sprays of delicate, often spurred flowers appear in late spring or early summer just above the foliage. Slowly spreading to form a broad mound or mat, they serve well as groundcovers in open woodland or in the foreground of borders and rockeries.

CULTIVATION
Frost hardy, most are tolerant of dry conditions, especially in the shade. All prefer a woodland environment and well-drained soil. Old leaves are best cut back in early spring to display the new foliage and flowers. Propagate from ripe seed or by division in autumn.

Epimedium grandiflorum
syn. Epimedium macranthum
BISHOP'S HAT, LONGSPUR EPIMEDIUM

This species from northern China, Korea and Japan is deciduous, except in mild climates. It has toothed leaflets often edged with red. Spidery pink or purple flowers with white spurs are held above the foliage on 12 in (30 cm) slender stems in spring. It is best displayed as a clump rather than as a groundcover. 'Rose Queen' bears clusters of cup-shaped rose-pink flowers with long, white-tipped spurs. 'White Queen' has large pure white flowers. **ZONES 4–9.**

Epimedium × perralchicum

This hybrid between *Epimedium pinnatum* subsp. *colchicum* and *E. perralderianum* was found in Wisley Gardens, England, where both parents were growing together. It grows to 18 in (45 cm) tall and has evergreen, spiny-edged leaflets up to 3 in (8 cm) long. Bright yellow flowers with short brown spurs are borne in spring. 'Fröhnleiten' has 1 in (25 mm) wide flowers and elongated leaflets. **ZONES 6–9.**

Epimedium pinnatum

Native to northeastern Turkey, this carpeting perennial grows to about 12 in (30 cm) high and wide. The leaflets are 3 in (8 cm) long and are somewhat leathery, evergreen and with spiny edges. The bright yellow flowers with purplish brown spurs are produced in late spring and early summer. *Epimedium pinnatum* subsp. *colchicum*, the Persian epimedium, has showy panicles of larger, yellow flowers with short brown spurs. **ZONES 6–9.**

Epimedium × versicolor

This hybrid of *Epimedium grandiflorum* and *E. pinnatum* is the best known of the epimediums. It is a carpeting perennial to 12 in (30 cm) high and wide. The green, heart-shaped leaves are tinted reddish when young. Clusters of pendent pink and yellow flowers with red spurs are produced in spring. 'Sulphureum' has sulfur-yellow flowers and reddish bronze-tinted young foliage. As summer advances it turns green, then russet again in autumn. **ZONES 5–9.**

Epimedium grandiflorum 'Rose Queen'

ERIGERON

FLEABANE

This large genus of about 200 species of annuals, biennials and perennials, some evergreen, occurs throughout temperate regions of the world but predominantly in North America. Some species were believed to repel fleas. The mainly erect stems are capped by masses of pink, white or blue, daisy-like flowers. They are well suited to the front of a mixed herbaceous border or rock garden. Flowers appear between late spring and mid-summer. There are many garden forms; 'Wayne Roderick' is just one example.

CULTIVATION

Frost hardy, they prefer a sunny position sheltered from strong winds and moderately fertile, well-drained soil. Do not allow to dry out during the growing season. Cut back immediately after flowering to encourage compact growth and prevent unwanted self-seeding. Some erigerons can become invasive. Propagate from seed or by division in spring.

Erigeron karvinskianus

Erigeron karvinskianus

syn. *Erigeron mucronatus*

MEXICAN DAISY, SANTA BARBARA DAISY, FLEABANE DAISY

This scrambling or mound-forming perennial from Mexico and Central America is useful as an informal ground-cover and in mild climates will bloom profusely throughout the year. The small, 1 in (25 mm) wide flowers open white, fading to various shades of pink and wine red. It grows to about 15 in (38 cm) tall with an indefinite spread, and has lax stems and narrow, often lobed, hairy leaves. It can be quite invasive in mild climates. Cut back hard from time to time. **ZONES 7–11.**

Festuca amethystina 'Superba'

FESTUCA

FESCUE

Native to temperate zones worldwide, this genus consists of 300 to 400 species of tuft-forming perennial grasses. They have evergreen linear leaves, often very narrow and sometimes rolled under. The panicles of flowerheads, composed of generally small and flattened spikelets, are produced from spring to summer. Several fescues are grown as fine lawns, others are grown for their ornamental gray-blue foliage which is attractive all year round.

CULTIVATION

Grow in any well-drained soil. They do best in full sun but will tolerate semi-shade and withstand dry conditions and the severest frosts. Propagate from seed in spring or autumn, or by division in spring. Disease and pests rarely affect them.

Festuca amethystina

LARGE BLUE FESCUE, TUFTED FESCUE

A native of the Alps and southern Europe, this fescue is named for its violet-tinged spikelets of flowers which appear in late spring and early summer. It grows to 18 in (45 cm) high and forms tufts of slender, blue-green, rough-edged leaves. *F. amethystina* 'Superba' has blue leaves and amethyst colored flowers. **ZONES 3–10.**

Festuca eskia

Festuca elatior

TALL FESCUE

This species from Europe and northern Asia has a tendency to clump, making it suitable for turf on playing fields and for controlling erosion. It grows to a height of 4 ft (1.2 m). Its leaves are tough and it will grow in compacted soil. As it does not send out runners, sow thickly for a close turf. **ZONES 5–10.**

Festuca eskia

syns *Festuca scoparia, F. varia* var. *scoparia*

BEARGRASS, BEARSKIN GRASS

This species from the Pyrenees reaches only 6 in (15 cm) high, but spreads to 10 in (25 cm) to form an attractive cushion of spiky, dark green, needle-like leaves. Slender, pendent flowerheads appear in summer. **ZONES 5–10.**

Festuca glauca

syn. *Festuca ovina* var. *glauca*

BLUE FESCUE, GRAY FESCUE

This clump-forming European grass reaches a height and spread of 12 in (30 cm). The very narrow leaves range in color from silvery white to blue-gray, and insignificant flowers bloom in summer. It is suitable as an edging or groundcover. Cultivars include **'Blaufuchs'** ('Blue Fox'), with vivid blue leaves; **'Blausilber'** ('Blue Silver'), with intensely silver-blue leaves; **'Elijah Blue'**, with paler silver-blue leaves; **'Seeigel'** ('Sea Urchin'), which forms a tight, compact tuft of soft, silver-blue leaves; and **'Golden Toupee'**, which has rounded tufts of bright green and yellow leaves. **ZONES 3–10.**

Festuca glauca 'Golden Toupee'

Festuca glauca

Festuca ovina
SHEEP'S FESCUE

Native to cooler temperate regions of the world, this clump-forming grass to 12 in (30 cm) high may form dense tussocks. It has stiff, very narrow green to gray-green leaves. In mid- to late summer it bears narrow open panicles with purple-tinged spikelets of 4 to 5 flowers. It is cultivated mainly as a forage and meadow grass. The New Zealand native *Festuca ovina* var. *novae-zelandiae* (syn. *F. novae-zelandiae*) has very narrow leaves to 18 in (45 cm) long and spikelets of 5 to 7 flowers. **ZONES 5–10.**

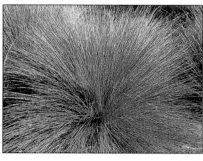

Festuca ovina var. novae-zelandiae

Festuca rubra
CREEPING RED FESCUE

A meadow grass native to Europe, this species is easily identified by the red or purplish sheath circling the base of the stem. Wiry slender green leaves rise to 6 in (15 cm), overtopped by narrow panicles of purple-tinged flowers. Rhizomatous and tolerant of dry conditions, it is suitable as a lawn grass and requires low maintenance. 'Commutata' is a tuft-forming cultivar that makes an appealing groundcover. It is also extensively grown as a lawn grass. *Festuca rubra* var. *pruinosa* is a popular variety. It has glaucous foliage with a whitish or bluish sheen. **ZONES 3–9.**

Festuca rubra var. pruinosa

Genista sagittalis

Genista sagittalis
syn. *Chamaespartium sagittale*

This prostrate shrub grows 6–12 in (15–30 cm) high with a spread of up to 3 ft (1 m). It has very distinctive, broadly winged stems, sparsely scattered with dark green oval leaves and dense clusters of deep yellow pea-flowers in early summer. **ZONES 4–9.**

GENISTA

Most of the species belonging to this genus are shrubs, and detailed information on the genus is given in the Shrubs chapter. However, *Genista sagittalis* is treated here as a ground-cover plant.

Glechoma hederacea

GLECHOMA

This genus consists of 12 species of low-growing, perennial plants. The stems root at the nodes, often forming extensive mats of coarsely toothed, rounded or broadly oval, soft hairy leaves. Ascending shoots bear pairs of small, tubular, 2-lipped flowers in the leaf axils in summer. They make good carpeting groundcovers, but can be very invasive and should be kept away from heavily planted beds. They are good for containers and hanging baskets.

CULTIVATION

They prefer full sun or part-shade and moderately fertile, moist but well-drained soil. Propagate from cuttings in late spring or by division in spring or autumn.

Helichrysum bellidioides

Glechoma hederacea

GROUND IVY, RUNAWAY ROBIN

This prostrate species often forms mats to 6 ft (1.8 m) or more across, producing an unpleasant smell when bruised. The opposite, almost kidney-shaped leaves have scalloped margins. Small violet flowers are borne in late spring and early summer. 'Variegata' has pretty, soft pale green leaves with white marbling. **ZONES 6–10.**

HELICHRYSUM

EVERLASTING, PAPER DAISY, STRAWFLOWER

As understood until recently, this is a genus of around 500 species of annuals, perennials and shrubs. Members of the daisy family, they all have typical flowerheads but with no ray florets or 'petals'. Instead, they have papery, mostly whitish bracts that are long-lasting when dried. But study by botanists has shown this to be an unnatural group, and they have been renaming some groups of species as distinct genera. This study is ongoing, and many species still in *Helichrysum* will eventually be reclassified. Some Australasian species have been reclassified as *Bracteantha, Ozothamnus* and *Chrysocephalum.*

CULTIVATION

Most species will tolerate only light frosts and are best suited to mild climates with low summer humidity, but a few are more frost hardy. They are mostly rock-garden plants, requiring gritty, well-drained soil that is not too fertile and a warm, sunny position. A few, such as *Helichrysum petiolare* and *H. splendidum* are more adaptable as border shrubs or groundcovers. Propagate from seed, cuttings, or rhizome divisions.

Helichrysum bellidioides

This prostrate perennial from New Zealand grows to a height of 6 in (15 cm), with a spread of up to 24 in (60 cm). It has tiny—¼ in (6 mm) long—spoon-shaped leaves that are light green above and clothed in cobweb-like white hairs beneath. The stems develop roots where they touch the ground. It produces many ¾–1¼ in (18–30 mm) white strawflowers on tall stems in spring and summer. **ZONES 7–9.**

HYPERICUM

ST JOHN'S WORT

This is a large and varied genus of 400 species of annuals, perennials, shrubs and a few small trees and is described in detail in the Shrubs chapter. The species described here is a good groundcover in temperate areas.

Juniperus horizontalis 'Douglasii'

Juniperus conferta
Left: *Juniperus horizontalis* 'Blue Chip'

JUNIPERUS

Most of the species belonging to this genus are trees, and detailed information on the genus is given in the Trees chapter. However, the ones included here are treated as groundcovers.

Juniperus conferta

JAPANESE SHORE JUNIPER

This prostrate, spreading shrub from Japan grows to a height of 6–12 in (15–30 cm) with a spread of 6–8 ft (1.8–2.4 m). The soft foliage is a mixture of fresh, clear green and pale blue, aromatic, needle-like leaves. The berries are pale green. It tolerates seaside conditions and grows rapidly, making it a first-rate groundcover. **ZONES 5–10.**

Hypericum calycinum

AARON'S BEARD, CREEPING
ST JOHN'S WORT

One of the best of all ground-covers for temperate climates, this species from Turkey is a low-growing evergreen shrub only about 15 in (38 cm) tall but spreading rapidly by creeping, runner-like stems to cover quite a large area. The mid-summer flowers are about the size of a rose and have long stamens. Any sort of soil suits and, though the plant will grow happily in the dry shade beneath deciduous trees, it flowers more pro-fusely if given sunshine. **ZONES 6–10.**

Juniperus horizontalis

This cold-climate prostrate shrub from northern North America is fast spreading and tough. Its branches form a mat of blue-green or gray leaves up to 18 in (45 cm) thick. Cultivars include 'Bar Harbor', with grayish green foliage, turning mauve in winter; 'Blue Chip', with blue-green foliage; 'Douglasii', with glaucous gray-blue leaves, turning plum purple in winter; 'Glauca', a prostrate form that exceeds 6 ft (1.8 m) in spread with a height of only 2 in (5 cm) or so, with blue-gray foliage often tinged purple in winter; 'Plumosa', which has an ascending habit unlike other forms of this species and spreads to about 10 ft (3 m) across by 24 in (60 cm) tall in a star-shaped pattern, with blue-gray foliage turning rich purple in winter; and 'Wiltonii', blue, with trailing branches. **ZONES 4–10.**

Lolium perenne
PERENNIAL RYE GRASS

This short-lived, clumping perennial species, originating in Europe and naturalized in most other temperate regions of the world, grows up to 18 in (45 cm) tall and 12 in (30 cm) wide. It has smooth, whippy stems that tend to lie down under the lawn mower, springing back up later. The flat blades are glossy and dark green. The tiny flowers, which appear in late spring and summer, are borne in narrow spikes 6 in (15 cm) long. It is a very coarse grass needing frequent mowing, and best for rough areas rather than for fine lawn. **ZONES 5–10.**

LOLIUM
RYE GRASS

There are about 8 species of annual or perennial grasses in this Eurasian genus. They have no ornamental value but are frequently cultivated as pasture grasses and are often found in lawns, although their presence may be unwelcome; they bear characteristic spikes with 2 appressed rows of green spikelets, that shed abundant pollen in late spring or early summer, a prime cause of hay fever in some parts of the world. The small grains that follow germinate freely.

CULTIVATION
These are adaptable grasses and will grow in most well-drained soils in full sun. Propagate from seed.

Lolium perenne

LUZULA
WOODRUSH

Luzula nivea

This genus of some 80 species of rushes is found in temperate regions of both the northern and southern hemispheres. They differ from most of the familiar rushes of the related genus *Juncus* in having grass-like, flat or channeled leaves with long silky hairs fringing the edges. Most are perennials and evergreen, forming tufts or clumps, some are stoloniferous and may be slightly invasive. The wiry, flowering stems extend above the foliage and bear clusters of tiny pale gray to golden-brown flowers, sometimes tinted pink. Several cultivars with variegated foliage are grown.

CULTIVATION
Most species prefer a moist position but are not fussy about soil type or aspect provided they are not in deep shade. Most species are frost hardy. Propagate from seed or by division.

Luzula nivea
SNOWY WOODRUSH

This slow-spreading evergreen perennial from central and southern Europe reaches 24 in (60 cm) in height and can spread to 24 in (60 cm) or more. The narrow grassy leaves are edged with white hairs and the flowers are borne in dense clusters of shining white. **ZONES 6–9.**

Lysimachia nummularia
CREEPING JENNY, MONEYWORT

Native to much of Europe and also Turkey and the Caucasus, this vigorous creeping perennial has become widely naturalized in North America. Various medicinal properties were attributed to it by herbalists. The prostrate stems take root wherever they touch damp ground, forming a dense, rapidly spreading mat usually no more than 3 in (8 cm) deep. The paired leaves are almost circular, hence *nummularia* from the Latin for coin-like, also the English 'moneywort'. The deep yellow bowl-shaped flowers are up to 1 in (25 mm) wide, borne singly on short stalks from the leaf axils over a long summer period. '**Aurea**', golden creeping Jenny, is a popular cultivar with pale yellow-green leaves and stems; when grown in shade it turns an interesting lime green. Both green and gold forms are useful ground-cover plants for moist or even boggy soil and can tolerate occasional light foot traffic. **ZONES 4–10.**

LYSIMACHIA
LOOSESTRIFE

Ranging through temperate and subtropical regions of the northern hemisphere, this genus of mainly evergreen perennials and shrubs of the primula family consists of around 150 species, of which about 130 are found in China. There are also a few species in Africa, Australia and South America. They vary greatly in growth habit from low, creeping plants to stately clumps with tall, spike-like racemes of crowded flowers. The 5-petalled flowers are mostly yellow or white, less commonly pink or purple. The botanical name is Latinized Greek for 'ending strife' and the English common name is a version of the same, though why these plants deserve such a name is now unclear.

CULTIVATION

They prefer slightly acidic soil with a good mix of organic matter and medium to moist conditions in sun or part-shade. Some species are marsh plants that grow best at the edge of a pond or stream. Propagate from seed or cuttings, or by division.

Lysimachia nummularia 'Aurea'

MAZUS

Consisting of around 30 species, this genus comes from usually damp habitats in lowland or mountain regions. Some plants are annuals but those grown in gardens are ground-hugging perennials that root at the nodes. This makes them ideal in between paving slabs and as low groundcover for rock gardens.

CULTIVATION

Most are reasonably frost tolerant and like fertile, moist but well-drained soil in full sun. Propagate by division in late winter or early spring.

Mazus pumilio

This almost completely prostrate species comes from Australasia. Its 2 in (5 cm) long leaves are spatulate and its summer flowers are usually blue with a yellow throat although a white-flowered form, **'Albus'**, exists. **ZONES 7–11.**

Mazus pumilio

Pennisetum clandestinum

KIKUYU GRASS

This species has both deep-running and surface rhizomes that form a dense, hard-wearing turf of a rich, slightly yellowish green. Its flowers are almost completely hidden among the sheathing leaf bases and appear briefly in summer. It is popular for its vigor and drought tolerance, but can be very invasive; un-mown, it will build into hummocks about 24 in (60 cm) high. It needs protection in winter. **ZONES 9–12.**

PACHYSANDRA

The 4 evergreen or semi-evergreen subshrubs in this genus are tough and thrive in dry shade where few others will grow. They form mats or mounding clumps of fleshy, rhizome-like stems clothed at the tips with whorls of 2–4 in (5–10 cm) long, oblong, deep green, toothed leaves. Small spikes of tiny, scented, cream flowers develop in spring.

CULTIVATION

Frost hardy, all species will grow in most soils in sun or part-shade. The more sun they receive, the more moisture they require. They are usually propagated by removing self-rooted layers or from cuttings.

Pachysandra terminalis

This creeping evergreen perennial, has leathery, ovate leaves with saw-tooth tips. Tiny white flowers, sometimes pink or purple tinted, appear in terminal clusters in early summer. It is frost resistant and makes a good groundcover, growing to 4 in (10 cm) high with a spread of 8 in (20 cm). **'Variegata'** has cream, gray-green and green variegated foliage. **ZONES 5–10.**

Pachysandra terminalis

PENNISETUM

Some species of this genus are ornamental grasses and detailed information on the genus is given in the Ornamental Grasses section of this chapter. However, *Pennisetum clandestinum* is treated here as a groundcover.

PERSICARIA

syns *Aconogonon, Bistorta, Tovara*

KNOTWEED

This genus of 50 to 80 species of annuals, perennials or subshrubs, have strong wiry stems with variously shaped leaves 1½–10 in (3.5–25 cm) long. The foliage often has purple-gray markings and may develop red and gold tints in autumn. The flowers, usually pink or cream, are small and are sometimes borne in showy panicles or spikes.

CULTIVATION

Most are vigorous and very frost hardy and easily cultivated in any well-drained soil in sun or part-shade. Some may become invasive: the stronger growers are best contained. Propagate from seed in spring or by division in spring or autumn.

Persicaria affinis

Persicaria affinis

syn. *Polygonum affine*

This evergreen perennial has small, shiny green, leaves that become bronze in winter. It forms a mat about 6 in (15 cm) deep and up to 3 ft (1 m) across. In late summer and autumn, it bears dense spikes 12 in (30 cm) or more high of small, red or pink funnel-shaped flowers. 'Darjeeling Red' has elongated leaves that turn bright red in autumn. 'Donald Lowndes' is a compact cultivar with salmon-pink flowers that age to deep pink. 'Superba' is a strong-growing cultivar with lusterous brown autumn foliage color and pink to red flowers. **ZONES 3–9.**

Phlox subulata

MOSS PHLOX

Throughout spring, this prostrate alpine perennial produces masses of 1 in (25 mm) wide, star-shaped flowers in blue, mauve, carmine, pink and white, the petals being notched and open. Its fine-leafed foliage grows carpet-like to 4 in (10 cm) high with a spread twice that. Fully frost hardy and evergreen, it is suitable for sunny rock gardens. 'Greencourt Purple' has a rich color; it likes a little shade. 'McDaniel's Cushion' (syn. 'Daniel's Cushion') is best in small groups among shrubs or taller perennials. 'Maischnee' (syn. 'May Snow') is a beautiful snow-white form. 'Marjorie' has glowing deep pink flowers, 'Oakington Blue Eyes' forms large mats and is smothered with light blue flowers. **ZONES 3–10.**

Phlox subulata

PHLOX

Most of this genus are annuals and perennials, and detailed information is given in the Annuals and Perennials chapter. However, *Phlox subulata* is treated here as a groundcover.

Phlox subulata 'Marjorie'

POA

This genus of some 500 species of mainly perennial grasses is widely used for sports fields and as tough lawn grasses. The species are widely distributed in the temperate regions and have narrow but strong stems, seldom more than 3 ft (1 m) tall. Their leaves, which are often thickened and jointed at the base, are narrow and usually bright green or blue-green. Short flower spikes appear throughout the growing season; they are often the same color as the foliage, but may develop red, brown or purple tints.

CULTIVATION

They are easily grown in full sun or part-shade in any well-drained garden soil. Most species are at least moderately frost hardy, some are very frost hardy. Propagate from seed or by division.

Poa pratensis
KENTUCKY BLUE GRASS, MEADOW GRASS

Although producing an appealing blue-green lawn, this perennial native of central Europe will not take the heavy traffic of playgrounds or playing fields and does not survive dry conditions. It does well in cooler climates. It has smooth, erect stems and small, flat, pointed leaves. If left ungroomed it will grow to 6 in (15 cm) in height and spread. In spring and mid-summer, it bears spikelets in spreading panicles. It is vulnerable to attack by rust and other diseases, including fusarium blight brought on by a hot summer. **ZONES 3–9,**

Polygala chamaebuxus

POLYGALA
MILKWORT, SENECA, SNAKEROOT

This genus consists of more than 500 species from warm areas all over the world. They include annuals, perennials and some shrubs, only a few of which are cultivated. Some species were used by the ancient Greeks to stimulate the secretion of milk in lactating mothers. The 2 biggest sepals of the pea-like flowers are rose-purple, petal-like and known as wings. The keel terminates in a crown-like tuft that is characteristic of polygalas. The flowers are carried in racemes and are followed by a 2-chambered seed pod.

CULTIVATION

They need light, well-drained soil in a sunny to part-shaded spot. They are suitable for pot culture. To keep the growth dense, prune any straggly stems after the main flowering has finished. Propagate from seed in spring or early summer, or from cuttings in late summer.

Polygala chamaebuxus
BASTARD BOX

This evergreen shrub grows to 8 in (20 cm) tall with a spread of 15 in (38 cm). Racemes of small yellow and white flowers appear in spring and early summer. It has tiny, oval, dark green leaves and is fully frost hardy. *Polygala chamaebuxus* var. *grandiflora* has larger flowers with purple wings and yellow petals. **ZONES 6–9.**

PRATIA

This genus includes 20 species of evergreen perennials. They have multiple branching stems and little toothed leaves. A profusion of starry flowers is followed by globular berries. Most are carpet forming and make excellent rockery specimens, but tend to overrun the garden.

CULTIVATION

Ranging from very frost hardy to frost hardy, they generally enjoy damp but porous soil, total sun or part-shade and protection from the elements. Water liberally during the growth period and sparingly in winter. Propagate by division or from seed in autumn.

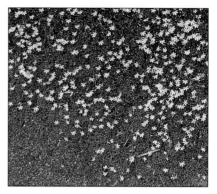
Pratia angulata

Pratia pedunculata

SAGINA

There are about 20 species in this genus of small tufted annuals and perennials. The paired linear leaves join where they meet at the stem. The flowers are white and small, with 4 or 5 petals.

CULTIVATION

Grow in a moist but well-drained soil in sun. Some midday shade in hot climates will be of benefit. Propagate from seed in autumn or by division in spring.

Sagina subulata
IRISH MOSS, SCOTCH MOSS

This plant is grown for its neat dense growth habit. Its short branches are self-rooting and bear bright green ¼ in (6 mm) leaves to form a compact spreading carpet with white flowers in late spring to summer. '**Aurea**' has yellow-green leaves. **ZONES 4–10.**

Pratia angulata

This very frost-hardy creeper has rounded, deep green leaves with roughly serrated edges. In spring, white starry flowers with purple veins appear in the leaf axils, followed in autumn by globular, reddish purple fruit. This species tolerates full sun and enjoys damp soil. **ZONES 7–10.**

Pratia pedunculata

From eastern Australia, this small-leafed, low-growing species makes a good groundcover, spreading and taking root at its nodes. In spring and early summer it bears profuse star-shaped, 5-petalled flowers, usually mid-blue to white, sometimes purple. These are followed by small berries. **ZONES 7–11.**

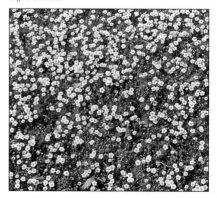
Sagina subulata

Scaevola 'Mauve Clusters'

This frost-hardy, perennial blooms profusely in spring and summer to present a mass of small mauve flowers against a backdrop of bright green leaves. Very low growing, it spreads as much as 6 ft (1.8 m). **ZONES 9–11.**

Scaevola 'Mauve Clusters'

SCAEVOLA

Most of the species in this genus are annuals and perennials, and detailed information on the genus is given in the Annuals and Perennials chapter. However, *Scaevola* 'Mauve Clusters' is treated here as a groundcover.

Scleranthus biflorus

Scleranthus biflorus

TWIN-FLOWERED KNAWEL

Found in alpine regions, this species may be covered with snow for 6 months in winter. It forms a spreading, tough, bright green mound 6 in (15 cm) high spreading slowly up to 24 in (60 cm). Tiny 2-pronged flowers appear during the summer. The bright green 'cushion' appearance makes it a very popular garden and container plant; it will grow quite happily for years given sun, moisture and a cool root system. **ZONES 7–9.**

SCLERANTHUS

KNAWEL

This genus consists of 10 species of small annuals and perennials. They have small, narrow, crowded leaves and tiny white or greenish yellow flowers. The tough calyces often persist for a long time.

CULTIVATION

These plants prefer full sun but midday shade and gritty, free-draining soil. They need protection from prolonged periods of frost and winter wet. Propagate from seed or cuttings, or by division.

SEDUM

STONECROP

This large genus contains about 400 species of succulent annuals, biennials, perennials, subshrubs and shrubs native to the northern hemisphere. They are described in detail in the Cacti and Succulents chapter. The species described here are popular groundcover plants.

Sedum kamtschaticum

syn. *Hylotelephium pluricaule*

KAMSCHATKA STONECROP

This carpeting semi-evergreen perennial grows 4–8 in (10–20 cm) high with 1 in (25 mm) long green leaves, bluntly toothed towards the tip. Yellow flowers appear in summer. It comes from northern China, eastern Siberia and Japan. 'Variegatum' has leaves edged with white; 'Weihenstephaner Gold' has a more trailing habit, with golden-yellow flowers ageing to orange. **ZONES 7–10.**

Sedum spurium

Sedum spurium

This summer-flowering, evergreen perennial from Turkey and northern Iran bears small blooms in big, rounded flowerheads; colors range from white to purple. Hairy stems carrying saw-edged, elliptical leaves spread widely into a carpet 4 in (10 cm) tall, suitable for covering banks and slopes. 'Schorbuser Blut' ('Dragon's Blood') is a creeping cultivar with plum-toned leaves and magenta flowers; 'Sunset Cloud' has deep pinkish orange flowers. *Sedum stoloniferum* is similar to *S. spurium* but its stems lie close to the ground and the flowers are pink. **ZONES 7–10.**

Sedum kamtschaticum

Thymus serpyllum 'Coccineus Minor'

THYMUS

Most of this genus are herbs, and detailed information on the genus is given in the Vegetables and Herbs chapter. However, the ones included here are treated as groundcovers.

Thymus pseudolanuginosus

syn. *Thymus lanuginosus*

WOOLLY THYME

This very low-growing, frost-hardy thyme, which reaches only 1 in (25 mm) in height, spreads to form broad, oval mats of densely hairy, gray-green foliage. It bears terminal spikes of tubular, 2-lipped, pale pink flowers in mid-summer and has tiny leaves. **ZONES 3–9.**

Thymus serpyllum

WILD THYME, CREEPING THYME, MOTHER OF THYME

This species grows to 10 in (25 cm) and spreads to 18 in (45 cm), forming a useful groundcover. Its creeping stem is woody and branching, and the scented, bright green leaves are elliptical to lanceolate. The bluish purple flowers are small and tubular with 2 lips, and are borne in spring and summer in dense terminal whorls. It is very frost hardy and will take moderate foot traffic. **'Annie Hall'**, has rounded leaves and pink flowers; **'Coccineus Minor'**, has crimson-pink flowers; and **'Pink Ripple'**, has bronze-pink flowers. **ZONES 3–9.**

Thymus serpyllum 'Annie Hall'

Tiarella cordifolia

TIARELLA

FOAMFLOWER

The foamflowers are a genus of 5 species of forest-floor perennials, which have been described in detail in the chapter on Annuals and Perennials. The following species makes an attractive groundcover plant.

Tiarella cordifolia

FOAMFLOWER, COOLWORT

This vigorous spreading plant blooms in early to late spring. Its terminal spikes of tiny, creamy white flowers with 5 petals look most effective in the garden. When in flower, it has a height and spread of 12 in (30 cm) or more. **ZONES 3–9.**

VINCA

PERIWINKLE

This genus contains 7 species of slender-stemmed, evergreen subshrubs and herbaceous perennials from Russia, Europe and North Africa. With their opposite, simple, lance-shaped leaves, they make useful groundcovers, although they may be invasive. The attractive flowers are widely flared and have 5 lobes. Ingestion of any part of the plant may cause a mild stomach upset.

CULTIVATION

Hardiness ranges from frost and drought resistant to fully frost hardy. Any soil is suitable provided it is not too dry. If groundcover is desired, provide these evergreens with shade to part-shade. If flowers are desired, let them have more sun. Propagation is usually by division in autumn through spring, or from cuttings in summer.

Vinca major
GREATER PERIWINKLE

This tenacious evergreen creeper from the Mediterranean has mid-green, glossy leaves that are heart-shaped to pointed ovate. Widely spreading with an erect woody stem, *Vinca major* reaches 18 in (45 cm) in height. The brilliant violet flowers, 2 in (5 cm) across, are borne in late spring through early autumn. Drought and moderately frost resistant, it can also be aggressive and invasive. The cultivar **'Variegata'** has leaves blotched and margined creamy white and large lavender-blue flowers. **ZONES 7–10.**

Vinca minor 'Gertrude Jekyll'
Right: Vinca major

Vinca minor
LESSER PERIWINKLE, DWARF PERIWINKLE

The slender, woody stems on this European evergreen creeper will cover ground over a distance of 10 ft (3 m) to lay down a mat of glossy, dark green leaves of pointed elliptical shape. The small flowers, produced in mid-spring through early summer, are bluish lilac, purple or white. This species, like *Vinca major*, is often aggressive and invasive if not trimmed back. *V. minor* has a number of very popular cultivars. **'Alba'** has white flowers and a more vigorous growth; **'Gertrude Jekyll'** has small white flowers and narrower foliage; **'Grape Cooler'** has deep pink flowers that become pale with age; and **'La Grave'** has large flowers and broad foliage. A variegated form is also available. **ZONES 4–9.**

Waldsteinia ternata
syn. **Waldsteinia trifoliata**

Native to central Europe through Russia to China and Japan, this herbaceous or semi-evergreen creeping perennial grows to a height of about 6 in (15 cm). Golden-yellow, buttercup-like flowers appear from late spring, mostly on the new growth. Each bloom is about ½ in (12 mm) across. It spreads quite fast and makes a thick groundcover in moist soil in part-shade beneath trees. In ideal conditions, *Waldsteinia ternata* can become invasive. **ZONES 3–9.**

Waldsteinia ternata

WALDSTEINIA

Found over much of the northern temperate zone, the 6 species in this genus are clump-forming, rhizomatous perennials. They are semi-evergreen, creeping groundcovers with 3-parted leaves resembling those of their close allies, the strawberries. The hairy leaves are usually bright green with bronze tints if grown in the sun. In spring and summer, bright yellow 5-petalled flowers are borne singly or in clusters of up to 8 blooms.

CULTIVATION

Most *Waldsteinia* species are quite frost hardy and easily grown in any well-drained soil in sun or part-shade. Propagation is usually by division or by self-rooted offsets from the runners.

ORNAMENTAL GRASSES & BAMBOOS

Acorus gramineus

Native to Japan, this species has soft, curved leaves under 12 in (30 cm) long and about ¼ in (6 mm) wide. The flower spikes are about 1 in (25 mm) long and emerge in spring and summer. 'Pusillus', popular in aquariums, is only about 4 in (10 cm) high; 'Variegatus' has cream-striped leaves; 'Ogon', more recently introduced from Japan, has chartreuse and cream variegated leaves.
ZONES 3–11.

ACORUS

SWEET FLAG

Acorus gramineus 'Ogon'

This unusual genus of only 2 species of grass-like evergreen perennials has inconspicuous flower spikes, and is grown mainly for its foliage. The leaves are in flattened fans like those of irises, crowded along short rhizomes. Both leaves and rhizomes are sweet-scented, most noticeably as they dry, and have been used in folk medicine, perfumery and food flavorings.

CULTIVATION

Sweet flags are easily grown in any boggy spot or in shallow water at pond edges, needing no maintenance except cutting back to limit their spread. They are fully frost hardy. Propagate by division.

Arundo donax

GIANT REED

This giant grass from the Mediterranean region is one of the most striking of summer foliage plants. Growing to a height of 20 ft (6 m) and a similar spread, it is an excellent ornamental plant for large gardens. The drooping leaves are up to 24 in (60 cm) long by 2½ in (6 cm) wide. In mild areas it can grow very vigorously and will need confining. In winter, when the foliage becomes untidy, it should be cut to the ground, creating luxuriant new spring and summer growth. 'Versicolor' is a popular variegated cultivar, the leaves with longitudinal cream stripes. The reeds used in musical instruments such as organs and clarinets all come from carefully selected and cured stems of the giant reed, as did the pipes of Pan.
ZONES 9–11.

ARUNDO

GIANT REED

Arundo donax

Found through much of the Old World subtropics and warm-temperate regions, the 3 species in this genus are large, rhizomatous, perennial grasses. They have strong, upright, leafy stems reminiscent of bamboo but lacking the twiggy side branches of most bamboos. Thin, flat leaves, drooping at the tips, alternate in 2 rows up the stems which terminate in summer in large, feathery panicles of minute, chaffy flowers.

CULTIVATION

Unlike most reeds and rushes, they do not need waterlogged soil although they tolerate it well. Any moist well-drained soil will do. They prefer full sun or light shade. Propagate from seed or by division.

Bambusa multiplex 'Alphonse Karr'

Bambusa multiplex

syn. *Bambusa glaucescens*

HEDGE BAMBOO

A native of southern China, this variable species has gracefully arching stems usually 10–30 ft (3–9 m) tall and 1–2 in (25–50 mm) in diameter topped with plumes of narrow, 6 in (15 cm) long leaves with silvery undersides. One of the more cold-tolerant species, it is mostly represented in gardens by yellow-leafed and variegated cultivars. **'Alphonse Karr'** has yellow-striped stems, tinted pink when young. **'Riviereorum'** is a relatively dwarf cultivar with 5–10 ft (1.5–3 m) stems.
ZONES 9–12.

CALAMAGROSTIS

REED GRASS

This genus of over 250 species of perennial grasses is native to temperate regions of the northern hemisphere where they occur mainly in damp places to form dense, robust clumps with narrow arching leaves; the plume-like seedheads are carried on tall stems in summer and can be quite decorative. A number of *Calamagrostis* species and cultivars are found among the more widely grown grasses.

CULTIVATION

Almost any moist soil in full sun or part-shade suits these plants. If conditions are to their liking, some may become invasive so are best given ample space, for example, beside a pond. Regular division of clumps serves to keep growth in check. seedheads and old leaves can be cut back to ground level in early winter. Propagate by division of clumps.

BAMBUSA

BAMBOO

This is a genus of around 120 species of clump-forming bamboos. Many are very large, up to 80 ft (24 m) tall or even more, with strong, woody, hollow stems. In their native lands they are put to all sorts of uses, especially in construction. The upper parts of the stems are often arching, and branch at the nodes into wiry branchlets with masses of grass-like leaves. The flowers are rather insignificant, often half-hidden among the foliage on slender, arching panicles, which are usually produced rather intermittently. *Bambusa* species are much less invasive than some other bamboos. Some of the most popular ornamental bamboos in this genus are cultivars with striped variegation of the stems or leaves.

CULTIVATION

They thrive in warm-temperate to tropical climates with humid conditions and deep, humus-rich soil. Propagate by division in spring.

Calamagrostis × *acutiflora* 'Karl Foerster'

Calamagrostis × acutiflora
FEATHER REED GRASS

A hybrid between the Eurasian species *Calamagrostis arundinacea* and *C. epigejos*, this clump-forming grass has a strong, upright habit with thin, arching leaves up to about 3 ft (1 m) long. The somewhat silky, brown seedheads are borne on erect, much branched panicles 3–5 ft (1–1.5 m) tall, and persist into winter. 'Karl Foerster' (syn. 'Stricta') is larger growing, to about 6 ft (1.8 m), with reddish pink seedheads that age more straw-colored. **ZONES 6–9.**

Carex elata 'Aurea'

Carex elata
syn. **Carex stricta**
TUFTED SEDGE

Native to Europe and North Africa, this deciduous sedge is useful for growing in damp places and beside ponds. It is a fast-spreading plant with new shoots springing from rhizomes to form broad-based tufts of foliage about 18 in (45 cm) high. In summer, erect flowering stems up to 3 ft (1 m) high with dark brown spikes also arise from the rhizomes. In gardens it is known by the cultivar **'Aurea'** (Bowles' golden sedge), with new yellow-green foliage changing to golden yellow in autumn. **ZONES 3–9.**

Carex albula

CAREX
SEDGE

This large genus of sedges contains over 1,500 species of deciduous or evergreen, usually clump-forming perennials. Most species have sharp-edged, grass-like leaves often with drooping tips, and tiny flowers arranged in catkin-like spikes. They occur worldwide but with the greatest concentration of species in cooler temperate parts of the northern hemisphere, including Arctic and subarctic regions. Most grow in bogs and swamps, and they form the characteristic vegetation of fens. With the growing interest in recent years in ornamental grasses and sedges, some species of *Carex* are now popular garden plants; east Asian and New Zealand natives are prominent among them. There are also a number of attractive cultivars including 'Everbright', which forms a tussock of long, narrow leaves that are creamy white with green margins, and 'Little Red', resembles a tuft of dry grass; its long, very narrow leaves a reddish brown.

CULTIVATION
Their cultivation requirements vary, although most species need full sun or part-shade and watering only when surface roots seem dry. Propagate from seed or by division of clumps.

Carex albula
syn. **Carex 'Frosted Curls'**

This is one of the most striking sedges by reason of its pale buff-colored or almost silvery white, very fine and curly foliage. An evergreen, Carex albula grows wild in very dry tussock grassland on hills in the north of New Zealand's South Island, one of the country's lowest rainfall areas. It forms a soft, rounded tussock of up to 12 in (30 cm) high, and the inconspicuous summer-flowering stems are hidden beneath the leaves. This plant was introduced to gardens under the cultivar name 'Frosted Curls' before its correct botanical identity was established. **ZONES 7–9.**

Carex morrowii
JAPANESE SEDGE

Native to Japan, this evergreen sedge makes a soft clump of recurving, fine-pointed leaves 8–12 in (20–30 cm) high. Insignificant flowers appear in summer on short stems. Variegated cultivars are more popular. '**Variegata**' has white-striped, rich green leaves; '**Bressingham**' and '**Fisher**' are very similar. These are especially well suited to rock gardens, or among poolside rocks. **ZONES 7–10.**

Carex morrowii 'Variegata'

CORTADERIA

This genus of giant tussock-forming evergreen perennial grasses contains around 20 species native to South America, 4 to New Zealand and one to Papua New Guinea. The leaves are long and finely tapering, of harsh texture and with sharp edges. The tall flowering stems are reed-like and carry long terminal plumes of white to silvery or pinkish seedheads. Several of the larger South American species are known as 'pampas grass', a reference to the *pampas*—the grass plains extending across that continent's central southern region. The genus name comes from these grasses' Spanish-American name *cortadera*, the 'cutter', from their sharp leaves. They make striking ornamental plants, though the fashion for them has waned as gardeners discover the difficulty of maintaining them. In temperate southern hemisphere countries in higher-rainfall areas, they have become ecological weeds, invading native vegetation even without any human intervention. Worst of the weeds are the well known *Cortaderia selloana*, which needs plants of both sexes to produce seed, and the very similar *C. jubata* which produces apomictic seed—seed that does not require fertilization.

Cortaderia selloana

Cortaderia selloana
syns *Cortaderia argentea, Gynerium argenteum*
PAMPAS GRASS

Native to Argentina and southern Brazil, this stately grass grows to a height of 10 ft (3 m) and similar spread, the pale green, rustling foliage forming a dense tangled clump about 6 ft (1.8 m) high. In summer and autumn the striking plume-like panicles appear above the leaves on pole-like stems, consisting of vast numbers of small silky spikelets varying in color from creamy white to purplish pink. In some regions this species has become very invasive. A number of clones have been named as cultivars. '**Aureolineata**' has bright green leaves with deep yellow edges. **ZONES 6–10.**

CULTIVATION

Pampas grass is easily grown in any open sunny position, in almost any soil as long as moisture is adequate. It tolerates exposure to strong winds and even to salt spray. With age a clump will build up unsightly dead leaves and old flowering stems; if circumstances allow, these can be disposed of by setting fire to the clump in autumn or winter, otherwise it should be cut back 12 in (30 cm) or so high, preferably with a motorized slasher. Propagate by division of selected forms or cultivars, or from seed if obtainable.

FARGESIA

This genus consists of about 4 species of evergreen, clump-forming bamboos from China and the northern Himalayas. They have narrowly oblong leaves, and grass-like flowers that are rarely produced in cultivation and then generally only on long-established specimens.

CULTIVATION

Grow these marginally to fully frost-hardy plants in fertile, moist soil in full sun or part-shade (depending on the species) and shelter from strong cold winds. Propagate from cuttings or by division in spring.

Fargesia nitida

Fargesia murieliae

syns *Arundinaria murieliae, Fargesia spathacea* **of gardens**
UMBRELLA BAMBOO

Native to China, this fully frost-hardy species grows to 12 ft (3.5 m) or more high and has bright green leaves to 4 in (10 cm) long. The canes, which are yellowish green when young, branch in the first year and turn yellow with age. This is an attractive specimen or accent foliage plant. **ZONES 6–10.**

Fargesia nitida

syns *Arundinaria nitida, Sinarundinaria nitida*
FOUNTAIN BAMBOO

Originating in China, this slow-growing bamboo can eventually reach about 12 ft (3.5 m) in height. It has small tapering mid-green leaves, purple canes, and after the first year a number of branches that grow out from the nodes. The insignificant flowers appear only rarely. *Fargesia nitida* is particularly effective as a screen or hedge and is fully frost hardy. **ZONES 5–10.**

GLYCERIA

MANNA GRASS

Around 16 species belong to this genus of aquatic and meadow grasses, distributed throughout the world with the majority in the northern hemisphere. They are vigorous growers with creeping rootstocks and flat, juicy leaf blades. The greenish flowers and seedheads are borne on narrow panicles, generally not rising above the leaves. The genus name comes from the Greek word for 'sweet', referring to the sweet-tasting seed grains of some of the European species; the name 'manna grass' also refers to this quality. Apart from their use as fodder, glycerias can be grown as aquatics in large ponds or lakes and their long-running rhizomes can stabilize muddy banks; occasionally their dense growth may be a nuisance in irrigation canals.

CULTIVATION

Grow in permanently boggy soil in full sun. Plants can also be grown at the edge of ponds in 6 in (15 cm) of water. To restrict spread, grow in containers. Propagate from seed or runners.

Glyceria maxima

syns *Glyceria aquatica, Poa aquatica*
REED SWEET GRASS, REED MEADOW GRASS

This species from temperate Eurasia, which spreads by rhizomes, has stems to 3 ft (1 m) or more tall with flat, arching leaves 24 in (60 cm) long and ¾ in (18 mm) wide. Branched panicles of green to purplish spikelets are produced in late summer. 'Variegata' is a popular ornamental grass with cream- or white-striped foliage, sometimes flushed pink when young. **ZONES 5–9.**

HAKONECHLOA

This tufted perennial grass genus occurs in Japan and has only one species. It grows to a height of 12–18 in (30–45 cm) and has bright green leaves that turn orange-bronze in autumn in cooler climates. There are a number of very attractive variegated forms.

CULTIVATION

This frost-hardy grass prefers full sun or part-shade and fertile, humus-rich, moist but well-drained soil. Propagate the species from seed, the cultivars by division.

Hakonechloa macra 'Aureola'

Hakonechloa macra 'Aureola'

GOLDEN VARIEGATED HAKONECHLOA

This slowly spreading, perennial grass from the mountains of Japan provides a striking accent to the garden. The narrow, 8 in (20 cm) long, bright yellow leaves are lined with fine green stripes with a pink-red tint in autumn. It can be used as a specimen or planted in drifts. Reaching heights of 24 in (60 cm), it is very good in a pot. **ZONES 5–11.**

Hordeum jubatum

HORDEUM

BARLEY

Hordeum is a genus of 20 or more species of annual or perennial grasses from temperate regions worldwide. They have flat or rolled, light to mid-green or blue-green leaves. The flowers are suitable for use in dried flower arrangements, but the plants are free-seeding and often weedy.

CULTIVATION

These grasses are frost-hardy. Any temperate climate suits, but they prefer well-drained, fertile soil and full sun.

Hordeum jubatum

SQUIRREL TAIL GRASS

Hordeum jubatum is quite densely tufted and has light green leaves growing to 15 in (6 in). The stems bear dense, nodding panicles of long-bristled, soft spikes in mid-summer. Place these ornamental grasses where the light can shine through them, emphasizing their delicacy. **ZONES 5–10.**

JUNCUS

RUSH

This genus contains about 225 species of grass-like plants from damp to wet habitats around the world, although they are rare in tropical countries. Most have little or no horticultural potential and some can become invasive weeds away from their natural habitats. If controlled, they can be used around the edges of ponds and lakes.

CULTIVATION

Most species grow well, perhaps too well, in any moist to wet position in heavy clay soil. Propagation, particularly of named cultivars, is by division.

Juncus effusus

COMMON RUSH, SOFT RUSH

This evergreen plant's range extends from Europe to North America. It grows to about 3 ft (1 m) tall and has little to offer the gardener. However, several cultivars are of some interest, including variegated plants such as '**Aureus Striatus**' and '**Zebrinus**'. The bizarre '**Spiralis**' has stems that are curled and twisted like a corkscrew; it rarely attains much height due to the curled leaves; any rhizomes that produce straight stems must be promptly removed to prevent the plant reverting to type. **ZONES 4–10.**

LAGURUS
HARE'S TAIL GRASS

Often found growing on coastal dunes, the single species of Mediterranean annual that makes up this grass genus is popular for dried arrangements and has naturalized in many other parts of the world. It is a wiry grass with very thin leaves up to 10 in (25 cm) long. The foliage is briefly green in late winter and spring but soon dries to a pale golden brown. The main feature is the mass of soft, downy seedheads carried on wiry stems just above foliage height; these last indefinitely when dried. Their shape and texture are reminiscent of a rabbit's or hare's tail, hence the common name.

CULTIVATION
Frost hardy, it is easily grown in any light, even sandy, well-drained soil in full sun. Propagation is normally from seed in late summer or autumn.

Lagurus ovatus
This ornamental, sparsely tufted grass grows to 18 in (45 cm) tall, spreading into a broad clump only if given ample space and nutrition. The panicles of downy spikelets begin pale green, sometimes with lilac tinges, and mature to a creamy white; they appear from mid-spring to summer. **ZONES 9–10.**

Lagurus ovatus

MELICA
MELICK

This genus of some 75 species of perennial grasses is native to most of the temperate regions except Australia. Most species are 2–5 ft (0.6–1.5 m) tall and form clumps of arching leaves with strong stems. The summer flowerheads, are erect spikes, usually with lax or drooping spikelets that often develop attractive pink or purple tints. Several species with variegated leaves and unusual flowers are cultivated.

CULTIVATION
Species of *Melica* will grow in any reasonably fertile, well-drained soil in full sun or very light shade. They are generally quite frost hardy. Propagate from seed in summer or by dividing large clumps.

Melica uniflora
Growing to 24 in (60 cm) tall but often less, this species makes an open clump or tuft of rich green, hairy leaves. The flowers are small and reddish brown in color and are produced in loose panicles. *Melica uniflora* occurs naturally from Europe to western Asia. The popular cultivar 'Variegata' has leaves striped white and darker colored flowers. **ZONES 7–10.**

Melica altissima
SIBERIAN MELICK

This is an elegant ornamental grass with tufted foliage to 8 in (20 cm) long. The leaves are mid-green and rough. The flower stems have spikelets hanging on one side of the stem. In the wild form these are green, while the cultivars have different colored spikelets: 'Alba' has pale leaves and greenish white spikelets; and 'Atropurpurea' has purple spikelets. **ZONES 5–10.**

MILIUM

Some 6 species of annual or perennial grasses native to Europe, Asia and eastern North America comprise this genus. The only species usually grown is *Milium effusum*, which in Europe has been planted in woods as a food plant for game birds. It is also grown as an ornamental.

CULTIVATION

They are easily grown in semi-shade, are frost tolerant and prefer moisture-retentive soil. Propagate by division or from seed in spring. The golden form described here comes true from seed as long as it isn't growing near the wild green form.

Miscanthus sinensis
'Gracillimus'

MISCANTHUS

This is a genus of ornamental grasses occurring naturally from Africa to eastern Asia. They are highly desirable and well-behaved herbaceous plants, ideal in a perennial border or by the edge of water. Most are tall-growing grasses that can reach up to 12 ft (3.5 m) or more. There are 17 to 20 species, usually neatly clump forming with upright reed-like stems and narrow arching leaves. The flowerheads are produced in late summer and autumn and make attractive fluffy plumes at the tops of the stems. They make good cut flowers.

CULTIVATION

Moderately frost hardy, they prefer full sun and fertile, moist but well-drained soil. Cut them down to ground level in late winter when the dead stems start to collapse. Propagate by dividing larger clumps in late winter.

Milium effusum 'Aureum'

BOWLES' GOLDEN GRASS, MILLET GRASS, GOLDEN WOOD MILLET

This evergreen, tuft-forming perennial grass is grown for its yellow foliage and flowers. It is good in perennial borders, water gardens or as a groundcover, and effective when planted under white-variegated shrubs. Its flat leaves are golden yellow in spring, fading to yellowish green in summer. Panicles of greenish yellow spikelets are produced in summer; they can be cut and used for dried arrangements. It grows to a height of 2–3 ft (0.6–1 m) and a spread of 12 in (30 cm). It self-seeds readily. **ZONES 6–10.**

Milium effusum 'Aureum'

Miscanthus sinensis

EULALIA

Probably one of the most beautiful and least invasive of ornamental grasses, this Asian species has undergone more selection of cultivars than probably any other grass. The wild form makes neat, upright to slightly arching clumps up to 12 ft (3.5 m) tall although usually less. Its leaves have a white midrib and die to a soft straw color in winter. The flowerheads are usually soft gray tinted purple-brown. 'Gracillimus' has very fine leaves that color well in autumn, have a white mid-rib and arch elegantly; it rarely exceeds 4 ft (1.2 m) in height. 'Kleine Fontaine' has arching leaves and flowers in early to mid-summer. 'Morning Light', similar to 'Gracillimus', has a fine silver variegated leaf edge. 'Silberfeder' (syn. 'Silver Feather') grows to 8 ft (2.4 m) and produces a generous crop of light, open, silvery pink flowers on slender, erect stems in autumn. 'Variegatus' has creamy white leaves with pale green bands. 'Yaku Jima' is a dwarf form to about 30 in (75 cm) or so with narrow arching leaves. **ZONES 4–10.**

Ophiopogon planiscapus 'Nigrescens'

syn. *Ophiopogon planiscapus* **'Ebony Night'**
BLACK MONDO GRASS

This cultivar is grown particularly for its distinctive purple-black rather stiff leaves about ¼ in (6 mm) wide, which form slow-growing, sparse clumps. Its lilac flowers appear in clusters along the flowering stem in summer. These are followed by black fruit. It reaches a height of 10 in (25 cm) and a spread of 12 in (30 cm). *Ophiopogon planiscapus* is native to Japan. **ZONES 6–10.**

Ophiopogon p. 'Nigrescens'

Panicum virgatum

SWITCH GRASS

Found from Central America to southern Canada, this 6 ft (1.8 m) tall perennial forms clumps of blue-green to purple-green stems with sticky, bright green leaves. Stiff, 18 in (45 cm) long flower panicles open from late summer. The leaves yellow in autumn, the flowers develop red to bronze tones. **'Heavy Metal'** has erect blue-green leaves that yellow in autumn. **'Rubrum'** has red-green leaves that turn bright red in autumn and fine sprays of deep brown flower spikelets. **ZONES 5–10.**

OPHIOPOGON

This genus contains about 50 species of perennials valued for their attractive, long-lived clumps of grass-like foliage. The summer flowers are small and can be white or blue through to purple. The berry-like fruits each contain one seed. Trouble-free plants, they are an excellent groundcover lasting indefinitely.

CULTIVATION

Most are fairly frost hardy and will tolerate sun or part-shade in moist, well-drained soil. Propagate by division of clumps in spring, or from seed in autumn.

Panicum virgatum

PANICUM

PANIC GRASS, CRAB GRASS

This is a genus of around 470 species of annual and perennial grasses found throughout the tropics and in warm-temperate parts of the northern hemisphere. Some are cropped, others are ornamental and more than a few are weeds. They range in size from 2–10 ft (0.6–3 m) tall and form clumps of fine stems with long, very narrow leaves often covered with fine hairs when young. Erect to nodding panicles of loose flower spikes open in summer. The flower panicles, which are up to 18 in (45 cm) long, are often bronze or red tinted.

CULTIVATION

They are easily grown in any moist, well-drained soil in full sun. Most of the perennial species will tolerate heavy frost. Propagate the species from seed and the cultivated forms by division.

PENNISETUM

This genus consists of about 80 species of tuft-forming, rhizomatous or stoloniferous, annual or perennial grasses found in tropical, subtropical or warm-temperate regions around the world. The leaf blades are usually flat. They are mostly grown for their dense flower clusters of brush-like spikelets, which appear in summer and autumn and are used in floral arrangements both fresh and dried.

CULTIVATION

Most species are very frost hardy and prefer full sun and fertile, well-drained soil. Dead foliage may be cut back when the plants are dormant. Propagate from seed or by division in spring.

Pennisetum alopecuroides 'Moudry'

PHALARIS

The 15 species of annual and perennial grasses that make up this genus are often rhizomatous and are found growing in damp areas. They form low clumps of narrow basal leaves up to 15 in (38 cm) long from which emerge upright, wiry flowering stems. These grow 4–5 ft (1.2–1.5 m) tall and are topped with plumes of tiny flowers.

CULTIVATION

They will grow in most garden soils that do not dry out in summer. The green-leafed species will grow in sun or light shade; variegated cultivars are best in full sun. Most species are very frost hardy. Propagate from seed or by division.

Pennisetum alopecuroides
syn. Pennisetum compressum
SWAMP FOXTAIL, FOUNTAIN GRASS

This perennial grass from Asia and parts of Australia has mid- to dark green leaves, which grow to 24 in (60 cm) long and form a dense clump. In summer to autumn, yellow-green to dark purple bristle-like spikelets appear. 'Hameln' is a shorter form, to 18 in (45 cm) high, flowering in early summer; its spikelets are white, tinted green. 'Moudry' is a low grower with wide, deep green leaves and purple to black flowerheads. **ZONES 7–10.**

Pennisetum setaceum
syn. Pennisetum ruppellii
AFRICAN FOUNTAIN GRASS, FOUNTAIN GRASS

This is a deciduous perennial grass from tropical Africa that grows into tufts 3 ft (1 m) high with a spread of 18 in (45 cm). It has rough stems and long, narrow leaf blades. In summer, it produces arching, coppery spikes with bearded bristles to form brush-like flower clusters that last into winter. It is not suitable as a lawn grass, but makes an attractive tall groundcover or a feature plant in a border. In warm climates it will self-seed freely and can become a nuisance. 'Burgundy Giant' grows to 4 ft (1.2 m) tall and has purple-red foliage. 'Rubrum' is tall-growing with bronze leaves and purple-red flower plumes. **ZONES 9–12.**

Phalaris arundinacea var. *picta*

Phalaris arundinacea var. picta
GARDENERS' GARTERS, REEDY GRASS

This clump-forming perennial grass is easily grown, bearing reed-like leaves with white stripes and, in summer, terminal panicles of purplish or pale green spikelets on stout, upstanding stems. Indigenous to North America and Europe, it can grow to 5 ft (1.5 m) tall, but is generally kept lower in a garden. It can prove invasive. **ZONES 4–10.**

PHRAGMITES

REED

This genus of the true reeds now includes just 4 widely distributed species of large, perennial, rhizomatous grasses with strong, erect stems 10–12 ft (3–3.5 m) or more tall. Their leaves are narrow, linear and flat, without ribbing, and around 24 in (60 cm) long. In summer and autumn, they produce large plumed panicles of flowers that mature into golden-yellow seedheads.

CULTIVATION

Although usually found in damp meadows or near standing water in temperate and tropical zones, they will grow in normal garden soil provided it does not dry out in summer. A position in full sun is best. They are very frost hardy. Propagate from seed or by division.

Phyllostachys aurea

Phyllostachys nigra

PHYLLOSTACHYS

Made up of 80 species of medium- and large-growing bamboos from Asia, these evergreen plants have spreading rhizomes that may sprout some distance from the parent plant. They are ideally suited to grove planting and are mainly grown for their decorative foliage and graceful habit. They are also useful for preventing soil erosion. The woody stems have nodes at intervals, and the insignificant flowers take several years to appear; as with most bamboos, the plants then die.

CULTIVATION

Temperate-climate plants, they thrive in a sheltered position that is not too dry. Propagate from seed in either spring or autumn, or by division in spring. If they must be confined to a specific area, they can be grown in large tubs.

Phragmites australis

syn. **Phragmites communis**

COMMON REED

This species has stems to 12 ft (3.5 m) or more tall and arching, 24 in (60 cm) long, 2 in (5 cm) wide leaves. The floral plumes are 18 in (45 cm) long and usually slightly pendent. They are brown with purple tints when young, ageing to golden yellow. 'Humilis' is a dwarf form that grows to around 4 ft (1.2 m) tall; 'Rubra' has red-tinted floral plumes; 'Variegatus' has yellow-striped leaves that fade to white; and *P. a.* subsp. *altissimus* grows to 20 ft (6 m) tall. **ZONES 5–11.**

Phyllostachys aurea

FISHPOLE BAMBOO, GOLDEN BAMBOO

This species has stiffly erect 6–30 ft (1.8–9 m) stems with crowded nodes at the base. It is a spreading species that soon forms large clumps and its dense foliage makes it a good screen or hedge. **ZONES 6–11.**

Phyllostachys nigra

BLACK BAMBOO

The slender canes of this species, growing to about 20 ft (6 m) tall with prominent joints, are green when young, turning black in their second year. The long, thin leaves are green and pointed. In cool climates, these plants need protection from cold winds, but can become seriously invasive in mild climates. *Phyllostachys nigra* var. *henonis* bears a mass of lush dark leaves and yellow-brown canes. **ZONES 5–11.**

PLEIOBLASTUS

This is a Chinese and Japanese bamboo genus of around 20 species. Most are dwarf to medium sized and seldom exceed 10 ft (3 m) tall. They have rhizomes and some are moderately invasive. They have slender, hollow stems and small narrow leaves that are seldom more than 8 in (20 cm) long, often considerably less and frequently with striped variegations. The leaf sheaths are conspicuous and often bristly.

CULTIVATION

Most species are very frost hardy and not difficult to cultivate. Plant in loose, moist, well-drained soil in sun or part-shade; water well in summer. Running species need to be contained. Propagate by division.

Pleioblastus variegatus

SASA

This genus of 40 to 50 species of small to medium, rhizomatous, woody bamboos is closely related to *Sasaella*. Native to eastern Asia, they have smooth, cylindrical canes with a waxy white bloom beneath the nodes. A variegated effect is achieved in winter when the large, toothed leaves wither at their edges.

CULTIVATION

Grow these fully frost-hardy plants in fertile, moist, well-drained soil in full sun or shade. They may need to be planted in containers to restrict growth. Propagate from seed in autumn or by division in spring.

Pleioblastus variegatus
DWARF WHITE-SHEATHED BAMBOO, CHIGO-ZASA

In common with several other species, this plant is known only from cultivation and has never been found in the wild. It has powdery white, 30 in (75 cm) tall stems with proportionally large, 4–8 in (10–20 cm) long, deep green leaves with variable cream stripes. The leaf sheaths have purple interiors and downy exteriors. **ZONES 7–10.**

Sasa palmata
syn. *Arundinaria palmata*

This spreading, evergreen bamboo from Japan grows to a height of 6 ft (1.8 m) with an indefinite spread. Its flowers are insignificant but the wide, rich green leaves make it an excellent foliage plant, adding grace and contrast to borders and rock gardens. Its hollow stems are streaked with purple and bear one branch at each node. It needs protection in winter and is suitable for container growing. **ZONES 7–11.**

STIPA
syn. *Achnatherum*
FEATHER GRASS, NEEDLE GRASS, SPEAR GRASS

This widely distributed genus consists of 300 species of perennial tufted and frost-hardy grasses. They are noted for their tall flowering spikes with large feathery panicles. The flowers borne in these large, loose panicles have one floret per spikelet, and as the seeds mature they develop long bristles or awns—in some cases as much as 4 in (10 cm) long—which give this genus its particular character. The leaves are narrow and straight-edged. The larger growing species, with flower spikes that can reach over 6 ft (1.8 m), are often grown as specimen plants.

CULTIVATION

Plant in full sun in well-drained soil. To propagate, sow seed in spring or autumn or divide the plants in late spring.

Stipa calamagrostis

The strong-growing clumps of this grass from southern and central Europe can reach 4 ft (1.2 m) tall. The leaves are 12 in (30 cm) long. Loose flowerheads grow to 30 in (75 cm) long with purplish spikelets and ½ in (12 mm) curved awns. **ZONES 7–10.**

Stipa calamagrostis

Stipa gigantea
GOLDEN OATS, GIANT FEATHER GRASS

Native to Spain and Portugal, this evergreen or semi-evergreen, clump-forming grass is best grown as a specimen plant. It is a long-lived species with narrow green leaves that can reach 30 in (75 cm). In summer the upright stems bear bristle-like, silver-purple flowers in large, open panicles up to 20 cm (8 in) long. These persist into winter, turning a deep golden color. Cut the flower stems in mid-summer for drying. **ZONES 8–10.**

Stipa tenacissima
ESPARTO GRASS

Found in Spain and North Africa, this grass yields a strong fiber that was used in paper manufacture in the nineteenth century. It was also used to make rope and matting. The plant forms a dense tuft of fine, smooth leaves with inrolled edges, and sends up flowering stems to about 6 ft (1.8 m) tall. **ZONES 8–10.**

TYPHA
BULRUSH, REEDMACE, CAT TAIL

This cosmopolitan genus includes some 10 similar species. They have tough, fiberous, spear-shaped leaves that form a dense thicket of foliage around the margins of ponds or slow-moving streams. Their most distinguishing feature is their cylindrical seedheads that develop on stems up to 10 ft (3 m) high.

CULTIVATION

These very frost-hardy plants demand permanently moist soil and will grow in shallow water. They tend to fill and drain a pond (they are an important source of peat), so plant only where they can be controlled. Propagate from seed or by division in spring.

Typha latifolia
REEDMACE, BULRUSH

This species from most temperate regions of the northern hemisphere is one of the tallest in the genus, reaching a height of 10 ft (3 m). It has large clumps of mid-green foliage and the erect stems carry leaves up to ¾ in (18 mm) wide. The flowers are cigar-like spikes 12 in (30 cm) in length, the male on the upper part and the female below. It can be extremely invasive. **ZONES 3–10.**

Typha latifolia

Chapter 6

FRUIT TREES, NUT TREES & OTHER FRUITS

Apricots drying in the sun. Many fruits can be enjoyed fresh, and can also be preserved or dried.

Anyone who has picked fruit from a tree or vine will understand that it is one of the subtle pleasures of gardening. It is easy to experience the flavor of home-grown fruit, no matter what size garden you have. And any excess which is not eaten fresh, to the precise degree of ripeness preferred, can be rewardingly put to good use in home cooking.

Many crops are suitable for a home garden

Generally, when anybody mentions home-grown fruit, thoughts immediately turn to stone fruit or citrus, but there are any number of other fruits that are equally suited. Berry fruits, for example, are ideal for the cool-climate garden, since they take up little space and a few plants can give a good yield. Nut trees, on the other hand, often grow into quite large shade trees, and have the convenient habit of shedding their fruit, which is easily gathered from the ground. Vines tend to be more demanding because they must be supported, but once this need is met, they give a bountiful yield for very little effort. Try passionfruit on a pergola for example.

A productive fruit and nut garden needs careful consideration

Like any other form of gardening, climate plays an integral part in the selection of the fruit we aim to grow. However, most gardens have micro-climate pockets, which can greatly extend the range of fruit a garden can accommodate. For example, citrus trees often do surprisingly well in colder climates when placed by a sunny wall, where they can revel in the extra heat created by reflected warmth. Further-more, many fruiting species also have a large range of cultivars, some of which may be more suitable to different cli-mates. However, it is usually more pro-ductive to choose a type of fruit you know does well in your area, or one your nursery can recommend, as this is is likely to be a specimen better able to resist pests and diseases.

Not every garden is large enough to have an orchard, so why not exper-ment with smaller, mixed plantings? A row of mixed citrus beside a drive-way is not only decorative, but also perfumed and productive. A pecan nut tree as a specimen on a lawn ensures that fallen nuts can be easily collected from the grass beneath, and a graceful persimmon illuminates the garden with its colorful orange fruit and brilliant orange autumn foliage. There are end-less examples.

A tree that can produce fruit without another of the same species nearby is known to be self-pollinating. Not all fruiting species have this ability. Some

Harvesting olives. The fruit is too bitter to be eaten fresh, and must be treated first.

fruit and nut trees have male and fe-male cultivars, which must be planted together if the females are to crop. With a little research, you can be sure that there will be fruit.

Another reason to mix different culti-vars of the same fruit is to maximize the fruiting period. This not only means that flavorsome fresh fruit can be enjoyed over a longer season, but also spaces the crop over a few months rather than appearing all at once. This reduces waste and gives time to use the crop productively. Finally, consider any specific regional peculiarities such as frost or seasonal pests. For example, a spring crop can be spoiled by late frosts in cold climates, but this can be avoided if a late-cropping variety is chosen. In warmer climates, damage by insect pests can often be minimized if fruit is ready for harvest by early summer.

Space-saving techniques for the smaller garden

When space is limited, there are alternatives to a 'mini orchard'. It is possible to graft more than one variety onto a single tree, although this may result in one of the grafted cultivars becoming more dominant. A popular way around this is to plant two or three fruit or nut trees into the same hole. Many of the deciduous cooler country trees, such as pears, apples and plums, can be grown

Some fruit trees make wonderful ornamental specimens. The blossom and fruit of this orange tree add beauty to the garden.

in this fashion, and as they grow on their own rootstock, each is equally dominant while giving the gardener a choice of fruit.

Trees planted in this way often become conversation pieces within a garden, but should not be treated as specimen trees and planted in a prime position. The blend of species can result in a somewhat lopsided appearance simply because they have different growth habits. To an extent, this can be overcome by selection and pruning, although it is best to seek the advice of a specialist fruit tree nursery in this instance.

The most popular space-saving idea is to espalier one or more deciduous fruit trees. Espaliered trees need only be 9–12 ft (3–4 m) wide, and can be spaced every 3 ft (1 m) or so along a fence or wall. Apples, pears and plums are good beginner plants, because the new growth is supple and easily trained with ties to a stout wire framework. As the tree matures, these main branches become self-supporting and the framework becomes unnecessary, so it is not essential that it be a long-lasting structure.

It is not too hard to espalier a fruit tree. Simply erect the training wires in the shape of the finished effect and remove any unwanted branches each winter or early spring. With most deciduous trees, fruit is produced on spurs or shortened branches, and the aim here is to encourage these spurs at the expense of unwanted water shoots; those springy, vertical branches that seem to appear right after pruning.

Cordons are very similar to espaliers, but even more space efficient: trees are planted close together and trained on wires set at a 45° angle to the required height, with each individual cultivar being pruned to produce maximum fruiting spurs.

For those who prefer not to prune on a regular basis, there are many naturally compact, dwarf deciduous fruiting trees. These and some of the smaller-growing citrus, such as Meyer lemons, limes and cumquats, make ideal container plants for a sunny position where both the blossom then the fruit can be appreciated before it is picked. While the nurture of any tree is important, it is especially so with potted plants as their roots are unable to forage far for nutrients and moisture. They need to have a moisture-retentive potting mix that should not be allowed to dry out, as this substantially checks their growth.

Vitis vinifera 'Cabernet Sauvignon'

ASIMINA

This genus consists of 8 species of deciduous and evergreen shrubs and small trees, all native to North America. The only species found in gardens is *Asimina triloba*, which is popular for its handsome leaves and unusual flowers. It bears edible fruit.

CULTIVATION

Plant in moist, well-drained, fertile soil and make sure it receives full sun. Propagate from seed in autumn.

Asimina triloba

Asimina triloba
PAWPAW

Unlike the tropical papaya, which is also sometimes known as pawpaw, this shrub or small tree from the southeastern USA is deciduous and very cold hardy, although it does need warm summers to ripen its fruit. Developing from striking maroon flowers, the oval fruits are up to 6 in (15 cm) long and are yellow-brown when ripe. They are aromatic, have a custard-like flavor and contain flat brown seeds. The flowers open from late winter and the fruit ripens from late summer. **ZONES 5–10.**

CARYA
HICKORY

These medium to large, deciduous trees are valued for their strong wood and edible nuts. Some 20 species occur in North America and Asia. They have large, pinnate leaves that turn yellow, orange or rich gold in autumn. Male and female flowers appear on the same plant in late spring. The fruit are enclosed in a leathery husk that is neatly divided into 4 segments. *Carya illinoinensis* is the most commonly cultivated species.

CULTIVATION

Cold hardy and fast growing, hickory trees prefer sheltered, fertile sites with deep, moist soil in regions with cold winters and long, hot, humid summers. They should be grown from seed *in situ*, or planted out as very young seedlings.

Carya illinoinensis

Carya illinoinensis
PECAN

This species produces one of the world's most popular edible nuts. From central USA, it occurs along broad river valleys and grows to 100 ft (30 m) tall with scaly gray bark. In cultivation it grows quickly to become an open-crowned tree of about 30 ft (9 m) within 10 to 15 years. Although quite frost hardy, it needs long, hot summers to set fruit and for the wood to mature. The leaves are long, with many glossy green leaflets, and the elongated nuts occur in clusters. Many selections have been named, propagated by grafting. **ZONES 6–11.**

Carya ovata

Carya ovata

SHAGBARK HICKORY, SHELLBARK HICKORY

This species has a similar striking bark to that of *Carya laciniosa*. In its native valley forests in central-eastern USA it grows as a tall, slender tree to 80 ft (24 m) with a long, straight trunk and high, narrow crown, but in the open it makes a much lower, broader column with foliage reaching almost to the ground. The leaves, of medium size with only 5 broad leaflets, turn a fine golden yellow in autumn. The smallish nuts are edible. **ZONES 4–9.**

CASTANEA
CHESTNUT, CHINQUAPIN

These cool-climate deciduous trees, mostly from North America, all bear edible nuts enclosed in a prickly, burr-like husk. The leaves are elliptical with regularly toothed margins and a feather-like arrangement of veins. In spring or early summer showy catkins of male flowers appear, and the less conspicuous female flowers on the same tree develop into the nuts. The larger species are highly valued for the fine timber they produce.

CULTIVATION
In a cool climate chestnuts are easily grown in full sun or part-shade in deep, fertile soil. Hot, dry summers suit them well as long as ample soil moisture is available in winter and spring. All species are readily propagated from fresh seed; plant out seedlings early to avoid disturbing the tap root.

Castanea sativa
SWEET CHESTNUT, SPANISH CHESTNUT

This species comes from countries around the Mediterranean, Black and Caspian seas, but has been planted throughout Europe for its edible nuts since time immemorial. Young trees are vigorous and have a pyramidal crown, but the lower limbs become massive and spreading with age, and the bark deeply fissured. In autumn, the leaves turn from yellowish green to gold and russet. When planting for nuts, buy grafted named varieties from a source certified free of disease.
ZONES 5–9.

Castanea sativa

CITRUS

Many of the cultivated forms in this genus of small evergreen trees are probably of ancient hybrid origin, first domesticated in China and India. While largely cultivated for their fruit, citrus plants are also attractive in the garden, with glossy evergreen leaves and fragrant flowers. Most species are frost tender to some degree: the lemon is the most cold resistant, especially when grafted onto the related *Poncirus trifoliata* rootstock, and the lime is the least cold resistant. Citrus can also be grown in pots, as long as the containers are large and they are grown on dwarf rootstocks.

CULTIVATION

Very well-drained, friable, slightly acid, loam soil is best. They need full sun, regular watering and protection from wind, especially during the summer. Citrus also need regular feeding, including large amounts of nitrogen and potassium for good fruiting. Prune only to remove dead, diseased and crossing wood. Subject to a range of virus diseases, they may also be invaded by scale, leaf miner, bronze orange bug, spined citrus bug and fruit fly. They are rarely propagated by home gardeners as this is done by specialist grafting. Citrus trees need protection in winter. Many are suitable for container growing.

Citrus aurantifolia
LIME

Best in tropical and subtropical climates, the lime is stronger in acidity and flavor than the lemon. It is an erect tree, growing 15–20 ft (4.5–6 m), with spiny, irregular branches, making it less ornamental than other citrus plants. The Tahitian lime, the most popular variety, bears fruit all year round. The Mexican lime has smaller fruit with high acidity and stronger flavor, and is a thornier tree. **ZONES 10–12.**

Citrus limon

Citrus limon 'Meyer'

Citrus aurantium
SOUR ORANGE, SEVILLE ORANGE

These marginally frost-hardy small trees are grown as ornamental shrubs or for their fruit, which are used to make marmalade and jelly. The heavy-fruiting 'Seville' is the premium marmalade orange. 'Chinotto' is excellent in containers or borders, with small, dark green leaves and a compact habit. The dwarf 'Bouquet de Fleurs' is a more fragrant, ornamental shrub. Watch for melanose (dark brown spots on the wood and fruit) and citrus scab. **ZONES 9–11.**

Citrus limon
LEMON

The lemon tree does best in warm Mediterranean climates with mild winters. It grows to a height of around 20 ft (6 m) and is prone to collar rot, so plant it with the graft union well above the soil and keep mulch away from the stem. 'Eureka' is probably the most commonly grown cultivar, producing fruit and flowers all year round. It is an attractive, almost thornless tree, the best variety for temperate locations and coastal gardens. The smaller, hardier 'Meyer' produces smaller fruit and is a suitable cultivar for growing in pots. 'Lisbon' is popular with commercial growers since it is reliable and heavy fruiting; it is good for hot areas but is thorny. **ZONES 9–11.**

Citrus × paradisi
GRAPEFRUIT

Easily grown in mild areas, the grapefruit can make a dense, rounded tree to 20–30 ft (6–9 m) or more. Its large, golden-skinned fruits are well known and widely appreciated all over the world. Popular frost-hardy cultivars include **'Marsh'**, **'Morrison's Seedless'** and **'Golden Special'**. The seedless and **'Ruby'** culti-vars are more tender, prefer-ring a frost-free climate. All grapefruit trees are usually grown from cuttings or grafts. **ZONES 10–12.**

Citrus reticulata
MANDARIN, TANGERINE

This is the most varied citrus species, and it has a wide range of climate tolerance: some varieties can survive an occasional light frost. Grow-ing to 12–20 ft (3.5–6 m) or so high, it is a good fruit tree for the suburban garden. Similar to oranges, the fruit are smaller and looser skinned. It is slow growing and has heavily perfumed flowers. **ZONES 9–11.**

Citrus sinensis
ORANGE

Attractive trees to 25 ft (8 m) or more tall with a rounded

Citrus sinensis

head. They have glossy foliage and sweet-scented white flowers, and will tolerate very light frosts. **'Valencia'** is perhaps the most frost hardy of all oranges, and produces fruit in spring and summer that is most commonly juiced but can also be eaten fresh. **'Joppa'** is a good variety for tropical gardens. **'Ruby Blood'** has oblong fruit with a reddish color to its rind, flesh and juice; it is the best known and best tasting of the 'blood oranges'. Navel oranges are mutated forms with a 'navel' at the fruit apex and no seeds: **'Washington Navel'**, which fruits through winter, has very large and sweet, bright orange fruit and is best suited to slightly cooler areas. New varieties may be found by gardeners at specialist nurseries. **ZONES 9–11.**

Citrus × tangelo
TANGELO

This evergreen tree grows 20–30 ft (6–9 m) high and 10 ft (3 m) wide. It is derived from a cross between the tangerine *(Citrus reticulata)* and the grapefruit *(C. paradisi)*. The tangelo is re-nowned for its juice and as a superb dessert fruit with a tart, yet sweet flavor. Plant in a warm site sheltered from frost. **ZONES 9–11.**

Citrus × tangelo

Citrus × paradisi

CORYLUS

HAZEL, FILBERT

The 10 or more deciduous trees and large shrubs in this genus are best known for their edible nuts. The genus has been described in detail in the Shrubs chapter. The species listed here is a popular fruit tree.

Corylus avellana

COMMON HAZEL, COBNUT, EUROPEAN FILBERT

This species occurs throughout Europe, western Asia and northern Africa. It typically makes a broad mass of stems to 12–15 ft (3.5–4.5 m) high. In winter the bare twigs are draped with catkins, which make quite a display. The nuts are half enclosed in a fringed tube. In autumn the leaves turn pale yellow. 'Contorta' is a bizarre cultivar with branches that wander in all directions; when leafless they are cut to be sold by florists. **ZONES 4–9.**

Corylus avellana 'Contorta'
Left: Corylus avellana

CYDONIA

QUINCE

These small deciduous trees are quite unusual and ornamental. Native to temperate Asia, they belong to the pome-fruit group of the rose family. They are small, crooked, very woody trees with smooth bark and simple, oval leaves, downy at least on the underside and clustered on short spur-shoots (as in apples) except on the long summer growths. The flowers are solitary at the ends of the spur shoots, and have downy calyces and pink petals. The large fruits have waxy or almost greasy skins that are pleasantly aromatic.

CULTIVATION

Quinces only thrive in cooler-temperate climates, although the Chinese species tolerates warmer, more frost-free areas than the common quince. They require moist, deep soil and a sunny position. Propagation is from seed, which is easily obtained from over-ripe fruit, or by grafting for named varieties.

Cydonia oblonga

COMMON QUINCE

A spreading, bushy tree of 12–15 ft (3.5–4.5 m), this species forks low down on its trunk into crooked limbs. The leaves are moderately large, deep green above but downy on the underside and on young twigs. The very attractive flowers, about 2 in (5 cm) in diameter and usually a clear pale pink, appear in late spring. The fruit, edible when cooked, ripen to pale or deep yellow and are up to 6 in (15 cm) long with hard flesh. **ZONES 6–9.**

Cydonia oblonga

Diospyros virginiana

DIOSPYROS
PERSIMMON, EBONY

This genus consists of several hundred species of mostly ever-green trees from the tropics and subtropics, as well as several deciduous species in temperate Asia and North and South America. The fruit of most species are edible. All have strong branches, and smooth-edged leaves. The flowers bear rolled-back petals and a leaf-like calyx that enlarges as the pulpy fruit develop. For a good crop of fruit, grow male and female plants together.

CULTIVATION
Fully frost hardy to frost ten-der, these trees prefer well-drained, moist soil, with ample water in the growing season and, being brittle, need shelter from strong wind. Propagate from seed.

Diospyros kaki
CHINESE PERSIMMON, KAKI

This native of China that has been cultivated in Japan for centuries, is a deciduous tree, which grows to about 20 ft (6 m) tall with spreading branches. Its dark green oval leaves turn yellow to deep orange in autumn. It has small cream flowers, which are followed by orange or yellow fruit about 3 in (8 cm) across. The fruit have delicious sweet flesh when ripe. There are many cultivars. *Diospyros kaki* grows well in containers.
ZONES 8–10.

Diospyros virginiana
AMERICAN PERSIMMON, POSSUM WOOD

This spreading tree can reach over 100 ft (30 m) in its native eastern USA, in alluvial river valley forests, but in cultivation it usually reaches 20–30 ft (6–9 m). It has cream flowers and sweet edible fruit, 1½ in (35 mm) across, ripen-ing to orange or purple-red. The timber (white ebony) is valued for its durability.
ZONES 5–9.

Diospyros kaki

Eriobotrya japonica
LOQUAT

Native to China and Japan, the loquat can grow to 20–30 ft (6–9 m) tall. It forms a shapely conical tree, but in gardens it can be kept considerably more compact if pruned after the golden yellow fruit have been harvested. The large, deep green leaves are pale and felty underneath. It blooms in late autumn and the fruit, which set in winter, ripen in spring. It is susceptible to fruit fly, and birds can also damage the crop. This is a plant for temperate areas where ample moisture is available as the fruit mature. In cool areas, provide winter protection. Plants can also be grown in containers. **ZONES 8–10.**

ERIOBOTRYA

This genus, which belongs to the rose family, includes 30 species of evergreen shrubs and trees. Only the loquat, *Eriobotrya japonica*, is commonly grown. Widely distributed through eastern Asia from the eastern Himalayas to Japan, they include trees growing to 30 ft (9 m). All species in the genus bear leathery, deeply veined leaves with silvery or felty undersides. The creamy white, scented flowers are held in loose sprays at the tips of the branches during autumn and are followed by edible, decorative fruits.

CULTIVATION

Easily grown, these plants are marginally frost hardy and will tolerate dry as well as coastal conditions. Grow in a fertile, well-drained soil in a sunny position. Propagate from seed or cuttings in early summer.

Eriobotrya japonica

Fortunella japonica

FORTUNELLA
KUMQUAT, CUMQUAT

The renowned Scottish plant collector Robert Fortune (1812–80) introduced the kumquat to the conservatories of the UK, where it has flourished ever since. The genus comprises 5 evergreen shrubs or small trees, most of which have a small spine at the junction of leaf and branch. They make compact shrubs that bear fragrant white flowers in spring and small, edible orange fruits from summer to autumn. They make perfect container plants for small gardens or sunny patios.

CULTIVATION

Frost tender, kumquats require an open position in full sun and fertile, moist but well-drained soil. Apply fertilizer and water well during the growing season, especially as the fruits are forming. In frost-prone areas grow in containers and overwinter in a greenhouse. Propagate species from seed or cuttings and varieties by budding onto rootstock in autumn or spring.

Fortunella japonica
ROUND KUMQUAT, MARUMI CUMQUAT

Reaching 8–12 ft (2.4–3.5 m), or smaller when container-grown, this species from China bears decorative, small, golden-orange fruit. They persist for a considerable time, but are best picked as they ripen to maintain the tree's vigorous growth. **ZONES 9–11.**

Juglans regia

JUGLANS
WALNUT

This genus, which consists of 15 species of deciduous trees, is distributed from the Mediterranean region and the Middle East to East Asia and North and South America. They are grown for their handsome form and elegant, aromatic foliage. All species bear edible nuts—produced on trees that are about 12 years or older—and several yield fine timber used in furniture making. Greenish yellow male catkins and inconspicuous female flowers

Juglans regia

appear on the same tree in spring before the large pinnate leaves. They are followed by the hard-shelled nuts. The fallen leaves are said to be toxic to several other plants, so do not put them on the compost heap. These are excellent ornamental trees for parks and large gardens.

CULTIVATION

Cool-climate trees, they prefer a sunny position. Although quite frost hardy, young plants and the new spring growth are susceptible to frost damage. Deep rich alluvial soil of a light, loamy texture is best, with regular water. Propagate from freshly collected seed in autumn.

Juglans cinerea

BUTTERNUT, WHITE WALNUT

From the rich woodlands and river valleys of eastern North America, this species reaches 60 ft (18 m) and has gray, furrowed bark. The dark green pinnate leaves are up to 18 in (45 cm) long and hairy on both sides. Male and female catkins, borne in late spring to early summer, are followed by clusters of 2 to 5 strongly ridged, edible, sweet-tasting, oily nuts, each enclosed in a sticky green husk. Native Americans used this tree as a digestive remedy and it was also widely used as a laxative in the nineteenth century. **ZONES 4–9.**

Juglans nigra

BLACK WALNUT, AMERICAN WALNUT

From central and eastern USA, this large, handsome, fast-growing tree reaches 100 ft (30 m) with a spread of 80 ft (24 m). It has a single, erect trunk and a broad, rounded crown. Greenish brown catkins appear in spring with the leaves, followed by dark brown edible nuts enclosed in a green husk. The leaves are made up of glossy, dark green leaflets. This species is valued for both its nuts and its dark wood. **ZONES 4–10.**

Juglans regia

COMMON WALNUT, PERSIAN WALNUT, ENGLISH WALNUT

From southeastern Europe and temperate Asia, this slow-growing tree reaches 50 ft (15 m) tall with a spread of 30 ft (9 m). It has a sturdy trunk, a broad, leafy canopy and smooth, pale gray bark. The leaves are purplish bronze when young, and yellow-green catkins appear from late spring to early summer. They are followed by the edible nut, enclosed in a green husk that withers and falls. The timber is valued for furniture making. Cultivars include **'Wilson's Wonder'**, which fruits younger than most at about 7 years old. **ZONES 4–10.**

Juglans nigra

Malus × *domestica* 'Ashmead's Kernel'

Malus × *domestica* 'Granny Smith'

MALUS

Most of the species belonging to this genus are trees, and detailed information on the genus is given in the Trees chapter. However, the ones included here can be treated as fruit trees.

Malus × *domestica* 'Discovery'

Malus × domestica
COMMON APPLE

This large hybrid group contains upright, spreading trees, usually with dark, gray-brown scaly bark and gray to reddish brown twigs. They can grow 30 ft (9 m) tall and 15 ft (4.5 m) wide. Their leaves are usually downy underneath and the white flowers are usually suffused with pink. The juicy, sweet fruit are green or yellow to red. These common orchard trees are distinguished from the wild crab *(Malus sylvestris)* by their downy shoots, blunter leaves and juicy fruit that sweeten on ripening. Apples are not completely self-fertile and for fruit production a different cultivar growing nearby is needed. Advice on compatible pollinating cultivars should be obtained before buying apple plants. There are hundreds of cultivars; some of the best known are 'Crofton', 'Cox's Orange Pippin', 'Discovery', 'Delicious', 'Golden

Malus × *domestica* 'Bramley's Seedling'

sweet white flesh; **'Blenheim Orange'** has yellow fruit with one-half flushed dull orange red; **'Bramley's Seedling'** has large, late-ripening fruit best suited to cooking; and **'Ellison's Orange'** bears light greenish yellow fruit with soft juicy flesh and a rich flavor.

Some apple varieties have been bred as single-stemmed columnar forms, enabling the trees to be grown close together in a row without

Delicious', 'Golden Harvest', 'Granny Smith', 'Gravenstein', 'James Grieve', 'Jonathan' and 'McIntosh Rogers'. Many relatively new varieties are grown for their greater disease resistance. **'Gala'** is a small dessert fruit with excellent flavor and good storage qualities; **'Jonagold'** has large, yellow, red-striped fruit with good flavor and crisp texture; and **'Liberty'**, a highly productive and especially disease-resistant tree bears striped dark red fruit with a pale yellow, crisp flesh.

All the apples so far mentioned are generally accepted varieties that are grown commercially to supply year-round fruit. But there are many fine old apples worthwhile growing in home gardens and small orchards with special markets. **'Adam's Pearman'** is a quality dessert apple with golden-yellow skin flushed bright red; **'Ashmead's Kernel'** is an upright spreading tree with light greenish yellow fruit and

Malus × *domestica* 'Jonathon'

occupying a lot of ground. Named varieties include **'Starkspur Compact Mac'** and **'Starkspur Supreme Red Delicious'**. Some tall forms such as **'Jonamac'** can be trained over a path to make an arch. **ZONES 3–9**.

Malus pumila

This tree grows 12–15 ft (3.5–4.5 m) high and half as wide. It bears oval leaves with serrated margins, and pink and white flowers. The small, attractive fruit are ideal for stewing and for making jellies and jams. **'Dartmouth'** is an open, spreading tree to 25 ft (8 m), with white flowers opening from pink buds and large crimson fruit. **ZONES 3–9**.

Malus pumila 'Dartmouth'

Malus × *domestica* 'Jonamac'

Malus × *domestica* 'Starkspur Supreme Red Delicious'

MESPILUS
MEDLAR

Allied to the pears, the medlar, the single species in this genus from Europe and southwest Asia, has been cultivated for hundreds of years. A deciduous, sometimes thorny tree, it is grown primarily for its brown fruit, edible only after they are 'bletted' (almost rotten), which remain on the tree until well into autumn. Its large hairy leaves form a dense canopy.

CULTIVATION

Slow growing, the medlar resents being transplanted, but is easy to cultivate; it needs a temperate climate, well-drained soil and shelter from strong wind. It must not be allowed to dry out. Lightly prune for shape in early winter. Propagate from seed or by grafting.

Mespilus germanica

Mespilus germanica

In early summer, this species bears large, single, unperfumed white flowers, and its gnarled branches make it look ancient even when young. Its dark green leaves turn russet in autumn, particularly if the tree is grown in full sun. It spreads to 25 ft (8 m).
ZONES 4–9.

MORUS
MULBERRY

There are about 10 species of deciduous shrubs and trees in this northern hemisphere genus. They bear broad, roughly heart-shaped leaves with closely toothed margins; the leaves on seedlings may be deeply lobed. Catkins of inconspicuous greenish flowers develop into tiny fruits, closely packed together to appear as a single fruit, the mulberry. Some species have been cultivated for centuries, for their edible fruits and for silk production; the silkworm larvae feed on the leaves.

CULTIVATION

They thrive under a wide range of conditions, but do best in fertile, well-drained soil in a sunny, sheltered position. Propagate from cuttings in winter, which can be quite large branches.

Morus alba
syn. *Morus bombycis*
WHITE MULBERRY, SILKWORM MULBERRY

This vigorous, low-branching tree has sustained the silk industry of China and Japan. It grows up to 40 ft (12 m) tall, with a broadly spreading crown and pendulous smaller branches. The almost hairless leaves are a fresh green-yellow in autumn, strongly veined, with sharp teeth. The rather rubbery fruit are cylindrical, sometimes lanceolate, and color varies from white through pink or red to purple-black. In east-coastal Australia a strain with purple-black fruit is regarded as the common mulberry. It prefers a climate with long, warm summers. **'Pendula'** is a mushroom-shaped weeping form usually grafted onto standards to give initial height. **ZONES 5–10.**

Morus nigra
BLACK MULBERRY

Grown primarily for its fruit, this is the common mulberry of Britain and northern Europe, believed to have come from China or central Asia. It is similar to *Morus alba* but has a thicker trunk, a more compact crown and darker leaves with velvety down underneath and bluntly toothed. The fruit are dark red or almost black, sweet when ripe. **ZONES 6–10.**

Morus alba

Morus alba

Morus nigra

Olea europaea

COMMON OLIVE

Olea europaea has a wide natural distribution through Africa, Arabia and Himalayan Asia. The cultivated olive, **O. e. subsp.** *europaea,* is believed to have derived from smaller-fruited plants thousands of years ago. A slow grower to about 30 ft (9 m), it is very long lived, and does not come into full fruit bearing until at least 10 years old. Its picturesque habit, rough, gray bark and leaves touched with silver on their undersides, make it a beautiful tree. **ZONES 8–11.**

Olea europaea subsp. *europaea*

OLEA

OLIVE

There are about 20 species in this genus, all long-lived, evergreen trees. They have leathery, narrow to broad leaves and tiny, off-white flowers which are followed by the fruits, known botanically as drupes. The most important species is the common olive *(Olea europaea)* which has many cultivars and is the source of olive oil. Since ancient times it has been cultivated around the Mediterranean for its nourishing oil-rich fruit. The fruits are too bitter to be eaten fresh; they must be treated with lye (sodium hydroxide) before being pickled or preserved in their own oil. The wood of the olive tree is prized by craftspeople for carving and turning.

CULTIVATION

Generally these plants require a frost-free climate, but the winters need to be sufficiently cool to induce flowering, while the summers must be long and hot to ensure development and growth of the fruits. Although olives can survive on poor soils, better cropping will result if the trees are given well-drained, fertile loam with ample moisture when the fruits are forming. Propagation is usually from seed in autumn, from heel cuttings in winter or from suckers.

Pinus pinea

PINUS

PINE

Pines are a very important genus of conifers. There are around 120 species of needle-leafed evergreens. The genus is discussed in detail in the chapter on Trees. The species listed below are often cultivated as nut trees.

Pinus edulis

ROCKY MOUNTAIN PIÑON

Native to southwest USA, this species grows to around 50 ft (15 m) and has a compact domed crown with silver-gray, scaly bark. Its stiff needles are in pairs, 1½ in (35 mm) long and dark green. *Pinus edulis* has small, light brown cones. It thrives in hot, dry areas and grows best in well-drained soil. **ZONES 5–9.**

Pinus pinea

ROMAN PINE, STONE PINE, UMBRELLA PINE

From southern Europe and Turkey, this attractive species can reach 80 ft (24 m) in the wild and has a flattened crown atop a straight, though often leaning trunk with furrowed, reddish gray bark. The rigid, paired needles, 4–8 in (10–20 cm) long are bright green. The globe-shaped cones are shiny and brown; the edible seeds are known as pine nuts and are very popular in the cuisines of the Middle East. Once established this pine copes with most conditions, including dryness and heat. **ZONES 8–10.**

Prunus avium

GEAN, MAZZARD, SWEET CHERRY,
WILD CHERRY

Native to Europe and western
Asia, this species is the major
parent of the cultivated sweet
cherries. It can reach 60 ft
(18 m) tall, with a rounded
crown and a stout, straight
trunk with banded reddish
brown bark. The pointed,
dark green leaves are up to
6 in (15 cm) long and turn
red, crimson and yellow before they drop. Profuse white
flowers appear in late spring
before the leaves and are followed by black-red fruit. The
cultivated cherries are rarely
self-fertile, so trees of 2 or
more different clones are often
necessary for fruit production.
Cherry wood is prone to
fungus so avoid pruning in
winter or in wet weather. The
ornamental cultivar 'Plena'
carries a mass of drooping,
double white flowers.
ZONES 3–9.

Prunus armeniaca 'Story'

PRUNUS

**Many of the species belonging to this genus are trees, and
detailed information on the genus is given in the Trees chapter.
However, the ones included here can be treated as fruit trees.**

Prunus armeniaca

APRICOT

Now believed to have originated in northern China and
Mongolia, the apricot was introduced to the Middle East more
than 1,000 years ago and thence to Europe. It grows to no more
than about 25 ft (8 m) tall, the trunk becoming characteristically
gnarled with age. White or pinkish blossoms are borne in early
spring before the leaves appear. The twigs are reddish, and the
smooth, heart-shaped leaves are about 3 in (8 cm) long. The
yellow-orange fruit contains a smooth, flattened stone that
separates easily from the sweet-tasting flesh. Prune moderately
after flowering to encourage a good fruit crop. '**Story**' is a
popular cultivar, fruiting mid-season. **ZONES 5–10.**

Prunus avium

Prunus cerasifera

CHERRY PLUM, MYROBALAN, PURPLE-LEAFED PLUM

Native to Turkey and the Caucasus region, this small-fruited thornless plum has long been cultivated in Europe. It grows to about 30 ft (9 m) and is tolerant of dry conditions, with an erect, bushy habit and smallish leaves that are slightly bronze tinted. Profuse, small white flowers appear before the leaves, in spring in cool climates and in late winter in milder ones, followed by edible red plums up to 1¼ in (30 mm) diameter in summer. There are many ornamental cultivars of this species, the most widely grown being those with deep purple foliage. **'Nigra'** is slightly smaller than the normal *Prunus cerasifera* and has vibrant, deep purple leaves turning more blackish purple in late summer; in spring it bears single, pale pink blossoms with red calyx and stamens. The cherry-size red fruit are edible but sour. **'Pissardii'** (syn. 'Atropurpurea') was the original purple-leafed plum, sent to France in 1880 by M. Pissard, gardener to the Shah of Persia. It has new foliage of a deep red color turning dark purple and its pink buds open white. Other purple-leafed cultivars include **'Newport'** and **'Thundercloud'**, of American origin. **'Elvins'** (syn. *P.* 'Elvins'), is an Australian-raised cultivar grown for its white blossom flushed flesh pink and densely massed on arching branches; it grows only to about 12 ft (3.5 m) and blooms in mid-spring. **ZONES 3–9.**

Prunus cerasus var. *austera*

Prunus cerasifera 'Elvins'

Prunus cerasus

SOUR CHERRY, MORELLO CHERRY

This tree has smaller, more bushy growth than *P. avium*; it suckers from the roots, and bears acid fruit. Its wild origin is unknown. The plants are self-fertile, so an isolated tree is capable of setting fruit, but like the sweet cherry, it needs cold winters for successful growth. *P. cerasus.* var. *austera*, has pendulous branches and blackish fruit with purple juice; the red amarelle cherries with clear juice belong to *P. c.* var. *caproniana*, while the famous maraschino cherries with very small blackish fruit are *P. c.* var. *marasca*. **ZONES 3–9.**

Prunus dulcis

Prunus × *domestica*

PLUM, EUROPEAN PLUM

This plum has numerous cultivars, most are grown for their sweet fruit, but some for their blossom. It is a vigorous grower to a height of 30 ft (9 m) or more, with a tangle of strong branches spreading into a broad, dense crown of foliage. The vigorous new growth are sometimes spiny and the flowers are white, borne in profuse small clusters in spring. The summer fruit are spherical to elongated, 1¼–3 in (3–8 cm) long, with a yellow, red or blue-black skin and green or yellow flesh. The fruit of most cultivars are not as juicy as the red-fleshed Japanese plums *(P. salicina)*, and are best cooked or dried for prunes; one of the best for eating is '**Coe's Golden Drop**' a sweet, juicy, amber-yellow plum with red spots. *P. domestica* subsp. *insititia*, the damson plum or bullace, forms a thornier tree, which often succeeds in districts that are too cold for the large-fruited varieties; it bears small purple-black fruit with tart acid flesh that are commonly used to make jams and jellies. **ZONES 5–9.**

Prunus dulcis

syn. *Prunus amygdalus*

ALMOND

Closely related to the peach, the almond is believed to have originated in the eastern Mediterranean region and requires a climate with hot dry summers and cool winters to bear well. It grows to well over 20 ft (6 m) high, with a moderately spreading habit. Stalkless pink blossoms are borne in clusters of 5 to 6 on the leafless branches in late winter or early spring. These are followed in summer by the flattened, furry fruit, like a small dried-up peach; this dries and splits to release the weak-shelled stone, which in turn contains the almond kernel. Almonds need a well-drained, salt-free soil and the young trees are frost tender; they are not self-fertile and two varieties that blossom at the same time are needed to produce fruit. They are prone to shot-hole disease, which appears on the fruit as purple spots, spoiling the nut inside. Prune to an open vase shape encouraging 3 or 4 main branches. **ZONES 6–9.**

Prunus spinosa
SLOE, BLACKTHORN

A species of plum, this small tree has already been described in the Shrubs chapter. Small white flowers are produced in spring; in summer the fruit appear. These are used to make jams and conserves. **ZONES 4–9.**

Prunus persica 'Klara Meyer'

Prunus persica
PEACH, FLOWERING PEACH, NECTARINE

Believed to have originated in China but introduced to the Mediterranean region over 1,000 years ago, the peach grows 12 ft (3.5 m) or more tall. It bears an abundance of pinkish red flowers in early spring (or late winter in mild climates). The narrow, 6 in (15 cm) long, mid-green leaves appear after the blossoms. Its delicious mid-summer fruit, which vary from cream and pale pink to yellow or scarlet, is covered with a velvety down and contain a stone that is deeply pitted and grooved. Many cultivars include both fruiting and flowering types, the latter mostly with small, hard fruit that are of little use for eating; the fruiting cultivars, though, can be quite showy in flower. Ornamental cultivars include the widely grown **'Alba Plena'**, with double white flowers ; **'Klara Meyer'**, with double peach-pink flowers with frilled petals; **'Magnifica'** is noted for its double, deep crimson blooms that cover the branches; and **'Versicolor'**, which bears semi-double flowers, white, pale pink or variably red-striped, all on the same tree. *P. persica* var. *nectarina*, the nectarine, is almost identical to the peach in habit and flowers, but its fruit are smooth skinned, mostly smaller and with a subtly different flavor. There are several named varieties and their seedlings often give rise to the normal, downy-skinned peaches. **ZONES 5–10.**

Prunus persica 'Versicolor'

Prunus persica

Punica granatum

This species, growing to 15 ft (4.5 m) tall and 3 m (10 ft) wide, has 3 in (8 cm) long, blunt-tipped, glossy leaves. Its large, 8-petalled, red-orange flowers appear at the branch tips in spring and summer; these are followed by the apple-like fruit, which have a thick rind and a mass of seeds in a reddish, sweet pulp. Many cultivars are available, the fruit varying from very sweet to acidic and the flowers from red to pink or white. *Punica granatum* var. *nana*, a dwarf cultivar to 3 ft 1 m) high, has single orange-red flowers and small fruit. The commercially grown 'Wonderful' has double, orange-red flowers and large fruit. **ZONES 9–11.**

Punica granatum

PUNICA
POMEGRANATE

This genus, originating from the Mediterranean countries and southern Asia, consists of just 2 species of deciduous shrubs or trees. They have opposite, entire leaves and trumpet-shaped, bright red flowers. *Punica granatum*, the only species cultivated, has been valued for centuries for its edible fruit.

CULTIVATION

Pomegranates can be grown in a wide range of climates, from tropical to warm-temperate, but the red or orange fruit will ripen only where summers are hot and dry. Plant in deep, well-drained soil preferably in a sheltered, sunny position. Propagate from seed in spring, from cuttings in summer or by suckers. They can be pruned as a hedge and are also good in tubs.

Pyrus pyrifolia
JAPANESE PEAR, SAND PEAR

This compact tree has been grown for centuries in China and Japan. It grows to 50 ft (15 m) and is valued for its beauty and for its fruit. Small flowers appear either just before or at the same time as the oblong, sharply toothed leaves. Glossy green when young, the leaves become a rich orange-bronze color in autumn. The small, round, brown fruit are hard and have a gritty texture. *Pyrus pyrifolia* var. *culta* is the name used for all the cultivated forms with larger, edible fruit, including the modern nashi pears. '**Kosui**' is a popular Japanese cultivar which bears russet-skinned, globular fruit. **ZONES 4–9.**

Pyrus communis 'Beurre Bosc'

PYRUS

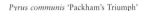

Most of the species belonging to this genus are trees, and detailed information on the genus is given in the Trees chapter. However, the following are treated here as fruit trees.

Pyrus communis
COMMON PEAR

The parent of many garden cultivars, the wild pear is grown for its beautiful single, pinkish white flowers with red stamens. Long lived, it reaches 50 ft (15 m) but its short branches can look unappealing when not covered in flowers. The bark is dark gray or brown and cracks into small plates. The dark green, leathery leaves have serrated margins and long stalks. The greenish fruit, up to 2 in (5 cm) long, ripen to yellow and are usually gritty with a dull flavor—the fruit of the cultivars are sweeter and best when picked before fully ripe. '**Beurre Bosc**' is widely cultivated for its heavy crops of large, soft, sweet, brown-skinned pears that are good for baking. '**Bon Chrétien**', cultivated since medieval times, has medium-sized, succulent, musky-flavored fruit: it is the parent of the famous English **Williams** pear; known in North America, Australia and New Zealand as the Bartlett pear and grown for canning—the red-skinned cultivar is known as '**Red Bartlett**'. '**Packham's Triumph**' is an Australian cultivar with large, sweet, green-skinned fruit. '**Conference**', an early flowering pear from Europe, produces the best quality fruit if cross-pollinated; its fruit start to ripen in mid-autumn and should be picked before fully ripe. **ZONES 2–9.**

Pyrus communis 'Packham's Triumph'

SORBUS

ROWAN, SERVICE TREE, MOUNTAIN ASH

This genus is made up of 100 species of deciduous trees and shrubs from cool climates of the northern hemisphere, grown for their foliage, timber and decorative fruits. The genus is described in detail in the Trees chapter. *Sorbus domestica* is grown for its edible fruit.

Sorbus domestica

ZIZIPHUS

This genus of about 80 or so species of deciduous or evergreen trees and shrubs occurs naturally in warm- to hot-climate areas of both the northern and southern hemispheres. Some have spiny branches. Their leaves are usually marked with 3 veins and there are spines at the base of each leaf stalk. The insignificant flowers are small, greenish, whitish or yellow, arranged in clusters in the leaf axils. The small, fleshy fruits of some species are edible.

CULTIVATION

Ziziphus species are frost tender, and should be grown in open, loamy, well-drained soil in full sun. Provide plenty of water, and tip prune to maintain compact growth. Propagate from seed or root cuttings in late winter, or by grafting.

Sorbus domestica

SERVICE TREE

This attractive 70 ft (21 m) high, spreading tree is indigenous to southern and eastern Europe and northern Africa. It has deeply fissured bark. The leaves are made up of 13 to 21 toothed leaflets. The 1 in (25 mm) long fruit are brownish green with a rosy tint. They are somewhat pear-shaped and edible when fully ripe. **ZONES 3–9.**

Ziziphus jujuba

Ziziphus jujuba

JUJUBE, CHINESE DATE

This deciduous tree, which is distributed from western Asia to China, grows to 40 ft (12 m) tall. Its oval to lance-shaped green leaves are 1–2 in (2.5–5 cm) long, with 2 spines at the base of the leaf stalk, one of which is usually bent backwards. Small greenish flowers are borne in spring. The dark red, oblong to rounded fruit are up to 1 in (25 mm) long: they ripen from autumn to winter on the bare branches and are apple-like in taste. They may be stewed, dried or used in confections. **ZONES 7–10.**

Actinidia arguta

This deciduous species from China, Japan and southern Siberia is not only one of the largest and most vigorous actinidias but also the most cold hardy. It can grow to 50 ft (15 m) or more high and has very broad glossy leaves 3–5 in (8–12 cm) long, with fine bristle-tipped teeth. Flowers are greenish white, fragrant, borne in clusters of three in leaf axils in late spring or early summer and are followed on female plants by 1 in (25 mm) long yellow-green edible fruit. 'Ananasnaya' is more cold hardy and has smaller fruit in larger clusters. **ZONES 4–9.**

Actinidia kolomikta
KOLOMIKTA

Grown mainly for its spectacular foliage, this slender deciduous twiner forms a large mound-like mass but can be very successfully trained in elegant espalier fashion against a wall. The young leaves are reddish green, changing to bright green splotched with white or deep pink. The faintly fragrant, small white flowers with pale yellow stamens are borne in late spring and summer, followed by small fruits. Plants color best in cool temperate climates. **ZONES 5–9.**

ACTINIDIA

In recent years this east Asian genus of woody climbers has become familiar in the guise of the fruit of one species, successfully promoted as 'kiwi fruit' by New Zealand orchardists who export them to many countries. An older generation first came across them as 'Chinese gooseberries', although the genus is quite unrelated to the gooseberry genus *Ribes* (or, for that matter, to kiwis). *Actinidia* also contains a few fine ornamentals, which are treasured by discerning gardeners in regions with a cool, moist climate. Mostly deciduous, they have tangled twining branches with widely spaced simple leaves. Both the leaves and branches are often covered with bristly hairs. Male and female flowers usually occur on separate plants, with white, green or reddish petals, and are quite showy in some species. The fruit is a fleshy oval berry containing numerous tiny seeds.

CULTIVATION

If fruit is desired it will usually be necessary to plant at least one male vine close to several other females. The vines need either a strong trellis, a strong support or even a dead tree on which to climb. They grow best in moist, fertile soil in a sheltered but sunny position. The most reliable method of propagation is normally from cuttings.

Actinidia kolomikta

FRAGARIA
STRAWBERRY

The dozen or so species in this genus are mostly native to temperate areas of the northern hemisphere. They are low-growing, creeping or tufted perennials grown as ornamental groundcovers and for their fleshy red fruits. The palmate leaves are composed of 3 toothed leaflets, and the white or pink, 5-petalled flowers appear in cymes. The strawberry itself is a false fruit; a large fleshy receptacle covered with tiny pips. Modern, more robust cultivars can fruit 6 months, or all year round in a warm climate. There are many named varieties with varying flavors.

CULTIVATION

Grow these frost-hardy plants in containers or beds lined with straw, in free-draining, acidic soil. The plants need full sun or light shade and protection from wind; in cold climates grow them in slits in sheets of plastic. Propagate from seed in spring or autumn or by runners and replant with fresh stock every few years. Protect them from snails, strawberry aphids and birds. Botrytis can be a problem in high rainfall areas.

PASSIFLORA
syn. *Tacsonia*
PASSION FLOWER, GRANADILLA

Passiflora quadrangularis

This genus of mostly evergreen or semi-evergreen, tendril-climbing vines, are grown for their ornamental blossoms and their pulpy fruit, notably the passionfruit. This genus is described more fully in the Climbers and Creepers chapter.

Passiflora edulis
PASSIONFRUIT

This frost-tender species is valued for its glossy, bright green leaves, purple-white flowers and flavorsome fruit. It grows to 15 ft (4.5 m) and has white flowers that are green beneath. Train on a pergola or trellis and prune to prevent tangling, which can be a cause of insect infestation. Pick fruit when the skin has turned purple and is still smooth, but do not eat until the skin is wrinkled. *Passiflora edulis* is self-fertile. **ZONES 10–12.**

Passiflora quadrangularis
GIANT GRANADILLA

This vigorous, scrambling vine grows to 50 ft (15 m) or more in height. It has bright green oval leaves and bears large, deep red flowers with a conspicuous ring of purplish filaments from mid-summer to autumn. The oblong to oval fruit, to 12 in (30 cm) long, have a thick yellowish rind and a sweet pulp. This frost-tender plant needs both high temperatures and high humidity to set fruit. **ZONES 10–12.**

Fragaria × ananassa
GARDEN STRAWBERRY

The name ananassa means 'pineapple-flavored', a curious description for the modern, large-fruited hybrid that arose from crossing American species. It has ovate leaflets that are glaucous above and white beneath. A wide range of garden strawberry cultivars have been developed to suit differing climates. **ZONES 4–10.**

Fragaria vesca
WOODLAND STRAWBERRY

Prior to the cultivation which began in the sixteenth century, this was the species gathered from European woodlands. It is a spreading perennial with white flowers and grows to 12 in (30 cm) high. 'Temptation' and 'Sweetheart' are just two of the many popular garden forms of this species. 'Semperflorens' (syn. *Fragaria alpina*) has few runners and bears small, tangy, red or yellow fruit from early summer to autumn. **ZONES 4–10.**

Passiflora edulis

PHYSALIS

GROUND CHERRY

This is a genus of about 80 species of annuals and perennials with a widespread distribution, especially in the Americas. Most form a clump of upright leafy stems 2–4 ft (0.6–1.2 m) tall. The leaves are variable in shape, usually lance-shaped, oval or deltoid (like a poplar leaf), often with lobes or shallow-toothed edges. The flowers are small, usually white or yellow blotched purple, and are backed by calyces that enlarge to enclose the fruit as they develop. The fruit are yellow, orange or red berries, and are often edible. They are ripe when the calyces start to dry.

CULTIVATION

Hardiness varies, but most species tolerate moderate frosts. They prefer moist, well-drained soil and a position in sun or part-shade. Propagate from seed or by division.

Physalis peruviana

CAPE GOOSEBERRY, GROUND CHERRY

This perennial species from South America grows to around 3 ft (1 m) tall. It is often treated as an annual and is grown for its crop of bright yellow to purple, edible berries. Its leaves are oval to heart-shaped and up to 4 in (10 cm) long. The yellow-blotched purple flowers are ½ in (12 mm) wide and are quickly enveloped by the calyces. **ZONES 8–11.**

Physalis peruviana

RIBES

CURRANT

This genus, from cool-temperate, northern hemisphere regions, contains some 150 species of evergreen and deciduous, ornamental and fruiting shrubs. The white, scarlet, purple, green or black berries are mostly edible. They can grow to 10 ft (3 m) and have long, arching stems. Some species have reddish brown branches, and some produce prickles on the stems or fruit, or on both. The lobed, mid-green leaves, sometimes with downy or felted undersides and toothed edges, may turn red and orange before dropping. Masses of yellow, red or pink blossoms, which are sometimes fragrant, appear in late winter or early spring.

CULTIVATION

These unisexual plants must be planted in groups to ensure vigorous fruiting. They are fully frost hardy and need to be grown in moist, rich soil with a site in full sun or semi-shade. In the USA, some species are host to white pine blister rust. The best method of propagation is from seed or cuttings.

Ribes nigrum

BLACKCURRANT

Ribes uva-crispa

Native to Europe and temperate Asia, this shrub reaches 6 ft (1.8 m) and bears greenish white flowers and sweet, black fruit. It thrives if fertilized with potash and nitrogen. Prune old shoots to promote new growth and harvest when the upper berries start to fall. Watch for currant borer moth, mites and leaf spot. 'Ben Lomond' is late-ripening, with a high yield of large fruit; and 'Jet' has a heavy crop of big fruit. ZONES 5–9.

Ribes silvestre

syns *Ribes rubrum, R. sativum*

REDCURRANT, WHITE CURRANT

Native to western Europe, this deciduous, prickle-free species is an erect 6 ft (1.8 m) shrub with 2½ in (6 cm) long, lobed leaves with silvery undersides. Racemes of small flowers open in spring, followed by clusters of small, juicy, round red or pale amber (white) fruit. They are rather tart and are excellent fresh or cooked. Cultivars of note include 'Viking'; 'Jonkheer van Tets', a vigorous, open redcurrant that flowers and fruits very early; 'Red Lake', vigorous, densely branched and disease-resistant with an early crop of dark red, rather small fruit; and 'White Grape' with large clusters of pale pinkish yellow fruit. ZONES 6–9.

Ribes uva-crispa

syn. *Ribes grossularia*

GOOSEBERRY, EUROPEAN GOOSEBERRY

This stiff, spiny, deciduous shrub is native to central Europe and North America. It grows about 3 ft (1 m) tall, with upright canes and small green leaves held at stiff angles from the stems. Pinkish green flowers are followed by greenish fruit covered with soft bristles. This species rarely fruits well in frost-free climates. There are many cultivars in a variety of sizes and shapes, bearing green, russet green or yellow-green fruit. 'Careless' is a spreading bush with few thorns, the fruit being yellow, elongated and bland; 'Invicta' (syn. 'Malling Invicta') is an early ripener with a heavy crop of large yellow fruit; 'Leveller' has well-flavored fruit and is fairly vigorous; and 'Whinham's Industry' is a slow-growing bush with a good crop of tasty, round, yellow berries with purple red bristles. *Ribes uva-crispa* var. *reclinatum* has bristly, round to slightly elongated fruit that may be yellow or red when ripe. ZONES 5–9.

Ribes silvestre

Ribes silvestre 'Viking'

RUBUS

This large genus of 250 or more species of deciduous and ever-green shrubs and scrambling climbers occurs in most parts of the world. The plants range in size from very small through to viciously armed, 12 ft (3.5 m) high thickets and high forest climbers. Their cane-like stems bear flowers and fruits in their second year. The leaves, usually felted underneath, are mostly compound with 3 to 7 leaflets arranged pinnately or palmately. The summer flowers are white, pink or purple, resembling those of a small single rose, for example, *Rubus* 'Navajo'. They are followed by the sweet, juicy fruits, a mass of tiny, usually red or black drupes.

CULTIVATION

These moderately to fully frost-hardy plants prefer moist, well-drained, moderately fertile soil in a sunny position. Some forms naturalize freely and become a menace. After fruiting, cut the canes back to ground level. Propagate by root division in winter, or from seeds, cuttings or suckers.

Rubus deliciosus

Rubus idaeus

Rubus deliciosus
ROCKY MOUNTAIN RASPBERRY

This 10 ft (3 m) deciduous shrub is found in western USA, especially the Rocky Mountains. Its leaves are rounded or kidney-shaped, 3- to 5-lobed and slightly less than 3 in (8 cm) wide. The stems are thornless with peeling bark. Spring-borne, 2 in (5 cm) wide white flowers are followed by purple-red fruit. **ZONES 5–9.**

Rubus fruticosus
BRAMBLE, BLACKBERRY

This widespread, northern European bramble grows wild in woods and hedgerows. It is an aggregate, consisting of over 2,000 micro-species, all differing in small details. The cultivated blackberry's prickly, arching stems grow to 10 ft (3 m) with a similar spread. They bear deep green leaves with 3 to 5 leaflets, white or pink flowers 1 in (25 mm) across, and delicious black-berries with purple juice. **'Himalayan Giant'** (syn. 'Himalaya') is very vigorous with dark, medium-sized berries which are produced over a long season; **'Loch Ness'** has spineless semi-erect canes. **ZONES 5–10.**

Rubus ideaus 'Killarney'

Rubus idaeus

RASPBERRY, RED RASPBERRY

The northern hemisphere raspberry is a cool-climate, deciduous, perennial shrub 5 ft (1.5 m) tall and wide. It has smooth, reddish brown stems bearing many or few prickles and serrated leaflets 6 in (15 cm) long. The small, 5-petalled white flowers appear on the side shoots of the branches produced over the previous summer. The succulent, aromatic berries are usually red, but can occasionally be white or yellowish. There are many cultivars. **'Autumn Bliss'** is an easily grown, repeat-fruiting cultivar with medium-sized red fruit; **'Taylor'** has large, strong canes with late season bright red, medium-sized fruit; and **'Killarney'** and **'Glen May'** produce full-flavored fruit in early summer. **ZONES 4–9.**

Rubus idaeus

Rubus × loganobaccus 'Boysen'

Rubus × loganobaccus

This popular, resilient evergreen shrub grows to about 15 ft (4.5 m) in height with upright stems and broadly oval leaves that are white beneath. The attractive white flowers are borne in prickly corymbs. **'Boysen'** (syn. *Rubus* 'Boysen'), the boysenberry, is a rampant grower with long canes that are either thorny or smooth and large, purple-red berries that take 6 weeks to ripen. **'Logan'** (syn. *Rubus* 'Logan'), the loganberry, is a hybrid between a blackberry and a garden raspberry said to have originated in the garden of Judge Logan in California in the USA in 1881; its crimson, tart fruit is highly suitable for cooking. **ZONES 5–10.**

VACCINIUM

This is a large and varied genus of about 450 species of deciduous and evergreen shrubs and occasionally small trees and vines. The species seen in gardens are shrubs valued for either their edible berries or their notable autumn color. The berries, known according to the species as bilberry, blueberry, cranberry, huckleberry or whortleberry, are red or blue-black and are often covered with a bloom when ripe. They are grown commercially for fresh fruit, as well as for juicing and canning. Vacciniums are indigenous mainly to the northern hemisphere in a wide range of habitats, stretching from the Arctic to the tropics. The leaves are bright green, often leathery and sometimes coppery red when young; their edges can be toothed or smooth. Small bell-shaped flowers, pale pink, white, purple or red, appear in late spring or early summer.

CULTIVATION

Vaccinium species are generally frost hardy and shade loving; many form dense, thicket-like shrubs. The plants need acidic, well-drained soil with plenty of humus and regular water; some, indeed, prefer boggy ground. Propagate by division or from cuttings in autumn.

Vaccinium ovatum

Vaccinium corymbosum
HIGHBUSH BLUEBERRY

This deciduous species from New England, USA, has a preference for boggy soils. It is grown mainly for its edible, blue-black berries. It also displays fine scarlet autumn foliage. Forming a dense thicket of upright stems with a height and spread of 6 ft (1.8 m), its new leaves are bright green. The clusters of pendulous flowers are pale pink. '**Blue Ray**' has delicious, sweet, juicy fruit. '**Earliblue**' is tall and vigorous with very large berries. For heavier cropping, grow two cultivars together. **ZONES 2–9.**

Vaccinium macrocarpon
syn. *Oxycoccus macrocarpon*
AMERICAN CRANBERRY

Native to eastern North America, this evergreen is commercially grown there and several cultivars are known. Prostrate in habit, it forms mats of interlacing wiry stems with alternate leaves spreading to around 3 ft (1 m) when fully mature. Pink, nodding flowers are produced in summer, followed by relatively large, tart red fruit. **ZONES 2–9.**

Vaccinium ovatum
EVERGREEN HUCKLEBERRY

Occurring naturally from Oregon through to southern California, this is a dense, compact shrub. Its dark green, glossy foliage is much in demand by florists as it lasts well in water; in fact, this demand has driven the wild plants very nearly to extinction. *Vaccinium ovatum* forms a spreading clump 3 ft (1 m) high and 5 ft (1.5 m) wide and can reach 8–10 ft (2.4–3 m) in shady positions. The attractive white or pink flowers appear in early summer. The plant bears tangy, edible red berries that mature blue-black. **ZONES 7–10.**

Vaccinium macrocarpon

Vaccinium corymbosum 'Earliblue'

VITIS

Most of the species belonging to this genus are climbers and creepers, and detailed information on the genus is given in the Climbers and Creepers chapter. However, *Vitis vinifera* is treated here as a fruit. It is popular around the world.

Vitis vinifera

GRAPE

This species is native to Europe and the Mediterranean and has been cultivated since antiquity. A vigorous, fully frost-hardy vine, it has given rise to a multitude of varieties with either black or white (pale green or yellow) fruit, some being better for wine, others for eating fresh or dried. It is best grown where summers are dry. '**Albany Surprise**' is a sweet white table grape; '**Cabernet Sauvignon**', a black wine grape, produces many of the best quality red wines; '**Chardonnay**' is a white wine grape that has become very popular in recent years; '**Merlot**' is a black wine grape often blended with 'Cabernet Sauvignon'; '**Pinot Noir**' is a black grape used in red wine manufacture and in the production of champagne; '**Purpurea**' has spectacular purple foliage in autumn; '**Riesling**', and its derivatives, is a white grape responsible for a range of wines depending on its degree of ripeness; '**Schiava Grossa**' (syn. 'Black Hamburgh') is a black table grape often grown in greenhouses in cool areas; '**Semillon**' is a white wine grape; and '**Shiraz**' (syn. 'Syrah') is a black wine grape. Other cultivars include '**Festivee**' and 'Perlette'. Wine grape cultivars are often grafted onto *Vitis labrusca* rootstock, resistant to the *Phylloxera* root aphid. **ZONES 6–10.**

Vitis vinifera

Vitis vinifera 'Festivee'

Vitis vinifera 'Purpurea'

Chapter 7

BULBS, CORMS & TUBERS

There is opportunity galore to garden with bulbs. Many wonderful species have been gathered from around the world, as well as from our own diverse habitats. Whether you live beside the sea or in 'true bulb' country, the trick is to plant those that are best suited to your particular area. That said, few gardeners can resist planting 'just one more' cool-climate daffodil when confronted with the evocative illustrations of them each autumn!

What is the difference between bulbs, corms and tubers?

Bulbs are thickened storage organs that lie beneath the soil surface. They consist mostly of swollen leaf bases and stalks that surround a central growing section, with a relatively small region at the base from which the roots protrude. The anatomy of a bulb can be seen very clearly when an onion is cut in half. As well as being used as a store of food, bulbs also 'insulate' the plant from unfavorable environmental conditions.

A corm is similar to a bulb, but it usually has its bud or growing tip on its flattened upper surface. After flowering, a new corm develops here, and the old corm shrivels and dies.

Tubers on the other hand, are swollen parts of stems. They produce

Massed plantings of tulips make a spectacular display—however, similar effects can be achieved in much smaller areas.

'Golden Pixie', an Asiatic Hybrid lily. These attractive bulbs grow very well in pots if they are not crowded.

'eyes' like those on a potato, from which new plants can be grown.

Whatever the structure of your favorite bulb, its primary function is to cope with the extremities of its natural habitat: environments that have long periods of cold or low rainfall followed by a brief growing period.

These plants escape from their harsh environment and survive underground as a dormant bulb, only to emerge during favorable conditions. This often coincides with a thaw, as seen in some crocuses, or after unexpected rainfall.

Bulbs for temperate gardens

Luckily, most gardeners living in temperate climates are able to grow a wide range of bulbs, even if they treat cold-country favorites as annuals in warm-temperate areas. Bulbs are invariably associated with spring, although there are tuberous types, like cannas, which give a blaze of scorching color to match the hottest summer's day. These can be coupled with the cooling colors of lilies. Bulbs like the nerines and belladonna suddenly signal the return of autumn, when it is time to plant bulbs again for the next spring display.

There are many bulbs that are hardy to hot, dry summer conditions, since most have evolved to withstand the hot, dry summers of their South African homeland. In areas where there are cool winters, it may be worthwhile to lift these after flowering, as in the case of dahlias, or to grow them in pots for seasonal display on patios. If your garden has a naturally moist area, make the most of it and incorporate a bog garden or pool. Here there is scope to grow the yellow-flowering flag,

'Sun and Sand' is a beautiful Louisiana Hybrid iris. They are popular for their beautiful colors and fine foliage. Louisiana Hybrid irises are basically swamp irises, so they need to be very well watered.

decorative Japanese irises, hostas, fairy fishing rods and wand flowers. In mature, warm-climate gardens, deep shade and matted tree roots are best overcome by undemanding clivias. In cooler areas, deciduous trees can be underplanted with drifts of bluebells, snowdrops and, of course, a myriad of daffodils and jonquils. Dwarf bulbs and less vigorous species can be grouped within well-drained rock garden pockets, where they do not have to compete with other plants.

There is an ever-expanding range of bulbs, tubers and corms with unusual names and growing habits. The glory lily, for example, is a decidedly different bulb that likes to climb to display its red and yellow reflexed petals in summer time. The paint-brush lily also has exceptional flowers. You may have to scan bulb catalogues or seek them out in specialist nurseries, but they certainly add an extra dimension of wonder to a gardener's world.

Bulb cultivation

Bulbs are not difficult to grow. With climatic requirements in mind, most need to be planted in a sunny spot. They only need to be assured of moisture during the growing season, then allowed to dry off as they become dormant. For best results, the soil needs to be well drained and rich in humus. Clay-based soils will need compost added to accelerate drainage, and all soils will be improved by the addition of complete, or specially formulated plant food a couple of weeks before planting.

Bulbs that flower in summer or autumn are planted in spring, while those that bring joy to the end of winter and early spring are best planted in autumn. Be patient to plant spring-flowering bulbs even if the nurseries begin to display them towards the end of summer—certainly buy them, the early shoppers are more likely to find what they want at the beginning of the season—but leave them in a cool, dry and airy position until the nights get cooler. Tulips will appreciate being placed in the crisper section of the refrigerator for up to 6 weeks before they are planted, especially in borderline areas. After the season's flowers have faded, always allow the foliage to die down naturally. Bulbs continue to manufacture food through their leaves, which is stored for next year's display.

One of the joys of the spring bulb season is to have them in pots. It can be a bit like spotting the first cuckoo in spring: the earlier they flower, the more appreciative we are of their glowing freshness. Pots can be either filled to the brim with one type of bulb, or grouped in a combination of favorites to prolong flowering time. Be careful to give bulbs a balanced diet, especially when grown in pots. If they are provided with too much nitrogen, they produce long, strappy leaves at the expense of the flowers. The pots can be kept in the shade initially, but once the first shoots appear, give them as much winter sun as possible. When flowering finishes, by all means remove them from the patio, but resist the temptation to lift them until the foliage has died back; exactly as you would treat those in the garden.

Not all bulbs need to be lifted each year, but tulips and hyacinths appreciate it in all but really cold areas. Some are vigorous growers and produce many offsets (bulblets formed beside the mother bulb), so to avoid overcrowded bulbs and subsequent weakness, lift and divide offsets approximately every 3 years. Others, such as rock cyclamens, belladonnas and the look-alike crinums, are happy to be left alone for years to multiply slowly.

Allium karataviense

ALLIUM

This large genus consists of more than 700 species of bulbous perennials and biennials that occur in temperate regions of the northern hemisphere and range in height from 4 in to 5 ft (10 cm to 1.5 m). Some species are edible, including onions, garlic and chives. The most ornamental species, which are brightly colored with beautiful flowers, mostly come from west and central Asia. Common to the genus is the oniony smell emitted when the leaves are bruised or cut. All species have flowers in an umbel terminating on a small, erect stalk and sheathed in bud by membranous bracts. Bulbs can be very fat or quite slender but generally produce new bulbils at the base, sometimes also in the flower stalks.

CULTIVATION

They prefer a sunny, open position in fertile, well-drained, weed-free soil. Watch for onion fly, stem eelworm, rust and onion white rot. Propagate from seed or bulbils.

Allium aflatunense

A large, summer-flowering species from central Asia, this grows to a height of 3–5 ft (1–1.5 m) or more. Over 50 tiny violet flowers, their petals with darker central stripes, are borne in 4 in (10 cm) diameter umbels. The semi-erect, bluish leaves die away before the flowers appear. It has a muted garlic smell that is hardly detectable. **ZONES 7–9.**

Allium caeruleum
syn. Allium azureum

This frost-hardy species from central Asia has very short, narrow leaves which wither by the time its 12–24 in (30–60 cm) flowering stalks have fully lengthened. These bear dense umbels of starry blue flowers in summer. **ZONES 6–9.**

Allium carinatum
KEELED GARLIC

Native to southern Europe, this species is also naturalized in parts of the USA. It produces numerous bulbils, which spread rapidly. Leaves are linear and the 12–24 in (30–60 cm) tall flowering stems bear umbels enclosed in very long narrow bracts which drop away to reveal purplish pink flowers with protruding stamens. **ZONES 7–9.**

Allium cernuum
LADY'S LEEK, NODDING ONION

The distinctive feature of this North American species is the way the slender 12–24 in (30–60 cm) flowering stem nods over at the top, as do the individual flower stalks, which bear white, pink or maroon bell-shaped flowers with protruding stamens. **ZONES 3–9.**

Allium christophii

Allium moly

Allium christophii

syn. Allium albopilosum

STAR OF PERSIA

Growing to 24 in (60 cm), this species has broad leaves, green and shiny on top and white beneath, and the sturdy stem bears a rounded umbel of flowers up to 15 in (38 cm) wide in spring. Star-shaped individual violet flowers turn black as the seeds ripen and are useful for dried flower arrangements. Plant bulbs in autumn, 2½ in (6 cm) deep. This species grows best in full sun. **ZONES 7–9.**

Allium cyaneum

Cyaneus is Latin for blue, cyanide being named thus because it turns the lips blue. In summer, this northern Chinese species bears nodding, bell-shaped flowers that are a bluish purple color, their petals with dark blue or green center stripes. The leaves sheathe the base of the flowering stems, which are up to 18 in (45 cm) tall. **ZONES 7–9.**

Allium giganteum

GIANT ALLIUM

Among the tallest of flowering alliums, this species has 4–6 ft (1.2–1.8 m) stems topped with dense, 4–6 in (10–15 cm) diameter umbels of violet to deep purple flowers in mid-summer. The leaves are gray-green, 18 in (45 cm) or more long. **ZONES 6–10.**

Allium karataviense

The most striking feature of this spring-flowering species from central Asia is the 2–3 broad flat leaves that spread widely from the base, dull gray-green in color, flushed with purple. The short flowering stems terminate in dense umbels of star-shaped white to pale purple flowers, their petals with darker central veins. The name is a latinization of Kara Tau, the mountain range in Kazakhstan where the species was first found. **ZONES 3–9.**

Allium moly

GOLDEN GARLIC

Native to southern Europe, in some parts of which its appearance in a garden was regarded as a sign of prosperity, *Allium moly* grows to 15 in (45 cm). Broad, gray-green basal leaves surround stems which each bear an umbel of up to 40 flowers. The bright yellow, star-shaped flowers appear in summer. *Moly* was the classical name of a magical herb, fancifully applied to this species by Linnaeus. **ZONES 7–9.**

Allium giganteum

Allium neapolitanum

Allium triquetrum

THREE-CORNERED LEEK,
THREE-CORNERED GARLIC

One of the most easily recognized alliums, on account of its sharply 3-angled thick flowering stems, *Allium triquetrum* is native to the western Mediterranean region. It can form dense clumps with flattish, soft green leaves rather like bluebell (*Hyacinthoides*) leaves, and the 10–18 in (25–45 cm) flowering stems bear small umbels of gracefully drooping ¾ in (18 mm) white, bell-shaped flowers in spring and early summer. It commonly naturalizes and may sometimes become a nuisance.
ZONES 7–10.

Allium neapolitanum

NAPLES ONION, DAFFODIL ONION

This easily grown flowering onion produces fragrant, usually white flowers in loose heads in early spring. Flowering stems are 12 in (30 cm) tall. The plant will spread from seed in favorable conditions. Plant 3 in (8 cm) deep in autumn. It can also be potted up and grown indoors.
ZONES 7–9.

Allium oreophilum

The name of this central Asian species means 'mountain loving'. A small clump-forming plant, its fine leaves are slightly longer than the 6 in (15 cm) flowering stems. Numerous bell-shaped pinkish purple flowers are borne in small, loose umbels in spring and summer. 'Zwanenburg' has deep carmine flowers.
ZONES 7–9.

Allium triquetrum

Alstroemeria haemantha
HERB LILY

This Chilean species has green leaves with a slightly hairy margin. The stiff flower stems up to 3 ft (1 m) tall carry up to 15 orange to dull red flowers during early summer, their upper petals splashed with yellow. The plants can spread by their fleshy rhizomes to form quite large patches. **ZONES 7–9.**

Alstroemeria haemantha

Amaryllis belladonna
syn. *Callicore rosea*
BELLADONNA LILY

This plant is a gardener's dream—moderately frost hardy, easy to grow and very beautiful as the name *belladonna* ('beautiful lady') implies. A sturdy, fast-lengthening stem up to 30 in (75 cm) high is topped with a glorious display of rosy pink, lily-like flowers about 4 in (10 cm) long. The strap-like basal leaves appear in a large clump after the long flowering period. Over a number of years the bulbs can multiply to form a clump up to 24 in (60 cm) or so in width. There are many cultivars, including 'Hathor', striking, large white flowers; 'Capetown', dark crimson-pink flowers; and 'Spectabilis', a many-flowered, rose-pink and white form. **ZONES 8–11.**

ALSTROEMERIA
PERUVIAN LILY

These tuberous and rhizomatous plants were discussed in detail in the Annuals and Perennials chapter. The species described here is a popular tuberous species.

Amaryllis belladonna

AMARYLLIS

These are some of the most beautiful of all flowering bulbs. Linnaeus' concept of *Amaryllis* was in fact a mixed one, including the American plants we now know as *Hippeastrum* as well as the familiar South African belladonna lily. As now recognized the genus consists of a single species, occurring wild only in southwestern Cape Province. Its notable feature is the way its long-stemmed umbels of magnificent rose-pink flowers appear in late summer and early autumn from leafless bulbs, the bright green, rather succulent leaves emerging after the flowers wither. Occasionally grown are generic hybrids between *Amaryllis* and some related genera: best known are × *Amarcrinum* (with *Crinum*) and × *Amarygia* (with *Brunsvigia*).

CULTIVATION

Plant large bulbs in late summer at soil level or just below, in well-drained soil. A fairly sunny position is best in cool areas, but they may need light shade in very warm areas. Cut down flower stalks once flowering is finished but ensure the plant is well watered through winter. Grown easily from seed, it often self-sows freely.

Anemone blanda 'Radar'

ANEMONE

Most species in this genus are perennials, and detailed information on the genus is given in the Annuals and Perennials
chapter. However, the ones included here are tuberous varieties.

Anemone blanda

This delicate-looking tuberous
species is frost hardy. Native
to Greece and Turkey, it grows
to 8 in (20 cm) with crowded
tufts of ferny leaves. White,
pink or blue star-shaped
flowers appear in spring. It
self-seeds freely and, given
moist, slightly shaded conditions, should spread into a
beautiful display of flowers.
Popular cultivars include
the large-flowered 'White
Splendour'; 'Atrocaerulea',
with deep blue flowers; 'Blue
Star', with pale blue flowers;
and 'Radar' with white-
centered magenta flowers.
ZONES 6–9.

Anemone coronaria
WIND POPPY, FLORIST'S ANEMONE

This very frost hardy species,
the most commonly planted
anemone, is one that dies
back to small woody tubers;
these are sold in packets just
like seeds, the plants being
treated almost as annuals.
They grow to about 10 in
(25 cm) high, and the poppy-
like flowers, up to 4 in (10 cm)
wide can range in color from
pink to scarlet, purple or blue.
The two best known strains
are the **De Caen** and **St Brigid
Groups,** with single and
double flowers respectively,
and colors ranging from pink
to purple to scarlet to blue.
ZONES 8–10.

Anemone hortensis

The finely dissected leaves of
this low growing rhizomatous
species from the Mediter-
ranean region, makes a
wonderful backdrop to the
mauve-pink flowers held
singly just above the foliage
in spring. **ZONES 7–9.**

Anemone blanda 'White Splendour'

Arisaema sikokianum

This Japanese native is probably the most widely cultivated species. Its flower stem
is around 18 in (45 cm) tall
and it has 2 trifoliate leaves
with leaflets up to 6 in (15 cm)
long. The spathe is 6–8 in
(15–20 cm) long, deep purple
on the outside with a stark
white interior. The spadix is
also pure white with an upright, club-shaped appendage.
ZONES 7–9.

Arisaema triphyllum

This is one of the most distinctive wildflowers of North
America's northeastern woodlands, flowering in spring
before the trees burst into
leaf. One or two medium
green leaves, each divided into
3 leaflets, expand to a height
of about 12 in (30 cm) after
the flowers fade. The slender
spadix is enclosed by a spathe
of pale green to purple-brown.
Bright scarlet berries ripen in
autumn when the leaves have
died down. **ZONES 4–9.**

Above: Arisaema triphyllum
Left: Arisaema serratum

ARISAEMA

JACK IN THE PULPIT

This genus of the arum family consists of around 150 species of
tuberous or rhizomatous perennials found in temperate to tropical parts of the northern hemisphere. Their foliage is variable
and they often have only one or two leaves per shoot. The
leaves are usually divided, sometimes very finely, and make a
frilled base to the erect, flowering stem that emerges through
the center of the foliage. The flowering stems vary considerably
in height depending on the species, and carry a single flower
spike in spring or early summer. The bloom is typical of the
arum family, with a central spadix of minute, fleshy flowers
surrounded by a greenish spathe. Size, color and shape of the
spathe vary widely. Heads of fleshy red fruit follow the flowers.

CULTIVATION

Most of the cultivated species tolerate moderate to severe frosts
and prefer to grow in woodland conditions with cool, moist,
humus-rich soil and dappled shade. Propagate from seed or offsets.

Arisaema sikokianum

Arisaema serratum

This northeast Asian species
has a flower stem up to 3 ft
(1 m) tall with 2 leaves each
divided into 7 to 20 leaflets
up to 6 in (15 cm) long. The
spathe is 3–4 in (8–10 cm)
long, pale green with purple
spotting or purple all over,
sometimes with white stripes.
The spadix has a 2 in (5 cm)
yellow appendage. **ZONES 5–9.**

Arisarum proboscideum

MOUSE PLANT

This is a charming miniature plant with little spathes, and round purplish hoods prolonged into slender 6 in (15 cm) 'tails' that never fail to arouse interest, though one may have to peer between the leaves to view them. Flowering in spring and dying back in autumn, the mouse plant is only about 6 in (15 cm) high but can spread to form a large patch. **ZONES 6–10.**

Arisarum proboscideum

ARISARUM

Species from this genus are densely clumping plants with long leaf stalks springing directly from the ground, ending in smallish arrowhead-shaped or heart-shaped blades. Much shorter than the leaves, the flowering stems bear a small but curiously shaped spathe, with the tip hooded over so as to completely hide the short spadix.

CULTIVATION

They are woodland plants that like a moist, sheltered situation, lightly shaded. Leave undisturbed except for lifting and dividing clumps every few years, in autumn or winter; propagate also from seed.

Arum italicum

ARUM

Many plants are called arums, but only a few truly belong to this genus. All are worth growing, but only 2 or 3 are widely available. They are tuberous perennials with broad, fleshy leaves, usually arrowhead-shaped and often variegated with a paler green along the veins. The true flowers are minute, carried in the finger-like spadix that terminates the thick flower stalk; the spadix in turn is encircled by the more conspicuous spathe, or bract.

CULTIVATION

The more leafy species, such as *Arum italicum*, are easily grown in part shade in moist but well-drained, humus-rich soil, and require no attention. Species from drier climates, such as *A. palaestinum*, require to be kept much drier during the dormant period. Propagate by division after the foliage dies back, or from seed in autumn.

Arum italicum

ITALIAN ARUM

Growing to 12 in (30 cm), this species has broad, arrow-shaped, marbled leaves in autumn. Appearing in early spring, the flower spike has a light green, hooded spathe with an erect yellow spadix in the center. It is followed by orange berries that last until late summer. **ZONES 7–10.**

Begonia, Tuberhybrida Group

The glorious large blooms of the Tuberhybrida Group come in almost every color except blues, as singles or doubles, with many variations of frills and ruffles. These hybrids are derived from a number of species native to South America. The tubers sprout in mid-spring, producing weak, brittle stems up to 24 in (60 cm) long with rather sparse, mid-green leaves. The summer flowers can weigh down the stems, which may need staking. After flowering, plants enter their dormant stage and the tubers are normally lifted in mid-autumn and stored dry. Several subgroups are recognized, based on growth form and flower type: most numerous are the **Camellia-flowered** and **Rose-flowered** cultivars, with very large, mostly double flowers up to 6 in (15 cm) across or even larger, in the full range of colors; examples are **'Fairy Lights'** and **'Mandy Henschke'**; their multiplicity of petals develop only in the male flower when the smaller single female flowers that grow on either side of the central male are removed. **Picotee** group cultivars are mostly double blooms with petal edges washed in contrasting or deeper shades of the flower color. Cultivars of the **Multiflora** type are usually single-flowered and are grown mainly for their effect en masse: available in the same color range and grown in the same way as the others, they need no bud removal. Plants can be floppy and will benefit from staking. The **Pendula**

BEGONIA

Most of the species belonging to this genus are evergreen perennials, and detailed information on the genus is given in the Annuals and Perennials chapter. However, the Tuberhybrida Group is included here.

Begonia, Tuberhybrida Group, 'Fairy Lights'

Group carry their flowers in pendent sprays; known sometimes as 'basket begonias', they look best cascading from hanging baskets. The single or double flowers are usually smaller than Camellia- or Rose-flowered types but come in the same color range and grow in the same way.
ZONES 9–11.

Begonia, Tuberhybrida Group, Picotee Type

CALLA

WATER ARUM, BOG ARUM

This genus, a member of the arum family, consists of a single species found in cool-temperate regions of the northern hemisphere. It is a semi-aquatic, deciduous or semi-evergreen perennial that grows in the boggy margins of lakes and swamps. It has thick rhizomes and long-stalked, smooth, heart-shaped leaves in a loose clump. The inflorescences are typical of the arum family, with a broad, rather flat white spathe and a short central spadix of very small fleshy cream flowers, which develop into closely packed small red fruits. The plants often called 'calla lilies' are in fact the African *Zantedeschia aethiopica*, not to be confused with the true genus *Calla*.

CULTIVATION

The water arum does best in boggy soil and will thrive when planted in up to 10 in (25 cm) depth of still or slow-moving water. It prefers full sun, but tolerates some shade in warmer areas. Propagation is normally by division in early spring, or from seed. Place seed in pots barely submerged in water. It will often self-seed if conditions are favorable.

Calla palustris

This very attractive plant grows to about 12 in (30 cm) high, and the dark green glossy leaves are up to 8 in (20 cm) long. The spathes, similar in shape to the upper stem-clasping leaves, are white flushed with green and appear through the summer months. Old spathes persist beneath the clustered head of bright red berries. **ZONES 2–9.**

CAMASSIA

CAMAS, QUAMASH, BEARGRASS

The edible bulbs of these North American lilies were called *kamas* by the Native Americans, written down variously as *camas, camash* or *quamash*, and this was Latinized to the generic name *Camassia*. The genus consists of 5 or more species, some divided into many subspecies and varieties, ranging in the wild from British Columbia to California and Utah, one extending to the upper Mississippi valley. They grow in moist meadows in very large numbers and the bulbs, like rather gummy potatoes when boiled, were an important food item of the indigenous people and indeed sustained the Lewis and Clark Expedition for part of their 1804–6 journey. From the midst of rather coarse leaf tufts rise the flower stems, studded along their length with clear blue, white or purple stars.

CULTIVATION

Camassias make attractive garden plants. Very frost hardy and easily grown in most temperate climates, bulbs should be planted in late autumn in well-drained, loamy, humus-rich soil. Position in part-shade, or full sun if the soil is very moist. Propagate by division or from seed; the latter may take up to 5 years to produce flowers.

Camassia quamash var. *brevifolia*

Camassia cusickii

A native of eastern Oregon, this species tolerates drier conditions than most others and is easily grown over a wide moisture and temperature range. In late spring and early summer it produces star-like blue flowers about 2 in (5 cm) across in spikes 24–36 in (60–90 cm) tall. **ZONES 5–9.**

Camassia cusickii

Camassia quamash

syn. Camassia esculenta

CAMASH, SWAMP SEGO

This is the most important edible species and also a fine ornamental. It occurs over a wide area of southwestern Canada and northwestern USA. The flowering stems are 12–36 in (30–90 cm) tall and are densely covered with 1 to 2 in (25 to 50 mm) wide star-shaped, pale to deep blue flowers in spring and early summer. This is a very variable species, 8 subspecies are recognized. *Camassia quamash* var. *brevifolia* has duller, more gray-green leaves and flowers that are a deeper shade of blue-violet. **ZONES 4–9.**

CARDIOCRINUM

Knowing a little of how a plant's name is formed may enable us to picture the plant itself and *Cardiocrinum* is a good example, as it is made up from the Greek *kardia* meaning heart and *krinon*, a type of lily. The leaves are heart-shaped and the magnificent flowers are lily-like. This genus includes 3 species from cool-temperate regions of eastern Asia, all of which are monocarpic (the plant dies after flowering); however, many offsets are produced.

CULTIVATION

The species occur naturally in moist forest areas, and this habitat can be duplicated in a woodland setting where deep soil and nutrient-rich humus is available, ideally on a gentle slope to ensure excess water drains away. Plant bulbs in autumn just below the surface, ensuring ample room between bulbs for best effect. Water and fertilize well once the shoots appear. The main bulb dies after flowering but propagation is possible from offsets (which flower in 3 or 4 years) and seed. Buying 3 sizes of bulbs will ensure some flowers each year.

Cardiocrinum giganteum
syn. *Lilium giganteum*
GIANT LILY

Native to mountains of central and western China, this is a magnificent, summer-flowering plant reaching up to 12 ft (3.5 m). The giant lily does not produce quick results: a small bulb planted today is unlikely to flower in less than 3 or 4 years. The tall, sturdy stem bears up to 20 trumpet-shaped flowers, each about 10 in (25 cm) long; they are cream, striped with maroon-red blotches in the throat and are heavily scented. **ZONES 6–9.**

Cardiocrinum giganteum

Chionodoxa luciliae
syn. *Chionodoxa gigantea*

Native to the same region of Turkey as *Chionodoxa forbesii*, this species resembles it in many respects but has only 2 to 3 flowers per stem and each flower has slightly broader, softer lilac petals and a smaller white central spot. **'Alba'** has all-white flowers. **ZONES 4–9.**

Chionodoxa sardensis

Sardes is a classical place-name from southwestern Turkey and *sardensis* is the Latin adjective referring to it. This species also comes from much the same region as *Chionodoxa forbesii*, and is a fairly similar plant but with narrower, more channeled leaves. The flowers are gentian-blue with a white eye, up to 12 per stem. It is rare in cultivation. **ZONES 4–9.**

Chionodoxa luciliae 'Alba'

Chionodoxa forbesii

CHIONODOXA
GLORY-OF-THE-SNOW

These small bulbs are relatives of the hyacinth. There are only 6 species in the genus, restricted in the wild to mountains of southern Turkey, Crete and Cyprus; they are all desirable garden plants. Plant them in quantity to show off the wonderful clarity of the rich blue flowers with their white centers; lilac-pink flowers are also available. The flowers appear in late winter or early spring, depending on climate.

CULTIVATION
They need full sun or light shade, well-drained soil and cold winter temperatures; in warmer climates they will languish and often fail to initiate flower-buds. Propagate from seed or offsets.

Chionodoxa forbesii
syns *Chionodoxa luciliae* of gardens, *C. siehei*

From the mountains of southwestern Turkey, this is the most widely grown species but has generally been misidentified as *Chionodoxa luciliae* in bulb catalogues. The plants are up to about 8 in (20 cm) high with broad, strap-shaped, fleshy leaves appearing with the flowers. The flowering stems can each carry up to 12 flowers about ¾ in (18 mm) across, very bright violet-blue except for the whitish center. **'Alba'** has pure white flowers. **ZONES 4–9.**

Colchicum 'Waterlily'

COLCHICUM

AUTUMN CROCUS

Colchicum consists of about 45 species, native to Europe, North Africa and west and central Asia, with the majority in Turkey and the Balkans; nearly all species have been cultivated by dwarf bulb and rock garden enthusiasts, but only a few are very widely grown. Despite the name 'autumn crocus', they bloom in either spring or autumn, depending on species. All have flowers with a very long tube, the ovary at or below soil level, the petals spreading at the top into a usually narrow funnel. There are six stamens (*Crocus* always has three). With few exceptions the leaves appear after the flowers and are mostly broad and fleshy. All parts of the plants are poisonous and even contact with the skin may cause irritation—the poisonous compound colchicine is used in the treatment of certain forms of cancer and in plant breeding.

CULTIVATION

Frost hardy, they are easy to grow as long as winters are sufficiently cold. Some Mediterranean species like hot dry summer conditions and need a warm spot in the rock garden with good drainage. Plant corms in late summer in well-drained soil in full sun or part-shade. Corms can be flowered once without any soil, so they can be kept inside for display. Propagate from seed or by division in summer.

Colchicum autumnale

AUTUMN CROCUS, MEADOW SAFFRON

This best known species comes from Europe. The flowers rise to about 6 in (10 cm) above the ground and are about 3 in (8 cm) across. Appearing from late summer to mid-autumn, they vary a little in color but are usually a delicate shade of lilac pink. This is one of the most moisture tolerant species, and the one occurring furthest north. '**Album**' has white flowers, and there is also a double-flowered form. **ZONES 5–9.**

Colchicum 'Waterlily'

'Waterlily' is striking for its large double flowers often with up to 26 petals and lilac rose in color. The late summer to autumn flowers may become top-heavy and flop over; the untidy effect may not please all gardeners, but they are eye-catching. **ZONES 6–9.**

Colchicum autumnale

COMMELINA

A widespread genus of about 230 species of perennial herbs from tropical and subtropical regions of the world, related to *Tradescantia*. They vary in growth habit, some sending up erect annual growths from tuberous roots, others with more evergreen and usually creeping stems which root at the nodes. Their distinctive features are the very asymmetrical boat-shaped bract that encloses each group of flower-buds, and the 3 petals of which often only 2 are conspicuous, each narrowed at the base into a fine 'claw', or stalk. Many species have petals of an intense, clear blue, though pinks and whites are also known.

CULTIVATION

A position in full sun is preferred and a well-drained soil is essential. Propagation is from cuttings or by division.

Commelina coelestis
MEXICAN DAYFLOWER

Native to Central and South America including Mexico, this species has vivid sky-blue flowers that close in the afternoon, each with 3 equal petals and about 1 in (25 cm) across. They open in late summer and autumn. The weak, semi-erect stems with broad green leaves spring from a deep tuberous rootstock and may reach a height of 3 ft (1 m). It needs a warm position in full sun. **ZONES 9–11.**

CRINUM

The bulbs of this genus are often quite large and may be deeply buried or sit virtually on the soil surface; in many species the bulb is elongated with a 'neck' of varying length on which the old, dead leaf bases persist as papery sheaths. The lily-like flowers are borne in umbels at the apex of thick flowering stems and usually open progressively; usually white or pink, they have six broad petals, often upward-curving, and long stamen filaments. Globular, thin-skinned fruits contain large fleshy seeds that have no dormancy and will begin to germinate dry. Only a few species and 2 or 3 hybrids are widely grown in gardens, but some enthusiasts have amassed larger collections. It can be very difficult to locate sources of supply for many of the species.

CULTIVATION

Bulbs should be planted in rich, moist soil with the neck of the bulb above ground level. Some species do best in full sun, others appreciate a light shade. Propagation is best from seed as dividing the plants is difficult. The flowers usually take a few seasons to develop with either method. In cold areas, they should be given good protection in winter. Most species are tender to frost and susceptible to caterpillars, slugs and snails.

Crinum asiaticum

Crinum asiaticum
ASIATIC POISON LILY, POISON BULB

This tropical Asian species can be a dramatic plant for a frost-free garden. It likes damp soil, and can be placed at the margins of a pond. Its long-necked bulbs sit on the surface and produce evergreen, fleshy, very broad leaves making a clump up to about 4 ft (1.2 m) high. The stout flowering stem can carry up to 50 sweetly scented white flowers with very narrow petals, opening through much of the year. There is a rare form with pale pink flowers, another with soft golden-yellow leaves, and one with its leaves boldly striped in green and cream. The poisonous bulbs were once used medicinally, as an emetic; they present little danger in the garden. **ZONES 10–12.**

Crinum moorei 'Cape Dawn'

Crinum × powellii

CAPE LILY

This easily grown hybrid between *Crinum bulbispermum* and *C. moorei* was bred in England in the nineteenth century. Strap-like foliage is produced from a long neck and dies back during late summer and autumn. At about the same time the 3–4 ft (1–1.2 m) flowering stems are each crowned with up to 10 deep pink, fragrant flowers, similar in shape and size to those of *C. moorei*. The flowers can become so heavy that the plant needs to be staked. '**Album**' has pure white flowers. **ZONES 6–10.**

Crinum moorei

MOORE'S CRINUM, BUSH LILY

This cold-hardy plant is popular for the delicate beauty of its large white to pale pink flowers, resembling those of some liliums. The very broad, weak leaves are usually beginning to die back as the flowers open in late summer and early autumn, finally leaving a clump of large, very long-necked bulbs protruding above the ground. Flowering stems are up to 3 ft (1 m) tall, and are topped by umbels of 4–5 in (10–12 cm) wide nodding flowers of very graceful appearance. It is easily grown in light to quite deep shade, preferring a friable, well-drained soil, but is highly prone to damage from snails and slugs. '**Cape Dawn**' is a delicate pink form. **ZONES 7–11.**

Crinum × powellii 'Album'

Crocosmia ×
crocosmiiflora

Growing to 36 in (90 cm), the stem of this hybrid raised in France in the 1880s bears a branching spike of up to 40 orange-red, gladiolus-like flowers about 1 in (25 mm) wide. This species is frost hardy but needs full sun in cold climates. In cold-winter areas, lift the corms for the winter and replant them in spring. Recently, larger flowered hybrids in a wider range of colors (yellow to red) have been raised in England. They have names like 'Bressingham Blaze' (bright orange-red) and 'Lucifer' (bright red) and are a little hardier than the species itself. **ZONES 7–11.**

Crocosmia masoniorum

This tall species grows up to 4 ft (1.2 m). The branched stem is topped with an arched display of tangerine flowers. The 6-petalled flowers are quite large, up to 3 in (8 cm) wide. **ZONES 8–11.**

CROCOSMIA
syns Antholyza, Curtonus

MONTBRETIA

These 7 species of South African cormous perennials have narrow, bayonet-shaped, pleated leaves. These fan out from the base of the plant, similar to a gladiolus. A branched spike of brightly colored flowers appears in summer.

CULTIVATION
Plant the corms in winter in rich soil with adequate drainage in a position that receives morning sun. Water well through summer. They will multiply freely and should not be divided unless overcrowded; if necessary, do this in spring.

Crocosmia × crocosmiiflora

Crocosmia masoniorum

Crocus gargaricus

CROCUS

CROCUS

This genus of cormous perennials has goblet-shaped flowers that taper at the base into a long tube that originates below the soil surface. Crocuses vary greatly in color, though lilac-blue, mauve, yellow and white are most usual. Spring-flowering species and hybrids bear flowers with or before the new leaves; autumn-flowerers bloom in full leaf. The foliage is grass-like, often with a central silver-white stripe.

CULTIVATION

Very frost-hardy, they do best in cool to cold areas. In warm areas corms may flower in the first season and not again. They can be grown in pots in warmer areas, in a cool spot. Plant corms in early autumn in moist, well-drained soil in full sun or part-shade. Clumps can be divided if they are overcrowded. Seed can be planted in autumn, but these plants will usually not flower for 3 years.

Crocus vernus 'Remembrance'

Crocus chrysanthus

syns *Crocus cannulatus* var. *chrysanthus*, *C. croceus*

This species has bright golden-yellow flowers feathered with bronze, and yellow anthers; they appear in late winter or early spring. Leaves up to 10 in (25 cm) long appear at the same time. Hybrid cultivars include: 'Cream Beauty', with creamy yellow flowers; 'Dorothy', with deep golden-yellow flowers; 'E. A. Bowles', with deep butter-yellow flowers with bronze feathering mainly at the base of the petals; 'Gipsy Girl' produces yellow flowers, striped purplish brown on the outside; and 'Ladykiller' has white flowers heavily suffused purple on the outside. **ZONES 4–9.**

Crocus gargaricus

This rare species from western Turkey bears golden-yellow flowers in spring, and rapidly builds into clumps by underground stolons. It tolerates slightly damper conditions than some other Asiatic crocuses. **ZONES 7–9.**

Crocus vernus

DUTCH CROCUS

This species grows to 4 in (10 cm) high and bears solitary white, pink or purple flowers from spring to early summer. The Dutch hybrids are vigorous plants with large flowers up to 6 in (15 cm) long, in a varied color range—white to yellow, purple or bluish; there are also some striped varieties. 'Remembrance' has violet flowers with purple bases. **ZONES 4–9.**

Crocus chrysanthus

Cyclamen coum

CYCLAMEN
CYCLAMEN

This genus consists of about 20 species of tuberous perennials, native to the Mediterranean region and southwest Asia. They belong to the primula family. The round tubers sit on or just below the soil surface and bear fleshy, heart-shaped leaves often with light or dark patterns on the upper surface. The very elegant flowers, borne singly on bare stalks, are downward-pointing, with 5 twisted petals sharply reflexed and erect. They come in colors varying from crimson red to pink or white and may be scented. Many smaller species are choice rock garden-plants; the larger florist's cyclamen *(Cyclamen persicum)* is grown indoors.

CULTIVATION

Cyclamens vary from frost tender to very frost hardy. Plant in light, fibrous soil, rich in organic matter with good drainage and in sun or part-shade. Water regularly during growth but allow to dry out during summer. Tubers are best left undisturbed and should grow larger and flower more abundantly each season. Propagate from seed in autumn. Some cyclamens are susceptible to black rot.

Cyclamen coum

This popular species from the Balkans, Turkey and Lebanon grows to 4 in (10 cm) with leaves that are round to heart-shaped, dark green and frequently marbled with light green or silver. The abundant winter or early spring flowers vary from pale mauve to deep pink, often crimson at the base. *Cyclamen coum* subsp. *caucasicum* has leaves marbled with silver; the dark pink flowers are stained crimson at the base. *C. c.* subsp. *coum* has elegant pink to crimson flowers.
ZONES 6–10.

Cyclamen hederifolium
syn. *Cyclamen neapolitanum*

This species flowers in autumn and can produce corms 6 in (15 cm) wide. Growing to 4 in (10 cm), it has dark green leaves heavily marbled paler green, with broad shallow toothing. The flowers are white to rose pink, darker at the base, and some strains are perfumed. It has a wide distribution in southern Europe and Turkey.
ZONES 5–10.

Cyclamen hederifolium

Cyclamen persicum cultivar

Cyclamen persicum

This occurs in woodlands from Greece to Lebanon and in North Africa. Selected strains are the florists' cyclamens, commonly grown indoors. These plants can be quite large, up to 12 in (30 cm) tall and of similar spread. From among the crowded heart-shaped leaves, which are often marbled light and dark green with silver bands, rise large waxy flowers in shades of white, pink, purple or red, sometimes ruffled or edged with a contrasting tone. It flowers profusely over a long winter season; cool nights will ensure that flowering continues. In areas with cold winters, grow under glass. **ZONES 9–10.**

Dahlia imperialis
syn. Dahlia excelsa
TREE DAHLIA

Native to Central America,
this tall woody perennial or
subshrub has thick, bamboo-
like stems to 15 ft (5 m) or
more high. The large bipinnate leaves to 24 in (60 cm)
long have up to 15 ovate
leaflets with toothed margins.
The large, single lavender-pink
flowerheads with yellow
centers are produced in
autumn. **ZONES 8–10.**

Dahlia imperialis

DAHLIA

This comparatively small genus of about 30 species from
Mexico and Central America has had a huge impact on gardens.
Only 2 or 3 species were used to create thousands of named
varieties. Progeny of *Dahlia coccinea* and *D. pinnata* originally
formed the nucleus of modern hybrid dahlias. Others are
derived from forms of *D. hortensis* such as the popular cultivar
'Ellen Huston'. Hybrids are classified into about 10 different
groups, determined by the size and type of their flowerheads.
Most of the groups have small-, medium- and large-flowered
subdivisions.

CULTIVATION

Dahlias are not particularly frost resistant so in cold climates the
tubers are usually lifted each year and stored in a frost-free place
to be split and replanted in spring. Most dahlias prefer a sunny,
sheltered position in well-fertilized, well-drained soil. Feed
monthly and water well when in flower. Increase flower size by
pinching out the 2 buds alongside each center bud. All, apart
from the bedding forms, need staking. Propagate bedding forms
from seed, others from seed, cuttings from tubers or by division.

Eranthis hyemalis

ERANTHIS
WINTER ACONITE

From Europe and temperate Asia, these 7 species of clump-
forming perennials have been grown for centuries and are
valued for their ability to naturalize under deciduous trees and
their habit of flowering in late winter and early spring. The
short-stemmed, yellow, buttercup-like flowers are surrounded
by a ruff of green leaves. They mix pleasantly with other early
flowering, bulbous plants.

CULTIVATION

Very frost hardy, these plants should be grown in full sun or
part-shade. Slightly damp conditions during the summer dormancy and an alkaline, well-drained soil are conducive to good
growth and plentiful flowers. Propagate from seed in late spring
or by division in autumn.

Eranthis hyemalis

Native to Europe, this
ground-hugging perennial
with knobbly tubers grows to
a height of 3 in (8 cm). The
yellow, cup-shaped flowers to
1 in (25 mm) across are borne
above a ruff of lobed leaves.
ZONES 5–9.

Eremurus aitchisonii

EREMURUS

FOXTAIL LILY, DESERT CANDLE

This is a genus of 50 or so species. It is de-scribed in detail in the chapter on Annuals and Perennials.

Eremurus aitchisonii

syn. *Eremurus elwesii*

From Afghanistan, this is a clump-forming perennial to 6 ft (1.8 m) tall with glossy, narrow, lance-shaped leaves to 24 in (60 cm) long and spikes of pale pink flowers in late spring to early summer. **ZONES 6–9.**

Eremurus × isabellinus, Shelford Hybrids

These frost-hardy perennials are grown for their lofty spikes of close-packed flowers, magnificent for floral displays. They produce rosettes of strap-like leaves and in mid-summer, each crown yields spikes of bloom with strong stems and hundreds of shallow, cup-shaped flowers in a wide range of colors including white, pink, salmon, yellow, apricot and coppery tones. **'Shelford Desert Candle'** is a particularly lovely pure white form. They grow to about 4 ft (1.2 m) in height with a spread of 24 in (60 cm). **ZONES 5–9.**

Eremurus robustus

The tallest of the foxtail lilies, this upright perennial from central Asia flowers profusely in early summer. The individual flowers are smallish stars in palest peach-pink and are produced by the hundreds in spires that can reach nearly 10 ft (3 m) in height. They need to be staked. **ZONES 6–9.**

Eremurus × isabellinus, 'Shelford Desert-Candle'

Erythronium revolutum

PINK TROUT LILY

The leaves are mottled and the stalks are often, but not always, suffused with a pink-ish glow. The petal color can vary between pink, purple and white with yellow central bands and yellow anthers. It reaches about 12 in (30 cm) in height. **'Pagoda'** has marbled green foliage and nodding, deep yellow flowers; **'Pink Beauty'** is a robust form with rich pink flowers. **ZONES 5–9.**

Erythronium tuolumnense

TUOLUMNE FAWN LILY

This native of central California grows on the foot-hills of the Sierra Nevada in open pine and evergreen oak woods. The leaves are mid-green to 8 in (20 cm) long and the flowers, which appear in late spring, are small, deep yellow and star-like. It reaches 12 in (30 cm) in height. **ZONES 5–9.**

Erythronium tuolumnense

Erythronium revolutum

ERYTHRONIUM

DOG'S TOOTH VIOLET, TROUT LILY, FAWN LILY

Native to temperate Eurasia and North America, these little perennial lilies bear delicate, reflexed, star-shaped flowers in spring. They come in shades of yellow or pink, and there are some very pretty hybrids available. The dark green foliage is often attractively mottled. The common name of dog's tooth violet refers to the shape of the tuber.

CULTIVATION

Frost hardy, they do best in cooler areas. Plant the tubers in autumn in part-shade in well-drained, humus-rich soil, and keep moist. They multiply easily and should be left undisturbed until overcrowding occurs. Propagate from offsets in summer or from seed in autumn.

EUCOMIS
PINEAPPLE LILY

The 15 species of pineapple lily, all deciduous and native to southern Africa, bear spikes of small, star-shaped flowers with crowning tufts of leaves like a pineapple. They grow from enlarged bulbs, and the basal rosette of glossy foliage is both quite handsome in itself and rather bulky—these are not bulbs to slip in among other plants but rather substantial border plants in their own right. The Xhosa people used the bulbs, boiled into a poultice, as a cure for rheumatism.

CULTIVATION
Marginally frost hardy, they do best in warm-temperate climates in full sun in moist but well-drained soil; they dislike water during the dormant winter months. Where there is a danger of frost reaching the bulbs they are best grown as pot plants and wintered safely indoors. Propagate from seed or by division of clumps in spring.

Eucomis bicolor

Eucomis bicolor
This summer-flowering bulb bears spikes of green or greenish white flowers with purple-margined petals; these are topped by a cluster of leaf-like bracts. It grows 18–24 in (45–60 cm) tall and 24 in (60 cm) wide. **ZONES 8–10.**

Eucomis comosa
syn. *Eucomis punctata*
This species grows to about 30 in (75 cm) in height. Dark green, crinkly, strap-like leaves surround the tall, purple-spotted scapes. The hundreds of flowers, white to green and sometimes spotted with purple, are borne in late summer and autumn. Water well through the growing season. It makes an excellent, long-lasting cut flower. **ZONES 8–10.**

Eucomis comosa

Fritillaria camschatcensis

BLACK SARANA

This pretty fritillary which grows to about
18 in (45 cm) high is found, in the wild, in
both northwestern USA and northeastern Asia
and grows in moist subalpine meadows, in
open woods and on lightly grassed slopes close
to the sea. The drooping, half-closed, bells-like
flowers vary in color between maroon-brown,
purple-green and black and are borne during
the summer months. **ZONES 4–9.**

Fritillaria imperialis

CROWN IMPERIAL

Native to Turkey, Iran, Afghanistan and
Kashmir, this is the tallest of the species, and it
is the easiest to grow. The leafy stems up to 5 ft
(1.5 m) high bear whorls of lance-shaped pale
green leaves. Pendent clusters of up to 8 yellow,
orange or red bell-shaped flowers appear in
late spring and early summer. The flowers have
an unpleasant odor. 'Lutea' bears bright yellow
flowers. **ZONES 4–9.**

Fritillaria meleagris

SNAKE'S HEAD FRITILLARY, CHEQUERED LILY

In spring, this common European species produces slender stems reaching 12 in (30 cm),
each with a few slender leaves and bearing one
nodding, goblet-shaped bloom that is maroon,
green or white, 1 in (25 mm) long, and
blotched or chequered. It thrives under
deciduous trees or in a rock garden, if kept
moist while growing. **ZONES 4–9.**

Fritillaria meleagris

Fritillaria camschatcensis

FRITILLARIA

FRITILLARY

There are about 100 species in this genus of
bulbs, native to temperate regions of the northern hemisphere. Hard to grow, their nodding,
bell- or goblet-shaped flowers borne mainly in
spring are worth the trouble.

CULTIVATION

Mostly quite frost hardy, they do best in areas
with cold winters. Plant bulbs in early autumn
in part-shade in rich, organic, well-drained soil.
Water well through the growing season but
allow to dry out after flowering. In areas with
high summer rainfall, lift bulbs gently and keep
them out of the ground for as short a time as
possible. Propagate from offsets in summer, but
leave clumps for a few years. Seed sown in
autumn will take 4 to 5 years to bloom.

Fritillaria acmopetala

This species, to 15 in (38 cm) high, comes from
southwestern Turkey, Cyprus, Syria and
Lebanon where plants are found in cedar
forests and on limestone escarpments. The bells
have 3 green outer segments and 3 inner
segments that are green stippled with brownish
purple. The inside of the bell is a glowing shiny
yellow-green. The foliage is a dull gray-green.
ZONES 7–9.

GALANTHUS
SNOWDROP

This genus of about 19 species of small bulbs is native to Europe and western Asia. Small, white, nodding, sometimes perfumed flowers appear above leaves like those of daffodils but much shorter. The 3 inner petals are much shorter than the outer 3 which usually have green markings. Snowdrops naturalize in grass or lightly shaded woodland. They also do well in a rockery and are excellent cut flowers. They flower in late winter and herald the coming of spring.

CULTIVATION

Very frost hardy, they do best in cooler climates. Grow in rich, moist but well-drained soil in part-shade. In very cold areas they may be planted in full sun. Water well during the growing period for good establishment and increase. Propagate from fresh ripe seed or divide clumps immediately the flowers fade, while still in leaf.

Galanthus nivalis
COMMON SNOWDROP

This most commonly grown species reaches 6 in (15 cm) tall. The erect leaves are bluish green. Each stem bears a nodding,

bell-shaped, 1 in (25 mm) wide scented flower in late winter. The outer petals are white, and the inner petals have a green marking at the tip. There are many cultivars, including the double-flowered 'Flore Pleno'. **ZONES 4–9.**

Galanthus nivalis 'Flore Pleno'

Galanthus plicatus
CRIMEAN SNOWDROP

This species from Turkey and eastern Europe is up to 8 in (20 cm) high with broadly strap-shaped, erect dull green leaves. The white flowers borne in late winter and early spring have a green patch at the tip of each inner petal. Flowers of *Galanthus plicatus* subsp. *byzantinus* differ in having green marks at both the base and tip of each inner petal. **ZONES 6–9.**

Galtonia candicans

GALTONIA

This genus of 4 species of frost-hardy bulbs is native to South Africa. Summer flowering, they are closely related to *Ornithogalum* though their more bell-shaped flowers set them apart. They have semi-erect, strap-like leaves in rosettes and elegant tall spikes of pendent, funnel-shaped flowers.

CULTIVATION

Plant in a sheltered site in full sun and fertile, well-drained soil; winter damp will rot them. They tend to die down in winter and may be lifted for replanting in spring. Propagate from fresh ripe seed in spring or by offsets in autumn or spring. Snails may be a problem.

Galtonia candicans
BERG LILY, SUMMER HNYACINTH

This species is up to 4 ft (1.2 m) high with fleshy gray-green leaves and erect stems bearing loose spikes of up to 30 pendent, bell-shaped white flowers, sometimes shaded or marked with green. They are produced for about 6 weeks from mid-summer. **ZONES 6–10.**

Gladiolus callianthus

syn. **Acidanthera bicolor var.**
murieliae

PEACOCK FLOWER,
ABYSSINIAN SWORD LILY

This beautiful species from the mountains of East Africa has flowering stems up to 3 ft (1 m) tall. The sweetly scented white flowers, borne few to a stem, often have a dull crimson blotch in the throat; they are 2–3 in (5–8 cm) wide with elegantly pointed, spreading petals and a tube about 6 in (15 cm) long. It flowers in autumn and the leaves die back in winter. In areas with cold winters, the corms should be lifted and stored until spring. **ZONES 9–11.**

Gladiolus communis

From spring to summer this vigorous species from southern Europe produces spikes of pink flowers streaked or blotched with white or red. It grows to a height of 3 ft (1 m) and has very narrow, tough leaves. *Gladiolus communis* subsp. *byzantinus* (syn. *G. byzantinus*) bears up to 15 pink to magenta blooms in late spring to early summer. **ZONES 6–10.**

Gladiolus communis subsp. *byzantinus*

GLADIOLUS

syns *Acidanthera, Homoglossum*

This genus of about 180 species of cormous perennials with sword-shaped leaves in fan-like tufts is native to Africa, Europe and the Middle East. The species with the most conspicuous and colorful flowers nearly all come from South Africa. Cultivated gladioli are mainly large-flowered hybrids, grown for their showy, funnel-shaped flowers. Plants vary greatly from very small and sometimes fragrant species to the spectacular florists' gladiolus. The 3 main hybrid groups are the Grandiflorus (or Large-flowered) Group, the Primulinus Group and the Nanus (or Butterfly) Group.

CULTIVATION

Plant corms about 4 in (10 cm) deep in well-drained, sandy soil in a sunny position. In cool areas plant in early spring; in warm areas plant from autumn. Water well in summer and cut off spent flower stems. Tall stems may need staking. When picking for indoors, cut when the lower flowers open. Lift corms over winter in cold climates; lift large-flowered corms in all areas, especially those with high winter rainfall; store when perfectly dry. Propagate from seed or cormlets in spring.

Gladiolus, Grandiflorus Group

These very large-flowered hybrids produce long, densely packed spikes of broadly funnel-shaped flowers in summer. The sometimes ruffled flowers are arranged in alternating fashion mostly on one side of a 3–5 ft (1–1.5 m) stem. Demanding in terms of pest and disease control, as well as requiring support to keep upright, they are grown mainly for exhibition or as commercial cut flowers. **'Green Woodpecker'** has medium-sized, ruffled greenish flowers with red markings at the throat; **'Red Majesty'** has lightly ruffled red flowers. **ZONES 9–11.**

Gladiolus, Grandiflorus Group, 'Red Majesty'

Gladiolus tristis

Gladiolus tristis

In late winter or early spring each 24 in (60 cm), slender stem of this species carries up to 6 white, cream or pale yellow 3 in (8 cm) wide flowers; strong fragrance is released only at night. It prefers rich soil, but is adaptable and in favorable conditions it self-sows freely. Many spring-flowering hybrids derive from this popular species. **ZONES 7–10.**

HYACINTHOIDES
syn. *Endymion*

BLUEBELL

The frost-hardy European bluebells, vigorous, bulbous perennials with attractive, scented flowers, are popular with gardeners in temperate regions worldwide. They have strap- to lance-shaped, basal leaves. The flowers are usually blue or white but sometimes pink. The 3 or 4 species are equally happy in a rock garden, naturalized under deciduous trees or in flower borders.

CULTIVATION
They thrive in moist, part-shaded conditions. Bulbs should be planted in autumn in rich, moist soil. Water well until the flowers start to die. They should multiply freely but are best left undisturbed for a few years, and then divided in late summer.

Hyacinthoides hispanica
syns *Endymion hispanicus*, *Scilla campanulata*, *S. hispanica*
SPANISH BLUEBELL

The most popular and most easily grown species, *Hyacinthoides hispanica* grows to about 12 in (30 cm) and flowers in spring. The 1 in (25 mm) wide, nodding, bell-shaped flowers are lilac to blue. The bright green foliage is strap-like. It multiplies freely. 'Azalea' is a compact, free-flowering form with many shorter spikes of pink-lilac flowers. **ZONES 5–10.**

Hyacinthoides non-scripta

Hyacinthoides non-scripta
syns *Endymion non-scriptus*, *Scilla non-scripta*
ENGLISH BLUEBELL

This plant flowers from early spring to summer. The fragrant, semi-pendulous, bell-shaped flowers in lavender blue, pink or white are about ½ in (12 mm) long and hang off one side of the fine, nodding stems that grow to about 12 in (30 cm) tall. The slender, strap-like foliage is glossy green. **ZONES 5–10.**

Hyacinthoides hispanica

Hyacinthus orientalis

HYACINTHUS
HYACINTH

There are 3 species in this genus of bulbs from Asia Minor and central Asia, all spring flowering. Bulbs are squat and have a tunic of fleshy scales. The glossy green leaves, which appear just as the flower spike is emerging, are narrow and strap-like while the blooms themselves are crowded onto a short spike. The individual flowers are either tubular or strongly reflexed and are sweetly and pervasively perfumed.

CULTIVATION
Plant bulbs about 4 in (10 cm) deep in autumn or at the start of winter in mild climates. Water in but do not keep watering unless winters are very dry. They do best in full sun except in climates with mild winters where some shade helps keep the bulbs cool. After bloom, bulbs can be left where they are but the following year's flowers are usually fewer and not so crowded on the spike. For a reliable display, replace bulbs in autumn every year.

Hyacinthus orientalis
Popular with gardeners all over the world, the many named varieties of hyacinth are cultivars of *Hyacinthus orientalis*, which originally comes from the Middle East and Mediterranean region. The wild form has far fewer flowers and rather more leaves than the cultivated varieties. A spike of flowers is massed atop a 12 in (30 cm) stem. The spring flowers vary enormously in color. 'King of the Blues' is a favorite cultivar, but many others are available in white, pale yellow, pink, red or purple. 'City of Haarlem' produces a strong spike of creamy yellow flowers late in the season. 'Columbus' has creamy white blossoms, long and tubular without reflexed petals. 'Lady Derby' has flowers in the softest pastel pink. **ZONES 5–9.**

Hyacinthus orientalis 'Lady Derby'

Hymenocallis caribaea

This evergreen species from the West Indies has strap-like leaves to 24 in (60 cm) long. The large flowers, about 6 in (15 cm) across, with long, narrow petals that look like white spiders perched atop glossy green foliage, appear from summer to autumn. **ZONES 10–12.**

Hymenocallis narcissiflora

syn. Ismene calathina

BASKET FLOWER, PERUVIAN DAFFODIL

Hymenocallis narcissiflora is the most widely grown species, often planted as a summer bulb like *Gladiolus*. It is native to the Peruvian Andes, and is at home in gardens of the southern hemisphere. Its broad, white flowers are very showy, with wide petals reflexed behind the green-tinged cup. The flowers appear in early summer; a pale yellow form exists. **ZONES 9–11.**

HYMENOCALLIS

syn. Ismene

SPIDER LILY, FILMY LILY, SACRED LILY OF THE INCAS

The unusual, beautiful white flowers of the spider lilies resemble daffodils except for the delicate, spider-like petals surrounding the inner corona. Native to Central and South America, there are about 40 species of *Hymenocallis*. Some are evergreen and all are deliciously scented.

CULTIVATION

Most species are tropical plants and prefer a warm, frost-free climate; in colder areas they need the shelter of a greenhouse. They can also be grown as indoor pot plants. Bulbs should be planted in winter, about 6 in (15 cm) deep in well-drained soil. A part-shaded position is best. Water very well during growth and never allow to dry out completely. Offsets form quickly and should be divided in winter.

Ipheion uniflorum

IPHEION

SPRING STARFLOWER

These small spring bulbs from Argentina present such a simple picture of starry pale blue flowers set among grassy leaves that it is hard to credit that for 160 years science has been unable to decide where they fit into the scheme of things and what their correct name should be. Since they were first described in 1830, they have been shunted from one genus to the next, been demoted to a subspecies or alternatively given a genus of their own, and been assigned no fewer than 8 generic names. Gardeners have barely had time to get used to each new name before botanists present them with a newer one.

CULTIVATION

Frost hardy, they are easily grown in any temperate climate. They prefer a sheltered position in dappled shade and well-drained soil, but can be grown in full sun in cooler areas. Propagate from offsets in late summer or early autumn.

Ipheion uniflorum

syns Brodiaea uniflora, Tristagma uniflorum, Triteleia uniflora

SPRING STARFLOWER

One of the longest blooming of the spring bulbs, each bulb of this plant produces a succession of dainty flowers on 4 in (10 cm) stems for several weeks from late winter to spring. The most common color is pastel blue, but forms are also available in white and deep, purple-tinted blue. The flowers are delicately and pleasingly scented; the grass-like leaves have a garlic odor when bruised. **ZONES 6–10.**

Iris danfordiae

IRIS

Most of the cultivated species belonging to this genus are perennials, and detailed information on the genus is given in the Annuals and Perennials chapter. However, the Dutch Hybrid irises and the other species described are included here with the bulbs, corms and tubers.

Iris aphylla

syns *Iris benacensis, I. bohemica, I. melzeri*

Native to central and eastern Europe, this bearded iris reaches only 6–12 in (15–30 cm) in height. It has broad deciduous leaves and branched flowering stems which produce up to 5 typical bearded iris flowers each in late spring and occasionally again in autumn. The flowers range in color from pale purple to a deep blue-violet, but are usually a rich dark purple. This is one of the species that have been used in the breeding of semi-dwarf and dwarf hybrids. Although it prefers good summer drainage, it is the most tolerant of winter wet of all the bearded irises. This species contains many regional varieties, some of which were once considered separate species. **ZONES 5–9.**

Iris bakeriana

Iris bakeriana

This bulbous Reticulata iris has narrow, almost cylindrical leaves that are very short at flowering time, but which grow longer later on. A solitary, pale blue flower with a dark blue blotch and a spotted, deep blue center is borne in late winter. A cold-climate species, it grows to 4 in (10 cm) in height and prefers an open, sunny, well-drained position. **ZONES 5–9.**

Iris bracteata

SISKIYOU IRIS

So called because its leaves on the flowering stems are short and bract-like, this native of Oregon inhabits dry conifer forests. Its flowers are usually predominantly cream or yellow, but some plants with reddish toned flowers exist. The falls are flared with reddish veins, and its standards are erect. The flowers are held on stems 12 in (30 cm) tall. Although frost hardy, this species is not easy to grow; it is best raised from seed. **ZONES 7–9.**

Iris danfordiae

DANFORD IRIS

This bulbous Reticulata iris, native to central Turkey, has narrow, quadrangular leaves which are very short during flowering, but later grow longer. It bears a usually solitary yellow flower with green spots on each fall in late winter. It produces masses of small bulblets and should be deeply planted. *Iris danfordiae* reaches a height of 2–4 in (5–10 cm). **ZONES 5–9.**

Iris, Dutch Hybrids

These bulbous irises of the Xiphium group derive their purity of color from the northern African *Iris tingitana*; their other main parent, *I. xiphium*, tends towards purple. They are very easy to grow and do well in temperate climates. They prefer sun and well-drained, slightly alkaline soil, but will also grow in acidic soil. Ranging in color from pale blue to almost violet, hybrids include **'Blue Magic'**, with flowers in the middle of the color range; the purplish blue **'Professor Blaauw'**, one of the most widely grown flower shop irises in the world and named for Professor A. H. Blaauw (1882–1942), whose pioneering studies led to the modern techniques of inducing irises to bloom every season of the year; and the pale, almost turquoise, **'Wedgwood'**. **ZONES 7–10.**

Iris, Dutch, 'Professor Blaauw'

Iris ensata

syn. *Iris kaempferi*

JAPANESE FLAG, HIGO IRIS

Native to Japan and cultivated there for centuries, this beardless iris grows to 3 ft (1 m) tall. It has purple flowers with yellow blotches on each fall, which appear from late spring to early summer; the leaves have a prominent midrib. The many named varieties bear huge flowers, up to 10 in (25 cm) wide, in shades of white, lavender, blue and purple, often blending 2 shades and some with double flowers. These plants prefer part-shade in hot areas, rich, acid soil and plenty of moisture, and can even grow in shallow water provided they are not submerged in winter; the foliage dies down for the winter. **'Exception'** has particularly large falls and deep purple flowers; **'Mystic Buddha'** has purple-blue flowers with red edging. **ZONES 4–10.**

Iris ensata

Iris foetidissima

STINKING IRIS, GLADWYN OR GLADDON IRIS, ROAST BEEF PLANT

This widespread European rhizomatous, beardless species is found growing in open woods, scrub and hedges. Its rich green foliage is evergreen and reaches a height of 30 in (75 cm) or more. The whole plant is fully hardy. The small flowers, which appear in late spring, are usually pale lemon to fawn or purple-gray in color and veined with brown. In winter, the plant's large green pods open to expose masses of orange seeds that are highly ornamental. Due to its ability to grow in dry shade, it is a very useful plant in cultivation. It also tolerates damp conditions. **ZONES 7–9.**

Iris germanica var. *biliottii*

Iris forrestii

A dainty, slender rhizomatous, beardless
Siberian iris, this species grows to 15 in (38 cm)
in height. Native to China and northern
Burma, it is fairly easy to grow and requires
little more than a sunny site with moist to
damp soil; it will even grow well on the margins of ponds. Its fragrant flowers, usually 2
per stem, are a soft yellow; the falls are marked
with black lines and dark brown spots along
the veins. The standards are erect or somewhat
closed in, and occasionally flushed with brown.
ZONES 6–9.

Iris germanica

COMMON FLAG, GERMAN IRIS

The putative ancestor of the modern bearded
irises, this rhizomatous, bearded species is easy
to grow in just about any temperate climate, its
creeping rhizomes multiplying rapidly into
large clumps. The sparsely branched stem produces up to 6 yellow-bearded, blue-purple to
blue-violet flowers in spring. *Iris germanica*
var. *biliottii* (syn. *Iris biliottii*) occurs naturally

in the Black Sea region of Turkey. It grows to
about 3 ft (1 m) tall and, like *I. germanica*, has
scented flowers. This variety has reddish purple
falls with standards of a more blue-purple
shade; the beard is white with yellow tips.
Another form of *I. germanica* is **'Florentina'**,
which has scented white flowers with a bluish
flush and a yellow beard. Its bracts are brown
and papery during flowering. This latter species
is cultivated in Italy, particularly around
Florence, for its perfume (orris root), which is
released when the roots are dried. An early
flowering variety, 'Florentina' prefers a position
with full sun. **ZONES 4–10.**

Iris laevigata

RABBIT-EAR IRIS

This rhizomatous, beardless species native to
Japan is similar to *Iris ensata*, but has slightly
smaller blooms and its leaves do not have a
prominent midrib. Its sparsely branched stems
bear 2 to 4 purple flowers with yellow blotches
from mid-spring to early summer. It thrives in
sun or part-shade in moist conditions, and will
also grow in shallow water all year. Both *I.
laevigata* and *I. ensata* feature in traditional
Japanese paintings. **ZONES 4–9.**

Iris germanica 'Florentina'

Iris pallida
DALMATIAN IRIS

This bearded iris from the Dalmatian region of Croatia has fragrant, pale blue flowers with yellow beards, which are borne on 4 ft (1.2 m) high stems in late spring. It is often grown as a source of orris (also obtained from *Iris germanica* 'Florentina'), a volatile substance that develops in the dried and aged rhizomes and is used in perfumes, dental preparations and breath fresheners. **'Variegata'** (syn. 'Aurea Variegata') has handsome leaves striped in gray-green and cream.
ZONES 5–10.

Iris pseudacorus
WATER FLAG, YELLOW FLAG

A robust beardless iris from Europe, the water flag has handsome, mid-green leaves and profuse bright yellow flowers on 3 ft (1 m) stems, which are borne in early spring. The flowers usually have brown or violet veining, with a darker yellow patch on the falls. It prefers to grow in shallow water and rich soil; plant in autumn in a box of rich earth and place in a sunny position in the garden pond. The cultivar **'Variegata'** has yellow- and green-striped foliage during the spring months, often turning green in summer; it is less vigorous than the species. **ZONES 5–9.**

Iris pallida

Iris pseudacorus 'Variegata'

Iris reticulata
NETTED IRIS, RETICULATED IRIS

Another highly variable species from the Caucasus region, this bulbous Reticulata iris grows to 4 in (10 cm) high when in flower. Several named varieties are available, differing mainly in the shade of blue of the showy flowers. The foliage is short during the late winter to early spring-flowering time, becoming longer after bloom. The leaves are quadrangular in cross-section and although these are often scarcely visible at flowering, some forms will have leaves taller than the flowers. It prefers sun and perfectly drained soil; it is very frost hardy and does best in cold winter climates. The flowers are scented and it makes a delightful pot plant. Some of its hybrids and forms (often crossed with *Iris histrioides*) include 'Cantab', with very pale Cambridge-blue flowers; 'Edward', which has a rich, dark blue flower with orange marks; 'Gordon', with its light blue flowers with an orange blotch on a white background; 'Joyce', which has lavender-blue standards and sky blue falls marked with gray-brown and yellow; and 'Purple Gem', which has flowers with violet standards and very dark purple falls blotched with lighter purple and white. **ZONES 3–10.**

Iris setosa subsp. *canadensis*

This subspecies of a more widely spread species is found from Newfoundland to Ontario and south to Maine in North America. It grows to 24 in (60 cm) tall, although it is often shorter. A beardless iris, it flowers from late spring to early summer. Its flowers are usually solitary and are lavender-blue in color. This is a tough, easy-to-grow plant ideal for rock gardens. **ZONES 3–9.**

Iris sibirica
SIBERIAN FLAG

Despite the name, this well-known species has a natural distribution across temperate Eurasia from France to Lake Baikal. It is one of the most popular beardless irises, usually found in gardens in one of its cultivars rather than its wild form. The plants make strongly vertical clumps of slender bright green leaves 2–4 ft (0.6–1.2 m) high. In late spring or early summer, flowering stems rise above the foliage with narrow-petalled, blue, purple or white flowers, often veined in a deeper color. It prefers full sun to very light shade (particularly in hot areas), a moderately moist, rich soil that may be slightly acid and water during the hottest periods. It will grow in a wet soil and does best in cold-winter climates. Some of the available cultivars include 'Cleave Dodge', with mid-blue flowers; 'Perry's Blue', which has rich lilac-blue flowers with yellow markings and netted brown towards the base of the falls; 'Ruby', with purplish blue flowers; 'White Swirl', which has pure white flowers with yellow at the base and flared, rounded petals; and 'Vi Luihn', with flowers in a rich violet shade. **ZONES 4–9.**

Iris sibirica

Ixia maculata
YELLOW IXIA

The yellow ixia is
the most commonly
grown species. It has
wiry stems and grows
to 18 in (45 cm) tall
and 1½–2 in (3.5–
5 cm) wide. The 2 in
(5 cm) flowers are
clustered along the
top, and have pur-
plish, brown or black
centers and orange to
yellow petals, some-
times with pinkish
red undersides. Gar-
den forms come in
white, yellow, pink,
orange or red.
ZONES 9–10.

Ixia maculata, garden form

IXIA
AFRICAN CORN LILY

This genus of 40 to 50 deciduous cormous perennials is confined to the
winter rainfall region of South Africa. They produce masses of delightful, star-shaped flowers on wiry stems in spring and early summer—these
flowers close in the evening and on cloudy days; the leaves are usually
long and slender. The tallest species grows to 24 in (60 cm).

CULTIVATION
Marginally frost hardy, they are easy to grow in temperate to warm
areas. In frost-prone areas, they should be grown in a cool greenhouse or
they can be lifted and stored during winter. Plant bulbs in early autumn
in well-drained soil. Bonemeal mixed into the soil before planting will
help produce good blooms. A sunny position is ideal, except in warm
areas where they need protection from hot sun. Water well through winter and spring, but allow to dry out after flowering. Plants are suitable
for containers. Propagate from offsets in autumn. If sown from seed in
autumn, they should flower in the third year.

LEUCOJUM
SNOWFLAKE

Leucojum autumnale

This genus consists of 10 species of bulbous perennials, resembling the snowdrop, which bear delightful flowers that bloom in spring and autumn. They are native to North Africa and the southern Mediterranean. The pendent, bell-shaped flowers consist of 6 petals, borne singly or in twos and threes at the top of a thin stem growing up to 24 in (60 cm). The mid-green to deep green leaves are narrow and strap-like. Bulbs multiply freely, and large clumps of nodding blooms make a glorious display.

CULTIVATION
Some of the species prefer part-shade in moist soil, while others thrive in sunny positions with well-drained soil; they are moderately to fully frost hardy. The bulbs should be planted in late summer or early autumn and only lifted for dividing when they produce few flowers and many leaves. Propagate from offsets in spring or early autumn or from seed sown in autumn.

Leucojum aestivum
SUMMER SNOWFLAKE, GIANT SNOWFLAKE

This dainty, spring-flowering bulb is native to Europe and western Asia. The fragrant flowers are white with a green spot near the tip of each petal and are borne in clusters atop 18 in (45 cm) stems. The blue-green leaves are long and slender. Frost hardy, the small bulbs are best planted under a deciduous tree. *Leucojum aestivum* var. *pulchellum* is found in the wild near or in water in the southern parts of Europe and western Asia. Growing to a height of 24 in (60 cm), it naturalizes freely in similar situations and climates and grows in sun or shade. The flowers, 3 to 6 per stalk, carry 6 white, green-spotted petals of equal length and appear in late spring and early summer. The strap-shaped leaves, which are poisonous to stock, form voluminous clumps. **ZONES 4–10.**

Leucojum autumnale
AUTUMN SNOWFLAKE

This species has delicate white flowers flushed with pink that appear singly or in twos and threes at the top of a thin, 10 in (25 cm) high stem. Its erect, very fine basal leaves, which usually follow the flowers, add to the plant's dainty air. As both common and scientific names imply, the flowers appear in late summer or early autumn. The bulbs should be planted 2 in (5 cm) deep in well-drained soil in a sunny position. **ZONES 5–10.**

Leucojum vernum
SPRING SNOWFLAKE

A native of central Europe that blooms in late winter and early spring, this species grows to a height of 18 in (45 cm). The plant naturalizes freely in damp conditions, in sun or shade, and survives dry summers in style. The attractive leaves are strap-like and the bell-shaped flowers, 2 to a stalk, carry white petals of equal length that are marked with either a green or yellow spot. **ZONES 5–10.**

Leucojum aestivum var. *pulchellum*

Lilium, Asiatic Hybrids

These have been bred from various central and west Asian species and form, by far, the largest hybrid group. They include most of the varieties grown commercially as cut flowers or potted plants as well as the widely grown Mid-Century hybrids. Most, however, lack fragrance. The group has been divided into 3 sub-groups: upward-facing, outward-facing and downward-facing. 'Red Carpet' is a strong-growing variety with deep red, upward-facing flowers. 'Connecticut Lemon Glow' is a popular cut-flower variety with bright yellow, unspotted, outward-facing flowers and quite short stems, usually only 18 in (45 cm) tall. 'Rosemary North' produces dull buff-orange, downward- facing flowers that are pendulous with recurving petals and are scented. **ZONES 5–10.**

LILIUM

LILY, LILIUM

Many plants are referred to as 'lilies', usually signifying that they belong to the lily family or one of its allied families, but in the narrowest sense this word means a member of the bulbous genus *Lilium*; this consists of around 100 species, native in temperate Eurasia (extending to high mountains of the Philippines) and North America, with the largest number found in China and the Himalayas. All species grow from buried bulbs consisting of overlapping fleshy scales which do not encircle one another as in the classical onion-type bulb. The stems are elongated with spirally arranged or whorled leaves that vary from narrow and grass-like to very short and broad. One to many 6-petalled flowers are borne in terminal sprays, the blooms erect, nodding or pendent and often with strongly recurved petals—the so-called 'Turk's cap' type.

Lilies vary both in their growth habit, their method of reproduction and the shape, size and color of their flowers. The great majority flower in summer. Lilies have been extensively hybridized, especially in recent years. A formal classification of hybrids was published in 1968 but more recent hybridizing and the introduction of tetraploid varieties has already blurred the distinctions between the various groups.

CULTIVATION

Lilium bulbs, unlike those of many other genera, have no outer protective coat so should be out of the ground for the shortest possible time. The most important requirement of lilies is good drainage. A few have a preference for an alkaline soil, others will not tolerate it. Almost all like sun but a cool root area, which means they should be planted quite deeply; a general guide is to plant so that there is a minimum of 4 in (10 cm) of soil over the bulb. Most can be left undisturbed for many years and allowed to multiply naturally. Liliums can be propagated by means of offsets from the main bulb, from bulb scales or seed or, in some species, from bulbils which form in the leaf axils up the stem.

Lilium, Asiatic Hybrid, 'Red Carpet'

Lilium bulbiferum

This species from southern Europe has upward-facing 4–6 in (10–15 cm) wide flowers, bright orange to fire red in color, with the inside of the petals spotted dark maroon. It grows to a height of 4 ft (1.2 m), bears 15 to 20 flowers on each stem, and produces bulbils in the leaf axils on the upper part of the stem. The leaves are short and dark green. *Lilium bulbiferum* var. *croceum,* from Italy, southern Germany and France, has orange flowers. **ZONES 7–10.**

Lilium bulbiferum

Lilium formosanum

Native to Taiwan, this species grows up to 6 ft (1.8 m) and flowers in late summer. The trumpet-shaped flowers have recurving, highly fragrant petals, pure white on the inside, pink or purple-brown on the outside. Up to 20 cm (8 in) long, the glossy, narrow leaves can cover the whole stem. It is easily grown from seed. **ZONES 5–11.**

Lilium formosanum

Lilium lancifolium

Lilium lancifolium

syn. Lilium tigrinum

TIGER LILY

This species from Japan, Korea and eastern China is one of the most widely grown and also one of the oldest in cultivation. It grows to a height of 4 ft (1.2 m) and produces numerous bright orange pendulous flowers, spotted with purple on the lower parts of the petals, in mid-to late summer. The stems are black and large quantities of dark purple bulbils are produced in the leaf axils. This vigorous lily thrives even in poor soils; its bulbs and flower buds are food items in Japan and China. **ZONES 4–10.**

Lilium martagon

COMMON TURK'S CAP LILY

This species grows to 6 ft (1.8 m) and can produce as many as 50 blooms. The flowers are pendulous and generally creamy white to pale purple with darker spots, although many forms exist, some with deep burgundy or mahogany-red flowers. It is fully frost hardy and will grow in sun or shade. *Lilium martagon* var. *album* bears pure white flowers. **ZONES 4–10.**

Lilium, Oriental Hybrid, 'Yasuko'

Lilium, Oriental Hybrids

Lilium martagon

Not to be confused with the so-called Asiatic hybrids, these are hybrids bred from East Asian species such as *Lilium auratum*, *L. speciosum* and *L. japonicum* and include hybrids between these and *L. henryi*. They are late flowering and may carry several flowerheads on one stem, which are inclined to make them top heavy and in need of support. All are intolerant of lime. There are 4 sub-groups: trumpet-shaped flowers, bowl-shaped flowers, flat-faced flowers and recurved flowers (rarely grown). 'Stargazer' has upward-facing, bowl-shaped flowers of rich crimson with darker spots, and paler on the margins of the petals, and is one of the most commonly grown of the Oriental hybrids. 'Yasuko' has flat-faced flowers, which are up to 10 in (25 cm) in diameter with a fine fragrance. 'Acapulco' has flat-faced flowers which are a vivid hot pink color. 'Shooting Star' is a variety with sturdy stems and recurved flowers with sharply reflexed petals, cerise in color and 4 in (10 cm) across. **ZONES 6–10.**

LYCORIS

SPIDER LILY, SURPRISE LILY

With spider-like flowers, these 10 to 12 species of
East Asian amaryllids are rather like the better
known nerines but are mostly more robust plants.
The strap-like foliage of these bulbs dies back during summer, reappearing after they bloom in summer or early autumn. Each smooth stem carries an
umbel of trumpet-shaped flowers with narrow,
strongly recurved petals that usually have wavy
margins; long, showy stamens and styles add to a
spidery appearance.

Lycoris radiata

CULTIVATION

Plant bulbs in a sunny position in rich, well-drained soil. Water
during their winter growing season but they need warm, dry
conditions when dormant. Only moderately frost hardy, they
need protection from cold winds. Clumps are best left undisturbed for a few years; they can then be divided when dormant
in summer. They may also be propagated from seed.

Lycoris radiata

RED SPIDER LILY

From China and Japan, this is
the most commonly grown
species. The red spider lily has
12–18 in (30–45 cm) stems,
and in late summer or early
autumn bears clusters of 4 or
5 rose red, 2–3 in (5–8 cm)
wide flowers with strongly
curled petals and very long,
slightly upward-curving
stamens. **ZONES 7–10.**

Mirabilis jalapa

Mirabilis jalapa

MARVEL OF PERU, FOUR-O'CLOCK FLOWER

This bushy tuberous perennial, indigenous to tropical
America, is grown for its
fragrant, trumpet-shaped,
crimson, pink, white or yellow
flowers that open in the late
afternoon and remain open all
night, closing again at dawn.
It is good as a pot or bedding
plant or as a dwarf hedge.
Summer flowering, it grows to
around 3 ft (1 m) high with a
spread of 24–30 in (60–75 cm).
ZONES 8–11.

MIRABILIS

UMBRELLA WORT

This Central and South American genus consists of about 50
species of annuals or herbaceous perennials that make showy
garden plants in virtually frost-free climates. Some can become
invasive and difficult to eradicate as they can be quite deep
rooted. The flowers are often brightly colored and in one case
at least, are variegated in bold colors like magenta and orange.
Most have a pleasant fragrance.

CULTIVATION

In frost-free and dry tropical climates, they are quite easy plants
to grow. All that is required is a sunny, well-drained aspect. In
colder climates, the tubers of perennial species can be lifted and
stored over winter like dahlias. Propagate from seed or by division of the tubers.

Muscari neglectum

MUSCARI

GRAPE HYACINTH

The 30 or so species of this genus are natives of the Mediterranean region and western Asia. The slender, strap-like leaves appear soon after planting, as the summer dormancy period is very short. Spikes 4 in (10 cm) long bear grape-like clusters of bright blue, pale blue, pale yellow or white flowers in early spring.

CULTIVATION

Frost hardy, they prefer cool areas. They look best in clumps and need rich, well-drained soil. Plant the bulbs in autumn in a sunny or part-shaded position, but protect from hot sun in warm areas. The rapidly multiplying clumps should spread freely and are best left undisturbed for a few years. Divide overcrowded bulbs or grow from seed.

Muscari armeniacum

Growing to about 8 in (20 cm) high and 2 in (5 cm) wide, *Muscari armeniacum* is one of the best loved of spring bulbs. The flowers may be blue or white and there are several named cultivars, of which **'Heavenly Blue'**, with its delicate, musky fragrance, is the best known; it is sometimes assigned to *Muscari botryoides*. **'Blue Spike'** bears clusters of rounded, bell-shaped double blooms; the flowers, borne on 8 in (20 cm) stems, are blue rimmed with white. **ZONES 4–10.**

Muscari botryoides

This species from central and southeastern Europe is one of several species that could be defined as a classical grape hyacinth. It grows to about 8 in (20 cm) tall with semi-erect, channeled, mid-green leaves and spherical, bright blue flowers with a white constricted mouth. **'Album'** bears racemes of scented white flowers. **ZONES 3–10.**

Muscari neglectum

syn. *Muscari racemosum*

COMMON GRAPE HYACINTH

This is a variable species native to Europe, North Africa and southwestern Asia. The tiny urn-shaped flowers are deep blue to blue-black with a white mouth. The leaves can be erect or spreading, and are bright green, sometimes stained red at soil level. **ZONES 4–10.**

Muscari armeniacum

Narcissus bulbocodium

NARCISSUS

DAFFODIL, NARCISSUS

Members of this well-known genus of bulbs from Europe, Asia and North Africa are easy to grow, multiply freely and bloom year after year. The wild species number about 50 and are mostly native to the western Mediterranean region. Many thousands of cultivars have been named, and horticultural authorities have grouped these into 12 divisions or classes, the first 4 of which are the most important: Trumpet narcissi (Division 1), which have trumpets as long as the outer petals or perianth; the Large-cupped narcissi (Division 2), with trumpets from one-third to two-thirds as long; the Small-cupped narcissi (Division 3), with trumpets less than one-third the length of the petals; and the Double-flowered narcissi (Division 4) with double flowers, either one or several per stem. Divisions 5 to 9 cover hybrids and cultivars of important species such as *Narcissus triandrus*, *N. cyclamineus*, *N. jonquilla*, *N. tazetta* and *N. poeticus* respectively; Division 10 covers the wild species (which in this book is listed separately); Division 11 the split-corona hybrids; and Division 12 consists of daffodils not included in any other division, such as *N. bulbocodium* hybrids. The flower colors range from white to yellow, although individual varieties may have white, yellow, red, orange or pink trumpets.

CULTIVATION

Frost hardiness of these bulbs varies, but all tolerate at least light frosts and they grow best in cool areas. Plant in autumn, 4–6 in (10–15 cm) deep in rich, well-drained soil. They enjoy full sun in cool areas, and some shade in warmer areas. Water well during growth and allow to dry out once the leaves die down. Remove spent flowers. Clumps will multiply freely and should be left undisturbed for a few years; thereafter lift and divide in autumn.

Narcissus bulbocodium
HOOP-PETTICOAT DAFFODIL

This species, widespread in the western Mediterranean, grows to 6 in (15 cm) and has many forms. Bright yellow flowers, with a long trumpet and sharply reflexed, usually insignificant petals, appear in spring. **ZONES 6–9.**

Narcissus Cultivars

Narcissus, Trumpet daffodils (Division 1)

These are the best known of all the daffodils with their solitary large flowers and long trumpets. They are derived mainly from the wild daffodil *Narcissus pseudonarcissus*. There are innumerable named cultivars, which may be all yellow, white with yellow trumpets, all white, or white with pale pink trumpets. They are the first of the big daffodils to flower. 'King Alfred', raised in 1890, is the classic cultivar, but its name has been very loosely applied. 'Arctic Gold', 'Las Vegas' and 'Dutch Master' are among the most popular. **ZONES 4–10.**

Narcissus, Division 1, 'Las Vegas'

Narcissus, Division 4, 'Tahiti'

Narcissus, Large-cupped daffodils (Division 2)

Flowering a week or two later than the trumpets, this large division has many named varieties. They originate mainly from the cross *Narcissus poeticus* × *pseudonarcissus* (or *N.* × *incomparabilis*). The popular pink-cupped cultivars with their white perianths mostly belong here, but there are many others in various combinations of white or yellow perianths with cups in white, yellow, orange or red. '**Exotic Pink**' and '**Ice Follies**' are popular. **ZONES 4–10.**

Narcissus, Small-cupped daffodils (Division 3)

Of similar origin to Division 2, these resemble the Trumpet and Large-cupped daffodils except for smaller cups. Like them, they come in many named cultivars. They flower at the same time as the Large-cupped types. The most popular include '**Merlin**', '**Amore**' and '**St Keverne**'. **ZONES 4–10.**

Narcissus, Double-flowered daffodils (Division 4)

These daffodils can have either a solitary large flower or several smaller ones, with the perianth segments or the corona, or both, doubled. The double-flowered daffodils are less popular than many other types because they tend to be late flowering and their buds will not open properly if they have undergone dry conditions while developing. '**Acropolis**', '**Tahiti**' and '**Unique**' are among the most popular. **ZONES 4–10.**

Narcissus, Triandrus daffodils (Division 5)

The type species *Narcissus triandrus* is native to Spain; it is rarely cultivated but this division includes garden forms of the species. All have pendent, nodding flowers, a straight-edged cup and slightly reflexed petals. There are usually several blooms per stem. The forms vary in height from 6 to 18 in (15 to 45 cm). '**Hawera**' and '**Thalia**' are among the most popular. **ZONES 4–9.**

Narcissus, Division 3, 'Amore'

Narcissus, Division 7, 'Suzy'

Narcissus, Cyclamineus daffodils (Division 6)

These hybrids bear the characteristics of *Narcissus cyclamineus* and grow to 15 in (38 cm) high. Their trumpet-shaped cups are longer than those of *N. triandrus*, and their petals are narrow and strongly reflexed. They flower in early to mid-spring. Popular hybrids are 'February Gold', 'Dove Wings', 'Tête-à-Tête' and 'Charity May'. **ZONES 6–9.**

Narcissus, Jonquilla daffodils (Division 7)

Possessing the characteristics of the wild jonquil of southern Europe and northern Africa, *Narcissus jonquilla*, these narcissi are scented, with the cups shorter than the flat petals. There are often 2 or more blooms on a stem, which grows to 15 in (38 cm). '**Suzy**', 'Trevithian' and 'Sweetness' are among the most popular. **ZONES 4–9.**

Narcissus, Division 9, 'Cantabile'

Narcissus, Poeticus daffodils (Division 9)

This is a late spring- to early summer-flowering division showing the features of *Narcissus poeticus* of southern Europe. The plants grow to 18 in (45 cm) and produce one, sometimes two, blooms per stem. The petals are white and the small cup often has a frilled red or orange rim. '**Actaea**' and '**Cantabile**' are among the most popular. **ZONES 4–9.**

Narcissus, Wild species and variants (Division 10)

Horticultural societies have decreed that all the wild *Narcissus* species be lumped under this division, at the tail end of the daffodils. In this book, though, the wild species included is listed separately. **ZONES 6–9.**

Narcissus, Split-corona daffodils (Division 11)

Characterized by having coronas or cups that are split along at least a third of their length, these narcissi are also referred to as Collar, Papillon, Orchid or Split-cupped daffodils. The edges of the split coronas bend back towards the petals, and are sometimes frilled. They all flower in spring. The best known include '**Baccarat**', '**Ahoy**', '**Palmares**' and '**Orangery**'. **ZONES 4–10.**

Narcissus, Division 11, 'Palmares'

ORNITHOGALUM

STAR-OF-BETHLEHEM

This large genus contains 80 or so species of spring- to summer-flowering bulbs native to Africa, Europe and western Asia. Star- to cup-shaped, mostly white and sometimes scented flowers are borne on short to tall stems. The leaves, occasionally striped silver down the center, are all basal. The sap may irritate the skin.

CULTIVATION
Marginally to moderately frost hardy, these plants are easy to grow. Plant bulbs in autumn or spring in well-drained soil. They like full sun but will need part-shade in warm areas. Keep the plants moist until the leaves begin to die off, and dry when dormant. Frost-tender species should be lifted in winter. They multiply quite freely and clumps should be divided every 1 to 2 years to prevent overcrowding. Propagate also from seed sown in autumn or spring.

Ornithogalum umbellatum

COMMON STAR-OF-BETHLEHEM

The leaves of this frost-hardy, clump-forming perennial are mid-green with a central white stripe. The loose clusters of white flowers with green striping appear at the top of the 12 in (30 cm), erect stems in early summer and open only in sunshine. This species can become invasive. **ZONES 5–10.**

Ornithogalum umbellatum

OXALIS

WOOD-SORREL

This is a large genus of 500 or so species of bulbous, rhizoma-tous and fibrous-rooted perennials and a few small, weak shrubs. Though found around the world, the greatest number of *Oxalis* species are native to South Africa and South America. Some have become garden and greenhouse weeds which, though pretty in flower, have given a bad name to the genus; the species listed here is more restrained in growth and makes a choice ad-dition to the garden. The leaves are always compound, divided into 3 or more heart-shaped or more deeply 2-lobed leaflets in a palmate arrangement (like clover). The funnel-shaped flowers are usually pink, white or yellow, and are carried in an umbel-like cluster on slender stalks.

Oxalis adenophylla

CULTIVATION

Most species grow from bulbs or corms, which multiply readily.
A position in sun or part-shade suits most of them, along with a
mulched, well-drained soil and moderate water. Propagate by
division of the bulbs or from seed in autumn.

Oxalis adenophylla

This bulbous species from the southern Andes of South America
makes a small mound to 3 in (8 cm) high. The leaves consist of
up to 12 two-lobed leaflets. Suitable for a rockery, it bears open,
purple-pink flowers with darker centers from late spring to early
summer. **ZONES 5–9.**

Paradisea liliastrum

In early summer, this species
bears racemes of 4 to 10, 1–
2 in (2.5–5 cm) long, scented,
white, funnel-shaped flowers
blooming on wiry, 12–24 in
(30–60 cm) stems. The
strappy, grayish green leaves
are arranged in a basal rosette. It is a beautiful plant
but not always amenable to
cultivation. **ZONES 7–9.**

PARADISEA

ST BRUNO'S LILY, PARADISE LILY

This genus consists of 2 species of rhizomatous perennials from
the mountains of southern Europe. They form small clumps of
grassy to strap-like, bright green leaves and from late spring produce erect stems topped with heads of 6-petalled, funnel- to bell-
shaped white flowers up to 1½ in (35 mm) long. The flower
stems are from 1 to 5 ft (0.3 to 1.5 m) tall, depending on the
species, and carry 4 to 25 blooms.

CULTIVATION

Both species will tolerate moderate frosts and prefer to be
grown in moist, humus-rich soil in full sun, though they do not
always respond well to cultivation. They must not dry out in
summer. Propagate from seed or by dividing well-established
clumps.

Paris tetraphylla
syn. *Paris quadrifolia*

This very frost-hardy species from Eurasia, which grows to 15 in (38 cm) in height, bears its star-shaped, green and white flowers in late spring. The mid-green leaves are 2–6 in (5–15 cm) long. **ZONES 8–10.**

PARIS
syn. *Daiswa*

This genus consists of 20 species of herbaceous, rhizomatous perennials and is closely related to the trilliums. It is found from Europe to eastern Asia. They form clumps and their leaves are carried in whorls at the top of stems up to 3 ft (1 m) long. Unlike trilliums, the 1–4 in (2.5–10 cm) long, oval to lance-shaped leaves are not always in 3s, but in groups of 4 to 12, depending on the species. The flowers, borne singly at the stem tips in spring and summer, have 4 to 6 petals and sepals that are usually green or yellow-green.

CULTIVATION
Plant in cool, moist, woodland conditions in dappled shade. Most species are vigorous and are not difficult to cultivate. They are very frost hardy. Propagate from seed or by dividing established clumps. Divide only every 3 to 4 years or the plants may be weakened.

Paris tetraphylla

PUSCHKINIA
STRIPED SQUILL, LEBANON SQUILL

This is a genus containing a single species, a strappy-leafed bulb native to the Caucasus, Turkey, northern Iran, northern Iraq and Lebanon. Resembling a small hyacinth *(Scilla)*, it has flower stems up to 8 in (20 cm) tall. The tubular flowers are pale blue with darker stripes and about ½ in (12 mm) long.

CULTIVATION
A tough little bulb well suited to rockeries or pots, squill prefers a climate with a distinct winter and a cool summer. Grow in full sun in well-drained soil. It naturalizes well where conditions suit it. Propagate from seed or by division of well-established clumps.

Puschkinia scilloides
syns *Puschkinia libanotica, P. sicula*

Reaching a height of 4–8 in (10–20 cm), this spring-flowering bulb has 2 semi-erect, mid-green, basal, strap-like leaves and a slim spike of up to 6 pale blue, star-shaped flowers with a darker line down the petals. The small, hyacinth-like flowers have a strong scent. **ZONES 5–9.**

Ranunculus ficaria, orange form

Ranunculus ficaria
LESSER CELANDINE, PILEWORT

From southwestern Asia, Europe and northwestern Africa, this perennial has single, almost cup-shaped, bright yellow flowers that appear in spring. It reaches only 2 in (5 cm) in height, and has glossy green leaves with silver or gold markings; the leaves die down after the flowers appear. 'Albus' has single, creamy white flowers with glossy petals. 'Brazen Hussy' has deep bronze-green leaves and shiny, deep golden-yellow flowers. **ZONES 5–10.**

RANUNCULUS

Most of the species belonging to this genus are perennials, and detailed information on the genus is given in the Annuals and Perennials chapter. However, *Ranunculus asiaticus* and *R. ficaria* are included here with the bulbs, corms and tubers.

Ranunculus asiaticus
PERSIAN BUTTERCUP

This frost-hardy perennial from the Mediterranean region is parent to many hybrids and cultivars. Masses of single or double flowers are borne on 15 in (38 cm) stems in spring, in many colors including yellow, orange, red, pink and white. The **Bloomingdale Hybrids** are an 8 in (20 cm) strain bred specially for growing in pots. **ZONES 9–10.**

Ranunculus a., Bloomingdale Hybrid

Roscoea cautleoides

Roscoea cautleoides

Bearing its yellow or orange flowers in summer, this frost-hardy species from China grows to 10 in (25 cm) tall with a 6 in (15 cm) spread. The glossy leaves are lance-shaped and erect and wrap into a hollow, stem-like structure at their base.

ZONES 6–9.

ROSCOEA

These 18 species of tuberous perennials from China and the Himalayas are related to ginger *(Zingiber)*, but in appearance are more reminiscent of irises. They are grown for their orchid-like flowers, which have hooded upper petals, wide-lobed lower lips and 2 narrower petals. The leaves are lance-shaped and erect. They are most suitable for open borders and rock and woodland gardens.

CULTIVATION

They prefer part-shade and cool, fertile, humus-rich soil that should be kept moist but well drained in summer. Provide a top-dressing of leafmold or well-rotted compost in winter, when the plants die down. Propagate from seed or by division.

SCHIZOSTYLIS

A single species of grassy-leafed, rhizomatous perennial makes up this genus. It is widely distributed in South Africa where it grows beside streams. The long, flowering stems terminate in clusters of bowl-shaped, 6-petalled flowers in deep scarlet and pink; it is an excellent cut flower.

CULTIVATION

Frost hardy, it prefers full sun and fertile, moist soil with shelter from the cold in cool-temperate climates. Divide every couple of years when it becomes crowded or propagate from seed in spring.

Schizostylis coccinea 'Grandiflora'

Schizostylis coccinea
CRIMSON FLAG

This variable species can fail in prolonged dry conditions. The sword-shaped leaves are green and are untidy unless pruned regularly and protected from thrips and slugs. It is valued for its late summer and autumn display, which in some climates, conditions and seasons can extend into winter and beyond. The flowers are usually scarlet. It is a dainty plant reaching a height of 24 in (60 cm) and spread of 12 in (30 cm). Several named varieties are available in shades of pink, including the rose-pink **'Mrs Hegarty'**, the salmon-pink **'Sunrise'** and the crimson **'Grandiflora'** (syns 'Gigantea', 'Major'). **'Viscountess Byng'** has pale pink flowers with narrow petals. **ZONES 6–10.**

Scilla peruviana 'Alba'

SCILLA

SQUILL, BLUEBELL

This genus of about 90 species of bulbous perennials from Europe, Asia and Africa has terminal racemes of usually blue flowers in spring, although they also come in pink, purple and white. Varying from 2 to 20 in (5 to 50 cm) in height, their tiny, usually star-shaped flowers are clustered above strap-shaped leaves. They look good naturalized under trees or in lawns.

CULTIVATION

Most are adaptable to cold-winter climates and naturalize with ease in lawns and gardens. All should be planted in autumn in average soil in full sun to light shade. Divide in late summer when clumps become crowded, or propagate from seed.

Scilla mischtschenkoana

syn. *Scilla tubergeniana*

This winter-flowering species from northwestern Iran, Georgia, Armenia and Azerbaijan has pale blue to white flowers with dark centers occurring on erect, terminal spikes. It reaches 4 in (10 cm) in height. The leaves are long, narrow and clump forming. **ZONES 6–9.**

Scilla peruviana

CUBAN LILY, WILD HYACINTH, PERUVIAN SCILLA

This plant has a dense cluster of up to 50 star-shaped flowers that are borne in summer on a 12 in (30 cm) long stem. The 1 in (25 mm) wide flowers are usually blue, sometimes white or purple. The dark to olive green foliage is glossy and strap-like. **'Alba'** bears white flowers. **ZONES 6–10.**

Scilla siberica

SIBERIAN SQUILL

In established patches of this Siberian species, rich blue flowers on loose racemes are produced in such quantity as to color the ground blue. The flowers appear in early to mid-spring on 6 in (15 cm) long stems. The foliage dies soon after flowering finishes. It spreads rapidly by division of bulbs and from seed, and does not do well where winters are mild. **ZONES 3–9.**

Scilla verna

SEA ONION, SPRING SCILLA

Blunt, concave leaves up to 8 in (20 cm) long appear before the heads of 6 to 12 bluish flowers on this species. The flowerheads are not as tall as the leaves, but the leaves arch away from the flowers so that the blooms are well displayed. **ZONES 6–9.**

Scilla verna

STERNBERGIA
AUTUMN CROCUS, AUTUMN DAFFODIL

This genus of 8 species of flowering bulbs ranges from Italy across to Iran. They have large, crocus-like flowers that appear in spring or autumn and are related to daffodils, the bulbs in fact looking like small daffodil bulbs.

CULTIVATION

They need a hot, sunny site in well-drained soil and should be planted against a sunny wall in cool climates. If left undisturbed they will form clumps. Propagate by division in spring or autumn.

Sternbergia lutea

Sternbergia lutea

This species is native to the Mediterranean region. The buttercup-yellow flowers are 2 in (5 cm) long and are borne singly on 6 in (15 cm) stems in autumn. The slender leaves are strap-like. It is only just frost hardy and needs warm, dry conditions when dormant in summer; it is best grown in pots in areas with wet summers and makes an excellent plant in a rock garden. **ZONES 7–10.**

TIGRIDIA
TIGER FLOWER

This genus contains about 35 species of cormous plants native to Central and South America. The distinctive flowers inspire admiration for their strikingly spotted centers and 3 bold outer petals in red, orange, pink, yellow, purple or white. They are short lived, usually each lasting only a day, but they make up for this by blooming in succession for weeks during summer.

CULTIVATION

Tigridias are subtropical plants but will tolerate light frosts. In cooler areas, the corms should be lifted and stored during winter or the plants grown in a greenhouse. They need a position in full sun in well-drained soil; water amply in summer. Propagate from seed in spring.

Tigridia pavonia

Tigridia pavonia
JOCKEY'S CAP LILY, PEACOCK FLOWER, TIGER FLOWER

This Mexican native blooms in summer. The 6 in (15 cm) triangular flowers are usually red with a purple-spotted, yellow center and are borne on 24 in (60 cm) stems. The foliage is iris-like, sword-shaped and pleated. **ZONES 8–10.**

Trillium grandiflorum

SNOW TRILLIUM, WAKE ROBIN

This showy, clump-forming trillium is the easiest to grow, reaching 12–18 in (30–45 cm) in height. The pure white flowers, borne in spring, fade to pink as they age. The double-flowered white form, 'Flore Pleno' has arching stems and oval, dark green leaves; this is a beautiful form but seldom found in gardens **ZONES 3–9.**

Trillium sessile

TOAD-SHADE, WAKE ROBIN

This upright, clump-forming perennial reaches 12–15 in (30–38 cm) in height with a spread of 12–18 in (30–45 cm). It has deep green leaves marbled with pale green, gray and maroon. They bear stalkless, maroon flowers with lance-shaped petals in late spring. *Trillium sessile* var. *californicum* bears white flowers. **ZONES 4–9.**

Trillium grandiflorum 'Flore Pleno'

TRILLIUM

WAKE ROBIN, WOOD LILY

This genus of the lily family is described in detail in the chapter on Annuals and Perennials. The bulbous perennials listed here are popular in gardens.

Trillium sessile var. *californicum*

TRITELEIA

The name of this bulb genus of 15 species comes from the Latin *tri* meaning 'three parts', and refers to the fact that the flowers are arranged in threes. The genus is closely related to *Brodiaea*, under which name species are often listed. Most are native to the west coast of North America. They usually produce grass-like foliage, with the onion-like leaves often dying before the flowerheads appear. The well-held umbels of starry flowers, usually borne in late spring, are blue and resemble alliums.

CULTIVATION

These bulbs like moist, well-drained soil, with drier conditions from late summer to early autumn; they should never be water-logged. Plant where there is full sun for at least part of the day during the growing period. In cold areas, they may need some winter protection. The corms, which should be planted in a sunny but sheltered position in autumn, can be dry-stored during the mid- to late summer dormancy.

Triteleia laxa
syn. Brodiaea laxa
GRASS NUT, TRIPLET LILY, ITHURIEL'S SPUR

This popular and easily grown plant has flowers varying between milky blue and purple blue. It has the largest flower umbels—up to 6 in (15 cm) in diameter—of any species in the genus. The umbels, however, are not as tight as in other species, with flower stalks over 2 in (5 cm) long. The flowers are borne from late spring to early summer; the stems are strong and wiry. '**Queen Fabiola**' is a little taller and has even stronger stems. **ZONES 7–10.**

Triteleia laxa 'Queen Fabiola'

Tulbaghia violacea 'Silver Lace'

TULBAGHIA

This is an African genus of 20 rhizomatous, tuberous or cormous perennials. The plants are generally evergreen with clump-forming, narrow leaves. The dainty flowers, which are carried in long-stalked umbels, appear spasmodically over a long period during the warmer months. Some species are onion scented; others smell pleasantly of hyacinths.

CULTIVATION

When consideration is given to their native habitat, these plants withstand moderate frost, provided the drainage is good and there is protection from cold, wet winds. They need full sun and moisture while the foliage is developing; water should be withheld once the flowers appear. Propagate from offsets, which can be removed while the plant is dormant.

Tulbaghia violacea
SOCIETY GARLIC

Robust and clump-forming, this plant grows to 30 in (75 cm) in height. It thrives in dry- or wet-summer climates, in a garden bed or container, and exudes a garlic-like odor. The flowers range from deep lilac to white and appear sporadically between mid-spring and late autumn. The narrow, gray-green leaves are more or less evergreen. It is good as a border plant or in a rock garden. The bulbs are edible. '**Silver Lace**' is a variegated form with leaves that are edged white. It is slightly less robust than the species. **ZONES 7–10.**

TULIPA

TULIP

Tulipa cultivars

Tulips are one of the world's major commercial flower crops, both for cut flowers and horticulture. Wild species of these bulbs come from central and western Asia. They were introduced into Europe in about 1554 and have been popular ever since. There are more than 100 species of *Tulipa*, but most of those we know are cultivars of only a few species, chiefly *Tulipa gesneriana*. Tulips sport freely and the origin of many very old tulips is unknown. Cultivars run into thousands, with new ones being developed every year. Their names sometimes vary between different countries. Modern revisions of cultivars have led to our present set of 15 groups or divisions. Characteristics are those which are produced in the Royal General Bulbgrowers' Association (KAVB) trial garden in Holland; they are classified according to characteristics such as stem length, flower features and time of flowering. By choosing bulbs from across the groups, you can have a sequence of flowering throughout spring. They range in height from 4 in (10 cm) up to 27 in (70 cm). The blooms come in many colors, including bronze, brown, black, yellow, white, red, pink, purple, lilac, violet, green and blue; these colors may vary with soil type or environmental conditions.

CULTIVATION

Climate crucially affects tulip flowering; they require dry, warm summers but cold winters and should not be grown in warm climates unless the bulbs have been suitably chilled. Plant in late autumn, preferably in a sunny position, about 6 in (15 cm) deep in rich, preferably alkaline, well-drained soil. Water well during their growth period. Remove spent flowers, but allow leaves to die off naturally in order to replenish the bulb. In areas with wet summers, lift bulbs and store under cool, dry, well-ventilated conditions. Tulips are prone to aphid attack and the fungal disease tulip fire, caused by *Botrytis tulipae*, which thrives under moist conditions. Propagate from offsets or seed in autumn.

Tulipa clusiana

syns *Tulipa aitchisonii, T. stellata*
LADY TULIP, PEPPERMINT STICK TULIP

One of the most graceful of all tulips, this lovely species produces elegant, star-like flowers, white inside with a violet base and outer tepals which are carmine on the outside. They grow to about 10 in (25 cm) tall and require minimal chilling, making them a delightful permanent garden plant, even in milder climates. Occasionally more than one flower per stem is produced. *Tulipa clusiana* var. *chrysantha* (syn. *T. chrysantha*) is also very popular. It is smaller than *T. clusiana*, reaching only 8 in (20 cm) in height, but its small flowers, deep yellow inside, are long and slimly elegant in bud. The outer petals may have a yellow edge. ZONES 5–9.

Tulipa gesneriana

This is not actually a species, but the collective name originally given to a large number of ancient cultivars in 1753 by the father of taxonomy, Carl Linnaeus. Cultivars and varieties of this 'species' are placed in different groups and are named as *Tulipa* cultivars. ZONES 5–9.

Tulipa clusiana var. *chrysantha*

Tulipa saxatilis

syn. Tulipa bakeri

This very showy species was first described
in 1825 in Crete. It reaches a height of 8 in
(20 cm) and usually produces 2 cups per stem.
They are rosy lilac with yellow bases. Minimal
chilling requirements make it very easy to grow
and suitable for naturalizing, although deep
planting is advisable. It spreads by underground stolons, rarely sets seed and has very
glossy, fresh green leaves which often appear in
late autumn and make it through the winter
unmarked. Its slightly smaller cultivar, '**Lilac
Wonder**', has an exterior of pinkish purple, the
inner ring of petals being somewhat lighter, and
a pale yellow base. The interior is pastel mauve
with a large, circular, lemon-yellow base and
yellow anthers. It grows to only 6 in (15 cm).
ZONES 5–9.

Tulipa saxatilis 'Lilac Wonder'

Tulipa cultivars

The **Single Early Group** has single-flowered
cultivars, mainly short-stemmed and early
flowering. They are mostly derived from *Tulipa
gesneriana*. The most popular examples include
'**Apricot Beauty**', '**Beauty Queen**' and
'**Keizerskroom**'.

The **Double Early Group** contains early
flowering, mainly short-stemmed cultivars.
They produce double flowers which look like
gardenias. '**Monte Carlo**', '**Murillo**', '**Peach
Blossom**' and '**Yellow Baby**' are among the
most popular.

Tulipa, Single Early, 'Beauty Queen'

Tulipa cultivars

The **Triumph Group** has single-flowered
cultivars, with medium stem lengths and mid-
season flowering. A feature of many of the
flowers is that they are edged or marked with a
contrasting color. '**Abu Hassan**', '**Merry Widow**'
and '**Rosario**' are among the most popular.

The **Darwin Hybrid Group** consists of
single-flowered, long-stemmed cultivars that
flower mid-season. They are the most frequently grown varieties for the cut-flower
market, including '**Apeldoorn**', '**Golden
Apeldoorn**' and '**Oxford**'.

The **Single Late Group** comprises late-flowering, single-flowered, mainly long-stemmed,
cultivars. Popular examples include '**Queen of
the Night**', '**Dreamland**' and '**Grand Style**'.

Tulipa, Darwin hybrids, 'Golden Apeldoorn' and 'Apeldoorn'

The **Lily-flowered Group** of single-flowered cultivars flowers in mid- or late season. The flowers form a star shape when open and have stems of variable length. '**Ballade**', '**Lilac Time**' and '**Red Shine**' are popular examples.

The **Fringed Group's** single-flowered cultivars have petals edged with crystal-shaped fringes. They flower mid-season or late, and stems are of variable length. '**Spring Green**' is popular.

The **Parrot Group** consists of unusually colored cultivars with curled or twisted petals. They are mainly late-flowering and stem lengths vary. '**Apricot Parrot**' and '**Flaming Parrot**' are examples.

The **Double Late Group** contains late-flowering, mainly long-stemmed cultivars similar to those of the Parrot Group. '**Granda**' and '**Angelique**' are among the most popular.

Tulipa, Single Late, 'Dreamland'

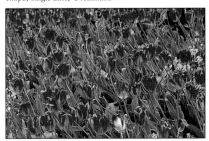

Tulipa, Double Late, 'Angelique'

Tulipa, Parrot, 'Flaming Parrot'

The **Kaufmannia Group** is very early flowering, with mottled foliage and flowers with a multi-colored base. '**Heart's Delight**' and '**Shakespeare**' are good examples.

The **Fosteriana Group** is early flowering. The stems are medium to long and the large long flowers have variable bases. The most popular examples include '**Golden Eagle**' and '**Robassa**'.

The **Greigii Group's** members have large flowers of variable shape. Heights too are variable, generally in the middle ranges. '**Plaisir**', '**Red Riding Hood**' and '**Sweet Lady**' are among the best known. **ZONES 5–9.**

Tulipa, Greigii, 'Sweet Lady'

Tulipa, Lily-flowered, 'Lilac Time'

UVULARIA

BELLWORT, MERRY-BELLS

The 5 species of rhizomatous perennials in this genus are native to eastern North America. These herbaceous woodland plants are usually found growing in moist but well-drained leafy soil in the shade of deciduous trees. The stems are either simple or branched, erect to arching and the leaves are perfoliate in some species. The pendulous, bell-shaped flowers are borne either solitary and terminal, or in axillary clusters. They usually come in shades of yellow and appear in spring.

CULTIVATION

Very frost hardy, they can be grown in rock gardens and beside water features, provided they are in at least part-shade and the acidic soil contains plenty of organic matter. Propagate by division in late winter or early spring, or from ripe seed.

Watsonia pillansii

Uvularia grandiflora

BELLWORT, MERRYBELLS

This easily grown herbaceous, clump-forming perennial has fresh green leaves on arching stems reaching about 30 in (75 cm) in height. The straw-yellow flowers, produced in spring, are 1–2 in (2.5–5 cm) long and hang delicately from the stems, rather like Solomon's seal *(Polygonatum)* to which it is related. It needs protection from slugs when young. **ZONES 3–9.**

WATSONIA

This genus of about 60 species of cormous perennials is allied to *Gladiolus* and native to South Africa and Madagascar. Their spikes of fragrant, tubular, red, orange, pink or white flowers resemble gladioli, although somewhat more tubular in form. Flowers usually appear from spring to summer. The leaves are also similar to those of gladioli, being sword-shaped and erect. There are evergreen and deciduous species available.

CULTIVATION

The corms should be planted in autumn in light, well-drained soil in a sunny spot. They like plenty of water during the growing season, and will tolerate only light frost. Clumps are best left undisturbed and allowed to spread freely. Propagate from seed in the autumn or by division when clumps become overcrowded.

Watsonia pillansii

syn. *Watsonia beatricis*

BEATRICE WATSONIA

This very pretty, evergreen species grows to about 4 ft (1.2 m) in height. The flower spike bears salmon pink, tubular, star-shaped flowers 3 in (8 cm) long in late summer to autumn. The foliage is sword shaped. Hardier than other species, it can withstand some frost. There is some doubt about whether this plant, common in nurseries under this name, is the true wild species. A number of hybrids have been developed from *Watsonia pillansii*, including 'Watermelon Shades'. **ZONES 7–10.**

Chapter 8

CACTI & SUCCULENTS

Cacti and succulents look most impressive when they are grown in groups, such as these silver torch cacti (Cleistocactus strausii).

Cacti are intriguing plants that have captured the imagination of gardeners throughout the world. They are native solely to the Americas, but contrary to popular belief, they are found in a variety of habitats. These range from high altitude areas of Mexico to the tropics of Central America.

All plants belonging to the Cactaceae family share the common need to conserve water. Most also need to protect themselves from the heat, and some, surprisingly, often need protection from the freezing conditions associated with high altitudes. Leaves have been dispensed with completely, in order to reduce the surface area from which water can evaporate, and their photosynthetic duties have been taken over by the stems and branches, which are often weird and wonderful, with mostly globular, ribbed shapes. The stems also act as water tanks, so that the plant has reserves to draw upon during periods of drought. The white hairs or spines that usually cover the body of a cactus act as insulators during hot or cold weather, and also protect the plants from harmful solar radiation.

True cacti fanciers often consider the flowers to be of secondary importance, because they are so fleeting. They are, however, truly magnificent, with their bright coloring and satiny sheen. Night-blooming cacti emit a perfume from their ephemeral, large, white or cream flowers to the delight of moths and gardeners within range. The bright pinks and yellows of the day bloomers do not have this perfume as the brilliance of their colors alone is sufficient to attract pollinating insects.

Although most casual observers think of cacti as the rounded, spiny plants remembered from childhood, they have many bizarre epiphytic counterparts, which thrive in the more shady areas of humid, tropical forests. They live on the trunks of trees or tucked into the niches and crevices created by branches, and their long, strap-like stems hold flowers of particular beauty. These cacti are best suited to greenhouse culture, or can be suspended in hanging baskets under a shady pergola. Popular hybrids have been raised from *Epiphyllum, Zygocactus* and *Schlumbergera* species.

Succulents have a different appeal

The cacti all come from one distinct plant family, but their allies, the succulents, are representative of many different plant families, mostly from Africa and subtropical areas of the Americas. However, their physiological demands, to conserve water, are the same as cacti, although succulents rely on their leaves to store moisture. It is the myriad variations of leaf shapes and coloring that give succulents their appeal, although their flowers can add immeasurably to their often striking architectural dimensions.

Succulents are also known for their great diversity of economic uses. Although the only commercially important product of the cacti family is the fruit of the prickly pear *(Opuntia)*, from among the succulents the sap of *Aloe vera* is renowned for healing the skin after burns, *Agave tequilana* forms the basis of the popular Mexican drink tequila, while other species are utilized in the manufacture of rope or modern medicines.

Cacti and succulents in the garden landscape

The special adaptations of these allied plant groups can be exploited by gardeners, and allows them great scope. Obviously, cacti and succulents are of great use in arid climates, where water conservation is of prime concern, but they will also forgive a forgetful, or otherwise busy, temperate-climate gardener, who tends to water plants erratically or infrequently. They are

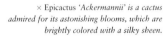

× Epicactus *'Ackermannii'* is a cactus admired for its astonishing blooms, which are brightly colored with a silky sheen.

The tall inflorescence of this spiky-leafed aloe adds to its already striking architectural dimensions.

spectacular effects. Success comes from meeting their native cultural needs: of primary importance are dry, hot summers in the growing season, and porous, well-drained soil. The winters should be dry, with only short periods of rain and cold, while the plants lie dormant. Whilst they may shrink or use other adaptive mechanisms when dormant or during long, dry spells, they will revive when it rains and the weather warms. In colder areas, particularly those with wet winters, succulents and cacti can be successfully grown in individual terracotta pots positioned out of the cold and rain. They will rot if left in cold, wet pots. In really cold areas, a warm greenhouse is ideal, provided a dry atmosphere is maintained.

Cacti and succulents look good and perform best when grouped like with like. For example, plants with succulent, fleshy leaves will be happiest together. There is an incredible diversity to choose from: large, spiky-leafed agaves and aloes, which are best positioned in the background away from passersby, rosette-forming species with gray-green leaves that are fine in a front row border, and low-growing

also very suitable for potted urns that stand on a sun-drenched balcony where there is plenty of air circulation and low humidity. For these situations, look to the adaptable *Echeveria* species for a low-growing, clumping effect.

A little more thought is needed to incorporate cacti and succulents into a general garden, than with other plants. With care, however, this can result in types with a more spreading nature, which makes them ideal weed and erosion suppressors. Many of these plants are long lived and look particularly effective in mature groupings. This maturity can be easily created in a short time; select species, say the deservedly popular *Agave attenuata,* and create a rather naturalistic family grouping of plants of varying ages. They can be given extra emphasis when placed beside rock outcrops or when the area is mulched with a distinctive gravel, which is better than having them become overgrown with quicker-growing shrubs. Quite often, it is this deliberate minimalist approach that sets cacti and succulents apart from most other plants.

How to cultivate cacti and succulents

The key to success with both terrestrial cacti and to the slightly less fussy succulents is to provide them with suitable soil. The soil in the natural habitat may be sandy, but it is usually very rich in minerals, which makes it rather different to the nitrogenous humus mixes that most other garden subjects demand. If your soil type is reasonably heavy, add a quantity of coarse river sand to provide the needed drainage while adding to the mineral content. Although they can tolerate a certain degree of neglect, most plants will respond to a scattering of slow-release fertilizer at the beginning of the growing period.

Epiphytes, those that live in trees, are somewhat different in their grow-ing requirements. These appreciate a higher atmospheric humidity and a richer soil mix, supplied by ample helpings of compost. They will repay you with a good display of flowers, especially when leaf fertilizer is applied during their growing period.

More than any other plant group, cacti are prone to aberrant mutations. Specialist collectors eagerly seek unusual, mutant cacti, and those new to cacti growing will find chlorotic mutations irresistible. These are quite common and are formed when there is a lack of chlorophyll in the seedlings, resulting in yellow or red plants. An affected plant can be grafted onto a closely related species to keep it alive. It is often when given such a grafted plant that gardeners become lured into the fascinating hobby of cacti growing.

While the results of grafting can give devotees pleasure, others prefer to propagate their cacti by the removal of offsets that cluster around the base of a mature globular plant. Always use gloves when taking cuttings, and in the case of the upright types, hold them with a cloth band while repotting or transplanting. Cacti are easily grown from seed, and are the ideal plant for a beginner gardener or one with limited space, as they make relatively undemanding pot plants when given a porous soil mix. If growing conditions are ideal, pests will rarely be a bother, but when growing cacti in containers keep a close watch around the collar, the section nearest the soil, for mealybug, which can decimate a plant.

Aeonium arboreum

AEONIUM

Native to the Canary Islands, the Mediterranean and northern Africa, this genus contains 40 species of short-lived, perennial or shrubby evergreen succulents. The plants develop either as one large (or several smaller), compact, stemless rosette, or branch into several long, thick stems terminating in leaves; some are more closely branched, with many smaller rosettes. Attractive, star-shaped, pink, red, white or yellow flowers appear in dense pyramidal sprays, from small to very large, from the center of the leaf rosettes, usually in spring.

CULTIVATION
They prefer full sun or partial shade, light, well-drained soil and warmer temperatures. Some species tolerate light frosts. Prune off dead flower panicles after the blooms wither, although the flowering rosette will usually die and single-rosette species will die out completely. Propagate from seed, stem or leaf cuttings during spring or summer.

Aeonium arboreum

Native to the Atlantic coast of Morocco, this species grows to 24 in (60 cm) and develops a number of branches with rosettes of bright green leaves. In spring, some branches produce dense conical clusters of golden-yellow flowers, the whole branch dying back when they are spent. The cultivar '**Zwartkop**' has striking, reddish black leaves. **ZONES 9–11.**

Aeonium arboreum 'Zwartkop'

Agave attenuata 'Nerva'

Agave americana

AGAVE

Native to the Caribbean region including southern USA, Mexico and the West Indies, these perennial succulents are grown for their dramatic, sword-shaped, often sharply toothed leaves. The small species flower only after 5 to 10 years and the taller species may take up to 40 years to flower. All agaves flower only once and then the flowering shoot dies, leaving offsets (in most species). These plants are popular for use in Mediterranean styles of landscape design and for large rockeries and dry embankments.

CULTIVATION

Plant in a well-drained, gritty soil in full sun. Once established, water only in summer. Frost hardiness varies from species to species, but all are adapted to surviving through very dry periods. Most species make excellent container plants. Propagate from offsets or from seed in spring or summer.

Agave americana
CENTURY PLANT, AMERICAN ALOE

From Mexico, this species consists of large, stemless rosettes of stiff, dull gray leaves with sharp tips and teeth. Each rosette grows to a height and spread of 6 ft (1.8 m) but an old clump may be 30 ft (9 m) or more across. The plant bears masses of yellow flowers on a branched flower stem rising to 20 ft (6 m) when about 10 years old. Popular cultivars include **'Marginata'**, with yellow-edged leaves, and **'Mediopicta'** with a broad yellow stripe down the center of the leaves. **ZONES 9–12.**

Agave attenuata

This spineless species has a thick stem to 5 ft (1.5 m) high, which is crowned by a compact rosette of broad, soft-textured, pale green leaves. Its flower spike grows to 10 ft (3 m) and bears crowded, greenish yellow flowers, which open in spring and summer. Lateral rosettes branch off the main stem making, in time, a large mound of rosettes. **'Nerva'** has bluish green leaves. **ZONES 9–12.**

Agave victoriae-reginae
ROYAL AGAVE

This slow-growing succulent is stalkless, up to 24 in (60 cm) in height and breadth, and its single rosette has dense, narrow, keeled leaves with white edges and surface lines. A flowering stem up to 12 ft (3.5 m) tall bearing pale greenish yellow flowers develops after 20 years. The royal agave tolerates light frosts, but prefers a frost-free climate. Some people consider it the most beautiful of the agaves, but it must be renewed from seed after flowering. **ZONES 9–12.**

Agave victoriae-reginae

Aloe arborescens 'Pearson'

ALOE

Occurring wild in Africa, Madagascar and the Arabian Peninsula, this genus of succulent-leafed plants consists of over 300 species, including trees, shrubs and perennials. The 'aloe' of traditional medicine is a bitter drug obtained from some shrubby African species. All are evergreen, mostly with distinct rosettes of sword-shaped leaves that terminate the stem or branches. Leaves vary greatly between species in size, color, degree of succulence, and presence and distribution of prickles on the margins or faces. The flowers are tubular to narrowly bell-shaped, in long-stemmed spikes on which they open progressively from the base. These are followed by oval fruits ¼–2 in (0.6–5 cm) long, usually ripening from green to brown. Aloes hybridize quite freely, some attractive examples include *Aloe speciosa* × *A. ferox* and *A. splendens* × *A. speciosa*.

CULTIVATION

Nearly all aloes prefer a warm dry climate and well-drained soil, but many will tolerate a few degrees of frost once established.

Aloe plicatilis

The larger species of aloes can be grown in full sun, the smaller types in part-shade. Propagation is from offsets or stem cuttings. Infestation by mealybug can be a problem.

Aloe arborescens
CANDELABRA ALOE, KRANTZ ALOE

This shrubby species from south-eastern Africa can mound from 6 to 10 ft (2 to 3 m) when in flower. The plants branch from the base into short, slender stems with both lateral and terminal rosettes, composed of rather narrow grayish blue leaves up to 24 in (60 cm) long, slightly downward curving and thorny edged. Branched spikes of scarlet red or yellow flowers appear from late winter to early spring. This species is both salt- and drought-resistant and marginally frost hardy. 'Pearson' and 'Compton' are just two of its cultivars.
ZONES 9–11.

Aloe aristata
TORCH PLANT, LACE ALOE

Native to South Africa, this miniature aloe forms long-lived, stemless clumps of rosettes only about 4 in (10 cm) high, and up to 12 in (30 cm) wide. Its finely tapering, deep green leaves have white surface spots, soft, serrated margins and are tipped by fine bristles. Loose spikes to 24 in (60 cm) high of orange-red flowers develop in spring. Marginally frost hardy, it grows well in pots on windowledges, or in rockeries.
ZONES 9–11.

Aloe vera

Aloe vera

syn. *Aloe barbadensis*

MEDICINAL ALOE, MEDICINE PLANT,
BURN PLANT

Renowned for its medicinal qualities, this short-stemmed species, its likely origin Arabia or northern Africa, grows to 24 in (60 cm) high. It has rosettes of narrow, thick, lance-shaped, green leaves with small whitish teeth on the margins. In summer, small orange-yellow flowers appear in spikes up to 3 ft (1 m) high. Its syrupy leaf juice is used in skin care products and for the treatment of burns. **ZONES 8–11.**

Aloe brevifolia

A miniature aloe from South Africa's Cape Province, *Aloe brevifolia* forms tight clumps of fleshy rosettes only about 3 in (8 cm) in diameter. Its bluish green leaves are armed with many rather soft prickles. In early summer it produces unbranched flower spikes up to 18 in (45 cm), carrying dull scarlet bells tinged with green at the base. It has long been popular for growing in pots, window boxes and in rockeries. **ZONES 9–11.**

Aloe plicatilis

FAN ALOE

With distinctive fan-like clusters of pale, blue-green succulent leaves, this shrub grows slowly to a height and spread of around 5 ft (1.5 m) with a stiff, multi-branched habit. Tubular scarlet flowers are borne in spring. Frost tender, it requires a sunny position with protection from hot afternoon sun and regular watering in winter and spring. **ZONES 9–11.**

Aloe saponaria

SOAP ALOE

Saponaria is Latin for 'soapy', and this well-known South African aloe was named thus because its leaf sap foams in water and can be used as a soap substitute. The plants form stemless rosettes of broad, flat, dark green leaves, usually closely flecked with white spots or streaks; the margins have close-set short teeth and the tips of the leaves soon die and curl, especially in dry conditions. The few-branched flowering stems are about 24 in (60 cm) high and bear very short head-like spikes of orange flowers in summer. This is one of the most easily grown aloes, surviving long periods without watering. **ZONES 9–11.**

Aloe brevifolia

Aloe saponaria

APOROCACTUS

RAT'S TAIL CACTUS

The name Aporocactus means the perplexing cactus, a comment on the difficulty of classifying these epiphytic cacti. Only two species comprise this genus from tropical Mexico; they have the usual round, spiny cactus branches, but so long, thin and weak that they cascade downwards. The pink or red flowers are large and showy, opening wide with a central small tuft of stamens; these are followed by small, reddish fruit.

CULTIVATION

Easy to grow, it is happiest in a hanging basket in fairly rich, freely draining potting soil with a place in the sun for about half the day, and no frost. Propagate from cuttings.

Aporocactus flagelliformis

Aporocactus flagelliformis

RAT'S TAIL CACTUS

The unflattering common name comes from the long round branches of this epiphytic cactus. Shocking-pink flowers are borne abundantly in spring and summer, crowded towards bases of stems. This species is one of the parents used in the colorful × *Epicactus* hybrids. **ZONES 10–12.**

Aptenia cordifolia 'Variegata'

Aptenia cordifolia

APTENIA

The two species in this genus of mesembryanthemum relatives are native to South Africa. They are prostrate succulents with fleshy, heart-shaped to oval leaves, their surfaces having a slight crystalline appearance. Solitary, small, pink to purplish red, daisy-like flowers open after rain in desert areas or in summer elsewhere.

CULTIVATION

They are surprisingly hardy for South African succulents. If kept dry over winter they will tolerate temperatures down to 20°F (–7°C) or lower. Plant in gritty, very free-draining soil in full sun. They do well in dry rockeries, on retaining walls and in hanging baskets. Propagate from seed or cuttings.

Aptenia cordifolia

This mat-forming succulent is quick growing, only about 2 in (5 cm) in height, but of indefinite spread. The creeping, weak stems bear green, heart-shaped leaves, up to 1 in (25 mm) long. Small magenta flowers (there is also a red-flowered form) appear mainly in summer, daisy-like in appearance with dense stamens. The leaves of 'Variegata' have greenish white margins. **ZONES 9–11.**

Astrophytum myriostigma

BISHOP'S CAP, BISHOP'S MITRE

Quite spineless, this odd-looking species grows up to 12 in (30 cm) high and 4 in (10 cm) wide. It has a grayish green body divided into 4 to 8 prominent ribs and typically is covered with tiny, white scales. Glossy yellow blooms appear in summer. It is quite variable and a number of varieties have been named. *Astrophytum myriostigma* var. *quadricostata* is distinctive for the fatness of each of its 4 ribs, separated only by shallow grooves.
ZONES 10–11.

Beaucarnea recurvata

syns *Nolina recurvata, N. tuberculata*

PONYTAIL PALM

This slow-growing, evergreen plant is commonly sold in pots for the novel appearance of its swollen stem base; this tapers upward to a palm-like trunk bearing at its apex a dense crown of strap-like, downward-curving leaves up to 3 ft (1 m) long. Mature plants bear large feathery panicles of cream flowers in spring, followed by pinkish, 3-winged fruit. **ZONES 9–12.**

ASTROPHYTUM

This popular genus contains six species of slow-growing cacti, all native to Mexico. They differ in size and their form varies from star-shaped—hence the Greek genus name (star-plant)—to elongated or globular. The mostly unbranched plants are divided into 5 to 10 prominent, smooth ribs, some covered in thick hair, others patterned with minute white scales. The large flowers with shiny, lemon-yellow to golden-yellow petals, sometimes red at the base, appear from the top of the plant in summer or autumn.

CULTIVATION
The plants are frost tender and prefer porous, alkaline soil and full sun. They should be kept fairly dry except during the mid-summer growing season. Propagate from seed in spring and summer. The tops of older plants can be grafted onto a hardier cactus, and the truncated base will then sprout new growths which can be rooted as cuttings.

Astrophytum myriostigma

BEAUCARNEA

Beaucarnea recurvata

This genus consists of 20 or more species of evergreen plants from semi-desert regions of Mexico and far southern USA, one of them widely sold as a potted plant. Related to yuccas, they are grown for their remarkable thickened stems and long, thin, grass-like leaves. The numerous small white flowers are borne in large panicles arising from the centers of the leaf rosettes, though only on plants with trunks more than 3 ft (1 m) or so in height, which are generally at least 10 years old. The plant usually remains single stemmed until at least this height, but if the top is cut off it will sprout many new shoots. Some botanists treat *Beaucarnea* as a synonym of *Nolina*, others prefer to maintain them as different genera.

CULTIVATION
They can be grown outdoors in mild to warm climates, in full sun and well-drained, fertile soil. Water well while growing, but sparingly in winter or the stem may rot. As indoor potted plants they can reach ceiling height, flourishing in the warm, dry atmosphere of centrally heated rooms, though needing high light levels. Propagate from seed in spring or from suckers.

CARPOBROTUS

PIGFACE, SOUR FIG, ICE PLANT

Valued for their abundance of vivid flowers, these 30 species of carpet-forming succulents are predominantly native to South Africa, growing mainly on seashores. The completely prostrate, angled stems may be 6 ft (1.8 m) or more in length and become leathery with age. The deep green to gray-green fleshy leaves, arranged in pairs, vary from round to triangular in cross-section, sometimes with finely serrated margins. The large, solitary, daisy-like flowers are in varying shades of pink, red, purple or yellow. These are followed by soft, sometimes edible fruits.

CULTIVATION

These marginally frost-hardy plants are easy to grow, requiring full sun and porous soil. They are very salt-tolerant, are suited to hanging baskets and make excellent sandbinders. Propagate from stem cuttings or seed in spring to early autumn.

Carpobrotus acinaciformis

CEPHALOCEREUS

Only 3 species of columnar cacti belong to this genus, both native to central Mexico. Their genus name means 'headed cereus', referring to the cephalium, an eruption of felt-covered tissue near the top of the stem from which flowers emerge year after year. Flowering generally occurs only on mature plants which may be decades old, and the average cactus grower may never see a cephalium develop. The main attraction of the genus is the snow white spines and bristles that cover the many-ribbed stems, especially near the apical growing point. The stems grow straight and erect and when they finally branch, it is from the base, to form a small group of parallel stems.

CULTIVATION

These are subtropical cacti and will only tolerate the lightest of frosts, and then only if the climate is warm and dry. In cool climates they are grown indoors, requiring a window position with strong light or a sunny conservatory. They demand much the same well-drained soil mix as most cacti, though some growers recommend the addition of limestone chips, and are sensitive to over-watering. They are susceptible to mealybug and spider mite. Propagate from seed.

Carpobrotus acinaciformis

GIANT PIGFACE

This species is native to South Africa. It can mound to a height of 12 in (30 cm) and a spread of 3 ft (1 m) or often more. The leaves are gray-green, saber shaped and up to 3 in (8 cm) long. From spring to autumn the plants bear purple-red flowers up to 6 in (15 cm) across, which open only in the sun. **ZONES 9–11.**

Cephalocereus senilis

Cephalocereus senilis

OLD MAN CACTUS

In the wild on dry scrubby hills of the Mexican plateau, this cactus grows to over 40 ft (12 m) tall with multiple stems, but in cultivation specimens taller than 4 ft (1.2 m) are rarely seen. But even as a very young plant this cactus attracts attention by virtue of its long, tangled white bristles that conceal the stem. The trumpet-shaped white or somewhat yellowish flowers open only at night in summer. **ZONES 9–11.**

CHAMAECEREUS

PEANUT CACTUS

If recognized as distinct, this genus consists of only one species, native to northern Argentina, but many botanists now prefer to treat it as just another species of the large genus *Echinopsis*. It is a clustering cactus with slender, weak stems that flop over as they elongate and become prostrate or pendulous. The small, weak spine clusters are closely spaced and give the stems a whitish appearance. It has showy orange or red flowers that open wide in the sun.

CULTIVATION

This is an easily grown cactus, popular as an indoor and balcony plant, and well suited to hanging baskets as well as pots. Grow in well-drained soil in a sunny spot and watch for infestations of mealybug, scale insects and spider mite. Propagate from offsets or seed.

Cleistocactus strausii

CLEISTOCACTUS

These 50 or so species occur widely from Ecuador to Uruguay. They are slender-stemmed, some columnar and reaching as much as 15 ft (4.5 m) tall, others with scrambling or almost prostrate stems. All species have ribbed stems, the ribs low and rounded and bearing numerous thin spines from closely spaced areoles. Flowers are often numerous, arising from the whole length of the stem or concentrated near the top, and are mostly rather narrowly tubular and slightly one-sided. The outside of the flower tube is usually bristly or spiny. Most species grow rapidly and flower readily.

CULTIVATION

They are mostly robust plants which are easily grown in well-drained soil in a sunny spot. They are moderately frost and drought resistant but may be susceptible to mealybug and spider mite. Propagate from cuttings or seed.

Chamaecereus silvestrii

syns *Echinopsis chamaecereus, Lobivia silvestrii*

This well-known cactus is composed of clusters of initially erect, finger-sized stems that are pale green with numerous soft, white bristles. Established plants can reach a height of 6 in (15 cm) and width of 12 in (30 cm), with many crowded stems. From an early age it flowers freely indoors if conditions suit it, producing vivid orange-red blooms about 2 in (5 cm) in diameter in spring and summer. **ZONES 10–12.**

Chamaecereus silvestrii

Cleistocactus strausii

SILVER TORCH CACTUS

This erect, columnar, 10 ft (3 m) cactus from Bolivia is easy to grow. Multiple, grayish green stems are covered with fine yellowish spines mixed with abundant, long white bristles. Profuse deep red, cylindrical flowers develop straight from the stems in late summer, but only on older plants. It likes full sun and very porous soil. Older plants need staking or they tend to fall over. **ZONES 9–11.**

Cotyledon orbiculata

COTYLEDON

This is a genus of the crassula family consisting of 9 species of evergreen succulent shrubs and subshrubs, from southern and eastern Africa and the Arabian Peninsula. In growth habit they range from highly succulent plants no more than 2 in (5 cm) high to larger shrubs that in rare cases can reach as much as 6 ft (1.8 m) high. They have fleshy leaves and tubular or bell-shaped, orange, yellow or red flowers.

CULTIVATION

Some species are marginally frost hardy, others quite frost tender. They prefer full sun or part-shade and humus-rich, very well-drained soil. Water only very lightly in winter. Propagate from seed, stem cuttings or leaf cuttings taken in spring or autumn.

Cotyledon orbiculata

Native to southwestern Africa, this species is very variable and has been divided into a number of botanical varieties. Typically, it is a succulent shrub growing 18–24 in (45–60 cm), branching just above the ground. Branches terminate in clusters of fleshy leaves that vary from paddle-shaped to almost circular in outline, and from quite green and glossy to almost pure white from a thick waxy or powdery bloom; the leaf margins are often red-lined. In autumn, long-stalked clusters of quite large, pendent orange flowers appear at the branch tips. **ZONES 9–11.**

Cotyledon orbiculata

PIG'S EAR

Cotyledon orbiculata

Crassula arborescens

SILVER JADE PLANT, SILVER DOLLAR

Widely distributed in South Africa including the summer-rainfall eastern parts, *Crassula arborescens* can exceed 10 ft (3 m) in height and spread, though 24–36 in (60–90 cm) is more usual in cultivation. It is a much-branched, succulent shrub with thick brown stems and red-edged, almost circular leaves about 1½ in (38 mm) wide with a powdery blue-gray coating peppered with small dark green dots. Panicles of small, starry, pale pinkish flowers dot the plant in autumn and winter. It is a favorite tub plant for any sunny spot, thriving on mini-mal attention. A common 'jade plant' of gardens often known as *Crassula arbor-escens* is actually *C. ovata* (see overleaf). **ZONES 9–11.**

CRASSULA

This diverse genus comprises about 300 species of annuals, perennials and evergreen shrubs, nearly all with succulent leaves. Some less highly succulent species are scattered widely around the world, but the great majority of species, including many of extreme succulent form, are confined to southern Africa. They range in habit from tiny prostrate or clump-forming plants to erect shrubs as much as 12 ft (3.5 m) high. A fairly constant fea-ture is the arrangement of the leaves in opposite pairs, some-times joining at the base around the stem. Flowers are grouped in terminal clusters or panicles and are only showy in a minority of species.

CULTIVATION

Species range from marginally frost hardy to frost tender. Some of the more vigorous growers are tough, adaptable plants that will survive with almost no attention in pots, tubs or window boxes as long as the soil is not waterlogged. At the other end of the scale are some of the more dwarf succulent South African species, which are grown mainly by succulent collectors willing to meet their specialized requirements. Propagate from stem or leaf cuttings, or from seed.

Crassula coccinea

Crassula arborescens

Crassula coccinea
syn. *Rochea coccinea*

From the mountains of South Africa's western Cape Province, this is a crassula grown mainly for its spectacular flowers. It is a succulent perennial up to 24 in (60 cm) high, branching from the base into several stems with crowded short green leaves sometimes tinged red. In late summer and autumn it bears an abundance of tubular, deep red flowers in dense, rounded panicles. It needs full sun and does best in a warm, dry spot in a rock garden with perfect drainage. Prune back stems to just above the base in late winter. **ZONES 9–10.**

Crassula multicava
FAIRY CRASSULA

One of the easiest of all crassulas to grow in mild climates, *Crassula multicava* is a spreading perennial 8–12 in (20–30 cm) high, its semi-prostrate stems taking root and spreading into a large patch. The thinly succulent gray-green leaves are densely dotted with dark green. Clusters of tiny star-shaped, pink and white flowers are borne on long, weak stalks in winter and spring, making a delicate gauze of color above the leaves when this species is grown as a groundcover. **ZONES 9–11.**

Crassula multicava

Crassula ovata
syns *Crassula argentea* of gardens,
C. portulacea
JADE PLANT, JADE TREE, FRIENDSHIP TREE

This South African species should not be confused with *Portulacaria afra*, also known as 'jade plant' but easily distinguished by its much smaller leaves, not in opposite pairs. *Crassula ovata* has also been much confused with *C. arborescens*, the silver jade plant. It is a fast-growing, shrubby succulent that can reach over 6 ft (1.8 m) in height, though 24–36 in (60–90 cm) is more usual. It has thick brownish stems and shiny, broadly wedge-shaped leaves that may be edged with red. In autumn and winter, small, white to pale pink, starry flowers appear. It prefers full sun, and makes a good tub plant for patios and balconies. 'Hobbit' is a dwarf cultivar. **ZONES 9–11.**

Crassula ovata

Cyphostemma juttae
syn. **Cissus juttae**

Native to southern Namibia, this long-lived, deciduous, succulent shrub grows eventually to about 6 ft (1.8 m) tall. It is a striking plant with a bloated, fleshy stem that branches near the top and is covered with brownish yellow peeling bark. The leaves are mostly divided into 3 pale bluish green leaflets that are quite fleshy and roughly saw-toothed, their downy undersides exuding droplets of resin. Small greenish yellow flowers appear in summer, followed by quite translucent red or yellow fruit that look very much like small bunches of grapes. **ZONES 9–11.**

Cyphostemma juttae

CYPHOSTEMMA

Closely related to *Cissus*, this genus consists of around 150 species of evergreen and deciduous climbers and shrubs, found in warmer parts of the world. Some of the many African species have swollen, succulent stems and are popular with succulent collectors. The leaves are usually compound, with several leaflets arranged in either a palmate or pinnate manner. Small flowers are borne on long-stalked, flattish panicles and are followed by grape-like fruits of varying size and degree of edibility.

CULTIVATION

These marginally frost-hardy to frost-tender plants need full sun and a very well-drained soil. They should be kept dry in winter. Propagate from seed in spring.

Drosanthemum candens
syn. **Drosanthemum floribundum**
ROSEA ICE PLANT

This is a low-growing, mat-forming plant reaching 4–6 in (10–15 cm) in height with an indefinite spread. Its creeping branches take root as they grow and are covered with pairs of pale, gray-green, cylindrical leaves. A profusion of pinkish purple, daisy-like flowers are borne in summer. Excellent for hanging baskets, pots or as groundcover, and it will drape over rocks and embankments. It thrives in exposed coastal situations. **ZONES 9–11.**

DROSANTHEMUM

This genus of the mesembryanthemum alliance contains approximately 95 species of perennial, mostly creeping succulents native to South Africa. *Drosanthemum* species have a spreading habit and vary in height, some reaching 3 ft (1 m). The fleshy leaves are densely covered in tiny protuberances and the daisy-like flowers range from pink and yellow to deep purple.

CULTIVATION

Frost tender, they require bright sunlight for the flowers to open fully. Pots can be kept indoors in winter in a warm, sunny position. Plant in well-drained, compost-enriched soil. Water sparingly in summer and keep fairly dry in winter. Propagate from seed or cuttings in spring or summer and replace plants about every 3 years.

Echeveria 'Baron Bold'

ECHEVERIA

Native to the Americas (mostly to Mexico), *Echeveria* takes its name from the Spaniard, Atanasio Echeverria Codoy, an eighteenth-century botanical artist. This large genus contains over 150 species of ornamental, perennial succulents valued for their habit, foliage and flowers. The leaves form symmetrical rosettes either sitting on the soil or as terminating erect stems; plants may form multi-stemmed bushes up to 3 ft (1 m) tall. They have fleshy, usually smooth-edged leaves that are particularly vivid during the colder months; some plants, for example, the hybrids 'Baron Bold' and 'Delight', have attractive crimped-edged leaves. The bell-shaped to cylindrical flowers bloom at different times of the year.

CULTIVATION

Marginally frost hardy to frost tender, these plants require full sun or semi-shade, very porous soil and plenty of water from spring to late summer, reducing to little or none in winter. Propagate from seed, offsets or cuttings, or by division in spring and summer.

Echeveria elegans
MEXICAN SNOW BALL

This marginally frost-hardy succulent forms a dense mound of small rosettes up to 2 in (5 cm) tall and 18 in (45 cm) in diameter. The leaves are frosted blue-green with red margins, and the bell-shaped, pinkish red flowers have yellow petal tips. '**Kesselringii**' has gray-blue leaves in a loose rosette. **ZONES 8–11.**

Echeveria × imbricata

Echeveria glavea and *E. gibbiflora* var. *metallica* are the parents of this attractive and widely grown hybrid. It has gray-green, obovate leaves and produces red, trumpet-shaped flowers in spring and summer. **ZONES 8–11.**

Echeveria 'Delight'

Echeveria elegans

Echeveria pulvinata
PLUSH PLANT, CHENILLE PLANT

This shrubby succulent produces loose, silvery gray-green rosettes up to 4 in (10 cm) across and short, brown downy stems. Leaves are dense, silky soft, inversely egg-shaped and covered with white down. Red or yellowish red flowers appear from winter to late spring on 12 in (30 cm) tall stems. It is rather frost tender. **ZONES 9–11.**

Echeveria × imbricata

Echeveria pulvinata

Echinocactus grusonii
GOLDEN BARREL CACTUS

Native to Mexico, this popular cactus reaches up to 3 ft (1 m) in height and spread. It has a single, globe-shaped, pale green body that elongates in maturity, becoming barrel-shaped. This stem is heavily ribbed with numerous areoles sprouting yellow radial spines. In summer, larger specimens produce a circle of vivid yellow flowers from a crown at the top of the plant. **ZONES 9–12.**

Echinocactus grusonii

ECHINOCACTUS

This is a genus of 12 species of very spiny cacti native to Mexico and southwest USA. Generally slow growing, they can eventually reach a height of 6 ft (1.8 m) and a width of 3 ft (1 m) and feature prominently spined ribs. Yellow, pink or red flowers are produced at the crown of mature plants in summer.

CULTIVATION

Frost tender but tolerant of very dry conditions, they grow best in well-drained soil and a position in full sun, which will help to maintain the luster of the spines and longevity of the flowers. Young plants are prone to mealybug and spider mite. Propagate from seed or cuttings.

ECHINOCEREUS

This large and popular genus of about 45 species of small cacti from Mexico and south to southwestern USA has a varying habit. The stems are many-ribbed and spiny with new stems bursting forth from inside existing ones. In spring and summer large, brightly colored, trumpet-shaped, enduring blooms appear, followed by small, spiny, globular fruits. The genus name comes from the Greek *echinos* meaning hedgehog.

CULTIVATION

Species range from marginally frost hardy to frost tender and need extremely porous soil with full sun. Propagate from seed or cuttings in spring and summer.

Echinocereus triglochidiatus

ECHINOPSIS

syns *Trichocereus, Lobivia*

SEA URCHIN CACTUS

This popular genus contains up to 120 species of cacti native to South America. Ranging from single, globe-shaped stems to readily colonizing, columnar and even tree-like plants, these cacti are mostly densely covered with spines and have pronounced ribs. Many species are valued for their funnel-shaped, brilliantly colored flowers, up to 8 in (20 cm) long. Some bloom at night and are very short lived. There are numerous hybrids.

CULTIVATION

In the garden these frost-tender cacti require full sun, a rich, well-drained soil and should be watered sparingly. Under glass they need bright light, a fairly dry atmosphere and warmth if they are to reach their full potential and bear flowers. Use a free-draining cactus potting mix and keep dry during winter. Propagate in spring and summer from seed or offsets.

Echinocereus triglochidiatus

This evergreen cactus is native to the southern USA and northern Mexico. The 4 in (10 cm) long green stems form large mats that spread along the ground. Funnel-shaped scarlet flowers are produced in summer and reach 2 in (5 cm) in diameter. The red fruit of this species can be made into jam when fully ripened. *Echinocereus triglochidiatus* var. *harvensis* grows to 6 in (15 cm) tall with a 5 ft (1.5 m) spread. **ZONES 8–11.**

Echinopsis oxygona

Echinopsis oxygona

syn. *Echinopsis multiplex*

EASTER LILY CACTUS, BARREL CACTUS

Originating in Brazil, this spherical, multi-branched cactus grows to about 6 in (15 cm) in maturity and with age forms dense clumps up to 3 ft (1 m) in diameter. The stems are covered with brown, black-tipped spines; these sprout fragrant, pinkish white flowers from the tips in summer. **ZONES 10–12.**

× *EPICACTUS*

This name, applied to many hundreds of cactus hybrids with flattened stems and large, brightly colored flowers, is used more as a matter of horticultural convenience than in the precise sense of a hybrid between two specified genera. What they have in common is that an *Epiphyllum* is one of the parents: other parent genera include *Echinopsis*, *Heliocereus* and *Nopalxochia*. The plants are semi-epiphytic, mostly only 12–24 in (30–60 cm) high, with a trailing habit. The large flowers, borne in spring and early summer, are basically funnel-shaped and come in a wide range of colors, from white to yellow, pink, orange, red or rosy purple. A few are night blooming and fragrant, but most are day bloomers.

CULTIVATION

Frost tender, they are nearly always grown in pots or baskets and require indoor or greenhouse conditions except in tropical or subtropical climates. They need a coarse, open mixture and strong light for flower production. Feed and water plants freely as soon as buds appear, reducing the amount of water in winter but never allowing plants to dry out completely. Propagate from cuttings.

× *Epicactus* 'Ackermannii'

syns *Epiphyllum ackermannii*, *Nopalxochia ackermannii*

This freely branching cactus grows up to 12 in (30 cm) tall with a spread of around 24 in (60 cm). Its succulent, arching stems are up to 18 in (45 cm) long with notched margins. Bright red, trumpet-shaped flowers arise from these notches from spring to summer. **ZONES 10–12.**

× *Epicactus* 'Bridesmaid'

This pendulous cultivar has flattened stems over 24 in (60 cm) in length. Its leaves have wavy edges. In early to mid-spring, flower buds appear along the leaves, opening into large, lightly fragrant mauve-pink flowers. **ZONES 10–12.**

× Epicactus 'Bridesmaid'

EPIPHYLLUM

ORCHID CACTUS

This genus from tropical and subtropical regions of the
Americas consists of 20 species of epiphytic cacti. They have
a shrubby, prostrate or pendent growth habit and are virtually
spineless when mature. The much-branched, flattened stems
have undulating margins and may be mistaken for leaves. In
spring or summer large, funnel-shaped flowers arise from the
edges of the stems. They may be nocturnal or diurnal.

CULTIVATION

Frost tender, they require a dry, cool spell during winter, a light,
sandy soil and strong light for optimum flowering. Ideal hanging
basket plants, their trailing stems seem to grow better if the
roots are restricted. Propagate from seed in spring, and cuttings
in summer.

Epiphyllum oxypetalum

Epiphyllum oxypetalum

BELLE DE NUIT

Ranging from Mexico to
Brazil, this popular species
has an upright growth habit
to 6 ft (1.8 m) in height. Its
multiple stems are up to 4 in
(10 cm) wide, tapering to
their bases and arching in
maturity. The nocturnal, 6 in
(15 cm) wide, white flowers
have long, slightly curved
tubes. They are intensely
fragrant. **ZONES 10–12.**

EUPHORBIA

MILKWEED, SPURGE

The genus is very large, with close to 2,000 species, among
numerous succulent species that at first sight look remarkably
like cacti. There is a great variety of forms, which suggests that
the genus should be divided, but the flowers of all species are
almost identical. They are very much reduced, consisting of only
a stigma and a stamen, always green, and usually carried in
small clusters. Many species have showy bracts, these are the
most widely cultivated; examples include *Euphorbia cognata*
and *E.* 'Excalibur'. Mainly tropical and subtropical, the genus
also includes many temperate species. All euphorbias have milky
sap which is corrosive to sensitive areas of the skin; some can
cause temporary blindness if sap contacts the eyes.

CULTIVATION

Plant species of *Euphorbia* in sun or part-shade in moist, well-drained soil. Cold tolerance varies greatly depending on the species; the more highly succulent species are generally frost tender. Propagate from cuttings in spring or summer, allowing succulent species to dry and callus before placing in barely damp sand, by division in early spring or autumn or from seed in autumn or spring.

Euphorbia caput-medusae

Euphorbia caput-medusae

MEDUSA'S HEAD

This South African succulent has a thick basal stem up to 6 in (15 cm) tall. Numerous thinner but still succulent branches up to about 18 in (45 cm) long radiate from the stem, like the tentacles of an octopus. Short-lived, narrow leaves grow only at the branch extremities, where green flowers with white, lacy margins appear in summer. **ZONES 8–11.**

Euphorbia milii

syn. **Euphorbia splendens**

CROWN OF THORNS

This slow-growing, ferociously thorny, semi-succulent shrub with bright green leaves is native to Madagascar. Deciduous in cooler areas, it tolerates dry conditions and grows to a height of about 3 ft (1 m). It is excellent in frost-free rock gardens or sunny courtyards, and is often used as a low hedge in coastal areas. Throughout the year, especially during spring, it carries tiny yellowish flowers among pink-red bracts, which are borne in showy flat sprays. *Euphorbia milii* var. *splendens* is a semi-prostrate variety with oblong leaves. **ZONES 10–12.**

Euphorbia milii

FEROCACTUS
syn. **Hamatocactus**

BARREL CACTUS

The name of this genus from North and Central America means 'fierce cactus', an apt title for plants protected by 4 in (10 cm) long sturdy spines that can be yellow, red, brown or white. There are about 30 species of these spherical cacti, which become columnar with age. They are slow growing and can take 15 years to produce flowers. The flowers are usually yellow, red, orange or brown. Plants vary in size and shape according to age and species, ranging in height from 12 in (30 cm) to 6 ft (1.8 m). When young they make excellent container plants.

CULTIVATION

They require full sun, porous, well-drained soil, free air circulation and protection from frost and excessive rain. Propagate from seed in spring.

Ferocactus haematacanthus

Not to be confused with the better known species *Ferocactus hamatacanthus*, this cactus native to eastern Mexico reaches 4 ft (1.2 m) high and 10 in (25 cm) wide. It is armed with short, reddish brown spines and has up to 27 ribs, patterned in slightly wavy lines. Medium-sized, purple-pink, daisy-like flowers appear in summer, and are followed by purplish oval seed pods in summer. **ZONES 10–11.**

Ferocactus haematacanthus

Graptopetalum paraguayense
syn. **Sedum weinbergii**

GHOST PLANT, MOTHER-OF-PEARL PLANT

In spite of its specific name implying it is native to Paraguay, the mother-of-pearl plant is now known to be native to Mexico. Dense rosettes of thick, blunt-tipped leaves are borne on fleshy stems, at first erect then bending down with age. The leaves are gray with a reddish cast and a silvery blue bloom. Showy sprays of white, star-shaped flowers bloom in spring, rising well above the rosette; they are very long lasting. **ZONES 9–11.**

Graptopetalum paraguayense

GRAPTOPETALUM

This genus of about 12 species of perennial succulents related to *Echeveria* is native to Mexico and Arizona, USA. They are mainly rosette-forming on short stems with bluish gray leaves, and bear star-shaped or tubular flowers in spring or summer. Frost tender, many of these species are grown as house plants or in temperate greenhouses. In frost-free areas they are ideal for rock and desert gardens.

CULTIVATION

Grow in very well-drained soil in full sun or very light shade. Propagate from seed or cuttings in spring or summer.

Gymnocalycium mihanovichii
PLAID CACTUS

This Paraguayan species has flattened, grayish green, globular stems 2 in (5 cm) in diameter. These have 8 ribs and horizontal grooves above and below the areoles which bear short brownish yellow spines. Pink or greenish yellow flowers appear in early summer. Cultivars with stems that are variegated or in different colors have become popular. Some lack chlorophyll and so must be grafted onto a normal green cactus to survive; the best known is the brilliant red **'Red Head'** (syn. 'Hibotan'). **'Variegatum'** has stems irregularly blotched red and bronzy green. **ZONES 9–11.**

GYMNOCALYCIUM
CHIN CACTI

This genus consists of about 50 species of low, round cacti with shallow, sometimes spirally arranged ribs and usually developing a protrusion or 'chin' below each areole. The spines are slightly curved and rather sparse, and the funnel-shaped flowers are large for the size of the plants. These small cacti are native to subtropical South America and make excellent house plants, although they can be grown outdoors in frost-free or near frost-free areas.

CULTIVATION
In the garden, chin cacti need full sun and poor, well-drained soil. Indoors use a cactus potting mix and provide plenty of light and water during spring and summer. Keep dry in winter. Propagate from seed in spring or from offsets in summer.

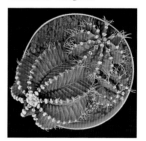

Left: Gymnocalycium mihanovichii
Below: Gymnocalycium mihanovichii 'Variegatum'

HAWORTHIA

This South African genus consists of 150 perennial succulents resembling miniature aloes, to which they are related. They are predominantly clump forming, developing in basal or short-stemmed rosettes. The small leaves vary in shape and may be marked with white dots or darker green translucent streaks. Racemes of insignificant white, or occasionally yellow, 6-petalled flowers appear in summer.

CULTIVATION
These frost-tender succulents require semi-shade to maintain healthy leaves, and porous, well-drained soil. Keep slightly moist during the hotter months and totally dry in winter. Propagate by division or from offsets from spring to autumn.

Haworthia fasciata
ZEBRA HAWORTHIA

This more or less stemless succulent is grown for its interesting leaves, which stand upright in neat rosettes, showing off the rows of white dots on their undersides and creating a gray and white zebra-like effect. The tiny white flowers are carried in early summer on 15 in (38 cm) tall bare stems. **ZONES 9–11.**

Haworthia fasciata

Kalanchoe blossfeldiana hybrid

KALANCHOE

This genus, native to subtropical and tropical Africa and Madagascar, with a scattering of species in Asia, consists of 150 species of perennial succulents, climbers or shrubs. These vary from small, leafy succulents to tree-like shrubs. They are mainly valued for their decorative foliage. Plants grow from 6 in (15 cm) to 12 ft (3.5 m) high and bear white, yellow or orange to brown, red or purple, tubular or bell-shaped flowers in early spring. These are followed by small seed-bearing capsules.

CULTIVATION

These succulents need full sun or part-shade and well-drained soil, with only light watering in the colder months; they range from marginally frost hardy to frost tender. Propagate from stem or leaf cuttings in late spring to summer, seed in late spring, or pot up plantlets that may form along leaf margins.

Kalanchoe blossfeldiana
FLAMING KATY

This small, shrubby African succulent reaches 12 in (30 cm) high and wide. Its multiple, upstretched branches are covered with round to rectangular, deep green leaves with red margins and notched tips. Thick racemes of small, deep red, cylindrical flowers appear from winter to early summer; cultivated strains may be pink, yellow or orange. Frost tender, it requires part-shade; it is a popular pot plant. **ZONES 10–12.**

Kalanchoe tomentosa
PANDA PLANT, PUSSY EARS

This erect, shrubby Madagascan succulent grows gradually to 3 ft (1 m) tall with a spread of 8 in (20 cm). Its spoon-shaped, light gray-green leaves, covered with white felt, often have rusty brown spots along the margins. Yellowish green flowers, tinged purple on the lobes appear in early spring, although flowering is rare in cultivation. **ZONES 11–12.**

Kalanchoe tomentosa

Kalanchoe blossfeldiana

Lithops turbiniformis

Lithops turbiniformis

This species of succulent forms in small clumps of paired leaves. Egg-shaped and orange-brown in color, they are up to 1 in (25 mm) in height. The flattened surface is scored with a shallow, transverse crevice and brown linear markings. Vivid yellow flowers up to 2 in (5 cm) in diameter bloom from white buds. **ZONES 9–11.**

LITHOPS

LIVING STONES, STONEFACE

Confined in the wild to the driest western part of South Africa's Cape Province and the adjacent part of Namibia, this fascinating genus of the mesembryanthemum alliance contains about 40 stemless succulents, which develop singly or in colonies. They are composed of pairs of extremely fleshy, upright leaves fused together to form a cylindrical or hemispherical mass with a deep crevice running across the top. New leaf-pairs and white or yellow daisy-like flowers grow up through the fissure. The plants look like smooth river stones, explaining the genus and common names, and often have translucent upper surfaces.

CULTIVATION

These frost-tender succulents are easy to grow but require very dry conditions, so need to be kept under shelter in all but arid climates. Plant in coarse, gritty soil and allow full sun. Water only in spring and propagate in summer from seed or by dividing bodies and treating them like cuttings.

Mammillaria pectinifera

MAMMILLARIA

PINCUSHION CACTI

This genus of cacti contains around 150 dwarf species, most of which are native to Mexico, although a few are from south-western USA. The short, globular or clump-forming, erect columns up to 12 in (30 cm) tall, bear stems with raised, horny tubercles and downy areoles, from which sprout silky bristles or tough, curving spines. In spring and summer, funnel- or daisy-shaped flowers appear in a circle around the crown. These are followed by light green or reddish fruits.

CULTIVATION

These marginally frost-hardy cacti require full sun for maximum flowering. Easy to grow, they prefer light, sandy soil and the occasional watering, particularly in the growing season. Most species will only tolerate frost in a dried-out state. Propagate from seed in spring and summer, or from offsets in summer. Mealybug and spider mite can be a problem.

Mammillaria bocasana

POWDER PUFF, SNOWBALL CACTUS

The white, hooked spines of this spherical cactus were used as fish hooks in its native Mexico. It grows 8–12 in (20–30 cm) high and 8 in (20 cm) across, with offsets measuring 2 in (5 cm) across each head. Off-white, daisy-like flowers appear in spring and autumn, and oblong red berries follow in summer. **ZONES 9–11.**

Mammillaria compressa

This species from central Mexico offsets freely into small pincushion clumps covered in long white spines. The body is a light bluish green to gray-green and the head of each offset can grow to 8 in (20 cm) high and 2–3 in (5–8 cm) wide. This cactus develops dark purple, daisy-shaped blossoms in spring, which are followed by large red berries in summer. **ZONES 9–11.**

Mammillaria pectinifera

syn. *Solisia pectinata*

From southeast central Mexico, the lovely flowers of this species are pale pink with a pale brown mid-stripe. They crowd around the stem in a lavish coronet. At 1 in (25 mm) across, they are nearly as wide as the stem itself. **ZONES 9–11.**

Mammillaria compressa

Mammillaria plumosa

FEATHER CACTUS

This Mexican cactus readily forms a thick, felty, mound-like cluster 6 in (15 cm) high and 15 in (38 cm) wide. The stems are blanketed with feather-like radial spines, which sprout from downy areoles. In winter, creamy green, pink or yellow flowers appear, but rarely under cultivation. It prefers fertile, alkaline soil. **ZONES 9–11.**

Mammillaria plumosa

OPUNTIA
PRICKLY PEAR, CHOLLA

This is the largest and most widespread genus of cacti. It numbers more than 200 species and occurs in the wild from southern Canada almost to the southern tip of South America, as well as the West Indies and Galapagos Islands. They range from tiny prostrate plants with tuberous roots to trees over 30 ft (9 m) tall. The branches are constricted at regular intervals to form 'joints' that may be broad and flattened, or cylindrical and sometimes covered in tubercles. All have small, fleshy leaves at the growing tips that usually fall off soon after they appear. Most species have sharp spines (sometimes barbed), as well as small bristles that are extremely hard to remove from the skin, so position these plants away from areas where children or animals play. The flowers are generally yellow or red, sometimes quite showy, followed by edible fruits (prickly pears), which range from green to yellow to red. Several species have become serious pests, with some being declared noxious weeds in some warmer countries. The spread of *Opuntia stricta* in Australia and South Africa was eventually checked by biological control, using the cochineal insect and the cactoblastus moth.

CULTIVATION

These plants thrive in hot, dry conditions in moderately fertile, gritty, humus-rich, well-drained soil and full sun. Many species, however, adapt to less optimal conditions indoors and can tolerate much neglect. Propagate from seed or detached joints in spring or summer. The cultivation of all or some of the species is prohibited in certain countries.

Opuntia microdasys var. *albispina*

Opuntia ficus-indica

Opuntia ficus-indica
INDIAN FIG CACTUS

Native to Mexico, this species has been cultivated in Mediterranean countries and India for centuries for its delicious fruit. It grows to 10–18 ft (3–5.5 m) tall and wide, each branch made up of several flat, oval segments that may be almost the size of a tennis racquet head. Rather attractive yellow flowers are borne in early summer: these develop into the oval, red or orange fruit 2–3 in (5–8 cm) in diameter, their skin studded with bristles that must be carefully stripped (wearing gloves) before the white sweet pulp can be enjoyed. Spineless cultivars exist, but connoisseurs insist they are not as sweet as the prickly ones. **ZONES 9–11.**

Opuntia microdasys
BUNNY EARS, DWARF PRICKLY PEAR

The crowded branches of this small cactus from Mexico, to only about 24 in (60 cm) tall, consist of flattened, oval, pale to mid-green pads densely dotted with small tufts of tiny golden spines. Each pad or segment is 3–5 in (8–12 cm) wide; in spring and summer they produce bright yellow flowers about 2 in (5 cm) across. These may be followed by reddish fruit more than 1 in (25 mm) in diameter, but they are rarely seen in cultivation. *Opuntia microdasys* var. *albispina* has clusters of white spines on darker green pads. Its flowers are also a paler yellow. Both are widely grown as pot plants, but the tiny spines pierce the skin at the slightest touch. **ZONES 8–11.**

Orbea variegata

syn. *Stapelia variegata*

TOAD CACTUS, STAR FLOWER, STARFISH FLOWER

Grown for its curious flowers, this South African succulent has much-branched, finger-shaped, creeping stems to 3 in (8 cm) tall with up-turned ends; they are often marked with purple and have pointed tubercles in 4 rows. From summer to autumn, striking, starfish-shaped, individual flowers appear, with a kaleidoscopic pattern of reddish brown, yellow and purple. **ZONES 9–11.**

ORBEA

This genus of about 20 species of curious, creeping succulents is closely related to *Stapelia*, and are native to drier parts of southern and eastern Africa. They are low plants, usually forming a cluster of leafless, semi-erect stems armed with ridges of soft fleshy spines. A milky sap exudes from cut or broken stems. In summer and early autumn, they produce flat, star-shaped flowers that are spotted or patterned and smell faintly of rotting meat in order to attract the flies that pollinate them.

CULTIVATION

Grow orbeas in full sun in sandy or gritty, very well-drained soil. Where summers are very hot and dry, the plants appreciate light shade in the afternoon. They do not require much water at any time of the year and outdoors will usually get by on rain. Frost tender, in cold climates they must be grown indoors, watering sparingly especially in winter. Propagate from cuttings, dried off for a few days before inserting in sand.

Orbea variegata

PARODIA

syns *Eriocactus, Notocactus, Wigginsia*

BALL CACTUS

Mostly native to the mountains of equatorial South America, the 50 or so species in this cactus genus vary from those that are singular and globe-shaped, to those that colonize in dense clusters of short cylindrical stems. These stems are ribbed with transverse rows of prominent tubercles with fleecy areoles that sprout brilliantly colored, curving spines. From a relatively young age, red, yellow and orange trumpet-shaped flowers bloom from the crown.

CULTIVATION

These frost-tender plants prefer full sun with protection from the midday heat. Easy to grow, they mostly require well-drained soil and plentiful water during the summer months, with a dry spell during winter. Propagate from seed in spring or from cuttings in summer.

Parodia haselbergii

syn. **Notocactus haselbergii**

This species from southern Brazil usually has a single stem up to 6 in (15 cm) in diameter with 30 to 60 or more ribs. Its spines, up to 60 per tubercle, are around ½ in (12 mm) long and white or yellow tinted. In winter and spring, the stem produces around 15 orange-red flowers, each about ½ in (12 mm) long. **ZONES 9–11.**

Parodia haselbergii

PEDILANTHUS

RICK RACK PLANT

This succulent genus, closely allied to *Euphorbia*, is native to the Caribbean, southern USA and northern South America. It consists of about 14 species, all bushy in appearance, that grow to a maximum height of 8 ft (2.4 m) with a spread of 5 ft (1.5 m). Species differ mainly in their inflorescence features: the flowers, borne in summer and autumn, are enclosed by oddly shaped bracts, which resemble a bird's head in some species. The foliage can be either green or variegated.

CULTIVATION

Ensure a sheltered spot as these plants are sensitive to cold. They prefer well-drained soil and part-shade. Propagate from cuttings.

Pedilanthus tithymaloides

ZIGZAG PLANT, DEVIL'S BACKBONE,
JACOB'S LADDER

This slow-growing succulent can reach a height of 6 ft (1.8 m) in cultivation. The fleshy, erect stems change direction at each node, hence the common name zigzag plant. The mid-green leaves sprout from the stems in 2 rows, resembling ribs on a backbone. Variegated cultivars are popular. Showy red bracts encase small scarlet flowers, but such flowers are rarely produced indoors. The stems, when cut, secrete a poisonous milky sap. **ZONES 9–11.**

Pedilanthus tithymaloides

Portulacaria afra

PORTULACARIA

JADE PLANT, ELEPHANT BUSH, ELEPHANT'S FOOD

The single member of this genus is a succulent, evergreen shrub with many branches that are often horizontal or twisted. It may reach a height of 12 ft (3.5 m) but looks like a twisted dwarf tree even when very young. In its native hot, dry habitat of southern Africa, it bears tiny pink flower clusters, followed by insignificant, pinkish, 3-cornered berries. In dry parts of South Africa the shrub is used to feed livestock and game, hence some of its common names.

CULTIVATION

It adapts well to a wide range of soils and climates. The soil should be well-drained and kept fairly dry, especially during winter. This plant thrives by the sea. It will grow in sun or shade and tolerates dry conditions but only the lightest frost. Propagate from cuttings in summer and from seed.

Portulacaria afra

The reddish to purplish branches on this species carry opposite pairs of lime green, round to oval, silky smooth leaves, ½ in (12 mm) across. Each leaf is set directly into the stem or into short spur-like twigs. The tiny pink flowers and berries are rare on cultivated plants. It makes an interesting rockery and tub plant; it is also a good subject for bonsai. 'Tricolor' has green, cream and pink tones, and 'Variegata' has green leaves edged with cream. **ZONES 9–11.**

Rebutia deminuta

This small, dark green, clustering cactus is from Argentina. Each individual plant grows to a height of 4 in (10 cm) and a width of 2½ in (6 cm). Attractive orange and red, funnel-shaped flowers grow from around the base of the body, lasting for about a week in summer. **ZONES 9–11.**

Rebutia senilis

This clump-forming species has a 2½ in (6 cm) wide stem matted with soft white spines. Trumpet-shaped red, yellow, pink or orange flowers 2 in (5 cm) wide appear in spring. **ZONES 9–11.**

REBUTIA

CROWN CACTUS, HEDGEHOG CACTUS

This genus, native to South America, contains about 40 very small, mostly cluster-forming cacti, varying from hemispherical to erect and cylindrical. The plants develop tubercles around their bases, from where the flower buds emerge after one or two years. Large, vivid orange, pink, purple, red, yellow or white flowers readily bloom in late spring to early summer.

CULTIVATION

Frost tender, rebutias prefer moderately fertile, very well-drained soil and full sun; they need water only during the budding and blooming period. Propagate from seed or cuttings in spring or summer.

Rebutia deminuta

Rebutia senilis

Schlumbergera 'Santa Cruz'

SCHLUMBERGERA

CHRISTMAS CACTUS

Schlumbergera 'Santa Cruz'

'Santa Cruz' is a relatively new cultivar of Christmas cactus, with showy, orange-red flowers. It was bred in California and introduced there in 1989. **ZONES 9–12.**

Christmas cacti are familiar flowershop pot plants. The genus consists of 6 species of bushy cacti from southeastern Brazil with flattened, spineless and rather weeping branches that have indented notches at the margins. While still marketed as *Zygocactus*, *Schlumbergera* has been the updated name now for several decades. Most plants sold are hybrids. The bright flowers appear at the stem tips and are an attractive, asymmetrical shape; they come in shades from palest pink to orange, magenta, scarlet and white. They are often grown in hanging baskets but do not cascade vigorously enough to cover the basket, looking their best in tall pots.

CULTIVATION

Species of *Schlumbergera* prefer mild, frost-free climates; in cooler areas they make excellent indoor plants. Plant in part-shade in rich, well-drained soil. Once they set their flower buds they do not like being moved to another position and could drop their buds. Propagate from stem cuttings in spring or early summer.

Sedum rubrotinctum
CHRISTMAS CHEER

This small and evergreen, sub-shrubby succulent grows up to 10 in (25 cm) in height and has yellow winter blooms. Its slender, readily branching multiple stems are wide-spreading and develop vivid green, pulpy, obovate leaves in grape-like bunches. The foliage turns red and yellow under arid conditions. A cold, damp climate will maintain the leaf luster. **ZONES 9–12.**

Sedum spectabile
syn. **Hylotelephium spectabile**
SHOWY SEDUM, ICE PLANT

Spoon-shaped, fleshy, gray-green leaves grow in clusters on the erect branching stems of this succulent perennial from China and Korea. Butterflies flock to the flattish heads of small, pink, star-like flowers, which bloom in late summer. It grows to a height and spread of 18 in (45 cm) and is resistant to both frost and dry conditions. 'Brilliant' bears profuse heads of bright rose-pink flowers. **ZONES 5–10.**

SEDUM
STONECROP

This large genus contains about 400 species of succulent annuals, biennials, perennials, subshrubs and shrubs native to the northern hemisphere. Quick-growing plants, they vary widely in habit, from carpet forming to upright plants growing 3 ft (1 m) tall. Their lush, whole leaves may be tubular, lanceolate, egg-shaped or elliptical, and the 5-petalled flowers appear in terminal sprays. Excellent as hanging basket or pot plants.

CULTIVATION
They range from frost tender to fully frost hardy. Fertile, porous soil is preferred; some types, however, are extremely robust and will grow in most soil types. They need full sun. Propagate perennials, shrubs and subshrubs from seed in spring or autumn, or by division or from cuttings in spring through mid-summer. Propagate annuals and biennials from seed sown under glass in early spring or outdoors in mid-spring.

Sedum morganianum
DONKEY'S TAIL, BURRO TAIL

Native to Mexico, this popular, readily branching, evergreen perennial succulent has a compact, upright habit, becoming weeping as the stems lengthen. The attractive stems grow to 12 in (30 cm) long and are composed of bluish green, inter-locking leaves that have a plump, lanceolate form. In culti-vation, clusters of long, pinkish red, starry flowers may bloom at the stem tips in summer. It makes an ideal hanging basket plant but should be handled with care as the leaves readily detach. **ZONES 9–12.**

Sedum morganianum

Sedum rubrotinctum

Sempervivum arachnoideum

SEMPERVIVUM

This is a genus of about 40 evergreen, perennial succulents originating in Europe and western Asia. They almost all have small yellow, pink or white, star-shaped flowers in summer, but their chief beauty resides in the symmetry of their rosettes of leaves and the way they spread to form carpets of foliage. This makes them ideal for rock gardens, walls and banks, and like all succulents they do not mind dry conditions. They take their common name from a custom dating from Roman times, which was to grow them on the roofs of houses—it was said that no witch could land her broomstick on a roof on which houseleeks were growing.

CULTIVATION

Plant in full sun in gravelly, well-drained soil. Flowering does not begin for several years; the rosettes die after flowering leaving offsets, from which they can be propagated.

Senecio serpens

Sempervivum arachnoideum
COBWEB HOUSELEEK

The web of white hairs covering the green, triangular-leafed rosettes of this species no doubt inspired its name. Through summer it produces pink to crimson flowers in loose terminal clusters. A native of the European Alps, it grows to a height of 3 in (8 cm) and spread of 12 in (30 cm). **ZONES 5–10.**

Sempervivum tectorum
COMMON HOUSELEEK, ROOF HOUSELEEK, HENS AND CHICKENS

The rosettes of this species are reddish tipped, sometimes red throughout. The flowers are purple to rosy red and appear in one-sided terminal clusters on 12 in (30 cm) high stems in summer. It reaches 4–6 in (10–15 cm) high and 18 in (45 cm) wide. Applying bruised leaves to the skin has a cooling effect and is said to relieve burns, insect bites, skin problems and fever; the juice is used on warts and freckles. 'Commander Hay' from the UK has large rosettes of red and green; 'Purple Beauty' has dark violet leaves; and 'Magnificum' has large rosettes and pink flowers. **ZONES 4–10.**

Sempervivum tectorum 'Purple Beauty'

SENECIO

Most of the species belonging to this genus are shrubs, and detailed information on the genus is given in the Shrubs chapter. However, *Senecio serpens* is treated here as a succulent.

Senecio serpens
BLUE CHALKSTICKS

The cylindrical blue-green leaves on this 12 in (30 cm) tall, shrubby succulent branch from the base. The white flowers appear in summer. It comes from South Africa. **ZONES 9–11.**

Stapelia gigantea

Stapelia gigantea

The specific name means 'gigantic', but this is a modest plant growing 8 in (20 cm) or so tall. It earns its name from the size of the flowers, the largest in the genus and often over 12 in (30 cm) across. They are star-shaped, yellow-brown marked with red and have white-haired, recurved edges. **ZONES 9–11.**

STAPELIA
CARRION FLOWER, STARFISH FLOWER

The 45 species in this genus are the carrion flowers *par excellence*. They are perennial succulents from southern Africa, like small cacti in growth habit but without thorns. The flowers are wide open stars, elegant in their symmetry, but they are pollinated by flies that think nothing in the world is more tasty than a piece of rotting meat. Stapelias pander to them both by the odor of the flowers and also by their color, which always includes some variation on the theme of red, brown and purple usually in marbled patterns and sometimes streaked with cream to resemble fatty meat. The flies are sometimes so thoroughly deceived that they lay eggs on them, but the larvae starve to death when they hatch—they can't eat the flower. There are several hybrids and cultivars, some featuring pinkish or yellow tints at the tips of their stems.

CULTIVATION
Plant these frost-tender species in full sun or part-shade and moderately fertile, very well-drained soil. Propagate from seed or stem cuttings in spring or summer.

Stapelia gigantea

Chapter 9

VEGETABLES & HERBS

Herbs can make attractive edible borders to both vegetable and flower gardens, or be interplanted to create intricate patterns.

Nothing compares to the satisfaction of harvesting a crop of flavorsome, home-grown vegetables and herbs. Apart from the obvious health advantages of really fresh ingredients, there is also that feeling of reward when you pick the crop that in a few short weeks has transformed from seed to edible produce.

What to plan before you plant

To provide a family's needs with a varied range of vegetables and herbs takes a little planning. A gardener who presents his or her family with a continuous supply of one particular vegetable all summer long will get no thanks at all. It may be better to plant a fraction of a packet of seeds over successive sowings, and keep what is left over for the following year.

The size of a crop is governed by the needs of the family. A small family will give most of the vegetables away if the whole back garden is given over to growing perishables such as zucchini (courgettes). However, delicious sauces can be made from an excess of tomtoes, and a glut of peas can be stored in the freezer. Herbs, of course, can be cut and dried. For really large crops, the upper limit is obviously determined by the ultimate size of the garden.

Choose the sunniest position the garden has to offer for the vegetable patch or herb garden. The soil can be improved, but sunlight is vital. Just like a tennis court, a vegetable garden is best positioned where it will receive at least 5 hours of sun each day, even in winter, when long shadows are cast from nearby trees or walls. With these shadows in mind, position the tall growers so as not to shade ground-hugging crops like lettuce.

Consider that vegetables are seasonal; some require warmth while others are better planted in cooler seasons. There may be vegetables in the local supermarket all year round, but most of these are imported from distant places where the seasonal climate may be completely different.

Cool season vegetables include broccoli, cauliflower, broad beans and spinach. They are best grown in temperatures between 50–70°F (10–20°C), and can be started from seed during the autumn. Vine crops, such as cucumbers, tomatoes and beans, grow best when planted out in spring after any likelihood of frost, where the temperature is above 70°F (20°C). Temperate growers, such as lettuce and Swiss chard (silverbeet and ruby chard), like the temperature to remain around 60–80°F (15–25°C); they are notorious for 'bolting' (running to seed) if grown on the cusp of their seasonal range.

Vegetables can also be grouped into three categories of food type: seeded, where the seeds are eaten, such as beans, tomato and sweet corn; leafy greens or stem, such as celery, rhubarb and spinach; and thirdly the root or bulbous types, the ones with their edible parts growing under the ground. These categories are of relevance when the time comes to choose fertilizers. Those vegetables that have edible roots will appreciate a higher concentration of phosphorous (shown as P on the back of a plant food packet), those that set fruit need greater amounts of potassium (K), while the leafy ones respond to a fertilizer high in nitrogen (N). This

Tomatoes are vine crops; they like to be planted out in spring and respond well to feeding with a high-potassium fertilizer.

is something to consider when planning the layout of a vegetable garden since it will be easier to manage when feeding different crops with specific fertilizer.

Good site preparation is the key to good vegetables

The best quality vegetables are produced when they are not checked in any way while growing. They should not be allowed to dry out or wilt on a summer's day, and must have sufficient nutrition. The simple answer is to maintain a good soil structure: soil that is well aerated, has a workable consistency in both damp and dry conditions and has the ability to absorb and retain moisture and fertilizers. The best way to do this is to add sufficient humus material to the soil before planting, which will also act as a temperature control for both excessive cold and heat. The more the soil structure is improved, the more enjoyable is the task of gardening and the more likelihood of the crop being able to resist both pests and diseases.

If the soil is improved each season then water use becomes more efficient. Many of the vegetables grown by the home gardener are the leafy green types. The larger the leaf, the quicker moisture transpires back into the atmosphere, and the gardener is often tempted to give a quick spray to alleviate the distressed look. It is better to water early or late in the day by a form of trickle or flood irrigation to ensure the ground stays moist but the foliage

Divide the vegetable garden into distinct sections for each crop. Taller plants should be sited where they do not cast shadows on low-growing plants.

remains dry. Damp foliage is attractive to fungus and other air borne diseases.

A layer of mulch in summer not only helps to conserve water and keep weeds to a minimum, but it can also be dug into the soil at the end of the season to provide well-composted nutrients for a winter crop. In really cold areas, the season can be extended by the application of a winter mulch to keep the chilling factor to a minimum.

There is often a need to enclose or screen a vegetable garden from strong prevailing winds. The best windbreaks are those that filter the wind. A solid wall will create turbulence and may also cast unwanted shadows, and a hedge of hungry and thirsty rooted plants will rob your crops of essential nutrients. It is better to erect a lattice, brush or wire-screened trellis and over it grow an edible vine or seasonable climbing peas or beans.

Remember to lay the vegetable garden out into distinct sections for different crops. As mentioned earlier, tall plants are best sited where they do not cast shadows. Equally, if planting successive seedlings of the same annual crop, begin where the maturing plants will not overshadow the newly planted seedlings. Perennial crops, such as rhubarb and long-lived asparagus, need to be given a section to themselves, and plants that mature at approximately the same time are best grouped together because when they are uprooted, the section can be revitalized and replanted with minimum disturbance to other plants still growing.

Herbs can be mixed with vegetables

For gardeners with a flair for design, grouping plants can be a fascinating pastime. Just as an annual garden invites experimentation with color, there is scope within a vegetable patch to coordinate both textured and colorful foliage into intricate patterns, either in a traditional manner or as a form of self-expression. There is seed available in vegetable catalogues that will never be found on supermarket shelves, such as multi-colored chards, red Brussels sprouts and climbing beans with bright scarlet flowers. Herbs can also be used with imagination to become edible borders to both vegetable and flower gardens or, in the manner of a cottage garden, they can be spot planted between perennials.

Many herbs have very similar growth requirements to vegetables. Some, like parsley, prefer a moist, fertile position, and chives will happily border a bed of onions. Others, the Mediterranean types such as rosemary, sage and the thymes with their gray-green, highly aromatic foliage, mix well with perennials in a drier well-drained position.

Abelmoschus esculentus

VEGETABLES

Abelmoschus esculentus

syn. *Hibiscus esculentus*

OKRA, GUMBO, LADY'S FINGERS

Long cultivated in parts of Africa and Asia where it originated, this 6 ft (1.8 m) tall species was taken to the Americas with slaves from West Africa, and has remained a traditional ingredient of many dishes in the USA's Deep South. It is an attractive plant with red-eyed yellow flowers. Both flower buds and the long starchy immature pods are eaten. Okra requires a long hot summer for successful growth, so in cold areas provide good protection over winter. **ZONES 9–11.**

Agaricus campestris

syn. *Psalliota campestris*

MUSHROOM

This common fungus is happy to grow indoors or outdoors, under houses or in sheds, as long as it is darkish, humid and the temperature is constant, ideally between 50–55°F (10–13°C). The mushroom lives on different sorts of compost, and most home gardeners are best buying a mushroom kit from their nursery and following detailed instructions. Mushrooms are usually ready to harvest within 5 weeks—they can be harvested at the button, cap or flat stage of growth. Pick them by twisting out, not pulling. **ZONES 5–11.**

ABELMOSCHUS

This is a genus of around 15 species from tropical Africa and Asia. They are annuals, biennials or short-lived perennials. Several species make attractive ornamentals and the vegetable okra or gumbo is grown for its edible young pods.

CULTIVATION

They are mostly grown as summer annuals, requiring fertile, well-drained soil, a sheltered position in full sun, and plentiful water.

AGARICUS

MUSHROOM

Mushrooms are among the few fungi actively cultivated. They are, of course, grown for their edible fruiting bodies, not their beauty. Mushrooms are all similar in general appearance but vary considerably in size: the white or pale pink to beige caps, with pink to brown undersides, range from ½ in (12 mm) to over 6 in (15 cm) diameter. As many fungi are highly toxic, take great care to accurately identify any collected in the wild before eating them—edible and inedible species are very similar in appearance.

CULTIVATION

Cultivating mushrooms is quite unlike growing any other garden crop. Generally grown in the dark, they require warm, moist conditions, a suitable growing medium, and care is needed with the compost mix to get the pH right. Once growing well, they are largely self sustaining, but can take considerable trial and error to get that first crop. Insects and rodents can be a problem, so it is important to keep the growing area clean.

Agaricus campestris

Allium porrum
syn. Allium ampeloprasum
var. porrum

LEEK

Of uncertain origin but now widely distributed in cooler parts of the northern hemisphere, the leek has broad concave leaves, the sheathing bases of which form a tight cylinder, this being the edible part. The flowering stem can be 3 ft (1 m) or more tall, with a large, spherical head of tiny gray-green to dull reddish flowers. Leeks are easier to grow than onions and more suited to cold climates. Seeds are sown in spring or summer, and plants are harvested as needed once the base of the leek is at least 1 in (25 mm) thick. 'Giant Winter Wila' is one of the blue-leafed cultivars that mature through winter; 'Mammoth Blanche' is typical of the very fat leeks, the bases of which can be up to 2½ in (6 cm) in diameter. **ZONES 5–10.**

Allium porrum 'Giant Winter Wila'

ALLIUM

Most of the species belonging to this genus are bulbs, and detailed information is given in the Bulbs, Corms and Tubers chapter. However, the ones included are treated as vegetables.

Allium cepa

ONION, SPRING ONION, SCALLION, SHALLOT

The onion was a popular vegetable among the Greeks and Romans but never eaten by the Egyptians who regarded it as sacred. The spring onion is an immature onion which has not yet made a bulb. This species has given rise to a vast number of cultivars, varying in size, shape, color and flavor. The standard onion belongs to the **Cepa Group**. Bunching onions or shallots belong to the **Aggregatum Group**, which is distinguished by the cluster of small bulbs; these have a more delicate taste than spring onions and can be used instead of chives. The tree onion belongs to the **Proliferum Group** which bears small bulbs at the top of the flower stalk. Harvest onions in late summer when the leaves have begun to yellow. **ZONES 4–11.**

Allium cepa, Proliferum Group

Allium cepa, Cepa Group

APIUM

CELERY, CELERIAC

Over 20 species of biennials and perennials make up this genus in the carrot family, occurring through Europe, temperate Asia and cooler parts of the southern hemisphere. It is known in the guise of one species, celery, grown as an annual in the garden for its stalk, or petiole, which can be eaten raw or cooked. The wild *Apium* species have leaves in basal tufts, or spread along creeping stems; these are divided to varying degrees into somewhat fleshy segments. Tiny white flowers are borne in umbels.

CULTIVATION

Plant in soil with ample moisture-retentive humus. They are relatively shallow-rooted plants and it is essential that both water and fertilizer be provided on a regular basis to ensure stalks remain tender and succulent. Today, many gardeners choose the self-blanching types which do not require trenching as was the case with earlier varieties. Sow seeds in a starter bed or tray and transplant seedlings to permanent beds ensuring that roots are disturbed as little as possible. Self-blanching types can be grown closer together to help keep light off stalks while the green or non-blanching types can be more widely spaced.

Apium graveolens

The wild celery of Europe is a strong-smelling biennial growing up to 3 ft (1 m). Occurring in marshy locations along the coasts, it has finely divided leaves; the late summer flowers are held in loose compound umbels. It has been domesticated for over 2000 years and selection and breeding has given rise to numerous cultivars which can be divided into 3 groups, traditionally designated as botanical varieties. *Apium graveolens* var. *dulce* is the common celery, characterized by its long, succulent, leaf stalks and limited leafy green tops. In a garden situation, it is cut before flowering, the timing of which to a great degree is governed by temperature, consequently it has quite a short growing season in many areas. *A. g.* var. *rapaceum* is celeriac and has a swollen, edible rootstock like a turnip and slender leaf stalks that are usually discarded. It requires similar growing conditions to celery but needs a long growing season to make a large root. Leaf celery or *A. g.* var. *secalinum* is the form from which the leafy tops are used in soups and stews. In China a similar type of celery is grown for its stalks and leaves. **ZONES 5–10.**

Apium graveolens var. *rapaceum*

Apium graveolens var. *dulce*

ASPARAGUS

This large genus not only includes the edible asparagus, *Asparagus officinalis*, but also up to 60 other perennial species. Many are commonly called ferns, but in fact they belong to the lily family in its broad sense, though botanists have recently recognized many smaller families in place of one large one, embracing very diverse elements. As interpreted here, the genus *Asparagus* includes only cool-temperate, herbaceous species, mainly from Europe and Asia. The shrubby and climbing species from Africa are removed to the genera *Protasparagus* and *Myrsiphyllum*.

CULTIVATION
For cultivation of the edible asparagus, the selection of a suitable garden bed is critical as the crowns can grow undisturbed for up to 20 years or more. The chosen bed, in full sun, should be well dug over, manured and have good drainage. They can be sown from seed, although crowns, if available, will produce earlier cropping. Give asparagus 12 in (30 cm) between each plant and do not harvest the young shoots or spears until the third spring so as to allow the crowns to mature; always allow a few shoots to elongate to build up the plant's food reserves. If white spears are preferred, cut well below the soil surface just as spears become visible.

Asparagus officinalis
ASPARAGUS

A frost-hardy perennial believed native to the Mediterranean region and western Asia, this vegetable seems to have been cultivated since before Christ, either for medicinal use or as a food crop. The emerging spear of asparagus will expand into a much-branched, ferny, erect stem with innumerable tiny, linear leaves if allowed to grow uncut. Female plants will produce many red-berried fruit, which should be removed before self-seeding occurs. '**Mary Washington**' is a variety well liked for its long, thick spears, but the newer F1 hybrids will often provide higher yields. **ZONES 4–9.**

Asparagus officinalis

A. officinalis 'Mary Washington'

BETA

BEET

This genus of 6 species of broad-leafed annuals, biennials and perennials, native to Europe, west Asia and North Africa, is most familiar in the form of several important garden and commercial vegetables, all cultivated races of the one species, *Beta vulgaris*. The genus belongs to the saltbush family, as do spinach *(Spinacia)* and orache *(Atriplex)*, and its species often grow in the wild in saline coastal habitats. They have a well-developed tap root and large basal leaves, from among which the flowering stems elongate, bearing numerous inconspicuous, greenish flowers followed by small, slightly prickly dry fruits, normally thought of as the 'seeds'.

CULTIVATION

All beets are relatively easy to grow, preferring a loose soil enriched with compost. Water well to encourage steady growth. Sow seeds in spring in cooler climates, all year round in warmer ones. Beetroot seeds are sown about 8 in (20 cm) apart; when the first leaves appear, weed out the weaker seedlings. Keep soil moist and harvest the beetroot by hand; in warm climates the beetroot can be harvested almost all year round, but in cold climates the roots are picked and stored over winter. Swiss chard (silverbeet and ruby chard) are fast growing, so plant further apart in an open position in deep, fertile soil that has been previously cultivated. Water frequently—any check in growth or sudden change of conditions can lead to bolting (premature flowering). Propagate from seed.

Beta vulgaris subsp. *cicla*

Beta vulgaris subsp. *maritima*

Beta vulgaris

The original wild form of this well-known species, now classified as **Beta vulgaris** subsp. **maritima**, is an erect or sprawling perennial of west European and Mediterranean seashores, with succulent, salt-resistant foliage that can be gathered as a vegetable. Domestication has led to a number of cultivated races of food plants, most of which behave as biennials or annuals. Botanists have divided them into two further subspecies, each containing two or more vegetable (or crop) types, which follow.

B. v. subsp. vulgaris—containing the familiar beetroot (and its cultivars such as **'Pablo'**), too well known to need description; sugar beet, similar but with pale roots that contain extremely high sugar levels; and mangel-wurzel, used mainly for livestock fodder.

B. v. subsp. cicla—containing the leaf vegetables, namely Swiss chard (including silverbeet and ruby chard), with large, puckered leaves, popular as a spinach substitute in warm climates, or grown partly for ornament if a red-stalked form; and spinach chard with smaller, flatter leaves that can be harvested over a long period. **ZONES 5–10.**

Beta vulgaris subsp. *vulgaris*

Beta vulgaris subsp. *vulgaris* 'Pablo'

Brassica oleracea, Acephala Group, Osaka Series

BRASSICA

This remarkable genus has produced a more diverse range of important vegetables than almost any other. It includes about 30 wild species of annuals, biennials and subshrubs, ranging through the Mediterranean region and temperate Asia. Thousands of years ago, botanists now believe, spontaneous hybrids between several of these appeared around human settlements and from one such hybrid arose all that major group of vegetables now classified under the name *Brassica oleracea*. Another large assortment are included under the name *Brassica rapa*. Then there are the mustards and rape, grown for the valuable oils in their seeds, hot-tasting in some. Yet other species are best known as common weeds of roadsides and crops: the wild mustards. The genus *Brassica* in its more primitive form is characterized by its usually lobed leaves, 4-petalled yellow to white flowers and small, spindle-shaped fruiting capsules containing rows of tiny seeds. Most parts of the plants have some hot-tasting mustard oils, which give the characteristic 'bite' to raw cabbage as well as the much more intense flavor to mustard.

CULTIVATION

Most brassicas love a lime-rich, moist, well-drained soil. Seedlings should be raised in seedbeds and then carefully planted out 6 to 8 weeks later in a sheltered, sunny spot in soil that has been previously used for a different crop. They are more prone to pests and diseases than other vegetables, and the use of insecticides is hard to avoid if undamaged vegetables are desired. Ensure soil is kept weed-free and not too wet. Club root is a common disease in these vegetables, and crop rotation should be practised.

Brassica oleracea

Thought to have originated as an ancient hybrid between two or more of the wild Mediterranean species, this is the most important of the *Brassica* species and one of the most versatile of all cultivated food plants. In its various forms it yields edible roots (kohlrabi), leaves (cabbage), shoots (Brussels sprouts) and flower buds (cauliflower and broccoli), as well as a few ornamentals, for example, the colored-leafed kales, and curiosities such as some forms of giant kale, the 'trunks' of which have been used as walking sticks! The vegetable brassicas associated with this species include thousands of named cultivars, which are most conveniently divided into the following cultivar groups.

Acephala Group, the kales and ornamental kales—these are flat-leafed or curly-leafed cabbages that do not form a head, popular in northern Europe because of their tolerance to cold. Some forms can grow thick, knobby stems up to 6 ft (1.8 m) or more tall. Sow the flat-leafed kales from seed, as they do not tolerate transplanting. In Scotland, the broth made from their leaves is a traditional Highland dish. 'Tall Scotch' is a typical cultivar, while '**Moss Curled**' is representative of the kales, with tightly curled leaves looking a bit like parsley. Ornamental kales, used for bedding and also sold in pots by florists, have leaves usually lobed or dissected, and strikingly veined with purple, pink, yellow or white. **Osaka Series** is a modern strain of mixed colors, the leaves undivided but with frilled edges.

Botrytis Group, the ordinary white cauliflower, is a popular vegetable with a history stretching back to the Renaissance. The densely massed, tiny, abortive flower buds and the stalk that bears them are white and tender, with a mild flavor. It is a vegetable that is not easy to grow to perfection, preferring a humus-rich soil for large, compact head production. The flower buds are easily bruised and damaged. Apart from white, cultivars with pale green, pink and purple heads are known. Typical white cultivars are '**Snowball**', large headed and late maturing, and '**Mini**', early maturing with heads of 4 in (10 cm) or so across. '**Early Purplehead**' is purple-green, but the purple disappears on cooking.

Capitata Group are the cabbages in all their diversity of form and coloring, possessing in common the tight, many-layered head of leaves. Innumerable cultivars, for example, '**Hardora**' and

Top right: Brassica oleracea,
Botrytis Group
Centre: B. o., Capitata Group, 'Hawke'
Right: B. o., Capitata Group, 'Hardora'

'Hawke', vary in their seasonal tolerance, and this ensures that they can be grown worldwide in many different climatic zones. Their nutritional value is high. 'Golden Acre' is a typical early-maturing, round-headed cultivar; 'Sugarloaf' a spring type with conical head; and 'Greengold' a large late-maturing F1 hybrid. Red cabbage, with its purplish leaves, is a slow-maturing cabbage that needs a long growing season, but its solid, chewy flesh makes it the best type for pickling and frying; 'Mammoth Red Rock' is one of the best red cultivars. The Savoy cabbages (**Sabauda Subgroup**) have wrinkled,

Brassica oleracea, Cymosa Group

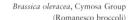

Brassica oleracea, Cymosa Group
(Romanesco broccoli)

strongly veined leaves: they are extremely frost hardy and will thrive in very cold conditions. They tend to be larger and more strongly flavored than ordinary cabbages. 'Drumhead' is a favorite Savoy cultivar, as is 'Karvoi'.

Cymosa Group includes all the broccolis which, like cauliflower, are grown for their densely massed flower buds and fleshy stalks, but the buds are further advanced and are not pure white but green, purplish or yellow-green. 'Broccoli' is Italian, coming from *brocco*, 'sprout', and it was in Italy that nearly all the different types of this vegetable evolved. Calabrese is the common type with broad, fleshy, green or purplish heads maturing in summer. 'De Cicco' is a pale green, early-maturing cultivar; 'Waltham 29' is also popular. Romanesco broccolis are more cauliflower-like in both appearance and flavor, with tight, hemispherical heads consisting of many neat conical points, maturing later than Calabrese; usually pale yellow-green in color, they are very decorative. Sprouting broccoli is different again, with many narrow-headed buds on long, asparagus-like stalks, appearing among the leaves—they develop over winter and can be picked over a long season in spring and early summer; 'Italian Green Sprouting' is the best known variety. All broccoli is best picked and eaten when young because once the yellow flowers begin to open it becomes coarse in both texture and flavor. It is ideally grown in raised beds. Do not allow the plant to flower, as it will stop growing. Grubs and waterlogging are two major problems.

Gemmifera Group equates with Brussels sprouts, cultivated as a biennial for the miniature cabbage-like heads which grow on the elongating stems, one below each of the large leaves. Timing is crucial when planting Brussels sprouts, since it needs to mature in the coldest part of the year in order to form compact hearts. In warm climates, sow the seed in

Brassica oleracea, Gemmifera Group, 'Troika'

Brassica rapa, Chinensis Group

summer, in cold climates, sow in mid-spring. In autumn, remove any yellowing leaves and make sure the soil stays firm around the stem of the plant. There are many cultivars, suited to different soils, yielding smaller or larger sprouts. 'Long Island', 'Jade Beauty', 'Icarus' and 'Troika' are widely grown cultivars; 'Ruby Red' has reddish sprouts.

Gongylodes Group is the name that covers kohlrabi (a word of German origin). This root vegetable resembles beetroot in its growth form with a swollen, bulb-like stem base. With a slightly nutty flavor reminiscent of both turnip and cabbage, it can be eaten raw or cooked. Young leaves are edible. Weed lightly as root disturbance will slow growth. 'Purple Vienna', 'White Vienna' and 'Earliest Erfurt' are established cultivars. **ZONES 6–11.**

Brassica rapa

After *Brassica oleracea*, this is the next most diverse of the brassica species in terms of the number of vegetables and crops it has given rise to. Its wild form, referred to as *B. rapa* subsp. *sylvestris*, is a common weed of road verges and crops. In common with most of the cultivated races it has quite large flowers, about ½ in (12 mm) across and bright yellow. There are also some lesser-known cultivar groups in *B. rapa*, including additional leaf vegetables and oilseeds.

Chinensis Group includes the Chinese vegetables known as pak-choi (bok-choi in Cantonese), annual plants with loose rosettes of bright green leaves with very broad white stalks, like silverbeet. The crisp stalks form the main bulk of the vegetable. The plants run to seed quickly, so should be sown in small groups every 10 days. Harvest the entire plant or take a few leaves as needed after 6 to 8 weeks. '**Joi Choi**' is a recent F1 hybrid with very white stalks.

Pekinensis Group equates to the Chinese pe-tsai, also known as wom-buk or Chinese cabbage. Somewhat resembling lettuce (especially cos lettuce) in growth form but with leaves strongly veined, this fast-growing vegetable was introduced to Europe only in the nineteenth century. It is easy to grow as long as it is kept moist. The leaves are commonly tied together around the developing heart, and the whole plant is harvested. '**Jade Pagoda**' and '**Hong Kong**' are modern, high-yielding F1 cultivars.

Rapifera Group, the turnips, is the best known cultivar group in the West. A moderately frost-hardy biennial, the turnip is grown as an annual for its fleshy roots. It was a staple food of the northern European working classes until the potato upstaged it. It is suited more to cooler regions of the world. To produce a quick crop, grow turnips in fertile soil in rows and keep young plants moist throughout the growing period. '**Scots Yellow**' is an old cultivar of carrot-like form; '**Purpletop White Globe**' is an early-maturing white turnip; '**Shogrin**' is exceptional in being grown primarily for its edible leaves. **ZONES 7–11.**

Brassica rapa, Pekinensis Group

CAPSICUM

Capsicum annuum, Conoides Group

PEPPER, CHILI

This genus of about 10 species of annuals and shrubs from tropical America is renowned for the hot taste of its fruits, some varieties contributing the fiery hotness considered an essential element in so many of the world's cuisines. There is debate about how and when they reached Asia from the Americas, some claiming that their arrival predated Columbus, but there is no denying that most present-day eastern and southern Asian dishes would not be the same without them. The plants have soft but tough branches and smooth green leaves; inconspicuous white flowers are borne singly or in small groups in the leaf axils, followed by fleshy, hollow fruits that vary greatly in size, shape, color and flavor—generally, the smaller the fruit the hotter the taste. There has been much debate among botanists as to how to classify the innumerable cultivated races into species, though most now divide them among 3 or 4 species only. Some chilies are grown as ornamentals for their brightly colored fruits, though some similar ornamental solanums with poisonous fruits are easily confused with these.

CULTIVATION

The larger-fruited chilies and sweet peppers, as well as the shorter-lived of the small chilies, grow in vegetable gardens as summer annuals, requiring a long, warm, humid season to ripen their fruit. Give plants a rich, friable soil as their roots are quite deep and ample water must be available to ensure growth is not checked. In warmer areas seed can be sown *in situ;* in colder areas sow under glass and transplant when frost danger is past. The shrubby chilies require only a sheltered spot against a wall in a warm climate, and are easily propagated from cuttings. In cold climates, make sure the plants are well protected in winter.

Capsicum annuum

PEPPER

This one species encompasses most of the variation in fruit characteristics found in the genus as a whole—from the large sweet bell peppers used in salads to some of the smallest and hottest of the

Capsicum annuum, Grossum Group

chilies. Despite the specific name, plants also vary from bushy annuals to quite long-lived shrubs up to 6 ft (1.8 m) tall. The species' main defining character is that the flowers are mostly solitary with recurved stalks. The many cultivars can be divided into a number of cultivar groups, depending on fruit size and shape. The well known **Grossum Group** includes the main salad peppers—pimento, bell and sweet peppers. The **Longum Group** includes the cayenne peppers and paprika and banana peppers, with elongated and usually curved, moderately hot to very hot fruits. The **Conoides Group** includes forms with erect, conical fruits, most small and hot, some grown as ornamentals with

multi-colored fruits—'**Red Missile**' is a typical example. Its fruit start out creamy white and ripen purple through red. The **Cerasiforme Group** (cherry peppers) have small, hot, globular to egg-shaped fruit; some of these are also used as ornamentals. The **Fasciculatum Group**, known as red cone peppers, have clustered, erect, elongated fruits. Within each group there is a range of cultivars of varying shades of red, yellow, green and purple, and in many shapes and sizes. **ZONES 8–12.**

Capsicum annuum, Fasciculatum Group

Capsicum annuum, Grossum Group

Cichorium intybus 'Palo Rosa Bella'

Cichorium endivia
ENDIVE, ESCAROLE

This close relative of chicory is an annual or biennial grown for its leaves, which are usually eaten green as a bitter salad; they resemble lettuce but are more sharply flavored. The plant typically is loose hearted, somewhat like a mignonette lettuce but all green. Most popular are varieties with more divided and crisped leaves, such as 'Sally' and 'Green Curled'. The wild origins of endive are uncertain, and it may be an old hybrid.
ZONES 4–10.

Cichorium endivia

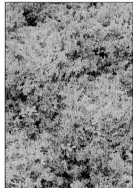

CICHORIUM

This genus of 8 species of annuals and perennials from Europe, western Asia and northern Africa is closely related to the lettuce genus *Lactuca*. Two species are grown in temperate-climate gardens mainly as salad plants, eaten in the same way as lettuce or sometimes blanched. The plants have slightly swollen taproots and basal tufts of large, crisp, tongue-shaped leaves, which exude pinhead drops of milky sap when broken. Their usually blue, dandelion-like flowerheads are borne on tall branched stems and open only for the morning.

CULTIVATION
Mostly very frost hardy, they need full sun. When growing as leaf vegetables plant in fertile, humus-rich, well-drained soil and keep moist, or the plants will run to seed early. Sow seeds from 12 to 15 in (30 to 38 cm) apart in a shaded position in late summer. Use liquid fertilizer every now and then as the plants are growing. Watch for attack by slugs and for rust-fungus and mildew. They can also be propagated from root division.

Cichorium intybus
CHICORY, WITLOOF, RADICCHIO

In some countries chicory is best known as a coffee substitute or adulterant, the roots being roasted and ground for this purpose. But in France, Belgium and Italy this species has produced a whole range of leaf vegetables that have a firm place in the cuisines of those countries. Grown like small lettuces, they vary greatly in leaf coloring and shape (see, for example, 'Palo Rosa Bella'). In cooler regions blanched shoots or 'chicons' are produced by forcing the roots into growth in a dark cellar in winter, or by tying the leaves around the growing shoot. The true 'endive' of the French belongs to this species, not *Cichorium endivia*. It has the same geographical range as the genus as a whole, and is widely naturalized along roadsides in temperate regions of other continents, conspicuous by its pale blue flowers.
ZONES 4–10.

Cucumis sativus

CUCUMIS
CUCUMBER, GOURD, MELON

Two genera of the cucurbit family are foremost in importance for the food plants they have produced, namely *Cucurbita* itself, and *Cucumis*. It is the latter genus that has given us most of the melons (except watermelon, which is *Citrullus*) and the cucumbers. It consists of 30 or more species and occurs wild in Africa, southern Asia and Australia. They are annual or perennial tendril climbers or prostrate scrambling vines with thin, lobed or angled leaves and white or yellow flowers, usually with both sexes on the one plant.

CULTIVATION
Plant in humus-rich soil and water generously. A dry climate is preferable as humid conditions can affect the quality of the fruits and make the plants more prone to the fungus anthracnose. Hand pollinate if growing melons on a small scale. Propagation is from seed.

Cucumis sativus
CUCUMBER, GHERKIN

A native of India, the cucumber is an annual trailing plant that grows to 18 in (45 cm) high with a 6 ft (1.8 m) spread. It has leaves with shallow, pointed lobes and yellow funnel-shaped flowers. The green-skinned fruit have a crisp white flesh with numerous seeds that are eaten with the flesh when immature. Cucumbers come in many different shapes and sizes, representing different cultivated races, though the flavor varies only slightly. Some smaller types have been developed for pickling and are known as gherkins. Some races have fruit with irregular rows of warty or prickly protuberances, others are completely smooth. In cool climates, cucumbers are normally grown in greenhouses, or the seedlings are raised under glass in winter or spring for summer planting. Train cucumber vines on a frame or trellis to keep the fruit away from the soil. They are quite vulnerable to downy mildew, though the long green kinds are more resistant than the short 'apple' cucumbers. All cucumbers are picked at an early stage of maturity, which encourages further fruit production as well as yielding tastier cucumbers.
ZONES 9–12.

Cichorium intybus

Cucurbita maxima

CUCURBITA

MARROW, PUMPKIN, SQUASH

All 27 species of this important genus are native to the Americas, mostly in the warmer, drier regions. Their history of domestication, established from archeological excavations, dates back to 7000 BC in Central America and 1000 BC in North America. Modern pumpkins and squashes come in a vast and bewildering array of shapes, sizes and colors and it is often difficult to assign a particular cultivar to a species. Some of the recognized species are believed to be of ancient hybrid origin. The cultivated species are annuals, generally with trailing stems radiating from a central root, and large, rough-textured leaves that are lobed in varying degree. The orange or yellow flowers are quite large and conspicuous, of different sexes but on the one plant; the fruits develop below the female flowers, which soon wither and drop off. Classification of cultivar groups is made difficult by the great variation in common names used in different countries: for example the 'pumpkin' of North America is usually one of the races of *Cucurbita pepo*, while in some other countries the most popular pumpkins are *C. maxima*. Some pumpkin varieties produce enormous fruits: some of those exhibited have exceeded 1,000 lb (454 kg).

CULTIVATION

Most species of this genus are easy to raise and have the same need of a warm, rich soil. In warm climates sow from early spring to late summer; in cold climates sow indoors in early summer, watering all seedlings well before planting. They do best planted on raised mounds of soil mixed with well rotted compost and manure. Keep well irrigated as they are water hungry. Harvest in autumn. Check for slugs.

Cucurbita maxima
AUTUMN SQUASH, WINTER PUMPKIN, WINTER SQUASH

Originating in subtropical South America, this species has long-running stems and large, nearly circular leaves that are hardly lobed. The feature by which it is recognized is the fruit stalk, which is large, not ridged, and of a soft corky texture. It includes a large group of pumpkins with very hard blue-gray or orange skins, including the gigantic show pumpkins, some of the pumpkins used for livestock feed, and some of the winter squashes including a great variety of shapes, sizes and colors, often with ornamented skins.
ZONES 9–11.

Cucurbita moschata
CROOKNECK SQUASH, PUMPKIN, WINTER SQUASH

Originating somewhere in Central America, this species was probably the earliest to be domesticated. The stems are long running or may climb by tendrils, and the leaves are shallowly 5-lobed. The fruits vary greatly but are often

Cucurbita pepo

Cucurbita moschata

elongated or bottle-shaped and some are bent over at the top (crookneck squashes); they include also the butternut and other pumpkins. Most cultivars of this species ripen their fruit in autumn or winter. **ZONES 8–11.**

Cucurbita pepo
GOURD, PUMPKIN, SUMMER SQUASH, VEGETABLE MARROW

Originating in Mexico and southern USA, and possibly an ancient hybrid, this species has given rise to a broader range of cultivars than any other. The plants can be either compact or have long trailing stems and the leaves are usually deeply lobed with overlapping lobes. The summer squashes vary from elongated to broad and flattened with scalloped rims, and may have ornamented skins, and there are also some crooknecked varieties. Vegetable marrows have long fruit with rather tender skins, usually green or yellow; a development from these, now of foremost importance among vegetables, are the zucchinis or courgettes, harvested when very immature and treated like a green vegetable. Vegetable spaghetti is a race of squashes with rather dry, shreddy flesh. Various kinds of pumpkin also belong to this species, some used mainly for stock food; they do not keep well and are normally eaten soon after picking. **ZONES 8–11.**

Cucurbita pepo

CYNARA

The 10 *Cynara* species of perennials, thistle relatives from the Mediterranean of statuesque proportions, are grown for their large silvery gray, deeply divided leaves and their thistle-like flowerheads. It includes the globe artichoke and the cardoon, both with edible parts, which in one are the immature flowerheads and in the other, the leaf stalks.

CULTIVATION

Cynara species should be grown in full sun and in a fertile well-drained soil. To be seen to best advantage they should be given plenty of space. Propagation is from seed by offsets that are formed around the crown.

Cynara cardunculus

CARDOON

Resembling its relative the globe artichoke, cardoon produces broad, fleshy, edible leaf stalks in a similar manner to celery. It also makes a fine ornamental, towering up to 8 ft (2.4 m) high with very coarse gray stems and leaves and multiple large mauve flowerheads. Most often grown from offsets, seed may be started indoors and planted out after all danger of frost has passed. Space plants 5 ft (1.5 m) apart in rows in well-drained, humus-rich soil. Leaf stalks can be blanched by enclosing them in cardboard tubes. Harvest stems by slicing under the crown through the roots. **ZONES 6–10.**

Cynara cardunculus

Cynara scolymus

Cynara scolymus

GLOBE ARTICHOKE

Once considered to be an aphrodisiac, the globe artichoke has delicate, gray-green leaves and is easy to grow in most soils and positions. Make sure it has enough space (one or two plants are enough in a small garden). A rich soil will mean better production. Plant suckers rather than seeds about 3 ft (1 m) apart in early spring. Remove yellowing leaves and stems in autumn. Cut the plump flower buds from the plants in spring and summer before the flowers begin to open. Watch for leaf spot disease. **ZONES 6–10.**

DAUCUS

This genus of about 25 species of annuals and biennials has a wide natural distribution and in the case of the carrot, *Daucus carota*, an even wider man-made distribution. The wild species can be found in Europe, temperate Asia, Africa, Australia and New Zealand. Only one form is found in cultivation, the root vegetable carrot, which is not a wild species as such but a form of one developed over centuries by cultivation.

CULTIVATION

Carrots are raised from seeds best sown where they are to grow in rows about 10 in (25 cm) apart in deep, warm loam, making sure the earth is firmly compacted around the seeds. Keep the ground moist and thin the rows out when the seedlings are about 1 in (25 mm) high. The carrot gives a high yield even in a small garden and can be stored in bins or boxes between layers of sand. Once they are big enough to pick, avoid leaving them in the ground during wet weather as the root will split. The carrot is vulnerable to carrot-root fly, greenfly and aphids. A sunny well-drained aspect with a deeply dug, fertile soil suits them best. Propagate from seed.

Helianthus tuberosus

HELIANTHUS

Most members of this genus are annuals and perennials, and detailed information is given in the Annuals and Perennials chapter. However, *Helianthus tuberosus* is treated here as a vegetable.

Daucus carota
subsp. *sativus*
CARROT

This everyday root vegetable is thought to have originated in Afghanistan and was introduced to Europe 600 years ago. Many varieties are available including '**Nantes**' and '**Touchon**' which have a longish, cylindrical root with a distinct orange-yellow core and orange-red skin.
ZONES 3–11.

Daucus carota subsp. *sativus*

Helianthus tuberosus
JERUSALEM ARTICHOKE

Native to the USA and Canada, this sunflower relative is sometimes regarded as a weed because it spreads rapidly, to make a forest of slender stems that terminate in small yellow flowerheads. It is a popular vegetable in parts of Europe, although the tubers contain the carbohydrate inulin, which is indigestible to humans. By fermenting tubers in pits, the native Americans converted inulin into digestible sugars. **ZONES 4–10.**

LACTUCA
LETTUCE

Lactuca sativa 'Black Seeded Simpson'

This widespread genus of around 100 species is best represented in temperate Eurasia. It includes a number of common weeds but is best known in the form of *Lactuca sativa*—the common lettuce—which appears to have been in cultivation for at least 5000 years and is thought to be derived from the weedy 'prickly lettuce', *L. serriola*, whose seeds also yield an edible oil. Species may be annual, biennial or perennial and range from 4 in (10 cm) to over 6 ft (1.8 m) high. If allowed to flower, this member of the daisy family has large sprays of small blooms, often mauve or yellow. The non-edible species contain very bitter compounds that have sedative properties and some have been used medicinally.

Lactuca sativa 'New Red Fire'

CULTIVATION
They are easily grown in any moist but well-drained soil in full sun or part-shade. In cool climates sow seed from early spring to late summer; in warm climates, from autumn to mid-spring, though some heat-tolerant varieties can be grown in summer. For tender, succulent leaves ensure soil remains moist. Shade young plants in hot weather and feed at intervals with weak liquid manure. Propagate from seed.

Lactuca sativa
COMMON LETTUCE

This leafy annual, grown for its succulent crisp leaves, comes in a large number of shapes and flavors. Popular types include the common iceberg or crisphead, with globular heads like pale green cabbages; cos or Romaine lettuce with tall, upright growth and crisp well-flavored leaves; butterhead, a small variety with waxy light green outer leaves and a firm heart; and the popular loose-

leaf varieties with leaves that can be picked a
few at a time as they mature. All come in an
array of cultivars. **'Black Seeded Simpson'**, a
loose-leaf variety with good vitamin C content,
is popular in the USA. **'Bubbles'** is a compact
semi-cos with blistered leaves, sweet and nutty.
'Frisby' has tight heads of bright green, crinkly
leaves. **'Green Salad Bowl'**, a loose-leaf variety
with bright green frilly leaves, is good for
cutting all summer. **'Lakeland'** is an excellent,
crisp-leafed iceberg variety that is similar to
'Great Lakes'. **'Lolli Bionda'** is a loose-leaf,
non-hearting variety with decorative frilly
leaves that can make an ornamental edging
plant. **'Lollo Rossa'** is another loose-leaf
variety; its rich reddish purple curly leaves
may be cut at any time of year. **'New Red Fire'**
is an iceberg with a green heart and reddish
bronze outer leaves. The **Oak Leaf** types are
loose-leafed, the leaves divided into narrow,
finger-like lobes: **'Red Oak Leaf'** has reddish
brown leaves. **'Red Salad Bowl'** has reddish
brown leaves with a hint of bitterness. The
Batavian loose-leaf **'Red Sails'**, with crinkled
dark reddish bronze leaves, is longstanding and
slow to bolt. **'Rouge d'Hiver'** is smooth-leafed
and among the hardier red lettuces for winter
cutting. **'Saladini'** is sold as a seed mixture of
many different types of loose-leaf lettuces and
lettuce-like greens. **'Simpson Flute'** has bright
green frilly leaves. **'Target'** is a tight-hearted,
almost cabbage-like lettuce. Celtuce, *Lactuca
sativa* **var.** *augustana* (syn. *L. s.* var.
asparagina), has an edible stem, similar to
celery stalk and edible bright green, curled
leaves. **ZONES 7–12.**

Lactuca sativa, Oak Leaf type

Lactuca sativa, 'Frisby'

Lycopersicon esculentum

LYCOPERSICON

TOMATO

There are 7 species in this Central and South American genus of annuals and short-lived evergreen perennials, closely allied to the much larger genus *Solanum,* which includes the potato and the eggplant. The plant known as the tomato was cultivated at the time of the Spanish conquest by the Incas in Ecuador and Peru and the Aztecs in Mexico. For centuries it was regarded with suspicion by Europeans; not until the early nineteenth century did it finally gain worldwide acceptance as a food plant. The genus name *Lycopersicon* is from the Greek meaning 'wolf peach' and applied originally to an unrelated Egyptian plant; Linnaeus somewhat arbitrarily named the tomato *Solanum lycopersicum* and the name stuck.

CULTIVATION

Tomatoes require a long, warm, growing season, and in cool climates the seedlings need to be started under glass in spring so fruit development can take place in the brief summer. Plant in fertile, well-drained soil that is warmed by at least 6 hours of direct sunlight. Position stakes before planting and set plants about 24 in (60 cm) apart when all danger of frost is over; in cool climates use cloches to protect young seedlings. Keep soil moist but not too wet and feed regularly while fruit are developing. A variety of pests and diseases attack tomatoes, and disease resistance is one of the main aims of breeders.

Lycopersicon esculentum
syn. *Lycopersicon lycopersicum*

This soft-stemmed, spreading plant up to 6 ft (1.8 m) high, has strong-smelling, deeply lobed leaves and yellow flowers followed by soft succulent fruit. The fruit are generally red or yellow and vary considerably in size and shape among the numerous cultivars. At harvest time, vine-ripened fruit are definitely the best. Among the most widely grown traditional red cultivars are '**Beefsteak**', tall, with large rounded fruit, '**Grosse Lisse**', very sweet with large, soft fruit, and '**Rouge de Marmande**' with large, ribbed fruit. '**Yellow Pear**' yields big crops of 2 in (5 cm), golden-yellow, pear-shaped fruit. '**Red Pear**' is similar except the fruit is red. The elongated Roma tomatoes, popular in Italy, include '**Super Roma**' and '**Plumito**'. A novel group in gardens of the West are the eastern European black tomatoes, an example being '**Black Russian**'. Cherry tomatoes, sometimes designated by the name *Lycopersicon esculentum* var. *cerasiforme,* bear long decorative strings of cherry-size red, orange or yellow fruit. The small-fruited species *L. pimpinellifolium* is sometimes cultivated and plant breeders have used it to introduce new genes to cherry tomatoes.
ZONES 8–12.

OXALIS

WOOD-SORREL

This is a large genus of 500 or so species of bulbous, rhizomatous and fiberous-rooted perennials and a few small, weak shrubs. Detailed information is given in the Bulbs, Corms and Tubers chapter. However, *Oxalis tuberosa* is treated here as a vegetable.

Oxalis tuberosa

Oxalis tuberosa

OCA

Believed to have originated in the northern Andes, this species is second only to the potato in importance as a root vegetable in the cooler parts of South America. Its knobbly translucent tubers are up to about 2 in (5 cm) in diameter and may be round or elongated with color varying from white to yellow or pink, sometimes with darker streaks. Only the white-tubered form will flower. Above ground, the plant forms a tangle of weak stems with plain green 3-pointed leaves; the small flowers are yellow. *Oxalis tuberosa* is hardy to most frosts. **ZONES 6–10.**

Pastinaca sativa

PASTINACA

Only one species is cultivated in this genus of 14 species of biennials or perennials found throughout Eurasia. It is the parsnip, grown for its fleshy white root with a distinctive flavor. It has simple or pinnate leaves and yellow flowers.

CULTIVATION

Grow in full sun in well-drained, deep, friable, stone-free soil that has been well dug. Improve poor soil with plenty of compost, but do not use fresh manure as it may cause misshapen roots. Propagation is usually from seed in spring. Watch for slugs, canker, celery fly or greenfly.

Pastinaca sativa

syn. **Peucedanum sativum**

PARSNIP

A hardy root vegetable related to the carrot, the parsnip is nutritious, sweet and can be grown year round in warm climates and from mid-spring in cold climates. A strong-smelling biennial that reaches 3 ft (1 m) in height, it has pinnate leaves 4–12 in (10–30 cm) long and flowers in summer. Harvest parsnips when their leaves start to yellow. **ZONES 7–10.**

PHASEOLUS

BEAN

This genus, native to warm-temperate to tropical regions of the Americas, contains 36 annual and perennial species, some familiar as garden crops. Twining climbers with thin, usually bright green, trifoliate leaves, they bear racemes of white, yellow, red or purple flowers, followed by long, narrow seed pods. In some species the pods are eaten, in others it is the beans within.

CULTIVATION

Beans thrive with a long, warm growing season, plenty of sunlight and ample moisture. They prefer a humus-rich yet light and well-drained soil. Some are also suitable for planting in tubs or flower beds. Propagate from seed in autumn or spring. They are prone to attack by slugs.

Phaseolus coccineus

SCARLET RUNNER BEAN

This vigorous climber comes in different varieties and can grow up to 12 ft (3.5 m) high. It needs a sheltered position. Sow seed in late spring in double rows 2 in (5 cm) deep and 12 in (30 cm) apart. Pick pods when they reach 6 in (15 cm) long. These perennials last for several years, though they bear most heavily in their first year. **'Achievement'** has larger leaves and the flower's keel is orange. **ZONES 9–11.**

Phaseolus vulgaris

FRENCH BEAN, KIDNEY BEAN, STRING BEAN, HARICOT BEAN

The major bean species both for green and dried beans, *Phaseolus vulgaris* displays great variation in pod and seed characters, as well as plant growth habit. Thought to be a cultivated derivative of a wild species *(P. aborigineus)* of the northern Andes, it was already widely planted in pre-Columbian times. An annual, it was originally a climber but many cultivated strains are 'dwarf beans' that are better adapted to mechanical harvesting. The beans can also be divided into those grown as pulses, including the borlotti, pinto, haricot and navy beans, and those grown as green beans (a few are dual-purpose); these go by many names, including French beans, snap beans, string beans and stringless beans. The pods vary in length, whether they are round or flat, and in color from cream to yellow, green, blue-green, red or purple; seed color may vary almost as much. Popular green bean cultivars include 'Tendercrop', a dwarf with straight, plump green stringless pods; **'Blue Lake'**, a climber with very plump, long, tender pods, slightly bluish green; **'Kentucky Wonder Wax'**, a climber with large golden-yellow pods; and **'Royal Burgundy'**, a dwarf with curved, deep purple pods and purplish foliage. **ZONES 7–11.**

Phaseolus coccineus 'Achievement'

Phaseolus vulgaris

Pisum sativum var. *macrocarpum*

PISUM
PEA

This genus originated in the eastern Mediterranean region and peas have been part of the human diet for at least 5000 years. Only 2 species are recognized in this genus, the wild pea and the garden pea, *Pisum sativum*, grown for its tender green peas. Garden peas come in dwarf, or bush and climbing forms. There are many varieties of each form including the sugar or snow peas which have tender, sweet, edible pods.

CULTIVATION
Peas are a cool-season crop that can be enjoyed both in spring and autumn. They need a sunny, well-drained, previously manured soil that contains some lime and dolomite. A support of stretched wire on short stakes helps keep the dwarf varieties off the ground and increases productivity. Propagate from seed in mild climates from autumn until spring. Young plants are not injured by frosts, but the blossoms and pods are. In cold winter areas sowing can be timed to give maturity when frosts have passed. Watch for mildew, mites and blight.

Pisum sativum
GARDEN PEA

This annual species grows to 6 ft (1.8 m) and has branched tendrils. There are from 1 to 4 pairs of leaflets and the flowers, to 1¼ in (30 mm) wide, are white, sometimes with pale or dark purple markings. Plant seedlings 2 in (5 cm) apart in rows 4 in (10 cm) apart. When seedlings are 3 in (8 cm) high stake them with short twigs. Keep weeds down and water when dry. Pick the pods from the lower stems. Popular cultivars include 'Alderman', 'Snow Flake' and 'Sugar Bon'. *Pisum sativum* var. *macrocarpum*, the snow pea or mange-tout pea, prefers a temperate climate and a moist sandy soil. Sow 2 in (5 cm) deep when the garden is frost free and use a trellis for climbing varieties. Pick the pods when they are still immature.
ZONES 3–10.

RAPHANUS

RADISH

Eaten by Egyptian slaves and the ancient Chinese, the well-travelled radish has been used for centuries as an important cooked vegetable (the winter variety) and in salads, pickles and garnishes (the summer variety). There are 3 species in the genus; many varieties are grown in different parts of the world and vary in form from globe-shaped, oblong to cylindrical or tapered. The outside of the root varies from white through pink, to red, purple and black; some are two-toned.

CULTIVATION
A friable, moisture-retentive, well-drained soil and a little shade for the summer varieties give best results. The summer varieties are sown directly into the soil in rows 12 in (30 cm) apart through summer at 14-day intervals. Thin out seedlings so that the roots are not competing. In hot weather, keep well watered. Harvest 4 weeks after sowing in warm climates. In cooler climates wait a further 3 weeks. Winter-maturing varieties may take up to 60 days to mature and are best sown later in summer or autumn. Do not leave in the ground too long as radishes turn woody. Propagate from seed.

Raphanus sativus

Raphanus sativus

This Chinese annual grows to 3 ft (1 m) and spreads to 18 in (45 cm). It has an erect, hollow stem and rough, alternate leaves. White or lilac flowers with strongly marked veins and 4 petals appear in branching clusters. 'Rex' and 'Tarzan F1' are both very popular cultivars. **ZONES 6–10.**

Rheum × cultorum

syns Rheum × hybridum,
R. rhabarbarum

RHUBARB

One of the few plants grown for its edible leaf stalks, rhubarb is a tough, vigorous perennial, now thought to be a hybrid of *Rheum rhaponticum*. In spring its large leaves quickly expand from the woody, winter-dormant rhizome. The stems, at first green, are ready to eat when they have reddened. Flowering stems, usually removed from cultivated plants, if left to develop grow to 5 ft (1.5 m) tall and are topped with heads of small red-flushed cream flowers. It is best grown from root divisions in fertile, phosphorous-rich soil. Eat the stalks only as the leaves are poisonous. **ZONES 3–9.**

Rheum × cultorum

RHEUM

All species in this genus are perennials and detailed information on the genus is given in the Annuals and Perennials chapter. However, *Rheum × cultorum* is treated here as a vegetable.

SOLANUM

Most cultivated species in this genus are climbers or creepers, and detailed information on the genus is given in the Climbers and Creepers chapter. However, *Solanum tuberosum* is treated here as a vegetable.

Solanum tuberosum

POTATO

Native to South America, this is one of the most widely eaten of all vegetables. A perennial plant, it grows to a height of 30 in (75 cm) with a spread of 18 in (45 cm). It has an erect, hairy, green stem and large—to 15 in (38 cm)—pinnate, dark green leaves with 3 or 5 pairs of heart-shaped leaflets. The flowers occur in pendent clusters of white or pale violet flowers. **ZONES 6–11.**

Solanum tuberosum

Solanum tuberosum

SPINACIA

SPINACH

The Chinese have the first record of the spinach plant in the seventh century; it was later introduced to Spain in the eleventh century and from there spread to the rest of Europe. The genus consists of 3 species of fast-growing annuals with large, delicate, rich green leaves that are eaten when young in salads or cooked. Two kinds are traditionally grown: the smooth seeded or marginally frost-hardy summer spinach and the fully frost-hardy prickly seeded winter type, which generally has more lobed leaves.

CULTIVATION

Spinach develops a long tap root so benefits from a deep, enriched soil with good drainage. It is a cool season, short-day crop and grows best during the cooler temperatures of spring and autumn. Space plants about 10 in (25 cm) apart. Keep the soil free of weeds and well watered so that the plants will not run to seed. Harvest the first leaves in 8 weeks. Propagate from seed. Watch for chewing insects and downy mildew.

Spinacia oleracea

Spinacia oleracea
ENGLISH SPINACH

Native to the Middle East and partial to cool climates, this species can be a challenge to grow well. It has stems to 3 ft (1 m) tall and bright green, entire or dentate leaves. The small flowers are unisexual. **ZONES 5–10.**

Vicia faba

VICIA
VETCH, TARE

This legume genus of around 140 species of annuals and perennials occurs wild mostly in temperate regions of the northern hemisphere, with a few species in the Andes of South America and mountains of East Africa. It is closely related to the sweet-pea genus *Lathyrus* and most species have the same tendrils at the ends of their pinnate leaves, by which they scramble through long grass or over shrubs and dead twigs; an exception is *Vicia faba*, the broad bean, which has an erect habit and lacks tendrils. The small flowers, usually borne in short spikes or clusters from the leaf axils, are typical pea-flowers in form though not opening very wide, and are mostly white, pink, purple or pale yellow. The pods that follow mature rapidly, are often hairy or downy and contain a row of small to large seeds. Many vetches are pasture plants or weeds of waste ground, but a few would make attractive additions to meadow or rock gardens.

CULTIVATION
Most vetches are easily grown in ordinary garden soil. They self-seed freely and can quickly become a nuisance, although the plants are easily pulled up. Propagate from seed; perennial species may also be divided in autumn. For cultivation of broad beans see under *Vicia faba*.

Vicia faba
BROAD BEAN, FAVA BEAN

Believed to be one of the earliest domesticated crop plants, broad beans are not known in the wild but may have been derived in cultivation from *Vicia narbonense*. An annual growing to about 30 in (75 cm) in height it has thick, erect stems and coarse, gray-green foliage. The white flowers (red in some cultivars) with a blackish central blotch are clustered in the upper leaf axils and are followed by large, downy green pods, up to 24 in (60 cm) long in some cultivars but usually much less; the large seeds, tender when immature, are white, green, or rarely crimson. As well as the vegetable strains there are races of this species cultivated for fodder, known as horse beans and tic beans. Broad beans are a winter to spring crop and successful cultivation requires a temperate climate. They are mostly sown in autumn in well-drained, limed and manured soil (mounded into ridges if necessary), preferably following a non-leguminous crop in the same plot; where frosts are very severe delay sowing until early spring. Young plants may need staking and should not be over-watered. Beans are harvested while still green and tender, usually 2 to 3 months after planting. Watch for aphids. Popular broad bean cultivars are '**Early Long Pod**', '**Green Windsor**', '**Red Epicure**' and '**Aquadulce Claudia**', an especially frost-hardy cultivar. **ZONES 7–10.**

Zea mays

Zea mays

SWEET CORN, MAIZE, MEALY

This robust annual grows to 12 ft (3.5 m) tall with arching, lance-shaped, waxy leaves. It produces terminal panicles of male flowers to 8 in (20 cm) long, and female inflorescences of the same length. The flowers are followed in late summer or early autumn by cobs with usually yellow, sweet, edible grains. 'Golden Beauty' is one of many much-admired cultivars. **ZONES 7–11.**

ZEA

The maize or sweet corn genus is now thought to include four species of annual and perennial grasses from Central America; the crop species may be an ancient hybrid, its grains found in archeological excavations up to 5,600 years old. They bear terminal male panicles with solitary 'ears'; the female inflorescences have numerous spikelets in rows on a thick axis enclosed within a 'husk', from which only the long silky styles emerge; these are followed by a 'cob' of fleshy kernels. Ornamental cultivars are grown for their variegated leaves and multi-colored cobs.

CULTIVATION

Grow in full sun in fertile, moist, well-drained soil. Propagate from seed in late winter or early spring. They may be prone to attack by aphids.

HERBS

Allium sativum
GARLIC

The common garlic is quite like an onion above ground but the bulb is compound, its tight papery sheath enclosing several to many daughter bulbs or 'cloves', whose pungent flavor is valued around the world for cooking, to say nothing of its renown as a remedy for and preventative of infections. It is unknown in the wild, but closely related plants are found in central Asia. Dainty deep pink to white flowers appear in summer in small umbels on a stalk about 18 in (45 cm) tall. Plant individual cloves 2 in (5 cm) deep in autumn in warmer areas or in spring where there is frost. Garlic takes up to 5 or 6 months to mature; harvest when the leaves have turned yellow. Garlic planted near roses helps to keep aphids away.
ZONES 7–10.

Allium schoenoprasum
CHIVES

The narrow, cylindrical leaves of this perennial plant are used for flavoring and garnishing savory dishes. Growing to 10 in (25 cm) in small, neat clumps, it bears numerous balls of mauve flowers in late spring and summer which are edible. Plant in full sun or part-shade and keep well watered. Propagate from seed or division of small bulbs. Lift and divide the clumps every 2 or 3 years to invigorate the tufts. Chives make an attractive edging for the herb garden and can be grown in window boxes, troughs and pots. Frequent cutting stimulates bushy growth and tender leaves. The vigorous cultivar, 'Forescate' has rose-pink flowers.
ZONES 5–10.

Allium tuberosum
CHINESE CHIVES,
GARLIC CHIVES

Cultivated for centuries in India and China, this edible species is now widely grown for its leaves, used as a green vegetable. It grows up to 18 in (45 cm) high and has flat, narrow leaves and angled flowering stems. Fragrant, star-shaped white flowers are borne from summer to autumn. Although grown in the tropics, it is fairly frost tolerant. Mature are easily clumps divided.
ZONES 7–11.

ALLIUM

Allium sativum

Most species in this genus are bulbs, and detailed information on the genus is given in the Bulbs, Corms and Tubers chapter. However, those included here are treated as herbs.

Allium tuberosum

Anethum graveolens
DILL

Originally from south-western Asia, this deliciously aromatic annual grows to about 3 ft (1 m) high with leaves divided into thread-like, fragile segments. Yellow flowers are borne in summer followed by the pungent dill seeds. Both leaves and seeds are used for flavoring. **ZONES 5–10.**

ANETHUM
DILL

This genus includes the commonly cultivated dill *(Anethum graveolens)*. Dill has a long, wiry root from which develops an upright, hollow stem with ferny foliage very similar to that of fennel *(Foeniculum vulgare)*. Umbels of tiny bright yellow flowers develop at the stem tip and are followed by the pungent seeds. Dill is widely used in pickling and fish dishes. Both the foliage and the seeds are used. The foliage is best used before flowering. It also has medicinal uses, most notably as an indigestion remedy.

CULTIVATION
Only moderately frost hardy, dill is easily grown in any moist, well-drained, humus-rich soil in sun. The seed is best sown in spring where it is to grow, as seedlings are difficult to transplant. Dill often self-sows.

ANTHRISCUS

A genus of 12 species of annuals, biennials and perennials from Europe and temperate Asia, one of them is used as a culinary herb. They are typical umbellifers, that is, members of the carrot family, with large, much-divided basal leaves and hollow, branched flowering stems terminating in umbels of tiny white or greenish flowers. The small dry fruits are narrow, with a terminal 'beak'.

CULTIVATION
Apart from chervil *(Anthriscus cerefolium)* the species are easily cultivated in any garden soil, and in fact may prove invasive. They prefer full sun. The annual chervil is best grown in a sheltered though moderately sunny position, in light, well-tilled soil. Sow seed directly into the beds in spring or late summer, harvesting leaves as soon as they are large enough and before the flowering stem begins to extend. If some plants are allowed to reach flowering size they will usually self-seed.

Anthriscus cerefolium

Anthriscus cerefolium
CHERVIL

Resembling parsley, chervil grows to about 24 in (60 cm) and is grown as a cool-season annual. The light green, finely textured leaves and stems are harvested 2–3 in (5–8 cm) above the crown and are used in French cooking to give a delicate licorice flavor. **ZONES 6–10.**

Armoracia rusticana

This is the only commonly grown species and the one used for horseradish sauce. Native to southeast Europe, it has 12–18 in (30–45 cm) long, bright to deep green leaves with a puckered surface, sometimes lobed towards the base. Panicles of white flowers develop in summer but are usually removed to encourage root development. 'Variegata', as the name suggests, is a variegated form. Japanese horseradish, or wasabi, is a different plant, from the genus *Wasabia*. **ZONES 5–10.**

ARMORACIA

HORSERADISH

This is a genus of 3 species of vigorous, taproot-forming perennials found naturally from southeast Europe to Siberia, only one of which is cultivated. Horseradish is an extremely vigorous grower. The tough, white roots are used to prepare the well-known condiment and also have some medicinal properties.

CULTIVATION

They are very easily grown in temperate climates, in any soil in sun or light shade. Propagate by dividing an established clump if necessary; it replicates itself freely.

Armoracia rusticana 'Variegata'

Borago officinalis

Borago officinalis

BORAGE

This annual herb is grown for its cucumber-flavored leaves and pretty, purplish blue star-shaped flowers. The plant grows to around 30 in (75 cm) high, with clusters of flowers in spring and summer. The fresh young leaves are used raw in salads and cool drinks or cooked with vegetables. The edible flowers have long been used to decorate salads. **ZONES 5–10.**

BORAGO

This is a European genus of 3 species of annuals and short-lived perennials. The plants are generally erect with rather coarse growth and are covered with bristly hairs. They form clumps of lance-shaped basal leaves that rapidly develop in spring into branched, leafy flowering stems. By late spring the plants bear semi-pendulous, starry, purple-blue or white flowers, which are quite ornamental. The flowers are a rich source of nectar and are popular with beekeepers.

CULTIVATION

These plants are easily grown in any light, moist, well-drained soil in full sun. Usually they are propagated from seed, which often self-sows, so plants may become slightly invasive. Seed of the annual species can be sown in late winter for an early crop. Protect from snails.

CALAMINTHA

CALAMINT

Seven species make up this genus of aromatic perennial herbs, occurring as natives mainly in Europe and temperate Asia but with two species confined to the USA. In growth habit they are quite like the true mints *(Mentha)*, with creeping rhizomes and leaves in opposite pairs on square stems, but the white, pink or purplish flowers are mostly larger and are borne in looser terminal sprays. The leaves of several species are used in herbal medicine, as well as being infused to make herbal teas. The name *Calamintha* (beautiful mint) goes back to ancient Greek, referring originally to an aromatic herb of this general kind but now not identifiable.

CULTIVATION

Mostly fairly frost hardy, calaminthas are easily grown in moist, but well-drained soil in a sheltered position; some species prefer woodland conditions in part-shade, others thrive best in full sun. Propagate by division of rhizomes or from seed sown in spring.

Calamintha nepeta

Calamintha nepeta

LESSER CALAMINT

Native to much of Europe, also North Africa and western Asia, this is an unassuming plant 12–24 in (30–60 cm) tall that favors dry, well-drained conditions in full sun. Its small leaves are hardly toothed and the small summer flowers, held in long, erect, rather open sprays, are pale mauve or almost white. The epithet *nepeta* was presumably given to indicate its resemblance to the catmint genus *Nepeta*. The forms, *Calamintha nepeta* subsp. *glandulosa* 'White Cloud' and 'Blue Cloud' are popular cultivars. ZONES 4–10.

CARUM

About 30 species belong to this genus of annuals, biennials and perennials, one of them being the well known herb caraway *(Carum carvi)*. The species are scattered through various temperate regions of the world, but caraway is the only one grown as a garden plant. They are typical umbellifers, with finely dissected basal leaves and hollow, branched stems bearing umbels of tiny white flowers, followed by aromatic, dry fruitlets. Caraway has been used as a condiment and medicinal herb since ancient Egyptian times. It is still widely cultivated for its aromatic seeds, used mainly to flavor bread, cakes, sauces and pickles.

CULTIVATION

These frost-hardy plants grow well in deep, fertile, moist, well-drained soil in full sun. Propagate from seed in early autumn in mild winter areas, otherwise in spring.

Carum carvi

CARAWAY

A native of Europe and western Asia, this is an attractive biennial or perennial that grows to about 3 ft (1 m) high. It has finely cut, lacy leaves. In its second year, small white flowers are produced in umbels in early summer. These are followed by a crop of seeds. **ZONES 5–10.**

Carum carvi

CHAMAEMELUM

Four species of weak annuals and perennials from the Mediterranean region and Europe make up this genus closely related to *Anthemis* and *Matricaria*. They have aromatic, finely divided leaves and smallish daisy flowerheads with white rays and a large, domed disc. Only one species is much cultivated, and it is used as a medicinal herb, and for herbal teas, and is also grown as an ornamental and for groundcover.

CULTIVATION

They need a sunny position and moist, well-drained soil of light texture. Propagate from seed sown in spring or autumn, or from cuttings.

Chamaemelum nobile

Chamaemelum nobile

syn. Anthemis nobilis

CHAMOMILE, ROMAN CHAMOMILE

This is a short-lived perennial growing to 12 in (30 cm) high, though inclined to flop over, with finely lobed leaves and white flowerheads a little over 1 in (25 mm) across, borne from late spring to early autumn. Chamomile tea is made from the leaves and blossoms and has a mild sedative and soothing effect. Chamomile is also grown as a lawn substitute, the prostrate cultivar 'Treneague' emits a wonderful odor when walked on. **ZONES 5–10.**

CORIANDRUM

Only 2 species make up this genus of annuals from the western Mediterranean, one of them renowned as a flavoring herb, now most widely employed in the cuisines of Southeast Asia and the Middle East. The plants have a fleshy tap root and much-divided leaves, the leaflets becoming much finer close beneath the umbels of numerous small white flowers.

CULTIVATION

Coriander is the only species grown, usually in the herb garden. It requires a light but fertile, well-drained soil and full sun. Propagate from seed in early spring.

Coriandrum sativum

CUMINUM

Only 2 species of annuals belong to this genus, native to the Mediterranean region and west and central Asia. They are slender plants with delicate, much-divided leaves and small umbels of tiny white or pink flowers. The small, oval, dry fruits or 'seeds' are very aromatic. One species, *Cuminum cyminum* (cumin) is grown for its seeds, which are widely used as a flavoring herb, or sometimes classified as a spice.

CULTIVATION

They are frost tender and grow best in warm climates. Grow in a light, well-drained soil in a sunny position. Propagate from seed sown in spring in a warm situation.

Coriandrum sativum

CORIANDER, KETUMBAR

This herb is grown mainly for its seeds and aromatic leaves, although in Thai cuisine the whole plant, including the roots, is used. It is a fast-growing annual to 30 in (75 cm) high with parsley-like leaves and umbels of tiny white flowers in summer, followed by small, round, aromatic seeds. Fresh leaves provide an exotic tang in Asian dishes. The dried seeds are used in curry powders, chutneys, confectionery, cakes and sauces. **ZONES 7–12.**

Coriandrum sativum

Cuminum cyminum

CUMIN

Cumin is grown commercially in India, China, Japan and the Middle East for its powerfully flavored seeds. It is a small annual which grows to 12 in (30 cm) high, with leaves finely divided into thread-like segments and small white flowers in summer, followed by aromatic seeds. The dried seed is an important ingredient in curry powders. The Dutch and Germans flavor cheese with it, and it is used in many Mexican and Middle Eastern dishes. **ZONES 9–12.**

Cymbopogon citratus

CYMBOPOGON

At least 50 species of rather coarse grasses, native to warmer regions of Africa, Asia and Australia, belong to this genus. A feature of many species is the aromatic foliage, from essential oils in the tissues. They are densely clump forming, mostly with long, flattened leaves, and send up long-stalked seedheads with clustered spikelets that are woolly or silky-haired in some species. The genus includes several species of economic importance for their aromatic oils, and some that are potentially ornamental in warm-climate plantings.

CULTIVATION

Their main requirement is a climate with a long summer growing season, and a well-drained, light-textured but fertile soil. Some species, including lemongrass, may not overwinter successfully if winters are cool and wet, and should be replanted each year in late spring in such climates. Propagate from seed or by division of clumps.

Cymbopogon citratus
LEMONGRASS

This valuable grass, believed to have originated in India, forms a dense clump of long, gray-green leaves reaching as much as 6 ft (1.8 m) high, though mostly smaller. It is rarely known to flower in cultivation, much less produce seed. The crushed or bruised leaves have a strong lemon fragrance but are very tough and inedible; it is the fleshy white bases of the shoots that are used in Southeast Asian cooking, collected and used fresh. The leaves can be dried to make a herbal tea.
ZONES 10–12.

Eruca sativa
ROCKET, ARUGULA, ROQUETTE

This low-growing annual to around 24 in (60 cm) high is native to southern Europe where it is very popular as a salad green. The plants are ready to harvest about 40 days after sowing. Younger leaves have a better flavor. Remove the flowering stems to prevent the spread of unwanted seedlings. **ZONES 7–10.**

ERUCA

Eruca sativa

Native to the Mediterranean region, this genus of cress relatives comprises 6 species of annuals. They form a rosette of deeply lobed leaves and bear flowers in terminal racemes. The narrow seed pod contains 2 rows of seeds. Only one species, *Eruca sativa*, is cultivated as a salad vegetable or herb and is now naturalized in various parts of the world.

CULTIVATION
They need cool weather and fast growth to promote tender, mild-tasting leaves. Grow in rich, moist soil with good drainage. Propagate from seed in spring or early autumn in mild areas.

Foeniculum vulgare

FOENICULUM

FENNEL

This genus of one species of aromatic biennial or perennial is grown for its yellow flower umbels and finely cut, aniseed-flavored leaves, which are used in cooking; it also has edible stems and seeds. Darker-leafed cultivars provide attractive contrast in the herb garden or flower border.

CULTIVATION

Grow this frost-hardy plant in full sun in fertile, moist but well-drained soil and remove spent flowers to prevent self-seeding. Propagation is from seed in spring or autumn.

Foeniculum vulgare

Foeniculum vulgare var. azoricum

Foeniculum vulgare

This tall, graceful perennial grows to 6 ft (1.8 m) tall with thick, hollow stems, masses of feathery foliage and flat clusters of yellow flowers on tall, erect stems during summer. The flowers are followed by brown seeds. Both the leaves and seeds have a strong aniseed taste and are used for flavoring fish and other savory dishes. *Foeniculum vulgare* var. *azoricum* (syn. *F. v.* var. *dulce*), Florence fennel, has a crisp white 'bulb' with the texture of celery. *F. v.* subsp. *piperitum* has fleshy leaves with segments less than ½ in (12 mm) long. Its lateral clusters of flowers are longer than those produced terminally. **'Purpurascens'** has finely divided bronze-purple foliage when young. **ZONES 5–10.**

Laurus nobilis

LAURUS

This genus consists of 2 species of evergreen shrubs and trees from the Mediterranean region, Canary Islands and the Azores. The common laurel *(Laurus nobilis)* has been grown as an ornamental since ancient times and has always had great symbolic significance. Its dark green leaves are used in funeral and remembrance wreaths. The highly aromatic leaves are also dried and used as a culinary herb (an essential ingredient in bouquet garni). Both species are useful evergreen screen plants and tub specimens, and can be used for topiary.

CULTIVATION

Cool- to warm-climate plants, they are moderately frost hardy and do best in sheltered positions in sun or part-shade in fertile, well-drained soil. They tolerate coastal conditions. Propagation is from seed in autumn or from cuttings in summer.

Laurus nobilis
SWEET BAY, BAY TREE, BAY LAUREL, LAUREL

A broadly conical tree, this species grows up to 40 ft (12 m) high and 30 ft (9 m) wide, but is generally smaller in cultivation. Its glossy, dark green leaves are smooth and leathery and in classical times were used to make the victor's 'crown of laurels'. The sweet bay produces small, star-shaped, fragrant yellowish flowers in late spring to early summer, followed by small, round, green berries that ripen to dark purplish black in autumn. This tree is suited to clipping and shaping. '**Aurea**' is a yellow-leafed form and '**Saratoga**' is best suited to training as a single-trunked tree. **ZONES 7–10.**

LEVISTICUM
LOVAGE

This genus consists of one species, a bright green perennial herb up to 6 ft (1.8 m) high, with celery-like leaves divided into wedge-shaped segments. Umbels of small greenish yellow flowers are borne in summer, followed by ribbed aromatic seeds in early autumn. When crushed, the leaves release a strong balsamic odor. This is a traditional cottage garden plant and its tall stature makes it a good background specimen in the herb garden.

CULTIVATION

Grow this fully frost-hardy plant in deep, humus-rich soil with good drainage in full sun or part-shade. Keep soil evenly moist, especially when grown in full sun. Protect from strong winds. Propagate by root division or from seed in spring.

Levisticum officinale

Levisticum officinale

This robust species from the eastern Mediterranean has dark green leaves and a thick, erect, hollow stem. The roots and shoots are used in salads. **ZONES 4–10.**

Matricaria recutita
syn. *Matricaria chamomilla*
GERMAN CHAMOMILE

This is an aromatic annual with stems to 24 in (60 cm) and finely divided, light green leaves. It has white daisy-like flowers with golden centres. The flowers appear in summer and autumn. The fully opened flowers can be harvested and dried. This species is used in a similar fashion to *Chamaeleum nobile*, chamomile. Use discarded tea flowers on the compost pile to activate decomposition. **ZONES 6–10.**

MATRICARIA

This extensively revised genus of aromatic annual herbs consists of 5 species, native to the temperate regions of the northern hemisphere. They have finely dissected leaves with numerous linear segments and produce terminal, white daisy-like flower-heads from spring to late summer. They can be grown in a rockery, herb garden or as a border edging. Some species produce good cut flowers and *Matricaria recutita* is valued for its herbal use.

CULTIVATION
These fully frost-hardy plants prefer well-drained, light sandy soil in full sun. Propagate from seed in summer.

Matricaria recutita

Melissa officinalis

MELISSA
BALM

This genus of 3 species of perennial herbs has representatives from Europe to central Asia. The name *Melissa* is derived from a Greek word meaning bee, owing to the abundance of nectar in the flowers which attracts bees. Borne in opposite pairs on square stems, the crinkled ovate or heart-shaped leaves emit a lemony odor when bruised. Axillary spikes of white or yellowish flowers appear in summer. These quick-growing, decorative foliage plants look good along paths, in herb gardens, among ferns and when grown in pots.

CULTIVATION
Very frost hardy, they prefer full sun or light shade if summers are hot. Slightly moist, well-drained soil is best. Propagate from seed sown in spring. Variegated forms are propagated by root division or from young spring cuttings.

Melissa officinalis
LEMON BALM, BEE BALM

This perennial to 24 in (60 cm) high is grown for its fresh, lemon-scented and lemon-flavored leaves. Small white flowers appear in late summer and attract pollinating bees into the garden. Lemon balm spreads rapidly, dies down in winter but shoots again in spring. The leaves are valued as a calming herbal tea. They also give a light, lemon flavor to fruit salads, jellies, iced tea and summer drinks, and can be used as a substitute for lemon peel in cooking. **ZONES 4–10.**

Mentha × piperita

MENTHA
MINT

Mentha × piperita
PEPPERMINT

This spreading perennial, grown for its aromatic foliage and culinary uses, grows to 24 in (60 cm) high and wide. Using underground stems, it forms a carpet of oval, toothed, mid-green and reddish green leaves. It has purple flowers in spring. **ZONES 3–10.**

Mentha spicata
SPEARMINT

Growing to 24 in (60 cm), this fast-growing mint with dark, crinkly leaves thrives in a sunny or part-shaded position. This is the mint used in mint sauce, mint jelly and to flavor and garnish new potatoes, green peas, fruit drinks and desserts. It is best grown in a container as it is highly invasive. **ZONES 3–10.**

This genus contains 25 species of aromatic, perennial herbs, some evergreen and some semi-evergreen, from Europe, Asia and Africa. Most are cultivated for their fragrance, some for their flavor or ornamental appeal. Several species make attractive groundcovers. They vary in size from tiny creeping forms to bushy plants, and vary in flavor from refreshing to very strong.

CULTIVATION

Mentha spicata

Most species are very frost hardy, like sunshine and rich soil and need lots of moisture. They are invasive, spreading rapidly by runners; to keep them under control, try growing them in large pots, watering regularly and repotting them annually. Propagate from seed or by root division in spring or autumn.

NASTURTIUM
WATERCRESS

There are 6 species of watercress. The one most commonly cultivated is *Nasturtium officinale*, an aquatic plant with longish stalks and dark green rounded leaf segments. White roots form on the leaf nodes. Originally a marsh plant from Europe and northern Asia, watercress is now a river weed in North America and temperate southern hemisphere regions. It is mainly used as a salad herb or cooked as a vegetable in Asian dishes. Rich in vitamins and minerals, watercress is a popular sharp-tasting garnish for salads. It is also used for stimulating the digestion and to ease severe headaches.

CULTIVATION
Watercress must have clean running water or be watered copiously to grow well; an old laundry tub is ideal as the old water can be regularly drained and the tub refilled with fresh water when needed. These plants flourish in damp, shaded corners of the garden as well as in ponds. Plant from cuttings about 4 in (10 cm) apart in early autumn, making sure the soil has been thoroughly and deeply manured. Prune the shoots to keep growth thick. Propagate from seed or cuttings.

Nasturtium officinale
syn. *Rorippa nasturtium-aquaticum*
COMMON WATERCRESS

This species has creeping stems up to 30 in (75 cm) in length that become erect with age. The small white flowers appear in racemes, but should be cut back when they appear in order to promote vegetative growth. **ZONES 6–10.**

A colorful assortment of *Ocimum* species

OCIMUM
BASIL

This genus of approximately 35 species of rather frost-tender annuals, perennials and shrubs is native to tropical Asia and Africa. They are now widely cultivated in many other countries for their aromatic leaves, which are used for medicinal purposes or to flavor food. They have mostly oval leaves in opposite pairs and small tubular flowers borne in whorls towards the end of the stems in late summer.

CULTIVATION
Grow in a protected, warm, sunny position in a moist but well-drained soil. Regularly pinch back plants to encourage bushy growth and to prevent them going to seed quickly. Propagate from seed in mid-spring. Protect from late frosts and check for chewing insects and snails.

Ocimum basilicum

Ocimum basilicum

BASIL, SWEET BASIL

This native of tropical Asia, together with its cultivars, is the most commonly grown and most widely used basil. A favorite with cooks, it is one of the most widely used herbs in Mediterranean cooking. Fresh leaves are best; freeze them for the winter as they lose their flavor when dried. It is a tender annual plant growing to about 18 in (45 cm) with light green, oval leaves that have a delicious warm, spicy fragrance. Small white flowers are carried in whorls towards the ends of the stems in late summer. There are a number of varieties of basil including a compact small leaf type; a crinkled, lettuce leaf variety and the beautiful '**Dark Opal**', which has rich purple stems and leaves. There are perennial varieties also, but their flavor is inferior. '**Minimum**' is a dwarf form with tiny leaves, used in the Greek Orthodox Church for sprinkling holy water. As a summer annual, basil can be grown in cooler climates. **ZONES 10–12.**

Ocimum tenuiflorum

Ocimum tenuiflorum

syn. *Ocimum sanctum*

HOLY BASIL

This flavorsome aromatic herb from India is an important sacred plant in the Hindu religion. It is a short-lived perennial that dies back to a few woody stems near ground level. It grows to about 3 ft (1 m) tall with many upright stems clothed in oval, toothed leaves. Small, not very showy flowers appear on a spike from the tips of the branches. It is not particularly frost hardy and in cooler areas is usually raised as a summer annual. **ZONES 10–12.**

ORIGANUM
syn. *Majorana*
MARJORAM, OREGANO

Native to the Mediterranean region and temperate Asia, these perennials and subshrubs in the mint family have aromatic leaves and stalked spikes or heads of small tubular flowers with crowded, overlapping bracts. Some species are grown as culinary herbs, while others are grown for their decorative pink flowerheads. With arching or prostrate stems arising from vigorously spreading rhizomes, they make useful plants for trailing over rocks, banks and walls.

CULTIVATION

These plants like full sun and a moderately fertile, well-drained soil. Trim excess growth regularly and propagate from seed in spring or by root division in autumn or spring.

Origanum majorana
syns *Majorana hortensis, Origanum hortensis*
SWEET MARJORAM

A highly aromatic plant up to 24 in (60 cm) high, marjoram originates in the Mediterranean, but has long been grown elsewhere in Europe for its sweet and spicy, small gray-green leaves. The tiny white flowers are borne in short spikes with very tightly packed bracts. The leaves are used fresh or dried for savory foods. Marjoram has a special affinity with tomatoes and goes well with many meats. **ZONES 7–10.**

Origanum vulgare

Origanum vulgare
COMMON OREGANO, WILD MARJORAM

The common oregano has a sharper, more pungent flavor than marjoram. It has a sprawling habit and grows to 24 in (60 cm) high with dark green, oval leaves and small, white or pink flowers in summer. The leaves are used, fresh or dried, in many Mediterranean-inspired dishes. In Italy, oregano is used in pizza toppings and pasta dishes. '**Aureum**' has a less sprawling habit and bright greenish gold leaves. '**Thumble's Variety**' is a low, mound-forming selection with yellow-green leaves. **ZONES 5–9.**

Origanum vulgare 'Thumble's Variety'

Petroselinum crispum var. neapolitanum

Petroselinum crispum

This clump-forming species, which grows to 30 in (75 cm) in height and 24 in (60 cm) in spread, has triangular leaves and minute, star-shaped flowers. For the best flavor, harvest the leaves before the plant flowers. The most commonly used are the curly leafed form and the stronger, flat-leafed Italian variety or French parsley *Petroselinum crispum* var. *neapolitanum*. **ZONES 5–11.**

PETROSELINUM

PARSLEY

This is a genus of 3 species of biennial herbs with a long rootstock and a rosette of bright green leaves, each divided into many leaflets with toothed margins. Very small pale greenish yellow flowers, borne on flat open umbels, are produced in the second year; these are followed by small light brown seeds. Cultivated for thousands of years, parsley is still one of the most popular herbs and makes a decorative foliage plant for edging, either alone or mixed with colorful annuals. It is also an ideal herb for pot culture.

CULTIVATION
Fully frost hardy, these plants do best in full sun or light shade in warm climates. They like moist, well-drained soil and regular feeding. Propagate from seed from spring to late summer; in frost-prone areas, seedlings can be raised indoors. Seed may take up to 6 weeks to germinate and it is helpful to soak in warm water overnight before sowing.

Petroselinum crispum var. neapolitanum

PIMPINELLA

This is a genus of around 150 species of mostly annuals and
perennials with entire or pinnate leaves and dainty, star-shaped
flowers borne in umbrella-like heads. These are followed by
small, oval-shaped fruits. Species occur naturally in Eurasia,
Africa and South America. *Pimpinella anisum* was cultivated by
the Egyptians, Greeks and Romans for its aromatic seeds used in
medicine and as a condiment.

CULTIVATION

All species are very frost hardy and easy to grow in a sunny,
protected position. Provide a moist but well-drained, fertile soil
for best results. Propagate from fresh seed in mid- to late spring;
seed can be sown directly into the garden. Germination may
take up to 3 weeks.

Pimpinella anisum

Pimpinella anisum
ANISE, ANISEED

Native to the eastern part of
the Mediterranean region, this
aromatic annual to 24 in
(60 cm) high has brilliant
green, fern-like leaves and umbels of tiny white flowers in
mid-summer. The light brown
seeds are used for flavoring
cakes, bread, confectionery
and liqueurs. Cut the whole
plant back in autumn and
hang the branches in a dark,
warm place until the seeds are
thoroughly dry. **ZONES 6–10.**

Prunella grandiflora

Prunella grandiflora
LARGE SELF-HEAL

Purple, 2-lipped flowers grow
in erect spikes above leafy
stubs in spring and summer
on this species. A native of
Europe, it is good for groundcover or rock gardens, having
a spread and height of 18 in
(45 cm). 'Loveliness' has soft
mauve flowers. **ZONES 5–9.**

PRUNELLA
SELF-HEAL

This is a genus of 7 species of semi-evergreen perennials from
Europe, Asia, North Africa and North America. They form low,
spreading clumps and bear opposite pairs of ovate to oblong,
sometimes deeply lobed leaves. Erect flowering stems bear
whorled spikes of 2-lipped tubular flowers in shades of white,
pink or purple.

CULTIVATION

Most species spread from creeping stems that readily take root
at the nodes, making them excellent groundcover plants for
creating large drifts. They are fully frost hardy and will grow
in sun or part-shade in moist, well-drained soil. Propagate from
seed or by division in spring or autumn.

Rosmarinus officinalis 'Prostratus'

ROSMARINUS

ROSEMARY

Some botanists recognize up to 12 species in this genus, but most suggest there is only one, an evergreen native to the Mediterranean. It has been valued for centuries for its perfume and for medicinal and culinary uses. A small shrub rarely growing more than 4 ft (1.2 m) tall, it has narrow, needle-like leaves that are dark green and aromatic. The blue flowers are held in short clusters.

CULTIVATION

Rosmarinus prefers a sunny site and thrives in poor soil if it is well drained; it is salt tolerant. Prune regularly to keep it compact and promote new growth. It can be grown as a specimen shrub or as a low hedge. Propagate from seed or cuttings in summer.

Rosmarinus officinalis

Widely grown as a culinary herb, this species is also ornamental. It is upright with strong woody branches densely clothed with narrow, 1 in (25 mm), deep green leaves. Simple, lavender-blue to deep blue flowers smother the bush in autumn, winter and spring. 'Benenden Blue' has vivid blue flowers; 'Huntingdon Carpet' is a low spreader with bluish flowers; 'Lockwood de Forest' has deep blue flowers and a spreading habit; 'Majorca Pink' is an upright grower with soft pink flowers; 'Miss Jessop's Upright' grows vigorously to 6 ft (1.8 m); 'Prostratus' (syn. *Rosmarinus lavandulaceus* of gardens), a groundcover form, is ideal for spilling over walls or covering banks; and 'Tuscan Blue' bears dark blue flowers.
ZONES 6–11.

Rosmarinus officinalis

R. o. 'Huntingdon Carpet'

RUMEX

DOCK, SORREL

Chiefly found in northern hemisphere temperate regions, this genus comprises around 200 species of annual, biennial and perennial herbs, usually with a deep tap root. Many species have been introduced to other parts of the world and have become invasive weeds. Docks are erect plants, usually with a basal rosette of simple leaves and with or without stem leaves. Flowers are borne in whorls in spikes or panicles, followed by small, oval, pointed fruits. A few species are cultivated for their ornamental foliage or as herbs mainly used as a vegetable.

CULTIVATION

Most docks thrive in full sun in moderately fertile, well-drained soil. They are marginally to fully frost hardy. Propagation is from seed sown in spring or by division in autumn; broken pieces of root will also sprout. Protect young plants from slugs and snails.

Rumex scutatus

Rumex acetosa

syn. *Acetosa sagittata*

GARDEN SORREL

This fast-growing, fully frost-hardy perennial grows to 3 ft (1 m) high and has bright green leaves shaped like arrowheads. Whorls of green flowers, which change to red, are borne during summer. The sour lemon-flavored leaves are eaten as a vegetable and in green salads. **ZONES 3–9.**

Rumex scutatus

SORREL, FRENCH SORREL

This low-growing perennial has pale green leaves and tiny flowers. French sorrel used to be eaten in the same way as spinach, but sorrel's tart flavor is more suitable for sauces, salads or in soups. Sow in spring or plant from divisions, leaving 12 in (30 cm) between plants. Remove flowers to encourage new, leafy growth. Sorrel contains oxalic acid, which is toxic in large amounts. **ZONES 6–10.**

Rumex acetosa

Ruta graveolens

Ruta graveolens
COMMON RUE

One of the bitter herbs of classical times believed to ward off disease, this species is also very decorative with attractive, blue-green, lacy leaves. It is a frost-hardy, evergreen shrub that grows 24 in (60 cm) high, with clusters of small yellow-green flowers in summer. The leaves and flowers make attractive posies. Common rue has been used in the past for medicinal purposes, but can be dangerous if taken in large doses and during pregnancy. **ZONES 5–10.**

RUTA
RUE

This genus consists of 8 species of subshrubs, shrubs and woody perennials with deeply divided aromatic leaves and small yellow flowers produced in terminal sprays. They are grown for their foliage and flowers and are sometimes used as a medicinal and strewing herb or as an insect repellent. The decorative blue-gray leaves make these plants outstanding in any garden where they can be used for low hedging. They look especially attractive when planted beneath tall-growing roses. Take care when picking or weeding around rue as the foliage can cause an irritating rash in hot weather.

CULTIVATION
Marginally to fully frost hardy, they prefer slightly alkaline, well-drained soil in full sun. Protect from strong winds and severe frost in cold climates. Trim after flowering to encourage compact growth. Propagate by division in spring or from stem cuttings in late summer.

Salvia officinalis

Salvia elegans

SALVIA

Detailed information on this genus is given in the Annuals and Perennials chapter. The Salvias included here can be treated as herbs.

Salvia elegans

PINEAPPLE-SCENTED SAGE

This open-branched perennial from Mexico and Guatemala reaches 6 ft (1.8 m) in milder areas and is grown for its light green foliage. It has a distinctive pineapple scent and flavor. Its whorls of small, bright red flowers are borne in late summer and autumn. The leaves are used fresh but sparingly in fruit salads, summer drinks and teas. The flowers are delicious, and are added to desserts and salads for color and flavor. '**Scarlet Pineapple**' (syn. *Salvia rutilans*) is more floriferous with larger scarlet flowers which, in milder areas, will persist to mid-winter and are attractive to honey-eating birds. **ZONES 8–11.**

Salvia officinalis

COMMON SAGE, GARDEN SAGE

From Spain, the Balkans and North Africa, common sage is a decorative, frost-hardy, short-lived perennial that grows to 30 in (75 cm) high and wide, with downy gray-green oval leaves and short racemes of purple flowers in summer. Its culinary merits are well known, and it has entered folklore over the centuries for its real and supposed medicinal qualities. '**Purpurascens**' has gray-green leaves invested with a purplish hue and pale mauve flowers; '**Tricolor**' is a garish combination of green, cream and beetroot-red leaves; '**Icterina**' has gold and green leaves; and '**Berggarten**' has larger leaves and blue flowers. **ZONES 5–10.**

Salvia officinalis 'Icterina'

SAPONARIA

SOAPWORT

The common name of this genus of 20 species of annuals and perennials comes from the old custom of using the roots for washing clothes. They contain a glucoside called saponin, which is just as good as any detergent for dissolving grease and dirt and which, being edible, has been used as an additive to beer to ensure that it develops a good head when poured. These are good plants for rock gardens, banks and for trailing over walls.

CULTIVATION

Fully frost-hardy, they need sun and well-drained soil. Propagate from seed in spring or autumn or from cuttings in early summer.

Saponaria officinalis

BOUNCING BET, SOAPWORT

While this species' pink flowers on their 24 in (60 cm) tall stems are not in the first rank of beauty, they do make an attractive show in their summer season and the plant grows almost anywhere; it is a very nice old-fashioned flower for a cottage garden. It has oval, smooth, mid-green leaves. Keep an eye on adjacent plants, as it spreads rapidly. **ZONES 5–10.**

Saponaria officinalis

Thymus vulgaris

THYMUS

THYME

This genus consists of over 300 evergreen species of herbaceous perennials and subshrubs, ranging from prostrate plants to 8 in (20 cm) high. Chosen for their aromatic leaves, these natives of southern Europe and Asia are frequently featured in rockeries, between stepping stones or for a display on banks. Some species are also used in cooking. The flowers are often tubular and vary from white through pink to mauve.

CULTIVATION

These plants are mostly frost hardy. For thick, dense plants, the flowerheads should be removed after flowering. Plant from early autumn through to early spring in a sunny site with moist, well-drained soil. Propagate from cuttings in summer or by division.

Thymus × citriodorus

syn. **Thymus serpyllum** var. **citriodorus**

LEMON-SCENTED THYME

This rounded, frost-hardy shrub grows 12 in (30 cm) high and has tiny, oval, lemon-scented leaves and pale lilac flowers. The leaves are used fresh or dried in poultry stuffings or to add lemon flavor to fish, meat and vegetables. 'Anderson's Gold' is a yellow-foliaged spreader that is inclined to revert to green; 'Argenteus' has silver edges to the leaves; 'Aureus' has golden variegated leaves; 'Doone Valley' is prostrate, with gold variegated leaves that develop red tints in winter; and 'Silver Queen' has silvery white foliage. **ZONES 7–10.**

Thymus vulgaris

COMMON THYME

This is the most popular culinary thyme, producing the strongest aromatic leaves. It is a frost-hardy subshrub that grows to 12 in (30 cm) high. White to pale purple flowers are produced in summer. The tiny, mid-green leaves are used in vinegars, butters and to flavor a variety of meat or vegetable dishes. Thyme tea is used to aid digestion, sore throats and coughs.
ZONES 7–10.

Thymus × citriodorus

Thymus × citriodorus 'Argenteus'

Chapter 10

CLIMBERS
& CREEPERS

The colorful flowers of the everlasting pea are very effective if it is allowed to climb through a late-flowering shrub.

Climbing plants use vertical space to give an added dimension, which opens up all sorts of possibilities within a garden landscape. This is especially applicable where space both for roots and foliage is limited. They are also unbeatable for the softening effect they give to a structure, whether it be a house wall, archway or pergola over a terrace.

The difference between climbers and creepers

These plants have many guises: some climbers have strongly arching canes that quickly scramble great heights, while other trailing types are ideally suited to steep banks to prevent soil erosion and to provide a weed-free cover. Although a creeper is generally defined as a plant that hugs the ground, there are any number of vines known by their common name which belie this term. Take for instance Virginia creeper *(Parthenocissus quinquefolia)*, many *Clematis* species and cultivars, and honeysuckle *(Lonicera)*, all vigorous climbers that happily clamber up a support. The lovely passion flower *(Passiflora)*, on the other hand, is suitable for a small container.

Climbers are as varied in their growth habits as any shrub or tree and many types are very rapid growers. In addition, horticulturists have hybridized a considerable number of species to provide even more spectacular displays. Care is therefore needed to select the correct climber for a particular site and the structure it is to cover. Unlike other plants, climbers have modifications to their lax-growing stems, which have evolved to help them reach for the light in their natural habitats. Understanding the difference between the main climbing mechanisms will help you choose the right vine.

First of all, there are those climbers that cling, needing a rock or brick wall for support. They produce tiny aerial roots, often with suckering disks, which attach to a flat surface or wend their way into moisture-retentive cracks in a wall or rockery. The creeping fig *(Ficus pumila)* and ivies *(Hedera* species) are well-known examples of this type of climber, as is Boston ivy *(Parthenocissus tricuspidata)*. Besides being useful to clothe walls, these plants are sometimes used as creeping groundcovers, but take heed, for all are very quick, once established, to outrun their welcome in a temperate zone garden bed unless constrained either by paths or unrelenting maintenance.

A more open framework of wire mesh, lattice or tripod-type structure is useful to support the second type of climbers that use delicate tendrils to climb, such as the deservedly popular sweet pea *(Lathyrus* species). Wonderful effects are achieved if a clematis for example, is allowed to climb through

a living structure, such as a shrub, in order to display its magnificent flowers to perfection.

Another group of climbers, the twiners, are those plants that have developed clockwise or anti-clockwise twisting stems. Consequently, twiners need similar supports to tendril climbers, but of a considerably more substantial nature. In maturity, twiners can completely engulf their original support as they develop tree-like branches. Many of these, such as wisterias, like to race away in the early years, and are ideal plants to cover a strongly constructed pergola through which their pendulous flower sprays can be admired.

Finally there are the lax-stemmed types, which unless tied to a pole or

Honeysuckle is a very reliable climber and attracts birds and bees to the garden.

wall plugs will not give their best. Many a rose or hooked bougainvillea will fend for itself if there is anything remotely resembling a support.

This should offer some insight as to why some climbers look good against a wall, while others provide a shady canopy of foliage and flowers that are best viewed from above. In some instances, these growth habits can be manipulated to give an entirely different plant. The versatile star jasmine *(Trachelospermum jasminoides)*, for example, can be pruned to encourage a mass of foliage and flowers on a given wall or garden bed space. Other climbers, such as wisteria and bougainvillea, that produce sturdy stems as they mature, can be trained as standards, either formally or in the evocative, branching manner of an eastern 'willow pattern'. These will provide a spectacular seasonal display.

One of the most entrancing ways to create an inviting atmosphere is to erect a supporting structure over the front gate and allow a couple of complementary climbers to bid a welcome. Alternatively, you could plant a not-too-rampant vine beside the front entrance. There are a great many fragrant types available, which will

Deciduous climbers, like this wisteria, are superb covers for an outside room. They provide shade in summer and let the sun through in winter.

extend the pleasure immeasurably.

Why not bring climbers into the main living areas of the great outdoors—the patio, the pool side or its surrounds—to add to this delightful attack on the senses? The eye-catching *Ipomaea alba*, with its apt common name of moon flower, is particularly good value for warm gardens. Coupled with its incredibly quick growth habit are its large white flowers, which shine at night without the aid of spot lighting. Cool-climate gardeners are quick to point out that roses, particularly those with recurrent blooms, are an unsurpassed cover for an outdoor room. Because roses are deciduous, the winter sun will pass through their bare stems and warm those sitting under its dormant structure during the cooler months of the year.

Many climbers may prove to be irresistible 'must haves', even if they are not suitable for your climate. However, most can be grown without resorting to greenhouse treatment. For those less hardy, gardeners can provide microclimates by planting them at the base of a sunny wall, and provide deep, moist soil and humus-enriched mulch to keep the chill of winter to a minimum. More delicate plants can be placed in pots and moved from site to site as the weather changes.

If a climber is needed, but there is an area of impenetrable paving adjoining a house wall, or the underlying soil is a disaster of builder's rubble or the like, a large tub that is filled with an enriched potting mix, and a gardener prepared to water and feed, can outwit both builders and the elements. Vigorous species can also be grown in tubs to confine their spread, but be sure to raise the base off the ground as roots will quickly forage through the bottom of the tub and negate the bonsai effect. As such potted specimens grow, the base can be planted with spillovers; less vigorous trailing types that add extra interest and help cool the root zone of the feature climber while it clambers up to the eaves on its supporting structure. Consider, too, that we can reverse the rules: climbers can be encouraged to act as a veil drooping verdantly from a tub placed on a balcony, to give shade below.

Climbers and creepers are prominent plants

Climbers and creepers occupy prime viewing positions, so there is no room here for lazy plants. Be sure to choose adaptable healthy growers, especially those grown in containers that may be moved about a lot. One quick-fix camouflage trick, to mask the bare branches of a deciduous climber in winter, is to hang baskets of trailing annuals, which will steal the scene until the treasured climber bursts into leaf again.

Of all the plants available to the gardener, climbers will reward a little time spent on their maintenance with a wonderful display, whether it be the fleeting blossoms of early spring, the turning of the leaves or the flamboyant flowers of the tropical vines.

Akebia quinata

CHOCOLATE VINE

Deciduous (or semi-evergreen in warm areas), this decorative, twining climber is grown for its attractive habit, leaves and flowers. The green leaves are divided into 5 leaflets and fragrant, purple-mauve, drooping flowers appear in late spring. Male and female plants are needed for the female plants to produce the interesting sausage-shaped, edible fruits. It grows to about 30 ft (10 m) or more and requires a strong support. **ZONES 5–9.**

AKEBIA

There are 4 species in this genus, all deciduous or semi-evergreen twiners with slender, twining stems, occurring wild in China, Korea and Japan. Their compound leaves have rounded, sometimes lobed leaflets, the number varying with the species. In spring they produce racemes of slightly fragrant reddish purple to brown flowers of separate sexes (females larger). Large pulp-filled—edible but bland-tasting—blue to purple, sausage-shaped fruit follow. Two or more plants are needed for fruit production.

CULTIVATION

Plant in cool, moist, humus-enriched soil with the base of the plant in partial shade. Moderately frost hardy, the extent of foliage loss in winter is dependent on how cold the weather is. Prune after flowering and cut to the base every 3 or 4 years to remove tangled growth. Propagate from seed, layers or cuttings.

Akebia quinata

Aristolochia macrophylla

syns *Aristolochia durior, A. sipho*

DUTCHMAN'S PIPE

This vigorous, eastern North American, deciduous, twining vine reaches a height of 20–30 ft (6–9 m), crowding out other plants as it matures. The large, glossy, dark green leaves tend to cover the pipe-shaped, purple-brown and yellow-green bicolored flowers, which are borne in the leaf axils in late spring and early summer. Tolerant of a wide variety of soil types, it grows well in sun or shade. **ZONES 4–9.**

ARISTOLOCHIA

DUTCHMAN'S PIPE, BIRTHWORT

This large genus of over 500 species comprises evergreen and deciduous, twining climbers and some herbaceous perennials, native to many different climatic regions. The climbers are most often cultivated, chosen for their heart-shaped leaves and unusually shaped tubular flowers, which have a swelling at the base and a hood above, usually with the tube between sharply bent. Insects are attracted into the mouth of the flowers by a strong scent, and pollen is scattered over their bodies. The fruit are curiously shaped, dangling from slender stalks and splitting at maturity to spill fine seed as they rock in the breeze.

CULTIVATION

The plants require well-drained, humus-rich soil in a sunny position with some shade in summer, and support for their climbing habit. Many have some degree of frost tolerance and grow vigorously in warm-temperate climates. In spring, prune the previous year's growth to 2 to 3 nodes. Propagate from seed in spring or cuttings in summer. Watch for spider mites.

BOUGAINVILLEA

Bougainvillea glabra

Bougainvilleas are valued for their glorious, flamboyant display of blooms and their ability to cover a large area, of either ground or wall. The genus consists of 14 species ranging through tropical and subtropical South America, but only 3 or 4 have been grown as ornamentals. The numerous cultivars include many different kinds and colors. They are evergreen in the wet tropics, but may be deciduous in cooler climates or where there is a severe dry season. In more temperate climates the main flowering period is summer and autumn, but in the tropics their finest display is in the dry season, though they may flower on and off all year. The true flowers are tubular and rather insignificant, but the surrounding bracts are brilliantly colored, often changing color or shade as they age. The plants are essentially scrambling shrubs, producing long canes armed with strong woody thorns that act as an aid for climbing. The simple, broad leaves are soft and usually finely hairy.

CULTIVATION
All species do best in warm to hot climates in full sun; they also do well in temperate frost-free areas. Only water when needed and do not over-fertilize, particularly with nitrogen, as this will produce luxuriant leaf growth but very little in the way of colorful bracts. Bougainvilleas need strong support for their vigorous growth, but can be controlled by pruning after flowering, when rampant plants can be ruthlessly cut back without harm. Flowers appear on the new wood. With regular heavy pruning, all bougainvilleas can be grown in large containers and kept to a height and width of about 3 ft (1 m) if desired. Propagate from cuttings in summer. In cool climates, they need winter protection indoors in bright light.

Bougainvillea × buttiana 'Mrs Butt'

Bougainvillea × buttiana

This hybrid is a cross between *Bougainvillea glabra* and *B. peruviana* and includes many cultivars. They are large, woody, vigorous growers with dark green leaves and spines. The bracts vary from white to orange-pink and deep red. '**Mrs Butt**', with purplish red bracts was the original of this popular group.'**Louis Wathen**' (syn. 'Orange King') has rounded, orange bracts that change to a bright rose pink. '**Golden Glow**' (syn. 'Hawaiian Gold') has bracts that are a magnificent shade of orange-gold, turning pinkish as they age. **ZONES 10–12.**

Bougainvillea glabra 'Alba'

Bougainvillea glabra 'Magnifica'

Bougainvillea glabra

A native of Brazil, this is one of the two common species that have been long established in gardens around the world. It includes many cultivars and is also one parent of the hybrid *Bougainvillea × buttiana*, which includes many more. It is a vigorous shrubby vine, growing to 30 ft (9 m), with masses of bright purple or white bracts. It has thin, curved spines and the leaves have tiny hairs. '**Alba**' (syns 'Snow White', 'Key West White') has white bracts with prominent green veins and smallish pale green leaves; it is not as vigorous as most other cultivars. '**Magnifica**' (syn. 'Magnifica Traillii') is the familiar bright magenta bougainvillea, blooming over a long summer season, with glossy, dark green leaves. **ZONES 10–12.**

Bougainvillea 'Scarlett O'Hara'

syns 'Hawaiian Scarlet', 'San Diego Red'

This popular free-flowering hybrid cultivar of uncertain origin is a large, vigorous grower. The large, dark green leaves are rather rounded, and the almost circular crimson bracts are very large, orange-tinted before they mature, and often appear before the leaves. **ZONES 10–12.**

Calystegia sepium
syn. *Convolvulus sepium*
HEDGE BINDWEED, WILD MORNING GLORY

Occurring wild through temperate regions of both hemispheres, this is a vigorous climber that can reach a height of 10 ft (3 m) or more. The heart-shaped leaves are up to 4 in (10 cm) long and the white or pinkish flowers, borne in summer, are 1¹/₂ in (35 mm) in diameter. It may be killed to the ground by cold winters but its hardy root system sprouts again in spring. **ZONES 5–10.**

CALYSTEGIA
BINDWEED

The English name bindweed is shared between this genus and the very similar *Convolvulus*, both consisting mainly of twining vines that wrap their cord-like stems around other plants. *Calystegia* includes about 25 species, found in most parts of the world, all perennial. The genus is easily distinguished by the large bracts covering the calyx, looking a little like extra sepals. The leaves are thin and vary from kidney- to heart- to arrow-head-shaped, while the flowers look like those of *Convolvulus*, and are mostly white or pink.

CULTIVATION

These plants are only occasionally cultivated and are inclined to become weedy and hard to eradicate. They require no special treatment other than a sunny position. Propagation is from seed or by division of the roots.

Campsis × tagliabuana

This plant is the result of a cross between two species: *Campsis grandiflora* and *C. radicans*. In some countries this hybrid is more commonly seen than either of its parents. It originated in Italy in the 1850s, in the nursery of the Tagliabue brothers near Milan. Often more shrubby in growth habit, it includes several attractive cultivars, most notably **'Madame Galen'** with spectacular salmon-red flowers with deeper veining clustered in loose, open sprays throughout the summer months. **ZONES 6–11.**

CAMPSIS
TRUMPET CREEPER, TRUMPET VINE

Campsis × tagliabuana

This genus, native to eastern USA and China, contains two species of vigorous, woody stemmed, deciduous vines that climb by clinging roots. They have pinnate leaves arranged in opposite pairs on the strong stems, and large, dull scarlet to orange trumpet flowers in summer and autumn in terminal panicles.

CULTIVATION

These plants require a sunny site, preferably with some shelter, with well-drained soil. Water well in summer. They can be propagated from cuttings or seed, or by layering. Established plants may be cut back hard in late winter or early spring.

CARDIOSPERMUM

This is a genus of 14 species of vigorous, fast-growing, ever-green climbers from tropical and South America, one of them naturalized in all warm regions of the world. They climb by ten-drils and need support. They have soft green foliage consisting of coarsely serrated leaflets and small white flowers, but it is the inflated, balloon-like seed pods that are their most distinctive feature—the pods split at maturity into three delicate segments, each with a hard black seed attached, that float to the earth with a spinning motion. Cardiospermums are grown as curi-osities in cool-climate conservatories, and one species is valued as a folk medicine in tropical Asia, but in some warm regions they can become troublesome weeds, smothering native trees and other vegetation.

CULTIVATION

In warm climates these vines self-sow and regenerate from very small sections of root, however, in colder climates seed can be planted *in situ*. They need well-drained, fertile soil and a reason-ably long, dry summer period to enable the seed cases to de-velop and dry to their attractive straw color.

Cardiospermum halicacabum
BALLOON VINE

Occurring widely through the world's tropics, this fast-growing vine climbs by tendrils and is usually treated as an annual in colder climates. It has hairy, pale green leaves with oblong, 3-lobed leaflets that are pointed and toothed. In summer, there are clusters of inconspicuous white flowers. These are followed by papery, inflated, straw-colored fruit enclosing black seeds. The balloon vine is used in Indian traditional medicine.
ZONES 10–12.

Cardiospermum halicacabum

Celastrus scandens

CELASTRUS

BITTERSWEET

Around 30 species of mostly deciduous shrubs and woody climbers from Africa, Asia, Australasia and North America belong to this genus, closely related to *Euonymus* but recognizable by their alternately placed leaves and distinctive capsular fruits that split open to reveal seeds enveloped in bright orange or red *arils*, oily edible appendages that attract birds. The most commonly grown species have the male and female flowers on separate plants, so one of each sex must be grown to produce the brilliantly colored fruits. Foliage color in autumn is quite good in some species. They are an excellent choice to cover an old tree stump or grow over a wall.

CULTIVATION

Celastrus species are easily grown in moist, well-drained soil in a sheltered position in full sun or part-shade. Plants will benefit from a spring trimming of the previous year's longer branches, and from occasional feeding. Propagate from seed or by layering in spring, or from cuttings in summer and autumn.

Celastrus orbiculatus
syn. ***Celastrus articulatus***
ORIENTAL BITTERSWEET

Native to China, Japan and eastern Siberia, this is a vigorous climber that can cover small trees or old stumps to a height of 30 ft (9 m) or more. The thin leaves, sometimes almost circular in outline, are 3–6 in (8–15 cm) long and widely spaced on the twining longer shoots. The flowers, borne in summer, are green and inconspicuous, but in late autumn the profuse small fruit ripen and split to reveal brilliant red, pea-sized seeds against the golden-yellow interior of the capsule, the display retained through winter on leafless twigs. **ZONES 4–9.**

Celastrus scandens
AMERICAN BITTERSWEET, STAFF VINE

Native over much of eastern North America and climbing to heights of around 20 ft (6 m) or more, this twining shrub has oval leaves up to 4 in (10 cm) long. The insignificant greenish yellow flowers appear in summer and are followed by bunches of pea-sized fruit which split to reveal orange insides and bright red seeds. The fruit mature in autumn and can persist on the plants well into winter. **ZONES 3–9.**

CLEMATIS

VIRGIN'S BOWER, TRAVELER'S JOY

The 200 or more species of mostly woody climbers in this genus
are scattered throughout the world's temperate regions, but most
of the popular, larger-flowered garden plants have come from
Japan and China. They climb by twisting their leaf-stalk tendrils
about a support and are ideal for training on verandah posts,
arbors, bowers and trellises. Showy, bell-shaped or flattish
flowers with 4 to 8 petals (*sepals* really) are followed by masses
of fluffy seedheads, often lasting well into winter.

CULTIVATION

The most important requirement for successful cultivation of
Clematis species and hybrids is a well-drained, humus-rich, permanently cool soil with good moisture retention. The plants like
to climb up to the sun with their roots in the shade. Prune old
twiggy growth in spring and propagate either from cuttings or
by layering in the summer months. In some areas where growing
clematis is a problem, plants are often grafted. Clematis wilt can
be a problem.

Clematis montana 'Tetrarose'

Clematis 'Barbara Jackman'

This large-flowered hybrid
is a vigorous and quite bushy
plant. Each flower has 8
petals which overlap and
taper to the tips; each about
4 in (10 cm) in diameter,
purple-blue with a magenta
bar but fading to a paler
mauve-blue. The stamens are
cream. **ZONES 5–9.**

Clematis 'Etoile Violette'

This is a hybrid from *Clematis
viticella*, very vigorous and
free flowering. The flowers
are 3–4 in (8–10 cm) in diameter and consist of 6 deep
purple petals with cream
stamens. It will reaches a
height of 10–12 ft (3–3.5 m).
ZONES 5–9.

Clematis 'Nelly Moser'

Clematis 'Barbara Jackman'

Clematis montana
ANEMONE CLEMATIS

This vigorous species from the Himalayas will reach up to 30 ft (9 m) or more. In late spring, it bears clusters of sweetly perfumed, white to pale pink flowers with yellow stamens. It is fast growing and very frost hardy, and ideal for covering a small shed or wall. The cultivars **'Elizabeth'**, **'Rubens'** and **'Tetrarose'** all produce pink flowers and purple-tinted leaves. Prune back hard after flowering. **ZONES 6–9.**

Clematis 'Nelly Moser'

Derived from *Clematis lanuginosa*, C. 'Nelly Moser' in early summer, bears large flat flowers, pale pink with a deeper pinkish stripe in the center of each of its 8 petals. Grow in a part-shaded position that receives morning sun. Reaching up to 15 ft (4.5 m), it is very frost hardy. **ZONES 4–9.**

Clematis viticella 'Minuet'

Clematis tangutica
LEMON PEEL CLEMATIS, GOLDEN CLEMATIS

This long-flowering species from China grows up to 20 ft (6 m). It bears curious, nodding, lantern-shaped flowers with clear yellow, 'thick-skinned' petals in summer and early autumn. The flowers are followed by decorative, silky seedheads. Grow in a protected, part-shaded position; it is frost resistant but dislikes dry conditions. **ZONES 5–9.**

Clematis viticella
VIRGIN'S BOWER

This deciduous climber from southern Europe can reach 12 ft (3.5 m). Its dark green, pinnate leaves have ovate, sometimes lobed, leaflets; the nodding, bell-shaped, violet or purple flowers appear in late summer and autumn. The plant dies back in winter and should be pruned to within 24 in (60 cm) of the ground. **'Purpurea Plena Elegans'** has double flowers, with a mass of narrow, recurved petals, soft rosy purple and lavender-gray on the reverse. *Clematis viticella* is the parent of many beautiful hybrids, including **'Abundance'**, light pink-purple; **'Alba Luxurians'**, white with a mauve tinge and dark stamens; **'Kermesina'**, deep crimson-purple; **'Madame Julia Correvon'**, burgundy-red, twisted petals; and **'Minuet'**, white with pink veins and edges. **ZONES 6–9.**

Clianthus puniceus

CLIANTHUS

Until recently this genus was regarded as including 2 species, one from Australia and one from New Zealand. The Australian species is the famous Sturt's desert pea, a prostrate hairy annual with spectacular red and black flowers; but recently it has been moved to the large Darling-pea genus, *Swainsona*. This leaves only the rather different New Zealand species in *Clianthus*. This is an evergreen shrub or scrambling climber with pinnate leaves; it bears elongated pea-flowers in stalked clusters on short side branches.

CULTIVATION

Easily grown in mild climates, *Clianthus* is moderately frost tolerant. Often rather short-lived, it is inclined to become woody and occasional cutting back helps to rejuvenate it. It is prone to attack by leaf miners. Propagation is from seed or from semi-ripe cuttings.

Clianthus puniceus
KAKA BEAK, PARROT BEAK

The kaka is a New Zealand parrot and the long-pointed flowers of this shrub are reminiscent of its sharp beak. This species is now rare in the wild but is widely cultivated. In gardens it often grows into a shrub of about 5 ft (1.5 m) but is capable of climbing to 20 ft (6 m) if supported by other vegetation or a wall. The flowers, borne in spring and early summer, are normally red, but pink forms and white forms such as 'Alba' are also available. 'Kaka King' flowers heavily with lush foliage. In cold climates it is essential to provide protection during winter. **ZONES 8–10.**

Clytostoma callistegioides
syn. *Bignonia lindleyana*
VIOLET TRUMPET VINE,
ARGENTINE TRUMPET VINE

This creeper, indigenous to southern Brazil and Argentina, has showy, trumpet-shaped flowers that may be borne in great profusion. Fast growing and densely foliaged, it climbs to around 12 ft (3.5 m) and needs good support. In late spring and summer the pale lavender flowers with purple streaks are carried on short, drooping stems. It can be trained over fences and tall tree stumps in warm areas, to very good effect.
ZONES 9–12.

CLYTOSTOMA

This South American genus consists of 9 species of evergreen, woody-stemmed climbers that were formerly included in the genus *Bignonia*. They have compound leaves with usually only 2 normal leaflets, and 2 others that are modified into tendrils, by which the plants climb. Showy, foxglove-like flowers are bornes in pairs or clusters at the leaf axils.

CULTIVATION
These frost-tender plants need well-drained soil and part-shade in summer, at least when young, they must be well-watered during hot weather. Growth can become rather congested after a while and may need some thinning, which should be done immediately after flowering has finished. Propogation is from semi-ripe cuttings taken in spring.

Clytostoma callistegioides

COBAEA

Although there are about 20 species of *Cobaea*, only one,
C. scandens, is ever seen outside their homelands in tropical
areas of the Americas. They are very fast-growing, somewhat
untidy vines with compound leaves, the terminal leaflet modified into a tendril. Bell-shaped flowers, usually green, bluish or
purplish, appear singly in the leaf-axils and have a prominent
disc-like calyx. It is thought that the flowers are pollinated by
bats as well as night insects.

CULTIVATION
Cobaeas are subtropical plants and they flower freely when
grown outdoors as annuals in temperate climates. They prefer a
sheltered, sunny position and fairly rich, moist but well-drained
soil. In cold climates, they need to be protected from winter
frosts. Propagate from seed in spring or cuttings in summer.

Cobaea scandens

Cobaea scandens
CUP AND SAUCER VINE

Native to Mexico, this
vigorous perennial vine, which
grows to a height of 12–15 ft
(3.5–4.5 m), has dense foliage
and abundant flowers to 2 in
(5 cm) wide, each with a large
calyx (the 'saucer'), that open
yellow-green and turn from
mauve to a translucent purple
with age; they appear throughout the year in mild climates.
In the evenings the young
flowers emit a rather un-
pleasant odor that diminishes
as they mature. '**Alba**' has
white flowers that age to
cream. **ZONES 9–11.**

ECCREMOCARPUS

GLORY FLOWER

There are about 5 species in this genus of climbing perennials, but only 2 are commonly seen away from their homelands of Chile and Peru. They have bipinnate leaves, each with a terminal tendril. The small, tubular flowers are constricted at the base and mouth. These rather dainty climbers can twine attractively around a pillar or trellis, enhancing it with handsome leaves and small, cheerful flowers.

CULTIVATION

Marginally frost hardy, glory flowers are short-lived vines usually grown as annuals in cold areas; they also grow well in temperate climates. They grow best in full sun in light, well-drained soil. Support plants with small sticks until attached to the main trellis. Propagate from seed in early spring.

Eccremocarpus scaber

Eccremocarpus longiflorus

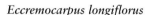

This evergreen vine will climb to a height of 10 ft (3 m). It has a woody, twining stem and heart-shape leaflets. The yellow flowers, which appear for a long time from summer, are 1 in (25 mm) long and occur in pendent clusters. As it is only marginally frost hardy, it can be treated as an annual in cold areas.
ZONES 9–11.

Eccremocarpus scaber

CHILEAN GLORY FLOWER

This evergreen, tendril climber is grown for its attractive flowers, which bloom over a long season from spring into autumn. It has dainty, heart-shaped leaflets and racemes of small, orange-red, tubular flowers, followed by fruit pods containing winged seeds. It grows sparsely to a height of 6–8 ft (1.8–2.4 m). In cold climates it can be grown as an annual.
ZONES 8–10.

Fallopia aubertii

syns *Bilderdykia aubertii*,
Polygonum aubertii

SILVER LACE VINE, MILE-A-MINUTE PLANT

This deciduous, vigorous, twining climber from China can reach 40 ft (12 m). The leaves are broad and heart-shaped, and panicles of small, white to green flowers, maturing to pink, are borne in summer. Small white fruit follow in autumn. Keep under control with hard pruning. Unlike other species in the genus, it can tolerate an alkaline soil. **ZONES 4–10.**

FALLOPIA

syns *Bilderdykia, Reynoutria*

This genus consists of 7 species of herbaceous annuals and woody-based perennials, with twining or trailing stems, from temperate regions in the northern hemisphere. Whitish flowers, borne in spike-like panicles in late summer or autumn, are followed by nut-like fruits. These vigorous but often invasive growers, ideal for covering a shed or old deciduous tree, need to be kept under control.

CULTIVATION
Very frost hardy, they will grow in any moderately rich, well-drained soil in full sun or part-shade. Plants like plenty of moisture. Propagate from seed or by division in spring. Trailing species are propagated from cuttings.

Fallopia aubertii

HEDERA

IVY

There are about 10 species of ivy from Europe, temperate Asia, North Africa, the Canary Islands and the Azores, but the most familiar and the only one to thrive indoors is *Hedera helix*, which is available in many named varieties. Evergreen, woody-stemmed climbers, ivies can be used for groundcover, clothing walls and fences, covering tree stumps and arches, growing up pillars and posts and edging borders, and for trailing from containers and as indoor specimens. Ivy topiary has been revived; as the ivy grows over the shape the side shoots are clipped regularly to produce a dense cover.

CULTIVATION

In sun or shade ivies are adaptable to a wide variety of conditions, soils and climates. Regular pruning is recommended so that the attractive, lobed juvenile leaves are retained and no flowers are produced. If the mature growth, which produces tiny green flowers in autumn followed by black berries, is struck as cuttings, the resultant plants remain as shrubs. Propagate from cuttings or rooted stems. Pests afflicting ivy include spider mites, scale, thrips and aphids.

Hedera colchica
PERSIAN IVY

This frost-hardy, vigorous creeper comes from the Caucasus region and has large heart-shaped, dark green leaves that are mostly lobed. It prefers a moist, well-drained position, and strikes readily from cuttings. 'Dentata' is densely foliaged with leaves that are paler than the species. 'Dentata Variegata' has cream variegation on the leaves. 'Sulphur Heart' is like the species but has attractive yellow variegation on the leaves. *Hedera colchica* is suitable for container growing. Provide protection during winter in cold areas. **ZONES 6–11.**

Hedera helix 'Goldheart'

Hedera helix
COMMON IVY, ENGLISH IVY

This very frost-hardy species from Europe will produce a dense, dark green cover. It is often used as a groundcover in shade where grass has difficulty thriving, and is also excellent for climbing up walls and hiding paling fences, although it may eventually damage woodwork or masonry that is not sufficiently strong. There are innumerable named varieties with a range of leaf shapes, some variegated. Many cultivars of ivy with variegated leaves are suitable for growing indoors. 'Atropurpurea' has purple stems and leaves that change from green to reddish purple in winter. 'Baltica' is a form from Latvia that differs from normal ivy in its smaller, more deeply cut leaves and paler veins. 'Buttercup' has beautiful golden new growth that shades to green with age. 'Erecta' is a form from Japan that has stout stems and broadly triangular pointed leaves arranged regularly up the stem. 'Glacier' has gray-green leaves with silver-gray variegations. 'Goldheart' is perhaps the best of the green and gold cultivars. 'Ivalace' is a very attractive branching vine with 5-lobed leaves with a lacy edge. 'Manda's Crested' has leaves with long undulate lobes that grow on erect red petioles; the overall effect rather resembles seaweed. 'Pedata' has elongated lobes and prominent veins. 'Pittsburgh' (syn. 'Hahn's Self-branching') has closely set, small, deep green leaves. 'Silver Queen' (syn. 'Tricolor') has shallowly lobed, triangular leaves that are gray-green with cream markings that are tinged pink in winter. **ZONES 5–11.**

HYDRANGEA

This is a genus of deciduous or evergreen shrubs, climbers and sometimes small trees. They are described in detail in the chapter on Shrubs. The species described here is a vigorous climber.

Hydrangea petiolaris

Hydrangea petiolaris
syn. *Hydrangea anomala* subsp. *petiolaris*
CLIMBING HYDRANGEA

This deciduous, self-clinging climber from Japan and northeast Asia grows to 50 ft (15 m) or more and bears beautiful flattened heads of small white flowers in summer. It has oval, finely toothed leaves and is very frost hardy. Provide some protection from hot afternoon sun, and water regularly in summer. Prune after flowering, trimming close to the support.
ZONES 5–9.

IPOMOEA
syns *Calonyction, Mina, Pharbitis, Quamoclit*
MORNING GLORY

This large genus of some 300 mostly climbing, evergreen shrubs, perennials and annuals is widespread throughout the tropics and warm-temperate regions of the world. It includes sweet potato and some of the loveliest of the tropical flowering vines. Most species have a twining habit and masses of funnel-shaped, flowers which in many species wither by midday. The flowers are usually short lived, lasting only one day (or night), but blooming prolifically and in succession. They are useful for covering sheds, fences, trellises and banks, and may also be grown in containers.

CULTIVATION
Marginally frost hardy to frost tender, they are best suited to warm coastal districts or tropical areas. They prefer moderately fertile, well-drained soil and a sunny position. Care should be taken when choosing species, as some can become extremely invasive in warm districts. Propagate in spring from seed which has been gently filed and pre-soaked to aid germination, or from cuttings in summer (for perennial species).

Ipomoea lobata

syns *Ipomoea versicolor*, *Mina lobata*, *Quamoclit lobata*

Native to Mexico and Central America, this vigorous, short-lived twining climber is a perennial usually grown as an annual. It is deciduous or semi-evergreen with 3-lobed bright green leaves, and bears racemes of small, tubular, dark red flowers fading to orange then creamy yellow. The flowers appear from late summer until late autumn. This marginally frost-hardy plant climbs to a height of 15 ft (4.5 m) and quickly provides a dense leafy cover over a suitable supporting structure. In cold climates it can be successfully grown in a large pot. **ZONES 8–12.**

Ipomoea tricolor

syns *Ipomoea rubrocaerulea*, *I. violacea*, *Pharbitis tricolor*

This Mexican perennial is more often grown as an annual. It can reach a height of 10 ft (3 m) with a spread of 5 ft (1.5 m), and has cord-like, twining stems and heart-shaped, light green leaves. From summer to early autumn, *Ipomoea tricolor* bears large blue to mauve, funnel-shaped flowers which open in the morning and gradually fade during the day. Widening to a trumpet as they open, they can reach 6 in (15 cm) across. The cultivar 'Heavenly Blue' is particularly admired for its color, as is the very similar 'Clarke's Himmelblau'. **ZONES 8–12.**

Ipomoea cairica

syn. *Ipomoea palmata*

This herbaceous perennial climber is from tropical and subtropical Africa and parts of Asia. It grows from a tuberous rootstock and reaches about 15 ft (4.5 m) in height. It can be used as a climber or trailing plant. The funnel-shaped flowers are red, purple or white, with purple inside the tube. **ZONES 9–12.**

Ipomoea tricolor 'Clarkes Himmelblau'

Ipomoea cairica

JASMINUM

JASMINE

The name jasmine is synonymous with sweet fragrance, although among this large genus of some 200 deciduous, semi-evergreen and evergreen shrubs and vines, mostly from Asia and Africa, there are many that offer nothing to the nose. The leaves are usually compound, the flowers white, yellow or more rarely reddish pink. Most of the species cultivated for their fragrance are climbing plants.

CULTIVATION

Some species are frost hardy, although most thrive best in subtropical to tropical areas. Plant in full sun in fertile, moist but well-drained soil. Prune as required after flowering. In cold climates, they can be grown in containers and kept indoors in a well-lit position. Propagate from cuttings in summer.

Jasminum polyanthum

Jasminum polyanthum

PINK JASMINE

This vigorous, scrambling, evergreen climber from China is fast growing but only marginally frost hardy, and best suited to mild climates. In cool areas, it is a pretty pot plant. Fragrant white flowers with pink buds are produced in spring and summer. Jasminum polyanthum grows to a height of 20 ft (6 m) and can become invasive. Prune after flowering to keep under control. ZONES 8–11.

Jasminum × stephanense

This evergreen hybrid between Jasminum beesianum and J. officinale is of garden origin, although it is said to also appear in the wild where both parents grow. Moderately frost hardy, it is a fast growing climber and reaches 20 ft (6 m) in height. Clusters of lightly scented, pale pink flowers are produced in summer; downy leaves are gray-green and composed of five leaflets. ZONES 7–11.

LAGENARIA

WHITE-FLOWERED GOURD

All members of this genus of 6 species of annual or perennial climbers from South America have soft hairy leaves, which are malodorous when bruised, and large white flowers. The various species have differently shaped gourds commonly named for their appearance or use, and edible when young.

CULTIVATION

Lagenarias require light, well-drained soil, regular water and part-shade. They tolerate little or no frost and are propagated from seed.

Lagenaria siceraria

TRUMPET GOURD

This annual vine grows to 10 ft (3 m) and has hairy, dark green leaves and white trumpet-shaped flowers in summer. The gourd is edible when young; the hard shell can be fashioned into a receptacle. The gourds vary in shape and it is sometimes possible to buy seed that produces a mixture of shapes. ZONES 10–12.

Lonicera japonica

LONICERA

HONEYSUCKLE, WOODBINE

This diverse genus, of wide occurrence in the northern hemisphere, consists of around 180 species of shrubs and woody twining climbers, both evergreen and deciduous. They have leaves in opposite pairs and mostly smooth-edged, and flowers that are 2-lipped with a short to long tube, usually sweetly scented and yielding nectar to visiting bees or birds. Many honeysuckle species and their hybrids are valued garden plants, hardy, long lived and disease free though often becoming straggly unless pruned annually.

CULTIVATION

They are plants of temperate climates, easily grown in sun or light shade and not fussy about soil. They benefit from regular pruning to keep them from becoming hopeless tangles. Propagate from seed in autumn or spring or from cuttings in summer or late autumn. Watch for aphids.

Lonicera × americana

Despite its name this deciduous, twining honeysuckle is a hybrid between 2 European species, *Lonicera caprifolium* and *L. etrusca*. It can grow up to 25 ft (8 m) high, though usually trimmed to lesser height. It has oval leaves and clusters of strongly perfumed yellow flowers flushed purple. **ZONES 6–10.**

Lonicera caprifolium

ITALIAN HONEYSUCKLE

Native to southern Europe and growing up to 20 ft (6 m), this species has light green, oval, pointed leaves that are joined at the base. Highly scented, yellow flowers tinted with pink on the outside appear in spring, followed by orange fruit that are very attractive to birds. **ZONES 5–9.**

Lonicera × heckrotti

EVERBLOOMING HONEYSUCKLE,
GOLDFLAME HONEYSUCKLE

Believed to have originated from a cross between *Lonicera × americana* and *L. sempervirens* this deciduous, woody vine is valued for its magnificent flower colors and exceptionally long bloom period: late spring through summer with an occasional recurrent bloom in autumn. In bud the flowers are brilliant carmine, revealing a lustrous yellow throat as the corolla opens. Once opened, the outside changes to a true pink. The fruit are red. The foliage emerges reddish purple and matures to a lustrous blue-green. It reaches 10–20 ft (3–6 m) in height. **ZONES 5–9.**

Lonicera × americana

Lonicera japonica
JAPANESE HONEYSUCKLE

This vigorous climber from eastern Asia, growing to 30 ft (9 m), has glossy, dark green leaves. Pairs of fragrant white flowers, ageing yellow or sometimes purple tinged, appear in late summer to autumn; black berries follow. This species can become an invasive weed, although it is very useful as a groundcover or to quickly hide fences and posts. '**Aurea-reticulata**' has attractive, gold-veined leaves but bears only a few flowers; '**Halliana**', with bright green oval leaves and perfumed, small white flowers that age to yellow, has been used in Chinese medicine since the Tang dynasty in 659 AD. **ZONES 4–10.**

Lonicera periclymenum
WOODBINE

This deliciously scented climber has long been a favorite for its delightful scent. It is a vigorous, twining, evergreen climber native to the UK and much of Europe, opening its small white and cream, sometimes pink and cream, flowers at mid-summer. It reaches 20 ft (6 m)

in height. '**Graham Thomas**' has oval to oblong leaves and fragrant white flowers; it has been used in folk medicine for many centuries but the red berries are harmful if eaten untreated. '**Serotina**', known as late Dutch honeysuckle, has fragrant, tubular, dark purple flowers with pink centers. **ZONES 4–10.**

Lonicera sempervirens
TRUMPET HONEYSUCKLE, CORAL HONEYSUCKLE

From eastern and southern USA, this twining, woody vine has pairs of glaucous, blue-green leaves, united to form a disc at least toward the ends of the thin stems, where clusters of long-tubed orange to red flowers are produced. The throat of the tube opens to reveal a bright yellow to yellow-orange interior. Bright red fruit follow. Climbing to 12 ft (3.5 m) or more, it is evergreen in milder climates but deciduous in colder regions. '**Superba**' produces brilliant crimson blooms, while '**Sulphurea**' produces a pure yellow flower. **ZONES 4–10.**

Lonicera sempervirens 'Superba'

Mandevilla sanderi 'My Fair Lady'

MANDEVILLA
syn. *Dipladenia*

Native to Central and South America, many of these fast-growing, woody-stemmed climbers come from the Organ Mountains forests near Rio de Janeiro, home of many exotic plants admired worldwide. They bear profuse pink or white, trumpet-shaped flowers, fragrant in some species. They were named after the British diplomat and gardener Henry Mandeville (1773–1861).

CULTIVATION

Although tropical, mandevillas grow at high altitudes so they prefer temperate, frost-free climates with part-shade in summer and deep, rich, well-drained soil. Provide ample water on hot days. In cool areas, they grow very well in greenhouses. Propagate from seed in spring or cuttings in spring or summer.

Mandevilla laxa
syn. *Mandevilla suaveolens*
CHILEAN JASMINE

From Argentina, this marginally frost-hardy vine reaches 20 ft (6 m) or more and is deciduous in cool areas. In summer it produces heavily perfumed white flowers in profusion—these make good cut flowers. The plant can be pruned heavily in early spring to shape it and to encourage new growth. **ZONES 9–11.**

Mandevilla sanderi
syn. *Dipladenia sanderi*
BRAZILIAN JASMINE

This vine climbs by twining around its support up to 15 ft (4.5 m) in warm, virtually frost-free climates. Its foliage is rich glossy green and up to 2½ in (6 cm) long. In the wild form, the flowers are usually rose pink and 3 in (8 cm) wide. Several named cultivars have recently been released, including 'My Fair Lady', which is pink in bud opening white with pink shadings; 'Red Riding Hood', with rich bright pink flowers from late spring to winter; and 'Scarlet Pimpernel', which can flower throughout the year in warm climates and is the darkest form so far discovered, with rich scarlet flowers and yellow throats. **ZONES 10–11.**

PARTHENOCISSUS

These 10 species of charming climbing plants from North America and Asia have deciduous, attractively cut leaves, some with magnificent autumn coloring. The genus name is from the Greek *parthenos*, meaning 'virgin', and *kissos*, meaning 'creeper'. They climb by tendrils with tiny disc-shaped suckers and are perfect for growing on building facades and walls.

CULTIVATION

Very frost hardy, they grow best in humus-rich, well-drained soil in filtered sunlight with protection from hot winds. Propagate from cuttings.

Parthenocissus tricuspidata

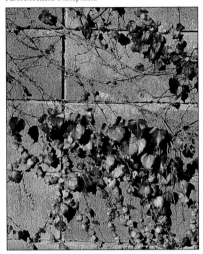

Parthenocissus quinquefolia

syns *Ampelopsis quinquefolia*, *Vitis quinquefolia*

VIRGINIA CREEPER, WOODBINE

This high climber from eastern North America grows to 50 ft (15 m) or more. It has handsome compound leaves with 5 leaflets and makes an attractive wall cover in all seasons. **ZONES 3–9.**

Parthenocissus tricuspidata

BOSTON IVY, JAPANESE IVY

Ideal for covering large walls, this ivy reaches up to 60 ft (18 m). The 3-lobed leaves, 8 in (20 cm) across, turn spectacular shades of red and purple in autumn; the tiny flowers are greenish yellow. The smaller leaves of **'Veitchii'** (syn. *Ampelopsis veitchii*) are purple when immature. **ZONES 4–9.**

Parthenocissus tricuspidata

Passiflora caerulea cultivar

PASSIFLORA
syn. *Tacsonia*
PASSION FLOWER, GRANADILLA

This genus contains over 400 species of mostly evergreen or semi-evergreen, tendril-climbing vines, primarily native to tropical South America. They are grown for their ornamental blossoms and their pulpy fruit, notably the passionfruit. Flowers range from pale pink to purple-red and fruits from pale yellow through to purple-black, depending on the species. Two examples of beautiful hybrids are 'Coral Seas', which is a deep red, and 'Lilac Lady' (syn. 'Lavender Lady'), with its delicate light lilac petals fading to white at their tips.

CULTIVATION
Very frost hardy to frost tender, these climbers are best suited to warm areas. Plant in rich, well-drained soil in full sun and provide support. In cold areas they are best grown in a warm greenhouse. Water regularly in summer. Prune congested or overgrown plants in spring. Propagate from seed in spring, or from cuttings or by layering in summer. They are susceptible to nematodes.

Passiflora caerulea
BLUE PASSION FLOWER,
BLUE CROWN PASSION FLOWER

In summer, this marginally frost hardy, fast-growing, 30 ft (9 m), evergreen or semi-evergreen climber produces beautiful flowers with pale pink petals, banded with blue or purple. These are followed by edible but not especially delicious, egg-shaped, yellow fruit. **ZONES 8–11.**

Passiflora coccinea
RED GRANADILLA, RED PASSION FLOWER

This robust, evergreen, woody-stemmed climber reaches 12 ft (3.5 m) in height. It bears brilliant, large, scarlet flowers with red, pink and white crowns in summer and autumn, set among large, dark green, crinkly leaves. It is frost tender; protect from hot winds. **ZONES 10–12.**

Passiflora caerulea

Passiflora coccinea

Passiflora mollissima

Passiflora mollissima
syn. *Tacsonia mollissima*
BANANA PASSION FLOWER

This attractive, fast-growing vine does well in cooler climates
and features pink flowers and long, golden-yellow fruit. Train
against a support to show the fruit and flowers to advantage.
Generous in its crop, it often fruits in the first year; the fruit are
not as sweet as the ordinary passionfruit. This vine can spread
like a weed if not controlled. **ZONES 8–11.**

Podranea ricasoliana

Podranea ricasoliana
syns *Bignonia rosea, Pandorea ricasoliana, Tecoma ricasoliana*
PINK TRUMPET VINE

This climber reaches 12 ft (3.5 m) high on a leathery, twisting stem. Its dark green, fern-like leaves consist of up to eleven finely serrated, lance-shaped to rounded leaflets. From spring until autumn light pink, funnel-shaped flowers with red markings appear on branched terminal clusters. They are suitable for container growing. **ZONES 9–11.**

PODRANEA
PORT ST JOHN CREEPER

This genus contains 2 species of evergreen shrubby climbers, both from South Africa and both very generous throughout summer with their pink or lilac trumpet-shaped flowers. These plants were once classified as bignonias and are related to the Australian pandoreas.

CULTIVATION
Podraneas are subtropical plants and grow strongly in warm, frost-free climates. Grow in part-shade in fertile, moist but well-drained soil. They need stout support and will soon cover a fence or pergola. Water liberally during the growth period. Dense foliage may be pruned in winter and at the beginning of summer. Propagate from cuttings in summer or from seed in spring.

Rosa banksiae var. *normalis* 'Lutea'

ROSA

Most of the species belonging to this genus are shrubs and detailed information on the genus is given in the Shrubs chapter. However, the ones included here can be treated as climbers.

Rosa 'American Pillar'

This rose is a perfect candidate for pergolas, pillars and for climbing into trees. The carmine-pink blooms have a white eye and golden stamens. They are 3 in (8 cm) in diameter, and are frequently borne in large clusters. The thick canes are vigorous, reaching 20 ft (6 m) in a season, and are easily trained. The foliage is leathery, glossy, and subject to mildew. It blooms on old wood later than other ramblers and hates hot, dry weather, but will tolerate partial shade. Although the single blossoms are uninteresting, collectively they are stunning. **ZONES 5–10.**

Rosa filipes 'Kiftsgate'

Rosa banksiae
DOUBLE WHITE BANKSIAN ROSE

This climbing species has thornless stems to 40 ft (12 m) in height and half that in spread. The double, rosette-shaped white flowers appear in clusters in spring. *Rosa banksiae* var. *banksiae* (syn. *R. b.* 'Alba Plena'), the Lady Banks rose, has long, arching, thornless canes and slender, pointed, dark green, smooth and leathery leaflets, 3 or 5 per stem; the foliage is ever-green and disease free. The sweetly scented, double white flowers appear in spring in clusters of 3 to 7 flowers. The hips, borne rarely, are small and dull red. *R. b.* var. *normalis* 'Lutea', from central and western China, has long, arching, thornless canes and grows to 12 ft (3.5 m) in height and spread. There are 3 to 7 evergreen, slender, dark green, leathery leaflets per leaf. The single, yellow spring flowers, with prominent stamens, are sweetly scented and grow in clusters of 3 to 7 flowers. The hips are small and dull red. **ZONES 7–10.**

Rosa filipes 'Kiftsgate'

This extremely vigorous climber can reach 50 ft (15 m) in height, although it is very slow to establish. The reddish tinted new growth has many hooked thorns and can grow to 20 ft (6 m) in a season. The foliage is large, profuse and glossy mid-green, tinted copper on the new growth and rich russet in autumn. Fragrant, single white flowers appear in spring in huge corymbs that can be 10 in (5 cm) across with upwards of 80 flowers. The hips are orange-red and round. **ZONES 5–10.**

Rosa 'American Pillar'

Rosa gigantea

syn. **Rosa** × **odorata gigantea**

A medium to tall climber up to 20 ft (6 m), taller in its natural habitat, *Rosa gigantea* has long, arching branches of purplish green that are randomly armed with hooked thorns. The leaves are made up of 7 prominently veined, long, narrow leaflets. The flowers are white, very large—up to 4 in (10 cm) in diameter at their best—sweetly scented and are produced in early summer. Yellow orange, pear-shaped hips about 1 in (2.5 cm) long appear after the blooms. This tender species is unsuitable for cold climates, but has been successfully grown in warm greenhouses. It is an ancestor of the early Tea Roses. **ZONES 9–11.**

Rosa laevigata

Rosa laevigata

syn. *Rosa sinica* 'Alba'

CHEROKEE ROSE

The Cherokee rose is a vigorous climber, reaching 20 ft (6 m) with green new wood and many hooked prickles; the old wood is silvery gray. The leaflets are smooth, shiny, light green and oval in shape with a long pointed apex. The large, late winter flowers are single, white with prominent golden stamens and slightly fragrant. **ZONES 7–11.**

Rosa helenae

Ever since this wild rose was discovered in Central China in 1907, *Rosa helenae* has been one of the most popular wild roses for the garden. A large scrambler for climbing up into the branches of trees and covering large expanses of wall, *R. helenae* attains a height of some 20 ft (6 m) in fertile soils. The thick, grayish green stems are heavily mottled brown and have numerous strong, hooked thorns. The bark of the older stems is inclined to flake. Dark grayish green leaves with 7 to 9 leaflets that are red when young, give good autumn color. The flowers are single, fragrant and white, and they appear in large corymbs in early to mid-summer. These are followed by drooping, oval, bright orange-red hips. Said to be tender, the species tolerates all but the most severe frosts. It is one of the most attractive tree scramblers, and is good in most soils. **ZONES 4–11.**

Rosa helenae

Solanum dulcamara

SOLANUM

syn. Lycianthes

There are over 1,400 species in this genus including trees, shrubs, annuals, biennials, perennials and climbers from a range of habitats worldwide. Some are evergreen, others semi-evergreen or deciduous. The genus includes important food plants like the potato and eggplant (aubergine), though many species are dangerously poisonous. Ornamental species are grown for their flowers and fruits. The leaves are arranged alternately, while the showy flowers are solitary or in clusters, star-shaped to bell-shaped, ranging in color from white and yellow to blue and purple. The fruits are berries that contain many seeds.

CULTIVATION

These warm-climate plants have a wide range of requirements; most prefer full sun and rich, well-drained soil. They are commonly grown from seed in spring or cuttings in summer. They are prone to attack by spider mite, white fly and aphids.

Solanum dulcamara

BITTERSWEET, CLIMBING NIGHTSHADE, POISONOUS NIGHTSHADE

This poisonous woody vine comes from Europe and Asia and has become naturalized in North America. It grows to 15 ft (4.5 m) and its leaves may be simple or quite deeply lobed. The flowers are lilac to blue, the fruit oval or spherical and bright red. **ZONES 4–9.**

Solanum dulcamara

Tecomaria capensis

Tecomaria capensis

syn. *Tecoma capensis*

CAPE HONEYSUCKLE

The Cape honeysuckle is a moderately frost hardy, scrambling shrub to 15–25 ft (4.5–8 m) tall. The branches are slender and sprawling, forming roots where they touch the ground. The glossy green leaves are 6 in (15 cm) long, divided into 5 to 9 rounded to oval leaflets with serrated edges. Orange-red to scarlet, curved flowers, each 2 in (5 cm) long are borne in short spikes from late spring to late summer. 'Aurea' has yellow flowers. **ZONES 10–12.**

TECOMARIA

A single, variable species of semi-climbing evergreen shrub constitutes this genus, native to southern and eastern Africa. Some botanists now merge it with the American *Tecoma*. It has showy trumpet-shaped flowers in shades of yellow, orange or scarlet, which appear in clusters at the ends of shoots. The pinnate leaves are arranged opposite each other or in whorls of 3, and have an odd number of leaflets. The fruits are oblong, narrow capsules.

CULTIVATION

Frost-tender, Tecomaria grows best in full sun in a position where it is protected from wind; it should be provided with some form of support. Thin out crowded stems in spring as necessary. The soil should be well-drained with added organic matter. Water regularly during the warmer months; less so at other times. In cold climates, grow in containers and move into a warm spot during winter. Propagate from seed in spring or cuttings in summer.

THUNBERGIA

This genus of 90 to 100 species of mainly twining climbers and evergreen, clump-forming shrubs, was named after the eighteenth-century Swedish botanist Dr Carl Peter Thunberg, who collected in Africa and Japan. Native to Africa, Asia and Madagascar, their leaves are entire or lobed, and the mostly trumpet-shaped blooms are borne individually from the leaf axils or in trusses.

CULTIVATION

The species prefer temperatures above 50°F (10°C) and protection from winter frosts. They grow in any reasonably rich soil with adequate drainage and are suitable for container growing. The plants like full sun, but if the weather is hot during the summer months, they need part-shade and liberal watering. Support the stems and prune in early spring. Propagate from seed in spring or from cuttings in summer.

Thunbergia alata

Thunbergia grandiflora

Thunbergia alata

BLACK-EYED SUSAN

Native to tropical Africa, this vigorous annual or perennial (in frost-free areas) climber grows quickly to 10 ft (3 m). It is marginally frost hardy. Its deep green, cordate leaves are up to 3 in (8 cm) long. It bears masses of 2 in (5 cm) wide orange flowers with black throats from early summer to autumn. **ZONES 9–12.**

Thunbergia grandiflora
BLUE TRUMPET VINE, SKY FLOWER

This fast-growing, vigorous, evergreen climber grows to around 15 ft (4.5 m) high. It bears drooping clusters of large, yellow-throated, sky-blue to deep violet, rarely white, trumpet-shaped flowers in summer and autumn. It has large-toothed, heart-shaped leaves up to 8 in (20 cm) long and looks best grown on a trellis, fence or pergola. It is frost tender. Protect from dry summer winds. **ZONES 10–12.**

Thunbergia grandiflora

Trachelospermum jasminoides

TRACHELOSPERMUM

This genus of about 20 evergreen species from east to Southeast Asia, with one from the USA, consists of twining or root-clinging shrubs suitable for all but the coldest climates. They bear sweet-scented, jasmine-like flowers in late summer. Both the stems and leaves exude a milky sap when cut.

CULTIVATION

Moderately frost hardy, they will grow in any fertile, well-drained soil in sun or part-shade. Prune congested or straggly branches in autumn. Propagate from seed in spring, by layering in summer or from cuttings.

Trachelospermum asiaticum

Trachelospermum asiaticum

This species from Japan and Korea grows to a height of 20 ft (6 m) or more with a similar spread. The oval leaves are 1–2 in (2.5–5 cm) long, dark green and glossy. The fragrant flowers, borne in summer, are creamy white with a buff yellow center that fades to yellow with age. More compact in its habit than *Trachelospermum jasminoides* and with smaller leaves and flowers, it will grow prostrate on the ground or cling to a wall, making a dense foliage cover in either case. **ZONES 7–11.**

Trachelospermum jasminoides

syn. *Rhynchospermum jasminoides*
CONFEDERATE JASMINE, STAR JASMINE

Valued for its perfumed, star-shaped flowers, this attractive evergreen, twining climber from China grows up to 20 ft (6 m). It has lance-shaped leaves, and hanging clusters of white flowers are produced in summer. This plant does best in a sunny position. Although slow-growing during the early stages, it will flourish once established and can be trained on pillars, pergolas and arches. It can also be used as a groundcover. **ZONES 8–11.**

Tropaeolum majus Alaska hybrid

TROPAEOLUM

NASTURTIUM

The 87 species of annuals, perennials and twining climbers in this genus from Chile to Mexico, are admired for their brightly colored flowers. In warm areas, nasturtiums can survive for several years, self-sowing freely and flowering all year. The flowers can be single or double, about 2 in (5 cm) across, and come in red, orange, russet, yellow, cream and even blue. In the nineteenth century a white cultivar was bred, only to be lost.

CULTIVATION
Frost hardy to frost tender, most species prefer moist, well-drained soil in full sun or part-shade. Propagate from seed, basal stem cuttings or tubers in spring. They make excellent pot plants. Watch out for aphids and cabbage moth caterpillars.

Tropaeolum majus
GARDEN NASTURTIUM, INDIAN CRESS

The stem is trailing and climbing on this fast-growing, bushy annual. Its leaves are rounded and marked with radial veins. It blooms in summer and autumn; its 5-petalled flowers spurred, open and trumpet-shaped, come in many shades from deep red to pale yellow. It grows to a spread of 3 ft (1 m) and a height of up to 18 in (45 cm). The hot-tasting leaves and flowers of this species are sometimes added to salads. There are several varieties with single or double flowers, and a compact or trailing habit. The **Alaska Hybrids** have single flowers in a range of colors. **ZONES 8–11.**

Tropaeolum peregrinum
syn. *Tropaeolum canariense*
CANARY CREEPER, CANARY BIRD FLOWER

This frost-tender vine climbs to more than 6 ft (1.8 m) in height. Its gray-green leaves have 5 broad lobes and radial veins. In summer to early winter, it bears small, trumpet-shaped yellow flowers; the upper pair of its 5 petals are bigger and are fringed. In cold climates, it is best grown as an annual. **ZONES 10–11.**

Tropaeolum peregrinum

Vitis coignetiae
CRIMSON GLORY VINE

This rapid-growing climber from Japan and Korea reaches 50 ft (15 m) in height, with green, slightly lobed leaves which turn deep crimson, orange and scarlet in autumn. Clusters of small black berries with a glaucous bloom are borne in late summer. The tendrils of this plant coil around supports and need plenty of room to spread. Fully frost hardy, the leaf color is shown to best advantage in cool climates. **ZONES 5–10.**

Vitis labrusca
FOX GRAPE

The parent of most of the non-*Vitis vinifera* grapes cultivated in the USA, this native of the eastern seaboard produces long, felty young shoots that require trellising for support. The large, shallowly 3-lobed leaves are deep green above and felty white beneath. Full sun and well-drained, fertile soil are ideal for the production of the large purple-black fruit which have a musky or 'foxy' flavor. 'Concord', 'Catawba' and 'Niagara' are among the more commonly grown cultivars in areas where winters are cold and summers are cool and short. **ZONES 4–9.**

VITIS
GRAPE VINE, VINE

This genus of around 65 deciduous, tendril-climbing shrubs and vines has huge commercial significance as the source of grapes. Only a few species yield fruits suitable for wine or the table, and almost all wine grapes are derived from *Vitis vinifera*. The foliage is standard through much of the genus—roughly heart-shaped with 3 to 7 lobes—and often colors well in autumn. Spring-borne sprays of small 5-petalled flowers develop into the familiar fruits popular all over the world.

CULTIVATION
Grow grape vines in humus-rich, moisture-retentive but well-drained soil in full sun or part-shade. Fully to marginally frost hardy, they need cool winters and low summer humidity or mildew will be a major problem. Train on a sturdy pergola or fence where it is sunny, and in deep soil so that the vine can dig its roots down. Pruning depends on both the grape type and upon the way the vine is being grown. For pergola vines, train on a single trunk until it reaches the horizontal beams, then allow it to spread out. Birds are a nuisance, so cover the vines with bird netting or put paper bags around the grape clusters. Cut the grapes with sharp scissors when fully ripe. Vines need annual pruning in mid-winter to control their growth and encourage heavy fruiting. Grape vines are traditionally propagated from cuttings in late winter.

Vitis labrusca

WISTERIA
WISTERIA

These deciduous, woody stemmed, twining climbers are among the most popular plants for pergolas, prized for their large, drooping sprays of perfumed flowers and the summer shade of their soft, light green, luxuriant foliage. This genus of legumes consists of about 10 species from China, Korea, Japan and the USA. Their leaves are pinnate and the plant bears pendent, bean-like, seed pods.

CULTIVATION
Wisterias like a sunny position and humus-rich, well-drained soil. Although they take some time to establish, they become large, vigorous plants and need strong support. Prune after flowering; prune again in winter only if really necessary to control size. With regular pruning and some support in the early years, a wisteria can be grown as a large, free-standing shrub or standard. All wisterias are frost hardy. Seedlings are easily raised but take many years to flower. Propagation is usually from cuttings or seed, or by layering or grafting in late summer or early autumn.

Wisteria floribunda
JAPANESE WISTERIA

From Japan, this vigorous climber grows up to a height of some 30 ft (9 m). It bears pendulous racemes of fragrant, purple-blue flowers 18 in (45 cm) or more long. These are often produced after the leaves expand, in spring. Large velvety oblong pods are produced in autumn. There are a number of very popular cultivars. 'Alba' (syn. 'Shiro Noda'), a beautiful, white-flowering form, has drooping sprays up to 24 in (60 cm) long. 'Domino' (syn. 'Issai') is a more dwarfed form with violet flowers and is suited to a more restricted environment. 'Honbeni' (syn. 'Rosea') has pale pink flowers with

Wisteria sinensis

purple tips. **'Macrobotrys'** (syn. 'Multijuga')
bears spectacular racemes of lilac flowers up to
3 ft (1 m) long. **'Violacea Plena'** (syn. 'Double
Black Dragon') produces its beautiful, double,
dark violet-blue flowers in the early summer
months. **ZONES 5–10.**

Wisteria floribunda 'Alba'

Wisteria sinensis
syn. *Wisteria chinensis*

CHINESE WISTERIA

Native to China and the most widely grown of
the wisterias, this vigorous deciduous climber
is known to reach 100 ft (30 m). The sprays of
slightly fragrant, lavender-blue flowers, up to
30 cm (12 in) long, appear in spring on bare
branches before the leaves, making a magnificent sight. The leaves are composed of 7 to
13 leaflets. **'Alba'** has strongly scented pea-like
white flowers, set in drooping racemes up to
60 cm (24 in) long. They are borne in early
summer. **'Caroline'** bears highly fragrant, dark
purple-blue flowers. **ZONES 5–10.**

Wisteria floribunda

Wisteria floribunda

Chapter 11

ORCHIDS

The heath spotted orchid is a fine choice for a cool-climate garden. It can be grown in a rockery or naturalized in a flower meadow.

in fact, distributed all over the world in cool, temperate and tropical areas. The orchids from the more temperate zones are generally terrestrial plants, with their roots foraging within the earth for their nourishment, while those from tropical regions are epiphytes, and cling to trees or rocks, storing moisture in pseudobulbs.

How to grow orchids in the garden

Orchids are easily grown once their environmental needs are understood. Growth requirements range from warm to intermediate and cool, which relates to the minimum nightly temperatures they are able to withstand. However, it is when these plants are grown in greenhouses that the major hazard, excessive summer heat, is encountered. Extra shading and good ventilation can overcome this.

Plant hunters of the eighteenth century were astounded by the flamboyant orchids that they found on their exploratory trips to inaccessible parts of the tropical world. These blooms created great interest then, and they have never ceased to fascinate.

New gardeners can therefore be excused for thinking of orchids as exotic, tropical-blooming plants. This family consists of almost 800 genera and is,

Many gardens in temperate climates can provide the right climatic conditions for growing orchids outdoors. For the epiphytes, all that is needed is a tree, one with not too thick a canopy and that doesn't shed its bark each year. Ideally, they should be positioned in a fork between branches at eye height, but they can also be attached to the trunk. In a new garden, or where a suitable tree is unavailable, many epiphytes can be mounted on a wooden slab then suspended or attached to a wall. Pack a little sphagnum moss between the roots, then position the plant and secure it with twine or copper wire. In a short time, new roots will attach themselves to the host.

Most gardeners like to place orchids in pots so they can be sheltered from rain and wind and brought indoors when flowering. Some, like the coelogynes with their cascading rhizomes, or others like the upside down orchids that flower from the base, are best displayed in hanging baskets.

Orchids planted in containers allow more control over watering. Many

× Odontocidium *Susan Kaufmann is derived from crossing specimens of* Odontoglossum *with* Oncidium. *The brilliant flowers display characteristics of both parents.*

Paphiopedilum insigne

to twist some temporary wires around the pot, tying them to some support, to ensure the pot is not accidentally knocked over. Young flower spikes are usually quite brittle and can be supported with a slender cane when they first emerge. Pendulous flower stalks are best supported by a stiff wire, which can be bent to allow for a naturally arching stem.

Propagate orchids when repotting

A pot that is too small can impede the growth of the roots and can easily impede drainage. It is very easy to repot an orchid, and is best done after flowering has finished. A pot-bound orchid will either send out roots over the edge of the pot, start to push itself upwards or, in the case of the cymbidiums, the plant begins to die back to leave a very noticeable cluster of back-bulbs (old pseudobulbs).

An orchid that is potbound should first be removed from its container. If the plant is hard to move, soak it for an hour or so in a bucket of water and it will come out cleanly. Then, shake or hose off all the old compost to reveal the roots. This will clearly show up those roots that are limp and shrivelled and need to be removed, and those that are plump, healthy and white. Cut the shrivelled roots off as close as possible to the base of the plant and discard them. With the compost removed and old roots discarded, the plant can be more easily divided and checked for pests and diseases, which should be

orchids like to have a moist growing period followed by a dry rest after flowering. Others, which include the mounted epiphytes and cymbidiums, adore an evening misting on hot summer evenings. None like to be continually waterlogged in heavy potting compost. Specially formulated orchid potting mixes are available from any good garden center. These special mixes are well aerated yet moisture retentive and while most include a large quantity of chopped pinebark, a basic mix for the terrestrial types often includes some coarse sand or grit.

It is often necessary, especially with the taller growers, to add ballast in the form of extra crocks or stones to the base of pots to prevent them toppling over. It may even be a wise precaution treated. Any backbulbs can be kept to propagate new plants.

The next step is to plant the orchid in a new container. Have on hand some clean pots, which should be partially filled with fresh compost, then hold the plant so that the base of the pseudo-bulbs or crown are just below the rim of the pot. Then, fill in and around the roots with additional compost. It is unnecessary to fill all air pockets as in the case of more conventional potting mixes, but it is a good idea to gently tap the pot a couple of times to ensure that there are no large air pockets, which can cause the plant to sink down into the pot. Finally, water the plant in to settle the roots, then allow the soil to dry out for a few weeks, which enables the plant to become established. However, remember to mist the leaves if the weather is dry during this period. Once growth is re-established, give the plants some fertilizer because orchid potting mix usually lacks nutrients.

Division has become the traditional method to increase orchid stock because germination of seed is somewhat difficult and best left in the hands of specialists. The relatively slow process of division kept many choice orchids in the higher price bracket until 1960 when propagation by meristem, and later tissue culture, made propagation of orchids on a large scale possible.

Orchids are the only plant family able to hybridize freely between different genera. This has given rise to entirely new plants that combine not only the best characteristics of each parent, but also the generic name: brassolaeliocattleyas, for example, are easily recognizable as containing the best of three genera. In the wild, hybridizing is quite rare for orchids, but in 1850 the first hybrid plant was bred by nurserymen. Since then thousands have been produced and recorded in a register that now contains over 100,000 plants.

Bletilla striata

Bletilla striata
syn. Bletilla hyacinthina
HYACINTH ORCHID

This charming plant makes broad clumps of foliage. Its broad, soft, pleated leaves, up to 18 in (45 cm) long, sprout abundantly from tubers in spring. In spring to early summer it bears 12–15 in (30–38 cm) tall sprays of tiny, bright magenta-pink flowers of typical orchid shape; the labellum, edged a darker purple-pink, is marked with white.
ZONES 7–10.

BLETILLA

This orchid genus of about 10 east Asian species is usually represented in gardens by the species, *Bletilla striata*, which is one of the most easily grown orchids in temperate climates, as well as being attractive in foliage and flower.

CULTIVATION

The plants prefer a part-shaded situation and undisturbed, good garden soil, and are best suited to a woodland-style garden. Keep soil moist in spring and summer; let leaves die back in autumn to build up food reserves in the root. Propagate by careful division in early spring, or leave undisturbed to develop into clumps.

Brassia verrucosa

This popular species makes a clump of elongated pseudo-bulbs with leaves to 18 in (45 cm) long and 2 in (5 cm) wide, above which horizontally arching flower spikes about 24 in (60 cm) long arise in early summer. Flowers are greenish white or cream with petals and sepals up to 6 in (15 cm) long, darker spotted at their base and on the short triangular labellum. The heavy perfume that develops as they age is definitely not to everyone's liking.
ZONES 10–12.

BRASSIA
SPIDER ORCHID

Brassia verrucosa

Around 25 species belong to this genus of easily grown epiphytic orchids from Central and South America and the West Indies. The plants form large clumps of cylindrical to conical pseudobulbs that arise at intervals from creeping rhizomes, each pseudobulb bearing 1 to 3 large, leathery leaves. They produce long, gracefully arching sprays of spidery flowers with long, narrow petals and sepals.

CULTIVATION

Brassias are happy growing outdoors in a frost-free climate, but need the warmth and shelter of a greenhouse in cooler areas. They are among the easiest of orchids to grow as house plants. In winter brassias can be allowed to dry out a little. Propagate by division, but they flower most freely when allowed to build up into sizeable clumps.

× *BRASSOCATTLEYA*

This hybrid orchid genus includes all crosses between the genera *Cattleya* and *Rhyncholaelia* and any later generations of seedlings. Orchids now classified in *Rhyncholaelia* were once in *Brassavola*, hence the name. They tend to have sumptuous flowers with the rich colorings of the cattleyas but with an extravagantly frilled and ruffled labellum. Often the flowers are fragrant, though usually only at certain times of the day.

CULTIVATION
Cultivate as for cattleyas; all require bright light and some will tolerate slightly cooler conditions than others.

CATTLEYA

The archetypal glamorous orchid flower is a cattleya, or one of its many hybrids with other orchid genera; *Cattleya* Angel Heart 'Pink Cloud' and *C.* Little Susie 'Orchid Glen' exemplify the beauty of these plants. The genus in its wild state consists of between 40 and 60 species of ephiphytes from Central and South America, however, from these have been bred countless hybrids, the flowers ranging from miniatures only 2 in (5 cm) or so across to giants of 6 in (15 cm) or more. Just about every color but blue is available. The flower characteristically has 3 fairly narrow sepals, in front of which are 2 broader upper petals often with frilled edges, and a showy central lip or labellum with frilled margin and variously marked and spotted, its edges folded over behind to form a tube. The plants have creeping rhizomes and narrow, erect pseudobulbs; in one group of species (the bifoliate cattleyas) there are 2 broad leaves arising from the top of each pseudobulb; in the other group (the unifoliates) there is only one leaf, usually narrower and more erect. The flower sprays, 1 or 2 to as many as 10 flowers, arise from the tops of the pseudobulbs. They appear in spring or autumn. Many

× *Brassocattleya* Hybrids
Some of these, depending on the parentage, have a compact, free-flowering habit, with narrow leaves, and flowers with narrow petals and sepals and a large oval lip; others develop into much larger plants producing a single leaf on each pseudobulb with large, often frilled flowers, for example, × *Brassocattleya* Donna Kimuna 'Susan'. On orchid labels, these hybrids usually have 'BC' before grex and cultivar names.
ZONES 11–12.

× *Brassocattleya* Donna Kimuna 'Susan'

Cattleya hybrids in the broad sense have other related genera in their parentage, for example × *Brassocattleya*, × *Brassolaelio-cattleya*, × *Laeliocattleya*, × *Sophrolaeliocattleya*.

CULTIVATION

In cool climates cattleyas must be grown in a heated greenhouse or conservatory, the bifoliate species and hybrids requiring lower temperatures than the unifoliates. All prefer good light but not strong sunshine, a coarse potting mix and a winter rest. They are propagated by division just as growth begins, which may be either in spring or in early autumn.

Cattleya Angel Heart 'Pink Cloud'

Cattleya, Bifoliate Hybrids

CLUSTER CATTLEYA

There are many of these hybrids available, with most of them having rather small flowers in clusters. They can be grown outdoors in a frost-free, humid summer climate and can be planted to good effect on low branches of trees, if the canopy is light and open. They can be spring or autumn flowering, and colors range from white through pink to magenta with some in the yellow to coral range. **Chocolate Drop** is of such a deep, glossy maroon, it almost looks like chocolate. It has a small flower and grows 18 in (45 cm) tall **Fascination** is about 24 in (60 cm) high and has 2½ in (6 cm) wide flowers. **ZONES 10–12.**

Cattleya bowringiana

This delightful bifoliate cattleya from Central America flowers in autumn and winter and is popular and easy to grow. The pseudobulbs, up to 24 in (60 cm) long, bear sprays of up to 15 flowers that are 3 in (8 cm) wide and deep pink in color. Allowed to make a large clump, it will bloom profusely. **ZONES 10–12.**

Cattleya, Bifoliate Hybrid, Fascination

COELOGYNE

This genus of epiphytic orchids, allied to *Cymbidium*, from tropical Asia and the Pacific Islands consists of over 100 species, though relatively few are in general cultivation. They have short, fat pseudobulbs, sometimes very smooth and cylindrical, closely to widely spaced on a creeping rhizome. Each pseudobulb bears one or two leathery leaves, and from the base come flowering stems that are usually arching or pendulous, though sometimes with a single flower only. The flowers come in many shapes and sizes, mostly in shades of green, cream, brown and dull purple, sometimes pure white, and often with orange markings on the labellum (lip).

CULTIVATION

Many of the coelogynes will grow into large, bulky plants, producing numerous sprays of blooms. Some do well in cool conditions and will happily grow outdoors in a sheltered spot protected from frost. They like a fairly coarse, soil-free compost and plenty of water while they are in active summer growth. However, they demand a winter rest if they are to flower freely. Propagation is by division after they have flowered.

Coelogyne cristata
ANGEL ORCHID

From the Himalayan hills, the angel orchid is the most popular member of the genus, and is one of the loveliest of all orchids. It makes a fine specimen plant with dozens of short sprays of scented white flowers touched with gold on the lip, among glossy, deep green leaves. Cool growing, it likes summer shade and is an easy orchid to grow as a house plant. It flowers from the end of winter into spring.
ZONES 10–11.

Coelogyne cristata

Cymbidium, Large-flowered Hybrids

These are the best known cymbidiums, and innumerable grexes (seedling families from the one cross) and cultivars (selected named seedlings) are available. The largest types can have flowers as much as 6 in (15 cm) wide, and their top-heavy, arching flower spikes benefit from staking. **Atlanta** has elegant cream and pink flowers about 4 in (10 cm) wide; **Claude Pepper** has clear crimson blooms, not like most red cymbidiums that tend more to mahogany, so it is much sought after. **Valley Furnace 'Chocolate'** is an outstanding seedling clone of the grex Valley Furnace with large brown flowers. **ZONES 9–11.**

Cymbidium, Large-flowered Hybrid, Atlanta

CYMBIDIUM

Although there are over 40 species of the orchid genus *Cymbidium*, ranging in the wild from south and east Asia to eastern Australia, few are found in orchid collections—it is their showy hybrids that are most widely grown. Long sprays of up to 30 graceful flowers come in combinations of green, yellow, white, pink, dull red or brown, with the labellum most commonly marked in red. *Cymbidium* species have long, arching leaves arising in 2 rows from the edges of a short, slightly flattened pseudobulb, though some species have a scarcely developed bulb, their leaves forming grass-like tufts. The erect to pendulous flower spikes arise from the bases of the bulbs, which build up into large clumps as the plants age. Wild species have pretty flowers with narrow, rather dull colored sepals and petals, and most have a spicy fragrance. The larger modern hybrids have bowl-shaped flowers 4 in (10 cm) or more across on stems more than 3 ft (1 m) long, appearing mainly in spring. Over the last several decades miniature cymbidium hybrids have become very popular, bred from east Asian species with narrow, grassy leaves and erect spikes of smallish flowers.

CULTIVATION

Advances in propagation techniques have increased the availability of cymbidium plants at reasonable prices. In warm climates, they are easily grown outdoors in sheltered spots, tolerating even very light frosts and some sun during the day (though sunlight can scorch pale-colored flowers). In cooler climates, they need a mildly warmed greenhouse. Plant in pots with large drainage holes, in an orchid compost with more finely chopped bark or fiber than that used for epiphytes such as cattleyas. Apply weak liquid fertilizer frequently in the summer growing season. After flowering, divide large plants into groups of 2 to 3 leafy pseudobulbs, carefully cutting apart with a sharp sterilized knife, trimming off all dead roots, and discarding the old, leafless 'backbulbs'; replant in a pot that is not too large. Propagation was traditionally from backbulbs, but commercially this has given way to production of seedlings and mericlones on sterile media in laboratory flasks.

Cymbidium, Miniature Hybrids

These cymbidiums are usually only about 18 in (45 cm) tall, with many flowers about 2 in (5 cm) wide or less; some have the broad petals and rounded shape of the larger types, others are more spidery. All are charming, cool-growing plants that look best when allowed to grow into large, many-flowered clumps, for example, *Cymbidium* Oriental Legend 'Temple Bells' and C. Lady Bud 'Drumm'. Some of them have rather weak flower spikes, which may need to be staked.
ZONES 9–11.

Cymbidium, Miniature Hybrid, Oriental Legend 'Temple Bells'

DENDROBIUM

This is one of the largest genera of orchids with about 1,200 species occurring from India to Japan, Australia, New Zealand and east to Fiji. The island of New Guinea, with at least 500 species, is particularly rich in *Dendrobium* species, as is the area from India across Thailand to southern China. Dendrobiums grow from hot steamy tropical lowlands to altitudes of 10,000 ft (3,000 m) and in semi-arid conditions in northern Australia. They grow epiphytically, on rocks and even in swampy ground, so it is difficult to generalize about cultivation. Clump formers make fat pseudobulbs; those with long, stem-like pseudobulbs often carry their flowers in sprays in the axils of the fallen leaves. There are innumerable hybrids, both natural and cultivated. It is likely that the genus will be split up in the near future.

CULTIVATION

Generally they are divided into warm, intermediate and cool growing. For warm-growing species the temperature should not drop below about 60° F (15° C); for intermediate species temperatures down to about 35° F (2° C) are tolerated; and cool-growing species will tolerate still lower minimums but do not grow well in hot climates. A very well-drained mixture of bark and charcoal, often with a little added sphagnum moss, is preferred and most species need a dry resting period during winter to ensure good flowering. Dendrobiums resent disturbance. Most species should be repotted when the new shoots appear, and plants may be divided at this time; cuttings may also be taken. Spider mites, aphids and mealybugs can be a problem.

Dendrobium kingianum

Dendrobium densiflorum

This spectacular epiphytic orchid is native to the Himalayas, Burma, Vietnam and Thailand. It forms dense clumps of erect, 4-angled pseudobulbs up to 20 in (50 cm) long with 3 to 5 narrowly elliptic leaves near the top. Pendent racemes to 10 in (25 cm) long bear many yellow flowers with fringed, golden-orange centers in spring. It prefers partly shaded intermediate conditions with plenty of water in summer and a dry rest in winter. **ZONES 10–11.**

Dendrobium kingianum

PINK ROCK ORCHID

From eastern Australia, this very variable clump-forming species has numerous pseudo-bulbs of varying lengths and thin-textured leaves to 5 in (12 cm) long. The perfumed flowers range in color from deep rose to pale pink or, rarely, pure white. They appear in short racemes of 5 to 20 blooms in late winter and spring. The plants should be given a dry rest during winter, intermediate to cool conditions, and strong light. **ZONES 9–11.**

Dendrobium, Yamamoto Hybrids

These soft-caned dendrobiums have undergone a great deal of development in recent years by Japanese gardeners. The general name, Yamamoto Hybrids, has been given to their creations, which are distinctive for their elegant shape and clear, brilliant colors. **ZONES 10–11.**

Dendrobium densiflorum

EPIDENDRUM

This is one of the largest of the orchid genera with about 1,000 species recognized, though in recent years several genera including *Encyclia* have been split from it. The genus is variable, with some species having cane-like stems and others having stout pseudobulbs. They range through the Americas from Florida to Argentina at a variety of altitudes, and in habitats ranging from rainforests to rocky, arid hills.

CULTIVATION

Epidendrums thrive outdoors in a warm, frost-free climate in sun or light shade; in colder climates they need the protection of a sunny room or greenhouse. Water and fertilize plants from spring to autumn. Propagate by division or by removing rooted offsets.

Epidendrum ibaguense
syn. *Epidendrum radicans*
CRUCIFIX ORCHID

This common species from Mexico to Colombia has slender, cylindrical stems to over 3 ft (1 m) long with short leathery leaves along most of their length. The orange, red or mauve flowers, which can appear at any time of year, are only about 1 in (25 mm) wide, but each flower stem will have up to 20 open at any one time. In cooler climates, it should be grown in a greenhouse and given strong light. The common name is inspired by the shape of the labellum, which looks like a tiny gold cross standing in the center of each flower. **ZONES 9–12.**

Laelia anceps

Epidendrum ibaguense

LAELIA

These orchids, found in Central and South America and the West Indies, are closely allied to the cattleyas and rather resemble them, both in growth and in the shape and colors of their flowers. Their reputation does not compare well with their more glamorous relatives but they are still an attractive group of epiphytes in their own right and many of the 50 species and their hybrids are well worth growing. Laelias bloom from autumn to spring, depending on the variety. Most bear their flowers in short sprays, although one group (formerly treated as *Schomburgkia*) has sprays of blooms up to 3 ft (1 m) long. They are spectacular for a large greenhouse.

CULTIVATION
Laelias like subtropical to warm-temperate, frost-free climates. Grow in strong light in a very open orchid compost in a small pot or, for some creeping species, establish the plant on a slab. In cooler climates grow indoors or in a cool to intermediate greenhouse. A dry resting period during dormancy is essential for many species. Propagate by division when the first roots appear on the new shoots.

Laelia anceps
This medium-sized species grows epiphytically or on rocks at moderate altitudes in Mexico where it is often exposed to full sunlight. The pseudobulbs are well separated, about 2½ in (6 cm) long and 1 in (25 mm) in diameter with a single, stiff, leathery leaf 8 in (20 cm) long. The 3 in (8 cm) wide lilac-pink flowers with purple labellums are carried several together on 3 ft (1 m) long flower stems in winter. There are several named clones available, chosen for their larger or more shapely flowers. **ZONES 10–12.**

× *LAELIOCATTLEYA*

Laelias have been much crossed with the cattleyas, giving rise to this hybrid genus of evergreen orchids. They vary from cool to intermediate growing, and can have dainty almost miniature flowers or enormous ruffled ones in the full range of cattleya colors. The pseudobulbs bear only one leaf; it is lance-shaped and leathery.

CULTIVATION

Grow these frost-tender plants in a very open orchid compost in bright, filtered light. Water well in summer, then sparingly in winter. Propagate by division and watch for aphids, spider mites and mealybugs.

× *Laeliocattleya* Hybrid 'Orange Crush'

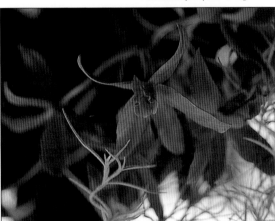

× *Laeliocattleya* Hybrids

These colorful hybrids of variable size and flower color have a large labellum (lip), often frilled and contrasting in color with the rest of the flower. Flowering primarily in spring and summer and occasionally through the year; they make good cut flowers. Among the wealth of hybrids are '**Chic Bonnet**', a bright pink flower with a magenta to crimson lip; and '**Orange Crush**', an overall orange flower with relatively narrow petals. **ZONES 11–12.**

LYCASTE

This orchid genus consists of about 45 species of epiphytes. The pseudobulbs are crowded into a compact clump, each with 2 to 4 large plicate leaves that are deciduous in many species. The showy flowers are borne singly, or occasionally 2 together, on many short stems arising from the bases of the pseudobulbs. Flower shape is more or less triangular dominated by the 3 sepals, the petals and labellum mostly smaller and of contrasting color. There is a wide range of flower colors with oranges and greenish yellows the most common, but pinks, reds, greens, and white also occur. There has been some hybridizing, for example, 'Diana' and 'Erin Harmony'.

CULTIVATION

Best in cool to intermediate conditions, no less than 50°F (10°C), a rather fine-textured orchid compost, and a well-lit position with good air movement. Water frequently in the growing period but let them almost dry out between waterings. Allow a dry period during winter. Propagate by division.

Lycaste cruenta

The pseudobulbs of this prolific flowerer are up to 4 in (10 cm) long and 2 in (5 cm) wide with several leaves 15 in (38 cm) long and 6 in (15 cm) wide. The greenish yellow flowers with bright orange petals and labellum are borne singly in spring on stems up to 6 in (15 cm) high; they are about 3 in (8 cm) wide and develop a sweetly aromatic scent like cinnamon toward the evening. A plant with several pseudobulbs can have up to 20 flowers and, as the leaves are shed before flowering, it is a spectacular sight. **ZONES 10–12.**

Miltoniopsis Hybrids

Numerous complex inter-
generic hybrids have been
made using *Miltonia, Miltoniopsis, Odontoglossum,
Oncidium, Cochlioda* and
Brassia. Most members of the
tribe Oncidiinae are inter-
fertile. These hybrids go by
names such as *Miltonidium,
Odontonia, Miltonioda* and
Miltassia. Among the resulting
multitude of forms and colors
have been the so-called pansy
orchids, which are derived
from *Miltoniopsis phalaenopsis*
and other species. Most of
these are cool-growing species
requiring shady, moist conditions. Hybrids include:
Anjou 'Red Mask', deep red
with a golden-yellow center
and dark markings; **Bel Royal,**
crimson with a white picotee
edge; **Charlotte's Delight,**
white with a large lower lip
and crimson markings;
Grouville, deep purplish pink
with fine white-edged, darker
markings and a golden center;
Hudson Bay 'Judith', deep
pink with a white-edged red
center; **Sao Paulo,** relatively
narrow, pale pink petals with
a large, deep pink lip and a
dark center; and **Rozel,** small
red petals with a large red-
veined and pink-edged lip.
Typical of the *Miltonia ×
Brassia* hybrids, × **Miltassia**
Anne Warne 'Alii' has strap-
like leaves and differs from
the *Miltoniopsis* hybrids in
having relatively narrow
petals and a prominent lower
lip. The magenta flower has a
darker throat and yellow
markings. **ZONES 10–11.**

Miltoniopsis Hybrid Grouville

MILTONIOPSIS

This genus was created for the pansy orchids, still commonly
called miltonias. With flat, almost circular flowers and vivid
markings, they resemble pansies, but are much larger—up to
6 in (15 cm) across—and come in stronger colors than pansies:
bright yellow, white, red, and pink, often with gold, purple or
brown flashes. Many are sweetly scented. Low-growing, clumping plants, they have round pseudobulbs and pale green, strap-
like leaves. Flowers, borne in small clusters, mostly in mid-summer, can appear any time from spring to autumn. Many flower
twice a year.

CULTIVATION

They like open compost and light shade and can grow outdoors
in the tropics and subtropics; elsewhere they need a greenhouse.
They do not take a winter rest. Propagate by division after
flowering.

Miltoniopsis Hybrid
× *Miltassia* Anne Warne 'Alii'

Odontoglossum crispum

This high-altitude epiphyte from Colombia is a variable species with many named forms, very popular in cultivation and with hybridists. The pseudobulbs are compressed, about 3 in (8 cm) long with 2 strap-like leaves to 15 in (38 cm) long and 1½ in (35 mm) wide. The inflorescence is arching or pendulous, with 8 to 25 showy flowers each 2½– 4 in (6–10 cm) across. Flowering occurs in autumn to winter. **ZONES 10–11.**

ODONTOGLOSSUM

The most widely grown plants of this genus of 200 species from Central and South America are epiphytes, although terrestrial species are known. They are admired for their usually ruffled flowers borne in long sprays, and the wonderful variety of colors and markings displayed thereon. They produce egg-shaped pseudobulbs, from the bases of which the flower stems appear; flowering is from early spring to autumn, depending on variety. The genus is closely related to *Oncidium*. Some well known *Odontoglossum* species are now separated off into the genera *Lemboglossum* and *Rossioglossum*.

CULTIVATION

Few odontoglossums are difficult to grow: most are cool growing, and need only the usual orchid cultivation of coarse compost, plenty of water in summer and light shade. They do not need as definite a winter rest as cattleyas, but do not overwater them. They can be divided after flowering.

Odontoglossum Hybrids

Thousands of colorful hybrids have been developed suitable for greenhouse culture using *Odontoglossum*. Many other genera have also been used in the production of hybrids including those with *Cochlioda* (× *Odontioda*), *Oncidium* (× *Odonticidium*) and *Miltonia* (× *Odontonia*). Virtually all are cool-growing species with similar requirements to the genus. 'La Houge Bie' is notable for its very broad, overlapping petals giving the bloom a full, rounded look. Extravagant **'Samares'** is another fine example. Its pure white petals are wavy with frilled edges and each is decorated with a few blood-red spots. **ZONES 10–12.**

Odontoglossum Hybrid 'Samares'

PAPHIOPEDILUM

SLIPPER ORCHID, LADY'S SLIPPER

The 60 orchid species in this genus extend from India through Southeast Asia, including southern China, to the Philippines and New Guinea. The plants grow mostly at moderate altitudes in dense shade on the rainforest floor or in leafmold on rock faces and occasionally as epiphytes. They are usually compact, consisting of fleshy roots, a short stem and a few large, often mottled leaves with a terminal inflorescence of one or a few large flowers with a characteristic pouched lip.

CULTIVATION

Requirements depend on the origin of the plants, but most are best grown in intermediate temperatures and part shade. They should be kept evenly moist throughout the year with well-drained potting mixture. Difficult to grow from seed, many species are threatened by over-collecting from the wild. They are propagated by division; mericlonal propagation does not suit them, and so selected clones and hybrids remain expensive.

Paphiopedilum Hybrid King Arthur 'Burgoyne'

Paphiopedilum Hybrids

Thousands of hybrids have been produced, many in an attempt to achieve a more rounded flower shape. Other goals include increased vigor and flower size, and interesting color combinations. Many will bloom several times a year. Another trend in hybridizing has been to produce novelties. Most of the hybrids come from about 25 species. **King Arthur 'Burgoyne'**, a typical hybrid, has flowers of a rich coppery red except for the white tip of the broad dorsal sepal. **Grande Jersey** is a hybrid grex of a quite different kind, bred from the small group of species with very elongated, twisted petals. **ZONES 10–12.**

Paphiopedilum insigne

This species occurs in Nepal and northern India at about 6,660 ft (2,000 m) in limestone soils. It is a vigorous grower, about 12–18 in (30–45 cm) tall, and often forms large clumps. The few strap-like leaves are up to 15 in (38 cm) long and 1 in (25 mm) wide. The inflorescence is 12 in (30 cm) long with 1 or 2 glossy flowers 4–6 in (10–15 cm) long, which appear in autumn and winter. This species is the basis of many hybrids. Named forms combine shades of green, russet, cream, and white in various patterns and markings. **ZONES 10–12.**

Paphiopedilum rothschildianum

Paphiopedilum rothschildianum

This large, clump-forming species occurs only on Mt Kinabalu in Borneo, where it grows at low altitudes terrestrially or on rock ledges. Regarded as one of the most threatened orchid species in the world, it is much sought after. There are several leaves, strap-like and up to 24 in (60 cm) long and 2 in (5 cm) wide. The inflorescence is up to 18 in (45 cm) long with 2 to 4 flowers about 12 in (30 cm) in diameter. Cultivation is as for the genus, but higher levels of light are recommended. Flowering occurs in spring. **ZONES 11–12.**

Phalaenopsis Hybrid
Longwood Gardens

Phalaenopsis Hybrid Plantation
Imp 'Moonglow'

PHALAENOPSIS

MOTH ORCHID

The pastel flowers, broad leaves and intricate petals of the nearly 50 species in this genus from tropical Asia to New Guinea and Australia look enough like fluttering butterflies to earn the common name of moth orchid. They do not make pseudobulbs; the leaves, plain green or spotted, spring directly from the rootstock and the arching flower stems rise clear above them. The stem can be 24 in (60 cm) tall, bearing as many as 20 shapely 4 in (10 cm) flowers. They are most commonly shining white, but are sometimes pale pink, and appear at almost any time of the year.

CULTIVATION

Phalaenopsis species need tropical and subtropical climates—elsewhere a warm but well ventilated greenhouse—and filtered light, constant moisture and a rich but open and perfectly drained compost. They are apt to send roots out over the top of the pot: these should be left undisturbed if possible. Their lives as house plants are limited unless they can be retired to a greenhouse when the flowers fade. Propagate by division in spring.

Phalaenopsis amabilis

This is an attractive, small-growing epiphyte from the humid tropical lowlands of Indonesia, Borneo, New Guinea, the Philippines and Australia. The short stem bears 2 to 5 pendulous, fleshy leaves to 15 in (38 cm) long and 4 in (10 cm) wide. The inflorescences are branched, arching to pendulous, up to 3 ft (1 m) long with 5 to 25 flowers. The flowers vary in size, up to 4 in (10 cm) across and appear in spring and summer. **ZONES 11–12.**

Phalaenopsis Hybrids

Thousands of hybrids have been produced from the species of this genus. Breeders have been striving to produce more floriferous plants with larger, more rounded flowers on upright flower spikes and colorful combinations such as striped flowers. Most hybrids are white or pink. Some notable examples are **Alice Gloria 'Cecil Park'**, which is pure white except for a small orange area at the lip; **Bill Smoothey**, pink with white edging; **'Carmela's Stripe'**, a striking hybrid with light pink petals with deep red veining and red lips; **Hiramatsua 'Ching Hua'**, with deep pink petals; **Longwood Gardens**, white with brownish yellow lips; and **Plantation Imp 'Moonglow'**, with pinkish orange stripes on whitish yellow petals, and pinkish orange lips. Some hybrids with *P. equestris* in their parentage have a multitude of smaller flowers on branched inflorescences. **ZONES 11–12.**

Pleione, Shantung Hybrid

PLEIONE

This is a small genus consisting of about 16 to 20 miniature orchids native to areas in southern and eastern Asia. They are epiphytic or terrestrial, with globose or flask-shaped, crowded pseudobulbs and one or two deciduous leaves. The flowers are large and showy, and arise from the base of the pseudobulb as the new growth is produced.

CULTIVATION

They like a mild, cool-temperate climate and protection from winter wet. They are usually grown in pots in good orchid potting mix and prefer part shade. Propagate by division.

Pleione bulbocodioides
syns *Pleione formosana, p. pricei*

This species from southern China, Taiwan and Burma grows on trees or rocks at moderate to high altitudes in moist forests. The pseudobulbs are clustered, pear shaped, about 1 in (25 mm) in diameter with a single leaf to 6 in (15 cm) long and 2 in (5 cm) wide. The shapely, 3 in (8 cm) wide flowers are borne in early spring before the new leaves appear. *Pleione bulbocodioides* var. *alba* (syn. *P. formosana* 'Alba') has white flowers. **ZONES 8–10.**

Pleione, Shantung Hybrids

Shantung is one of the most desirable of the fairly new hybrid pleiones. It comes in a number of clones that differ slightly in their blends of cream and pale pink. **'Muriel Fisher'**, named for a New Zealand botanist, is fairly frost hardy but needs a sheltered spot. Enrich its soil liberally with leafmold or compost. **ZONES 8–10.**

× *Sophrocattleya* and × *Sophrolaeliocattleya* Hybrids

It is the infusion of genes from the brilliantly colored *Sophronitis coccinea* that has most influenced these hybrids, the first cross having been made in England as early as 1886; the resulting grex, × *Sophrocattleya* Bateman-iana, is still in cultivation. Since that time thousands of hybrids have been registered, the sophrolaeliocattleyas now greatly outnumbering the sophrocattleyas. Typical modern hybrids are × *Sophrolaeliocattleya* Jannine Louise 'Orange Glow', with orange-yellow flowers tinged reddish on the frilled edges and × *Sophrolaelio-cattleya* Jewel Box 'Scheherazade', a compact plant with clusters of rich, shining red flowers. **ZONES 10–12.**

Vanda Miss Joachim × *Phalaenopsis laycockii*

× *SOPHROCATTLEYA*

This orchid generic hybrid name covers all crosses between any members of the genera *Sophronitis* and *Cattleya*, including all later generation seedlings and back-crosses. They mostly have slightly smaller flowers than the average *Cattleya* or × *Laelio-cattleya* hybrid. × *Sophrolaeliocattleya* is the equivalent tri-generic name for crosses involving *Sophronitis*, *Laelia* and *Cattleya*, in practice these are much the same as sophrocattleyas.

CULTIVATION

All these generic hybrids require much the same conditions as the cooler-growing cattleyas, though perhaps with a little more water supplied during the winter resting period. Propagate by division, though commercial production is usually from flasked seedlings or mericlones.

VANDA

The most celebrated species of this epiphytic orchid genus from Southeast Asia to northern Australia is *Vanda caerulea* from the mountains of Thailand and Burma, where it was once quite common. Sadly, the greed of Western collectors has brought it to an endangered state—and it is not often seen in gardens either, its place having been taken by more easily grown hybrids. Some of the 35 or so species of this genus are spring or summer flower-ing, and the color range is from white through cream and pink to orange—blue is rare. Many have interesting markings and mottlings of other colors. These orchids range from miniatures to large robust plants.

CULTIVATION

They are all warm-growing epiphytes, liking a very coarse com-post and strong light, though preferably not full sunshine; they are outdoor plants only in the tropics. Keep them warm and watered all year, as they rarely take a winter rest. Most need staking: on a piece of tree fern trunk they will cling to it by aerial roots. Feed regularly during the growing season. Propagate by removing rooted offsets.

Vanda Hybrids

Vanda species have been used to develop a large number of hybrids over the past 100 years. Many of these have been used in the cut flower industry as the flowers are large and long lasting, and are readily grown in tropical countries. Major trends have been with the terete-leafed species (now usually regarded as a separate genus—*Papilonanthe*) and with the larger-flowered species such as *V. sanderiana* (now *Euanthe sanderiana*) and *V. caerulea*. There are also many intergeneric crosses with other genera like *Ascocentrum*, *Phalaenopsis* and *Euanthe*. **Nellie Morley, Josephine van Brero** and **Miss Joachim** × *Phalaenopsis laycockii* are popular hybrids. *V. rothschildiana*, the blue orchid, is a hybrid between *V. caerulea* and *Euanthe sanderiana*. It is easier to grow than its parents are—and hence more often encountered in gardens than other hybrids. It bears sprays of 6 in (15 cm), or larger, long-lasting flowers in winter. They range in the different clones from light to deep violet blue, the flowers being distinctly veined with a deeper shade; a well-grown plant can carry several sprays of flowers. It has itself given rise to further hybrids. **ZONES 11–12.**

ZYGOPETALUM

This orchid genus consists of 12 or so rather similar species of evergreen epiphytes from Central and South America. The fragrant flowers are admired for their unusual color—the petals and sepals are usually green, spotted with red, and the labellum finely striped in purple and white. These tones may be distributed in different patterns in some species. Zygopetalums are low-growing, clumpy plants with glossy, mid-green leaves. Their flower stems grow to 24 in (60 cm) long and can carry up to a dozen blooms. Flowering occurs in autumn or early winter.

CULTIVATION

Zygopetalums prefer subtropical and frost-free, warm-temperate climates when grown outdoors; under these conditions, they are very easy to grow in a shaded position. In cooler climates, they need to be protected in a greenhouse. Grow in orchid compost with filtered light and water freely. Propagate by division.

Zygopetalum mackaii

This is an epiphytic species from Brazil and bears long sprays of perfumed, brown-spotted, green flowers with purple-veined, white lips to 3 in (8 cm). It grows to 30 in (75 cm) tall and has oval, ribbed leaves. **ZONES 10–12.**

Zygopetalum mackaii

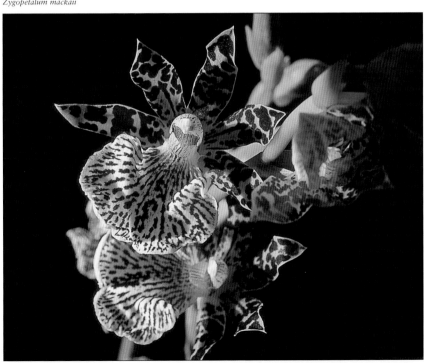

Chapter 12

FERNS, PALMS
& CYCADS

Although unrelated botanically, palms, ferns and cycads share many horticultural attributes that gardeners find wonderfully compatible. All three rely entirely on their foliage for ornamental effect. Ferns evolved a long time before flowering plants and have a unique reproduction structure as a consequence.

The cycad family emerged shortly after the flowering plants, and relies on cones similar to those of conifers to survive from generation to generation. Palms, however, are a relatively modern group of plants.

Regardless of how they evolved, all three plant types group together well as low-maintenance foliage plants. There is great variation in leaf or frond shapes, textures and coloring, and height and outline. Combine these with a water feature, and you create one of the most tranquil forms of garden design: that of a rainforest.

Dicksonia antarctica

What are Palms?

Palms are unique trees with a very distinctive growth habit, which can be divided into three groups. The majority are single trunked, called solitary palms, and can grow very tall. They grow naturally in large colonies amongst other trees.

The second group of palms sucker to form a clump of shrub-like proportions, and the third group likes to climb amongst tropical growth in the quest to reach the light. Very rarely do any species have branches. The leaves, often called fronds, can be either long or rounded, and palms are referred to as feather leafed or fan shaped respectively. The foliage grows at the top of the shaft, and leaves either fall naturally or persist on the trunk in a withered state for many seasons.

Palms in the garden

While there are many palm species of commercial value, including date and coconut, the home gardener is much more interested in their decorative uses. They have a distinct advantage over many other trees in that they have a predictable nature and shape. A warm-climate garden is needed to display the magnificent foliage of the more tropical species, otherwise they may need to be grown indoors or where they can be given shelter. A large number, however, are suitable for more temperate gardens.

Most of the solitary trunked species look particularly good when grouped, although one of the few exceptions, unless used in an avenue, is *Phoenix canariensis*. When young, many of these tall growers will also welcome light shade, but they prefer to be in full sun when mature. The lower-growing palms, native to the forest understorey, always prefer a shady habitat where they are happy to share their space with ferns and cycads.

Although palms are not unduly worried about soil, the better the soil texture and quality, the healthier and quicker growing the palm. If the soil is particularly heavy or sandy, it may be impossibly expensive to overcome. In these instances, it is best to seek advice on what to plant from a specialist palm grower, rather than rely on the sort of species that are seen as mature specimens in established parks or gardens. These are residues from fashionable plantings in the early 1900s, and today there are many more species from which to choose. For example, not many palms will tolerate boggy conditions, but the native Australian *Livistona australis* is not only adaptable to the margins of such

a position, but also to quite a wide climate range.

Palms are easily grown from seed, but gardeners who want to create an instant garden atmosphere can easily transport quite large palms. The procedure is not really any different from that used for trees or shrubs. It pays to dig the hole a little larger than the pot size to allow the roots to penetrate easily, and to dig in some well-rotted manure or slow-release fertilizer. Once the palm is in position, water it in well. It is sometimes advisable to insert support stakes until the plant becomes established.

Doodia aspera

Fashionable ferns and their decorative uses

Ferns happily tolerate moist conditions, in fact they rely on moisture for reproduction. Not surprisingly, their popularity with gardeners was delayed until reliable methods of propagation and cultivation become known. Once this was understood, there was no stopping their popularity. In Victorian times, fern collecting become known as 'pteridomania' and continued unabated for years. Many wild species completely disappeared as their natural habitats were denuded. Then, like all fashions, the craze faded once it became commonplace.

Ferns are a vast range of plants that exist from sea level to the highest mountain ranges. They are found in three habitats: woodland or rainforest, where they revel in the moist atmosphere; in rocky, well-drained pockets in mountain areas; and arid zones where seasonal rainfall ensures their survival. The latter two groups are usually only sought by collectors, since the first group contains more than enough hardy species for the generalist.

Both terrestrial and epiphytic types are readily available to the home gardener who wants to create a fernery. In warmer climates, this conjures up images of a green cavern, which could be in a shaded area beside a patio where palms and ferns mingle, and if there is a mature tree with well-positioned branches, so much the better for the epiphytes. A pond can be used to accommodate aquatic ferns. In cooler areas, a greenhouse may be necessary, with potted ferns rotated indoors, or it can be fun to plant out an unused aquarium in the style of a Wardian case. These containers with a controlled humid environment were particularly popular in Victorian times.

Fern care

Ferns rely on a primitive vascular system, which is generally unable to cope with dry conditions. In the garden, this means ferns should be well protected and given a humid atmosphere, while those grown in pots may need to be sprayed or misted on a regular basis during summer. The soil should remain moist, although most species resent sitting in waterlogged soil. Coarse sand will help with drainage where garden soil tends to be heavy. Supply plenty of humus in the form of rotted manure, compost or peatmoss, and they respond well to fertilizer. Diluted solutions of a general nature can be used, although specially formulated fertilizers for ferns and palms are available. In the garden, fern aftercare is surprisingly simple, as they resent being disturbed by digging and weeding.

Cycads, while completely unrelated to both palms and ferns, nevertheless look best when combined with these two plants. Many ferns have fine, surface-creeping rhizomes and roots, and quickly establish to form a dense groundcover that blends particularly well with trunked cycads—*Dicksonia* and *Cyathea* species for example.

These, in turn, can be shaded by the taller-growing palms. Cycads require very similar conditions to palms and ferns, but take much longer to mature; you could wait a lifetime, in fact, to notice any real growth. The *Macrozamia* species with their deep green leaves, however, make good pot plants and are easily transported should you ever move house.

Fan palms make a splendid solitary trunked specimen for a lawn; they also look good planted in small groups.

FERNS

Adiantum aethiopicum

COMMON MAIDENHAIR

Occurring through much of
Asia, Africa and Australasia,
common maidenhair has some
of the most delicate fronds of
the genus with very rounded,
pale green leaflets ¼ in (8 mm)
or less in diameter. Its wiry
rhizomes are deeply buried,
and a plant can spread extensively. It often appears
spontaneously in moist, shady
spots in the garden, from
wind-carried spores. It also
flourishes in containers and
hanging baskets, with
frequent repotting.
ZONES 9–11.

ADIANTUM

MAIDENHAIR FERN

Adiantum raddianum 'Triumph'

Among the best known ferns, maidenhairs in their typical guise
are recognizable by their billowy fronds of many delicate, membranous, almost circular fresh green leaflets, each connected by
a very fine, smooth, blackish stalk to a repeatedly branched
main stalk of the same color. Sporecases appear as tiny inden-
tations with curled-over 'lips' around the edges of leaflets. With
over 200 species in all but the coldest parts of the world (the
majority in the American tropics), this genus is very varied and
not all species conform to this frond pattern: some have larger,
thicker, oblong or triangular leaflets without individual stalks.

CULTIVATION

Hardier species will thrive outdoors in shady areas, spreading
by deep or shallow rhizomes to form a dainty groundcover, but
they resent root disturbance so transplanting may be difficult.
Tropical species, most with fronds in dense tufts, are usually
grown indoors in pots or hanging baskets, appreciating strong
light but not direct sun, and high humidity—the bathroom is
a popular site; they don't like the dry atmosphere of heated
rooms. Plant in a humus-rich, indoor potting mix in a container
that is not too large for the roots, which do not like too much
wetness. Remove old fronds. Propagate from spores; division of
rhizomes is possible.

Adiantum raddianum

DELTA MAIDENHAIR

Larger and coarser than
Adiantum aethiopicum, this
tropical American species has
vigorous, arching fronds making a dense, cascading tuft,
the pale green, fan-shaped
segments are borne on fine,
dark purple stems. Frost tender, it reaches a height and
spread of 12–18 in (30–45 cm).
Cut the old fronds away in
autumn to encourage new
growth. The most popular
species for indoor use, it has
given rise to numerous cultivars; '**Triumph**' is one example. **ZONES 10–12.**

ASPLENIUM
SPLEENWORT

This genus of some 700 species of mainly evergreen ferns is found around the world. They include terrestrial and epiphytic species as well as many that grow on rocks. Some make dense tufts of fronds or rosettes, others creep across the surface with thick, scaly rhizomes. Most have feathery pinnate or bipinnate fronds but in some they are large and undivided: the 'bird's nest ferns' are one such striking group. The fronds of many species develop small plantlets along the ribs. The spore-bodies are typically arranged in parallel or radiating lines on the undersides of the fronds.

CULTIVATION

Most species prefer woodland conditions with cool, moist, humus-rich soil and dappled shade. A few species, however, need sunnier locations and are reasonably tolerant of dry conditions. Propagate from spores, by division of established clumps, removing rooted pieces of rhizomes, or from frond-borne plantlets.

Asplenium australasicum
BIRD'S NEST FERN

Found in Australia and the South Pacific, this species has leathery, undivided fronds, up to 5 ft (1.5 m) long by 8 in (20 cm) wide forming a dramatic large 'nest' or funnel. In the wild it grows on tree trunks or rocks. It is frost tender and requires warm, humid conditions to thrive. *Asplenium nidus* is a very similar species widespread in the tropics. **ZONES 10–12.**

Asplenium bulbiferum
HEN AND CHICKEN FERN, MOTHER FERN

This Australian and New Zealand native is one of the more widely cultivated species, easily grown in pots or hanging baskets. Typically fern-like in appearance, it has a tuft of arching, deep green, finely divided fronds up to 3 ft (1 m) long and 12 in (30 cm) wide. Small plantlets form on the fronds, mainly on the midrib. **ZONES 9–11.**

Asplenium australasicum

Blechnum nudum

BLECHNUM

WATER FERN

This genus of over 200 species is found around the world, the majority in the southern hemisphere. Most species have very short rhizomes or vertical stems with rosettes of fishbone-type fronds. In a few species a short trunk develops. New fronds are usually pink, red or bronze. In many species the spore-bearing fronds are sharply distinct from the vegetative ones, more erect and with much narrower, thicker segments.

CULTIVATION

Blechnums are generally easy ferns to grow, especially outdoors in sheltered, moist areas. The edges of ponds and streams are favored spots. Most are ground dwellers that prefer humus-rich soil and part-shade, and form clumps that spread by runners. Most are frost tender and thrive in subtropical climates. Propagate from spores in late summer, or by division.

Blechnum discolor

CROWN FERN, PUI-PUI

So called because of the attractive crown of bright green radiating fronds, this New Zealand native has adapted well to gardens. Mature plants have trunks up to 12 in (30 cm) tall and a total height of 3 ft (1 m); they spread in time to produce large colonies of rosettes. The fronds are long and narrow with closely spaced segments, and the spore-bearing fronds are distinct with thicker, narrower segments. It likes a lot of water and will grow in sun, although it prefers a position in shade. **ZONES 8–10.**

Blechnum nudum

FISHBONE WATER FERN

Native in southeastern mainland Australia and Tasmania, this species is a vigorous spreader with shuttlecock-like rosettes of fresh green fronds 24–36 in (60–90 cm) high. The new fronds are delicately tinted pink. The frond midrib is blackish towards the base, and the rosettes often develop a short trunk. Spore-bearing fronds are much narrower and thicker, growing erect from the center of the rosette. It grows in damp places, often beside water, and will tolerate full sun. **ZONES 9–11.**

Blechnum penna-marina

ALPINE WATER FERN

A low-growing species native to New Zealand, southern Australia, South America and the subantarctic islands, this fern is often found in sub-alpine bogs where snow and frost are common. Growing in quick bursts in summer from creeping rhizomes, its narrow, dark green fronds, pink-tipped when young, are only about 8 in (20 cm) long and may form extensive mats. It prefers bright light and needs a temperate climate with cold periods. It makes an ideal groundcover. **ZONES 6–9.**

Blechnum discolor

CYATHEA
TREE FERN

Apart from *Asplenium* this is the largest genus of ferns, with over 600 species scattered throughout the humid tropical and subtropical regions of the world. *Cyathea* species vary greatly in size, but most are single-stemmed with a trunk up to 50 ft (15 m) tall and an umbrella-like crown of very large fronds. The frond bases are usually covered in hairs or chaff-like scales which may be quite prickly. In warm-climate gardens, few plants create such dramatic effects as these tree ferns, some of which grow relatively quickly under ideal conditions.

CULTIVATION

They prefer a humid atmosphere, part-shade, and a moist, humus-rich soil. In warm weather they need plenty of water and may need frequent mist-spraying during hot dry spells. When young, many species make attractive indoor plants in a suitably humid environment. Propagate from spores in spring. Transplant established plants with care.

Cyathea dealbata
syn. *Alsophila tricolor*
SILVER TREE FERN, PONGA

This attractive New Zealand species has distinctive silver-white undersides to its fronds. It is slow growing to about 15 ft (4.5 m) in cultivation. The slender erect trunk is topped by a crown of fronds up to 10 ft (3 m) long. One of New Zealand's national symbols, it is marginally frost hardy and needs shelter from wind. ZONES 9–11.

Cyathea medullaris
syn. *Sphaeropteris medullaris*
BLACK TREE FERN

From New Zealand and other islands of the South Pacific, this species is one of the largest, most robust tree ferns known in cultivation. The trunk can reach 50 ft (15 m) or even more and 12 in (30 cm) in diameter, with widely spaced frond scars. The fronds can reach 20 ft (6 m) long, and more than 6 ft (1.8 m) wide, with black stalks up to 3 in (8 cm) thick covered in blackish chaff-like scales. It needs a sheltered position and grows rapidly with an abundant supply of water and nutrients. ZONES 9–12.

Cyathea dealbata

CYRTOMIUM

This genus of about 12 species of evergreen ferns is from eastern and central Asia. They are clump-forming, terrestrial ferns with pinnate fronds radiating from short erect rhizomes covered with scales. The broad segments may be toothed or cut, and on fertile fronds the rich brown spore-bodies are sprinkled densely over their undersides.

CULTIVATION

Most species are frost tender to moderately frost hardy and easy to grow. They grow well indoors in a well-lit position or in a conservatory or greenhouse. Propagate from spores, which germinate readily on moist bricks or mossy stones, or by division of clumps.

Cyrtomium falcatum
syn. **Phanerophlebia falcata**
HOLLY FERN

A native of East Asia, this species is easily recognized by the holly-like form and texture of its tough, glossy frond segments, though their shape differs in some varieties. It forms a dense clump 24–36 in (60–90 cm) high, and has naturalized in countries with mild climates, mainly on coastal cliffs. It tolerates light frosts though the upper fronds can burn. It will grow in quite deep shade, yet is one of the most sun-tolerant of the ferns. **ZONES 9–11.**

Cyrtomium falcatum

Dicksonia antarctica

DICKSONIA
TREE FERN

Tree ferns are common in the wet tropics, among mountains where mist and drizzle are frequent. They are true ferns, distinguished from other ferns by their single bud terminating a vertical stem, at the core of which is a convoluted system of conducting and strengthening tissues, often clothed in matted aerial roots. The fronds are usually large and multi-pinnate, with downy bases. This genus of 30 large, evergreen to semi-evergreen species, ranges from Malaysia to Australia. A New Zealand species, *Dicksonia squarrosa*, occurs up to latitudes equivalent to central Europe.

CULTIVATION

Fully frost hardy to frost tender, they need shelter and prefer peaty, damp soil in full or part-shade; they will not tolerate a dry atmosphere. Propagate from spores in summer.

Dicksonia antarctica
SOFT TREE FERN, TASMANIAN TREE FERN

Native to southeastern Australia, this tree fern can grow to 50 ft (15 m) with a trunk diameter of 3 ft (1 m) in the wild, with lacy, dark green fronds up to 10 ft (3 m) long. In cultivation, it rarely exceeds 10 ft (3 m) in height. It is a marginally frost-hardy species requiring a moist, sheltered position. Its erect trunk is densely covered with fibrous roots and is an excellent host for epiphytic orchids and other ferns. **ZONES 8–10.**

Doodia aspera
PRICKLY RASP FERN

Native to eastern Australia, Norfolk Island and New Zealand, this small fern proliferates in open forests. It has a short, creeping rhizome and grows to about 12 in (30 cm) tall. The upright fronds, which widen at the base, have serrated margins and a harsh, raspy texture. New growth is pink or red. It thrives in shade or sun if kept moist. **ZONES 9–11.**

DOODIA

This fern genus was named after English chemist and botanist Samuel Doody and contains 11 species of tufted, terrestrial ferns native to Australia, New Zealand and some Pacific islands. The slender, pinnate fronds are harsh to the touch and have heavily serrated leaflets, vivid red-pink when immature. They are attractive small ferns suitable for gardens or containers.

CULTIVATION

Species range from frost tender to marginally frost hardy and prefer a cool, not cold, climate. Plant in fertile, damp soil and avoid direct sunlight. They thrive in humidity, but tolerate dry conditions once established. Propagate from spores or by division in spring.

Doodia aspera

Lycopodium phlegmaria
LAYERED TASSEL FERN

This elegant species is widely distributed in the rainforests of tropical Asia and the South Pacific. It features small, shiny, lacquered leaves that line the long, pendent stems in 4 rows. In this and many related species the ends of the stems branch into groups of fine, elongated, strobili-like green tassels, earning this group the name tassel ferns. They form large clumps of hanging stems that look very good in baskets. **ZONES 11–12.**

LYCOPODIUM
CLUBMOSS

Widespread throughout most moister regions of the world, there are 100 or more species in this genus. Considered more primitive than the ferns but more advanced than the mosses, they range from tiny thread-stemmed plants that grow in boggy ground below heath, to large epiphytes that form curtains of ferny foliage on the limbs of tropical rainforest trees. All share similar cord-like stems clothed with overlapping, bright green or golden-green, scale-like leaves. Club mosses do not flower but instead bear tiny spore capsules between the scales of delicate small cones (strobili).

CULTIVATION

Only the epiphytic species are cultivated to any extent, mainly by fern enthusiasts. Outdoors in the tropics they prefer part-shade and a permanently moist niche in the fork of a tree. Elsewhere they require a greenhouse or conservatory maintained at high humidity, and can make dramatic specimens in hanging baskets. Hang in positions with some air movement; they are sensitive to excess water around the roots. Propagate from cuttings or by layering fertile stem tips.

LYGODIUM

CLIMBING FERN

About 35 to 40 unusual climbing fern species
make up this genus, scattered widely through
warmer and moister regions of the world.
Including both deciduous and semi-evergreens,
they have much-branched rhizomes beneath the
soil. Young plants at first produce short pinnate fronds, but they soon send up fronds with
the unusual ability to grow indefinitely from
the tips. Their mid-stalks twining around twigs,
shrubs and saplings and sometimes forming
large masses of foliage. The leaflets vary from
almost circular to narrow and lobed, and fertile
portions of the frond are usually edged with
narrow, comb-like teeth bearing small spore-
bodies. In some regions the tough 'stems' are
used for cordage, nets, mats or baskets.

CULTIVATION

Grow in moist, humus-rich, peaty soil in sun
or part-shade. Frost hardiness varies with the
species. Provide support or drape from hanging
baskets. Propagate by division in spring or
from spores in summer.

Lygodium japonicum

JAPANESE CLIMBING FERN

This deciduous species can climb to more than
12 ft (3.5 m) and the fronds are bright green
and divided into many long leaflets that are
toothed and basally lobed. The spore-bearing
leaflets are sharply distinct. **ZONES 10–12.**

Lygodium japonicum

PELLAEA

BRAKE FERN, CLIFF BRAKE

This genus of ferns is widespread in tropical to
warm-temperate areas and includes some 80
species. They are rhizomatous, creeping and
usually evergreen, and have generally pinnate
fronds in a wide variety of forms. The rhizomes are usually brown and scaly and spread
across the surface of the ground or through
crevices in rocks. The fronds, which are rarely
over 18 in (45 cm) tall, are often leathery and
are held erect.

CULTIVATION

Although hardiness varies with the species,
these ferns are generally quite sun tolerant
provided they do not dry out. They often thrive
in exposed positions in fairly poor soil or hard
clay that would defeat most ferns. Propagate
by breaking off rooted pieces of rhizome.

Pellaea falcata

Pellaea falcata
SICKLE FERN, AUSTRALIAN CLIFF BRAKE

Found from Australia to India, this species has 12–15 in (30–38 cm) fronds with 1–2 in (2.5–5 cm) leaflets. They have dark green upper surfaces, brownish undersides and are carried on 2–6 in (5–15 cm) stems. **ZONES 10–12.**

Pellaea rotundifolia
BUTTON FERN, ROUND-LEAFED FERN, TARAWERA

Native to Australia and New Zealand, this species is a very popular garden plant. It is a small, dark green, ground-dwelling fern found in damp, open forests or drier woodlands. It has pinnate fronds with deep green, glossy, oblong to round leaflets and long-creeping rhizomes. Suitable for a garden or fernery with filtered sunlight and protection from drafts, it also does well in rock gardens. **ZONES 9–11.**

Pellaea rotundifolia

PLATYCERIUM

This genus is common to the tropics and subtropics of Africa, Southeast Asia and Australia, although some species can tolerate quite cool temperatures. The 15 species are epiphytic ferns with hanging, spore-bearing divided fronds up to 8 ft (2.4 m) long. They are valued for their dramatic appearance.

CULTIVATION
These ferns can either be grown as epiphytes by tying them onto boards that are then attached to a post or tree, or grown in baskets. The sterile nest leaves catch leaf litter and other vegetable matter so that the roots eventually grow into the debris and are protected from wind. The base of the plants should be kept moist. Fertilize the plants with dilute liquid manure. Propagate by division in spring. Check for beetle and moth larvae.

Platycerium bifurcatum
ELKHORN FERN

Native to the northeast coast of Australia, Papua New Guinea and New Caledonia, the elkhorn fern is an easily grown plant that does well in sheltered gardens. It grows to a height and spread of about 3 ft (1 m). **ZONES 9–12.**

Platycerium superbum
syn. *Platycerium grande*
STAGHORN FERN

In the wild, clinging to a rainforest tree, this epiphyte can reach up to 6 ft (1.8 m) in height and spread, and its sheer weight can make it fall to the ground. It does well in a fernery or garden, where it grows to about half its natural size. **ZONES 10–12.**

POLYSTICHUM

SHIELD FERN

This genus of 200 species of ground- or rock-dwelling ferns is found worldwide from tropical to subantarctic regions. Their fronds are either pinnate or simple and ribbon-shaped. They are known as shield ferns because groups of the spores are covered with a fragile, shield-shaped growth. Ornamental species have become very popular.

CULTIVATION

They prefer part- to full shade and fertile, humus-rich, well-drained soil. The frond tips usually bear an abundance of small buds that become plantlets in their own right when conditions are favorable. Otherwise, propagate by sowing spores in summer or by division of the rhizomes in spring.

Polystichum proliferum

MOTHER SHIELD FERN

From southeastern Australia, this shield fern is one of the most reliable and easy to grow. It grows to 3 ft (1 m) tall and is longlasting in both tubs and in the ground. **ZONES 5–9.**

Polystichum proliferum

Pteris umbrosa

PTERIS

BRAKE FERN

This genus consists of 280 deciduous, semi-evergreen and evergreen ferns native to the shady, damp gullies of subtropical and tropical rainforests. They are also found growing out of rock crevices in full sunlight. They have closely spaced fronds and spores that form at the frond edges. Brake ferns do well as feature plants.

CULTIVATION

These adaptable ferns need a great deal of water when young, and should be kept out of direct sunlight. Often grown indoors, they are best propagated from spores or by division. Some are frost tender, others frost hardy. Watch for aphids on the leaf stalks.

Pteris umbrosa

JUNGLE BRAKE

This Australian species has 12–24 in (30–60 cm) fronds on 4–12 in (10–30 cm) stems. Its creeping rhizome spreads quickly and enables the plant to colonize large areas. **ZONES 10–12.**

Archontophoenix cunninghamiana

BANGALOW PALM,
PICCABEEN PALM

This species is similar in appearance and requirements to the Alexandra palm, but with green undersides to the fronds, a rusty scurf coating the crownshaft, and longer, vertically pendulous panicles of pale lilac flowers. It is usually taller than the Alexandra palm at first flowering, and prefers slightly cooler climates. It can also tolerate extremely light frosts and is more tolerant of shade. **ZONES 9–11.**

PALMS

ARCHONTOPHOENIX

Majestic, subtropical palms from the rainforests of eastern Australia make up this genus of 6 species. All have tall, solitary trunks topped by a green crownshaft from which the long, gracefully arching fronds radiate. Old fronds fall cleanly from the trunk, leaving ringed scars. Large panicles of tiny, fragrant flowers burst from massive green buds that emerge at the base of the crownshaft, later becoming laden with cherry-sized red fruit.

CULTIVATION

These palms are not at all frost hardy but will grow in most fertile soil where organic matter and moisture are sufficient, even tolerating boggy conditions. They prefer part-shade when young, full sun as the crown gains height. They can also be grown as potted plants, but are not as satisfactory for this purpose as many other palms. Propagate from seed, which germinates readily in summer.

Archontophoenix alexandrae

ALEXANDRA PALM

This tall and elegant species has a straight trunk up to 50 ft (15 m) and arching fronds 10–12 ft (3–3.5 m) long. The silver-gray undersides of the fronds catch the light, especially when the sun is low. The cream flowers appear mostly in autumn. It thrives in the wet tropics, but adapts well to warm-temperate climates. **ZONES 10–12.**

Archontophoenix alexandrae

BRAHEA

syn. *Erythea*

This genus of 16 species of fan-leafed palms is related to *Washingtonia*, and comes from the same dry regions of Mexico. They range from low-growing plants that develop no trunk, to quite tall, solitary-trunked palms with compact crowns. Panicles of tiny flowers hang below the crown and, as the date-like fruits develop, may exceed the fronds in length.

CULTIVATION

Most species can grow in inhospitable places, some even tolerating light frosts once established. Plants in containers should be watered frequently in summer. Propagation is from seed only, with rapid germination as palms go, but seedling growth is slow. Plants are prone to attack by scale insects and spider mites.

Brahea armata

syn. **Erythea armata**
HESPER PALM

The pale blue-gray color of the stiff fronds is the outstanding feature of this species. It grows slowly to a height of 20 ft (6 m), with a crown 10 ft (3 m) wide. In flower and fruit it is even more dramatic, with arching panicles 15 ft (4.5 m) long. It takes decades to reach flowering size, but even young plants are notable for their foliage. *Brahea edulis* differs from *B. armata* in having light green leaves and a stout trunk. It also grows taller: to about 30 ft (9 m). The flowers are similar but are more likely to be held within the crown of fronds, and the 1 in (25 mm) long dark brown fruit have a sweet, sticky, edible flesh like dates. **ZONES 9–11.**

Brahea armata

BUTIA

This small genus of marginally frost-hardy palms comes from central South America and is related to the coconut palm. They have short, thick trunks and thick-textured, elegantly arched fronds of the 'feather' kind (pinnate). They periodically produce among the fronds large panicles of fruit-scented, small cream or purplish flowers, which are enclosed while in bud in a very long, woody bract; these are followed by abundant fruits with juicy but fibrous flesh around a very hard stone.

CULTIVATION

These tough palms are adaptable to a range of climates and soils. They are at their best when planted in full sun but will tolerate part-shade perfectly well. They are deeper rooted than most palms, and once established need little watering as long as summer rainfall is not too low. Dead fronds can be cut off close to the trunk, but not before they turn brown. Propagate from seed in spring.

Butia capitata

syn. **Cocos capitata**
BUTIA PALM, JELLY PALM, PINDO PALM

This palm can be variable in shape, reaching a height of up to 20 ft (6 m). It has a rough gray trunk and long, gray-green fronds, which are arching and recurved. The fragrant, yellow or purplish flowers are borne in very large panicles on a strong stalk, emerging among the frond bases, and may be followed by a large weight of juicy, yellow or orange fruit up to 1 in (25 mm) in diameter; their sweet, edible pulp is used for jellies or fermented to make wine. A vigorous and easily grown palm, it is useful for landscaping. **ZONES 8–11.**

Butia capitata

CARYOTA

FISHTAIL PALM

Very unusual palms with bipinnate fronds make up this genus of 12 species from tropical Asia and Australasia. 'Fishtail' refers to the shape of the leaflets, which are usually wedge-shaped with the corners drawn out into points and veins radiating from the stalk end. Flowering panicles first appear at the top of the trunk and continue opening successively lower down; after the last one sets fruit, the whole stem dies. Marble-sized fruits, usually ripening dark red, form on female flowers and contain 1 to 3 black seeds in a fibrous flesh that is quite irritating to the skin.

CULTIVATION

Coming from very moist tropical rainforests, they require a sheltered, humid environment, but most will tolerate a surprising degree of cold as well as poorly drained soils. They are easily propagated from seed.

CHAMAEDOREA

This genus consists of over 100 species of small to very small palms, most of them native to rainforests of Central America, with a minority in northern South America. They include many very ornamental species with smooth, green, bamboo-like stems which can grow singly or in clusters; some species are virtually stemless. The fronds are mostly few to each crown and consist of thin segments arranged pinnately (in feather fashion), or in some species undivided apart from a shallow to deep notch at the apex. Flowering stems are mostly branched, appearing among or below the fronds, the tiny male and female flowers are carried on different plants; females in particular often have stems that are bright red, orange or yellow, often contrasting with the color of the developing fruits, which are small berries.

CULTIVATION

They make first-class indoor plants, tolerating low humidity and dry soil better than many other palms and survive for years in small containers. Plant in a humus-rich soil and keep in good light but out of strong sun. Water freely in summer, keep barely moist in winter. Outdoors, plant in humus-rich soil, in full sun or part-shade. Propagate from seed.

Caryota mitis

CLUSTERED FISHTAIL PALM

This rainforest understorey palm consists of a number of closely crowded stems up to about 30 ft (9 m) tall and 3–4 in (8–10 cm) in diameter, nearly always with a thicket of sucker growth at the base. The fronds are rather erect, up to about 8 ft (2.4 m) long, with widely separated leaflets. The flowers and fruit appear in succession throughout the year. It is the most widely grown species for ornament.
ZONES 10–12.

Caryota urens

TODDY PALM, WINE PALM

This handsome, single-stemmed species is commonly grown for the drink toddy in its native India, Burma and Malaysia. Toddy is obtained by cutting off the young flower clusters and collecting the sugary, vitamin-rich sap that flows from the wound. It grows to about 40 ft (12 m) and is a popular ornamental tree in tropical countries.
ZONES 10–12.

Chamaedorea cataractarum

Chamaedorea cataractarum
CASCADE PALM

This species grows along banks of fast-flowing streams, sometimes half-submerged. Its stems are prostrate and branching, like thick green rhizomes, and each oblique shoot has only 4–5 dark green pinnate fronds up to 6 ft (1.8 m) long. The short, green inflorescences are half-hidden by the leaves and bear small, yellow flowers followed by tiny, reddish fruit on female plants. It is easily cultivated in a moist, sheltered spot, forming quite large clumps with age. **ZONES 10–12.**

CHAMAEROPS
MEDITERRANEAN FAN PALM

Noteworthy as the only palm indigenous to Europe (except for a rare date palm on Crete), the single species of this genus occurs along all the warmer Mediterranean coasts, growing in seashore scrubs often on limestone and in northwest Africa on rocky slopes of the Atlas and Rif Mountains. Cultivated plants develop multiple trunks clothed in shaggy fiber and stubs of leaf stalks. Flowers are of different sexes on different plants: the males are yellow in dense, short panicles, and the females are green in even shorter but sparser clusters, followed by shiny orange-brown fruit like short dates.

CULTIVATION

Easily cultivated in milder temperate climates, this palm will tolerate sun or shade and a wide range of soil types, but does best in warm, sunny positions. It takes many years to reach a respectable size and big specimens are prized for transplanting. Propagate from seed, which germinates readily, or by careful division of a clump.

Chamaerops humilis

Old plants of this palm have trunks up to about 12 ft (3.5 m) tall and 8–10 in (20–25 cm) in diameter, including the coating of fibers and old stalks. The fronds (leaves) are small for a fan palm, with stiff segments only 12–18 in (30–45 cm) long radiating from a stalk of about the same length, its edges fiercely armed. Fronds vary from olive green to a strong blue-gray shade in different races. The perfumed male flowers appear in late spring. **ZONES 8–11.**

CHRYSALIDOCARPUS

These feather palms from Madagascar and nearby islands are very graceful plants, which are happiest in tropical and subtropical areas. Although there are 22 species, only one, *Chrysalidocarpus lutescens*, is widely grown. The branched sprays of simple yellow flowers and fruit are unremarkable, but the foliage is very luxuriant.

CULTIVATION

All species are frost tender, but adapt well to warm-temperate climates as well as tropical. Plant in moist, well-drained soil in sun or light shade. Water freely in the summer, and keep the soil slightly moist all year. Propagate from seed in spring; seeds can take up to 5 months to germinate.

Chrysalidocarpus lutescens

Chrysalidocarpus lutescens

syns *Areca lutescens, Dypsis lutescens*
BUTTERFLY PALM, GOLDEN CANE PALM

This species is one of the most widely cultivated ornamental palms. It is a clump-forming feather palm with fairly short fronds that arch elegantly from cane-like stems 10–20 ft (3–6 m) high. The basal sheaths and frond stalks are yellow and the fronds them-selves are yellowish in sun but when grown in shade are a beautiful light green. It responds well to container cultivation and can be grown as a house plant. **ZONES 10–12.**

COCOS

COCONUT

As now recognized, the only species in this genus of tropical feather palms is the coconut *(Cocos nucifera)*, though many other palms were once included in it (for example, *Butia* and *Syagrus*, among others). It is the epitome of the tropical palm tree and a plant with many commercial and local uses. The genus is distinguished from its relatives, which share the hard blackish inner fruit shell with 3 pores or 'eyes', by the large size of the seed and the fact that its endosperm, or stored food mat-erial, is partly liquid (the 'coconut milk').

CULTIVATION

It is strictly a tropical plant and will not grow well where the temperature regularly falls below 60° F (15°C); it is occasionally grown in heated greenhouses in cooler climates but seldom achieves any size. It does best in full sun in deep, porous soil with ample moisture but will of course tolerate coastal condi-tions. It is propagated from seed, which take a few months to germinate once the whole unhusked nut is laid on its side on moist sand.

Cocos nucifera

Cocos nucifera

COCONUT PALM

The coconut has now become distributed throughout most tropical lowland regions, both through human agency and because its nut can survive for a month or so floating in the ocean. It is characterized by its slender, often curved trunk, up to as much as 100 ft (30 m) high, topped with a head of long, gracefully drooping fronds. It bears, continuously, large panicles of small creamy yellow flowers, a few of which develop into the familiar yellow-green fruit that dries and browns as it ripens. There are many selected strains, in-cluding **'Malay Dwarf'** with a much shorter trunk and abun-dant golden-yellow nuts. **ZONE 12.**

Cyrtostachys renda
syn. Cyrtostachys lakka
SEALING WAX PALM, LIPSTICK PALM,
MAHARAJAH PALM

The contrast between the rich green of the leaves and the brilliant scarlet of the glossy leaf bases makes this clumping feather palm from swampy lowlands of Malaysia and western Indonesia one of the most ornamental of all palms. Needing constant hot weather for the color to develop properly, it grows to about 20 ft (6 m) tall and has the reputation of being rather difficult to transplant. **ZONE 12.**

Cyrtostachys renda

Howea forsteriana
KENTIA PALM, THATCH PALM

Growing singly but in natural groves, the kentia palm is best known as an indoor plant. Outdoors in warm climates it is slow growing to about 30 ft (9 m) with a slender trunk; it can withstand coastal conditions. This palm is most effective when planted in groups, it needs to be protected from the sun when young. Water regularly during dry periods. **ZONES 10–11.**

CYRTOSTACHYS

This genus has 8 species, occurring wild in the Malay Peninsula, Sumatra, Borneo and New Guinea, which generally grow in coastal swamps. All are tall, slender, mostly clumping palms that will grow outdoors only in the tropics. The trunks are ringed with leaf scars and terminate in smooth 'crownshafts' of furled frond bases. The fronds are of the feather type (pinnate) with arching midribs. Branched inflorescences emerge below the fronds bearing numerous small flowers, followed by small, single-seeded fruits. Only one species is widely cultivated, prized for its brilliantly colored crownshaft.

CULTIVATION
They require a tropical climate with year-round humidity to grow well, and rich, constantly moist soil. Outside the tropics they will only succeed in a heated greenhouse with a winter temperature no lower than about 60° F (15°C). They should be propagated from freshly gathered seed.

HOWEA
syn. Kentia

This genus of palms has only 2 species, both native to Lord Howe Island off eastern Australia and both widely cultivated. They have graceful, feather-like fronds on long, smooth stalks and a smooth, ringed, single trunk. The flowers are small and fleshy, borne in long, arching spikes that emerge among the frond bases and are followed by small red fruit. Lord Howe Islanders successfully export the seeds.

CULTIVATION
These palms are frost tender and need moist, humid conditions and some shade if they are to be kept outdoors. They are more commonly grown indoors, tolerating less light and needing less heat than most other palms. They can be kept in the same pot or tub for years, as long as the potting mix is well drained and contains some humus. Provide part-shade while they mature. They are propagated from seed in spring; constant warmth is required for successful germination.

Howea forsteriana

JUBAEA

CHILEAN WINE PALM, COQUITO PALM

Consisting of one species of palm, this genus is named after King Juba of the old African kingdom of Numidia, although the plant itself comes from coastal Chile. It is now very rare in its natural habitat as it has been consistently cut for its sugary sap.

CULTIVATION

Slow growing when young, this palm's growth is much quicker once a trunk has formed. More frost tolerant than most palms, and widely grown in temperate climates, it needs full sun and deep, fertile, well-drained soil. As both male and female flowers are held on the same plant, fertile seed is easily obtained in autumn; it must be sown while fresh, but can take 6 to 15 months to germinate.

Jubaea chilensis

syn. Jubaea spectabilis

With maturity, this handsome palm reaches 80 ft (24 m), with a distinctive thick, cylindrical gray trunk topped with a dense mass of long, straight, feathery, deep green fronds. The yellowish flowers are borne in spring and are followed in autumn by woody, yellow fruit that look like small coconuts. **ZONES 8–11.**

Jubaea chilensis

LICUALA

There are around 100 species in this genus of fan palms from the wet tropics of Southeast Asia and Australasia, varying greatly in stature. Their fronds are very distinctive, from circular to fan-shaped in outline with regularly radiating ribs and toothed around the perimeter; in most species they are divided by splits into pie-wedge segments, often of unequal widths and with few to many ribs each. Slender panicles arise from the frond axils, bearing numerous tiny yellowish flowers followed by small red or orange berries.

CULTIVATION

Frost tender, they prefer part-shade and sandy, well-drained soil. Where temperatures fall below 60° F (15°C) most species need the shelter of a warm greenhouse, though the Australian Licuala ramsayi is able to survive night-time temperatures only slightly above freezing-point. Propagate from seed or suckers.

Licuala spinosa

This is a Southeast Asian evergreen species reaching 20 ft (6 m) with a 10 ft (3 m) spread. *Licuala spinosa* has clumps of slender stems and frond segments like the spokes of a wheel, 3 ft (1 m) across. The fruits are bright orange berries carried on an arching inflorescence growing up to 8 ft (2.4 m) long. **ZONES 10–12.**

Licuala spinosa

Livistona chinensis

LIVISTONA

This genus has about 30 species of medium to tall fan palms, about half of them endemic to Australia, the remainder scattered through the Malay Archipelago and southern Asia with a single species recently identified in desert oases of southern Arabia and Djibouti. Most feature large, almost circular, pleated fronds up to 5 ft (1.5 m) across forming a dense crown from which dead fronds may remain hanging for some time. The frond stalks are usually long and are edged with sharp prickles. These palms are widely used for outdoor landscaping; their clusters of blue, black or rarely reddish fruits and tapering frond segments are shown to great effect.

CULTIVATION

Some species will tolerate frosts down to about 25°F (-4°C), although they do best in subtropical, frost-free areas. Slow growing, they prefer deep, sandy soil and, while they tolerate full sun, they produce more vigorous, deeper green foliage in dappled shade. They make excellent indoor or outdoor container plants. Propagate from seed in summer.

Livistona australis

AUSTRALIAN FAN PALM,
CABBAGE-TREE PALM

Widely distributed along the east coast of Australia south of the Tropic of Capricorn, this is one of the tallest species, growing to 80 ft (24 m) in the wild. The slender brown trunk shows the scars left by the shed fronds. The large, rounded leaves are held at the apex of the trunk, allowing understorey plants such as ferns to grow under mature specimens. Long sprays of small yellow flowers appear in spring. The common names refer to the highly nutritious apical bud, which was eaten by Aborigines and early European settlers. **ZONES 9–12.**

Livistona chinensis

syn. *Livistona oliviformis*
CHINESE FAN PALM,
CHINESE FOUNTAIN PALM

This palm from islands to the south of China and Japan will reach 20–40 ft (6–12 m) tall; it is quite fast growing in the tropics, slow in temperate climates. Its single trunk is rough textured, and the large fronds held on relatively short stalks have very long, attractively drooping segments giving a curtain-like effect. The fruit are somewhat elongated, about ¾ in (18 mm) long and ripen to china blue. A useful container specimen, it is one of the most frost-hardy palms and has been grown outdoors in sheltered gardens in southern England. **ZONES 8–11.**

Livistona australis

PHOENIX

These evergreen feather palms are native to subtropical and tropical parts of Asia, Africa and the Canary Islands. There are 17 very different species; some are an important source of food (dates and palm sugar derived from dates), others are popular as house plants or avenue trees. *Phoenix* includes species with a single trunk as well as some that form clumps of stems. The long fronds have stiff, sharp spines at the base and form a dense crown. The small yellow flowers grow in clusters and are followed by the fruits.

CULTIVATION

Male and female plants are needed to ensure pollination. The plants prefer full sun, although they will tolerate part-shade, hot winds and poor soil if given good drainage. Hybrids between species are common. Trim off dead fronds. Propagate from seed in spring.

Phoenix reclinata

Phoenix reclinata
SENEGAL DATE PALM

This African species reaches only 20–30 ft (6–9 m) in height. It is distinctive for its multiple trunks, each gracefully curving out from the center of the clump. The small fruit are yellow to red.
ZONES 10–11.

Phoenix roebelenii
DWARF DATE PALM

The dwarf date palm is suitable for a hot-climate garden or as a potted specimen indoors. Growing to 10 ft (3 m) tall with a similar spread, its dark green, arching fronds give it an elegant, lacy effect. The short, slender stem is rough. The fruit are small, black, egg-shaped drupes.
ZONES 10–12.

Phoenix canariensis
CANARY ISLAND DATE PALM

This large palm from the Canary Islands grows to 50 ft (15 m) tall with a spread of 30 ft (9 m). It has a sturdy trunk up to 3 ft (1 m) across and arching, deep green fronds up to 12 ft (3.5 m) long. The small yellow flowers, borne in drooping clusters in summer, are followed by inedible, orange-yellow, acorn-like fruit. This palm needs plenty of room to show off its dramatic symmetrical shape. In areas that are prone to frosts, plant a relatively mature specimen when the danger of frost has passed.
ZONES 9–11.

Phoenix canariensis

RHAPIS

LADY PALM

Rhapis is a small genus of about 12 species of low-growing palms ranging from southern China to Thailand. They form clumps of slender, bamboo-like stems carrying small, deeply divided, fan-shaped fronds. New stem growth is covered with interwoven fibers arising from the base of each frond. The yellow male and female flowers occur on separate plants. The fruits are small berries containing a single seed.

CULTIVATION

These frost-tender palms are often grown in tubs, as ornamental clumps, or as hedges in warm, humid climates. Elsewhere they are favorite house plants. They require some shade and rich, moist soil, are usually propagated by division, but can be reproduced from seed.

Rhopalostylis sapida

RHOPALOSTYLIS

The 3 species in this genus of palms are indigenous to New Zealand, Norfolk Island and the Kermadec Islands. The trunks are topped by a swollen shaft made up of the leaf bases, called the crownshaft. The pinnate leaves, obliquely erect and feather-like, give these palms their distinctive outline. The flowers, carried in a cluster below the leaves, are followed by red berry-like fruit

CULTIVATION

Choose a sunny, sheltered spot in a frost-free climate. A moist but well-drained, light to medium soil enriched with organic matter is ideal. Propagate from fresh seed in spring.

Rhapis excelsa

MINIATURE FAN PALM

The many stems of this palm form a dense clump up to 15 ft (4.5 m) tall. The fronds, light to rich green, divide into 5 to 8 stiff, finger-like segments. The tiny, bowl-shaped, creamy flowers appear in small panicles among the fronds in summer. It will grow outside in warm climates, but slowly; its leaves may burn in full sun. **ZONES 10–12.**

Rhopalostylis sapida

NIKAU PALM, FEATHER DUSTER PALM

This slow-growing New Zealand species is the world's most southerly wild palm. It has a stout 30 ft (9 m) trunk, a shiny green crownshaft bulging at the base, and a mass of short-stalked fronds 10 ft (3 m) long, each divided into many lanceolate leaflets 3 ft (1 m) long. Cream to mauve flower clusters 12 in (30 cm) long appear below the crownshaft. **ZONES 10–11.**

Rhopalostylis sapida

Sabal minor

DWARF PALMETTO,
SCRUB PALMETTO

This shrub-sized palm is usually about 6 ft (1.8 m) tall and half as wide. The stem is mostly underground, and leaves appear from the crown at ground level. Each frond is green to bluish green, stiff and almost flat and cut into regular ribbed segments. Flowers are small, white and scented, on slender erect panicles projecting high above the foliage. The small fruit are black and shiny. **ZONES 8–12.**

Sabal palmetto

CABBAGE PALM,
CABBAGE PALMETTO

This species thrives in swampy coastal areas. It can reach a height of 80 ft (24 m) with a sturdy trunk, scarred where the frond bases have been. The fronds are dark green above and grayish underneath, and up to 6 ft (1.8 m) long. Each characteristically twisted frond is divided into regular segments cut two-thirds of the way to the main axis and split at the tips. The small, whitish flowers are held in long, branched clusters while the fruit are small black berries. **ZONES 8–12.**

SABAL

PALMETTO

These 14 species of fan palms are indigenous to southeastern USA and the Caribbean. Some have tall trunks, others feature very short stems. The fronds are fan-shaped and deeply cut into segments: the stalks often persist for years after the fronds have fallen. Tiny whitish flowers appear in long sprays among the fronds, their stalks enclosed by tubular bracts at the base. The fruits are rounded to slightly pear-shaped berries. The buds of some species are one source of hearts-of-palm, also known as millionaire's salad.

CULTIVATION

These palms suit warm to hot climates and moist or dry conditions. They prefer a sheltered, sunny spot in well-drained soil rich in organic matter. Propagate from fresh seed.

Sabal palmetto

SERENOA

SAW PALMETTO, SCRUB PALMETTO

This genus contains just a single palm species which occurs naturally in southeastern USA. It is an evergreen fan palm with creeping or, rarely, short upright stems. It forms immense colonies in its natural habitat.

CULTIVATION

This palm prefers full sun or part-shade and dislikes frost. It grows best in well-drained soil and is very tolerant of exposed coastal locations; it also tolerates boggy conditions. Propagate from seed or suckers.

Serenoa repens

This palm has stems that are mostly prostrate or creeping and grows to 24–36 in (60–90 cm) high and twice as wide, but occasionally grows an upright 10 ft (3 m) stem. The fan-shaped leaves are held stiffly upwards and vary from green to bluish green or even silver; each leaf is 18–30 in (45–75 cm) across and is divided into about 20 strap-like segments. The leaf stalks are toothed along the edges. In summer, creamy white, perfumed flowers are hidden among the foliage. The fruit that follow are egg-shaped and blackish when ripe. **ZONES 8–11.**

TRACHYCARPUS

WINDMILL PALM, FAN PALM

This genus consists of 6 species of highly ornamental palms bearing large, fan-shaped leaves. They are valued for their ability to tolerate cooler climates than most other palms. Indigenous to southern China and the Himalayas, they often occur at high altitudes. They are small to medium palms, and their trunks are usually covered with coarse, shaggy fiber. The dark green fronds are divided into narrow, pointed segments and can be up to 5 ft (1.5 m) across. Small yellowish flowers, borne in summer, are followed by dark-colored berries.

CULTIVATION
Provided with adequate moisture, these palms will adapt to any free-draining soil in part-shade or full sun. Protect plants from cold winds, especially when young. These palms are shallow-rooted and easily transplanted. They make excellent tub specimens for patios and larger greenhouses. Propagate from seed.

Trachycarpus fortunei

Trachycarpus fortunei

CHINESE FAN PALM, CHUSAN PALM, WINDMILL PALM

Moderately frost hardy, this remarkable palm has been cultivated in Europe for 160 years, where it is prized for its exotic appearance and tolerance of cold. It reaches 30 ft (9 m) tall and the trunk is swathed in brownish fiber. The leaves are held on long stalks and are dark green above, blue-green below; dead leaves tend to persist as a 'skirt' on the tree. Dense, showy clusters of small yellow flowers precede the marble-sized, dark blue berries, which have a coating of whitish wax. **ZONES 8–11.**

WASHINGTONIA

WASHINGTONIA PALM

The two species of this genus are made up of fan-leafed palms from arid parts of western Mexico, southern California and Arizona. Their stately appearance makes them ideal specimen or avenue trees. They have an upright, single trunk, and are sometimes called petticoat palms because the dead fronds hang down in a mass around the trunk. The large fronds have many long, tapering segments and spiny stalks. The small white flowers cluster at intervals on long flowering branches that arch out well beyond the fronds. The fruits are small dark drupes.

CULTIVATION
These palms do best in warm to hot climates, well-drained soil and an open position in full sun. Propagate from seed in spring.

Washingtonia filifera

syn. *Washingtonia filamentosa*
CALIFORNIA FAN PALM, COTTON PALM

From southern California and Arizona, this palm develops a fat trunk and grows 20–60 ft (6–18 m) tall. The grayish green fronds form a broad, spherical crown about 15 ft (4.5 m) across. The common name cotton palm comes from the white, cotton-like threads on and between the frond segments. Its small, hard, black berries ripen in winter. **ZONES 9–11.**

Washingtonia robusta

MEXICAN WASHINGTONIA PALM, MEXICAN FAN PALM

This species, taller and more slender than *Washingtonia filifera* and with a more tapering trunk, occurs naturally in northwestern Mexico. It grows to 80 ft (24 m) and its crown is 10 ft (3 m) across. The shiny, bright green fronds, almost circular, are less deeply segmented than those of *W. filifera*. The fruit are tiny dark brown berries. **ZONES 10–11.**

CYCADS

CYCAS
SAGO PALM

Cycas armstrongii

This species from the tropical 'Top End' of Australia's Northern Territory occurs in flat, sandy country in open eucalypt woodland. It is usually unbranched, with a straight, slender trunk 6–15 ft (1.8–4.5 m) tall, from the top of which emerges a circle of delicate, new, pale green fronds at the start of each wet season; during the dry season they gradually shrivel, drooping in a brown 'skirt'. Plants in moister positions may retain fronds for longer. Female trees mostly sport another 'skirt' of seed-bearing organs, each with 2 to 4 large, orange-brown seeds. **ZONES 11–12.**

This geologically ancient genus of cycads has about 60 species from Australia, Southeast Asia, Madagascar and eastern Africa, as well as many of the islands in between, and out into the Pacific. They are palm-like plants with pinnate fronds that spread from the top of a thick trunk. The top of the trunk is also packed with starchy tissue; male and female organs are on different plants, the male in long, narrow cones terminating the stem, the female on the margins of furry, leaf-like organs that ring the trunk apex and may eventually hang in a 'skirt' below it, as the hard, egg-like seeds mature. Growth of the trunk is normally very slow, so large specimens are prized and fetch high prices from collectors and landscape contractors.

CULTIVATION

With the exception of *Cycas revoluta*, most *Cycas* species do not thrive outdoors except in tropical and warmer subtropical areas. They like sunny positions but with some shade when young, and deep, well-drained soil. There are various methods of propagation; from seed, by detached offsets, or by cutting off a whole cross-section of the trunk and plunging the base in a trench filled with gravel and organic matter.

Cycas revoluta

Cycas revoluta
JAPANESE SAGO PALM

Endemic to the islands of southern Japan, this cycad is a popular ornamental plant. It grows slowly with short, single or multiple trunks to 10 ft (3 m) high, with a compact crown of stiff, pinnate leaves that have closely crowded, very narrow, spine-tipped leaflets. It is the most widely cultivated cycad in the world and is valued as a landscape subject, especially suited to courtyards and plazas. Slow growing, it is capable of living for 50 to 100 years or even more and is readily transplanted. **ZONES 9–12.**

ENCEPHALARTOS

The 60 or more species of slow-growing cycads in this genus come mostly from southern Africa with a minority scattered through tropical Africa. They are commonly found on rocky outcrops, among coastal dunes or on mountainsides. They appear as large tufts of spiky fronds for many years before eventually developing a stout trunk, which grows 10–12 ft (3–3.5 m) high. The stiff, palm-like leaves are pinnate, with leaflets that are spine tipped and often toothed. Female and male plants bear spectacular cones either singly or in groups of up to five from the center of the crown.

CULTIVATION

These plants tolerate an occasional frost, but will do best in subtropical areas with full sun and plenty of moisture; they can withstand strong winds. Propagate from seed, which germinates easily, although seedlings take many years to develop.

Encephalartos altensteinii
PRICKLY CYCAD, BREAD TREE

This cycad from moist coastal areas of South Africa is extremely slow growing. The rigid, palm-like fronds are about 6 ft (1.8 m) long, with numerous stiff, spiny-toothed leaflets. A female specimen may produce cones that resemble giant, elongated pineapples 18 in (45 cm) long. **ZONES 10–11.**

Cycas armstrongii

LEPIDOZAMIA

Four species have been named in this cycad genus, but 2 of them exist only as fossils, while the remaining pair can be found growing in the moist forests of Australia's east coast. Among the tallest known cycads, they are palm-like in appearance with a usually unbranched, straight trunk and dark green, glossy pinnate fronds that are produced in annual whorls, with 3 to 5 years' whorls present at any one time. Like all cycads they produce male (pollen) and female (seed) cones on separate plants, and both are exceptionally large in this genus, sitting singly and erect in the center of the circle of fronds: the female cones are coated in brown felt, with pointed flaps projecting, while the narrower males are green, releasing vast quantities of pollen through a spiral split when mature.

Lepidozamia peroffskyana

MACROZAMIA

This genus consists of about 24 species of cycads from Australia. Their stems vary from cylindrical to almost globose, above or below ground level, and are topped with palm-like fronds of evergreen foliage reaching up to 8 ft (2.4 m) long. The trunks are clothed in persistent dead frond bases. They produce large, light green, pineapple-shaped, male and female cones, the individual cone scales tipped with a sharp spine; the mature female cones contain bright orange, red or yellow seeds. The starchy kernels cannot be eaten fresh.

CULTIVATION

Marginally frost hardy, they prefer temperate to subtropical areas and open, well-drained soil in part-shade. Propagate from fresh seed, which may take up to 18 months to germinate. Growth is very slow in cooler areas.

Macrozamia communis
BURRAWANG

Extensive stands of this species occur in coastal New South Wales. The trunk, though usually underground, may reach 6 ft (1.8 m) high. The crown carries up to 100 bright green, palm-like fronds about 6 ft (1.8 m) long. It produces multiple male and female cones 18 in (45 cm) long; the female cones contain oblong orange or red seeds. It tolerates light frosts and transplanting. **ZONES 9–11.**

CULTIVATION

Attractive garden and container plants in warm climates, they tolerate an occasional very light frost. Grow in moderately fertile, moist but well-drained soil. They transplant easily and are best grown in the shelter of taller trees, as the leaves become faded and yellowish in full sun. Propagate from seed in spring or summer.

Lepidozamia peroffskyana
syn. *Macrozamia denisonii*
PINEAPPLE ZAMIA

Named for a Russian patron of botany, the pineapple zamia from subtropical eastern Australia will in time grow to more than 25 ft (8 m), but in gardens it is more commonly seen with no trunk or a very short one. The glossy fronds are about 5 ft (1.5 m) long with curved, smooth-edged leaflets about ½ in (12 mm) wide. The huge female cones are up to 30 in (75 cm) long. The second species, *Lepidozamia hopei* from tropical Queensland rainforests, differs mainly in its broader leaflets and is known to reach a height of over 60 ft (18 m). **ZONES 10–12.**

Macrozamia communis